DICTIONARY OF

BRITISH SCULPTORS

1660—1851

NEW REVISED EDITION

DICTIONARY OF
BRITISH SCULPTORS

1660—1851
NEW REVISED EDITION
BY
RUPERT GUNNIS

THE ABBEY LIBRARY

146/152 HOLLOWAY ROAD
LONDON

GVLIELMO BARONI DE LISLE ET DUDLEY

NECNON IACOLINAE VXORIS SVAE

ITINERVM DOMI PEREGREQUE

FORTVNA BONA CONFECTORVM

COMITIBVS DILECTIS

PREFACE

THIS book should perhaps have been called an "attempted dictionary of British sculptors, 1660–1851," for it is obvious that no one person working on his own could ever hope to cover completely so wide and so vast a field. The chief object has been to give the lives and known work of the craftsmen and I have avoided any attributions on stylistic or other grounds. All the statues, busts, monuments, etc., given here are either signed works or sufficiently documented from MS. or printed sources. It is to be hoped, therefore, that this book may serve as a foundation and that the lists of the various artists' certain works may enable other students to identify those which are unsigned.

The writing of this book, however, has not been an easy task, and indeed, looking back, I wonder at my temerity in thinking that I could ever hope to achieve anything. And yet something may have been accomplished, for the great majority of the biographies which follow are not to be found in any printed book of reference; some of these, however, are of men who have played a large part in the artistic life of England.

The sculpture of the eighteenth and nineteenth centuries has for many years past been unpopular and neglected, for all that there is so much of it in Britain. There is hardly a village church or churchyard which has not a monument, a tablet or gravestone by craftsmen whose names are often unknown and whose lives are buried in obscurity. It has been my desire to discover, however imperfectly, something about them which has driven me on to finish this book—a task which has taken more than fourteen years of hard work.

The idea of such a work had been in my mind for a long time; indeed, I recently found a postcard, written to a relation more than forty years ago, proudly announcing the fact (which was probably of no interest to her) that I had found the sculptor's signature on a monument in a London church. It was, perhaps, because no one was able to tell me anything about these statuaries that I decided to start collecting information on the subject. Other work and interests, however, intervened, and it was not until much later that I began in earnest to make a large card-index containing facts and dates regarding sculptors and their works.

Having collected the information, it was difficult to know how to present it to the public or how to plan it. I had had little experience of such work and was uncertain on many points. For example, which craftsmen were to be included and which excluded; what period should be covered and how many works by each sculptor should be given. In the end I have thought it wisest to include all those who could be called artists or fine craftsmen, though of some who figure here it may well be said that I have made "a fond attempt" to write about "names ignoble born to be forgot."

As to the period covered, I had originally intended to write a complete dictionary of British sculpture from the earliest times until the close of the last century. But I quickly discovered that such a task was utterly beyond my powers, nor would any publisher have printed so large a volume. It has, therefore, seemed best to confine myself to the period between the Restoration and the opening of the Great Exhibition, a period less than two hundred years in length, though even so it has meant writing more than seventeen hundred separate biographies.

The next thing to decide was how much to write about each artist and how many of his works to list. Again it seemed best to give a considerable amount of information about those sculptors who have, as yet, found no biographer, and less about those (such as Gibson, Nollekens or Roubiliac) of whom lives already existed. For the more important artists I have given a fairly complete list of their works, and with the minor craftsmen have only mentioned their best productions. As to the dates of these, in the case of statues or busts it is the date of execution, in the case of monuments or tablets the date of death of the person commemorated, unless the sculptor has not only signed, but dated, the work itself.

It has not, however, been an easy task to collect this information. It has entailed visits to more than six thousand churches all over Britain (besides a number in Eire), and numberless hours have been spent reading through archives and documents in public and private collections. With the exception of works overseas, I have seen practically every monument and tablet mentioned in this book, and the great majority of the statues and busts.

The work has certainly been of the greatest interest and has had all the excitement of a detective story. One finds a signed monument in a church, or a stone-carver mentioned in some building accounts, and one begins with a name. Then comes the hunt to find out more about the man, and by searching in places likely and unlikely, in books and MSS. obvious and obscure, one slowly begins to rediscover his life and work. And what was once a mere name in the card-index may in the end grow into a more or less complete figure. How can one ever tire of the moment when one opens the door of a parish church, not knowing whether in the next few minutes an unrecorded monument by Rysbrack or an unnoticed bust by Nollekens may come to light.

Of course, the checks and disappointments are frequent. It is maddening how many volumes are missing in the archives of provincial cities and towns—those books of apprentices, freemen, or ratepayers which would help to fill in the gaps. Nor has the fate of private collections of muniments been happier. Taxation has forced owners to sell their family homes, and the papers, the bills, the letters of interest, have all been scattered, sold or destroyed.

It is impossible to attempt to mention the very large number of sources from which information has been obtained, extending as they do from lists of bankrupts to the muniments at Chatsworth, but I have, in most cases, stated where or how I have obtained my information, though where the facts about London masons obviously come from the archives of the Company I have not thought it necessary always to state that fact.

The chief source has indeed been the archives of the Masons' Company; valuable too were the minute books and lists of students at Burlington House, and the papers of the Society of Arts. I am deeply grateful to the Worshipful Master of the Masons' Company, the President and Secretary of the Royal Academy, and the Secretary of the Society of Arts for permission to search through these muniments, and also to the Secretaries of the Artists' Annuity Fund, the Artists' General Benevolent Institution and the Suffolk Street Galleries.

The Court minute books, list of apprentices, etc., of the Masons' Company have proved the foundation to many of the biographies, for from them it has been possible to discover the parentage, apprenticeship, etc., of a very large number of statuaries, and they had, so far as I am aware, hardly been examined for this purpose before. The papers at Burlington House provided invaluable information, including the dates of birth of those sculptors who had been students at the Royal Academy Schools, while the minute books of the Society of Arts gave a number of facts about those artists who had received premiums from the Society.

I must also offer my thanks to the Masters of the City Companies for the readiness with which they have granted my requests to examine their records; the Headmasters of Eton, Christ's Hospital and Stonyhurst; the Custodians of the Archives of St. Bartholomew's Hospital, St. Thomas's Hospital, Guy's Hospital and to the Secretary of the Foundling Hospital. I would also like to thank Messrs. Coutts and Messrs. Child, and especially the Directors of Messrs. Hoare, not only for permission to examine their own most important family archives, but also for the help they gave me when the muniments of the Masons' Company were in their custody. Nor must I forget Messrs. Christie, who allowed me to look through all their sale catalogues.

To librarians all over England I am grateful for so courteously answering my questions concerning their local sculptors, but especially to Dr. Hollaender of Guildhall Library, who has never failed to let me know of any manuscript acquired by his library which he thought might be of interest to me; to Miss Dorothy Stroud of the Soane Museum, for her guidance, advice and help about manuscript material in her charge, and to the Director of the Museum for allowing me access to it; to Mr. Beard, of the Birmingham Library; Mr. Hodgkinson, of the Victoria and Albert Museum; Mr. Erith, late of the Essex Record Office; and to Mr. Marcus Whiffen, Mr. Laurence Whistler, Mr. Edmund Esdaile and Mr. Frederick Burgess.

My list of personal obligation and thanks is especially long. First and chiefly I shall always remember with deep gratitude the help I received from the late Mrs. Arundell Esdaile, and recall with pleasure the many days we spent visiting churches together and discussing the authorship of the monuments we found in them. Her friendship and encouragement meant a great deal to me and for these I can never be sufficiently grateful. Her works on English sculpture are too well known to mention here. She was the first person to realize the importance of the eighteenth-century monuments in British churches, and as she wrote on post-Reformation sculpture so did many begin to realize for the first time that the later monuments were worth looking at, even if neglected by guide-books, whose authors scornfully dismissed them as ugly and pretentious.

I cannot mention all those who have helped me to collect the information for this book. There are so many scattered all over Britain who have assisted me, giving up valuable time and taking an infinite amount of trouble to answer the questions and deal with the problems with which I have bombarded them. But there are, however, some whom it would be the grossest ingratitude not to thank. To Mr. John Whitehead, the Town Clerk of my own town of Tunbridge Wells, I am particularly grateful, for he has furnished me with letters of introduction to his fellow Town Clerks, so that I have been able without difficulty to search the archives of most of the chief cities and towns of England. To my friends who have accompanied me in my numberless journeys to visit churches, and who have with unfailing patience, good nature and kindness read maps, found keys of locked churches, climbed ladders to read skied monuments and, indeed, made this book possible, I can never be grateful enough.

To Mr. Howard Colvin I owe an especial debt. Not only did he accompany me on several of my more extended tours, but during his own researches for his forthcoming Dictionary of Architects he was unfailing in sending me any information he found bearing on English sculpture.

Many of the photographs in this book I owe to the kindness of Mr. Alan Lamboll, who took them specially for me, and I must also thank Mr. Richard Brain for reading through the typescript.

This list could be extended much further, but space, not ingratitude, forbids. The heads and librarians of Oxford and Cambridge colleges, the incumbents I have met during my tours, the mayors, town clerks and other borough officials, the heads of County Record Offices and Cathedral Libraries, the directors of Art Galleries and Museums, and the authorities at Somerset House, all I should wish to thank and, at the same time, to apologize for the valuable time which I must have so frequently wasted during my unceasing and, indeed, almost remorseless, search for information.

In conclusion, may I again repeat that this is but an "attempted" dictionary, and I hope that younger and more experienced hands will add to it as the years pass. If it has formed a foundation for others to build on it has served its purpose. Finally I shall be most grateful to anyone who will send me any further information or correct the inevitable mistakes which must have crept into a work of this nature, consisting, as it does, so largely of names of places and persons.

To hear of any new discoveries will assure me that there are some at least who have looked at works of sculpture in churches and public and private buildings with greater delight and interest since this book was published, and I shall count that a further reward after the many years of work from which I myself have drawn similar pleasure.

1951

PREFACE TO THE NEW EDITION

I HAVE left the original preface more or less as I wrote it save that in it I thanked a very large number of owners of Archives for their kindness in allowing me to go through their papers in the twenty years that I collected the material for the first edition of this book. Since then it is inevitable that not only a number of those, who were so generous in letting me go through their muniments have died, but County Archive Offices have been formed; therefore, the majority of the documents that were in private hands while I was doing research for this book have, in the great majority of cases, been deposited in Archive Offices and are no longer in the houses from which once I saw them. It is sad to think that in a number of cases the houses themselves have been pulled down or passed out of the hands of the original owners. I am, none the less, eternally grateful to all those who allowed me free access to their papers but as these have now passed from their hands it is wrong to give the idea that they are still in the houses as I originally stated. For students may be disappointed when they write to these previous owners and find that the papers are no longer in their possession or care.

It is also obvious that in the thirteen years that have passed since I first published my book I should have collected a great deal more information on many of the sculptors mentioned, or about the new ones I have discovered. It is quite impossible to add all this information, for had I done so the book would have been more than twice its original size. However, I am always pleased to answer, as far as I can, any questions from those interested in any particular sculptors. I am fully aware that there is yet a great deal to be discovered and that there are many churches, especially in India, which I have neither seen nor yet got full and complete lists of the monuments which they contain.

I would like to thank Mr. Edmund Esdaile for allowing me to make use of his annotated copy of my book and thus being able to correct a number of mistakes that were in the first edition.

I am also most grateful to Dr. Margaret Whinney, Mr. Bruce Bailey, Mr. Howard Colvin, Mr. H. S. Haden and Mr. Lawrence Stone who have sent me lists of suggested corrections.

There are a great many more persons, some known, some unknown, who have written to me giving me information, but as this has been spread over so many years it is impossible for me to list all of them, though I am, none the less, conscious of the debt I owe.

As I have said before, I look on this book only as a foundation and hope that in the years to come somebody else may be able to build more completely and produce a book (though I fear it will have to be in several volumes) which will give a comprehensive list of the many sculptors and statuaries who worked in England from 1660 to 1851 and thereby fill in the many gaps I have left, not only in their lives but also in the lists of works that they produced.

There is one detail that I would like to make clear. The dates of the monuments of various sculptors are not necessarily the dates of death.

9

LIST OF PLATES

PLATE I   *facing page* 16

JAMES ANNIS
Sir George Fettiplace, 1743, Swinbrook, Oxon
By kind permission of Mr. Derek Sherborn

JOHN BACON THE YOUNGER
William Markham, Archbishop of York, 1813, Windsor Castle
By gracious permission of Her Majesty the Queen

JOHN BACON THE ELDER
George III, 1775, Windsor Castle
By gracious permission of Her Majesty the Queen

PLATE II   *facing page* 17

JOHN BUSHNELL
William Ashburnham, 1675, Ashburnham, Sussex
By kind permission of the late Lady Catherine Ashburnham

E. H. BAILY
Viscount Brome, 1837, Linton, Kent
By kind permission of Mr. Alan Lamboll

PLATE III   *facing page* 32

WILLIAM BEHNES
Princess, later Queen, Victoria, 1829, Windsor Castle
By gracious permission of Her Majesty the Queen

THOMAS BANKS
Sir Clifton Wintringham, 1794, Westminster Abbey
By permission of the Warburg Institute

BELTHASAR BURMAN
Rachel, Countess of Bath, 1680, Tawstock, Devon

PLATE IV   *facing page* 33

SAMUEL CHANDLER
Edmund Humfrey, 1727, Rettendon, Essex
By kind permission of Mr. Alan Lamboll

SIR HENRY CHEERE
Charles Apthorp, 1758, King's Chapel, Boston, U.S.A.
By kind permission of Mr. Henry Wilder Foote

ANDRIES CARPENTIÈRE
Sir John Thornycroft, 1725, Bloxham, Oxon
By permission of the National Buildings Record

PLATE V   *facing page* 112

AUGOSTINO CARLINI
George III, 1773, Burlington House
By kind permission of the President of the Royal Academy

SIR FRANCIS CHANTREY
Lady Frederica Stanhope, 1823, Chevening, Kent
By kind permission of Earl Stanhope, K.G.

PLATE VI   *facing page* 113

THOMAS CARTER
Colonel Thomas Moore, 1735, Great Bookham, Surrey
By permission of the National Buildings Record

THOMAS DUNN
Edward Colman, 1739, Brent Eleigh, Suffolk
By kind permission of Mr. Alan Lamboll

PLATE VII   *facing page* 128

JOHN DEARE
"Venus," 1787, Parham Park, Sussex
By kind permission of the Hon. Clive Pearson

ANNE SEYMOUR DAMER
"Two Dogs," Goodwood, Sussex
By kind permission of the Duke of Richmond and Gordon

PLATE VIII   *facing page* 129

CLAUDE DAVID
Philip Carteret (*d.* 1710), Westminster Abbey
By permission of the Warburg Institute

JOHN DEVAL THE YOUNGER
Thomas Spackman, 1786, Cliffe Pypard, Wiltshire

PLATE IX   *facing page* 160

JOHN FLAXMAN
Earl Howe, 1803, St. Paul's Cathedral
By permission of the Warburg Institute

PLATE X   *facing page* 161

G. B. GUELFI
James Craggs, 1725, Westminster Abbey
By permission of the Warburg Institute

GRINLING GIBBONS
Part of the monument of John, Lord Coventry, 1690, Croome D'Abitot, Worcestershire

JOHN GIBSON
"Narcissus," 1838, Burlington House
By kind permission of the President of the Royal Academy

PLATE XI   *facing page* 176

JOHN HUNT
Cilena l'Anson Bradley, 1726, Long Buckby, Northants
By permission of the National Buildings Record

RICHARD HAYWARD
Lord Botetourt, 1773, Williamsburg, Virginia, U.S.A.
By permission of the Williamsburg College, Virginia

PLATE XII   *facing page* 177

PETER HOLLINS
Mrs. Thompson, 1838, Malvern Priory
By permission of the National Buildings Record

PLATE XIII   *facing page* 224

ROBERT HARTSHORNE
Sir Thomas Powys, 1720, Thorpe Achurch, Northamptonshire
By permission of the National Buildings Record

JOHN HANCOCK
Joseph Mellish, 1703, Blyth, Nottinghamshire
By permission of the National Buildings Record

CHRISTOPHER HORSNAILE THE ELDER
Sir Jacob Garrard, 1730, Langford, Norfolk
By kind permission of Mr. Marcus Whiffen

PLATE XIV   *facing page* 225

SAMUEL JOSEPH
William Wilberforce, 1838, Westminster Abbey
By permission of the Warburg Institute

11

PLATE XV   *facing page* 240

J. F. MOORE
William Beckford, *c.* 1767, Ironmongers' Hall
Photographed by Mr. Alan Lamboll by kind permission of the Master of the Ironmongers' Company

PLATE XVI   *facing page* 241

CHARLES MANNING
Captain George Hardinge, 1808, St. Paul's Cathedral
By permission of the Warburg Institute

EDWARD MARSHALL
Lady Culpeper, 1638, Hollingbourne, Kent
By kind permission of Mr. Alan Lamboll

PLATE XVII   *facing page* 272

JOHN VAN NOST
The Duke of Queensberry, 1711, Durisdeer, Dumfries
By kind permission of Mr. Alan Lamboll

PLATE XVIII   *facing page* 273

ARNOLD QUELLIN
Sir John Cutler, 1683, Grocers' Hall
Photographed by Mr. Alan Lamboll, by kind permission of the Master of the Grocers' Company

JOSEPH NOLLEKENS
George III, 1773, Royal Society
By kind permission of the Royal Society

J. M. RYSBRACK
Mr. and Mrs. Knight, 1733, Gosfield, Essex
By kind permission of Mr. Alan Lamboll

PLATE XIX   *facing page* 288

NICHOLAS READ
Part of the monument of Admiral Tyrrell, 1766, Westminster Abbey
By permission of the Warburg Institute

PLATE XX   *facing page* 289

J. C. F. ROSSI
Lord Heathfield, 1825, St. Paul's Cathedral
By permission of the Warburg Institute

L. F. ROUBILIAC
Part of the monument of the Duke of Argyll and Greenwich, 1748, Westminster Abbey
By permission of the Warburg Institute

PLATE XXI   *facing page* 336

HENRY ROSSI
"The Bowler," 1825, Woburn Abbey, Bedfordshire
By kind permission of the Duke of Bedford

PLATE XXII   *facing page* 337

JOSEPH ROSE THE ELDER
Richard Ladbroke, 1730, Reigate, Surrey
By kind permission of Mr. Alan Lamboll

PLATE XXIII   *facing page* 352

ABRAHAM STOREY
Lord and Lady Crofts, *c.* 1678, Little Saxham, Suffolk
By kind permission of Mr. Alan Lamboll

PLATE XXIV   *facing page* 353

R. W. SIEVIER
Earl Harcourt, 1832, Stanton Harcourt, Oxon
By permission of the National Buildings Record

WILLIAM STANTON
Sir John and Lady Brownlow, *c.* 1679, Belton, Lincs

THOMAS SCHEEMAKERS
Part of the monument of Ralph Freman. *c.* 1773, Braughing, Hertfordshire

PLATE XXV   *facing page* 368

HENRY SCHEEMAKERS
Sir Francis and Lady Page, 1730, Steeple Aston, Oxon

PLATE XXVI   *facing page* 369

PETER SCHEEMAKERS
and L. DELVEAUX
Sir Samuel Ongley, 1726, Old Warden, Bedfordshire

ROBERT SINGLETON
Colonel Edmund Soames, 1706, West Dereham, Norfolk
By permission of the National Buildings Record

PLATE XXVII   *facing page* 384

EDWARD STANTON
Sir Francis Russell, 1705, Strensham, Worcestershire
By permission of the National Buildings Record

THOMAS STAYNER
Dr. Turner, 1714, Stowe-Nine-Churches, Northants
By kind permission of Mr. Derek Sherborn

CHARLES R. SMITH
Rev. Thomas Whitaker, 1822, Whalley, Yorkshire
By kind permission of Mr. Derek Sherborn

PLATE XXVIII   *facing page* 385

WILLIAM TYLER
Samuel Vassall, 1766, King's Chapel, Boston, U.S.A.
By kind permission of Mr. Henry Wilder Foote

JOHN WALSH
Bust of Lady Lechmere, part of the monument of Sir Thomas Robinson and his wife, the Dowager Lady Lechmere, *c.* 1778, Westminster Abbey
By permission of the Warburg Institute

HENRY WEEKES
Robert Southey, 1843, Westminster Abbey
By permission of the Warburg Institute

PLATE XXIX   *facing page* 416

R. J. WYATT
Part of the monument to Ellen Legh, 1831, Winwick, Lancashire
By permission of the National Buildings Record

PLATE XXX   *facing page* 417

JOSEPH WILTON
Admiral Holmes, 1761, Westminster Abbey
By permission of the Warburg Institute

PLATE XXXI   *facing page* 432

—. WESTON
Part of the monument to Jonathan and Elizabeth Ivie, 1717, St. Petrock's Church, Exeter

PLATE XXXII   *facing page* 433

RICHARD WESTMACOTT THE ELDER
James Dutton, 1791, Sherborne, Gloucestershire
By permission of the National Buildings Record

A

ABBOTT, C., of Aylsham
fl. 1805–1830

His work is typical of the early nineteenth-century Norwich school and he signs tablets in Norfolk to Charles Smith, 1802; and Anne Bond, 1803, at Southrepps; Edward Piggon, 1805, at Aylesham; Charles Hornor, 1811, at Irstead; and Robert Doughty, 1817, at Hanworth. Another to Sir John Lubbock, 1823, at North Walsham is signed "Abbott and Thompson."

ABBOTT, GEORGE
b. 1803, *d.* 1883

He was born in London on 18 July, 1803. Although he had exhibited a bust of Mrs. George Abbott at the Royal Academy in 1834, it was not until five years later that Abbott joined the Academy Schools on the recommendation of Benjamin Wyon (Royal Academy Archives). In 1850 he executed bronze cabinet busts of Wellington and Peel. A large number of replicas was made of both these works, those of Peel being manufactured by Messrs. Hetley of Soho Square; an example of the Duke's bust is at Stratfield Saye.

At the Great Exhibition of 1851 Abbott showed a group entitled "Alexander the Great Crossing the Granicus." In 1862 he modelled for Copeland small seated figures of the Prince Consort and Wellington for mass production in "Parian" (*Art Journal*, 1852, page 211). He exhibited a number of busts at the Academy between 1829 and 1867, including those of Dr. Solomon Herschell (1838); Thomas Blizard (1840), now at the Royal College of Surgeons; Lord Raglan (1857) and Miss Maria Dickson (1858).

ABRAHAM, CHARLES J.
b. 1816

He was the son of an architect named Robert Abraham and attended the Royal Academy Schools in 1833 (Royal Academy Archives). In 1841 he carved in stone "an admirably executed statue" of the Duke of Wellington for J. N. Franklyn. This work which, with its pedestal, was 14 ft. high, was erected by Mr. Franklyn on the lawn in front of his house at Henbury Hill, near Bristol (*Gentleman's Magazine*, 1841, Vol. II, page 407).

ABRAHAM, NICHOLAS
fl. 1678–1688

He signs the magnificent monument with its kneeling life-size figures of Mr. and Mrs. Langdon, 1678, at St. Martin by Looe, Cornwall. In 1688 he obeyed the summons of the London Masons' Company to appear before them as "a foreigner of the Mason's trade" and "to be sworn of the company." His son, Nicholas Abraham the Younger, was apprenticed to Thomas Shadbolt and died in 1727 (Archives, Masons' Company).

ADAMS, GEORGE GAMON
b. 1821, *d.* 1898

He attended the Royal Academy Schools in 1840 on the recommendation of William Wyon, chief engraver to the Royal Mint, and studied there both as a sculptor and as a medallist. In the same year he won a Silver Medal from the Academy, and in 1841 exhibited a medallion of "Melpomene." In 1844 he showed a statue of "An Ancient Briton" at Westminster Hall. *The Literary Gazette* (1844, page 483) called this "a capital figure for an aspirant, great decision in the muscular development, as well as in character and drawing," adding that "Mr. Adams has done this well, but he'll live to do better."

In 1845 another competition was held for sculpture for the new Palace of Westminster and Adams submitted a work entitled "The Contest between the Minstrel and the Nightingale." The *Art Union* (1845, page 258) thought this had "much grace and elegance," although the effect was "in some degree diminished by the lines formed by the arms of the figure."

In the following year Adams went to Rome where he studied under J. Gibson (q.v.), but by 1847 he was back in England, for in that year he won the Royal Academy Gold Medal for his group of "The Murder of the Innocents." This was one of the works which he showed at the Great Exhibition of 1851, the others being "The Combat of Centaurs and Lapithae" and a "Figure With a Torch."

In 1852 Adams was the sculptor chosen to take the death-mask of the Duke of Wellington. From this he executed a marble bust which was apparently very successful, for the second Duke wrote to say that it was "considered by myself and those gentlemen who knew him best, as well as by his servants, as the best by far that has appeared, and we are obliged to you for thus making a likeness which hereafter will be considered as authentic."

(Wellesley's *Iconography of the First Duke of Wellington*.)

Adams carved a number of public statues of unequal merit, the one of General Napier in Trafalgar Square being described by the *Art Journal* (1862, page 98) "as perhaps the worst piece of sculpture in England." For the Baroness Burdett Coutts he made a number of red-marble pedestals each with a white marble bas-relief set in front, the object of the latter being to represent an appropriate scene from the life of the person whose bust was to stand on the pedestal. Three of these pedestals, including the one intended for the bust of Sir Francis Burdett, which shows him arriving at the Traitors' Gate in a wherry, are in the possession of the writer; another is at Stratfield Saye.

Adams signs the monument with a portrait-medallion to Augustus de Burgh, 1864, at West Drayton, Middlesex. As a medallist he designed and cut a number of medals, including the prize ones for the Great Exhibition of 1851, the funeral medal of the Duke of Wellington, and that of the S.P.C.A. in 1880. He exhibited at the Royal Academy, 1841–1885, and at the British Institution, 1864–1865. Plaster-casts of his busts of the Prince Consort, Lord Brougham, Sir Henry Havelock, Sir Charles Napier, Lord Palmerston, Lord Seaton, Sir Harry Smith, and Sumner, Archbishop of Canterbury, are in the National Portrait Gallery. (Various references *Art Union*, *Art Journal* and *Builder*.)

STATUES, etc.

1851	Duke of Wellington	Norwich
1856	General Sir Charles Napier	St. Paul's Cathedral
1856	General Sir Charles Napier	Trafalgar Square
1858	The Good Shepherd	For St. Stephen's, Westminster
1860	Sir William Napier	St. Paul's Cathedral
1862	Richard Cobden	Stockport
1862	Night	Exhibited International Exhibition, 1862
1866	Lord Seaton	Devonport
1868	Admiral Sir Charles Napier	St. Paul's Cathedral
1868	Youth Diving	Sold Christie's, 23 April, 1900
1871	Hugh McNeile, Dean of Ripon	St. George's Hall, Liverpool
1875	Music's Martyr	For Mr. Greenall of Walton Hall, Lancs

BUSTS

1849	Sir Harry Smith	United Service Club, London
1850	Viscount Gough	National Portrait Gallery (plaster-cast)
1852	Duke of Wellington	Corsham Court, Wilts
1852	Duke of Wellington	Stratfield Saye, Hants (replicas possession Viscount Hardinge and Marquess of Exeter)
1853	Sir Charles Napier	Scottish National Portrait Gallery
1853	Duke of Wellington	Stratfield Saye, Hants (bronze)
1855	William Brown	St. George's Hospital
1855	Lord Clyde	National Portrait Gallery (plaster-cast)
1855	Sir John Pennefather	Chelsea Hospital
1855	Sir William Napier	Scottish National Portrait Gallery
1855	Duke of Beaufort	Badminton, Glos
1855	Sir William Napier	National Portrait Gallery
1861	Lord Charles Wellesley	Apsley House, London
1861	Lord Clyde	Scottish National Portrait Gallery
1863	Lord Seaton	United Service Club, London
1864	Sumner, Archbishop of Canterbury	Exhibited Royal Academy
1867	Lord Palmerston	Exhibited Royal Academy
1869	Baroness Burdett Coutts	Possession author
1869	Lord Brougham	Guildhall (destroyed by enemy action, 1940)
1876	Thomas Proctor	Mansion House, Bristol
1878	Lord Cottesloe	Exhibited Royal Academy
1882	Second Duke of Wellington	Stratfield Saye, Hants
1888	Duke of Cambridge	Windsor Castle
?	Samuel Graves	Walker Art Gallery, Liverpool

MONUMENTS

1856	Capt. Thompson	St. Paul's Cathedral
1862	Sir Duncan MacDougall	St. Paul's Cathedral
1882	Hon. and Rev. Gerald Wellesley	Stratfield Saye, Hants

ADDISON, ROBERT

He was described in 1726 as "a freemason of King's Meaburn" when he made the font for Bampton Church, Westmorland (M. E. Noble's *History of Bampton*, chapter xi).

ADKINS, JOHN, see ATKINS, JOHN

ADRON, WILLIAM
fl. 1792–1838

He may be the son of "William Adron, mason",

of King Street, Golden Square, who is listed in the Westminster poll-book for 1748. Adron received £220 for marble chimney-pieces for Glevering Hall, Suffolk, in 1792 (Archives, Soane Museum) and, in 1812, £314 for chimney-pieces for Longleat (Archives, Marquess of Bath). In 1825 and 1826 he and his son Charles were employed on decorative work at Buckingham Palace (P.R.O. Works 5/125). Between 1810 and 1813 he was paid £318 by the Duke of Bridgewater for chimney-pieces for Ashridge Park (Archives, Lord Brownlow).

As a statuary Adron is uninspired, though the details of his tablets are carefully carved. His best work commemorates Henry Bewes, 1793, at Duloe, Cornwall, which has a relief of a woman mourning by a pillar bearing a portrait-medallion of the dead man. Other signed works by Adron (although the last three may be by his son Charles who assisted his father) include those to William Golding, 1800, in Southwark Cathedral; Thomas Manning, 1805, at Diss, Norfolk; Sir James Musgrave, 1814, at North Leigh, Oxon; Aretas Akers, 1816, at Yalding, Kent; Thomas Easton, 1835, at Ryton, Durham; Clare Thornhill, 1836, at Riddlesworth, Norfolk; and Major-General Adye, 1838, in Woolwich Parish Church.

ADYE, or ADY, THOMAS
fl. 1730–1753

From 1737 until 1744 he held the post of sculptor to the Society of Dilettanti, for which he carved a ballot-box in 1738. This was the so-called "Bacchus' Tomb" in which the books and papers of the Society were kept (Cust's *History of the Society of Dilettanti*, page 31).

When the Mansion House was being furnished in 1752, Adye submitted estimates for various lamp-stands, "six rich carved frames with looking-glasses," and "six brackets richly carved." These do not seem to have been accepted, though he was paid later in the year for "atlases and globes of glass for lights" (City Corporation MSS., Mansion House Box 2, Nos. 644 and 663).

In 1742 he made the marble bust of the seventh Earl of Westmorland. There are two signed versions of this work, one at West Wycombe Park and another in the Victoria and Albert Museum. The terra-cotta model of the base, which is also signed is in the possession of the Earl Fortescue, of Ebrington Park, Gloucestershire; this has Lord Westmorland's arms in front and trophies of "War" and "The Arts" on each side.

Adye's monuments are of first-rate importance and all have large medallion portraits either unveiled or held by a cherub. The grandest are those which commemorate Charles Sergison, 1732, at Cuckfield, Sussex, and William Mitchell, 1745, at Fowlmere, Cambs. The former has a life-size figure of "Truth," who sits on a sarcophagus, a mirror in one hand while the other supports one side of the medallion of Sergison, the other side being held by a cherub. The latter, an even larger work, is of practically the same design, although in this case the seated figure represents Mitchell's widow. Other signed works by Adye include those to Hugo Raymond, 1737, at Beckenham, Kent; Lane Harrison, 1740, at Perivale, Middlesex; and Humphrey Hall, 1742, at Bengeo, Herts.

The sculptor apparently left his widow badly off, for in 1762 she had to apply for financial assistance to the Society of Artists (Archives, Society of Artists).

AGLIO, AUGOSTINO
fl. 1831–1838

He was the son of Agostino Aglio, of 36, Newman Street, a painter who exhibited at the Royal Academy, 1807–1834.

In 1831 the younger Aglio received a Silver Isis Medal from the Society of Arts for a bust, while in the following year he exhibited a "bust of a gentleman" at the Manchester Academy.

AIREY, —, of Kendal

Signs a well-carved marble tablet to Anne Stewardson, 1815, in Kendal Parish Church, Westmorland.

ALCOTT, JOHN, of Coventry
fl. 1820–1850

He was presumably the son of "Mr. Alcott, mason of Coventry," whose wife died in 1803 (*Monthly Magazine*, 1803, Part II, page 387), and who was employed from 1796 until 1802 on the rebuilding of Arbury, Warwickshire, where he carved a great number of Gothic Strawberry Hill pinnacles, panels, coats of arms, etc., in stone for both the exterior and interior (Newdegate Archives).

John Alcott, who had yards at Coventry and Rugby, signs a number of tablets, mostly Gothic in design. They include those to the Rev. Arthur Mill, 1831, at Over Whitacre, Warwick; Maria Powys, 1833, at Achurch, Northants; the Rev. Henry Walpole, 1840, at Winslow, Bucks; and Thomas Eagle, 1847, at Alsley, Warwick.

ALKIN, or ALKEN, SEFFERIN, of London
fl. 1744–1783

In 1744 he was working at Stourhead, Wiltshire, where he was paid £187 for decorative carving. In 1753 he received an order from Sir Richard Hoare for a marble chimney-piece which cost £67 16s., but this was destroyed when Stourhead was burnt down in the early part of the present century.

In the same year Alkin was paid £59 for a chimney-piece by Mr. Arnold, a partner in Hoare's Bank, while in 1754 he received £67 for work in connexion with the house Mr. Henry Hoare was building at Clapham (Archives, Hoare's Bank). Also in 1754 he made "a richly carved pier-glass" for Lady Dungarvon, Henry Hoare's daughter, which was sent to her home at Marston House, Somerset (Archives, Stourhead).

In the Fitzwilliam papers there are payments to Alkin in 1750 and again in 1774 for unspecified work at Milton Hall, near Peterborough. In 1757 he was employed at St. Margaret's, Westminster. A pamphlet, written four years later and dealing with the repairs carried out in the church, notes that "directly under the window is placed in a square moulding our Saviour at Emaus (*sic*), represented in *basso-relievo* and well executed by Mr. Alkin, of St. Anne's Westminster, from the famous painting by Titian." In 1759 Alkin carved capitals for Longford Castle and was paid £50 8s. for six Portland stone "termes," which can still be seen in the garden (Archives, Earl of Radnor).

In 1770 he was at Blenheim Palace making chimney-pieces (British Museum, Ad. MS. 41133), while from 1777 until 1783 he was working at Somerset House, carving five "fronts of Corinthian capitals to pilasters," and, in 1778, twelve more "fronts" in Portland stone, for which he received £117. In 1781 he was paid £261 for "twenty-nine faces in Portland stone of composite capitals" (Building Accounts, Somerset House, R.I.B.A. Library), and he also carved a number of wooden chimney-pieces for the interior of the building (P.R.O., A.O.1/2495).

In 1767 Sir William Chambers, writing to Lord Charlemont about the furnishing of "Marino," the latter's seaside villa near Dublin, informs him that "Alkin has carved one of the little heads for the corner of the doors of the medal-cases. It is very fine, but as he tells me that he cannot do them under three guineas and a half a head, I have stopped his further progress till I hear from your Lordship." Later in the same letter Chambers says: "Alkin I have set about a head of Plato to match that of Homer" (*Historical Manuscripts Commission*, Earl of Charlemont, Vol.1, page 283).

In Mortimer's *Universal Directory* for 1763 Alkin is listed as living in Broad Street. He may have died in 1783, for all payments for work done at Somerset House after that date are made to his son Samuel (q.v.).

ALKIN, or ALKEN, SAMUEL
b. 1756.

Son of Jefferin Alkin (q.v.), he was born on 22 October, 1756, and attended the Royal Academy Schools in 1769, winning a Silver Medal in 1773 (Royal Academy Archives). Ten years later he received £151 for "sixteen composite capitals in Portland stone for the east front of the west return building" of Somerset House. In 1784 he carved in the same material nine goats' heads above the windows of the principal floor of the building, and he also carried out a good deal of wood-carving for the interior (Building Accounts, Somerset House; R.I.B.A. Library).

ALLCOTT, or ALCOT, JOSEPH
fl. 1796–1815

He began life as a carpenter and was sent to Stoke Park to prepare wooden pillars for the Italian artists to cover with scagliola, but being an ingenious man he watched the workmen and soon learnt the secret of the process. "He then obtained a piece of marble and imitated it so well as to please the architect (Wyatt), more than what had been done by the Italians" (*Builder*, 1845, page 50).

Allcott now set up on his own account as a maker of scagliola. In 1796 he was paid £70 for twenty scagliola columns of "yellow antique marble," and £14 for four "of jasper" for Arbury, Warwickshire. In a letter to Sir Roger Newdegate, written in 1799, Allcott tells him that he has "received an order from his Grace the Duke of Bridgewater for an imitation of a very fine porphyry table in his Grace's possession." In the same year he made a chimney-piece for Arbury with "twenty small Doric flutes in each column" and a year later the porphyry columns for the saloon chimney-piece (Newdegate Archives).

In 1811 the Earl of Coventry paid Allcott £180 for scagliola columns for Coventry House, Piccadilly (Archives, Earl of Coventry), and four years later he made the noble columns with their elaborate composite capitals for the entrance-hall of Goodwood, Sussex (Mason's *Goodwood*, page 7).

ALLEN, —

He signs the monument to Sir Thomas Allen, 1681, at Finchley, Middlesex. This large work is 8 ft. high, with Corinthian pillars and an open pediment with an urn in the centre. The only craftsman of this name who was a member of the Masons' Company at the time was Peter Allen, so the monument is possibly his work.

Peter Allen, who became free by redemption in 1674, had a son Theophilus. The latter was

PLATE I

JAMES ANNIS
Sir George Fettiplace, 1743, Swinbrook, Oxon.

JOHN BACON THE YOUNGER
William Markham, Archbishop of York, 1813,
Windsor Castle.

JOHN BACON THE ELDER
George III, 1775, Windsor Castle.

PLATE II

JOHN BUSHNELL
William Ashburnham, 1675, Ashburnham, Sussex.

E. H. BAILY
Viscount Brome, 1837, Linton, Kent.

apprenticed to John Thomson (q.v.) in 1686, but did not become free until 1694, when a "General Search" was made by the Masons' Company.

ALLEN, —, of Plymouth
fl. 1795–1802

He signs a few tablets in Devon, the best of which commemorate James Luce, 1795, and Sir Thomas Byard, 1798, both in St. Budeaux Parish Church; and William Forbes, 1802, at Plympton.

ALLEN, JAMES, of Bristol
fl. 1756–1780

His tablets are well carried out, the design in most cases being the conventional one of a semi-urn set against a pyramid. Signed examples of his work commemorate Ann Taylor, 1765, in St. Mary Redcliffe, Bristol; Priscilla Colley, 1775, at Barnstaple, Devon; and Samuel Smith, 1775, at Powick, Worcestershire.

Allen became a Freeman of Bristol on 23 February, 1756, by marriage with Ann, daughter of John Weaver, gentleman. He was dead by 18 September, 1780, the date on which his son James became a Freeman of Bristol. It is presumably the younger Allen who signs the tablet to John Bennett, 1780, at Camerton, Somerset. James Allen the younger became a bankrupt in 1793; he was living in 1810.

(Bristol City Archives and Directories.)

ALLEN, WILLIAM, of Norwich
fl. 1820–1845

According to the *New Monthly Magazine* (1827, Part III, page 405), he was responsible for the monument to the Rev. Charles Chapman, designed by Arthur Browne and erected in St. Peter Mancroft, Norwich, in 1826.

ALLWOOD, THOMAS, or ALWOOD
fl. 1769–1772

He attended the Royal Academy Schools in 1769, and between 1771 and 1772 exhibited three unnamed busts at the Society of Artists. In the latter year he was elected a Fellow of the Society.

ANDERSON, —
fl. 1760–1770

Between 1760 and 1770 he did a great deal of decorative carving at Penicuick House, Midlothian (private information). A "Mr. Anderson" (who may be the same person) exhibited at the Free Society of Artists in 1761 "a tripod, from an original design of Mr. Stuart's."

ANDERSON, DAVID
b. 1804?, *d.* 1847

He was a self-taught Perthshire sculptor who had a considerable local success with his statue of "Tam O'Shanter." In 1847 he went to Liverpool to exhibit his groups in stone of "Tam O'Shanter and Kirkton Jean" and "The Parting Between Watty and Meg," but died of typhus there in October of the same year. The *Gentleman's Magazine* (1847, Vol. II, page 668), considered him "a man of great ability as an artist," while the *Liverpool Mercury* (October, 1847), in its obituary, stated that "like most men of genius he was modest, retiring, plain and unassuming."

Anderson was buried at Perth. A number of his groups illustrating Scottish poems, including Scott's "Last Minstrel" and "The Highland Drover," Burns's "Three Jolly Boys," and Alexander Wilson's "Watty and Meg," now stand in the grounds of Fingask Castle, near Perth.

ANDERSON, EDWARD
b. 1696, *d.* 1781

He was the son of Edward Anderson (1673–1749), of Chelsea, farmer, and was apprenticed in 1720 to Benjamin Denny, "citizen and mason of London." He became free in 1731 and set up for himself at the "Horse-ferry near Chelsea" (Archives, Masons' Company). Between 1747 and 1749 he was employed on stonework for the theatre at Surgeons' Hall (Archives, Royal College of Surgeons) and a year later became Master of the Masons' Company.

It was during Anderson's term of office that the Company began to go downhill, as in their Court Book for that year is a note that it was to be "a frugal dinner next election day and to have neither ladies or musick." In 1751 Anderson was appointed churchwarden of Chelsea Old Church. Shortly after this he was appointed Master Mason to Chelsea Hospital and later held the same post for three of the Royal Palaces (Royal Kalendar).

In 1778 he was paid £157 for three stone obelisks for the use of the observatory at Richmond (P.R.O. Works 5/66). He died on 17 June three years later, and was buried in Chelsea Old Church, where a slab of touch in the floor of the porch commemorated him and his father. Here he was described as mason "to His Majesty's Palaces at Hampton Court, Richmond and Kew."

ANDERSON, WILLIAM, of Perth
fl. 1845–1859

He was the son of David Anderson (q.v.) and showed at the Great Exhibition of 1851 a figure of a Highlander throwing the "putting-stone," while on the pedestal were reliefs of figures "further illustrative of Highland games" (*Exhibition Catalogue*, Vol. II, page 831).

In 1853 Anderson carved the bust of Peel for the memorial erected at Forfar (*Builder*, 1853, page 152). In the following year he executed a heroic statue of Burns, which he presented to his native town, and which was described by the *Builder* (1854, page 295) as of "manly make." It now stands above a public-house in County Place.

Anderson's statues of Prince Charles Edward and Flora Macdonald, carved about 1845, are in the grounds of Fingask Castle, near Perth.

ANDREWS, JAMES, of Olney
b. 1735, *d.* 1817

When William Cowper lived at Olney, Andrews taught him drawing. The poet called him "my Michelangelo," and in a letter to Mr. Newton said that "James Andrews pays me many compliments on my success in the art of drawing, but I have not yet the vanity to think myself qualified to furnish your apartment" (Wright's *Town of Cowper*, page 32).

Andrews signs a number of local monuments and tablets in Buckinghamshire, the most important commemorating Alexander Small (*d.* 1752) at Clifton Reynes. The fine terra-cotta bust of Small, which is set on the monument against a pyramid, is known from the parish records to have been executed by P. Scheemakers (q.v.).

Other signed tablets and tombstones by Andrews include those to Ann Buck, 1776, and Bartholomew Higgins, 1778, both at Weston-Underwood; William Lambry, 1779, at Olney; John Campion, 1787, at Sherrington; Charles Small, 1787, at Clifton Reynes; and Thomas Skevington, 1793, at Newton Blossomville.

ANDREWS, SAMUEL, of Wisbech
fl. 1801–1840

His tablets are of provincial workmanship, the best commemorating M. Smith, 1801, at Yaxley, Hunts; Robert Wing, 1824, at Walsoken, Norfolk; and James Smith, 1835, at Wisbech, Cambs. In Yaxley Church there is also a large wall-tablet to Captain William Papp, 1797. This has an urn and military trophies and is signed by "S. Andrews, of Yaxley," who is presumably identical with S. Andrews, of Wisbech.

ANGELINI, GIUSEPPE
b. 1742, *d.* 1811

Wilfred Whitten, in a footnote to his edition of J. T. Smith's *Nollekens and His Times* (Vol. II,

page 58), says that Angelini was born in 1735, but when the latter joined the Royal Academy Schools in 1772 he gave his age as thirty, which would make the year of his birth 1742 (Royal Academy Archives).

Angelini was a Roman sculptor who had studied under Cavaceppi and who came to England about 1770. As already stated, he joined the Royal Academy Schools and in 1775 exhibited a group entitled "Chastity Rejecting Profane Love" at the Society of Artists. He was employed by J. Nollekens (q.v.) and was often mistaken for his master from "his dashing method of dressing in a fashionable coat and red morocco slippers." One of the works executed by him in England was a life-size marble group of the Virgin and Child, but he was unable to sell it and was forced to dispose of it by means of a lottery (op. cit., page 58).

Angelini was apparently in financial difficulties by 1777, for in that year he applied for assistance to the Royal Academy, who granted him a "charitable donation" of twenty-five guineas (Royal Academy Archives). By 1787 he was back in Rome, where he modelled for Wedgwood various works, including "Apollo With the Muse Erato," "Pluto Carrying Off Proserpine," "Victory," "Mercury" and "The Whole Fable of Meleager" (Meteyard's *Wedgwood*, Vol. II, page 591).

ANNIS, JAMES
b. c. 1709, *d.* 1775

He was the brother of John Annis (q.v.), to whom he was apprenticed in 1723 and whom he succeeded as mason to the Ironmongers' Company in 1740, ten years after gaining his freedom. He also worked as a mason for St. Bartholomew's Hospital, receiving a total sum of £361 between 1754 and 1767 (Hospital Archives).

Annis was a competent statuary, but his monument to Sir George Fettiplace, 1743, at Swimbrook, Oxon, is of real importance, for the modelling and cutting of the portrait-bust is magnificent and not unworthy of a Rysbrack. He also signs a monument, with a cherub unveiling a medallion portrait, to Zachariah Foxall, in St. Botolph's, Aldersgate.

In 1756 Annis married Sarah Shapman, of the parish of St. Dionis Backchurch (Parish Register). His yard was in Aldersgate Street, and he was Renter Warden of the Masons' Company in 1764, Upper Warden in 1765, and Master a year later. His death is noted in the Court Book of the Company. In 1748 he took as an apprentice his nephew William, son of John Annis.

ANNIS, JOHN
b. c. 1699, *d.* 1740.

He was the son of John Annis of Beckenham and was apprenticed to William Holland (q.v.) in 1714. He was free in 1721 and soon set up on his own account in Aldersgate Street (Archives, Masons' Company). As a mason he was employed at the College of Physicians in Warwick Lane in 1727 (Archives, Royal College of Physicians). He was mason to the Ironmonger's Company from 1730 until his death ten years later, as the payment for 1740 is made to his executrix, Elizabeth Annis. For the Company he built three houses in Old Street in 1731 (Company Archives).

Annis signs a number of monuments. That to William Lytton Strode, 1732, at Knebworth, Herts, has two small kneeling figures each side of a sarcophagus, while above is a relief of a family group. The monument to John Styleman, 1734, at Bexley, Kent, is a large architectural work, while one commemorating Thomas Hawes and family, *c.* 1740, at Leyton, Essex, has a broken pediment on which cherubs recline. It is possible, however, that this last monument may be the work of his brother James (q.v.).

ANSPACH, the Margravine of
b. 1750, *d.* 1828

She was Elizabeth, daughter of the fourth Earl of Berkeley, and married the sixth Earl of Craven in 1767. A fortnight after the latter's death in 1791 she became the wife of Christian, Margrave of Brandenburg-Anspach.

In 1806 the Margravine received the Silver Medal from the Society of Arts for a marble bas-relief of her second husband, who had died in the previous year. An illustration of this work forms the frontispiece of the second volume of her autobiography, published in 1826.

ARCHER, FREDERICK SCOTT
b. 1814, *d.* 1857

He was the second son of a butcher in Bishop's Stortford, and as a young man worked as an assistant to a silversmith of Leadenhall Street, named Massey. In 1836 he attended the Royal Academy Schools on the recommendation of Edward Hawkins (Royal Academy Archives) and in 1844 exhibited "Alfred the Great With the Book of Common Law" at Westminster Hall. The *Builder* (1844, page 367) considered it "a very good work," a view not shared by the *Literary Gazette* (1844, page 466), who considered that "to fulfil our idea of Alfred the figure should be grand and powerful, but Mr. Archer seems to think that a tame, spiritless specimen of vulgarity will do."

In 1850 Archer carved the monument to Lady Albert Conyngham for Mickelham Church, Surrey, which was illustrated in the *Gentleman's Magazine* of that year (Part II, page 510). He exhibited at the Royal Academy, 1836–1851, showing, among other works, a group entitled "A Young Briton Receiving Instruction"; a statue of Gertrude Hanson (1851); and busts of Sir George Smart (1839), the Dean of Manchester (1848) and the Marquess of Northampton (1850).

Archer's chief claim to fame is based, not on his work as a sculptor, but as the inventor of the collodion process in photography, but his activities in that field are, of course, outside the scope of this book. He died in May, 1857, and was buried in Kensal Green Cemetery. A subscription list was opened for the benefit of his family, who had been left ill-provided for, and over £600 was raised; but as his widow died in the following year, the money was used for the benefit of his children. The latter were also granted a pension of £50 by the Crown, on the grounds that their father's photographic discoveries had been of no benefit to him, although they had been extremely profitable to others.

(Various references: *Art Journal, Builder,* etc.)

ARMINGER, WILLIAM
b. 1752, *d.* 1793

He was born on 22 November, 1752, and attended the Royal Academy Schools in 1774 (Royal Academy Archives). J. T. Smith (*Nollekens and His Times,* Vol. I, page 51) describes Arminger as "a raw-boned man, full six feet in height," who came to Nollekens one day saying that he was a "cutter of funeral inscriptions come from the City of Norwich, and would be glad of a job." Nollekens took him into his employment and allowed him to cut the inscription for the monument to Goldsmith, which was to be erected in Westminster Abbey. Arminger carried this out so well that Nollekens gave him regular work, and he afterwards cut many of his employer's busts.

Arminger later set up for himself as a carver of tablets for chimney-pieces. He died in 1793 and was buried at Paddington (Lyson's *Environs of London,* Vol. IV, page 603). After his death Messrs. Greenwood held a sale of his effects on 6 March, 1794, disposing, among other works, of the following chimney-piece tablets: "Aurora, stained upon marble"; "Adam and Eve Conducted by St. Michael Out of Paradise"; and "The Slaughter of the Innocents." (Sale Catalogue, Victoria and Albert Museum.)

ARNALD, SEBASTIAN WYNDHAM
b. 1806

He was the son of George Arnald, A.R.A. (1763–1841), the landscape painter, and attended the Royal Academy Schools in 1824, winning the Gold Medal in 1831 for his group of "The Massacre of the Innocents" (Royal Academy Archives). He exhibited this work, and also "War in Heaven," at Burlington House in the following year. The former was considered by the *Literary Gazette* (1832, page 395) as "not a subject for the public eye," as it could "be viewed by the artist or amateur only as an academic exercise"; the latter, however, was described by the *Library of Fine Arts* (Vol. I, page 430) as "a composition in no way discreditable to the English school."

Arnald exhibited at the Academy, 1823–1841, showing both ideal works and busts, including those of G. Garrard, A.R.A. (1828); the Rev. E. Irvine (1831); and S. T. Coleridge (1836). At the Birmingham Society of Artists in 1834 he exhibited "The Iron Age," "Bacchus" and "Design from Revelations."

He later seems to have abandoned sculpture for painting, as he did not exhibit at the Academy for some years after 1840, and when he did finally send in a work in 1846 it was a picture of "Christian and Pliable in the Slough of Despond."

ASHCROFT, EDMUND, of Liverpool
fl. 1819–1831

He may have been the son of "Mr. Henry Ashcroft, of Liverpool, stonemason," who died in 1810 at the age of seventy (*Gentleman's Magazine*, 1810, Part II, page 493). He signs a large wall-tablet at Rostherne, Cheshire, to Thomas Hewitt, 1820.

ASHMORE, JOHN

In 1662 he was paid £4 7s. for the font in Wirksworth Church, Derby. This is described by Cox (*Churches of Derbyshire*, Vol. II, page 552) as of "octagon design and ornamented with patterns of unusual style, having more resemblance to Egyptian art, than anything that pertains to either Gothic or Renaissance."

ASHTON, HENRY, of London
fl. 1813–1814

He was the son of Robert Ashton the Elder (q.v.), and from 1813 until 1814 was the mason responsible for building 18, Park Lane.

A "Thomas Ashton, of London," who signs a monument to James Bennett, 1815, at North Cadbury, Somerset, is perhaps a member of the same family.

ASHTON, ROBERT, the Elder
fl. 1770–1792

He was first the pupil and later the assistant of W. Tyler, R.A. (q.v.), and together they sign a number of monuments. All these are large and important works and include those to Martin Folkes (died 1754: erected 1783), in Westminster Abbey; Elizabeth Yorke, 1779, at Marchwiel, Flint; William Pym, 1788, at Sandy, Beds; and William Franks, 1790, in the parish church of Kentish Town.

Ashton also carved chimney-pieces and in 1788 supplied several to the Duke of Devonshire for Chiswick House, including those for the drawing-room (£94), the dining-room (£73), the Duchess's dressing-room (£73), the Duke's dressing-room (£40), and the Duke's bedroom (£36). In 1790 he made a chimney-piece for John Weyland, of Woodeaton Hall (Notebook, Soane Museum).

In 1788 Ashton put in a tender for building the Freemasons' Tavern, quoting as his figure the sum of £7,283. As the lowest tender was under £5,000 he very naturally did not get the work, although he was afterwards employed on decorative carving for the building from 1791 until 1792 (Freemasons' Archives).

ASHTON, ROBERT, the Younger
fl. 1795–1836

He was the son of Robert Ashton the Elder (q.v.), and in 1813 was employed by Lord Ashburnham at his house in Dover Street, for which he may also have carved a chimney-piece (Ashburnham Archives).

The younger Ashton signs a number of monuments and tablets, the best being that commemorating Christian Gosselin, 1824, at Faversham, Kent, which has a finely cut relief. The tablet to Anne Norton, 1796, at Little Gaddesden, Herts, has a relief of a mourning woman seated by a sarcophagus, a broken lily in her hand. Other signed memorials by Ashton include those to Mrs. Dinwiddie, 1795, in the Grosvenor Chapel; John Bailey, 1813, at Great Wenham, Suffolk; the Rev. B. Barnard, at Peakirk, Northants; Earl Beauchamp, 1816, at Madresfield, Worcs; William Edmonds, 1818, at Wendover, Bucks; the Houghton family, 1818, in St. Botolph's, Aldersgate; and Mrs. Zenogle, 1836, at Farnham Royal, Bucks.

ASSITER, THOMAS,
of Maidstone
d. 1826

His tablets are good for a provincial statuary, the best being that to Sir John Twisden, Bart., 1810, at East Malling, Kent, which has a relief not unlike the work of John Bacon the Younger (q.v.). Other signed tablets by Assiter in Kent include those to William Jewell, 1778, at Seal; William Bowles, 1814, at Aylesford; William Bryant, 1816, at Maidstone; and Robert Foote, 1818, at Boughton Monchelsea.

Assiter was also employed by Lord Romney on mason's work during the rebuilding of "The Mote," near Maidstone (Building Accounts, Maidstone Museum). He was buried in the graveyard of Maidstone Parish Church.

ATHOW, JOHN, of Norwich
b. 1742, *d.* 1822

He lived in the precincts of Norwich Cathedral and in 1788 married Mrs. Waller, widow of a linen-draper, who died in 1808 at the age of sixty-one.

Athow signs tablets in Norfolk to Thomas Wright, 1775, Kilverstone; Robert Tilyard, 1786, at Hemsby; William Bullock, 1792, at Walsingham; and the Rev. W. Enfield, 1797, in the Octagon Chapel, Norwich.

ATKINS, or ADKINS, JOHN
fl. 1761–1783

In 1761 he received a premium of £31 7s. from the Society of Arts for a bas-relief in stone entitled "Regulus Returning to Carthage," and exhibited the work in the same year at the Society of Free Artists (Archives, Society of Arts).

Atkins was a pupil of L. F. Roubiliac (q.v.) and his name is noted on the list of those attending the latter's funeral in 1762. He then became assistant to J. Wilton (q.v.), and according to J. T. Smith (*Nollekens and His Times*, Vol. II, page 110) it was Atkins and Nathaniel Smith who modelled and carved the statuary on Somerset House for which Wilton received the payment and the credit.

ATKINS, ROBERT
fl. 1800–1815

His yard was in Charlotte Street, Brompton, and he signs a very pretty little tablet at Buntingford, Herts, to Edward Saunders, 1800. Another, commemorating Major Chambers, 1815, is in Lowestoft Parish Church, Suffolk.

ATKINS, WILLIAM

In 1720 he made several chimney-pieces for the Duke of Wharton's house, "The Wilderness" (Archives, Lord Braye).

ATKINS, WILLIAM

In 1761 he made a marble chimney-piece for the second Earl of Ashburnham which he sent down to Ashburnham Place, Sussex, with his man, Joseph Gilliam. The latter was paid £2 10s. "subsistance allowance" during the time he spent erecting this in the drawing-room (Ashburnham Archives).

ATKINS, WILLIAM, of Ludlow
fl. 1800–1817

He signs a wall-tablet to Richard Harper, 1817, at Ashford Bowdler, Salop.

ATKINSON, CHARLES,
of London
fl. 1750–1770

At the time of the erection of Holkham Hall, Norfolk, Atkinson was responsible for most of the chimney-pieces. He also signs the large monument, 20 ft. high, of the Earl of Leicester, 1760, at Tittleshall in the same county, although the busts of Lord and Lady Leicester which form part of it are the work of L. F. Roubiliac (q.v.).

According to the *London Directory* of 1768, Atkinson's yard was in Leadenhall Street.

ATKINSON, JOHN, of London
fl. 1800–1830

His yard was at 100, Goswell Street, and he and his partner, Thomas Whitfield Browne, were the masons for building Salters' Hall, 1823–1827. Their tender of £17,362 was the lowest submitted, although in the end, owing to various alterations and additions, they exceeded this figure by over £10,000. As early as August, 1823, the Clerk of the Company wrote to them to express the great dissatisfaction of the Building Committee "at the extreme slowness and want of energy with which they had hitherto proceeded." In addition to the building itself, they were also responsible for most of the carved stonework, and for the marble chimney-pieces for the Court Room, dining-room, breakfast-room and drawing-room (Company's Archives).

The partners also built the New Hall of Christ's Hospital in 1824, where they also executed all the carved stonework (Archives, Christ's Hospital).

Atkinson signs tablets to Johanna Howland, 1815, at Haverhill, Suffolk, and to John Kipling, 1830, at Overstone, Northants.

ATKINSON, THOMAS,
of London
fl. 1790–1804

Between 1790 and 1804 he was working at Stourhead, Wiltshire, where he built the wings of the house and was also responsible for the decorative stone-carving. These wings were saved when the rest of the building was destroyed by fire in the early part of the present century. (Stourhead Archives.)

ATKINSON, THOMAS, of York
d. 1798

Atkinson took his son James as an apprentice in 1761, a year after he had become a Freeman of York. Another son, Joseph, had been apprenticed to Samson White, "stonecutter of York," in 1757 instead of to his father, probably because the latter at that time was classed as a "foreigner" (York City Archives).

Between 1763 and 1769 Atkinson designed the Gothic front and the gate-house of Bishopthorpe for Archbishop Drummond, and also made chimney-pieces for the drawing-room and dining-room. His monuments, which are of good provincial workmanship and carried out in coloured marbles, include those to John Dixon, 1782, in Leeds Parish Church, Yorks; Sir Henry Vane, 1794, and Lady Vane, 1795, both at Long Newton, Durham; and Elizabeth Scarisbrick, 1797, in Holy Trinity, York. In 1778 James Atkinson sent in an estimate for repaving Lincoln Cathedral with marble (Cathedral Archives).

ATKINSON, W., of London
d. 1766

From 1756 until 1759 he and his partner, Joseph Pickford (q.v.), were building the New Library at Cambridge, where they received nearly £5,000. Atkinson himself seems to have been responsible for most of the decorative stone-carving and was paid £333 for work which included "four large heads representing the Seasons, £32"; "twenty-two large festoons of fruits and flowers, £159"; and "two vases, £9" (Vice-Chancellor's Accounts). In 1765 he made the chimney-piece in the alcove bedroom at Corsham Court, Wiltshire (Methuen Archives).

Atkinson signs a large rococo monument to the Rt. Hon. Walter Cary, 1757, at Heston, Middlesex. The words "Guls. Atkinson, Londini, *fecit*" are cut on the medallion of a man mourning over an urn which forms part of the monument to Mrs. Osborne (*d.* 1798) at Fiddown, Co. Kilkenny. As the work itself is signed by Carew of Waterford, it seems possible that the medallion originally came from another of Atkinson's memorials.

After his death a sale of the contents of his studio was held at his yard in Piccadilly on 2 April, 1767. Among the lots was the bust of "Champion Dymoke." This was the model for the bust (a very fine work) on Lewis Dymoke's monument, dated 1760, in Scrivelsby Church, Lincolnshire. Other lots were "Garden terms in Portland stone 7 ft. high of Alcibiden (*sic*) and a Grecian Venus"; "bust of Lord Westmorland" and "a large and magnificent vase in Bath stone, designed by Mr. Kent." Among the furniture was "a most beautiful and magnificent table inlaid with horses' teeth and different rich marbles in fret and with a statuary marble border."

There had been a previous sale on 24 and 25 July, 1766, when among the lots sold were a "Head of Apollo"; "two side frizes (*sic*) of statuary carved with Diana's trophies"; "5 figures in Portland stone (the Stuart family) and one pedestal"; "Figures of Peace, Plenty and Cleopatra" and "a fine cast of dolphin and boys by Rysback."

AURIOL, —

In 1697 he was making statues for Chatsworth. Some of these were for the fountain, so he may have been a worker in lead (Chatsworth Building Accounts).

AUSTIN, FELIX
STATUARY AND TERRA-COTTA WORKER
fl. 1828–1850

About 1800 Van Spangen (q.v.), a Dutchman, founded a manufactory of artificial stone at Bow. He later went into partnership with a Mr. Powell, but the firm was broken up about 1828 and the moulds were purchased by Felix Austin, who set up in the New Road works to produce "artificial stone" which, according to the *Builder* (1868, page 546), was made from Portland cement, broken stone, pounded marble and coarse sand. The process proved successful, and among the works produced by Austin in this material were oriental vases (designed by S. Smirke) for the Pantheon Bazaar (1833) and a pedestal for Ironmongers' Hall (1834).

Like his predecessor, Mrs. Coade (q.v.), Austin was shrewd enough to get the leading architects and designers to work for him. Besides S. Smirke, already mentioned, he employed J. Papworth, and these two and others designed a number of large fountains, including those for the Pantheon Bazaar; for Earl Amherst, at Montreal House, Sevenoaks; and for the Earl of Shrewsbury, at Alton Towers (*Architectural Magazine*, 1834, page 295; and 1835, page 123).

As a statuary, Austin signs a number of tablets, including those to William Ruddiman, 1826, in St. John's Wood Chapel; the Countess of Athlone, 1830, at Sacombe, Herts; the Hon. Catherine Petre, 1830, at Selby, Yorks; and Lieutenant-Colonel Dashwood, 1832, at Kirklington, Oxon. About 1840 Austin went into partnership with John Seeley (q.v.) and together they sign tablets to Frances Samwell, 1841, at Upton, Northants, and to Sophia Pym, 1841, at Willian, Hertford-shire, the latter being designed by a "B. Watson."

AYRAY, ROBERT, of York

He signs the monument at St. Crux, York, commemorating Sir Tancred Robinson who was twice Lord Mayor of York and who died in 1754. This fine work has a cherub holding a medallion portrait of Sir Tancred; behind it are naval trophies and below the emblems of a Lord Mayor.

B

BACON, CHARLES

b. 1821, *d.* 1885 (?)

Bacon first exhibited at the Royal Academy as a gem-cutter when, in 1842, he showed a cornelian intaglio of "Eve," and it was not until four years later that he attended the Academy Schools on the recommendation of Alarick Watts, the poet and writer (Royal Academy Archives). In 1847 he showed a bust of his friend Watts, and in 1853 offered for sale at the British Institution a group entitled "Helen Veiled Before Paris," for which he asked five hundred guineas.

In 1861 Bacon was given the commission for a statue to be erected at Spilsby, Lincolnshire, to the memory of Sir John Franklin, the Arctic explorer. The sculptor was apparently unknown at that time, for the *Art Journal* (1861, page 29), on hearing who had been chosen for the work, asked: "Who is Mr. Bacon? We do not know of any living sculptor of that name."

In 1864 Bacon made a bust of Shakespeare for the Agricultural Hall, Islington. In 1874 Mr. Charles Oppenheim offered to present a statue of the Prince Consort to the City of London, and Bacon was chosen to execute it for a fee of £2,000. The result was the poor equestrian bronze statue at Holborn Circus, which shows the Prince, cocked hat in hand, on a prancing horse. The granite pedestal on which the work stands is 15 ft. high; on the east and west sides are seated figures of "Commerce" and "Peace," while to the north and south are bronze reliefs showing the Prince laying the foundation-stone of the Royal Exchange, and Britannia distributing awards for the 1851 Exhibition. The *Art Journal* (1874, page 61) was kind when it wrote that "on the principle that one must not too narrowly examine a gift horse, we abjure criticism."

In 1875 Bacon carved the statue of John Candlish for Sunderland. His bust of George Grote, 1855, is in Westminster Abbey, and he also executed others of Warren Stormes Hale, Lord Mayor in 1864, and the Rev. G. F. W. Mortimer, both of which are at the City of London Schools. He exhibited at the Royal Academy, 1842–1884, where his busts included those of Henry Faudel (1864); Sir George Barrow (1865); the Rt. Hon. B. S. Phillips (1866); the Duke of Edinburgh (1867); and the Bishop of Chichester (1884). Bacon probably died in 1885 as his name is no longer noted in *The Year's Art*

after that date. He was then living at the Bolton's Studios, South Kensington, London, S.W.

According to Graves's *Royal Academy Exhibitors*, a "G. Bacon" (of whom there is no other trace) showed heads of "Minerva," "Antinous" and "Ariadne" between 1846 and 1848. As his address is the same as that given for Charles Bacon, he may be a brother or some other relation (unless, of course, the "G." in the catalogue is a misprint for "C.").

BACON, JOHN, R.A.

b. 1740, *d.* 1799

He was born in Southwark on 24 November, 1740, the son of a clothworker in that district, and at the age of fourteen was apprenticed to a Mr. Crispe of Bow Churchyard. Crispe, a maker of porcelain, also had a china factory at Lambeth and it was with him that Bacon first learnt to model figures. He was so apt a pupil that he was soon able "to make all the models of 'The Deer and the Holly Tree,' 'The Bird and the Bush,' and 'The Shepherd and the Shepherdess,' which were required for his master's factory" (Allan Cunningham, *Lives of the Painters*).

In 1759 Bacon received a premium from the Society of Arts for a figure of "Peace," and between 1760 and 1778 he received ten further awards (Archives, Society of Arts). About 1767 he became a modeller for the manufactory of artificial stone which Mrs. Coade (q.v.) had just opened at Lambeth. For her he made a great variety of works, the most important being "A Tiger" for Sir Francis Bassett; "Charity" for the Marine Society of London; "Contemplation" for Dr. Lettson of Camberwell; and reliefs for Hooton Hall, Cheshire. In 1768, Bacon entered the Royal Academy Schools and removed from the City to lodgings in Wardour Street, although he still continued in Mrs. Coade's employment.

One of the first works from his chisel which caught the attention of the public was a colossal head of "Ossian," and in 1769 he won the first Gold Medal for sculpture ever awarded by the Academy for a bas-relief, entitled "Aeneas Escaping From Troy." In 1770 he was elected an Associate of the Royal Academy and seven years later a full member.

In 1769 Bacon was employed by Wedgwood, for whom he modelled two reliefs of "The Good of Day" and "The Good of Night." Peter Swift, Wedgwood's London agent, in a letter dated

21 March, 1769, tells his master that "Mr. Bacon brot a model of Apollo and Daphne which I have got a cast of. He asks for your future instructions, since which I have found a paper with two drawings of vases and some references for modelling— went with them tonight but did not find him at home" (Wedgwood Archives). In the Royal Collection are three Derby biscuit groups modelled by Bacon, made in 1772 and based on the picture by Zoffany of George III, Queen Charlotte and their children.

In 1770 the sculptor executed a statue of "Mars" which he showed at the Royal Academy in the following year, but which did not find a purchaser. He accordingly presented it, with a companion statue of "Venus," to the Society of Arts in 1778 and was awarded their Gold Medal. It was the statue of "Mars" that so impressed Benjamin West and caused him to exclaim: "If this is his first essay, what will this man be when he arrives at maturity?" It also attracted the attention of the Archbishop of York, who arranged for Bacon to model a bust of the King for the Hall of Christ Church, Oxford. The bust was so successful, and the King so delighted with it, that he ordered another to be made for the University of Göttingen, while a third was subsequently executed for the Prince of Wales and a fourth for the Society of Antiquaries.

The King's friendship was to bear fruit later, for it was owing to his influence that Bacon received the commission, in 1779, for the monument to Chatham in Westminster Abbey. This towering mass of marble, with its picturesque magnificence and riot of figures, was greatly admired at the time of its unveiling. The *European Magazine* (1790, page 84) considered that it would "at all times remain a proof of the genius of the artist who produced it; an artist who has acquired his fame without foreign instruction or study in the schools of Italy, and who may be produced as a proof that genius is the growth of the British Isles unassisted by such aids." Cowper wrote in "The Task" that

". . . Bacon there
Gives more than female beauty to a stone
And Chatham's eloquence to marble lips."

Apparently the inscription, which the sculptor wrote himself, was not so successful, for the King remarked: "Now, Bacon, mind you do not turn author, stick to your chisel."

Bacon was now fairly launched, and from then on his career was one of unbroken prosperity. He was a shrewd, perhaps almost grasping, man of business and at one period had the audacity to propose to the government that he should execute all the national monuments at a certain percentage below the price fixed by Parliament. This extra-ordinary suggestion naturally infuriated his fellow-artists and called forth from Fuseli, the painter, the acid retort that: "If Bacon is to do all the stone-work for the Army and Navy, they ought also to give him the contract for hams and pork." It is, however, only fair to the sculptor to add that his son, J. Bacon, the Younger (q.v.), called this story "a gratuitous, unqualified falsehood" in a letter written to Peter Cunningham in 1854.

Bacon was largely a self-taught artist and was accused by his enemies of having no knowledge of the antique or ability to produce works of a classic character. In reply he modelled a head of "Jupiter" to which he carefully gave the appearance of antiquity before producing it among the connoisseurs. They were completely deceived and inquired from what ancient temple the work had come.

As a sculptor Bacon lacked the true fire of genius, but he knew what the public wanted and gave it them in full measure. According to the *New Monthly Magazine* (1816, page 27), he "was singular in never setting his draperies, but executing them according to his ideas as the work came out," while, perhaps because of his early training with Crispe, the delicately cut details of his monuments have the appearance of porcelain. The symbolism, however, is always obvious and he was too fond of repeating certain designs. The "Pelican in its Piety," for example, appears with remorseless frequency and bears out Cunningham when he says that if Bacon could think of nothing else he would fall back on what he used to call "our old friend the Pellican" (op. cit.).

In 1773 the sculptor had married a Miss Wade and moved to more commodious premises in Newman Street; his wife died in 1783 and he re-married in October of the same year, his second wife being a Miss Martha Holland. He was still living in Newman Street at the time of his death, which took place on 7 August, 1799. He was buried in Whitefield's Tabernacle, where his grave bore the following epitaph written by himself: "What I was as an artist seemed of some importance while I lived; what I really was as a believer in Jesus Christ is the only thing of importance to me now."

Of the various accounts of Bacon, the best is given in his obituary which appeared in the *Gentleman's Magazine* of 1799, and which was the work of "one who had a long and intimate acquaintance" with him. His life by Cunningham was considered by his family to be coloured by personal dislike, while the "Memoir" by Robert Cecil is over-flattering and deals more with his activities as a pillar of the Methodist Church than as a sculptor.

(Authorities cited in text: *Universal Magazine*,

1800, Part II, page 184; *Builder*, 1862, page 692, and 1863, page 167; J. T. Smith's *Nollekens and His Times*.)

STATUES AND GROUPS

1770	Mars	Presented later by the Sculptor to the Society of Arts
1770	Venus	Presented later by the Sculptor to the Society of Arts
1772	Mars	For Lord Yarborough
1775	Minerva	In Coade's show-room in that year (terracotta)
1776	Narcissus	Presented by the Sculptor to the Society of Arts
1776	Figures, reliefs, etc.	Façade of Guy's Hospital (£762) (Hospital Archives)
1778	Colossal group of Fame and Genius of England supporting the British Arms, with a festoon of laurel and the insignia of the Order of the Garter. (R.I.B.A. Library. MS. 335A)	Somerset House (£376 10s.)
1778	"Two Tritons supporting British Arms, adorned with coral and other marine productions." (R.I.B.A. Library, MS. 335A)	Somerset House (£307 10s.)
1778	Sickness	Presented by the Sculptor to the Royal Academy
1782	Lord Chatham	Guildhall (£3,421 14s.)
1784	Sir William Blackstone	All Souls, Oxford
c. 1784	Hercules	Observatory, Oxford (bronze)
c. 1784	Atlas	Observatory, Oxford (bronze)
1786	Lord Rodney	Spanish Town, Jamaica (model in Victoria and Albert Museum)
1786	Henry VI	Upper Chapel, Eton College
1789	Group of George III and the River Thames	Somerset House (£2,000, bronze)
1793	Marquess Cornwallis	India Office (£525)
1795	John Howard	St. Paul's Cathedral
1796	Sir William Jones	Calcutta
1796	Samuel Johnson	St. Paul's Cathedral
1799	Sir William Jones	St. Paul's Cathedral
1799	William III	St. James's Square (finished by the sculptor's sons)

BUSTS

1770	George III	Christ Church, Oxford
1770	John Guise	Christ Church, Oxford
1770	Richard Trevor, Bishop of Durham	Christ Church, Oxford
1770	Robinson, Archbishop of Armagh	Christ Church, Oxford
1775	George III	Windsor Castle
1778	Samuel Foote	Exhibited Royal Academy
c. 1780	Inigo Jones	Carpenters' Hall
c. 1780	Sir Francis Dashwood	Mausoleum, West Wycombe, Bucks
1790	Professor Shepherd	Trinity College, Cambridge
1793	John Howard	Shrewsbury Prison
1793	Thomas, Bishop of Rochester	Westminster Abbey
1793	Duke of Portland	Mausoleum, Wentworth Woodhouse
1798	Dean Colet	St. Paul's School
1798	Marquess Cornwallis	Exhibited Royal Academy

VARIOUS

1762	Interview between Coriolanus and Volumnia	Exhibited Free Society (model in clay)
1768	A Bacchanalian	Exhibited Society of Artists
c. 1769	The Elements	Casts formerly at the Crystal Palace (four oval bas-reliefs)
1769	Aeneas Escaping from Troy	For Sir William Chambers' house, 53, Berners Street. Now Royal Society of Medicine, Henrietta Street (medallion)
1770	The Good Samaritan	Exhibited Royal Academy (bas-relief)
1770	Coat of Arms	For front of Skinners' Hall (Company's Archives)
1773	Design for his own door-plate	Exhibited Royal Academy (artificial stone)
c. 1776	Sculptures	For façade of Coade's manufactory, Lambeth (terra-cotta)
1777	Chimney-piece	For the Duke of Richmond, Goodwood
1778	Keystone	Great arch of Embankment front, Somerset House (R.I.B.A. Library, MS. 335A)
1780	Bas-relief	Carpenters' Hall (Company's Archives)
1780	Urn	For Lady Chatham, now Chevening, Kent (marble)

1784	Designs for a pediment	For Chapel of Greenwich Hospital (two models, £31 10s.) (P.R.O. Ad. MS. 86/813)
1785	Two angels	For East End of Chapel of Greenwich Hospital (£630) (P.R.O. Ad. MS. 86/816)
1789	Frieze	For doorcase of the Chapel of Greenwich Hospital (£168) (P.R.O. Ad. MS. 86/824)
1789	Clock case, with figures of "Vigilance" and "Patience"	Now at Buckingham Palace
1790	Chimney-piece	For ante-room at Fonthill (Rutter's *Fonthill Abbey*)
1792–1794	The Winds	Observatory, Oxford (reliefs)
1793	Chimney-piece	For Warren Hastings, Daylesford House (£63) (British Museum Ad. MS. 29227)
1795	Sculpture	Façade of Trinity House, Tower Hill (Richardson's *Vitruvius Britannicus*, page 7)
1797–1799	Pediment, etc.	For East India House (£2,342; completed by J. Bacon the Younger) (Company's Archives, India Office)
?	Mason Chamberlain, R.A.	National Portrait Gallery (portrait relief)
?	Chimney-piece	Pishiobury, Herts (Neale's *Views of Seats*, Vol. II)

MONUMENTS

c. 1767	Widworthy, Devon	James Marwood
c. 1770	Worcester (St. Swithin's)	Joseph Withers
1771	Westminster Abbey	Earl of Halifax
1771	Westminster Abbey	Thomas Gray
1778	Bristol (Cathedral)	Mrs. Draper
1778	Westminster Abbey	Lord Chatham (£6,000)
1779	Guy's Hospital Chapel	Thomas Guy (model at Burlington House). The Governors had a private plate of the monument engraved by Bartolozzi
1780	Salisbury (Cathedral)	Jacob Harris
1781	Macclesfield (Christ Church)	Charles Roe

1781	Warboys, Hunts	John Leman
1781	Cork, Eire	Lord Tracton
1783	Woodford, Essex	Charles Foulis
1784	Eastry, Kent	John Broadley
1784	Jersey (St. Helier)	Major Peirson
1784	Bath (Abbey)	Lady Miller
1784	Rostherne, Cheshire	Jonas Brooke
1784	Berkhamsted, Herts	John Dorrien
1785	Ashby St. Ledgers, Northants	John and Jane Ashley
1786	Leicester (Cathedral)	John Johnson
1786	St. Edmund's, Lombard Street	J. Milles (*Gentleman's Magazine*, 1786, Part II, page 480)
1786	Jamaica (Montego Bay)	George McFarquhar
1787	Newcastle (Cathedral)	Matthew Ridley
1787	East Barnet, Herts (churchyard)	General Prevost (*Gentleman's Magazine*, 1787, page 660)
c. 1787	Dunkeswell, Devon	Admiral Graves (designed by Miss Burgess)
1788	Westminster Abbey	Miss Whytell
1788	Canford, Dorset	Samuel Martin (medallion portrait)
1789	Deptford (St. Paul's)	Henry Sayer
1789	Simpson, Bucks	Sir Waldon Hanmar, Bart.
1789	Jamaica (Kingston Cathedral)	John Wolmer
1790	Warboys, Hunts	Elizabeth Strode
1790	Jamaica (Kingston Cathedral)	Dr. Fortunatus Dwarris
1790	Canterbury (St. Mildred's)	William Jackson
1790	Great Canford, Dorset	Miss Henrietta Wilkie
1791	Aberdeen (West Church)	Mrs. Allardyce (*d.* 1787)
1791	Speen, Berks	Thomas Wyld
1791	Stanmore, Middlesex	Jacob Forbes
1791	Grosvenor Chapel	Colonel Francis Robertson
1791	Stamford (St. George's)	Sir Richard and Lady Cust (£510) (Archives, Lord Brownlow)
1792	Burnham, Bucks	Mr. Justice Willes
1792	Rostherne, Cheshire	Samuel Egerton
1792	Runcorn, Cheshire	Sir Richard Brooke (4th Bart.)
1793	Hawstead, Suffolk	Lucy Metcalfe
1793	St. Giles, Cripplegate	John Milton
1793	Watton, Herts	Sir Thomas Rumbold
1793	Astley, Worcs	Sarah Winford
1793	Belton, Lincs	Hon. Etheldred Cust
1793	Westminster Abbey	General Hope
1794	Godstone, Surrey	Mrs. Sarah Smith
1794	Berkswell, Warwick	Lady Eardley
1794	Jamaica (Montego Bay)	Rosa Palmer
1794	Lymington, Hants	Captain Rogers

1794	Sherborne, Glos	William Naper
1794	Buckland Monac-horum, Devon	Sir Francis Drake
1794	Tackley, Oxon	Hon. George Morton
1794	North Mimms, Herts	Rev. John Hickson
1794	Eastry, Kent	Captain John Harvey
1794	Jamaica (Kingston Cathedral)	Malcolm Laing
1795	Hillingdon, Middlesex	Thomas Lane
1795	Buckland Monac-horum, Devon	Lord Heathfield
1795	Tregynon, Montgomery	Arthur Blayney
1796	Westminster Abbey	Sir George Pocock
1796	Eton College Chapel	Earl Waldegrave
1796	Bottesham, Cambs	Soame Jenyns
1796	Runcorn, Cheshire	Sir Richard Brooke (5th Bart.)
1796	St. Andrew-by-the-Wardrobe	Rev. William Romaine
1796	Jamaica (Spanish Town Cathedral)	Earl and Countess of Effingham
1797	Shalford, Surrey	Robert Austen
1797	Finningham, Suffolk	Sir John Fenn
1797	Reading (St. Giles's)	Hon. and Rev. William Cadogan
1797	Ridge, Herts	Joseph Bushman
1797	Westminster Abbey	William Mason
1798	Pott, Cheshire	Peter Downes
1798	Wimpole, Cambs	Lord Dover
1798	Jamaica (Spanish Town Cathedral)	Richard Batty
1798	Jamaica (Spanish Town Cathedral)	Lady Williamson
1799	Cardington, Beds	Samuel Whitbread (finished by John Bacon the Younger)
1799	Great Yeldham, Essex	Gregory Way
1799	Jamaica (Spanish Town Cathedral)	Francis Broadbelt
1799	Tackley, Oxon	Sir John Gardiner
1799	Great Canford, Dorset	Catherine Willett
1799	Jamaica (Kingston Cathedral)	Mary Carr

BACON, JOHN, the Younger
b. 1777, *d.* 1859

He was the second son of John Bacon, R.A. (q.v.), and was born at his parents' house in Newman Street on 13 March, 1777. His father trained him in sculpture and, to quote the *European Magazine* (1815, page 3), "put the tools so early in his hands that there are now in various parts of the kingdom monumental figures executed completely by him when only eleven, twelve or thirteen years of age." In 1789 Bacon entered the Royal Academy Schools and four years later won a Silver Medal; in 1797 he received the Academy Gold Medal for a statue of "Cassandra."

It was in 1792 that he had first exhibited at the Royal Academy, showing a relief of "Moses Striking the Rock," while a figure of "Providence"

for Trinity House appeared in 1796. In 1799, on the death of his father, he took over the conduct of the business and completed the unfinished works in the studio. Bacon received so many commissions, mostly for monuments, that he decided in 1803 to have a public exhibition of his larger works, a plan, according to the *European Magazine*, "never before adopted in the same way by any artist."

In 1806 Bacon competed for the statue of Pitt to be erected in Cambridge and the model he submitted is now in the possession of the Earl of Normanton. In 1809 he made for the island of Antigua a group in memory of Lord Lavington, a work later destroyed by a hurricane. The sculptor, before he sent it to the West Indies, gave the following description of it to Prince Hoare: "A representation of his Lordship habited (agreeably to the wish of the Council) in his robes as Knight of the Bath. He is seated and elevated to convey the idea of vice-regal authority. His sarcophagus is also introduced. The island of Antigua, personified, pays a tribute of sorrow to his memory" (Hoare, *Academic Correspondence*, 1809, page 42).

In 1814 Bacon restored Cibber's famous figures of "Madness" and "Melancholy" at Bethlem Hospital. Till about 1830 his life was untroubled and prosperous. He had more than enough work and he never lacked commissions, but for the last thirty years of his life he practically retired from active business and produced, as far as I know, only two major works. One was the reredos of St. Laurence, Exeter, described by Miss Cresswell in her *Churches of Exeter* (page 76) as "very remarkable, not to say remarkably ugly." It represented "an Angel holding a cross, rising from clouds towards a crown." The other work is also in Exeter and is a recumbent figure of the sculptor's daughter, Mrs. Medley (1842), in the Church of St. Thomas, of which her husband was Vicar. Even that severe critic, the *Ecclesiologist*, approved of the tomb and was "glad to be able to present to our readers the following instance of true and Catholick taste and feeling." The writer continues with a description of the recumbent effigy of which "it is not too much to say that few of the best ages of Christian art surpass it."

It is a curious commentary and shows how utterly the once famous Bacon was forgotten that the *Art Journal*, that repository of information on contemporary art and artists, hardly troubles to mention his death. Bacon was not as great a sculptor as his father, and it is perhaps significant that though his name was put forward he never secured sufficient votes to be elected an Associate of the Royal Academy. Nor apparently did his fellow-artists think highly of his work. Smirke told Farington (*Diary*, Vol. III, page 173) that if Bacon's model of the statue of Lord Wellesley was carried out "he would shun the place where it was to be seen"; while N. Marchant, R.A. (op. cit., page 182), said of Bacon's work that he finished it with care but was "deficient in taste and knowledge of the antique," and that he designed "his parts in a petite manner."

Bacon exhibited at the Royal Academy from 1792 to 1824 and at the British Institution in 1806 and 1807. His portrait by Russell, R.A., is reproduced in the *European Magazine* for 1815. (Authorities quoted in text.)

STATUES

1803	Marquess Cornwallis (designed by his father)	Calcutta
1808	William III (designed by his father)	St. James's Square
1809	Marquess Wellesley	Calcutta
1809	Marquess Wellesley	Bombay
1810	Marquess Cornwallis	Bombay
1813	George III (designed by T. Kirk)	Bank of Ireland

BUSTS

1793	Thomas, Bishop of Rochester	Westminster Abbey
1798	John Bacon, R.A.	Exhibited Royal Academy
1804	William Markham, Archbishop of York	Christ Church, Oxford
1804	Dr. Garthshore	Exhibited Royal Academy
1804	Lady Ribblesdale	Exhibited Royal Academy
1808	Marquess Wellesley	National Portrait Gallery
1810	Canning	Exhibited Royal Academy
1810	Hon. Mrs. Lee	Exhibited Royal Academy
1810	Lord Le Despencer	Exhibited Royal Academy
1811	R. Payne Knight	British Museum
1812	Earl of Aberdeen	Exhibited Royal Academy
1812	Pitt	British Museum
1813	Duke of Kent	Windsor Castle
1813	William Markham, Archbishop of York	Windsor Castle
1816	Mrs. Arbuthnot	Exhibited Royal Academy
1817	Sir Joshua Reynolds	Exhibited Royal Academy
1818	Two unnamed busts	For Carlton House (£315) (P.R.O., L.C. 9/367)
1820	Hon. Antonia Stapleton	Exhibited Royal Academy

MONUMENTS

1793	West Drayton, Middlesex	Fysh de Burgh
1794	Ottery St. Mary, Devon	William Williams
1794	Westminster Abbey	Captain Harvey and Captain Hutt
1795	Amersham, Bucks	Rachel Drake (*d.*1784)
1795	Harefield, Middlesex	Charles Parker
1796	St. James's, Hampstead Road	Anna Rhodes
1797	Hull (Holy Trinity)	Joseph Milner
1798	Leek, Staffs	John Daintry
1798	**Chesham, Bucks**	**Nicholas Skottowe**
1799	St. Clement, Cornwall	Samuel Thomas
1799	Westminster Abbey	Captain Edward Cooke
1799	Newington, Kent	Rev. Ralph Brockman
1800	Harefield, Middlesex	Hester, Lady Newdegate
1800	Twickenham, Middlesex	George Gostling
c. 1800	Theydon Garnon, Essex	Lady Mary Archer (*d.* 1776)
1800	Brecon (Cathedral)	Sir John Meredith
1800	Prestwould, Leics	Francis Andrew
1800	Hatfield, Herts	Joseph Bland
1800	West Drayton, Middlesex	Fysh de Burgh
1800	Ockham, Surrey	Hon. George Murray
1800	Bradford (Cathedral)	William Northrop
1800	Ware, Herts	Francis Shephard
1800	Jamaica (Cathedral)	Dr. Anderson
1800.	Abbots Langley, Herts	Countess of Northampton
1801	Barbados (Cathedral)	Mrs. Austin
1801	Amersham, Bucks	Elizabeth Drake
1801	Stapleford, Notts	George Borlase Warren
1801	**Astley, Worcs**	**Harriet Winford**
1801	Brentford (St. Laurence's)	Ann Clitherow
1801	Windsor (Parish Church)	William Heberden
1802	Harefield, Middlesex	Charles Parker
1802	Westminster Abbey	Admiral Totty
1802	Wrenbury, Cheshire	Thomas Starkey
1802	Shepperton, Middlesex	Barbara Barron
1802	Stratton Audley, Oxon	Miss Warren
1802	Tooting, Surrey	John Rice
1802	St. Stephen's, Walbrook	Griffin Stonestreet
1802	Eccles, Cheshire	Thomas Bayley
1802	St. Mary Aldermary	Margaret Bearsley
1802	Armagh (Cathedral)	Lord Rokeby
1802	Amersham, Bucks	William Drake
1803	Sandwich (St. Clement's)	William Boys
1803	St. Kitts (Trinity, Palmetto)	Captain John Garvey
1803	Reigate, Surrey	Robert Petrie
1803	Sudbury (St. Gregory's)	John Newman

1803	Westminster Abbey	John and Richard Forbes
1803	Deane, Hants	John Harwood
1803	Welford, Berks	John Archer
1804	Worcester (Cathedral)	Richard Solly
1804	Friern Barnet, Middlesex	Children of Richard Down
1804	Acton, Middlesex (Churchyard)	John Way (obelisk)
1804	Wells (Cathedral)	John Burland
1804	Stoke, nr. Guildford, Surrey	Elizabeth Creuzé
1805	Beddington, Surrey	William Bridges
1805	Otford, Kent	Charles Polhill
1805	Calcutta (St. John's)	J. A. Kirkpatrick
1805	Stanstead Abbots, Herts	Paul Feilde
1805	Banstead, Surrey	Mrs. Burr
1805	Totteridge, Herts	John Puget
1805	Sprowston, Norfolk	Lady Maria Micklethwait
1805	Blunham, Beds	Godfrey Thornton
1805	Speldhurst, Kent	John Yorke
1805	Speldhurst, Kent	Martin Yorke
1805	St. Paul's Cathedral	General Dundas
1806	St. Paul's Cathedral	Captain George Duff
1806	Hanmer, Flint	Lord Kenyon
1806	Clapham (Parish Church)	John Castell
1806	Astley, Worcs	Sarah Freeman
1806	Rochester (Cathedral)	John, Lord Henniker
1806	Sherborne, Glos	Princess Bariatinsky
1806	Standish, Lancs	Richard Watt (d. 1796)
1806	Bunny, Notts	Sir Thomas Parkyns
1806	Ormesby St. Michael, Norfolk	Elizabeth Upcher
1806	Stanstead Abbots, Herts	Robert Jocelyn
1806	Marylebone (Parish Church)	Elizabeth Towry
1806	Hampstead (Parish Church)	Charles Duncan
1806	Stoke, nr. Guildford, Surrey	Charlotte Smith
1806	Thames Ditton, Surrey	Sir Richard Sullivan
1807	Cuckfield, Sussex	Percy Burrell
1807	Hungerford, Berks	Charlotte Willes
1807	Hainton, Lincs	Frances Heneage
1807	Melton Constable, Norfolk	Rhoda and Sofia Astley
1807	Cottesbrooke, Northants	Lady Langham
1807	Paddington (Parish Church)	General Crosbie
1807	Harlestone, Northants	Robert Andrew
1807	Odell, Beds	Thomas Alston
1807	Bombay (Cathedral)	Captain Warden
1807	Bath (Abbey)	Herman Katencamp
1807	Wanstead (Parish Church)	Hannah Doorman
1808	Edwardstone, Suffolk	Thomas Dawson (d. 1807)
1808	St. Peter's-in-Thanet, Kent	Anthony Calvert
1808	Winchester (Cathedral)	Colonel Morgan
1808	Reading (St. Mary's)	Colonel Charles Taylor
1808	Wollaton, Notts	5th Lord Middleton
1808	Wrenbury, Cheshire	John Jennings
1808	Beverley (St. Mary's)	William Hutchinson
1808	Burton-on-Stather, Lincs	Penelope Sheffield
1808	Calcutta (Cathedral)	Lt.-Colonel James Kirkpatrick
1808	Madras (St. Mary's)	Jane Russell
1808	Bombay (Cathedral)	Captain G. Hardinge
1808	Westminster Abbey	Admiral Kempenfelt (d. 1782)
1809	Bletchingley, Surrey	Sir William Bensley
1809	Great Bromley, Essex	Henry Hanson
1809	Navestock, Essex	Hon. Edward Waldegrave
1809	Kirk Ella, Yorks	Joseph Sykes
1809	South Stoneham, Hants	Lt.-General Stibbert
1809	Crayford, Kent	John Jackson
1809	Westminster Abbey	Captain Bryan
1809	Hampstead (Parish Church)	Hon. Frances Erskine
1809	Monkton, Pembrokeshire	Sir Hugh Owen
1809	Cottesbrooke, Northants	Marianne Langham
1809	Croome, D'abitat	Earl of Coventry
1809	West Drayton, Middlesex	Catherine de Burgh
1809	St. James's, Hampstead Road	Henry Evelyn
1809	St. Paul's Cathedral	Sir John Moore
1809	Westminster Abbey	General Manningham
1810	Rye, Sussex	Elizabeth Woollett
1810	Hawstead, Suffolk	Viscountess Carleton
1810	Amersham, Bucks	Thomas Tyrwhitt Drake
1810	Winchester (Cathedral)	John Littlehales
1810	Manchester (Cathedral)	Charles Lawson
1810	Woodnesborough, Kent	Thomas Godfrey
1810	Tooting, Surrey	Mary Rice
1810	Walmer, Kent	Sir Henry Harvey
1810	Chesham, Bucks	Nicholas Skottowe
1810	Epsom, Surrey	Jane Rowe
1810	Cottesbrooke, Northants	Lady Langham
1810	Norwich (St. George Colegate)	John Herring
1810	Faxton, Northants	Mrs. Raynsford
1811	Nowton, Suffolk	Elizabeth Oakes
1811	Bombay (Cathedral)	J. Duncan
1811	Hampstead (Parish Church)	Louisa Lownds
1811	Madras (St. Mary's)	George Keble
1811	Westminster Abbey	Dr. Plenderleath
1811	Eydon, Northants	Rev. Francis Annesley
1812	Marlow, Bucks	Mary Clayton

1812	Cottesbroke, Northants	Sir William Langham
1812	St. Paul's Cathedral	General Crawfurd and General Mackinnon
1813	Stoke-by-Nayland, Suffolk	Admiral Sir William Rowley
1813	Canterbury (Cathedral)	George Fraser
1813	Bidborough, Kent (Churchyard)	Baron de Roll
1813	Leicester (St. Mary's)	Rev. Thomas Robinson
1813	Buckland Monachorum, Devon	2nd Lord Heathfield
1813	Walton-on-Thames, Surrey	Henry Skrine
1814	Westminster Abbey	Sir Thomas Trigge
1814	Westminster Abbey (Cloisters)	Lutterell Wynne
1814	Westminster Abbey (Cloisters)	Mary Markham
1814	Thames Ditton, Surrey	Sir Henry Sullivan
1814	Letheringsett, Norfolk	Henry Jodrell
1815	Great Bromley, Essex	William Hanson
1815	Ash, Kent	Thomas Lambard
1815	Bocking, Essex	Josias Nottedge
1815	Worcester (Cathedral)	Sir Henry Ellis
1815	Wrenbury, Cheshire	Eleanor Starkey
1815	Rostherne, Cheshire	Thomas Brooke
1815	Burton-on-Stather, Lincs	Sir John Sheffield
1815	Richmond, Surrey	Major George Bean
1815	Westminster Abbey	Earl of Normanton
1815	Edwardstone, Suffolk	William Shepherd
1816	Amersham, Bucks	Rev. Charles Drake
1816	Madras (St. Mary's)	Charles Ross
1816	Battersea (Parish Church)	Thomas and William Crowther
1816	Chew Magna, Somerset	Sir Henry Strachey
1816	Abingdon Pigotts, Cambs	Mary Pigott
1816	St. Andrew by the Wardrobe	Rev. William Goode
1816	Worlingworth, Suffolk	Duchess of Chandos
1817	Bylaugh, Norfolk	Sir John Lombe
1817	Bombay (Cathedral)	Jonathan Duncan
1817	Assington, Suffolk	Rev. Philip Gurdon
1818	Stoke-by-Nayland, Suffolk	Francis Fortescue
1818	Hampstead (Parish Church)	Marianne Beresford
1818	West Molesey, Surrey	Hon. George Berkeley
1818	Oxford (Balliol College Chapel)	John Parsons, Bishop of Peterborough
1818	Madras (St. Mary's)	Thomas Davies
1818	Mildenhall, Suffolk	Elizabeth Swale
1818	Westminster Abbey	Warren Hastings (bust)
1818	Bagshot, Surrey	Mrs. Abraham
1819	Peasmarsh, Sussex	Elizabeth Delves
1819	Chichester (Cathedral)	Edward Madden
1819	Markyate, Herts	James Howell
1819	Hanwell, Middlesex	Louisa Lushington
1821	Mildenhall, Suffolk	John Swale
1822	Chester (Cathedral)	Augusta Slade
1822	Great Bromley, Essex	Laetitia Mangles
1822	Stratton Audley, Oxon	Admiral Sir John Borlase-Warren
1825	St. Pancras	Samuel Foyster
1825	Ovingham, Northumberland	Mary Blackett
1832	St. Peter's-in-Thanet, Kent	Captain Richard Burton

BACON, JOHN, and MANNING, SAMUEL

Partnership *fl.* 1818–1843

John Bacon the Younger (q.v.) and his former pupil, Samuel Manning, later went into partnership as monumental masons, and the firm turned out a large number of dull and second-rate monuments and tablets. As most of this work was produced when Bacon had practically retired from business, it seems doubtful if he had much to do either with designing or carving the monuments; indeed he can have been little more than a sleeping partner. To the public, however, the name "Bacon" stood for the prolific and popular statuary whose works could be admired, not only in Westminster Abbey and St. Paul's, but also in a hundred village churches. The widow, ordering a modest tablet from the firm, felt that she was employing the sculptor of national monuments. In reality all she would get would be either some stock "Bacon" design, which had been in use since the end of the eighteenth century, or the not very original one showing a widow in flowing weeds bowed over a funeral urn; extra carving, in the form of branches of yew or cypress, cost a little more.

Manning, save on the rarest of occasions an inferior sculptor, doubtless ran the firm; and a prosperous one it must have been, to judge by the very large number of works it produced. Peter Cunningham wrote in the *Builder* (1863, page 167) "that Bacon should die worth £60,000 without making busts seems to be inexplicable, and I cannot see how Bacon acquired by sculpture alone the large sum he was unable to take with him." The answer is that Bacon found turning out endless similar memorial tablets far more paying than cutting busts.

As the years pass so do the firm's tablets get duller, and as one enters a church it is only occasionally that the eye lights on one of their works which has a fresh, original or well-thought-out design. To Bacon and Manning, therefore, must go much of the blame for the mass-produced memorials which, by the middle of the last century, had become so lamentable and frequent a blot on the wall of aisle and chancel. A list of their better works is given below:

TABLES

c. 1818	Heckfield, Hants	Sir William Pitt (d. 1809)
1818	Adderley, Salop	Robert, Viscount Kilmorey
1818	Stanstead Abbots, Herts	Philip Booth
1818	Hawstead, Suffolk	Philip Metcalfe
1818	Rye, Sussex	John Woollett
1819	Upper Sheringham, Norfolk	Abbot Upcher
1820	Ulcombe, Kent	Marquess of Ormonde
1820	Hawstead, Suffolk	Christopher Metcalfe
1820	Britford, Wilts	Richard Jerveys
1821	Itchen (Pear Tree Green) Hants	Catherine Short
1823	Bloomsbury (St. George's)	Sir Charles Grant
1823	Stockport, Cheshire	James Newton
1823	Eltham, Kent	Arthur Pott
1824	Adderley, Salop	Francis, Earl of Kilmorey
1824	Marylebone (Parish Church)	William Gurdon
1825	Warfield, Berks	Sir John Walsh
1825	Wartling, Sussex	Caroline Curteis
1827	Tuxford, Notts	Ann Dollond
1828	Bisham, Berks	Augustus East
1830	Hawstead, Suffolk	Frances Metcalfe
1831	Rotherfield Greys, Oxon	Lord Despencer
1831	Amersham, Bucks	Arthur Tyrwhitt
1833	Langham, Essex	Margaret Maude
1843	Tenbury Wells, Hereford	William Godson

BACON, THOMAS

b. 1773

Eldest son of John Bacon, R.A. (q.v.), he worked in his father's studio and himself exhibited at the Royal Academy, 1793–1795, showing a few religious works. After his father's death he assisted his younger brother John (q.v.) in the completion of the unfinished works in the studio, including the statue of William III, but soon after 1800 all trace of him is lost.

BAILY, EDWARD HODGES, R.A.

b. 1788, *d.* 1867

He was born on 10 March, 1788, at Bristol, his father being a ship's carver and a man of considerable artistic talent. At the age of fourteen Baily was taken from school and placed in a merchant's counting-house where he worked for two years, although even at this time he felt a strong leaning towards art. For this reason he began to take lessons from a modeller in wax, and made such rapid progress that by the time he was sixteen he had given up all idea of a commercial career. He started his artistic work by executing portraits in wax, and even considered making this his medium for the rest of his life until he saw Bacon's monument to Mrs. Draper, in Bristol Cathedral, and felt "the first emotion of a higher aspiration" (*Art Union*, 1847, page 230).

Baily now determined to study sculpture and received help from a young surgeon named Leigh, who not only lent him Flaxman's designs for Homer's Iliad, but also gave him a commission for two small groups to be executed from the drawings. The result was so satisfactory that Leigh sent one of these groups to Flaxman himself, urging him to give the artist a chance. Flaxman must have been equally impressed, for he summoned Baily to London and accepted him as a pupil in his studio. Here the young man remained for seven years and in 1808 won a Silver Medal from the Society of Arts for a plaster-cast of "Laocoon." He joined the Royal Academy Schools in the same year and was awarded a Silver Medal by the Academy in 1809.

In 1811 Baily won the Academy Gold Medal and a purse of fifty guineas for his "Hercules Restoring Alcestis to Admetus." In 1817 he accepted the post of chief modeller to the firm of Rundell and Bridge, the best-known gold- and silversmiths of the period, and for twenty-five years designed for them a very large number of works, including presentation plate, candelabra, racing trophies, etc., for other goldsmiths he designed the Doncaster Cup in 1843, and the Ascot Gold Cup in the following year.

Baily's first exhibited work to attract attention was a figure of "Apollo Discharging his Arrows Against the Greeks," which he showed at the Royal Academy in 1817, and which made so favourable an impression on the members that it procured him election as an Associate. It was a year later that he showed a model of his most celebrated work, "Eve at the Fountain," which at once gained him a European reputation; it is curious to reflect that he had made the original design as the handle of a cover for a soup-tureen for one of the City Companies. In 1821 "Eve" was executed in marble and purchased by the citizens of Bristol for their Literary Institute. In the same year the sculptor was elected a Royal Academician, and he deposited as his diploma work a bust of Flaxman. In 1825 he made the frieze for the portico of the Masonic Hall at Bristol, and in the following year the relief for General Picton's monument at Carmarthen.

In 1826 Baily also received extensive orders for sculpture for the Marble Arch; this consisted of four trophies upon columns (£3,200); two square

PLATE III

WILLIAM BEHNES
Princess, later Queen, Victoria, 1829, Windsor Castle.

THOMAS BANKS
Sir Clifton Wintringham, 1794, Westminster Abbey.

BELTHASAR BURMAN
Rachel, Countess of Bath, 1680, Tawstock, Devon.

PLATE IV

SAMUEL CHANDLER
Edmund Humfrey, 1727, Rettendon, Essex.

SIR HENRY CHEERE
Charles Apthorp, 1758, King's Chapel, Boston, U.S.A.

ANDRIES CARPENTIÈRE
Sir John Thornycroft, 1725, Bloxham, Oxon.

panels (£600); six spandrels with "Victories" (£900); three keystones (£300); and four statues of "Victories" (£1,200) (P.R.O. Works 20 4/1). All this work was apparently finished and paid for by the Government, although it was not all placed on the Marble Arch and some was probably used for other Government buildings. The statues on the façade of the National Gallery were also executed by Baily, though they were originally commissioned by George IV either for Buckingham Palace or the Marble Arch. In 1829 the sculptor agreed to execute eight statues for the gateway at Hyde Park Corner, but owing to the King's death they were never carried out. Apparently he found it difficult to get the Government to pay him for his work, for in 1831 he and Sir Richard Westmacott (q.v.) wrote a letter to the Treasury in which "as the principal sculptors employed on the Arch now erecting in St. James's Park, in honour of the late military and naval achievements," they asked for payment of the "third and last instalment due to us." They ended by asserting that "the greatest part of these works have been executed nearly three years ago" (P.R.O. Works T.1/3489).

In 1833 Baily wrote to the Royal Academy "representing the depressed state of sculpture and urging the Council to adopt some measures for its assistance," but though the Academy agreed with all he said they were unable to suggest any remedy (Academy Archives).

Baily also worked at Buckingham Palace, being responsible in 1828 for the relief of "Britannia Acclaimed by Neptune and Tritons Being Drawn in her Chariot" which formed the pediment of the portico of the quadrangle. In the same year he made four friezes for the throne-room depicting incidents in the Wars of the Roses from designs by Stothard.

As a monumental sculptor he had a large practice, though his work was never as popular as Chantrey's. His recumbent figure of Lord Broome at Linton, Kent, is, however, far more moving and beautiful than Chantrey's much better-known and applauded effigy of Lady Frederica Stanhope at Chevening in the same county, which is starred in every guide-book. On the other hand, he could produce works of utter bathos; for example, his monument to Sir William Ponsonby in St. Paul's, which a contemporary critic described as a "vulgar combination of nature and art, a confused idea wrought with a heavy hand" (Smyth's *Monuments of St. Paul's*, page 789).

Baily's monuments were undoubtedly much admired during his lifetime. After seeing one of them, the Rev. J. Eagles wrote in his *Rhymes Latin and English* a poem which ends as follows:

"And by his last Will and Testament
Provide for his own monument.
Baily's his man, in spite of death
To chisel in again his breath,
Make blood reflow in marble vein
And set him on his legs again."

In 1847 the sculptor exhibited his statue of Chief Justice Tindal which aroused a great deal of unfavourable comment in artistic circles, where it was alleged that he had patched up an old model by J. Bacon, R.A.—"Sir William Blackstone's statue made to do new duty," as the *Art Journal* put it (1867, page 170). He did very little work for some years prior to being made an "Honorary Retired Academician" (with a pension of £200) in 1863, and after this he exhibited no more.

Though Baily must have made a large sum of money during his career, he seems to have been extravagant and the last years of his life were much embarrassed; indeed in 1857 he applied to the Royal Academy for assistance. The *Art Journal* in its obituary (1867, page 110) said that "the years of his prolonged life were actively passed in upholding the dignity and purity of his art, and in its annals his name must always be referred to as one of the most successful sculptors of the nineteenth century" The *Builder* on the same occasion (1867, page 387) wrote that "his 'Eve' was a marble inspiration softened into life," though they were forced to remark that his portrait statues "were luckily few in number and did not add to his reputation." Busts they considered to have been "little understood by Mr. Baily, save that of Douglas Jerrold," which was "very fine in conception and execution and true to the man and his wit."

Baily exhibited at the Royal Academy, 1810–1862, and at the British Institution, 1812–1840, where he showed in the latter year a confused design for the Nelson monument with an obelisk and figures of Nelson, "Victory," "Neptune" and "The Nile," while "the subordinate deities of the ocean form a triumphal procession round the rock on which the monument is placed." This gained the second prize, but there was a good deal of controversy over the memorial and two competitions had to be held before it was finally decided that William Railton's column should be chosen, while Baily should execute a simple figure of the Admiral without any "subordinate deities." The model for this statue is now in Admiralty House, London.

A number of Baily's works were in Mr. Elkanah Bicknell's sale held at Christie's on 25 April, 1853. They had originally been made for Mr. Bicknell's gallery at Herne Hill, and the chief lots sold were

"Paris" (£161); "Helen" (£162); "Psyche" (£315) and "Cupid" (£254). At the Manchester Art Treasures Exhibition held in 1857, Douglas Jerrold and Professor Owen lent their own busts by Baily, while the Duke of Newcastle sent the sculptor's "Head of Eve."

At the Royal Academy in 1843 T. Mogford exhibited a portrait of Baily, and a drawing of him by T. Bridgeford appeared in the *Art Journal* four years later.

(Authorities cited in text; Royal Academy Archives; Chilcot's *Bristol*; H. Clifford Smith's *Buckingham Palace*; Catalogue of Sir Thomas Lawrence's Sale, 1830.)

STATUES

1825	Jenner	Gloucester Cathedral
1827	Justice	Council House, Bristol
1830	Minerva	Exterior Athenaeum Club
1836	Jebb, Bishop of Limerick	Limerick Cathedral
1837	Earl Grey	Newcastle
1838	Admiral Sir Pultney Malcolm	St. Paul's Cathedral
1839	Telford	Westminster Abbey
1840	Earl of Egremont	Petworth Church, Sussex
1841	Sir Richard Bourke	Sydney, New South Wales
1842	Nelson	Trafalgar Square (model at the Admiralty)
1842	Sir Astley Cooper	St. Paul's Cathedral
1843	Dr. Wood	St. John's College, Cambridge
1844	Lord Metcalfe	Jamaica
1844	Bishop Butler	St. Mary's, Shrewsbury
1844	Dr. Dawson	St. Patrick's Cathedral, Dublin
1845	Isaac Watts	Abney Park Cemetery
1846	David Hare	Calcutta
1846	Duke of Sussex	Freemasons' Hall
1847	Chief Justice Tindal	Chelmsford, Essex
1849	Flaxman	University College, London
1851	Thomas Fleming	Manchester Cathedral
1852	Sir Robert Peel	Bury, Lancs
1857	Charles James Fox	Palace of Westminster
1857	Lord Mansfield	Palace of Westminster
1858	Turner	Illustrated in *Art Journal*, 1858, page 340
n.d.	George IV	Windsor Castle (small equestrian bronze)

BUSTS

1818	B. R. Haydon	Exhibited Royal Academy
1818	Mr. Baily (artist's father)	Exhibited Royal Academy
1823	Flaxman	Burlington House
1823	R. Hart-Davis	Exhibited Royal Academy
1824	H. Fuseli, R.A.	For Sir Thomas Lawrence (fetched £35 at his sale in 1830)
1825	Master Emilius Watson Taylor	Formerly Erlestoke Park
1825	Peter Dobree	Trinity College, Cambridge
1825	Joseph Munden	For Drury Lane
1825	Thomas Bewick	Newcastle Literary and Philosophical Society
1826	Thomas Stothard	Burlington House
1826	Lord Byron	Harrow School
1826	Sir W. Beechey	Burlington House
1827	Samuel Dobree	Merchant Taylors' Hall
1827	Duke of York	Freemasons' Hall (after Nollekens)
1827	Thomas Campbell	Glasgow Art Gallery
1828	Robert Smirke, R.A.	For Sir Thomas Lawrence (fetched thirty guineas at his sale in 1830)
1828	Lord Bacon	Magdalen College, Oxford
1829	Rev. W. Turner	Newcastle Literary and Philosophical Society
1829	Sir Richard Glyn	Exhibited Royal Academy
1830	William Wilkins, R.A.	Trinity College, Cambridge
1830	Michael Faraday	University Museum, Oxford
1830	Sir Thomas Lawrence (posthumous)	Bristol Institution (replica National Portrait Gallery)
1830	John Waller	Bristol Art Gallery
c. 1830	Canning, Newton, Wellington and Johnson	For Robert Vernon
1831	J. Northcote, R.A.	Exhibited Royal Academy
1831	Lord Brougham	Exhibited Royal Academy
1833	G. Clint, R.A.	Exhibited Royal Academy
1837	Earl Grey	Exhibited Royal Academy
1837	Sir William Knighton	Exhibited Royal Academy
1837	Admiral Sir Michael Seymour	Exhibited Royal Academy
1838	Rev. T. Biddulph	St. James's Church, Bristol
1840	Sir Robert O'Callaghan	Compton Place, Eastbourne
1842	Thomas Biddulph	St. James's Church, Bristol
1842	Lord George Bentinck	Russell-Cotes Museum, Bournemouth

1844	Lord Metcalfe	Metcalfe Hall, Calcutta
1844	James Lonsdale	National Portrait Gallery
1845	Lord Fitzgerald	Exhibited Royal Academy
1845	Robert Southey	Bristol Cathedral
1846	Sir John Jeremie	Sierra Leone Cathedral
1846	Professor Owen	Royal College of Surgeons
1847	Sir Henry la Beche	Exhibited Royal Academy
1848	Hon. Frederick Methuen	Exhibited Royal Academy
1850	Sir John Herschel	St. John's College, Cambridge
1850	Lord Gough	Exhibited Royal Academy
1851	William Whewell	Trinity College, Cambridge (plaster-cast National Portrait Gallery)
1851	Alderman Donkin	Newcastle Public Library
1851	Joan Lever	Guy's Hospital
1851	William Smyth	Fitzwilliam Museum, Cambridge
1852	Arthur Blakestone	Foundling Hospital
1853	Douglas Jerrold	National Portrait Gallery
1856	John Estlin	Bristol Art Gallery

IDEAL WORKS AND GROUPS

1811	Neptune Drives off the Winds	Exhibited Royal Academy
1813	Hercules Restoring Alcestis	Exhibited Royal Academy
1815	Apollo Discharging his Arrows Against the Greeks	For Joseph Neeld
1817	Flora	For Earl of Darnley
1819	Hercules Throwing Lycus into the Sea	For Joseph Neeld
1822	Eve at the Fountain	Bristol Art Gallery (replica dated 1845 at Glyptotek, Copenhagen)
1827	Maternal Love	For Joseph Neeld
1827	Painting drawing Inspiration from Poetry	Exhibited Royal Academy
1833	Caius Marius and the Ruins of Carthage	Exhibited Royal Academy
1836	Sleeping Nymph	For Lord Monteagle
1842	Eve Listening to the Voice	Bethnal Green Museum
1843	Psyche	For E. Bicknell
1843	Helen Unveiling Herself for Paris	Exhibited Royal Academy
1848	The Tired Hunter	For Joseph Neeld
1849	Eve	For Robert Vernon
1850	The Graces, Grittleton House (Wilts)	For Joseph Neeld

1850	Sleeping Girl	Bristol Art Gallery
1851	A Youth and his Dog	Exhibited Great Exhibition
1851	Nymph Preparing for the Bath	Exhibited Great Exhibition
1852	Infant Bacchus	Exhibited Royal Academy
1854	Morning Star	Mansion House
1855	The Circassian Slave	Royal Collection
1856	The Pet Bird	Exhibited Royal Academy
1858	Genius	Mansion House (destroyed by enemy action, 29 November, 1940)
?	Mother and Child	Manchester Art Gallery

MONUMENTS

1812	Much Hadham, Herts	Archibald Randolph
1813	Westminster Abbey	Sir Richard Fletcher
1815	Newcastle (Cathedral)	Calverly Bewicke
1819	Uffington, Berks	Elizabeth Hughes
1820	St. Paul's Cathedral	Sir W. Ponsonby (designed by William Theed, R.A.)
1820	Devizes, Wilts	William Salmon
1821	Little Torrington, Devon	Sarah Fortescue
1821	Moseley, Birmingham	Elizabeth Russell
1823	Thames Ditton, Surrey	Robert Taylor
1823	Newcastle (Cathedral)	Joseph Bainbridge
1823	Culford, Suffolk	2nd Marquess Cornwallis
1823	Linton, Kent	Maria Mann
1823	St. Paul's Cathedral	Earl St. Vincent (statue)
1824	Madras (Cathedral)	William Parry
1824	Lichfield (Cathedral)	Earl Cornwallis
1824	Tottenham (Parish Church)	Rev. Thomas Roberts
1824	Oxford (Cathedral)	Francis Bayley
1825	Dolgelley, Merioneth	Sir Richard Richards
1826	Bristol (Cathedral)	Mrs. Middleton
1826	Exeter (St. Martin's)	Eliza Mortimer
1827	Middle Claydon, Bucks	Catherine Verney
1827	Heston, Middlesex	Lt.-General John Skinner
1827	Buckden, Hunts	Bishop Pelham
1828	Egham, Surrey	Lydia Gostling
1829	Hawstead, Suffolk	Clare Colville
1830	Ecton, Northants	Rev. Thomas Whalley
1830	Easton Neston, Northants	George, 3rd Earl of Pomfret
1831	Whalton, Northumberland	John Ogle
1831	Potterne, Wilts	John Spearing
1832	Trowbridge, Wilts	Rev. G. Crabbe
1833	Llanbadarn Fawr, Cardigan	Matthew Williams
1833	Wrington, Somerset	Hannah More
1833	Wotton-under-Edge, Glos	David Taylor

1833	Clapham Parish Church	Jebb, Bishop of Limerick
1834	Bristol (Cathedral)	Bishop Gray
1835	Shuckburgh, Warwick	Gertrude Shuckburgh
1835	Easton Neston, Northants	Peter Denys
1835	Linton, Kent	Lieutenant C. J. Mann
1835	St. Edmund the King	Mr. Horne
1836	Linton, Kent	Lady Jemima Wykeham-Martin
1837	Linton, Kent	Viscount Brome (recumbent figure)
1838	Bristol (St. James's)	Rev. Thomas Biddulph
1838	Wimbledon (Parish Church)	Sir James Park
1840	Bristol (Cathedral)	Dr. Elwyn
1840	Fulbeck, Lincs	Sir Henry Fane
1840	Westminster Abbey	3rd Lord Holland
1841	Bristol (Cathedral)	William Brame
1841	Colwich, Staffs	Elizabeth Sparrow
1842	Handsworth (Parish Church)	Sarah Russell
1843	Hopton Wafers, Salop	Thomas Botfield
1844	Stoke, nr. Guildford, Surrey	Eliza Paynter
1844	Richmond, Surrey	Samuel Paynter
1845	Abbots Leigh, Somerset	Philip Miles
1845	Sisted, Essex	Caroline Savill-Onley
1846	Westminster Cemetery	John Jackson
1846	Whalton, Northumberland	Sara Ogle
1846	Baldock, Herts	Georgiana Caldecott
1846	Fareham (Holy Trinity), Hants	Sophia Dixon
1846	Cheam, Surrey	4th Earl of Carrick
1847	Linton, Kent	Julia, Countess Cornwallis (recumbent figure)
1847	South Stoneham, Hants	George Fullerton
1850	South Stoneham, Hants	Mary Fullerton
1850	Aldenham, Herts	Rev. Edward Benbow
1851	Lewisham (Parish Church)	John Thackeray
1853	Whalton, Northumberland	John Ogle
1853	Camborne, Cornwall	Edward Pendarves (with bust)

BAKER, ANDREW, of London

He signs the monument of Colonel Robert Bridges (d. 1717) at Finglas, Co. Dublin.

BAKER, BENJAMIN, of Liverpool

fl. 1828–1845

He signs Hellenic wall-monuments to Thomas

Brooks, 1831, at Whalley, Lancashire, and to the Rev. Samuel Sewell, 1833, at Prescot in the same county. With his partner, Earle, he made the tablet with military trophies to George Vernon, 1844, at North Mimms, Herts.

BAKER, ROBERT CHARLES, of Southampton

fl. 1836–1851

At the Great Exhibition of 1851 Baker showed the model of "A Cemetery Memorial." He signs a small wall-tablet to Charles Baker (d. 1836) at Upton, Bucks.

BALDWYN, STEPHEN

In the Worcester audit of account-books (No. 3, 1640–1669) is the bill for the statue of Charles II. This was erected at the Worcester Guildhall in 1661 by Baldwyn, who was paid £20 "for cutting and setting up the King's statue, according to the agreement." There is also a later payment to him of £8 12s. for his "men's wages in settinge up the Pediston and the Arch." The statue must either have been damaged or become very worn, for Thomas White (q.v.) was paid for repairing it in 1712.

A Samuel Baldwin of Stroud signs the important monument with its recumbent figures of Sir John and Lady Young, 1606, in Bristol Cathedral. He died in 1645 and was buried at St. Nicholas, Gloucestershire (Fosbrooke's *Gloucestershire*, page 309).

BALLANT, THEODORE

In 1767 he received a premium of twenty-five guineas from the Society of Arts for a bas-relief of "The Sacrifice of Iphigenia" (Archives, Society of Arts). There is no further mention of him, so he apparently never exhibited again.

BALLARD, FRANCIS

b. 1751, d. 1811

He signs a tombstone to Mary Gibbs, 1804, at South Littleton, Worcs.

BALLY, WILLIAM, of Manchester

fl. 1832–1846

At the Manchester Exhibition of 1832 he showed a bust of the Rev. R. Newton and, in 1846, "Two busts of Clergymen." His busts of Samuel Hope (1832) and Thomas Henry Illidge (1837) were shown at the Liverpool Academy. His wax portrait of Lord Eldon is in the Victoria and Albert Museum.

BANKES, HENRY
b. 1679, *d.* 1716

He was the son of Matthew Bankes (*d.* 1706), who became His Majesty's master-carpenter under Charles II in 1683 and was reappointed by William and Mary in 1689. Young Bankes was apprenticed to Edward Strong (q.v.) in 1695, and from 1705 until 1709 was working at Blenheim Palace, where he built part of the colonnade of the Great Court. He was employed at Marlborough House, 1709–1712 (Malcolm's *Londinium Redivivum*, Vol. IV, page 317), while in the following year he received £41 for work at the Royal Mews, Charing Cross (*Wren Society*, Vol. XVIII, page 164), and in 1715 went to Windsor Castle, where he was paid for a Portland-stone chimney-piece (P.R.O., A.O.1, 2448/149). He died in 1716 and was buried at Hampton, Middlesex, where a much-worn slab on the floor of the church tower commemorates him.

A Mr. John Banks (who may be a member of the same family) received £25 for "5 staggs heads for ye Hall" of the banking house built by Sir Robert Clayton in Old Jewry. They were presumably carved in wood and the payment for them is entered in Sir Robert's ledger in the Guildhall Library.

There is also a Richard Bankes, described as *3 Bus Regibus Lapicidae* on the tablet commemorating his son-in-law and daughter, the Rev. and Mrs. Francis Clerke, in Shoreditch Parish Church. Sarah Clerke died in 1709 at the age of sixty-four, and her husband six years later. The monument not only bears his arms but also those of the Bankeses—"on a cross or, between four fleur de lys or, a cross patty gules."

BANKS, CHARLES
b. 1745 (?)–1792

Son of William and Mary Banks and brother of Thomas Banks, R.A. (q.v.), he was probably born about 1745. In 1764 he was a pupil of L. Holm (q.v.) and, a year later, was working with a Mr. Powell of Oxford Road. In 1765 he was also awarded a premium of fifteen guineas by the Society of Arts (Archives, Society of Arts), and in 1769 attended the Royal Academy Schools. Here he won a Silver Medal in 1771 and three years later was awarded the Gold Medal for his group entitled "The Story of Pygmalion" (Archives, Royal Academy).

Banks exhibited at the Royal Academy, 1774–1792, showing various models, a design for a monument (1783) and a bas-relief in wax. His niece, Mrs. Foster, afterwards wrote to Allan Cunningham, giving her reminiscences of him, as well as of her more famous father, Thomas Banks. Of her uncle she says: "He was principally instructed by my father, but he died young and was not, I believe, very industrious, therefore nothing remains of his talents in his profession" (*Builder*, 1863, page 4). To describe Charles Banks as having "died young" is hardly accurate, as he must have been at least forty-seven.

BANKS, THOMAS, R.A.
b. 1735, *d.* 1805

He was the son of William Banks, steward to the Duke of Beaufort and surveyor of the works while Kent was building Badminton. Banks was sent to school at Ross-on-Wye, Hereford, but at the age of fifteen was apprenticed to W. Barlow (q.v.), with whom he served his full term of seven years. His master lived near Peter Scheemakers (q.v.), and it was to that sculptor's studio that Banks would go to study when his day's work was over. He was also employed by William Kent, the architect, who must have known his father well.

In 1763 Banks received a premium from the Society of Arts for a relief of "The Death of Epaminondas" in Portland stone; a second came two years later for a marble relief of "The Redemption of the Body of Hector"; while in 1769 he won two more for a life-size model of "Prometheus" and "A Design for Ornamental Furniture" respectively (Archives, Society of Arts).

At that time Banks may have been working or studying with R. Hayward (q.v.), for Nollekens addresses a letter to "Mr. Thomas Banks, Sculptor, at Mr. Hayward's, Piccadilly, London" (Whitley's *Art in England, 1821–1837*, page 40): He was certainly studying at the Royal Academy, where in 1770 he received the Gold Medal for a bas-relief of "The Rape of Proserpine." He also exhibited there, and the talent shown in his works, especially a "Mercury, Argus and Io," shown in 1772, decided the Academy to grant him a travelling studentship. In the summer of that year Banks and his wife (for he had married a Miss Elizabeth Hooton in 1766), set out for Rome. Mrs. Banks was an heiress and owned property in London, so they were able to remain in Rome for seven years, untroubled by financial considerations, although the Academy grant was only for three.

While in Italy, Banks carved the grand relief of "The Death of Germanicus" for Mr. Coke, which is now at Holkham, and also a smaller one of "Thetis and Her Nymphs Rising From the Sea to Console Achilles for the Loss of Patroclus," a work which Mrs. Foster, the sculptor's daughter, afterwards presented to the National Gallery; it is now in the Victoria and Albert Museum.

In 1779 Banks returned to London and took a house in Newman Street. In the following year he exhibited a marble bas-relief of "Caractacus Before Claudius" at the Royal Academy. The commission for this had been given when Mr. Grenville (later Marquess of Buckingham) was in Rome in 1774 and, indeed, had been finished and dispatched from Italy in 1777. The work was placed on the west wall of the entrance-hall at Stowe, where it still remains. While in Rome Banks had also modelled a statue of "Cupid" and, on his return to England, carved it in marble. "The artist, being then unemployed, embarked with it for Petersburg in June, 1781, and, arriving there in August, it was by the recommendation of Lord Malmesbury and Prince Potemkin showed to the Empress who purchased it for four thousand roubles and ordered it to be placed in a building called the Grotto in the gardens at Sczarsco-Zelo" (*European Magazine*, 1790, page 24). Banks remained for a year in Petersburg and made a model of a statue of the Empress for Prince Potemkin; he also, according to Mrs. Foster (*Builder*, 1863, page 4), carved the relief of "Armed Neutrality" for the Empress.

Finding that the Russian climate did not suit him and that he was unlikely to receive any more commissions, Banks returned to London in 1782 and almost at once was employed by Mrs. Newton on a large monument of her late husband, Bishop Newton, which was to be erected in St. Paul's Cathedral. Permission not being granted for its erection in the Cathedral, Banks made a smaller version, which was placed in St. Mary-le-Bow. Though damaged and calcined when that church was burned during the Second World War, the monument still remains and it is to be hoped that one day it may be restored.

In 1783 Banks made stone statues of "The Four Quarters of the Globe" for the attic of the north front of the Dublin Customs House, but these were destroyed when the building was shelled and burned during the Irish Rebellion in 1916. In 1784 he carved for Somerset House two trophies with naval and military ornaments, one for the centre of the north front and the other for the centre of the building next the river, receiving a total sum of £144 15s. (P.R.O., A.O.1/2497). In the same year he was elected an Associate of the Royal Academy and, in 1786, became a full member. He deposited as his Diploma work "The Falling Titan," which J. T. Smith considered "far superior to any that produced in England and perhaps which will never be surpassed" (*Nollekens and His Times*).

In 1789 Banks executed the alto-relievo of "Shakespeare Between the Dramatic Muse and the Genius of Painting" for the exterior of Alderman Boydell's gallery in Pall Mall; it is now in the gardens of New Place, Stratford-on-Avon. In 1790 Boydell, then Lord Mayor, presented to the sculptor the statues of "Religion," "Temperance" and "Fortitude," originally on the front of the Guildhall. These he repaired in his studio, and at the sale held after his death they were bought by Mr. Bankes, M.P., for Corfe Castle (*Athenaeum*, 1846, page 1223).

Between 1787 and 1792 Banks made various chimney-pieces, including one (£93 3s. 6d.) for the Egyptian Hall at Fonthill (Britten's *Beauties of Wilts*, Vol. I, page 214), and several for the house of Richard Cosway, R.A., at 20, Stratford Place (Wheatley's *London*, Vol. III, page 327). In 1790 he carved one for the Bank of England with a "rich ornamented tablet, a festoon of laurel leaves and ribbons on the frieze; Vitruvian scrolls and flutes on the architrave; angular columns with staff and ribbon and twisted flutes" (Building Accounts, Bank of England, Soane Museum). Two years later he made the famous chimney-piece for Daylesford House, to the order of Warren Hastings.

In 1793 Banks executed his most admired monument, that commemorating Miss Penelope Boothby for Ashbourne Church, Derbyshire. This was first exhibited at Somerset House, where a crowd of enthusiastic spectators, including Queen Charlotte and her daughters, was often moved to tears by the simple figure of the sleeping child.

There is a puzzling note in the *Gentleman's Magazine* in 1794 (Part I, page 410) to the effect that the large monument of Lady Henniker "lately erected in Rochester Cathedral" was the work of "Mr. Banks." The work, save for an unimportant marble sarcophagus, is entirely carried out in Coade's artificial stone, the chief feature being two magnificently modelled life-size figures of "Time" and "Eternity." This is the only statement I have found which indicates that Banks was employed by Mrs. Coade (q.v.). The report may be incorrect, but if so it seems strange that so widely read a journal made no attempt to contradict it in a later number.

The rest of Banks's life was passed in executing commissions mostly for busts and monuments. Colonel Johnes, of Hafod in Cardiganshire, was one of his chief patrons, but his works formerly in that house have now been scattered and dispersed.

Banks died on 2 February, 1805, and was buried in Paddington Churchyard. A small cenotaph to his memory was erected in Westminster Abbey with the lines: "Whose superior abilities in his profession added a lustre to the arts of his country, and whose character as a man reflected honour on human nature."

In the *Builder* of 1863 (pages 3–5) are published letters between Allan Cunningham and Mrs. Foster. They give a great many details of her father's career and of his friendship with Horne Tooke and their discussions on politics, "which at that period engaged his attention almost exclusively and even endangered his liberty." After Tooke's arrest for high treason "an officer came to my father with an order from the Secretary of State for him to accompany him to his office." Banks, however, returned a few hours later honourably acquitted.

Mrs. Foster gives this sketch of her father: "He was remarkably taciturn and spoke but little, yet that little was ever to the purpose. . . . He was a most minute observer of nature. . . . He spent much time and was at a considerable expense in forming a collection of drawings and engravings. . . . Simple and frugal in his general style of living, from which he did not deviate, even when fortune began to smile on his talents. . . . Latterly he became very strict in his religious tenets, which opened the way to numberless applications from those who attended the same place of worship which he did. . . . Yet notwithstanding he left a handsome provision for his widow."

At the sale of "a nobleman," held by Mr. Christie on 17 May, 1782, the following lots by Banks were sold: a model in terra-cotta of a "design for a monument of the late Earl of Chatham," a head of Agrippina, "a bas-relief of Doctor Watts, dictated by Divine poetry" and "a mould of Mr. West's bust."

At the sale of Banks's effects held by Mr. Christie on 22 May, 1805, the casts of a number of busts by him were sold, these included "Bonaparte, Mrs. Cosway, Horne Tooke, Mrs. and Miss Johnes, Mrs. Campbell, Miss Rose, Mr. West (terra-cotta), Mr. Home the artist (modelled at Rome), Mr. Palmer, Duchess of Gloucester (terra-cotta modelled in Rome), Dr. Egerton and Dr. Warner (both in clay), Felix Vaughan, J. C. Schroeter, General Martin and another of him when young, Marquis Cornwallis, Lord Camden, Sir R. and Lady Lawley, Mr. West's dog, and Mrs. Taylor." The busts of Warren Hastings included two in "different drapery" and another "in Roman drapery executed in marble for the late Marquis of Lansdowne." Other lots included bas-reliefs of the heads of Lord Daer and Cipriani; and a "circular bas-relief allegorical of the Revolution of King William III" and a "terra-cotta of the death of Hector."

A large number of the original models of Banks's monuments were sold, including those of Sir Eyre Coote, Earl Howe and "Captain Cook, never executed," and "an original model for a monument to Lord Chatham, a great composition of five figures, modelled at Rome. N.B.—This model arrived in England too late for the decision of the Judges." (Archives of Messrs. Christie.)

The original terra-cotta busts of Warren Hastings and Mr. Schroeter belonged to William Tassie and were lots 207 and 208 in his sale held by Mr. Christie on 12 July, 1805.

(C. F. Bell's *Annals of Thomas Banks*, 1938, a full and admirable biography of the sculptor; *European Magazine*, 1790, Vol. XVIII, page 23; *Builder*, 1872, page 483; *Gentleman's Magazine*, 1811, page 617; *Monthly Magazine*, 1807, Vol. I, page 486.)

STATUES

| 1784 | Sir Eyre Coote | India Office |
| 1798 | Marquess Cornwallis | Madras |

BUSTS

1777	Duchess of Gloucester	
1780	Benjamin West	Burlington House (terra-cotta)
1783	Mrs. Cosway	Exhibited Royal Academy
1785	Sir Joshua Reynolds	Watson Taylor Sale, 1832 (Lot 162)
1785	Sir Joseph Bankes	Watson Taylor Sale, 1832 (Lot 165)
1790	Warren Hastings	India Office
1792	Mrs. Johnes	Possession H. Lloyd-Johnes, Esq. (plaster)
1794	Warren Hastings	National Portrait Gallery (bronze)
1798	Dr. Addington	Possession Lord Sidmouth
1800	Marquess Cornwallis	Possession Major Warde
1800	John Horne Tooke	Formerly possession Baroness Burdett Coutts
1803	Oliver Cromwell	
1804	George Soane	Soane Museum

MONUMENTS

1774	Westminster Abbey	Isaac Watts
1782	St. Mary-le-Bow	Bishop Newton
1783	Westminster Abbey	Sir Eyre Coote
1785	St. Giles, Cripplegate (des. 1941)	Anne Hand
1787	Chester (Cathedral)	Dean Smith
1787	Hatfield, Herts	John Heaviside
1787	Carlisle (Cathedral)	Bishop Law
1788	St. Mary, Whitechapel	Robert Markham
1789	Marylebone (Chapel)	Giuseppe Baretti
1790	Flitton, Beds	Earl of Hardwicke
1790	Wimpole, Cambs.	Earl of Hardwicke
1791	Plymouth (St. Andrew)	Samuel Northcote (archives Earl of Iddesleigh)
1791	Westminster Abbey	William Woollett

1792	Hungarton, Leics.	Shukburgh Ashby
1793	Ashbourne, Derby	Penelope Boothby
1793	Stoke Newington (Parish Church)	Joseph Hurlock
1793	Chester (Cathedral)	Anna Matthews
1793	Westminster Abbey	General Loten
1794	Westminster Abbey	Sir Clifton Wintringham
1795	Ewell, Surrey	Mrs. Hallifax
1795	Lewisham (Parish Church)	Margaret Petrie (d. 1791)
1796	Marylebone (Parish Church)	Stephen Storace
1796	Calcutta (Botanical Gardens)	Colonel Kyd
1796	Croft, Yorks	Cornelia Millbank
1797	Halesowen, Worcs	John Halliday
1800	Ickenham, Middlesex	John Clarke
1802	St. Paul's Cathedral	Captain Richard Burgess
1805	St. Paul's Cathedral	Captain Westcott

BAQUET, —

His address was given as 8, Bartholomew Close, when, in 1773, he exhibited two portrait models in wax at the Society of Artists.

BARBER, —

He signs a monument, in the form of sarcophagus with a scroll hanging from it, to Mary Bennett, 1835, at Martock, Somerset.

BARLOW and MULLEY, of London
fl. 1830–1840

They sign a small monument, with a cherub mourning by an urn, to John Miles, 1834, at Cheshunt, Herts.

BARLOW, WILLIAM, of London
fl. 1733–1754

He became free of the Masons' Company by redemption in 1751, and a year later received £350 for chimney-pieces for the Mansion House, including those for the Lady Mayoress's apartment, the Lord Mayor's ante-chamber, and the Lord Mayor's bedchamber. He was also paid £16 for a marble cistern. (City Corporation MSS., Mansion House Box.)

Between 1740 and 1754 Barlow was employed on wood-carving at the house of the Rt. Hon. Henry Pelham in Arlington Street, where in 1749 he received £109 for the carving in the "great room" (R.I.B.A. Library, MS. 728.3).

Barlow, who took Thomas Banks (q.v.) as an apprentice in 1750, signs the monument to Sir George Savile, 1743, in Thornhill Church, Yorkshire. This is a large architectural work, with a triangular pediment and central sarcophagus.

BARNARD, JOHN
fl. 1760–1762

He was "under twenty-two and trained by his father when, in 1760, he received a premium from the Society of Arts for a model of ornaments in clay" (Archives, Society of Arts). Two years later he exhibited at the Society of Free Artists a "model in clay, piece of flowers" and "piece of ornament with two swans."

Graves, in his *List of Exhibitors*, wrongly gives Barnard's initial as "P."

BARRATTA, JOSEPH

At the sale of a "Gentleman" held by Mr. Christie on 25 April, 1804 one of the lots was his "beautiful whole length statue of the Great Duke of Marlborough in the character of Mars, executed for his youngest daughter Lady Mary, who was married to the Duke of Montagu. It was lately the ornament of the Hall of Entrance at Ditton Park." The statue fetched 180 gns. (Archives, Messrs. Christie.) There are a number of Italian sculptors called "Barratta" or "Baratta" and I am uncertain which carved this statue, though it may possibly be Giovanni Di Issidoro Baratta (1670–1747).

BARREL, or BARRELL, HENRY
fl. 1775–1805

In 1775 he received £85 from Lord Radnor in part payment for the "capitals of the chapel columns" at Longford Castle (Archives, Earl of Radnor). In 1777–1778 he was paid £72 10s. for "statuary work" at Guy's Hospital on the centre building. This work included "12 faces" (£50) and "5 pattern's for ye frieze" (£6 6s.) (Archives, Guy's Hospital). In 1780 he was paid £138 for the carving in the library, dressing-room and drawing-room at Gorhambury, Herts (Hertford County Archives, B.12). Between 1786 and 1791 he was working at the "new building next the Admiralty," receiving £139 for wood-carving and chimney-pieces. The latter came from a demolished house at Blackheath belonging to Sir Gregory Page, so Barrel only had to reset most of them, though he did recut one (P.R.O., Ad. Ms. 17/1).

From 1788 until 1805 he was employed by Sir John Soane on mason's work at the Bank of England, where he did a great deal of ornamental stone-carving. In the former year he was paid £4 for a mask-head and, in 1789, £75 for four Corinthian capitals, besides other sums for carving various roses, honeysuckles, runs of moulding, etc., in stone. In 1798 Barrel made for the same architect chimney-pieces for the offices of the Commercial Commissioners at 7, Austin Friars (Soane Note-books, Soane Museum).

His son, Henry Barrel, was apprenticed to Emmanuel Williams, mason, in 1781 and became free in 1788.

BARRETT, B., of London

He carved the monument, designed by L. N. Cottingham, erected to the memory of Lady Boothby, 1838, at Ashbourne, Derby.

BARRETT, G.
fl. 1846–1849

In 1846 he exhibited "Mercury and Pandora" at the Royal Academy, and three years later showed "Mercury and Argus."

BARRETT, JAMES, of Norwich
b. 1701/2, *d.* 1769

He signs the monument to Augustine Curtis (q.v.), 1732, in St. Peter Mancroft, Norwich. This work, which is about 8 ft. high, takes the form of a central Corinthian pillar with a curtain behind it, while to left and right hang curtains supported by cherub-heads. The unusual and curious design almost exactly resembles that of the monument at Dersingham, Norfolk, to Mrs. Hodgson, 1743, though here the statuary was Francis Stafford (q.v.). Barrett also signs the monument to George Warren, 1728, at Horstead, Norfolk.

BARTOLI, DOMINICK
fl. 1764–1813

Bartoli was a worker in scagliola who was employed at Gorhambury, Herts, where in 1785 he was paid sixteen guineas (Hertford County Archives, MS. XI. 71). He later went to the Earl of Darnley's seat at Cobham, Kent, receiving, in 1793, £301 for the twenty-four pilasters and the frieze in the Great Hall (Archives, Earl of Darnley). He also worked at Stowe, and here he was responsible, not only for "the beautiful scagliola columns in imitation of Sienna marble" for the music-room, but also for those in imitation jasper for the saloon (Lipscombe's *Buckinghamshire*, Vol. III, page 90). According to Britton's *Beauties of England* (Vol. III, page 414) he made the pilasters of verd antique for the saloon at Kedleston, Derbyshire. (See also "Richter, John Augustus.")

BARTOLINI, LORENZO
b. 1777, *d.* 1850

He was born at Voria in Tuscany and died at Florence. His "Venus" is in the Walker Art Gallery, Liverpool, and he also signs (in Greek)

the monument with a fine relief which commemorates Sir Vyell Vivian, 1820, at Mawgan in Meneage, Cornwall. His bust of Master Henry Hope was formerly at Deepdene, Surrey, as was his "Venus Coming From the Bath." His bust of The Marchioness of Bristol is at Ickworth Park, Suffolk.

BARTON, WILLIAM, of Derby

In 1839 he exhibited various works at the Derby Mechanics' Institute, including a bust of John Gibson (q.v.), a greyhound in alabaster, and medallic portraits of Queen Victoria, Sir Richard Arkwright and the Rev. William Falkner.

BASTARD, BENJAMIN, of Blandford
b. 1698, *d.* 1772

He was born in 1698, the son of Thomas Bastard and Bridget Creech, and during his lifetime worked as a statuary, architect and builder. In the cloisters of Wells Cathedral is his large monument to Peter Davis, 1749, which is 14 ft. high, and consists of a cherub standing in front of a pyramid and leaning his elbow on a down-turned smoking torch. Bastard died in 1772 and was buried at Castleton, Dorset (Hitchens's *Dorset*, Vol. IV, page 205).

BASTARD, JOHN
b. 1687, *d.* 1770

His brothers were Benjamin (q.v.) and William (1689–1764), the builder of Blandford Church. John Bastard signs a large architectural monument, with a delightful circular relief of angels' heads at the base, to Henry Dirdoe, 1724, at Gillingham, Dorset.

BASTARD, JOHN, the Younger
b. 1722, *d.* 1778

He was the nephew of John (q.v.) and Benjamin Bastard (q.v.) and worked for Lord Winterton in 1764 and also at Stoneleigh Abbey.

In 1770 he made "126 bannisters" for Greenwich Palace, and between 1771 and 1772 received £1,081 for masonry-work on the south-west pavilion of King Charles's building. In the following year he was paid £686 for further work at the Palace, including a "run of very large, fully enriched Corinthian block cornice" (P.R.O., Ad. MS. 68/876).

BATCHELOR, RICHARD, of Buckingham
fl. 1750–1760

In 1759 Mrs. Purefoy of Shalstone, Bucks,

signed an agreement with Richard Batchelor, of Buckingham, "mason and statuary," for a marble monument to herself, which was to be made in a "good, sound and substanial (sic), firm, neat and workmanlike manner." This monument, which was erected in Shalstone Church, is an architectural work with Corinthian capitals, and a broken pediment with a bust of Mrs. Purefoy in the centre. There were originally two cherubs on the pediment, but a nineteenth-century vicar, disliking their nakedness, caused them to be removed. The work cost altogether £98, of which £30 went on the carving of the "bosto" (sic) and the "two boys" (i.e., the offending cherubs) in marble. As a mason, Batchelor was employed on repairs to Buckingham Church between 1754 and 1757 (*Records of Buckinghamshire*, Vol. XII, page 261, et seq.; C. Eland's *The Purefoy Letters*).

A "George Batchelor of Buckingham," who was working between 1825 and 1845 and may be a descendant, signs a number of small tablets in churches in the county, including those of Oakley, Padbury and Buckingham (Parish Church).

Another member of the same family may be John Batchelor of Oxford, who was born in 1734 and apprenticed to Jacob Hayfield, mason, of Oxford. He became free in 1762 (Oxford City Archives) and died in 1810 (*Gentlemen's Magazine*, 1810, page 91).

BATE, RICHARD, of Shrewsbury
fl. 1814–1825

Bate, who became a Burgess of Shrewsbury in 1814 (Town Archives), signs the large wall-tablet to the Birch family which was erected in 1823 in the village church at St. Martin's, Shropshire. At first sight this appears to be a typical London production of the late eighteenth century, and is interesting as showing how slowly new designs reached the more distant counties.

BATESON, WILLIAM, of York
fl. 1729–1750

In 1729 he made a chimney-piece for York Guildhall and in 1731 became, with his partner, William Ellis, master-mason for the York Assembly Rooms on the dismissal of Leonard Smith (q.v.). Bateson and Ellis took over the shell of the building and "worked all the columns," which were finished before the year was out, although the hall was not roofed until 1736. These columns, forty in number, with very fine Corinthian capitals, are closely spaced and divide all the four sides of the main room, or Egyptian Hall, from its aisles. A year later, besides executing a great deal

of masonry-work, the partners carved "the cornice stone of ye Corinthian order," but for some reason or other they were not allowed to finish the building, which was completed by the reinstated Leonard Smith.

Bateson died some time before 1757, for in that year his widow, "Elizabeth Bateson, mason," took a Richard Waddington as an apprentice (York City Archives and Assembly Room accounts).

BAX, JOHN, of Deal
fl. 1830–1837

He signs two unexciting wall-tablets to Henry and Richard Harvey (erected *c.* 1830) and to Sir Richard Lee (*d.* 1837), both in Walmer Parish Church, Kent.

BAYES, ROBERT, of Kettering
fl. 1810–1845

The firm consisted of Robert Bayes and his son Joseph, who later succeeded him. They sign a wall-tablet with a semi-urn to Robert Stanley, 1821, at Weekley, Northamptonshire, and another in the form of a hatchment to the Rev. James Hogg, 1844, at Geddington in the same county.

BAYLIFF, —, of Kendal

In 1832 he made chimney-pieces for Mr. Dunslay's house at Micklegate Bar, York, including one of Italian marble for the drawing-room and another in black Kendal marble for the dining-room (Account-book of Peter Atkinson, architect, in private possession).

BAYLISS, EDWARD, of Helmdon
fl. 1738–1740

He signs an architectural marble monument with a broken pediment and well-carved details to Job Hanmer, 1738, at Simpson, Buckinghamshire. In 1739 he was employed to set up at Shalstone in the same county the "turkey marble" chimney-piece which Mr. Henry Purefoy had bought from William Palmer (q.v.) (Eland's *Purefoy Letters*).

BAYLISS, NATHANIEL

At Flitton in Bedfordshire there is a wall-tablet to George Hadley, 1768, which is signed "Bayliss." This is probably Nathaniel Bayliss, who was working in the county at Woburn Abbey from 1762 until 1768 and who, according to the building account-books, died in 1768 (Bedford Archives). He is buried at Woburn.

BAZZANTI, PIERRE and NICHOLAS, of Florence
fl. 1823–1843

Although there is no record that they ever came to England, the Bazzantis must have had English patrons, for there are several monuments by them in Britain. Those to Isabella Cave, 1827, at Henbury, Glos., and Mary Jones, 1829, at South Stoneham, Hants, are signed by Nicholas and both have reliefs in the classical tradition; the monument commemorating Lady Sophia Pierrepont, 1823, at Holme Pierrepont, Notts, is the work of Pierre. The model for this last-named work, and the correspondence concerning its dispatch to England, are in the possession of the Duke of Wellington. The letters are signed by Pierre Bazzanti and his partner, Joseph Moise, and their address is given as *"près du Palais Corsini."*

Nicholas Bazzanti carved a marble statue of Orcagna for the Uffizi in 1843.

BEAL, F., of Barnstaple
fl. 1790–1800

The best of his tablets, commemorating John Palmer, at Torrington, Devon, measures 10 ft. by 4 ft. and has an urn of coloured marble against a pyramid. Beal also signs tablets to Colonel M —— (rest of name illegible), 1790, and Henry Tippitts, 1796, both in Barnstaple Parish Church.

BEAL, J., of Exeter
fl. 1789–1793

His tablets, like those of F. Beal of Barnstaple (q.v.), are in marble and well carried out. Two of them commemorate the Rev. John Penneck, 1789, and William Harris, 1792, both at Gulval, Cornwall.

BEAL, JOHN, of Doncaster
fl. 1713–1750

He became a freeman of Doncaster on 19 September, 1713. In 1744 the Town Council decided that he should be employed to do "the inside masons' work at ye Mansion House" which was then being built from Paine's design. His son, John Beal, the Younger, became a freeman on 28 December, 1742, and William Beal, presumably also a relation, on 1 October, 1750; both being described as "masons" (Doncaster Corporation Archives).

BEARD, THOMAS
b. 1727, *d.* 1803

He was the son of Robert Beard, a barber of Navestock, Essex, and was apprenticed to William Hoathly in 1739. He was afterwards turned over to William Spratt (q.v.) and became free of the Masons' Company in 1747; he was later appointed Renter Warden in 1779, Upper Warden in 1780, and finally Master of the Company in 1781 (Archives, Masons' Company). Beard, who took his son Robert as an apprentice in 1774, died in 1803 and was buried at Islington, where his tombstone describes him as "citizen and mason of London" (Nelson's *Islington*, page 329).

He signs two large architectural tablets to Owen Phillips, 1748, at St. Thomas Haverfordwest, Pembroke, and Katherine Masters, 1760, at Meopham, Kent.

BEARD, WILLIAM
fl. 1674–1680

In 1674 he was paid for work on the great model of St. Paul's Cathedral (*Wren Society*, Vol. XVI, page 202) and, four years later, as a "stone-cutter of London," he repaired "the breeches and decays in the Earl of Leicester's and Ambrose Earl of Warwick's monuments" in St. Mary's Church, Warwick (Anon, *Churches of Warwick*, 1837, Vol. I, page 63).

Sir William Dugdale, the Garter King of Arms, in his diary (edited by W. H. Hamper, 1827, page 143) has "June 15th, 1680, delivered to Mr. William Beard, stone cutter, the summe of ten pounds in part of the summe of £20 for a monument of white marble for Mr. Edward Bonham, which summe of £20 Mrs. Eliz. Dilke is to pay to my son at Coventre." This monument is in Ryton-on-Dunsmore Church, Warwickshire.

It was presumably his son, another William Beard, who was apprenticed to Edward Pearce (q.v.) in 1686.

BEATTIE, WILLIAM
fl. 1829–1864

He exhibited at the Royal Academy, 1829–1864, and at the British Institution, 1834–1848, his work including busts, chased silver medallions, and a bronze statue of Lord Bacon. At the Great Exhibition of 1851 he showed a vase with a statuette of the Prince Consort, which was 4 ft. high and made of solid silver.

In 1855 Beattie exhibited "A Group of Boys" at the Birmingham Society of Artists; his bronze statuette of Newton is at Windsor Castle. He was also employed by the firm of Wedgwood, modelling for them "The Finding of Moses," "The Flute Player," and statuettes personifying England, Scotland, Ireland and America (Wedgwood Archives).

BEAUCHAMP, EPHRAIM
b. 1660, *d.* 1728

He was made free of the Masons' Company in 1684, and later became Renter Warden in 1697, Upper Warden in 1698, and Master in 1701. Beauchamp and his partner, Christopher Kempster (q.v.), were the master-masons responsible for a great deal of building and carved stonework at St. Paul's between 1691 and 1707, while in 1699 Beauchamp was working at Greenwich Palace, either as partner or assistant of Edward Strong the Elder (q.v.). He was also employed at St. Dunstan's-in-the-East in 1696, and at Sir Edward de Bouverie's London house two years later (Longford Castle Archives).

Beauchamp seems to have retired from business and left London in 1708, for in that year his address is given as "Tottenham High Cross" in the Court book of the Masons' Company. He was buried in All Saints' Church, Tottenham, where his tomb bore a long inscription stating that he died on 16 September, 1728, that he was for many years one of the Governors of Christ Church, Bethlem and Bridewell Hospitals, and that his widow, Laetitia, daughter of John Coppin of Pullox Hill, Bedford, died in 1739, at the age of seventy-two (Cansick's *Epitaphs*, Vol. III, page 53). A Thomas Beauchamp built Founders' Hall, 1669–1671 (Archives, Founders Company).

(Wren Society's Publications.)

BEAUPRÉ, —
fl. 1764–1783

Beaupré was a Frenchman who "came over to try his fortune in England" and lived for a time in Covent Garden (Angelo's *Reminiscences*, Vol. I, page 113). He exhibited various works at the Society of Artists, 1764–1767, and at the Free Society in 1766 showed "a sketch for a monument to Mr. Churchill."

In the same year, under the direction of J. Wilton, R.A. (q.v.), he executed a lead statue of George III, which was erected by Princess Amelia, the King's sister, in Berkeley Square. According to J. T. Smith (*Nollekens and his Times*, Vol. II, page 112), Beaupré was an excellent carver of flowers and had been recommended to Wilton by the French sculptor Pigalle, under whom Wilton had studied in Paris. To be a carver of flowers, however excellent, does not necessarily mean that a sculptor can execute a successful equestrian statue in lead, and though this was much praised at the time it was in a state of collapse by 1827 and had to be supported with props. Shortly afterwards it was removed and presumably melted down.

In 1777 Beaupré went to Dublin, where he remained for six years. He does not seem to have exhibited in Ireland, and no work by him is known there (Strickland's *Dictionary of Irish Artists*).

BEAUCLERK, G.
fl. 1848–1851

In 1848 he exhibited at the Royal Academy "Cupid and Psyche," while at the Great Exhibition of 1851 he showed "A Female Figure on a Couch" and "A Sleeping Nymph."

BEDBOROUGH, JAMES,
of Windsor
fl. 1808–1830

He was much employed at Windsor Castle under Wyattville, becoming chief mason in 1808 on the death of John Slingsby (q.v.), and thereafter describing himself as "statuary and stonemason to His Majesty." He received £1,042 for building part of the terrace walk at Windsor in 1810, and two years later constructed the Royal vaults beneath St. George's Chapel, for which he was paid £3,626 (P.R.O. A.O.1/2501).

Bedborough signs a few tablets, including those commemorating John Mackie, 1818, at Feltham, Middlesex; Henry Neech, 1823, in Windsor Parish Church; Maurice Swabey, 1826, at Langley Marish, Bucks; and Mrs. Wagstaffe, 1826, at Horton, Bucks.

BEDFORD, J., of London
d. 1875

He was a popular monumental mason with a yard at 256, Oxford Street, and though most of his work is apt to be obvious and conventional in design on a few occasions it is not too unfortunate. His monument commemorating William Tallents, 1837, at Newark, Notts, has a well-cut portrait relief, and he also signs three Naval ones, to Edward Long (died 1809, though the memorial was erected later) at Seale, Surrey; Mrs. Dawson, 1843, at Barnes, Surrey; and Captain Ellice, 1853, in Hampton Parish Church. The first two respectively have reliefs of the wreck of the *Isis* and a mourning naval officer, while the Ellice monument shows the figure of the Captain in full naval uniform, standing against a white ensign, his telescope tucked under his arm and his cap at his feet.

Other signed works by Bedford include those to John Hope, 1821, at St. Ewe, Cornwall; Sir Thomas Metcalfe, 1822, at Winkfield, Berks; Sarah Bedford, 1832, at Penzance, Cornwall; Sir

Richard Jones, 1835, at Broadwater, Sussex; Sarah Bott, 1836, at Bromfield, Salop; Harriot Cotton, 1837, at Birchington, Kent; Jane Bonnell, 1841, at Walthamstow, Essex; Sir Edward Page-Turner, 1846, at Bicester, Oxon; Francis Price, 1853, at Overton, Flint; Sophia Greaves, 1857, at Tooting, Surrey; the Officers and Men of the 84th Regiment, 1859, in York Minster; and Arthur Saltmarshe, 1864, at Howden, Yorks. Bedford's monument to Earl Grey, 1849, at Howick, Northumberland, was designed by J. Francis (q.v.).

BEHNES, WILLIAM
b. 1795, *d.* 1864

There seems to be some confusion about the date of Behnes's birth, for the *D.N.B.* and his obituary notice in the *Art Journal* both say it is unknown, while Redgrave in his *Dictionary of Artists* gives it as "before 1795." Behnes himself, however, gave his age as eighteen when he joined the Royal Academy Schools in 1813, so we may take it that 1795 is correct.

He was born in London, the son of a pianoforte-maker from Hanover and his English wife. The elder Behnes had come to London when his apprenticeship in Germany had ended, probably because he already had a link with Britain, for his elder brother had joined the British Navy and served as a surgeon in H.M.S. *Cumberland*. When William was quite young the family went to live in Ireland. Here the father, assisted by his sons, worked at his craft, though William himself was never happy unless he had a pencil in his hand and spent his spare time in a public drawing-school, where he distinguished himself by the accuracy and finish of his work.

Piano-making in Ireland, however, did not prove a paying proposition, so the family returned to England and settled near the Tower of London, where they still continued with the manufacture of musical instruments. In 1812 they moved again, this time to Charles Street, near the Middlesex Hospital. William and his brother Henry (who later changed his name to Burlowe, q.v.) had in the meantime continued to study art, and in 1813 the former joined the Royal Academy Schools. In his spare moments he painted portraits on vellum which, according to the *Art Journal* (1864, page 83), were "among the most beautiful we have ever seen on that material."

In the same house in Charles Street lodged the sculptor, P. F. Chenu (q.v.), whom William and Henry used to watch at work. Seeing that he had a considerable practice and a number of clients, they decided to adopt the same profession,

although towards the end of his life William sometimes regretted his choice and was heard to say thoughtfully: "I should like to paint a picture before I die."

In 1816, 1817 and 1819 Behnes won Silver Medals at the Royal Academy. He also received a Silver Medal from the Society of Arts in 1814, and, in 1819, was awarded the Society's Gold Medal for inventing "an instrument for transferring points to marble" (Archives, Society of Arts). He first exhibited at the Royal Academy in 1815 when he showed a bust of a Mr. Badger; after that date success came swiftly to him and in three years he was an established and sought-after artist. One of his earlier patrons was Barrington, Bishop of Durham, of whom he made a bust in 1818. This led to other commissions from the County Palatine, including one from Lord Durham for a statue of his son, the "Master Lambton" of Sir Thomas Lawrence's famous picture.

Work now came in so fast that Behnes felt he was justified in moving to larger premises and bought a house in Dean Street, Soho. This was a fatal mistake, for the building was totally unsuited to his purpose and it was the expense incurred in trying to adapt it, and in building on a modelling room high enough to admit statues of heroic proportions, that crippled him financially. His extravagant habits caused him to fall into the hands of moneylenders, and he later began to neglect his pupils and be off-hand with his clients. Nor was this all, for the *Art Journal* hints darkly that "his moral reputation began to suffer from irregularities which mark a man even among the 'indifferently honest' " (1864, page 83).

In 1829 Behnes received a contract for a group of figures in Roche Abbey stone for the clock-tower of Buckingham Palace, the amount named being £700 (P.R.O. Works 19/3). In 1837 he was appointed Sculptor in Ordinary to the Queen, probably because he had already executed a very successful bust of her in 1828 (a plaster-cast of which is in the Bethnal Green Museum). The appointment, however, was purely honorary and did not produce a single Royal commission, although before that date he had executed busts of the Duke of Cumberland, Prince George of Hanover, the Duchess of Cambridge, the Duke of York and the Duchess of Kent. In 1843 he carved the head of "Queen of Beauty," the horse ridden by Lord Seymour in the Eglinton tournament (*Illustrated London News*, 30 September, 1843).

Behnes's last years were sad. His financial troubles grew worse, and in 1861 culminated in a bankruptcy which swept from him all his belongings and mementoes of a lifetime. He was forced to move to miserable lodgings in Charlotte

Street, but later fell ill and died in the Middlesex Hospital on 3 January, 1864, indeed, according to S. C. Hall's account he was "Found one night literally in the gutter with threepence in his pocket, somewhere close to the Middlesex Hospital" (S. C. Hall, *Retrospect of a Long Life*, Vol. II, page 238).

He was buried in Kensal Green Cemetery, and a Committee was formed, with George Cruikshank as secretary, to raise money to erect a monument and bust over his grave and to present a bronze bust to the National Gallery. Later, in 1864, however, the *Art Journal* regretted that "the fund was not making the progress it deserved" and part of the scheme was afterwards abandoned.

Behnes was a great artist. He was particularly successful with busts; indeed, the *Art Journal* considered that they had "never seen anything finer in modern or ancient art" than his bust of Clarkson, while H. Weekes (q.v.), when lecturing on art, was inclined to rate him as the superior of Chantrey in the field of portrait sculpture. The reliefs on some of his monuments at times reach the highest level of true art, and no one who sees the memorial to Mrs. Botfield at Norton, Northamptonshire, can fail to be moved by the figure of Beriah mourning by his mother's coffin. The figure is not only superbly carved, but conveys the grief of a son for the death of a beloved mother in a finer, nobler and more touching manner than any other monument in England.

Behnes's statues, with the exception of his Dr. Babington in St. Paul's, are less happy. For his statue of Sir Henry Havelock in Trafalgar Square he relied on a photograph to obtain a likeness, the first time that photography had been used for such a purpose.

Behnes exhibited at the Royal Academy, 1815–1863, and at the Great Exhibition of 1851 showed his colossal statue of Sir William Follett and a figure of Lady Godiva. To the International Exhibition of 1862 he sent his "Cupid with Two Doves." He also modelled a work in mezzo-relievo, with half-sized figures, illustrating Shakespeare's "Seven Ages of Man," which, according to Palgrave (*Essays on Art*, page 221), was "of great ingenuity and beauty, but never produced in marble."

(Authorities cited in text.)

STATUES

1822	George IV	For Dublin
1823	Hon. Charles Lambton	Lambton Castle
1824	Alexander Hope	Formerly at Deepdene
1837	Dr. Babington	St. Paul's Cathedral
1839	Earl of Egremont	Petworth
1840	Baron Joy	Dublin
1843	Sir John Jones	St. Paul's Cathedral
1844	Lady Emily Somerset	(*Builder*, 1844, page 368)
1845	Sir Thomas Gresham	Royal Exchange
1850	Sir William Follet	Westminster Abbey
1852	Henry Hall	Leeds Infirmary
1852	Peel	Leeds
1855	Peel	Formerly Cheapside, now Police College, Hendon
1855	Peel	Bradford
1858	Edward Barnes	Leeds
1861	Sir Henry Havelock	Trafalgar Square
1861	Sir Henry Havelock	Sunderland

BUSTS

1817	Henry Earle	Foundling Hospital
1818	Lady Sophia Kent	Exhibited Royal Academy
1818	Admiral Lord Radstock	Exhibited Royal Academy
1818	Sir Thomas Plumer	Exhibited Royal Academy
1819	Lord Eldon	Inner Temple
1820	Benjamin West, P.R.A.	For Lord De Tabley
1820	Duchess of Cambridge	Windsor Castle
1821	Lord Barrington	Exhibited Royal Academy
1822	George Tierney	National Portrait Gallery
1824	Lord Stowell	Inner Temple (exhibited Royal Academy; replica Middle Temple)
1824	Joseph Marryat	St. George's, Grenada, B.W.I.
1825	Lord Stowell	National Portrait Gallery
1825	Earl Grey	Exhibited Royal Academy
1825	Mrs. Fitzgerald	Exhibited Royal Academy
1825	James Northcote	Exhibited Royal Academy
1826	James Christie	Exhibited Royal Academy
1826	Colonel Thomas Perkins	Athenaeum, Boston, U.S.A.
1826	Sir Isaac Coffin	Athenaeum, Boston, U.S.A.
1826	Lady Beresford	Exhibited Royal Academy
1826	Earl of Egremont	Petworth, Sussex
1826	Duke of Kent	Buckingham Palace
1827	Mr. Young, of Covent Garden	Exhibited Liverpool Academy
1827	Lord and Lady Southampton	Exhibited Royal Academy
1827	Oliver Goldsmith	Trinity College, Dublin
1827	Countess of Jersey	Exhibited Royal Academy

1828	Prince George of Cumberland	Windsor Castle
1828	Duke of Cumberland	Windsor Castle
1828	Duchess of Cleveland	Raby Castle
1829	Princess Victoria	Windsor Castle
1830	1st Earl Camden	Bayham Abbey (based on a work by J. Wilton, R.A.)
1830	Lord Ebrington	Barnstaple Infirmary
1830	Beriah Botfield	Longleat
1831	Lady Ebrington	Castle Hill, Devon
1831	J. Nash	Exhibited Royal Academy
1831	Marquess of Bristol	Possession Viscount Mersey
1831	Prince George of Cambridge	Royal Collection
1831	Sir Richard Keats	Windsor Castle
1832	Earl of Harrowby	Sandon Hall
1832	Marquess of Bristol	Ickworth
1832	Lord Eldon	Middle Temple
1833	Richard Whately	Oriel College, Oxford
1834	Lord Brougham	Lincoln's Inn
1835	Martin Tupper	Exhibited Royal Academy
1836	William Hey	Leeds Infirmary
1836	Sir Thomas Hardy	Greenwich Hospital Chapel (replica Royal Collection)
1836	Sir Benjamin Brodie	Royal College of Surgeons (plaster-cast)
1836	Lord Morpeth	Castle Howard
1837	John Paris	Royal College of Physicians
1837	Lord Brougham	Exhibited Royal Academy
1838	Marquess of Bristol	Ickworth Park, Suffolk
1838	Henry Earle	St. Bartholomew's Hospital
1838	John Tomlinson	Stoke-on-Trent Parish Church
1838	Joshua Bates	Public Library, Boston, U.S.A.
1839	William Babington	Royal College of Physicians
1839	Thomas Clarkson	Guildhall, London (destroyed by enemy action 29 September, 1940)
1840	Colonel Leake	Fitzwilliam Museum, Cambridge
1842	Lord North	Eton College
1842	Sir William Molesworth	Reform Club
1843	George Grote	Exhibited Royal Academy
1843	Duke of Newcastle	Eton College
1843	Edward Copleston	Oriel College, Oxford
1844	Lord Lyndhurst	Trinity College, Cambridge
1845	Richard Porson	Upper School, Eton College
1846	Lord Howe	Eton College
1846	Count D'Orsay	Royal Collection

1846	Earl Camden	Eton College
1846	Bishop Wilson	St. Paul's Cathedral Calcutta
1847	Chatham	Upper School, Eton College
1847	Dr. Carpue	St. George's Hospital
1847	Benjamin Disraeli	Hughenden Manor, 'Bucks
1847	Richard Jones	Guildhall, London (destroyed by enemy action, 29 September, 1940)
1848	Captain Marryat	Exhibited Royal Academy
1849	Thomas Arnold	National Portrait Gallery
1849	Lord Hammond	Upper School, Eton College
1849	Charles Barry	Exhibited Royal Academy
1851	Wellington	County Buildings, Winchester
1851	Wellington	For the King of Prussia
1855	George Cruikshank	Kensal Green Cemetery
1857	Isaac Hargraves	Tunbridge Wells Hospital
1857	George Norman	Guildhall, Bath
1858	Sir David Salomons	City of London School
1858	Benjamin Travers	Royal College of Surgeons
1858	Sir Henry Havelock	Guildhall
1861	Earl of Elgin	Exhibited Royal Academy
n.d.	William Maltby	Fitzwilliam Museum, Cambridge
n.d.	George and Mary Lucy	Charlecote Park, Warwick
n.d.	Duke of York	Royal Collection
n.d.	Earl Fortescue	Powderham Castle, Devon

MONUMENTS

1819	St. John's Wood Chapel	John Tunno
1821	Bodmin, Cornwall	Michael Bennet
1822	Streatham (Parish Church)	James Strachan
1823	Paddington (Parish Church)	Joseph Nollekens, R.A.
1823	Old Alresford, Hants	Esther North
1824	Penang (St. George's)	John Macalister
1825	North Ockenden, Essex	John Russell (with bust)
1825	Navestock, Essex	Lord Radstock
1825	Norton, Northants	Charlotte Botfield
1826	Benacre, Suffolk	Sir Thomas Gooch, Bart.
1827	Wangford, Suffolk	1st Earl of Stradbroke
1828	North Ockenden, Essex	Joseph Russell

1828	West Wickham, Kent	Isaac James
1829	Stoke-on-Trent (Parish Church)	Josiah Spode
1829	Hull (Holy Trinity)	John Alderson
1832	Westminster Abbey	Dr. Andrew Bell
1832	Westminster Abbey	Sir Henry Blackwood
1833	Stoke-on-Trent (Parish Church)	Woodhouse, Dean of Lichfield
1833	Stoke-on-Trent (Parish Church)	John Bourne
1833	Tunbridge Wells (Holy Trinity)	Maria Thomas
1833	Bristol (St. Michael's)	Richard Seyer
1833	Lambeth (St. Mary)	Rev. S. Pope
1833	Clifton Campville, Staffs	Rev. John Watkins
1834	Grafton Regis, Northants	Lord James FitzRoy
1834	Tyringham, Bucks	William Praed
1835	South Warnborough, Hants	Richard Harrison
1835	Bodmin, Cornwall	Captain Oakley
1836	Swallowfield, Berks	Sir Henry Russell
1837	Tyringham, Bucks	James Praed
1839	Crowan, Cornwall	Sir John St. Aubyn
1840	Cambridge (Trinity College Chapel)	John Wordsworth
1840	Great St. Helen's, Bishopsgate	Thomas Blenkarne
1840	Sulacoats, Hull	Mr. and Mrs. Spaldin
1842	Warwick (St. Nicholas)	Alexander Trotter
1843	Clifton Campville, Staffs	John Mousley
1843	Corrington, Lincs	Rev. George Beckett
1846	Navestock, Essex	7th Earl Waldegrave (bust)
1854	Charterhouse Chapel (London)	Oliver Walford (medallion portrait)
1855	Hornsey (Parish Church)	Samuel Rogers
1858	Highgate (Cemetery)	Mrs. Elsworth

BELL, ALEXANDER,
of Newcastle-upon-Tyne

fl. 1764–1773

From 1764 until 1768 he was employed at Seaton Delaval House, returning there in 1776 to build the mausoleum which took two years to complete. He also received £211 for the carved stonework, the capitals of the columns costing £7 4s. each and the frieze around the entrance-door £15 3s. 8d. (Archives, Lord Hastings).

BELL, JOHN
b. 1812, *d.* 1895

According to the *D.N.B.*, Bell was born in 1811, but in the 1862 edition of *Men of Our Times* (of which he presumably saw the proof) it is stated that he was born a year later. His birthplace was Hopton in Suffolk, and he was educated at the village school of Catfield in Norfolk. He attended the Royal Academy Schools in 1829 on the recommendation of H. Sass, and in 1833 won a large Silver Medal from the Society of Arts for a model of a bust. In 1839 he competed for the Nelson memorial, but his design was rejected and he afterwards presented it to Greenwich Hospital.

In 1844 Bell sent his statues of "The Archer" and "Jane Shore" to Westminster Hall. The former, which had already been shown at the Royal Academy in 1837, was described by the *Literary Gazette* (1844, page 466) as "a performance so striking and masterly that it at once fixes the attention, not only by the novelty of the subject, but by the ability of the treatment"; the latter, however, it considered "not so successful." In 1848 the sculptor executed the figures on the Corn Exchange at Newark (*Builder*, 1848, page 391), and also designed a number of objects for the exhibition of "British Manufacture and Decorative Art." These included fish-knives, a door-stop in the form of Cerberus, and a match-box in the shape of a Crusader's altar-tomb, which even moved the *Art Union* to remark that they "were unable to appreciate it."

Bell had first exhibited at the Royal Academy in 1832, when he showed a religious group. Ten years later came his "Babes in the Wood," which was a great success and caused the *Art Union* (1842, page 128), to say of the sculptor: "His mind is deeply imbued with poetic feeling, he is one of the few artists who attempt higher efforts than mere busts."

His best-known work in London is the Crimea monument of the Brigade of Guards at the junction of Pall Mall and Waterloo Place. The work soon came to be known somewhat irreverently as "The Quoit Player," from the figure of "Honour" with outstretched arms and a pair of coronals in each hand. On its unveiling in 1861 the *Art Journal* (1861, page 158) wrote regretfully: "We have tried in every possible way to like this work and consider it the right thing, but we have failed signally." Another critic was more outspoken when he declared that it "looked best in a fog."

Bell was employed by Blashfield (q.v.) from 1854 and in the following year modelled a figure of "Hibernia" for him, which was carried out in terra-cotta. His "Una and the Lion" was reproduced in miniature in "Parian" by Copeland. In 1845 he had designed for the Colbrookdale Company a fearsome object called "the deerhound hall table," which consisted of four life-sized deerhounds, cast in iron and seated on their haunches, supporting a table decorated with "emblems of the chase and with the leaves and fruit of the vine." This canine monstrosity, which was illustrated in the *Art Union* of 1845 (*Appendix*, page 6), had a great success and in the same year appeared at the Paris Exhibition. Nor do the statues of Queen Victoria and the Prince Consort "in bronze and ormolu," which the sculptor sent to the Great Exhibition of 1851, seem in better taste.

In 1858 Bell modelled heads of various animals which were cast in iron and used as part of the railings for the Metropolitan Cattle Market at Pentonville. Five years later he made a fountain for Kew Gardens with the figure of a child raising a shell to its lips. In 1859 he was awarded a medal by the Society of Arts for a treatise on "The Origination of the Principle of Entasis as Applied to the Obelisk," a form for which he apparently had a passion. The *Art Journal* of 1861 (page 30), comments on the fact that "Mr. John Bell, who has been eagerly and rather unnaturally striving to erect an obelisk somewhere, is at length to be gratified. We are not sorry to say it will be placed far off, at Bermuda, to the memory of Sir William Reid." His model of "Peace," originally designed in 1876 for the main hall of the Foreign Office, was presented to the Guildhall in 1888.

As a monumental sculptor, Bell signs the tablet with a medallion portrait erected in 1868 to the memory of John Crome, the landscape painter, in St. George's, Norwich. He also exhibited "a monument to Miss Legard" at the Royal Academy in 1847.

He died on 14 March, 1895, at 15, Douro Place, Kensington, where he had lived for more than forty years. His early works of sculpture had shown vigour and imagination, but his later groups exhibited at the Academy were remarkable for nothing but bad taste and sickly sentimentality. Among these may be included "Cherub with Primroses" (1865), "Mother and Child" (1867), "The Last Kiss" (1868), and "The Dove's Refuge" (1871). They were much admired at the time and are typical of the work which has brought the sculpture of the late Victorian era so deservedly into disrepute.

(*Magazine of Art*, 1894, page 16; authorities cited in text.)

STATUES, GROUPS, etc.

1833	The Quarterstaff Player	Exhibited Suffolk Street Galleries
1837	Infant Hercules	Formerly Crystal Palace
1841	The Eagle Slayer	Bethnal Green Museum
1842	Babes in the Wood	Sold Christies 22 June, 1861 (£210)
1844	Dorothea	For Lord Lansdowne
1844	The Archer	For Lord Fitzwilliam
1845	The Child's Own Attitude	Royal Collection
1845	William Shakespeare	Exhibited Westminster Hall (original model given by the sculptor to Crystal Palace)
1851	Andromeda	Osborne. (Exhibited Great Exhibition and purchased by Queen Victoria)
1851	Una and the Lion	Exhibited Great Exhibition
1853	The Maid of Saragossa	Formerly Crystal Palace
1853	Four colossal statues of California, Australia, etc.	For Terrace of Crystal Palace
1853	Eve	For Lord Truro
1854	Lord Falkland	St. Stephen's Hall
1854	Sir Robert Walpole	St. Stephen's Hall
1855	Lord Clarendon	Foreign Office
1855	Armed Science	Woolwich (replica for Lord Waveney)
1855	Omphale mocking Hercules	Art Gallery, Salford
1856	Lalage	For Lord Fitzwilliam
1856	Wellington Monument	Guildhall
1860	Guards' Memorial	Waterloo Place
1860	Crimea Artillery Memorial	Woolwich
1861	Monument to James Montgomery	Sheffield Cemetery (model in Cutlers' Hall, Sheffield)
1861	Monument to Sir William Reid	Bermuda
1864	America	Albert Memorial
1869	Imogen	For Lord Coleridge
1871	Monument to Lady Waveney	Flixton Church, Suffolk
1875	Cursetjee Manockjee	Bombay (statue)

BUSTS

1848	Sir Fowell Buxton	Freetown Cathedral, Sierra Leone
1858	Sir Robert Walpole	Eton College
1866	Dr. Clark	Anatomical Museum, Cambridge
1867	Dr. Hugh Falconer	Madras
1867	Mr. Cooper	Town Hall, Cambridge
1877	Lord Byron	Exhibited Royal Academy

BELL, LADY
d. 1825

She was Maria, sister of William Hamilton, R.A., and studied painting under her brother and Sir Joshua Reynolds, many of whose works she copied. These were much admired by the *Gentleman's Magazine* (1825, Part I, page 570), which considered them "the more valuable because they retain their fine colouring of which time has deprived the originals."

She later married Sir Thomas Bell, Sheriff of London, and exhibited at the Royal Academy in 1816 and 1819, showing pictures and, in the latter year, busts of her husband and daughter. She died on 9 March, 1825, in Dean Street, Soho.

BELL, R.

He signs a marble monument with a curved pediment, and a skull with bats' wings at the base, to Samuel Walford, 1746, at Stratford-on-Avon, Warwick.

BELLAMY, THOMAS
b. c. 1699, *d. c.* 1754

Son of Richard Bellamy, tailor, of St. Botolph's, Aldgate, he was apprenticed to James Paget or Padgett on 12 March, 1714, becoming free of the Masons' Company in 1721 (Archives, Masons' Company). His workshop was in Camberwell, but in 1754 he wrote to the Company asking to be allowed to resign from the post of Assistant to the Court, "being obliged, on account of my health, to live in the country."

Bellamy signs large architectural monuments to Sir Thomas Halton, 1733, at Long Stanton, Cambridgeshire, and to Sir Henry Fetherston, Bart., 1746, at Stanford-le-Hope, Essex. In 1753 he was employed at the house of James West in Lincoln's Inn Fields (Archives, West of Alscot Park).

BENNIER, JOHN

The Historical Manuscripts Commission in their seventh report (Part II, page 816) publish the articles of agreement between John Bennier and the Earl of Longford, dated 23 December, 1681, for casting four large and sixteen small statues for the Duke of Ormonde.

BENNIER, or BESNEIR, PETER
d. 1693

He was the brother of Isaac Besneir, whom he succeeded as Sculptor in Ordinary to Charles I, for a Royal Warrant issued in 1643 orders him to "take into his custody and keeping all the moulds, statues and modells which were heretofore committed to the charge of Isaac Besneir."

Peter lost his office during the Commonwealth, but in May, 1660, petitioned to be reinstated on the grounds that the late King had granted him the "place of sculptor to His Majesty and the custody of his statues, etc., "but by reason of the most unhappy distraction befallen since, hee injoyed not the same place, but was reduced into very great poverty and want through his faithfulness and constancy" (*Calendar of State Papers Domestic, Charles II,* Vol. II, page 66). Charles II granted his request and he held the post until 1692–1693. On 30 May, 1693, C. G. Cibber (q.v.) was appointed on the "decease of Peter Bennier" (Faber's *C. G. Cibber*, page 12).

Bennier signs the monument with a noble portrait-bust of Sir Richard Shuckburgh (died 1656) in Shuckburgh Church, Warwickshire. In 1655 he was employed at Lamport Hall, Northants, where he carved the shield-of-arms on the garden front of the house (Isham Archives).

BENNIER, or BENIERE, THOMAS
b. c. 1663, *d.* 1693

Vertue (*Walpole Society*, Vol. I, page 89) wrote of him: "Thomas Beniere is a curious ingenious Statuary. Born in England of French parents, his works in small in Marble from the Life or modells are very fine. The anatomy figure commonly seen at apothecarys was from his Original model many other things are in the hands of the Curious of his doing. he was much imployd by Mr. Salmon for the wax work figures shown in Town. he us'd to cutt in Marble from the Life a Portrait for 2 guineas, being industrious & young & very quick at his work. he livd & died near fleet ditch aged about 30 ano 1693. (Buried in Black Fryers. St. Annes Sep. 18. 1693)."

BENNISON, APPLETON, of Hull
fl. 1778–1821

His yard was in Mytongate in Hull. He signs monuments to Sir James Pennyman, Bart., 1808, at Stainton, Yorks, and to Henry Legard, 1819, and William Williamson, 1821, at Kirk Ella in the same county.

BERCHETT, or BURKETT
fl. 1692–1706

He did a good deal of work for Chatsworth, and in 1692, with his partner Carnall, supplied busts for the great hall. In the following year he and another partner, Mr. Finch, made the bases for the west terrace on which C. G. Cibber's (q.v.) sphinxes now stand, and in 1694 they executed a marble basin for the Great Stairs (Francis Thompson's *A History of Chatsworth*).

Berchett later worked at the Inner Temple, and in 1706 received £21 10s. for "the eight figures at the end of the Robert Sawyer's building" (Inderwick's *Inner Temple Records*, Vol. III, page 399).

BERNASCONI, FRANCIS
d. 1841

He may have been a son of Bernato Bernasconi, who was employed as a plasterer by the second Earl Verney at Claydon Hall, Bucks, between 1770 and 1784. Bernato seems to have settled in the county, for it is as "a poor man with a large fameley (*sic*) in the town of Buckingham" that he asks to be paid by Lord Verney, who was then on the verge of bankruptcy (Verney Archives).

Francis Bernasconi was mostly employed on scagliola work and decorated the Royal Palaces and many of the great houses in London and the country. Under Wyattville he worked at Windsor Castle, where in 1805 he was paid for "Gothic elliptical arches, elliptical soffits, Gothic compo mouldings, twelve enriched spandrels, the Royal Arms, thirteen angels with plain shields, etc." (P.R.O. Works 5/93). Between 1800 and 1809 he received a total of £1,556 for plaster-work, Gothic mouldings, etc., at Cobham Hall (Earl of Darnley's Archives). In 1813-1815 he was paid £879 for work at Ashridge Park (Archives, Lord Brownlow). In 1810 he repaired with Roman cement the east side of the great court of Trinity College, Cambridge, while five years later John and Peter Bernasconi (who one imagines were his brothers) agreed to cover the exterior of Jesus College with the same material (Willis and Clarke's *Architectural History of Cambridge*, Vol. II, pages 147 and 420). In 1816 Bernasconi was at Chicksands Priory, where he made Gothic ornaments (Notebook, Soane Museum). Between 1814 and 1818 he repaired the screen at York Minster (Allen's *Yorkshire*, Vol. I, page 284), and, in 1819, the canopy of Wolsey's statue at Christ Church, Oxford (Hiscock's *A Christ Church Miscellany*, page 206).

About 1820 he modelled four groups, designed by Stothard, for the grand staircase at Buckingham Palace, and, in the same year, repaired the sedilia at Southwell Cathedral, Nottinghamshire. In 1825 he executed the altar-piece for Westminster Abbey which "consisted of a series of shrines, or rather ornamental niches, canopied with a profusion of delicate tabernacle work" (*Gentleman's Magazine*, 1825, Part II, page 226). He was also employed by The Duke of Bridgewater to decorate the chancel of Gaddesden Church, Herts, in 1817 (Archives, Lord Brownlow). As a plasterer, his contract (dated 1803, for £826) for stucco-work in "The Great Tower" of Westminster Abbey is in the Abbey Archives.

BERRY, JOHN, of Barnstaple
fl. 1755-1790

He carved a number of sundials for churches in Devon, the best of these being the elaborate one, dated 1757, above the south door at Tawstock Church. Berry, who was later assisted by his son Thomas, signs a tablet to John Thorn, 1763, at Marwood in the same county.

BIDFORD, W. MANLEY

He signs a marble tablet in the form of a curtain, bunched and corded at the corners, to William Smith (*d.* 1818) at Alcester, Warwickshire.

BIELFIELD, C. F.
fl. 1821-1832

He received a Silver Isis Medal in 1821 from the Society of Arts for an "original bust." He exhibited at the Royal Academy in 1832 a "medallic portrait of J. Thrupp."

BIENAIMÉ, ANGELO
fl. 1829-1851

He was born at Carrara and had studied under Thorwaldsen before he came to London about 1828. In the following year he showed busts of Sir Astley and Lady Cooper at the Royal Academy, and in 1838 exhibited a statue of "Innocence Lamenting the Loss of Her Dove." Another statue "Innocence" had been commissioned in Italy by the Marchesa Somareva, but was unfinished when she died and was accordingly sent over to London. It was exhibited at the Colosseum in Regent's Park in 1829 and was later bought by Sir Matthew Ridley. At the Great Exhibition of 1851 Bienaimé showed his "Love Triumphant."

The sculptor's "Recumbent Bacchante" is at Powerscourt, Ireland, and was executed in 1836, a replica being made in the following year for the Emperor of Russia. Bienaimé also made another replica later for his patron, Sir Augustus Clifford, for whom he carved statues of "Narcissus" and "The Four Seasons," as well as six marble vases for Clifford's house at Westfield, in the Isle of Wight (Privately printed description of Westfield, 1862).

For the Duke of Devonshire he made eight statues and two vases which are now at Chatsworth. His signed bust of Sir Robert Peel (*c.* 1840) is at Felbrigg Hall, Norfolk.

BIGÉE, NICHOLAS
fl. 1705-1712

In 1712 he and his partner, John Woodward, carved the two eagles on the gate adjoining the bridge at St. John's College, Cambridge (Willis and Clarke's *Architectural History of Cambridge*, Vol. II, page 277).

Bigée signs two monuments at St. Leonard's, Buckinghamshire; the first, erected in 1707, commemorating Mr. and Mrs. Seth Wood, and the second their son, Colonel Cornelius Wood, who died in 1712. The Colonel's monument has a portrait-bust set against a great baroque trophy-of-arms, in the centre of which is Hercules's club, crowned by a plumed helm. A curious feature is provided by the skulls with bats' wings, placed on either side of the trophy, and holding in their teeth heavy fringed curtains which fall in thick folds.

BIGGS, JOSIAH, of Bath
fl. 1821–1840

He was a minor local statuary whose tablet to Theodore Haultain, 1832, in St. Mary's, Bath, is inscribed: "This marble came from Pompeii." He also signs tablets to Thomas Morgan, 1821, at Hinton Charterhouse, Somerset; the Rev. Benjamin Richardson, 1832, at Farleigh Hungerford, Somerset; William Whipham, 1835, at Calne, Wilts; and Susanna Manifold, 1836, at Brackley, Northants.

BIGGS, RICHARD, of Bath
fl. 1744–1758

He was apprenticed to his father, Richard Biggs, of Bath, in 1735 and became free in 1744 (Bath Corporation Archives). He signs a tablet in Bath Abbey to Sir Everard Fawkener, who died in 1758.

The younger Biggs also worked in London, for in 1749 he was employed as a mason at St. Bartholomew's Hospital (Hospital Archives).

BIGGS, WILLIAM, of Bath
fl. 1732–1764

He was employed on the new buildings of St. Bartholomew's Hospital between 1731 and 1739 and was responsible for most of the carved stonework. He also executed three chimney-pieces for the "Great Room," for which he received £68 in 1734 (Hospital Archives).

Biggs was living at Monkton Combe, near Bath, and gave Ralph Allen as his security when, in 1741, he was engaged by John Wood for the building of Bristol Exchange. He continued working there until 1744, but does not seem to have given entire satisfaction for, as early as 4 September, 1741, "being summon'd to attend the Committee, Mr. Wood told him great complaints were made of his work and admonished him to keep strictly to his contract" (Exchange Minute Book, Bristol Archives).

He described himself as "citizen and mason of London" on the tomb he erected to two of his children in Monkton Combe churchyard (*Church Rambler*, Vol. I, page 105).

Another member of the same family was Benjamin Biggs, who was the mason responsible for building Bath Guildhall, 1760–1770.

BINGHAM, EDWARD,
of Peterborough
d. 1796

In 1750 he carved chimney-pieces for Lord Fitzwilliam at Milton Hall (Fitzwilliam (Milton) Archives), while in 1773 he was employed under Sir William Chambers on marble carving for the same house (R.I.B.A. Library, Chambers' Correspondence).

Bingham was an excellent provincial statuary, producing architectural monuments and tablets in coloured marbles. He died on 16 July, 1796 (*Gentleman's Magazine*, 1796, page 621).

MONUMENTS

1751	Stamford (All Saints)	Mr. and Mrs. Denshire
1751	Titchmarsh, Northants	Colonel John Creed
1754	Gamlingay, Cambs	Ralph Lane
1756	Oundle, Northants	Jane Squire
1758	North Luffenham, Rutland	John Digby
1760	Cotterstock, Northants	John Simcoe
1764	Elton, Northants	Jane Forster
1767	Peterborough (Cathedral)	Richard Tryce
1767	Clinton, Northants	James Edings
1769	Grantham, Lincs	Edmund Turnor
1771	Sleaford, Lincs	Richard Moore
1782	Stamford (All Saints)	George Denshire
1783	Peterborough (St. John's)	William Bowker
1786	Peterborough (St. John's)	Rev. John Image (*d.* 1759)
1788	Peterborough (Cathedral)	William Gery
1788	Stamford (St. Martin's)	John Truman
1790	Ufford, Northants	Lord James Manners
1792	Clinton, Northants	Richard Arnold
1793	Stamford (St. Martin's)	Henry Fryer
1795	Peterborough (St. John's)	Thomas Sambrook

BINGHAM, JAMES,
of Peterborough
fl. 1800–1820

Presumably the son or grandson of Edward Bingham (q.v.), he signs a tablet to William

Harper, 1803, in St. Martin's, Stamford, and a ledger to Eleanor Wing, 1816, at Sedgbrook, Lincolnshire.

BINGLEY, JOHN, of London
fl. 1773–1802

About 1790 he went into partnership with J. C. F. Rossi (q.v.) and together they executed a number of works in terra-cotta. The partnership, however, does not seem to have been a success and was later dissolved (for details, see under "Rossi, J. C. F."). In 1796 he was paid £145 17s. for chimney-pieces by the Duke of Bridgewater for Cleveland House, London; they included a marble reeded one (£46 15s.) for the drawing-room and a dove-grey marble one (£18) for the ante-room (Archives, Lord Brownlow).

In 1801 Bingley was working for Mr. Henry Peters, carving a veined marble chimney-piece, inlaid with black marble, for the latter's country seat at Betchworth Castle, Surrey, and another marble one costing £38 for his London house in Park Street (Notebooks, Soane Museum). In the following year he was employed by Lord Radnor at 6, Grosvenor Street (Longford Castle Archives).

Bingley, whose studio was in John Street, Tottenham Court Road, signs monuments to Mary Darker, 1773, and John Darker, 1784, both in St. Bartholomew's the Less; Jacob Evelyn, 1793, at Godstone, Surrey; James Blicke, 1793, in Twickenham Parish Church; and John Davenport, 1796, at Teddington, Surrey.

BIRCH, ROBERT
fl. 1736–1747

In 1746 he made marble chimney-pieces for Welbeck Abbey, including those for the Duke's bedroom and dressing-room, and for the Duchess's bedroom. In the following year he supplied three more for the same house (Welbeck Abbey Archives).

BIRCH, WILLIAM
fl. 1749–1751

In 1749 he received over £1,000 or mason's work at Welbeck Abbey, while two years later he was paid a further £944 for building the riding-house, stables, etc. (Welbeck Abbey Archives).

BIRD, EDWARD CHAPMAN
d. 1792

From his names he would appear to have been a son of Francis Bird (q.v.), whose father-in-law was Edward Chapman; if so, he was probably born about 1716 and may well be the E. C. Bird

of Westminster who died 22 February 1792. E. C. Bird became as "a mason" bankrupt in 1770 and a sale of his stock-in-trade was held at his yard at Millbank on 4 April, 1771, by Mr. Christie. Among the lots sold were a "Head of Venus"; reliefs of "The Crucifixion" and the "Death of Lucretia" and "Sicilian Jasper marble tablets." As a number of marble chimney-pieces, marble vases, etc., were sold it seems as if Bird must have had a considerable business.

BIRD, FRANCIS
b. 1667, *d.* 1731

He was born in the parish of St. James's, Westminster, and, when he was about eleven years old, was sent to Flanders, where he studied under the sculptor Cozins. He then went on to Rome and worked in the studio of Le Gros, but returned home about 1689, though he had been so long abroad he found he could hardly speak English. In London he worked under Grinling Gibbons (q.v.) and C. G. Cibber (q.v.), but after a few years went back to Rome for a further nine months' study under Le Gros.

Bird, who was again in England by 1700, is best known for his work at St. Paul's Cathedral. In March, 1706, he was paid £329 for the panel over the west door, and, in December of that year, £650 for carving the "Conversion of St. Paul," 64 ft. long and 17 ft. high, for the great pediment. This contained "eight large figures, six whereof on horseback and several of them two and a half feet imbost" (*Wren Society*, Vol. XIV). Between 1712 and 1713 he executed the two panels over the west portico for £339, but it was not until 1721 that he carved the statues of various apostles and evangelists (each nearly 12 ft. high) for the west front and south side of the Cathedral. For these he received a total sum of £2,040 (*Wren Society*, op. cit.).

Between 1711 and 1712 Bird made a marble statue of Queen Anne to stand in front of St. Paul's. This work had a chequered career, for it was mutilated by a mad lascar (who considered it a reflection on his mother) in the eighteenth century and, though it was afterwards repaired by John Henning the younger (q.v.), by 1885 it had become very dilapidated. There was, however, little excuse for removing it in that year, and none at all for employing Mr. Richard Belt, one of the worst of the late Victorian sculptors, to make the "copy" which now stands in its place. Mr. Augustus Hare rescued Bird's original statue from the yard of the City's stone-mason and transported it with considerable difficulty to his house, Holmhurst, near Hastings, in the grounds of which it still remains (Hare's *Story of My Life*).

Bird was also a prolific statuary and the "many lofty tombs and magnificent monuments in Westminster Abbey and other churches" (*Gentleman's Magazine*, 1731, page 83) for which he was responsible range from the vast erection commemorating the Duke of Newcastle in the Abbey, to the fantastic and macabre tablet, with its two skeletons tearing in half an ancient oak, to the memory of Elizabeth Benson in Shoreditch Church. This is unsigned, but is included in the list given by the sculptor to his friend, Le Neve, for the latter's *Monumenta Anglicana*. Many other monuments noted by Bird have been identified by Mrs. Esdaile (*Antiquaries' Journal*, Vol. XXII), while one which has been traced even more recently is that to the Rev. John Cawley. This, according to an MS. note made in 1751 by Richard Rawlinson in his copy of *Le Neve* (now in the library of St. John's College, Oxford), is at Henley, Oxfordshire.

Bird was for many years accused of having executed the monument to Sir Cloudesley Shovel in Westminster Abbey. All writers on the Abbey have attacked it; the *D.N.B.* considers it "one of the worst works in the world"; it often gave Addison "great offence"; while Horace Walpole wrote of it that "Bird bestowed busts and bas-reliefs on those he decorated, but Sir Cloudesley Shovel's and other monuments by him made men of taste to dread such honours." Because nobody has ever had a good word for the monument, writers on English sculpture have hastened to condemn other works by Bird, but the main reason for these attacks now no longer holds good, for the late Mrs. Esdaile's researches have proved conclusively that the work is not Bird's, but was carried out by Grinling Gibbons. Henrietta, Countess of Oxford, mentions Bird's monument to John Holles, Duke of Newcastle, also in Westminster Abbey, when in 1742 she writes to her trustee, Mr. West, that she thinks "the model of my father's monument may sometime hence be properly disposed at Welbeck" (Archives, West of Alscot Park).

Lot 412 at Sotheby's sale on 6 November, 1951, was an undated letter to Bird from Alexander Pope ordering a monument to be erected to his father who had died in 1717. This was to "be entirely white marble," and the poet also indicated on the scale drawing the inscription he wanted. This tablet is in the north gallery of Twickenham Parish Church.

In the minute book for the building of Greenwich is "April 5th, 1718, resolved that the great marble block, bought by the Hospital some time since, should be cut into a statue of King William and that Mr. James do write to Mr. Bird the statuary to attend here next Board Meeting." Bird attended on 19 April and brought a sketch, but the work was never carried out (*Wren Society*, Vol. VI, page 71).

At Christmastide, 1729, Bird had a serious accident. He was coming out of a tavern near his home one frosty night when he slipped and broke his leg, and this was badly set by the surgeon. In January, 1730–1731, "he became swelled, his body and legs like a dropsy and this continued to his death on 27 February, 1730–1731, aged sixty-five. He was buried in a vault in the church of St. Andrew's, Holborn." (*Walpole Society*, *Vertue Notebook*, Vol. III, page 49.) He left a considerable sum of money and also an estate near Windsor, which he had inherited from his father-in-law, Edward Chapman (q.v.). Three of his five daughters were educated by the Blue Nuns and one son was 15 when his father died.

Bird's workshop was in Lincoln's Inn Fields. Many years after his death a mason named William Green wrote to Lord North in 1770, with reference to recutting an inscription on a monument at Amesbury, Wiltshire. Green asked a penny a letter and undertook for this price to do it "as it should be done, which is what ye old one never was, nor indeed was any of those things performed as they ought to be in Mr. Bird's shop from my knowledge" (Bodleian, MS. North, C.11, F.222).

For some reason or other the sale of Bird's belongings was not held till twenty years after his death. The auction took place on 30 April, 1751, by Langford of Covent Garden. Many of the lots were prints, drawings, etc., but among the models sold were those of the monument of Congreve in the Abbey and the statue of Queen Anne outside St. Paul's.

(Authorities cited in text.)

STATUES, etc.

1703	Henry VIII	St. Bartholomew's Gate, Smithfield
1706	Queen Anne	Kingston-on-Thames (£47 18s. 6d., Borough Archives)
1712	Queen Anne	Formerly outside St. Paul's Cathedral, now at Holmhurst, nr. Hastings
1717	John Radcliffe	University College, Oxford
1719	Henry VI	Eton College (£443 17s. 11d., bill in possession of Buckinghamshire Archaeological Society)

1719	Cardinal Wolsey	Christ Church, Oxford
1720	Queen Mary	University College, Oxford
1721	Lord Clarendon	Clarendon Building, Oxford (£55, Vice-Chancellor's Accounts)
1721	Statuary	Clarendon Buildings, Oxford (£300, Vice-Chancellor's Accounts)

MONUMENTS

c. 1690	West Wycombe, Bucks	Hugh Darrell
1692	Westminster Abbey	Thomas Shadwell (with bust)
1695	Westminster Abbey	Dr. Richard Busby
1699	Tissington, Derby	Mrs. Fitzherbert
1701	Chenies, Bucks	Duke of Bedford
1702	St. Paul's Cathedral	Jane Wren (*Gentleman's Magazine*, 1783, page 637)
1704	St. James's, Piccadilly	Earl of Huntingdon
1705	Isleworth, Middlesex	Sir Orlando Gee
1705	Salisbury (Cathedral)	Mrs. Eyre
1707	Westminster Abbey	Robert Killigrew
1709	Henley, Oxon	Rev. John Cawley
1710	St. Leonard's, Shoreditch	Mrs. Benson
1711	Westminster Abbey	Duke of Newcastle
1711	Westminster Abbey	W. E. Grabe
1712	Westminster Abbey	Admiral Henry Priestman
1712	Westminster Abbey	Earl of Godolphin
1713	Westminster Abbey	Sprat, Bishop of Rochester
1714	York (Minster)	Archbishop Sharp
1714	Stonham Aspal, Suffolk	Anthony Wingfield
1716	Westminster Abbey	Admiral Baker
1728	Bolsover, Derby	The Cavendish family
1729	Westminster Abbey	William Congreve

BIRD or BYRD, WILLIAM, of Oxford

b. 1624

He was born in 1624 in the parish of St. Nicholas, Gloucester, and was baptized in the church on 1 June of that year (Parish Registers). When he gave evidence in a lawsuit on 7 June, 1681, he told the Court his age and place of birth, and also that he "had worked in Oxford for thirty-four years"; that he was "an accepted Mason and served an apprenticeship of eight years to one Walter Nicholls, of Gloucester, an accepted mason"; and that, since he had been "a Master Workman," he had "in diverse Counties work'd

severall noble buildings too many to be here mentioned and lately in Oxford he built the Arch at New College and Edmund Hall Chappell." He also mentioned that he was responsible for the "dorecase of the Divinity School" and for a chimney-piece "of Burford stone in Mr. Lentall's house at Hasely" (University Archives, Vice-Chancellor's Court, 1681, Mich.).

At "the latter end" of 1658 Bird discovered the art of "paynting or stayning of marble." He presented specimens of his work to Charles II and his Queen when they visited Oxford, and to Cosmo, Prince of Tuscany, when he came to the city in 1669 (Wood's *Life and Times*, Vol. I, page 241).

In 1659 he made a sundial for All Souls, and in 1665 and 1670 was working at Christ Church, first carving the Royal Arms for the Canons' lodgings, and later a statue of Mercury (Hiscock's *A Christ Church Miscellany*, page 201). In 1664 he was paid £11 7s. for restoring the monument of William of Wykeham at Winchester (Kirby *Annals of Winchester College*, page 353). Between 1666 and 1667 he received £307 for all the stone-carving at the Sheldonian Theatre and was also paid for making a model of the building (Vice-Chancellor's Accounts).

In 1668 payment of £24 0s. 6d. was made to Bird "for repairing and setting up the remainder of the marbles given by my Lord Howard and Mr. Selden," and he also received £28 15s. 0d. for the two inscriptions intended for them (Vice-Chancellor's Accounts). This, of course, refers to the Arundel Marbles. For the Ashmolean he carved "the coat of arms of the founder, twelve terms, trophies, the King's arms and six cartouches in the front" (Vice-Chancellor's Accounts, 1679–1682). On 19 November, 1683, he signed a contract with Sir Christopher Wren, under which he agreed to execute carved stonework at Winchester Palace (*Wren Society*, Vol. VII, page 34–36).

Bird's monuments are important, especially that commemorating Brideoake, Bishop of Chichester, 1678, in St. George's Chapel, which has a life-size figure in full vestments. His monument to the Fettiplace family, 1686, at Swinbrook, Oxon, is a curious work, apparently based on an earlier one in the same church, with life-sized effigies of three of the Fettiplaces lying one above the other on shelves, for all the world as if they were in bunks on board ship.

Other monuments signed by Bird include those to M. Dunch, 1679, at Pusey, Berks; William Guise, 1683, in St. Michael's, Oxford; William Wilmot, 1684, at Wantage, Berks; and Samuel Sandys, 1685, at Ombersley, Worcs.

BISHOP, EDWARD, of Tenterden
b. 1757, *d.* 1822

He signs a tablet to William Stringer, 1817, at Goudhurst, Kent. Bishop is buried at Tenterden, where a stone in the churchyard commemorates him and his wife, Ann Cloake.

BISWICK, —
fl. 1743–1745

Probably a Bristol mason, he was employed by Maynard Colchester as a "stone-carver" during the building of Westbury Court, Gloucestershire, between 1743 and 1745. In February–March, 1744–1745, he was also paid for carving "Lions." These were probably heraldic beasts for a shield-of-arms, or for the gate-piers (Archives, Sir Francis Colchester-Wemyss).

BLACKBURN, JOHN, of Norwich
d. 1814

In 1788, the year he became a Freeman of Norwich, he put an advertisement in the *Bury Post* "informing his friends and the public (not being generally known) that the articles which existed between Mr. Ivory and him confining him from executing marble business has been for some time by mutual consent entirely dissolved. He now executes every article in the stone and marble branches. Monuments, ornamental and plain chimney-pieces in the most improved taste, best manner and on reasonable terms."

As a mason, Blackburn was employed by Sir Thomas Proctor Beauchamp on repairs to Langley Park, Norfolk, in 1796 (Beauchamp Archives). He died in 1814 "aged about fifty years, after a lingering illness" (*Bury Post*, 18 May, 1814). He signs monuments to John Woodbine, 1786, and Richard Pillans, 1793, both at East Dereham, Norfolk; and to William Powell, 1810, in St. Saviour's, Norwich.

BLAGDEN, JOHN, of Sheffield
fl. 1792–1805

He signs a tablet to Elizabeth Bagsnaw, 1792, at Chesterfield, Derbyshire, and another to Elizabeth Jackson, 1805, at Badsworth, Yorkshire.

BLAKE, WILL, of Basingstoke

He agreed with Anthony Chute in 1753 for £91 13s. 4d. to lay a pavement of Portland stone and black and white marble in the gallery at the Vyne (Archives, Sir Charles Chute, Bart.).

BLANCHARD, M. H.
fl. 1839–1870

A terra-cotta worker, served his apprentice-ship with Coade and Sealy (q.v.) and, in 1839, set up his own manufactory in the Blackfriars Road, buying some of the Coade moulds, etc.

His principal works include the enrichments on the Brighton Aquarium; the South Kensington Museum; the Charing Cross, Cannon Street and Star and Garter Hotels; and the Grand Hotel, Cairo. He also made the twelve panels representing the months of the year on the Wedgwood Institute at Burslem.

At the Great Exhibition of 1851 Blanchard showed Ionic capitals for Clifden House, and "pinnacles and tracery windows for the new chapel, Tottenham and for Kingston Church" at the Architectural Exhibition of the following year (*Builder*, 1852, page 34).

(Various references, *Art Journal* and *Builder*.)

BLAND, THOMAS

A self-taught artist, he carved in 1842 the statue of Britannia and the bas-reliefs on the octagonal column which was erected at Shap Wells Spa, Westmorland, to commemorate Queen Victoria's accession (*Builder*, 1842).

BLASHFIELD, J. M.
fl. 1830–1870

Having purchased some of Coade's moulds when W. Croggon (q.v.) closed down the original factory in 1836, Blashfield opened terra-cotta works at Poplar. In 1858 he moved to Stamford, but shortly afterwards left the firm he had founded, which was then formed as a limited company and became insolvent in 1875.

Blashfield employed the sculptors Bell (q.v.), Nixon (q.v.), Woodington (q.v.) and Weigall (q.v.) to model for him, and it was the first-named who was responsible for the statue of a Triton, executed in 1857 for the fountain at Oxford Infirmary.

Works turned out by Blashfield's firm during his régime include the urns for the Royal Mausoleum at Windsor; vases for Buckingham, Kew and Hampton Court Palaces; and a heroic "Apollo Belvedere" for the Earl of Normanton. He was also responsible for the terra-cotta enrichments for Alford House, Dulwich College, the Sun Fire Office at Charing Cross, the Duke of Cornwall's Hotel at Plymouth, and Farnham Town Hall. For the Crystal Palace he supplied a statue of Australia, four colossal Tritons, and a fountain in the Rennaissance Court. In 1863 he made a terra-cotta portico for Viscount Strangford's house in Cumberland Street, Hyde Park, and, in 1868, the gate-piers for Castle Ashby, Northants. (Various references, *Art Journal* and *Builder*.)

BLAXLAND, H., of Milton-next-Sittingbourne, Kent

fl. 1802–1828

He signs a few small tablets in churches in the neighbourhood of Faversham and Milton.

BLAYNEY, J., of Chester

fl. 1820–1840

Signed examples of his tablets, which are mostly Hellenistic, include those to John Corser, 1822, at Moreton Say, Salop; Elizabeth Panton, 1833, and Edward James, 1834, both in Chester Cathedral; Mary Boydell, 1835, at Gresford, Denbigh; and Harriet Evans, 1837, at Tarvin, Cheshire.

BLORE, ROBERT the Elder and ROBERT the Younger, of Piccadilly

Firm *fl.* 1786–1835

It is difficult to distinguish between the monuments carved by the elder Blore and those for which his son was responsible, for the firm seems to have been styled "R. Blore and Son" from about 1790. The firm also made chimney-pieces, and in 1806 supplied one for Ramsey Abbey (Soane Notebooks).

The senior partner became bankrupt in 1818 and apparently retired about two years later. His son carried on the business and, some time after 1830, went into partnership with George Wilcox, a former pupil.

Monuments and tablets executed by the firm were sent all over England; they are always well carved, but the designs are dull and uninteresting. However, they cannot be held responsible for the monument to Edward Foley, 1805, at Stoke Edith, Hereford, for this large and very ugly erection, 18 ft. high, was executed to a design by Tatham (*Gentleman's Magazine*, 1805, Part I, page 278). In 1826 Blore brought an action for defamation against the notorious Hariette Wilson on the publication of her "Memoirs." He was awarded £300 damages.

MONUMENTS AND TABLETS

1786	Ryton, Durham	John Simpson
1791	Ramsbury, Wilts	Ann Reaa
1799	Paddington (Parish Church)	Elizabeth Coghlan
1799	Chertsey, Surrey	John Escott
1802	Northampton (St. Peter's)	Rev. Edward Lockwood
1803	Barbados (Cathedral)	The Mayers family
1805	Barbados (Cathedral)	Sir W. Myers
1805	Hampton, Middlesex	Lady Edwards
1806	Appleton, Berks	Anne Southby
1807	St. Paul's Cathedral	John Wasdale
1807	East Bedfont, Middlesex	William Sherborn
1807	Alberbury, Salop	Richard Lyster
1808	Forthampton, Glos	Hon. and Rev. James Yorke
1809	Catherington, Hants	John Todd
1810	Cromer, Norfolk	George Wyndham
1811	Evenley, Northants	H. Browne
1811	St. Mary Abbots, Kensington	Hon. William Murray
1812	Betley, Staffs	Sir Thomas Fletcher
1818	St. Mary Abbots, Kensington	Thomas Chase
1819	St. John's Wood (Chapel)	Charles Stratton
1819	St. John's Wood (Chapel)	Martha Cherry
1819	Pott, Cheshire	Edward Downes
1821	Methley, Yorks	Countess of Mexborough
1821	Chester (Cathedral)	Edward Wrench
1822	Burwash, Sussex	Mrs. Christian Mackenzie
1823	Oxford (St. Peter's-in-the-East)	Thomas Winstanley
1824	Winchester (Cathedral)	Thomas Rennell
1828	Methley, Yorks	Hon. Henry Savile
1831	Iver, Bucks	Martha Jadis
1833	Stoke Rochford, Lincs	Sir Montagu Cholmeley

BLORE, ROBERT, of Derby

b. 1810, *d.* 1868

He was born in Derby, the son of Joseph Blore, a monumental mason of that city. About 1837 he modelled a figure of the "Sleeping Endymion," based on a work by Canova, and copies of this were later made in biscuit porcelain by the Derby china works. Blore also made the ornamental vases in the Arboretum in Derby and, in 1839, a bust of the Rev. Noah Jones.

In 1841 he moved to Middlesbrough, where he worked for Moss, Isaac Wilson and Co., who had opened a pottery there in 1838. In 1851 he carved a bust of Sir Joseph Paxton.

(Information from Public Library, Derby.)

BLUNDELL, WILLIAM, of Daventry

b. ca. 1780, *d.* 1865

He signs tablets in Northamptonshire with well-cut details to John Lucas, 1810, at Dunchurch; John King, 1816, at Long Buckley; and Colonel David Rattray, 1820, at Daventry.

BOAG, MAITLAND, of London
b. 1759, d. 1817

In 1809 he and his son David were the principal stone-carvers engaged on the restoration of Henry VII's Chapel in Westminster Abbey (Brayley's *Westminster Abbey*, Vol. I, Part II, page 26; *Gentleman's Magazine*, 1817, Vol. II, page 630).

BOHSE, —

He was an assistant of J. F. Moore (q.v.) and exhibited a tablet for a chimney-piece at the Free Society of Artists in 1773.

BONE, CHARLES
b. 1791

He attended the Royal Academy Schools in 1811 and exhibited at the Academy, 1815–1826. His principal work seems to have been "Ulysses Throwing the Rocky Fragments," for he showed this at the Academy in 1815 and at the British Institution in the following year. (Royal Academy Archives.)

BONOMI, JOSEPH
b. 1796, d. 1878

He was born in Rome on 9 October, 1796, the son of the architect, Joseph Bonomi (1739–1808). In 1815 he won a Silver Medal from the Society of Arts for an original bas-relief in plaster and, in the following year, joined the Royal Academy Schools, where he was awarded Silver Medals in 1817 and 1818. He also studied under Nollekens (q.v.) and was, indeed, the only pupil the sculptor ever accepted. His monument in the old Cathedral at Calcutta, which commemorates Captain C. L. Showers (d. 1815) is signed "Bonomi, Nollekensi Discipulus fecit, 1819." This is a fine work with a bas-relief of the action at Malown, in which the Captain was killed in 1815, together with his companions, Lieutenants Bagot and Broughton. Bonomi also signs a tablet with a medallion portrait in the same Cathedral, in memory of Lieut.-Colonel John Weston, who died in 1819.

Nollekens was extremely attached to Bonomi, whom he took with him on his Sunday evening walks. According to J. T. Smith (*Nollekens and His Times*, Vol. I, page 39), "it was generally supposed that he would have left a considerable part of his immense property" to his ex-pupil "from his long continued attachment to him from his birth." As a matter of fact, Nollekens did nothing of the kind and only left Bonomi £100, though he did bequeath a similar sum to each of the latter's five brothers and sisters.

In 1823 Bonomi returned to Rome, where he made a bas-relief of a "Dancing Bacchanal" and a small statue of one of the Muses. A writer in the *Literary Gazette* (1824, page 668) who saw them considered that "this accomplished and intelligent artist is particularly distinguished by animation, freedom and simplicity in his works, very different from the usual manner of his countrymen."

From 1824 until 1844 Bonomi lived almost entirely in Egypt and the Near East, where he worked at drawing and Egyptology, and was also engaged in exploration. Between 1852 and 1853 the sculpture and modelling for the Egyptian Court at the Crystal Palace was executed under his direction and in great part by his own hand (*Handbook to the Crystal Palace*, 1853). In 1861 he was appointed Curator of the Soane Museum, a post he held until his death on 3 March, 1878.

Bonomi exhibited at the Royal Academy, 1820–1838, and at the British Institution in 1820. His group of "Jacob Wrestling With the Angel" was sent to the Academy in 1820, and he later showed busts of James Northcote (1821), Joseph Hume (1822, now in the possession of the New York Historical Society) and Henry Parks (1838). A cast of his bust of Prince Hoare (1822) was formerly at the Crystal Palace, and a smaller undated one of Dr. John Lee is in the Aylesbury Museum.

(Authorities cited in text.)

BOOBYER, JAMES, of Bath
fl. 1780–1790

Boobyer, who was succeeded in the business by his son James, signs a tablet to James Moutray, 1785, in Bath Abbey.

BOOL, GEORGE M.
b. 1812

In 1831 he attended the Royal Academy Schools on the recommendation of J. Francis (q.v.) and won a Silver Medal three years later. He exhibited at the Academy, 1832–1836, showing various medallic portraits, busts and bas-reliefs. The *Literary Gazette* (1834, page 299) considered Bool's bust of William IV, which he showed at the Academy in 1834, "one of the most perfect resemblances of the King that has yet been executed; the effect of it is very grand."

BOOTH and JOHNSON, of Nottingham
fl. 1770–1800

They sign tablets in a good eighteenth-century style to John Bulstrode, c. 1770, at Keyworth, Notts; Elizabeth Cripple, 1778, at Ruddington,

Notts; the Hawksley family, 1780, in St. Nicholas's Church, and Robert Wright, 1799, in St. Mary's Church, Nottingham; and Elizabeth Bambrigge, 1797, at Lockington, Leicestershire.

BOSSOM, CHARLES, of Oxford
b. 1788, *d.* 1830

His tablet to Dr. Loveday, 1828, at Magdalen College, Oxford, is illustrated in the *Gentleman's Magazine* of that year (Part I, page 209). He also signs tablets to Mrs. Deane, 1822, at Kingston Bagpuize, Berks, and to John Oglander, 1825, in Merton College Chapel.

Bossom died on 14 June, 1830, and was buried in the churchyard of St. Giles's, Oxford, where his tombstone referring to him as a "sculptor" can still be seen. He was succeeded in the business by his son, who signs the tablet to Lord Stavordale, 1837, at Farley, Wilts.

BOSSOM or BOSON, JOHN
d. 1743

Bossom, whose yard was at Greenwich, was the carver employed at St. George's, Bloomsbury, 1720–1730; St. Luke's, Old Street, 1727–1733; St. John's, Horsleydown, 1728–1733; and St. Olave's, Southwark, 1737. With his partner, John How, he was responsible for all the carved wood-work on the façade of the East India House in Leadenhall Street, and also for the chimney-pieces in that building (Archives, East India Company).

In 1732 Bossom carved the reredos in Canter-bury Cathedral, for which he received £242 (Fabric Account Book, Cathedral Library). Three years later he was paid £61 by the Hon. Francis Godolphin, of Baylies, Stoke Poges, for carving which included the chimney-piece in the "great room" (Archives, Duke of Leeds). In 1740 he made a chimney-piece for Culverthorpe Hall, Lincolnshire, the seat of Sir Michael Newton.

In 1729 he was paid £33 for carved woodwork for the screen and organ gallery of Westminster Abbey. In 1741 he was paid a further £95 which was also presumably for the organ case (West-minster Abbey Archives).

Vertue (*Walpole Society*, Vol. III, page 116) refers to Bossom as "a man of great ingenuity and undertook great works in his way for the prime people of quality and made his fortune very well in the world." He also records that he "dyd about April, 1743, of an age not considerably above middle age." (Authorities mentioned in the text; information from Mr. H. M. Colvin.)

BOTTOMLEY, CHARLES, of Bury and Cambridge
fl. 1729–1749

His signature is to be found on the obelisk, made about 1739, which was placed on a hill between Shelford and Newton in Cambridgeshire, in memory of Gregory Wale. He also signs the ledger to Elizabeth Wenyade, 1747, at Brettenham, Suffolk. The cartouche tablet to John Stevenson (*d.* 1749) at Newton, near Cambridge, is said by William Cole, the antiquary (*fl.* 1742–1782), to be the work of "Bottomley, a mason in Cam-bridge, who was to have thirty guineas for it" (W. M. Palmer's *Monumental Inscriptions from Cambridgeshire*).

In 1749 Bottomley married Susannah Flowerday at St. James's Church, Bury St. Edmunds. She seems to have carried on the business after his death, for in 1757 she was paid for "mason's work to the back of the Senate House" (Vice-Chancel-lor's Accounts).

BOTTOMLEY, GEORGE
fl. 1728–1735

About 1729 he went into partnership with R. Singleton (q.v.), and together they sign archi-tectural monuments in Norwich to Thomas Batchelor, 1729, in the Cathedral, and to Daniel Fromanteel, 1734, in St. Mary Coslany.

BOUQUET, W. V.
fl. 1782–1798

He exhibited a large number of unnamed wax portraits at the Royal Academy, 1782–1798, and at the Free Society in 1783.

BOWER, JOSEPH the Elder and JOSEPH the Younger
Firm *fl.* 1714–1759

The Bowers, father and son, were the master-masons for building Wentworth Castle between 1714 and 1722, and they were also responsible for the carved stonework.

In 1725 the younger Bower was paid £92 for making "the cascade in the menagerie," and two years later he built three miniature towers named after Lord Strafford's daughters, the Ladies Lucy, Anne and Harriett Wentworth. In 1734 his work included an obelisk erected in the Park to the memory of Queen Anne; in 1739 he built a temple copied from one at Tivoli; and in 1742 he made a column with a carved capital (British Museum, Ad. MS. 22241).

In 1744 "Mr. John Bower ye carver and stone-cutter" was employed at Westbury Court, Gloucestershire, then being built by Mr. Maynard Colchester (Archives, Sir Francis Colchester Wemyss).

BOWLES, RICHARD

In 1765 Trevor, Bishop of Durham, who was building a church at Glynde in Sussex, paid Bowles £20 for a "handsum veined marble font, properly ornemented." This charming work is still in the church (Archives, Brand of Glynde).

BOZZONI, LUIGI
fl. 1838–1847

He was a native of Florence and had studied under Finelli in Rome before he came to England in 1838, where he took for his studio part of the ground floor of the Imperial Hotel in Covent Garden. Here, between 1839 and 1844, he executed for Mr. Constable Maxwell, of Everingham Park, Yorkshire, life-sized statues of the Twelve Apostles, four martyrs, and eighteen bas-reliefs of religious subjects. All these were intended for the Roman Catholic Church which Mr. Maxwell had built at Everingham (*Art Union*, 1839, page 106).

Before the statues went to Yorkshire, Bozzoni exhibited those of St. Andrew and St. John in Westminster Hall in 1844. The *Literary Gazette* (1844, page 466), described them as having "good modelling about the drapery, though as much cannot be said for the figures."

In 1847 Bozzoni exhibited a subject from the Aeneid at the Royal Academy. He probably died in the same year.

BRADLEY, —, of Coleford

He signs a large wall-tablet in coloured marbles to Thomas Hopkins (*d.* 1793) at Weston, Herefordshire.

BRADLEY, ROGER, of Hertford
fl. 1790–1815

Between 1790 and 1815 he did a good deal of masonry work for Lord Grimston at Gorhambury, Herts (Herts County Archives, XI, 74), and he was also employed by Lord Melbourne at Brocket Hall. He was one of the master masons for building Ashridge Park, Herts, being paid over £2,000 between 1815–1817 (Archives, Lord Brownlow).

BRADLEY, WILLIAM, of Selby
fl. 1806–1840

He signs tablets in Halifax Parish Church to Joseph Hulme, 1806; William Norris, 1807;

James Waddington, 1820; and Joshua Jackson, 1832. His tablet to the children of Edward Russell, 1835, is at Snaith, Yorkshire, and he also signs another to John Dobson, 1837, at Selby, in the same county.

A number of other Yorkshire statuaries and masons were named Bradley, including William, a master mason at York Minster in 1505; John, a freemason, who became a Freeman of York in 1739; and Robert, who describes himself as "sculptor" in the York directory of 1841.

BRADSHAW, —, of South Molton

In 1739 the Mayor and Corporation of South Molton, Devon, decided to build a Town Hall and accordingly sent a Mr. Joshua Bawden to buy some materials from Stowe (the famous house of Granville, Lord Bath, near Kilkhampton), which was then being demolished. Mr. Bawden spent £129 and purchased, among other things, four Corinthian capitals and pilasters, the "ornaments of three windows," a "carved architrave," a picture of "The Triumph of King Charles II," and a ton of lead.

The building was erected between 1740 and 1741 to the plans of a Mr. Cullen, and into it were incorporated the fragments from Stowe. Bradshaw, however, was responsible for the rest of the carved stonework, including shields, festoons, Corinthian capitals, etc., and the result is undoubtedly one of the most charming town halls in England (South Molton Town Archives).

BRADSHAW, W., of Manchester
fl. 1735–1772

He signs large wall-tablets to William Lawson, 1735, in Wakefield Cathedral, and to the Massey family, 1765, at Rostherne, Cheshire.

Hilbert, in his *Foundations of Manchester* (Vol. II, page 316), describes Bradshaw's monument to William Clowes, 1772, in Manchester Cathedral as "a mural monument which for elegance is not exceeded by any one within the church."

BRAITHWAITE, WILLIAM
b. 1757

He was born on 13 October, 1757, and in 1776 attended the Royal Academy Schools, where he won a Silver Medal in 1782. After that date, however, all trace of him is lost.

BRANWHITE, CHARLES, of Bristol
b. 1817, *d.* 1880

In 1836 he received the Silver Medal from the

Society of Arts for a bas-relief. His bust of W. J. Muller, 1845, is in Bristol Cathedral.

BRAYNE, T., of London

According to the *Gentleman's Magazine* (1812, Part II, page 221), the monument to Sir George Booth (*d*. 1797) at Cotterstock, Northants, is the work of Brayne.

BREAMER, FREDERICK CHRISTIAN, of London
fl. 1793–1816

In 1793 he exhibited "a tablet of flowers in marble" at the Royal Academy, and in 1801 made a chimney-piece for the London house of Rt. Hon. Henry Dundas, in Charles Street, Berkeley Square (Soane Notebooks). In 1816 he made nine chimney-pieces; two of dove-grey marble for the Royal Pavilion at Brighton and five of statuary and two of veined marble for Mr. Nash's house in Langham Place (R.I.B.A. Library, Shide Ledger).

Breamer signs tablets in Kent to Sir Richard Clode, 1804, at Orpington, and to Mrs. Oswald Smith, 1809, at Bexley.

BREWER, FRANCIS, of Petersfield
fl. 1820–1830

He signs tablets to John Clement, 1820, and to the Baker family, 1823, both at Steep, Hants.

BREWER, W., of Box and Colerne
fl. 1777–1813

He carried out monuments and tablets in marble and stone, and frequently executed a charming wall-tablet with a bow of ribbon at the top; another design for a circular one has crossed torches at the base. His signed tablets in Wiltshire commemorate James White, 1787, and Fanny Warner, 1779, both in St. Peter's, Marlborough; Richard Legg, 1778, and William Merewether, 1783, both at Market Lavington; Anne Cullurne, 1778, Thomas Pinnell, 1787, and William Fry, 1799, all at Malmesbury; Elizabeth Millington, 1783, at Cliffe Pypard; Rachel Neate, 1794, and John Neate, 1812, both at Aldbourne; and Lucia Pyke, 1813, at Great Somerford. The tablet to John Painter, 1809, at Hinton Charterhouse, Somerset, is also his work.

BRICE, E., of London

He exhibited a bas-relief of "Innocence" at the Royal Academy in 1780.

BRIDGENS, RICHARD, of Liverpool
fl. 1811–1826

He was a pupil of G. Bullock (q.v.) and exhibited a statue of "A Nymph Attiring" at the Liverpool Academy in 1811.

About 1813 he moved to London, and from that year until 1826 exhibited architectural drawings at the Royal Academy.

BRIDGES, —

His workshop was at Knightsbridge, and on 26 May, 1775, a sale of "the remaining stock in trade of artificial stone at the manufactury in Knightsbridge" was sold by Messrs. Christie on the occasion of his "quitting business." Among the lots sold were medallions of Alfred and Ethelred; busts of Homer and Pitt, statues of Ceres, Flora, Sampson and a Druid. There were also two statuettes of "Rubens and Vandyke." A number of the lots were purchased by Mrs. Coade (q.v.).

BRIDGES, —

He signs a tablet of good workmanship to H. Bale, 1796, at Bishops Waltham, Hants.

BRINE, JOHN, of London
Firm *fl*. 1800–1851

Brine was assisted, and later succeeded, by his sons George and James. In 1824 the firm received £2,265 for statuary marble chimney-pieces for the Quadrant, Regent Street, and £155 for chimney-pieces for the Royal Pavilion at Brighton (R.I.B.A. Library, Shide Ledger). They also showed chimney-pieces at the Great Exhibition of 1851. In 1826 the elder Brine made statues for Lady de Grey's gardens at Wrest Park, Bedfordshire (Archives, Lady Lucas and Dingwall).

The firm's monuments include those to John Elmslie, 1829, in Windsor Parish Church; the Dick family, 1837, at Chilham, Kent; John Rogers, 1840, in Streatham Parish Church; and Lady Preston, 1846, at Beeston St. Lawrence, Norfolk.

BRISLEY, THOMAS WILLIAM, of Rochester
b. 1800

Brisley's name is given as "Thomas" when he was apprenticed to his father in 1814, but the local directory of 1828 calls him "William." He was the son of Thomas Brisley, a mason who became a Freeman of Rochester by purchase in 1795 (Rochester City Archives).

The younger Brisley made a chimney-piece for Cobham Hall, Kent, in 1834 (Archives, Earl of

Darnley), and he also signs the monuments to William Burke, 1836, and James Forbes, 1837, in Rochester Cathedral. The medallion on the Forbes monument is a charming and competent work, surprisingly good for a local statuary.

BROAD, DAVID
fl. 1787–1792

Broad, who also worked as a surveyor, received £10 in 1787 for the font in Manchester Collegiate Church (Hilbert's *Foundations of Manchester*, Vol. II, page 247).

BROAD, RICHARD, of Box
fl. 1710–1730

In 1710 he was working at Longleat, where he was paid for building the "two great Pallisados" (Archives, Marquess of Bath).

Broad signs the large monument with Corinthian columns and weeping cherubs to William Tipler, 1710, at Seend, Wiltshire, and another to the wife and children of Thomas Smith in Melksham Church in the same county. Smith, in his diary for 1720, notes that he "walked this morning, being frosty, to Broad, the stone-cutter near Bath, to see a monument he has just finished to be put up in memory of my dear spouse and children" (Diary of Thomas Smith, reprinted in J. A. Neale's *Charters and Records of Neale*, page 207).

BROAD, RICHARD, of Worcester

He signs a large tablet in coloured marbles to Mary Wolstenholme (*d.* 1749), at Stoke Edith, Herefordshire.

BROADBENT, Messrs., of Leicester
fl. 1840–1862

In 1847 they carved the marble cenotaph of Latimer, Bishop of Worcester, in Thurcaston Church, Leicestershire (*Gentleman's Magazine*, 1847, Part I, page 539). In the same year they were also working as builders on the restoration of Anstey Church in that county.

BRODIE, ALEXANDER
b. 1830, *d.* 1867

Like his brother, William Brodie (q.v.), he lived at Aberdeen. In 1863 he carved the statue of the Duke of Richmond to be erected at Huntley and, two years later, one of Queen Victoria for his native city. His "Oenone" was exhibited at the International Exhibition of 1862. Brodie died by his own hand on 30 May, 1867.

(Various references, *Art Journal.*)

BRODIE, WILLIAM
b. 1815, *d.* 1881

He was the son of John Brodie, a ship-master of Banff, and was about six years old when his family moved to Aberdeen. He was later apprenticed to a plumber, but in his spare time studied at the Mechanics' Institute, where he amused himself by casting lead figures of well-known people. He soon began to model small medallion portraits which attracted the attention of a Mr. John Hill Burton, and it was Burton who encouraged him to go to Edinburgh in 1847. Here Brodie studied for four years at the Trustees' School of Design, learning to model on a larger scale, and also executing a bust of one of his earliest patrons, Lord Jeffrey.

About 1853 he went to Rome, where he studied under Laurence Macdonald (q.v.), and it was with the latter's assistance that he modelled "Corinna, the Lyric Muse," a work which Copland reproduced in miniature in "Parian" four years later. Brodie was elected an Associate of the Royal Scottish Academy in 1857, becoming a full member in 1859. In 1876 he was appointed Secretary of the Scottish Academy, a post he held until his death. In 1875 he made the group of "A Peer and His Lady Doing Homage" for the Prince Consort Memorial in Edinburgh.

Brodie exhibited at the Royal Academy, 1850–1881, and at the Royal Scottish Academy, 1847–1881; at the Great Exhibition of 1851 he showed a group of "Little Nell and Her Grandfather." He died on 30 October, 1881.

(Various references, *Art Journal; The Times*, 1 November, 1881.)

STATUES

1856	Hecamede	For the Rt. Hon. Henry Labouchère
1858	Oenone	Avington Park, Hants
1862	Lord Cockburn	Parliament House, Edinburgh
1862	Dr. Alexander	Prestonpans
1864	Prince Consort	Perth
1866	Lady Kinnaird	Exhibited Royal Academy
1870	John Graham Gilbert	Kelvingrove Art Gallery, Glasgow
1872	Dr. Thomas Graham	Glasgow
1872	St. Andrew	Life Insurance Building, Glasgow
1877	Sir David Brewster	Edinburgh
1878	Sir James Simpson	Edinburgh
1880	George Brown	Toronto, Canada

BUSTS

1847	Sir Thomas Dick-Lauder	Exhibited Royal Scottish Academy
1850	Lord Jeffrey	Exhibited Roya Scottish Academy

1855	Lord Cockburn	Diploma Work, Royal Scottish Academy
1855	Duke of Argyll	Dunrobin Castle
1857	Lord Tennyson	Exhibited Royal Scottish Academy
1858	Lord Dunfermline	Scottish National Portrait Gallery
1858	"Laura"	Bowood
1858	Hugh Miller	Scottish National Portrait Gallery
1860	Lord Kinnaird	Dundee Corn Exchange
1863	Professor Blackie	Scottish National Portrait Gallery
1868	Queen Victoria	Balmoral
1868	Dr. Adams	Aberdeen University
1868	John Philip, R.A.	Exhibited Royal Academy
1869	Miss Ada Barclay	Scottish National Gallery
1871	John Graham Gilbert	Glasgow Corporation
1873	Rev. John Paul	Edinburgh (St. Cuthbert's)
1873	Mrs. Farquharson of Invercauld	Exhibited Royal Scottish Academy
1874	Baroness Burdett-Coutts	Coutts Bank
1875	Dr. Guthrie	Inverary Manse, Argyle
1877	Sir James Simpson	Edinburgh
1877	Dr. Crawford	Edinburgh University
1879	Thomas Carlyle	Scottish National Portrait Gallery
1879	Henry Irving	Exhibited Royal Academy
1879	Sir James Simpson	Westminster Abbey
1879	David Livingstone	Possession (1917) of Mr. Livingstone-Bruce
1880	Ellen Terry	Exhibited Royal Academy
1880	William Nelson	Scottish National Portrait Gallery
n.d.	James Nelson	Glasgow Art Gallery
n.d.	Professor Blackie	Scottish National Portrait Gallery

MONUMENTS

1864	Edinburgh (St. Giles)	Officers and Men of the 93rd Sutherland Highlanders
1868	Edinburgh (Warriston Cemetery)	Alexander Smith
1875	Edinburgh (St. John's)	Dr. Guthrie

BROMFIELD, BENJAMIN, of Liverpool
fl. 1757–1790

In 1773 he carved the large and imposing red-marble chimney-piece for the saloon at Chirk Castle (Chirk Castle Accounts), and in 1788

received £400 from Sir Corbet Corbet for chimney-pieces for Adderley Hall, Salop. The date of his death is uncertain, but he was buried in a vault in Holy Trinity Church, St. Anne's Street, Liverpool.

All Bromfield's monuments and tablets have good details and are obviously influenced by those of Sir Henry Cheere (q.v.). That to Robert Lloyd, 1769, at Oswestry, Salop, is a fine work in coloured marbles with delicately carved angels' heads, while others commemorate George Coytmore, 1757, at Conway, Carnarvon; Mary Eyton, 1764, in St. Mary-on-the-Hill, Chester; the Rev. L. Richmond, 1769, at Stockport, Cheshire; Philip Puleston, 1776, at Wrexham, Denbigh; George Warrington, 1770, at Gresford, Denbigh; Robert Comberbach, 1771, in St. Michael's, Chester; William Tomkinson, 1771, at Davenham, Cheshire; Richard Thelwall, 1775, in St. Asaph Cathedral; Robert Howard, 1776, at Conway, Carnarvon; Nathaniel Wettenhall, 1776, at Audlem, Cheshire; John Stanley, 1781, at Winwick, Lancs; and Francis Parry Price, 1787, at Overton, Flint.

BROOKSHAW, GEORGE

He manufactured marble chimney-pieces in Curzon Street, Mayfair, and in 1780 exhibited at the Free Society. Here he showed, among other works, "Two figures from Herculaneum; these are marble in a new species of painting"; and "A Sacrifice to Cupid; a frieze for a chimney-piece."

BROOMHALL, THOMAS, of Fleet Ditch, London
fl. 1677–1718

He became free of the Masons' Company in 1677 and between 1705 and 1707 made several marble chimney-pieces for Mr. Samuel Tufnell's house, Langleys, near Chelmsford (Tufnell Archives). In 1717 Broomhall made, for the parish churches of Fetcham and Great Bookham in Surrey, marble tablets recording the benefactions of Sir George Shiers (Aubrey's *Surrey*, Vol. II, page 262).

In the list of Members of the Masons' Company for 1708 are the names of James and Samuel Broomhall, both of whom are described as "working for Mr. Cartwright." James was the son of "Richard Broomhall of Madley, Hertford, husbandman," and was apprenticed to Jasper Latham (q.v.) in 1679.

BROTHERS, P., of London

He signs a Hellenic tablet to Robert Laurence 1838, in Marylebone Parish Church.

BROUGH, JOHN, of London
fl. 1779–1782

In 1779 he made chimney-pieces for Greenwich Hospital to replace those destroyed in the fire and, in 1781, rebuilt the north colonnade. In 1784 he built a school near the hospital and in 1791 made the pedestals for the Coade (artificial stone) figures in the vestibule outside the Hospital chapel. A year later he erected the south-west staircase in King William Building (P.R.O. Ad. MS. 68/825–30 and 68/880).

BROWN, ALFRED
fl. 1845–1856

In 1845 he won the Royal Academy Gold Medal for a relief entitled "The Hours Leading Out the Horses of the Sun," and exhibited at the Academy from that year until 1855. He made marble chimney-pieces for the Army and Navy Club in 1848, and showed a statue of "David Before Saul" at the Great Exhibition of 1851.

Brown was also a designer of silver. He modelled the trophy presented by the Emperor of Russia for Ascot Races in 1845 and, five years later, a large candelabrum presented to the Marquess of Tweedale by his friends in India. In 1856, when working for Roskell and Hunt, he designed and modelled a silver centre-piece costing £2,500 for the Earl of Stamford. This represented "Stags in Bradgate Park" and must have been one of the largest ever made, for it weighed 112 pounds. (Various references, *Art Journal.*)

BROWN, F., of Salisbury
fl. 1775–1806

In 1804 he was appointed master-mason to Salisbury Cathedral and, two years later, was paid for "two Portland-stone columns and capitals" for the Cathedral (Cathedral Archives). He signs monuments of good workmanship in Wiltshire to William Batt, 1775, at Nunton; John Mayne, 1779, at Teffont; Thomas King, 1787, at Alvediston; William Brooker, 1799, at West Dean; and John Wyche, 1805, in St. Martin's, Salisbury.

His son, F. Brown the Younger, was responsible for a few minor tablets, but his chief work, executed about 1835, was an imposing marble chimney-piece, with two life-sized female figures on each side, for the saloon at Somerley, Hampshire, the seat of the second Earl of Normanton. The drawing for this is in the possession of Lord Normanton.

BROWN, GEORGE
b. 1803, *d.* 1877

In 1795 he made "a veined-marble chimney-piece" for the Hon. Mrs. Yorke, of Sydney Lodge, Hamble, Southampton. A year later he executed a similar one for the house of a Mr. Thomas Lewis at Palmer's Green, near London (Soane Notebook, MS. 5).

BROWN, or BROWNE, J., of London
fl. 1830–1850

In 1844 he exhibited a group entitled "Caractacus Before Claudius" at Westminster Hall, a work disliked by the *Literary Gazette* (1844, page 466), which considered the Britons "abominably bad" and advised the artist to "break the whole thing up."

Brown signs a number of monuments and tablets, including those to the tenth Lord Saye and Sele, 1830, and the eleventh Lord Saye and Sele, 1846, both at Broughton, Oxon; General Chowne, 1834, and Mrs. Tremaine, 1836, both in Kensal Green Cemetery; Charles Lefevre, 1836, Heckfield, Hants; Emma Sparkes, 1842, at Shalford, Surrey; and the Church family, 1848, at Hatfield, Herts. His monument to Philip Saltmarshe, 1848, at Howden, Yorkshire, is a large Gothic work with standing figures of "Hope" and "Charity."

BROWN, JOHN, of Colchester

He signs a Hellenic tablet to Robert Torrin, 1823, at Kelvedon, Essex.

BROWN, L., of London
fl. 1846–1848

He exhibited at the Royal Academy wax models of "A Dog Setting a Hare" (now in possession of the author) in 1846, and "Caesar Crossing the Rubicon" in 1848.

BROWN, or BROWNE, RICHARD, and Sons of Derby
Firm *fl.* 1735–1830

The firm was founded in 1735 by Richard Brown, whose advertisement in the *Derby Mercury* of that year stated that he "performed monuments, gravestones, chimney-pieces on reasonable terms." In 1759, and again in 1782, he was paid for paving the floor of All Saints' Church, Derby (Cox's *Chronicles of All Saints', Derby*). In 1765 he made a pair of "purple obelisks" for Kedleston, probably the magnificent pair of "blue john" which is still in the house (Kedleston Archives).

At a sale held by Mr. Christie on 7 November, 1797, of "a statuary and mason going abroad" one lot was a chimney-piece of Derbyshire Spar "manufactured at considerable expense at Mr.

Brown's of Derby for the late Mr. Harris of the Strand." (Charles Harris, q.v.)

The first Richard Brown died before 1785 and was succeeded by his son, Richard the Younger (1736–1816). He, in his turn, was followed by a third Richard Brown, grandson of the founder of the firm; the latter, having no son, sold the business to J. Hall (q.v.) about 1830.

Work carried out by the Browns included the altar-piece at Stapleford, c. 1783 (Nichols's *Leicestershire*, Vol. II, Part I, page 340), and chimney-pieces for Derby Prison. They did marble-carving for the great north wing of Chatsworth, and also did a good deal of work in the local marble, which they quarried at Monyash and Ashford in Derbyshire. Richard Brown the Elder signs the monument to Samson Bulkeley, 1761, at Leek, Staffordshire (Glover's *Derby*, Vols. I and II).

BROWN, RICHARD, of London
fl. 1817–1830

Signed examples of his tablets, which are mostly Hellenistic, commemorate John Thornhill, 1817, at Stanmore, Middlesex; the second Earl of Roden, 1820, at Sawbridgeworth, Herts; and William Dodd, 1822, at Sutton Valence, Kent.

BROWN, ROBERT, of London
fl. 1830–1857

At the Great Exhibition of 1851 he showed "a sepulchral monument of the Decorated period." His monuments and tablets are mostly Gothic in style, though that to Archibald Little, 1844, at Chipstead, Surrey, has a classical relief of a mourning woman, not unlike a minor work by Chantrey.

Signed tablets by Brown commemorate James Foster, 1833, in Streatham Parish Church; Lieut.-Colonel Richard Boteler, 1833, at Eastry, Kent; Richard Bucker, 1837, in Chichester Cathedral; Nathaniel Baron, 1841, at North Cave, Yorks; Charles Williams, 1842, Gwennap, Cornwall; Lady Shuckburgh, 1846, at Shuckburgh, Warwick; George Watlington, 1848, at Aldenham, Herts; Benjamin Biddulph, 1849, at Burghill, Hereford; Caroline Williams, 1849, Gwennap, Cornwall; and Henry Kemble, 1857, at Bray, Berks.

BROWN, RICHARD RUSHTON, of Manchester
d. 1851

In 1812 he exhibited at the Liverpool Academy figures of "Cupid" and of "Young Bacchanals." At the Exhibition of Contemporary Art at Man-

chester in 1827, he showed five works, including "The Infant Hercules Strangling a Serpent" and the "Posthumous Bust of a Gentleman." He continued to exhibit busts and ideal works until 1833. From 1841 to 1851 he was employed modelling for Messrs. Austin and Sealy (q.v.) (Archives, Artists' General Benevolent Institution).

BROWN, WILLIAM, of Liverpool
d. 1836

He exhibited at the Liverpool Academy in 1812 and 1813, showing a figure of "Diana" in the latter year. His widow, Elizabeth, when she applied for help to the A.G.B.I. in 1837, said that her husband had died of apoplexy on 31 December, 1836.

BROWN, W., of London
b. 1799

He joined the Royal Academy Schools in 1820 and signs a large monument to the second Viscount Sidney, 1845, at Chislehurst, Kent.

BROWN, W., of Stonehouse
fl. 1808–1835

His tablets, which are mostly classical in design, include those to Margaret Nesham, 1808, at Anthony, Cornwall; William Rowe, 1820, at Liskeard, Cornwall; Sarah Body, 1835, at Wonersh, Surrey; and Charles Mathews, 1835, in St. Andrew's Church, Plymouth.

BROWNE, —, and YOUNG, —
Firm *fl.* 1816–1820

Their tablets have delicately carved details, a good example being one commemorating Sir Felton Harvey-Bathurst, 1819, at Egham, Surrey, which has reliefs of the numerous medals and decorations won by Sir Felton during the Napoleonic Wars. They sign other tablets to John Kirkpatrick, 1816, in Windsor Parish Church; John Bovill, 1816, in Streatham Parish Church; and Ann Drury, 1817, at Upton, Bucks.

In 1819 the firm agreed to supply for £742 the scagliola columns for the east end of St. Pancras Church (Britton and Pugin's *Public Buildings of London*, Vol. I, page 154).

BROWNE, JOSEPH
fl. 1815–1848

In 1815 he was employed by the Duke of Bridgewater at Ashridge Park making scagliola columns and verd antique stands (Archives, Lord Brownlow).

In 1823 he made chimney-pieces for a house in Carlton House Terrace, and from 1827 until 1830 was employed at Buckingham Palace. Here he received over £6,000 for marble chimney-pieces, including those for the drawing-room, and five for the picture-gallery at £250 each. For a chimney-piece with "pilasters, profiles and frieze carved with Greek leaf and ogee" for an unnamed room, he received £145 (P.R.O. Works 5/119).

His scagliola work at the Palace included "six scagliola Corinthian columns, shafts and bases and six pilasters ditto" for the picture gallery; "twenty-eight pilaster shafts with sunk panels on the face and large ogee moulding round" costing £1,278, for the Bow drawing-room; and the "scagliola columns of lapis lazuli" for the blue drawing-room (P.R.O. Works 5/119).

Browne was the chief marble contractor for the Marble Arch and, in 1827, received £1,077 for "six cornices, sixty-four modillions, fifty-eight coffers and six very large laurel wreaths in solid ravaccione marble" (P.R.O. Works 19/3, etc.).

In 1830 he carved chimney-pieces for Stafford House, and also received £37 for a French marble chimney-piece for Lord Sherborne's room at Sherborne Court, Gloucestershire (Archives, Lord Sherborne). In the same year he held an exhibition at his premises in University Street of his collection of antique marble and other works, "forming together nearly two thousand elegant specimens of ancient and modern art" (*Library of Fine Arts*, Vol. I, page 178). In 1848 he made the chimney-piece for the music-room of Westfield, Isle of Wight (Sir Augustus Clifford's *History of Westfield*).

Browne's tablets are dull, the best being that to William Kay, 1845, at Tring, Herts, which has a neo-Hellenistic relief of a woman seated by an amphora. Other monuments and tablets executed by him commemorate William Bray, 1832, at Shere, Surrey; Elizabeth Pughe, 1833, in St. Mary Aldermary; the Hon. Mrs. Cox, 1836, at Mistley, Essex; the Rankin family (an altar-tomb in the churchyard), 1838, at Royston, Cambs; the Hon. Lionel Damer, 1839, and the Countess of Portarlington, 1839, both at Winterbourne Came, Dorset; Jane Mills, 1842, at Barford, Warwick; and the Hon. Cassandra Graves, 1845, at Burnham, Bucks.

BRYAN, JOHN and JOSEPH, and Sons, of Gloucester

Firm *fl.* 1749–1802

The firm was founded by John (1716–1787) and Joseph (1718–1780), sons of Joseph Bryan (1682–1730). John, the elder, survived his brother by seven years and died on 21 March, 1787. He was buried under a large pyramidical monument at Painswick, Gloucestershire, and in his will left bequests to his two daughters, Anne Bryan and Mrs. Loveday. The business then passed to his nephew John, the son of Joseph Bryan, who had married his first cousin Anne and went into partnership with George Wood (q.v.) about 1795.

Masonry-work executed by the firm includes the tower of Great Whitcombe Church in 1749, and the spire of St. Nicholas, Gloucester, in 1784. Their monuments have charming and well-carved details, while a delightful and intelligent use is made of coloured foreign marbles. Among these works may be included those commemorating Noble Pitts, 1770, at Much Marcle, Hereford; William Smart, 1772, at Winchcomb, Glos; Alexander Colston, 1775, at Fairford, Glos (there is another in the same church dated 1754, but the name is illegible); Abigail Carter, 1776, at Eldersfield, Glos; Charles Coxe, 1779, at Rodmarton, Glos; James Pitt, 1784, at Maisemore, Glos; Mary Smith, 1787, at Bishop's Cleeve, Glos; Mary Morse, 1788, Samuel Hayward, 1790, and John Webb, 1795, all in Gloucester Cathedral; Anne Coxe, 1790, at Kemble, Glos; Frances Turner, 1793, at Chadlington, Oxon; Mary Milborne, 1793, at Abergavenny, Mon; Mrs. Hughes, 1794, at Cheltenham, Glos; Lucy Dolphin, 1801, at Upper Slaughter, Glos; the Rev. D. Pritchett, 1801, in St. David's Cathedral; and Mary Probyn, 1802, in Pershore Abbey, Worcs. The last-named is the joint work of Bryan and George Wood.

(Information from Mr. H. M. Colvin; Gloucester City Archives.)

BRYSON, DANIEL

fl. 1800–1805

Bryson, who did a good deal of wood and stone carving under Sir John Soane, modelled a figure in 1800 for Bentley Priory, the seat of the Marquess of Abercorn. In 1801 he received £65 for carved stonework on the façade of Messrs. Praed's offices in Fleet Street, and four years later was paid for decorative details in stone for the offices of Messrs. Peters in Fountain Court. Bryson also worked at Mr. Robert Knight's house in Charles Street, Berkeley Square, in 1802 (Soane Account-books), and, in 1804, he was paid £53 for carving at Aynho, Northamptonshire (Cartwright Archives).

BUBB, JAMES GEORGE

b. 1782, *d.* 1853

He attended the Royal Academy Schools in 1801, winning a Silver Medal in 1805, and also worked with Bingley (q.v.) and Rossi (q.v.). In

1806 he was given the commission for the monument to Pitt which was to be erected in the Guildhall, not apparently because of the excellence of his model but because "his estimate of expense was some hundred pounds less than that of any other candidate, which influenced many of the citizens to vote for it" (*Farington Diary*, Vol. IV, page 1). Later in the same year Farington (op. cit., page 55) again stresses the fact that the cheapness of the monument was the first consideration and mentions that Bubb had "canvassed the Members of the Common Council and gave cards on the back of which he put the mark which he put on his model that it might be known."

The sculptor was not at all popular among his fellow-artists, and L. Gahagan (q.v.), an unsuccessful competitor, referred to "Tobacconist Bubb" when he wrote to the committee asking for the return of his rejected model for the Pitt monument. Before being definitely given the commission, Bubb was asked to produce references, and he accordingly requested Bingley and Rossi to supply them. The former stated that "during the partnership with Mr. Rossi and myself, Mr. Bubb did studiously attend to the duties of his profession and was employed in the several works carried on during that period, particularly in marble, viz. Captain Faulkener's monument in St. Paul's" (City Corporation Records, MS. 95.2). Rossi, however, wrote rather differently and his letter is quoted elsewhere (see under "Rossi, J. C. F."). Bubb seems to have taken his time over the work, for the statue was not unveiled until 1813.

In 1809 Bubb made a stone statue for the Hope Insurance Office on Ludgate Hill. Two years later he executed a delightful bas-relief of "Britannia, Neptune and Minerva" for the portico of the Commercial Rooms at Bristol, and for the exterior of the same building carved statues of "Bristol," "Commerce" and "Navigation."

About 1818 Bubb started to manufacture terra-cotta in partnership with Rossi, for both had been employed at Mrs. Coade's (q.v.) artificial-stone works at Lambeth. The venture began well, for they received a contract for over £5,000 for reliefs, etc., for the façade of the London Customs House, the work to include "a marine shell of large dimensions to be placed over the clock," and a "basso-relief of Commerce, represented by a number of groups of figures, the size of life and in the costume of their respective countries, and another of Prosperity, Britannia, etc., accompanied by Strength, Justice, etc." (P.R.O. Works 5/144).

The result when all was completed does not seem to have been a success. The *New Monthly Magazine* (1818, page 154) found fault with the material, remarking that "the process of baking which it undergoes frequently distorts and injures the work, it is of a brick-like ferruginous colour and the general effect is very unpleasing," while the works they considered "entirely devoid of all that is requisite in art; they possess no sentiment, they express nothing, they are seen and forgotten." Forgotten they certainly have been, for the badly constructed building had in a short time to be demolished, and Bubb's contribution to it disappeared with the rest.

In the same year he also made other terra-cotta reliefs for the pediment of the Italian Opera House in the Haymarket. These, according to Allen's *London* (1827, Vol. IV, page 296), represented "the progress of Music from the earliest attention to sound. Into the groups, dancing is introduced, as associated with its advancement from the rudest ages to the extraordinary accomplishments of the modern ballet."

Notwithstanding the money he seems to have made for his work at the Customs House, Bubb became a bankrupt and his business was taken over by Joseph Browne (q.v.), who employed him as a designer and modeller. While he was working for Browne, Bubb was responsible for a large number of works in terra-cotta, including the portico of the Harmonic Institution, Regent Street, in 1820, and the statues of "The Four Quarters of the Globe" for the Royal Exchange two years later (Elmes's *Metropolitan Improvements*, Vol. I, pages 103 and 158). About 1823 he made terra-cotta statues and reliefs for the Bristol Exchange (Evans's *Bristol*, Vol. II, page 353), and, in 1824, the composition ornaments for the Salters' Hall. He also carved the Company's arms on the exterior of the building (Archives, Salters' Company). In 1826 he executed the figures of British Worthies for Chester Terrace, Regent's Park, while in the following year appeared the pediment with forty figures for Cumberland Terrace, a work which the *Literary Gazette* (1827, page 65) considered to be "on so large a scale that it is only exceeded in size by that on St. Paul's Cathedral."

About this time Browne abandoned the manufactory and Bubb returned to sculpture. In 1830 and 1831 respectively he exhibited statues of "Poetry" and "Vertumnus" at the Royal Academy, and in 1839 carved a figure of "Pomona," which had been commissioned by Sir William Middleton, of Shrublands, Suffolk.

In 1833 Bubb held a sale of his architectural and sculptural casts, etc. Among the lots sold was Zoffany's famous picture of the Royal Academicians which was bought by Joseph Browne (q.v.) for £37 16s. (*Gentleman's Magazine*, 1833, Part I, page 252). In 1839 Bubb was employed by Blashfield (q.v.) on experimental terra-cotta work at Canford, Dorset, where Sir John Guest was trying to build inexpensive model cottages for agricultural workers. A small quantity of moulded bricks, tiles and ornaments were made from sketches by Mr. (afterwards Sir Charles) Barry, but Bubb's health seems to have failed about this time, and he fell on hard times. Indeed, as early as 1835 he had applied to the A.G.B.I. and stated that having had scarcely any employment for the last two years his circumstances had become impoverished and that his complete stock had been taken by his landlord and sold to pay the rent; also that he had to support a wife and two children. A later note states that his wife had eloped with a young man who had been living with him as a pupil. The erring wife was Margaret Alice, second daughter of Henry Blakey of Scots Yard, Bush Lane, whom he had married on 9 May, 1812 (The *News*, 31 May, 1812). Bubb left a son, Francis, who was employed by Messrs. Seeley, of New Road (q.v.).

Bubb exhibited at the Royal Academy, 1805–1831, where his work included busts of Mrs. Furniss (1805), W. Shield (1811), and M. Wood, M.P. (1818). His bust of Lord Nelson (1810) is in the possession of the author. He also signs monuments to George Children, 1818, at Tonbridge, Kent; Henry Manley, 1819, at Halberton, Devon; and Margaret Pounsett, 1820, and Richard Rothwell, 1821, both in Battersea Parish Church.

(*Builder*, 1868, page 547; authorities cited in text.)

BUCK, JOHN
fl. 1817–1821

Between 1817 and 1821 he exhibited three reliefs at the Royal Academy, including one entitled "David [*sic*] Slaying the Lion."

BUCKHAM, GEORGE

The only signed work of his I know is the large monument to the Earl and Countess of Kerry, 1799, in Westminster Abbey.

BUCKINGHAM, EDWARD
fl. 1681–1728

Buckingham was apprenticed to Nathaniel Turner in 1672 and became free in 1681. He was the chief mason for the Inner Temple between 1693 and 1711, and in 1696 (the year in which he took his son Jeremiah as an apprentice) he received £115 for "repairs to the Temple Church" (Inderwick's *Inner Temple Records*, Vol. III).

In 1701 Buckingham was at Knole, Sevenoaks, where he was paid £100 for unspecified work (Sackville Archives). In 1708 he was living in "Clements Lane by Clare Market," according to the Court Book of the Masons' Company. He became Master of the Company in 1716.

A "John Buckingham," who may have been a relative, built a house in London before 1730 for Richard Woolley, one of the directors of the South Sea Company (Inventory of Directors, South Sea Company).

BULL, THOMAS
d. 1751

Son of Henry Bull, goldsmith and citizen of London, he was admitted to the Masons' Company by patrimony in 1712 and was later Master of the Company in 1746. His yard was in Plum Tree Court, Shoe Lane. Bull signs the fine architectural monument with a portrait-bust of Sir Roger Hill, 1729, at Denham, Bucks, and another to Mary Eccleston, 1732, at Redbourn, Herts. Bull died in 1750–1751 and was buried in St. Helen's, Bishopsgate.

In the Quarterage Book of the Masons' Company there are references to another Thomas Bull, who was apprenticed to Thomas Crowther in 1725, free in 1732, and living in Broad Street two years later.

BULL, WILLIAM
d. 1762

He was apprenticed to his father, Thomas Bull (q.v.), in 1726, and became free of the Masons' Company in 1735. In 1737 he received £231 for alterations to Skinners' Hall (Archives, Skinners' Company) and, in 1742, repaired a house at Cripplegate for a Mr. Pinch. Bull became a bankrupt in 1752 (*Gentleman's Magazine*, 1752, page 536), and his death is noted ten years later in the Court Book of the Masons' Company.

He signs monuments to John Lloyd, 1740, in the private chapel of Aston Hall, Salop, and to Sir Robert Godschall, 1742, at Albury, Surrey.

BULLOCK, GEORGE,
of Liverpool
d. 1818

He was born in Liverpool and worked there as a sculptor and modeller, exhibiting both at the Royal and Liverpool Academies between 1804 and 1816, and acting as President of the latter body, 1810–1811. According to *The Stranger in Liverpool* (printed 1812), "the showrooms of Mr. George Bullock contain statues, figures, tripods, candelabras, antique lamps, sphinxes, griffins, etc., in marble, bronze and artificial stone. There is also a good collection of busts, among them many of the most distinguished characters in Liverpool and its neighbourhood, modelled by himself."

Bullock also worked, under the name of "Mona Marbles," quarries which he had discovered in the centre of the island of Anglesey. These contained two beds of marble, one resembling "in colour and effect oriental porphyry and the other verd antique." For some time he conducted the business from Liverpool, sending the blocks of marble to London, where they were made into chimney-pieces. One of these is illustrated in Ackermann's *Repository of Arts,* for 1816 (Vol. XV, page 19). The material seems to have been much admired and "when enriched with brass work of ormolu" exceeded "in splendour the most elaborate carvings in statuary," according to a writer in *Scott's Magazine* (1815, page 255). In 1813 Bullock left Liverpool for London to become a director of the Mona Marble Works.

The busts which he exhibited in Liverpool and at Burlington House included those of W. Roscoe (1804), W. Stevenson (1804), Master Betty (1805), the Duke of Gloucester (1806), Sir W. Elford (1807), Mrs. Siddons (1808), Sir James Smith (1810), Dr. Wilkinson (1810), Lord Tamworth (1811), Mr. Sadler (1812), Colonel Fraser (1813) and W. Hey (1816). In 1812 he exhibited a bust of Kemble at the Egyptian Hall. In 1807 he executed a statue of Lord Nelson in artificial stone which was erected in Liverpool (*Monthly Magazine,* 1807, Vol. I, page 396), and in 1814 he made a cast of the bust of Shakespeare in Stratford-on-Avon Church. The design for the statue was used for the frontispiece of the first volume (1807) of the *Literary and Fashionable Magazine,* while a number of copies were made of the Shakespeare bust. Some of them may still be seen outside inns or public buildings in country towns. On 3 May, 1819 Mr. Christie held a sale of the contents of "the late Mr. George Bullock's house at 4, Tenterden Street, Hanover Square." Among the lots were a number of Mona Marble chimney-pieces. (Archives, Messrs. Christie.)

(Authorities cited in text.)

BULLOCK, Miss SYBELLA

While living in Sloane Street she was awarded, in 1825, the large Silver Medal of the Society of Arts for "a bust from life."

BULMER, WILLIAM, of Stockton
fl. 1833–1858

Bulmer was a minor statuary who signs tablets commemorating Elizabeth Wedderburn, 1833, and the Rev. William Fountaine, 1837, both at Middleton St. George, Durham; John Rockliffe, 1842, at Topcliffe, Yorks; and Viscountess Falkland, 1858, at Rudby, Yorks.

BUMPSTEAD, JOHN
fl. 1673–1683

In 1679 he carved statues of Charles I and James I, in wood, for the Clothworkers' Hall (Company Archives).

In 1673 he received £47 for "carving work about the public stairs at Queenhithe," and, in the same year, was employed on masonry work at the Guildhall (Guildhall Library, MS. 184/4). In 1683 he was paid £17 for carving at the Mathematical School at Christ's Hospital (Christ's Hospital Account Books).

Bumpstead was Upper Warden of the Masons' Company in 1676 and Master two years later. According to Robert Hooke (*Diary,* page 329), he made, in 1677, the monument to Miss Garaway for the Church of St. Peter-le-Poor.

BURCH, E., R.A.
b. 1730, *d.* 1814

According to the *New Monthly Magazine* (1816, page 417), Burch was originally a waterman and "his first effort in painting was exercised in the imitation of a gold band round his hat and the superior style of the interior of his wherry."

He is chiefly known as a gem-engraver and wax-modeller and entered the Royal Academy Schools in 1769, becoming an Associate a year later and a full member in 1771. He was the first Royal Academician to be elected by his fellow-members, all of whom had been nominated by the King.

In 1788 Burch was appointed engraver to the King and the Duke of York for "medals and seals in stone." Two years later he was given a similar appointment by the King of Poland, and he also worked for Wedgwood, for whom he modelled portraits of George III and Queen Charlotte. He became the Academy Librarian in 1794 and held the post until his death, although after a few years illness prevented him from carrying out his duties. By 1796 he was in financial difficulties, for in that year the Academy made him a gift of £100; later on they also granted him a pension (Royal Academy Archives).

Burch exhibited at the Academy, 1771–1808, and at the Society of Artists, 1760–1769, showing various works, including engraved gems, sulphur casts and models in wax. Among the last-named were portraits of Dr. Robinson, Primate of Ireland

(1775); the Empress Catherine of Russia (1776) and General Paoli (1791). An "E. Burch, Junr., gem engraver," exhibited at the Society of Artists in 1790 (Sandby's *Royal Academy of Arts*, Vol. I, page 216).

BURCHARD, C.
fl. 1716

Possibly a pupil and assistant of John Nost (q.v.), he modelled for the Duke of Chandos a large equestrian statue of George I (cast and gilded by Nost), which was set up at Canons about 1716. When that house was demolished the statue was purchased in 1748 by the inhabitants of Leicester Fields, who erected it on a stone pedestal in the centre of the square. Here it remained until 1851, when it was removed to make room for an exhibition. It was replaced in 1862, much damaged and disfigured, and was finally sold in 1872 for £16. It was the ill-treatment of this statue that determined the Government in 1854 to bring in a Bill placing all statues in public places under the care of the Board of Works.

(*Gentleman's Magazine*, 1748, page 521; *Notes and Queries*, Fifth Series, Vol. II, page 46 et seq.)

BURGESS, CLEMENT,
of Petworth
d. 1855

In the Sussex directory of 1828 Burgess describes himself as "Statuary and Architect." He made Portland-stone pedestals for Petworth House in 1830 (Archives, Lord Leconfield). He signs a tablet to John Salter, 1820, at Fittleworth, Sussex.

BURGESS, D., of Sandbach

He signs a square tablet with well-cut lettering to John Wilkins, 1740, at High Offley, Staffordshire.

BURGISS, JOHN, of Uxbridge
fl. 1800–1830

In 1802 he was employed under Sir John Soane on masonry-work at the Treaty House, Uxbridge (Soane notebooks). He signs tablets to John Bell, 1800, Harefield, Middlesex; Peter Parker, 1804, Chalfont St. Giles, Bucks; Alexander Stewart, 1820, Wingrave, Bucks; Mrs. Tillyer, 1827, Harmondsworth, Middlesex; Thomas Allen, 1829, Chalfont St. Giles, Bucks.

He was succeeded by his son, E. Burgiss, who signs a number of tablets, including those to Charlotte Raine, 1832, Little Missenden, Bucks, and Thomas Clarke, 1840, Ickenham, Middlesex.

BURLOWE, HENRY BEHNES
b. 1802, *d.* 1837

He was the brother of William Behnes (q.v.) and took the name of Burlowe at the suggestion of the art critic, S. C. Hall. The reason given was that he did not wish his work to be confused with that of his more famous brother, but the *Art Journal* of 1864 attributed the change to his desire to dissociate himself in the public mind from William, whose irregular life was apparently well known.

Burlowe attended the Royal Academy Schools in 1821 and won a Silver Medal two years later; he exhibited at the Academy, 1831–1833. In 1834 he went to Rome, where he had many patrons among the English residents, but died there during the cholera epidemic of 1837 and was buried in the English Cemetery at Monte Testaccio. The *Art Union* said in its obituary (1840, page 193) that "no person ever had more friends or earned them and merited them better. A more upright, manly or straightforward person never lived; and it will not be too much to say that no one with means so limited ever did more good to those who required assistance."

(*Art Journal*, 1859, page 201.)

BUSTS

c. 1827	James Christie II	Possession Messrs. Christie
1829	Miss Josephine Bache	Possession Miss C. Clive
1831	G. Clint, A.R.A.	Exhibited Royal Academy
1831	John Pye	Plaster cast at National Portrait Gallery
1831	Henry Graves	Exhibited Royal Academy
1831	Richard Hart-Davis	Exhibited Suffolk Street Galleries
1832	Sir James Mackintosh	(*Literary Gazette*, 1832, page 364)
1833	Samuel Carter Hall	Bethnal Green Museum
1833	Dr. Lushington	Exhibited Royal Academy
1834	D. Roberts	Exhibited Royal Academy
1834	Female head	For Lord de Clifford
1837	George Clifford	Stonyhurst College
1837	Sir Peter Hesketh-Fleetwood	Fleetwood, Lancs

MONUMENTS

1828	Carshalton, Surrey	Robert Houstoun
1832	Kirkby Mallory, Leics.	Katherine Noel

BURMAN, BELTHASAR
fl. 1678–1688

Son of Thomas Burman (q.v.), he became free of the Masons' Company in 1678 and two years later carved the magnificent standing figure of Rachel, Countess of Bath, in Tawstock Church, Devon. This, except for the pedestal, is a replica of the elder Burman's statue of the Countess of Shrewsbury at St. John's College, Cambridge, but owing to a misreading of the sculptor's name in the Wrey Archives it was for many years quite mistakenly assigned to Bernini (1598–1684). Belthasar Burman also signs the monument to Brian Duppa (d. 1662) in Westminster Abbey.

BURMAN, THOMAS
b. 1618, *d.* 1674

Burman, who was bound apprentice to Edward Marshall (q.v.) in 1633, is chiefly remembered as the master of John Bushnell (q.v.), though the few works he is known to have executed show him to have been an artist of considerable merit. The most important of these is the statue of the Countess of Shrewsbury, 1671, at St. John's College, Cambridge (Willis and Clarke's *Architectural History of Cambridge*, Vol. II, page 320), and in the same year he was paid £38 for a marble chimney-piece for Alderman (afterwards Sir) Robert Clayton's banking-house in Old Jewry (Sir Robert Clayton's ledger, Guildhall Archives).

Burman signs the large monument with a life-size standing figure of John Dutton (d. 1656) at Sherborne, Glos; according to Vertue (*Walpole Society, Vertue IV*, page 169), he was also responsible for the monument to the Rev. and Mrs. Beale, 1672, at Walton, Bucks, which has portrait-busts set in oval niches.

He was buried in the churchyard of St. Paul's, Covent Garden, where a stone surrounded by an iron railing bore the inscription: "Thomas Burman, sculptor of St. Martin's, died March 17th, 1673/4." His widow, Rebecca, seems to have carried on the business after his death, for Martin Johnson was bound apprentice to her in 1679 (Archives, Masons' Company).

BURNARD, NEVIL NORTHEY
b. 1818, *d.* 1878

He was born at Altarnun, Cornwall, the son of George Burnard, a mason, and the only education he received was from his mother, who kept a dame's school and made straw bonnets in her spare time. When he was old enough he worked as mortar-boy to his father and, at the age of fourteen, made his grandfather's tombstone for the village churchyard. Two years later he carved in slate a group depicting the death of Laocoon and his sons and sent it to the exhibition of the Royal Cornwall Polytechnic Society at Falmouth, where it won a Silver Medal.

Sir Charles Lemon, M.P., became interested in Burnard and took him to London, where he prevailed upon Chantrey to employ the young man in his studio. In 1848 the influence of the same patron secured permission from Queen Victoria for Burnard to model a bust of the Prince of Wales. This was exhibited at the Royal Academy in the same year and afterwards sent to the Polytechnic Hall in Falmouth.

Burnard, who continued to exhibit at the Academy until 1873, married when he was in London and for a time all went well. On the death of his wife, however, he took to drink and deteriorated so rapidly that by the end of his life he was living like a tramp, wandering about Cornwall and earning a pittance by drawing portraits and sketches at farms and public-houses, for he seems to have been equally skilful with his pencil. He died in Redruth Workhouse on 27 November, 1878.

In his younger days Burnard appears to have been regarded as a local celebrity. Caroline Fox, in her *Memories of Old Friends*, writes that on "4 October, 1847, Burnard our Cornish sculptor dined with us. He is a great powerful, pugilistic-looking fellow at twenty-nine." There is a small profile self-portrait of him at Penpont House, and he also executed the relief of John Wesley (1834) on Altarnum Methodist Church. He signs monuments to the Rev. Robert Newton, 1854, in the Wesley Chapel, City Road, and the Rev. Hugh Rogers, 1858, at Camborne, Cornwall.

(*D.N.B.*; *Art Union*, 1848, page 180; *Builder*, 1852, page 205, and .1854, page 467; S. Baring Gould's *Cornish Characters and Strange Events*, page 186.)

STATUES

| 1852 | Richard Lander | Truro |
| 1854 | Ebenezer Elliott | Sheffield |

BUSTS

1849	J. C. Adams	Exhibited Royal Academy
1849	Sir Charles Lemon	Exhibited Royal Academy
1851	The Prince of Peace	Exhibited Great Exhibition
1859	George Greenough	Geological Museum
1859	Lord Macaulay	Westminster Abbey
1866	Richard Cobden	Exhibited Royal Academy
1867	Thackeray	For Plymouth Library
1867	Professor Edward Forbes	Exhibited Royal Academy
1869	Rt. Hon. John Bright	Exhibited Royal Academy
1871	W. E. Gladstone	Exhibited Royal Academy
1873	Prince of Wales	Truro Town Hall

BURNELL, —
fl. 1733–1750

He signs monuments to Elinor Phillips, 1733, at Haverfordwest, Pembroke, and to John Warden, 1750, at Cuckfield, Sussex. It has been impossible to discover whether he was any relation to Thomas Burnell (q.v.).

BURNELL, THOMAS, and Sons, of London
Firm *fl.* 1761–1841

The firm consisted of Thomas Burnell, his son Henry, and the latter's son Thomas, who was apprenticed to his father and became free "by patrimony" in 1792. In the late years of the eighteenth century they were also joined by a George Burnell, who had been summoned to "take up his Freedom" in 1772 by the Court of Assistants of the Masons' Company (Court Book, Masons' Company).

The elder Thomas was born about 1740, the son of John Burnell, "citizen and joiner," and was apprenticed to Edward Anderson (q.v.) in 1754. He became free in 1761 and was Master of the Masons' Company in 1783. In 1790 he and his cousin, a Mr. Tibbs, were left £60,000 between them by their uncle, John Burnell, who had been Lord Mayor two years previously (*Gentleman's Magazine*, 1790, page 89).

On 9 May, 1792, Burnell was appointed mason to the Inner Temple, a post in which he was succeeded by his grandson Thomas, who was employed under Savage to carry out the drastic "repairs" to the Temple Church. The estimate for the work, however, was exceeded by no less than £6,000; inquiries were made and, as a result, the Committee of Members resolved on 30 April, 1841, that "Mr. Burnell be discharged from his present employment as Mason at the Temple Church."

The monuments executed by the firm in the eighteenth century have finely cut and beautifully finished details, the two most important being those which commemorate John Blencowe, 1777, at Marston St. Lawrence, Northants, and the D'Anvers family, 1790, at Culworth, in the same county. The former has a fine urn, while the latter (a large work, 16 ft. high) has a sarcophagus with a cherub standing on either side.

The Burnells also sign monuments to Benjamin Wheeler, 1783, at Ewelme, Oxon; Mr. Baldwin, 1785, at St. Leonards, Bucks; Major Richard Boorn, 1795, at Romsey, Hants; Stephen Wright, 1797, in Hammersmith Parish Church; Captain John Barfott, 1807, in St. Matthias, Poplar; and Joseph Peel, 1821, at Burton-on-Trent.

BURNS, —

At the Robert Adam sale in 1818, Lot 3 is described in the catalogue as "ten tablets and parts of friezes modelled by Burns."

BURT, JOHN, of Callington

He signs a large slate ledger with a relief of a woman kneeling by a prayer-desk to Ann Holiday, 1753, at Callington, Cornwall.

BURTON, —

Probably a local craftsman, he signs a ledger with a fine coat of arms and mantling to Ann Wigley, 1786, at Scraptoft, Leicestershire.

BUSHNELL, JOHN
d. 1701

Bushnell, who was the son of a plumber, was apprenticed to T. Burman (q.v.), but before his seven years' service was up was entrapped into marrying a servant-maid, who declared that he was the father of her illegitimate child, whereas she had in reality been seduced by Burman. Bushnell was disgusted by the trick which had been played upon him, and when Burman sent him down to the country to supervise the erection of a monument, seized his chance to escape. He fled overseas, taking £15 of his master's money with him.

The young man first travelled to Rome, where he studied for a time, and then wandered across Europe. He had worked in Flanders and France, as well as in Italy, before he finally settled in Venice, and it was here that he carved the vast monument of Alviso Moncenigo for the Church of S. Lazaro di Mendicanti. He had been living abroad for twenty-two years when an English nobleman, who was visiting Venice, persuaded him to return to his native country.

Bushnell accordingly returned to England, where he was presented to Charles II, who received him courteously. He apparently considered, however, that his fame in Italy made him the superior of all English artists and, "being of a haughty mind," expected "to have particular honours done to him, according to his extraordinary merit, by all the courtiers and nobles as well as the King, which (as) they did not, he soon grew disgusted" (*Walpole Society, Vertue*, Vol. I, page 86). The only person Bushnell had any right to treat with disgust was his former master, who had treated him so shabbily and who now had the effrontery to sue him for breaking his apprenticeship and stealing the £15.

Bushnell's first public works in England were the statues of the King and Queen which he made for Temple Bar in 1670, and for which he received

£440 (City Corporation MSS., Temple Bar, B.5/27). In the same year he made the effigy for the Duke of Albemarle's state funeral in Westminster Abbey, executing the face and hands in wax and the rest in "stucko." In 1671 he carved the statues of Charles I, Charles II and Sir Thomas Gresham for the Royal Exchange which are today housed in the Old Bailey. The bill for the last-named is in the City Corporation Records (Gresham Account Ledger, 1665–1680) and reads: "Paid to John Bushnell £37 the City moiete in full for making and setting up the figure of Sir Thomas Gresham over the South entrance of the Royal Exchange by order dated Nov. 7th 1671." Bushnell had agreed to do other Royal statues for the Exchange, but when he discovered that another sculptor had "made interest to make some of them, contrary to agreement . . . though he had begun six of them, he would not proceed and (they) are unfinished to this day" (Walpole Society, op. cit.).

Vertue (op. cit.) describes Bushnell as a haughty man who could not bear to be contradicted and who used to say "that this nation was not worthy of him, nor his works; when any nobleman had once slighted him he would never have anything to do for him or say to him." When he heard that his fellow-sculptors had declared that he could not model a naked statue, he proceeded to make one of Alexander the Great. Vertue saw this many years afterwards and declared that it had "the beautifullest body and limbs possible to be imagined," but that the head was "the most wretched to the neck, the hands ill-formed, the feet crippled" (op. cit.).

As time went on the sculptor became more and more eccentric and unbalanced. On one occasion, hearing some courtiers discussing the wooden horse of Troy and declaring that it would be impossible to construct such an animal, he set about making one of wood covered with stucco. The head was so large that there was room for twelve men to sit round a table inside it, the eyes forming the windows. The work was practically completed when a sudden gale blew it over and smashed it to pieces.

In the reign of James II Bushnell began to build himself a house near Hyde Park, but it was unfinished in 1701 when he died there of gout in the stomach. He was buried in Paddington, where the curious entry in the Parish Register reads: "May 15th, 1701. Buried John Bushnell, an image-maker." He was survived by a widow (Mary died on 22 July, 1704) and several children, including two sons who lived in their father's unfinished house "like hermits or brutes," refusing to allow anyone to enter or to see their father's works,

which, indeed, they proceeded to destroy. One son, Robert Bushnell, was paid a small pension by the Masons' Company until 1717. He presumably died in that year, for the payment for 1718 is made to "Widow Bushnell" (Archives, Masons' Company).

As a statuary Bushnell could either be extremely good or maddeningly bad. Dallaway, writing in the *Gentleman's Magazine* (1818, Vol. I, page 595), attributes to him the monument of Lady Henrietta Wentworth, 1686, at Toddington, Bedfordshire. If this is correct he must have been a very great sculptor, for though the work is sadly mutilated it is still one of the loveliest of its kind in England. Mrs. Esdaile (*Archaeological Journal*, 1930, page 161) ascribes it to William Stanton (q.v.), but I am inclined to think it is far beyond Stanton's powers.

Of Bushnell's other monuments, that commemorating Sir Palmes Fairborne, 1680, in Westminster Abbey, was "originally of greater importance than it now appears, it having been ornamented with relievos of Moorish towns and other sculptures" (Brayley's *Westminster Abbey*, Vol. II, page 240). The most dramatic is the great baroque group of William Ashburnham and his wife, 1675, at Ashburnham, Sussex, with its kneeling figure of the husband, his hands outstretched in agonized entreaty towards the dying woman, whom cherubs beckon to the skies. Notes concerning Bushnell and the black-marble background to the monument are among the Ashburnham Archives. Magnificent also is the proud standing figure of Lord Mordaunt, 1675, in Fulham Parish Church. Three years later the sculptor was paid "for taking down and setting up part of the monument" when Lady Mordaunt was buried with her husband (Churchwardens' Accounts).

In the Chirk Castle archives an entry in the accounts for 1676 notes that "John Harrys" was paid "for his journey to Weston for my Lady's picture for Bushnell the stone-cutter to draw a pattern to make her monument at Chirk." Besides this monument to Elizabeth, Lady Myddelton, he also made in the same year another with two busts in memory of Sir Thomas and Lady Myddelton. Both these monuments are still to be seen in Chirk Parish Church. Another of Bushnell's monuments, with a life-size effigy of Dame Mary May, was formerly in Mid Lavant Church, Sussex, but was interred in a vault during a Victorian restoration. Dallaway, writing in 1815, described it as "capricious, but the portrait exact and the execution good" (*Western Sussex*, Vol. I, page 115).

The sculptor's monument to Abraham Cowley (d. 1667) in Westminster Abbey was paid for by the Duke of Buckingham. The latter's finances, however, were so involved that they were taken over by Alderman Sir Robert Clayton, and it was he who made the disbursements to Bushnell amounting to £100 between 5 June and 15 September, 1674. These payments for "setting up Mr. Cowley's monument" are noted in Sir Robert's banking ledger in the Guildhall Library.

Two other monuments known to be the work of Bushnell are those to Henry Stanley, 1670, at Little Gaddesden, Herts, and Lord Thomond, 1700, at Great Billing, Northants. He also executed the busts of Charles II in the possession of Lord Hastings, and of Mrs. Pepys, wife of the diarist, formerly in St. Olave's, Hart Street. A terra-cotta bust of Charles II in the Fitzwilliam Museum, Cambridge, has also been attributed to him, while Vertue (*Walpole Society*, Vol. I, page 129) says that he cut "a fine bust in marble of Mr. Talman, architect."

One statue by Bushnell now no longer appears to be in existence; it is that of James II, and was carved in 1685 for the façade of Southwark Town Hall. The payment for it is noted in the Rentals of the Bridge House for 1686 (Corporation of London Records Office): "June 12th, 1686 paid Mr. Bushnell £80 in full for making the King's statue at St. Margaret's Hill."

Southwark Town Hall and Court House were pulled down in 1793 and the statue was bought by some local inhabitants. In 1834 it was standing in a garden in St. George's Road, Kent Road, but I have failed to trace its history after that date. Two other statues by Bushnell have also disappeared, those of St. Peter and St. Paul which he made for the Chapel at Somerset House. (Mrs. Esdaile, *Walpole Society*, Vols. XV and XXI; *Walpole Society, Vertue Notebooks: Archaelogia*, Vol. LX, Part II, pages 559 and 563.)

BUSHROD, WILLIAM,
of Weymouth

Son of H. Bushrod of Weymouth, mason, he signs a large marble tablet to Charlotte Chaning, 1791, at Maiden Newton, Dorset.

BUSSELL, WILLIAM,
of Gloucester
fl. 1830–1842

He signs a tablet to Sophia Morris, *c.* 1830, at Kidwelly, Carmarthenshire.

BUTLER, TIMOTHY
b. 1806

He won a large Silver Medal from the Society of Arts in 1824 and in the following year attended the Royal Academy Schools on the recommendation of W. Behnes (q.v.); two years later he was awarded the Academy Silver Medal.

Butler was a popular portrait-sculptor and his busts seem to have been excellent likenesses. In 1842 he executed one of Sir James Eyre which the *Art Union* of that year (page 128) described as "a work which would do honour to the greatest of our sculptors, a finer bust than this we have never seen, it will bear comparison with any of modern times."

In 1863 Butler made a memorial to Professor Narrien for the Staff College at Farnborough. In 1870 he designed lamp-standards for the Thames Embankment to be set up on the landing-place between Hungerford and Waterloo Bridges, and also the lions' heads which "appear on the river front of the pedestals both on the north and south sides of the river" (*Builder*, 1870, page 210).

He exhibited over one hundred busts at the Royal Academy between 1828 and 1879. His statue of the Earl of Leicester (1858) is on Dereham Town Hall, Norfolk, and he also executed one of Cobden (1877) for Bradford.

BUSTS

1839	Musgrave, Bishop of Hereford	Exhibited Royal Academy
1841	Earl of Granard	Exhibited Royal Academy
1842	Sir James Eyre	For the Corporation of Hereford
1844	Charles Kemble	Exhibited Royal Academy
1844	Hon. Mrs. Norton	For R. B. Sheridan, Jnr.
1846	Dr. Wolff	Exhibited Royal Academy
1851	Samuel Cooper	Royal College of Surgeons
1860	J. W. Bazalgette	Exhibited Royal Academy
1862	Sir Richard Kirby	Exhibited Royal Academy
1865	Mr. Thomas and Mr. Eton	Bristol General Hospital
1866	Dr. William Clark	Trinity College, Cambridge
1867	Lord Rollo	Exhibited Royal Academy
1868	C. H. Cooper	Town Hall, Cambridge
1870	Arthur Purvis	Cocanada, Madras
1878	T. Hughes	Exhibited Royal Academy
n.d.	Hugh Falconer	Royal Society

MONUMENTS

1829	Hadley, Herts	James Ince
1831	Horsmonden, Kent	Anne Marriott
1833	Fareham, Hants	Lady Thompson

1836	Hendon, Middlesex	William Prescott
1841	Kensal Green	Lord Douglas
	(Cemetery)	Hallyburton
1845	Hadley, Herts	James Ince
1846	Goudhurst, Kent	Edward Miller
1849	West Brompton	Jackson, the Pugilist
	(Cemetery)	
1850	Hadley, Herts	Charles Ince
1861	Kensal Green	General Peter de la
	(Cemetery)	Motte

BUTLIN, W.
b. 1794, *d.* 1836

When his widow applied for help to the A.G.B.I. after her husband's death she stated that: "He had been sent to visit Rome by the assistance of Lord Spencer to perfect his art." Between 1828 and 1835 he exhibited various works at the Royal Academy, including a model for a statue of Lord Althrop to be executed in bronze, which the *Gentleman's Magazine* (1834, Part I, page 631) considered "wanted proportion."

In 1836 Butlin applied to the Academy for assistance and was granted eight guineas (Royal Academy Archives). He died in the same year, and his widow, who was left with seven children, was granted a pension in 1837.

BUTTON, BENJAMIN
fl. 1791–1802

Button, who was probably a local Northamptonshire statuary, signs a tablet with excellent details to George Ashby, 1802, at Hazelbeach, Northants. Another tablet in this church commemorates Mrs. Alcock, 1798, and he also signs a tombstone to Joseph Hearne, 1791, in Kelmarsh churchyard in the same county.

A "John Button" was paid £789 between 1769 and 1777 for masonry work at Bowood (Archives, Marquess of Lansdowne).

BYRD, WILLIAM. See Bird.

C

CACCIATORI, B., of Milan
b. 1794, *d.* 1871

He signs the monument, with a relief of a woman holding an infant, to Lady Mildmay, 1840, at Dogmersfield, Hants.

CACKETT, W.

In 1793 he received £225 from Lady Twisden for carving and erecting a tomb in the churchyard at Newington, Kent, to Isaac Wildash, the family steward (Archives, Twisden, of Bradbourne).

CAESAR, ANTHONY

In 1727 he carved a coat of arms over the hall door of Lord Bingley's house in Cavendish Square, and also made some mirror-frames for the same patron (Lane-Fox Archives, Bramham Park, Yorks).

CAKEBREAD, GEORGE,
of Bloxham
fl. 1806–1848

He worked both in marble and stone, and his tablets, considering that they were executed by a village mason, have careful and well-cut details. Monuments by him in Oxfordshire include those to the Woolston family, 1806, in Adderbury churchyard; Mary Hitchcock, 1818, in Dedington churchyard; Richard Kirby, 1823, at Bicester; and Richard Austen, 1836, at Bodicote. Northamptonshire examples of Cakebread's work include monuments to Elizabeth Blencoe, 1814, and John Blencowe, 1830, both at Marston St. Lawrence; and to the Rev. Moses Bartholomew, 1838, at Edgcote.

CALDWELL, GEORGE,
of Chester

In 1824 he exhibited a bust of "Mr. Harrison the Architect" at the Liverpool Academy.

CALVERT, JAMES
fl. 1765–1783

In 1766 he was a pupil of J. F. Moore (q.v.), and in the same year received a premium of fifteen guineas from the Society of Arts for a relief of the "Death of Socrates" in Portland stone. In 1770 he deserted sculpture for the stage and appeared in Dublin in Otway's "Venice Preserved," but though favourably received he did not remain an actor for long, but returned to his old profession and started to model wax portraits in Dublin.

Calvert later came back to England and was apparently employed by J. Wilton (q.v.), for in 1780 he went to Jamaica to erect his master's monument to Sir B. Keith in the Cathedral. By 1783 he had returned to Britain. He exhibited wax portraits at the Free Society and the Society of Artists, 1765–1783.

(Strickland's *Dictionary of Irish Artists;* MS. Notes in Minute-books of Society of Artists.)

CAMPBELL, THOMAS
b. 1790, *d.* 1858

He was born in Edinburgh of humble parents on 1 May, 1790, and at an early age was apprenticed to John Marshall, a marble-cutter, later transferring to James Dalzell, who took over the business on Marshall's death. Campbell's first patron was Gilbert Innes, who was struck by the young man's intelligence when he was putting up a chimney-piece in the latter's house in St. Andrew's Square, Edinburgh. This proved a fortunate encounter, for it was Innes who provided him with money to go to London and study at the Royal Academy Schools. Campbell also seems to have worked for E. H. Baily at this time. B. R. Haydon, the painter, notes in his autobiography that when he was lodging in Somers Town in 1817 it was near "where Baily the sculptor was living and where he made his first bust. Campbell, the sculptor, was then his journeyman."

In 1818 Campbell, again assisted by Innes, went to Rome. Here he studied and later began to carve busts, for which he received a number of commissions from fellow-countrymen visiting Italy. He apparently possessed "the peculiar felicity of seizing the individual likeness of his sitters and of giving them a sentiment and expression highly characteristic," though he had not "a ready imagination" and was "slow in creation." When he had "conceived an idea he studied with patience every detail and, having a certain mistrust of his own judgment upon his work, he willingly listened to advice and comment and spared no pains to give it the utmost perfection of finish" (*Art Journal*, 1858, page 107).

One of Campbell's earliest patrons was the Duke of Devonshire, by whom he was commissioned to execute a statue of Princess Pauline Borghese, sister of Napoleon, and famous for the beauty of her hands and feet. Of these the sculptor took casts and afterwards reproduced them in bronze and silver. Campbell while he was in Rome mixed very little with his fellow-artists. He was of a retiring and sensitive nature and preferred to work in his studio rather than to go into society. By 1830 he had commissions to the value of £30,000 and decided to return to England, though he retained his studio in Rome for many years, frequently returning to Italy to purchase marble, etc. In London he first lived in Leicester Square, and afterwards took a house in Marlborough Street, where he remained until his death on 4 February, 1858. He was buried in Kensal Green cemetery.

"In person he was of the middle stature, of a robust frame, lively in temperament, although occasionally subject to depression of spirits. He was never very sanguine and naturally reserved and shy, which he habitually tried to conceal and carry off by a brisk and somewhat boisterous manner. No appeal was unsuccessfully made to him in any case of distress" (*Art Journal*, 1858).

Campbell exhibited at the Royal Academy 1827–1857 and at the Great Exhibition showed "Portrait of a Lady as a Muse." (*D.N.B.*; Authorities cited in text.)

STATUES, MONUMENTS, etc.

1821	Ganymede	For Lord Kinnaird, Rossie Priory
1827	Duchess of Buccleuch	Warkton Parish Church, Northants
1828	Duke of Wellington	Dalkeith Palace
1828	Princess Pauline Borghese	Chatsworth
1829	Duke of York	Senior United Service Club
1830	Psyche	For R. N. Hamilton
1831	Mrs. Siddons	Westminster Abbey
1831?	Countess of Harrowby	Sandon Park
1833	4th Earl of Hopetoun	Royal Bank of Scotland, Edinburgh
1834	Sir William Hoste	St. Paul's Cathedral
1836	Hon. A. Kinnaird	Rossie Priory
1838	Earl Grey	Howick
1839	Countess of Courtown	Courtown Church, Co. Wexford (recumbent effigy)
1839	Duke of York	Edinburgh
1842	Duke of Gordon	Aberdeen
1843	Earl of Dalkeith	Dalkeith Palace
1847	Lady Whichcote	Aswarby Church, Lincs (relief)
1851	Lord George Bentinck	Cavendish Square, London
n.d.	Mrs. Siddons	National Portrait Gallery (relief)

BUSTS

1823	Duke of Devonshire	Chatsworth (bronze)
1824	Lady Cullum	Town Hall, Bury St. Edmunds
1825	Duke of York	Stratfield Saye
c. 1825	Earl and Countess of Shrewsbury	Formerly Alton Towers
1826	Cardinal Gonsalvo	Formerly Alton Towers
1827	Duke of Wellington	Stratfield-Saye
1827	Sir Henry Raeburn	Scottish National Portrait Gallery
1828	Duke of Wellington	Brynkinalt, Denbigh (bronze)
1828	Lady Caroline Sackville	Drayton, Northants
1830	Earl of Belfast	Exhibited Royal Academy
1834	Duke of Devonshire	Castle Howard
1835	Duke of Buccleuch	Boughton, Northants
1836	Earl Grey	Royal Collection
1836	Duke of Gordon	Windsor Castle
1841	Marchioness of Douro	Stratfield Saye
1844	Lord Wallace	For Sir Charles Monck
1845	Sir Robert Smirke	British Museum
1845	Duke of Wellington	For Lord Westmorland
1848	Lord George Bentinck	National Portrait Gallery
1849	Sir Henry Lawrence	National Portrait Gallery
1851	Robert Liston	Royal College of Surgeons
1853	John Dalrymple	Royal College of Surgeons
1853	Lord Denman	Eton College
1853	Henry Drummond	Exhibited Royal Academy
n.d.	Anna Maria Stanhope	Woburn Abbey
n.d.	Earl of Newburgh	Chatsworth (bronze)
n.d.	Princess Pauline Borghese	Chatsworth

CAMPLLEMAN, ROBERT and RALPH

Probably York masons. In 1784 they built the stable block at Castle Howard, including the carved work (Archives, Castle Howard).

CANE, R.
b. 1796

He attended the Royal Academy Schools in 1818, and in the same year exhibited a bust of a Mr. Brindle at the Academy.

CANOVA, ANTONIO
b. 1757, *d.* 1822

Canova exhibited at the Royal Academy, 1817–1823. A list of works executed by him for English patrons is given in *The Works of Antonio Canova* by the Countess Albrizzi (London, 1824).

His three monuments in England are those of the Margrave of Anspach, 1806, at Speen, Berks, and of Sophia, Countess Brownlow, 1814, at Belton, Lincs, and Lord Harrington, 1829, at Elvaston, Derby.

CANSICK, H.

Signs a tablet to James Redfern, 1826, in Kentish Town Parish Church.

CAPIZZOLDI,
or CAPITSOLDI, —
fl. 1755–1774

He was born in Italy and worked in Florence, but yielded to the persuasion of J. Wilton (q.v.), whom he met in Florence, and accompanied him to England in 1755. On his arrival in London Capizzoldi took the attic storey of a house in Warwick Street, where he proceeded to improve the appearance of his poorly furnished sitting-room by painting chairs, pictures and curtains on the bare walls.

During his stay in England he worked with Wilton, and when the latter received the commission from Parliament to execute the Abbey monument to Wolfe, it was Capizzoldi who carved the bronze relief of the General's death. The work was unveiled in 1772, but it is not known whether the Italian was still in this country at the time. He had certainly returned home by 1774, for in that year T. Banks (q.v.) met him in Rome and received instructions from him on marble-cutting (J. T. Smith's *Nollekens and his Times*, Vol. II, pages 102 and 122).

C. F. Bell (*Annals of Thomas Banks*, page 20) thinks that the sculptor's real name was Giovanni Battista Capezzuoli, who was working in Florence about 1760 and again in 1782 and who seems to have come to England. J. T. Smith stated that Capizzoldi had been a pupil of the Italian sculptor Algardi, but this, as Mr. Bell (op. cit.) points out, is impossible as Algardi died in 1653.

CARDELLI, DOMINICO,
of Rome
fl. 1786–1810

He signed the monument, erected in 1789 in St. Mary Aldermanbury, to the memory of Lieutenant John Smith, drowned off Staten Island, U.S.A.

A "P. Cardelli" (who may be a son) exhibited busts, etc., at the Royal Academy, 1815–1816, and at the British Institution in the latter year.

CARDWELL, HOLME
b. 1815

He was born in Manchester, and in 1834

attended the Royal Academy Schools on the recommendation of Chantrey (q.v.), winning a Silver Medal in 1839. In 1841 he went to Paris, where he studied for three years under the sculptor P. J. David (q.v.) and also distinguished himself at the Académie Royale. From Paris he moved to Rome and remained there for some considerable time. A writer to the *Gentleman's Magazine* in 1844 (Vol. II, page 71), who had just visited Cardwell's studio, mentions that he was engaged on a group for a Mrs. Beaumont, of Yorkshire, and was also executing another entitled "Greyhounds Playing" which "showed a keen observation of nature and great powers." In 1852 Cardwell sent to England his colossal marble group of "The Good Samaritan," which had taken him two years to complete. This work, which had been "highly praised by Gibson and other sculptors in Rome" (*Art Journal*, 1853, page 297), was placed in the hospital at Cheltenham. In 1855 he made a statue of "Sabrina" (now in the Hove Museum) for J. Murray.

Cardwell exhibited at the Royal Academy, 1837–1856, where his busts included those of John Kennedy (1837), Thomas Henshaw (1840) and Dr. Dalton. In 1840 he also showed a bust of Dr. Marsh at the Birmingham Society of Artists and, four years later, won the Heywood Medal at Manchester. The sculptor's "Shepherd Paris" was lent by Mr. J. Pender, and his "Venus Victrix" and "Huntsman and a Stag" by Mr. R. Openshaw to the Exhibition of Art Treasures of the United Kingdom held in Manchester in 1857. The "Venus Victrix" is now in Manchester Art Gallery. In the William Leech Sale at Christie's on 21 May, 1887, Cardwell's "Nydia" fetched two hundred and forty guineas and his "Nymph with Bow and Quiver" a hundred guineas.

CAREW, JOHN EDWARD
b. 1785(?), *d.* 1868

He was born at Tramore, near Waterford, and is said to have been the son of a local statuary. He apparently studied art for a time in Dublin before, about 1809, he went to London and was engaged as an assistant by Sir Richard Westmacott (q.v.). Carew afterwards stated that, during the latter part of his time with Westmacott, he earned as much as £1,500 to £1,800 a year, besides another £800 from his practice in his own studio. An income of over £2,000 seems an incredibly large sum for a minor sculptor in those days, but even if Carew exaggerated it does explain the large fortunes left by men of the status of Bacon, Chantrey and Nollekens.

About 1822 the Earl of Egremont invited

Carew to work entirely for him to the exclusion of all other commissions. The sculptor accepted the offer and the arrangement lasted until his patron's death in 1837. During this time he received generous help, not as definite payment for his services, but to keep him going and to pay expenses incurred for marble, etc., but he also seems to have made up his mind that he was going to be left a large legacy under Lord Egremont's will. When he found that he had been left nothing, he proceeded to bring an action against the Earl's executors, claiming the fantastic sum of £50,000 from the estate for works executed.

The executors, anxious that no slur should rest on the name of a man who in his lifetime had been one of the most distinguished and generous patrons of British art, decided to allow the case to go for trial. They were even generous enough to supply Carew with money when he declared he could not afford the legal expenses. Their attitude was, however, amply justified, for when the case was heard at the Lewes Assizes in 1840 it was proved that Carew had received no less than £20,000 while working for his patron and he was non-suited. In the following year he was declared a bankrupt, and it was during these proceedings that he gave the following version of the arrangement between himself and the Earl: "The late Earl of Egremont proposed my leaving Sir Richard Westmacott, his Lordship agreed to settle £1,700 a year upon me. I was eight years in town after that period, during which Lord Egremont occupied the greater portion of my time, and from that period to the present (upwards of seven years) having been induced to quit London on purpose, I devoted the whole of my time and services to his Lordship, sacrificing all the prospects which a residence in town and competition with other sculptors held out and during the best period of my life. I built a house and large studio at Brighton at the desire of Lord Egremont and expended upon those, and also with my changes of residence, considerable sums."

Besides executing statues and busts, Carew also made two marble chimney-pieces for Buckingham Palace in 1829 (P.R.O. Works 19/3). His contract for these was £800, but for some reason he seems to have received only £500. In 1830 he made other chimney-pieces for Lord Egremont's seat at Petworth in Sussex and, five years later, the altarpiece for the Roman Catholic Chapel at Brighton. As he was working for Lord Egremont at the time it was thought that his patron must have paid for this, an idea which the latter hastened to contradict when he wrote to the Press that he had "never given, never thought of giving, and never intend to give, one shilling for the building or decoration of any Roman Catholic Chapel in England."

In 1841 Carew exhibited a "Descent from the Cross" which the *Literary Gazette* of that year (page 252) called a "noble, affecting and sublime production" which placed the sculptor "in the very highest order." Three years later he carved the Royal Arms for the Royal Exchange (*Builder*, 1844, page 419) and, in 1850, executed the great bronze relief of "The Death of Nelson" for the base of the column in Trafalgar Square. In 1853 he made the reredos for the Royal Bavarian Chapel in London (*Builder*, 1853, page 624), now in the Chapel of the Assumption, Warwick Street.

Carew exhibited at the Royal Academy, 1821–1846, and at the British Institution, 1824–1843. At the latter he showed in 1842 a figure of a "Boy Playing at Marbles" which the *Art Union* (1842, page 77) considered "a noble and beautiful statue, satisfactory to the anatomist and most valuable to the lover of art. Mr. Carew is an artist of the rarest powers."

At the Great Exhibition of 1851 Carew showed an "Alto-relievo for a Temple in Sussex." Towards the end of his life he presented his statues of "Meleager" and "Diana" to the Royal Hibernian Academy. By that time he had become partially blind and he died on 30 November, 1868, and was buried in Kensal Green Cemetery. His son, F. Carew, exhibited at the Royal Academy in 1834.

(Report of case of Carew *v*. Burrell and other Executors of the late Earl of Egremont; Strickland's *Dictionary of Irish Artists*; *Art Union*, 1840, page 50.)

STATUES

1822	Arethusa	Petworth
1826	Adonis and the Boar	Petworth
1827	Vulcan and Venus	Petworth
1829	Dog of Alcibiades	Petworth
1829	The Falconer	Petworth
1830	Group of Boys	For Lord Grantham, Wrest Park
1831	Prometheus	Petworth
1832	William Huskisson	Chichester Cathedral
1833	Edmund Kean	Drury Lane
1844	Henry Grattan	St. Stephen's Hall
1844	Sir Richard Whittington	Royal Exchange
1856	John Curran	Palace of Westminster

BUSTS

1812	Dr. Roche	Exhibited Royal Academy
1813	Marquess of Wellington	Exhibited Royal Academy
1818	Rt. Hon. George Ponsonby	Exhibited Royal Academy

1820	George III	Exhibited Royal Academy
1830	Lord Thurlow	Mentioned in Carew v. Burrell
1830	General Brown	Mentioned in Carew v. Burrell
1831	Earl of Egremont	Petworth
1831	Henry Wyndham	Petworth
1831	Lord John Townshend	Woburn Abbey (replica at Petworth)
c. 1832	Miss Harriet King	Petworth
c. 1833	Mrs. King	Petworth
1834	Dr. Wagner	For School in Church Street, Brighton
1834	Captain Marryat	Exhibited Victorian Exhibition, 1891
1843	Edward Cooke	Exhibited Royal Academy
1844	Father Matthew	Exhibited Adelaide Gallery
1846	Lady Georgiana Fane	Exhibited Royal Academy

MONUMENTS

1818	St. James's, Hampstead Road	General Sir John Floyd
1823	Marlesford, Suffolk	Rev. Henry Williams
1825	Hackney (Parish Church)	Mary Field
1825	Sevenoaks, Kent	1st Earl Whitworth (with bust)
1828	Morden, Surrey	Henry Hoare
1828	Tillington, Sussex	Dr. Clarke
1829	Petworth, Sussex	Admiral Richard Willis
1834	Chichester (Cathedral)	Edmund Woods
1834	South Burstead, Sussex	Canon James Clarke
1837	Petworth, Sussex	The Percy family
1837	Brighton (Roman Catholic Church)	Mrs. Fitzherbert
1845	Tichborne, Hants	Sir Henry Tichborne
1846	Kensal Green Cemetery	Michael Nugent
1847	Alnwick, Northumberland	Duke of Northumberland
1850	Brighton (Roman Catholic Church)	Rev. Edward Cullin

CARLINE, JOHN, the Elder, and John, the Younger, of Shrewsbury

b. 1730, *d.* 1793   *b.* 1792, *d.* 1862

The elder Carline and his partner Tilly designed and built the bridge over the Rea brook at Coleham Head in 1771, and the Welsh Bridge at Shrewsbury between 1792 and 1795. They were also responsible for Montford Bridge, which was designed by Telford, and in Shrewsbury itself for St. Alkmund's Church and Claremont Buildings. In 1788 Carline built the portico of Adderley Hall,

Salop, for Sir Corbet Corbet, while father and son later erected Pelwall House, Market Drayton, between 1822 and 1828.

In 1817 the elder Carline executed the four couchant lions at the base of the column erected to the memory of Lord Hill at Shrewsbury (*Gentleman's Magazine*, 1817, Part II, page 393). In the same year his son became a Freeman of the town. It was the younger Carline who exhibited at the Royal Academy in 1825 and who, in 1839, built Grinshill Church, Salop.

The firm was responsible for a large number of monuments, and, in 1815, ordered a figure of "Fame" from Sir Francis Chantrey (q.v.) for one which they were making for a Mrs. Hill (Chantrey's ledger, Burlington House). Their monument to Edward Poore, 1817, in Salisbury Cathedral was designed by the Rev. Hugh Owen, according to the *New Monthly Magazine* (1817, page 563), which described it as "perhaps one of the most perfect specimens of florid Gothic in the Kingdom."

In 1828 the younger Carline prepared a "most elegant and chaste design" for a monument to the Rev. J. B. Blakeway. This "noble and splendid" work was later carried out in Grinshill stone and erected in St. Mary's, Shrewsbury (*Gentleman's Magazine*, Part II, page 316). The epitaph on their monument to John Simpson (*d.* 1815) in St. Chad's Church, Shrewsbury, declares that Simpson "superintended the building of St. Chad's, the bridges of Bewdley, Craig Ellachie, Dunkeld and Bonar, and the aqueducts at Pontcysylte and Chirk, and the locks and basins of the Caledonian Canal." Other works by them in this church commemorate Richard Scott, 1821; the Rev. George Scott, 1832; and William Hazledine, 1840. The first two have beautifully carved details, and the last a portrait-bust.

MONUMENTS

1789	Llanyblodwell, Salop	Francis Cunliffe
c. 1790	Kinlet, Salop	Catherine Baldwyn
1790	North Lydbury, Salop	Hester Bright
1794	Oswestry, Salop	R. W. Lloyd
1806	Ruyton, Salop	William Kinaston
1806	Shrewsbury (St. Julian's)	Robert Laurence
1808	Hodnet, Salop	Sir Richard Hill
1808	Shawbury, Salop	Lucy Minor
1810	St. Martin's, Salop	Richard Phillips
1811	Bishops Castle, Salop	John Oakley
1813	Moreton Corbet, Salop	Mary Corbet
1813	Chester (Cathedral)	Stephen Leake
1813	Shrewsbury (St. Chad's)	Francis Leighton
1813	Llanfair, Denbigh	Maurice Lloyd
1814	Hodnet, Salop	John Hill
1814	Market Drayton, Salop	Charles Groby
1817	Battlefield, Salop	John Corbet

1822	Moreton Say, Salop	Elizabeth Clive
1823	Adderley, Salop	Sir Corbet Corbet
1824	Kinlet, Salop	William Childe (with medallion portrait)
1827	Wellington, Hereford	Joseph South
1828	Willey, Salop	Lord Forester
1829	Shrewsbury (St. Alkmund's)	Sir Thomas Jones
1834	Hodnet, Salop	Mary Heber
1844	Baschurch, Salop	Rev. John Basnett

CARLINE, THOMAS,
of Shrewsbury

b. 1799, *d.* 1868

Carline, who was the second son of John Carline the Elder (q.v.), attended the Royal Academy Schools in 1821, and in the same year won the Isis Silver Medal for a single figure from the Society of Arts. He exhibited at the Academy between 1825 and 1828, showing in 1826 a figure of a sleeping child, Henry, son of the Hon. Thomas Kenyon. This "interesting and expressive" work was "fortunate enough to obtain one of the best situations in the sculpture room," according to the *Gentleman's Magazine* (1826, Part II, page 589). The same critic also considered the relief of a funeral procession on Carline's monument to Sir John Hill, 1826, at Prees, Salop, "admirably executed," declaring that "never did sculpture tell its tale more forcibly."

CARLINI, AUGOSTINO, R.A.

d. 1790

A native of Genoa, he settled in London as a young man and later became one of the Foundation Members of the Royal Academy. He exhibited there between 1769 and 1787 and, in 1783, succeeded Moser as Keeper.

About 1760 Carlini made a statue of his friend Ward, the quack doctor and inventor of friar's balsam (a nostrum which the sculptor assisted him to concoct). Ward, to advertise himself and his remedies, paid Carlini £200 a year simply to keep the statue in his studio and appear to work at it when visitors or patrons were about. After the doctor's death his executors promised to continue this annuity, but they failed to do so, and "the figure lay for some time disregarded in a stable at Westminster" (*New Monthly Magazine*, 1816, page 418). It now stands in the entrance-hall of the Royal Society of Arts, to whom it belongs.

In 1783, Paul Sandby, R.A., wrote to James Gandon, the architect, that he had "had the pleasure of seeing the models which Carlini has made for you, and think they possess great merit" (C. F. Bell's *Annals of Thomas Banks*, page 54). The models referred to were of eight statues for the north and south fronts of the Dublin Customs House; they were destroyed by fire and bombardment during the Irish Rebellion of 1916. From 1776 until 1778 the sculptor was making statuary for Somerset House, where his work included three colossal keystones for the Strand front, in the form of masks representing the Rivers Dee, Tyne and Severn. He also received £240 for two Portland-stone statues over 7 ft. high of "Justice" and "Prudence" for the same building (P.R.O. A.O.1/2495).

In 1768 Carlini executed in wax an "Emblematical Figure Representing Maritime Power and Riches," and advertised in the Press that he could supply reproductions of it in plaster-of-Paris at six guineas each. About a year later he sold for ten guineas each a number of models he had made of an equestrian statue of George III. One of these he presented to the Royal Academy, another is at Windsor Castle, while a third was formerly at Audley End, Essex. His bust of the King, executed in 1773, is at Burlington House.

Carlini died unmarried on 15 August, 1790, in Carlisle Street, and administration of his will was granted to "Elizabeth Watton, spinster," his maid-servant and sole heiress. A sale of his effects was held on 13 January of the following year, and among the models sold were those of a "Colossal Head of George III," the "Old Duke of Cumberland," "The Death of Wolfe" and "A Dog."

His monuments are on a heroic scale, the finest being those to the Countess of Shelburne, 1771, at High Wycombe, Bucks, and to the Earl and Countess of Dorchester, 1775, at Milton Abbey, Dorset. He also signs the monument to his friend, Dr. Ward, 1774, once in Westminster Abbey. His monument with a life-size statue of Lady Bingley, 1771, in the private chapel at Bramham Park, Yorkshire, is unsigned, but the model for it was Lot 54 in the sale already mentioned. He submitted a design for Alderman Beckford's monument in the Guildhall which was not accepted, though a fine engraving of it was made by Bartolozzi (*Gentleman's Magazine*, 1819, Part I, page 43). He was again unsuccessful in 1784 when he sent in a model for a statue of Admiral Lord Rodney, which it was proposed to erect in Jamaica (Royal Academy Archives).

Carlini also seems to have been of an inventive turn of mind, for the Court Book of the Royal Academy has the following entry: "19 March, 1771. Resolved that the apparatus for the use of the Academy according to a Design delivered by Mr. Carlini be carried into execution and that Mr. Carlini be desired to order and superintend making the Machine."

(J. T. Smith's *Nollekens and His Times*, Vol. II; authorities cited in text.)

CARPENTER, AARON,
of London
fl. 1762–1767

According to the *London Magazine* of 1762 (page 173), he showed in that year a "marble statue of Acteon" at the Society of Free Artists, a work not mentioned by Graves in his list of Exhibitors. Carpenter continued to exhibit until 1767, showing impressions of seals, etc.

CARPENTER, ANDREW. See
Carpentière, Andries

CARPENTER, EDMUND

In 1688 he was employed by Sir John Brownlow, who was then building Belton. From the prices he received he almost certainly worked in wood. Payments to him include £26 for "a very rich chimney-piece in the withdrawing roome to the great parlor, done with a varietie of fish and shells with birds, fouliage, fruit and flowers"; £25 for "one rich chimney-piece with birds, fruits and flowers in the withdrawing roome in ye little parlor," and £18 for "one chimney-piece in the great parlor with fruit and flowers." (Archives, Lord Brownlow.)

CARPENTER, SAMUEL,
of London
fl. 1712–1729

In 1712 he made the statue of Queen Anne, formerly on the front of the Moot Hall at Leeds, and now in the possession of the City Corporation. The statue was given by Alderman Milner and "was generally esteemed the best that was ever made, not excepting the celebrated one in St. Paul's Churchyard" (Whitaker's *Ducatus Leodiensis*, Vol. II, page 249).

In 1729 Carpenter executed the statues for the façade of Moulsham Hall, near Chelmsford, and also the "lyons over the great piers" (Account-book of the first Earl Fitzwalter).

CARPENTER, SAMUEL, of York
b. 1660, *d.* 1713

He became free of the Masons' Company of York in 1684 and, in the following year, was made a Freeman of the city (York Corporation Archives). In 1702 he received £72 3s. 3d. for the "carving on the obelisk at Ripon" (Ripon Corporation Archives). Between 1705 and 1706 he was working at Castle Howard, where he was responsible for "a dragon" costing £10, two stone vases, and the very fine "satyr gate" in the garden.

For the exterior of the house Carpenter executed "thirty-six pilaster capitals of the Corinthian order and seventeen pilaster capitals for the West Wing." He also carved the shield on the south front, and a shield and cherubim over the middle window. His bill for carved stonework on the north and south fronts, including festoon and busts, came to £206. For the interior he made twenty-six capitals of the composite order for the great hall and six scallop shells in a passage (Castle Howard Archives).

In 1710 Carpenter was commissioned by Ralph Thoresby to execute a bust of the elder Thoresby for Leeds Parish Church, and a monument to Ralph's friend, Mr. Thomson, for St. John's Church in the same city, but both these works have long since disappeared (Atkinson's *Ralph Thoresby*, Vol. II). He signs the monument, with a lovely bust, to Lady Elizabeth Stapleton, 1684 at Snaith, Yorkshire; the contract for this is published in *The Ancestor*, Vol. III, page 161. He also made a cartouche tablet in St. Mary's, Bishophill Senior, York, but here the date and the inscription are now illegible.

Carpenter died 27 June, 1713 and was buried in St. Lawrence's, York. His wife, Frances, died in 1731, aged sixty-nine, but for some reason was not buried with her husband, but in the church of St. Dennis in the same city.

CARPENTER, STEPHEN,
of Blandford
fl. 1770–1775

Between 1770 and 1775 he was the master-mason responsible for building Milton Abbey in Dorset, a house designed by Sir William Chambers. Lord Milton seems to have been very dilatory in settling his accounts, for in 1774 Chambers was forced to write and inform him that "Carpenter has been with me and is much distressed for money to pay debts contracted" (British Museum, Ad. MS. 41136).

CARPENTIÈRE, ANDRIES
b. 167?, *d.* 1737

Carpentière, who anglicized his name to "Andrew Carpenter" soon after his arrival in England, first worked as principal assistant to John Nost (q.v.), but later set up for himself. Vertue (*Walpole Society*, Vol. III, page 83) says that "he was a man in his time esteemed for his skill and made many works for noblemen and others of distinction in stone and marble." In 1722 he began working at Canons for the Duke of Chandos, but later quarrelled with him and lost his patronage. According to Vertue (op. cit.) the trouble was caused by Carpenter building some houses and an inn not far from the mansion and then putting up a statue as a sign in the middle of the road close to the main entrance. The Duke, very annoyed, ordered him to take the statue down, which he firmly refused to do.

Carpenter had started to make lead statues at his yard at Hyde Park Corner before 1722. This yard was situated more or less where No. 94, Piccadilly stands today. At first the venture was a success, but "he had much ado to hold up his head at last," owing to being undersold and having to lower his prices (Vertue, op. cit.).

One of his earliest patrons was Lord Carlisle, to whom he sent a price list of his lead figures. They included the following:

	HEIGHT IN FEET	PRICE
Narcissus	7½	£25
Hercules and Wild Boar	6	£20
Cain and Abel	6	£20
Diana and Stag	6	£20
Venus de Medici	6	£15
Antinous	6	£18
Bacchus sitting	6	£18
Faunus	6	£20
Melagor	6	£20
Adonis	6	£18
Apollo	6	£18
Flora	6	£16
Gladiator	6	£12
Duke of Marlborough	6	£28
Roman Wrestlers	6	£20
Neptune	5½	£9
Bagpiper	5	£7
An Indian	5	£8
Cleopatra	5	£7
Daphne	5	£8
French paisant and paisanne	4 ft. 2 in.	£12
Winter and autumn	4½	£8 8s.
4 Signs of ye Zodiac	4	£16
Faunus and Nymph	4 ft. 2 in.	£8 8s.

From this price list Lord Carlisle ordered, in 1723, "Hercules of Farnese, Spartan Boys, sitting Venus, and Faunus," paying £84. The cases to send these figures from London came to £9 7s. 9d. It took a man nine and a half days to make the cases and besides the wood twenty-one pounds of "spike" and a thousand "double-tenns" nails were used (Archives, Castle Howard).

Another patron was the Duke of Kent, and on 9 August, 1730, the Duchess wrote to her husband that "the carrier will be at Mr. Carpenter's for the statues on Tuesday morning." This almost certainly refers to the magnificent lead groups still in the gardens at Wrest Park, Bedfordshire. A later letter mentions that Carpenter was also making a "blackamoor" and a "gladiator" for Wrest (Archives, Lady Lucas and Dingwall).

Other works in lead executed by Carpenter include a head of Cicero in 1716 for Lord Ashburnham (Ashburnham Archives), and two flower-pots and four figures of "The Seasons" for the first Earl of Bristol in the same year (Archives, Ickworth Park). In 1720 he was working for two directors of the South Sea Company, supplying figures and flower-pots costing £128 for Mr. Francis Hawes, of Purley Hall, Berks, and vases for Mr. Robert Chester, of "Briggens," Herts (Inventory of Directors of the South Sea Company). In the Bodleian (Gough, Maps, 46) is a drawing of a vase designed by Gibbs and executed by Carpenter for Wimpole in Cambridgeshire.

In the minute book for the building of St. Paul's Cathedral is, "Feb. 13th, 1716/17. Ordered that Mr. Bird and Mr. Carpenter, statuaries, do proceed to make Statues for St. Paul's according to the direction and agreement made with them by Mr. James." There is, however, no trace of any payment to Carpenter, and Bird alone was probably employed (*Wren Society*, Vol. XVI, page 128).

Carpenter's monuments are important, the finest of them commemorating the Earl and Countess of Warrington at Bowden, Cheshire. The work, erected in 1734 and costing £389, has a large sarcophagus in the centre, while at either end sit figures of "Learning" and "Truth." In the same church is his large monument, 20 ft. high, to Langham and Henry Booth, 1727, with lovely portrait-medallions of the two youths. Other portrait-medallions appear on the monument to Montagu Drake, 1724, at Amersham, Bucks. According to the Shardeloes Archives, this cost £180 and was executed by Carpenter from a design by James Gibson. He also signs monuments to Sir John Fermor, 1722, at Sevenoaks, Kent; Sir John Thornycroft, 1725, at Bloxham, Oxon; and the Bertie family, *c.* 1730 at Theddlethorp All Saints, Lincolnshire.

Carpenter died in 1737 and, according to Vertue (op. cit.), was buried at St. George's, Hanover Square. Vertue describes him as a "gross, heavy man," and his son John as an "idle fellow." This is probably true, for Carpenter in his Will cut him off with a shilling and left everything, including his property at Edgware, to his wife.

(Authorities cited in text; Archives, Earl of Stamford.)

CARR, JOSEPH, of London
fl. 1754–1768

Between 1754 and 1758 he built part of the

Horse Guards in Whitehall, where his work included "a marble frieze carved and polished with cables, flutes and tongues" (R.I.B.A. Library, MS. 725/18). He also signs the large architectural wall monument in coloured marbles to Francis Fawkes, 1754, at Otley, Yorks. In 1765 he was paid £18 for the ledger to Charles Monson in Broxbourne Church, Herts. The carving of the coat of arms came to £3 6s., and the cutting of 153 letters to £1 5s. 6d. (Archives, Lord Monson).

Carr became a bankrupt in 1768 and on 13 September a sale of his stock-in-trade was held at his yard at "Mill Bank, Westminster." Among the lots were a number of marble chimney-pieces. A note on the sale catalogue reads: "The business will be continued as usual by Joseph Carr, Junior, who begs the favour of his father's friends and customers."

A contemporary was William Carr, son of Edward Carr, "citizen of London and barber-surgeon," who was apprenticed to Henry Daintry in 1741 and became free in 1748.

CARRECK, or CARRICK, WILLIAM, of Ashford

He signs a tablet to Captain Thomas Smart (d. 1815) at Ashford, Kent. A "Charles Carrick" of Canterbury showed "a loo table, inlaid with various coloured woods" at the Great Exhibition of 1851.

CARTER, BENJAMIN
d. 1766

He worked chiefly as a maker and carver of marble chimney-pieces sometimes in partnership with his brother, Thomas Carter (q.v.), and sometimes on his own account. Both partners sign the bills for the chimney-pieces they executed for 18, Cavendish Square (the house of Thomas Bridges) in 1757. Here they received £144 for a "Doric" and a "French" chimney-piece, the former having "columns and the ground of frieze of jasper, the rest statuary, the columns whole, the tablet lion and boys," and the latter "statuary astsagal (sic), mantel and jambs, carved black marble coverings, veined slab, the rest of wood, carved as the drawing." The chimney-piece they supplied for the parlour of this house had a tablet of Cybele and cost £52 (Middlesex Record Office, 85/223).

On his own account Benjamin Carter made chimney-pieces for Longford Castle (1739), Stourhead (1759–1761), Bowood (1764), and Saltram, Devon (Archives of houses mentioned). In 1762 he carved a marble one for the second Earl of Ashburnham and sent down his workman, Robert Stavely, to set it up at Ashburnham Place,

Sussex (Ashburnham Archives). He also supplied nine for Blair Castle, including one with a head of Apollo, the bill being paid after his death and receipted by his widow, Mary.

Carter also made for Stourhead a pedestal of coloured marbles costing £30 for the "Florence box," and another at £40 of "Sienna, Genoa green, and black marble," but these are no longer there and were presumably destroyed when so much of the house was burned down early in this century. In 1761 he made the eight alto-relievos for the Pantheon at Stourhead, for which he received £268. The reliefs have always been attributed to Rysbrack, but the existence of the detailed bills in the archives of Hoare's Bank proves that they were executed by Carter.

In 1752 he made the model for the famous lion on Northumberland House in the Strand, which is now at Isleworth (Gentleman's Magazine, Vol. 82, Part I, page 341), and, with his brother Thomas, signs the monuments to Sarah Currer, 1757, in Bath Abbey, and Colonel Townshend, 1759, in Westminster Abbey. His son was John Carter (1748–1817), the architect and draughtsman.

CARTER, CHARLES
fl. 1815–1820

His yard was in Dean Street, Soho. In 1816 he was paid £237 3s. 11d. by the Duke of Bridgewater for "stone carving," probably for a London house (Archives, Lord Brownlow).

CARTER, JOHN
fl. 1762–1780

He was "under twenty-two" when, in 1762, he won a premium from the Society of Arts. In 1765 he was a pupil of Henry Cheere (q.v.) and in that year gained another premium of fifteen guineas for a model of "A Slave Taking a Thorn from a Lion's Foot." The Minute Book of the Society of Arts states that he died before 1782.

CARTER THOMAS the Elder
d. 1756?

According to the European Magazine (1803, Vol. II, page 178), Carter as a young married man, had his own yard in Shepherd's Market, and about 1729 received a loan of £100 from Jervase the artist, a kindness which enabled him to hire an assistant, buy marble and generally enlarge the business. The assistant he hired was L. F. Roubiliac, according to Mrs. Esdaile's biography of that sculptor, but there is always the possibility that Roubiliac worked for Carter's brother Benjamin (q.v.) for we only know that he was apprenticed to a "Mr. Carter". Like his brother Carter was chiefly known as a maker of chimney-pieces.

In 1746 he carved some for Welbeck Abbey and sent down two of his best men, Kay and Wild-smith, to set them up. While they were there they apparently had a quarrel, for Carter wrote to Mr. Thompson, Lady Oxford's agent, that "if it is not too much trouble to you, I would take it as a great favour of a line or two from you what you think may make the disturbance between Kay and Wildsmith, for at this time I have more than forty men under me and, thank God, without any disturbance in the least." Later in the year he wrote to Kay that he had "sent her Ladyship a drawing of a Gothick chimney-piece." This was accepted and two years later he was paid for "three Gothick chimney-pieces of several sorts of English marble" for the dining-room (£526) drawing-room (£281) and bedchamber (£249) respectively (Archives, Duke of Portland). In 1745 Carter had also supplied two chimney-pieces of "black and yellow marble" and "black and gold marble" for Mr. James West's house in Lincoln's Inn Fields (Archives, West of Alscot Park). In 1746 he made several for Moulsham Hall, Essex, including those for the north-west dressing-room, the west bedroom and the "Great Room." The last named costing £201 (Fitzwalter Archives.)

Other houses for which he supplied chimney-pieces include Longford Castle in 1739 (£70) (Earl of Radnor's Archives) and Milton Hall near Peterborough in 1750 (£23 19s.) (Earl Fitz-William's Archives). Carter made a considerable number of chimney-pieces for Blair Castle, Perth-shire, where he was working from 1748 till his death, indeed, all the best chimney-pieces in the castle are by him. He was also paid £52 10s. in 1754 for "two figures," and these may well be those of "Piece and Plenty" over the door of the Ante-Room. In 1756 he received an order for three chimney-pieces which were to be the same as the ones in "Lord Townsend's house" (this probably refers to Lord Townsend's London home and not to Raynham). He provided chimney-pieces for Oakover Hall, Staffs., 1747, and Belhus, Essex, 1752.

At Holkham, Norfolk, he received a consider-able amount of employment, being responsible, about 1740, for the chimney-pieces in the Saloon, Great Dining-Room, State Bedroom, North State Bedroom etc. (Matthew Brettingham "Plan of Holkham" 1773). Between 1747 and 1756 Sir Matthew, Featherstonehaugh paid him nearly £1,000 for chimney-pieces for Uppark, Sussex, the two finest being in the Hall. In 1737 he made

another for General Dormer for Rousham Park, Oxfordshire (Archives of Houses Named).

His monuments are of considerable importance; perhaps the grandest is that of the Speaker Conolly who died in 1729. This monument must have been one of the first commissions Carter received, and it was set up in a large mausoleum in the graveyard of Celbridge, Co. Kildare, and shows full length reclining figures of the Speaker and his wife in a vast architectural setting.

An unsigned monument by Carter is that with its life sized figure of Colonel Thomas Moore, 1735, at Great Bookham, Surrey. Evidence that he was the sculptor is to be found in the North Archives (Bodleian, C. 14, F. 19) here, in a list of "Family pictures of William Moore Esq. left to go with the estate and not yet delivered to Lord North" is included "a half length picture of Colonel Moore left to Mr. Carter, the stonemason, who is making a monument". Monuments signed by him include those to Mary Carew 1731 at Antony, Cornwall, and to Sir Cecil and Lady Wray 1736, with two portrait busts at Branston, Lincs.

The monument to Sir Henry Every (died 1709) at Newton Solney, Derby, is also a fine work. The Victorian restoration of the church has destroyed its background and removed the dis-membered monument to the West End. It does not seem to have been erected till about 1734 as in that year Sir Henry's brother, Sir Simon Every, writes to his sister-in-law (now by a second marriage Lady Guise) his "most humble thanks for ye Beautiful Monument you have given my brother "(Archives, Sir Edward Every Bart.)

In his will made August 1st, 1756 and proved in the same year, Carter states that his yard was in the Parish of St. George's Hanover Square, and appoints as his Executors John Cheere (q.v.) and John Phillips "Carpenter". Mentioned in his will are his wife Mary and his daughters Elizabeth and Ann, the former being the wife of his nephew Thomas Carter the Younger (q.v.).

CARTER THOMAS
the Younger

d. 1795

He was a nephew of Thomas Carter the Elder (q.v.) and also his son-in-law, having married his eldest daughter. His father-in-law left his stock to his brother Benjamin (q.v.) but the younger Thomas seems to have gone into partnership with his Uncle and when Thomas died in 1766 he acquired the whole family business and moved to a yard in Piccadilly. Like the elder Carter he made a very large number of chimney-pieces and must have had a considerable number of workmen to carry out all the commissions he received, nor were all his assistants Englishmen for John Eckstein (q.v.) worked for him. Whilst still in partnership with Thomas the firm made chimney-pieces for Sir Edward Knatchbull's house at Mersham, Kent; Benjamin died before the work was finished and Thomas wrote to Sir Edward asking him to advance payment on the grounds that "the Executors of my late partner have advised me to settle all my accounts." The reply he received was the reverse to encouraging, for Sir Edward declared himself "a stranger as to what engagements you have entered upon concerning your partner" and added, rather unkindly, "you may have heard of buying a pig in a poke" (Archives, Lord Braborne). Two years before this the Carters had made two chimney-pieces costing £46 and £53 respectively for Sir Richard Lyttleton's house in Piccadilly (Archives, Lord Brownlow). Other houses for which Thomas made chimney-pieces include Saltram, Devon, about 1760; Shardloes, Bucks, where in 1761, he was paid £147 for the one in the Library. In 1765 he made the chimney-pieces for the Dressing-Room and Ante-Room at Croome Court, Worcs., receiving £150 for the first named room, and in 1769 he was paid £260 for the Drawing-Room chimney-piece. Between 1774 and 1776 he made a number for Milton Abbey, Dorset, though none of these seem to have been of great importance. From designs by Robert Adam he carved, in 1763, several very grand chimney-pieces for Bowwood, Wilts., and also some minor ones from his own designs. In 1774 he carved one in the Library in the same house, though on this occasion the design was provided by James Stuart. He was also employed at Lansdowne House, Berkeley Square, in 1768, making one for the Ante-Room, and returned in the same year to Mersham where he executed two large ones in Portland stone for the hall and another of marble for the Drawing-Room which cost £155. The Duke of Bedford employed him in 1791 to make a number of chimney-pieces for Woburn Abbey (Archives of houses named). The Prince Regent employed him for Carlton House about 1785 (Pyne's *Royal Residences* Vol. III).

Carter also did a good deal of work for the architects Henry Holland and Sir John Soane. Under the former in 1777 he made a chimney-piece costing £70 for the Museum at Bussbridge, the seat of Sir Thomas Marker, and others in the same year for General Smith of Chiltern, Hungerford, and Mr. Nicholas Henny's house in St. James' Street where he received £935. Under Soane he provided chimney-pieces in 1782 for Lord Delavel in Hanover Square, and in 1791 for Messrs. Ransome, Morland, and Hammersley of Pall Mall at a total cost of £444 (Archives, Soane Museum). Like his Uncle he worked at Halkham making the scrolls in "open pilasters" for the archway of the North Dining-Room (Archives, Earl of Leicester), and in 1763, Horace Walpole paid him £31 for "marbles" for the Gallery at Strawberry Hill (Toynbee's *Strawberry Hill Accounts*).

Carter's monuments are of the greatest importance; indeed that to Challoner Chute in the tombhouse attached to the chapel of the Vyne in Hampshire is one of the noblest works of late eighteenth century sculpture in England. This monument, or rather cenotaph, the model for which is the Victoria and Albert Museum, was planned by John Chute to the memory of his ancestor, Chaloner Chute, Speaker of the House of Commons in the Long Parliament. It was erected 1775–1776 and shows the Speaker, a life-sized figure, reclining on a woven pallet, his head resting on his right hand, his hat and a book by his side.

The sarcophagus on which he lies is a most unusual work, with its fluted Ionic columns dividing the panels in which are coats of arms in elaborate cartouches. The design of the whole monument and its modelling are beyond praise and doubtless owes much to the taste and guidance of John Chute, sited by his friend, Horace Walpole, in his essay on gardening, as a leading example of the fact that architecture at that time owed as much to learned amateurs as to professionals.

John Chute died in 1776, when only part of the sarcophagus had been carried out, and Carter's bill to him (in the Vyne Archives) is chiefly concerned with the marble and some of the carvings. It is dated 29th November 1775; The cost of the marble itself came to £186 1s. 6d., while among the charges for carving are £51 16s., for "fluting" and £66. 15s., for "moulded work". The cost of the slab of black marble on which the effigy lies was only £4 9s. 3d. The total came to £335 19s. 11d., and a note on the bills states that the work so far carried out had been measured by a William Barker.

CARTWRIGHT, THOMAS, the Elder
b. c. 1617, *d.* 1702

He was born about 1617 and was apprenticed to David Chaloner in 1631; he did not, however, finish his time with Chaloner, but was turned over to Christopher Kingsfield in 1637. Cartwright became Warden of the Masons' Company in 1671, and was twice Master, first in 1673 and again in 1694. As a mason-contractor he was employed on building, or repairs to, the Inner Temple in 1657 (Inderwick's *Inner Temple Records*), the Royal Exchange between 1668 and 1671 (*Builder*, 1846, page 2), and Moorgate in 1674 (Guildhall MS. 184).

After the Great Fire, Cartwright built, or helped to build, a number of City churches. At St. Bennet Fink his carved stonework included "four draperies and two festoons, 4 ft. long, £9," and "six capitals, £27"; at St. Antholin's, "eight capitals and two cherub-heads, £46," and "eight flambeaus on the outside of the spire, £36"; and at St. Mary-le-Bow, "ten Corinthian capitals, £8." In his work on the steeple of the last-named church he was assisted by John Thompson, receiving £250 for "four pinnacles and carving," and £20 for "four urns with flames" (Bodleian, Rawlinson, MSS. 387). Robert Hooke in his diary (page 219) records how he "agreed with Cartwright for Bow tower for £2,500," and also mentions (page 183) that the latter made the statues on Bedlam Gate in 1675. In the following year he also carved statues of "Justice," "Mercy," "Truth" and "Liberty" for Newgate.

Between 1668 and 1670 Cartwright was the mason employed for the rebuilding of Drapers' Hall after the Great Fire. In 1669 he made the chimney-piece for the "Lady's chamber" and in the following year carved a pair of gate-pillars which so pleased the Company that they paid him £6, instead of the £4 for which he had asked. In the Court Minute-book of that year it is recorded that "Mr. Thomas Cartwright (is) to have a lease of the land unbuilt upon by the late Mr. Thynne" (Archives, Drapers' Company). Cartwright was also employed as master-mason for the rebuilding of the Weavers' Hall, 1667–1669; the Haberdashers' Hall, 1669–1671; and the Tallow Chandlers' Hall, 1672–1673 (Companies' Archives). In 1673, in partnership with J. Young (q.v.), he was working at Mercers' Hall, where they received £150 for "stone and workmanship about the porch and columns," and a further payment of £350 later in the same year (Company's Court-book). Two years later, on his own account, he was the mason for building Sir William Turner's house in Warwick Lane (Guildhall Library, MS. 5107/1).

In 1667 Cartwright had supplied black-marble chimney-pieces for the Duke of York's Lodging, the Duke of Kendal's bedchamber and the Countess of Rocheford's lodging at Whitehall (P.R.O. Works 5/9), and in 1682 Lord Ailesbury paid him £30 for "two lions" and "for setting them up on the gate of Ailesbury House, Clerkenwell" (Archives, Marquess of Ailesbury).

From about 1680 till 1702 Cartwright was engaged on the building of St. Thomas's Hospital. According to the Minute-book of the Court of Governors it was decided on 11 November, 1681, that "the plan of a scheme or frontispiece to bee made of Purbeck stone before the front of our hospitall to the High Streete, prepared by direction of the said Committee, containing pillars and the Kings Armes and the effigies of King Edward the Sixth and fower cripples to be carved in stone, was approved of and ordered to bee made accordingly. It is further ordered that Mr. Thomas Cartwright, mason, being the person that made the draft should be imploied in the performance of the work." Cartwright asked £190 as the work "could not well be done for less." The statues of the "fower cripples" are now outside the modern main entrance of the hospital, and the statue of Edward VI faces the river.

Cartwright was also the master-mason for building the parish church of St. Thomas at Southwark in 1700 and the hospital chapel—for the latter he carved in 1696 "2 large urns" and "a sun dyall with scroul's inriched with carving." By 1730, however, there is a minute of the Grand Committee that "one of the urns over the chapel is ready to fall," and the Treasurer was authorized to arrange for the removal of both the urns and the sundial.

Cartwright signs the very fine monument at Ledsham, Yorkshire, with its two reclining figures of Sir John and Lady Lewys. This cost £100, and the bill, dated 4 April, 1677, is in the ledger of Lewys's banker, Sir Robert Clayton (Guildhall Library). An earlier entry reads: "1676, July 21st: paid Mr. Thomas Cartwright, by order of Sir Stephen for the monument for Sir John Langham —£290." This magnificent work, with recumbent figures in white marble of Sir John and his wife, stands in Cottesbrooke Church, Northamptonshire. It is of great artistic importance and proves conclusively that its creator was one of the foremost sculptors of the seventeenth century. Cartwright also signs a tablet to John Polhill, 1689, at Burwash, Sussex.

(Authorities cited in text.)

CARTWRIGHT, THOMAS, the Younger

b. 1655, *d.* 1711

In 1672 he was apprenticed to his father, Thomas Cartwright the Elder (q.v.), and was later Renter Warden of the Masons' Company in 1704, Upper Warden in 1705, and Master in 1710 (Archives, Masons' Company). He continued his father's work at St. Thomas's Hospital. He died on 15 November, 1711, and was buried in Rickmansworth Parish Church, where a stone, long since vanished, commemorated him and his wife, daughter of Roger Touchet, of Rickmansworth (Cussan's *Hertfordshire*, Vol. III, Part II, page 157).

Cartwright signs tablets to Edward Sulyard, 1692, at Runwell, Essex, and Benjamin Dodd, 1706, in Hackney Parish Church.

CARTWRIGHT, THOMAS, the Third

d. 1740

He was the son of Joseph Cartwright and presumably the grandson of Thomas Cartwright the Elder. His father, who had become free of the Masons' Company by patrimony in 1673, died before 1702, the year in which Thomas himself (also by patrimony) was admitted to the freedom of the Company. In 1733 Mr. Henry Hoare employed him at one of his houses, possibly Stourhead (Archives, Hoare's Bank), and in 1739 he made a chimney-piece costing £53 for Longford Castle (Archives, Earl of Radnor).

Thomas's son, Newman Cartwright, was apprenticed to his father in 1723 and was working with him in 1731, the year in which he became free (Court-book, Masons' Company). Thomas died in 1740 and was survived by his widow Elizabeth, who received a pension from the Masons' Company until her death in 1770 (Company Archives).

CASS, CHRISTOPHER, the Elder

b. 1678, *d.* 1734

He was apprenticed to Henry Parker in 1692, and in 1704 (three years after he had become free) was one of the chief masons employed under Edward Strong (q.v.) at Greenwich (Guildhall MS. 233). As a master-mason Cass built, or helped to build, the tower of Greenwich Church and the churches of St. George's, Hanover Square; St. Luke's, Old Street; St. John's, Westminster; St. Anne's, Limehouse; and St. Martin-in-the-Fields. On 16 December, 1719, he wrote to the Bishop of Carlisle that Mr. Tufnell, late mason to Westminster Abbey, having died, he offered himself for the post "having been bred in the buildings part of the Masons Trade in ye most considerable Publick Buildings lately advanced, which I have conducted where I have been concerned so farr as related to ye immediate executive part, and from that experience doubt not to do ye same work equally well at £20 pr. cent. cheaper than the Abbey have paid for ye same." Cass added that he

had been "ye lowest Bidder among many competitors for ye Balistrades to St. Paul's which I have just finished" (Archives, Westminster Abbey). In 1733 (though the work was done in 1726) he received £1,623 for "the portico with eight pillars, entablature and pediment upon the same, and carving His Majesty's Arms thereon" (St. Martin-in-the-Fields, Parish Records).

For the University of Cambridge Cass built the south-east and north sides of the Senate House, where he was responsible for all the carved stonework, including the "shields with palm branches 20 ft. long" in the tympana of the two pediments and, in 1731, "the stone posts before ye theatre" (Vice-Chancellor's Accounts). In 1724 he was working at King's College and, three years later, at Trinity Hall (Willis and Clarke's *Architectural History of Cambridge*, Vol. I, page 503; Vol. III, page 46).

About 1719 he built "Briggens," a house in Hertfordshire, for Robert Chester, one of the directors of the South Sea Company. In 1720, when the "Bubble" burst and the directors were arrested and forced to give an account of their financial position, Chester wrote that he was "indebted to Christopher Cass, mason, for stone and marble used and work done in building my house in Hertfordshire, £928 3s. 7d., as by his accompts, which not being according to agreement, I cannot adjust it at present" (Inventory of the Estates of the Directors of the South Sea Company). Other houses where Cass was employed include Canons, the seat of the Duke of Chandos, in 1724 (Collins Baker's *Duke of Chandos*); the London house of the architect, Nicholas Hawksmoor, in 1727 (British Museum, Ad. MS. 27587); and the house in St. James's Square belonging to Lord Bristol, in 1732 (Diary of the first Earl of Bristol, Ickworth Park). The Court Book of the Masons' Company notes in 1708 that he was working at Woodstock, so it seems possible that he may have been employed on the building of Blenheim.

Cass, who was also master-mason to His Majesty's Ordnance, took Andrews Jelfe (q.v.) and Thomas Shepherd as partners at various times to assist him with his building work. He died in London and was buried in the cemetery of St. John's, Westminster, where his heavy granite monument, with its inscription "Chr. Cass, master-mason to his Maj. Ordnance. Dy'd Ap. 21, 1734," may still be seen. C. H. Smith (q.v.) is reported in the *Builder* (1851, page 215) as saying that this monument was the first work in England to be carried out in granite, and that "its mouldings though such as would now be considered rude in form and execution, were highly esteemed in his

(Mr. Smith's) boyhood." In his will Cass had originally expressed a wish to be buried in a vault beneath the portico of St. Martin-in-the-Fields, but substituted St. John's burial-ground in a codicil, To Edward Strong (q.v.), "my friend and benefactor," he left £50, declaring that he owed him what "I and my family, under the good providence of God, have." To Andrews Jelfe (q.v.), whom he named his executor, he bequeathed one hundred guineas, and to his foreman, T. Gayfere (q.v.), £20 and "all his wearing apparel, linen and woollen of all kind."

Cass's widow survived him and died in 1742. Andrews Jelfe, writing in that year to William Dixon, tells him that "Mrs. Cass was buried last week. She had left all her part to Mr. Bright, a young lawyer, who married her daughter" (British Museum, op. cit.).

(Authorities mentioned in text.)

CASS, CHRISTOPHER, the Younger
d. 1732

He was the son of Christopher Cass the Elder (q.v.), to whom he was apprenticed in 1721 and assisted him in a number of works. Young Cass seems to have carved in marble, for his father bequeaths to his daughter (Sarah Gilbert) "a marble pedestal done by my late son, Christopher Cass."

CASTLE, J., of Oxford
fl. 1840–1852

He exhibited a figure of Abel at the Royal Academy in 1849, and a font in Caen stone at the Great Exhibition two years later. He also executed in 1851 two statues on the façade of St. Mary's Church, Oxford.

CATHERWOOD, THOMAS
In 1806 the Marquess of Buckingham paid him one hundred guineas for a chimney-piece for the "Gothic" library at Stowe (Soane Notebooks).

CATTERNS, JOSEPH
fl. 1678–1684

When a "General Search" was carried out by the Masons' Company in 1678 there was found at "Mr. Tompson's" (i.e., John Thompson, q.v.) "Joseph Katernes, not free, bound at Joyners Hall"—that is, a member of the Joiners' Company. Catterns signs the lovely monument, his only known work, with medallion portraits of Sir John Finch and Sir Thomas Baines in the Chapel of Christ's College, Cambridge; this was erected to their memory in 1684 by the second Earl of Nottingham.

CERACCHI, or CIRACHI, JOSEPH
b. 1751, *d.* 1801

He came to England from Rome in 1773 and worked for Carlini (q.v.) and also for the architect Robert Adam. For the latter he modelled a large bas-relief in composition of the "Sacrifice of Bacchus" for the back front of Mr. Desenfans's house in Portland Place, while at Adams's sale held on 22 May, 1818, Lot 1 was "a piece of foliage and various other models by Ceracchi," and Lot 13 "figures sacrificing, a bas-relief in three parts designed by A. Zucchi, modelled by Ceracchi." About 1777 the sculptor made the statue of the Hon. Mrs. Dawson Damer (q.v.) which is now in the British Museum and, in the following year, the figures of "Temperance" and "Fortitude" in Portland stone for the Strand front of Somerset House (P.R.O. A.O.1/2495). In 1779 his name was put forward as an Associate of the Royal Academy, but he only received four votes (Royal Academy Minute-book).

Ceracchi later left London for America and arrived in Philadelphia in 1791. Here he hoped to get a commission for a statue of "Liberty," but the project fell through. He did, however, model busts of a number of prominent Americans, including Benjamin Franklin, now in the Pennsylvania Academy of Fine Arts; John Jay, in the Supreme Court at Washington; Thomas Jefferson, at Monticello, Virginia; George Washington, in the Metropolitan Museum, New York; and two of George Clinton, now in the Boston Athenaeum and at the headquarters of the New York Historical Society respectively. His bust of Alexander Hamilton, now in the New York Public Library, was reproduced on the thirty-cent stamp by the United States Government in 1877. Another bust executed during his stay in America was that of Amerigo Vespucci, which is also in the possession of the New York Historical Society. About 1794 Ceracchi returned to Florence and, after a short time, moved to Paris, where he joined the anti-Bonaparte faction and plotted to murder Napoleon. The conspiracy was discovered, however, and the sculptor was one of those arrested. He was condemned to death and guillotined in 1801, going to the scaffold, it is said, in a triumphal chariot of his own design. J. T. Smith (*Nollekens and His Times*, Vol. II, page 56) describes him as "a short thin man with a piercing black eye and a very blue beard."

During his stay in England Ceracchi exhibited

busts at the Royal Academy between 1776 and 1779, including, in the latter year, those of Count Belgiosa and General Paoli. Other busts of his are those of Admiral Keppel (1777) and the Marquess of Granby (1778), both at Belvoir Castle; Napoleon I and George Washington in the Museum at Nantes; and Pope Pius VI in the Palace at Munich. His marble bust of Sir Joshua Reynolds and the original terra-cotta from which it was modelled in 1778 are both at Burlington House, the former being signed "Cirachi." He also made a portrait of Dr. Priestly for Wedgwood.

In the catalogue of the Stowe Sale of 1848, Lot 126 to be sold on the thirty-sixth day was described as "a marble statue of Britannia by Ceracchi." Before the time came, however, it was discovered that the figure was made, not of marble, but of plaster, and it was consequently withdrawn.

(Information, Frick Art Reference Library, New York; authorities cited in text.)

CEUNOT, JOHN
b. c.1740, d. before 1782.

He was the son of the French sculptor John Ceunot, and in 1762 received a premium of seven guineas from the Society of Arts for a "model in clay of ornaments" (Archives, Royal Society of Arts). He exhibited a "piece of flowers" at the Free Society in the same year.

CHADWICK, WILLIAM, of Pentonville
fl. 1808–1826

He was the master-mason employed for building the Board of Trade Office in Whitehall in 1825, and the hospital of St. Katherine, Regent's Park, in the following year (P.R.O. Works 5/119).

Chadwick signs tablets to Robert Hinde, c. 1808, and Robert Hinde the Younger, 1819, both at Hitchin, Herts; and to John Smith, 1821, in St. Giles-in-the-Fields.

CHALKLEY, EDWARD, of Portsea
He signs a tablet to William Bowles, 1824, at Boarhunt, Hants.

CHALLIS, JOHN, of Braintree
fl. 1790–1820

In 1805 he was appointed by the Vicar of Great Waltham to supply tombstones for the parish (Parish Records). His tablets have pleasant classical details, and signed examples, all in Essex, include those to Sarah Jones, 1790, Bernard Seale, 1819, and Joseph Lucas, 1820, all at Braintree; the Rev. John Harrison, 1797, at Faulkbourn; and the Rev. Jeremy Pemberton, 1811, at Belchamp St. Paul's.

CHAMBERLAIN, R., of Newark
He signs a charming altar tomb with a well-carved urn in the churchyard of Winthorpe, Notts. The monument is in memory of Sarah Thompson, d. 1809, and her epitaph begins: "This monitor of human instability . . ." A charming, but unexpected, way to begin a funeral inscription.

CHAMBERS, ROBERT
b. 1710, d. 1784

Mendes da Costa, who collected notes on various "literati" between 1747 and 1788, mentions "Mr. Robert Chambers, a mason, who painted arms, flowers, fruit, Hebrew and other characters on marbles." He also states that Chambers, whom he calls "a very curious person," was "a Gloucestershire man and about seventy-four when he died," and adds that "he painted, or stained, on marble, several roses, exquisitely well for me, and the blazoned arms of the present Duke of Norfolk on a marble slab for his Grace" (Gentleman's Magazine, 1812, Part I, page 517).

In 1759 Chambers received a bounty of ten guineas from the Society of Arts for "staining marble." Vol. LI of Philosophical Transactions for the year 1760 contained an account of "experiments on several pieces of marble stained by Mr. Robert Chambers," though the exact method employed is not disclosed.

As da Costa records, Chambers was a Hebrew scholar; indeed, he had almost a mania for the language, even inscribing a Hebrew word on his monuments. Among the large number of works in stained marble which he exhibited at the Society of Free Artists between 1761 and 1783 were "the most sacred names in Hebrew," "the Hebrew alphabet," etc.

The memorial to John Howard, Earl of Stafford, 1762, in Westminster Abbey is signed "invented and stained by Robert Chambers." It is described by Brayley (Westminster Abbey, Vol. II, page 160) as a "white tablet stained with the arms and ancient badges of the families connected with the Howards," while the widowed Lady Stafford not only considered it "simple and noble, which is just what I wished, and what my Lord himself would have chosen for any friend," but also that "Chambers has executed it in perfection" (Nichols' Literary Anecdotes, Vol. VIII, page 107).

Chambers also signs monuments to Joseph Iles, 1749, at Minchinhampton, Glos; Peter Eaton,

1769, in Dover Parish Church, Kent; Richard Savage, 1772, at Boughton Monchelsea, Kent; and Sir John Evelyn, 1778, at Wotton, Surrey. His monument to Bishop Zachary Pearce was formerly in Bromley Parish Church, but was destroyed with the church in the Second World War. His bill (1087/22/73) for the monument to Colonel Molyneux, 1782, in St. Nicholas, Guildford, is in the Loseley Archives, Guildford Record Office.

CHAMMOLL, THOMAS
fl. 1660–1667

He worked as a mason at the Palaces of Whitehall and Westminster, and for the former building made three black-marble chimney-pieces in the Duke of York's lodgings in 1667 (P.R.O. Works 5/9).

CHANDLER, SAMUEL
d. 1769

His chief signed monument is the towering mass of marble which commemorates Edmund Humfrey, 1727, at Rettendon, Essex. This has a reclining figure of the dead man, while above him in niches stand life-size figures of his parents and grandparents; it is overpowering for a village church, but is nevertheless one of the most important early-eighteenth-century monuments in England.

Chandler, who lived at Wanstead, also signs a monument, with Corinthian pillars supporting a broken pediment, to William Taylor, 1741, at Broadway, Worcestershire. In 1730 he was paid for the stone tablet over the doorway of Walthamstow Workhouse, a building now used as a museum (Workhouse Archives).

CHANTREY, SIR FRANCIS LEGATT, R.A.
b. 1781, *d.* 1841

He was born on 7 April, 1781, at Norton, near Sheffield, the son of a carpenter who died when Francis was twelve years old. The boy began work with a grocer, but later, at his own request, was apprenticed to a Mr. Ramsay, a carver and gilder of Sheffield.

Raphael Smith, the mezzotint engraver, used to visit Ramsay's shop and here he met young Chantrey, who interested him and to whom he gave lessons in drawing. The boy gradually became dissatisfied with wood-carving as a form of art and, when he was twenty-one, he paid his master £50 (all the money he had) to cancel his indentures, this in spite of the fact that he had only six more months to serve.

As soon as Chantrey was free, he turned to painting and began to paint portraits in Sheffield. In this way, and by borrowing from friends, he collected enough money to try his fortune in London, but, knowing that he could not hope to hold his own as a portrait-painter, he found work as assistant to a wood-carver. He then went to Ireland in the hope of finding employment, but caught a fever from which he nearly died and which left him completely bald. On his recovery he went back to London, resumed wood-carving and executed some figures which were at one period in the possession of Mr. Hope, the banker. He also made a table for Rogers, the poet.

Finding that there was no money in woodcarving, Chantrey again tried portrait-painting, and also began to model figures in clay in his spare moments. In 1805 the parishioners of Sheffield Parish Church commissioned him to execute a bust of their late vicar, the Rev. J. Wilkinson, but they had so little faith in his ability that they insisted on his completing the work under their supervision in Sheffield. Three years later he exhibited his first imaginative work, a head of Satan, at the Royal Academy. About the same time his friend, Mr. Tappin, the architect, introduced him to a Mr. Daniel Alexander, who commissioned him to make four colossal busts of the Admirals Duncan, Howe, Nelson and St. Vincent for Greenwich Hospital. Shortly afterwards he executed similar ones for Trinity House.

It was not until 1811, however, that Chantrey found fame with his bust of Horne Tooke, which he exhibited at the Academy in that year (the marble is now in the Fitzwilliam Museum, Cambridge). Many years later, when he was giving evidence in 1840 in the case of Carew *v.* Burrell (q.v. under "Carew"), the sculptor gave some details of his early life. He was reported as saying "that he had never worked for any other sculptor and had never had an hour's instruction from any sculptor in his life; he established a studio as soon as he could afford it, that was eight years after he had entered the Metropolis, and during those eight years he never made five pounds in his profession. The bust by which he first got his reputation he made for nothing. It was a bust of Horne Tooke; it went to the exhibition in model, for neither Tooke nor he could afford to make it in marble. He got £12,000 of commissions by that bust at the exhibition." He ended his evidence by remarking: "so you see how uncertain the rise of a sculptor is."

This picturesque story is a little difficult to reconcile with certain facts. In 1806 Chantrey left his lodgings in Charles Street and went to live with his uncle and aunt, a Mr. and Mrs. Wale, who were in service with Mrs. D'Oyley of 24, Curzon Street; and there later Chantrey married his cousin, Mary Ann Wale. The *D.N.B.* says the marriage took place in 1807, while George Jones in his biography of the sculptor states that it was in 1811. In the writer's copy of Jones's book is a manuscript note by G. A. Sala (to whom the book had belonged) that the real year of the marriage was 1809. All authorities, however, agree that his wife brought Chantrey a fortune of £10,000 which had enabled him to "purchase a house and grounds on which he built two houses, a studio and offices, also to buy marble" (George Jones, R.A.'s *Life of Sir Francis Chantrey*, page 9). So it is rather hard to understand Chantrey's assertion that he could not afford marble for Tooke's bust.

In any case, Chantrey was now on the road to fame, and as his reputation grew greater so also did his prices. He started by asking eighty or one hundred guineas for a bust, but at the end of three years raised his fees to 120 and 150 guineas. By 1822 he was charging 200 guineas, and, when he made a bust of George IV the King insisted on paying 300 guineas for it.

In 1811 Stothard, the R.A., introduced Chantrey to Mr. Johnes, of Hafod, who commissioned him to execute a monument to his beloved only child, Marianne. This work (unfortunately destroyed when Hafod Church was burned in 1932) was the sculptor's noblest monument and, like everything else connected with Mr. Johnes, was conceived on a heroic scale. It showed the dying girl lying on a couch attended by her sorrowing parents, while at her side lay all the objects she had loved in life—her palette and brushes, her lyre and a scroll bearing the words and music of her favourite song. When it was finished the monument was too large to be exhibited at the Academy, and it was many years before it finally reached Hafod. Chantrey noted in his ledger (now at Burlington House) that the price agreed upon was £3,150, but that he did not receive the final payment until 1835 (long after Johnes's own death), and that even then he was £231 out of pocket.

In 1817 Chantrey executed what has always been his most popular monument, that to the children of the Rev. W. Robinson, in Lichfield Cathedral (the well-known "Sleeping Children" who died in 1812). His personal preference was for his figure of Lady Frederica Stanhope in Chevening Church, while he considered that his finest statue and bust were those of James Watt, at Handsworth, and Sir Walter Scott respectively. Of the Scott bust the sculptor made two replicas,

one for Sir Robert Peel, the other for the Duke of Wellington; the former fetched £2,250 at the sale of the Peel heirlooms in 1900.

In 1814 Chantrey went to Paris and, five years later, to Rome, where he visited the studios of Thorwaldsen and Canova and also purchased marble at Carrara. He exhibited at the Royal Academy, 1804–1842, becoming an Associate in 1815 and a full member in 1818. In 1835 he was knighted by William IV. He died suddenly of a spasm of the heart on 25 November, 1841, and was buried in his native village of Norton, beneath a tomb which he had himself prepared. An obelisk to his memory was later erected on the village green.

Chantrey left his fortune of £150,000 to his wife for life and, after her death, to the Royal Academy to found what is known as the Chantrey Bequest. In 1842 Lady Chantrey presented all his original models of busts, statues, etc., to the University of Oxford. The sculptor's ledger (which he bequeathed to the Academy) contains, not only a mass of business details, but also a few more personal notes in his own hand. From these may be quoted his remarks about Lord Ilchester, who had ordered a monument to his wife's memory in 1819 and had agreed to pay £1,100. Chantrey obviously had a great deal of difficulty with this client, for he firmly records that "in consequence of extreme disappointment from Lord Ilchester's extraordinary behaviour, I have determined to disarm his Lordship of all possibility of complaint and to charge only £840 for executing the monument." From the ledger also comes the information that the five marble monuments erected in 1832 by the Marquess Camden to the memory of his family and ancestors in Seal Church, Kent, are the work of Chantrey, though, contrary to his usual practice, he did not sign them. N. N. Burnard (q.v.) told Caroline Fox that on Chantrey's death "Lady Chantrey came into the studio with a hammer and knocked off the noses of many completed busts, so that they might not be too common." (S. Baring-Gould, *Cornish Characters*, page 288.)

The sculptor also notes payments for a number of busts whose present whereabouts I have been unable to discover, including those of Lady Gertrude Sloane (1812), William Vaughan (1813), Mrs. Simson (1816), George Phillips (1817), J. H. Frere (1818), the Hon. Charles Wemyss (1818) and Lady Nugent (1819).

In the British Museum (E.G. 1911) is another ledger which gives various details of works executed by Chantrey. These include "four dolphins in lead for a fountain ordered by Mr. Simpson, Engineer" in 1815, and a tombstone in 1816 in memory of R. B. Sheridan for Westminster Abbey.

In 1818 there is an entry for another tombstone, this time for a Mr. Brenton, to be sent to the Cape of Good Hope, and, two years later, a wall-tablet commemorating Colonel Canning to be erected in the church at Waterloo, Belgium. Among the busts is mentioned one of Sir Spiridon Foresti of Zante which was made in 1816.

Though a man of little education, Chantrey possessed great native intelligence and sagacity which undoubtedly helped him to amass his large fortune. He built his own foundry in Eccleston Place, and here his bronze statues, including those of Sir Thomas Munro, Pitt, George IV and Wellington, were cast. His manners were rough and his language strong, but he never willingly hurt the feelings of others. He was an excellent host, gave good dinners and was devoted to shooting and fishing. The brace of woodcock which he killed with one shot at Holkham in 1834 have become legendary. He carved them in marble and presented the work to his host, Mr. Coke, afterwards the Earl of Leicester. The epigrams composed to celebrate the occasion were collected and published in 1857 under the title of "Winged Words on Chantrey's Woodcocks." Lord Jeffrey wrote:

"Their good and ill from the same source they drew,
Here shrined in marble by the hand that slew."

According to the *Georgian Era* (1834, page 179), Chantrey produced what was luckily "an unexecuted design" for a statue of Nelson, 130 ft. high, to be erected at Yarmouth on a pier projecting far out into the sea. The statue was to be illuminated at night and was to stand "on a pedestal made of the bows of vessels taken from the enemy." He also designed the Minerva seal for the Athenaeum Club.

(Holland's *Memorials of Sir Francis Chantrey*; *Art Union*, 1842, page 6; *Gentleman's Magazine*, 1844, page 99; *European Magazine*, 1822, page 3; *Builder*, 1863, pages 91 and 112; authorities cited in text.)

STATUES

1811	George III	For Guildhall (destroyed 29 September, 1940)
1815	Dr. James	Rugby
1815	President Blair	Edinburgh
1816	Countess St. Vincent	Caverswall Church, Staffs
1816	Sir Robert Gillespie	St. Paul's Cathedral
1818	Lady Louisa Russell	Woburn Abbey
1818	Spencer Perceval	Town Hall, Northampton
1818	Lord Melville	Sessions House, Edinburgh
1818	Sir Alexander Boswell's daughter	(British Museum, MS. E.G. 1911)
1819	James Watt	Westminster Abbey (£6,234)
1819	Dr. Anderson	Madras
1820	Francis Horner	Westminster Abbey
1820	Dr. William Hey	Leeds Infirmary
1821?	George IV	Windsor Castle
1821	Countess of Liverpool	Kingston-on-Thames Parish Church
1824	Robert Dundas	Sessions House, Edinburgh
1824	Cyril Jackson	Christ Church, Oxford
1824	James Watt	Handsworth Parish Church (£2,000)
1826	Bishop Heber	St. Paul's Cathedral
1826	George Washington	Boston State House, U.S.A.
1827	Stephen Babington	Bombay
1827	Mr. Coutts	Coutts' Bank, Strand
1827	Sir Joseph Banks	For British Museum
1827	Henry Grattan	City Hall, Dublin
1828	George IV	Brighton
1829	George IV	For Marble Arch, now Trafalgar Square
1829	Sir Edward Hyde East	Calcutta
1830	James Watt	Greenock (£1,030)
1830	James Watt	For Glasgow College (£1,000)
1830?	Bishop Heber	Calcutta
1830?	Canning	Athens
1830	George IV	Windsor Castle
1831	George IV	Edinburgh
1831?	Mrs. Jordan	Possession of the Earl of Munster
1831	William Pitt	Hanover Square
1832	Sir Stamford Raffles	Westminster Abbey
1832	Canning	Town Hall, Liverpool
1832	James Watt	Glasgow (£3,454)
1833	William Pitt	Edinburgh
1833	Mountstuart Elphinstone	Bombay
1833	Sir John Malcolm	Westminster Abbey (replica, Bombay)
1834	Canning	For the Duke of Sutherland
1837	Duke of Sutherland	Dornoch, Sutherland
1837	Lord Downe	Snaith Parish Church, Yorks
1837	John Dalton	Royal Institution, Manchester
1838	Duke of Sutherland	Trentham Parish Church, Staffs
1838	Sir Thomas Munro	Madras (£8,012)
1840	William Roscoe	Liverpool
1840	Duke of Wellington	Royal Exchange (completed by Weekes)
1841	Sir Charles Forbes	Town Hall, Bombay
1841	Bishop Bathurst	Norwich Cathedral
1841	James Northcote, R.A.	Exeter Cathedral

1841	Bishop Ryder	Lichfield Cathedral
n.d.	Endymion (bronze)	Chatsworth

BUSTS

1805	James Wilkinson	Sheffield Cathedral
1808	Richard Porson	Trinity College Chapel, Cambridge
1810	William Pitt	For Trinity House
1810?	George III	Belton House, Lincs
1811	John Browne	Royal Infirmary, Sheffield
1811	Benjamin West	New York Historical Society
1813	John Simpson	St. Chad's Church, Shrewsbury
1813	Henry Cline	St. Thomas's Hospital
1814	George III	Royal College of Surgeons
1816	Sir William Blizard	Royal College of Surgeons (£126)
1816	Sir Everard Hone	Royal College of Surgeons
1816	Edward Bird	Plaster-casts, National Portrait Gallery and Bristol Art Gallery
1817	Francis Mundy	Town Hall, Derby
1817	Henry Bone, R.A.	Burlington House
1817	Rt. Hon. Spencer Perceval	Charlton Church
1817	Charles Townshend	St. John's College Chapel, Cambridge
1818	Nollekens	British Museum (replica for the Duchess of Bedford)
1818	Rev. Alexander Mackenzie	St. Paul's Church, Sheffield
1818	Sir Benjamin Hobhouse	Art Gallery, Bath
1818	Sir Joseph Banks	Royal Society (replica at Petworth)
1818	Francis Horner	National Portrait Gallery, Edinburgh
1818	John Rennie	National Portrait Gallery, Edinburgh
1818	Benjamin West	Burlington House
1819	Charles Herries	Westminster Abbey
1819	John Fuller	Brightling Parish Church, Sussex
1819	Canning	For Mr. Bolton of Liverpool
1820	John Hunter	Royal College of Surgeons
1820	George IV	Buckingham Palace
1820	Sir Walter Scott	Abbotsford
1820	Bishop King	Corpus Christi, Oxford
1820	Sir A. Hamond	Private Possession
1820	Henry Colebrooke	India Office
1820	Sir Walter Scott	Stratfield Saye
1820	Lord Farnborough	National Portrait Gallery

1821	Viscount Castlereagh	National Portrait Gallery (replica at Apsley House)
1821	Canning	National Portrait Gallery
1821	Wordsworth	For Sir George Beaumont
1822	Charles Hutton	Newcastle Literary and Philosophical Society
1822	Lord Castlereagh	Windsor Castle
1822	George IV	Chatsworth
1823	Duke of Wellington	Apsley House
1823	Dr. Matthew Baillie	Westminster Abbey
1823	George IV	Royal College of Surgeons
1824	Granville Sharp	Guildhall (destroyed 29 September, 1940)
1824	Cyril Jackson	Christ Church, Oxford
1824	E. D. Clarke	Fitzwilliam Museum
1824	Marquess of Abercorn	For Earl of Aberdeen
1825	J. T. Smith	Victoria and Albert Museum
1825	Sir Henry Halford	Royal College of Physicians
1826	Canning	Chatsworth
1827	Henry Cline	Royal College of Surgeons
1827	George IV	For Jesse Russell of Ilam Hall
1828	Marquess of Stafford	Dunrobin Castle
1828	Sir Walter Scott[1]	For Sir Robert Peel
1828	Lord Melbourne	Private Collection
1828	Wellington	Windsor Castle
1829	Lewis Bagot	Christ Church, Oxford
1829	Dean Ireland	Bodleian Library, Oxford
1829	Duke of Sutherland	For British Gallery
1829	T. W. Coke	Holkham, Norfolk
1830	Thomas Lett	Lambeth Parish Church
1830	Marquess Camden	Bayham Abbey, Kent
1830	Sir John Soane	Soane Museum
1830	Duke of Sussex	Freemasons' Hall
1831	Earl of Lonsdale	Apsley House
1831	J. Northcote	Pynes, Devon
1831	William IV	Penshurst Place, Kent
1831	Earl of Lauderdale	Apsley House
1832	Baron Hume	Sessions House, Edinburgh
1832	Princess Louise of Saxe-Weimar	Exhibited Royal Academy
1833	John Abernethy	Royal College of Surgeons
1833	Nelson	Royal Collection
1833	Pitt	Pembroke College, Cambridge

[1] This bust and the ones at Abbotsford and Stratfield Saye (see 1820) are the *only* marble busts of Scott made by Chantrey. All the others are the work of copyists. (See *Gentleman's Magazine*, 1842, page 259.)

1835	William IV	Greenwich Palace Chapel
1835	Sir Robert Peel	Royal Collection
1835	James Watt	For National Institute of Paris (replica Tew Park)
1836	William IV	Eton College
1837	George III, George IV and William IV	For Temple at Kew, now Buckingham Palace
1837	Mary Somerville	Royal Society
1837	Sir Jeffrey Wyatville	Windsor Castle
1837	Robert Southey	For John Murray
1837	Professor Wilson	Calcutta
1837	Wellington	Buckingham Palace
1837	George IV and William IV	Formerly Herrenhausen, Hanover
1838	Marquess of Westminster	Eaton Hall
1838	Wellington	Belton, Lincs
1839	Dr. Mill	Asiatic Society of Bengal
1839	William Murdock	Handsworth Church
1839	Queen Victoria	Windsor Castle
1840	William Hazeldene	St. Chad's Church, Shrewsbury
1841	Lord Melbourne	Windsor Castle
1841	Queen Victoria	National Portrait Gallery
1841	William IV	Burlington House
n.d.	Sir Stamford Raffles	Raffles Institution, Singapore
n.d.	Duke of York	Junior United Service Club (copy of bust by Nollekens)
n.d.	Francis Cunningham	Scottish National Portrait Gallery
n.d.	James Watt	Scottish National Portrait Gallery

RELIEFS

1816	Plenty	For Mr. D. Brammall, Sheffield (stone mezzo-relievo)
1828	"Hector Recommending his Son to the Protection of the Gods"	Woburn Abbey
1828	"Penelope's Reluctance to Produce the Bow of Ulysses"	Woburn Abbey
1832	"Signing of Reform Bill"	Holkham

VARIOUS

1818	Altar dedicated to Peace	For Archbishop of Canterbury (marble) (Ledger at Royal Academy)
1819	Two pedestals for busts of Banks and Newton	For Royal Society
1830	William IV	Medallion for coinage
1832	Death Mask, Sir Walter Scott	National Portrait Gallery, Edinburgh

| 1841 | Lord Eldon and Lord Stowell | Law Society (medallions) |
| n.d. | Queen Adelaide | Oxford Museum (medallion) |

MONUMENTS

1806	Cambridge (St. John's College Chapel)	Henry White
1807	Kelmarsh, Northants	William Hanbury
c. 1808	Westminster Abbey	Sir George Staunton
1809	Madras (Cathedral)	James Anderson
c. 1811?	Exeter (Cathedral)	Lord Daer
1811	Topsham, Devon	George Duckworth
1811	Liverpool (Christ Church)	William Lewis
1811	St. Paul's Cathedral	General Hoghton
1812	North Stoneham, Hants	Rev. Stephen Sloane
1812	Lichfield (Cathedral)	Children of the Rev. W. Robinson
1812	Cults, Fife	Rev. David Wilkie
1812	St. Paul's Cathedral	General Bowes
1813	Chelsea (St. Luke's)	Colonel Henry Cadogan
1813	Westminster Abbey	Granville Sharp
1814	Easebourne, Sussex	Hon. Elizabeth Poyntz
1814	St. Paul's Cathedral	General Gore and General Skerrett
1814	St. Paul's Cathedral	Colonel Henry Cadogan
1815	Orpington, Kent	William Gee
1815	Edington, Wilts	Sir Simon Taylor
1815	Oxford (Brasenose College Chapel)	Rev. Hugo Cholmondley
1815	Christchurch, Hants	John Baines
1816	Orpington, Kent	Richard Carew
1816	Chiswick, Middlesex	Thomas Tomkins
1816	Aberystwyth, Cardigan	Mr. Bonsal
1816	Westminster Abbey	Richard Brinsley Sheridan
1816	Glasgow (Cathedral)	Mr. Lowndes
1817	Chislehurst, Kent	William Selwyn
1817	Shillingston, Dorset	Elizabeth Acton
1817	Orpington, Kent	Gee Family
1817	Cape of Good Hope	Mrs. Wardon
1817	Wanstead (Parish Church)	George Bowles
1817	Topsham, Devon	Admiral Sir John Duckworth
1818	Badger, Salop	Isaac Browne
1818	Bristol (Cathedral)	Mrs. Elwyn
1818	Bristol (Lord Mayor's Chapel)	Henry Bengough
1818	Charterhouse Chapel	Lord Ellenborough
1818	Owston, Yorks	Frances Cooke
1818	Hoxne, Suffolk	Sir Thomas Hesilrige
1819	Winchester (Cathedral)	Lt.-General Sir George Prevost
1819	Waterperry, Oxon	Anna Greaves
1819	Cambridge (All Saints)	Henry Kirke White
1819	Stoke Doyle, Northants	Hannah Roberts

1820	Winchester (Cathedral)	Bishop North	
1820	Salisbury (Cathedral)	1st Earl of Malmesbury	
1820	Penn, Bucks	Viscount Curzon	
1820	Wombourn, Staffs	Richard Marsh	
1820	Cromford, Derby	Mrs. Arkwright	
1820	Burley-on-the-Hill, Rutland	Lady Charlotte Finch	
1820	Whittlebury, Northants	Charlotte Bradshaw	
1821	Walton-on-Thames, Surrey	Mr. and Mrs. D'Oyly	
1821	North Cray, Kent	Lady Ellenborough	
1821	Melbury Sampford, Dorset	Countess of Ilchester	
1821	Epsom, Surrey	Susan Warre	
1821	Derby (Cathedral)	Richard Bateman	
1822	Chilham, Kent	James Wildman	
1822	Alcester, Warwick	Marquess of Hertford	
1822	Armagh (Cathedral)	Archbishop Stuart	
1823	Chevening, Kent	Lady Frederica Stanhope	
1823	Wragby, Yorks	John Winn	
1823	Bristol (Cathedral)	Emma Crauford	
1823	Croxall, Staffs	Eusebius Horton	
1823	Westminster Abbey	Sir George Staunton	
1823	Weybridge, Surrey	Duchess of York	
1823	Sheffield (Cathedral)	Thomas Harrison	
1824	Rugby (School Chapel)	Thomas James	
1824	Shelford, Notts	Lady Georgina West	
1825	Withyham, Sussex	Arabella, Duchess of Dorset	
1825	St. John's Wood Chapel	Sarah Capel	
1825	Ingestre, Staffs	John Talbot	
1825	Worcester (Cathedral)	Charlotte Digby	
1826	Erith, Kent	Lord Eardley	
1826	Ilam, Derby	David Pike Watts	
1826	Ashley, Staffs	Thomas Kinnersly	
1826	Ingestre, Staffs	Lord Ingestre	
1826	Lichfield (Cathedral)	Sir Charles Oakley	
1826	Bayford, Herts	William Baker	
1827	Orton Longueville, Hunt	Lady Mary Seymour	
1827	Madras (St. Thomas's)	Colonel John Noble	
1828	Bath (Abbey)	William Hoare	
1828	Trinidad (Cathedral)	Sir Ralph Woodford (replica in Roman Catholic Cathedral)	
1828	Hodnet, Salop	Bishop Heber	
1829	Wiston, Sussex	Charles Goring	
1830	Owston, Yorks	Bryan Cooke	
1830	Durham (Cathedral)	Bishop Barrington	
1831	Itchen (Pear Tree Green), Hants	William Chamberlayne	
1831	Exeter (Cathedral)	James Northcote	
1832	Derby (St. Werburgh's)	Mrs. Whinyates	
1833	Guernsey	The Le Marchant family	
1833	Tardebigge, Worcs	Lord Plymouth	

1833	Great Brington, Northants	Captain Sir Robert Cavendish-Spencer
1834	Bath (Abbey)	Sir Richard Bickerton
1834	St. Albans (Cathedral)	Frederica Mure
1834	Great Tew, Oxon	Mrs. Boulton (d. 1829)
1834	Liverpool (St. James's Chapel)	William Nicholson
1834	Hartburn, Northumberland	Lady Bradford
1834	Westminster Abbey	Rev. Evelyn Sutton
1835	Clapham (St. Paul's)	John Wilson
1835	Itchen (Pear Tree Green), Hants	Charlotte Chamberlayne
1836	Tichfield, Hants	Hornby Family
1836	Kentish Town (Parish Church)	William Minshull
1836	Lichfield (Cathedral)	Bishop Ryder
1837	Hanbury, Worcs	Thomas Vernon
1837	Wells (Cathedral)	John Pheleps
1837	Redbourne, Lincs	Duchess of St. Albans
1837	Longbridge Deverill, Wilts	Marquess of Bath
1837	Plympton, Devon	Richard Rosdew
1837	Calcutta	Mr. Palmer
1838	Iver, Bucks	Edward Ward
1838	Harwell, Bucks	Christopher Smith

CHAPLING, J.

Probably a Norwich carver, he signs the monument of Sir Horatio (d. 1730) and Lady Pettus (d. 1746) at Rackheath, Norwich.

CHAPMAN, EDWARD
fl. 1696–1706

He was the son of Edward Chapman, mason, and in the Company's "search" carried out in 1696 was reported as working with his father. His yard was in Red Lion Square and in 1706 he was employing William Palmer (q.v.) as an assistant.

In 1699 Chapman made five coloured-marble chimney-pieces for Ampthill House, Bedfordshire (Account-book, Ashburnham Archives). Between 1699 and 1705 he made chimney-pieces for Burley-on-the-Hill, Rutland (Finch's *History of Burley-on-the-Hill*, Vol. I, page 72), and others for Winslow Hall, Bucks, between 1699 and 1702 (*Wren Society*, Vol. XVII, page 555). In the latter year he also made "Italian figures" for Chatsworth costing £60 (Account-book, Chatsworth).

Chapman was the father-in-law of Francis Bird (q.v.), to whom he bequeathed an estate near Windsor (*Walpole Society, Vertue Notebooks*, Vol. III, page 48).

CHAPMAN, JOHN

In 1833 he exhibited "David With the Head of Goliath" at the British Institution.

CHAPMAN, JOSEPH, of Frome
fl. 1806–1832

His signed tablets are not very exciting and include those in Wiltshire to Thomas Tayler, 1809, Devizes; James Carpenter, 1824, Beckington; William Crumbleholme, 1830, Horningsham; and Thomas Latimer, 1832, Mere. In Somerset he signs two tablets at Midsomer Norton to John Parsons, 1806, and John Smith, 1829.

His son, Joseph Chapman the Younger, also a statuary, utterly destroyed in 1863 the house known as "King Ina's Palace" at South Petherton, Somerset. Built by Sir Giles Daubeny in the reign of Henry VI, it was a magnificent and untouched example of a fifteenth-century manor-house till Mr. Chapman got possession of it and, having pulled most of the house down, rebuilt it in Cockney Gothic.

CHARDINI, P. J.
fl. 1842–1843

Between 1842 and 1843 he exhibited at the Royal Academy various busts and medallions, including those of the Duke of Wellington and the King of Holland, and also equestrian statuettes of Queen Victoria and the Prince Consort. His address in the latter year is given as Cleveland Street, Fitzroy Square.

CHARLES, WILLIAM, of Nottingham
fl. 1720–1763

His tablets are usually carried out in the local slate and have well-carved armorial bearings. In Nottinghamshire they include those to Henry Fawks, 1730, in the churchyard of Stanford-on-Soar; the Rev. John Wood, 1752, and the Rev. Henry Wood, 1755, both at Wilford; and James Bryans, 1757, in the churchyard of Willoughby-on-the-Wolds. Charles's gravestone to Ann Bonner, 1763, is in the churchyard of St. Nicholas, Deptford.

CHARLTON, WILLIAM, of Cambridge and King's Lynn

In the *Ipswich Journal* of 17 May, 1760, he advertised that he had taken a wharf and shop near Lady Bridge at Lynn Regis and that he could execute orders "both in the ancient and modern taste, viz. statuary, monuments, chimney-pieces, sconces, chandeliers, girandoles, etc."

CHEERE, SIR HENRY, Bart.
b. 1703, *d.* 1781

He was the son of John Cheere, of Clapham (*d.*

1756) and his wife, Sarah (*d.* 1738), and was probably the pupil of John Nost (q.v.). He later may have joined with Henry Scheemakers (q.v.) for together they sign the great monument of the Duke of Ancaster, 1728, at Edenham, Lincolnshire. Faussett the antiquary, in a manuscript dated 1757 (in private possession), states that the monument to Hammond Twyman, 1727, at Westbere, Kent, is also the work of both sculptors, and is indeed signed by them.

Cheere's yard was near St. Margaret's, Westminster, and here he worked in marble, bronze, stone and lead. The three Portland-stone statues of "Law," "Physic" and "Poetry" which he made for Queen's College, Oxford, cost £135 each, according to the contract signed in 1734, which also stipulated that they were "to be cut out of ye solid stone and not pieced as those at ye end of ye west wing." On 23 April, 1735, Sir Thomas Lee paid Henry Cheere £42 for a "Portland statue of King William" (Hartwell Archives). I am uncertain whether this statue was erected at Hartwell House or not; Admiral Smyth in his *Aedes Hartwellianae.* (page 71) only mentions statues of Frederick, Prince of Wales and George II as being in the Park. Lipscombe in his *Buckinghamshire* (Vol. II, page 315) says that formerly there were many statues in the garden but they disappeared when "an improved taste began to prevail." In the Vice-Chancellor's Oxford accounts 1737/8 is a payment to Cheere of £223 7s. 10d. for two statues "for the theatre." These are presumably those of Archbishop Sheldon and the Duke of Ormonde. In 1746 he received £137 for his life-size statue of Sir William Pole. This cost £25 12s. to send to Devonshire, and Cheere's own man, Richard Breach, went down to set it up in Shute Church (Cambridge University Library, MS. 6292). In 1770 the sculptor executed the lead statue of the Duke of Cumberland for Cavendish Square. This no longer exists, for it was removed and melted down by order of the fifth Duke of Portland in 1868.

Cheere also carved chimney-pieces, and in 1739 supplied some for Ditchley, Oxon, the seat of the second Earl of Lichfield. These included one for the drawing-room with a "Bacchus Head" which cost a hundred guineas, and others for "the little room within the Great Room" (£100), the Velvet Room (£100) and the Tapestry Room (£84). From the bills it is clear that the designs in some cases were supplied by Henry Flitcroft, the architect (Dillon Archives). Cheere also executed chimney-pieces for Sir John Trevelyan, of Wallington, Northumberland, *c.* 1740; for Lord Folkestone at Longford Castle between 1741 and 1742, where he received £800 (Archives, Earl of Radnor); for the Duke of Manchester, for whom he made a chimney-piece for the drawing-room at Kimbolton Castle costing £54 in 1747; for Kilnwick Hall, Yorkshire (Archives of Lady Waechter de Grimston), in 1752; and for John Trotter, of Soho Square (*Beauties of England*, 1815, Vol. X, Part IV, page 60). In 1746 he was paid over £200 by Sir James Dashwood for chimney-pieces for Kirtlington Park, Oxon (Dashwood Archives).

The rococo details of Cheere's monuments are often very similar to those of his chimney-pieces, but they must have been much admired in their day. The first Earl Verney in his will (dated 1752) left £200 "for erecting a monument to my late dear wife in Middle Claydon Church after the model of the monument set up in Westminster Abbey for Archbishop Boulter" which had been executed by Cheere, but his wishes never seem to have been carried out.

In 1749 Cheere was appointed Controller of Duties for the Free Fish Market in Westminster. In 1755 he was one of the committee of artists who met to discuss the scheme which was to result in the founding of the Royal Academy of Arts. He was knighted in 1760 when he presented a congratulatory address to George III from the County of Middlesex, and was created a baronet six years later.

He retired from business in 1770, and on 26 and 27 March in the same year a sale of the contents of his yard was held. Among the lots mentioned in the catalogue are reliefs in marble and Portland stone, tablets, for chimney-pieces, friezes, busts, models of monuments, etc., but as no details are given it is impossible to identify any of the models or busts with certainty. The only item of which any description at all is given is that of a model of a monument with a "perspective of Westminster Abbey." This, of course, is the monument of Dean Wilcocks in the Abbey.

Cheere died on 15 January, 1781, and was buried in the family vault at Clapham with his wife, Helen Randall, who had predeceased him on 25 October, 1769 (not 1760, as stated in *D.N.B.*), (*Gentleman's Magazine*, 1769, page 511). Lady Cheere was apparently an ill-educated and stupid woman, for there are a number of anecdotes about her and her gaucheries in eighteenth-century memoirs. At the sale of Sir Robert Ainslie, held by Mr. Christie on 10 March, 1809, two of the lots were Cheere's "small sitting figures of Vulcan and Venus." They fetched 40 guineas. (Archives, Messrs. Christie.)

(*London Magazine*, 1769, page 592; *Notes and Queries*, Fourth Series, Vol. VI, page 525; Registers of Clapham Parish Church; Archives of Queen's College, Oxford.)

STATUES

1733	Queen Caroline	For the Queen's College, Oxford (£120)
1734	Christopher Codrington	All Souls College, Oxford (100 guineas; contract in College Archives)
1734	William III	Bank of England

BUSTS

1738	Lord Clarendon	Clarendon Buildings, Oxford
1742	Three unnamed busts	For Lord Folkestone (Archives, Longford Castle)
1756	Twenty-four Fellows of the College	All Souls College, Oxford
?	Duke of Cumberland	Belton, Lincs

MONUMENTS

1725	Shoreham, Kent	Anne Borrett (with bust)
1728	Mold, Flint	Robert Davies (life-sized standing figure)
1731	Towyn, Merioneth	A. Owen
1731	Hampton, Middlesex	Miss Thomas
1731	Westminster Abbey	Bradford, Bishop of Rochester
1732	Oxford (Cathedral)	Henry Aldrich (medallion portrait)
1732	Westminster Abbey	Admiral Sir Thomas Hardy
1732	Abbots Langley, Herts	Lord Raymond (life-size reclining figure; the monument is also signed "Westby Gill, Ar. invenit")
1733	Hillesden, Bucks	Sir Alexander and Lady Denton (with busts)
1734	Winchester (Cathedral)	Bishop Willis (reclining figure)
1738	Esher, Surrey	Lady Fowler
1738	Whitchurch, Middlesex (St. Laurence's)	Countess of Carnarvon
1739	Shoreham, Kent	Mr. and Mrs. Borrett (busts)
1739	Westminster Abbey	John Conduitt
1740	Writtle, Essex	Sir John Comyns (bust)
1741	Westminster Abbey	Sir Edmund Prideaux
1742	Westminster Abbey	Boulter, Archbishop of Armagh
1742	Norwich (St. Giles)	Thomas Churchman
1743	Dublin (Christ Church Cathedral)	Earl of Kildare (with reclining and standing figures)
1746	Westminster Abbey	Sir John Chardin (d. 1713)
1747	Westminster Abbey	Captain Philip de Sausmarez
1747	Grantham, Lincs	William Cust

1747	York (Minster)	Admiral Medley (with bust)
1750	Westminster Abbey	Edward Atkyns
1752	Kilnwick, Yorks	Thomas Grimston
1754	Belton, Lincs	Viscount Tyrconnel (life-size figure)
1756	Grantham, Lincs	Sir Dudley Ryder (portrait medallion)
1756	Westminster Abbey	Wilcocks, Dean of Westminster
1757	Amersham, Bucks	Elizabeth Drake
1758	Boston, U.S.A. (King's Chapel)	Charles Apthorp

CHEERE, JOHN
d. 1787

He was first in partnership with his brother, Sir Henry Cheere (q.v.), but took over John Nost's (q.v.) yard and his moulds for lead figures, etc., about 1739. The writer of *Leaves in a Manuscript Diary* (London, 1772) describes Cheere's place of business as follows: "I came out at the Lodge" (i.e., of the Green Park) "and stepped into Mr. Cheere's yard, which, on account of numberless figures in stone, lead and plaster you would swear was a country fair or market, made up of spruce squires, haymakers with rakes in their hands, shepherds and shepherdesses, bagpipers and pipers and fiddlers, Dutch skippers and English sailors enough to supply a first-rate man-of-war."

J. T. Smith in *Streets of London* (page 11) gives the following description of Cheere's yard: "The figures were cast in lead as large as life and frequently painted with an intention to resemble nature. They consisted of Punch, Harlequin, Columbine and other pantomimical characters; mowers whetting their scythes, haymakers resting on their rakes, gamekeepers in the act of shooting and Roman soldiers with firelocks, but above all that of an African, kneeling with a sundial on his head found the most extensive sale."

Cheere's works in lead include a figure of "Mars" made in 1752 for Hampton Court (P.R.O. A.O.1/2467); statues of "Augusta" and "Flora," 1759, and seven others of mythological subjects, 1768, all executed for Longford Castle (Archives, Earl of Radnor); and two great wyverns for Trevor, Bishop of Durham, for which he received £48 5s. in 1759 and which still adorn the brick gate-piers of the entrance to Glynde, Sussex (Archives, Brand of Glynde). For Bowood between 1762 and 1763 he made lead figures of "Apollo," "Venus," "Mercury," "Livia," "Augusta" and "Flora," and busts of Fortina and Antinous; for Blenheim he supplied sphinxes for the bridge in 1773 (British Museum, MS. 41133), while he made four other large sphinxes for Somerset House five years later (P.R.O. A.O.1/2495). In 1774 Wedgwood bought from him busts of Shakespeare, Plato, Homer and Aristotle (Wedgwood Archives). The lead statues, the lion and the lioness, the sphinxes, etc., at Castle Hill, Devon, are also the work of Cheere, who tells Lord Clinton (the builder of the house) in an undated letter that he hopes "your Lordship will be so good as to excuse me not answering your letter sooner, for the man that made the drawings for you has been out of town so I was obliged to wait his return. He has been at Lord Burlington's and measured it" (a sphinx?) "again and it is just ten foot. I have sent it as he measured it and gave it to me" (Archives, Earl Fortescue).

In 1769 he made a lead statue of Shakespeare which was presented to the Corporation of Stratford on Avon by Garrick in the same year and was erected in a niche on the north side of the Town Hall.

Cheere also did a great deal of work for Stourhead. One of his figures (that of the "River God" in the grotto) has been for some reason perversely and consistently attributed to Rysbrack by every writer, but the bill for it, dated 7 August, 1751, and amounting to £98, is quite definitely Cheere's (Archives, Hoare's Bank). For Stourhead he also made in 1766 lead statues of "Pomona," "Minerva," "Urania," "Venus," "A Vestal," "Mercury," "Apollo" and "Bacchus." Ten years later he was paid for a bas-relief for the same house, but as it only cost ten guineas it was probably of plaster. In 1776 he received £104 and, in 1778, £97 for unspecified work for West Wycombe Park, possibly lead statues (Dashwood Archives).

In 1742 he made eight busts for Sir John Evelyn at Wotton, including Brutus and Seneca. In 1745 he made five more (Evelyn Archives).

Cheere also made statues and busts in plaster as well as in lead. In 1743 he supplied eight busts to Earl Fitzwalter for Moulsham Hall, Essex, and, in 1753, made others for Mr. Henry Hoare's houses at Clapham and Barnes (Archives, Hoare's Bank). His plaster statues include one of "Flora" made in 1754 for Maisters' House, Hull (*Country Life*, 13 January, 1950), while he also executed life-size figures for Mr. Du Cane, of Boreham Hall, Essex, in 1756 (Essex County Archives D/DDC. 118), and four casts of classical figures costing £223 for the Pantheon at Stourhead in 1766.

In 1754, writing to a client in Yorkshire on the subject of plaster statues for his house in High Street, Hull, Cheere explains there has been some delay because he has been "out of a new mold—I cast three of each which did not prove so white as I could wish for, but the fourth proved quite white and I finish't them very neat." He concludes that he has "sent the names of several other statues of the same size if you should want any more you may depend on having them in less than a month." At the end of the letter he gives a list of stock statues and busts, including those of Homer, Virgil, Horace, Demosthenes, Socrates, Shakespeare, Chaucer, Milton, Dryden, Spencer, Locke, Newton, Tillotson and Boyle (*Country Life*, 13 January, 1950). In 1748 he made chimney-pieces for Kirtlington Park, Oxon (Dashwood Archives).

In the Castle Howard Archives is his undated bill for two lead figures, a Dancing Faun £17 17s. and a Roman gladiator £14 14s.

The monument with a fine portrait-bust of James Lawes (*d.* 1733) in Halfway Church, Jamaica, is apparently the only one signed by Cheere.

The sculptor's first wife, Theodosia Maria, came from the parish of St. George's Hanover Square. She died on 1 May, 1767, "of a broken heart for the death of her father and only son" (*Gentleman's Magazine*, 1767, page 280), and the widower married Mary Wilmot of Clapham, on 30 June of the following year (*Gentleman's Magazine*, 1768, page 349). Cheere died in 1787 and in his will desired to be buried at Clapham with his first wife. To his nephew, Charles Cheere, he left "the leases of the house and grounds in Piccadilly which were granted to my brother Sir Henry Cheere" and "all the statues with the models, moulds, patterns."

In 1788 Charles Cheere offered to the Royal Academy any figure they liked to choose from his uncle's collection, and they accordingly selected one of "Susannah" (Royal Academy Archives). Samuel Whitbread purchased a number of the lead statues, including figures of "Pluto and Persephone," "Samson," "Daphne," "The Four Seasons," etc., for Southill Park, Bedfordshire, where they still remain. The figure of Shakespeare, however, he presented to Drury Lane Theatre; it formerly stood in the portico, but is now in the entrance hall.

(J. T. Smith's *Nollekens and His Times;* Clapham Parish Registers; authorities cited in text.)

CHENEY, BARTHOLOMEW

He acted as assistant to Sir Robert Taylor (q.v.) and carved the figures of "Fame" and "Britannia" on his master's monument to Captain Cornewall, 1742, in Westminster Abbey. Taylor paid him £4 15s. a week, according to J. T. Smith (*Nollekens and His Times*, Vol. I, page 151).

CHENU, PETER FRANCIS
b. 1760

He was born on 8 October, 1760, and attended the Royal Academy Schools in 1784. Here he won a Silver Medal in 1785, and in the following year was awarded the Gold Medal for his "Restoration of the Torso." In 1810 he did decorative work for the building erected in St. James's Park for the Grand National Jubilee of that year (P.R.O. Works 5/112).

Chenu exhibited at the Royal Academy, 1788–1822, and at the British Institution, 1811–1822, showing at the former a bust of Dr. Herschell in 1788 and models of candelabra, figures designed to hold lights, etc. His monuments are of unequal merit, some have extremely well-cut reliefs, while others are not nearly so successful. The relief on his tablet to Thomas Gorsuch (*d.* 1821) at Barkway, Herts, is almost comic. It shows Time, who is knocking down an obelisk, while he holds in one hand what appears to be a wine-jar bearing the words "All sink to re-ascend." The sculptor exhibited the design for this at the Academy in 1822. He was alive in 1833 as in that year he exhibited a bronze figure of "Aurora" at the Suffolk Street Galleries.

Other monuments signed by Chenu include those to Walter Strickland, 1788, in Beverley Minster; Lord Pigot, *c.* 1795, and Sir Robert Pigot, 1796, both at Patshull, Staffs; James Andrew, 1796, at Barkway, Herts; Peter Smith, 1796, in Ely Cathedral; Charles Nairn, 1797, at Cranbrook, Kent; Henry Rice, 1797, in Dover Parish Church, Kent; John Beaufoy, 1809, at Upton Grey, Hants; Mary Golding, 1809, at Ditton, Kent; Sir Thomas Style, Bart., 1813, at Wateringbury, Kent; and Mary Watten, 1817, at Woodchester, Glos.

A "D. Chenu," who attended the Royal Academy Schools in 1794 and exhibited two busts in the same year, was presumably a relation.

CHICHLEY, RICHARD
fl. 1726–1730

Between 1726 and 1728 he and his partner, J. Wade (q.v.), carved the pediment of the west middle front of Greenwich Palace. Chichley was also responsible for the stone-carving of the South Pavilion of Queen Anne's Court in 1730, receiving "£98 for twelve faces of capitals, £20 for forty modillions and £9 for forty flowers." In the same year he carved "two mask-heads over the chimney in the kitchen" of the South-west Pavilion (P.R.O. Ad. MS. 68/706–68/710).

CHISLET, JOHN, of Beaminster
fl. 1823–1830

According to the *Gentleman's Magazine* of 1829 (Part II, page 478), he carved the "chaste and elegant" monument erected in that year to Sir William Domett in Hawkchurch Church, Dorset. In the Pigot's Directory for 1830 he describes himself as "Sculptor and Professor of Music." He also signs a monument to Joseph Bishop, 1823, at Corscombe, Dorset.

CHITQUA, —
d. 1796

He was a Chinese modeller who arrived in England from Canton in August, 1769. According to the *Gentleman's Magazine* (Vol. XLI, pages 237–238), he had obtained leave from his Government to go to Batavia, but instead took passage for Great Britain. He was described as "a middle aged man, of a proper stature; his face and hands of a copperish colour, is elegantly clothed in silk robes . . . and speaks the Lingua Franca mixt with broken English; is very sensible and a great observer. He is remarkably ingenious in forming small busts with a sort of China clay, many of which carry a striking likeness of the person they are designed to represent. He steals a likeness, and forms the busts from memory" (op. cit.).

In 1771 he decided to return to his country and embarked at Gravesend, but the sailors considered him a Jonah who would bring bad luck to the ship, and their treatment of him, coupled with the fact that he fell overboard and had been nearly drowned, induced him to beg the Captain to put him ashore at Deal. The Captain did so and also asked the pilot to see Chitqua to London, but on arrival in the City "a mob gathered round the hackney coach and began to abuse and beat the pilot, for having, as they supposed, kidnapped a foreigner" (op. cit.).

Chitqua finally left London in 1772 and returned to Canton, where he died in 1796. "The news of his death, and of its having been occasioned by his taking poison, was brought to Madras by ships that arrived there in December, 1796." (*Gentleman's Magazine*, Vol. LXVII, page 1,072.)

Chitqua is responsible for the model of Dr. Anthony Askew in the Royal College of Physicians. He exhibited at the Royal Academy in 1770. Chitqua's portrait by J. H. Mortimer was exhibited at the Society of Artists in 1771.

CHUKE, MICHAEL,
of Kilkhampton, Cornwall
b. 1679, d. 1742

He was the son of Stephen Chuke, a London carver, who was employed on decorative work at Grenville, Lord Bath's great house at Stowe, near Kilkhampton, and married and settled down in the village. As a boy Michael Chuke was sent to London and apprenticed to Grinling Gibbons (q.v.), but he returned home later and, like his father, went to work at Stowe, where he carved a pulpit and the cedar wainscoting in the chapel. When the house was pulled down in 1739 Lord Cobham bought the woodwork and moved it to the private chapel of Stowe in Buckinghamshire.

Chuke married Elizabeth Braginton in 1713 and died in 1742. He was buried in Kilkhampton churchyard on 24 September of that year. His widow survived him for twenty years, dying at the age of seventy-eight on 1 November, 1762.

The Royal coat of arms in Kilkhampton Church, and those in the neighbouring churches of Marhamchurch, Launcells and Stratton, are all the work of Chuke. His monuments include those to John Warminster, 1700; Richard Westlake, 1704; John Courtis, 1705; and Sir Bevil Grenville, 1714, all in Kilkhampton Church, and he also made one in memory of his father in the churchyard (Rev. R. Dew's *Kilkhampton Church*).

CIBBER, CAIUS GABRIEL
b. 1630, d. 1700

Cibber was born at Flensborg in Slesvig, the son of a cabinet-maker employed at the Danish Court, and went to Italy when he was about seventeen. Here he remained for several years and then moved on to the Netherlands. Towards the end of the Commonwealth he arrived in England, where he was employed by John Stone, the youngest son of Nicholas Stone, master-mason to Charles I. When his master died in 1667 Cibber started to work on his own and, in 1693, was appointed "sculptor in ordinary unto His Majesty" by William III.

Nothing is known of the sculptor's first wife, but his second, whom he married in 1670, was an heiress and brought him a dowry of £6,000. She was Jane Colley, daughter of William Colley of Glaston, Rutland, and it was she who became the mother of Colley Cibber, the future actor, playwright and poet laureate. In spite of his wife's fortune Cibber was always in financial difficulties. He was arrested for debt and confined in the King's Bench at the time he was cutting the reliefs on the Monument, but continued his work from the prison, to which he was forced to return every night.

From 1687 until 1690 he worked for Lord Devonshire at Chatsworth and, in the former year, gave his new employer an account of the work he had previously done for Lord Kingston at Thoresby (a house afterwards burnt down in 1745). The memorandum, which is in Cibber's own handwriting, is pasted in the beginning of one of the Chatsworth building account-books and runs thus:

"The rates I had at my Lord Kingstone were as follen.

"The two figures flat in the pediment each of them having four tunn of stone in them. I had seventy pounds for one & for both one hundred & forty pounds.

"For one round statue, having a boy upon its shoulders I had three score pounds.

"For four statues which were not wrought round, I had forty-two pounds ten shilling per statue.

"For two doggs I had eight pound apeice.

"For twelve Caesar's heads I have five pounds per head.

"After this my Lord did pay for my board & wine for me & my man & then I did two sphinx at ten pounds a peice, having in them but three quarters of a tunn.

"For two statues as big as the life I had thirty-five pounds a peice & all charges born. And at this rate I will doe my endeavour to serve any nobleman in Freestone."

Cibber's work at Chatsworth included the altar and figures of "Faith" and "Justice" for the chapel, and statues of "Lucrece" and "Apollo" which are now on the grand staircase. His original drawings for the two last-named are in the possession of the writer. For the garden he made two sphinxes, a triton for the fountain, a figure of "Flora," etc.

In 1694 he began building the Danish Church in Wellclose Square, the greater part of the cost being borne by Christian V of Denmark, who subscribed £4,600. The church, which was consecrated on 15 November, 1696, was demolished in 1869. In 1700 Cibber himself was buried there, in the grave of his second wife who had died three years before.

Cibber was not responsible for many monuments, but one of them is undoubtedly one of the finest in England. This commemorates Thomas Sackville (d. 1677) at Withyam in Sussex. The boy lies on a sarcophagus, his left hand resting on a skull, while on either side kneel life-size figures of his parents, Lady Dorset in prayer, Lord Dorset gazing at his son. The look of frozen sorrow on the father's face makes this group one of the most moving in England. According to the original contract drawn up between the sculptor and the boy's mother, the monument was to cost £350, while the work was to be "substantiall, rare and artificially performed" to "ye well liking of Mr. Peter Lilly, his Maty's painter, or any other artis who should be desired to give their judgment

thereof" (Phillips's *History of the Sackville Family*, Vol. I, page 420).

Cibber also executed two monuments for the Earl of Rutland at Bottesford, Lincolnshire, one of the eighth Earl and his Countess, the other of Lord George Manners. In a letter written in 1682 to Mr. Herbert, his patron's secretary, on the subject of these monuments, Cibber mentions that the marble for them is to come from Lyme Regis in Dorset. He also refers to repairs to the church, remarking that "to make cedar seates for groomes and footmen as well as in the quire is werry redical," and offers to Lord Rutland two half-finished stone figures of gladiators, larger than life, which he had begun at Ketton (Historical Manuscripts Commission, Duke of Rutland, Vol. II, page 67). These may be the figures which are still in the garden at Belvoir.

In the Isham archives at Lamport Hall is a drawing by Cibber of a simple monument, consisting of three panels, which was to cost £44. The specification on the back, dated 12 March, 1670, states that this work is to be "all brought safe to Lamport in Northamptonshire and then to be sett up in a Chappell for Sir Justinian Isham before ye 24th of June, 1670," but apparently the design was not accepted and the monument was never executed.

In the Court Minute-book of the Skinners' Company is the following entry dated December, 1684: "James Smith, the mason to the Company recommended one Gabriel Cibart, a stone-cutter of St. James's, for the setting of the statue of Edward the third on the Exchange for this Company." In the following March another entry records that the sculptor had asked £70 for work and that he was invited to bring the model to the Hall. Apparently the Company did not like it, or perhaps considered his charges too high, for they gave the commission to Edward Pierce (q.v.), who agreed to make a statue for £60.

(Harald Faber's *C. G. Cibber*; *Walpole Society*, Vertue Notebooks; *Builder*, 1862, page 835; *Art Journal*, 1903.)

STATUES

1676	Statues on West Side	Newgate (Guildhall MS. 184/4)
1680	Four Seasons, The Two Senses and Juno	Belvoir Castle, Rutland
1680	"Melancholy" and "Raving Madness"	Bethlem Hospital (now in Guildhall Museum)
c. 1680	"Boy Playing Bag-pipes"	Victoria and Albert Museum. Formerly at Welcombe, Stratford on Avon
1681	Statues on Library (£80)	Trinity College, Cambridge

1681	Charles II	For Soho Square
1692	"Flora," "Pomona," "Ceres" and "Diana"	For Hampton Court (now at Windsor Castle). (P.R.O. Works 5/145.)
1695	"Faith," "Hope" and "Charity"	For Danish Church, Wellclose Square (now in Ny-Carlsberg Glyptothek, Copenhagen)
1697	William of Wykeham	Winchester College

VARIOUS

1660	Capitals of pillars, etc.	For Chesterton, Warcs. (demolished 1802)
1669	Chimney-piece	For Sessions House, Westminster (marble)
1670	Eagle	For gate of Steelyard (now in Guildhall Museum)
1673– 1675	Reliefs	For the Monument (£600)
1674	City Arms	For Newgate (P.R.O., E. 101/475/2)
1674	King's Arms	For Newgate, west side (Guildhall Library, MS. 184/4)
1690	Marble vase and urn (former with relief of "Meleager hunting the Calydonian Boar")	For Hampton Court (£755), (now at Windsor Castle)
1691	"Four great flowerpots of Portland stone"	Kensington Palace (P.R.O. E. 351/3467)
1692	"Two great coats of arms with two boys to each, bigger than the life"	Over the windows on the south front of Hampton Court (£100), P.R.O. Works 5/145)
1694	Pediment	East front of Hampton Court
1698– 1700	Various works, including keystones of the arches of the great dome; the phoenix on the south pediment; and four "incence pots" upon the piers of the south entrance	St. Paul's Cathedral (Wren Society's Publications)

CLARK, J., of Hereford
fl. 1805–1830

He signs tablets in Herefordshire to Benjamin Holland, 1805, at Wellington, and to Susannah Davies, 1830, at Pembridge. George Clark, his son and assistant, became a Freeman of Hereford in 1832 (City Archives).

CLARK, T., of Bristol
b. 1764, *d.* 1829

Clark, who was assistant to Sir Richard Westmacott (q.v.) and the principal stonecarver employed during the building of Eaton Hall in Cheshire, also did a good deal of work in his native city. In 1821 he executed a "very elegant canopy in the perpendicular style" for the effigy (copied from the original dated 1629) of John Whitson, Mayor of Bristol, in St. Nicholas's Church. In the following year he made the tracery of the west window in the Lord Mayor's Chapel and, in 1823, received £40 for the decoration of the stone gallery in the same building. The window-tracery was removed from the chapel by Pearson the architect in 1890, and now stands in the grounds of a private house at Henbury, near Bristol. In 1825 Clark was paid a total sum of £160 6s. 4d. for carving the coat of arms on the front of Bristol Council House and for four marble chimney-pieces.

Clark signs a tablet to Mark Howell, 1810, at Long Ashton, Somerset. He died in 1829 and was buried in the Lord Mayor's Chapel in Bristol, where there is a monument to his memory.

(Roper's *Effigies of Gloucestershire*, page 134; City Archives.)

CLARKE, —, of Wigmore Street
fl. 1829–1845

Between 1829 and 1830 he was the mastermason responsible for the additions to Lambeth Palace, where the total sum paid to him (£8,315) included £335 for stone-carving (Cambridge University Library, MS. 3928).

Clarke signs two large and very ugly "Gothic" tablets to Lord Western, 1844, at Rivenhall, Essex, and to the Rev. William Way, 1845, at Denham, Bucks. He also signs a simpler work to Adolphus Meetkerke, 1841, at Rushden, Herts.

CLARKE, GEORGE, of Birmingham
b. 1796, *d.* 1842

He was a pupil of Chantrey (q.v.) and set up for himself in Birmingham after leaving his master's studio. In 1829 he went to London and rented premises in Charles Street, Covent Garden, where he executed a colossal head of the Duke of Wellington, and busts of Dr. Miller, Stanfield the artist and Braham the singer.

In 1832 Clarke became a bankrupt, and ten years later, on 12 March, 1842, he died very suddenly in the shop of a Birmingham chemist, leaving a family of nine children totally unprovided for. At the time of his death he was engaged in the arduous task of casting the leaves for the capital of the Nelson Column in Trafalgar Square, but had only completed two of them.

Clarke exhibited at the Royal Academy, 1821–1839. He showed considerable promise as an artist and would probably have become eminent in his profession had he lived.

(*Gentleman's Magazine*, 1842, Vol. I, page 453; *Art Journal*, 1850, page 8; *Literary Gazette*, 1829, page 586.)

STATUES

1829	Lt.-Colonel Hercules Pepper	St. Mary's, Madras
1831	Major Cartwright	Cartwright Gardens, Euston
?	Children of E. G. Barnard, M.P., of Gosfield Hall	Sold at Christie's, 7 July, 1877 (anonymous owner)

BUSTS

1822	Will Hamper	Birmingham Reference Library
1825	W. Macready	Exhibited Royal Academy
1827	Rev. S. Parr	Exhibited Birmingham Society of Arts
1827	John Johnstone	Exhibited Birmingham Society of Arts
1827	Mr. Rolfe	Exhibited Birmingham Society of Arts
1829	Colonel Shorte	Exhibited Birmingham Society of Arts
1829	Rev. Dr. Blomberg	Exhibited Birmingham Society of Arts
1830	Rev. Dr. Butler	Exhibited Birmingham Society of Arts
1832	Lady Sutherland	Exhibited Birmingham Society of Arts
1832	Rajah Ramohum Roy	Calcutta
1833	Sir Charles Cockerell	Exhibited Royal Academy
1833	Charles Sylvester	Derby Art Gallery
1834	Earl of Guilford	Exhibited Royal Academy
1834	Lady Burrell	Exhibited Royal Academy
1834	Lord Encombe	Exhibited Birmingham Society of Arts
1841	George Muntz	Exhibited Royal Academy

CLARKE, JOHN
fl. 1667–1708

Clarke, who was apprenticed to Timothy Townsend and became free in 1669, was Warden of the Masons' Company in 1693 and Master four years later. In 1677 he was employed at Greenwich Palace (British Museum, Harleian 1658), and in 1686 was working with George Pile at Windsor Castle. For their work here (which

included a number of marble chimney-pieces) they received a total sum of £6,127 (Hope's *Windsor Castle*, Vol. I). In 1687 Clarke built Windsor Guildhall (Town Archives).

During the extensive additions to Hampton Court made between 1689 and 1696 Clarke acted as one of the principal masons and was paid over £7,000 for his work (P.R.O., E.351/3463). Between 1688 and 1691 he also built the New School at Eton, receiving £1,050 (*Wren Society*, Vol. XIX, page 109). In 1694 he was there again to carry out repairs to the Upper Chapel (Willis and Clarke's *Architectural History of Cambridge*).

He is described in the list of Members of the Masons' Company for the year 1708 as living at Windsor.

CLARKE, RICHARD, of Reading
fl. 1811–1836

A popular provincial statuary who also had yards at Wallingford and Watlington. His work is in no way distinguished. Signed tablets by him include those to Richard Jervoise, 1811, at Shalstone, Bucks; Elizabeth Parker, 1812, and Henry Fludyer, 1817, both in St. Leonard's Church, Wallingford; John Bushnell, 1816, at Blewberry, Berks; Samuel Rudge, 1817, at Wheatfield, Oxon; Henry Hopkins, 1828, at Basildon, Berks; Lady Caroline Kerr, 1829, at Arundel, Sussex; and John Beaufoy, 1836, at Upton Grey, Hants.

CLERUCI, CHARLES
fl. 1769–1783

For Wentworth Woodhouse he made, in 1772, an inlaid coloured marble chimney-piece, and a white-marble hearth inlaid with ivy-leaves in 1783 (Wentworth Woodhouse Archives).

CLEVELY, —

Presumably a Gloucester statuary, he signs the large tablet in memory of Lucy Stokes, 1732, in the Cathedral.

CLIFFORD, RICHARD WILLIAM, of Stow-on-the-Wold
fl. 1828–1834

There were several masons of this name in the neighbourhood of Stow, including Richard Clifford (1734–1797) and William Clifford of Bourton-on-the-Water (1747–1833), the latter being the mason employed by Warren Hastings to build Daylesford Church in 1816.

I am uncertain which of these was the father of

Richard William Clifford, who signs three monuments in Stow Church. The earliest, that to Leonard Hayward, 1828, takes the form of a classical urn and is a copy in marble of a Coade (q.v.) terra-cotta erected in 1780 on the same wall. The other two tablets are to Ann Knight, 1829, and Elizabeth Cornbill, 1834.

CLIFFORD, THEOPHILUS,
of Marlow
fl. 1823–1842

He signs tablets at Hurley, Berks, to Commander Hippolyte da Costa, 1823, and at Bray, Bucks, to Mary Waghorne, 1826.

CLINT, SCIPIO
b. 1805, *d.* 1839

He was the son of George Clint, A.R.A., and was appointed medallist to William IV in 1831 and seal-engraver to Queen Victoria in 1838. Clint worked chiefly as a medallist and gem-engraver, but he did carve a few marble busts, including those of Margaret Watson and Mrs. Robert Graves, which he exhibited at the Royal Academy in 1835 and 1837 respectively. His busts of Peter Barlow and Olinthus Gregory, both shown in the former year, were formerly at the R.M.A., Woolwich, while that of the Very Rev. Dr. Wiseman was exhibited at the Liverpool Academy in 1837.

Clint also acted as secretary to a Roman Catholic society established to forward a Government plan of education. He died on 6 August, 1839, leaving four children. He had married at St. Clement Danes on 20 August, 1828, Miss Ann Anderson (Archives, Artists' Annuity Fund).

CLOUD, R.

He signs a large tablet to John Knight, 1801, at Axminster, Devon.

CLUTTEN, HENRY,
of Framlingham
fl. 1830–1840

His monument to John Sheppard, 1830, at Campsey Ash, Suffolk, is an exact copy of one by Sir Richard Westmacott (q.v.) in the same church. Clutten also signs a tablet to George Edwards, 1839, at Framlingham, Suffolk.

COADE, MRS. ELEANOR
Firm *fl.* 1769–1820

There were other manufactures of artificial stone in London before Mrs. Coade set up hers at Lambeth. Lloyd's *Evening Post*, 18–21 December, 1767, has a notice that Mr. Christie will sell by auction "all this year's produce of the Artificial Stone Manufactury, consisting of about a hundred different subjects including antique bustos, figures, vases, tables, friezes, medallions and chimney-pieces, both antique and modern." In the catalogue the manufactury is said to be at Goldstone Square, Whitechapel, and the warehouse at 18, Long Acre. Among the lots sold were a pair of medallions of Jupiter and Hercules, busts of Marcus Aurelius and Faustina, "a curious chimney-piece, French taste" and a model of flowers in wax by Voyez. Among the buyers was Lord Rockingham, who purchased "a pair of river gods, six key stones and a bust of Antoninus Pius."

On 29 June, 1771, Messrs. Christie's held another sale of objects in artificial stone, though neither the name of the vendor nor that of the manufactury is given. Among the lots were large medallions of Baron Montesquieu, chimney-pieces, keystones with masks, medallions of the twelve seasons and another of George III. Out of the eighty-eighty lots sold, seventeen were purchased by Sir J. Delaval and these may have been taken to Seaton Delaval, Northumberland, as in the ruins of that house can still be seen the remains of terra-cotta chimney-pieces (Archives, Messrs. Christie).

About 1769 Mrs. Eleanor Coade, a native of Lyme Regis in Dorset, came to London and opened a manufactory for artificial stone at Pedlar's Acre, Lambeth. The process is supposed to have been discovered either by her father or her husband, but in any case little use had been made of it commercially, until Mrs. Coade, a remarkable business woman, set about popularizing a material which, to quote one of her advertisements, had "a property peculiar to itself of resisting the frost and consequently of retaining that sharpness in which it excels every kind of stone sculpture."

The venture was an instantaneous success and the works at Lambeth were kept busy turning out all manner of objects. Mr. George Coade died in 1769, but he never seems to have taken any part in the business, which was run by his wife and her nephew and partner, John Sealy (1749–1813) (q.v.). They were shrewd enough to engage only first-class modellers and designers for their products, and among the sculptors who worked for them at various times may be mentioned the elder Bacon, De Vaere, Rossi, Flaxman, Bubb and Banks. The architects, James Paine, James Johnson and S. Robinson, were three of the designers employed, and it was the last-named who made the sketches for the monument to

Edward Keeble. This lovely work is dated 1782 and takes the form of a sarcophagus with an angel standing at each corner. It still stands (although badly damaged) in the churchyard at Woodford, Essex.

From the firm's price-lists, which they issued at frequent intervals, it is possible to see how inexpensive was their work. A figure of a Charity School child, more than 4 ft. high, was sixteen guineas, while a bust of Edward VI or Queen Elizabeth was only three. For a very little more one could buy portrait-busts of the Rev. Rowland Hill, Voltaire, the Abbé Raynal, Lord Chatham, Lord Nelson or Dr. Mead. The most expensive item in the 1784 catalogue was a River God at one hundred guineas, although a clock-case cost but five, and a garden-seat three and a half. Architectural items were equally reasonable. Ionic capitals were thirteen shillings each and a "frieze of griffins" ten shillings a foot. As can easily be imagined, the output from Lambeth was vast, and examples of Coade terra-cotta are to be found in Poland, Russia and the West Indies, while for North America the firm supplied Corinthian capitals to Boston, chimney-pieces, friezes and keystones to Washington, and ornamental details for the houses of William Bingham and John Dorsey. In 1784 Samuel Coade transferred "Bunter's Castle," Lyme Regis, to his niece, Mrs. Coade. The building (later known as "Belmont") was redecorated by the firm, and here may still be seen the Coade coat of arms (which embodied a coot), carried out in their terra-cotta, while the north front has a profusion of enrichment in Coade stone.

In 1772 the firm made some gate-piers for Horace Walpole at Strawberry Hill. The bill came to £150, which Walpole considered excessive, and it was decided to settle the dispute by arbitration. Sir William Chambers, the architect, agreed to act for the aggrieved client, and Mr. Kemble Watley for Mrs. Coade. Chambers took a great deal of trouble in the course of the investigation, not only making a thorough examination of the works and the firm's ledgers, but also talking with the workmen who made the piers. He finally signed the following certificate jointly with Mr. Watley: "Upon examination of the books, models, casts, moulds, etc., and upon questioning the men of the manufactory and inspecting into the nature of the work, we are of opinion that the piers made and erected at Twickenham for the Hon. Mr. Walpole cost Mrs. Coade £151 14s. 10d., exclusive of profit" (British Museum, Ad. MS. 41133).

In 1804 the firm made the model of a West Indiaman which was placed over the entrance of the West India Docks. The "extraordinary dimensions and elegant execution" of the ship afforded "a very superb and handsome spectacle," according to the *Monthly Magazine* of that year (page 75). About 1809 they executed the great west window of Exeter Cathedral from designs by John Carter (1748–1817), the architectural draughtsman (*Gentleman's Magazine*, 1817, Part II, page 365).

Their most ambitious work, however, was the tympanum of the west pediment of Greenwich Palace, which was begun in 1810 and not finished until 1813. The relief, designed by Benjamin West, was 40 ft. long and the principal figures 8 or 9 ft. high. West wrote in the latter year that the horses alone had taken him a week to draw and that he had attended daily at the King's Mews to study the anatomy of the animals there. He received £1,000 for the work and his employers £2,584 (Streatfeild's *Hundred of Blackheath*, page 73).

By this time a second Eleanor Coade was the senior partner of the firm, for Mrs. Coade herself had died in 1796 at the age of eighty-eight and had been succeeded by her daughter. The latter continued in partnership with Sealy until his death in 1813, when she took as her partner her cousin, William Croggan (q.v.), who was soon in complete control. She was at that time over eighty and died in 1821 at the age of eighty-nine. The family were presumably Baptists by religion, for both she and her mother were buried in Bunhill Fields.

Mrs. Coade's claims, however, have been amply justified by time, for many of the figures and friezes, monuments and statues, plaques and ornaments are as fresh today as when they first left Lambeth. At the sale of an "Eminent Publisher retiring from Business," held by Mr. Christie on 24 February, 1809, two of the lots were Coade busts of Venus and Caracalla.

(*Survey of London*, Vol. XXIII, Part I, pages 58–61; authorities cited in text.)

STATUES AND FIGURES

1772–1777	Statues for Library	Audley End, Essex, £64 (Essex Records D/DBY, A.204)
1773	"Urania"	Stourhead, Wilts.
c. 1785	Flora	Tehidy Park, Cornwall (Britton's *Cornwall*, page 506)
c. 1788	Two Charity Children	St. Mary's School, Leicester
1789–1792	"Charity," etc.	Fishmongers' Hall, London, £205 (Company Notebook, No. 5)
1790	"Hope," "Meekness," "Charity" and "Faith"	Greenwich Palace, Ante-chapel (Designed by Benjamin West)

1793	Statues for Staircase	Marquess of Buckingham's house, Pall Mall (Soane Archives)
1795	Twelve statues, for Dome of the Rotunda	Bank of England, £200 (Soane Archives)
1799	Twelve Statues for Transfer Office	Bank of England, £252 (Soane Archives)
1799	Statue of Britannia (designed by Rossi)	Liverpool Exchange
1800	"Justice"	Thetford Guildhall, Norfolk
c. 1800	"Temperance" and "Justice"	Hothfield Place, Kent
c. 1800	Statues of the Virgin and Child, St. George, and King Edward	St. George's Chapel, Windsor, West Front
1801	"Europe," "Asia," "Africa" and "America"	Bank of England, £88 each (Soane Archives)
1808	Nelson	Montreal, Canada
1809	George III	Weymouth (see Hamilton, James)
1810	George III	Dunston Pillar, Nocton, Lincs (destroyed)
1811	George III	Portland Square, Bristol (destroyed, 1817)
1812	Captain George Bettesworth	St. Michael Carehays, Cornwall
1812	Two Egyptian Figures	For Bullocks Museum, Piccadilly
1816	Lord Hill	Shrewsbury
1817	Britannia	On the Nelson Column at Yarmouth, Norfolk
1819	Caryatids and other decorations	New Church, St. Pancras (designed by Rossi)

VARIOUS

1771	Gothic Gateway	For Horace Walpole, Strawberry Hill
1771	Two chimney-pieces	Boreham House, Essex (Archives, Hoare's Bank)
1780	Reliefs on façade	Watermen's Hall, London (Company's Archives)
1782	Capitals of Corinthian Portico, etc.	Gorhambury, Herts (£342, Hertford County Archives MS. XI. 71)
1783	Chimney-piece	Argyll House, Twickenham
1783	Fireplace in Lord Harborough's pew	Stapleford Church, Leicestershire
1784	Thirty-two capitals for pilasters	Greenwich Palace Chapel
1784	Death-mask of Dr. Johnson	(*Gentleman's Magazine*, 1796, page 298)

1787	Trophies of war for centre of screen; four naval and military trophies for end of screen; copies of six vases from collection of Sir William Hamilton	Carlton House (£150, £300 and £45 respectively). Two of the vases are now in the Soane Museum (P.R.O., H.O. 73/18)
1787	Twenty-nine vases	Somerset House (£193)
1787	Reliefs of "Ceres" and "Erin"	Stratfield Saye
1788	Four "pannels of Tritons"	Admiralty, London (P.R.O., Ad. MS. 17/1)
1788	"Fortitude"	For Royal Pavilion, Brighton
1788	Reliefs of "Agriculture" and "Commerce"	Entrance-gates of Perdiswell Hall, Worcestershire
1788	Plaques in saloon	Sledmere, York
1789	Six medallions of scenes from the life of St. Paul; four medallions of Prophets	Greenwich Palace Chapel
1789	Chimney-pots	Woburn Abbey
1789	Medallion of Elymas the Sorcerer	Greenwich Palace Chapel (P.R.O., Ad. MS. 68/824)
1789	Font	Parish Church, Debden, Essex (*European Magazine*, 1789, page 4)
1789	Ornamental decoration	For Lord Aldborough's house, Dublin (*Monthly Magazine*, 1798, page 545)
1790	Four chimney-pieces; two medallions of Nereids and Dolphins	Fishmongers' Hall, London
1790	Font	Milton Abbey, Dorchester
1790	Duke of Richmond's Fountain	Merion Square, Dublin
1790	Reliefs on façade	Chelmsford Town Hall, Essex (£141, designed by J. Bacon the Elder)
c. 1790	Four torchères	West Wycombe Park, Bucks
c. 1790	Gothic screen	St. George's Chapel, Windsor
c. 1790	Ten life-sized female figures designed as lamp-holders (usually known as "The Wise and Foolish Virgins")	Burghley House, Northants
1791	Ornamental work	Belview House, Co. Galway

1791	Porch (modelled on the Temple of Miletus)	For Mr. John Weyland, Woodeaton Manor, Oxon
1792	Screen and vaulting of Harvey Chapel	Langley Marish Parish Church, Bucks
1792	Font	Hafod, Cardigan
1793	Decorative details	For Mr. W. B. Simond's house, Reading
c. 1793	Font	Pentonville Chapel (*Londinium Redivivum*, Vol. III, page 243)
1794	Vase	For James Templer of Stover (7 ft. 3 in. high)
1795	Pair of urns on entrance-gates	Coopers Hill, Ampthill, Beds
1796	Two Corinthian capitals (£16 16s.)	For Ffynone, Pembroke
1799	Urns on entrance-gates	Croome Park, Worcs
1799	Decorative Details	Henham Hall, Suffolk
1800	Two Egyptian figures	At Mr. Crowther's, Isleworth (7 ft. high)
1800	Decorative work (£182)	Grocers' Hall, London (Company's Archives)
c. 1800	Pair of swans	Vintners' Hall, London
c. 1800	Fountain in the dairy	Ashburnham Place, Sussex
1801	Relief of "Saxon Monarch instituting Trial by Jury"	Arundel Castle, Sussex
1801	Pair of Vases with classical reliefs	Garden of Cobham Hall, Kent
1802	Caryatids for dining-room, statues on façade, etc.	Sir John Soane's house, Pitzhanger Manor, Ealing Grove
1802	Royal Arms	Vintners' Hall, London
1804	Relief of a West Indiaman	West India Dock
1804	Font	Foundling Hospital Chapel
1804	Royal Arms for drawing-room	Windsor Castle
1805?	Reliefs on Dome	Ickworth Park, Suffolk (designed by Flaxman)
1808	Balustrade	Moggerhanger House, Bedford
1808	Royal Arms (£21 10s.)	County Hall, Lewes
1809	Three large reliefs (£94 10s.)	County Hall, Lewes, Sussex (designed by James Johnson)
1810	Tympanum of west pediment	Greenwich Palace
1812	Two caryatids on façade (£40)	Sir John Soane's house, Lincoln's Inn Fields

1812	Capitals and friezes	Royal Palace, Rio de Janeiro
1813	Two large vases	Elvaston Castle, Derby
1815	British Lion and French Eagle	For Palmer's Exhibition, Pall Mall
1818	Ornamental details (£419)	Battle Abbey, Sussex
1819	Ornamental decoration	Union Assurance Office, Cornhill
?	Large shield with twelve quarterings	Allington Parish Church, Lincs

MONUMENTS

1779	Desborough, Northants	Mary Pulton
1781	Lambeth (Parish Church)	James Moore
1784	Marston Lea, Warwick	Lettice Adderley
1786	Soulbury, Bucks	Eleanor Lovett
1787	Westminster Abbey	Edward Wortley Montagu
1788	Langley Marish, Bucks	David Harvey
1789	Bramber, Sussex	Thomas Green
1790	Roch, Pembroke	Rev. John Grant
1792	Battersea (Parish Church)	John Camden
1792	Keynsham, Somerset	Margaret Simpson
1793	Rochester (Cathedral)	Dame Ann Henniker (see "Banks, Thomas")
1793	Great Dunmow, Essex	Lady Henniker
1794	Ponteland, Northumberland	Richard Ogle
1796	Lawhitton, Cornwall	Richard Coffin
1797	Montserrat (St. Andrew's)	Emma Saunders
1797	Aston, Yorks	Rev. W. Mason (medallion portrait)
1798	Fen Stanton, Hunts	Francis Brown
1798	Wiston, Sussex	Sarah Goring
1799	Laugharne, Carmarthen	George Elliot
1799	Stamford (St. John's)	John Booth
1799	Lambeth (Parish Church, churchyard)	Robert Wilmot
1800	Tonbridge, Kent	Rev. Henry Harpur
1800	Lambeth (Parish Church)	Charles Carsan
1800	Lambeth (Parish Church, churchyard)	William Sealy
1800	St. James's, Hampstead Road	William Hillman
1801	Buckland, Berks	Elizabeth Perfect
1801	Plympton, Devon	William Symons
1801	Lee, nr. Lewisham (churchyard)	Sir John Call
1803	Great Dunmow, Essex	Lord Henniker
1804	Bunhill Fields Cemetery	Henry Hunt
1804	Lambeth (Parish Church)	James Bryan

1805	Teigngrace, Devon	Captain Templer
1805	Teigngrace, Devon	Lord Nelson (Cenotaph)
1806	Bassalleg, Mon	Sir Charles Morgan
1806	St. Michael's, Cornhill	Mrs. Asperne
1807	Lee, nr. Lewisham (churchyard)	William Chivers
1807	Speldhurst, Kent (churchyard)	William Nesbitt
1808	Streatham (Parish Church, churchyard)	Joseph Hay
1809	Capel St. Mary, Suffolk	William Piess
1810	Brentford (St. Laurence)	Rev. William Cooke
1810	Paddington (Parish Church)	Joseph Johnston
1810	Thorpe, Norfolk	Elizabeth Martineau
1810	St. Michael Carehays, Cornwall	Charlotte Trevanion
1812	Coleshill, Berks	Mark Stuart-Pleydell
1812	Beverley (Minster)	Major-General Bowes
1812	Melton Constable, Norfolk	Lady Stanhope
1813	Teigngrace, Devon	James Templer
1815	Aylesford, Kent (churchyard)	Spong Family
1817	Lambeth (Parish Church, churchyard)	Admiral Bligh
1817	Old Windsor (churchyard)	Mrs. R. B. Sheridan

COFFEE, H.,
of Derby and London
b. 1795

He was born in Lambeth, 14 May, 1795 (Archives, Artists' Annuity Fund).

He was probably a son of William Coffee (q.v.) and exhibited at the Royal Academy, 1819–1845, showing various works in marble and wax. In his "Boy and Foliage, part of a chimney-piece executed for His Late Majesty George IV," the *Literary Gazette* considered he had shown "judgment and taste." His last exhibited work, "Death of a Boar," was afterwards carried out in silver.

Coffee was elected a member of the Committee of the "Artists' Annuity Fund" in 1840. He was alive in 1863.

COFFEE, JOHN THOMAS
fl. 1815–1869

Coffee, who also worked for Coade and Sealy (q.v.), exhibited a "Candelabrum in terra-cotta" at the Royal Academy of 1816. In the same year he emigrated to Charleston, South Carolina, and later went to New York, where he died after 1869.

One of his busts, that of General Scott, was reproduced in 1877 on the twenty-four-cent stamp of the United States, and another, of Edward Ratchford Williamson, M.D., is in the Fort Beauséjour Museum, New Brunswick. The museum also has a bust of John Watts by "Thomas Coffee," who was probably the same artist.

COFFEE, WILLIAM
b. 1746, *d.* 1840

When in 1829 he applied to the A.G.B.I. for help he stated that he had "carved several coats of arms and figures about different parts of England; at Greenwich College Chapel he worked the apostles and prophets around the pulpit and reading desk, and also the angels under the communion table." He also stated that he was responsible for the Royal Arms at Windsor Castle, outside Hatchett's in Long Acre, figures and coats of arms for Lord Abergavenny, Lord Darnley, Lord Essex, the Duke of Buckingham, the Honourable Mr. Villers, Squire Bedford, etc.

In 1831 he again applied for help, stating that "having lost his hearing he is now so feeble that he cannot earn one penny."

COFFEE, WILLIAM JOHN,
of London and Derby
fl. 1790–1846

Coffee was employed by Miss Coade (q.v.), but left Lambeth about 1792 after a disagreement with her manager and junior partner, John Sealy (q.v.) (Jewitt's *Ceramic Art in Great Britain*, Vol. I, page 141). He then went to Derby where he found work as a modeller at the china factory, being specially successful with figures of animals.

Coffee apparently did not stay long at the Derby works, but set up for himself in the town as a sculptor and worker in terra-cotta. In 1810 he made a statue of Aesculapius for the Derby Infirmary and also busts of Sir Richard Arkwright, Mr. Robertshaw, Daniel Parker and C. J. Fox; another, of William Strutt, is in the Derby Museum. His bust of Dr. Darwin, made of artificial stone and dated 1804, is in the Derby Art Gallery. "The materials of which it is composed not being liable to be injured by the properties of atmospheric air, it is admirably calculated to convey to posterity the image of one of the greatest physicians and philosophers of the age," according to the *Monthly Magazine* of that year (page 557).

The sculptor later emigrated to the United States, where he lived in New York from 1816 to 1826, and in Albany between 1827 and 1846. In America he also executed a number of busts, including those of General Pinckney, now at the College of Charleston, South Carolina; Cornelia Randolph, in the possession of Mrs. Page Kirk; Thomas Jefferson, in the possession of Miss Olivia Taylor; Hugh Williamson, at the headquarters of the New York Historical Society; and Pierre van Cortlandt, in the New York Museum.

(Information from Derby Public Library and Frick Art Reference Library, New York.)

COFFIN, EDMOND, of Exeter
fl. 1753–1767

Coffin, who may have been a brother of Thomas Coffin of Exeter, Alderman and goldsmith, became a Freeman of his native city in 1769. In 1759 he received £116 for work at the Mayoralty House and was working at the Guildhall in 1767 (Exeter City Archives). He signs the large wall monument to Thomas Bolithoe, 1753, in St. Stephen's, Exeter.

A "William Coffin," son of Thomas the goldsmith, was apprenticed to William Barlow (q.v.) in 1755.

COFFIN, EDMUND, of London
b. 1761

He exhibited busts and wax portraits at the Royal Academy, 1783–1803, and also attended the Academy Schools in 1785, winning a Silver Medal ten years later.

Coffin's wax portraits show great delicacy of treatment. A beautifully modelled example (a likeness of Louis XVI, dated 1793) is in the possession of the writer, while a wax model for a medal is in the Victoria and Albert Museum. He signs a large wall tablet at Milborne St. Andrew's, Dorset, to John Cole, 1790.

COLBOURNE, WILLIAM, of Lymington
fl. 1819–1830

He signs monuments to Charles St. Barbe, 1819, and John Nike, 1827, both at Lymington, Hants. His father, William Colbourne, a local statuary and mason, died in 1804 (*Monthly Magazine*, 1804, page 277).

COLE, J., of Stamford
b. 1735, *d.* 1797

Cole, whose death is noted in the *Gentleman's Magazine* of 1797 (page 534), signs a tablet to the Rev. Richard Knowles, 1796, at Tinworth, Rutland.

A Robert Cole, son of Thomas Cole of Stamford, became a Freeman of the borough by birth in 1749 (Town Archives).

COLEBOURNE, or COLBOURNE, WILLIAM, of London
fl. 1694–1727

When the Masons' Company made a "general search" in 1694 they found that "William Colbourn works at Mr. Nest's (John Nost, q.v.), in the Haymarket, bound to Mr. Bumstead (John Bumpstead, q.v.), not yet free." Colebourne, who also worked for William Kidwell (q.v.), signs a fine and important monument, in the form of a great urn in an architectural setting, to Jacob Holte, *c.* 1722, at Rochdale, Lancashire. His other signed monument to Jefferay Gilbert, 1726, in the Temple Church, was presumably destroyed when the building was bombed.

COLECOM, SAMUEL, of Merstham
fl. 1812–1843

His tablets and monuments are above the usual standard of the provincial mason. Signed examples in Surrey include those commemorating Mrs. Bury, 1812, at Nutfield; James Eldridge, 1817, in Bletchingley churchyard; Harriet Clements, 1831, at Reigate; Richard Dendy, 1832, at Leigh; and Sir E. Banks, 1838, in Chipstead churchyard. Colecom also signs tablets to General Robert Morse, 1824, in Marylebone Parish Church, and to Hilton Joliffe, 1843, at Petersfield, Hants.

COLES, JOHN, of London
fl. 1790–1833

He was the son of John Coles, who had a yard at 21, Fleet Street in 1768. The younger Coles signs tablets to Maria le Geyt, 1795, in Canterbury Cathedral; the Rev. Thomas Marston, 1800, at Hatfield, Herts; the Rev. Thomas Marsham, 1817, at Kew, Surrey; and Mrs. Maitland, 1823, at Hartfield, Sussex. In his later works he was assisted by his son Thomas. In 1796–1797 John Coles was paid £216 for marble chimney-pieces for Henham Hall, Suffolk (Archives, Earl of Stradbrooke).

COLES, JOHN and JAMES, of Thrapston and Huntingdon
John: *b.* 1763, *d.* 1816
James: *b.* 1791, *d.* 1834

The Coles, father and son, sign tablets to Mrs. Creed, *c.* 1800, at Titchmarsh, Northants; the Rev. C. Sherard, 1803, at Glatton, Hunts; Edward Ashton, 1807, at Old Weston, Hunts; and George Maule, 1812, in St. Mary's Church, Huntingdon.

They were buried at Islip, a village a mile from

Thrapston, where their tombstone is still to be seen in the churchyard.

COLLETT, NICHOLAS
fl. 1760–1765

Collett was a great friend of Thomas Gainsborough, and also of Waldron the actor, who used to call him a "Garrick of a carver." He made a number of tablets illustrating incidents from Aesop's fables, but his chief work was the decorative wood-carving on the State coach, which Sir William Chambers had designed for George III. He also executed a horse for "the late Mr. Hackett of Long Acre, as large as the life, for the purpose of showing the harness upon; and this he modelled from actual admeasurement, from one of the King of Hanover's stud called Beauty. He also carved a portrait of the same animal for the armoury of the Tower of London" (*Builder*, 1854, page 72).

COLLINGWOOD AND SONS,
of Grantham
Firm *fl.* 1806–1836

They sign tablets, mostly with Hellenistic designs and all in Lincolnshire, to Margaret Brudenell, 1806, at Hougham; John Turney, 1823, at Sedgebrook; Maria Kelly, 1826, at Grantham; and Sir John Thorold, 1836, at Marston.

COLLINGWOOD, H.
b. 1797, *d.* 1825

He attended the Royal Academy Schools in 1820 and gained the Silver Medal two years later. He exhibited two unnamed busts at the Academy in 1824 and died in the following year.

COLLINS, JOB, of Warwick

About 1750 he made a stone vase for Lady Luxborough, which she placed in her garden at Barrells, Warwickshire. He also carried out similar work for William Shenstone at the Leasowes (Letters of Lady Luxborough to William Shenstone).

COLLINS, JOHN, of London
fl. 1779–1786

He was the master-mason for building the Middlesex Sessions House, 1779–1782.

He exhibited a bust of Mr. Barrymore at the Royal Academy in 1806.

COLLINS, WILLIAM,
of Driffield

About 1731 he made the life-size lead statues of St. John of Beverley and King Athelstan at the entrance to the choir of Beverley Minster. Oliver (*History of Beverley*, page 320) says: "He was a clever man. His models of animals well managed. He was a native, either of Driffield or some village in its immediate neighbourhood, but for want of patronage he passed his days in obscurity and wretchedness and was frequently reduced to absolute indigence."

COLLINS, WILLIAM
b. 1721, *d.* 1793

He was a pupil of Sir Henry Cheere (q.v.), and was much employed as a modeller of bas-reliefs and tablets for chimney-pieces. J. T. Smith describes these tablets as consisting of "pastoral scenes which were understood by the most common observer; such, for instance, as a shepherd-boy eating his dinner under an old stump of a tree, with his dog begging before him; shepherds and shepherdesses seated upon a bank surrounded by their flocks; anglers, reapers, etc." (*Nollekens and His Times*, Vol. II, page 243). A chimney-piece by Collins with a tablet depicting "The Bear and the Beehives" is in one of the offices in Ancaster House, Lincoln's Inn Fields. He also worked for Robert Adam, and two of his tablets, "Bacchus and Ariadne" and "Cupid," were Lots 11 and 20 at the architect's sale held in 1818.

About 1760 Collins made the altar-piece for St. Mary's Church, Warwick, described by Hands in his Guide to the church (published *c.* 1770) as "a fine bas-relievo of the Salutation, under a Gothic canopy, the whole exceedingly well executed." In the following year Collins executed a similar relief in plaster-of-paris for the chapel of Magdalene College, Cambridge, a work "reckoned well worth the observation of the curious," according to the author of *Cambridge Depicta* (1764, page 77). It is now in the College library. The designer in both cases was the architect Lightoler.

In 1760 Collins was working at Harewood House, Yorkshire, making medallions of "Liberty" and "Britannia" on the right, and "Agriculture" and "Commerce" on the left wing of the building, besides figures of "Mars" and "Neptune" for the great hall (Hargraves' *History of Knaresborough*, page 157). In the following year he went to Kedleston, where he executed the medallions on the main façade (Curzon Archives).

The sculpture in the pediment of Worksop, Nottinghamshire, is also the work of Collins and was carried out by him in 1765; it is illustrated in Paine's *Plans* (Plate CI). In 1770 he made the relief in the pediment of Sandbeck Park, Yorkshire (Paine, op. cit., Vol. I, page 14). In 1767 Robert Adam, in a letter to Sir Rowland Wynn, for whom he was designing a chimney-piece, tells him that "Mr. Collins promised me to have the tablet for the library chimney sent to my house, end of last week, but has likewise disappointed me." (Brockwell's *The Nostell Collection*, page 16.)

At the sale of a "statuary and mason, quitting business" held by Mr. Christie on 15 March, 1798, the following models in terra-cotta by Collins were sold: "a frieze for a chimney-piece, the subject Romulus and Remus" and "a tablet for a chimney piece Tame and Isis, for the Margrave of Anspach." (Archives, Messrs. Christie.)

Collins was one of the original members of the Incorporated Society of Artists in Great Britain, founded in 1759, and showed works at the Society's exhibitions between 1760 and 1768. He died at his home in Tothill Fields on 24 May, 1793, and was buried in the old cemetery in King's Road, Chelsea (Authorities cited in text).

COMELLI, J. B.
fl. 1821–1837

Comelli, who was a pupil of Canova and later Professor of Sculpture to the University of Milan, came to England about 1820 and rented a studio at 1, Seymour Terrace. In the following year he carved the altar (costing £1,000), columns, etc., for the Roman Catholic Chapel in Moorfields (Britton and Pugin's *Public Buildings of London*, Vol. II, page 9).

His busts of the Duke of Gloucester, Lord Grenville and Thomas Grenville were in the Stowe sale of 1848; his undated bust of the last named is in the British Museum, and he also executed the fine one of Napoleon now in the Junior United Service Club.

CONNEY, CHRISTOPHER,

The large architectural monument to Richard Prynce (*d.* 1665), in the Abbey Church, Shrewsbury, is signed "Cony arc. et proj^r." In 1708 he made the altar-piece of St. Mary's, Shrewsbury.

CONSTANCE, —

In the account-book of the first Duke of Kent a payment is made in 1726 to "Mr. Constance, figure-maker," for two heads for Wrest Park, Bedfordshire (Archives, Lady Lucas and Dingwall).

CONTE, —

He was an Italian sculptor living in London when, in 1848, he made a marble statue of the Marquess of Stafford in highland dress. Apparently this was not an original work, but a copy of the original bronze by a French sculptor (*Art Union*, 1848, page 343).

COOKE, JAMES, of Gloucester
fl. 1800–1836

He was the son of John Cooke, of Gloucester, "parjiter," who had become a Freeman of that city in 1770, and he signs a number of tablets in the county, including those to Susanna Colchester, 1811, at Brockworth; Thomas Turner, 1820, at Down Hatherley; Elizabeth Williams, 1823, at Dursley; John Daylis, 1825, at Winchcombe; Catherine Hodges, 1825, at Pauntley; and William Wakeman, 1836, at Beckford. His tablets in Worcestershire commemorate Lady Lyttleton, *c.* 1800, at Malvern, and the Agge family, 1824, at Overbury; while two others in Herefordshire are those to Anne Skipp, 1810, at Ledbury, and George Little, 1826, at Goodrich.

Cooke's partner was James Millard, also of Gloucester, and together they sign a number of tablets (for these see under "Millard").

COOKE, RICHARD, of London
fl. 1796–1810

Between 1803 and 1809 he received £205 for "marble work" at Cobham Hall, Kent. This almost certainly included the two large alcoves at each end of the dining-room (Archives, Earl of Darnley).

COOKE, ROBERT, of London
fl. 1780–1817

In 1793 he received £39 17s. 6d. for a chimney-piece for Salisbury Guildhall (City Archives) and, six years later, made another for Lord Radnor (Longford Castle Archives). Between 1807 and 1808 he did similar work at Longleat, where he was paid £86 12s. (Archives, Marquess of Bath).

Cooke's monuments are important, one of his finest commemorating Henry, second Earl of Darlington (*d.* 1792), at Staindrop, Durham. This has a high relief of Lord Darlington on his deathbed, while in the background is a charming vignette of Raby Castle. The monument to John Smeaton, 1792, at Whitkirk, Yorks, has a model of the Eddystone Lighthouse, while that to Mary Styleman, 1807, at Snettisham, Norfolk, takes the form of an urn standing on a wreathed pillar.

Other signed monuments by Cooke include those to Margaret Loveden, 1786; Elizabeth Loveden, 1788; and the Rev. Robert Ready, 1791; all in Buscot Church, Berks; Edward Ives, 1786, at Titchfield, Hants; Miss Meade, 1790, in St. Botolph's, Aldersgate; Elizabeth Richmond, 1795, at Thorpe, Surrey; Richard Millington, 1796, at Coln Roger, Glos; Robert Meade, 1796, in Christ Church, Philadelphia, U.S.A.; Margaret,

PLATE V

AUGOSTINO CARLINI
George III, 1773, Burlington House.

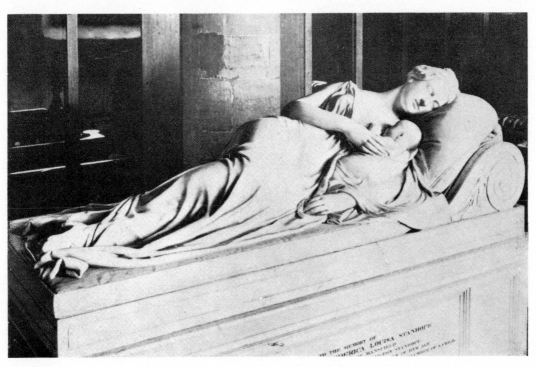

SIR FRANCIS CHANTREY
Lady Frederica Stanhope, 1823, Chevening, Kent.

PLATE VI

THOMAS CARTER
Colonel Thomas Moore, 1735, Great Bookham, Surrey.

THOMAS DUNN
Edward Colman, 1739, Brent Eleigh, Suffolk.

Countess of Darlington, 1800, and Katherine, Countess of Darlington, 1807, both at Staindrop, Durham; John White, 1802, at Newington, Oxon; Jane Caygill, 1807, in Halifax Parish Church; and Elizabeth Baily, 1817, at Gamston, Notts.

COOKE, THOMAS, of London
fl. 1796–1820

Cooke, whose yard was in Fitzroy Square and later in the New Road, signs a monument with a portrait-bust of Aaron Morgan, 1818, in Southwark Cathedral. An earlier one to Richard Stevens, 1796, at Frome, Somerset, has a relief of two Charity children and their school, which was endowed by the dead man.

Other monuments by Cooke include those commemorating William Selwin, 1800, at Hatfield Broad Oak, Essex; Walwyn Graves, 1813, at Mickleton, Glos; Samuel Weston, 1817, at Wyke Regis, Dorset; Viscountess Ranelagh, 1820, in Fulham Parish Church; and John Twemloe, 1820, in Finchley Parish Church.

COOLEY, WILLIAM, of Chelmsford
fl. 1732–1746

He was the son of Benjamin Cooley, a mason of Chelmsford, who helped to build part of Boreham Hall for Mr. Benjamin Hoare in 1736 (Archives, Hoare's Bank). Between 1744 and 1746 the younger Cooley was employed by Earl Fitzwalter at Moulsham Hall, where he made a marble chimney-piece and also carried out various other works (Fitzwalter Archives).

COOPER, GEORGE, of Canterbury
fl. 1818–1851

His father was John Cooper, a builder of Canterbury, who added the aisles to Ashford Church in 1827. George Cooper signs a number of tablets in Kent, including those to Robert Deane, 1818, in Holy Cross, Canterbury; the Rev. Thomas de Lannay, 1830, at East Langdon; Mary Davies, 1832, at Cranbrook; and John Sutton, 1836, at Chartham. According to the *Builder* of 1851 (page 23), the tablet to George Neame erected in Sellinge Church in that year was from "the atelier of Mr. George Cooper and executed by H. J. Day, a student in the Royal Academy."

COOPER, JOHN, of Maidenhead
fl. 1757–1777

Cooper, who married a Miss Emlyn in 1757, was possibly a son of Thomas Cooper, of Henley

DES—H

(q.v.). He was the master-mason for building the Town Hall at Maidenhead in 1777, and was also employed on repairs to Marlow Church (Churchwardens' Accounts).

COOPER, THOMAS, of Henley
fl. 1740–1754

Cooper, who was later employed on repairs to Stonor Park, Oxon, in 1754, signs a large monument to William Sidney, 1740, at Turville, Bucks. The original bill for this is in the archives of Lord De L'Isle and Dudley.

COOPER, THOMAS, of London

At Burghley, the seat of Lord Exeter in Northamptonshire, is Cooper's large bust of Queen Elizabeth, signed and dated 1838.

COOPER, WILLIAM
b. 1700, *d.* 1754

William Cooper was the son of John Cooper, a mason of the parish of St. James's, Clerkenwell, who had been apprenticed to William Savory in 1685. He was apprenticed to his father in 1714, and became free of the Masons' Company in 1722, although he had apparently already taken over the family yard at London Wall on the elder Cooper's death about two years previously.

In 1720 Sir Harcourt Masters paid £150 to "Mr. William Cooper, the mason, in part for a monument to Mrs. Mary Masters in St. Paul's Church at Canterbury" (Declared Accounts of the Directors of the South Sea Company). The monument is no longer in existence, but it must have been of some importance judging from the size of the part payment. Cooper's death is noted in the Court-book of the Masons' Company.

CORBETT and MARSHALL, of Bromley

They sign a large tablet to Susannah Hunter, 1797, in Lewisham Parish Church.

CORNMAN, H.
fl. 1799–1821

He was the son of P. Cornman (q.v.) and between 1799 and 1821 exhibited a large number of wax portraits and busts at the Royal Academy, including those of Lord Carlisle, Mr. Downs, Benjamin West, the Princess Charlotte, Lord Dudley and T. Valentine.

CORNMAN, P.
fl. 1788–1792

He was a wax-modeller who exhibited portraits in that material at the Royal Academy between 1788 and 1792.

COSTA, PIETRO, of Florence
fl. 1840–1880

Costa, who was chiefly known as a carver of monumental statues for cemeteries, was born in Genoa, but moved to Rome in 1848. He signs the monument to Thomas Waller, 1845, at Luton, Bedfordshire.

COSTOLI, ARISTODEME, of Florence
b. 1803, *d.* 1871

He was Professor of the Academy of Fine Arts in Florence, and in his work imitated the style of the fifteenth century. As a sculptor he was "skilful in design and in all the technique of his art, but before his work the heart remains placid and the pulse is not quickened" (Clement and Hutton's *Artists of the Nineteenth Century*, Vol. I, page 162).

In 1845 Costoli exhibited "The Gladiator" at the Royal Academy, a figure whose "masterly modelling" the Art Union considered "worthy of the antique." At the Great Exhibition of 1851 he showed a terra-cotta model of a dog which he had executed for the Rev. Mr. Sanford, of Nynehead, Somerset.

His figure of "A Wounded Gladiator," signed and dated 1837, is at Corsham Court, Wiltshire, and he also signs large monuments in the florid Italian style of the period to Richard Jodrell, 1835, at Lewknor, Oxon; Mrs. Sanford, 1837, at Nynehead, Somerset; and Eliza, Lady Rendlesham, 1840, at Rendlesham, Suffolk.

COTTERILL, EDMUND
b. 1795

He attended the Royal Academy Schools in 1820 and exhibited at the Academy, 1822–1858; at the British Institution, 1832–1855; and at the Suffolk Street Galleries in 1829–1836, showing busts of Sir Edward Banks in 1832 and of Mr. R. S. Kirby in 1836. In 1829 he had exhibited a bas-relief of "Theseus and Hippodamia."

The works he showed included small bronze equestrian statues of Queen Victoria, the Duke of Wellington, and Lord Anglesey, and an "alto-relievo, descriptive of the name of Buccleugh" (*Literary Gazette*, 1834, page 361).

COTTON, —, and HUMPHREYS

In 1773 the Syndics agreed with them for £64 to make the Doric columns for the Divinity Schools at Cambridge University (Vice-Chancellor's Accounts).

COTTRELL, T.
fl. 1830–1832

He exhibited a "miniature model of Samuel Cottrell" at the Birmingham Society of Artists in 1830, and busts of Earl Grey and Lord Brougham two years later.

COULMAN, —, of London
fl. 1809–1818

Coulman, whose yard was in Portland Road, signs dull tablets to Porteus, Bishop of London, 1809, in Fulham Parish Church; James Hatsell, 1812, at Godstone, Surrey; Frances Hoskins, 1812, at Appleton, Berks; John and Elizabeth Ball, 1813, at Berry Pomeroy, Devon; and George Lovibond, 1818, at Hatfield Peveril, Essex.

COULTON, J., of Braithwell

He signs a large marble tablet to Joseph Tomlinson, 1792, at Tickhill, Yorks.

COX, HENRY, of Northampton
b. 1725, *d.* 1810

He was the son of Samuel Cox (q.v.), but for some reason did not become a Freeman of his native town until 1752 (Town Archives). His monuments and tablets have well-carved details and he makes an ingenious use of coloured marbles. Examples of his work occur very frequently in Northamptonshire churches, one of the most delightful being the tablet commemorating Dr. John Shipton, 1748, at Wollaston, Northants, which shows a number of books lying on a ledge, with a pot of ink and a most realistic quill. Other well-executed tablets in the county include those to George Palmer, 1758, Edmund Bateman, 1731, and Sarah Mansel, 1751, all in St. Giles's Church, Northampton; Henry Chester, 1726, at East Haddon; Samuel Keynton, 1753, at Bugbrooke; George Evans, 1757, in St. Peter's Church, Northampton; Sir Thomas Samwell, 1757, at Upton; Colonel James Money, 1785, at Pitsford; Henry Locock, 1761, and John Newcombe, 1765, both in All Saints' Church, Northampton; Thomas Lucas, 1756, at Guilsborough.

Cox also signs a tablet to Robert Atkinson, 1756, at Ware, Herts.

COX, J. R., of Deptford
fl. 1822–1840

He was the son of John Cox, a mason who had been apprenticed to George Drewett in 1765 and who had set up for himself in Deptford after becoming free in 1774. The younger Cox was master-mason to Woolwich Dockyard and he also signs a tablet to Elizabeth Dobson, 1838, in St. Paul's Church, Deptford.

COX, SAMUEL, of Northampton
b. 1690, *d.* 1749

Cox was a native of Northampton, for he became a Freeman of the town "by birth" in 1715. He had previously been apprenticed to John Lumley, a "stone-cutter," who had himself become a Freeman in 1703 "gratis," in repayment of a debt owed to him by the Corporation.

Cox's work is greatly superior to that turned out by his contemporary provincial statuaries. His monument at Abington, Northants, to William Thursby, 1730, has a life-size figure in barrister's robes, while another in the same church to Downhall Thursby, 1736, has a portrait-bust. Cox died on 19 November, 1749, and was buried in St. Giles's Church, Northampton, where there is a tablet to his memory in the sanctuary.

Other signed works by him in the county include those to Ann Woolston, 1726, and William Price, 1727, both in St. Giles's Church, Northampton; Dorcas Sargeant, 1729, and Mrs. Sargeant and Mrs. Beckett, 1748, both in All Saints' Church, Northampton; Richard Thursby, 1736, and Henry Lowth, 1737, both at Abington; and George Tompson, 1737, and Nicholas Jeffcutt, 1740, both in St. Peter's Church, Northampton. He also signs tablets to William Ashton, 1722, at Kimbolton, Hunts; and to Mrs. Robb, 1733, at Milton Ernest, Beds.

COX, SAMUEL, the Younger, of Northampton and Daventry
b. 1767, *d.* 1851

He was a grandson of William Cox of Northampton (q.v.). Some of his monuments have eighteenth-century designs, though erected in the early nineteenth century.

Cox signs tablets in Northamptonshire to John Portington, 1789, in All Saints' Church, Northampton; William Mayo, 1801, at Great Brington; Margaret Fremeaux, 1802, at Kingsthorpe; Edward Swinfen, 1802, at Long Buckby; and John Clarke, 1805, at Welton.

COX, WILLIAM, of Northampton
b. 1717, *d.* 1793

He was born 29 June, 1717. In 1762 an advertisement in the *Northampton Mercury* shows that he worked in London. He made the marble chimney-pieces for the "Great Parlour" and the "Sprig'd Room" at Lamport Hall, Northants (Isham

Archives). In 1787 a John Cox applied to William Cowper for some verses for his "Bill of Mortality" and was referred by the poet to William Cox, "a statuary and a first-rate maker of verses." Cox (who was apparently a parish clerk) replied that he had already borrowed help from that source, but that William "was a gentleman of so much reading that the people of the town could not understand him" (*Quarterly Review*, 1857, page 13).

William Cox, who was buried in St. Giles's Church in his native town, had a yard in Daventry as well as in Northampton. His tablets have delightful details and he frequently makes use of a pyramid with rococo flaming lamps on either side.

MONUMENTS AND TABLETS

1745	Orlingbury, Northants	Charles Sturges
1754	Spratton, Northants	Thomas Malcher
1757	Welton, Northants	Isaac Ashley
1761	Orlingbury, Northants	Mary Young
1763	Faxton, Northants	Mrs. Raynsford
1764	Abington, Northants	J. H. Thursby
1765	Northampton (All Saints)	Richard Backwell
1766	Noseley, Leics	Sir Arthur Hesilrige
1766	Spratton, Northants	Benjamin Okell
1769	Weston Favell, Northants	Mrs. Halford
1769	Geddington, Northants	Thomas Maydwell
1769	Courteenhall, Northants	Sir Charles Wake
1770	Spratton, Northants	Mrs. Benyon
1770	East Haddon, Northants	Clarke Adams
1774	Yelvertoft, Northants	Thomas Wills
1774	Northampton (All Saints)	Edward Whitton
1778	Northampton (St. Peter's)	Mrs. Treslove
1779	Welton, Northants	John Wainwright
1785	Northampton (St. Peter's)	Thomas Treslove (*d.* 1749)
1788	Catworth, Hunts	Matthew Maddock
1792	Soulbury, Bucks	Robert Lowndes

COX, WILLIAM
fl. 1725–1750?

Cox, who may have worked at Deptford, signs two very fine, but unfortunately undated, portrait-busts of Thomas Bacon and William Horsmonden Turner (1678–1753). The first stands above the entrance to the Free School at Bermondsey, founded by Bacon *c.* 1710, though the bust is dated 1703. The second, an admirable work by a skilled hand, is in the Maidstone Museum. Turner was Recorder of Maidstone in 1747, but he would have been nearly seventy at that date, and the bust is of a younger man.

CRAKE, —, of Chelsea
fl. 1825–1834

He signs a number of tablets in St. Luke's Church, Chelsea, the two best being those to William Terwin, 1826, and Richard Lee, 1833.

CRAKE, MATTHIAS JOHN, of London
b. 1805

In 1825 he attended the Royal Academy Schools on the recommendation of H. Sass, and won the Silver Isis Medal from the Society of Arts in the following year. In 1837 he was carrying out repairs to the Royal College of Physicians in Cockspur Street, for which he received £70.

Crake signs tablets to Lady Harriet Capel, 1837, at Watford, Herts; and to John Payne, 1840, in St. Margaret's, Lothbury. He exhibited a bust of Mr. M. G. Dowling at the Society of British Artists in 1832.

CRAKE, MICHAEL, of London
fl. 1800–1825

Between 1815 and 1819 he was working at the Royal Pavilion, Brighton, where he received £643 for statuary work. Three years later he was paid £244 for chimney-pieces executed for 7, Langham Place (Soane Archives).

Crake, whose yard was in Portland Road, produced a very large number of monuments and tablets, none of them particularly outstanding, though three of them, to Harriet Sweetland, 1813, in Exeter Cathedral; William Acton, 1814, at Stoulton, Worcs; and Grice Smith, 1816, at Youghal, Eire, have reliefs.

Other signed works by Crake include those to Sir William Green, *c.* 1811, at Plumstead, Kent; Mrs. Schreiber, 1801, at Laxton, Northants; Martha Pybus, 1802, at Cheam, Surrey; John Bye, 1809, in St. Giles-in-the-Fields; Walter Booth, 1810, at Goostrey, Cheshire; John Hallam, 1811, in St. George's Chapel, Windsor; Captain Charles Rand, 1812, in St. Michael's Church, Lewes, Sussex; Ann Butt, 1816, at Buntingford, Herts; Sir William Essington, 1816, at Wandsworth, Surrey; the Rev. John Hargreaves, 1818, at Burnley, Lancs; Sir Charles Price, 1818, at Richmond, Surrey; the Countess of Cardigan, 1823, at Navestock, Essex; and the Hon. Mary Denny, 1823, at Aldenham, Herts

CRAMPHORN, WILLIAM
b. 1788

He attended the Royal Academy Schools in 1806, winning a Silver Medal in 1808, and exhibiting wax portraits at the Academy, 1807–1819. A note in the Academy Council Minute-book dated 1807 records that a model by Cramphorn, which he valued at seventeen guineas, had been stolen from the Exhibition Room. Four years later it was decided to pay him this sum, as there was no chance of the model ever being recovered.

He signs a monument with a fine relief to Mrs. Cumberbatch, 1818, in Paddington Parish Church.

CRASHLEY, or CHRASHLEY, —
fl. 1774–1777

Crashley, who had a "figure-shop" in Long Acre in 1774, exhibited a number of reliefs at the Society of Artists between 1775 and 1777, some of these being executed from models by J. Durant (q.v.).

CROAD, JOHN, of Plymouth
fl. 1756–1769

He signs two large architectural marble tablets in Cornwall to Sir John Trelawney, 1756, at Pelynt, and to the Rev. Samuel Deeble, 1761, at Sheviocke. He was master-mason of the Ordnance at Plymouth.

CROGGAN, WILLIAM
fl. 1814–1840

Croggan was a cousin of Miss Eleanor Coade (q.v.) and became her partner in the artificial stone manufactory at Lambeth on the death of John Sealy (q.v.) in 1813. As she was then over eighty he was soon in complete control, and signs himself "W. Croggan, for Coade" in a letter to General Imhoff on the subject of the terra-cotta heads and corbels which they were supplying for the church Warren Hastings was building at Daylesford (British Museum, Ad. MS. 39902).

On Miss Coade's death in 1821 he purchased the business and continued at Lambeth until about 1836. During those years the output from the works was very large, and Croggan received £5,290 between 1826 and 1828 for decorative work at Buckingham Palace alone. Here he supplied six vases for the terrace and statues of 'Neptune," "Commerce" and "Navigation" for the Grand Entrance in 1827 and, in the following year, statues from designs by Flaxman representing "Sculpture," "Architecture," "Painting" and "Geography," which cost £157 10s. each. Also in 1828 he made reliefs of "King Alfred Expelling the Danes" and "King Alfred Delivering the Laws" for the West Front of the Palace, and the capitals, pillars and trophies for the Quadrangle.

Other works in terra-cotta and artificial stone carried out by Croggan include the capitals of the columns for All Souls', Langham Place, in 1822, and decorative details for the New Courts of Judicature and the Board of Trade buildings in 1824 and 1827 respectively. In 1835 he made the statue of Sir John Crosby for Crosby Hall, Bishopsgate, and he signs a large plaque of a lion on the front of Northwick Park, Gloucestershire. The material of this may be marble, but it is impossible to be certain, for the work is placed so high.

Croggan also dealt in scagliola and made three doorcases in that material for the picture-gallery of Buckingham Palace, at a total cost of £220 (P.R.O. Works 19/3). In 1836 he supplied scagliola pillars, etc., for the Royal College of Surgeons.

As a statuary he produced a number of marble tablets, including those commemorating Lovell Badcock, 1821, at Little Missenden, Bucks; Lord Henry FitzGerald, 1822, in Paddington Parish Church; Nicholas Parry, 1823, at Little Hadham, Herts; the Rev. Charles Hawtrey, 1831, in Christ Church, Spitalfields; Francis Browne, 1833, at Frampton, Dorset; and Wither Bramston, 1834, at Deane, Hants.

Croggan was succeeded in the business by his son, Thomas John, in 1836, but the days of the artificial-stone manufactory were numbered, and a year later the premises were let to Thomas Routledge (*Builder*, 1868, pages 525, 546).

CROOKE, or COOKE, RICHARD
d. 1697

Crooke was Warden of the Masons' Company in 1667 and 1672 and Master in 1674. Between 1670 and 1673 he and his partner, John Shorthose (q.v.), received £1,300 for work at Ludgate and, in 1683, he built part of the Mathematical School at Christ's Hospital, for which he was paid £396 (School Archives). In 1692 he was again at Christ's Hospital, this time with his partner, Samuel Foulkes (q.v.), and together they built the Writing School, which was finished three years later at a total cost of £1,159.

Crooke was the master-mason for the rebuilding of the Grocers' Hall from 1680 until 1682, while in 1688 he was responsible for part of the library of the Royal College of Physicians in Warwick Lane (College Archives). He apparently died in 1697, for in the account-book of the Grocers' Company, under the date 1697–1698, is entered a payment to "Sarah Crooke, executrix to Richard Crooke." Crooke's son John succeeded him as mason to the Company, but only held the post for five years. (Wren Society Publications.)

CROOME, JOHN, of Salisbury
fl. 1771–1796

In 1771 and again in 1773 he was working at Longford Castle (Longford Castle Archives). Between 1789 and 1796 he was the master-mason responsible for building Salisbury Guildhall, where he also executed the carved stonework (City Archives).

CROWE, M., of Norwich

He signs a tablet to William Crowe, 1778, in Lakenham Church, Norfolk.

CROWLEY, PETER LAWRENCE
b. 1824(?), *d.* 1860

There seems some confusion about the date of Crowley's birth. When he joined the Royal Academy Schools he stated he was born in 1818, but in 1859, when he applied for help to the A.G.B.I., he gave his age as 35.

In 1839 he attended the Royal Academy Schools on the recommendation of J. Loft (q.v.), and in 1844 exhibited "Edward I Presenting His Son to the Welsh" at Westminster Hall. The *Art Union* of that year (page 217) thought that the King was "a fine chivalrous figure, but rather easy than dignified in movement," but the *Literary Gazette* (page 483) remarked that "the standing leg is several inches too short and we must confess until now our ignorance of His Majesty's physical defect."

In 1846 Crowley exhibited his figure of "The Drowned Leander" at the Royal Hibernian Academy. At the Royal Academy he showed various busts between 1847 and 1859, including those of T. H. Illidge (1850) and Sheridan Knowles (1859).

CRUTCHER, RICHARD
b. c. 1660, *d.* 1725

He was bound apprentice in 1674 to William King, citizen and mason, and six years later "by consent of both parties" was turned over to Edward Pierce (q.v.) for the remainder of his time. He became free of the Masons' Company in 1681, Steward in 1691, Renter Warden in 1707, and Master in 1713. His yard was in Billiter Lane, and between 1716 and 1719 he was the mason responsible for the rebuilding of Bakers' Hall (Company's Archives).

Crutcher's son Michael, who had become free in 1712 and worked as his father's assistant, died in the latter's lifetime. His business was apparently carried on by his widow, Mary, for in 1722 the Court-book of the Masons' Company has the following entry: "William Crutcher, son of Peter Crutcher, late of Mersham, Surrey, yeoman deceased. Late apprentice to Michael Crutcher, late citizen and mason deceased. By indenture dated 23 February, 1713 (his mistress Mary Crutcher, a widow, testifying for his services), was made free."

In his will Richard Crutcher left most of his property to his two daughters, Mrs. Wilmot and Mrs. Saunders, and his silver to his grandson, Richard Crutcher. His only signed monument is the superb one at Bletchingley, Surrey, to Sir Robert and Lady Clayton, which is not only the most important early-eighteenth-century monument in England but, according to Mr. Sacheverell Sitwell, "one of the most entirely satisfying works of art in the whole kingdom." He considers: "The architectural composition in which the statues are framed is really and truly magnificent and one of the splendours of the age . . . in the Corinthian manner, that is, yet not Roman at all, and still less Italian, but only English and of Queen Anne's reign" (Introduction to Mrs. Esdaile's *English Church Monuments*, page 30).

CUMBERWORTH, —
d. 1852

He was born in America, the son of an English officer and a Frenchwoman, but was brought to Paris as an infant and later studied sculpture there under Pradier (1792–1852). In 1842 he won from the Paris Academy the prize which would have enabled him to study in Rome, but on the eve of his departure it was discovered that he was not a Frenchman, and therefore not eligible for the award.

As the son of an Englishman, Cumberworth then decided to send work to the Royal Academy in London in 1846, but unfortunately his group of "Paul and Virginia" arrived two days after the official receiving date and could not be accepted. It was, however, later reproduced in "Parian" china by Copeland and a large number of copies sold. The same firm also showed at the Great Exhibition of 1851 figures of "The Indian Fruit Girl" and "The Water-bearer" in statuary porcelain, both from models by Cumberworth.

(*Art Journal*, 1846, page 299; 1852, page 316.)

CUNDY, JAMES, of Pimlico
b. 1793, *d.* 1826

He was the second son of Thomas Cundy (1765–1825), an architect and builder, and attended the Royal Academy Schools in 1812. Cundy, who exhibited at the Royal Academy in 1817 and at the British Institution, 1817–1823, was employed as a designer and modeller by Rundell and Bridge the

silversmiths, "and at the time of his death he was engaged in the design of one of the largest and most sumptuous vases ever made in England" (*Gentleman's Magazine*, 1826, Part I, page 569).

He died on 2 May, 1826, from the effects of an accident in Regent Street, where he was struck by the shaft of a butcher's cart which was being "driven at a furious rate from Piccadilly." The driver was later convicted of manslaughter and imprisoned. (*Op. cit.*)

Tablets by Cundy include those to Lemuel Shuldham, 1815, at Marlesford, Suffolk; George Tate, 1822, at Mitcham, Surrey; and Dr. Benjamin Tate, 1823, in the Chapel of Magdalen College, Oxford. The last named was designed by Buckler and was illustrated in the *Gentleman's Magazine* of 1823 (Part I, page 135). He exhibited a statue of "Musidora" at the Suffolk Street Galleries in 1825.

CUNDY, SAMUEL
b. 1816, *d.* 1867

Samuel Cundy, son of James Cundy (q.v.), was the mason responsible for the repairs to Fulham Church carried out in 1845, and also built, in 1851, the staircase of Northumberland House, Charing Cross.

Under Mr. (afterwards Sir Giles) Scott he worked on repairs to various churches at St. Albans, including the Abbey Church and St. Stephen's, while under the same architect he was allowed to restore the monument of Philippa of Hainault in Westminster Abbey. Large fragments of this, including two entire alabaster canopies, had been purchased from T. Gayfere (q.v.), the Abbey mason, about 1822, but were found and returned to the Dean by Cottingham the architect (*Builder*, 1852, page 33).

In 1845 Cundy made the large Gothic tomb of the first Lord Bateman in Kelmarsh churchyard, Northants, and ten years later the reredos in North Marston Church, Bucks. Tablets by him include those to William Gell, 1838, in Westminster Abbey; General Sir William Clinton, 1846, at Barkway, Herts; Frederick Anson, 1848, in St. Luke's Church, Chelsea; and the tomb of Sir Michael Hicks Beach, 1855, at Coln St. Aldwyn, Glos.

CUNNINGHAM, PATRICK
d. 1774

Cunningham spent nearly all his life and did practically all his work in Ireland. He did not come to London until 1772, and two years later died there and was buried at Paddington. In 1773 he exhibited wax portraits and a bust in clay at the Society of Arts.

For details of his work in Ireland, see Strickland's *Dictionary of Irish Artists*, Vol. I.

CURRIE, JOHN
fl. 1830–1860

He was a self-taught Scottish sculptor and a native of Dumfries who carved a statue of Mungo Park for Selkirk in 1839. In 1860 he made a statue of James Hogg, "the Ettrick Shepherd," which was erected on the banks of St. Mary's Lake, at the head of the vale of Yarrow.

Currie also executed a sandstone figure of "Old Mortality" which he decided to raffle. The winner, a Dr. Sinclair, was killed in Chatham on the very day of the draw and his executors presented the work to the Observatory at Dumfries, where an octagonal temple was built to receive it.

Currie's group entitled "Old Mortality Renewing the Inscription on the Gravestones of the Covenanters" was exhibited at Liverpool, and in 1840 the sculptor also showed "Edie Ochiltree and Douster Swivel" in London. His figures of "Dominie Sampson" and "Meg Merrilees" are, or were, in the grounds of Carlton House, near Kirkcudbright (*Builder*, 1851, page 30).

CURTIS, AUGUSTINE, the Elder, and AUGUSTINE, the Younger, of Norwich

Augustine the Elder, *b.* 1661, *d.* 1731
Augustine the Younger, *b.* 1701, *d.* 1732

The Curtises, father and son, sign the monument to Abigail Jenny, 1728, in St. John Maddermarket, Norwich. They died within a year of one another, and were both buried in the Church of St. Peter Mancroft. Blomefield's *Norfolk* (Vol. II, page 631) describes their monument as "an unusual, but a well-looking composure, at the top is a shield, on which are the arms of Curtis, supported by a neat pillar, surmounting a piece of marble, cut in the form of a pyramid." The epitaph refers to them as "carvers" and as "son and grandson of John and Frances Curtis, late of this city."

CURTIS, F., of Bristol
fl. 1737–1743

Curtis's monuments, which are large and important, somewhat resemble those of the contemporary London sculptor, William Palmer (q.v.), for both placed a large acanthus leaf with out-turned leaves at the base of their monuments.

Signed works by Curtis commemorate Henry Walker, 1737, in the Lord Mayor's Chapel, Bristol; Thomas Rouse, 1737, at Wotton-under-Edge, Glos; and Thomas and Catherine George, 1743, at Croscombe, Somerset.

CURTIS, LAURENTIO

In 1672 he made a marble chimney-piece for the banking-house built by Alderman (afterwards Sir Robert) Clayton in Old Jewry (Ledger of Sir Robert Clayton, Guildhall Library).

CUSHING, JOSHUA, of Norwich
b. 1775, *d.* 1824

He was the son of Samuel Cushing, a church-carver of Norwich, and became a Freeman of his native town in 1797. Ten years later he exhibited there a model in stone for a proposed monument to Lord Nelson. This took the form of a "hexagonal temple with three triumphal arches of entrance," ornamented with a statue of the Admiral and "terminated with a hexagonal obelisk" (*Gentleman's Magazine*, 1807, page 126).

Cushing died at Norwich in 1824. He was survived by his wife, whose death took place, at the age of sixty-nine, in the same town in 1850. He signs a few tablets in Norfolk, including those to John Kerrison, 1804, at Ranworth; John Baseley, 1806, in St. Saviour's, Norwich; Charles Garneys, 1808, at Hadenham; and Harriet Stracey, 1817, at Rackheath.

CUSWORTH, JOHN
of Stoke Newington
fl. 1830–1842

His monument, or rather mausoleum, to Andrew Ducrow, the equestrian, erected in 1837, is a fantastic work in the Egyptian style, decorated with reliefs of horses, angels, sphinxes, etc. Ducrow had it built in his lifetime to contain the body of his first wife. He himself was buried in it in 1842, leaving in his will the sum of £800 further to "decorate" the tomb. Among the many strange and curious monuments which throng Kensal Green Cemetery this is by far the most bizarre. His address in 1830 is given as "Near the bridge," Stoke Newington.

D

DAINTRY, or DAINTEE, JOHN
fl. 1760–1764

In 1760, when "under twenty-two" and an apprentice of T. Carter (q.v.), he won a premium from the Society of Arts for a model of birds and, in 1764, a further premium for a bas-relief in clay of "Mucius Scaevola Burning His Hand." Carter later employed him to carve tablets for chimney-pieces.

DAMER, ANNE SEYMOUR
b. 1749, *d.* 1828

Mrs. Damer, who was the only child of Field-Marshal Conway and his wife, Lady Caroline Campbell, daughter of the 4th Duke of Argyll, showed artistic talent at an early age. The story goes that when she was still a child David Hume rebuked her for laughing at the work of an itinerant Italian plaster-modeller and told her she could not do the like, a remark which at once prompted her to go home and model a head in wax, a performance she afterwards repeated in stone. She later studied under Ceracchi (q.v.) and John Bacon, R.A. (q.v.), and in 1767 married John Damer, eldest son of Lord Milton (afterwards Earl of Dorchester). Her husband, who was heir to a great fortune, was unfortunately a hopeless spendthrift; in 1776 he committed suicide in a tavern in Covent Garden.

After his death his widow devoted herself to sculpture, a pursuit in which she was encouraged by her lifelong friend, Horace Walpole, who had a most exaggerated idea of her talents. In a letter to Sir Horace Mann in 1781 on the subject of Mrs. Damer's intended visit to Naples he wrote enthusiastically: "In Italy she will be a prodigy. She models like Bernini, has excelled the moderns in the similitudes of her busts and has lately begun one in marble."

Farington the painter, however, was not so impressed when he visited the Tuileries in 1802 and saw Mrs. Damer's busts of Charles James Fox and Nelson, which she had presented to Napoleon, whom she greatly admired. He merely considered them "not very good likenesses but they might be known" (*Farington Diary*, Vol. II, page 20).

Horace Walpole, who died in 1797, bequeathed to Mrs. Damer his beloved Strawberry Hill for life and also a sum of £2,000 to keep it in repair. She lived there until 1811, when she parted with it, according to a provision in the will, to Lord Waldegrave. She died in Upper Brook Street on 28 May, 1828, and was buried at Sundridge, Kent. In her will she desired that her mallet, chisel and apron and the ashes of a favourite dog should be placed in her coffin. As a young woman she was, according to her portraits, good-looking, but Farington describes her in 1798 as "wearing a man's hat and shoes and a jacket like a man, thus she walks about the field with a hocking stick" (*Diary*, Vol. I, page 232).

It is a little difficult to place Mrs. Damer as an artist. She was absurdly over-praised by Walpole, who went to the length of having the words "*Non me Praxiteles finxit at Anna Damer*" cut on the terracotta model of a fishing-eagle which she presented to him in 1787. Her detractors, on the other hand, whispered that she was assisted by "ghosts" and professional sculptors. Had she been of humble birth she might well have remained unnoticed. What was exceptional in the eighteenth century was, as Gould (*Sketches of Eminent Artists*, 1834) rather heavily said, that a woman of her beauty and rank should "disdain the frivolous and frequently vicious pursuits by which females in the higher circles of society are unhappily absorbed and occupy herself with studies of an intellectual character."

Her best-known works are the Portland-stone heads of the Rivers Thame and Isis for Henley Bridge, which she executed in 1785. In 1792 she made a statue of Apollo for Drury Lane Theatre (destroyed in the fire of 1809) and in 1795 one of George III, which is now in the Registrar's Office, Edinburgh. Her busts of her husband and herself are now at Drayton, Northants, while another self-portrait is in the British Museum. Other busts by her include those of Lady Melbourne; Miss Farren; Nelson (one version in the London Guildhall and another, dated 1816, at Windsor Castle); the Duchess of Argyll and Lady Caroline Conway (both in Sundridge Church, Kent); Sir Joseph Banks; the Duchess of Devonshire; Mrs. Freeman as "Isis" (in the Victoria and Albert Museum); the Duke of Richmond (a plaster-cast at Goodwood); Sir Humphry Davy; the Hon. Peniston Lambe; and Mrs. Siddons.

Other works by Mrs. Damer included "Two Sleeping Dogs," now at Goodwood, Sussex; "Two Kittens," at Came House, Dorset; and reliefs of "Antony and Cleopatra" and "Coriolanus" for Boydell's Gallery. Of her few wax portraits, those of Lady Ailesbury and the Emperor Augustus were in the Strawberry Hill sale of 1842. Shortly before her death in 1828 she made a replica of her bust of Nelson, a work which in 1829 was presented by her kinsman, Sir Alexander Johnston, to the Rajah of Tanjore on his becoming the first Honorary Member of the Royal Asiatic Society (*Literary Gazette*, 1829, page 427).

Mrs. Damer exhibited at the Royal Academy, 1784–1818. There is a list of her works in Walpole's *Anecdotes of Painting* (edited by Dallaway, Vol. IV, page xix).

(Percy Noble's *Anne Seymour Damer*; Allan Cunningham, *Lives of the Painters*, Vol. III; authorities cited in text.)

DANCE, GILES
1713–1751

As a master-builder he was responsible in 1720 for Carshalton House, the home of Sir John Fellowes, one of the Directors of the South Sea Company (Inventory of the Directors). He signs a large architectural monument to Richard Dawes, 1712, at Wotton-under-Edge, Gloucestershire. Thomas Dance built Guy's Hospital in 1733 (Hospital Archives).

A "G. Dance" was the master-mason in 1783 for building the mausoleum at Cobham Hall, Kent (Archives, Earl of Darnley).

DANIELL, Mc.

He signs a monument with a large, well-carved relief of "Hope" mourning over an urn to Mrs. Hare, 1801, at Stow Bardolph, Norfolk.

DARBEY, JOSEPH, of Dudley

He signs a large tablet to Joseph Amphlett, 1821, at Enville, Staffordshire.

DARBY, THOMAS
fl. 1712–1746

From 1712 until 1724 he was one of the carvers employed at St. Anne's, Limehouse, while he also worked at St. Mary Woolnoth, 1716–1727, and St. John Horsleydown, 1728–1733. In 1746 he was paid £161 for stone- and wood-carving at Welbeck Abbey, which included £39 for six stone Corinthian capitals (Archives of Welbeck Abbey).

A "John Darby," who may be a relation, was the carver employed at Christ Church, Spitalfields, 1723–1729, and at St. Luke's, Old Street, 1727–1733.

DAVID, CLAUDE
fl. 1706–1722

David, a Burgundian by birth, who came over to work in England, made a design for a fountain to be erected in Cheapside. This was apparently seen by Vertue who described it as having figures of River Gods, an equestrian statue of the Duke of Marlborough, while the whole structure was to be surmounted by a statue of Queen Anne (*Walpole Society, Vertue*, Vol. II, page 87). David must have been in England in 1706, as the first Lord Ashburnham on 16 November, 1706, writes to his architect, Captain Winde, from Ampthill Park: "Monsieur La Guerre and Le Chavalier Davy have obliged me by a visit to this place, we had a good deale of discourse about matters relating to their several professions in knowledge, but we have adjourn'd the debate till we meete and see you in Towne." In 1721 the sculptor tried to raise by subscription a sum of £2,500 for an equestrian statue of George I (to be executed by himself). The work was to be erected in the centre of St. James's Square, but only £100 was collected and the plan had to be abandoned.

David's monument to the Hon. Philip Carteret (*d.* 1710) in Westminster Abbey has a beautifully modelled figure of "Time" and is signed "*Cldius David eques sculpsit.*" He also executed the "Prometheus Chained to a Rock" which is, or was, on the staircase of Narford Hall, Norfolk (Blomefield's *History of Norfolk*, 1781, Vol. VI, page 64).

DAVID, PIERRE JEAN (DAVID D'ANGERS)
b. 1788, *d.* 1856

David, who paid a visit to England in 1816, showed a bust of Jeremy Bentham at the Royal Academy in 1829, a work which was in the possession of Dr. Bowring in 1844 (illustrated *Times*, 1844, page 377).

Other busts of British clients by David (dates, where known, in brackets) include those of Lady Morgan (1830), Arthur O'Connor (1833), and Amelia Opie (1836). He also executed medallions of Lord Byron, Canning (1827), John Flaxman (1828), Sir John Franklin (1829), Amelia Opie (1829), Sir Sidney Smith (1830), Joseph Pentland (1832), Daniel O'Connor, Sir John Bowring (1832), George Pitt-Rivers (1834), John Wilkes (1834), James Watt, Sir John Ross (1836), Mrs. Somerville, and William Temple (1838).

DAVIES, —, of Chelsea

He signs a tablet to Countess Winterton, 1841, in St. James's, Hampstead Road.

DAVIES, R., of Newcastle
fl. 1777–1800

Davies, who could possibly have been the father of R. G. Davies (q.v.), signs a tablet at

Grindon, Durham, to Thomas Peacock (*d.* 1762) and another, larger one to William Christopher, 1797, at Norton in the same county.

DAVIES, R. G.,
of Newcastle-upon-Tyne

fl. 1820–1857

He exhibited "Actaeon Devoured by His Hounds" at Westminster Hall in 1844, not apparently with great success, for the *Literary Gazette* (1844, page 482) remarked: "We wish the unfortunate hunter had been entirely devoured, so that we might have been spared the sight of so disgusting a group." The *Illustrated London News* of the same year (pages 188 and 326) published woodcuts of his newly erected monuments to Grace Darling in St. Cuthbert's Chapel, Farne Islands, and to Luke Clennell in St. Andrew's Church, Newcastle.

Other monuments signed by Davies include those to Robert Jopling, 1820, in St. Peter's, Bywall; Margaret Clavering, 1821, and Francis Johnston, 1822, both in Newcastle Cathedral; Jane Gowland, 1821, at Bedale, Yorks; and to Elizabeth Woodifield, 1831, in Durham Cathedral.

Davies, who married at St. Andrew's, Newcastle, in 1812, later took C. Tate (q.v.) into his studio. The latter died in 1841, leaving unfinished a statue of the Duke of Northumberland which was completed by his former master and erected at Tynemouth. It is not known when Davies left Newcastle, but by 1857 he had moved to Chester-le-Street in Durham.

DAVIES, SAMUEL

In 1759 he received £13 for a marble chimney-piece for Hoare's Bank in Fleet Street (Bank Archives).

DAVIES, or DAVIS, THOMAS

fl. 1680–1712

In 1687 he made for Lord Melfort the cross which was set up in the Cross Bath at Bath (Wood's *Bath*, Vol. II, page 259). In 1695 and 1696 he executed statues of "Faunus" and Mark Antony for Chatsworth, receiving £23 and £24 respectively (Chatsworth Building Accounts). Also in 1696 he carved seven marble chimney-pieces for Hampton Court (P.R.O. A.O. 297/2482).

In 1712 Davies was the master-mason employed for building Lord Ashburnham's house in St. James's Square (Ashburnham Archives). He also signed monuments to Humphrey Levins, 1681, in St. Mary-le-Bow, and Sir Thomas Hanmer, 1689,

in the Temple Church, but both of these have been destroyed by enemy action.

In 1700 he took his son Edward as an apprentice.

DAVIS, EDWARD
b. 1813, *d.* 1878

Davis, who was a native of Carmarthen, attended the Royal Academy Schools in 1833 and also trained in the studio of E. H. Baily (q.v.). In 1844 he exhibited "The Power of the Law" at Westminster Hall, a work which is now in the Assize Courts at Cambridge. It did not meet with a very enthusiastic reception at the time, for the *Art Union* considered it "heavy in character, coarse in execution," while the *Literary Gazette* succinctly remarked: "Would that this gentleman had the power of doing something better." Nor did the statue of the Duke of Rutland, executed in 1850 for Leicester, meet with more favourable criticism, for the *Builder* (1851, page 715) thought that "His Grace is made to appear positively intoxicated."

In 1851 Davis made a statue of Sir William Nott for Carmarthen, and, in 1860, one of Wedgwood for Stoke-on-Trent. At the Great Exhibition of 1851 he showed a marble group entitled "Venus and Cupid" (now in the Salford Art Gallery), and at the International Exhibition of 1862 a figure of "Rebecca."

Davis exhibited at the Royal Academy, 1834–1877. His busts of Daniel Maclise and John Constable, now at Burlington House, were commissioned by the Academy in 1870 and 1874. He died on 14 August, 1878.

BUSTS

1836	Charles Kemble	Exhibited Royal Academy
1837	William Tooke	Exhibited Liverpool Academy
1838	David Salomons	Exhibited Royal Academy
1838	F. Raincock	Exhibited Liverpool Academy
1838	Benjamin Aislabie	Marylebone Cricket Club
1843	Duchess of Kent	Royal Collection
1849	Sir John Jervis	Middle Temple
1850	Duke of Rutland	Belvoir Castle
1857	George Guthrie	Royal College of Surgeons
1857	William Rathbone	St. George's Hall, Liverpool
1862	Dr. E. Parkes	University College, London
1867	Thomas Hood	Royal Society
1876	Thirlwall, Bishop of St. David's	Westminster Abbey
n.d.	Sir Francis Ronalds	Royal Society

DAY, CHARLES, of Cambridge

In 1781 he was the master-mason responsible for building Cambridge Town Hall (Town Archives).

DAY, JOHN

In 1818, he built, from the designs of Sir John Soane, the mausoleum of Sir Francis Bourgeois, which was attached to the Dulwich Picture Gallery (Soane Notebooks).

DAY, JOSEPH C.
fl. 1835–1842

In 1835 and 1836 he exhibited reliefs at the Royal Academy, and in the following year won a Silver Isis Medal from the Society of Arts for a "Model of a Faun's Head." He was awarded another Silver Medal in 1842 for a figure of Moses, while his brother, F. S. Day, also received the Isis Medal in 1839 for a portrait-bust.

There seem to have been other contemporary artists named Day, for a Henry John Day (born in 1825) attended the Royal Academy School of Sculpture in 1844, and in 1851 was working as assistant to George Cooper of Canterbury (q.v.). There was also W. Day, who won the Academy Silver Medal in 1840 for a clay model of a group, but who never exhibited and of whom there is no further trace.

DAY, R., of Camberwell
fl. 1822–1851

As a very young man Day was in partnership with his father, D. Day, a mason who became bankrupt in 1822 (*European Magazine*, 1822, page 277). After this he worked on his own, and did a good deal of stone-carving for Buckingham Palace between 1827 and 1828. Here he made capitals for the building itself, "rockwork bases, cornices and balustrades" for the terraces, and "wreaths for the four pediments of the conservatory." Nash refers to him in a letter as an "extraordinarily excellent workman" (P.R.O. Works 19/3).

Day exhibited at the Royal Academy, 1827–1841, showing models and designs of buildings. His chief monumental work is the mausoleum of Richard Budd, 1824, in the churchyard of St. Matthew, Brixton. Allen, in his *History of Lambeth* (1826, page 414), describes it as "the finest sepulchral monument in the open air in the metropolis and perhaps not equalled by any one in the kingdom."

DAYMOND, J.

He was the son of William Daymond, a London statuary, and showed a vase of flowers in marble at the Great Exhibition of 1851.

DEAN, H.

In 1794 he exhibited at the Royal Academy a bas-relief illustrating the parable of "The Good Samaritan."

DEANE, JOHN
d. 1706

Deane served as City Mason between 1696 and 1705 and, in 1701, was responsible for all the masonry work (including the stone cartouches, coats of arms, etc.), for the Emmanuel Hospital in Tothill Fields (City Corporation Records, Rep. 106). Just before his death he was working at the Guildhall, and at a meeting of the Building Committee it was reported that he had offered to "do the whole front of the porch and chapel both as to imagery and masonry work for £60."

In 1703 he received £26 from Mr. Tufnell of Langley's, Chelmsford, "for a marble monument and gravestone," a work which I have so far been unable to trace (Account-book of Samuel Tufnell).

Deane's widow, Mary, who carried on the business, received £400 in 1708 for work at the Guildhall, though part of this sum was owing to her husband at the time of his death (City Cash Account 1/25).

DEARE, JOHN
b. 1759, *d.* 1798

He was born in Liverpool on 26 October, 1759, the son of a jeweller, and displayed from childhood an interest in art. When he was only ten years old he cut from a lump of wood with a penknife a model of a skeleton, exact in every detail. At the age of sixteen he was apprenticed to Thomas Carter (q.v.), who employed him on carving tablets for chimney-pieces.

In 1777 Deare attended the Royal Academy Schools and, three years later, won the Gold Medal for a subject from "Paradise Lost," being the youngest artist to whom that honour had so far been awarded. However, he still continued to work for Carter and carved a tablet so well that "the sculptors allow me to be the first young fellow in the kingdom and sometimes come with a model for me to do them the very great favour of giving it a touch," as he wrote to his father in 1783. For John Cheere (q.v.) he modelled a figure of Cupid and he describes how, when he was working there, "Mr. Bacon came after me and wanted me to model him some figures for a monument, which I agreed to do at the rate of two guineas a week."

Deare's ardour and enthusiasm for his art was unbounded and he seldom went to bed before three in the morning. He was interested, not only in anatomy, but also in facial expression as supplying the key to the human mind and its passions. He was especially fascinated by the faces of criminals and once actually prevailed upon the relatives of an executed man to lend him the body for a few hours. He then proceeded to cut off the head and took it into the wash-house behind Cheere's workshop, where he sat up all night making a cast of his grisly trophy.

Towards the end of 1783 Deare set up on his own, his first independent work being executed for George Gosling of Whitton Park, Middlesex. This was a bas-relief in plaster, 21 ft. long, for the pediment of the house and depicted "The Destruction of the Titans by Jupiter" (Brewer's *Beauties of England*, Vol. X, Part V, page 432).

In 1785 the Royal Academy sent him to Rome for three years. Almost as soon as he arrived in the city commissions of all kinds crowded in upon him, and it was with difficulty that he found time to execute each year a work for exhibition at the Academy, an obligation which, as a travelling student, he was bound to fulfil.

Among Deare's patrons were Lord Cloncurry and Sir Richard Worsley. For the former he made a small statue of "Faunus," "noticed by Canova in warm terms of commendation" (Brewer's *Beauties of Ireland*, Vol. II, page 77), and for the latter a relief of a "Marine Venus," while for Sir George Corbett he executed a group of "Edward and Eleanor," a cast of which is, or was, in the Royal Liverpool Institution. Other patrons were Lord Berwick, who paid £700 for a statue of Apollo; the Prince of Wales and Lord Bristol, for whom Deare carved chimney-pieces; and Mr. Penn, who purchased a relief of "Caesar Invading Britain" to stand over the chimney-piece at Stoke Poges House (Hakewill's *Windsor*, page 257). Another went to the picture-gallery of Northwick Park, Gloucestershire (*Art Union*, 1846, page 273), while a third (a lovely relief of "Venus") was bought in 1787 by Sir Cecil Bysshopp, who brought it home in triumph and set it at the head of the staircase of Parham Park, Sussex, where it still remains; it is now the property of the Hon. Clive Pearson. The sculptor also received commissions from Henry Blundell, Lady Webster and the Duke of Sussex.

By the time the three years had elapsed Deare had so much work that there was no necessity for him to return to England. He accordingly settled down in Rome and married into a Roman family in 1791. He died in his thirty-ninth year on 17 August, 1798, and was buried in the Protestant Cemetery near the pyramid of Caius Cestius. Several accounts were given of the cause of his death. One story alleged that he had died as the result of being imprisoned in a dungeon, where he had been thrown, an unwanted husband, by the amorous commander of the French troops then in Rome, while another had it that he had literally "caught his death of cold" by sleeping all night on a block of marble, in the hope that he would learn in a dream how to execute his greatest masterpiece.

(J. T. Smith's *Nollekens and His Times*, Vol. II, pages 232–259; authorities cited in text.)

DEARE, JOSEPH
b. 1803, *d.* 1835

Nephew of John Deare (q.v.), he attended the Royal Academy Schools in 1822, winning a Silver Medal in 1823 and the Gold Medal two years later for his group of "David and Goliath." The Society of Arts twice awarded him the Silver Isis Medal, for a model of "Bacchus" in 1823, and for a bas-relief in the following year.

About 1832 Deare went to Liverpool, where he had a studio in the old Excise Office in Hanover Street and where he worked both as a sculptor and as a portrait-painter. Late one night in 1835 he was trying to reach his studio by climbing a wall when he fell and died shortly afterwards from his injuries.

Deare exhibited at the Royal Academy, 1826–1832, showing a group of "Virginius and Virginia" (1831), and busts of Thomas Kearsey (1830), Francis Thomas (1831) and the Rev. H. S. Cotton (1832). At the Liverpool Academy he exhibited busts of Dr. Raffles, Charles Nicholson ("Professor of the Flute"), Dr. Gall and Master W. Patton in 1832, and others of John North, Thomas Rodick and Dr. Stewart Traill in 1834. His bust of Lord Brougham was formerly at the Crystal Palace. (J. T. Smith's *Nollekens and His Times*, Vol. II.)

DE CARLE, BENJAMIN,
of Norwich
b. 1788, *d.* 1864

Son of John De Carle, of Norwich (q.v.), he was assisted by his relation, Mary (1787–1848), as some of the payments for work which he executed are made to her. In 1829 they supplied a marble chimney-piece for the Norwich Branch of the Bank of England.

De Carle's tablets include two in Norfolk, to the Rev. Ligonier Treadway, 1834, at Gayton, and to William Killett, 1846, at Kenninghall; and two in Suffolk, to William Scott, 1831, at Mildenhall, and to Mary Gataker, 1839, at Worlington.

DE CARLE, JOHN, of Norwich
b. 1750, *d.* 1828

He was the son of a bricklayer named Robert De Carle, and in 1766 was apprenticed to John Ivory, of Norwich (q.v.). In 1774 he became a Freeman of his native city, and in 1783 built the Blackfriars Bridge there, carving the city arms in the centre.

De Carle was also employed on building, or rebuilding, various houses in the eastern counties from designs by Sir John Soane. These included Burnham Hall, Norfolk, for Lord Camelford in 1783; Earsham Hall, Bungay, Norfolk, for William Windham in 1785; Saxlingham Hall, Norfolk, for Archdeacon Gooch in 1786; and Letton Hall, Norfolk, for Mr. Dillingham in 1787 (Soane Archives).

In his later works he was assisted by his brother, Robert, who became a Freeman of Norwich in 1785, and in 1790 they were the masons responsible for alterations, costing £3,905, to Norwich Castle (City Archives). Two other members of the family who became Freemen of the city were John De Carle's sons, James (who acted as his father's assistant) and Charles, the elder in 1797, the younger in 1804.

De Carle signs tablets to the Duchess of Norfolk, 1791, in St. John Maddermarket, Norwich; William Wollaston, 1797, at Great Finborough, Suffolk; Edmund Tyrell, 1799, at Stowmarket, Suffolk; the Earl of Clermont, 1806, at Little Cressingham, Norfolk; and William Stevenson, 1821, in St. Stephen's, Norwich.

DE CARLE, ROBERT
the Younger, of Bury
St. Edmunds and Norwich
fl. 1795–1842

The two De Carle families of Norwich and Bury St. Edmunds are impossible to disentangle. Robert of Bury may be either a grandson of Robert De Carle the Elder, a mason and architect of the town (1724–1796), or the son of Robert De Carle, the bricklayer of Norwich, and therefore brother of John De Carle (q.v.). Nor is the confusion lessened by the fact that the two monuments to George Stone, 1808, at Woodton, Suffolk, and Bedingham, Norfolk, are signed "R. De Carle and Son." It is, however, quite certain that Robert De Carle, of Bury, built the obelisk in memory of Frederick, Earl of Bristol and Bishop of Derry, which was erected in Ickworth Park, Suffolk, in 1803.

De Carle also signs a number of large wall tablets, including those to Lieut.-Colonel Collier, 1814, in St. Mary's, Bury St. Edmunds; Gertrude Dawson, 1820, at Bardwell, Suffolk; Sir James

Affleck, 1833, at Dalham, Suffolk; George Weller-Poley, 1840, at Boxted, Suffolk; Emma Colvile, 1840, at Hawstead, Suffolk; and Lady Pilkington, 1841, at Dedham, Essex. His monument to the Robinson family, 1822, at Denstone, Suffolk, takes the form of a large altar-tomb in stone, marble and touch, the design being a copy of a sixteenth-century work.

DE CARLE, ROBERT BRETTINGHAM
d. 1791

Probably the nephew of Robert De Carle the Elder, architect and mason of Bury St. Edmunds (1724–1796), and exhibited wax portraits at the Royal Academy in 1785. His obituary in the *Bury Post* of 11 February, 1791, refers to him as "an eminent modeller whose skill was unrivalled."

Matthew Brettingham (1699–1769) was superintending the building of Holkham from 1748 until 1764, and it seems possible that the elder De Carle may have worked under him, which would explain his choice of his son's second name; indeed, the architect may have consented to stand godfather to the child.

DE COUCY, JACINTHE

De Coucy was an Italian who was brought to Britain by Sir Thomas Cullum to decorate his seat of Hawstead Hall in Suffolk, and he also signs his patron's monument, dated 1675, in Hawstead Church. Gage in his *Hundred of Thingoe* (page 459) describes this as "plaster, painted in colours and full of ornament."

DEEVE, THOMAS,
of Bury St. Edmunds
fl. 1705–1715

He signs box-tombs dated 1705 and 1715 in the churchyard of St. Gregory's, Sudbury, Suffolk.

DEITERICH, GEORGE

A pupil of Sir Henry Cheere (q.v.), he won a premium in 1758 from the Society of Arts for a model in clay.

DELAISTRE, F. N., of Paris
b. 1746, *d.* 1832

He was responsible for the lovely monument to Lord Boringdon, 1817, at Plympton St. Mary, Devon. Lord Morley, the boy's father, had wished to employ an English sculptor and had asked four London artists to submit designs, but only Sir Richard Westmacott (q.v.) agreed to the proposal, the other three refusing to engage in what they regarded as a competition. Lord Morley accordingly decided to look elsewhere and engaged Delaistre. The medallion which forms part of the monument was executed by the sculptor from a wax model of the child made by his mother.

(*Some Account of Lord Boringdon's Accident*, published 1818.)

DELL, J.

Between 1793 and 1797 he exhibited portraits in ivory and wax at the Royal Academy, the most interesting being a "portrait of an English sculptor in Rome in ivory," dated 1793. Dell's signed wax portrait of Robert Burns is on loan from Mrs. Bate at the Victoria and Albert Museum.

DELVAUX, LAURENT

b. 1696, *d.* 1778

Born in the Low Countries, he came to London in 1717 and worked for a short time for F. Bird (q.v.) and F. Plumière (q.v.). He then joined Peter Scheemakers (q.v.), and together they carried out a number of works, including the "Apollo and Venus" at Stowe and the monuments of Sir Thomas Grantham, 1718, at Bicester, Oxon; Sir Samuel Ongley, 1726 (with a life-size standing figure) at Old Warden, Beds; and Dr. H. Chamberlen, 1728, in Westminster Abbey. Delveaux also carved the figure of "Time" for the Duke of Buckingham's monument in the Abbey, though the rest of the work was carried out by Scheemakers.

In 1724 he received £400 in three separate payments for the monument of the Earl of Rockingham at Rockingham, Northants. The first two payments are to Delveaux alone, the third being to "Delveaux and partner." In the same bill are payments to a "Mr. Moore" who received £31 for "surveying the work" and three guineas was given to Dr. Stanhope's servant for "transcribing the inscription" (Lincoln County Archives, Monson 28b/14/1).

In 1726 thirty works by the two partners were offered for sale at Covent Garden and, two years later, they went to Rome together. However, Delveaux only remained there two months and then left for Brussels where he was appointed sculptor to the Archduchess Marie Elizabeth of Austria. He revisited England for a short time in 1733 and then returned to the Continent. He died at Nivelle in 1778.

Among the chief works carried out by the sculptor on his own account during the eleven years he spent in England may be included the statue of George I for the Rolls Chapel in London, and a statue of "Hercules," "six foot high and finely done in marble" for Lord Castlemaine. This was Lot 267 on the fifth day of the Wanstead House sale of 1822, when it fetched £21 10s. 6d.

In the Sculpture Gallery at Woburn Abbey are statues of a "Crouching Venus," "David" and "Salmacis and Hermaphroditus," and a bust of Lucius Verus, all by Delveaux. According to the catalogue of 1822, his head of Caracalla was also in the gallery at that date. This was presumably the "bust of Caracalla cut in marble from the antique" which Vertue calls "a fine and just imitation" and notes that it was "done by him at Rome, 1732, and brought to England with him" (*Walpole Society, Vertue*, Vol. III, page 66). At Narford Hall, Norfolk, is the sculptor's statue of a "Sleeping Venus" which is described as "in female softeness and delicacy. . . exceedingly beautiful" (Blomefield's *Norfolk*, Vol. VI, page 61).

Two vases by Delveaux, one with a relief of a Bacchanalian and the other with a heroic subject, were also in the Wanstead House sale of 1822, where as Lots 371 and 372 they fetched £80 17s. and £78 15s. respectively. At West Wycombe Park are his groups of "The Four Seasons," which are said to have come from Nocton, Lincolnshire. His "Vertumnus and Pomona," and the terracotta model of the Abbey monument to Dr. Chamberlen already mentioned, are both in the Victoria and Albert Museum.

Models by Delveaux included in Scheemakers' sale of 1756 were "Head of Lucius Verus," "Faun and Goat," a group of "Papyrius and his Mother" and "The Calydonian Boar." Two models by the same sculptor, which were presented to the Royal Academy in 1769 by Lord Bessborough, may also have come from this sale (Royal Academy Archives).

At the sale of the Earl of Bessborough's collection at Roehampton, held by Mr. Christie on 7 April, 1801, one of the lots was "a bust of Lucius Verus, terra-cotta, modelled by Delveaux at the Villa Borghése" (Archives, Messrs. Christie).

(Georges Willame's *Laurent Delveaux*, published Brussels, 1914.)

DENER, JOHN, of Marston

b. 1646

Dener, who was called to give evidence in 1681 in the suit between Thomas Wood (q.v.) and Richard Frogley, told the court "that he served an apprenticeship of nine years to his father and during that time worked at Brazenose College Chapel" and "likewise at the Vestry and Vault of St. John's College and also at the Theater in Oxford." Under William Bird (q.v.), he had been employed "at the making of the dorecase of the Divinity School in Oxford" and he had undertaken and finished the new stonework in the quadrangle of New College since he had become a master workman. He also stated that "now he is and hath been employed in the building of the Elaboratory within the University of Oxford" (Vice-Chancellor's Court, 1681, Mich.).

DENHAM, JOSEPH,
see Dinham, Joseph

DENMAN, MISS MARIA
b. 1776, d. 1861

She was born on 2 February, 1776, and baptized at St. Mary's, Whitechapel, her parents being Ann and William Denman, of Mansell Street. She was the sister-in-law and adopted daughter of John Flaxman (q.v.), who at his death left her his casts, models, etc., which are now in the library of University College, London, though a number of them were damaged by enemy action.

In 1807 Miss Denman received a Silver Medal from the Society of Arts for the model of a Cupid's head, which may be the plaster of "Cupid Bacchus," now in the Soane Museum.
(British Museum, Ad. MS. 39791.)

DENMAN, THOMAS
b. 1787

Son of William and Ann Denman, of Mansell Street, London, and brother of Maria Denman (q.v.), he attended the Royal Academy Schools in 1807 and in the same year won the Lesser Silver Palette from the Society of Arts for a model of Antinous. In 1813 he gained a Silver Medal from the Royal Academy. He worked for many years in the studio of his brother-in-law, John Flaxman (q.v.), and on the latter's death was commissioned to complete his unfinished works. These included the statue of the Marquess of Hastings for Calcutta, and the monument to James Watson at Heston, Middlesex.

In 1829 Denman was employed on decorative work at Buckingham Palace, receiving £600. In 1833 he exhibited at the Royal Academy the sketch of a "Colossal Group executed for General Anderson's Institution at Elgin." In 1836 he showed a statue of Thomas Telford. He became a bankrupt in 1847.

Denman exhibited at the Royal Academy, 1815–1836, where, besides the works already mentioned, he also showed busts of John Flaxman (1830) and the Marquess of Hastings (1835). At the Birmingham Society of Artists in 1830 he showed "Menelaus Defending the Body of Patroclus"; he also exhibited at the British Institution, 1818–1827.

Denman was a prolific statuary, but most of his monuments and tablets are uninspired and dull, except when they borrow a Flaxman design. The list which follows is of the best of these.

MONUMENTS AND TABLETS

1817	Chertsey, Surrey	Sir Joseph Mawbey
c. 1817	Snitterfield, Warwick	George Lloyd
1818	Fighledean, Wilts	William Dyke
1820	South Mimms, Herts	William Adams
1825	Helston, Cornwall	John Trevenen
1828	Leicester (St. Mary's)	Paul Benfield
1828	West Drayton, Middlesex	General Arabin
1829	Cheam, Surrey (churchyard)	Henry Farmer (obelisk)
1830	Marlow, Bucks	George Ellison
1833	Sandy, Beds	Francis Pym
1834	Wimpole, Cambs	Rt. Hon. Charles Yorke
1834	Writtle, Essex	Lt.-Colonel Booth
1836	Speldhurst, Kent	William Raymond
1837	Fareham, Hants (Holy Trinity)	Elizabeth Kelsall
1837	Trumpington, Cambs	Helen Anstey
1837	Helston, Cornwall	Peter Hill
1837	South Weald, Essex	Admiral Tower
1838	Wartling, Sussex	Charlotte Curteis
1840	Shrivenham, Berks	Hon. Russell Barrington
1840	Yelverton, Norfolk	Peter Nichols
1840	Madras (Cathedral)	Lt.-Colonel Thomas MacLean
1841	Hartfield, Sussex	Henry Jackson
1841	Nacton, Suffolk	Sir Philip Broke
1842	Normanton, Rutland	Lady Heathcote
1842	St. John's Wood Chapel	Sir John Lawford
1843	Canterbury (Cathedral)	Officers and Men of the 13th Light Infantry
1843	Terrington St. Clement, Norfolk	Mary Morphew
1843	Marylebone (Holy Trinity)	Lieutenant James Fuller
1844	Hertingfordbury, Herts	Sir Gore Ouseley
1847	Berkswell, Warwick	Sir John Eardley-Wilmot

DENT, ISAAC, of Rochester

He was the master-mason for building the Travellers' House at Rochester in 1771, and also carved the large urn on the central apex of the roof (Account-book, Travellers' House).

DERMOTT, T. M.

A local statuary, he signs the large wall-tablet to John Postlethwaite, 1818, in the Parish Church of Ashton-under-Lyne. This is decorated with masonic emblems, the number of Postlethwaite's Lodge, etc., and is one of the earliest monuments embodying such details that I have so far encountered.

DE VAERE, JOHN
b. 1755, *d.* 1830

He was born at Ghent, his name being originally spelt "De Vaare," but he changed this slightly on coming to England. Here he attended the Royal Academy Schools in 1786, giving the date of his birth as 10 March, 1755. He also seems to have modelled for Wedgwood about this time, for the latter gave him ten guineas in 1787 towards the expenses of his journey to Rome.

While in Rome, de Vaere assisted Flaxman (q.v.) and with him executed a group of "The Fury of Athamas." On 15 March, 1788, the latter wrote to Byerly asking him to inform Wedgwood that "Mr. De-veare has been at work with the utmost diligence ever since he has been here on the bas relief of the Borghese vase in which he has succeeded very well, but it will still take him some weeks to finish and after he has done, I also shall have something to do to it." "Mr. Wedgwood," Flaxman continued, "will easily conceive as this is new work to Mr. D. he must needs be slow at first especially as he takes so much pains. As a proof he follows his studies well he has already gained the Pope's first silver medal for a figure modelled at night in the Roman Academy" (Wedgwood Archives).

On his return to England in 1790, De Vaere went to work for Wedgwood at Etruria, where he succeeded H. Webber (q.v.) as one of the chief modellers. His original wax models for the medallions of the Admirals St. Vincent, Duncan and Nelson are now in the Etruria Museum. He left the firm after Wedgwood's death in 1795 and entered the employment of Mrs. Coade (q.v.), for whom he modelled in 1797 a large group for the cornice of the Pelican Life Insurance Office in Lombard Street. This work, which was illustrated in the *European Magazine* (Vol. 39, page 262), is now in the grounds of the Jeffrye Museum. He seems to have set up for himself about 1800, but left England for Flanders in 1810 and was appointed Professor of Sculpture to the Royal Academy of Ghent. His bust by P. J. Farmer (q.v.) was exhibited at the Royal Academy in 1826. De Vaere died four years later.

De Vaere exhibited at the Royal Academy, 1797–1809, where his works included "a candelabra in Coade artificial stone" (1798); a statue of "Apollo" (1800); and a design for a monument to General McPherson of Charlestown, South Carolina, who had been drowned off New York in 1806. His statue of "Mercury" was formerly in the collection of Mr. Hope of Deepdene.

Tablets signed by De Vaere commemorate the Countess of Kenmare, 1806, in St. Giles-in-the-Fields; William Drake, 1806, at Amersham, Bucks; Hannah Shirley, 1808, in Bristol Cathedral; and Edmund Irby, 1809, at Whiston, Northants.

(J. T. Smith's *Nollekens and His Times*; Meteyard's *Wedgwood*; authorities cited in text.)

DEVAL, JOHN, the Elder
b. 1701, *d.* 1774

He was the son of "George Deval, yeoman of Ensham, Oxon, deceased," and was bound apprentice in 1718 to Joshua Fletcher (q.v.). After he became free in 1727 he worked for Andrews Jelfe (q.v.), but afterwards set up for himself and was later assisted by his son, John Deval the Younger (q.v.). Both father and son executed a good deal of work for the Crown, and were the chief masons for the Royal Palaces, the Tower of London, the Royal Mews, etc. In 1760 the elder Deval became Master of the Masons' Company. He died in 1774 and was buried at Isleworth.

As a mason Deval was employed at St. Olave's, Southwark, in 1737; Kimbolton Castle in 1738; the Mansion House and Guy's Hospital in 1739; and Cornbury House, London, in 1744. Between 1742 and 1752 he was also the mason responsible for building the Foundling Hospital and its chapel. In 1747 he informed the Committee that, on the demolition of Canons, he had purchased for £24 10s. "two Venetian windows which would be fit for the chappell of this hospital" and that he was prepared to part with them at cost price. His offer, however, was regretfully refused on the ground that the windows were too large. Two years later he presented to the hospital a marble chimney-piece and a marble surround for a relief by Rysbrack, both of which are now in the office of the hospital in Brunswick Square (Archives, Foundling Hospital). In 1769 he was the mason for building Newgate Prison.

Besides the chimney-piece for the Foundling Hospital, Deval made in 1739 one costing £85 for Sir Richard Hoare for Barn Elms House, and others for the house at Clapham belonging to Mr. Arnold, a partner in Hoare's Bank (Bank Archives), and for Charles Lowndes of Chesham Bury, Bucks. In 1755 he made a chimney-piece for Christopher Tower of Weald Hall, Essex (Tower Archives), and in 1767 another for Sir Rowland Winn, of Nostell Priory, Yorkshire.

PLATE VII

JOHN DEARE
"Venus," 1787, Parham Park, Sussex.

ANNE SEYMOUR DAMER
"Two Dogs," Goodwood, Sussex.

PLATE VIII

CLAUDE DAVID
Philip Carteret (died 1710), Westminster Abbey.

JOHN DEVAL THE YOUNGER
Thomas Spackman, 1786, Cliffe Pypard, Wiltshire.

Deval was working at Woburn in or before 1751, for in that year Horace Walpole visited the house and noticed that "the Hall has two reliefs by Duval" (Walpole Society, Vol. XVI, page 17). In 1756 also he made the chimney-pieces for the gallery and state-rooms (Bedford Archives). In 1738 he made marble tables for Lord Folkestone at Longford Castle (Archives, Earl of Radnor), while in 1756 he supplied a chimney-piece costing £289 to Lord Fitzwilliam for Milton Hall.

(Archives of houses, etc., mentioned in text.)

DEVAL, JOHN, the Younger
b. 1728, *d.* 1794

He was the son of John Deval the Elder (q.v.) and was admitted to the Masons' Company by patrimony in 1777. In 1784 he became Master of the Company, and in 1793 was joined in the business by his son, a third John Deval. Deval, who was also much employed by the Crown, succeeded his father as master-mason to the Royal Palaces, etc., on the latter's death in 1774.

As a mason-contractor, the younger Deval built the north and south fronts of Somerset House, 1777–1786; Coutts' Bank in the Strand, 1780–1789 (Bank Archives); the King's Bench Prison, 1780–1784, at a total cost of £4,590; the house for the Marshal of the Prison, 1781–1782, for £546; Argyll House, 1783; the Government building next the Admiralty, 1786–1791, for which he received £1,875; the Temple at Audley End, 1791, at a cost of £300 (Essex Records, D/DBY.A.222); and the new Guardroom at St. James's Palace, 1793.

He was also employed on additions, or repairs, to Cobham Hall, Kent, between 1776 and 1778 (Archives, Earl of Darnley); Audley End in 1785, where he was paid £790: and Carlton House, where he received, in 1788, £931 for chimney-pieces and statuary work (P.R.O. H.O. 73/18). Between 1784 and 1789 he rebuilt the Queen Mary block of Greenwich Palace after it had been destroyed by fire (P.R.O. Ad.MS. 68/813), and, in 1791 and 1792, carried out work at Woburn Abbey for a total sum of £1,653. In 1779 he was also responsible for the mausoleum of the Earls of Radnor in Britford churchyard, Wiltshire.

In addition to the work at Somerset House already mentioned, Deval carved "twenty-five faces of rich Corinthian capitals of columns" for £213 and, in 1786, made Portland stone chimney-pieces for the building. Two years later, when the Royal Chapel at Greenwich was being rebuilt after the fire, he executed all the marble-work. The £1,897 which he received included £64 for "591 feet of antique galloches of statuary in black

marble," and £390 for "four circular flowers of statuary and black marble and two large flowers" and a marble doorcase. In the same year he was paid £73 for marble-work in Prince Edward's apartments in St. James's Palace. In 1791 he was paid £163 for carving the great Portland stone capital of the column erected at Colne Park, near Colchester.

Chimney-pieces executed by Deval, in addition to those at Carlton House and Somerset House, included one in the Long Parlour at Longford Castle, which cost £66 in 1780, and others for William Windham of Earsham Hall, Norfolk, in 1783; for Lord Berwick at Attingham Park, Salop, in 1785; for Bedford House, London, in 1787; and for the waiting-room in St. James's Palace in 1793.

Deval's most important monument commemorates Thomas Spackman, 1786, at Cliffe Pypard, Wiltshire. This exciting and arresting work is 18 ft. high and has for its chief feature a life-size figure of Spackman with one hand outstretched. At his feet lies a straw basket of carpenter's tools, while to left and right stand a boy and a girl, pupils of the Charity School he endowed out of the fortune he made as a carpenter. More emblems of his trade are in relief at the base of the monument. The excellence of this work, in its obscure village church, shows that Deval deserves greater recognition than he has had hitherto, for he was undoubtedly a fine artist in the best English tradition.

(Archives of houses, etc., mentioned in the text.)

DE VEAUX,
or DE VAUX, JOHN
fl. 1821–1836

De Veaux, who also spells his name De Vaux, exhibited intaglio portraits at the Royal Academy between 1832 and 1834. His wax medallions of William IV and the Duke of York are in the National Portrait Gallery.

DEVIGNE, or DEVISNE
fl. 1706

He was employed by Mr. Thomas Coke of Melbourne Hall, Derbyshire, in 1706, carving the bases for lead figures and the "Vase of the Seasons," all made by John Nost (q.v.). Mr. Sergeant, Coke's Derbyshire agent, writing to his master, says: "Mr. Devigne will come about them (the pedestals) by next week. They are to be made from stone from the new quarry. Mr. Devigne and all the workmen think it will work as fine or finer than Donington." Mr. Coke paid Devigne, whom he refers to as "ye French carver," £27; his work included, besides the sculptured pedestals for the great vase and the groups of amorini, two baskets of flowers and fruit, which still stand in front of Melbourne Hall. Devigne seems to have returned to France, as late in 1706 Sergeant writes to Mr. Coke: "Mr. Devigne desires to know if you have any more occasion for him, for he thinks to leave this country in a little time."

(Archives, Marquess of Lothian.)

DE VILLE, JAMES S.
b. 1776, *d.* 1846

As a young man he was employed by Nollekens (q.v.) to make casts from moulds (J. T. Smith's *Nollekens and his Times*, Vol. I, page 321) and he later seems to have set up on his own account. In 1809 the Rev. James Hall wrote to J. Flaxman (q.v.) on behalf of Lord Buchan who "desired a cast from the face of Newton." Flaxman replied that he could not supply one himself, "but the original mould from it belongs to Mr. de Ville figure maker in Newport Street, who sells them at two shillings or half a crown each" (Wedgwood Archives). The *European Magazine* (Part II, page 344) states that de Ville purchased "the original moulds of busts from the models made by the late Mr. Nollekens of all the distinguished characters who honoured that artist with sittings for the same" and that he also prepared casts from "the original busts by Roubiliac of Hampden, Sidney and Cromwell." "His large collection of busts and casts from nature for the illustration of phrenology," the paragraph ends, "cannot fail to gratify every visitor to his establishment."

De Ville died on 6 May, 1846, and his obituary in the *Gentleman's Magazine* (1846, Part II, page 104) describes him as "a plaster figure-maker, lamp manufacturer and phrenologist in the Strand." He exhibited at the Royal Academy, 1823–1826, showing busts of General Maitland (1823), Captain Lyon (1824), and Sir Harford Jones (1826). His bust of Thackeray (1822), illustrated in the *Magazine of Art* in 1891 (page 289), is now in the National Portrait Gallery, together with a plaster-cast of the life-mask of William Blake, executed in the following year. In 1825 he made a bust of J. S. Duncan, now in the Radcliffe Camera, Oxford, while his bust of the Rev. Rowland Hill is described by Edward Sidney as "one of the most beautiful casts of Hill's features I ever saw" (*Life of the Rev. Rowland Hill*, page 322).

DICKINSON,
or DICCONSON, RICHARD
fl. 1719–1724

In the account-book of the first Duke of Kent (Archives, Lady Lucas and Dingwall) he is described as a "figure-maker" when, in 1719, he was paid for plaster statues for Wrest Park, Bedfordshire. In the same year he also received £32 8s. from Lord Derby for statues for Knowsley (Derby Archives, 2005/5).

According to J. T. Smith (*The Streets of London*), Dickinson's yard was on the site of Gloucester House, Piccadilly.

DICKINSON, G., of Newark

He signs a slate headstone with delightful decorative details and a relief of "Hope" to Elizabeth Dickinson, 1776, at Scrooby, Nottinghamshire.

DIEMAR, JOHN EMMANUEL
fl. 1761–1790

Diemar, whose address is given as "opposite the Lying-in Hospital, Westminster Bridge," was appointed one of the directors of the Society of Artists in 1769. He exhibited models in wax at the Free Society in 1761 and at the Society of Artists between 1768 and 1783.

DIEMAR, EMMANUEL MATTHIAS
b. 1720

Presumably a brother of J. E. Diemar (q.v.), he exhibited wax models, mostly of flowers, at the Society of Artists, 1768–1790. A flower-piece in wax, signed by him, is in the Victoria and Albert Museum.

DIEVOT, A., of Mechelen
d. c. 1715

Dievot worked for Grinling Gibbons (q.v.) and, according to Vertue (*Walpole Society, Vertue*, Vol. I, page 61), he and Laurens Vandermeulen (q.v.) "modelled and made" the statue of James II commissioned from their master. This assertion seems to be contradicted by Sir John Bramston in his autobiography (Camden Society, 1845), for he mentions that "on New Year's Day, 1686, a statue in brass was to be seen (placed the day before) in the yard at Whitehall made by Gibbons at the charge of Toby Rustick (*sic*) of the present King James II."

Vertue says that Deviot gave up "his business of carving" and left England in the "troubles of the Revolution," retiring to Antwerp and dying "at a good age" at Mechelen (Vertue, op. cit., page 106).

DINHAM, or DENHAM, JOSEPH

b. 1803, *d.* 1854

He attended the Royal Academy Schools in 1820 and gained Silver Medals in 1821 and 1824. On leaving the schools he was for some time employed in the studio of Chantrey (q.v.) and then set up on his own. He exhibited at the Royal Academy, 1823–1852, where his busts included those of Harriet Gouldsmith (1825), E. H. Baily, R.A. (1826), Sir Richard Birnie (1827), Sir James Wigram (1849), and the Marquess of Hastings (1851). His "Sleeping Nymph" (1826) is, or was, at Blagdon, Northumberland, and he signs the monument of Elizabeth Mackenzie (*d.* 1840) at St. James's, Bermondsey. Dinham died in December, 1854, leaving a widow and five children.

DIPPLE, HENRY, of Richmond

He signs the monument of Mrs. Elizabeth Theobald, 1796, in Kew Parish Church. In 1808 the firm was known as "Dipple, Hudson and Dipple," of Red Lion Street, Richmond, but by 1827 was owned by Henry Dipple of the same address.

DIXON, JOHN

fl. 1754–1766

He was born in St. Botolph-without-Aldgate, and in 1754 was apprenticed to Henry Gregory; he became free in 1761.

Dixon signs the monuments of Bishop Sherlock, 1764, in Fulham churchyard; the first and second Earls Waldegrave, 1765, at Navestock, Essex; and the Rev. Henry Trotter, 1766, at Graveley, Cambs.

A sale of a "Mr. Dixon, mason" (presumably John Dixon) was held at "his yard at Pedlars Acre, Lambeth," on 13 December, 1766, and the two following days. Among the lots were models for tablets and monuments, various busts and figures, terra-cottas of Briseis and Agamemnon, and a large statue of Mercury. Also sold were four marble busts of Inigo Jones, Seneca, Dr. Stukely and Palladio, all by "Steff. Domine-Ceti" and "two vases in statuary marble inlaid with sienna."

DIXON, JOSEPH

d. 1787

In 1760 he became free of the Masons' Company "by virtue of an order of the Lord Mayor and Court of Aldermen" and in the same year began to build Blackfriars Bridge, which was completed in 1768. He was also the mason responsible for the bridge at Exeter (*Gentleman's Magazine*, 1817, Part II, page 363), and in 1762 was employed on alterations to Woburn Abbey (Bedford Archives).

As a mason-contractor under the architect Henry Holland, Dixon built, or altered, houses for Baron Atkinson at Putney, in 1767; for Sir Thomas Robinson at Chelsea, in 1769; for Philip Stephens at Fulham, in 1770; and for Mrs. Crawford in Hertford Street and Sir Samson Gideon in St. James's Square. In 1769 he carved the dining-room chimney-piece, costing £48, for Lord Warwick's house in the same Square, and also received £100 in that year for chimney-pieces for Colonel Scott, of Charlton, Kent (Notebook of Henry Holland, Soane Museum).

As an architect Dixon designed Battersea Church, built between 1775 and 1777, where he was buried "without a fee" in the crypt in 1787 (J. G. Taylor's *Our Lady of Batersey*), nine years after he had been declared a bankrupt (*London Magazine*, 1778, page 190).

In 1764 one of his pupils was John Carter, who later made a name for himself as an architectural draughtsman, and who in 1768 began to make drawings for Henry Holland, the employer of his former master (*Builder*, 1850, page 303).

DOE, JOHN, of London

d. 1772

Chief assistant to Anthony Hart (q.v.), he carved a number of marble chimney-pieces for Dudley North, of Glenham Hall, Suffolk. His contract, dated March, 1722–1723, stated that "Mr. Doe shall do all the chimneys in the house at Glenham as Mr. North shall order at 5 shs. a foot, and the marble paving in ye middle of ye chapell at 2 shs. a foot." The rooms for which chimney-pieces were made included "The Great Roome," "Roome next ye Chapell," and the "Roome next ye Great stairs." In 1727 Doe also carved the capitals of the gate piers. (North Archives.)

DORMAN, JOSEPH, of Chelmsford

fl. 1801–1840

From 1801 until 1813 he acted as foreman to G. Wray, a mason of Chelmsford, but in the latter year set up for himself. He signs tablets to the Rev. William Harty, 1823, at Great Leighs, Essex, and to John Poole, 1839, at Bovinger in the same county.

D'ORSAY, COUNT ALFRED

b. 1801, *d.* 1852

It is difficult to assess d'Orsay's work as a sculptor, for it has always been hinted that he employed "ghosts" to execute most of his work. The *Art*

Journal, in its obituary of Thomas Henry Nicholson (1870, page 204), states definitely that it was Nicholson who carved for the Count, and that he used to leave the studio when visitors were announced. The same article also mentions that he used to complain bitterly of his employer's attempts at modelling, which apparently took him weeks to correct. W. Behnes (q.v.), when in need of money, is also said to have assisted d'Orsay, but on the other hand, it is only fair to add that the latter's supporters always maintained, not only that he did all his work unaided, but that it equalled, if it did not surpass, the productions of professional sculptors.

D'Orsay exhibited at the Royal Academy, 1843–1848, and in the following year (when he and Lady Blessington left England) a number of his works were included in the sale held at Gore House. These were bronze busts of Lord Lyndhurst, Lord Brougham, the Emperor of Austria, and Count d'Orsay the elder; marble busts of Wellington, Sir F. Grant and Lady Blessington; bronze statuettes of Louis Napoleon (afterwards the Emperor Napoleon III), the Emperor of Russia, and Daniel O'Connell; a marble statuette of Jenny Lind; and equestrian statuettes of Wellington and Napoleon Bonaparte.

DOVELL, N., of Barnstaple

He signs a tablet to Augustus Willett, 1813, at Westleigh, Devon.

DOWYER, JOHN

An entry made in 1726 in the private account book of the first Duke of Kent (Archives, Lady Lucas and Dingwall) reads: "Paid Dowyer, the carver, third payment, on account of Lord Harold's monument, £40"; a fourth payment of £20 is later noted in the same book.

The monument referred to is in Flitton Church, Bedfordshire, and consists of a life-size reclining figure on a sarcophagus. The workmanship is generally clumsy, the attitude of the figure is awkward and the head is too big for the body; in fact, the only features of the monument worth noting are the curious feet of the sarcophagus, which are in the form of eagle's claws. It seems strange that the Duke should have engaged so obscure and second-rate a sculptor to execute the monument to his deeply loved, only surviving son.

DRAPER, JOHN

In 1746 he was working at Welbeck Abbey, and with his partner, William Wilson, carved "a large ornament with festoons of fruit and flowers and a keystone with a lion's head in front" (Archives, Duke of Portland)

DRAWATER, JAMES
fl. 1766–1775

Drawater, who was described as "of St. Mary le Bonne, Middlesex, mason," became a bankrupt in 1770 (*London Magazine*, 1770, page 112), but apparently continued in business, for he was the mason employed six years later on repairs to Sir John Griffin's London house (Essex Record Office, D./DBY.A.1./27). He also signs the tablet to Richard Canning, 1775, in St. Helen's, Ipswich. As a contractor he built two houses in Harrow Road in 1768 (Middlesex Building Affidavits).

His father could have been the "Barnwall Drawater, mason" employed in 1747 by the Hon. George Fox at his house in Cavendish Square (Archives, Bramham Park).

DREW, —, of London

He signs a tablet with charming details to Mrs. Lloyd, 1767, in Marylebone Chapel.

DREW, CHARLES, of Bedford
d. 1826

Between 1808 and 1812 he was the mason responsible for building Moggenhanger House, Bedfordshire, from designs by Sir John Soane. He also worked as a statuary and his tablets usually have carefully carved details. Examples of these in Bedfordshire include those to Henry Sharp, 1791, at Flitton; William Edwards, 1800, at Arlesey; Carter Shavington, 1805, at Kempton; and John Osborn, 1814, at Campton. Drew also signs others in Buckinghamshire to Alexander Small, 1816, at Clifton-Reynes, and to John Higgins, 1819, at Weston Underwood.

(Soane Archives.)

DREW, THOMAS, of Bury St. Edmunds

In 1706 he made the black-marble monumental ledger of Isabella, Countess of Bristol, in Ickworth Church, Suffolk (Account-book, first Earl of Bristol).

DREWETT, WILLIAM, of Bristol
fl. 1789–1810

He apparently had various partners for, although he signs most of his monuments alone, others are signed "Jones, Dunn and Drewett" or "Dunn and Drewett." His monument to Mary Teast, 1790, at Henbury, Glos, is about 14 ft. high and has a figure of "Hope," while that of Sir Robert Mackworth, 1794, at Neath, Glamorgan, has a large draped sarcophagus.

Tablets signed by this firm include those commemorating Morgan Evans, 1789, at Lydney, Gloucestershire; Samuel Webb, 1799, at Widford, Somerset; Hannah Hughes, 1799, in St. Mary Redcliffe, Bristol; Eleanor Kemeys, 1803, at Newport, Monmouth; William Wheeler, 1803, in St. Augustine's, Bristol; and John Lloyd, 1810, in Carmarthen Parish Church. In 1794 Drewett agreed with John Colby to build for £84 a Painswick-stone staircase for Ffynone House, Pembroke, and to supply a marble chimney-piece for £5 17s. 6d. (Colby Archives).

DREWIT, HENRY

He was the son of Henry Drewit (or Druit), who was apprenticed to John Cooper in 1721, and the grandson of Henry Druit, "stone-carver" of Goodman's Fields. In 1763 he received a premium from the Society of Arts for an "ornamental tablet in clay."

DRUIT, JOSEPH, of London
fl. 1825-1827

His tablet to the Townsend family, erected in 1826, is at Godmanchester, Hunts. Druit is listed as a "statuary" in the *London Directory* of 1827.

DU CHAIME, GIDEON

During the building of Castle Howard, Yorkshire, he received, in 1706, £53 for carved stonework (Castle Howard Archives).

DUCKETT, THOMAS, of Preston
b. 1804, *d.* 1878

He was a self-taught artist, the son of a farmer and a native of Preston, who first worked as an apprentice to a local plasterer. However, he soon changed his occupation for that of wood-carver to a firm of cabinet-makers, and later went to Liverpool where he was employed by Messrs. Franceys (q.v.), and exhibited a bust of the Rev. J. Dunn at the Liverpool Academy in 1828. From there he moved to Kendal and joined the firm of Webster (q.v.) of that town, ultimately becoming manager of their sculptural department. His first large work was the "St. George and the Dragon" in limestone for the pediment of Kendal Roman Catholic Church in New Road. Shortly afterwards he returned to Preston and lived there until his death in 1878.

Duckett did a good deal of work in his native town and in 1838 won a prize for a design for a statue of John Horrocks. In 1846 he executed the carved stonework on the front of the Literary and Philosophical Institute and, in 1851, made a statue of Sir Robert Peel in Westmorland limestone, the general effect of which was "injured by the incongruous character of the drapery of the lower limbs" (Hardwicke's *History of Preston*, 1858, page 434). He also carved a marble altar for St. Augustine's Church.

Duckett also made a group of two children over the entrance to an infants' school in Lancaster, and designed and executed in plaster a colossal seated statue of Sir Richard Arkwright. This was eventually demolished as no funds were available to carve it in marble. The sculptor competed for the statues of Peel for Bolton, and the Duke of Wellington for Leeds, but in neither case was his model selected.

Duckett's bust of Thomas German (1851) is in Preston Town Hall, and in the Art Gallery are those of T. B. Addison (1844), the Rev. Robert Harris (1845), Thomas German (1847), William Taylor (1852), John Addison (1861), Thomas Miller (1870) and Miles Myres (1874). His tablets to T. Lowndes (1854) and Thomas Hart (1861) are respectively in the churches of St. George and St. John. Outside Preston he signs tablets to Richard Gell (1841), at Walton-le-Dale, and Giles Thornton (1860), at Poulton-le-Fylde, Lancashire, while the large marble coat of arms of the Brockholes family in the same church is also his work. (Information, Preston Public Library.)

DUDLEY, CORNELIUS,
of Bristol

He signs the monument to Anna Maria, daughter of Morgan Lloyd, 1738, at Llangadock, Carnarvon.

DUGDALE, THOMAS
fl. 1677–1678

In 1678 he carved in stone "four sculpture or figures" for the top of Sir Kenrick Eyton's house at Wrexham and, in the same year, executed the magnificent panelling of the long gallery at Chirk Castle. This is still in its original position, although the "fifteen capitals" previously made for the drawing-room by Dugdale in 1677 were removed during a Georgian restoration (Myddelton Archives).

He may be the same "Thomas Dugdale, of Liverpool, carver," whose will was proved in 1714.

DUNBAR, DAVID, the Elder,
of Carlisle
fl. 1815–1838

Dunbar was living in London in 1815, but two years later removed to Carlisle, where he apparently spent the rest of his life. He exhibited at the Royal Academy, 1815–1823, and at the Northern Society's Exhibition at Leeds in 1826 showed a statue of Mr. W. Hey and a bust of "Isis," while two years later he showed figures of "A Sleeping Child" and "Love." In 1829 he exhibited "A Nymph" at the Birmingham Society of Artists.

Dunbar's statue of Robert Williamson (1835) is in Newcastle Cathedral and that of the Rev. Robert Gray (1838) at Sunderland. His bust of the Earl of Lonsdale (1834) was formerly at Lowther Castle. He also signs monuments to the Rev. Edward Stanley, 1834, at Workington, Cumberland; Robert Anderson, 1833, Carlisle Cathedral; Elizabeth Connell, 1825, St. Cuthbert's, Carlisle; and the Rev. Alexander Scott, with a portrait bust, at St. Michael's, Dumfries. In Carlisle Cathedral is the small sleeping figure of the artist's infant daughter who died in 1825, and a similar monument commemorates Edith Dunbar (also a daughter of the artist?) in St. Michael's, Dumfries.

DUNBAR, DAVID, the Younger
d. 1866

Son of David Dunbar the Elder (q.v.), he went to study in Rome, and on his return to England was employed by Sir Francis Chantrey (q.v.). He later went to Newcastle, where he lived for some years, but came back to London about 1840. In 1844 he exhibited a statue of Robert Burns in Westminster Hall, which "would have been very pleasing," according to the *Literary Gazette* of that year (page 482), "had the execution been equal to the intention."

In 1850 Dunbar carved the recumbent figure of Miss Catherine Losh in Wreay Church, Cumberland, while in the following year he repaired some of the statues on the exterior of St. Mary's, Oxford.

He exhibited at the Royal Academy, 1840–1859, where his busts included one of Sir Martin Foulkes in 1844. He also made another of Alderman Wilson, which is now at Gateshead, but his most popular works were the medallions and busts (of which he executed a number of replicas) of Grace Darling and her father, William.

(*Builder*, 1866, page 638; *Art Journal*, 1866, page 320.)

DUNCKLEY, SAMUEL,
of Warwick

About 1757 John Sabin, the Parish Clerk of St. Mary's Collegiate Church, Warwick, wrote a "brief description" of the building, in which he mentioned that Dunckley, "a poor mason of Warwick," "designed, carved, built and finished that August Frontispiece in the Gothic Taste" in 1704. He is, of course, referring to the entrance to the Beauchamp Chapel in the south transept of the church.

DUNN, CHARLES, of Greenwich
d. 1762

He assisted his father, Thomas Dunn (q.v.), and, after the latter's death in 1746, carried on the family business. Under Dance the Elder he was the master-mason for building Shoreditch Parish Church, the foundation-stone of which was laid on 15 November, 1736 (*Gentleman's Magazine*, 1736, page 682).

In 1757 Dunn became a bankrupt (*London Magazine*, 1757, page 44), but a year later he was working with his partner, John Townesend— son of his father's old partner, John Townesend of London (q.v.)—on repairs at Greenwich Palace (P.R.O. Ad. MS. 68/767). Dunn's death is recorded in the Court Minute-book of the Masons' Company.

DUNN, THOMAS
b. c. 1676, *d.* 1746

Apprenticed to David Farmer, of Southwark, in 1692, he became free in 1699 and was Renter-Warden of the Masons' Company in 1722. As a mason-contractor he was much employed by Nicholas Hawksmoor and built the churches of Spitalfields, 1714–1729, and St. Mary Woolnoth, 1716–1727, being assisted in both cases by his partner, Thomas Bray. In 1710 he was the mason for Clapham Church (Churchwardens' Accounts), and in 1729 built the church of Stratford-le-Bow.

Dunn did a considerable amount of work at Greenwich Palace, where he and his partner, John Townesend the Younger (q.v.), built the south, north, north-east and north-west pavilions of Queen Anne's Court between 1729 and 1731 (P.R.O. A.D. 68/708–710). In 1720 he had been appointed mason to the Grocers' Company (Company's Archives); in 1739 he was one of the mason-contractors for the Mansion House.

In 1729 he was paid £37 by "Mr. Hayes" for building a wall and balustrade for a house at Wimbledon. (Surrey Records 19/20/100.) This must have been a large work as the iron railings and gate cost £65.

As a statuary Dunn is of considerable importance. He signs two monuments, the first to Edward Peck, 1736, at Christ Church, Spitalfields, which has a fine portrait-bust; and the second to Edward Colman, 1739, at Brent Eleigh, Suffolk, which is a dramatic and important work with its life-sized reclining figure in an elaborate architectural setting.

He also made a number of chimney-pieces, including fourteen for the north-west pavilion of Greenwich Hospital (P.R.O. A.D. 68/709); one of Dr. Mead's apartments at the Royal College of Physicians in 1732 (Archives, Royal College of Physicians); and one in 1733 for Mr. Benjamin Hoare, of Boreham Hall, Essex, which cost £43 (Archives, Hoare's Bank).

Dunn's yard was in Blackman Street, Southwark. He died on 30 April, 1746 (*Gentleman's Magazine*, 1746, page 272).

DURANT, JOHN
fl. 1757–1774

He was apprenticed to J. Wilton (q.v.) and later employed by Chrashley or Crashley (q.v.). In 1757 he sent a model of "Marsyas" to the Society of Arts and in 1774 exhibited an alto-relievo of "Minerva Judging the Arts" at the Society of Artists.

DURANT, MISS SUSAN
d. 1873

She first studied sculpture in France under the Baron de Triqueti, but had then no intention of adopting it as a profession. However, she later changed her mind and was a frequent exhibitor at the Royal Academy from 1847 until her death. She was also one of Queen Victoria's favourite sculptors, and not only made busts and medallions of the Royal Family, but was also permitted for a time to take Princess Louise, Duchess of Argyll, as a pupil in her studio. In 1856 and 1857 she assisted her old master, the Baron de Triqueti (1804–1874), to execute the monument of Leopold, King of the Belgians (uncle of the Queen), for St. George's Chapel, Windsor (now Esher), and carved for it a number of portrait-medallions.

In 1851 Miss Durant showed statues of "The Chief Mourner" and "Belisarius" at the Great Exhibition. In 1857 she lent her statue of "Robin Hood" to the exhibition of Art Treasures of the United Kingdom, held in Manchester, and in 1863 made a figure of "The Faithful Shepherdess" for the Mansion House. Her medallions of the Prince Consort and Queen Victoria, now at Windsor Castle, were executed in 1860 and 1866 respectively, and she also carved a bust of the Queen for the Inner Temple in 1872.

Miss Durant exhibited various works at the Royal Academy, 1847–1873, including "Negligent Watch-boy of the Vineyards Catching Locusts" in 1858 and "Ruth" in 1869, the former being described by the *Art Journal* as an "elaborate and very admirable composition." Among her busts were those of Miss Allwood (1847), Daniel Harvey (1851), a self-portrait (1853), Mrs. Beecher Stowe (1857), Lady Killeen (1858) and the Baron de Triqueti (1864). She also exhibited at the British Institution in 1860. She died in Paris on 1 January, 1873.

DURHAM, JOSEPH
b. 1814, *d.* 1877

Durham, who was born in London and apprenticed to J. Francis (q.v.), worked in the studio of E. H. Baily (q.v.) after becoming free, and first exhibited at the Royal Academy in 1835.

In 1858 his model of "Britannia Presiding Over the Four Quarters of the Globe" was awarded the first prize in a competition to select a memorial for the Great Exhibition, and in 1863 he executed a statue of the Prince Consort. This was first erected in the gardens of the Royal Horticultural Society, but later placed on the front of the Albert Hall. In the following year came his group entitled "Santa Filomena," which included a figure of Florence Nightingale, while in 1871 he made the memorial of the Building Committee for the Freemasons' Hall. His statue of "Sunshine" was shown at the Exhibition of Art Treasures of the United Kingdom held in Manchester in 1857.

He also made a number of fountains, including those at St. Lawrence Jewry in 1866; Somerleyton Hall, Suffolk, in 1868; and Gloucester Gate, Regent's Park, in 1878.

Durham exhibited no less than one hundred and twenty-eight works at the Royal Academy between 1835 and 1878, the last being shown after his death. He was elected an Associate of the Academy in 1868 and died in London after a long illness in 1877. His pair of statues, "Master Tom" and "Miss Ellie," fetched 180 guineas at the sale of his works, held at Christie's on 18 March of the following year, while a similar sum was paid for his group of "The Sirens and the Drowned Leander." Other works of his were later sold at Christie's, including "Go To Sleep" at the Joseph Arden sale of 26 April, 1879; "The First Dip" at the Edward Brooke sale of 4 March, 1882; and "At the Spring" at the Joseph Harrison sale of 10 May, 1884. The prices in each case were 120 guineas, 200 guineas and 220 guineas respectively.

(Various references, *Art Journal* and *Builder*; *Athenaeum*, 3 November, 1877.)

STATUES

1859	Caxton	For Westminster Palace Hotel
1861	Frank Crossley	Halifax
1863	Prince Consort	Guernsey

1865	Prince Consort	Agricultural College, Framlingham
1866	Queens Victoria, Anne, Elizabeth	Record Office
1867	Mary and Richard Redhead	Exhibited Royal Academy
1867	Stephenson and Euclid	University Museum, Oxford
1867	Lord John Scott	Dunchurch
1869	Newton, Milton, Bentham and Harvey	Façade of Burlington House

IDEAL WORKS AND GROUPS

1849	Il Penseroso	Exhibited Royal Academy
1858	Hermione	Mansion House
1860	Chastity	*Illustrated Art Journal*, 1860
1862	Go to Sleep	For F. Bennoch
1865	Alastor	Mansion House
1866	Waiting for his Innings	City of London School
1868	Peace	For G. Fox, of Harefield, Cheshire
1868	Paul and Virginia	Exhibited Royal Academy
1870	Perdita and Florizel	Walker Art Gallery, Liverpool
1871	Hero	For G. Fox, of Harefield, Cheshire

BUSTS

1848	Sir Frederick Pollock	Exhibited Royal Academy
1848	Jenny Lind	Exhibited Royal Academy
1849	Thomas Hunt	Exhibited Royal Academy
1850	Captain R. J. Elliott	For the Sailors' Home, Wells Street
1850	F. W. L. Ross	Art Gallery, Exeter
1856	Queen Victoria	Guildhall (destroyed 29 September, 1940)
1857	Thomas Hall	Guildhall (destroyed 29 September, 1940)

1857	W. H. Smith	Exhibited Royal Academy
1859	Sir Edward Sabine	Royal Society
1862	Prince Consort	Guildhall (destroyed 29 September, 1940)
1863	James Bunning	Guildhall (destroyed 29 September, 1940)
1864	Lady Beatrice Clinton	Exhibited Royal Academy
1864?	W. M. Thackeray	Garrick Club
1866	The Duke of Newcastle	Exhibited Royal Academy
1867	Lord Palmerston	Guildhall (destroyed 29 September, 1940)
1867	Lord Romilly	Record Office
1869	Leigh Hunt	Chelsea Town Hall (replica at Kensal Green)
1870	Sir George Pollock	National Portrait Gallery
1871	Mr. Havers	For Freemasons' Hall
1874	Charles Knight	National Portrait Gallery
1875	Rev. John Barlow	Royal Institution
1875	Hogarth	Leicester Square
1876	Edward Wakefield	Colonial Office
1876	Sir William Grave	Exhibited Royal Academy
1877	Thomas Webster, R.A.	Exhibited Royal Academy

MONUMENTS

| 1861 | Madras (Cathedral) | Thomas Dealtry, Bishop of Madras |
| 1874 | Bushey, Herts (churchyard) | William Jerdan |

DURRANT, EUSTACE

He was apprenticed to G. Hart, of London, but set up for himself in Ipswich in 1735, announcing in the *Ipswich Gazette* that he made "monuments, gravestones, coats of arms and chimney-pieces of the newest fashion," and that he was also prepared to make "designs for any manner of building at reasonable rates."

E

EAMES, or EMES, M., of Exeter
fl. 1788–1812

Though his tablets feature rather too often the draped urn against a pyramid, he was a careful, if uninspired, craftsman. Towards the end of his career he went into partnership with W. Stephens (q.v.), and was succeeded in the business by his son, W. Eames, who signs a tablet to Elizabeth Penton, 1829, at Bampton, Devon.

Tablets signed by Eames in the same county include those to Richard Blake, 1788, at Farway; Rebecca Burrows, 1792, at Tawstock; Margaret Graham, 1794, at Littleham; Samuel Needham, 1797, at Dawlish; Egerton Filmore, 1799, at Lympson; and William Holmes, 1812, at Shobroke. His tablet to Lady Charlotte Carr, 1801, is at Menheniot, Cornwall.

EARLE, JOHN, of Hull
b. 1779, *d.* 1863

Earle was born in Hull, where he seems to have spent most of his life and for which he executed a number of works. In 1830 he carved the relief of the "Sea and River Gods" for Smith's Bank in Whitefriars Gate, and a statue of Dr. Alderton for the Mechanics' Institute, while in the following year he made a relief of "Oceanus" for the Trinity Almshouses.

He was also responsible for a number of monuments and tablets, the best commemorating the Etherington family, 1819, in North Ferriby Church, Yorkshire; a work executed in coloured marbles and having delightful decorative details. Other signed works by Earle in the same county include those to Henry Maister, 1812, in Holy Trinity, Hull; John Foster, 1816, and the Rev. Robert Todd, 1830, both at North Cave; George Gibson, 1821, at Sigglethorne; and Mary Howard, 1838, at Sutton-on-Hull. He also made the tablets commemorating Harriot Abbey, 1810, at Aswarby, Lincolnshire, and the Rev. John Beevor, 1820, at Staunton-in-the-Vale, Nottinghamshire.

(Sheahan's *History of Hull.*)

EARLE, THOMAS
b. 1810, *d.* 1876

He was born in Hull, the son of John Earle (q.v.), and in 1830 went to London, where he was employed by Chantrey (q.v.). In 1832 he attended the Royal Academy Schools, and in 1839 was awarded the Gold Medal for a group entitled "Hercules Rescuing Hesione." He later returned to Chantrey and, when the latter died in 1841, finished the equestrian statue of George IV for Trafalgar Square, which had already been partially modelled.

In 1844 Earle exhibited at Westminster Hall "An Ancient Briton Protecting His Family," a work much admired by the *Literary Gazette* (1844, page 483) which considered that nothing could "surpass the arrangement and composition of the female and children, the modelling of the young ones most exquisite and masterly." At the same time Earle showed "Edward I Presenting the Prince of Wales," and both groups were afterwards purchased by George Gee, of Hull. At a second exhibition, held at Westminster Hall in the following year, the sculptor showed "Sin Triumphant," the idea of which was "original, but not very happily realized," according to the *Art Union* (1845, page 258).

Earle exhibited at the Royal Academy, 1843–1873, and at the British Institution, 1843–1865, but many of his works were rejected, and it is said he died of a broken heart on hearing that his "Alexander the Great" (which had taken him three years to execute) had not been accepted by the Royal Academy. As a writer in *The Times*, (3 May, 1876) put it: "His death was a melancholy termination to the career of an artist who for nearly forty years had been before the public and most creditably."

A number of Earle's works were lost when Hull Central Museum was destroyed by enemy action in 1943. These included "Alexander Before Mounting Bucephalus" and "Genius Receiving the Award of Merit." He is commemorated in Holy Trinity, Hull, by a large monument of his own workmanship, which has a fine relief of a mourning mother and daughter.

(*Art Journal*, 1876, page 236.)

STATUES

1843	Miss Todd	For Tranby Park, Yorks
1861	Queen Victoria	Hull
1863	Prince Consort	Licensed Victuallers' Asylum, Kennington
1864	Harold	Mansion House
1866	Edward I	Hull

GROUPS, etc.

1845	The Morning Ablution	Exhibited Manchester Institution

1847	Pastorella	Exhibited Royal Academy
1851	Ophelia	Exhibited Great Exhibition
1852	L'Allegro	Exhibited National Exhibition
1853	Happy as a Queen	For the Earl of Yarborough

BUSTS

1837	James Brothers	Exhibited Royal Academy
1843	John Todd	Exhibited Royal Academy
1845	Richard Bethell	Exhibited Royal Academy
1846	Earl of Zetland	Minerva Lodge, Hull
1848	Earl of Yarborougl	Exhibited Royal Academy
1850	Samuel Warren	Exhibited British Institution
1854	Rt. Hon. Thomas Sydney	Exhibited Royal Academy
1861	Queen Victoria	Buckingham Palace
1867	Thomas Teale	General Infirmary, Leeds

MONUMENTS

1832	Kirk Ella, Yorks	The Sykes family
1833	Barsham, Suffolk	Elizabeth Flavell
1834	Hull (Holy Trinity)	Ann Earle
1835	South Cave, Yorks	Mary Burland
1840	Hull (St. Mary's)	Joseph Pease
1845	Sculcoates (St. Mary's)	Charles Bamford the Elder
1846	Lea, Lincs	Sir Charles Anderson
1850	Hull (Holy Trinity)	Alderman Ferres (with a fine relief)
1858	Hull (Holy Trinity)	John Gray
1860	Sculcoates (St. Mary's)	Charles Bamford
1860	Sculcoates (St. Mary's)	John Holmes
1860	Hull (Holy Trinity)	John Appleyard

EARLEY, JOHN

In 1762, when "under twenty-two," he won a premium from the Society of Arts. He lived at Datchet and modelled a number of tablets for chimney-pieces (Archives, Society of Arts).

EARLEY, or EARLY, THOMAS

He was presumably a brother of John Earley (q.v.) and, when "under nineteen," won a premium from the Society of Artists for a model of "Neptune." He afterwards worked for Thomas Carter (q.v.).

EARLSMAN, RICHARD, the Elder, of Salisbury

fl. 1730–1750

He was employed on stone- and wood-carving at Longford Castle between 1737 and 1750. In 1742 he received £8 for "ye carving over ye green damask door," while in 1750 he was paid £16 for "several ornaments." His father, Edward Earlsman, was paid for carving "urns and a mitre" for Salisbury Cathedral in 1713 (Cathedral Archives).

EARLSMAN, RICHARD, the Younger, of Salisbury

b. 1745, *d.* 1831

Son of Richard Earlsman the Elder (q.v.), he was also employed as a mason at Longford Castle between 1776 and 1792, and in 1796 was working as a stone-carver at Salisbury Cathedral. He died in 1831 and is buried in St. Martin's, Salisbury.

Earlsman signs a monument to Sir Alexander and Lady Powell, 1786, in St. Thomas's, Salisbury. Other signed works by him commemorate Samuel Foot, 1792, and Philip Pinchnay, 1807, both at Berwick St..John, Wilts, and Edward Doyle, 1795, in All Saints, Colchester, Essex.

EASTON, CHARLES

d. 1786

Charles Easton, who was the son of Robert Easton (q.v.), became free of the Masons' Company by redemption in 1728, and was Upper Warden in 1753 and Master in the following year. He succeeded his father as mason to the Fishmongers' Company and later became City Mason in 1762. In this capacity he was employed on various repairs to the Mansion House between 1762 and 1777. His death in 1786 is noted in the Court Book of the Masons' Company.

In 1730 he was paid £50 for the monument, in Rochester Cathedral, to Richard Watts, which had a portrait-bust, a copy of an earlier work (Archives, Watts Charity, Rochester). He also signs monuments to Thomas Lewis (*d.* 1722) in All Hallows, Twickenham, and Richard Ansell (*d.* 1726) at Ickleworth, Herts, and Rev. G. Morton, 1722, St. Margaret's, Lothbury.

EASTON, ROBERT

d. 1722

Easton, who was apprenticed to Charles Cotton, had a yard in Bow Street, Covent Garden, in 1708. He was mason to the Fishmongers' Company, for whom he executed in 1721 a marble statue of Mr. James Hulbert for their almshouses at Newington. The payments for this are entered in the accounts of the Prime Warden and the first one reads: "Paid Robert Easton in part for the effigie of Mr. Hulbert to be set up in the New Square £80." The second, made after Easton's death in 1722, is to "the widow Easton in full of the Company's agreement with her late husband for the marble effigies (*sic*) of the late Mr. Hulbert set up in the square £102 10s." In 1724 a "Mr. Skeat" was paid £7 for "ironwork set round the effigie" (Guildhall MS. 5561/3 and 5561/4).

The statue, a fine work showing Hulbert (who founded the Newington Almshouses) in contemporary costume, stood "on a pedestal in the centre of the enclosure," according to Walford's *London* (Vol. VI, page 258), which describes the buildings as "a neat and imposing little pile consisting of three courts with gardens behind, together with a dining-hall and chapel." In 1851, however, they were pulled down and the inmates taken to new accommodation at Wandsworth. The statue remained there until 1923, when it was removed to the Company's almshouses at Bray, where it still stands. At some period the lettering on the base and the sculptor's signature must have been re-cut, for the latter now appears as "Daston."

Easton's widow, Mary, to whom the second payment for the figure was made, seems to have carried on the business after her husband's death, for a Robert Green was apprenticed to her in 1727.

EASTON, THOMAS
b. 1704

Son of Robert Easton (q.v.), and brother of Charles Easton (q.v.), he was bound to his father in 1718, but on the latter's death in 1722 finished his apprenticeship with Bartholomew Woolfe. He became free in 1724, his mother, "Mary Easton, widow, testifying for his service," and set up for himself "against the Weigh House, Little Eastcheap" (Archives, Masons' Company). He signs the monument to Sir Edward Betenson, 1733, at Chislehurst, Kent.

In 1756 Robert Easton, Thomas's son, was apprenticed, not to his father, but to Charles Easton, which seems as if the former were already dead. Robert became free of the Masons' Company in 1763.

ECKSTEIN, GEORGE PAUL
b. 1739, *d.* 1828

He was born at Poppenruth in Germany, but left for the Hague in 1760, and five years later came to London. Here he settled in Marylebone, and in 1770 married in Faversham Church a Miss Ann Mitchell of that parish. The two elder children of their family of twelve were born at Ospringe, in the same district, the others in London.

Eckstein, who died in London in 1828, exhibited at the Royal Academy, 1777–1802, showing various reliefs in marble and wax, and also models of animals. About 1775 he made two greyhounds in Portland stone for Ashburnham House in Dover Street. These were later moved to Ashburnham Place in Sussex, where they still remain.

ECKSTEIN, JOHN
b. 1735, *d.* 1818

Elder brother of G. P. Eckstein (q.v.), he visited England as a young man and remained there for seven years, winning a premium from the Society of Arts in 1761 for his relief of "The Death of Epaminondas," which he exhibited at the Society for the Encouragement of Arts in the following year (*London Magazine*, 1762, page 173). In 1764 he was awarded a further premium for a marble relief of "The Rape of Cassandra." During this period of his life Eckstein worked for Thomas Carter (q.v.), and together they made the monument of Lieut.-Colonel Roger Townshend (who had died in 1759) in Westminster Abbey, Eckstein being responsible for the relief, a work which Flaxman considered one of the best pieces of sculpture in the church.

In 1765 Eckstein accepted an invitation from Frederick the Great to go to Prussia, where he became the King's principal sculptor and executed numerous works at Potsdam and Sans Souci. He was next employed by the Duke of Mecklenburg, who in 1770 sent him to England on a special mission. Here he met with a most flattering reception and exhibited wax portraits both at the Royal Academy and the Society of Artists. On the conclusion of his mission he returned to the Grand Ducal Court at Ludwigs Lust and stayed there until 1774. He then went back to Prussia and remained at Potsdam until the death of Frederick the Great in 1786.

In 1794 Eckstein emigrated with his family to America and settled in Philadelphia, where he lived until 1818, and where in 1812 he exhibited a model of an equestrian statue of George Washington in Roman costume (Dunbar's *History of the Arts in the United States*, Vol. II, page 149). In 1818 he set out for Cuba, but died as soon as he had reached Havana. His last recorded work was a marble bust of Swedenborg.

John Deare, in a letter written in 1780 and quoted by J. T. Smith in *Nollekens and His Times* (Vol. II, page 238), refers to "a German," who had been employed by Carter and who had worked with Deare to make a proof sketch in clay in competition for the Gold Medal, offered annually by the Royal Academy for the best historical design. Deare goes on to say that the German "shamefully lost both in large model and sketch." Smith, in a footnote to this letter, says that "the German" was Eckstein. This is impossible.

Fifteen years earlier Eckstein had been in partnership with Carter (for both sign their names on the Townshend monument) and it seems quite incredible that in 1780 the former (who in any case was in Prussia) could have returned to England and be so forgotten that Carter's apprentice did not even know his name. It is equally impossible that he should have failed so miserably in a test set for apprentices by the Academy where he had triumphantly exhibited twenty years before.

Graves, in his *Royal Academy Exhibitors*, says that John Eckstein exhibited portraits at the Academy, 1787–1802. This should be his son, also John, who died in 1838.

(The information given in the sketches of George Paul and John Eckstein is taken from a privately printed but undated history of the Eckstein family by Louisa V. Adlerstein, daughter of G. P. Eckstein.)

EDMONDSON, J.

He exhibited bas-reliefs at the Royal Academy, 1790–1792, his address being given as 14, Warwick Street, Golden Square.

EDWARDS, ALEXANDER WILSON, of Wrexham
fl. 1806–1820

He signs charming wall-tablets in coloured marbles to William Travers, 1806, at Gresford, Denbigh; to Christiana Smith, 1811, at Holt, in the same county; and to Susan Price, 1813, at Overton, Flint.

EDWARDS, EDWARD
b. 1803, *d.* 1827 (?)

He attended the Royal Academy Schools in 1820 and gained a Silver Medal a year later. In 1823 he received from the Society of Arts their Gold Isis Medal for a group of "Ulysses and Calypso," while in 1824 he gained their large Silver Medal for another relief and the Silver Isis Medal for a bust.

Edwards exhibited at the Royal Academy 1825 and 1826, showing a bust and a relief of "David and Goliath." After this date there is no further trace of him.

EDWARDS, JOHN
fl. 1719–1722

Probably a native of Wrexham, he received £25 in 1719 for the "capitals and urns upon ye stone pillars by ye iron gates" at Chirk Castle. The "iron gates" are the famous pair which originally stood at the entrance of the north court of the Castle, but which were moved in the nineteenth century to form the main entrance to the Park.

Two years later Edwards also made for Chirk the stone pedestals for John Nost's (q.v.) lead figures of "Atlas" and "Hercules." Both these figures once stood in the north court, but "Atlas" has long disappeared and "Hercules" (with his pedestal) has now been banished to a hill in the Park (Archives, Chirk Castle).

EDWARDS, JOSEPH
b. 1814, *d.* 1883

He was born at Merthyr Tydfil, the son of a stone-cutter, and went to London in 1835. In 1837 he joined the Royal Academy Schools on the recommendation of Chantrey (q.v.) and won a Silver Medal in the following year.

Edwards's first important commission came in 1839 from the seventh Duke of Beaufort, who engaged him to execute the monument to the sixth Duke to be erected in Badminton Church. Both this work and the Hellenic altar in memory of Eleanor Estcourt (*d.* 1829) at Shipton Moyne, Gloucestershire, were carved by the sculptor from designs by T. H. Wyatt. In 1846 he made a statue of William Williams for Aberystwyth, and in 1866 the figure of "Religion" on the grave of Mrs. Vaughan in Highgate Cemetery. This last-named work was much admired in the Victoria era and was engraved for various periodicals.

Edwards showed three bas-reliefs at the Great Exhibition of 1851, where his work was praised by H. Weekes (q.v.), who wrote: "We have the highest possible respect for his talents; he rarely exhibits largely, but in all that he does there is a delicacy of feeling which indicates a refined mind. . . . We believe he is capable of great things and only requires to be brought forward more prominently to be appreciated as he deserves" (*Treatise on the Fine Arts in the Great Exhibition*, page 75). His relief of G. G. Ferrari (undated) is at Castle Howard.

At the Royal Academy he showed a number of busts between 1838 and 1878, including those of the Rev. John Guthrie (1845), Lord Raglan (1857), and Archdeacon Williams (1860). His bust of the Duke of Beaufort (1857) is at Badminton, those of Sir John Guest (1864) and G. T. Clerk (1873) are at Merthyr Tydfil, while that of Lord Palmerston (1867) is in Tiverton Town Hall.

A number of works by Edwards were engraved by the *Art Journal*, including "Religion Consoling Justice" (1856), "The Last Dream" (1858), "A Vision" (1864) and "The Spirit of Love and Truth" (1867). He died in London in 1883 and was buried in Kensal Green cemetery.

Signed monuments by Edwards include those to Lieut.-Colonel Henry Booth, 1841, at Northallerton, Yorks; Mrs. White, 1848, at Berechurch, Essex; William Hawkins, 1854, in St. Botolph's, Colchester; Sir J. Bosanquet, 1856, at Dingestow, Monmouth; Charles Bosanquet, 1856, at Rock, Northumberland; Charles Warren, 1857, at Market Drayton, Salop; Mrs. Morley, 1858, at Newton, Montgomery; Miss Hutton, 1858, at North Otterington, Yorks; the Duchess of Beaufort, 1859, at Badminton, Glos; Mrs. Davis, 1860, at Tredegar, Monmouth; Lewis Morgan, 1861, at Graig, Glamorgan; George Virtue, 1870, in Walton-on-Thames cemetery; and the Rev. Evan Owen, 1870, at Bryncoed-Ivor, North Wales. (Chilcott's *Bristol*, page 311; various references *Art Journal*.)

EGART, DANIEL
fl. 1762–1763

In 1763 he received a premium from the Society of Arts for a relief in marble of "Iphigenia Released," a work he had exhibited at the Society of Free Artists in the previous year, and of which he also made a replica in Portland stone.

EGLINGTON, —, of Birmingham

A large wall-tablet, about 10 ft. high with a pyramid and well-carved details, in the Parish Church of Aston, Birmingham, commemorates Edward Brandwood (*d.* 1731), and is signed "Eglington Snr. Birmingham." The sculptor is presumably the father of the Samuel Eglington "mason" who received £37 18s. for work carried out in the same church between 1789 and 1790 (Churchwardens' Accounts).

A "Joseph Eglington" of Birmingham made an Italian marble chimney-piece for Arbury, Warwickshire, in 1794 (Newdigate Archives).

EGLINGTON, JAMES, of Walsall

Probably a descendant of Eglington, of Birmingham (q.v.), he signs a tablet to Joanna Goodall, 1790, in Walsall Parish Church, Staffs.

ELDERTON, JAMES, of Southampton
fl. 1807–1827

He signs tablets (both in Hampshire) to Anna Lintott, 1807, at Woolston, and to the Rev. Charles Phillipson, 1826, at Eling. He was succeeded by his son, Charles Harben Elderton.

ELDREDGE, or ELDRIDGE, WILLIAM, of King's Lynn
b. 1749, *d.* 1819

He was the son of Joseph Eldredge, a mason who had been apprenticed to John Fellowes (q.v.) in 1725. He signs tablets (all in Norfolk) to Francis Dalton, 1796, at West Bilney; Ann Lancaster, 1805, at Pentney; William Benezet, 1814, at Swaffham; and to the Rev. Horace Hammond, 1815, at South Wooton.

ELLIOT, THOMAS, of Hull

He signs a tablet at Lawford, Essex, to Edward Green, *d.* 1814.

ELLIS, JOHN, of Portsea
fl. 1803–1835

He signs tablets to Solomon Ferris, 1803, at Southwick, Hants, and to Sir Thomas McMahon, 1835, in Portsmouth Cathedral.

ELLIS, WILLIAM
b. 1824, *d.* 1882

He was born in Sheffield and studied under Edward Law (q.v.), but went to London about 1850, where he was associated with Alfred Stevens. He later returned to his native city and set up on his own account as a sculptor, but the venture failed and he died in 1882 of "exhaustion, disappointed and in poverty" (Odom's *Hallamshire Worthies*).

Ellis's busts in Sheffield include those of Thomas Sale (1874) in the Cathedral, William Overend (1875) and Alfred Stevens (1876) in the Art Gallery, and Arthur Roebuck (1881) in the Cutlers' Hall. His bronze medallion of James Montgomery (1852) is also in the Art Gallery.

ELSWORTH, JOHN, of York
fl. 1703–1715

He and his partner, William Smith, were the chief masons for building Castle Howard between 1703 and 1714. They also built the bridge in the Park and the obelisk, receiving for these £80 and £168 respectively.

Their carved work at the house itself included the cornice and capitals of the cupola, "the south modilion cornich" for £137; vases on the north wing at £8 each; and some of the less important chimney-pieces (Archives, Castle Howard). (See also "Smith, William.")

EMETT, or EMMETT, WILLIAM
fl. 1680–1700

He was probably born in 1641, for he was aged about thirty when as a "citizen and joiner" he married Jane Brown at St. Margaret's Westminster, in 1671 (*Wren Society*, Vol. XIV, page xxiii). *Vertue* (*Walpole Society*, Vol. XVIII, page 129) notes that "William Emett was sculptor to the Crown before Gibbons," and that "Phillips, uncle to Emett, had that place before him."

Emett was employed on decorative carving in wood and stone at Whitehall, Kensington Palace, and Chelsea Hospital. He also worked at the Temple Church, St. Bartholomew-by-the-Exchange, St. Bride's, Fleet Street, and St. Mary Abchurch. In 1693 he carved for Whitehall the keystone in Portland stone "for the new portico to the waterstairs" (P.R.O., Works 5/46), and in the same year received £220 for work which he had carried out at Hampton Court. This included "eleven round windows of Portland stone with a compartment of lyons' skins and lorrell leaves" and "4 Keystones of Portland stone in the arches of the portico in Fountain Court." (P.R.O., Works 5/46.)

William had four younger brothers, including Maurice (*b.* 1645), bricklayer to the king; and Henry (*b. c.* 1657), a painter stainer (visitation of London, 1687). In the archives of General Norman, of Bromley is an account book kept by William Emett, son of Maurice, in which is noted: "My father Maurice Emmett dyed Monday ye 26th day of November, 1694, aetatis 49 and was buried on Friday the 30th of ye same month." William also records the death of his mother, Elizabeth, on 18 August, 1703, "aetatis sua 51 wanting six days." In William's inventory (1741) of his Bromley House is "in the study model of a house designed by my father Emmett."

ENGEL, J.
b. 1805

Engel, who was a pupil of W. Behnes (q.v.), attended the Royal Academy Schools in 1832. In 1846 he executed "The Amazon and the Argonaut" for the Prince Consort, who lent it to the Great Exhibition of 1851. He exhibited at the Academy, 1840–1847, showing works in ivory, and busts of Mr. Colnaghi (1844) and W. G. Rogers, the wood-carver (1845).

ENGLEHEART, THOMAS
b. 1745, *d.* 1786

Son of Francis Engleheart of Kew, and elder brother of George Engleheart, the miniature-painter, he attended the Royal Academy Schools in 1769. In 1771 he gained a Silver Medal, and in the following year won the Gold Medal, defeating Flaxman (q.v.) with a relief of "Ulysses and Nausica." In 1777 he was awarded a premium of twenty-five guineas by the Society of Arts for a model, 6 ft. high, of "John the Baptist in the Desert."

Engleheart exhibited at the Royal Academy, 1773–1786, showing a bust of Thomas Fluelling (1773) and portraits in wax. His wax portrait of Edward, Duke of Kent (1786), is in the National Portrait Gallery, while those of George III and Queen Charlotte are in the Royal Collection.

A "J. Engleheart," of Richmond, exhibited a wax portrait at the Academy in 1783.

ESSEX, CHARLES
fl. 1847–1853

He exhibited busts and medallions at the Royal Academy, 1847–1853, the busts, including those of Alfred Essex (1847); Captain Maconochie (1849); and William Essex, the painter (1852).

EVANS, E. F., of Derby
fl. 1797–1802

He was probably a son of Joseph Evans (q.v.), and his monuments in design and execution are better than those of the average provincial statuary of the time. Signed examples in Derbyshire include those to George Bansall, 1797, at Alfreton, and William Stevens, 1800, at Repton.

EVANS, ENEAS, of Derby
fl. 1761–1765

Evans, who may have been the father of Joseph Evans (q.v.), was working as assistant to J. Hall (q.v.) at Kedleston in 1761. In 1765 he made chimney-pieces of black and yellow marbles for some of the bedrooms (Curzon Archives).

EVANS, JOSEPH, of Derby

He signs a tablet with a finely fluted urn to Thomas Peach, 1770, at Dingley, Northants.

EWING, W, or EWINGS
fl. 1820–1825

In 1820 he was in Rome, where he carved ivory portraits of Canova and Pope Pius VII. Two years later he exhibited these, and other examples of his work in ivory, at the Royal Academy.

Ewins signs the monument to Owen Lewis, 1824, at Laugharne, Carmarthen; this has a fine relief of a mourning woman in the manner of Chantrey (q.v.).

EYKYN, ROGER,
of Wolverhampton
b. 1725, *d.* 1795

He signs a monument at Broseley, Salop, to Elizabeth Crompton, 1747, and a large undated one with a sarcophagus to George Weld at Willey in the same county.

F

FARMER, P. J.

He exhibited a bust of John de Vaere, the sculptor (q.v.), at the Royal Academy in 1826.

FARMER, RICHARD,
of Swindon

He was probably the son of James Farmer of Chippenham and was apprenticed to Richard Smith, mason, of the same town in 1719 (P.R.O. INL/1/6.)

He signs a very pretty marble cartouche-tablet to Jane Scholes, 1733, in St. Mary's, Marlborough.

FARRELL, JAMES
b. 1821, *d.* 1891

Son of Terence Farrell (q.v.), he studied in his father's studio in Dublin and first exhibited at the Royal Hibernian Academy in 1836. Most of his life was spent in Ireland, but he sent over works to the Royal Academy in London between 1843 and 1869. He was elected an Associate of the Royal Hibernian Academy in 1880, and a full member two years later. He died on 20 November, 1891.

For a list of his works in Ireland see Strickland's *Dictionary of Irish Artists.*

FARRELL, TERENCE
b. 1798, *d.* 1876

He was born at Creve, Co. Longford, and in 1810 was brought to Dublin, where he was placed in the modelling school of the Dublin Society, receiving instruction from the Irish sculptors, Edward and John Smyth. On leaving the school he entered the studio of Thomas Kirk (q.v.), first as a pupil for seven years and later as the sculptor's assistant.

About 1828 Farrell set up for himself. Most of his life was spent in Dublin and for a list of his works in Ireland see Strickland's *Dictionary of Irish Artists.*

Farrell's work in England includes four statues for Lord Petre's chapel at Thorndon Park, Essex; figures of the Seasons which were executed for Earl de Grey and placed on the terrace of Wrest Park, Bedfordshire; and groups of "Children and Dogs" and "Children and Goats" for the same patron, which are now at Studley Royal, Yorkshire. At the Great Exhibition of 1851 he showed "Early Sorrow."

Farrell signs the monuments of Lord Vivian, 1842, in Truro Cathedral, and of Henrietta, Countess de Grey, 1853, at Flitton, Bedfordshire. He was elected an Associate of the Royal Hibernian Academy in 1851 and a full member in 1859. He died on 19 March, 1876.

FARRINGTON, WILLIAM,
the Younger

A tablet in memory of Mary Farrington, 1715, in Brereton Church, Staffordshire, is signed "William Farrington, Jnr."

FARROW, THOMAS, of Diss
fl. 1824–1842

He signs the monument to Lady Sophia Macdonald, 1824, at Quidenham, Norfolk, and another to Susanna Frere at Roydon, Norfolk. In 1842 he married a "Mrs. Maskett," of Palgrave Place in the same county.

FAULKNER, MATHEW
of Twickenham

In 1725–1727 he carved chimney-pieces and decorative details for a house called "Little Deene" which was built in the grounds of Deene Park, Northants. It was a building of some pretensions with enriched ceilings, etc. Apparently Faulkner got into trouble as in the Brudenell accounts is a note about "poor Matt Faulkner's bill and letter from Prison" (Brudenell MSS ASR 118/209).

FELLOWS, JOHN,
of King's Lynn
fl. 1714–1742

As a "free stone-mason" he became a Freeman of his native town in 1714, and between 1714 and 1717 built the library at the west end of the south aisle of St. Margaret's Church, which was destroyed in 1874 (Town Archives).

In 1723 Fellows made the chimney-piece of black and grey marble (now in the smoking-room) for Rainham Hall, Norfolk. With John Parsons, of Wells, Norfolk, he built in 1742 the nave of St. Margaret's Church, King's Lynn, from designs by Matthew Brettingham. (Churchwardens' Accounts.)

He signs monuments to Vokes Walsham, 1714, and John Dickinson, 1730, both at Woodstone, Hunts, and to Richard Dashwood, 1738, at Cockley Cley, Norfolk.

FELLOWS, WILLIAM,
of King's Lynn
fl. 1721–1765

He was the son of John Fellows (q.v.) and was apprenticed to his father in 1721, becoming a Freeman of his native town in 1758. He signs monuments to William Browne (*d.* 1735) at Westacre, and to Christopher Adamson, 1765, at Wereham, Norfolk.

FENELLA, JOHN BAPTISTA

In the *Dom. Entry Book*, Car. II, Vol. IX, page 334, is a copy of the Royal Warrant (dated April, 1663) to John Baptista Fenella, "our sculptor," granting him "ye sum of £40 pr. ann. for and towards ye charge, and of providing a fit and necessary working-place, & other accommodations for ye performance of our service in his profession."

FENTIMAN, JOHN,
of Stoke Newington

In 1789 he received £4,116 for building Lewes Prison (Town Records).

FICKER, —, of Piccadilly

He exhibited a tablet for a chimney-piece at the Free Society of Artists in 1765.

FIELD, JOHN, of Hampstead

He signs tablets in Hampstead Parish Church dated 1825 and 1833.

FILLANS, JAMES
b. 1808, *d.* 1852.

He was born at Wilsontown, Lanarkshire, and was apprenticed in Paisley, first to the weaving trade and then to a stone-mason. He later moved to Glasgow, where, without studying under any master, he adopted sculpture as a profession, producing a number of successful busts and also carving the capitals of Glasgow Royal Exchange.

In 1835 he produced a small bust in wax of William Motherwell and also visited Paris, where he copied pictures in the Louvre. On his return to England in the following year he became acquainted with Allan Cunningham, whose bust he modelled and who introduced him to Chantrey (q.v.). The latter introduced Fillans to various patrons, including Archibald Oswald, and when Oswald was staying in Vienna the sculptor visited him there and executed his bust. From Vienna Fillans travelled in 1841 to Italy, where he spent some months. In 1848 he was living in Baker Street, London, and in the same year was entertained at Paisley on the occasion of the unveiling

of his statue of Sir James Shaw at Kilmarnock, being "invited to a public banquet" where "homage was rendered to him by all the leading persons of the town and neighbourhood" (*Art Union*, 1848, page 314).

Two years later Fillans returned to Glasgow, where he died on 27 September, 1852, of rheumatic fever, leaving a widow and eight children unprovided for. He was buried at Paisley, and the figure of "Grief," which he had designed for the grave of his father, was placed over his own. He exhibited at the Royal Academy, 1837–1850, and at the British Institution, 1847. At the Academy he showed busts of William Walkinshaw (1837), Mrs. Charles Tennant (1837), Allan Cunningham (1837), John Burnet (1840) and Robert Napier (1840). His busts of Archibald Campbell (1839) and Professor Wilson (1848) were executed for the County Hall, Paisley, and that of Colonel Mure (1848) for the County of Renfrew. He signs the monument to William Motherwell, 1851, at Glasgow Necropolis.

(*Art Journal*, 1852, page 350; *Building Chronicle*, 1854, Vol. I, page 114; *Gentleman's Magazine*, 1852, Part II, page 654.)

FINES, C.
fl. 1833–1846

He exhibited wax portraits at the Royal Academy, 1833–1846, including those of E. Jesse and Mr. Chabot.

FIRMADGE, WILLIAM,
of Leicester

b. 1755, *d.* 1836

He was a son of William Firmadge, "slater," and became a Freeman of Leicester in 1778. In 1809 he was Mayor of Leicester.

As a mason he built Leicester Gaol in 1792. His tablets have well-carved designs and he makes intelligent use of coloured marbles; his slate ledgers are equally good.

He signs tablets in Leicestershire to the Rev. Richard Wynne, 1778, at Gumley; to Henry Coleman, 1779, and to Miss Lee, 1792, both at Burton Overy; to John Rowland, 1790, at Enderby; to the Rev. Barton Shuttleworth, 1792, at Laughton; and to Anne Firmadge, 1793, at Scrapton. He also signs a tablet to William Kemp, 1787, at Belton, Rutland; and a ledger to Samuel Soames, 1792, at Rolleston, Staffordshire.

FISHER, JAMES, of Camberwell
b. 1682, *d.* 1722

The only signed work of his which I know is the

magnificent monument at Marholm, Northants, with its life-size standing figures of the First Earl Fitzwilliam and his wife, 1719.

The contract for this monument is in the Fitzwilliam (Milton) Collection of the Northamptonshire Record Society. It is endorsed: "Mr. Fisher the stone-cutter of Camberwell his bill and acquittance for making and setting up the monument at Marham Church and for the little monument at North Runcton Church in Norfolk." For this monument the sculptor received £900, and for the one in Norfolk £24 10s.

The contract is dated 28 August, 1718, and besides giving a full specification of the monument, also states that when finished the work is to be conveyed by Fisher to some "wharf or stairs below London Bridge and shipped and put on board some vessel at his own cost and charges." Fisher's witnesses are Richard Dixon and Robert Harper.

The sculptor died on 30 March, 1722, and was buried in Camberwell churchyard, but the tombstone commemorating him has since been destroyed (Seymour's *London*, Vol. II, page 833).

FISHER, JOHN, and CHARLES, of York

John Fisher: *b*. 1786

Charles Fisher: *b*. 1790, *d*. 1861

They were sons of John Fisher the Younger (q.v.) and carried on the family business, but their tablets are inferior to those produced by their father and grandfather. Charles became a bankrupt in 1823 (*European Magazine*, 1823, Part II, page 284).

The Fishers sign a number of tablets, the best in Yorkshire being those to Robert Hotham, 1806, in St. Dennis's, York; Mary Lister, 1809, in Bradford Cathedral; Julia Cooke, 1811, at Owston; George Coates, 1821, in Ripon Cathedral; Simon Kettlewell, 1823, at Kirklington; the Earl of Mexborough, 1830, at Methley; and the Rev. James Geldart, 1839, at Kirk Deighton. Other tablets executed by them commemorate Richard Prosser, 1809, in Durham Cathedral; John Hopwood, 1813, at Rochdale, Lancs; and Mary Fortescue, 1814, at Ketton, Rutland. The tablet to Mary Wilks, 1817, at Sowerby, Yorks, is signed by Charles alone.

FISHER, JOHN, the Elder, and JOHN, the Younger, of York

John Fisher the Elder: *b*. 1736, *d*. 1804

John Fisher the Younger: *b*. 1760 (?), *d*. 1839

In 1761 the elder Fisher exhibited at the Free Society of Artists a figure of "Our Saviour With the Cross" in white marble and "A Statue of Jupiter." The former is now in the Lady Chapel of York Minster, and the latter in the museum of the Philosophical Society, York. These works attracted the attention of the Marquess of Rockingham, who persuaded the sculptor to settle in York, where he met with instantaneous success. In 1768 he carved for his patron, at Wentworth Woodhouse, chimney-pieces for a bedroom and dressing-room which cost £164 and £88 respectively, while in 1783 he made one in white marble for the Museum (Fitzwilliam Archives). According to Paterson's *Roads*, the chimney-piece in the dining-room at Farnley Hall, Yorkshire, was of the "finest Italian marble and superbly executed by Fisher, of York."

Fisher, who settled down in York, and later became a Freeman of the city, was chiefly known as a monumental sculptor. He was a fine artist, though his obituary in the *Monthly Magazine* (Vol. XVIII, page 173) is perhaps over-flattering when it says that "his merit as a sculptor ranked him high in the annals of the arts, and so long as the works of genius remain the objects of our admiration, the purity and classic originality of his design, as well as the spirit and elegant chastity of its execution prove the justice of his claim to eminence."

Fisher was later assisted by his son John, whom he took as an apprentice in 1785. Apparently he was an unbusinesslike and not very satisfactory employer. In 1795 J. Carr, the architect, wrote from York to Benjamin Hall, Lord Fitzwilliam's steward, on the subject of a monument in memory of Edmund Burke which Fisher was making for Lord Fitzwilliam. In the course of the letter the writer remarks that he wishes "you would apply to Nollekens just to have done the head, the rest might have been done here. . . . All Fisher's best men have left him. They cannot get their wages of him" (Fitzwilliam Archives).

The elder Fisher's most important works are a figure which presumably personifies "Religion" on the monument to Sir Charles Sheffield, 1780, at Burton-on-Stather, Lincs, and the fine statue of Sir George Savile, 1784, in York Minster; though his monument to Sybil Wilson, 1773, in Lancaster Parish Church has a relief of great charm, which shows the child's parents in classical costume mourning by her death-bed.

All the monuments executed by the Fishers, however, reach a very high standard of craftsmanship. Their use of coloured marbles is intelligent and sympathetic, while the frequent "Adam" details are beautifully carved. A number of their works feature a medallion-portrait, and that in memory of John Dealtry, 1773, in the Lady Chapel of York Minster has a lovely figure of "Hygeia." As all are signed "Fisher" or "Fishers," it is difficult to assign any particular monument to father or son, and their works are accordingly given together in the following list.

(Authorities cited in text; York City Archives.)

MONUMENTS

1766	Brayton, Yorks	Robinson Morley
1769	Burton Agnes, Yorks	Ann Cayley
1771	Ripon (Cathedral)	G. Staines
1772	Exeter (St. Thomas's)	James Buller
1772	Whitby, Yorks	Catherine Cholmley
1772	Clarborough, Notts	Thomas Outybridge
1773	Masham, Yorks	William Danby
1773	Chesterfield, Derby	Godfrey Heathcote
1773	Harpham, Yorks	Mary Darby
1776	Norton, Derby	Richard Bagshaw
1777	York (St. Crux)	Thomas Bowes
1778	Thirsk, Yorks	Amelia Sparre
1780	York (St. Crux)	Henry Waite
1780	Howden, Yorks	John Dunn
1784	York (St. Michael's)	William Hutchinson
1784	Newcastle (Cathedral)	Hannah Mosley
1784	Thorne, Yorks	Edward Forster
1784	Stillington, Yorks	Rev. John Varley
1785	York (Minster)	Rev. George Anderson
1785	Owston, Yorks	Mary Cooke
1786	York (Minster)	Mary Pulleyn
1786	York (Minster)	Sir Thomas Davenport
1786	Otley, Yorks	Francis Fawkes (medallion portrait)
1786	Skipton, Yorks	John Birtwhistle
1786	Lichfield (Cathedral)	Dr. Simpson
1787	Howden, Yorks	Mary Rawson
1788	Swillington, Yorks	Sir W. Lowther
1789	Whalley, Lancs	Elizabeth Whalley
1791	Harewood, Yorks	The Fairfax family
1791	Whitby, Yorks	Nathaniel Cholmley
1792	Alfreton, Derby	George Morewood
1792	Skipton, Yorks	Walter Fawkes
1792	Rudby, Yorks	Hon. George Cary
1792	Thornton-le-Street, Yorks	Roger Talbot
1793	York (Minster)	Pelsant Reeves
1794	York (Minster)	Richard Wharton
1794	Richmond, Yorks	Fowler Hickes
1794	Sand Hutton, Yorks	Deborah Read
1795	Beverley (Minster)	Henry Roxby
1796	Halifax (Parish Church)	John Royds
1799	Escrick, Yorks	Beilby Thompson
c. 1800	Lowther, Westmorland	Richard, Viscount Lonsdale (d. 1751)
1800	Brayton, Yorks	Joseph Thompson
1805	Lowther, Westmorland	Jacob, Viscount Lonsdale (d. 1802)
1809	York (Minster)	Henry Whittam
1809	Kendal, Westmorland	William Richardson
1811	Howden, Yorks	Elizabeth Saltmarshe
1814	Otley, Yorks	Mrs. Laconwood

FISHER, RICHARD
b. 1690

He seems to have settled in Ripon about 1716, and came from Scotland. (In an MS history of the family of Fisher (Poss. Miss Porteous of York) it is said "he was of a very stern and reserved nature and never revealed his early history".)

FISHER, WILLIAM
b. 1777, *d.* 1815

In 1793 he was apprenticed to his father, John Fisher the Elder, of York (q.v.). He worked for a short time in the family firm and signs a few tablets with his brother Charles (q.v.).

In 1806 William Fisher left York and set up for himself in London. In the same year he submitted a model (which was rejected) for the Guildhall monument to Pitt and offered to complete the work for £5,700 (City Corporation Records, MS. 95.2). He exhibited at the Royal Academy, 1801–1811, showing reliefs of "A Greyhound Course" (1801) and "A Stag Chase" (1806), and various busts including those of Mr. Fothergill (1808), Miss Smith of Covent Garden Theatre (1808), and Sir Charles Turner (1811). His bust of Earl Fitzwilliam was formerly at Wentworth Woodhouse.

Fisher's address is given as "15, Great Castle Street, Cavendish Square," in the *London Directory* of 1809.

FITZGERALD, J.
At the British Museum there is a bust of W. S. Vaux, dated 1845, and signed by Fitzgerald, but he does not seem ever to have exhibited.

FLAXMAN, JOHN, the Elder
b. 1726, *d.* 1795

The elder Flaxman was born at Aston Clinton in Buckinghamshire, the son of Robert and Elizabeth Flaxman (British Museum, Ad. MS. 39791), and later earned his living by making and selling plaster-casts and figures. He also worked as a modeller, and in this capacity was employed by Roubiliac (q.v.), Scheemakers (q.v.) and Wedgwood.

For the last named he produced a number of reliefs, etc., including in 1775 those of "Thalia," "Terpsichore," "Euterpe," "Sappho," "Hercules With the Lion," "Hercules With the Boar," "Bacchus," "Ariadne," "The Seasons," "Jupiter," "Juno," "Minerva," "Justice" and "Hope." For Wedgwood he also supplied busts of Rousseau and Sterne in 1781, and received £1 4s. for "moudling a bust of Dr. Fothergale," while in 1782 and 1784 he executed busts of Mrs. Siddons and "Hercules" respectively (Wedgwood Archives).

Flaxman also made busts of Milton and Pope and figures of "Flora" and "Zingara" for Mr. James West in 1767 (Archives, West of Alscot Park). In 1782 he supplied busts costing £20 for Wolverley House, Worcestershire (Knight MSS., Kidderminster Public Library), while his plastercasts of "Venus" and "Cupid" for Audley End were executed in 1794 (Essex Records, D/DBY.A 225). His bust of Handel in the same material is now at Windsor Castle.

Flaxman was living in York when his second son, John (q.v.), was born in 1755, but he returned to London six months later and opened a shop in New Street, Covent Garden.

(Authorities cited in text.)

FLAXMAN, JOHN, R.A.
b. 1755, *d.* 1826

He was born in York, the second son of John Flaxman the Elder (q.v.), but was taken to London by his parents when he was six months old. He was a puny child, so weak and ill-shaped that he could not walk without crutches; indeed, for some time he was not expected to live and it was not until he was about ten years old that his health began to improve.

From an early age the boy had spent his time in modelling and drawing figures in his father's shop, where he soon began to attract the attention of the customers. Some of his earliest friends were Romney the artist; Frederick Montagu, for whom he later modelled "The Death of Caesar in the Capitol" (*Gentleman's Magazine*, 1781, page 65); and a clergyman named Mathew, whose wife used to invite the sickly child to her house and read to him from translations of the early poets, while he made sketches to illustrate passages which took his fancy.

Flaxman's first commission came from a friend of the Mathews, a Mr. Crutchley, of Sunninghill Park, for whom he made six drawings in black chalk with figures about 2 ft. high. In 1766 and 1769 he was awarded premiums by the Society of Arts, and in the following year won their Gold Palette for modelling a statue of Garrick (Archives, Society of Arts). In 1770 also he joined the Academy Schools and gained a Silver Medal in 1771, but was defeated by Thomas Engleheart (q.v.) in the competition for the Gold Medal in 1772.

In 1775 Flaxman joined his father in working for Wedgwood, for whom he designed cameos and made wax models of classical friezes, portraitmedallions, etc. Examples of his friezes include "The Dancing Hours," in 1775; "The Muses," in 1777; "The Sacrifice to Ceres," in 1779; "Blind Man's Buff," "Sacrifice to Cupid" and "Psyche Bound and Attacked by Cupid," all in 1782; and "Hercules in the Garden of the Hesperides," in 1787. Among his portraits may be mentioned those of Sir Joseph Banks and Dr. Solander, both in 1777; the Duchess of Devonshire, Sir William Herschell and C. J. Fox, all in 1783; Captain Cook, Sir Joshua Reynolds, John Philip Kemble, Dr. Johnson, and Mrs. Siddons, all in 1784; and William Franklin, in 1785. (Information, Wedgwood Museum, Barlaston.) For a full discussion of the work Flaxman executed for Wedgwood, see W. G. Constable's *John Flaxman* (1927).

Flaxman also gave Wedgwood advice and assistance over the decoration of Etruria Hall. In a letter to his employer dated 12 November, 1781, he tells him that "as soon as Mr. Byerly" (Wedgwood's partner) "communicated your workmen's want of the drawings at large for the cornice and vestibule, I began them immediately to prevent delay; but as some of the mouldings will be enriched in a manner not very likely to be well executed by a Country Plaisterer from a drawing only, I will, if you please, send two or three patterns cut in plaister for eggs and darts, water-leaf, etc. You will probably," he continues, "have an ornamental frieze for the saloon, if that is not already determined on, I would recommend the Lions and Foliage you admired so much in the chimney-piece I was carving for Mr. Knight" (Wedgwood Archives).

In 1782 Flaxman married Miss Ann Denman, the daughter of a gunstock maker of Whitechapel, a match which met with no approval from that sturdy bachelor, Sir Joshua Reynolds, who remarked: "So, Flaxman, I am told you are married. If so, you are ruined for an artist." Two years later he received one hundred guineas "for a tomb to the memory of Rousseau in Portland stone erected on Mr. Fierville's estate near Stanmore" (Wedgwood Archives), and in 1787 left with his wife for Rome. In this venture they had Wedgwood's assistance, for he needed someone to supervise the work of the designers and modellers employed by his firm in Italy. On 29 September of the same year Flaxman wrote to Byerly that "the Duke of Bouillon made kind enquiries after you and desired me to tell you he wishes to see you at the Castle of Navarre on matters of business."

The young couple had originally intended to spend only two years in Rome, but for various reasons their stay was extended to seven. Flaxman's patrons at this time included Edward Knight of

Portland Place, Mr. Hope of Deepdene, and Hervey, Earl of Bristol and Bishop of Derry. For the last-named he carved a marble group entitled "The Fury of Athamas," a work which caused him a great deal of trouble; indeed, one of the reasons for his remaining so long in Italy was the difficulty in finishing it. The price originally fixed was £600, but the Earl was extremely unpunctual in his payments, and in the end the sculptor was considerably out of pocket over the transaction.

While he was in Rome, Flaxman also started work on his designs for monuments to the poet Collins and Lord Mansfield, the former for Chichester Cathedral, the latter for Westminster Abbey; but it was, however, as an illustrator, rather than as a sculptor or modeller, that he gained a reputation at this time. Mrs. Hare Naylor commissioned him to illustrate the *Iliad* and the *Odyssey*, Thomas Hope the works of Dante, and the Dowager Countess Spencer the tragedies of Aeschylus, and, when all four series had been engraved in Rome by Thomas Piroli in 1793, Flaxman's fame was established throughout Europe, so that "he acquired a higher reputation than any artist of our country, excepting Sir Christopher Wren and Sir Joshua Reynolds" (*Gentleman's Magazine*, 1827, page 273).

In 1794 Flaxman decided to return to England, and on his way home was elected a member of the Academies of Florence and Carrara. On landing in this country, however, he found that he had to pay duty on all the models, etc., which he had brought with him from Rome, not only for his own use, but also for his friend Romney and other artists, and so warmly did he resent this imposition that he forthwith petitioned the Government to have the duties removed. This they agreed to do, and Flaxman later received a letter signed by all the English artists studying in Italy thanking him for his public-spirited action. Apparently this does not seem to have been his first attempt to get rid of the obnoxious duties, for among the Wedgwood archives there is a petition on the same subject (undated, but probably *c.* 1787) signed by Flaxman and his countrymen then in Rome and addressed to the Government.

On his return to England, Flaxman and his wife took a house in Buckingham Street, Fitzroy Square, and here he lived until his death, devoting himself chiefly to monumental sculpture and producing comparatively few statues and portrait-busts. In 1797 he was elected an Associate of the Royal Academy and, in 1800, a full member. In 1810 the Academy appointed him Professor of Sculpture and in that capacity he delivered a number of lectures which were published in book form after his death. In 1816 he became a member

of the Academy of Painting and Sculpture in Rome. Four years later he suffered a heavy blow by the loss of his wife, to whom he was devoted, from which he never really recovered.

From George IV Flaxman received commissions to make drawings for sculpture for the exterior of Buckingham Palace and for the Marble Arch. The King's original idea for the Arch was that it should constitute a memorial to Nelson, and with this end in view the sculptor executed a seated figure of Britannia with spear and shield, the latter bearing a prominent head of the Admiral. This was finished when the King died, but had not yet been placed on the top of the Arch, and, as the rest of the plan never matured, it remained for some time in obscurity. It was later placed on the St. Martin's Lane end of the National Gallery, not, however, as Britannia, but as Minerva, the change being easily effected by chipping off the head of Nelson from the shield (*Art Journal*, 1868, page 51).

Flaxman died on 7 December, 1826, and was buried in the churchyard of St. Giles-in-the-Fields in the old St. Pancras Road, where the following inscription was placed on his tomb: "John Flaxman, R.A., Professor of Sculpture, whose mortal life was a constant preparation for a blessed immortality, his angelic spirit returned to the Divine Giver on 7 December, 1826, in the seventy-second year of his age." The unfinished works in his studio were completed by E. H. Baily (q.v.).

He left a comparatively small sum, his will being proved at about £4,000, the principal beneficiary being his sister-in-law, Miss Maria Denman (q.v.), who had looked after him since the death of his wife. In 1851 she presented all his models, casts, etc., to University College, London, where they were placed in what was ultimately known as the Flaxman Hall. Unfortunately many of them were damaged by enemy action in the Second World War. There are also a number of his models in the Soane Museum.

Allan Cunningham, who knew the sculptor towards the end of his life, gives the following description of him in *Lives of the Painters* (Vol. III): "He was small in stature, slim in form: he walked with something of a sidling gait and his hair dark and long was combed down carelessly on either side of his head. . . . His forehead was fine: his large eyes seemed to emit light while he spoke: and the uncommon sweetness of his smile softened a certain proud expression of mouth and some coarseness of physiognomy. His dress was plain but not mean. He kept neither coach nor servants in livery and considered himself more the companion than the master of his men, treated them to a jaunt in the country and a dinner twice a year." A fellow Royal Academician said of Flaxman: "He is inaccessible to either censure or praise; he is proud but not shy, but I wish he would not bow so low to the lowly, his civility oppresses."

Sir Richard Westmacott, who became Professor of Sculpture at the Royal Academy on Flaxman's death, said of him in a lecture that he was "the greatest of modern sculptors" and that he "not only had all the fine feeling of the ancient Greeks, but united to it a readiness of invention and a simplicity of design truly astonishing." Flaxman's two small whole-length figures of "Raffaelle and Michelangeolo" [sic] were in Sir Thomas Lawrence's sale held by Messrs. Christie on 17 June, 1830. They fetched £74 (Archives, Messrs. Christie).

Flaxman exhibited at the Academy, 1781–1827. His account-book dating from 1794 until 1810 is in the British Museum (Ad. MS. 39784), and from this, and from an article on it by Edward Croft Murray (Walpole Society, Vol. XXVIII), it has been possible to discover the actual date of erection of a number of the monuments in the following list.

(D.N.B.; Art Journal, 1867 and 1868; Builder, 1863, pages 37 and 60; Monthly Magazine, 1802, page 362; the brief memoir attached to Flaxman's lectures, 1838; Gentleman's Magazine, 1781, page 65; W. G. Constable's John Flaxman; authorities cited in text.)

STATUES

1803	Rajah of Tanjore	Tanjore, India
1812	Pitt	Glasgow
1813	Sir Joshua Reynolds	St. Paul's Cathedral
1819	Sir John Moore	Glasgow
1822	Burns	National Portrait Gallery, Edinburgh
1823	Warren Hastings	India Office
1826	Marquess of Hastings	Calcutta (finished by Denman)
1826	John Kemble	Westminster Abbey (finished by Hinchcliffe and Denman)
?	Apollo	For Mr. Thomas Hope of Deepdene, Surrey

BUSTS

1778	Self-portrait	Sold at Christie's, J. W. Brett sale, 1864 (£161). Purchased for the Victoria and Albert Museum
1798	Sir George Yonge	Terra-cotta
1803	Josiah Wedgwood	Stoke-on-Trent Parish Church (£93 19s.)
1805	John Hunter	Royal College of Surgeons
1806	Second Earl of Guilford	Examinations Schools, Oxford

1807	Pasquale di Paoli	Westminster Abbey
1809	Matthew Boulton	Handsworth Parish Church (replica Tew Park)
?	Nelson	United Service Club
?	Henry Howard	Soane Museum
?	Pitt	Soane Museum

GROUPS

1786	Venus and Cupid	For Mr. Knight, of Portland Place
1790	Fury of Athamas	Ickworth House
1791	Cephalus and Aurora	For Mr. Thomas Hope
1821	St. Michael and Satan	Petworth
1824	Pastoral Apollo	Petworth

VARIOUS

1772	Miss Flaxman	Victoria and Albert Museum
c. 1772	Figures of Architecture and Painting	Raby Castle, Durham (3 ft. high)
1779	Self-portrait	Victoria and Albert Museum (terra-cotta)
1781–1782	Chimney-pieces	Wolverley House, Worcs
1783	Sir William Herschel	Art Gallery, Bath (medallion)
1785	Vase	For Wolverley House, Worcs (19 guineas)
1787	Two chimney-pieces	For Josiah Wedgwood (£25 4s. and £31 3s. 6d. respectively)
c. 1787	Chimney-piece	For Fonthill Abbey
1798	Hercules in the Garden of the Hesperides	For Josiah Wedgwood (bas-relief, £23)
1800	Apollo and Marpessa	Diploma Work, Royal Academy
1801	Bacchanalian relief	Wolverley House, Worcs
1802	Chimney-piece	Albury Park, Surrey
1803	Pediment of Temple of Liberty	Woburn Abbey
1803	Chimney-piece	Luscombe Castle, Devon
1805	Mercury and Pandora	Glyptotek, Copenhagen (relief, replica Royal Collection)
1808	Statue of Comedy and relief of Ancient Drama	Façade of Covent Garden Theatre
1818	Shield of Achilles	For George IV, replica for the Duke of York
?	Chimney-piece	For Samuel Rogers, St. James's Place
?	Lord Howe	National Portrait Gallery (wax relief)

MONUMENTS

1780	Lydd, Kent	Ann Russell

1781	Lambeth (Parish Church)	James Morris
1782	Great Gaddesden, Herts	Agatha Halsey
1783	Petworth, Sussex	John Wickins
1784	Gloucester (Cathedral)	Sarah Morley
1794	Basing, Hants	6th Duke of Bolton
1795	Chichester (Cathedral)	William Collins (d. 1759)
1795	Westminster Abbey	Earl of Mansfield (d. 1793)
1795	St. Paul's, Covent Garden	John Bellamy (d. 1794)
1795	Cherry Hinton, Cambs	Captain Serocold (d. 1794)
1795	Kingston, Surrey	Lady Frances Meadows
1796	Rickmansworth, Herts	The Earle family
1796	Island of St. Helena	Sarah Mapletoft (d. 1792)
1796	Lewisham (Parish Church)	John Petrie
1796	Bradford (Cathedral)	Abraham Balme
1797	Christ Church, Spitalfields	Sir Robert Ladbroke
1797	University College, Oxford	Sir William Jones (d. 1794)
1797	Cuckfield, Sussex	Sir William Burrell
1797	West Grinstead, Sussex	Sir William Burrell
1797	Ruscombe, Berks	Richard Neville (d. 1793)
1797	Shorwell, Isle of Wight	Catherine Bull (d. 1795)
1797	Market Lavington, Wilts	Thomas Sainsbury (d. 1795)
1797	Chichester (Cathedral)	Jane Smith (d. 1780)
1797	Rye, Sussex	Thomas Owens
1797	Epsom, Surrey	Rev. John Parkhurst
1798	Salisbury (Cathedral)	William Earle (d. 1796)
1798	Lyndhurst, Hants	Sir Charles Jennings-Clerke
1798	Shuckburgh, Warwick	Lady Shuckburgh-Evelyn
1798	Chichester (Cathedral)	Agnes Cromwell (d. 1797)
1798	Lewisham (Parish Church)	Mary Blackshaw
1798	Rochester (Cathedral)	Sir Edmund Head (d. 1796)
1798	Old Radnor, Radnorshire	John Lewis (d. 1797)
1798	Grosvenor Chapel	John Wilkes (d. 1797)
1798	Westminster Abbey	Captain James Montagu (d. 1794)
1798	St. James's, Piccadilly	James Dodsley
1799	Kirkthorpe, Yorks	Lady Georgina Smyth
1799	Kirkthorpe, Yorks	Sarah Smyth
1799	Kirkthorpe, Yorks	John Smyth
1799	Bath (Abbey)	Dr. Sibthorpe
1799	West Grinstead, Sussex	Elizabeth Woodward (d. 1797)

1799	St. Paul's, Covent Garden	Edward Hall
1799	Ashurst, Sussex	Sarah Wilson
1799	Lucea, Jamaica	Sir Simon Clarke (d. 1777)
1799	Barbados (St. John's)	Mr. Pinder
1800	Wroxton, Oxon	Earl of Guilford
1800	Hurstpierpoint, Sussex	Rev. Christopher Dodson
1800	Thirkleby, Yorks	Children of Sir Thomas Frankland
1800	Epsom, Surrey	John Braithwaite
1800	Poplar (St. Matthias)	George Steevens
1800	Eartham, Sussex	Thomas Hayley
1801	Ashton Keynes, Wilts	Charlotte Nicholas
1801	Lambourne, Essex	Matilda Maydwell (d. 1800)
1801	Stapleton, Glos	Mary Harford (d. 1798)
1801	Vaudreuil, Quebec	Madame Tonnancour
1801	Stoke, nr. Guildford, Surrey	William Aldersey
1801	Shrivenham, Berks	Admiral Barrington
1801	Winchester (Cathedral)	Joseph Warton
1801	St. Paul's Cathedral	Captain Ralph Miller
1801	Temple Church	Anthony Champion
1801	Petersfield, Hants	John Sainsbury
1801	Oxford (St. Mary's)	Sir William Jones
1801	Dawlish, Devon	Lady Pennyman
1801	Beckenham (Parish Church)	Lady Hoare
1801	Epsom, Surrey	John Warre
1801	Winchester (Cathedral)	Hon. Mrs. North
1801	Fareham (Holy Trinity)	Admiral Sir Charles Thompson
1801	Lambeth (St. Mary's)	Lt.-Colonel Roger Morris
1801	Wolverley, Worcs	Helen Knight
1802	Shellingford, Berks	3rd Viscount Ashbrook
1802	East Dereham, Norfolk	William Cowper (d. 1800)
1802	Holme Pierrepont, Notts	Hon. Evelyn Pierrepont
1802	Badger, Salop	Jane Browne
1802	Epsom, Surrey	Eleanor Belfield
1802	Chichester (Cathedral)	Francis Dear
1802	Barbados (Cathedral)	John Brathwaite
1802	Upper Penn, Staffs	John Marsh
1802	Edinburgh (St. Cuthbert's)	Children of Franci Redfearn
1803	St. Paul's Cathedral	Earl Howe
1803	Burnham Thorpe, Norfolk	Rev. Edmund Nelson
1803	Wortley, Yorks	John Stuart Wortley
1803	Campsall, Yorks	The Yarborough family
1803	Ledbury, Hereford	William Miles
1803	Oxford (University College Chapel)	Sir Robert Chambers
1803	Madras (St. Mary's)	Rev. Christian Gericke

1804	Salisbury (St. Martin's)	John Blake
1804	Stratfield Saye, Hants	Lord Rivers
1804	Cambridge (Trinity College Chapel)	Isaac Browne
1804	Romsey Abbey, Hants	Viscount Palmerston
1804	Esher, Surrey	Hon. Mrs. Ellis
1804	Broome, Worcs	Anne Hill
1804	Lower Basildon, Berks	Sir Francis Sykes
1804	Windsor (St. George's Chapel)	Hon. Mrs. Brudenell
1804	Peterborough (St. John's)	Agnes Squire
1804	Kensington (St. Mary Abbot's)	Elizabeth Godfrey
1805	Tanjore, India	Christian Schwartz
1805	Madras (St. Mary's)	Josiah Webbe
1805	Wortley, Yorks	Hon. James Stuart-Wortley
1805	Shuckburgh, Warwick	Sir George Shuckburgh-Evelyn
1805	Bristol (All Saints')	Troth Blisset
1805	Brentford (St. Laurence's)	William Ewin
1805	Holywell, Flint	Paul Panton
1805	Dawlish, Devon	Rev. Charles Robinson
1805	Kirby-Fleetham, Yorks	Anna Laurence
1805	Twyford, Hants	Mrs. Shipley (d. 1803)
1805	Twyford, Hants	Anna Maria Shipley (d. 1796)
1805	Twyford, Hants	Amelia Sloper (d. 1800)
1805	Westminster Abbey	William Buchan
1805	Farnham, Surrey	Frances Timson
1806	Canterbury (Cathedral)	Thomas Lawrence
1806	Richmond, Surrey	Hon. Barbara Lowther
1806	Hendon, Middlesex	Charles Colmore
1806	Milton, Cambs	Elizabeth Knight
1806	Bath (Abbey)	William Bingham
1806	Burwash, Sussex	Rev. John Courtail
1806	Steeple Aston, Oxon	Francis Page
1806	Madras (St. Mary's)	Archdeacon Leslie
1806	Dawlish, Devon	Frances Hunter
1806	Wragby, Yorks	Sir Rowland Winn
1807	Penang, F. M. S.	Marquess Cornwallis
1807	Rotherham, Yorks	Samuel Buck
1807	Leyton, Essex	Children of Edward Hillersdon
1807	Bangor (Cathedral)	Rev. Pearce Mealy
1808	Newcastle (Cathedral)	Rev. Hugo Moises
1808	Salisbury (Cathedral)	Walter Long
1808	Wortley, Yorks	Hon. Mrs. Wortley-Mackenzie
1808	Oxford (University College Chapel)	Rev. Nathan Wetherell
1808	Grafton Regis, Northants	Countess of Euston
1809	St. Paul's Cathedral	Viscount Nelson
1809	Micheldever, Hants	Lady Baring

1809	Reading, Berks	John Monck
1809	Leeds (Parish Church)	Captain Walker and Captain Beckett
1810	Hurley, Berks	Deborah, Viscountess Ashbrook
1810	Cookham, Berks	Sir Isaac Pocock
1810	Newcastle (Cathedral)	Sir Matthew Ridley
1811	Chichester (Cathedral)	Sarah Udney
1811	Holme Pierrepont, Notts	William Saltean
1812	Great Billing, Northants	Caroline Elwes
1812	Camberwell (Parish Church)	Nicholas Wanostrocht (now destroyed)
1812	Madingley, Cambs	Admiral Sir Charles Cotton
1813	Llanbadarn Fawr, Cardigan	Hon. Harriet Pryse
1813	Leyton, Essex	William Bosanquet
1813	Brecon (Cathedral)	William Morgan
1813	Madras (St. Mary's)	Major-General Sir Barry Cole
1813	Westminster Abbey	George Johnstone
1814	Chichester (Cathedral)	Admiral Frankland
1814	Throwley, Kent	Hon. Charles Harris
1814	Tattingstone, Suffolk	Admiral Western
1814	Wath, Yorks	Rev. T. Brand
1814	Great Brington, Northants	Countess Spencer
1815	Christchurch, Hants	Viscountess Fitzharris
1815	Sharnbrook, Beds	William Antonie
1815	Harrow, Middlesex	John Lyon
1815	Buckland Filleigh, Devon	Ann Fortescue
1815	Sacombe, Herts	Elizabeth Caswell
1816	Hatfield Broad Oak, Essex	Lady Ibbetson
1816	Stoke Poges, Bucks	Nathaniel Marchant
1817	Rufford, Lancs	Lady Hesketh
1817	Kingsbridge, Devon	Frances Drury
1819	Chichester (Cathedral)	Rev. Thomas Ball
1819	Chertsey, Surrey	Emily Mawbey
1820	Egham, Surrey	George Gostling
1820	Wimpole, Cambs	Hon. Mrs. Charles Yorke
1820	Esher, Surrey	Elizabeth Ellis
1820	Manchester (St. John's)	Rev. John Clowes
1823	Broxbourne, Herts	Edward Christian
1823	Madras (Cathedral)	Archdeacon Mousley
1823	Madras (Cathedral)	James Lushington
1823	Gaze Dore, India	Marquess Cornwallis
1824	Streatham (Parish Church)	Sophia Hoare
1825	Ketteringham, Norfolk	Harriot Peach
1825	Cambridge (Jesus College Chapel)	Edward Clarke

FLAXMAN, WILLIAM

b. 1753 (?); d. 1795 (?)

Elder brother of John Flaxman (q.v.), he

exhibited a bas-relief of "Venus" at the Free Society in 1768, and also showed wax portraits at the Royal Academy, 1781–1793, including one oɪ his famous brother in 1781. In the same year he received £30 10s. for "carving" at Wolverley House, Worcestershire (Knight MSS., Kidderminster Public Library).

FLETCHER, ANGUS
b. 1799, *d.* 1862

He was born in Edinburgh, where he began to study law, but later abandoned it in favour of sculpture. In 1825 he attended the Royal Academy Schools on the recommendation of Chantrey (q.v.), and exhibited at the Academy, 1831–1839, showing busts of the Duke of Argyll (1831); J. S. B. Morritt, of Rokeby (1834); and Charles Dickens (1839). At the Liverpool Academy he exhibited two busts of Felicia Hemans, the poetess, one in 1830 and the other in 1832. His bust of Mrs. Lawrence of Studley (1834) is in Ripon Town Hall.

Fletcher was a great friend of Charles Dickens, who used to call him "Mr. Kindheart."

FLETCHER, JOSHUA, the Elder
d. 1725

Fletcher, who became free of the Masons' Company on 20 April, 1699, was living at Woodstock in 1708, according to the list of members in the Company's Court Book, and in 1716, as foreman to Henry Banks (q.v.), was one of the master-masons for building Blenheim Palace.

Between 1721 and 1723 he was the mason responsible for the erection of "the new church in George Street, London." The Court Book of the Company also notes his death in 1725.

FLETCHER, JOSHUA, the Younger
d. 1749

Son of Joshua Fletcher the Elder (q.v.), he was apprenticed to his father in 1723 and was admitted to the Masons' Company in 1730. In 1734 he was living in Grosvenor Square and in 1748 in Mount Street. In the Westminster Poll Book of the latter year he is described as a "statuary," but I know of no works by him. His death is noted in the Court Book of the Masons' Company.

FLETCHER, Z., of Stockton

He signs tablets, with nicely carved details, to Frances Brewster, 1818, at Greatham, Durham, and to Alice Barras, 1819, at Norton in the same county.

FLINTOFT, JOHN, of York
fl. 1813–1841

He signs tablets to John Eadon, 1828, at Snaith, Yorkshire, and to Mr. Richardson, 1829, at St. Michael-le-Belfry, York. In the York Directory for 1841 he is described as "sculptor."

FLORY, JAMES
fl. 1663–1680

He was employed as a mason at St. Dunstan's-in-the-East in 1671, and at St. Michael Bassishaw in 1680, carving for this church, besides other decorative details, the cherubim-heads at the east end. The payment for this work was made to his widow, Alice Flory, which indicates that he must have died in 1680 or shortly afterwards. Mrs. Flory also received the money for her husband's work at St. Michael's, Greenhithe, which included "ten windows with ornaments, £110" (Bodleian, Rawlinson MSS. 387).

Flory was mason to the Bakers' Company from 1672 until his death (Company's Archives). In 1676 he was paid £50 for paving in marble the chapel of Emmanuel College, Cambridge (Willis and Clarke's *Architectural History of Cambridge*, Vol. II, page 707).

FOLEY, EDWARD ARLINGTON
b. 1814, *d.* 1874

He was the elder brother of J. H. Foley (q.v.), and was born in Dublin. At the age of twelve he joined the Royal Dublin Society's Schools and, in the following year, was apprenticed to the Irish sculptor, John Smyth.

Though he was a good student, Foley found that his master could not provide him with work, and he therefore decided to try his luck in London without waiting to finish his apprenticeship. For some time he had little success there, but his fortunes improved when W. Behnes (q.v.) engaged him to carve a coat of arms, for he did this so well that the sculptor offered him permanent employment at a salary of £4 a week.

In 1844 Foley showed "Canute Reproving His Courtiers" at Westminster Hall, a work which won the approval of the *Literary Gazette* (1844, page 482), which considered that "in this sitting figure there is much sarcastic dignity and appropriate action."

He exhibited at the Royal Academy, 1834–1873, where his busts included those of Mrs. Edward Tyrrell (1842), Professor Murphy (1851), Miss Catherine Hayes (1855), the Rev. David Laing (1860), and Douglas Jerrold (1862). Copies of the Laing bust—suitable "for a boudoir or drawing-room ornament"—were made by Overhead of

Haverstock Hill in the same year as the original appeared at the Academy (*Art Journal*, 1860, page 319). His bust of Samuel Lover, the artist (1839), is in the National Portrait Gallery.

Foley committed suicide on 10 May, 1874, being found drowned in the Regent's Canal.

(Strickland's *Dictionary of Irish Artists;* various references, *Art Journal; Annals of Our Time*, page 1152.)

FOLEY, JOHN HENRY, R.A.
b. 1818, *d.* 1874

He was born in Dublin on 24 May, 1818, the second son of a grocer named Jesse Foley who gave him very little education. However, fired by the example of his brother Edward (q.v.), the boy joined the Royal Dublin Society's Schools in 1831 and two years later won their principal medal for modelling and drawing. In 1834 he left Dublin and went to his brother in London. Here he entered the Royal Academy Schools and was later awarded a large Silver Medal.

In 1839 Foley exhibited "The Death of Abel" and "Innocence" at the Royal Academy, both works being favourably received. In the following year he was commissioned by Lord Ellesmere to carve in marble a group of "Ino and Bacchus," which was later engraved for the *Art Journal*. The editor's action in reproducing the figure of a semi-nude female, however, was much deplored by many readers, who considered that he would thereby "endanger the minds of the young."

"Youth at the Stream," which Foley showed at Westminster Hall in 1844, was an instantaneous success. The *Art Union* of that year (page 216) considered it the most beautiful work in the whole exhibition—"the head is modelled in fine taste and had such a figure been dug up in Rome, or near Naples, somewhat mutilated, it would have been pronounced a valuable specimen of classical art." As a result the sculptor secured a commission to execute a statue of John Hampden for the Palace of Westminster.

Commissions for busts and statues now began to flow in and Foley soon found himself in the front rank of British contemporary sculptors. In 1849 he was elected an Associate and, in 1858, a full member of the Royal Academy. Three years later he became a member of the Royal Hibernian Academy and, in 1863, was similarly honoured by the Belgian Academy of Arts. He continued to send works to the Royal Academy until 1861, but never submitted anything after that date, owing to a difference of opinion with the Committee concerning the arrangement of his sculpture for that year's exhibition. He was a most conscientious and fastidious worker, spending as long as twelve years on his statue of "Outram," and "even after it had been cast he continued his work upon it and, where he thought his modelling defective, had pieces of bronze cast and let in" (Strickland's *Dictionary of Irish Artists*).

If Foley's finest work is the equestrian statue of Viscount Hardinge in Calcutta—which the *Art Journal* (1859, page 36) described as "a masterpiece of art, one that for grandeur of design, for truth of action and for power and beauty of execution, has scarcely, if at all, a parallel in the world"—his best-known one is the seated figure of the Prince Consort which forms the centre of the Albert Memorial. He received the commission for this after the death of Baron Marochetti, but never lived to finish it, and the work was completed by his pupil, G. F. Teniswood, who was also responsible for some of the chasing. The statue, which weighed ten tons, was not gilded until after it had been placed in position, this supplying the finishing touch to a monument which had cost £120,000 to erect, and which one critic described as "a confection of gingerbread which ought to be under a glass shade on a giant's mantelpiece."

As a designer of silver-work, Foley was responsible for the testimonial to Samuel Courtauld which was illustrated in the *Art Journal* of 1866 (page 28). He also designed the seal of the Confederate States of America.

Besides the figure of the Prince Consort, Foley was also responsible for the group representing "Asia" for the Albert Memorial, and it was while he was modelling this in the open air that he caught the chill which ultimately affected his lungs. He died after some years of ill health at "The Priory," his home in Hampstead, on 27 August, 1874, and was buried in the crypt of St. Paul's Cathedral on 5 September. In his will he left the bulk of his property to the Artists' Benevolent Fund, and his casts to Ireland, for the Schools of the Royal Dublin Society. According to the author of his obituary in the *Art Journal* (1874, page 306), "no sculptor living or dead has produced works more grand than the Lord Hardinge and Sir James Outram. There exists no statue more perfect than that of Oliver Goldsmith in which he has untoward' materials to deal with, and which is beyond question a triumph of genius over difficulties, such as I think is unparalleled in art of any period." The editor of the *Art Journal* (S. C. Hall) gives this picture of the sculptor: "Slight, but well-formed, the face long and sallow, pensive almost to melancholy; and I do not think he was outwardly of what is called a genial nature. He was not 'robust,' either in body or in mind; all his sentiments and sensations were graceful;

so in truth were his manners. His leisure was 'consumed by thought.' He seemed to me to be at work when apparently doing nothing. He was never idle, though his hands were at rest."

Foley exhibited at the Royal Academy from 1839 until 1861, a number of his works also being shown there in the year following his death. He also exhibited at the British Institution, 1840–1854. At the Jonathan Nield sale of 3 May, 1879, at Christie's, his figures of "Winter" and "Summer" fetched £273 and £183 respectively. At the same room, on 29 May, 1880, his "Egeria," the property of J. Banstead, fetched £178.

(*Art Journal*, 1849, page 49; W. Cosmo Monkhouse's *Works of J. H. Foley*; authorities mentioned in text.)

STATUES

1847	John Hampden	St. Stephen's Hall
1848	Innocence	Illustrated in *Art Journal*, 1851
1851	The Wanderer	Great Exhibition
1853	Selden	St. Stephen's Hall
1856	Egeria	Mansion House
1857	Caractacus	Mansion House
1858	Viscount Hardinge	Calcutta
1860	The Elder Brother in 'Comus'	Diploma Work (Diploma Gallery, Royal Academy)
1862	Earl Canning	Westminster Abbey
1863	John Fielden	Todmorden
1863	Oliver Goldsmith	Dublin
1864	Sir Charles Barry	Palace of Westminster
1864	Youth at the Stream	For Royal Horticultural Society
1864	Father Matthew	Cork
1864	Lord Elphinstone	Bombay
1864	Sir James Outram	Calcutta
1865	Manochjee Nesserwanjee	Bombay
1866	Sir Henry Marsh	Royal College of Physicians, Dublin
1866	Daniel O'Connell	Dublin
1866	Prince Consort	Fitzwilliam Museum, Cambridge
1867	Lord Herbert of Lea	Waterloo Place, London
1867	Prince Consort	City Hall, Birmingham
1867	Archbishop of Tuam	Mayo
1868	Lord Clyde	Glasgow
1868	Edmund Burke	Dublin
1868?	Prince Consort	Dublin
1869	Sir Dominic Corrigan	Royal College of Physicians, Dublin
1870	Earl of Carlisle	Dublin
1870	Earl of Carlisle	Carlisle
1873	Sir Benjamin Lee Guinness	Dublin
1873	Henry Grattan	Dublin
1873	Lord Dunkellin	Galway
1874	General Jackson	Lexington, Virginia
1874	Prince Consort	Albert Memorial, Kensington Gardens (unveiled 1876)
1874	William Rathbone	Liverpool (unveiled 1877)
1874	Lord Gough	Dublin (unveiled 1880)
1874	Earl Canning	Calcutta
1874	Earl of Rosse	Birr, Ireland (unveiled 1876)
1874	Prince Consort	Cambridge

The statues dated 1874 were unfinished at the time of Foley's death and were completed by his pupils.

BUSTS

1843	Miss Helen Faucit (Lady Martin)	National Portrait Gallery
1848	Sir James Annersley	Exhibited Royal Academy
1852	Rev. Andrew Reed	Exhibited Royal Academy
1852	Viscount Hardinge	South Park, Penshurst
1856	Sir Charles Hulse	Exhibited Royal Academy
1858	Major-General Forbes	The Mint, Calcutta
1860	Viscount Hardinge	Windsor
1864	Lord Ashburton	Sold at Christie's, 5 December, 1950
1865	Lord Herbert of Lea	Harrow School
1870	Sir Herbert Edwardes	National Portrait Gallery
1871	7th Earl of Carlisle	Morpeth Town Hall
?	William Carpenter	British Museum
?	B. W. Proctor	National Portrait Gallery
?	Michael Faraday	Royal Society

MONUMENTS

1839	Madras (St. Mary's)	Catherine Prendergast
1848	Kensal Green Cemetery	Lt.-General Morris
1852	Melfield, Hants	Sir William Cornwallis
1854	Colombo, Ceylon	Hon. J. Stuart
1859	Guilsfield, Montgomery	John Jones
1862	Lisburne, Co. Antrim (Cathedral)	Brigadier Nicholson
1866	Kensal Green Cemetery	James Ward
1866	Dunfermline (Abbey)	General the Hon. Robert Bruce
1872	Farnham, Surrey	William Cobbett

FORD, JOHN, the Elder, of Bath
b. 1711, *d.* 1767

He was the master-mason responsible for building Bath Grammar School in 1752 and almost certainly executed some of the earlier monuments listed under his son, John Ford the Younger (q.v.).

The elder Ford was buried at Colerne in Wiltshire, where his epitaph declares that "his abilities and enterprise in business in a great measure contributed to the erection of the handsome buildings and streets" of Bath.

FORD, JOHN, the Younger, of Bath
b. 1736, *d.* 1803

Ford, who was the son of John Ford the Elder (q.v.), exhibited a marble bust of "Young Mr. Worlidge" at the Free Society in 1764. Three years later he was working as a "statuary" (presumably a carver of chimney-pieces) at the Royal Crescent in his native city. He died in 1803 and, like his father, was buried at Colerne, where a monument was erected to his memory.

His monuments are usually carried out in coloured marbles with large reliefs, a favourite design consisting of a female figure mourning by an urn with an obelisk or pyramid in the background. It may have been the sight of just such a work that inspired an anonymous correspondent to send a sonnet to the *Gentleman's Magazine* in 1787. The poem (which appeared on page 352) contains the following lines:

"Then, sculptor, sparing of thy marble graces,
    Let thy taught chisel from my tombstone spurn
All dove-winged cherubs with fat baby faces,
    And Christian faith squat by a Roman urn."

In the list of works given below some of the earlier ones are almost certainly by the elder Ford.

MONUMENTS

1746	Steeple Ashton, Wilts	Henry Long
1750	North Bradley, Wilts	Henry Long
1750	Seend, Wilts	George Husey
1755	Combe Hay, Somerset	Robert Smith
1758	Wheathampstead, Herts	Thomas Garrard
1758	Castle Cary, Somerset	John Russ
1759	Bathford, Somerset	Elizabeth Phillips
1761	Wheathampstead, Herts	Sir Samuel Garrard
1763	Bromham, Wilts	John Andrew
1763	Bathampton, Somerset	Charles Holder
1770	Mickleton, Glos	Morgan Graves
1770	North Stoke, Somerset	The Ward Family
1771	Steeple Ashton, Wilts	Anne Wainhouse
1771	Frampton, Dorset	John Browne
1772	Frampton, Dorset	Robert Browne
1772	Jamaica (Cathedral)	Charles Inman and Ralph Preston
1773	Batcombe, Somerset	Thomas Coward
1773	Marlborough St. Peter's	Elizabeth and Robert Clavering

FORREST, ANDREW HUME
b. 1813

In 1839 he attended the Royal Academy Schools on the recommendation of William Behnes (q.v.). At the Great Exhibition of 1851 he showed a work entitled "The Forsaken."

FORREST, ROBERT, of Lanark
b. 1790, *d.* 1852

He was an entirely self-taught sculptor who began life as a stone-mason in the quarries of Clydesdale. His first patron was a Colonel Gordon, who in 1817 lost his way when out shooting and by chance discovered the young man in an old quarry, carving figures of animals out of the local stone. Gordon was so impressed that he ordered a figure of "Bacchus" from the sculptor, and also recommended him to various friends, one of whom (a Mr. Robertson) commissioned him to execute a life-size figure of a Highland chieftain. Enough orders followed to justify Forrest adopting sculpture as a profession. He fixed on a quarry near Lanark for his studio, and here he executed figures of "Old Norval," "Falstaff" and "Rob Roy."

In 1830 he exhibited in Edinburgh equestrian groups of the Duke of Wellington, the Duke of Marlborough, Queen Mary and Lord Herries, and Robert the Bruce and the Monk. In course of time this exhibition became one of the most popular sights in the city, and before Forrest died he had executed thirty groups and statues for it.

His chief work was the statue of Sir William Wallace for Lanark. This is 7 ft. 6 in. high and somewhat unexpectedly shows the national hero of Scotland dressed in "a Roman costume with sword and buckler." The people of Lanark, however, were immensely pleased with it, and, on the day of the unveiling, carried the sculptor "in triumph through the streets, preceded by music and the banners of the different trades" (*The Georgian Era*, 1834, Vol. IV, page 180).

Other statues by Forrest (who died on 29 December, 1852) include a colossal one of Lord Melville (1822), in Edinburgh; John Knox (1825), in the Glasgow Necropolis; Mr. Ferguson, of Raith (1843); and the Duke of Wellington (1851), at Falkirk. The Melville statue was executed from a design by Chantrey (q.v.).

(MacVeigh's *Scottish Family History*, Vol. III, page 710; Swan's *Views on the River Clyde*.)

FOSS, WILLIAM, of Richmond, Yorks
fl. 1812–1822

He was probably the son of John Foss of

Richmond, who died in 1827 and whose tombstone in the churchyard describes him as "architect and Mayor and Alderman of this Borough."

The younger Foss signs pretty tablets in coloured marbles to Sophia Milbanke, 1818, and William Milbanke, 1821, both at Well, Yorks; Eleanor Milbanke, 1819, at Croft, Yorks; Thomas Colpitts, 1819, at Barnard Castle, Durham; and Henry Blegborough in Richmond Parish Church, Yorks.

FOSTER, EDWARD, of Hull

He signs a large wall-tablet with delicately carved details to William Bethell, 1799, at Rise, Yorks.

FOSTER, JAMES, of Bristol
fl. 1795–1825

He was assistant to W. Paty (q.v.) and took over the yard on his master's death in 1801. Here he continued in business, executing (to quote his advertisement) "monuments and chimney-pieces in marble with peculiar grace and elegance."

Signed works by Foster include those to John Maxse, 1798, at Brislington, Somerset; Richard Oakley, 1801, at Carmarthen; and John Kernan, 1804, at Stanton Drew, Somerset. The tablet to Amelia Burges in St. Augustine's, Bristol, is signed "Foster and Walker." Foster was joined by his son, also James, in 1806, and together they built the upper and lower arcades, Bristol, in 1825.

FOX, CHARLES
d. 1854

In 1847 he received the Silver Isis Medal from the Society of Arts for a model of a group of children. At the Great Exhibition of 1851 he showed a model of a design in sculpture for a pediment, which had a relief representing "The Arts, Commerce and Manufactures promoted by the Great Exhibition." Two years later he executed a set of decorative panels for a building in North Street, Brighton.

Fox's brother Edward showed statuettes of Chaucer and Spenser at the Great Exhibition.

FOXHALL, EDWARD
fl. 1783–1794

He was the son of Martin Foxhall, and was responsible for decorative carving for various houses designed and built by his father's friend, Sir John Soane. In 1783 he received £1,069 for all the carved woodwork, etc., in Philip Yorke's house in New Cavendish Street, and ten years later was again employed by Yorke (now Earl of Hardwicke) at Wimpole in Cambridgeshire. Under Soane he also worked at Malvern Hall for Sir Henry Lewis in 1786, in Grosvenor Square for the Marquess of Abercorn in 1787, and in Pall Mall for Lady Louisa Manners in 1788. He also carved four Ionic capitals for the Marquess of Abercorn at Bentley Priory.

Other work by Foxhall included a chimney-piece for Burnham Hall, Norfolk, in 1783, while two years later he carved the snake round the base of the stone column erected to the memory of Edward and Julia Evelyn at Felbridge, near East Grinstead. This was taken down after the First World War and now stands at Lemmington in Northumberland.

(Soane Notebooks.)

FOY, or FOYE, MICHAEL

In 1777 he sent a "Bust of an Artist" from Rome to the exhibition of the Society of Artists. He may be the Michael Foy who worked in Dublin and who received premiums from the Dublin Society for two out of the three bas-reliefs which he exhibited there between 1767 and 1770. A bas-relief of the head of "Durno, by Foy" was sold by Mr. Christie at the sale of the effects of Thomas Banks (q.v.), on 22 May, 1805 (Archives, Messrs. Christie).

FRANCEYS, SAMUEL, and F., of Liverpool
Samuel Franceys: *b.* 1762, *d.* 1829

There was a Samuel Franceys who was employed on decorative stucco-work at Melbourne Hall, Derbyshire, in 1760 who may belong to the same family, or, indeed, be the father or grandfather of the Liverpool statuaries (Archives, Marquis of Lothian).

The firm of Franceys, besides being the leading statuaries of Liverpool, also manufactured marble chimney-pieces "in the Egyptian, Grecian, Gothic and modern taste," which they exhibited in their "marble-rooms," together with "various figures in marble, bronze and artificial stone to support dials and lamps" (*The Stranger's Guide to Liverpool*, 1812).

Their most distinguished apprentice was John Gibson (q.v.), who, while working for them, designed and carved a monument to Henry Blundell about 1813. The work was erected in Sefton Church, Lancashire, but it is signed by the firm and not by Gibson (Gregson's *Fragments*, page 224).

Samuel left the business in 1819 and the partnership was dissolved (*European Magazine*, 1819, page 282), his place being taken by W. Spence (q.v.). The reconstructed firm of Franceys and Spence continued working until about 1844, many years after Samuel's own death, which took place on 20 May, 1829. He was buried in the graveyard of the Wesleyan Chapel in Brunswick Street, Liverpool.

The firm's most ambitious monument is the large stele at Garstang, Lancashire, with its figure of Alexander Butler (*d.* 1811) as a Roman warrior, with a sword in his hand. Another, to the Rev. Joseph Venables, 1810, at Oswestry, Salop, has a most curious life-size portrait silhouette of black marble inlaid on white. A third, commemorating the Rev. Josias Dawson (*d.* 1807), is also signed "John Foster del."

MONUMENTS BY S. AND F. FRANCEYS

1783	Gresford, Denbigh	William Pate
1800	Selattyn, Salop	Rev. Thomas Edwards
1801	Chirk, Denbigh	Thomas Lovett
1806	Rochdale (Parish Church)	Thomas Smith
1807	Chester (Cathedral)	John Ford
1809	Rochdale (Parish Church)	Benjamin Smith
1809	Penwortham, Lancs	Rev. William Loxham
1811	Llanbedr, Denbigh	Rev. Robert Morgan
1813	Stockport, Cheshire	Frances Bower
1813	Manchester (St. Ann's)	Rev. Samuel Hall
1813	Burnley, Lancs	Rev. John Hargreaves
1813	Broughton, Staffs	Sir Thomas Broughton
1814	Davenham, Cheshire	Elizabeth France
1817	Audlem, Cheshire	Hannah Hale
1818	Chester (St. Peter's)	George Johnson

MONUMENTS BY FRANCEYS AND SPENCE

c. 1820	Congleton, Cheshire	John Lownes
c. 1820	Ruabon, Denbigh	Anne Rowland
1823	Ruthin, Denbigh	Rev. E. Jones
1823	Holt, Denbigh	Rev. Thomas Blackburne
1827	Ormskirk, Lancs	Joseph Brandreth
1833	Colne, Lancs	Robert Reynolds
1844	Sefton, Lancs	Rev. Richard Rothwell

FRANCHESCHI, B.
fl. 1842–1844

He exhibited busts of Queen Victoria (1842), and the Prince Consort (1844) at the Royal Academy.

FRANCIS, JAMES, of Clapham
b. c. 1751, *d.* 1833

As a mason he was working at Clapham Parish Church in 1802, and in the same year rebuilt the tower of St. Anne's, Soho (Churchwardens' Accounts).

He signs monuments to the Carpenter family, 1798, at Tavistock, Devon, and to Elizabeth Davidson, 1798, in St. George the Martyr, Southwark.

FRANCIS, JOHN
b. 1780, *d.* 1861

He was born in Lincolnshire on 3 September, 1780, and began life by training as a farmer in his native county. His decided talent for art, however, made his friends advise him to study it seriously, and he accordingly went up to London in 1810 to work under Chantrey (q.v.).

About 1815 Francis attracted the attention of Mr. Coke (afterwards Earl of Leicester) and he later carved a successful bust of his patron which he exhibited at the Royal Academy in 1820. Coke introduced him to various political friends, and in a short time he found himself the unofficial sculptor of the Whig party. He became a great favourite of William IV and also worked for the Duke of Sussex, making between 1830 and 1840 small (or cabinet) marble busts of the latter's family and political associates. On the Duke's death seventeen of these were sold at Christie's in 1843 and fetched prices varying between two guineas for George IV to five for Lord Melbourne. Others sold included those of Princess Augusta, the King of Prussia, Earl Spencer, Canning, Earl Grey, Fox, and Bathurst, Bishop of Norwich.

Francis's busts of the Duke of Sutherland and Lord Holland, both dated 1838, are at Buckingham Palace, together with one of the Duke of Saxe-Coburg which he modelled in 1846 "under the guidance of Prince Albert." Other busts executed by him include those of Leopold, Prince Royal of Belgium (1830); Lord John Russell (1838); Lord Holland (1838); Queen Louise of Belgium (1840); and the Duke of Saxe-Coburg and Gotha (1844), all at Windsor Castle; the Duke and Duchess of Saxe-Coburg, at Osborne; and the second Duke of Sutherland, at Sutton Place, Guildford. His statue of the Prince Consort exhibited at Westminster Hall in 1844 was, in expression, "deficient of intellectual life," according to the *Art Union* of that year.

Francis exhibited at the Royal Academy, 1820–1857. He had a large studio and numbered among his pupils the sculptors, J. Durham (q.v.) and M. Noble (q.v.). He married a relation of Lord Nelson and was the father of Mrs. Thornycroft (q.v.). He died on 30 August, 1861.

(*Art Journal*, 1861, page 312.)

STATUES AND STATUETTES

1834	Lord Brougham	Exhibited Royal Academy
1836	Lord John Russell	Exhibited Royal Academy
1843	Duke of Sutherland	Dornoch Cathedral

BUSTS

1818	Marquess Wellesley	Apsley House
1822	Miss Horatia Nelson	Exhibited Royal Academy
1824	Mr. Coke	Woburn Abbey
c. 1825	Cicero	Woburn Abbey
1829	Lord Holland	Formerly Holland House
1830	Wellington	Woburn Abbey
1832	William IV	Mansion House
1832	William IV	Freemasons' Hall
1832	Duke of Kent	Mansion House
1832	Wellington	Stratfield Saye (after Nollekens)
1832	Duke of Bedford	Woburn Abbey
1832	Lord John Russell	National Portrait Gallery
1833	Duke of Kent	Freemasons' Hall
1834	Duke of Sutherland	Dunrobin Castle
1840	Queen Victoria	Reform Club
1844	Earl of Leicester	Longford Church, Derby
1844	Prince Albert	National Portrait Gallery
1848	Hon. Edward Petre	Exhibited Royal Academy
1850	Queen Victoria and Prince Albert	Geological Museum
1851	W. Lascelles (Plaster)	Castle Howard
1851	Queen Victoria and Prince Albert	Mansion House
1852	Queen Victoria and Prince Albert	Drapers' Hall
1852	Wellington	National Portrait Gallery

MONUMENTS

1823	Stockport, Cheshire	Hon. Frances Warren
1827	Oundle, Northants	William Walcot
1829	Great Oakley, Rutland	Sir Richard Brooke
1835 and 1837	Sudbury, Derby	Lord and Lady Vernon
1843	Colwich, Staffs	Anne, Viscountess Anson

FRANCIS, MISS MARY.
See under Thornycroft, Mrs.

FRANKLIN, JOSEPH and of Stroud and Purton
fl. 1789–1850

His monuments and tablets are uninteresting, the best in Gloucestershire being those to Richard Aldridge, 1789, at Woodchester; Mary Naylor, 1790, in St. John's, Gloucester; William Carruthers, 1790, at Painswick; and William Hewer, 1792, at Cirencester. Other examples in Wiltshire commemorate John Bryant, 1802, and John Sadler, 1811, both at Purton; Richard Broome, 1803, at Cliffe Pypard; Henry Wilson, 1812, at Wootton Bassett; and William Stratton, 1822, at Brinkworth. He also signs tablets to Thomas Pearce, 1791, and Catherine Tarrant, 1807, both at Ashbury, Berks.

FRANKS, of Brentford

A "stone cutter," he was paid £14 by William Lowndes in 1700 for a "pair of Plints, a pair of Necks carved and Acornes to Sett up betweene the two gardens." These were for Winslow Hall, Bucks, designed by Sir Christopher Wren (Wren Society, Vol. XVII, page 62).

FREEBAIRN, RICHARD G.
b. 1797, *d.* 1825

He attended the Royal Academy Schools in 1814 and later studied in Rome, returning to England in 1821. He exhibited at the Royal Academy, 1818–1835, and at the British Institution, 1819. In 1822 he showed a bust of George III at the Academy. This must have been a most curious production, for it showed the late King "under his afflicting malady" (*Literary Gazette*, 1822, page 346).

Freebairn's most important work, carved just before his death in 1825, was a marble statue of "Psyche." The *Literary Gazette* of that year (page 428) considered that he had "wrought it with sufficient variation to entitle him to credit for a very successful work."

FREEMAN, WILLIAM
fl. 1824–1828

Between 1824 and 1828 he was employed on the building of the east wing of the British Museum, and received £100 for carving four 5-ft. Ionic capitals (P.R.O. Works 5/119-5/125).

FRIEND, or FREND, JOHN, of Canterbury
fl. 1704–1747

In 1704 he was apprenticed to John Broxup of Canterbury, and was appointed chief mason to the Cathedral in 1731, a post he retained until 1747. Between 1734 and 1735 he repaired most of the tracery of the windows, a task for which he received £500 (Cathedral Library Archives). He also signs the architectural monuments to John Barrett and Paul Lukin, both of whom died in

1709, in St. Margaret's Church, Canterbury. These are well executed and typical of their period, with weeping cherubs on either side, etc.

In 1732 Francis made a sideboard with a marble slab for Lord Folkestone's house at Bifrons, in Kent (Longford Castle Archives).

Hutchins, in his *History of Dorset* (Vol. III, page 570), says that the monument to Thomas Chafin (*d.* 1691) in Chettle Church is "curiously sculptured and was made at Canterbury and erected in 1708," so it might be the work of Friend.

FULKES, SAMUEL
fl. 1664–1711

Under Wren he was responsible for a considerable amount of masonry work at St. Paul's Cathedral, where he executed shields and festoons, keystones and cherub-heads, Corinthian capitals, the great tribune at the west end, four scrolls in the library, the capitals on the north-west tower, the decorative work of the west portico and part of the great upper portico. The sum he finally received for masonry and carved work in connexion with the building amounted to no less than £23,115 (*Wren Society's Publications*).

Fulkes was also employed at St. Bride's, Fleet Street; All Hallows', Bread Street; and St. Mary Aldermanbury. For St. Swithin's, Cannon Street, he made the font, costing £15; for St. Margaret Pattens, "three Corinthian capitals," for £39; while he received £40 for "eight freestone pillar-capitals and five pilaster-capitals" for St. Margaret, Lothbury (Bodleian, Rawlinson MSS. 387).

In 1695 he was the master-mason for building Aske's Hospital at Hoxton, and on 28 May of that year the Minute-book of the Haberdashers' Company notes that Mr. Fulkes was ordered "to go on with the figures for the Great Gate." These apparently stood on the piers of one of the entrance-gates to the building and are described in Stow's *London* (Strype Edition, 1720, page 212) as "two stone statues representing two of Aske's hospital men in full proportion." In the same year the sculptor was paid for "bassos, capitals and pineapples according to the modell" (Archives, Haberdashers' Company).

Fulkes's daughter married Edward Stanton (q.v.), and died in 1712 at the age of thirty-eight. The epitaph on her tomb in the churchyard of St. Andrew's, Holborn, is given by Le Neve in his *Monumenta Anglicana* (Vol. IV, page 104).

FURNISS, B. C.
fl. 1829–1833

He exhibited at the Royal Academy, 1829–1833, showing a bust of Lord Cosmo Russell and a medallion of W. Martin Coates.

G

GAFFIN, THOMAS, and EDWARD

Firm *fl.* 1805–1865

Edward Gaffin and his son Thomas were the most prolific statuaries of the first half of the last century. From their workshop in Regent Street poured forth an apparently unceasing flood of tame, dull and uninteresting monuments and memorial tablets. The number they produced must have run into thousands, the majority of which have a strong family likeness; unfortunately it was such a very plain family.

The firm, however, sometimes employed good designers, for the monument of John Willis, 1835, at Greatford, Worcestershire, has a lovely relief. It was, indeed, during the 1830s that their best work was produced, but the memorials become duller and plainer as the years go on, with the result that, stuck on the walls of aisle and chancel like postage-stamps, many of our parish churches have white-marble tablets with square, black-marble surrounds which look exactly like the mourning-cards of our grandparents. There follows a brief list of the best works of the firm.

MONUMENTS AND TABLETS

1814	South Weald, Essex	Sir Richard Neave
1819	Chichester (Cathedral)	Duke of Richmond
1827	Coltishall, Norfolk	Sophia St. John
1827	Langley Marish, Bucks	Jemima Harvey
1828	Stanstead Mount-fitchet, Essex	William Torriano
1833	Christow, Devon	2nd Viscount Exmouth
1834	Tyringham, Bucks	Sarah Winfield
1834	Reading (St. Mary's)	John Monck
1836	St. Mellion, Cornwall	William Coryton
1836	Bourne, Lincs	James Digby
1837	Adlestrop, Glos	Hon. Emily Wingfield
1838	Ulcombe, Kent	Lady Sarah Wandesforde
1840	Stanford-on-Soar, Notts	Caroline Dashwood
1843	Hartfield, Sussex	Admiral the Hon. Jacob Henniker
1847	Wartling, Sussex	Herbert Curteis
1849	Congleton, Cheshire	Sir Thomas Reade
1863	Westminster Abbey	Lord Clyde

GAHAGAN, C.

fl. 1825–1844

He assisted Flaxman (q.v.), who paid him three guineas a week (British Museum, Ad. MS. 39784),

and he later exhibited busts at the Royal Academy between 1831 and 1836.

In 1844 Gahagan showed at Westminster Hall "An Allegorical Representation of the Union of the Three Kingdoms." The art critic of the *Literary Gazette* said of this production: "If the Union conferred as little benefit upon the Kingdom as this gentleman does upon the Arts, the dissolution were most devoutly to be wished for."

GAHAGAN, EDWIN

d. 1858

Like his kinsman, C. Gahagan (q.v.), he also exhibited at Westminster Hall in 1844, showing a statue of Newton, which the *Art Journal* thought possessed "marked merit and gives promise of future excellence." Even the *Literary Gazette* was kinder, mentioning their "pleasure when we come to speak of that which can be admired."

Gahagan exhibited at the Royal Academy, 1831–1837. His son Stephen, born in 1832, attended the Academy Schools in 1850 and showed a medallion portrait at Burlington House in 1857. Edwin died 5 July, 1858.

GAHAGAN, LAWRENCE

fl. 1756–1820

He was born in Ireland, and in 1756 won a premium from the Dublin Society "for a piece of sculpture," probably a statuette of Rubens. Shortly after this he went to London, where he changed his name from Geoghegan to Gahagan.

In 1777 he was awarded a premium by the Society of Arts for a relief 6 ft. high of "Alexander Exhorting His Troops." In 1801 he was employed on decorative work at Castle Howard (Castle Howard Archives), and in 1806 submitted a model for the proposed Guildhall monument to Pitt. His design was rejected, however, and he later wrote to the Committee that he had "made four applications at your office for my model, but could not obtain it until last Saturday and then in a very mutilated state" (City Corporation Records, MSS. 95.2).

Gahagan seems to have made a speciality of small bronze portrait-busts, and one, dated 1812, in the possession of the writer, is a charming, carefully modelled work. He exhibited at the Royal Academy, 1798–1817, and at the British Institution in 1809. At the Academy his busts included those of Admiral Sir Thomas Paisley (1798);

PLATE IX

JOHN FLAXMAN
Earl Howe, 1803, St. Paul's Cathedral.

PLATE X

G. B. GUELFI
James Craggs, 1725, Westminster Abbey.

GRINLING GIBBONS
Part of the monument of John, Lord Coventry, 1690,
Croome D'Abitot, Worcestershire.

JOHN GIBSON
"Narcissus," 1838, Burlington House.

Nelson (1798), afterwards engraved in mezzotint by Barnard; William Pitt (1800); the Bishop of St. Pol de Leon (1809); Dr. Hawes (1809); and Sir Samuel Romilly (1816). Another bust of Nelson, shown in 1804, is now in the Bath Art Gallery, while a bronze one of Wellington, exhibited seven years later, is at Stratfield Saye.

Gahagan also signs monuments to the Hon. George Napier, 1804, in Redland Chapel, Bristol, and Joseph Baldwin, 1810, at Cholebury, Bucks.

In 1840 the contents of Chandos House, Bath (which had belonged to a Miss Fenton), were offered for sale and among the lots were a number of models, etc., catalogued as by Lawrence Gahagan, although some of them must have been the work of his son Lucius (q.v.). They included reliefs of "George IV presenting Peace to the Goddess of the Earth, in background equestrian figure of Wellington," "The Death of Spencer Perceval," and "A Missionary Preaching to the South Sea Islanders," a figure of "William IV Seated in a Chair"; statuettes of Lady Hood, Princess Cariboo and Hannah Moore; and "A Large Model of the Murdered Figure of Maria Bagnell and Gillingham the Murderer." Busts in the sale attributed to the same hand (some apparently small bronze portrait-busts or the terra-cotta models for them) included those of the Emperor Alexander I (the only portrait for which he sat when in England), Lord Byron, Sir Edward Parry, Gabriel Goldney (Mayor of Chippenham), Madame Catalini, General Blücher, the Marquess of Albuquerque, the Rev. — Jay, Mr. Tottenham and Mr. Trevor (Sale Catalogue, possession of author).

GAHAGAN, LUCIUS, of Bath
d. 1866

He was the son of Lawrence Gahagan (q.v.) and settled in Bath about 1820, where he lived in a house named "Lo Studio." For Bath he carved in 1824 statues of "Commerce" and "Genius" for the façade of 9, Quiet Street, and the head of Garrick for the exterior of the Garrick Head Hotel in 1831. His bust of Caleb Parry is in the Art Gallery.

Other works by Gahagan included a bust of the Rev. J. Hyatt, which he showed at the Royal Academy in 1817, and a medallion plaque of Wellington dated 1832, which is now at Stratfield Saye. He also signs the monument to Viscountess Bridport, 1831, at Cricket St. Thomas, Somerset.

GAHAGAN, MISS SARAH
d. 1866

She was the daughter of Lawrence Gahagan (q.v.), and in 1817, the year she showed a bust of a child at the Royal Academy, was living in Bristol. Later on, however, she joined her brother Lucius (q.v.) at Bath.

GAHAGAN, SEBASTIAN
fl. 1800–1835

He was the brother of Lawrence Gahagan (q.v.) and was born in Dublin, but later went to work in England where he was employed by Nollekens (q.v.). He carved a number of his master's works, including the statue of Pitt for Cambridge in 1809, but for this "Mr. Nollekens paid him, I am sorry to say, a miserably small sum," says J. T. Smith (*Nollekens and His Times*, Vol. I, page 368). "I really think," Smith continues, "those who now bask in the sunshine of Mr. Nollekens' immense wealth should take into consideration the letter he addressed to the executors shortly after the death of his old master."

Nollekens did leave Gahagan £100, but for some reason he did not receive it "till several years had elapsed, during which time he had undergone many serious vicissitudes of ill fortune" (op. cit., Vol. II, page 354). Apparently ill-luck continued to dog his footsteps, for in 1835 he was forced to apply for assistance to the Royal Academy, which granted him a small "charitable donation" (Archives, Royal Academy).

In 1809 Gahagan had received a premium from the Society of Arts for his group of "Samson Breaking his Bonds," and three years later he made the statues of "Isis" and "Osiris" for the front of the Egyptian Hall in Piccadilly. His best-known work, however, is the statue of the Duke of Kent, erected in 1825 at the top of Portland Place "by the supporters of the numerous charities he so zealously and successfully patronized."

Gahagan exhibited at the Royal Academy, 1802–1835, showing busts of Sir Thomas Picton (1816), George Cholmondeley (1822) and Sir Peter Laurie (1824). His bust of William Windham (1821) is at Felbrigg Hall, Norfolk, while another of Dr. Hutton (1832) is in the possession of the Newcastle Literary Society. According to Hutton's obituary in the *Gentleman's Magazine* (1823, Vol. I, page 232), "casts of his bust have been already obtained by many of Dr. Hutton's friends, and still continue to be supplied by the sculptor, Mr. Gahagan, at his premises in King Street, Edgware Road."

Gahagan's most important monument, with its life-sized figures, commemorates Sir Thomas Picton, 1815, in St. Paul's Cathedral. His monument to Dr. Charles Burney was unveiled in Westminster Abbey on 16 February, 1819, and he also signs tablets to Thomas Wyndham, 1814, at St. Bride's, Glamorgan, and Archdeacon Thomas, 1820, in Bath Abbey. In 1815 he made a bust of Sir Thomas Picton for John Colby, of Ffynone, Pembroke (Colby Archives).

GAHAGAN, VINCENT
fl. 1804–1832

He was probably the brother of Lawrence (q.v.) and Sebastian Gahagan (q.v.) and settled in England before 1804. In 1811 the Count of Funchal, the Portuguese Ambassador, asked the Royal Academy to arrange a competition for a royal equestrian statue to be erected in Rio de Janeiro, and offered prizes of two hundred guineas each for the two best models and fifty guineas for the third.

The Academy took considerable trouble over the matter and asked a number of sculptors to submit models, although some of the best known did not trouble to do so. Long before the works were ready to be judged in 1815 the Ambassador began to repent of his bargain, but the Academy refused to allow him to go back on his word and awarded the two first prizes to C. Rossi (q.v.) and Vincent Gahagan. When they hurried round to show their models to the Count he was, or pretended to be, disappointed and wrote to the Academy that they were "but little worthy to be sent to his Court." To this the Academy firmly replied that they were the best sent in and must therefore be accepted. The correspondence dragged on in a desultory way for a year or two and then ceased, but it is not clear whether the successful sculptors were ever paid for their trouble (Royal Academy Archives).

Gahagan exhibited at the Royal Academy, 1804–1833, and also showed an equestrian statue of the Duke of York at the British Gallery in 1832. The *Literary Gazette* (1832, page 170) considered it "both in feature and in figure an admirable resemblance of His Royal Highness," but could not "praise the nag."

Vincent died in 1832, being, as his widow stated in her application to the Artists' General Benevolent Institution, "Frightfully destroyed at Pimlico by the falling of the statue of the Right Hon. George Canning while working on the statue." Gahagan was, at the time of his death, employed by Sir Richard Westmacott (q.v.). He left a widow and six children totally unprovided for. It is curious how most writers, including J. T. Smith, have stated that it was Edwin Gahagan (q.v.) who was killed by the fall of the statue, but this is clearly impossible, as Edwin exhibited at Westminster Hall twelve years after his supposed death.

GALLAGHER, JOHN
b. 1805

He was born in Ireland and studied sculpture at the Schools of the Royal Dublin Society, where he won several prizes. Indeed, he showed so much promise that when William Behnes (q.v.), himself an old student of the Schools, offered to take two of the boys into his studio for instruction, Gallagher was one of the two chosen, the other being Panormo (q.v.).

Before going to Behnes, however, Gallagher first attended the Royal Academy Schools in 1824, gaining a Silver Medal in 1825, and entering the sculptor's studio in the following year. He later went to Rome at the expense of the Dublin Society, but the promise of his early years does not seem to have been fulfilled, for very little more is heard of him.

He exhibited at the Royal Academy, 1834–1844, and at the Great Exhibition of 1851 showed a design for a fountain.

(Strickland's *Dictionary of Irish Artists*; Royal Academy Archives.)

GARDENER, —
His fine contemporary wax portrait of David Garrick is in the Royal Collection.

GARDENER, or GARDNER, GEORGE, of Tewkesbury
fl. 1793–1838

He signs tablets to John Hancock, 1793, and John Jones, 1813, both at Chastleton, Oxon; James Olive, 1826, at Twyning, Glos; and the Rev. Joseph Baugh, 1838, at Ripple, Worcs.

GARDENER, W. M., of Cheltenham
fl. 1812–1843

He signs monuments to William Hill, 1812, at Leigh, Glos; Charlotte Edwards, 1838, at Laugharne, Carmarthen; and Lieutenant-Colonel Cyprian Bridge, 1843, at Harwich, Essex.

GARDIE, LOUIS
fl. 1850–1854

He exhibited at the Royal Academy, 1850–1854, showing busts of H. Wilde (1850), Charles Wilkins (1853), and the Duke of Wellington (1854). In 1851 he executed a bust of the Marquess de la Roche Jacquelin, and also showed a bronze one of Sir Robert Peel at the Great Exhibition of the same year. His terra-cotta bust of John Speke is in the National Portrait Gallery.

GARLAND and FIELDWICK, of Camberwell

Firm *fl.* 1807–1847

In 1816 they were the masons responsible for building the portico of Camberwell Church. Their tablets are dull, except for one commemorating Joseph Newcomb, 1841, in Brixton Parish Church, which has a fine relief of a mourning woman.

Other monuments and tablets executed by the firm include those to Mary Walter, 1807, at Crayford, Kent; the Hichens family, 1815, at St. Ives, Cornwall; Ann Hedges, 1820, at Whitchurch, Bucks; Ellen Caldecott, 1828, at Shimpling, Suffolk; William Old, 1833, in St. Mary-at-Hill; and Captain Borlase, 1836, at Fareham, Hants. They also sign the large sarcophagus of William Morris, 1847, in the churchyard at Woodford, Essex.

A "Garland" signs the busts of John Dollond (1843) and an undated one of George Dollond, both in the possession of the Royal Society.

The partners sign a large sarcophagus tomb to Louisa Schroder d. 1824 in the Old Burial Ground, Dulwich Village and also tablets to Admiral Maitland, d. 1839 in Bombay Cathedral and Arthur Teagle, who died in the same year in Antigua Cathedral, British West Indies.

GARRARD, CHARLES

b. 1798

He was the son of George Garrard (q.v.) and attended the Royal Academy Schools in 1816, winning a Silver Medal two years later. He exhibited a number of busts at the Academy between 1816 and 1829, including those of Mr. Raymond, of Drury Lane Theatre (1818), J. Watts (1826) and Mr. Mitchell (1831). He also exhibited at the British Institution, 1824–1825. His bust of a girl is at Powderham Castle, Devon.

GARRARD, GEORGE

b. 1760, *d.* 1826

He was born on 31 May, 1760, and as a boy studied under Sawrey Gilpin, the painter and Royal Academician. In 1778 he joined the Academy Schools, and three years later had pictures of horses and dogs accepted for exhibition at Burlington House. He continued to show pictures of horses and other sporting subjects until about 1795, when he deserted painting for sculpture.

In his new profession Garrard soon became well known for his reliefs and accurate small-scale models of animals, particularly of dogs and cattle, which he executed both in plaster and bronze. There are large collections of such models at Woburn Abbey, Southill and Burghley, while others were made for Lord Petre and Sir John Soane.

He lived in George Street, where "he executed his sculptured imitations of animals, which he exhibited in his gallery, forming a collection of models that have raised him in this department to a competition with the greatest statuaries of Greece" (Ackerman's *View of London*, 1816, page 49).

As a portrait-sculptor he must also have been considered competent, for he was one of the five artists invited by Cambridge University in 1806 to send in models for the proposed statue of Pitt (*Cambridge Chronicle*, 28 March, 1807). J. T. Smith, in his *Book for a Rainy Day* (page 289), mentions that he went to Garrick's villa at Hampton in 1829, and in the temple there found a cast which Garrard had made of Roubiliac's statue of Shakespeare. This, he continues, "was similar to the one he furnished the late Mr. Whitbread for the hall of Drury Lane Theatre."

In 1814 Garrard proposed to erect a statue of Wellington, but the scheme fell through owing to lack of funds. Perhaps this was just as well, for the work was to be 48 ft. high, and was to show the Duke "in the costume of a Roman general, resting on his truncheon; the horse in the gallop, under which the Furies are represented sinking to the earth" (*New Monthly Magazine*, 1814, page 249).

Garrard exhibited at the Royal Academy, 1781–1826, and at the British Institution, 1806–1825, showing altogether over two hundred works. In 1800 he was elected an Associate of the Royal Academy. Three years previously he and his fellow-sculptors had petitioned Parliament to introduce a Bill to secure copyright in works of plastic art. Their efforts were successful and resulted in the passing of the Act of 1798 (38 Geo. III, c. 71) "for encouraging the art of making new models and casts of busts, and other things therein mentioned."

Garrard died at Queen's Building, Brompton, on the morning of Sunday, 8 October, 1826, while kneeling at prayer with his family. At the subsequent sale of his works one of the lots was a bust of Thomas Girtin, the well-known painter in water-colours, "taken from a cast made after death." Apparently the sculptor left very little money, for his widow, a daughter of his old master, Sawrey Gilpin, was forced to write and ask the Royal Academy for assistance, "as she had been left in very necessitous circumstances and with a daughter, incapable from illness of doing anything for her subsistance." In reply the Academy granted her a pension of £45 a year and a donation of £50 (Royal Academy Archives).

(*D.N.B.*; Authorities cited in text.)

BUSTS

1803	Benjamin West	Exhibited Royal Academy
1803	Henry Holland	Woburn Abbey
1803	Thomas Adkin	Southill, Beds
1804	Rev. Dr. Willis	Burghley
1804	Lord Somerville	Exhibited Royal Academy
1804	Duke of Bedford	Uppark, Sussex
1804	Sir J. Banks	Burghley
1805	William Batton	Uppark, Sussex
1805	Napoleon	Uppark, Sussex
1806	Sawrey Gilpin, R.A.	Burghley
1806	Henry Holland	Southill, Beds
1807	C. J. Fox	Uppark, Sussex
1807	Rt. Hon. J. Foster	Exhibited Royal Academy
1807	Earl of Egremont	Petworth
1808	Pitt	Fitzwilliam Museum, Cambridge (terra-cotta)
1810	Humphrey Repton	Exhibited Royal Academy
1810	William Wilberforce	Exhibited Royal Academy
1813	R. B. Sheridan	Soane Museum (plaster-cast)
1814	Wellington	Althorp
1815	Prince Hoare	Exhibited Royal Academy
1816	Wellington	Southill, Beds
1818	Princess Charlotte	Exhibited Royal Academy
?	Arthur Young	Petworth
?	Thomas Girtin	Lot 68, Sale of Garrard's Works, 1827

VARIOUS

1799	Two pointers	Southill, Beds (bronze)
1805?	Four large plaques of animals	Southill, Beds (over doors out of main hall)
c. 1805	Reliefs of sporting scenes	Uppark, Sussex (bronze)
1806	Plaques of animals	Burghley (in corridor, etc.)
1806	Two dogs	Southill, Beds (marble)
1811	Lion	Woburn Abbey (for west front)
1811	Eagle grasping a Fulmen	Woburn Abbey (over architrave of Temple of the Graces; bronze)

1812	Bacchic Bull	Woburn Abbey (pediment of south front of Sculpture Gallery)
1812	The Boxers	Southill, Beds (plaster)
1812	Sir John Moore	Southill, Beds (bronze mounted figure, model for a statue)

MONUMENTS

1799	Bocking, Essex	Anne Nottidge
1809	Lymington, Hants	Paul Burrard
1816	Wiviliscombe, Somerset	John Weech
1816	Hughenden, Bucks	Countess Conyngham
1816	Bocking, Essex	Thomas Nottidge

GARRATT, —
fl. 1710–1711

He worked under William Townsend (q.v.), and between 1710 and 1711 carved the pediment on the west side of the quadrangle of Queen's College, Oxford (Hiscock's *A Christ Church Miscellany*, page 43).

GARRETT, GEORGE, and JONATHAN, of Southampton

They sign a large tablet to Anne Northage, 1832, at Itchen (Pear Tree Green), Hants

GATES, HENRY
fl. 1684–1722

He was the son of William Gates of Kingston-on-Thames and in 1684 was apprenticed to Thomas Broomhall (q.v.). He later became free of the Masons' Company and was living at Vauxhall in 1708, according to the list of members for that year. In 1722 he made a marble chimney-piece for Stourhead, Wiltshire (Hoare Archives).

GATES, WILLIAM
fl. 1731–1761

Son of Henry Gates (q.v.), he was apprenticed to his father in 1713 and became free in 1722. He was Renter Warden of the Masons' Company in 1760, and in the following year was living near Fishmongers' Hall. He signs a large monument to John Wise, 1746, at Totnes, Devon.

Gates' son, another William, was apprenticed to Samuel Stretton in 1740, and became free in 1747.

GATLEY, ALFRED
b. 1816, *d.* 1863

Gatley came from a family which had long been settled in Cheshire, where his father owned quarries in the Kerridge hills. In 1837 he came to London with the help of friends and obtained work in the studio of E. H. Baily (q.v.). Two years later he joined the Royal Academy Schools, gaining a Silver Medal and exhibiting for the first time at the Academy in 1841.

In 1834 he left Baily to become assistant to M. L. Watson (q.v.), and in the same year showed his bust of "Hebe" at Burlington House, a work which was bought by the Art Union of London, who reproduced it in bronze for one of their prizes.

In 1852 Gatley went to Rome, where he met John Gibson (q.v.), whose enthusiasm for Greek art he shared. He does not seem to have been very successful in Italy, for practically his only patron was Mr. Christie Miller, who commissioned him to design a mausoleum which was to be erected near Edinburgh to the memory of Mr. W. H. Miller.

Of all Gatley's works the one which attracted the most attention was his bas-relief of "Pharaoh and His Hosts," shown at the International Exhibition of 1862. *The Queen* of August, 1863, considered it among "the noblest productions of modern art," while the *Art Journal* of the same year (page 181) declared that "there is not a sculptor in Europe who would not consider it an honour to have been its author." Gatley himself visited England for the last time in 1862, but to his great disappointment failed to sell any of the works he had sent to the Exhibition. He returned to Italy and died of dysentery in Rome on 28 June of the following year. He was buried there in the Protestant Cemetery, where a marble lion (one of his own works) was placed over his grave.

The *Art Journal* (1863, page 322), in its obituary of the sculptor, said of him that "he had a mind of singular independence. The style he chose," the article continued, ' admitted of no facile compromise of the classic with the pictorial. It descended not to seek an easily purchased popularity by softly blended forms after the manner of the Romantics. The school to which he belonged was stern and strict. The English public failed to comprehend the largeness of this manner."

Gatley's chief work, after the "Pharaoh," was "The Song of Miriam," which was also a commission from Mr. Christie Miller and which he began in 1855 but did not complete until just before his death. His group of "Greek Hero and the Bull" and his statue of "Echo" (1861) are both in the Salford Art Gallery. At the Royal Academy, where he exhibited between 1841 and 1853, he showed busts of Thomas Legh of Lyme (1845), the Duke of Vittoria (1846), Mrs. Smith Barry (1847), William Hulton (1848) and A. J. Coffin (1852). In 1851 he executed a bust of Richard Hooker for

the Inner Temple, while in 1862 (besides the relief already mentioned) he sent to the International Exhibition a statue of "Night" and four small marble figures of recumbent animals.

He signs tablets to Bridget Downes, 1840, at Pott Shrigley, and Thomas Legh, 1857, at Disley, both in Cheshire; and another, with a medallion portrait, to John Lowe, 1846, at Mottram, Lancs; and a monument to Mary Legh, 1846, at Newton-in-Makerfield, Lancs.

(*D.N.B.*; Authorities cited in text.)

GAWEN, JOSEPH
b. 1825

He joined the Royal Academy Schools in 1847, on the recommendation of E. H. Baily, and exhibited at the Academy, 1850–1882. Here his works included busts of W. Blanchard Jerrold (1850), George Cruikshank (1868) and the Rev. Samuel Smith (1882).

GAY, M. L., of London
fl. 1818–1821

Gay, who was declared a bankrupt in 1818, signs a tablet to Mrs. Knipe, 1821, in Bath Abbey.

GAYFERE, THOMAS, the Elder, and THOMAS, the Younger
Thomas Gayfere the Elder: *b.* 1720, *d.* 1812
Thomas Gayfere the Younger: *b.* 1755, *d.* 1827

Thomas Gayfere the Elder was the eldest son of Thomas Gayfere, a mason of Wapping, and his wife, Mary Townsend of Burford (probably a member of the family of Oxford masons). Old Gayfere, who had been foreman to Christopher Cass (q.v.), moved to Westminster after the child's birth and remained in business there for many years. In 1748 he was described as "of Westminster, mason," when another son, Richard Gayfere, was apprenticed to a mason named George Mercer. In 1756 he built 18, Cavendish Square for Thomas Bridges (Middlesex Record Office 85/223), and in 1774 became Master of the Masons' Company.

In 1734 Thomas Gayfere the Elder was apprenticed, not to his father the Westminster mason, but to Andrews Jelfe (q.v.). He became free in 1741 and, about 1760, was appointed mason to Westminster Abbey. Between 1768 and 1769 he carried out repairs to Harefield Church, Middlesex, for which he received £53 (Newdigate Archives), while in 1773 he made the Portland-stone front of Horace Walpole's chapel at Strawberry Hill, and also the chimney-piece in the great north bedroom (Toynbee's *Strawberry Hill Accounts*, pages 156–157).

The elder Gayfere, who had lost his wife on 22 March, 1770, died on 4 April, 1812, and was buried on 10 April in the west cloisters of the Abbey. His estate, which was sworn at under £10,000, was administered by his only surviving child, Thomas Gayfere the Younger, who had been appointed master-mason of the Abbey jointly with his father on 7 December, 1802, and who had superintended the repairs to Henry VII's Chapel which were begun in 1809.

After his father's death Gayfere undertook the repair of the great rose window in 1814. He signs the Abbey monument to Mrs. Vincent, 1807, while other work executed by him in the neighbourhood was the restoration of the north front of Westminster Hall between 1810 and 1812. In the former year he was also employed at Somerset House (P.R.O., A.O. 1/2499).

Gayfere died on 20 October, 1827, and was buried at Newton-Solney in Derbyshire. His obituary in the *Monthly Magazine* of the following year (page 224) declared that "the faithfulness of his workmanship will be a lasting testimony to his abilities and it is by no means too great praise to aver that to no other individual could the interests of that edifice" (i.e., Westminster Abbey) "have been better entrusted. At its completion the antiquary rejoiced and the fears which had been long entertained gave way to feelings of gratification."

Owing to the fact that three generations of the family had the same Christian name, it is not very easy to disentangle their works, but it was probably the first Thomas Gayfere, assisted by his son (Thomas, the Elder), who was the mason for Westminster Bridge, which was opened in 1750.

(Chester's *Westminster Abbey Registers*; Brayley's *Westminster Abbey*, Vols. I and II; Authorities cited in text.)

GEERTS, CHARLES, of Louvain
b. 1807, *d.* 1855

Geerts, a Belgian, was responsible for the modelling of the sculpture in the Byzantine Court at the Crystal Palace, where in 1856 an exhibition of sixty of his works was held (*Art Journal*, 1856, page 376).

He also signs the monument to Harriot Rushout, 1852, at Burford in Shropshire.

GEORGE, GEORGE
fl. 1762–1764

He was "under twenty-two" when in 1762 he gained a premium from the Society of Arts for a "model of ornaments," winning further premiums in the two following years.

George was apprenticed to John Wildsmith (q.v.), but was free by 1764 and working on his own account as an ornamental carver, probably of tablets for chimney-pieces.

(Archives, Society of Arts.)

GERAERSTEN, JAN
fl. 1688–1692

He was an assistant to C. G. Cibber (q.v.), and from 1688 until 1692 was employed at Chatsworth, making figures and statues for the fountains (Francis Thompson's *A History of Chatsworth*).

GHEYS, JAMES
b. 1749

Gheys was born on 6 August, 1749, the son of a statuary. In the following year his father asked the Barber Surgeons' Company for the skeleton "that used to hang up in the theatre," offering an "ornamental figure in plaster-of-Paris in exchange." A bargain was struck, and the Barber Surgeons received a head of Inigo Jones in return for their skeleton (Archives, Barber Surgeons' Company).

James Gheys attended the Royal Academy Schools in 1773 and in 1775 received a premium of fifteen guineas from the Society of Arts for a model of Lucretia. He exhibited at the Academy, 1774–1778.

The monument to the Lort family at Tenby, Pembrokeshire (erected 1778), is signed "Gheys, Marylebone," and it is, therefore, impossible to say whether the work is by James Gheys or his father.

GIANNELI, J. B.
fl. 1777–1809

He was chiefly employed in making plaster busts, vases and statues, and in 1777 made a plaster-cast of a dog's head for Lord Shelburne. In the same year he exhibited at the Great Rooms by Exeter Exchange, London, showing figures of "Flora," "Hebe," "Mercury" and "Venus," and busts of King Alfred and Socrates, while his wife contributed "a dish of fruit in coloured wax."

In 1789 Gianneli executed four statues—"Isis, Flora, Antinous and a Discobalon"—for the great hall of Carlton House. Four years later he made vases for Lord Hardwicke, both for Wimpole in Cambridgeshire and for his patron's London house in New Cavendish Street. In 1794 he made a bust for Lord Abercorn at Bentley Priory, and in 1806 one for Lord Bridport. On 14 December, 1841, died Dominico Giannelli, a minor sculptor and perhaps a brother of J. G. Giannelli (q.v.). His daughter Rosa applied to the Artists' General

Benevolent Institution, for assistance in the following year.

GIANNELLI, J. G.
fl. 1808–1829

He was the son of J. B. Gianneli (q.v.) and exhibited at the Royal Academy, 1809–1820, showing busts of J. C. Saunders, the oculist (1810); Mr. Baldwin (1812); and Dr. Wachul (1820).

His very fine bronze bust of Professor Porson, executed in 1809, is in the College library at Eton, and in 1814 he made "a very faithful bust" of John Nichols (*Gentleman's Magazine*, 1826, Part II, page 502). Another in wax of an unknown man, signed and dated 1829, is in the Victoria and Albert Museum.

GIBBONS, GRINLING
b. 1648, *d.* 1721

Grinling Gibbons was the son of James Gibbons who was admitted to the freedom of the Drapers' Company on 12 September, 1638. Grinling was born at Rotterdam in 1648, where his father continued to live until after 1659. James married about 1638–1639 Elizabeth Gorlings, or Gurlings, and it has been suggested that the singular christian name Grinling is a corruption of his mother's maiden name. Grinling was admitted by patrimony to the Drapers' Company in 1672. In 1704–1705 he became Renter-Warden, in 1712–1713 Second Master-Warden, and in 1714–1715 First Master-Warden. He stood for the Mastership in 1718, 1719 and 1720, but was not elected. (*The Genealogists' Magazine*, Vol. V, 1929–1930, page 322); and *Notes and Queries*, (Vol. 161, page 56.)

According to Vertue (Walpole Society, Vol. I, page 125) he "was born in Holland of English parents and came into England about nineteen years of age." The young man then went to Yorkshire, where, Vertue continues, "he was first employed and afterwards came to London, settled with his family at Deptford and followed ship-carving. About that time the playhouse in Dorset Gardens, called the Duke's House, being a-building, Mr. Betterton finding him an ingenious man, employed him to carve for him the ornaments and decorations of that house, particularly the capitals, cornishes and eagles, with which Sir Peter Lilly was well pleased and inquiring after the artist that performed them, Mr. Gibbons by his means was recommended to King Charles II, who then had ordered the beautifying of the Palace of Windsor in which work he was employed."

It is John Evelyn the diarist, however, who is usually given the credit for discovering Gibbons in the cottage at Deptford, which was close to Evelyn's seat of Sayes Court. On 18 January, 1671, he notes in his diary how he found Gibbons carving in wood a copy of "The Crucifixion" of Tintoretto, which "for curiosity of handling, drawing and studious exactness, I had never before seen in all my travels. I questioned him why he worked in such an obscure and lonesome place: he told me it was that he might apply himself to his profession without interruption."

Evelyn, who found the young man "very civil, sober and discreet in his discourse," took his protégé to Whitehall on 1 March to show his carving to the King. His Majesty inspected it and then desired them to take it to the Queen, but they arrived at an unpropitious moment to find her closeted with a French peddling-woman from whom she was buying baubles. The latter, fearful that the sight of the carving might distract attention from her wares, began "to find fault with several things in it which she understood no more than an ass or a monkey," and the Queen, therefore, refused to buy it. It was later sold for £80 to Sir George Vyner, a goldsmith and son of the Lord Mayor.

Undismayed, Evelyn next recommended Gibbons to Hugh May and Sir Christopher Wren and he was given employment on wood-carving at Windsor, where he made a chimney-piece "representing a festoon of many fishes, shells and other ornaments" (*Walpole, Vertue,* Vol. I, page 136).

Gibbons's failure at Court, however, was not permanent, for Charles II, recognizing his genius, appointed him Master Carver in Wood to the Crown, a post he held until the reign of George I. It is, of course, chiefly as a wood-carver that he is remembered today, but this branch of his art is outside the scope of this book. Having once found fame, he proceeded to employ a number of skilled assistants, so that much of the work in wood, marble, stone and brass for which he received the pay, and later the credit, was, in fact, carried out by others. Wood seems to have been his favourite medium, for Vertue (op. cit.) says that "he was neither well-skilled or practised in marble or bronze, for which work he employed the best artists he could procure."

On 23 March, 1682, Gibbons wrote to John Evelyn asking him to see Sir Joseph Williams again, "you woold be pleased to speak to him that hee wold get me to carve his ladies sons house, my Lord Kildaer, for I understand it will be very considerable." Evelyn drafted a letter to Lord Kildare saying that Gibbons was "well known for what he had done at Windsor and other places, he is the most excellent in his profession not only in England but in the whole world." In his draft answer to Gibbons Evelyn says: "when we next meet we will consult about the monument to be erected at our church for Sir Richard Browne (Evelyn Archives). The monument referred to, which was a grey-marble tablet with cornice, urn and shield of arms, was erected in St. Nicholas', Deptford, and it is to be hoped has survived the burning of the church during the Second World War.

In 1692 Gibbons carved a marble chimney-piece for Evelyn's house at Wotton, receiving £18 (Evelyn Archives).

In 1683 Gibbons (with or without the help of collaborators) made a statue of Charles II for the Royal Exchange. The manuscript diary of Sir Edward Deering, Bart. (in private possession), notes on 11 July of that year that "the Hamburg Company were desirous to express their gratitude to the King and therefore intend to set up a marble statue for him in the midst of the Royal Exchange and this day the King was pleased to see the model of it as it is prepared by Mr. Gibbon, a most famous artist in carving and eminent also for working in marble." The figure, which was to be 6 ft. 10 in. high, was to stand on a pedestal "8 ft. high, with eight marble steps upon the four faces of the marble pedestal. Ye front is to have the inscription and the other three sides ye arms of England, Scotland and Ireland."

About two years later the sculptor also supplied statues of Edward VI, Queen Mary, James I and James II for the same building, but these were all damaged or destroyed in the fire of 1838. The figure of the Queen was ordered by the Mercers' Company, and their Court Book records that Gibbons was to receive £50 for it and "that he is to finish the statue in three months from Thursday, being ye nineteenth of June, 1685" (Company's Archives).

In 1672 Gibbons was made free of the Drapers' Company and five years later he moved to Bow Street, Covent Garden. In 1701 the house collapsed, although no one was hurt, and it was in the new building erected on the same site that he died on 3 August, 1720. A week later he was buried in St. Paul's, Covent Garden.

As far as I know he only signs one monument, that of Robert Cotton, 1697, at Conington, Cambridgeshire, though an inscription on the base of Miss Beaufoy's monument, dated 1705, in Westminster Abbey, states that the work is by "Mr. Gibbons." However, a number of bills or contracts survive relating to other monuments, and particulars of four of these are given below.

In the Coventry archives at Croome Court is the indenture, dated 30 April, 1690, between Gibbons and Margaret, Lady Coventry, for the tomb of her husband, John, Lord Coventry. This was to be made of the "best and purest white Italian marble" and was to consist of "three statues as big as life," the central one to be "the semblance and perfect figure of Lord Coventry in all his Baron's robes lying upon a tomb properly adorned, with his coronet tumbled at his feet, his right hand outstretched to catch at a starry crown presented towards him by the statue of Faith." It was to be finished in a year and "the name of the said Grinling Gibbons to be engraved in some prominent place as the artificer of the said monument." The sculptor entered into a bond of £500, though the monument was only to cost £215. On signing the indenture he was paid £107 10s. by Lady Coventry and in the end received a total sum of £322.

The appearance of Lord Coventry's monument today would hardly meet with the approval of his widow or "the said Grinling Gibbons." When the church at Croome D'Abitot, Worcs, was rebuilt the "starry crown presented towards him by the statue of Faith" disappeared altogether, while his own coronet, instead of being allowed to remain "tumbled at his feet," was perched on his head in a most ludicrous way, for it was far too small to fit. Thus later restorers have not only turned a dramatic design into bathos, but have also provided a weapon for the detractors of English seventeenth-century sculpture.

One item in the contract was apparently omitted, for a careful search has failed to reveal the name of the sculptor engraved in any place, "prominent" or otherwise.

The contract between Sir Richard Newdigate and Gibbons, dated 22 July, 1693, is preserved in the family archives and is for a monument costing £10 to the memory of Henry Newdigate who had died more than seventy years before. The work, "5 ft. high and 3 ft. broad," was to be erected in Ashtead Church, Surrey. Gibbons was also responsible for the memorial to Lady Newdigate, 1693, in Harefield Church, Middlesex, and his receipt for £170 and a letter he wrote to Sir Richard on the subject are still extant. The latter runs as follows: "I ombly thanck you for youer great faver and extrorney ponuallity I receifed the £50 wich I shall allwaes aknoligs as a pertickler faver. As for the grait I will not imply the Smich till I hear youer comands. I shoeld thnick that it shoeld be of it self and goe round the monnemint but howsoever I will send to my man hoem is not kom hoem to a gost akount off both the monnemints." At the end of it the writer's "wiffe begs her sarvis to the Ladie and youer honred sealf."

It must have been open to question whether Gibbons's correspondents understood him, for his spelling is atrocious, even by seventeenth-century standards. A possible reason for this may be the fact that he spent his early life in Holland and probably spoke and wrote Dutch more easily than English.

In the Fitzwilliam Museum is his drawing for a monument showing two linked cartouche tablets and endorsed "15th January, 1696 agreet. for Monument in St. Paul's." On the back of the drawing is the name of Doctor Holder, for whom the monument was intended.

In 1717 he executed the monument of the Duke of Chandos and his wives for St. Lawrence, Whitchurch, Middlesex, a work often wrongly attributed to Andrew Carpenter (q.v.). Apparently the Duke thought the price was too heavy, for he wrote to Gibbons on 10 January, 1718, as follows: "Sir, I have ye favour of yours, and must own I think ye monument and statues to be excessive high, however Since you Say, you have never yet in any dealings you have had had any abatement made in your prices, I have directed Mr. Zollicoffre to pay you ye £350 remainder of your bill. You'l forgive me if I can't but add that I believe there never was so much reason from ye workmanship to allow of an abatement in this case, from ye judgment of everyone who has seen ye figures" (Huntington Library, California, St. 57. Vol. 15, page 103).

In 1705–1706 he was paid £35 "for carving" by the third Earl of Carlisle. This was presumably for work at Castle Howard, and there was always a family tradition that the carving above the chimney-piece in a room west of the saloon (destroyed in the 1940 fire) was the work of Gibbons (Castle Howard Archives).

(*D.N.B.*: Allan Cunningham's *Lives of the Painters*; H. Avray Tipping's *Grinling Gibbons*; Notes and Queries, Fourth Series, Vols. III and IV; Archives, Christ's Hospital and St. Thomas's Hospital; Vice-Chancellor's Accounts, University of Cambridge; authorities cited in text.)

STATUES

c. 1682	Charles II	Chelsea
1686	James II	Outside National Gallery (see also Dievot, A.)
1691	Duke of Somerset	Trinity College, Cambridge (£200)
1695	Sir John Moore	Christ's Hospital, now at Horsham, Sussex (£90, Hospital Archives)
1701	Sir Thomas Clayton	St. Thomas's Hospital
1701	William III	For College Green, Dublin

VARIOUS

1678	Pedestal of Charles II's statue	Windsor Castle
1678	Sundial	North Terrace, Windsor Castle
1684	Font	St. James's, Piccadilly
1686	"Marble holy-water pott" in the Chapel, and chimney-piece in the Queen's lodging	Whitehall Palace (P.R.O., Works 5/54)
1688	Bas-relief of Goliath in marble "over great bed-chamber chimney"	Whitehall Palace (P.R.O., Works 5/42)
1688	"Two great marble figures as big as the life, crown and cushion and a pedestal over the chimney in the drawing-room"	Whitehall Palace (P.R.O., Works 5/42; £180)
1690	Four plaster busts above the book-cases	Trinity College Library, Cambridge
1689–1695	Work which included nineteen festoons under the windows of the east end, seven festoons on the outside, and the bas-relief on the north pediment	St. Paul's Cathedral (Wren Society Publications)
1700–1712	Work in freestone which included six Ionic capitals at £14 each; four statues for the west quadrangle at £25 each; the great doorcase in the west wall of the saloon, £179; statues of "Peace" and "Truth" for the quadrants; the Duke's coat of arms, £75; two statues of slaves on the upper pediment, £56; a figure of "Charity" with three children, £35; three figures on the quadrant; forty-eight Corinthian capitals for the south front, £420; two lions on the great front; and two "basons" of flowers for the top of the garden piers	Blenheim Palace

1701	Seven chimney-pieces	Dalkeith Palace
1701	Chimney-piece, with a bas-relief of "Neptune and Galatea"	For Moor Park, Hertford (£80), now Dalkeith Palace
1701	Lion and unicorn, 3 ft. long, for gates	Hampton Court Palace (P.R.O., Works 5/52)
1706	Eight capitals	House of Commons (P.R.O., E.351/3312)

MONUMENTS

1683	Radbourne, Derby	German and Anne Pole (Archives, Col. John Chandos-Pole)
1683	Exton, Rutland	Viscount Campden
1689	Rochester (Cathedral)	Sir Richard Head (Collins's *Baronetage*, 1741, page 599)
1689	Clifton-on-Teme, Worcs	Henry Jeffreys (Wren Society, Vol. IV, page 14)
1691	York (Minster)	Archbishop Lamplugh
1693	Harefield, Middlesex	Lady Newdigate
1695	Fulham (Parish Church)	Dorothy, Lady Clarke (Brewer's *Beauties of England*, Vol. X, Part IV, page 101)
1695	Harefield, Middlesex	Sarah Newdigate
1697	Conington, Cambs	Robert Cotton
1699	Soulbury, Bucks	Robert Lovett
1702	Henbury, Glos	Sir Edward Southwell
1702	Kensington (St. Mary Abbot's churchyard)	William Courten (Faulkner's *Kensington*, page 230)
1705	Westminster Abbey	Miss Beaufoy
1707	Westminster Abbey	Admiral Sir Cloudesley Shovel
1710	Westminster Abbey	Admiral Churchill (drawing and contract, Westminster Public Library)

GIBBONS, JOHN, of Bristol

In 1743 he was working at Bristol Exchange, where he carved "two coats of arms" and "two Venetian window pedestals" (Bristol Archives, Exchange Building-Accounts).

GIBBS, SAMUEL, of Axminster
Firm *fl.* 1773–1821

His work is well above the average of the contemporary small-town statuary of the period.

He signs monuments and tablets in Dorset to Robert Coade, 1773, at Lyme Regis; to William Drake, 1775, Jane Steer, 1779, and John Ellard, 1816, all at Axminster; to Benjamin Studley, 1775,

at Broadwindsor; to the Rev. Maurice Hopkins, 1819, at Stoke Abbott; and to Elizabeth Cozens, 1821, in St. Peter's, Dorchester. In Somerset monuments by Gibbs include those to Christopher Jolliffe, 1799, at Kingsdon; and to Samuel Sparks, 1813, at Crewkerne.

GIBBS, W., of Basingstoke
fl. 1803–1842

His best work is the monument of Sarah Debary, at Hurstbourne-Tarrant, Hants, which has a well-carved relief. Other monuments and tablets signed by him include those to Peter Waldo, 1803, at Worting, Hants; Thomas Mathew, 1814, at Upton Grey, Hants; Lady Ashley, 1824, at Evesley, Wilts; and John Ker, 1842, at Weyhill, Hants.

GIBSON, BENJAMIN
b. 1811, *d.* 1851

Youngest brother of John Gibson (q.v.), he was born in Liverpool in 1811. In 1837 he joined his brother in Rome, sending from there to the Liverpool Exhibition in 1840 a "Psyche borne off by the Zephyrs" (a copy of a work by his brother), and an original composition entitled "Shepherd Boy and Dog" (*Gentleman's Magazine*, 1840, Part I, page 404). In 1848 he carved a "Bacchante Listening to Pan" for Mr. Lousanda; "Cupid Disguised as a Shepherd Boy"; "Innocence," for a Mr. W. Jackson, of Birkenhead; and a bas-relief of "A Wounded Amazon" (another copy of a work by his brother) for Mrs. Huskisson (*Art Union*, 1848, page 50).

Benjamin Gibson died at the Baths of Lucca on 13 August, 1851, and was buried in the Protestant Cemetery there. The monument over his grave is the work of his brother John, with whom he spent all the time he was in Italy, "assisting him in his professional engagements and contributing to his domestic circle an unvarying amiability of disposition and cheering and pleasing manners" (*Gentleman's Magazine*, 1851, Part II, page 522).

He also wrote a number of articles on Italian antiquities for the *Gentleman's Magazine* and for the Society of Antiquaries. His remarks on the Lycian Marbles were published by Sir Charles Fellows.

Gibson signs a few monuments, including those to Mrs. Clough, 1826, at Mold, Flint; to John Hodson, 1827, Standish, Lancs; and to Major Hilton, 1829, in Chester Cathedral. According to the *Gentleman's Magazine* (1829, Part II, page 652), he was also responsible for the tablet to Matthew Gregson, 1829, in St. John's, Liverpool.

(Authorities mentioned in text.)

GIBSON, JOHN, R.A.
b. 1790, *d.* 1866

Gibson was born near Conway, the son of a market-gardener, but his parents moved to Liverpool when he was nine years old and, when he was fourteen, apprenticed him to a firm of cabinet-makers. A year later the boy met F. A. Legé (q.v.), who was then working for Messrs. Franceys (q.v.), the Liverpool statuaries. Legé had made a head of "Bacchus" which Gibson proceeded to copy, and he also carved a small marble head of "Mercury." These works so impressed Messrs. Franceys that they offered to pay his employer £70 to cancel his indentures, and, after considerable difficulty, it was arranged that Gibson should become their apprentice. He soon attracted the attention of William Roscoe, of Liverpool, for whom he carved a bas-relief for a chimney-piece, but his first important independent work was the monument to Henry Blundell. This was erected in Sefton Church, Lancashire, in 1813, and though signed by Gibson's firm was entirely executed by himself (Gregson *Fragments of Lancashire*, page 224).

In 1816 Gibson had work accepted by the Royal Academy, and in the following year went to London with introductions to Lord Brougham and to Christie, the well-known auctioneer. The latter introduced him to Mr. Watson Taylor, who commissioned, not only a bust of Roscoe, but also those of himself, his wife and all his children down to the baby, "a little thing of no shape at all." Four of these were included in the Erlestoke Park sale of 1832.

At the sale of Nollekens's effects held by Mr. Christie on 23 July, 1823, one of the lots was "Theseus & Centaur, modelled by Mr. Gibson in Mr. Nollekens's studio" (Archives, Messrs. Christie). This would seem to show that Gibson may have had some training under Nollekens.

Gibson, however, had set his heart on going to Italy, even "if he went there on foot," and on 20 October, 1817, he at last arrived in Rome. Here he was received with great kindness by Canova, who gave him instruction in his own studio and in the Academy of St. Luke, while he also received assistance from Thorwaldsen, who was living in Rome at that time. The young sculptor's first original work was a life-size figure of a "Sleeping Shepherd," and his first patron the Duke of Devonshire, for whom he carved "Mars and Cupid"; another early patron was the King of Bavaria. About 1822 Sir George Beaumont wrote to Sir Francis Chantrey (q.v.) from Rome that he had "given a commission to Gibson, he seems to me to have great merit and his composition will,

I think, please you. He is modest and assiduous with much taste," the writer added, "and I think will do England great credit" (*Builder*, 1866, page 77).

Gibson was now on the road to success and was urged by his friends to return to London, where they felt he would make more money. This, however, he steadfastly refused to do, for, as he wrote in a letter, "I thank God for every morning that opens my eyes in Rome." In 1833 he was elected an Associate and, five years later, a full member of the Royal Academy; he exhibited there from 1816 until 1864.

It was not until 1844 that he at last revisited England, for he had been commanded by Queen Victoria to execute a statue of herself. It was on this statue that he introduced the touches of colour of which he was so fond, and which he claimed had been the practice of the Greeks. In a letter written in 1846 he told a correspondent that "my eyes have now become so depraved and I cannot bear to see a statue without colour." Most art critics regarded such a departure with considerable suspicion, although the *Roman Advertiser* (July, 1847) did admit that "the application of colour is so delicate, the tone so subdued, that no effect of glaring contrast is produced, and the pale purity of the marble does not as a whole suffer from the partial tinting." Apparently Gibson's experiment with the Queen's statue was not his first effort in this direction, for as early as 1839 the *Art Union* (page 106) reported that he had gilded the narrow band on the head of the central figure in his group "Psyche Borne on the Shoulders of Two Youths," which had been commissioned by Prince Torlonia. This unorthodox proceeding deeply shocked the editor, who could "scarcely conceive it to be other than a dangerous departure from true art."

Gibson was living in Rome during the political troubles of 1847–1849, though he and his brother Benjamin (q.v.) did move for a short time to Lucca. In 1850 he again returned to England in order to model another statue of the Queen, this time for the Houses of Parliament, and took five years to complete the work. It was during this period that he began for Mr. Preston the celebrated statue known as "The Tinted Venus." The sculptor himself described it as "the most carefully laboured work I ever executed . . . I tinted the flesh like warm ivory scarcely red, the eyes blue, the hair blonde, and the net which contains the hair golden."

After this Gibson never revisited England, and he died in Rome on 27 January, 1866. He was buried in the English cemetery there, while French soldiers fired a volley over his grave, in recognition of the fact that he had been granted the Legion of Honour. His friend, Lord Lytton, who composed the inscription on his tomb, had some years previously paid another tribute in the dedication of his book, *Zanoni*, when he alluded to Gibson as "the man whose noble ambition has never been depraved by the appetite for wealth or the appetite for praise; the sculptor whose love of Grecian art has never betrayed him into servility or plagiarism."

Gibson's life was one of great happiness, simplicity and purity; as he said of himself: "I worked on all my days happily and with ever new pleasure, avoiding evil and with a calm soul; making images, not for worship, but for the love of the beautiful." With his mind set entirely on his art, he was as guileless as a child and quite as helpless. He could not travel alone, for he not only lost his luggage and his ticket, but even forgot his destination and had a habit of alighting at the wrong station. "Pray, Sir, are you a foreigner?" a porter asked him on one occasion. "No," answered Gibson, "I am not a foreigner, I am a sculptor." As his pupil, the American sculptor, Miss Hosmer, succinctly remarked: "He is a god in his studio, but God help him out of it." In middle age he was "of prepossessing appearance, with greyish hair and a peculiarly grave, immovable expression of countenance," according to a visitor who saw him in 1854.

In his will Gibson left the bulk of his fortune of £32,000 and the contents of his studio to the Royal Academy, including marble statues or groups of "The Wounded Warrior," "Hebe," "Bacchus," "Narcissus" and "Venus." In the list of his works sold at Christie's, which is given below, the name of the sale, and in some cases the amount, have been added in brackets:

"The Hunter and the Wounded Fawn," 27 March, 1863 (Lord Herbert of Lea); "Bust of Helen," 1875 (H. de Burgh); "Wounded Amazon," 7 July, 1875 (Anonymous, 300 guineas); "Shepherd and Dog," 2 March, 1878 (Miss Webb, £65); "Venus," 20 March, 1880 (H. Roe, 280 guineas); "The Hunter," 29 May, 1880 (George Moore, £246); "The Tinted Venus," 28 July, 1890 (Walter Long, £1,837); and "Venus and Apple," 22 July, 1893 (R. C. Naylor, £918). At the sale of the Peel heirlooms held by Messrs. Robinson and Fisher on 10 May, 1900, Gibson's "Shepherd Boy" fetched 160 guineas.

(Lady Eastlake's *Life of Gibson*; *Literary Gazette*, 1829, page 649; *Art Journal*, 1853, page 63, and 1857, page 273; *Builder*, 1847, pages 223 and 540; *Art Journal*, 1866, pages 90 and 113; Watson Taylor Sale Catalogue, 1832; T. Matthews, "Biography of John Gibson", (authorities cited in text.)

STATUES

1823	Augusta Pierrepont	Stratfield Saye
1824	"Sleeping Shepherd Boy"	For Lord George Cavendish (replicas for Duke of Northumberland and Mr. Lenox, of New York)
1824	"Nymph"	For Count Schonberg of Bavaria
1824	"Paris"	For George Watson Taylor
1824	"Endymion"	For Duke of Devonshire
1826	"Cupid"	For Sir Watkin Williams Wynn
1829	"Narcissus"	For Lord Barrington (replicas for Mr. Evrington, and Mr. Fort, of Manchester)
1830	"Flora"	For Earl of Dudley (replica Walker Art Gallery, Liverpool)
1831	"Nymph Untying her Sandal"	For Earl of Yarborough
1832	"Proserpine"	For Mr. Ablett, of North Wales (replica for Dwarkanath Tagore, of Calcutta)
1833	Dudley North	Little Glenham Church, Suffolk
1836	W. Huskisson	Pimlico Gardens, London
1836	Bishop Van Mildert	Durham Cathedral
1838	"Narcissus"	Burlington House (Diploma Work)
1839	"Cupid Tormenting the Soul"	For Lord Selsey (replicas for Richard Yates and Mr. Holford)
1840	"Wounded Amazon"	For Lord Grosvenor
1840	W. Huskisson	Liverpool Necropolis
1840	"Cupid Disguised as a Shepherd Boy"	For Sir John Johnstone (replicas for Emperor of Russia; Mr. Appleton, of Boston, U.S.A.; Lord Crewe; Mr. Alleson, of Liverpool; Mr. Farnham, of Philadelphia, U.S.A.; and Sir R. Peel)
1845	Hon. Mrs. Murray	Exhibited Royal Academy
1846	Kirkham Finlay	Merchants' Hall, Glasgow
1847	W. Huskisson	Customs House, Liverpool

1848	"Aurora"	For Mrs. Sandbach, of Liverpool (replica for Mr. D. Henry)
1850	"Venus"	For J. Neeld (replicas for Marquess of Sligo, Mr. Uzielli, and Mr. Preston)
1851	George Stephenson	St. George's Hall, Liverpool
1852	Sir Robert Peel	Westminster Abbey
1856	"Bacchus"	For Marquess of Londonderry
1856	"Pandora"	For Lady Marian Alford, now Victoria and Albert Museum (replica for Mr. Penn, of London)
1863	Queen Victoria	Royal Collection
?	"Sappho"	For Patterson Ellams, of New York
?	"Venus"	For Drapers' Hall, London
?	"The Graces"	Walker Art Gallery, Liverpool
?	"The Young Augustus"	For Elkanan Bicknell

BUSTS

1814	John Philip Kemble	National Portrait Gallery
1816	H. Park	Exhibited Royal Academy
1816	William Roscoe	For Royal Institution, Liverpool
1820	George James	Possession Lord Northbourne
1822	C. Ellison	Exhibited Royal Academy
c. 1826	"Helen of Troy"	Derby Art Gallery
1828	W. S. Landor	National Portrait Gallery (plaster-cast)
1830?	"A Greek Girl"	Formerly Ilam Hall, Staffs
1843	"Grazia"	Royal Collection (replica Victoria and Albert Museum)
1857	Duchess of Wellington	Apsley House
1863	Princess of Wales	Buckingham Palace
?	Sir Charles Eastlake	National Portrait Gallery
?	Mrs. Jameson	National Portrait Gallery
?	"The Young Augustus"	Walker Art Gallery, Liverpool
?	"Flora"	For Mr. Rogers; sold Christie's, 12 May, 1871

GROUPS

| 1821 | "Mars and Cupid" | Chatsworth |

1822	"Psyche Carried off by the Zephyrs"	For George Beaumont (replicas for Emperor of Russia, and for Prince Torlonia, 1839)
1826	"Hylas and the Naiads"	For Mr. Vernon, now Tate Gallery
1847	"Hunter and his Dog"	For Henry Sandbach (replica for Earl of Yarborough)
?	"Hunter and Wounded Fawn"	For Lord Herbert of Lea

RELIEFS

1822	"Hero and Leander"	For Duke of Devonshire
1826	"The Hours Leading Forth the Horses of the Sun"	For Earl Fitzwilliam
1826	"Phaeton Driving the Chariot of the Sun"	For Earl Fitzwilliam
1839	"Venus and Cupid"	Burlington House
1840	"Amalthea"	For the Earl of Carlisle
1844	"Cupid and Psyche"	For Queen Victoria (replica for Duke of Northumberland)
1862	"Christ Blessing Little Children"	For Henry Sandbach

MONUMENTS

1823	Barbados (Cathedral)	Frances Bovell
1830	Liverpool (St. James's Chapel)	William Earle
1832	Liverpool (St. James's Chapel)	William Hammerton
1833	Whitchurch, Bucks	John Westcar
1837	Madras (Cathedral)	Anne Chamier
c. 1840	Badger, Salop	Harriet Cheney
1851	Rome (Protestant Cemetery)	R. J. Wyatt
1852	Badger, Salop	Harriet Pigot
1856	Chichester (Cathedral)	Mrs. Huskisson
1856	Fawsley, Northants	Lady Knightley
?	Pulborough, Sussex	William Hammond
?	Liverpool (Renshaw Chapel)	Mrs. Roscoe

GIBSON, SOLOMON,
of Liverpool
b. c. 1796, *d.* 1866

He was the younger brother of John Gibson (*q.v.*), and at the age of sixteen modelled a figure of "Mercury," his best-known work. Of this he made a number of replicas, including one which he presented to Sir Thomas Lawrence, who sent him a £10 note as "an encouragement."

Gibson exhibited at the Royal Academy in 1816 and 1822, while at the Liverpool Academy he showed in 1812 "Cupid and Psyche" and

"Venus Lamenting the Death of Adonis," and busts of Miss Traill and Dr. T. S. Traill in 1822 and 1824 respectively. His marble bust of Mr. Rosson dates from 1822. He died in Paris on 29 January, 1866, two days after his brother John. He had heard of the latter's illness and had set out to join him in Rome, but never reached his destination.

Gibson signs a few monuments, including those to Pudsey Dawson, 1817, in St. George's, Liverpool; the Rev. Hope Eyton, 1824, monument, 1826, at Mold, Flint; Scrope Colquitt, 1825, at Childwall, Lancs; John Hughes, 1830, at Llanfair, Denbigh; and Dr. John Davies, 1844, at Mallwyd, Montgomery. In St. Michael's Church, Charleston, South Carolina, U.S.A., is his tablet to General Charles Pinckney, 1825, and he also signs four others (with very inferior lettering) in Dudleston Church, Salop. These are to Charles Morrall, 1822; Mrs. Edwardes, 1825; William Challnor, 1825; and Mary Hilton, 1826.

As an architect he produced a plan for the restoration of Trajan's Forum when he was in Rome in 1829. This, the *Literary Gazette* (1829, page 649) considered, showed "great research and knowledge," but was "very defective in drawing and perspective."

In addition to his artistic work Gibson was also a classical scholar and had a good knowledge of ancient Welsh literature, a subject on which he wrote many papers. In spite of all these activities there was an "absence of purpose in the direction of his studies," and "he passed through life a strange and useless, though not a commonplace, man," according to the *Dictionary of National Biography*. His brother John supported him for many years and bought him an annuity of £100, which was probably the reason why he left him practically nothing in his will.

GILBERT, JOHN, of Cambridge
fl. 1824-1830.

His signed tablets are commonplace and include those to Mary Hurrell, 1824, at Newton, Cambs; Josiah Neale, 1826, in St. Clement's, Cambridge; and the Rev. Thomas Kerrich, 1828, at Dersingham, Norfolk.

GILBERT, JOHN, of Stamford
Firm *fl.* 1812–1837

There is, for some reason, no mention in the Stamford "Hall Books" of his ever having become a Freeman of the town. He was succeeded in the business by his son, Henry Gilbert, who carved the later tablets, but neither of them produced any outstanding work.

Tablets executed by the firm include those to Sally Mounsay, 1812, at Greystock, Cumberland; Mary Graham, 1816, at Belton, Rutland; John Bailey, 1822, at Thorney, Cambs; Susanna Pailliet, 1822, at Yaxley, Hunts; Mrs. Bonney, 1824, at Kingscliffe, Northants; William Belgrave, 1824, at Preston, Rutland; the Rev. Stephen Wright, 1824, at Castor, Northants; the Rev. Richard Lucas, 1827, at Great Casterton, Rutland; and Joseph Phillips, 1837, in St. Martin's Church, Stamford.

GILES, —, of Wakefield

He signs a classical wall-tablet to Samuel Haxley, 1834, at Brotherton, Yorks.

GILL, JOHN, of London
fl. 1808–1812

In 1808 he received £113 for marble chimney-pieces for the Bank of England (Soane Notebooks), and three years later was one of the principal masons for building Mr. Coutts's house in Stratton Street, Piccadilly (Archives, Coutts Bank).

GILLIAM, JOHN
fl. 1776–1798

As the junior partner of John Deval the Younger (q.v.) he was employed on building work at Somerset House between 1776 and 1795, though for the last year of that period he was in partnership with Thomas Wood (q.v.), Deval having died in 1794. Gilliam also worked on his own account for the same building, carving "three ox-skulls and drapery to the back of the keystones to the arches in the vestibule," while in 1777 he received £85 for "rich shells" above the windows of the principal floor. For the interior he supplied chimney-pieces in 1780 and again six years later (Shide Ledger, R.I.B.A. Library).

In 1782 he was the master-mason responsible for building the Fleet Prison, where he received a total sum of £2,211 (P.R.O., A.O.1/2495).

There were a number of other masons of this name, including some in Lincolnshire. A William Gilliam, of Welburn in that county, was apprenticed in 1718 to his father, Thomas Gilliam, mason. There was also a Joseph Gilliam, assistant to William Atkins (q.v.), who was sent down to Ashburnham Place, Sussex, in 1761 to set up a chimney-piece made by his master (Ashburnham Archives).

GILLINGHAM, JAMES, of Winchester
fl. 1814–1838

He signs tablets in Hampshire to Chaloner Ogle,

1814, in Winchester Cathedral; to John Terry, 1835, at Dummer; and to Sarah Wickham, 1838, at Wonston.

GINN, JOHN
b. 1813

In 1830 he attended the Royal Academy Schools, to which he had been recommended by John Constable, R.A., and in the same year won the large Silver Medal from the Society of Arts for a model of a bust.

Ginn exhibited at the Academy in 1832 and 1833, showing "Psyche Borne by Zephyrs," a bust, and a group of "Adam and Eve." He showed a bust of Lord Brougham at the Suffolk Street Galleries in 1833.

GOBLET, LEWIS ALEXANDER
b. 1764

He attended the Royal Academy Schools in 1792 and, after winning a Silver Medal two years later, became assistant to Nollekens (q.v.). He ultimately became the sculptor's principal carver, though his master paid him only £24 for each bust he executed. He was also responsible for the figures on the monument to Mr. Coke and for the statue of "Religion" on the tomb of Mrs. Howard.

Goblet, who was present at his master's death-bed, received under the latter's will the working tools and all the marble in the sculptor's yard, while his children, Henry and Louisa, were bequeathed £100 and £30 respectively. He seems at one time to have had a studio of his own, for his address is given as "20, Upper Marylebone Street" in the London Directory of 1809.

Goblet exhibited at the Royal Academy, 1799–1822, showing busts of Lord Nelson (1808), Madame Catalini (1808), Henry Goblet (1811), Nollekens (1816), the Duke of Norfolk (1817), the Rt. Hon. Mr. Ponsonby (1818), and Mr. Lonsdale, R.A. (1818). His bust of Dr. Burney, dated 1818, is in Westminster Abbey.

Monuments signed by Goblet commemorate the Rev. J. Boucher, 1804, at Epsom, Surrey; and Dr. Charles Burney, 1818, in St. Paul's, Deptford.

At the sale of Nollekens's effects which was held by Mr. Christie on 3 July, 1823, the following works by Goblet were sold: "A Fawn," a bust of Mr. Nollekens and a relief of "Joseph & Potiphar's Wife." (Archives, Messrs. Christie.)

(J. T. Smith, *Nollekens and His Times.*)

GODDARD, JAMES,
of King's Lynn

fl. 1801–1823

He signs a number of tablets in Norfolk, including those to Elizabeth Postlethwaite, 1794, at Dersingham; and to the Rev. William Atkinson, 1822, at Hillington.

GODFREY, WILLIAM,
of Abingdon
fl. 1811–1843

Probably son or grandson of William Godfrey, of Abingdon, who was apprenticed to Gilbert Burgess, of Oxford, and became a Freeman of that city in 1756. The younger Godfrey signs a number of tablets in Berkshire, including those to Mary Anthony, 1800, and Robert Sellwood, 1801, both at Appleton; Bernard Bedwell, 1811, Thomas Lintall, 1820, and Charles King, 1842, all in St. Helen's, Abingdon; and Thomas Humfrey, 1836, at Blewberry.

GOLDEN, JOHN, of Holborn
fl. 1781–1808

His monuments are carried out in coloured marbles and frequently have charming "Adam" details. His yard was in Upper North Place, Gray's Inn Road. Monuments and tablets signed by him include those to John Williamson, 1781, at Finningham, Suffolk; Henry Doughty, 1781, at Mapledurham, Oxon; John Badcock, 1784, at Paul, Cornwall; John Bates, 1785, at Beaconsfield, Bucks; John Carpender, 1790, at Watford, Herts; Dorothy Filmer, 1793, at East Sutton, Kent; and Joseph Brooke, 1796, at Southfleet, Kent. In 1781 he carried out repairs to Mr. Wood's house in Red Lion Square (Archives, Lord Brownlow).

GOODLIFF, —

A local statuary, he signs a wall-tablet to Francis Pochin, 1806, at Morcott, Rutland.

GOODWIN, ROBERT,
of Stamford

He signs a tablet to Samuel Allen, 1796, in St. John's, Stamford, while his son, Robert Goodwin the Younger, signs one to William Pears, 1823, at Barnack, Northants.

Another member of this family of masons was James Goodwin, who died in 1803 at the age of forty-five.

GOOLD, —, of Swindon

He signs a wall-tablet to Walter Brind, 1816, at Liddington, Wiltshire.

GOSSET, ISAAC
b. 1713, *d.* 1799

Gosset, who was one of the best of the eighteenth-century wax-modellers, belonged to a family which had fled from Normandy to Jersey at the time of the revocation of the Edict of Nantes and had later settled in London. He invented a composition of wax, and in this, according to his obituary in the *Gentleman's Magazine* (1799, page 1,088), "he modelled portraits in the most exquisite manner." "He was one of those ingenious men," the article later declares, "so rarely met with, who are at the same time equally amiable and inoffensive. In the line of his art he may be said to have been unique, as the inventor of the inimitable materials with which he worked, and of which the secret is in the possession of his son, the learned and reverend Isaac Gosset, D.D."

Gosset exhibited at the Society of Artists and at the Free Society, 1760–1778. During his long life he modelled likenesses of most of the famous people of his time, his list of sitters including George III; Queen Charlotte; Lord Thurlow; the Duke of York; Lord North; Gideon Gosset; Dr. Harris; David Garrick; General Wolfe; the Duke of Sussex; the Prince Regent; Henry Pelham; George Grenville; the Duke of Grafton; Lord Bathurst; Louth, Bishop of London; Lord Maynard; Trevor, Bishop of Durham; Francis Hutcheson; the Earl of Mansfield; Mrs. Delany; George Selwyn; General Conway; Thomas Townshend; Lord Camden, and Sir Jeffery Amherst.

There is a collection of his works in the small drawing-room at Stourhead, Wiltshire, where they have remained since they were purchased by Henry Hoare between 1753 and 1755. At this period Gosset does not seem to have been well paid, for the Stourhead portraits only average £1 each (Stourhead Archives). He also worked for Wedgwood, modelling for him likenesses of George I, George II, William, Duke of Cumberland and Henry Dundas.

Horace Walpole had at Strawberry Hill Gosset's portraits of Hoadley, Bishop of Winchester; Frederick, Prince of Wales; Lady Mary Coke; and Charles Townshend, the last-named being now in the National Portrait Gallery. In the Newdigate Archives is the artist's bill for ten guineas for wax portraits of Miss Conyers and Miss Palmer, both executed in 1763. Four years later Trevor, Bishop of Durham, paid him £1 11s. 6d. for a portrait of the Duke of Newcastle (Archives, Brand of Glynde). Gosset's portrait of the Fourth Earl of Bristol is at Ickworth Park, Suffolk.

Works by Gosset which are still extant include a set of Roman Emperors in the possession of his direct descendants; a portrait of General Maclean, dated 1779, at Buxted Park, Sussex; and others of Earl Granville and the Countess of Shelburne

at Bowood. At Hartlebury Castle, the palace of the Bishop of Worcester, are those of Charles Yorke, Prince Octavius, Bishop Hurd (dated 1778), Fisher Littleton, Lord Mansfield and Ralph Allen.

His finest works, however, are in the library at Windsor Castle, and include wax portraits of George I; George, Prince of Wales; Ferdinand, Duke of Brunswick; Edward, Duke of York; and Frederick, Prince of Wales, and his wife, Princess Augusta of Saxe-Gotha. Other likenesses of the Royal Family, including George I; George II; Queen Caroline; Frederick, Prince of Wales; Princess Augusta, and the Duke of Cumberland, are in the Schreiber Collection at the Victoria and Albert Museum. At the National Portrait Gallery, besides the portrait of Charles Townshend already mentioned, there is another of Henry Seymour Conway by the same artist.

(*D.N.B.*; *Notes and Queries*, Third Series, Vol. VI, page 516; Strawberry Hill Sale Catalogue, 1842; information from Messrs. Wedgwood.)

GOSSET, MATTHEW
b. 1683, *d.* 1744

Uncle of Isaac Gosset, he was French by birth but was naturalized after his family had fled from Normandy. He was later one of the Gentlemen of the Band of Pensioners of George II and, in 1728, was elected a member of the Spalding Society.

Gosset, who made a number of wax portraits, was also a statuary with a yard at St. Anne's, Westminster, and here in 1714 he took as an apprentice "Rodney, son of Joseph Stone" (P.R.O., I.R.1/3).

He died in 1744 and was buried at St. Marylebone, where his marble monument bore "specimens of his work," according to his epitaph, which alludes to him as a "statuary," and also adds "that he was well known for his superior skill in the polite arts."

(Nichols's *Literary Anecdotes*, Vol. VI, page 83.)

GOTT, JOSEPH
b. 1786, *d.* 1860

He was born at Calverley, near Leeds, and worked in John Flaxman's (q.v.) studio as an apprentice for two or three years (British Museum, Ad. MS. 39,784). In 1805 he joined the Royal Academy Schools, where he won a Silver Medal in 1806 and the Gold Medal in 1807. In the following year he was awarded the Greater Silver Palette by the Society of Arts for an original plaster-cast of "Samson," while in 1819 he received a second Gold Medal from the Academy for his "Jacob Wrestling with the Angel."

PLATE XI

JOHN HUNT
Cilena l'Anson Bradley, 1726, Long Buckby, Northants.

RICHARD HAYWARD
Lord Botetourt, 1773, Williamsburg, Virginia, U.S.A.

PLATE XII

PETER HOLLINS
Mrs. Thompson, 1838, Malvern Priory.

One of Gott's patrons was Sir Thomas Lawrence, in whose sales on 17 June and on 7 July, 1830, were included the sculptor's models of a "Sleeping Venus," of a "Group of Four Figures, a Man, a Woman, and two Infants" and of "A Female at the Bath." Another was Benjamin Gott, of Armley House, Leeds, and it was he who sent Gott to Rome in 1824. Here the latter lived until his death, executing a number of works for Armley House and also a recumbent figure for the tomb of his benefactor, to whom, curiously enough, he was in no way related. In 1824 he also sent a group in plaster to the Academy, as he wished "to be considered for the vacant appointment of travelling student" (Royal Academy Archives).

Gott died in Rome in January, 1860, and was buried in the Protestant Cemetery. He exhibited at the Royal Academy, 1820–1848, and at the British Institution, 1821–1822, while he showed "Ruth Gleaning" at the Paris Exhibition of 1855. His plaster group "The Dying Spartacus" is in the Soane Museum, and in the Leeds Art Gallery are his busts of John Barran, and Miss Beckitt, together with a seated statue of George Banks. His "Ragazzo" fetched £129 at the Schlotel sale held at Christie's on 25 April, 1885.

His monuments are nearly all fine, the best being one in memory of Thomas Lloyd, 1828, in Leeds Parish Church, which has a portrait-bust and an inscription-tablet flanked by two beautifully cut figures of officers in full regimentals. The most surprising commemorates Colonel Edward Cheney of the Scots Greys, in Gaddesby Church, Leicestershire, and shows him (almost life-size) at the supreme hour of his life, when "four horses were killed under him and a fifth wounded and the command of the Regiment devolved upon him" at the Battle of Waterloo. The sculptor has chosen to portray the moment when the Colonel's horse (presumably his fifth) sinks beneath him with a bullet-wound in its throat, a disaster which does not appear to perturb him unduly, save that he has lost his shako, which lies with a broken strap among the down-trodden corn into which horse and rider are floundering. On the pedestal of the monument is a relief showing the Colonel defending the regimental colours, which a French officer is trying to seize.

The whole work gives the impression of being correct in every detail, and one feels that the Colonel himself must have directed every stroke of the chisel. The result is interesting from a documentary point of view, although artistically it leaves much to be desired. Nevertheless it has the almost fatal attraction which a second-class work sometimes exercises on the beholder, though he is forced to admit later that the whole effect was faintly comic.

(Taylor's *Worthies of Leeds*; various Sale Catalogues.)

WORKS

1820	Head of a Bacchante	Chatsworth
1821	"Sisyphus"	Exhibited Royal Academy
1825	"Dog and Puppies"	Chatsworth
1826	"Girl with a Basket"	Lot 1092, Peter Norton's sale, Christie's, 1869
1828	"Pug-dog and Cat"	For Earl of Shrewsbury
1831	"Venus Dissuading Adonis From the Chase"	Exhibited Royal Academy
1831	"Boy and Greyhound"	For Earl Cadogan
1832	William Ewart	St. James's Chapel, Liverpool (seated statue)
1834	"Italian Greyhound"	Exhibited Northern Society, Leeds
1834	"Hagar and Ishmael"	Exhibited Northern Society, Leeds
1834	"Boy with a Bird"	Exhibited Northern Society, Leeds
1835	"A Spaniel"	For General Ramsay
1841	"Dog Scratching for a Rat"	For Earl Cadogan
1841	"Ruth"	Possession Messrs. Crowther, Isleworth
1845	"Dancing Girl"	For E. Bicknell
1847	"A Vintager"	Exhibited Royal Academy
1848	"Calypso"	Exhibited Dublin
1848	"Mary Magdalen"	Exhibited Royal Academy
?	"Musidora"	Chatsworth
?	"Greyhound and Pups"	Formerly Normanhurst Court, Sussex
?	"Boy with a Rabbit"	Walker Art Gallery, Liverpool

BUSTS

1824	Hogarth	For Sir Thomas Lawrence
1856	Benjamin Gott	Leeds Literary Society
?	Columbus	Capitoline Museum, Rome
?	"Ariadne"	Chatsworth

MONUMENTS

1824	Walton-on-Thames, Surrey	Lady Williams
1828	Gilling, Yorks	Thomas Fairfax
c. 1830	Durham (Cathedral)	Emily Cadogan
1833	Bradford (Cathedral)	Samuel and Mary Hartley
c. 1835	Bradford (Cathedral)	William Sharp

1840 Armley, Yorks	Benjamin Gott (life-size reclining figure)
1847 Halifax (All Saints, Mortuary Chapel)	Jonathan Ackroyd (recumbent figure)

GOUDE, ANTHONY,
of Chelmsford
fl. 1726–1741

Goude, who had been assistant to Christopher Cass (q.v.), set up for himself in Chelmsford before 1726 and was the mason employed on the building of Boreham House, Essex, from 1726 until 1731. From 1729 till 1741 he was working for Earl Fitzwalter at Moulsham Hall, in the same county, making the hall chimney-piece in 1732 and a "veined-marble chimney-piece" in the following year. In 1737 he cut the stone capitals for the piers of the stable court, receiving £30.

In 1741 he was paid £7 13s. 6d. for the six milestones between Ingatestone and Chelmsford. (Hoare and Fitzwalter Archives.)

GOULD, I., of Barnstaple
fl. 1800–1835

The best of his monumental works is the tablet to Thomas Gay, 1802, at George Nympton, Devon, which has a most unusual relief of butter-flies leaving the chrysalis. Other monuments and tablets in Devon carried out by Gould include those to Ann Newbold, 1800, at Shirwell; Walter Robins, 1818, at South Molton; Major Glaze, 1828, at Bishops Tawton; Thomas Stevens, 1832, at Little Torrington; and Thomas Hogg, 1835, at Northam.

GRAHAM, WILLIAM
fl. 1845–1872

He exhibited at the Royal Academy, 1845–1872, showing busts which included those of Sir Robert Peel, George Peabody and Lord Brougham. Of the first of these the *Art Union* (1847, page 200) said: "We cannot think Sir Robert sat for this bust, it is unlike, and in every way much too heavy."

GRANT, BENJAMIN
fl. 1775–1809

Grant, who in 1775 was in partnership with James Hoskins (q.v.), was plaster-figure maker to the Royal Academy. He apparently got into difficulties, for the Academy Minute-book records in 1808 that a letter had been received "from Mr. Flaxman with a petition from Mr. Benjamin Grant praying assistance from the President and Council."

On this occasion the Council gave him ten guineas, but when Grant wrote to them again later in the same year "stating his wretched situa-tion," they accompanied another donation of the same amount with a letter saying that he "was not to expect any relief in the future."

This display of firmness seems to have made no impression, for Grant petitioned twice for help in 1809 and each time the Academy relented and gave him ten guineas.

GRAVENOR,
or GRAVENER, JAMES

In 1763 he made the model of "four medallions" for the exterior of Kedleston. In the same year there is a payment of £54 to Joseph Hall of Derby (q.v.) for "carving two medallions" for the outside of the house, and this may refer to Gravenor's work. It seems hardly likely that he could have modelled the great circular plaques on the exterior of the main front (which in any case were executed by William Collins, q.v.).

Gravenor was also paid £16 for "altering" four alabaster capitals and £5 9s. 6d. for "altering" figures in the drawing-room chimney-piece (Curzon Archives).

GRAY, —, of Weymouth

He signs tablets in Dorset to Priscilla Awdry, 1814, at Wyke Regis, and to Robert Cope, 1818, at Weymouth.

GRAY, WILLIAM
b. 1818

In 1839 he attended the Royal Academy Schools, to which he had been recommended by William Behnes (q.v.), and in 1844 received a Silver Medal for a bust of the Rev. John Williams ("murdered by savages on the island of Acro-manga"), which he had exhibited at the Academy three years previously.

Gray showed busts and paintings at the Academy from 1841 until 1857, and at the British Institution in 1848, the busts including those of Sir Robert Peel and Sir Augustus Clifford.

GREEN, —, of Warwick

He signs a tablet to John Knightley, 1814, at Offchurch, Warwick.

GREEN, ALEXANDER
b. c. 1670

He was the son of Richard Green of the County of Oxford, yeoman, and was apprenticed to Peter Powell, of London. In 1691 he became free and in 1713 was employed with Thomas Davies (q.v.) on the building of Lord Ashburnham's house in St. James's Square (Ashburnham Archives).

GREEN, HENRY

Presumably a local mason, he built the very pretty little dovecote at Melbourne Hall, Derbyshire, in 1708 (Archives, Marquess of Lothian). The building has now been adapted as a muniment room.

GREEN, JOHN HIPPISLEY
b. 1753

He was born on 30 June, 1753, the son of Jane Hippisley, afterwards Mrs. Green, the famous actress, who died in 1791.

Green, who attended the Royal Academy Schools in 1774 and gained a Silver Medal in 1780, was afterwards employed by Nollekens, "being among his best workmen," according to J. T. Smith. He exhibited at the Academy 1775–1820, but ceased to show sculpture after 1793 and confined himself to landscapes. Works in the former class included "Hercules and Omphale," 1775; a medallion of the Rev. J. Wesley, 1791; and "a design for a monument for a late comic actress to be erected in St. Paul's, Covent Garden," 1793 (J. T. Smith, *Nollekens and His Times*).

GREEN, THOMAS,
of Camberwell
b. c. 1659, *d. c.* 1730

He was bound apprentice to John Fitch in 1673, and later turned over to William Hind, becoming free in 1681. In 1694 he was journeyman to Thomas Cartwright the Elder (q.v.) and later to William Holland, but by 1697 had settled in Camberwell where he worked on his own account.

Green is one of the outstanding statuaries of the first quarter of the eighteenth century, and his monument at Redgrave, Suffolk, to Lord Justice Holt (*d.* 1709), with its seated figure flanked by Justice and Truth, is superb. Equally noble is the standing figure of Judge Powell (*d.* 1713) in Gloucester Cathedral. Grandiose, but rather overpowering, is his towering monument at Waldershare, Kent, to Sir Henry Furnese, which rises like a wedding-cake tier by tier to the very ceiling of the chapel built to contain it. One cannot but have an affection, too, for Green's monument at Denton, Lincs, with its full-length figure of Richard Welby (*d.* 1704) in the square-cut coat and square-toed shoes of the period, while an unexpected touch is provided by the two cherubs who, flying down, place a heavenly crown on the top of his full-bottomed wig.

Other monuments signed by Green (or given by him to Le Neve for the latter's *Monumenta Anglicana*) include those to William Chew, 1712, at Dunstable, Beds; George Courthope, 1714, at Ticehurst, Sussex; Sir Peter Seaman, 1715 (a half figure), in St. Gregory's, Norwich; Maynard Colchester, 1715, at Westbury, Glos; Thomas Hall, 1715, in St. George's, Colegate, Norwich; and Bishop Cumberland, 1718, in Peterborough Cathedral.

He was also responsible for carving a number of coats of arms on barracks and other Government buildings. In April, 1717, he agreed for £26 to cut the Royal coat of arms on the Royal Foundry at Woolwich and in July of the same year agreed for the Duke of Marlborough's arms on the keystone beneath the King's arms for £7 (P.R.O., W.O. 47/30). The King's arms are still on the front of the foundry.

In the same year he was also responsible for the King's arms on the New Storehouse at Chatham, being paid £18 (P.R.O., op. cit.). There are other payments to Green in this year for work at Chatham and it seems fairly certain that he was responsible for the magnificent Royal Heraldry over the main gate of the dockyard. In November he was ordered to "sett up" the Royal arms on St. Martin's Tower of the Tower of London.

In 1718 he was paid £34 for the Royal arms on the New Storehouse at Portsmouth and £50 for the King's Cypher and Crown on keystones which are to "put over the gate at the Gun Wharfe" (P.R.O., W.O. 47/31). The storehouse and gate are no longer in existence.

GREEN, W.
fl. 1731–1737

He worked in the neighbourhood of Rotherham, Yorkshire, and signs a number of monuments which are usually carried out in stone. The designs are based on London work of the period, with cartouche inscription-tablets, architectural details, mourning cherubs, etc., but the carving is first-rate, far above the level of the ordinary provincial statuary, while an unusual touch is also given to each monument by a curious and individual emblem in the centre of the gadrooned base. In the monument to John Spencer, 1732, at Cawthorne, Yorkshire, this takes the form of a skull, with a snake holding an apple in its mouth crawling out of one eye-socket, while a seated cherub with its arm resting on an hour-glass figures on the memorial to Thomas Beaumont, 1731, at Darton, in the same county.

Green only painted his signature on his works, with the result that, in some cases, it has become so faded as to be almost indecipherable. Other signed monuments by him in Yorkshire include those to Richard Green, 1733, and Christiana Spencer, 1737, both at Cawthorne, and to Lord Darcy of Navan, 1733, at Gilling, near Richmond.

GREENSHIELDS, JOHN,
of Lanark
b. c. 1792, *d. c.* 1838

He was a mason by trade, but when he was about thirty he was employed by Robert Forrest (q.v.), who was working at that time on a statue of Melville. This gave Greenshields an interest in sculpture and he accordingly began to study and to model in clay, though he had no idea that he had any talent in this direction. His first work was a figure of a dog carved in stone, and he also modelled likenesses in clay of his father and brother.

He next executed a small stone statue of Lord Byron, while in 1827 he made a figure of Canning and followed this with a colossal statue of the Duke of York in 1828. "It is truely surprising what a degree of dignity and grace has been given the figure and how admirably the most minute parts of the dress and decorations are executed" (Leighton's *Views on the River Clyde*, 1830, page 24). The statue was made for "Mr. Greenwood of Charing Cross the Army Agent." It was cut "from a block of freestone belonging to Mr. Lockhart of Cambusnethan who has kindly permitted Mr. Greenshields to have another for a statue of His Majesty" (*Naval and Military Magazines*, Vol. IV, page XLIII).

In 1834 Greenshields carved the statue of Prince Charles Edward for Glenaladale, Inverness, and in 1835 made a figure of Sir Walter Scott for a Mr. Cadell. His last work was a group of "The Jolly Beggars," executed in 1836. His small-scale model for a seated statue of Sir Walter Scott, 1832, is at Powderham Castle, Devon.

(Authorities cited in text.)

GREENWAY,
BENJAMIN and DANIEL,
of Bath

They were presumably sons of Thomas Greenway (q.v.), and worked as "marble and free-stone masons, carvers and vase-makers" for John Wood the architect, when he was building the Bristol Exchange in 1745.

Two years later Daniel Greenway married a Miss Anne Winslow, of Bath.

(John Wood's *A Description of the Exchange at Bristol*, 1745.)

GREENWAY, JOHN, of Bristol
fl. 1800–1833

He signs tablets in Somerset to Copplestone Bampfylde (*d.* 1791), at Kingston; Caleb Pointing, 1828, at Midsomer Norton; and Benjamin Millard, 1833, at Keynsham. His tablet to Samuel Prosset, 1818, is at Mathern, Monmouth.

The name of the firm is given as "John and Olive Greenway" in a directory of 1830, and it is the latter who signs a tablet to Elizabeth Palmer, 1830, at Paulton, Somerset.

GREENWAY, THOMAS, of Bath
fl. 1707–1720

John Wood, in his *Essay Towards a Description of Bath* (1729, page 424), says that Thomas Greenway, having built about 1720 in St. John's Court a house "so profuse in ornament as to tempt the King to Bath to make part of it his palace, particularly applied himself to small ornaments in freestone, such as crests, vases, fruits, etc., and several that served their apprenticeship to him pursued the business till they brought it to such a perfection as to merit publick encouragement and render their work a rising branch of the trade of Bath."

Earlier in the book (page 225) he also mentions that Greenway, acting on the advice of Dr. Oliver, made "a handsome bath" about 1707 "in one of the rooms of a house built by him upon the beach."

GREENWOOD, JOHN

In 1791 he received £116 for chimney-pieces which he had made for Somerset House (P.R.O., A.O.1/2498).

GREGG, SIDNEY, of Ledbury
fl. 1824–1834

He signs tablets to Charlotte Ballard, 1824, and John Spencer, 1834, both in Ledbury Parish Church, Herefordshire.

GREY, —, and JOYNES,
of London

The firm's yard was in Park Lane and they sign a tablet to Hester Manning (*d.* 1805) at Ormesby St. Michael, Norfolk.

GRICE, ELIAS

In 1662 he made the octagon font for All Saints', Derby (Cox's *Churches of Derbyshire*, Vol. IV, page 95).

GRICE, PHILIP
fl. 1671–1684

In 1671 the Minute-book of Blacknall's Charity

at Abingdon, Berkshire, records that "Philip Grice should have seaven pounds for setting up Mr. Blacknall's statue, his wife and children, and if he did them well with gilt and good colors to their liking, he was then to have eight pounds." For some reason, however, the monument was not set up until 1684, and in the same year Grice received £17 11s. from the Charity, perhaps because the work was on a larger scale than had been at first intended.

As Blacknall had died as early as 1625, a Jacobean design was chosen for the monument. He and his wife are shown kneeling *vis-à-vis*, while the two daughters kneel behind their mother.

GRIGGS, W.
fl. 1830–1840

Griggs, who was an assistant to Sir Richard Westmacott (q.v.), was called as a witness in the case of J. E. Carew (q.v.) *v.* the Executors of the Earl of Egremont.

He exhibited at the Royal Academy and at the British Institution, 1830–1835, showing a number of ideal works and a medallic portrait of the Hon. Charles FitzRoy. At the Suffolk Street Galleries he showed the figure of "An Archer" in 1835.

GRIMBALSTON, WILLIAM
fl. 1769–1778

He lived at "Silver Street opposite Great Pulteney Street," and exhibited wax portraits at the Free Society, 1769–1778.

GRIMSLEY, THOMAS,
of London and Oxford
fl. 1827–1847

In 1829 he received £220 for "six sculptured vases" which he had executed for Buckingham Palace (P.R.O., Works 19/3). At Westminster Hall in 1844 he showed a figure of Cardinal Wolsey, which the *Literary Gazette* considered gave "more idea of the butcher's son than of the great Cardinal," and in the same year made for Oxford Town Hall a statue of Alderman Rowney, carved from a block of Caen stone weighing more than three tons (*Gentleman's Magazine*, 1844, page 630).

Grimsley exhibited at the Royal Academy, 1827–1840, showing a number of works, including a bust of George IV in 1831. His bust of the Duke of Wellington, executed in the previous year, is at Stratfield Saye, while another of Christopher Codrington, dated 1843, is at Codrington College, Barbados.

He signs tablets to Viscountess Valentia, 1843, and the Rev. Robert Brown, 1847, both at Bletchington, Oxon.

GRINDROD, TIMOTHY,
of Liverpool
d. 1817

He originally came from Rochdale, but was in partnership with W. Hetherington (q.v.) at Liverpool when he built the New Exchange there in 1803. He also signs tablets with good details to John Cooper, 1797, and John Bankes, 1817, both at Runcorn, Cheshire.

Grindrod died himself in 1817. His widow, who only survived until the following year, is buried in the churchyard of St. Nicholas, Liverpool, while their son, Robert, who acted as his father's assistant, died in 1820, aged about thirty-two (Liverpool City Archives).

GROVES, WILLIAM
b. 1809

He first exhibited at the Royal Academy in 1834, when he showed a statue of "Psyche," "full of lively and appropriate expression," according to the *Literary Gazette*, and three years later joined the Academy Schools on the recommendation of J. T. Smith.

Groves continued to exhibit at Burlington House until 1861, showing a bust of Charlotte Gaskell in 1857. His bust of John Abernethy is in St. Bartholomew's Hospital.

He also signs a few tablets, including those to Samuel White, 1840, in Hampstead Parish Church; Hannah Cooper, 1843, in St. Michael's, Cornhill; and Lieutenant Thomas Cubitt, 1848, at Catfield, Norfolk. In 1842 he sent to the Academy monuments which were to be erected at "St. Benet Finck, London," and "Shouldham Church, Norfolk."

GRUBB, EDWARD,
of Birmingham
b. 1740, *d.* 1816

He is said to have been born at Towcester, but early in life he moved to Stratford-on-Avon with his two brothers, one, Samuel, a stone-mason and carver, the other a tailor. Although Grubb himself trained, and later worked, as a stone-carver and statuary, he afterwards turned to portrait-painting, "and his numerous paintings on canvas, however coarse in execution, show his success in delineating the human face" (*Warwickshire Worthies*, page 303).

Before 1769 he left Stratford-on-Avon for Birmingham, where he rented from the Corporation a house near the top of Henley Street. In the same year he, and his brother Samuel, carved figures of a boy and girl for the front of the Birmingham Bluecoat School, taking "likenesses of two children then residing in the establishment." When the school moved to Harborne Hill in 1932 replicas of these statues were made for the exterior of the building, while the originals—"no despicable memorial of his ability"—were erected inside (op. cit.).

Grubb died at Stratford-on-Avon on 8 April, 1816 (*Gentleman's Magazine*, 1816, Part I, page 475), his son George, who was also a portrait-painter, having predeceased him.

He signs a few monuments, those in Warwickshire commemorating the Earl of Carhampton, 1788, at Kingsbury; William Ash, 1789, and the Rev. Richard Riland, 1790, both at Sutton Coldfield; and Peter Judd, 1796, at Stratford-on-Avon. In Oxfordshire is his monument to Edward Taylor, 1797, at Steeple Aston.

GRUMBOLD, ROBERT, of Cambridge

b. 1639, *d.* 1720

Grumbold, whom Nicholas Hawksmoore refers to as "our honest and skilful artificer" (*Wren Society*, Vol. XIX, page 105), was the master-mason responsible for a great deal of building at Cambridge during his long life. His works included, for Trinity College, the Library in 1676, and the rebuilding of the great fountain, while at Clare Hall he built the New Hall in 1684, and at St. John's College the bridge between 1696 and 1698 (Willis and Clarke's *Architectural History of Cambridge*).

In 1687 and 1688 Grumbold was working for the Earl of Elgin at Houghton House, Ampthill, where he made chimney-pieces and a door-case for the great hall (Archives, Marquess of Ailesbury). Three years later he was at Wrest Park, Bedfordshire, building the garden terrace with the stairs, coping, etc. In 1694 he received £69 for "a pair of stone peers with Wyverns on them," and in 1695 made two fountains for the garden, for which he was paid £86 (Account-book of the tenth Earl of Kent; Archives, Lady Lucas and Dingwall).

Another member of the same family was John Grumbold who rebuilt the north aisle of Ely Cathedral between 1700 and 1702 (*Wren Society*, Vol. XIX, page 148).

GRUNDY, THOMAS

d. 1829

He became free of the Masons' Company "by redemption" in 1802, and later as a master-mason, worked under Sir John Soar.e on a number of buildings designed by that architect. With Nelson (q.v.) as his partner, Grundy was employed on the building of the Bank of England from 1807 until his death, executing, among other things,

two veined-marble chimney-pieces for £48; 39 ft. of Vitruvian scrolls costing £79; fifty shells in Portland stone for £29; and four carved roses, ten carved flowers in the arch, and nine carved flowers enriched, for £10 10s., £20, and £36 respectively—all this being carried out between 1809 and 1812.

In 1818 and 1819 he was responsible for alterations to the houses of Lord St. Germans and Samuel Thornton in St. James's Square, and also to Fife House, the home of Lord Liverpool, the Prime Minister. In 1821 he built four houses in Regent Street and, between 1827 and 1830, branches of the Bank of England at Bristol, Hull, Liverpool, Newcastle and Norwich.

Among other works which Grundy executed for Soane may be included the sarcophagus ordered for Sir Francis Bourgeois in 1807, to be erected in the mausoleum in the Charlotte Street graveyard, Portland Place. In 1825 Soane employed him at the New Courts of Judicature in Westminster, where he executed three marble chimney-pieces for £78; sixteen corbel-heads for £51; and twenty-four bosses and the cornice, costing £38 altogether (P.R.O., Works 5/125). In the following year, still under the same architect, he was working at Pelwall House, Market Drayton, Salop, where he made the black-and-gold chimney-piece in the dining-room, the statuary and gold chimney-piece in the small drawing-room, and the carved marble one in the large drawing-room for £49, £58, and £140, respectively.

In 1828 Grundy was employed by the Freemasons, for whose Hall in London he supplied four Ionic columns and capitals costing £50, and four veined-marble chimney-pieces for which he was paid £100 (Freemasons' Archives).

In the Soane MSS. is Grundy's bill dated 1818: "To the Executors of Signora Storace for a statuary marble wall-piece fixed in Lambeth Church, £30," the lady referred to being Ann Storace who had died at the age of fifty-one in the previous year. She was the sister of Stephen Storace (1763–1796), whose monument in Marylebone Chapel is the work of Banks (q.v.). A careful search in Lambeth Church, however, has failed to discover Ann Storace's tablet, and I can only conclude that it was destroyed when the building was restored later in the nineteenth century. It is referred to as a "neat marble tablet" in Allen's *History of Lambeth*, published in 1836.

After Grundy's death in 1829 his widow Jane carried on the business.

(Soane MSS.)

GRYLLS, —, of Devonport

He signs large wall-tablets to Gertrude Hawkins,

1823, at Saltash, Cornwall, and to John Newton, 1827, at Bridestowe, Devon.

GUELFI, or GUELPHI, GIOVANNI BATTISTA
fl. 1715–1734

Guelfi, who worked in Rome under Cavalier Camillo Rusconi, was brought to England about 1714 by Lord Burlington, by whom (according to Vertue) "he was much employed for many years in his house in London and made many statues for his villa at Chiswick, being much, continually almost, employed for him several years, also several busts he did" (*Walpole Society, Vertue,* Vol. III, page 73). Faulkner's *Brentford,* published in 1848 (page 412), mentions that Guelfi's statues of Venus and Mercury were then in the gallery of Chiswick House, together with two small heads by the same hand.

The sculptor was also employed by Lord Pomfret to restore the Arundel Marbles and his work is mentioned in a letter written in 1775 to Sir Roger Newdigate by Joseph Pickford (q.v.). Lady Pomfret had just presented the marbles to Oxford University and Pickford recalls that he "was at the placing and repairing of them with Signor Guelfi when first he came from Italy, as well as moving them lately to Towcester, and I know it will be attended with a great deal of trouble and expense before they are properly fixed" (Newdigate Archives).

There is considerable confusion about the authorship of the busts ordered by Queen Caroline for her Grotto or Hermitage at Richmond. The building was designed by Kent, and Vertue (*Walpole Society,* Vol. III, page 51), writing in 1731, has "four busts in stone are to be made by Signr. Guelphi for the Queen's . . . at Richmond. Sir I. Newton, Lock, Dr. Clarke and Mr. Woolaston." Two years later a writer in *The Free Briton* attributed the busts to Rysbrack, but his assertion is corrected in the issue of 6 September, which states that they "unfortunately happened to be the work of another, and as some think a much inferior, hand." Vertue, however, in 1733 definitely says that there are now to be six busts, Bacon and Boyle being added, and that they "imploy the hand of Rysbrack." What probably happened is that Guelfi received the commission but for some reason or other it was transferred to Rysbrack, though he certainly carved one of the busts—that of Dr. Clarke—as Rysbrack writing to Sir Edward Littleton in 1756 says he did not make "the bust of Dr. Clarke in the Hermitage; it was done by Mr. Guelphi, an Italian who is dead." Guelfi also executed a bust of Newton for Pope,

who left it in his Will to Mr. Murray (afterwards Lord Mansfield), together with "the marble head of Homer by Bernini" (*Gentleman's Magazine,* 1744, page 313). The bust of Newton is now at Scone Palace.

Vertue (op. cit.) also says of Guelfi that Lord Burlington "much commended him to the nobility for an excellent sculptor" and "procured him many works." One of these commissions was for the monument to James Craggs erected in 1727 in Westminster Abbey, a "graceful and simple" production, according to Horace Walpole, but who also remarked that it showed Guelfi to be "a very indifferent sculptor."

In 1730 Guelfi made the monument, with its life-size figure of the Earl of Warwick, in St. Mary Abbots, Kensington, and the bill for this, dated 14 October of the same year, is now in the British Museum (MS., E.G.1973). About this time he was responsible for the bust to Anne, Duchess of Richmond, at Deene, Northants. The terra-cotta model of the bust of the Duchess was formerly at Goodwood, but is now in the Victoria and Albert Museum.

In the Earl of Westmorland's archives (Northampton Record Society, Misc. Vol. I, folio 94) is the following entry: "March 26th, 1731. Paid Mr. Guelfi statuary upon signing the articles for a monument of my father Stringer and mother in pursuance of the order in my dear wife's last Will, to be set up in Kirkthorp Church; for the first payment £150." The sixth Lord Westmorland is here referring to the monument of Thomas and Katherine Stringer, the parents of his late wife, which is still in Kirkthorp Church, Yorkshire. On 16 April of the same year Lord Westmorland notes that he "paid Mr. Guelfi statuary as per agreement signed this day the first payment for Mr. Beaumont's monument £100." Richard Beaumont was Lady Westmorland's first husband, and his monument stands in Kirkheaton Church, near Leeds. Also about this time Guelfi made and signed a large monument commemorating T. Watson Wentworth in York Minster.

The sculptor left England in 1734, "after residing nearly twenty years," and returned to Italy, where he settled at Bologna. "It is thought that Lord Burlington parted with him very willingly," says Vertue (op. cit.). The same writer describes him as "a man of slow speech, much opiniated and as an Italian thought nobody could be equal to himself in skill in this country. Yet," he adds, "all his works seem to the judicious very often defective, wanting spirit and grace."

(Authorities cited in text, M.I. Webb, "Busts of Sir Isaac Newton," *Country Life,* 25 January, 1952.)

H

HACKER, JAMES
fl. 1826–1839

In 1826 he won the Silver Palette from the Society of Arts for a bust. He exhibited at the Royal Academy, 1829–1839, showing in the latter year busts of Mr. Back and the Rev. Lancelot Sharpe.

HACKER, JOHN, of Canterbury
fl. 1803–1847

He is probably the son of James Hacker o. Canterbury, mason, who in 1789 was paid £407 for building the market-place in Canterbury (City Archives). John signs a number of dull tablets in Kent, including those to the Rev. William Gregory, 1803, in Canterbury Cathedral; Robert Stains, 1806, in Holy Cross, Canterbury; and Vincent Wood, 1814, at Chilham. A tablet to William Price, 1826, at Allesley, Coventry, is signed "J. and C. Hacker fecit [*sic*]. London and Canterbury."

HACKWOOD, JAMES
fl. 1770–1790

One of the best of the modellers employed by Wedgwood, he agreed with the firm on 11 November, 1778, to work for them for four years, his wages to be a guinea and a half a week and a house rent free. He modelled a large number of busts, cameo-portraits, etc. (Wedgwood Archives).

HAGBOLT, T., of London
b. 1775, *d.* 1849

His wax statuette of Lady Caroline Gordon, dated 1829, is in the Victoria and Albert Museum, while his bust of James Rennell (died 1830) is in Westminster Abbey.

Hagbolt exhibited at the Royal Academy, 1826–1833, showing busts of the Hon. Lady Cust (1826) and the Rt. Hon. John Sullivan (1830), and a medallic portrait of William Tassie (1833).

HALFPENNY, WILLIAM,
alias MICHAEL HOARE
fl. 1742–1785

Halfpenny was mason to Lincoln's Inn between 1752 and 1785. In 1757 he made the sundial for the west end of the Garden Row, receiving £21. In 1782–1785 he built the north wing of the Stone Buildings (Archives, Lincoln's Inn). Halfpenny was not only a mason, statuary, architect and carpenter, but is also chiefly remembered as a writer on architecture. His work in this connexion is, however, outside the scope of this book.

In May, 1742, he agreed to take over the building of Redland Chapel at Bristol and to oversee the workmen. He also undertook "to visit said work six days in evry week, and for evry day neglect I do agree to forfeit three shillings and sixpence and to measure all said work when required, both within and without" (Charlton and Milton's *History of Redland*, page 67).

Halfpenny signs a very fine monument with portrait-busts and a medallion, to Mrs. Ann Dash, *c.* 1750, in Isleworth Parish Church.

HAINES, EDWARD

In 1743 he made the chimney-pieces for the "new hall and the eating room" of Hampden House, Buckinghamshire, and in the same year was responsible for the wood-carvings in the "alcove" (Archives, Earl of Buckinghamshire).

HAKEWILL, HENRY JAMES,
of London
b. 1813, *d.* 1834

He was born on 11 April, 1813, third son of James Hakewill (1778–1843), the architect, and studied under Richard Sass. In 1830 he joined the Royal Academy Schools and in the following year won a Silver Medal for a figure of "Apolino."

In 1832 Hakewill made figures of the founders, Sir Richard and Lady Beaumont, for the alms-houses at Cheshunt, Hertfordshire. In the same year he modelled a figure of Earl Grey, and a committee, under the chairmanship of Lord Duncannon, was formed to raise money to have it carved in marble and erected in Marylebone. The project, however, was later abandoned as there was not enough money forthcoming to carry it out.

Hakewill died of consumption on 13 March, 1834. His obituary in the *Literary Gazette* of the same year (page 249) stated that "in person he was tall and elegant and his face eminently beautiful, his manners and address were modest and unassuming but collected." He exhibited at the Royal Academy, 1832–1834, showing a few busts, including one of Lord Brougham which he had modelled when his subject was dispensing justice in the Assize Court.

(Authority cited in text.)

HALL, JOSEPH, the Elder, of Derby

fl. 1745–1763

He was the master-mason for building Kedleston and was also responsible for nearly all the carved stone, alabaster and woodwork in the house. His most important contribution to it—the famous alabaster columns in the Great Hall—was made in 1760. For these he received £536, while the material and carving of the capitals together came to another £648. In the same year he was also paid £744 for building the portico and £186 for carving its capitals and pilasters.

In 1761 Hall went into a partnership for a short time with a Mr. Chambers, and together they built the east wing, but he was working on his own in 1763, when he was responsible for the west wing and for the main staircase. In the same year he received £54 for "two modillions on the south front," and he also carved "Corinthian modillions to the large cornice round the building" for £121, the coat of arms on the pediment of the main lodge, a stone pedestal for a statue of Venus and piers for the churchyard gate.

For the interior of the house Hall made chimney-pieces for Lord Scarsdale's dressing-room and Lady Scarsdale's bedroom, costing £21 and £37 respectively, while he received a further £100 for the alabaster Corinthian capitals in the drawing-room. (Archives, Lord Scarsdale.)

In 1745 Hall was paid £31 10s. for a marble chimney-piece for "The great dineing room" at Melbourne Hall, Derbyshire (Archives, Marquess of Lothian).

HALL, JOSEPH, the Younger, of Derby

fl. 1819–1852

Hall, who was presumably a grandson of Joseph Hall the Elder (q.v.), succeeded Richard Browne (q.v.) in the Derby Marble and Spar Works. Glover, in his *History of the County of Derby* (Vol. II, page 606), says that Hall was "a person well qualified from his knowledge of mineralogy and long experience of the business to continue improving in taste and elegance the innumerable articles he manufactures." Apparently he was also a benefactor to his native town, for he built "swimming and other baths for the accommodation of the inhabitants" some time before 1830 (op. cit.).

He exhibited at the Royal Academy in 1838, showing "a fawn, the colour of the marble being entirely natural," and he also sent various ornamental items to the Great Exhibition of 1851. In the following year he repaired the effigy of Archbishop Sandys in Southwell Cathedral, Nottinghamshire (Archives, Lord Sandys).

Hall signs a number of monuments. Those to the Rev. George Robinson, 1837, at Tutbury, Staffs, and John Macaulay, 1840, at Repton, Derbyshire, have well-carved reliefs, while in the latter county he also signs others commemorating John Hope, 1819, in Derby Cathedral; Martha Twigge, 1827, at Bakewell; Josiah Crammer, 1836, at Heanor; Walter Evans, 1839, at Darley Abbey; Shirley, Bishop of Sodor and Man, 1842, at Shirley; and the Earl of Leicester, 1844, at Longford (the bust in this case being the work of J. Francis). Hall signs monuments in Staffordshire to Thomas Grosvenor, 1831, at Leek; the Rev. John Mosley, 1834, at Rolleston; and Samuel Allsopp, 1838, in Burton-on-Trent Parish Church. Others executed by him include those in memory of Francis Launder, 1822, at Elton, Notts; Lady Welby, 1826, at Allington, Lincs; and Miss Linwood, 1845, in St. Margaret's, Leicester.

HAMILTON, DAVID, and SONS, of Glasgow

fl. 1816–1817

They sign monuments to Colonel Cadogan, 1816, in Glasgow Cathedral, and Colonel Cunynghane, 1817, at Kirkmichael, Ayrshire.

HAMILTON, J.

A tablet at Otterden, Kent, to Sibylla Wheler, 1844, is signed "J. Hamilton successor to Peter Rouw" (q.v.). Hamilton must have taken over the yard in Rouw's lifetime, as the latter did not die until 1852.

HAMILTON, JAMES, of Weymouth

fl. 1784–1816

In 1784 he designed and erected the obelisk to the memory of James Frampton at Moreton, Dorset (*Gentleman's Magazine*, 1787, page 49). In 1785 he was the mason for building Bridport Town Hall (Town Archives). In 1795 he rebuilt the south-east wall of the "Cobb" at Lyme Regis (Town Archives), and in 1809 designed the statue of George III carried out in artificial stone by Coade and Sealy (q.v.) for Weymouth.

Hamilton also carved a monument which was erected in 1816 in Wyke Regis churchyard to commemorate the passengers and crew of the *Alexander* (*New Monthly Magazine*, 1816, page 81).

HAMILTON, JOHN

The monument to Sir Robert Napier, 1700, at Puncknowle, Dorset, is signed "Johannes Hamiltonus Scoto-Britannus fecit."

HAMLETT, JOHN, of Stroud

A small bronze bust of the Duke of Sussex, signed by Hamlet and dated 1826, is at Ombersley Court, Worcestershire.

HAMLETT, J., of Stroud

His stone wall-tablet to Robert Griffin, 1835, at Eastington, Gloucestershire, repeats a design frequently used by W. Paty (q.v.).

HAMMOND, H.

fl. 1850–1852

He showed busts, etc., at the Royal Academy between 1850 and 1852, including one of Dr. Cholmondeley in the latter year. He also exhibited at the British Institution in 1851.

HAMMOND,
or HAMON, WILLIAM

fl. 1670–1690

Between 1670 and 1679 Hammond was the mason employed for rebuilding the Vintners' Hall, and in 1671 carved "twenty stone scutcheons with the Company's arms for the Company's houses" (Archives, Vintners' Company). From 1674 until 1678 he was working at the Royal College of Physicians, where he received £210 for the gateway in 1675 (Archives, Royal College of Physicians). Robert Hooke has the following entry in his diary: "Back to Physicians' College. Met Hammond. Disliked carvings" (*Diary of Robert Hooke*, page 157).

Hammond was also employed as a mason at the City churches of St. Michael's, Crooked Lane, between 1684 and 1690; St. Anne and St. Agnes; and All Hallows the Great, where his carved stonework included "six pilasters with capitals, £107" (Bodleian, Rawlinson MSS. 387).

HAMSTON, J. S., of Kensington

He signs a Gothic tablet to John Torriano, 1832, in St. Mary Abbots, Kensington.

HANCOCK, JOHN

fl. 1703–1718

He was probably a York mason and his monuments (of which I have discovered only three examples) are on the grand scale, with life-size figures and architectural backgrounds. Though they may have a slight air of country clumsiness, they are nevertheless impressive witnesses to the high standard of craftsmanship attained by good provincial work in the first quarter of the eighteenth century.

Hancock's monument to Joseph Mellish, 1703, at Blyth, Nottinghamshire, is about 18 ft. high, with a semi-reclining figure in contemporary costume. The second monument, to George Pashley, 1708, at Stainton, Yorkshire, is a large architectural work with a central urn, but the grandest of the three commemorates Sir Edward Blacket, 1718, in Ripon Cathedral. This work, with its architectural background, has a total height of nearly 24 ft. and, in addition to a reclining figure of Sir Edward himself, has also life-size figures of his two wives to left and right.

It was extremely difficult to find Hancock's signature on any of these works; indeed, in the case of the Mellish monument I was only able to discover it by climbing a ladder, for it was tucked away at the top of the right-hand Corinthian pilaster supporting the carved pediment.

HANCOCK, JOHN, of London

b. 1825, *d.* 1869

He was born at Fulham and was largely a self-taught artist, although he studied for a short time at the Royal Academy Schools in 1842, exhibiting at the Academy "The Prodigal Son" in the following year.

In 1844 he showed a statue of Chaucer at Westminster Hall, which the *Art Journal* thought "not in good taste," while the *Literary Gazette* considered that "Mephistopheles would have been a better title." Two years later he made a portrait-medallion of Dante Gabriel Rossetti, while in 1853 he modelled the bronze relief of "Christ led to Crucifixion" for the Art Union of London.

Apparently Hancock's best work was the plaster statue of "Beatrice" which he showed at the Great Exhibition of 1851 and later made in marble for the Baroness Burdett Coutts. Henry Weekes in his treatise entitled *Fine Arts at the Great Exhibition* (page 65) asked: "Will he" (i.e., the visitor) "not stop before the beautiful spiritualized figure of Beatrice by Hancock and become for a moment as absorbed in expression as is the plaster itself?"

Hancock exhibited "Beatrice" again in Paris in 1855, showing at the same time another statue of "Maidenhood." Of this a French critic said "the expression and movement in it are remarkable," but also added that it was "covered by a thick coat of paint which is barbarous." Another distinguished French critic said that both statues "possessed what Gibson's works require—life" (*Builder*, 1856, page 406).

At the Royal Academy of 1858 Hancock showed a bronze figure entitled "Ariel Released from the Tree" which the *Art Journal* considered to be "ot infinite grace and lightness."

He exhibited at the Royal Academy, 1843–1864. His statue of "Il Penseroso" (1857) is at Osborne, while another version of the same work (1864) is at the Mansion House.

In 1849 he carved a bas-relief of the "Entry into Jerusalem" for the Art Union and again in 1853 a companion work of "Christ led to Crucifixion" for the same society. He died on 17 October, 1869.

(*Builder*, 1870, page 44; authorities mentioned in text.)

HANSON, JOB, of Newbury
d. 1874

He signs tablets at Chalton, Hants, to the Rev. Henry Hall, 1829, and at Speen, Berks, to Mary Wyld, 1831.

HARDCASTLE, ROBERT
fl. 1739–1768

He became a bankrupt in 1739 and in the Westminster poll-book of 1748 is described as "mason of John Street, Westminster." In the "List of Artists" in Mortimer's *Universal Directory* of 1763, however, he appears as a "carver in wood and stone," living on the "Surrey side of Westminster Bridge." I know of no work by him.

HARDEN, T., of Burton-on-Trent
He signs a large classical tablet to George Hutchinson, 1818, at Tutbury, Staffs.

HARDENBERG, B. F., of London
fl. 1800–1823

Hardenberg executed a number of busts, including one of Prince Blücher for Carlton House in 1817, for which he received £150 (P.R.O., L.C.9/367). His busts of the Princess Charlotte (1818) and of Lord Ellenborough (1820) are in the Royal Collection, while another undated one in plaster of George IV is at Brynkinalt, Denbigh. His busts of three Roman Emperors, Nero, Vespasian and Claudius, executed between 1819 and 1820, were formerly at Kimbolton Castle, Huntingdonshire, and that of General Morgan (1821) is at Corsham, Wiltshire. His bust of the Second Earl of Liverpool is at Ickworth Park, Suffolk. He also made a bronze statuette of Wellington which is now at Stratfield Saye.

In 1800 Hardenberg exhibited at the Royal Academy "The Four Seasons Decorating an Urn, intended for the Centre of a Green Room." In 1822 he took the death-mask of Stuart, Archbishop of Armagh (*Gentleman's Magazine*, 1822, Part I, page 470), for whose monument at Luton, Bedfordshire, he was also responsible. He also signs one to Thomas Brooke, 1820, at Runcorn, Cheshire.

Hardenberg, whose studio was in Mount Street, went into partnership with P. Nicoli (q.v.) later in his career.

HARDING, CHARLES, of Sudbury
fl. 1830–1837

He signs tablets in Suffolk to the Rev. John Bigg, *c.* 1830, at Glemsford; to Captain Rodney Sims, 1834, in St. Gregory's, Sudbury; and to Walter Westropp, 1837, at Long Melford. His tablet to Mrs. Pemberton, 1834, is at Belchamp St. Paul, Essex.

Harding's wife, Charlotte, died in 1831 at the age of forty-three.

HARDING, JAMES, of Farnham
fl. 1816–1837

He signs four undistinguished tablets in Farnham Parish Church between 1816 and 1837.

HARDMAN and ILIFFE, of Birmingham
According to the *Gentleman's Magazine* (1842, Vol. I, page 266), they made the monument of the Rev. Samuel Hopkinson (*d.* 1841) at Hacconby, Lincolnshire.

HARDY, JAMES
*b. c.*1632, *d. c.*1721

Son of William Hardy, of Kirby, Northumberland, he was apprenticed to Robert Bridles, citizen and mason of London, in 1669, becoming free in 1676. Two years later he was acting as assistant to Jasper Latham (q.v.), but by 1696 he was a master-mason with an apprentice and journeyman. He was Steward of the Masons' Company in 1691, Renter Warden in 1705, Upper Warden in 1707 and Master in 1711. His workshop was in Piccadilly.

Hardy never signs his monuments, but fortunately gave to his friend Le Neve a list of a few of his works for the latter's *Monumenta Anglicana*. That he was considered to be one of the leading statuaries of the day is shown in a letter written in 1706 by the First Lord Ashburnham to his steward, Mr. Lanion, concerning statues for the "attick" of

Ampthill House. In it Lord Ashburnham remarks that he has "considered the papers in yours of the 26th and do find Mr. Hardy more reasonable in his demands than Mr. Nost. Perhaps you may yet happen upon some other more reasonable than Mr. Hardy, if not, you will please bring Hardy as much lower as you can and to strike a bargaine with him to perform in a month or six weeks' time." (Ashburnham Archives.)

Unfortunately the writer never lived to finish his house, but it is obvious from his letters that it was to be on the grand scale. Considering that he intended to engage Tijou and La Guerre (the most important artists in England in their different fields) for the ironwork and frescoes respectively, it is plain that Hardy at that time had a high reputation as a statuary.

Hardy married for the second time in 1668 and his grandson, another James—was born in 1717. James Hardy the Younger was apprenticed to William Hale, citizen and mason, in 1731. In 1755, according to a Minute in the Court Book of the Masons' Company, he was summoned before the Lord Mayor "to show cause why he should not serve the office of Livery and Steward of the Company to which he had been duly elected."

The elder Hardy, whose yard was in Piccadilly, gave the following list of monuments to Le Neve: Sir Henry Puckering, 1700, at Warwick; Mrs. Cradock, 1704, at Berkhamsted, Herts; Mrs. Duncumb, 1705, at Horsham, Sussex; Viscount Kilmorey, 1710, at Adderley, Salop; Alicia Stede, 1710, and Constance Stede, 1714, both at Harrietsham, Kent; Viscount Ikerrin, 1712, at Silchester, Hants; Thomas Maule, 1714, in Edmonton Parish Church; and Reynolds Calthorpe (with bust), 1714, at Elvetham, Hants.

He married (lic Vic. Gen. Jan. 28 1687/8) "Elizabeth Johnson of Ebisham, Surrey, Spinster, abt. 30". Hardy is described as "of St. Giles in the Fields, Mason, Widr. abt. 36".

HARDY, JOHN

He signs a marble sundial, dated 1800, with cherub-heads in the corners, on the south wall of the church at Horne, Surrey.

HARDY, WILLIAM, of Norwich

He signs the monument to James Watt, 1788, in St. John de Sepulchre, Norwich.

HARGRAVE, JEREMIAH, of Hull

He carved the very fine, large rococo relief in the pediment of Trinity House, Hull, in 1753 (account-books, Trinity House, Hull). Hadley, in his *History of Hull*, published in 1788, says that Hargrave was the father of Joseph Hargrave, "an ingenious artist, who designed the drawings in this book."

HARGRAVES, ISAAC, of Lewes
fl. 1792–1796

He signs a large wall-tablet with an oval inscription panel to Elizabeth Scrase, 1792, at Stanmer, Sussex.

HARMER, JAMES, of London

He exhibited a "sculptured frieze in plaster of Paris" at the Great Exhibition of 1851.

HARMER, JONATHAN, of Heathfield
b. 1762, *d. c.* 1841

He was the son of Jonathan Harmer the Elder, mason, and in 1796 went to America where he followed the same calling, working as a journeyman. On his father's death in 1800 Harmer returned to England and began the manufacture of small terra-cotta bas-reliefs, which he used principally in his monumental work, inserting them into the upper part of a tablet or tombstone. He also used them for the exterior decoration of houses and there was in existence a terra-cotta coat of arms of the Second Duke of Newcastle made by him.

Harmer's principal designs included a vase or basket of flowers, an urn with rams' heads, an angel, a basket of fruit, Charity, etc. The best examples of his work *in situ* are in the interior and churchyard of Cade Street Chapel, Sussex. Other examples can be found in the churches or churchyards of Hailsham, Mayfield, Wadhurst, Warbleton, Heathfield, etc., all in Sussex. There is also a collection of these bas-reliefs in the Sussex Archaeological Museum at Lewes.

(Lucas's *Heathfield Memorials*, pages 104–108.)

HARMER, T., of Snettisham

He signs a large wall-tablet in coloured marbles at Heacham, Norfolk, to Nicholas Styleman, 1830.

HARPER, R., of London

He exhibited busts of Lord Brougham and the Rev. Rowland Hill at the Society of British Artists in 1833.

HARRIS, CHARLES, of the Strand, London
d. 1795 (?)

His monuments have great charm, being in the best eighteenth-century tradition, with a lavish use of coloured marbles and reliefs. His most important work is that to the third and fourth Dukes of Ancaster at Edenham, Lincs, which has a life-size standing figure of the Third Duke in Roman costume, while the fourth Duke is seated, dressed in full peer's robes and holding a medallion portrait of his wife.

In the archives of Stourhead is the account for Harris's monument to Henry Hoare (*d.* 1787) which was erected at Stourton, Wilts, and cost £75. The final payment of £35 is made in 1795 to Elizabeth Harris, who is presumably the sculptor's widow.

Harris signs monuments in Sussex to the Rev. Thomas Wrench, 1778, at Stedham; and to Sarah Peckham, 1784, and the Rev. George Farhill, 1790, both in Chichester Cathedral; in Surrey to Henry Allcraft, 1779, to Benjamin Tate, 1790, and Miss Sophia Tate, 1790, all at Mitcham; and to Lady Fletcher, 1791, at Cheam; in Berkshire to Francis Stonehouse, *c.* 1779, at Hungerford; to William Jennens, 1784, at Long Wittenham; and to Robert Palmer, 1787, at Hurst; and in Hampshire to George Dewer, 1786, at Knights' Enham, and to Henry Lloyd, 1792, at Christchurch. He also signs a monument in Buckinghamshire to Barbara Reepington, 1775, at Stony Stratford, and another in Devon to Mrs. Tucker, 1788, at Kilmington.

HARRIS, CHARLES,
of Wallingford

He signs a tablet at Hambledon, Bucks, to Richard Mason, 1776. In 1797 he took his son, another Charles, as his apprentice.

HARRIS, H., of Poole

In the *Gentleman's Magazine,* 1825 (Part II, page 135), it is stated that the monument of Admiral Russell, recently erected at Canford Magna, Dorset, was carved by Harris and was "highly creditable to his abilities."

HARRIS, JOSEPH, of Bath
fl. 1808–1836

Harris was one of the least successful of the Bath school of statuaries. His absurd monument to Henry Haffey, 1836, at Bathampton, Somerset, has, for its chief decoration, a marble copy of the large silver trophy presented to Haffey by the inhabitants of Jamaica.

Other signed monuments and tablets by him include those to John Butt, 1808, at Warminster, Wilts; Captain Maxwell, 1809, at Twyning, Glos; Josiah Patrick, 1818, at St. John in Bedwardine, Worcs; Emily Roe, 1819, at Walcot, Berks; the Rev. John Selwyn, 1823, in Salisbury Cathedral; and Adam Wrags, 1835, at Seend, Wilts.

HARRIS, SAMUEL, of Jacobstow

He signs a ledger with a fine coat of arms at Whitstone, Cornwall, to Thomas Cogcombe, 1712.

HARRISON, ELIZABETH,
of Chester
fl. 1827–1835

Possibly the widow or daughter of Daniel Harrison who became a Freeman of Chester in 1801. She signs a Hellenic wall-monument at Bruera, Cheshire, to John Colley, 1835. With her partner, John Wright of Chester, she signs a similar one with good details to John Edgworth, 1827, at Marchwiel, Flint.

HARRISON, JAMES, of Devizes
fl. 1811–1816

He signs tablets at Pewsey, Berks, to Thomas Pike, 1811, and at Bromham, Wilts, to Andrew Rolt, 1816.

HARRISON, RICHARD,
of Buckingham
fl. 1817–1836

He signs tablets in Buckinghamshire to Mary Aubrey, 1817, at Middle Claydon; and to the Rev. John Dayrell, 1832, and to Richard Dayrell, 1836, both at Lillingstone Darell.

HARRISON, THOMAS
b. 1815, *d.* 1841

In 1836 he attended the Royal Academy Schools, to which he had been recommended by C. Rossi (q.v.). He exhibited busts at the Academy, 1838–1840, showing in the latter year one of Mrs. Hinton Baverstock, of Norwich. He died at Old Windsor in 1841.

HARRISON, WILLIAM,
of Stamford
b. 1776

Harrison was apprenticed to John Cole, of Stamford, in 1790, becoming a Freeman of that town in 1797. In St. Martin's, Stamford, are his tablets to Elizabeth Plumptree, 1806, and Thomas Truman, 1810, while he signs another at St. Mary's (in the same town) to George Stevenson, 1808.

HARSTON, H.
fl. 1795–1811

Harston signs a small monument in Newark Parish Church to Garret Ordoyne, 1795. In 1811 the firm was known as "Harston, Marshall and Co."

HART, ANTHONY
fl. 1686–1734

He was the son of Anthony Hart, citizen and brewer of London, and after serving an apprenticeship with Abraham Storey (q.v.) became free of the Masons' Company in 1686.

Hart was chief assistant of John Nost (q.v.) and was working with him in 1708, as in that year he is described in the archives of the Masons' Company as "working with Mr. Nost a carver at Hyde Park Corner."

In 1723 his chief assistant, John Doe (q.v.), carved chimney-pieces for Dudley North of Glenham Hall, Suffolk. In 1727 North wrote to Hart: "I have at last examined Mr. Doe's late bills and reduced the articles where they differ from my agreement with him." North goes on to quote the contract and adds: "You have in some places charged more. I have with due help measured out all the chimney-pieces which I hope are very exactly done" (North Archives). In 1734 Hart was living at Cripplegate.

HART, JOSEPH
fl. 1724–1765

The son of Edward Hart, of Hackney, husbandman, he was apprenticed to John Annis (q.v.) in 1724. He signs the monument of Mrs. Mabletoft, 1765, at Weybridge, Surrey.

I have not been able to discover whether Hart was any relation of Clement Hart, who was apprenticed in 1719 to Thomas West, and who became Renter Warden of the Masons' Company in 1751, the year of his death.

HARTLEY, HENRY ROBERT
fl. 1820–1827

He signs monuments in St. George-the-Martyr, Southwark, to Susan Pigeon, 1822, and to William Toulmin, 1826. His monument of Anne Brocas, 1824, at Banbury, Oxon, has a life-size kneeling figure of Faith, and is signed "Jos. Gwilt, arch. S.A.S. London invt. H. R. Hartley excud."

HARTSHORNE, ROBERT,
of London
fl. 1715–1728

Hartshorne was an assistant of William and Edward Stanton (q.v.). His masterpiece is the noble monument of Sir Thomas Powys, 1720, at Thorpe Achurch, Northants, which is 20 ft. high and has an architectural setting of Corinthian columns, supporting a broken pediment. To left and right stand figures of Justice and Truth, while in the centre is the semi-reclining figure of Sir Thomas in his judge's robes.

In the "Inventories of the Directors of the South Sea Company," 1721, are bills for the sum of £149 owed by Sir John Fellowes to Hartshorne. These are either for work carried out at Sir John's house at Carshalton, Surrey, or possibly for a monument erected in Carshalton Church. Between 1718 and 1727 Hartshorne made a number of chimney-pieces for Ditchley Park, Oxon (Dillon Archives).

Other signed monuments by him include those to John Rogers, 1715, in St. Mary's, Leicester; Bishop Burnet, 1715, in St. James's, Clerkenwell; and Mark Kirby, *c.* 1728, in Holy Trinity, Hull.

HARVEY, —, and SON,
of Stonehouse
Firm *fl.* 1830–1850

They sign uninteresting tablets in Devonshire to Edward Hockin, 1836, at Hartland; Charlotte Pierce, 1836, at Ipplepen; and Catherine Butter, 1837, at Woodbury. Their tablet to Hugh Hockin, 1837, is at Stoke Climsland, Cornwall.

HARVEY, or HERVÉ, DANIEL,
of York
b. 1683, *d.* 1733

Harvey was born in France and anglicized his name soon after his arrival in England. He did a great deal of work at Castle Howard, carving four statues on the north front at £14 each in 1709. Three years later he was paid £89 "for sculpture." In 1721 he carved for the avenue of Castle Howard stone vases and pedestals, the latter decorated with "frost work," while the former must have been gilded as there are various payments for "gold for ye vase." Between 1726 and 1727 he carved all the stonework for the Temple of the Winds at a total cost of £276. This included twenty-eight capitals (£56) and twelve vases (£21) (Castle Howard Archives).

In 1720 he made an agreement with the Earl of Strafford "to carve, perform and finish 4 capitals after ye Corinthian order which are to be fitted in just proportions to 4 marble columns which have already been shewn to the said Daniel Harvey." The capitals, which were to be of Roche Abbey stone, were intended for the gallery at

Wentworth Castle, and Harvey was to receive £50 for the work (B.M. Ad. MS. 22241, folio 11). In 1725 he carved four more capitals, this time in wood, for the same house (op. cit., folio 29).

In 1730 Harvey made the monument of Hugh Ripley in Ripon Cathedral (Ripon, Mayor's accounts). This was apparently a copy or restoration of the original, for the inscription on it read "the former monument having been defaced in the times of the Civil Wars, this new one was erected by the Corporation 1730."

He died on 11 December, 1733, and was buried in St. Olave's, York, where his epitaph describes him as "*sculptor. architector etiam peritus, ingenio acer*" (Drake's *York*, Vol. I, page 260).

(Authorities mentioned in text.)

HARVEY, FREDERICK, of Ipswich and Diss
fl. 1830–1840

As a mason he built a house for a Major Walker at Lavington, Suffolk (Clerke's *Ipswich*, page 377). He signs a tablet to Elizabeth Bunny, 1836, at Diss, Norfolk, and another to Sharan Shorting, 1836, at Brome, Suffolk.

HARVEY, JOHN, the Elder, and JOHN, the Younger, of Bath
Firm *fl.* 1687–1740

The Harveys of Bath seem to have followed a variety of callings, being architects, statuaries, painter-stainers and stone-cutters. As an architect, the elder Harvey built the first Pump Room in 1706, while his son was responsible in 1734 for the church of St. Michael extra Muros.

In 1687 the former was paid £270 for "carving" at Longleat. Unfortunately the bill gives no details of this work, but it may have been for the great fountain of which there is a drawing in the Longleat archives. In 1694 he was again at Longleat, carving "13 figures of boys" and "2 shields at the end of the walk." In 1701 he made a fountain, being paid £6 for each figure of a boy (Archives, Marquess of Bath).

The younger Harvey carved the trophy of arms, etc., on the Lansdowne monument above Bath in 1720. According to Wood's *Bath* (Vol. I, page 231), he pretended that Lord Lansdowne had never given him a penny for the work, for he was extremely mean and wanted an excuse for not paying his workmen, especially John Pitcher, the freestone mason. The latter, however, "he [i.e., Harvey] amused to the day of his death with a promise of payment as soon as he should receive his money from Lord Lansdowne, protesting he had not received a shilling when in truth he had

had the full value of the monument from him in three blocks or more of fine marble which his Lordship procured him from abroad."

The Harveys sign monuments to John Tiley, 1703, in St. Mary Redcliffe, Bristol; to Elizabeth Inceldon, 1717, at Barnstaple, Devon; and to Mary Coghill, 1733, in St. Peter's, Marlborough.

HARVEY, SAMUEL, of London
fl. 1762–1765

Between 1762 and 1765 he executed three life-sized marble statues for the Society of Arts. These were "Ceres" (£52 10s.), "Bacchus and a Young Satyr" (£73 10s.) and "Victory" (£84). His address is given as Masham Street, Westminster.

(Archives, Royal Society of Arts.)

HARWOOD, FRANCIS
fl. 1748–1769

All his statues and busts which I have seen are either copies of, or based on, Greek and Roman originals, but they are none the less fine works. For Gordon Castle he carved in 1762 a bust of Marcus Aurelius and in 1765 a bust of "A Vestal." He also supplied in the latter year statues of "Apollo" and a "Marine Venus." These, together with the busts from Gordon Castle, were in 1950 at Messrs. Crowthers' of Isleworth, who also had Harwood's busts of Seneca (1763), Homer (1764) and Cicero (1768).

Other busts by Harwood include Faustina (1748) at Castle Ashby, and Caracalla (1762) at Finchcox in Kent.

Harwood is probably the "F.H." referred to by Nollekens in a letter (in his inimitable spelling), written from Rome to Thomas Banks (q.v.) in 1769, in which he says that "there is F.H. at Florence who is knocking the marbil about like feway & belive he as got more work to do than any One Sculptor in England" (Whitley's *Art in England*, 1821–1837, page 41).

HASKOLL, J.
fl. 1824–1840

In 1824 he was living in the Isle of Wight. He exhibited busts at the Royal Academy, 1824–1835, and at the Suffolk Street Galleries in 1832, including those of Algernon Jones (1831) and Augustus Perkins (1832). In 1835 he applied to the Artists' General Benevolent Institution stating that "he had passed many years on the Continent and had made a bas-relief for a church in the Isle of Wight." This bas-relief is probably part of the monument of Sir L. Worsley Holmes which was erected in Arreton Church and of which Haskoll exhibited the model at the Suffolk Street Galleries in 1829.

His bust of Isaac Newton, dated 1834, is in Lincoln Public Library, while that of the 1st Countess of Yarborough, 1836, is at a Brocklesby Park, Lincolnshire.

HASLEWOOD, RICHARD

While apprenticed to "Mouchet a Chaser" he received in 1762 a premium from the Society of Arts for "ornaments in clay."

HASWELL, GEORGE, of Chester

About 1840 he carved the coat of arms of the County of Cheshire surrounded with foliage on the pediment of the Chester Lunatic Asylum (*Builder*, 1850, page 94).

HATCHARD, JAMES
b. 1793

He attended the Royal Academy Schools in 1814, having previously exhibited at the Academy in 1811 a bust of "Mr. Hatchard, Architect," possibly his father.

He signs the monuments of Captain Thomas Fraser, 1823, at Checkheaton, Oxon, and Sarah Smith, 1835, in Holy Trinity, Marylebone.

HATTON, EDWARD
fl. 1779–1785

Samuel Smiles in his *Lives of the Engineers* (Vol. II, page 311) quotes a letter from Thomas Telford written in 1785 when he was working as a journeyman-mason at Somerset House.

Telford says of Hatton that: "He has been six years at Somerset House and is esteemed the finest workman in London and consequently in England. He works equally in stone and marble. He has excelled the professed carvers in cutting Corinthian capitals and other ornaments about the edifice. . . . He may be half-a-dozen years older than myself at most. [Telford was then twenty-six.] He is honesty and good-nature itself and is adored by both his master and fellow-workmen."

HAWKE, J.
fl. 1777–1784

From 1777-1784 he was the master-mason and builder of Gorhambury in Hertfordshire. He received altogether £2,621, which sum included payment for all the carved stonework (Hertford County Archives, B.XI. 66).

HAWKE, WILLIAM
fl. 1789–1790

He was extensively employed during the rebuilding of Woburn Abbey, 1789–1790, receiving £900 for masonry and carved Portland stonework (Woburn Abbey Archives).

HAWKINS, B. W.
fl. 1847–1851

Hawkins exhibited at the Royal Academy, 1847–1849. In 1851 he showed at the Great Exhibition a group in bronze of "The European Bison," which the Zoological Society of London were to present to the Emperor of Russia.

HAWKINS, J. B.
fl. 1842–1844

He exhibited at the Royal Academy in 1842, and two years later showed the "Hesitation of Pandora" at Westminster Hall. This latter work the *Literary Gazette* (1844, page 466) called "an accurate copy of bad nature, or a cast filled up, cannot be worth anything."

HAWORTH, WILLIAM
b. 1759

Haworth was born on 21 June, 1759. He attended the Royal Academy Schools in 1777 and four years later exhibited at the Academy a terra-cotta bust of the Rev. Dr. Giffard.

His younger brother Henry (born on 14 September, 1760) also attended the Royal Academy Schools in 1779 (Academy Archives).

HAY, JAMES, the Elder, of Portsea
fl. 1782–1813

His most ambitious work was the monument "in a pyramidal form ornamented with marine trophies, arms and sculptured urns" which was erected in Portsea churchyard to the memory of Admiral Kempenfelt and the crew of the *Royal George*. This was unveiled in March, 1783, and a description of it, together with a plate, is given in the *Gentleman's Magazine* for that year (page 368).

According to the *Monthly Magazine* (1810, page 613), Hay was "an eminent naturalist and a fellow of the Linnaean Society."

He signs monuments in Hampshire to Mrs. Sarah Reid, 1785, in Fareham churchyard; to William Feilding, 1789, in Portsmouth Cathedral; to Catherine Moody, 1802, at Porchester; to Gavin Kempt, 1810, at Bishops Waltham; to James Norris, 1813, and Alexander Cameron, 1813, both at Warblington; and to David Renaud, 1813, at Havant.

HAY, JAMES, the Younger, of Portsea
b. 1772, *d.* 1810

Son of James Hay the Elder (q.v.), he first studied painting under Benjamin West, but later turned to sculpture and became a pupil of J. Flaxman (q.v.), studying anatomy under Sheldon and Brookes. At the time of his death at Portsea in 1810, Hay was acting as assistant to his father. According to his obituary in the *Gentleman's Magazine* (1810, Part I, page 498) "his too intense applications to the various branches of science brought on a lingering disease which terminated by a premature death, the life and labours of a rising genius."

The *Monthly Magazine* of the same year (page 613) also mentions that "he left many drawings of the most remarkable antiquities in Hampshire; and a much greater number of almost the whole zoology of Great Britain, particularly a complete arrangement of all the shells, beautifully drawn and coloured from nature."

I know of no independent works by him.

HAYDON, SAMUEL JAMES BOUVERIE
b. 1815, *d.* 1891

He was born at Heavitree, near Exeter, on 29 April, 1815, and, after being educated at Mount Radford School, was articled to a lawyer. He later began to practise on his own account in Exeter, but the love of art proved too strong and he abandoned the law and went to London, where he studied sculpture under E. H. Baily (q.v.). He apparently showed great promise in his new profession, for B. R. Haydon, the painter, wrote of him as "one capable of taking the place of Chantrey," while Pyecroft in *Art in Devonshire* (page 58) says that his works were "so good that it is more the pity they are so few. It was not from want of genius, power or personal merit that he failed to make for himself a far greater name."

Haydon exhibited at the Royal Academy, 1840–1876, and at the British Institution, 1847. At the former he showed groups of "Hermia and Helena" (1844), "Charity" (1862), and "Ophelia" (1865), and busts of Sir Henry Goldfinch (1842), John Dickens (1843), H. Bridges (1860) and Lady Mason (1864). In 1840 he executed the busts of Sir Robert Newman and Thomas Newman for Mamhead House, Devon, and nine years later those of the Earl of Radnor and Admiral the Hon. D. Bouverie for Longford Castle. His bust of the Rev. J. W. Gleadall is in the offices of the Foundling Hospital, while another in wax of an unknown man, signed and dated 1843, is now at the Victoria and Albert Museum.

(Authority cited in text.)

HAYES, T., of Beverley
fl. 1832–1845

He signs a tablet to John Soane, 1832, in Beverley Minster, and a large Gothic wall-tablet to James Atkinson, 1845, in St. Helen's, York.

HAYLER, HENRY
b. 1824

He joined the Royal Academy Schools in 1840, on the recommendation of Sir Richard Westmacott (q.v.). He exhibited at the Academy, 1849–1859, showing various works, including a cameo portrait of George Godwin in 1854.

HAYLEY, THOMAS ALPHONSO
b. 1780, *d.* 1800

Hayley, a young man of much ability, was the natural son of William Hayley the poet, and studied sculpture under John Flaxman (q.v.), and modelled busts of his master, Lord Thurlow and J. S. Clarke. He died when he was only twenty and was buried at Eartham in Sussex, where there is a monument to his memory carved and erected by Flaxman, with an epitaph composed by his father. Redgrave says that young Hayley's death took place in 1810, but this is incorrect as the date on the monument is 2 May, 1800.

In 1823 appeared a life of William Hayley and his son edited by John Johnson. This consisted of two volumes of nearly a thousand pages and the *Literary Gazette* (1823, page 405) rightly remarked that "the Genius of Humbug never produced a more gross piece of absurdity."

(Horsfield's *Sussex*, Vol. II, page 62.)

HAYNES, WILLIAM, of Bury St. Edmunds

In 1729 he made the tombstone or ledger of the Hon. Barbara Hervey at Ickworth Church (account-book of John, First Earl of Bristol).

HAYTER, SIR GEORGE
b. 1792, *d.* 1871

Hayter is chiefly remembered as a fashionable portrait-painter of the period, and his work as such is outside the scope of this book.

As a sculptor he signs a marble bust of the sixth Duke of Devonshire (1858) at Chatsworth and also exhibited a figure of "Atalanta" at the

International Exhibition of 1862. These are, however, the only examples I know of works of sculpture executed by him.

HAYWARD, JOHN, of Lincoln
fl. 1767–1787

In 1767 he built for Lord Monson the stables at Burton Hall, Lincolnshire. He was master-mason to Lincoln Cathedral and was in charge of the repairs carried out to that edifice. In 1787 he was paid £867 for the restoration of the west front and other parts of the Cathedral (Lincoln Cathedral Archives; Archives, Lord Monson).

HAYWARD, RICHARD
b. 1728, *d.* 1800

He was born at Bulkington in Warwickshire and apprenticed to Christopher Horsnaile (q.v.), becoming free of the Masons' Company in 1749. In 1752 he was Renter Warden of the Company, and in 1753 went to Rome, where he remained for about a year.

Hayward was a friend of Thomas Jenkins, who, on 30 March, 1755, wrote from Rome to Lord Dartmouth: "It is said your Lordship is about building a house at Westminster. If such a person as Mr. Hayward, sculptor, should be recommended to your Lordship, I believe I may venture to say that he is a deserving young man. I knew him sometime here and he behaved well" (H. M. C., Earl of Dartmouth).

Another friend was Charles Jennens, the patron of Handel, for whom he carried out various works at his seat at Gopsall in Leicestershire, including, in 1764, the reliefs and busts on the Ionic temple on the roof of which stood the statue of "Religion" by Roubiliac (q.v.) (Nichols's *Leicestershire,* Vol. IV, page 858; *Gentleman's Magazine,* 1791, page 305). According to Dodsley's *London* (Vol. V, page 96), "a Bacchanalian Boy, Bust of Aratus, and a Vestal," all by Hayward, were to be seen at Jennens's London house in Great Ormond Street in 1761.

In 1771 Hayward made a marble chimney-piece. for Woburn Abbey (British Museum, Ad. MS. 41133). The bill for it was sent to the Duke of Bedford by Sir William Chambers, who remarked in his covering letter that he considered the charge reasonable, "as the work is well done and the chimney-piece very large." In the following year the sculptor was at Blenheim, where he executed "termes" for the gallery (British Museum, Ad. MS. 41133), and in 1774 he was needed again, for the Duke of Marlborough wrote to Chambers that he wanted "much to have this fountain settled. You must let Hayward or one of his

foremen meet you here and I'll have the parts of the fountain put out ready for him to see" (British Museum, Ad. MS. 41136). This almost certainly refers to the famous Bernini fountain which was "set up" by the fourth Duke in the park at Blenheim and rescued by the ninth Duke, who had it repaired and erected in a place of honour on the terrace below the west front of the Palace.

In the Newdigate archives is Hayward's bill for £70, dated 1776, for the monument to Lady Newdigate (*d.* 1765) in Harefield Church, Middlesex. For Arbury Park, Warwick, the Newdigates' family seat, he made "two marble plinths for candelabras."

Besides the Woburn chimney-piece, Hayward also made one for Kedleston in 1760 (Archives, Lord Scarsdale), and another for Ingres Abbey in Kent in 1771 (British Museum, Ad. MS. 41133). He also made a large number for Somerset House, beginning in 1778 with two for which he was paid £212 (P.R.O., A.O. 1/2497). In 1784 he made another two of statuary and Sicilian marble, costing £51 each, for the Stamp Office and the Board Room of the Salt Office at Somerset House, while six years later he received £262 for more chimney-pieces, one with "a frieze of Persia marble, three small ovals and broad flutes" at £60, and another with a "long frieze carved with two oval flowers and three small figures" for £66. Others for Somerset House included one with "leaves and oval flowers in centre" costing £30; a second with "three medallions on frieze, vases on breaks" at £40; and a third with "a long tablet veneered with oriental alabaster and carved with waterlily leaves" (R.I.B.A. 335A).

To the church at Bulkington (his birthplace) Hayward presented a font carved by himself with an enchanting series of Bartolozzi-like reliefs and inscribed "this fragment of ancient Numidian marble was imported from Rome by Richard Hayward and given to this church in 1789."

His statue of Lord Botetourt, erected in 1773 at Williamsburg, Virginia, is the oldest public statue in North America still in existence. Lord Botetourt, the most popular Governor the colony had ever had, died on 15 October, 1770, and on 20 July of the following year the House of Burgesses unanimously decided to erect at the public expense an "elegant statue in marble" to his memory. They then chose one of their number, John Norton, to go to England and make arrangements with a suitable sculptor, and in this task he was given every assistance by the Duke of Beaufort, the dead man's nephew. As there was no recent picture of Lord Botetourt in existence, the Duke produced a wax medallion by Isaac Gosset (q.v.) to be lent to the chosen sculptor and, on 10 March, 1772, Norton wrote to a relative in Yorktown that he had "fixed on an artist to execute the statue for L. Botetourt since the Duke of Beaufort came to town, his name is Hayward and lives in Piccadilly. He's to be finished in 12 months completely," Norton continued, "with iron rails, packed, and to be put into a ship for £1,700." Hayward kept to his bargain for the statue duly arrived in Virginia in May, 1773.

Hayward, who exhibited at the Society of Arts, 1761–1766, died on 11 August, 1800, in Half Moon Street. "His performances in the line of his profession dispersed throughout the kingdom show him to have been an admirable master of the old school," according to his obituary in the *Gentleman's Magazine* (1800, page 909).

His sister erected a monument to his memory at Bulkington, the epitaph of which reads, "the surviving sister of Richard and Mary Hayward placed this marble as a memorial of the taste and genius of one, of the virtue and affection of both." The best and most unusual of his signed monuments, all of which have delicate and carefully cut details, commemorates the Rev. Sloughter and Mrs. Clarke, 1772, at Theddingworth, Leicestershire. This has a standing figure of the Rev. Stephen in a flowing cassock, while his wife is shown seated with her arm resting on an urn.

Works by Hayward in Westminster Abbey are in memory of William Levinz, 1765; Susannah Davidson, 1767; Mrs. Pritchard, 1768; General Strode, 1776; John Roberts, 1776; and Sir James Oughton, 1780. Other signed monuments by him include those to Harriot Whitbread, 1769, at Cardington, Beds; Charles Jennens, 1775, at Nether Whitacre, Warwick; Mary Miles, 1781, at Nackington, Kent; John Hamilton, 1781, and George Ogden, 1788, both in Chester Cathedral; the Hayward family, 1781, at Bulkington, Warwick; and William Wyldbore, 1781, in St. John's, Peterborough.

(Authorities cited in text; information from Williamsburg Library.)

HAYWARD, SAMUEL, of Lichfield
fl. 1799–1822

He signs unimportant tablets to Lieut.-Colonel Philip Bainbridge, 1799, at Ashbourne, Derby; William Booth, 1812, at Ecclesfield, Yorks; and the Rev. William Vyse, 1816, and Mercy Woodhouse, 1826, both in Lichfield Cathedral.

HAYWARD, WILLIAM
fl. 1820–1825

His yard was first at Pentonville and later in the Borough. He signs a large wall-monument with a draped urn to the Hon. Michael Nolan, 1822, at Bradwell, Essex.

HEAP, WILLIAM, of Manchester
fl. 1820–1830

He signs a tablet with well-carved details to the Rev. John Haughton, 1828, at Middleton, Lancs, and another to Holland Watson, 1819, at Congleton, Cheshire.

HEARNDEN, JOHN

In 1726 he repaired Aylesford Bridge, Kent. His bill for the work includes "erecting a pillar on and repairing Aylesford Bridge, cutting an oval to place ye marble inscription in, cutting ye old inscription anew, consisting of 43 letters."

(Kent County Records.)

HEDGES, NATHANIEL
d. c. 1784

In 1772 the Court of Assistants of the Masons' Company wrote him a letter to the effect that "not being free of this Company" he did "use and exercise the trade of masonry within the City of London or the liberties thereof." He was directed to attend the next Court "in order to accept and take upon him the freedom and to become free of this Company" under a penalty of £10 (Courtbook, Masons' Company).

Hedges was mason to the Stationers' Company from 1738 until 1784, in which year he apparently died, for it is then the last payment is made to his widow. He was mason to Hoare's Bank (1764–1775) and was employed by Henry Hoare at Stourhead in 1753 and 1757. He also worked for Richard Hoare at Boreham Hall, Essex, in 1767, for both houses executing chimney-pieces, etc. (Archives, Hoare's Bank).

Hedges' monuments are important; that of Moses Ashley, 1740, at Ashby St. Ledgers, Northants, has a fine portrait-bust, while the monument of Sir Thomas Denison, 1765, at Harewood, Yorks, consists of a sarcophagus with curious rococo legs on which stands a bust of Sir Thomas.

Other signed monuments by him include those to Joseph Ashley, 1739, at Ashby St. Ledgers, Northants; to Ephraim Chambers, 1748, in the cloisters of Westminster Abbey; and to Heigham Bendish, 1746, in East Ham Parish Church.

HEFFERNAN, JAMES
b. 1788, *d.* 1847

He was born in Londonderry, the son of a marble-carver employed by the fourth Earl of

Bristol, who was also Bishop of Derry. According to Strickland's *Dictionary of Irish Artists*, the date of his birth was 1785, but Heffernan himself gave it as 1788 when he later joined the Royal Academy Schools.

When he was only eleven his father died and Lord Bristol apprenticed him to a Cork architect. This man also owned marble works and there the boy began to learn sculpture, being employed on cutting chimney-pieces and tombstones.

Heffernan came to London when he was twenty-two and, after being employed by C. Rossi (q.v.) for a few months, entered Chantrey's (q.v.) studio. In the following year he attended the Royal Academy Schools, gaining Silver Medals in 1815 and 1817, and then went to study in Rome. On his return to England he might well have set up for himself, but was lured back to Chantrey's employ by promises which that sculptor never fulfilled, although he made every use of Heffernan. This fact was well known at the time, for a writer in the *Library of Fine Arts*, 1831 (page 432), regretting that Heffernan exhibited so few independent works at the Royal Academy, did not scruple to add that he "was wasting the summer of his life to increase the already overgrown reputation of another."

Heffernan remained with Chantrey until the latter's death in 1841 and afterwards completed some of the sculptor's unfinished works. His master had said he would leave him money, but this promise, like all the others, was never fulfilled. Heffernan returned to Cork about 1843 and died there of dysentery on 21 October, 1847.

Peter Cunningham said of him that "he was a consummate master in transferring a look from dull, dead clay to semi-transparent Carrara marble; he saw and caught and translated Chantrey into another material" (*Builder*, 1863, page 112). The *Gentleman's Magazine* (1842, Part I, page 163), in its obituary of Chantrey, said that "Heffernan has cut in marble almost every one of Chantrey's busts literally from the first to the last."

Heffernan exhibited at the Royal Academy, 1816–1830, and at the British Institution, 1817–1822. At the former he showed groups of "Musidora" (1822) and "Ino and Bacchus," and busts of J. Stark (1818); Miss E. W. Hill (1825); H. P. Briggs (1828) and James Morrah (1832). His bust of James Watt (1834) was exhibited at the Art Treasures Exhibition in Manchester in 1857, and is now in the possession of the Royal Society. His groups of "Susannah at the Bath" (1825) and "Girl Caressing a Child" (1832) are at the Cork School of Art, and his medallion of Sir Francis Chantrey (1842) at the National Portrait Gallery in Edinburgh.

He signs monuments to Dr. McCarthy, 1808, in South Parish Church, Cork; to William Bennett, Bishop of Cloyne, 1823, in Cloyne Cathedral; to William Forrester, 1832, in All Saints, Leicester; and to Sir Francis Chantrey, 1842, at Norton, Sheffield.

(Authorities cited in text.)

HELBY, JOSEPH
fl. 1692–1700

He signs a very fine cartouche-tablet to Mrs. Papillon, 1692, at Acrise, Kent. The "mort" or skull at the base of it has a wreath of ivy-leaves, which is most unusual.

When the London Customs House was rebuilt in 1700 Helby received £45 8s. for carved work (P.R.O., T.11/4).

HELLYER, ISAAC, of Dorchester and Weymouth
fl. 1820–1834

He signs tablets in Dorset to Jane Love, 1820, at Weymouth; John Swaffield, 1825, at Wyke Regis; and Sarah Perkins, 1834, at Melbury Osmond.

HENDERSON, J.
fl. 1782–1797

He exhibited a number of wax portraits at the Royal Academy between 1782 and 1797, including one of "Mr. Morceau, Master of the Ceremonies at Cheltenham," in 1794. A portrait-bust of "Mr. Henderson, modeller in London, cut on a sardonyx," is mentioned by J. Tassie in his *Engraved Gems* (Vol. II, page 743).

HENDERSON, ROBERT
fl. 1820–1832

He exhibited bronze statuettes, models of animals, etc., at the Royal Academy, 1820–1832, and at the British Institution, 1825–1828. These included figures of the racehorses "Risk" and "Sober Robin," and statuettes of George IV and the Duke of York.

Henderson's bronze statuette of George III, signed and dated 1821, is in the Victoria and Albert Museum.

HENNING, JOHN, the Elder
b. 1771, *d.* 1851

He was born at Paisley on 2 May, 1771, the son of Samuel Henning, a carpenter and builder, and, by assisting his father, learnt to draw plans and elevations. In 1799 he went to an exhibition of waxworks in his native town and became fired with the idea of making wax busts himself. His first sitter was one of his father's workmen, but the result was not particularly successful, and Henning would have given up his efforts had not the decline of his father's business forced him to seek some other means of livelihood.

In 1800 he therefore went to Glasgow and set up as a modeller of wax portraits. Here he was fortunate enough to attract the attention of the Duke of Hamilton, and the fact that the Duke not only was good-natured enough to sit for his own portrait, but also commissioned others of his wife and daughters, established Henning's reputation as an artist. He then moved on to Edinburgh, where he made likenesses of many of the leading inhabitants, including the Earl of Buchan, Sir William Forbes, Hector MacNeill and Mr. Allison. In 1803 he finally decided to settle in the city and to study at the Trustees' Academy. He also made a number of drawings, busts, and portraits in enamel and wax of various distinguished Scotsmen, including Sir Walter Scott, Graham, Jeffrey, Lord Frederick Campbell, the Earl of Lauderdale, the Duke of Gordon and Lord Glenbervie.

In 1811 Henning went to London, but was at first disappointed with the city and its inhabitants. Chance, however, led him to Burlington House where the sight of the Elgin Marbles greatly influenced his future career. On 19 October, two years later, he described the impression they made on him in a letter to Josiah Wedgwood, for whom he was working at the time. "Arriving in London," he said, "about the beginning of July, 1811, I had the good fortune to see the Athenian marbles and felt my mind transfixed with admiration of them. In hope of improving myself in art I began to draw from them. It struck me forcibly that from their superior excellence they might some time or other become such an object of public curiosity that models of them, while they might be very improving to myself, might become objects of pecuniary advantage" (Wedgwood Archives).

It took Henning twelve years to complete his models (with the missing portions restored) of the Parthenon and Phigaleian friezes, and a number of small plaster copies of these were later produced. He also executed large friezes based on them for the exterior of the Athenaeum Club in 1830. In 1838 he made a relief on the same theme round the staircase hall of the Royal College of Surgeons, while there is a similar one at Terling Place, Essex, which is also his work.

During his early years in London Henning made portraits and busts in wax or enamel of various notabilities, including the Duke of Wellington and the Princess of Wales. In some cases these were executed for Wedgwood, to whom he wrote on 13 September, 1813, about a medallion he had just made of the Princess Charlotte, "which I have cast as I do my other works in Enamel-paste." "Having," he continued, "shown H.R.H. a small bust in bronze metal she signified a wish to have one of her own head in the same stile which I have nearly completed and intend making some casts of it in bronze, however I find of those who speak of taking casts of it that it will please more generally in bisque than in bronze" (Wedgwood Archives).

Henning also sent Wedgwood a list of his "medallion portraits done from life," which included likenesses of the Dukes of Gordon and Devonshire; the Marchioness of Lansdowne; the Marquess of Douglas; Lords Archibald Hamilton, Frederick Campbell and Webb Seymour; the Earls of Lauderdale and Rosslyn; Viscount and Viscountess Hampden; Lord Glenbervie; Colonel Cadogan; Sir Samuel and Lady Romilly; Sir Humphry Davy; Thomas Telford; Henry Brougham; Francis Horner; Thomas Campbell; Mrs. Siddons; Sir William Forbes; the Rev. Sidney Smith; James Watt; and Miss Smith, of Drury Lane Theatre. He also added that he charged from seven to ten guineas for a wax portrait.

Between 1820 and 1822 Henning produced a series of small plaster copies of the Raphael cartoons, executed with amazing delicacy and sharpness. The originals were exhibited at Leeds in the year of their completion, while replicas are at the Palace, Bishops Auckland, and in the possession of the writer. In 1848 when he applied to the A.G.B.I. for assistance he stated that: "The nature of his principle property (the restoration of the frieze of the Parthenon and the Cartoons and Transfiguration of Raphael) rendering it easy of piracy, has been the total ruin of his work which occupied 12 years labour."

Henning, who in most of his later works was assisted by his elder son, John Henning the Younger (q.v.), was one of the founders of the Society of British Artists. He died in London on 8 April, 1851, and was buried in the St. Pancras cemetery at Finchley. His obituary in the Art Journal (1851, page 212) commented on "the multiplicity and attractive character of his works" which, it asserted, had "assisted in diffusing a taste for fine art."

He exhibited at the Royal Academy, 1821–1828; at the British Institution, 1816–1823; at the Edinburgh Society of Artists, 1808–1813; and at the Royal Scottish Academy, 1827–1829.

His medallions in the Scottish National Portrait Gallery include those of Lord Jeffrey, 1801; Ebenezer Macome, 1801; Rev. Alexander Carlyle,

1802; Mrs. Fletcher, 1802; Sir William Forbes, 1802; Hector MacNeil, 1802; Rev. Sidney Smith, 1803; Sir Henry Wellwood, 1803; Francis Horner, 1806; Lord Lauderdale, 1806; Lord Seymour, 1807; Mrs. Siddons, 1807; Lord Glenbervie, 1808; Rev. James Grahame, 1810; Professor Dugald Stewart, 1811; William IV, 1827. Undated medallions by him include Rev. Archibald Alison, Lord Campbell, Queen Caroline, Baron Dundas, Lord Robertson.

His medallions of Sir Alexander Gordon and Francis Horner (1806) are in the National Portrait Gallery, while as a statuary he signs monuments to John Heaton, 1818, at Havering-atte-Bower, Essex, and John Ellis, 1836, at Wyddial, Hertfordshire.

(*New Monthly Magazine*, Part I, 1820, pages 455–459, which has a very full account of Henning's life up to that date; *Builder*, 1851, page 297; *Art Journal*, 1849, page 112, and 1851, page 212; Rinder and McKay's *Royal Scottish Academy*.)

HENNING, JOHN, the Younger
b. 1801, *d.* 1857

He was the eldest son of John Henning the Elder (q.v.) and received in 1816 the Silver Isis Medal from the Society of Arts for a relief of "The Good Samaritan." About 1825 he repaired the statue of Queen Anne outside St. Paul's Cathedral which had been damaged by hooligans.

Three years later, assisted by his father, and brother Samuel (q.v.), Henning produced his most famous and lovely work, the classical reliefs on Decimus Burton's triple screen at Hyde Park Corner. In 1836 he carved the reliefs of "Architecture, Painting and Sculpture" and "Wisdom, Astronomy and Mathematics" for the front of the Manchester Art Gallery (City Archives, R.M.I. Minute-Book), and in 1844 sent a statue of Lord Bacon and a group of "Boadicea" to the exhibition in Westminster Hall. The *Literary Gazette* (1844, page 466) was not particularly complimentary about either of these productions, for though they conceded that there was "much of spirited composition in the Queen," they also noticed that "the pelvis is large enough for the life-size," while Bacon's figure was dismissed as "poor," though the head was admitted to be "full of character."

In 1845 Henning executed the reliefs, etc., on the column erected at Holkham to the memory of the Earl of Leicester (*Illustrated London News*, Vol. VII, page 112), and in the same year the reliefs round the Colosseum, Regent's Park. In 1850 he made, for the Freeman's Orphan School in Brixton, reliefs based on Hogarth's pictures of the industrious and the idle apprentices. In the

same year he made for Lord Northwick a "Homeric table," which was Lot 657 in the Northwick sale of 1859. The reliefs of "The Vintage" and "Music and Painting" were executed in 1852 for the drawing-room and the long parlour of the Mansion House (*Illustrated London News*, 30 October, 1852).

Henning showed a bust of "Achilles" at the Society of British Artists in 1825 and exhibited at the Royal Academy, 1828–1852, where his works included busts of his father and George Rigby in 1848 and 1849 respectively. At the Suffolk Street Galleries he showed busts of John Galt and Dr. Maltby in 1824 and one of Dr. James in 1834. His bust of Ann, Duchess of Bedford, is at Woburn Abbey, and that of the first Duke of Marlborough at Windsor Castle. His monument to Charles Heaton Ellis, 1857, is at Wyddial, Hertfordshire.

(Authorities cited in text.)

HENNING, SAMUEL
d. 1832

He was the younger son of John Henning the Elder and assisted his father both in the restoration of the Elgin Marbles and at Hyde Park and the Athenaeum. In 1818 he received a Silver Palette from the Society of Arts and he later exhibited at the Royal Academy, 1823–1831, and at the British Institution, 1825–1826, showing intaglios, gems, etc. He also carved "two tablets for the New Buckingham Gate" (presumably the Marble Arch?) (A.G.B.I. Archives).

J. T. Smith (*Nollekens and his Times*, Vol. I, page 256) gives an account of Henning's taking impressions of the best Italian medals in Flaxman's collection. From these he made casts which he sold "at a price accommodated to the limited resources of the economical student." He was also responsible for the sarcophagus of Duncan Sinclair, *c.* 1832?, in Kensal Green Cemetery.

Henning died of cholera on 2 November, 1832, apparently in poor circumstances, for his widow, Ann, was granted a pension by the Royal Academy which she continued to draw until 1851 (Royal Academy Archives). Mrs. Henning, in 1834, had a stall at the Soho Bazaar, selling "Patent candle lamps and bronze articles."

(Authorities cited in text.)

HENSHALL, WILLIAM,
of London

Henshall, whose studio was in Mortimer Street, signs a large tablet with an "Adam" semi-urn against a pyramid to Joseph Ashley, 1798, at Ashby St. Ledgers, Northamptonshire.

HENSON, W., of Kettering
fl. 1841–1843

He signs a pretty little tablet to Sir George Robinson, 1841, at Cranford St. John, Northamptonshire, and a plainer one to the Rev. William Layng, 1843, at Great Harrowden in the same county.

HENWOOD, JOHN, of Plymouth
fl. 1815–1830

He signs a tablet in the shape of an anchor to Arthur Edgcumbe, 1815, at Milton Abbot, Devon.

HERRMAN, CARL, of Dresden
b. 1791, *d.* 1845

He signs a lovely stele to Charles Lucas, 1831, at Filby, Norfolk.

HETHERINGTON, WILLIAM, of Liverpool
fl. 1803–1810

With his partner, G. Grindrod (q.v.), he built the New Exchange at Liverpool in 1803. He signs a tablet to Anne Walmley, 1808, at Runcorn, Cheshire.

HEWETSON, CHRISTOPHER
b. 1739, *d.* 1799

He was born in Ireland, the son of Christopher Hewetson, of Thomastown, Co. Kilkenny, but his talent for sculpture led his friends to send him to study in Rome. Here he executed, between 1772 and 1781, the magnificent monument of Dr. Baldwin for the Examination Hall of Trinity College, Dublin, a work for which he received £1,000. He died in Rome in 1799.

Hewetson exhibited at the Royal Academy, 1786–1790, showing a bust of Gavin Hamilton in 1786 and another of "A Nobleman" in 1790. His bust of the Duke of Gloucester, executed in 1772, is at Windsor Castle, while that of Pope Clement XIV, signed and dated 1776, is in the Victoria and Albert Museum.

(*Notes and Queries*, Tenth Series, Vol. VI, page 285; Strickland's *Dictionary of Irish Artists*.)

HEWETT, —, of Camberwell

He signs a pretty wall-tablet in coloured marbles to Maria Hammond, 1820, in Brixton Parish Church, and also a sarcophagus of the same date to M. Bentley McLeod in the churchyard.

HEWLETT, —
fl. 1847–1856

He exhibited at the Royal Academy, 1847–1856, showing various works, including a bust of the Hon. M. Berkeley in 1847, and a medallion of Lord Macaulay in 1856.

HEWLETT, DANIEL, of Gloucester
fl. 1808–1829

He signs tablets, dated 1808 and 1829 respectively, in the Gloucestershire village churches of Brockworth and Staunton.

HEWS, —

He signs a circular wall-tablet of good workmanship to Mary Greetham, 1787, at Petersfield, Hampshire.

HIBBINS, THOMAS, and family, of Stamford

There was a large family named Hibbins centred at Ketton in Rutland who worked as masons and stone-carvers for over two hundred years. The earliest of them I have been able to trace is William Hibbins, who became a Freeman of Stamford in 1686. Another William of a later generation was paid for work at the Town Hall in 1755 (Chamberlain's Accounts) and was the father of Thomas Hibbins, Freeman of Stamford by patrimony in 1754.

This Thomas signs a tablet at Langtoft, Lincs, to Mrs. Handley, 1755, and yet another Thomas signs tablets in Ketton Church, 1834–1835. In the same churchyard William Hibbins, who died young, is commemorated by a tombstone decorated with the tools of the mason's craft.

A member of this family was still working as a mason at the beginning of the present century.

HICKEY, JOHN
b. 1751, *d.* 1795

He was born in Dublin, the fourth son of Noah Hickey, a confectioner, and entered the Dublin Society's Schools in 1764. Here he gained several prizes before he left to become a pupil of Richard Cranfield who worked as a carver in the city.

In 1776 Hickey went to England, where he joined the Royal Academy Schools, giving the date of his birth as 7 November, 1751 (not 1756, as stated by Strickland). Two years later he won the Academy Gold Medal for his relief of "The Slaughter of the Innocents."

In 1782 it was proposed to erect in Dublin a monument to Henry Grattan, and Hickey applied for the commission. In this he was supported by Edmund Burke, who wrote from Whitehall to Lord Charlemont that: "it will be a pleasure to you to know that at this time a young man of Ireland is here, who I really think, as far as my judgment goes, is fully equal to our best statuaries. If you employ him, you will encourage the rising arts in the decoration of the rising virtue of Ireland. . . . The young man's name who wishes to be employed is Hickey" (*Historical Manuscripts Commission*, Earl of Charlemont, Vol. I, page 61).

Though the project fell through and the monument was never erected, Burke still continued to do everything in his power for his fellow-countryman. Not only did he sit to him for two portraitbusts, but he also secured him the commission for the Abbey monument to Garrick. Hickey, however, died before he could begin the work and Burke wrote to Albany Wallis : "if poor Hickey had been spared to us, I should not have preferred any sculptor living to him" (*Farington's Diary*, Vol. I, page 86, q.v. Webber H.).

Another of Hickey's patrons was Lord Loughborough, of whom the sculptor made a bust in 1785. Loughborough, too, seems to have been anxious to help him, for in the same year he recommended him to Lord Berwick as a carver of chimney-pieces, adding in his letter that he had "employed Hickey on work of that nature with complete satisfaction." Here again Hickey was unfortunate, for Lord Berwick replied that he had already engaged another artist (Berwick Archives), but he did make a few chimney-pieces under Soane, including one costing £54 for Mr. Branthwayt of Norfolk in 1783, and another of black and veined marble in 1791 for Messrs. Ransom and Morland of Pall Mall (Soane Notebooks).

Hickey, who had been appointed sculptor to the Prince of Wales in 1786, died in Oxford Street on 12 January, 1795. Farington (op. cit.) attributed his death "to having lain in a damp bed," but Strickland (*Dictionary of Irish Artists*, page 482) asserts that "his intemperate habits hastened his end." He exhibited at the Royal Academy, 1777–1794, showing busts of Mrs. Siddons as "Cassandra" in 1786 and Mr. Thickness of St. Paul's School in 1792. One of his busts of Edmund Burke, already mentioned, was formerly at Wentworth Woodhouse and there is a replica of it in the British Museum. In 1788 he designed a colossal statue of "Time" supporting a clock for Carlton House.

Hickey's most important monuments, with their statues, busts and medallions, commemorate Henry Singleton, 1788, in St. Peter's Church, Drogheda, and David La Touche, 1790, at Delgany, Co. Wicklow, while his finest monument in England is that to Mrs. Hawkins, 1780, in St.

Helen's Church, Abingdon. Other signed works by him include those to William Dowdeswell, 1775, at Bushley, Worcs; Samuel Foster, 1778, at Grantham, Lincs; Lord Archer, 1778, at Tanworth, Warwick; Mary Child, 1782, in St. Nicholas's, Abingdon; General William Haviland, 1784, at Penn, Bucks; John Spencer, 1786, at Cawthorne, Yorks; Sir Richard Hoare, 1787, in Barnes Parish Church; John Story, 1787, at Leyton, Essex; Joseph Baker, 1789, in Chichester Cathedral; and Mrs. Burrell, 1789, in Beckenham Parish Church.

At a sale held by Mr. Christie on 15 March, 1798, of a "statuary and mason quitting business" two of the lots were "a large bas-relief of 'Herod's cruelty' for which the late Mr. Hickey obtained the gold medal of the Royal Academy" and a small marble statue "a tragic figure of Mrs. Siddons in the character of Cassandra after the original by Mr. Hickey in the collection of Earl Fitzwilliam." (Archives, Messrs. Christie.)

(Authorities cited in text.)

HICKS, JOHN, of Newbury
b. 1726, *d.* 1768

He is possibly a son of Jonathan Hicks (q.v.) and signs monuments to the Rev. Joseph Wells, 1750, at Hungerford, Berks, and to the Sainsbury family, 1765, and Robert Hayward, 1768, both at Market Lavington, Wilts.

The younger Hicks is buried at Speen, Berkshire.

HICKS, JONATHAN
b. 1675, *d.* 1743

He was employed by Henry Viscount Bolinbroke in 1712–13 at Bucklesbury House in Berkshire. He, too, is buried at Speen Church in the same county, where his monument in the chancel describes him as "Freemason and carver." This monument, a very fine cartouche tablet, is possibly his own work.

(*Berkshire Archaeological Journal*, Vol. 38, No. 2, pages 148–149.)

HILL, EDWARD, of Hill Street, Berkeley Square
d. 1799

In 1790 he received £719 for mason's work, including carved Portland stone, for Woburn Abbey, and in the two following years he and his partner, Thomas Oldfield, made a number of chimney-pieces for the building. For these they were paid a total sum of £449, which included £48 for the chimney-piece in the south-front west bedroom and £35 for one in the eating-room (Woburn Abbey Archives).

Hill died on 25 December, 1799 (*Gentleman's Magazine*, 1799, page 1094). As contractors Hill and Oldfield built houses in Sloane Street in 1789 (Middlesex Building Affidavits).

HILL, GEORGE, of London
fl. 1731–1747

In 1731 he made chimney-pieces for Mr. Benjamin Hoare of Boreham Hall, Essex, while in 1744 he was employed by a Mr. Christopher Arnold, a partner in Hoare's Bank, at his house near London (Archives, Hoare's Bank). In 1747 he was paid four guineas for "festoons."

Hill figures as a "carver in wood and stone" in the *London Directory* of 1740.

HILL, J., of Barnet
fl. 1818–1832

Between 1818 and 1832 he made three dull tablets in the Parish Church of Monken Hadleigh, Hertfordshire.

HILL, JAMES, of London
fl. 1761–1770

In Mortimer's *Universal Directory* for 1763 he is noted as "statuary in the Strand." He exhibited at the Society of Artists, 1761–1770, showing bas-reliefs of classical subjects, models in wax, etc.

HILL, JOHN, of Reading
fl. 1782–1788

In the *Reading Mercury* of 9 January, 1786, is an advertisement of "John Hill, stone-mason, and carver, on the High Bridge, London Street . . . executes Monuments, chimney-pieces in different kinds of coloured marbles in the most elegant and modern taste—tombs and headstones, and all kinds of ornaments in stone." In the voters' lists of 1782 his name is given as "John Flewell Hill, stone-mason."

Hill signs a wall-tablet at Shinfield, Berks, to Edward Waite, 1788. He also carved the font in Basildon Church in the same county, which had been designed by the Vicar, the Rev. George Bellas.

HILL, THOMAS
d. 1713

He became free of the Masons' Company in 1670, and later held the offices of Renter Warden in 1694, Upper Warden in 1695, and Master in 1699. In 1708 his address is given as "Chelsea" in the books of the Company.

Hill, who was several times employed at White-hall, also worked at the Chelsea Royal Hospital, 1686–1702; St. Paul's Cathedral, 1686–1707; Kensington Palace, 1689–1690; Greenwich Palace, 1698; and Hampton Court. At St. Paul's he and his partner, Thomas Wise (q.v.), executed much of the stone-carving, while for Kensington he, and two other partners, John Thompson and Richard Walters, supplied twenty-five marble chimney-pieces and two hundred and twenty-one of Portland stone (P.R.O., E.351/3466), payment for these being made to them between 1689 and 1691.

It is impossible to give a full list of all the carved and statuary work carried out by Hill and his partners for the Royal Palaces and St. Paul's, but they range from four stone troughs made in 1701 for the lions at the Tower to marble chimney-pieces. At Whitehall they supplied one of Egyptian marble for the apartment of "Duchess Mazarin" in 1685 (P.R.O., Works 5/46), six others for unspecified rooms in 1686, and one for Queen Mary's bedroom in 1693 (P.R.O., Works 5/47). In 1687 they made one for the Council Chamber at Chelsea Hospital, while for Kensington, besides the large number already mentioned, they executed in 1697 one of dove marble for Lord Albemarle's lodgings (P.R.O., Works 5/49). Another of black and yellow marble was made for the Presence Chamber at Hampton Court in 1700 (P.R.O., Works 5/50). Also for Hampton Court, Hill made in 1699 "two large urns with festoons and four mask faces" and the piers for them to stand on.

Hill, who died in 1713, is mentioned in a letter written by Sir John Vanbrugh to Lord Godolphin, wherein Sir Christopher Wren is quoted as calling him "a whimsical man and a piece of an astrologer and would venture on nothing till he had consulted the stars" (*Wren Society*, Vol. VII, page 140).

In 1681 he made for £8 a marble font for the Church of St. Anne and St. Agnes (Church-wardens' Accounts), and he also signs monuments to William Levinz, 1698, in St. John's College, Oxford; Mrs. Frances Ball, 1704, at Hampton, Middlesex; and Mr. Jordan, 1706, in Barbados Cathedral.

Hill's son, Thomas Hill the Younger, was apprenticed to him in 1695, but was later turned over to William Stanton (q.v.). He became free in 1702 and died in 1724.

Another Thomas Hill, son of William Hill, "citizen and mason," was apprenticed to Edward Maslin in 1710, but was later turned over to his father; he became free in 1720. His son, another Thomas, was apprenticed to J. Rose (q.v.) in 1737.

(Authorities cited in text.)

HILL, WILLIAM

Between 1656–1658 he built Brasenose College Chapel (College Archives).

HILLS, S.

He signs a large and elaborate Gothic monument, 15 ft. high, to Dugdale Dugdale (*d.* 1836) at Merevale, Warwickshire.

HINCHLIFFE, or HINCHLIFF, JOHN, the Elder and JOHN, the Younger

John Hinchliffe the Elder: *d.* 1796
John Hinchliffe the Younger: *b. c.* 1760

The elder Hinchliffe was the son of John Hinchliffe, a barber of the parish of St. George's, Bloomsbury, and after being bound apprentice to Richard Buddle (*d.* 1796) was turned over to Lewis Cockran, citizen and mason, in 1748. He took up his freedom in 1755 and later became Master of the Masons' Company in 1790.

In 1774 Hinchliffe took his son, John Hinchliffe the Younger, as an apprentice. The latter, who afterwards assisted his father, was alive in 1801, for in that year his nephew Samuel, son of William Hinchliffe, was apprenticed to him.

The elder Hinchliffe exhibited at the Society of Artists in 1768 a "specimen of a new manner of ornamenting chimney-pieces, tables, etc., with scagliola inlaid with marble," while four years later he showed "a statuary marble table inlaid with scagliola."

His signed monument to Ann Herney, 1771, is in the triforium of Bristol Cathedral. This is a curious work, in the form of a large wreathed triumphal column. For Kensington churchyard he made in 1784 the mausoleum of the Earl of Bellamont, costing £159 3s. 8d., and also carved a sarcophagus for Miss Johnstone which had been designed by Soane (Soane Note-books).

The younger Hinchliffe's signed monuments and tablets include those to the Rev. Richard Southgate, 1795, in St. Giles-in-the-Fields; Mrs. Worral, 1795, at Wisbech, Cambs; and Milward Row, 1804, at Tillington, Sussex.

The family lived "at the King's Place Farm near the Baldfaced Stag, Epping Forest," and it was here that the elder Hinchliffe died in 1796. As a contractor Hinchliffe built houses in Tottenham Court Road (1777); Gower Street (1785) and Devonshire Place (1793) (Middlesex Building Affidavits).

HINCHLIFFE, or HINCHLIFF, JOHN ELY

b. 1777, *d.* 1867

He was born in 1777, the son of William

Hinchliffe, and in 1791 was apprenticed to John Hinchliffe the Elder (q.v.), who may have been his grandfather. In 1796 he became free of the Masons' Company by patrimony, but did not attend the Royal Academy Schools until 1808.

Two years previously he had entered the employment of John Flaxman (q.v.) and for the last twenty years of the sculptor's life acted as his faithful, devoted and confidential assistant. When Flaxman died in 1826 Hinchliffe helped to complete the unfinished works in the studio, including the statue of John Philip Kemble for Westminster Abbey.

He exhibited at the Royal Academy, 1814–1847, showing mostly designs for memorials and a few portrait-busts. His monuments are not, in spite of the years he spent with Flaxman, very inspired or exciting works, and are mostly in the neo-Hellenic tradition.

Hinchliffe, who was the father of John James Hinchliffe (1805–1875), the engraver, died in 1867. The *Art Journal* in its obituary (1868, page 48) said of him that: "in private life he had long enjoyed the sincere regard of a large number of friends who found in the integrity of his nature many of the highest social qualities."

Signed monuments and tablets by him include those to John Quantock, 1820, in Chichester Cathedral; John Pusey Edwardes, 1822, in the Grosvenor Chapel; Sir Harry Goring, 1824, at Washington, Sussex; Joseph Watson, 1829, in Bermondsey Parish Church; James Smith, 1832, at Udimore, Sussex; Edward Biggs, 1833, in Barking Parish Church; Lord Gambier, 1833, at Iver, Bucks; Margaretta Ewbank, 1833, in Marylebone Parish Church; Mary Norris, 1836, at Taunton, Somerset; General Sir George Cooke, 1837, at Harefield, Middlesex; William Wickham, 1840, in York Minster; Mary Graves, 1843, in St. Margaret Pattens; and General Taylor, 1846, in Canterbury Cathedral.

(British Museum, Ad. MS. 39,784; authority cited in text.)

HIND, JOHN, of Swithland

fl. 1718–1761

Hind, who was one of the best of the Leicestershire slate-carvers, was apprenticed to William Heafford, a slater of Leicester, in 1718. He signs a large number of works in churchyards in the county, two of his best tombstones being those of Robert Hall, 1754, at St. Margaret's, Leicester, and the Armston family, 1761, at Cosby, but his finest monument is that to Sir Joseph Danvers, 1745, at Swithland, which has large reliefs of an agricultural landscape, an African sea-port, etc.

He was succeeded by his son, who signs monuments to Edward Dawson, 1788, at Long Whatton, and George Doughty, 1792, at Mount Sorrel.

HIORN, FRANCIS, of Warwick
b. 1744, *d.* 1789

His family came from Great Tew in Oxfordshire, where they had been masons since the early seventeenth century, or perhaps earlier. Francis Hiorn, who was born in 1744, was the elder son of William Hiorn (q.v.). In 1771 he built the gateway at Wroxton Abbey for Lord Guilford (Bodleian, North MSS, *c.*64), while he was also employed as a mason at St. Michael's, Coventry, in 1788 and at St. Mary's, Warwick, in the following year.

(Authority cited and information, Mr. H. M. Colvin.)

HIORN, JOHN, of Warwick
fl. 1724–1727

He was presumably a brother of William Hiorn (q.v.) and worked under Francis Smith (q.v.) between 1724 and 1727 on the building of Ditchley Park, Oxfordshire, for the second Earl of Lichfield (Dillon Archives). During the same period he was also employed under Smith at Ombersley, Worcestershire (Archives, Lord Sandys).

HIORN, WILLIAM, of Warwick
b. 1712, *d.* 1776

He made a number of chimney-pieces, including one for a Mr. Weaver of Morville Hall, Salop, in 1748, and seven marble ones for Edward Pitts of Kyre Wyard, Worcestershire, four years later (Ass. Art. Society's Report 28, 1905–1906, page 796). In 1751 he executed some carving at Arbury Park, Warwick, where he also made a chimney-piece for the dressing-room (Newdigate Archives).

Hiorn signs the monument to Thomas Crossfield, 1744, in Rugby Parish Church, while in 1751 he made one commemorating Edward Acton for Acton Scott Church, Salop. He received £100 for this work, which was carried out according to a design by William Baker.

He died in 1776 and is buried in St. Mary's, Warwick, where there is a tablet to his memory.

HISCOCK, J. S., of Blandford
fl. 1805–1827

Hiscock, who had a yard at Poole as well as one at Blandford, was declared a bankrupt in 1827 (*New Monthly Magazine*, 1827, page 360).

His best tablets, which are all in Dorset, commemorate Mary Wright, 1805, at Wareham; John Bastard, 1809, at Blandford; George Churchill,

1814, in St. Peter's, Dorchester; and Mary Slade, 1816, at Poole.

HISCOCK, WILLIAM, of Christchurch
fl. 1798–1820

In 1809 he was employed on repairs to Christchurch Priory, Hampshire. All his best tablets are there and include those to Augusta Bullock, 1798; Philip Norris, 1806; and J. Penleaze, 1819.

HITCH, WILLIAM, of Hertford
b. 1793, *d.* 1832

He signs tablets in Hertfordshire at Ware, between 1821 and 1829, and also at Datchworth in 1824.

HOARE, PRINCE, of Bath
d. 1769

He was probably born in Suffolk, and was the brother of William Hoare, R.A. Vertue, writing in January 1749/50, has the following paragraph about Hoare: "As soon as a young statuary came to England from Italy, where he had been to make his studyes about seven or eight years, it was advertised in the newspapers that Prince Hoare, statuary, being at Bath, some of the citizens there had proposed by subscription to erect a sta ue of marble to the memory of Richd. Nash, Esq., who had for forty years past so much encouraged the interest and welfare of that place. This project, no doubt, was also much encouraged by his brother Hoare, an ingenious and well-esteemed painter of portraits, principally in crayons, who had great success in his way and much esteem for his skill and his conduct. This young statuary, his brother, was educated under Mr. Scheemaker, and in early dayes, groweing a tall handsom agreeable person, and somewhat skill'd in music, bids fair for a great man (*Walpole" Society, Vertue,* Vol. III, page 152). Hoare's statue of Beau Nash, which Vertue mentions here, was erected in the Pump Room at Bath, but does not seem to have been unveiled until about 1752.

A much earlier work by Hoare was a bust of Lord Chesterfield. This must have been executed before 1741, for on 15 February of that year Chesterfield wrote to the Bishop of Waterford that "Lady Chesterfield has sent you from Bristol a busto of your humble servant, cast from a marble one done by Mr. Hoare at Bath" (Chesterfield's *Works,* 1777, Vol. IV, page 241).

In 1759 Hoare made statues of "Helen," "Paris," "Diana" and "Venus" for Stourhead (Archives, Hoare's Bank). He was also employed at Corsham Court, Wiltshire, where, between

1760 and 1762, he made chimney-pieces, including those for the library and a bedroom. Three years later he supplied others, for which he received £75 (Methuen Archives). His "Copy of the Wild Boar at Florence" and "Bust of a Vestal" were made for Sir Robert Throckmorton, probably in 1754, for there are payments to him entered in Sir Robert's account-book in that year, and these two works are specifically mentioned in the inventory, drawn up by the latter in 1788, of the contents of his houses at Buckland and Coughton.

Hoare also carved a few busts, including three in Bath of Ralph Allen (1757) at the Hospital; Richard Nash (1761) in the Guildhall; and Pope in the Art Gallery.

He died at Bath on 8 November, 1769 (*London Magazine*, 1769, page 593), having previously married on 4 May, 1751, an heiress—Miss Coulthurst, of Melksham, Wiltshire—with a fortune of £6,000 (*Gentleman's Magazine*, 1751, page 284).

Hoare's monuments, lavishly adorned with coloured marbles, are typical of the period, the finest of them commemorating Bishop Maddox, 1743, in Worcester Cathedral. This has a life-size female figure with a down-turned torch in her hand, while on the sarcophagus is a relief of "The Good Samaritan." His monument to Pope, who died in 1744, was erected in Twickenham Parish Church in 1761 to the order of the poet's friend, William Warburton.

Other signed monuments by Hoare include those to Jacob Selfe, 1730, at Melksham, Wilts; Mary Hilliard, 1745, at Kilmerdown, Somerset; John Long, 1746, at Hedington, Wilts; Lady Cobb, 1749, at Newton St. Loe, Somerset; Jacob Barclay, 1750, Weston, Somerset; the Eyles family, 1757, in Devizes Parish Church; Thomas Dawtrey, 1758, at Petworth, Sussex; Thomas Collins, 1761, in St. Leonard's, Exeter; Anne Carey, 1762, at Steeple Aston, Wilts; and John, Lord Trevor, 1764, at Bromham, Beds.

HOBDAY, SAMUEL, of Evesham

He signs a tablet to Bernard Baldwyn, 1816, at Aston-sub-Edge, Gloucestershire.

HOBSON, AARON, of Enfield
fl. 1826–1830

He signs a large wall-tablet to James Meyer, 1826, in Enfield Parish Church. His yard was in London Lane. He was also a dealer in "Welch black marble."

HOCKLEY, DANIEL

He signs a large tablet to Thomas Wolfe, 1819, at Arkesden, Essex.

HOCKLEY, JOHN, of London
b. c. 1731

He was a son of Thomas Hockley, a tallow-chandler of Godalming, Surrey, and was apprenticed to Thomas Bull the Elder (q.v.) in 1745. Five years later, however, he was turned over to Thomas Bull the Younger (q.v.) and finally became free in 1752.

By 1760 Hockley had set up on his own and his address appears in the Court Book of the Masons' Company as "Old Broad Street, opposite the Pay Office." In 1774 he succeeded to the post of Assistant to the Company on the death of J. Deval (q.v.).

He signs large and curious monuments of an architectural type to Mrs. Gildart, 1758, and John Hayley, 1763, in the churchyards of Totteridge, Hertfordshire, and Hendon, Middlesex, respectively.

HODGES, WILLIAM

His father, William Hodges, became free of the Masons' Company in 1734. The younger Hodges received a premium from the Society of Arts in 1759 for a clay model of birds.

HODGSON, J., of Driffield

He signs a large wall-tablet to William Schoolcroft, 1805, at Hovingham, Yorkshire.

HOGAN, JOHN
b. 1800, *d.* 1858

He was born at Tallow, Co. Waterford, on 14 October, 1800, the son of a carpenter named John Hogan, and in 1816 was apprenticed to Thomas Deane, a builder and architect, for whom he worked as a carpenter and woodcarver. In 1823 he attracted the attention of W. P. Carey, the Irish engraver, who recognized his genius and resolved to help him.

Carey not only interested Lord de Tabley in his protégé, but also appealed for funds to allow him to study in Rome. A sum of £250 was collected and Hogan set out for Italy, where he remained, except for brief intervals, until 1848. He soon made a name for himself, and Thorwaldsen, when he was leaving the country, is supposed to have said: "My son, you are the best sculptor I leave after me in Rome." In 1840 he was elected a member of the Society of "Virtuosi al Pantheon," the first British subject to be so honoured since its foundation in 1500 (*Art Union*, 1840, page 41).

In 1845 Hogan sent from Rome a marble statue of Mr. Crawford, but unfortunately it was packed in tan and resembled an Egyptian mummy when it finally arrived at Cork. In the following year the *Art Journal* (page 153) described his bust of Lord Cloncurry as "one of the happiest works of the kind ever conceived and one of the most beautiful ever executed in Rome."

Ten years after he finally left Italy, Hogan died in Dublin on 27 March, 1858. Nearly all his works are in Ireland and lists of them are given in Strickland's *Dictionary of Irish Artists* and also in Volume I of the *Journal of the Cork Historical and Archaeological Society* (pages 200–218). He exhibited a few works at the Royal Academy between 1833 and 1850, while his statue of "Eve Startled at the Sight of Death," which he had executed in 1825 for Lord de Tabley, was lent by its owner to the exhibition of Art Treasures of the United Kingdom held at Manchester in 1857.

(Authorities cited in text.)

HOLBERT, —

Holbert, who was assistant to John Nost (q.v.), carved a chimney-piece in purple marble for the long gallery at Hampton Court in 1701 (P.R.O., Works 5/52).

HOLDER, JAMES, of Emsworth
fl. 1818–1824

His best tablet, in a delightful neo-Hellenic style, commemorates John Campbell, 1818, at Westbourne, Sussex. He also signs others to Miles Monk, 1821, at Funtington in the same county, and to John Walker, 1824, at Warblington, Hampshire.

HOLDER, T., of Tewkesbury
fl. 1793–1820?

He signs a tablet to Thomas Hill (*d.* 1793) in All Saints Church, Evesham. Another to William Gredge, 1820, at Orpington, Kent, which may also be his work, is signed "T. Holder sculp. John Mullins arc."

HOLLINS, PETER
b. 1800, *d.* 1886

He was born on 1 May, 1800, in Great Hampton Street, Birmingham, the eldest son of W. Hollins (q.v.), and trained in his father's studio until about 1822, when he went to London to work under Chantrey (q.v.). On his return to Birmingham he assisted his father who was then working at Alton Towers, carving much of the ornamental work in the grounds.

Hollins's first independent work was the bust of Edward Grainger, referred to by Mr. Elkington

in his letter to the Editor of *Aris's Gazette*, published in the issue of 20 December, 1824. After expressing surprise at its "masterly execution," the writer added that "it certainly would not disgrace the chisel of the most experienced artist." In 1828 the sculptor returned to London with his friend, Harry Room, a Birmingham portrait-painter, and together they shared a studio at 17, Old Bond Street. Here in 1833 Hollins held an exhibition of his works, which included a "Colossal Group of the Murder of the Innocents," and busts of Thomas Bateman, William Macready, T. Telford, and the Hon. Mrs. Norton. In the same year the *Annals of the Fine Arts* said of him that: "there is not a young artist of the present day whose efforts deserve greater encouragement. Every subject undertaken by him is executed with great care and fidelity and in a most refined taste." Two years before this he had been awarded the "Sir Robert Lawley" Prize by the Birmingham Society of Arts for his group entitled "Conrad and Medora."

In 1835 or 1836 Hollins visited Italy and, on his return, received various important commissions. In 1843 he went back to Birmingham and took over the family business on the death of his father, which occurred shortly afterwards. He exhibited at the Royal Academy, 1822–1871, and sent his "Murder of the Innocents" to the Great Exhibition of 1851. He died on 16 August, 1886, in the house in which he was born. About twelve years before his death he had been forced to give up work, being practically disabled by rheumatism, the result of working in wet clothes (*Birmingham Daily Post*, 18 August, 1886).

Hollins at his best was a very great artist and his monuments to Lady Bradford and Sophia Thompson are as fine as anything executed by Chantrey. Of the two, that commemorating Lady Bradford, 1842, at Weston, Staffs, is the more beautiful; she is portrayed lying on her death-bed, while behind her is a large relief of angels receiving her into Heaven. The figure of Mrs. Thompson, 1838, in Malvern Priory, is superbly carved and shows her reclining on a couch. At first sight this monument appears to have been influenced by the work of Chantrey, but a closer examination soon proves its complete individuality.

Hollins's statue of Sir Rowland Hill, which he made for his native city, has had a chequered career. It was erected in 1868 in the Birmingham Exchange, but was removed to the new General Post Office in 1874, and again to newer Post Office headquarters in 1891. In 1940 it was taken down and sent away "for safety," but has apparently been mislaid (information from Birmingham Public Library).

(Langford's *Modern Birmingham*, Vols. I and II; Authorities cited in text.)

STATUES

1825	Marquess of Anglesey	Exhibited Royal Academy
1834	Daughter of Vincent Thompson	Exhibited Royal Academy
1840	Rev. Dr. Warnford	Warnford Lunatic Asylum, nr. Oxford
1846	"Sabrina"	For the Earl of Bradford
1846	Dr. Jephson	Leamington
1855	Peel	Calthorpe Park, Birmingham
1859	Thomas Attwood	Calthorpe Park, Birmingham
1859	Thomas Holloway	Exhibited Royal Academy
1868	Sir Rowland Hill	For Birmingham

BUSTS

1825	Edward Grainger	Royal College of Surgeons
1827	Nero	Exhibited Birmingham Society of Artists
1831	Charles Lloyd	Birmingham General Hospital
1831	Gabriel de Lys	Edgbaston Church
1833	Joseph Grice	Handsworth Parish Church
1833	Nathaniel Clarke	Handsworth Parish Church
1835	H. Earle	Exhibited Birmingham Society of Artists
1836	Percival Pott	Royal College of Surgeons
1839	Lord John Russell	Exhibited Royal Academy
1839	William Phipson	Exhibited Birmingham Society of Artists
1842	Rev. Samuel Warnford	Birmingham School of Medicine
1843	William Hollins	St. Paul's Church, Birmingham
1845	Rev. Vaughan Thomas	Queen's College, Birmingham
1846	George Barber	Birmingham General Hospital
1850	Mendelssohn	Birmingham Town Hall
1851	William Hutton	Ward End Church, Birmingham
1853	W. Congreve Russell	Exhibited Birmingham Society of Artists
1853	James Foster	Old Swinford, Worcs
1860	David Cox	Birmingham Art Gallery
1860	William Scholefield	Birmingham Art Gallery
1867	Recorder Hill	Birmingham Art Gallery
1867	M. Davenport Hill	Formerly Birmingham Central Library

VARIOUS

1830	Group of "Cupid and Psyche"	Aston Hall, Birmingham
1833	Group of figures	Façade of Blue Coat School, Birmingham
1848	Font	Darleston Church, Staffs
1862	Font	Bodelwyddan Church, North Wales

MONUMENTS

1826	Marston Lea, Warwick	Charles Adderley
1827	Ansty, Warwick	The Ludford family
1828	Wednesbury, Staffs	Samuel Addison
1828	Birmingham (St. Martin's)	John Home
1829	Birmingham (Cathedral)	Rev. George Breay
1829	Ansty, Warwick	John Ludford
1830	Lichfield (Cathedral)	Rev. John Newling
1831	Claines, Worcs	Sir Henry Wakeman (with bust)
1832	Wednesbury, Staffs	Edward Crowther
1833	Market Drayton, Salop	Rev. John Stubbs
1835	Dudley, Worcs	Samuel Bennitt
1835	Ecclesfield, Yorks	John Booth
1835	Birmingham (Cathedral)	Edward Wilkes
1836	Yardley, Warwick	Edmund Greswolde
1837	Chester (Cathedral)	Elizabeth Buchanan
1838	Stone, Staffs	Thomas Unett
1839	Hanbury, Staffs	John Wilson
1839	Wellington, Salop	Martha Oliver
1841	Malvern (Priory)	Thomas Woodyatt
1848	Birmingham (St. Margaret's)	William Hulton
1850	Moseley, Birmingham	William Russell
1850	Lichfield (Cathedral)	Officers and Men of the 80th Regiment
1852	Aston Flamville, Leics	Sir Edward Hartopp
1854	Longdon, Staffs	C. S. Foster
1855	Kensal Green (Cemetery)	John Hollins
1856	Dudley, Worcs	Thomas Badger
1860	Wednesbury, Staffs	Rev. Isaac Clarkson (with bust)
1865	Ashley, Staffs	Elizabeth Kinnersly
1870	Dudley, Worcs	John Badley

HOLLINS, WILLIAM
b. 1763, *d.* 1843

There seems to be a certain amount of confusion concerning the date of Hollins's birth. He was the son of John and Mary Hollins, of Shifnal,

Salop, and was born in 1754, according to the *Dictionary of National Biography*. Langford, in his *Modern Birmingham* (Vol. I, page 31) makes it ten years later, but both are wrong, for the date is given as 18 March, 1763, on Hollins's monument in the graveyard of St. Paul's Church, Birmingham.

Hollins was a self-taught artist who passed practically all his life in Birmingham. Here he carved the figures over the doorway of the Dispensary in Union Street and carried out the "Gothic" restoration of Handsworth Parish Church in 1820. With his son Peter (q.v.) he also prepared the south chapel for Chantrey's statue of James Watt.

As an architect he did a good deal of work in Birmingham, designing Soho House and the Institution for Promoting the Fine Arts. For Lord Shrewsbury's seat at Alton Towers he planned the garden-buildings and executed the stone-carving, and he was also, rather strangely, the architect of the Royal Mint in St. Petersburg. In 1806 he produced a design for the Birmingham memorial to Nelson. This was to consist of a pillar, 100 ft. high, based on "an appropriate building with two fronts suitable for a dispensary and a post-office," but fortunately the Selection Committee preferred the simpler design submitted by Westmacott (*Birmingham Gazette*, 9 July, 1806). In the following year Hollins designed the "Egyptian Conduit" in the Bull Ring.

Hollins exhibited at the Birmingham Society of Artists, 1827–1840, showing in 1827 "a medallion of James Watt" and "Thetis," and also busts of the Marquess of Anglesey and E. J. Littleton. In 1830 he exhibited a bust of George IV, and in 1840 a marble statue of Catherine Jenner. At the Royal Academy he showed busts of Archdeacon Outram (1821), the Earl of Shrewsbury (1822) and the Marquess of Anglesey (1822). He also modelled a number of wax portraits.

His monuments are not as fine as those of his son, although that to Alexander Forrester, 1817, in All Saints', Leicester, is a fine classical stele. He died on 12 January, 1843, and was buried under a granite obelisk in the churchyard of St. Paul's, Birmingham. A window in the south aisle of the same church commemorates him and his family. The stained glass is insignificant, but the sculptured marble surround is most arresting. The carving represents flowing foliage, which forms cartouches containing the names and dates of the various members of the family; on the right-hand side is a bust of William Hollins himself by his son Peter, who may be presumed to be responsible for the whole design. Hollins's wife, Catherine, died in 1831. They had another son named

William, born on 20 December, 1788. He acted as assistant to his father and died on 22 August, 1831.

Hollins signs monuments to John Freer, 1808, in Handsworth Parish Church; to William Withering, 1808, at Edgbaston; to Joseph Wainwright, 1810, at Dudley, Worcs; to Samuel Addison, 1817, at Wednesbury, Staffs; and to Mary Sayer, 1823, at Moseley, Worcs. His monuments to James Goddington, 1821, and Benjamin Spencer, 1823, are both at Aston, Birmingham; and those of Thomas Cooper, 1818, Edmund Outram, 1821, and David Owen, 1823, are all in Birmingham Cathedral.

HOLLIS, J., of London
fl. 1820–1836

He seems to have had an unfortunate career, for he became a bankrupt in 1821 and again in 1828. He signs a neo-Hellenic tablet at Clerkenwell to Thomas Greatrex, 1824, while his tablet at Lutterworth, Warwick, to Henry Ryder, Bishop of Lichfield, 1836, has a medallion portrait.

HOLLOWAY, THOMAS
fl. 1773–1792

He exhibited at the Royal Academy from 1773 until 1792, showing wax portraits, pictures in oils and crayons, and engraved gems, the most interesting in the last category being a "portrait of the Rev. Mr. Wesley, impression of a seal from life" (1773).

HOLM, or HOLME, LAWRENCE ANDERSON
fl. 1760–1774

He came to Britain from Denmark some time before 1760, and in 1762 made the model of the State Coach which had been designed by Sir William Chambers (*Builder*, 1854, page 72). Two years later he was working as assistant to William Atkinson (q.v.), and also received a premium from the Society of Arts for a bas-relief in marble of "Hector Parting with his Wife." Between 1765 and 1767 he was paid nearly £200 by the same society for two large statues in marble of "Oedipus Expounding the Riddle to the Sphinx" and "Sophonisba with a Cup of Poison" (Archives, Society of Arts).

In 1771 Holm received £408 for the decorative sculpture and the chimney-piece for the "Great Room near Exeter Exchange" which the Society of Artists were then building so that they could hold exhibitions in a place of their own (Archives, Society of Artists). Three years later the Vintners'

Company paid him £87 for "carving and gilding large figures" (Archives, Vintners' Company), and shortly afterwards he apparently returned to Denmark.

Holm exhibited at the Society of Artists, 1761–1773, showing a number of works, including busts of Sir Edward Hulse and George Grenville in 1763 and 1768 respectively. He signs three monuments—to Thomas Prowse, 1767, and to Abigail Prowse, 1763, both at Axbridge, Somerset, and a third to Sir Edward Hulse, 1759, in the churchyard of Wilmington, Kent.

(Authorities cited in text.)

HOLMES, SARAH, of Brentford
fl. 1811–1835

Her work is dull and conventional and consists of a semi-urn or similar design. She signs tablets in Middlesex to Herbert Swyer, 1811, at Isleworth; John Howard, 1818, in St. Laurence's, Brentford; Thomas Smith, 1823, in Ealing Parish Church; and George Engleheart, 1833, at East Bedfont. Her tablet to Viscount Falkland, 1827, is at Rudby, Yorkshire.

HOLT, JOHN, of Brixworth

He signs a tablet at Spratton, Northamptonshire, to Thomas Chapman, who died in 1826. Another John Holt (born in 1808) joined the Royal Academy Schools in 1830.

HONE, ALFRED
fl. 1836–1882

He may have been a son of the writer, William Hone (1780–1842), as Alfred exhibited his bust at the Suffolk Street Galleries in 1836.

He exhibited at the Royal Academy, 1836–1852, showing a number of busts, including those of Joseph Parkes (1836); Thomas Slingsby Duncombe (1843); and T. Pollock (1852). His bust of Thomas Addison, executed in 1838, is at the Royal College of Physicians, and another of Mrs. Duppa, dating from the following year, at Sharsted Court, Kent.

HONEYBONE, —, of Shrivenham

He signs a tablet with a relief of "Faith" to Elizabeth Batson, 1808, at Ramsbury, Wilts.

HOOKEY, JOHN, of Southampton
fl. 1792–1808

He was the son of G. Hookey, a mason of Southampton, whose widow died in 1802 (*Monthly Magazine*, 1802, page 1951). His large wall-tablets in coloured marbles are well above the average work of the provincial statuary of the period.

Hookey signs two tablets at Lymington, Hampshire, to Jeremiah Meylor, 1792, and James Allen, 1808. His tablet to John Stewart, 1796, is at North Stoneham in the same county.

HOOPER, JOHN
fl. 1761–1768

He was employed at Audley End, 1761–1764, not only as a mason, but also to execute a considerable amount of carved Gothic stonework (Essex Record Office, D/DBY. A243).

In 1762 Hooper built, from a design by Leadbitter, the temple in the park at Ditchley, Oxon, the seat of the Earl of Lichfield. He also carved all the stone columns, the capitals, pilasters, cornice, etc. In 1768 he built the lodge in the "New Park" at Ditchley (Dillon Archives).

HOPE, SAMUEL and J., of Manchester
fl. 1780–1801

Their monuments and tablets, which are well designed and quite ambitious works with well-carved details, include those to Anna Legh, *c.* 1780, at Rostherne, Cheshire; Mary Sayer, 1781, and John Caygill, 1787, both in Halifax Parish Church; Hugh Hall, 1788, at Bowden, Cheshire; John Glegg, 1789, at Goostrey, Cheshire; Margaret Toosey, 1795, at Stockport, Cheshire; Thomas Drinkwater, 1797, at Salford, Lancs; and James Brown, 1801, in the Parish Church of Ashton-under-Lyne. The later works are signed only by Samuel Hope.

HOPKINS, —, of Bath

He signs a square memorial with an oval inscription tablet to Ann Bathurst, 1804, at Lydney, Monmouthshire.

HOPKINS, JORDAN, of Swindon

He signs a tablet to John Stratton, 1718, at Brinkworth, Wiltshire.

HOPKINS, WILLIAM ALEXANDER
b. 1815

He attended the Royal Academy Schools in 1840 on the recommendation of Eastlake, and four years later exhibited at the Academy a bust of "the infant son of H. E. Kendall, Esq., Jnr." After that date, however, all trace of him is lost.

HOPPER, HUMPHREY
b. 1767

He did not attend the Royal Academy Schools until 1801, gaining a Silver Medal in 1802 and the Gold Medal in the following year for a group of "The Death of Meleager."

Hopper was a competent, indeed occasionally a very good, sculptor, but he was at his very worst when given a commission for a large national monument. The responsibility seems to have paralysed his invention, as the lamentable mass of marble commissioned by the House of Commons to commemorate General Hay (1814) in St. Paul's Cathedral only too clearly shows. The figure of the falling General is merely absurd, while Smyth in his *Genii of St. Paul's* (Vol. II, page 76) notes that "the man upon whom Hay falls is naked" and goes on to remark rather pompously that "this is a most perverse licence, and what is more provoking, he seems to be placed as he is merely for the sake of a display of art and the effect of attitude. There is not an expression about him to indicate concern for the melancholy charge he happens to support."

Some of Hopper's smaller monuments, however, have charm and distinction and well-carved reliefs, although the majority of his later tablets are unfortunately poor works in spiky "Gothic." He also designed lamps, and one in the possession of Mr. Derek Sherborn is dated 25 December, 1820. It is in plaster, standing about 4 ft. high, and takes the form of a draped female figure with an eagle at her side, her right hand holding the lamp.

In 1812 Hopper made terra-cotta or plaster statues, apparently representing four of the Muses, for the Ballroom in the County Hall at Lewes, where they still remain, though now relegated to passages.

He exhibited at the Royal Academy, 1799–1834, showing busts of Dr. Thornton (1815); Lord Beresford (1815); Lord Hill (1815); John F. Johnstone (1817); C. C. Western (1825); and Wellington (1828). A plaster-cast of the last-named is in Lewes Town Hall.

MONUMENTS

1800	Addington, Bucks	Lady Tynte
1803	Chingford, Essex	Esther Cook
1810	Etwall, Derby	Joseph Green
1814	St. Paul's Cathedral	General Hay
1815	Windsor (St. George's Chapel)	Robert Packe
1819	Steveton, Hants	Rev. James Austin
1821	Merstham, Surrey	Lady Ann Simpson
1823	Cookham, Berks	Caroline Coney
1824	Sherborne St. John, Hants	William Chute
1826	Aston Rowant, Oxon	Susan Mangin
1827	Stoke-on-Trent (Parish Church)	Josiah Spode
1828	Hillington, Norfolk	Lady West
1829	Ramsgate, Kent	Sir William Curtis
1829	Warfield, Berks	Captain Digby
1829	Exeter (Cathedral)	Rev. Joseph Palmer
1830	Great Amwell, Herts	William Duncan
1830	Hempsted, Essex	Admiral Sir Eliab Harvey
1831	Harrow (Parish Church)	John North
1831	St. Blazey, Cornwall	Thomas Carylon
1831	Tillington, Sussex	Charles Mitford
1831	Ashtead, Surrey	Rev. William Fawssett
1831	Teddington, Middlesex	Juliana Coulson
1832	Bucklebury, Berks	Rev. W. Hartley
1832	Maidstone, Kent	Colonel Noel Hill
1832	Dawlish, Devon	Mrs. Chichester
1832	Sunbury, Middlesex	C. Musgrave
1832	Stoke Doyle, Northants	Thomas Capron
1832	St. Katherine's, Regent's Park	Emily Wynyard
1833	Podington, Beds	Richard Orlebar
1833	Chobham, Surrey	Thomas Bainbridge
1834	Haselbury Plucknett, Dorset	Martha Best
1835	Shoreham, Sussex	Robert Hooper
1835	St. Anthony in Roseland, Cornwall	Admiral Spry
1835	Milborne Port, Somerset	Sir William Medlycott
1835	Worlington, Suffolk	Rev. William Coop
1836	Goathurst, Somerset	Elizabeth Tynte
1836	Oxford (New College Chapel)	Charles Burlton
1836	Whitkirk, Yorks	John Wilson
1836	Marylebone (Parish Church)	Hon. Eileen Fletcher
1838	Liston, Essex	John Campbell
1838	Tunbridge Wells (Holy Trinity)	Sarah Poynder
1838	Edgcote, Northants	Rev. George Wasey
1838	Aylsham, Norfolk	Rev. Philip Hunt
1838	Marylebone (Parish Church)	Admiral Sir John Hood
1840	Corfe, Somerset	Sir Frederick Cooper
1841	Elmstead, Kent	Lady Honywood
1842	Fulham (Parish Church)	Thomas Ravenshaw

HORSNAILE, CHRISTOPHER, the Elder
fl. 1700–1742

He became free of the Masons' Company in 1700 by service with Herbert Paine, and eight years later was living at "Blackfriars, at the Bell in Glasshouse Yard" (Archives, Masons' Company).

Horsnaile was a partner of Edward Stanton (q.v.) who, in his will (1734), leaves to "Mr. Christopher Horsnaile, my honest and industrious co-partner, £40." Together they had been appointed masons to Westminster Abbey in 1719–1720 and after his partner's death Horsnaile carried on by himself until 1737. The partners made a number of chimney-pieces for Ditchley Park, Oxon, the seat of the second Earl of Lichfield, in 1725. These included one of "agate marble, consisting of architraves, moulded mantel and jambs," and, for the hall, one with a "Portland architrave and two termes of fine statuary marble, standing at each side, each terme being 6 ft. high curiously carved." For the library in the following year they made two, one of black and yellow marble, which cost £60 and the other of purple marble. They also made "two fine agate tables" (Dillon Archives).

As a mason, Horsnaile was employed at Hoare's Bank, 1726–1738 (Bank Archives). In 1727 he was paid £17 16s. 6d. by Lord Folkestone for a chimney-piece for his London house (Archives, Earl of Radnor). In 1722 he had been employed at the Royal College of Physicians in Warwick Lane (College Archives), and in 1733 he rebuilt Bishopsgate, receiving £300 and an extra £80 for "the City arms in a shield, with a cap of maintenance and dragons to stand on the attick over the great arch" (*Journal Committee City Lands*, Vol. XXV, page 166, and Vol. XXVI, page 180). In the same year he was paid £214 for work at the dormitory of Westminster School.

Horsnaile was also mason to the Inner Temple from 1737 to 1742, repairing in 1737 the south side of the Temple Church, and in 1741 the front of the Hall for which he was paid £767 (Roberts' *Inner Temple Records*, Vol. IV). In 1737, in partnership with John Deval the Elder (q.v.), he rebuilt St. Olave's, Southwark, and also provided the "communion table" at a cost of sixteen guineas (*Builder*, 1844, page 253).

As a statuary Horsnaile is important. The finest monument made by him without the assistance of Stanton is that to Sir Jacob Garrard, *c.* 1730, at Langford, Norfolk, with its recumbent figure of the knight, while figures of his two sons stand to left and right. His other two independent works—those to William Rogers, 1731, at Dowdeswell, Glos, and to Sir John Philipps, 1736, at Haverfordwest, Pembroke—both have portrait-busts. The monuments which he signs with Edward Stanton are all important works and are always signed with the latter's name first. The best is that to Thomas Vernon, 1721, at Hanbury, Worcs, which has a life-sized reclining effigy and seated figures of "Justice" and "Learning."

Another, to William East, 1726, at Witham, Essex, has a portrait-bust.

Other signed works by the partners include monuments to Bartholomew Layton, 1702, at Ringwood, Hants; Anne, Lady Hodgson, 1719, at Marston, Lincs; Robert Pleydell, 1719, at Ampney Crucis, Glos; Alice, Lady Brownlow, 1721, and William Brownlow, 1726, both at Belton, Lincs; Thomas Renda, 1722, at Wallingford, Berks; George Cressiner, 1722, at Earls Colne, Essex; Jacob Wishart, 1723, at Leatherhead, Surrey; Bishop Fleetwood, 1723, in Ely Cathedral; Sir John Sherard, 1724, and Sir Richard Sherard, 1730, both at North Witham, Lincs; Sir John Blencoe, 1726, at Marston St. Lawrence, Northants; Lady Benet, 1727, at Warminghurst, Sussex; and William Beaumont, 1729, at Great Dunmow, Essex.

HORSNAILE, CHRISTOPHER, the Younger
d. 1760

Son of Christopher Horsnaile the Elder (q.v.) he was apprenticed to his father in 1708 and became free on 8 January, 1719, the same day as William Stanton, son of his father's partner, Edward Stanton (q.v.)

The younger Horsnaile was given considerable employment at the Mansion House, to which he put some of the finishing touches, supplying all the chimney-pieces on the lower floor at a total cost of £900. Apparently some of these were unsatisfactory, for Dance, architect of the building, wrote in his report of 1753 that "the slabs of the chimney-pieces are not entire, but made out with some little pieces in the breaks thereof"; also that "the marble of two of the chimney-pieces is pretty much stained and the carving but indifferently performed." Horsnaile was also paid for busts, but of these Dance says that "the bustos in all the rooms are but indifferent casts." Nor was this the only trouble over Horsnaile's work. There had been a previous discussion in 1752 about "the regalia at the front of the Mansion House." Horsnaile refused to alter anything, except the "handle of the sword," but a year later agreed that if Dance would redraw the shield, he would make the model. This was accordingly done and the new model laid before the Committee, who found, however, that "the mace had not relievo enough" and ordered Horsnaile to make it bolder "by raising the said mace three-quarters of its substance." He was also paid £88 for marble tables, but these apparently survived the scrutiny of both Dance and the Building Committee without mishap. In 1755 he was paid £450 for "fluting the pillars" (City Corporation Records, Mansion House Building Accounts).

Horsnaile was also employed by Mr. John Nicholl, father of Lady Carnarvon, at his house in Red Lion Square in 1748 (Chandos Archives, Middlesex Record Office). He died 31 January, 1760 (*London Magazine*, page 107). His son, another Christopher Horsnaile, became free in 1747 "by service with his father."

HORSON, EZRA,
and WARRINGTON, JOSEPH

In 1686 they were employed at Grimesthorpe, making windows, cornices, chimney-panels and a doorcase of hewn stone (Wentworth, Woodhouse Archives).

HORWELL, CHARLES
b. 1754

He was born on 1 April, 1754, and attended the Royal Academy Schools in 1777. Here he won a Silver Medal in 1784, while the Gold Medal was awarded to him four years later for his group of "Achilles' Grief at the Death of Patroclus." In 1787 he had gained the Silver Palette from the Society of Arts for a figure of "Psyche." In 1796 he was employed on decorative work at the house of Lord Mornington in Park Lane (Soane Note-books).

Horwell exhibited at the Royal Academy, 1785–1807, showing busts, designs for monuments, and tablets for chimney-pieces. He signs the monument to Christopher Anstey, 1805, in Westminster Abbey.

In 1809 his daughter married Richard Woodman, the engraver (*Art Journal*, 1860, page 47).

HOSKINS, JAMES
d. 1791

In 1772, with his partner, Samuel Euclid Oliver (q.v.), he made two statues for Mersham Hatch in Kent, one in plaster of "Apollo" for the parlour, and the other, a lead figure of "Mercury," for the "mount" (Archives, Lord Brabourne).

In 1770 Hoskins and Oliver had started working for Wedgwood, for whom they modelled "16 round basso relievo's, busts of Cicero and Horace, a relief of Ganymede and Bacchus," as well as "a tail of a Dolphin" and "the rock for the Neptune." By 1775 the firm had become "Hoskins and Grant" (See Grant, Benjamin) and supplied Wedgwood with busts of "Swift, Milton, Spenser, Chaucer, Addison, Pope, Locke, Dryden, Dr. Johnson, Ben Jonson, Sir William Reigley, Prior, Congreve, Fletcher, Beaumont, Bacon, Boyle, Harvey and

Newton." Four years later they made busts of "Garick and Sterne" (Wedgwood Archives).

Hoskins, who held the post of "moulder and caster in plaster" to the Royal Academy from its foundation until his death, made "casts of two lions" in 1773 for which the Academy paid him twenty guineas (Royal Academy Archives). In 1790 he supplied four enriched Etruscan vases and eight small bronze figures for the house of Lord Delaval in Portland Place (Soane Note-books). He also executed a plaster bust of Robert Adam, the architect, which was Lot 10 at the latter's sale, held on 22 May, 1818.

HOWARD, ISAAC

In 1699 he made brass figures of a "Tartar on horseback, a large Mercury and a head of Oliver Cromwell" for Thomas Coke, of Melbourne Hall, Derbyshire (Archives, Marquess of Lothian).

HOWE, J.
fl. 1829–1842

Between 1829 and 1842 he exhibited busts and medallic portraits at the Royal Academy, including those of a Mr. Gardener in 1829, and of Andrew Ducrow, the equestrian, in 1842.

HUGGINS, WILLIAM
b. 1756

He was born in March, 1756, and joined the Royal Academy Schools in 1773, winning a Silver Medal two years later. In 1790 he exhibited at the Academy a bas-relief of "Commerce Presenting Abundance from the Four Quarters of the World to Britannia" (Royal Academy Archives).

HUGH, J.

He signs a tablet to William Graffitt, 1799, at Laugharne, Carmarthen.

HUGHES, ROBERT BALL
b. 1804, *d.* 1868

He attended the Royal Academy Schools in 1818, giving the year of his birth as 1804—not 1806, as stated by the *Art Journal* in its obituary notice. In 1819 and 1822 he was awarded Silver Medals and, in 1823, the Academy Gold Medal for a bas-relief of "Pandora Brought to Earth by Mercury." In 1820 he also received a Silver Medal from the Society of Arts for his copy of the Barbarini Faun. On leaving the Schools he entered the studio of E. H. Baily (q.v.), where he studied and worked for seven years.

In 1829 Hughes left England for New York and

remained in the United States until his death, which took place at Dorchester, near Boston, on 5 March, 1868. Soon after his arrival in the city he executed a marble statue of Alexander Hamilton for the Merchants' Exchange, a building which was burnt to the ground shortly afterwards. This was the first portrait-statue to be executed in America and a small model of it is now in the Boston Athenaeum, together with the sculptor's group of "Uncle Toby and the Widow Wadman."

Other works by Hughes include a bust of John Trumbull, now in the Yale Art Gallery, Newhaven, Connecticut, and the monument to Bishop Hobart in Trinity Church, New York. His seated statue of Nathaniel Bowditch, the navigator, was cast in bronze and was also the first of its kind to be made in the United States. It stands over Bowditch's grave in Mount Auburn Cemetery, Cambridge, Massachusetts, and is inscribed on the base "Executed by Ball Hughes, 1847" and "Recast by Gruet Jne. Fondeux." The original casting was so inferior that the family had to have it redone in Paris, which explains the double inscription.

Hughes exhibited at the Royal Academy, 1822–1828, showing various busts, including those of the Dukes of Wellington and Sussex in 1826, and a statue of "The Shepherd Boy" two years later. In 1851 he made a statue of "Oliver Twist" for the Duke of Devonshire.

(Lorado Taft's *American Sculptors*; *Art Journal*, 1868, page 128.)

HUGHES, THOMAS
b. 1809

In 1825 he received from the Society of Arts a large Silver Medal for a model of a bust, and in the same year joined the Royal Academy Schools on the recommendation of E. H. Baily (q.v.), in whose studio his brother, Robert Ball Hughes (q.v.), was then working.

The younger Hughes exhibited at the Royal Academy, 1826–1836, where his works included several busts. He also sent his figure of "Eve" to the Great Exhibition of 1851.

He showed a bust of Theodore von Holst at the Suffolk Street Galleries in 1829.

HULL, SAMUEL of Leicester
fl. 1818–1850

Hull's monuments, whether signed by himself alone or with his partner, Pollard, are nearly always neo-Hellenic in design, the best being one to Stephen Peet, 1834, at Mount Sorel, Leicestershire, which has a relief of a cherub with a downturned torch.

Other signed works by Hull include those to the Rev. Auley Macaulay, 1818, at Rothley, Leics; Henry Bickley, 1820, in the churchyard at Peckleton, Leics; George Pochin, 1831, at Barkby, Leics; James Swan, 1831, at Ridlington, Rutland; Mary Miles, 1837, and Mary Clare, 1838, both at Cosby, Leics; the Rev. Henry Sheild, 1840, at Preston, Rutland; and the Rev. Samuel Heyrich, 1840, at Brampton Ash, Leics.

Monuments signed by Hull and Pollard (all in Leicestershire) commemorate Elizabeth Corrance, 1818, at Foxton; John Heyrick, 1822, in Leicester Cathedral; Colonel William Hulse, 1825, at Cossington; and Mary Wood, 1828, in St. Mary's Church, Leicester.

HUMPHREY, THOMAS, of London
fl. 1786–1815

Humphrey, who was apprenticed to William Vere (q.v.) in 1786, signs two tablets in memory of John Charrington, who died in 1815. One of these is in Stepney Parish Church, and the other at Aldenham, Hertfordshire.

HUNT, JOHN, of Northampton
d. 1754

Hunt was a pupil of Grinling Gibbons (q.v.) for Sir Justinian Isham, writing to his son in 1714 on the subject of a family monument, suggests that it should be entrusted to him, as "he is accounted a good workman, being apprenticed to Gibbons ye carver" (Isham Archives).

Hunt was the leading sculptor and statuary in Northamptonshire for many years. He became a Freeman of Northampton on 25 September, 1712, being admitted "gratis for carving King Charles's statue," the same statue which is now above the portico of All Saints' Church. (Town Archives.)

Two years previously he had carved the large triangular relief of Diana on the garden front of Hinwick House, Bedfordshire (Orlebar Archives). This shows the goddess in her chariot and is a spirited work, though perhaps a little rustic and naïve in treatment.

His best piece of sculpture is the delightful alabaster bust of Cilena l'Anson Bradley, 1726, in Long Buckby Church, Northants, which is quite equal to London craftsmanship of the period. Baker in his *Northamptonshire* (Vol. I, page 226) states that there was a bust of Hunt himself (whom he wrongly alludes to as "Henry") at Upton Hall, Northants, in 1822. This apparently is no longer in existence. In the archives of General Norman of Bromley is the inventory dated 1714 of the contents of the house at Bromley, Kent, belonging to

Mr. William Emmett, the younger (nephew of William Emmett, q.v.)—among the objects in the hall is noted "a very good piece of carving done by Hunt."

In the interior of the church at Normanton, Rutland, is the following inscription: "Built by Sir Gilbert Heathcote, 1764; William Cantrel, Rector; Mason, carpenter and joiner, Jon Hunt, Matw. Fancourt." This is rather a puzzling state-

Hunt was a popular statuary. His most important monument, that to Sir William and Lady Boughton, 1716, is at Newbold-on-Avon and has life-size standing figures of the baronet and his wife. Other signed monuments by him in Northamptonshire include those to Sophia Whitwell, 1711, at Oundle; Frances Stratford, 1717, and Edward Stratford, 1721, both at Overstone; Samuel Knight, 1721, at Wellingborough; William Wykes, 1721, at Hazelbeech; John Perkens, 1728, at Kislingbury; Rebecca Ivory, 1728, Benjamin Kidd, 1731, Anthony Eynead, 1741, and Dorcas Stratford, 1744, all in All Saints', Northampton; Richard Cumberland, 1731, at Peakirk; Mary Shortgrave, 1732, and John Smith, 1742, both in St. Peter's, Northampton; Thomas Peace, 1732, at Hardingstone; Elizabeth Trimmell, 1737, at Brockhall; William Watson, 1738, at Spratton; John Raynsford, 1740, at Faxton; and Samuel Pennington, 1743, in St. Giles', Northampton. He also signs two monuments in Bedfordshire—to Diana Orlebar, 1716, at Podington, and William Carter, 1728, at Turvey; and one in Warwickshire—to Sir John Shuckburgh, 1724, at Shuckburgh.

He died September 25th, 1754, and the *Northampton Mercury* says "he was found dead in his bed; he ate a hearty supper the evening before and went to bed seemingly in good Health, not complaining of any illness".

HUNT, WILLIAM, of London
fl. 1668–1718

Hunt, who was apprenticed to William Stanborow in 1668 and became free in 1677, made a sundial for Sir Charles Kemeys in 1692 for which he received ten guineas (Account-book of Sir Charles Kemeys, possession author).

He is presumably the William Hunt who was paid £30 in 1718 for "carving the stone doorcase" of Aylesbury Free School, a building which is now the Aylesbury Museum (Free School Archives).

HUNTER, HUGH, of London
fl. 1782–1796

He signs large tablets with good detail to William Lyne, 1782, in All Hallows', Twickenham, and Thomas Bush, 1791, at Broxted, Essex. In 1796 he built Cleveland House, London, for the Duke of Bridgewater, being responsible for all the carved stone-work, Portland stone chimney-pieces, etc. (Archives, Lord Brownlow).

HUNTINGDON, JOHN
fl. 1731–1740

Between 1737 and 1740 he was working at Lord North's London house, his address being given as "Henrietta Street" (Bodleian, North MSS. C.58). The large and imposing architectural monument to Miss Elizabeth Cromwell, 1731, at Hursley in Hampshire, is signed "G. Sampson, architect, John Huntingdon fecit." Sampson was the architect of the first Bank of England, but I know of no other monumental work by Huntingdon.

HURLE, J., of Frome

He signs a tablet to Elizabeth Hooper, 1808, at Westbury, Wiltshire.

HURST, EDWARD
fl. 1698–1714

He made the large monument to Sir Gilbert Lort, 1698, in Westminster Abbey. This is now dismantled, but there is an illustration of it in Dart's *Westmonasterium* (Vol. II, page 121).

Hurst signs the monument with portrait-busts of John and Mary Bohun and their daughter Mary, erected *c.* 1709 in Holy Trinity, Coventry. The monument to Elizabeth Saunderson, 1714, at Glentworth, Lincolnshire, is also signed.

HUSKINSON, or HUSKISSON, SAMUEL, of London
b. c. 1706

He was a son of William Huskinson, of Little Appleby, Leicestershire, and was apprenticed to Francis Commins, of London, in 1720, becoming free seven years later.

His monuments are large, architectural works, the most important being that to Catherine Joliffe, 1731, at Petersfield, Hants, which is about 14 ft. high. Huskinson also signs monuments to Ann Thirkell, 1738, at Kinsbury, Warwick, and to Hester Probert, 1742, at Denham, Bucks.

HUTCHINSON, EDMUND, of Spalding

He was a pupil of William Sandes, an architect, and carved in 1751 the monument of his master erected in Spalding Church (Nichols' *Literary Anecdotes*, Vol. 6, page 72).

I

IBACK, JOSIAS
fl. 1679–1694

He made the equestrian bronze statue of Charles II at Windsor Castle, and cut into one of the horse's hoofs are the words "*Josias Jback Stadti Blarensis 1679 Fudit*." The words "*Stadti Blarensis*" are difficult to understand, but they may mean that Iback came from Bever in Hanover (for a discussion on this point, see Hope's *Windsor Castle*, Vol. II, page 555).

Sir Christopher Wren in a letter to the Bishop of Oxford, written in 1682 on the subject of a bronze statue for Tom Tower, Christ Church, tells him that "the horse at Windsor was at first cut in wood by a German and then cast by one Ibeck a founder in London, but this is the dearer way, if wee can find a good statuary for brasse it will be better" (*Wren Society*, Vol. V. page 22).

Iback's name appears in the list of Denizations for 22 June, 1694 (*Huguenot Society Publications*, Vol. XVIII, page 234).

INCE, ANTHONY

He was probably a Mansfield mason and signs a tablet to Peter Bayston, 1753, at Tuxford, Nottinghamshire. He may also be a son of that Thomas Ince of Mansfield who, in partnership with James Osborne (q.v.), was one of the master-masons for building Welbeck Abbey in 1743 (Archives, Duke of Portland).

IRELAND, SAMUEL, of London
fl. 1775–1805

He was the son of John Ireland, a carpenter of Horsham, and in 1768 was apprenticed to William Ireland (q.v.), who was probably a relation. In 1775 he became free and later set up on his own in Cannon Street. In 1800 Ireland was working at Vintners' Hall (Company's Archives), and five years later became Master of the Masons' Company. He was mason to the Cordwainers Company from 1788–1798 and again from 1800–1805 (Company's Archives).

IRELAND, WILLIAM, of London
fl. 1764–1783

Ireland, who was a Freeman of the Masons' Company, exhibited a figure of "The Young Bacchus" at the Society of Artists in 1769. Graves, in his *Exhibitors at the Society of Artists*, says that Ireland also showed a number of pictures there between 1764 and 1783, but I am uncertain whether the artist and the sculptor were the same person.

IREMONGER, THOMAS
fl. 1744–1751

In 1744 he was appointed master-mason for building Hampden House, Buckinghamshire. In 1751 he built the "Gothic" porch, for which he also executed the stone-carving (Archives, Earl of Buckinghamshire).

IRESON, NATHANIEL,
   of Wincanton
b. 1672, *d.* 1769

He was the master-builder appointed for the erection of Redlynch House in Somerset, and from 1744 onwards was working in the same capacity at Stourhead in Wiltshire (Stourhead Archives). In 1748 he gave the altar-piece to Wincanton Church (Phelps's *Somerset*, Vol. I, page 162), while in the churchyard is the monument with a life-size statue of himself, which he "executed in his lifetime and kept it ready to be erected after his death" (op. cit., page 167).

Ireson almost certainly carved the cartouche-tablet in memory of his daughter, who died in 1723, which he erected in Stourton Church, Wiltshire. He also signs a tablet to Robert Kingston, 1748, in St. Cuthbert's, Wells.

ISBELL, JAMES, of Truro
fl. 1797–1837

He was the son of Robert Isbell (q.v.), and in 1837 carved the coat of arms on the Market House at Penzance (Town Archives). He is responsible for a number of monuments and tablets in Cornwall, including those to John Wallis, 1797, at Sheviocke; Silvanus Jenkins, 1802, at St. Michael Penkevil; Grace Marrack, 1810, at Paul; Captain John Haswell, 1811, at Mylor; and Captain James Bull, 1821, at Falmouth. Also at St. Michael Penkevil is his monument to Viscount Falmouth, 1808, which is inscribed "Falmouth invent. Isbell sculpt."

ISBELL, ROBERT, of Stonehouse
fl. 1769–1824

His monuments are delicately carved, while a favourite type of tablet is oval in shape and carried out in coloured marbles. His most unusual work is the monument to Joseph Sawle, 1769, at St.

Austell, which consists of a delightful black-and-white marble "Adam" urn set on a square base. The reliefs on some of his tablets somewhat resemble the work of T. King, of Bath (q.v.).

Isbell's signed monuments and tablets in Cornwall commemorate William Williams, 1785, at St. Ewe; Edmond Hearle, 1796, at St. Columb Major; Edward Bewes, 1806, and Sir Edward Buller, 1824, both at Duloe; Thomas Hall, 1806, at Lostwithiel; and Lieutenant Hawkey, 1809, at Liskeard. Louisa Barlow, 1796, in St. Nicholas, Saltash; Sarah Traill, 1806, in St. Stephen's, Saltash. He also signs works in Devon to Admiral Cotton, 1794, at Plympton St. Maurice; Elizabeth Docton, 1801, at St. Budeaux; the Radcliffe family, 1805, at Tamerton Folliott; and Thomas Strode, 1817, at Plympton. The monument to Thomas Holliday, 1793, in Carmarthen Parish Church, is also his work.

IVORY, JOHN, of Norwich
d. 1805

He was apprenticed to Robert Page (q.v.) and became a Freeman of Norwich in 1752. His wife died in 1805 at the age of seventy-four "after fifty-five years of married life" (*Monthly Magazine*), 1805, Part I, page 413), and Ivory did not long survive her, dying "suddenly of a fit" in the same year. His stock was sold in October, 1806.

His monument to Thomas Moore, 1779, in Norwich Cathedral, has a portrait-relief and is signed in conjunction with J. de Carle (q.v.), as is that to Cyril Wyche, 1780, at Hockwold. Other monuments in Norwich signed by Ivory alone include those to the Rev. Thomas Scott, 1746, and John Dawson, 1756, both in the Old Meeting House; Charles Mackerell, 1747, in St. Stephen's; William Clarke, 1752, in St. George's; Thomas Hurnard, 1753, in St. Mary Coslany; and John Chambers, 1788, and Philip Lloyd, 1790, both in the Cathedral. Signed works by him in Norfolk commemorate Mary Slater, 1748, at Hingham; Elizabeth Wiggett, 1768, at South Pickenham; Clement Francis, 1792, at Aylesham; Ralph Caldwell, 1792, at Hilborough, and Mary Evans, 1798, at Sall.

J

JACKSON, —
fl. 1764–1770

He was the master-mason responsible for building Lord Petre's seat, Thorndon Hall, Essex, between 1764 and 1770, and also executed the carved stonework of the capitals, etc. (Archives, Lord Petre).

JACKSON, BENJAMIN
d. 1719

He was a native of Grove, near Retford in Nottinghamshire, and in 1687 was appointed master-mason for the building of Chatsworth. Here he worked until 1699, when he was dismissed by the Duke of Devonshire who was dissatisfied with the slow progress of the work.

Among payments made to Jackson during this period were £25 for a marble chimney-piece for "The Queen of Scots' closet," £50 for four other chimney-pieces, and £60 for "four vases on ye east side." In 1692 he also received £265 for carving the grotto (Chatsworth Archives).

After his dismissal Jackson went to London and was employed at Hampton Court, where he was paid £226 in 1700 for "the building and workmanship of the great basin in the Fountain Garden." He also carved in the same year eighty-one capitals of Portland stone for Fountain Yard (P.R.O., Works 5/51). In 1702 he was working at Whitehall, where he made a white-and-veined marble chimney-piece for Sir John Stanley's room, and also received £85 for "ten new Doric columns with capitals and bases for the same palace" (P.R.O., Works 5/53).

From 1702 to 1704 Jackson was working at Drayton, Northants, for Sir John Germain, building part of the house. He agreed "to finish ye front of ye house against ye coming into Drayton Hall with heads, vauses and fflames on pine Aples upon pedistalls in all points according to ye draft or designe drawn by Mr. Talman and to perform all his work, well rought, strong and fine" (Archives, Colonel Stopford-Sackville). His carved-stone work in the Inner Courtyard is beyond praise; how admirable is the cutting of the capitals, busts, vases, caryatids, heraldry, pineapples and trophy of arms which adorn and decorate the doorway and centre of the façade designed by Talman.

In 1701 Jackson had succeeded John Oliver (q.v.) as master-mason to William III and he continued to hold the appointment under Queen Anne. Apparently the Duke of Devonshire was not the only person to be dissatisfied with him, for Sir John Vanbrugh, writing to Lord Godolphin in 1704, is extremely outspoken on the subject. The letter was written to protest against Jackson's doing the mason's work for the greenhouse at Kensington, contrary to the Order of the Board of Works issued 1662–1663, and in it Vanbrugh says:

"As for Jackson my Lord, besides this Crime, the highest the nature of his Office will admit of, I must acquaint your L'dship he is so villainous a Fellow and so Scandalous in every part of his Character; and that in the unanimous opinion of all Sorts of People he is known to; that he is indeed a disgrace to the Queen's service and to everybody that is oblig'd to be concer'd with him." (Knoop and Jones's *The London Mason in the Seventeenth Century*, page 37).

Jackson died in May, 1719, a wealthy man, though in his will he refers to money owed to him from the time of Queen Anne, who had died in 1714. He is buried in Hampton Parish Church (Authorities mentioned in text).

JACKSON, BENJAMIN, and WILLIAM, of Reading
fl. 1776–1809

They sign two tablets, dated 1805 and 1809, at Shinfield, Berkshire.

JACKSON, EDWARD, of Doncaster
fl. 1769–1779

On 2 May, 1769, it was ordered that Jackson should "be admitted his freedom for his trouble in drawing a plan of the gaol and for his attendance to see the work properly executed." In 1770 he made the cross for Doncaster market-place (Corporation Archives).

JACKSON, HENRY, of Lincoln

He signs a tablet in coloured marbles to George Wakefield, 1816, at East Stoke, Nottinghamshire.

JACKSON, ISAAC, of Liverpool
fl. 1831–1850

Jackson, who lived in Liverpool until about 1850, when he seems to have gone to Rome, exhibited in the former city from 1831, showing busts of Admiral Murray (1831), John Johnson (1831), Charles Taylern (1832), Dr. Raffles (1832), the Rev. A. Campbell (1834), William Rathbone (1838), George Syers (1840) and J. Bostock (1841). He also showed a "copy of a Colossal Statue of W. Roscoe, Esq.," in 1834, and an "Alto-relievo from the 137th Psalm" in 1840. Another bust, of the Rev. Thomas Raffles, is in the Walker Art Gallery.

At Manchester in 1833 Jackson exhibited statues of "Psyche" and "Narcissus," while at the Royal Academy he showed busts of J. A. Paris and James Smith in 1836 and 1837 respectively.

JACKSON, JOHN

An Oxford craftsman, he made in 1659 the Royal coat of arms of Burford stone over the cloister door at Brazenose College, Oxford (College Archives). He was dead by 1664 as in the Vice-Chancellor's accounts 1663/64 is a payment of £10 19s. 3d. to "Mrs. Jackson, the stone-cutter's widow for work done by her husband."

JACKSON, JOHN, of Oxford
fl. 1789–1797

He signs tablets to Eleanor Rusbridge, 1789, in St. Mary's, Oxford, and Richard Smith, 1797, in St. Giles', Reading. A Jackson of Windrush signs a rather crude stone monument to William Bateman, 1810, at Asthall, Oxon.

JACKSON, PHILIP, of Edensor

In 1695 he received £446 for building the Bowing Green House at Chatsworth, this payment including the carved stonework and also "four potts standing upon ye front of ye battlement at forty shilling each" (Chatsworth Archives).

JACKSON, ROBERT
fl. 1840–1878

He was the chief assistant to John Thomas (q.v.) with whom he executed the statues, ornamental sculpture, etc., for the Houses of Parliament. In 1860 he was working in Rome, but was back in England three years later when he made a fountain for the south side of St. James's Park and another erected in Regent's Park near Gloucester Gate. The *Art Journal* (1863, page 167), however, disapproved of a spout in the shape of an animal's head, remarking that "the association of ideas is far from agreeable."

Also in 1863 Jackson executed the monument to Lieutenant Robert Anderson in Glasgow Cathedral (op. cit., page 157), and in 1865 made the statue of Lord Palmerston for Westminster Abbey. He exhibited at the Royal Academy, 1851–1878,

showing busts of Henry Gurney (1860), the Rt. Hon. F. W. Cowper (1862), Lord Cawdor (1874) and Henry Irving (1874). His bust of the Rev. Dr. Raffles (1860) is in Liverpool Public Library, and that of Lord Palmerston (1870) in the Speech Room at Harrow.

JACKSON, WILLIAM
b. 1820

He attended the Royal Academy Schools in 1844 and, in the same year, showed in Westminster Hall a statue of Newton, concerning which the *Art Union* remarked "the proportions of this figure do not appear to be sufficiently just and the drapery is mannered and untrue."

Jackson exhibited at the Royal Academy, 1848–1854, and busts by him of General Napier and Lord Nelson were in the W. J. Broderip sale of 1859. In 1862 he made a chimney-piece for Dorchester House (*Builder*, 1862, page 574), and in 1875 a statue of Sir Robert Clifton for Nottingham. He signs the monument of the Rev. John Fawcett, 1851, in St. Cuthbert's, Carlisle.

JACKSON, WILLIAM, of Melton Mowbray
fl. 1740–1744

He was the master-mason for the re-building of Melbourne Hall, Derbyshire, being paid £1,500 (Archives, Marquis of Lothian).

JAMES, C.

He exhibited "a portrait of a gentleman in wax" at the Royal Academy in 1792.

JAQUES, JOHN, the Elder, and JOHN, the Younger
Firm *fl.* 1781–1796

They carved a number of tablets for chimney-pieces and, in 1781–1782, made artificial ornaments for Inverary Castle.

The firm became bankrupt in 1795, but in the following year Jaques was working in Holborn, for he put an advertisement in Aris's *Birmingham Gazette* on 28 November, offering to supply "chimney-pieces and composition ornaments of the newest designs, suitably adapted for rooms of every denomination, from the greatest elegance to the neatest simplicity." The firm was employed at Cordwainers' Hall in 1786 (Company Archives).

(R. S. Mylne, *The King's Master Masons*, page 277.)

JARVIS, C., of Birmingham
fl. 1807–1837

He signs tablets at Packwood, Warwickshire, in 1830, and at Coleshill in the same county in 1832.

JEANS, —, of Edinburgh
fl. 1769–1771

He exhibited at the Free Society, 1769–1771, showing models in terra-cotta and clay. There are two statues of "Dacian Captives" signed by him in the portico of Penicuik House, Midlothian.

Jeans was in Rome in 1767. (B.M. Print room A.5.G.S.C.), and was also an artist, as his signed drawing of John Brown (1752–1787) is in the Scottish National Portrait Gallery.

JELFE, ANDREWS
d. 1758

He was apprenticed to Edward Strong and became free of the Masons' Company in 1711. Later he went into partnership with Christopher Cass (q.v.) and took over the business on the latter's death in 1734.

In 1726 Jelfe erected a sarcophagus to his family at South Weald, Essex, and ten years later made the black-marble tombstone of Nicholas Hawksmoor, the architect, in the churchyard of Shenley, Herts. In 1734 he made a sundial for Lord Godolphin at Gogmagog, Cambridgeshire, and in the following year carved a door-case for a Mr. Francis Sheppard. Another employer was Lord Macclesfield, for whom he worked at Sherborn Castle, and Sir John Evelyn for whom, in 1740, he built a house in St. James's Square.

Jelfe was a friend of Matthew Brettingham, the architect, and in 1742 carved a shield and festoon for Holkham where Brettingham was then working. In 1744 he made "two enriched pieces of frieze" for Houghton Hall, Norfolk.

As a mason Jelfe is best known as the builder, in conjunction with his partner Tuffnell (q.v.), of Westminster Bridge.

He had apparently two sons, one a naval officer, named Andrew. Writing to a friend in 1741, the elder Jelfe says that: "My son Andrew wrote me from St. Helena. I am afraid he is a great distance from a Captain's commission. It hath already cost me an incredible sum to carry him on in the Service" (British Museum, Ad. MS. 27587).

On his retirement Jelfe bought a house at Bletchingley in Surrey.

(Authority cited in text.)

JELFE, WILLIAM
d. 1771

He was apprenticed to his uncle, Andrews Jelfe (q.v.), in 1739, but did not become a member of the Masons' Company until twenty years later. From 1750 until 1758 he and the elder Jelfe were the masons for building the Horse Guards.

In 1753 William Jelfe built a house at Clapham for Henry Hoare and in 1767 made the pavement for the Temple of Apollo at Hoare's seat at Stourhead in Wiltshire (Archives, Hoare's Bank). He was also stonemason to George III, and in that capacity was employed on the rebuilding of Greenwich Palace in 1770.

His death is noted in the *London Magazine* under the date 3 September, 1771. A sale of his "stock in trade" was held, 9 and 10 January, 1772.

JENKINS, JOHN

He signs a pretty tablet at Byford, Herefordshire, to Uvedale King, 1774.

JENKINSON, EDWARD

Possibly a son of Matthew Jenkinson (q.v.), he made a veined-marble chimney-piece for St. James's Palace in 1796.

JENKINSON, MATTHEW
fl. 1790–1808

He was the mason for the Tower of London, Greenwich Palace, the King's Mews, etc., in 1790, in which year he also built a colonnade at St. James's Palace at a total cost of £398, including "all carved and moulded work."

In 1808 Jenkinson was paid £148 for work at the Duke of Clarence's apartments in St. James's Palace and a further £26 for a marble chimney-piece.

JENNINGS, BENJAMIN, the Elder, of Hereford
fl. 1825–1850

He was possibly a son of James Jennings, mason of Hereford, and in 1846 repaired the monument to Sir Thomas Vaughan at Kington in the same county (*Builder*, 1846, page 440).

Jennings signs tablets in Herefordshire to the Hon. Mrs. Dew, *c.* 1800, at Sellack; the Rev. John Clutton, 1830, and John Clutton, 1838, both in Hereford Cathedral; the Rev. Harry Williams, 1830, at Goodrich; John Collins, 1831, at Walford; Sir James Kyrle Money, 1843, at Much Marcle; and the Rev. George Woodhouse, 1846, at Leominster. None of these, however, are of any particular interest.

JENNINGS, BENJAMIN, the Younger, of Hereford

d. 1875

He was the son of Benjamin Jennings the Elder (q.v.) and studied in Rome under Gibson (q.v.).

In 1849 and 1850 he exhibited at the Royal Academy, showing busts and a statue of "Cupid, the Birth of a Rose." This latter work gained immediate popularity and was illustrated in the *Art Journal*, as well as in books on contemporary sculpture. Jennings lent it to the Exhibition of Art Treasures of the United Kingdom, held at Manchester in 1857, and at a sale held after his death it was purchased (together with a "Head of a Madonna") by a gentleman from Gloucester. It is now in Hereford Museum. Jennings also exhibited at the Great Exhibition. He signs the monument of William Thompson, 1855, at Kirkby, Westmorland. (Various references, *Art Journal*.)

JEWELL, THOMAS, the Elder, of Barnstaple

d. 1728

He signs a very lovely cartouche tablet at Tawstock, Devon, to Lady Rolle, 1705. This work, with its swags of flowers in the Grinling Gibbons manner, is almost worthy of the master himself. Three other cartouche tablets in the same church are practically identical in design with the one to Lady Rolle, and are obviously also by Jewell. They commemorate Sir Boucher Wrey, 1696; Florence, Lady Wrey, 1726; and Robert Lovett, 1710; but on none of them, after very careful inspection, could I find a signature.

Neighbouring churches contain similar tablets. At Braunton, for example, there is a delightful cartouche to Margaret Allen, 1709, which has winged cherubs at the top.

JEWELL, THOMAS, the Younger, of Barnstaple

b. 1676, *d.* 1758

He was presumably a son of Thomas Jewell the Elder (q.v.) and became a Freeman of Exeter in 1734. He signs a large monument in Tawstock Church to Sir Henry Northcote, 1732, but the workmanship, which can only be called provincial, already shows a deterioration from the carefully carved details and delicate cutting of his father. The younger Jewell signs other tablets in Devon to Robert Hales, 1740, at Braunton, and to Richard Bennett, 1750, at Bishops Tawton.

He died at the age of eighty-two on 29 September, 1758, and his wife Joanna on 1 September,

1762, aged seventy-seven. These details come from a list in manuscript of the tombstones which were formerly in the churchyard of Barnstaple Parish Church. According to this list, the tomb was situated in the south-eastern corner, but no trace of it remains today.

According to the Barnstaple Parish Registers, there was a third Thomas Jewell, a mason and maker of tombstones, and presumably a son of the second Thomas. He became a Freeman of Exeter in 1761 (City Archives).

JOANES, JOHN, of Worthing

He was presumably the son of Ralph Joanes (q.v.) and signs a neo-Hellenic tablet to Thomas Nash, 1814, in St. George's, Bloomsbury.

JOANES, RALPH, of Horsham

fl. 1760–1801

In 1760 he was paid for repairs to Lewes Prison and in 1778–1779 he received £393 for building the Gaoler's House at Horsham, which was designed by Henry Joanes of Horsham, presumably a relative (Sussex County Archives).

He signs a box-tomb at Ifield, Sussex, to George Hutchinson, 1801. This rather curious work has relief panels of Christ with the woman of Samaria, and of angels bearing an urn heavenwards. On top of the tomb is an urn signed by Coade (q.v.).

Joanes also supplied stone to the Duke of Norfolk for his house at Horsham in 1787 (Horsham Archives).

JOHNSON, A.

fl. 1848–1852

He exhibited various works at the Royal Academy, 1848–1852, including busts of George Trower (1848) and Mr. Henry Melton (1850).

JOHNSON, JAMES, of Stamfordham

fl. 1750–1770

He cut in stone a large number of life-size figures which were placed on the battlements of Alnwick Castle. These represented men "in the act of defense, wielding such arms as were then used; some of them are disposed with great propriety" (Mackenzie's *Northumberland*, Vol. I, page 450). Johnson began this work about 1750 and took twenty years to complete it.

JOHNSON, JOHN

In the Kimbolton Archives is a long agreement dated 1710, between the Earl of Manchester (afterwards the first Duke) and John Johnson "free mason of London." In it the latter agrees to a considerable amount of work at Kimbolton Castle, including the carving of decorative details and the ciphers and coronets, etc., on the keystones above the "windows of the inner court."

JOHNSON, JOHN

He exhibited at the Royal Academy in 1773 "a tablet of the dining-room chimney-piece at the Jockey Club Room, Newmarket." This showed "two centaurs running a race and whipping themselves," and was described as "absurd" by Horace Walpole.

JOHNSON, MATTHEW WHARTON, of London
fl. 1820–1860

Johnson was a prolific but dull statuary whose work may be found all over England. His most successful monument commemorates Joseph Somes, 1845, in Stepney Parish Church, his worst, Augustus Cleveland, 1849, at Westleigh, Devon. The former has an amusing relief of merchant-ships moored at a quay, the latter a relief of a woman lying prone at the foot of an impossible weeping-willow.

Other monuments signed by Johnson include those to the Rev. Holford Cotton, 1822, at Adderbury, Oxon; Sarah Holroyd, 1823, in Walthamstow Parish Church; Mrs. Hale, 1829, at Brede, Sussex; Elizabeth Price, 1829, at Llandovey, Brecon; Sir John Farnaby, 1831, at West Wickham, Kent; the Hon. Frederick Robinson, 1831, at Flitton, Beds; Samuel Greg, 1834, at Wilmslow, Cheshire; the Rev. James Sedgwick, 1834, at Currey Rivel, Somerset; General Thornton, 1842, at Brockhall, Northants; Sir Francis Hammond, 1850, Whepstead, Suffolk; and Lord Carew, 1856, in Waterford Cathedral.

JOHNSTON, —, of Belfast

In 1845 he carved a statue of Sir Robert Gillespie for Comber, Ulster.

JOHNSTON, J., of Lichfield
fl. 1836–1845

In 1836 he exhibited a bust of John Rosson at the Liverpool Academy. He also signs a neo-Hellenic wall-tablet to Edward Gore, 1845, at Shenstone, Staffordshire.

JONES, HENRY, of Canterbury
fl. 1819–1847

His best monument commemorates William Hopson, 1819, at Milton Regis, Kent. This has figures of two cherubs, one holding a flaming heart in his hand, and is the latest example I know of imagery popular during the seventeenth and early eighteenth centuries, but which had gone out of fashion in the rest of England long before 1800.

Jones, who was the mason responsible for building Seasalter Church in Kent in 1844 (*Builder*, 1844, page 460), signs other tablets in the same county to Hannah Woolley, 1819, at Smarden, and John McDivitt, 1839, at Bishopsbourne.

JONES, JAMES, of Abergavenny

He signs a large tablet with an open pediment to Mrs. Jenkings, 1781, at Abergavenny.

JONES, JAMES, of Bristol
fl. 1774–1794

He was the son of William Jones, a mason of Bristol, and became a Freeman of that city in 1774. In 1782 he received £18 from Lord Radnor for work carried out at Longford Castle (Archives, Earl of Radnor), and he also signs monuments to Sarah Exon, 1788, at Creech St. Michael, Somerset, and Peter Coates, 1794, at Stanton Drew in the same county.

Jones was first in partnership with Dunn and Tyley, and the firm signs the tablet to Ann Hillhouse, 1786, in the Church of St. Philip and St. Jacob, Bristol. By 1793, however, the name had been changed to Jones, Dunn and Drewett, the Dunn in both cases being William Dunn, son of a mason of the same name, who had become a Freeman of Bristol on 11 March, 1768.

(Bristol City Archives.)

JONES, JOHN EDWARD
b. 1806, *d.* 1862

He was born in Dublin on 2 May, 1806, the son of Edward Jones, a miniature-painter, and was trained as an engineer. In this capacity he carried out many important works in Ireland, including the building of Waterford Bridge, and he later went to England to follow his profession in London. In 1840, however, he abandoned engineering for sculpture and made "within a marvellously short space of time wonderful progress in that art" (*Literary Gazette*, 1844, page 738).

Jones exhibited at the Royal Hibernian Academy, while at the Royal Academy, 1842–1862, he showed over one hundred works, mostly portrait-busts. These included likenesses of Louis Philippe (1844), M. Balfe (1846), the King of Holland (1848), Thomas Brassey (1850), the

Empress Eugenie (1852), Lord Clarendon (1852), the Duke of Cambridge (1853), Queen Victoria (1854), and Lord Palmerston (1861). The *Art Journal* of 1846 (page 189) considered that there were "few works of this kind which in severe eloquence are at all comparable" with the bust of Sir Henry Pottinger, exhibited in that year, while the bust of Signora Favanti was shown at the Louvre in 1845 and one of the Earl of Carlisle at the International Exhibition of 1862.

Other busts by Jones are those of Lord Denman (1834) at Lincoln's Inn, Daniel O'Connell (1843) in the National Gallery of Ireland, Sir William Magnay (1844) in the Palace of Versailles and Dr. Alderson (1847) in Hull Hospital. His undated bronze bust of Sir Robert Peel is in the Birmingham Art Gallery, and that of John Fitch, Jnr., in the Walker Art Gallery, Liverpool.

Other works by Jones include a group of "Children and Animals" which he sent to the Great Exhibition of 1851; a statue of Mr. Dargan, executed in 1853 and shown at the Industrial Exhibition in Dublin; and another of Sir Robert Ferguson made for Londonderry in 1862.

The sculptor died at Finglas, near Dublin, on 25 July of the same year. The *Art Journal* in its obituary (1862, page 207) described him as possessing " a kind, courteous and generous disposition," while "in wit, humour and vivacity he was a thorough Irishman." (Strickland's *Dictionary of Irish Artists*; Authorities cited in text.)

JONES, R., of Swindon
fl. 1778–1780

He signs a wall-tablet in coloured marbles to Thomas Cox, 1778, at Shrivenham, Berkshire. In 1780 he was working as a mason at Longford Castle (Archives, Earl of Radnor).

JONES, RICHARD, of Wapping
fl. 1718–1720

Between 1718 and 1720 he was working at St. Alphege, Greenwich, where he carved the stone capitals. An Oliver Jones, who may be a relation, was in 1773 apprenticed to his father, Richard Jones of Wapping, "citizen and mason" (Archives, Masons' Company).

JONES, ROBERT
d. 1722

He was employed from 1698 until his death twenty-four years later on stone and marble carving at Greenwich Palace, where he seems to have done all the important work of this kind. A full list of everything he did is too long to give here, but among the more important items were, in 1698, "a large ornament, being festoons of drapery and flowers on the west front of the new building" and "a large pediment in basso-relievo over the west entrance containing the King's Arms held up by genii with trophies and ornaments relating to marine affairs, 30 ft. long and 7 ft. 9 in. high." For the latter Jones received £80 (P.R.O., Ad. MS. 68/672).

In 1702 he made four large Ionic capitals "with large festoons hanging out of the scrolls cut with several sorts of shellfish containing eight sides at £20 a side," and also four large keystones, costing £44, "being riverheads dressed with flags and water-flowers." In the following year he was paid £20 for the two large spandrels in the cupola (P.R.O., Ad. MS. 68/676).

Jones continued his work at Greenwich until his death, carving capitals, columns, pilasters, scrolls, festoons, ornaments for chimney-pieces and coats of arms (P.R.O., Ad. MS. 68/677–699).

He died in 1722 and his will was proved on 9 May of the same year. He was a Captain in the City trained bands.

JONES, WATKIN D.
fl. 1846–1861

He was born at Merthyr in Wales, the son of the Parish Clerk. He exhibited at the Royal Academy, 1846–1859, showing various works, including a bust of T. E. Evans, the tragedian, in 1854.

JONES, WILLIAM
fl. 1840–1850

He was the brother of Watkin Jones (q.v.) and, after leaving Merthyr for London, found employment in the studio of Joseph Edwards (q.v.). In 1845 he made for, and exhibited at, the Eisteddfod (held that year at Abergavenny) a statue of "The Prince of the Bards" (*Illustrated London News*, 1845, page 265).

Jones exhibited at the Royal Academy, 1843–1847, where he showed, among other works, busts of Thomas Bevan, M.D. (1845); John Fothergill (1845) and Mohun Lall, Persian Secretary to the British Government (1846).

JOPLING, J., of Gateshead
Firm *fl.* 1780–1822

The death of Jopling's wife is noted in the *Monthly Magazine* of 1801 (page 362), and ten years later his son Isaac won a Silver Palette from the Society of Arts for a plaster-cast of "A Gladiator."

Isaac Jopling assisted his father and, indeed, signs some of the later monuments and tablets, which are pleasant, simple works with good details. Works executed by them in Durham include those commemorating Anne Williamson, 1782, Jacob Clavering, 1792, and John Carr, 1817, all at Whickham; Richard Brewster, 1797, at Greatham; Anne Musgrave, 1799, at Chester-le-Street; Richard Dawes, c. 1800, at Heworth; Margaret Maxwell, 1807, at Bishop Auckland; and the Hon. Mary Smith, 1820, and Thomas Headlam, 1821, both at Gateshead. There is also another tablet in Northumberland to Ralph Carr, 1806, at Ponteland.

JORDAN, JOHN
fl. 1699–1706

Probably a local mason, he was responsible for the stonework of the gardens of Melbourne Hall, Derbyshire, in 1699. His work included the pedestals, staircases, pillasters, etc. (Archives, Marquess of Lothian).

JOSEPH, SAMUEL
b. 1791, *d.* 1850

He was a pupil of Peter Rouw (q.v.) and attended the Royal Academy Schools in 1811, gaining a Silver Medal in the same year and another in 1812. Three years later he won the Gold Medal for a group entitled "Eve Supplicating Forgiveness." In 1823 he went to Edinburgh, where in 1826 he became one of the foundation-members of the Royal Scottish Academy. J. M. Graham (*British Literature and Art*, page 448) described his busts as "superior to any examples of sculptural art that had been produced in Scotland previous to his practice."

In 1828 Joseph returned to work in London, but he never received, either in his lifetime or posthumously, the credit he deserved. William Scott, in his *English Schools of Sculpture*, written in 1871, gives an engraving of Joseph's statue of Wilberforce, but adds that "of the sculptor we are unable to give an account, and also unable to point out any other works of his, having looked in vain through the literary and artistic journals in the hope of finding at least an obituary notice."

This statue of Wilberforce is the sculptor's masterpiece. It was erected in Westminster Abbey in 1838 and, though much criticized at the time, is now generally agreed to be a magnificent work. There is also a plaster-cast of it in the chapel of St. John's College, Cambridge. Joseph became bankrupt for £450 in 1848, and a forced sale of all his belongings was held.

Joseph exhibited at the Royal Academy, 1811–1846, and at the Royal Scottish Academy, 1827–1835. He died in London on 1 July, 1850 (*Literary Gazette*, 1850, page 508), leaving seven children and very little money. The Royal Academy granted a pension to his widow, which was continued until her death thirteen years later (Archives, Royal Academy). A wax portrait of Joseph was exhibited by T. Smith (q.v.) at the Royal Academy in 1828.

(Rinder and McKay's *The Royal Scottish Academy*; A.G.B.I. Archives; Authorities cited in text.)

STATUES

1838	William Wilberforce	Westminster Abbey
1843	Sir David Wilkie	Tate Gallery
1844	Hon. Elizabeth Elliot	Exhibited Royal Academy
1845	Sir Hugh Myddelton	Royal Exchange

BUSTS

1811	Master T. Rouw	Exhibited Royal Academy
1815	Edmund Kean	For Drury Lane
1819	Lord Beresford	Exhibited Royal Academy
1819	General Sir Lowry Cole	Exhibited Royal Academy
1821	Michael Angelo Taylor	Exhibited Royal Scottish Academy
1822	Henry Mackenzie	Scottish National Portrait Gallery
1822	Charles Mathews	National Portrait Gallery (plaster-cast)
1824	Mr. Liston	Exhibited Royal Academy
1824	Lord John Campbell	Exhibited Royal Academy
1825	Sir Walter Scott	Preston Hall, near Edinburgh
1825	Sir Henry Wellwood	National Gallery, Edinburgh
1827	Professor Stewart	Edinburgh University
1828	Robert Stevenson	For Library of Bell Rock Lighthouse
1830	Duke of Argyll	Exhibited Royal Academy
1830	Sir Herbert Taylor	Exhibited Royal Academy
1830	Flaxman	York Art Gallery (small bronze)
1831	George IV	Exhibited Suffolk Street Galleries
1831	Davies Gilbert	Exhibited Royal Academy
1832	Rev. Jonathan Brooks	Exhibited Liverpool Academy
1833	Lord Brougham	Exhibited Royal Academy
1833	William Wilberforce	School for the Blind, York
1834	William IV	Penshurst Place, Kent
1835	William IV	United Service Club
1837	Sir William Franklin	Rochester Cathedral

1838	Lady De l'Isle and Dudley	Penshurst Place, Kent	
1840	Colonel Gurwood	Apsley House	
1841	Rev. Archibald Alison	Scottish National Portrait Gallery	
1842	Sir David Wilkie	National Gallery of Scotland	
1844	Earl of Shannon	Exhibited Royal Academy	
n.d.	Professor Dugald Stewart	National Portrait Gallery, Edinburgh (bronze)	
n.d.	William Huskisson	Petworth	

n.d. Voltaire	Elvetham Hall, Hants

MONUMENTS

1800	Battersea (Parish Church)	William Vassall
1812	Otterden, Kent	Rev. John Tattershall
c. 1820	Otterden, Kent	Rev. Granville Wheler
1833	Great Brickhill, Bucks	Rev. Latham Wainwright
1834	East Farleigh, Kent	Agnes Wilberforce

K

KACHLER, H., of London
fl. 1837–1844

He exhibited at the Royal Academy, 1837–1844, where his works included busts of Miss Elphinstone (1839) and James Sheridan Knowles (1842).

KARN, GEORGE, of Chichester

He signs wall-tablets in Chichester Cathedral and at Warblington, Sussex, both dated 1830.

KELLOW, JAMES, of Winchester
fl. 1830–1839

He may be a member of the same family as the "Kellow, stone-mason," who was employed at Salisbury Cathedral in 1785 (Cathedral Archives). In 1839 he made the monument to Sir Thomas Dyer in the churchyard of Ovington, Hampshire, which was of "highly creditable workmanship and designed by Owen Carter" (*Gentleman's Magazine*, 1839, Part II, page 160).

Kellow also signs monuments in Winchester Cathedral to Sarah Rennell, 1830, and to the Earl of Banbury, 1834. Two others executed by him (both in Hampshire) are those commemorating William Nevill, 1831, at Titchfield, and Elizabeth Gomm, 1836, at Bramsdean.

KELLY, THOMAS, of Chester
fl. 1826–1833

In 1826 he was employed on the building of Chester Bridge (Hemingway's *Chester*, Vol. I, page 373), and three years later was responsible for a "marble monument handsomely executed" to Lord Chancellor Ellesmere, which cost £100 and was erected at Dodleston, Cheshire (*Gentleman's Magazine*, 1829, Part II, page 495).

Kelly also signs tablets to Ann Truslove, 1833, in St. John the Baptist's, Chester, and to Mrs. Drake, 1829, at Thornton Le Moors, Cheshire.

KELSEY, CHARLES SAMUEL
b. 1820

He joined the Royal Academy Schools on the recommendation of W. Etty, R.A., in 1843 and won a Silver Medal two years later. In 1844 he exhibited figures of the Earl of Shrewsbury and the Venerable Bede at Westminster Hall. The former was described by the *Literary Gazette* as "a portrait of a suit of armour carefully put on," while the latter was considered "very heavy and unmeaning."

About this time Kelsey executed the large Gothic monument in memory of William Rolls (*d.* 1840) in St. George's, Bloomsbury, and a tablet with a medallion-portrait of Henry Corbould (*d.* 1845), for Etchingham Church, Sussex. In 1846 he was awarded a Silver Medal by the Society of Arts for "a design for a ticket of admission to the Society's Rooms" and two years later carved the sculpture above the doorway of the Royal Insurance Office in Liverpool (*Builder*, 1848, page 614). For Liverpool also he executed the decoration above the windows of St. George's Hall in 1854 (*Building Chronicle*, 1854, page 84).

In 1868 Kelsey made two large stone figures of women for the entrance to Smithfield Market, while in 1870 he modelled and carved the tripod on top of the memorial column to Lord Carlisle at Castle Howard (*Builder*, 1870, page 349). The poor relief on the monument which replaced Temple Bar in the Strand is also by Kelsey and was executed in 1880. It shows Queen Victoria and the Prince of Wales attending St. Paul's on 27 February, 1872, for the thanksgiving service after the Prince's recovery from typhoid fever.

Kelsey exhibited at the Royal Academy, 1840–1877, showing in 1846 a statue of "A Greek Youth Examining His Sword," and a bas-relief of "Christ Blessing Little Children" and a marble relief of "Music" in 1877.

(Authorities cited in text.)

KELSEY, W. T., of Brompton
fl. 1830–1846

He signs two surprisingly good tablets at Flitton, Bedfordshire, one to Lady Grantham, 1830, which is a copy of an early eighteenth-century cartouche, the other to her sister, the Countess de Grey, 1833, which is also in the style of that period.

In 1846 Kelsey made two chimney-pieces of green Irish marble for Wyndham's Club (*Builder*, 1846, page 477).

KEMPSTER, CHRISTOPHER
b. 1627, *d.* 1715

He was born at Burford, the son of William Kempster of that town, and went to London in 1659, becoming free of the Masons' Company by redemption in 1670. He afterwards became Master of the Company in 1700.

In 1672 Kempster was working as assistant to

PLATE XIII

ROBERT HARTSHORNE
Sir Thomas Powys, 1720, Thorpe Achurch,
Northamptonshire.

JOHN HANCOCK
Joseph Mellish, 1703, Blyth, Nottinghamshire.

CHRISTOPHER HORSNAILE THE ELDER
Sir Jacob Garrard, 1730, Langford, Norfolk.

PLATE XIV

SAMUEL JOSEPH
William Wilberforce, 1838, Westminster Abbey.

Edward Strong (q.v.) at St. Stephen's, Walbrook, and as a master-mason he was extensively employed under Sir Christopher Wren, who thought highly of him. For Wren he built the churches of St. James's, Garlickhithe, 1674–1687, where he was paid £20 .or the font in 1683; St. Mary Somerset, 1686–1694, where his work included six cherub-heads in Portland stone and the keystones to the three outward doors; and St. Mary Abchurch in 1686, where he was responsible for the font and "seven pilaster-capitals and corbels." He was also one of the principal master-builders of St. Paul's Cathedral, where he worked from 1692 until 1709.

Outside London Kempster built the Market House at Abingdon for Wren between 1678 and 1681 and in the latter year he was working on Tom Tower at Christ Church, Oxford, where he was assisted by his son and namesake (W. G. Hiscock's *A Christ Church Miscellany*, page 232). Wren had previously written to the Bishop of Oxford in 1681 recommending Kempster as a "very able man, modest, honest and treatable and one that your masons will submit to worke with because of his interest in the quarries at Burford." "Therefore," he added, "you will have the stone from him at first hand" (*Wren Society*, Vol. V, page 18).

Kempster later retired from business and went to live at Burford, his birthplace. His wife Joan had died in 1701 at the age of eighty-two, and his own death took place on 12 August, 1715. He was buried in the parish church, where his epitaph on a tablet describes him as "a person eminent in his profession and built several churches in the said City" (London) "and was many years employed in building the Cathedral and Dome of St. Paul's." A ledger in the church also commemorates his son John who died on 18 February, 1733, aged seventy-five, while two other sons were the Christopher mentioned above and William (1678–1717), who assisted his father in his later works, especially at St. Paul's.

Another distinguished mason of the same family was Kempster's brother, William, who became free of the Masons' Company by redemption in 1677. He was afterwards Renter Warden in 1700, Upper Warden in 1701 and Master of the Company in 1705. His death took place in 1707 (Wren Society's Publications; Bodleian, Rawlinson MS.B.387).

KENDALL,
or KÉNDAL, EDWARD,
of Exeter
d. 1796

Kendall, who was the mason responsible for building the Exeter Guildhall, 1776–1792, died on 28 November, 1796, "at an advanced age," according to the *Gentleman's Magazine* of that year (Part II, page 1059).

His monuments have charm and are usually carried out in coloured marbles. Examples of his work in Devon commemorate Paul Orchard, 1764, at Hartland; Edward Hanbury, 1767, at Dartmouth; Thomas Morrison, 1778, at Torrington; Mary Cross, 1785, at Cullompton; Mrs. Churchill, 1785, at Dawlish; Mary Heathfield, 1791, at Woodbury; Charlotte Morrison, 1791, at Alwington; and the Rev. John Newte, 1792, at Tiverton. He also signs monuments to Joseph Hunt, 1761, and Edward Hunt, 1787, both at Maker in Cornwall.

KENDALL, J., of Exeter
b. 1766, *d.* 1829

He was the son of Edward Kendall (q.v.) and also worked in his native city, rebuilding the south-west angle of the west front of the Cathedral and restoring the statues of Edward III and Alfred the Great in 1817 (*Gentleman's Magazine*, 1817, Part II, page 358). He also made the altar-piece for the Cathedral and published an essay on "The Principles of English Architecture" (*Gentleman's Magazine*, 1829, Part II, page 572). He died in October, 1829.

Kendall's monuments are less ambitious than those of his father though some of them have quite pleasant reliefs. He also has a rather curious individual trick of making the capitals of some of his pilasters in the form of rams' heads, a motif which he probably copied from the work of Robert Adám. His best monument, surrounded by a wreath of sibthorpia, commemorates Humphrey Sibthorp, 1801, at Instow, Devon, while his tablets to the Lyne family, 1805, at Launceston, Cornwall, and Henry Brutton, 1816, at Cullompton, Devon, have pretty reliefs of a woman wreathing an urn and of a mourning youth respectively.

Other tablets in Devon signed by Kendall include those to Andrew Quicke, 1793, at Newton St. Cyres; Lord Hawarden, 1803, at Teigngrace; Thomas Galsworthy, 1805, at Hartland; James Rudman, 1805, in Exeter Cathedral; George Buck, 1805, at Bideford; Henry Downe, 1805, at Northam; the Cann family, 1807, at Spreyton; Elizabeth Marshall, 1809, at Barnstaple; William Matterface, 1814, at Dawlish; Richard Kingdom, 1816, at Holsworthy; the Rev. John Swete, 1821, at Kenton; and Mary Peel, 1825, at Littleham. Other works by him commemorate Lucretia Putt, 1813, at Trent, Somerset; Richard Ivyleafe, 1814, at Syston, Glos; and John Barker, 1819, at Wareham, Hants.

KENDRICK, JOSEPH
b. 1755

He was born on 4 June, 1755, and attended the Royal Academy Schools in 1771. He seems to have had some connexion with Wateringbury in Kent, for he signs the pedestal of the sundial in the churchyard. The dial itself is the work of Thomas Crow, a Wateringbury craftsman, one of whose children was christened "Kendrick."

Emma Kendrick the miniaturist (1788–1871) was Kendrick's daughter. The *Dictionary of National Biography* states, however, that her father was Josephus Kendrick (q.v.), whereas he was in reality her younger brother.

The elder Kendrick seems to have moved from London to Portsea, for he signs a monument in Warblington Church, Hampshire, "J. Kendrick of Portsea." This delightful work commemorates Elizabeth How, 1806, and has a pretty relief which resembles the work of Flaxman (q.v.).

Other monuments and tablets signed by Kendrick include those to Charles Style, 1774, at Wateringbury, Kent; Frances Champneys, 1800, at Boxley, Kent; Geoffery Hornby, 1801, Samelsbury, Lancs; William Bleamire, 1803, in Hampstead Parish Church; William St. Quintin, 1805, at Harpham, Yorks; and George Grigby, 1811, at Drinkstone, Suffolk.

KENDRICK, JOSEPHUS JOHN PINNIX
b. 1791, *d.* 1832

He was the son of Joseph Kendrick (q.v.) and joined the Royal Academy Schools in 1808, winning a Silver Medal in 1811, and the Gold Medal for his relief of "Adam and Eve Lamenting Over the Dead Body of Abel" in 1813. He had also received in 1811 the Silver Isis Medal from the Society of Arts for a plaster-cast of "A Gladiator," a work which he exhibited two years later at Liverpool.

Kendrick was a competent minor sculptor, whose smaller monuments and bas-reliefs are harmless and even pleasing. A good example is the relief of the Battle of Copenhagen on the monument to Sir George Murray, 1819, in Chichester Cathedral, while there are delightful medallion-portraits on those of Sir Francis Molyneux, 1812, at Teversal, Nottinghamshire, and Lord and Lady Henniker, 1821, at Thornham Magna, Suffolk.

When he was chosen as the sculptor for the national monument to Sir William Myers, 1816, in St. Paul's Cathedral, he attempted, however, a task far beyond his powers and produced one of the most unfortunate memorials in the whole building.

The design—one of complete bathos—shows Hercules and Minerva warmly shaking hands in front of a tomb surmounted by a bust of Myers. Nor is the monument to General Ross, *c.* 1820, in the same Cathedral, much happier. The sculptor described his design for it as "Valour lays an American flag on the tomb of the departed warrior, on which Britannia is recumbent in tears, while Fame is descending with a laurel to crown his bust."

Kendrick exhibited at the Royal Academy, 1813–1829, showing in 1826 a statue of Sir James Leith "for Barbados." This was presumably the statue which the inhabitants of Barbados had subscribed for; in 1819 Kendrick had written in to the Dean and Chapter of Westminster Abbey stating that the subscribers wished to erect the statue "immediately against the next column of the church to that where Mr. Addison's stands being of the same dimensions." He also showed busts of Fisher, Bishop of Salisbury (1813); the Hon. W. Lamb (1818); Lord Selsey (1825); and Lord Henniker (1825). His tablet to James Bindley, 1819, now destroyed, was the first monument which was allowed to be erected in the church of St. Mary-le-Strand. At the Suffolk Street Galleries he exhibited in 1828 the model of a "Proposed Statue of Carl Maria von Weber for St. Paul's Cathedral."

When he applied to the A.G.B.I. in 1831 asking for money "to enable him to complete some marble busts ordered by Lord Minto, Lord Selsey and gentlemen of the highest class of society," he added that "his financial difficulty had arisen from gentlemen not honouring their accounts." His widow, Frances, also applied for help on 24 March, 1832, saying that "the many disappointments which chequered his unfortunate career preying upon his mind caused his early decease." She was granted a pension by the Royal Academy which continued until 1851. Kendrick had an only son who had been born in 1828 who emigrated to Australia in 1852. (Archives, Royal Academy and A.G.B.I. Archives.)

Signed monuments by Kendrick include those to Colonel Stables, 1815, at Great Hormead, Herts; Sir George Thomas, 1815, at Madehurst, Sussex; Lord Selsey, 1816, at Barkway, Herts; the third Earl Stanhope, 1816, at Chevening, Kent; Major-General Churchill, 1817, in Lewisham Parish Church; Thomas Clark, 1818, and George Pring, 1824, both in Hammersmith Parish Church; Sir Thomas Bloomfield, 1822, and Lady Bloomfield, 1826, both in Plumstead Parish Church; Martha Rudding, 1823, in Hampton Parish Church; Thomas Leverton, 1824, at Waltham Abbey, Essex; Janet Maude, 1824, in

Wakefield Cathedral; Henry Mash, 1825, in Stanstead Abbotts Parish Church; and Thomas Hardwick, 1829, in St. Laurence's, Brentford.

KENNEDY, MRS. E.

In 1842 she exhibited at the Royal Academy an alto-relievo of "Scenes at a Fair in the North of Ireland." The *Art Union* of that year gave it a long notice and described it as "a work of rare value."

KENT, —, of London

He signs a large neo-Hellenic monument with a figure of "Hope" to Ann Elverson, 1840, at Oadby, Leicestershire.

KESSELS, M., of Denmark
b. 1784, *d.* 1836

The favourite pupil of Thorwaldsen, he carved the monument of Georgiana Naylor, *d.* 1806, which was erected in 1829 at Hurstmonceaux, Sussex. The first monument was lost at sea and the Hare family ordered another version from the sculptor.

KEYWORTH, WILLIAM DAY, the Elder, of Hull
b. 1817, *d.* 1897

His father, a marble mason of Hull, moved to London in 1826 and worked in the studio of Sir Francis Chantrey (q.v.). In 1831 William Keyworth became a pupil of H. Weekes (q.v.) and studied under that sculptor for three years. He then returned with his father to Hull and set up on his own account.

Keyworth produced a number of works for his native town, including busts of William Woolley (1837) for Holy Trinity Church; George Lee (1838) for the Mechanics' Institute; the Rev. Thomas Dykes (1840) for St. John's Church; Dr. George Fielding (1848) for the Infirmary; and Henry Blundell (1860) for the Town Hall. He also made those of an Eskimo and his wife who were brought to Hull in a whaling-ship in 1845. He exhibited at the Royal Academy, 1837–1844, showing busts of Dr. Ayre (1837); the Rev. William Ellis (1839); and the Rev. Walter Hook (1844).

Keyworth later practised as an architect and also made casts of medieval architecture for the Great Exhibition of 1851. These were afterwards taken to the Crystal Palace. He died in 1897 and in his will left a number of works to his native town, but they were destroyed when Hull Central Museum was bombed in 1943.

Of Keyworth's few monuments, those in Hull itself commemorate John Parker, 1841, in Holy Trinity; R. Craven, 1850, in Christ Church; Robert Roach, 1855, in St. James's; and Robert Glossop, 1863, in St. Paul's. He also signs others in Yorkshire to Joseph Sykes (with a medallion-portrait), 1857, at Kirk Ella, and Mary Heslewood, 1856, at Preston.

His son, William Day Keyworth the Younger, was born in Hull in 1843, but as a sculptor his work is outside the scope of this book.

(Information Hull Central Library; various references, *Art Journal.*)

KIDWELL, ROBERT
b. c. 1675, *d.* 1747

Kidwell, who was apprenticed to his father William Kidwell (q.v.) in 1689, became free in 1703, and in 1716 was living in Channel Row, Westminster. In 1713 he was working as a mason at Lord Ashburnham's house in St. James's Square (Ashburnham Archives), and he was also employed at the London house of the Duke of Newcastle in 1738 and 1742, receiving £118 (British Museum, MS. 33,322), and at Canons, the seat of the Duke of Chandos. His death in 1747 is recorded in the Court Book of the Masons' Company.

Kidwell had two sons, Oliver and Robert the Younger, who were apprenticed to him in 1713 and 1715 respectively. Oliver became free in 1723, was Warden of the Masons' Company in 1734, and died in 1739. Robert had a son, Thomas, who was apprenticed to his grandfather in 1741. A Mary Kidwell, presumably a daughter-in-law of the elder Robert, applied successfully for financial assistance to the Masons' Company in 1767 (Court Book, Masons' Company).

KIDWELL, WILLIAM
d. 1736

Kidwell, whose yard was at "Westminster Hall Gate" in London, was a member of the Painter Stainers' Company. Quite early in his life he went over to Ireland and was taken up by Sir John Perceval, who employed him to work the marble quarry on his estate in County Cork and to be in charge of the Irish workers. Perceval notes in his account book that in 1712 he had advanced Kidwell £2 15s. 6d. for "going to England for work." In 1713 Kidwell was back in Ireland with a number of orders and made two marble chimney-pieces, also marble tables for his patron's house at Duncarrey. In 1713 Kidwell made two chimney-pieces of Irish marble for "Mr. Southwell" and Perceval gave the same gentleman a present of a chimney-piece "of my own white marble" for his house (King's Weston, near Bristol). By 1719 the works were in full swing and Perceval, who by now had become Earl of Egmont, had many customers, and chimney-pieces were made for Lord Barrymore, Lord St. George, Sir Richard Meade, Sir Matthew Deane, Lord Doneraile and Alderman Edward Hoare, while Mr. Floyd of Newcastle and Mr. Thornwell ordered marble monuments (British Museum, Ad. MSS. 46984 and 47047).

Kidwell apparently passed the rest of his life in Ireland though towards the end he removed to Dublin where he died in 1736. His will, in which he describes himself as "of the city of Dublin, stonecutter" was signed on 7 August of that year and proved on the following 13 September.

Kidwell's monuments in England are important. The finest, commemorating Sir Robert Bernard, c. 1690, at Brampton, Huntingdonshire, has a noble portrait-bust, while one to the Hon. Francis Coventry, 1699, in Mortlake Parish Church, is curiously designed with two male caryatids supporting a pediment. A very similar, though unsigned, monument to Sir Henry Coventry, 1686, is now at Croome in Worcestershire. It was originally erected in St. Martin-in-the-Fields, but was moved to his family church by the ninth Earl of Coventry. Kidwell also signs other monuments to John Harvey, 1700, in St. Mary-at-Hill, and Henry Herringman, 1703, at Carshalton, Surrey.

His works in Ireland (which are usually signed "of London") commemorate Mrs. Fry, 1698, in Waterford Cathedral; Boyle, Archbishop of Armagh, 1702, at Blessington, Co. Wicklow; Sir Donat O'Brien, 1717, at Kilnasoola, Co. Clare; and Viscount Duncannon, 1724, at Fiddown, Co. Kilkenny.

KING and SONS, of London
Firm *fl.* 1775–1811

The firm's best monument commemorates Sir Robert and Lady Lawley, 1779, at Hints, Staffordshire. There is a charming relief on this work, and also on one in memory of Lord Calthorpe, 1798, at Edgbaston, near Birmingham.

The Kings also sign monuments to another Sir Robert Lawley, 1793, at Hints, Staffs; Frances Cattell, 1795, at Barford, Warwick; Sir John Croft, 1797, at Highworth, Wilts; and George Schultz, 1802, at Holton, Oxon.

KING, BENJAMIN
fl. 1744–1783

In 1755 he was employed at Arbury Hall, Warwick, being paid £39 9s. 6d. for work in the library (Newdigate Archives). Between 1755 and 1758 he did all the stone-carving of the exterior and interior of the Warwick Shire Hall, for which he received £220.

Apparently there was some trouble about the carving of the pediment, for David Hiorn (q.v.), the mason in charge, writing to the architect, Sanderson Miller, on 3 February, 1758, says:

"I was a little surprised one even as came in Mr. Lightholder and Mr. Lowe and desired I would get them up a scaffold to do the pediment, for that you had given them orders so to do, which I hope is not true. For as I shall be glad of yours and Mr. Prowses approbation in the disposition of ye ornaments, and what they should be, but own I shall be very sorry to have any other persons come to do the work, unless it cannot be done by the people who have been already concerned; and as I a little doubt the veracity of Mr. Lightholder, I ask my Lord Brooke, who said something of the kind had been shown to him, but that he thought it was doing Mr. King a great injury if it [i.e., the pediment] was executed by others" (Warwick County Records, A.C.C.R. 125/33).

KING, CHARLES, of London
fl. 1809–1840

He was probably a junior partner in the firm of King and Sons (q.v.), for in both cases the address of the yard is given as Chenies Street. In 1823 he was employed as a mason on repairs to the tower of St. Anne's, Soho (Westminster Public Library, A.2312).

King's tablets are dull, the best of them commemorating the Douce family, 1809, at West Malling, Kent. Others signed by him include those to John Martin, 1813, in Plumstead Parish Church; Joseph Kirkwood, 1815, in St. George's, Bloomsbury; John Wardle, 1825, at Wardington, Oxon; Pierre Clerc, 1825, in St. Pancras Parish Church; the Rev. Peregrine Bingham, 1826, at Berwick St. John, Wilts; William Micklefield, 1826, at West Tilbury, Essex; Sir William Rush, 1833, in Wimbledon Parish Church; and Peter Gilkes, 1833, in St. James's, Piccadilly.

KING, G. E., of Ware
He signs a tablet to the Adams family, 1826, at Ware, Herts.

KING, H.
He exhibited a number of unnamed portrait-busts at the Royal Academy, 1828–1845.

KING, J., of York
fl. 1811–1840

He signs a large neo-Hellenic wall-tablet to

Marmaduke Hodgson, 1834, in Ripon Cathedral. In the same Cathedral there are various other tablets by him, but these are either insignificant or of the same design as the one already mentioned.

KING, THOMAS, and SONS, of Bath

Thomas King the Elder: *b.* 1741, *d.* 1804

Thomas King, the founder of the firm, was the son of Henry King, a clockmaker of St. Dunstan's. He was apprenticed in 1752 to Charles Saunders, mason, of London, but settled in Bath soon after becoming free, dying there in 1804. He married a daughter of Thomas Paty (q.v.).

He is buried at Woolley, near Bath, where his epitaph says that he was "many years an eminent statuary in the parish of Walcot, and after sustaining a long and painful illness with exemplary fortitude and resignation, calmly departed this life 5 December, 1804, aged 63."

King was also a wood-carver, for in Charles Morgan's account-book (Tredegar Archives) there are various payments for picture-frames to "Mr. King, carver, of Lansdowne Road, Bath." In 1810 the firm received £76 for marble chimney-pieces for Longleat, and two years later a further £28 for several of "Keinton stone" (Archives Marquess of Bath).

"King and Sons" lasted for nearly a hundred years and the firm was the most prolific and popular of all the West Country statuaries. Their monuments and tablets are to be found scattered, not only over all England, but in India and in the West Indies. It is true that there was a certain sameness of design and execution, but the work is always in good taste and I have yet to find an ugly or grotesque monument by them. Their early work is particularly good. The monuments of James Quin the actor, 1761, in Bath Abbey, and of Bishop Warburton, 1779, in Gloucester Cathedral, both have medallion portraits, while the great oval monument in coloured marbles to John Burgess, 1772, at North Molton, Devon, is well up to the level of the best London work of the period.

MONUMENTS

c. 1760	Birdbrook, Essex	James Walford
c. 1760	Bath (Abbey)	Thomas Brocas
1764	Dinton, Bucks	Elizabeth Vanhattem
1764	Tyberton, Hereford	William Brydges
1769	Bath (Abbey)	Dr. Butt
1769	George Nympton, Devon	William Karslake
1770	Hinton Charterhouse, Somerset	Mrs. Baxter
1771	Steeple Aston, Wilts	Thomas Beach
1772	Debden, Essex	Richard Chiswell
1782	Salisbury (Cathedral)	Bishop John Hume
1783	Stanton Drew, Somerset	Elizabeth Lyde
1785	Debden, Essex	Peter Muilman
1787	Tetbury, Glos	John Paul
1787	Bath (Abbey)	Sir Nigel Gresley
1788	Bath (Abbey)	Robert Walsh
1789	Gloucester (Cathedral)	Rev. William Adams (medallion portrait)
1791	Tawstock, Devon	Anne, Lady Wrey
1792	Wells (Cathedral)	Dodington Sherston
1792	Eastington, Glos	Nathaniel Stephens
1792	Lydney, Monmouth	Poole Bathurst
1793	Tyberton, Hereford	Frances Brydges
1795	Bath (Abbey)	Andrew and Alexander Sutherland
1795	Wells (Cathedral)	Thomas Linley
1796	Great Horkesley, Essex	John Codd
1796	Astbury, Cheshire	Peter Shakealey
1796	Salisbury (St. Martin's)	Edward Baker
1797	Great Somerford, Wilts	William Pyke
1797	Ramsbury, Wilts	Mary Burdett
1797	Clovelly, Devon	Lady Hamlyn
1799	Warrington (Parish Church)	Dorothea Patten
1801	Beckington, Wilts	Harry Edgell
1801	Bishop's Lydiard, Somerset	Thomas Slocombe
1802	St. Gluvias, Cornwall	John Enys
1804	Bath (Abbey)	Jane Clootwyk
1805	Draycot Cerne, Wilts	Sir James Long
1806	Langford Budville, Somerset	William Wade
1807	Dudley, Worcs	Edward Dixon
1813	Stroud, Glos	Ann Tyres
1820	Wells (Cathedral)	Peter Sherston
1821	Charlton Kings, Glos	William Prinn
1823	Langley Burrell, Wilts	Thermuthis Ashe
1824	Woolley, Somerset	Richard Bendyshe
1826	Bath (Abbey)	Lt.-Colonel North (*New Monthly Magazine*, 1826, page 168)

KING, WILLIAM

fl. 1769–1782

He exhibited at the Free Society, 1769–1782, showing reliefs and, in the latter year, "a monumental figure in marble." His brother, G. King, also exhibited models at the Free Society, 1771–1776.

KING, WILLIAM, of Islington

He signs a large tablet with carefully cut details to Aeneas Barkly, 1836, in St. Mary's, Holloway.

KING, WILLIAM, of Oxford

In 1734 he agreed with All Souls College to

build "the gate leading out of the North Quadrangle" and "also the Cloister on the south side." The carved stonework was to include the "arms of the benefactors upon the shields in the Gateway" (Archives, All Souls College, Oxford).

KINGWILL, WILLIAM,
of Sidmouth

He signs a small monument with a relief of "Hope" to Charlotte Temperance, 1810, at Sidmouth, Devon.

KINSON, THOMAS A.

He signs a wall-tablet in coloured marbles with a charmingly carved design to Elizabeth Scarisbrick, 1797, in Holy Trinity, Hull.

KIRK, JOHN, of Dumfries
b. 1832

He joined the Royal Academy Schools in 1847, and two years later won a Silver Medal for the "Best Model from the Antique." In 1850 he was working at the Birmingham School of Design.

Kirk exhibited at the Royal Academy, 1847–1854, and at the British Institution, 1849–1854, showing busts, etc., and a marble group entitled "Feeding-time" in 1853.

KIRK, JOSEPH ROBINSON
b. 1821, *d.* 1894

He was the fifth son of Thomas Kirk (q.v.) and studied in his father's studio. In 1840 he exhibited at the Royal Hibernian Academy, becoming an Associate five years later and a full member in 1854. He went to Rome in 1843, but remained there for only a year.

Most of Kirk's work is in Ireland and a full list is given in Strickland's *Dictionary of Irish Artists.* He exhibited at the R.A., 1846–1862, showing marble groups of "Ruth and Naomi" (1849) and of "St. John and the Virgin" (1862). His bust of Francis Burton (a copy of Chantrey's) is at Christ Church, Oxford.

KIRK, THOMAS
b. 1781, *d.* 1845

Kirk was born in Cork and studied at the Dublin Society's Schools. In 1808 he was chosen to execute the figure of Nelson for the column in Sackville Street, Dublin. Most of his life was spent in Ireland and his principal works are in that country; a list of these is given in Strickland's *Dictionary of Irish Artists.*

The most important work executed by Kirk in England is the statue of Sir Sidney Smith (1845) in the National Maritime Museum, Greenwich. He also made two statues for Wrest Park in Bedfordshire, which Earl de Grey had ordered when Viceroy of Ireland. These were "The Young Champion" (1840) and "The Young Suppliant" (1843). His bust of the Duchess of Dorset (1818), a very pretty work, is at Knole, Kent, while that of Countess Talbot (1819) is in Ingestre Church, Staffordshire. A third bust, that of John Wilson Croker, executed in the same year, was formerly in the collection of Sir Robert Peel, but was sold with the other heirlooms in 1900.

Kirk exhibited at the Royal Academy, 1825–1839, and at the British Institution in 1840. At the Liverpool Academy of 1822 he showed busts of George IV and Thomas Moore.

KIRK, WILLIAM BOYNTON
b. 1824, *d.* 1900

The second son of Thomas Kirk (q.v.), he attended the Schools of the Royal Dublin Society in 1839 and later worked in his father's studio. In 1848 he went to England, where he remained for nine years, and it was while he was living at Worcester in 1851 that he designed the Shakespeare dessert-service for the famous china-works.

Kirk exhibited at the Royal Academy, 1848–1857, and at the Great Exhibition of 1851. His statue of "Iris Ascending," executed in 1844, is now at Marlborough House. In 1860 he entered the Church and later held livings at Birkenhead and Ashton-under-Lyne.

A list of Kirk's works in Ireland is given in Strickland's *Dictionary of Irish Artists.*

KIRKBRIDE, —, of Carlisle
fl. 1823–1838

Signs monuments to William Thurnham, 1823, in Carlisle Cathedral, to George Mounsey, 1838, in St. Cuthbert's, Carlisle, and Edward Grave, 1838, at Penrith, Cumberland.

KNAPP, JOHN, of London
fl. 1810–1830

Knapp, whose yard was in Foley Street, signs monuments to John de Coussmaker, *c.* 1810 (?), in Staines Parish Church; Gilbert Hare, 1820, in Marylebone Parish Church; and Sir Andrew Hammond, 1828, at Terrington St. Clement, Norfolk. His monument to Urban Vigors, 1815, also in Marylebone Parish Church, has a medallion-portrait.

KNIGHT, SAMUEL, of Exeter
fl. 1835–1841

In 1841 he made the altar-piece, altar-table and

pulpit for Bickleigh Church, Devon (*Gentleman's Magazine*, 1841, Part I, page 87), and he was also responsible for carrying out decorative carving in Honiton Church when it was being rebuilt after a fire.

Knight signs a classical tablet to James Coleridge, 1836, at Ottery St. Mary, Devon.

KNIGHT, THOMAS, of London
b. 1637, *d.* 1680

Knight was appointed the City mason in 1666 and in 1670 received £260 "for stone workmanship in and about the Guildhall Chapel, Newgate and other places." In the same year he and Joshua Marshall (q.v.) were responsible for the building of Temple Bar (City Corporation Records, 159/16), while between 1674 and 1675 he was paid £600 for further work at Newgate (P.R.O., E.101,475/2). In 1679 he cut the lettering on the Monument. Hooke notes on 10 April how "Knight cut wrong 'R' for 'P' for the 'Fish Street Piller.'"

Knight died on 11 June, 1680, leaving a widow, Sarah, and one daughter. He was buried in Sanderstead Church, Surrey, under a "black coarse marble tomb," the verses on which began as follows:

"Stay Reader here, and leave one groan
If not for my sake, for thy own.
Since impartiall Death that mee
Hath overtaken, followes thee.
Hast thou wealth, strength, art and industry
Yet dye thou must, for those had I. . . ."
(Manning and Bray's *Surrey*, Vol. II, page 576.)

KNOLTON, S.
He signs a large monument to Edward Austen, *c.* 1750, at Bexley, Kent.

KNOWLES, THOMAS, of Oxford
d. 1826

Knowles was foreman to Stephen Townsend of Oxford, and took over his master's yard in 1799. He later went into partnership with his son, Edward, in 1816, and it was the latter who received £135 for carving eagles and work on the pediment of Queen's College, Oxford (College Archives).

The elder Knowles signs tablets to the Messrs. Mapletoft, 1799, at Byfield, Northants; and Mr. Kipling, 1802, at Chilton, Bucks. Others executed by him in Oxfordshire include those to the Rev. W. Breeres, 1804, at Hampton Gay; Lady Elizabeth Spencer, 1812, and Lord Charles Spencer, 1820, both at Wheatfield; and William Fletcher, 1826, at Yarnton.

L

LAKE, J.

He signs a marble cartouche tablet to Gilbert White, 1728, at Selborne, Hants.

LAMB, FRANCIS
fl. 1749–1756

He signs a ledger to Edward Solomon, 1749, in Grantham Church, Lincolnshire, and a slate tombstone in the churchyard dated 1756.

LAMB, FREDERICK HERBERT
d. 1852

When his widow applied for assistance to the A.G.B.I. she stated that her husband had been employed by Hunt and Roskell, the silversmiths, and had modelled a number of original works for Queen Victoria, and also a bust of Mr. Fisk for General Goodfellow. Lamb also designed and executed the figure for the top of a flower stand, a work which gained the prize medal at the 1851 Exhibition. Mrs. Lamb also stated that her husband had exhibited at the Royal Academy, but I can find no trace of this in contemporary catalogues. Lamb died 31 October, 1852.

LAMBERT, JAMES
fl. 1761–1773

He exhibited a "Bust of a Gentleman" at the Society of Artists in 1763.

LANCASHIRE, FRANCIS, and SON, of Bath
Francis Lancashire: *b.* 1740, *d.* 1814

Francis Lancashire, who died in 1814, is referred to as "an ingenious statuary" in his obituary in the *Gentleman's Magazine* of that year (Part I, page 204). He was apparently assisted at one time by his elder brother, Richard (1736–1813), who was "formerly a statuary and a pupil of Mr. Prince Hoare" (*Gentleman's Magazine*, 1813, Part II, page 502). The business was carried on by Francis's son, William, who went into partnership with Tyley of Bristol (q.v.), and later with a Mr. Walker of the same city. Queen Charlotte paid a visit to the firm when she was staying in Bath in 1817.

Tablets executed by the Lancashires (which are not as good as those of their rivals, the Kings of Bath, q.v.) include those to Mrs. Jubb, 1790, at Ringwould, Kent; Mary Parsloe, 1792, at Great Somerford, Wilts; John Seare, 1792, at Marsworth, Bucks; Elizabeth Curtis, 1793, Sydling, St. Nicholas, Dorset; John Dowson, 1797, at Greystock, Cumberland; Edward Read, 1798, at Gillingham, Dorset; the Earl of Cork, 1798, at Frome, Somerset; William Moody, 1798, at Steeple Langford, Wilts; John Gunning, 1798, at Cold Ashton, Glos; James Montagu, 1798, at Lacock, Wilts; Sir John Smyth, 1802, at Long Ashton, Somerset; the Rev. Charles Gatley, 1821, at St. Brides, Glamorgan; and the Rev. R. W. Howell, 1822, at Mere, Wilts.

LANCASHIRE, RICHARD
b. 1736, *d.* 1813

In 1763 he received twenty guineas for carving eight stone Ionic capitals for Ditchley, Oxfordshire (Dillon Archives). See Lancashire, Francis.

LANDER, F. M.
fl. 1840–1855

Of all his monuments in Kensal Green Cemetery, that commemorating General Sir William Casement, 1844, is the most extraordinary. This consists of a sarcophagus, over which is flung the General's cloak. On this lie his cocked hat, sword, etc., while the canopy above is supported at each corner by four heroic caryatids in the form of turbaned Indians wrapped in long cloaks. Fantastic as the tomb appears at first sight, it must be admitted that the details, especially the modelling of the figures of the Indians, are well carried out. One cannot, however, say as much of all Lander's work in the cemetery.

LANDRÉ, MARY
fl. 1769–1774

She was employed by Wedgwood, who paid her in 1769 for models of "6 passions or vices," "4 groups of boys," "3 female virtues," "Moses and the Serpent," "Josep," and "Apolow and Dafnee" (*sic*). Five years later she received another payment from the firm for "12 signs of the Zodiack" and "4 boys in metal" (Wedgwood Archives).

LANE, JOHN

In 1722 the Rt. Hon. Thomas Coke of Melbourne Hall, Derby, paid him £6 6s. for "four solid vauses like ye Earl of Burlington's porphyry" (Archives Marquess of Lothian).

LANE, RICHARD JAMES
b. 1800, *d.* 1872

He is best known as an engraver and lithographer, but at one time he did try his hand at sculpture and executed, about 1835, a life-size seated statue of his brother, Edward, in Egyptian dress. His bust of this brother (*c.* 1833) is in the Bodleian, Oxford.

Lane acted as assistant to J. E. Carew (q.v.) and gave evidence for his master in the lawsuit of 1840.

LANE, WILLIAM, the Elder, and WILLIAM, the Younger, of Norwich
William Lane the Elder: *b.* 1729, *d.* 1798
William Lane the Younger: *b.* 1756, *d.* 1806

The elder Lane, who became a Freeman of Norwich in 1769, made chimney-pieces for Mr. Dillingham's house at Letton, Norfolk, in 1788 (Soane Notebooks). He and his wife died within a few days of one another in 1798, and the business was taken over by their son, William Lane the Younger (*Monthly Magazine*, 1798, page 234).

Lane signs monuments to Jeremiah Berry, 1767, at Acle, Norfolk, and to P. Browne, 1773, in St. Mary's, Bungay, Suffolk. Two tablets in Norwich churches are signed "Lane and Son." These commemorate William Foster, 1783, in St. Stephen's, and John Marks, 1784, in St. Simon and St. Jude's.

LANGLEY, BATTY
b. 1696, *d.* 1751

As a writer on architecture Langley is well known, but he was also the inventor (about 1731) of a kind of artificial stone. Vertue (*Walpole Society*, Vol. III, page 51) describes it as "a new invention of casting in stone or a hard composition, busts, statues, columns, etc., or any frieze or cornice work for building in imitation of free stone and said to be more durable." He also says that statues from 1 ft. to 7 ft. high could be supplied at prices varying according to size and adds: "These are made near Lambeth and sold by one Batty Langley, a bold-faced undertaker."

In the *Daily Journal* of 10 March, 1731, there is a notice referring to a "Mr. Langley, sculptor, at the stone warehouse at Bankside at the sign of the Hercules Head in Southwark." It will be noticed that Vertue says "Lambeth" and the advertisement "Bankside," but it hardly seems possible that two statuaries of the same name could have set up on the south bank of the Thames in the same year.

The only payments made to a Langley which I know of are in the Longford Castle account-books,

where the following items are listed as having been supplied by him to Lord Folkestone: "1748: a sundial stone, £1 13s.; 1757: carving capitals, £10 15s. 6d.; 1758: stucco ornaments to ye Venetian seat, £7 7s.; 1758: for four shields on ye piers, £12 12s.; 1758: a carved head in ye passage, £4 12s. 6d." From the date of four of these five payments, it would seem that either Batty Langley's business was carried on after his death, or that there were, after all, two Langleys.

Batty Langley also did some building for the Duke of Kent at Wrest Park in 1735. In that year, in a long letter to his employer about the new brewery, he ends on a pathetic personal note: "This afternoon my dearest son Euclid, a child of about two years and a half age, the most manly child that nature ever form'd departed this life, as did my daughter Caroline, a child of one year old, on ye last Monday that I was at Wrest" (Archives, Lady Lucas and Dingwall).

LANGLEY, WILLIAM
W. H. Hamper in his edition (1827, page 145) of the diary of Sir William Dugdale (1605–1686), the Garter King of Arms, quotes the bill for Sir William's altar-tomb (erected in his lifetime) in Shustoke Church, Warwickshire: "Payd to Wm. Langley, 17 Feb., 1681 for worke done by him in making the monument in the chancell of Shustoke Church (excepting the tablet of marble, and the armes which were done at London), and setting it up, £3 12s."

In 1724 he was paid £12 8s. for the two large stone figures of a boy and girl on the front of the Charity School at Frome, Somerset (Churchwarden's Accounts). The statues, known as "Nancy Guy" and "Billy Ball," are still *in situ*.

LANGSTAFF, THOMAS
As "carver and mason of Edward Street, Marylebone," he became a bankrupt and a sale of the contents of his yard was held on 10 March, 1778. Among the lots were a number of chimney-pieces, including two "in green and Sienna marble" and one "very beautiful and highly finished, with dentals fitted with green, carved tablet, etc."

LARSON, WILLIAM
His equestrian statue of James II which he made for Newcastle was erected in 1685, but three years later was torn down by the mob and thrown into the Tyne. According to Brand's *History of Newcastle* (Vol. I, page 31), it was "cast in copper of the size of the famous equestrian statue of

Charles I at Charing Cross," was "approved by Sir Christopher Wren and cost the town eight hundred pounds sterling."

The statue was later taken up out of the river, melted down and cast into a peal of bells. A miniature copy of it is in the National Gallery of Ireland (*Country Life*, 1950, page 1007).

LATHAM, JASPER
d. 1693

Under Wren, Latham was the master-mason for building St. Mildred's, Poultry, 1677–1679, where his carved stonework included a door with "scrolls, cherubim-heads, deathsheads and bones." He was also employed as one of the master-builders at St. Paul's Cathedral where, between 1679 and 1690, he received over £10,000 for work which included carving "the great wreath of bay-leaves and berries" for the north side of the Cathedral, "four laurels with the arms of the Deanery," seventy-five faces of capitals, four festoons, 10 ft. long, etc. In 1682 he was paid £300 for carving the moulding of the flowers for the tribune windows. He also worked at Temple Bar in 1684 and at the Royal Exchange between 1691 and 1693.

In 1670 Latham built offices for Mr. Morris and Alderman (afterwards Sir Robert) Clayton in Austin Friars and Old Jewry, and two years later carried out the masonry work for Clayton's banking-house in Hand Alley (Clayton ledgers, Guildhall Library). He also executed the stone-work of Watlingford House for a Major Wildman, for which he was paid £200 in 1678.

According to Vertue (*Walpole Society*, Vol. I, page 129), Latham made, in 1672, the head of the equestrian statue of Charles II presented to the City of London by Sir Robert Vyner. This statue had a curious history. In all books on London it is stated that the Polish Ambassador to the Court of St. James's ordered in Italy an equestrian statue of his master, John Sobieski, showing him trampling a Turk under his horse's feet. When it was finished, however, the Ambassador could not pay for it, so Vyner, hearing of this, asked his agent at Leghorn to buy it and ship it to England, where on its arrival he engaged Latham to alter the head.

The real story, however, seems rather different. In 1737, when the building of the Mansion House was under consideration, the question arose of moving the statue, and a Mr. Huggins, agent of the Vyner family, wrote to the Corporation protesting against this suggestion. In his letter he made the following statement about Sir Robert's gift: "The pedestal cost him upward of £700, besides the horse which he bought at Rome and

the figure of King Charles II, which was there placed thereon in memory of that Restoration which is still commemorated in our liturgy; and on the day Sir Robert was sworn Lord Mayor of your City, I saw that conduit run with claret" (City Corporation Archives, Mansion House Committee Papers, Box I).

From this letter it seems that only the horse was bought in Rome, so that the pedestal and the figure of Charles II may both be the work of Latham. In spite of Mr. Huggins's protests, the statue was taken down and for forty years lay neglected in a yard. In 1779 it was given to a descendant of the donor, who took it to his country house at Gautby, Lincolnshire; in 1885 it was moved to Newby Hall, near Ripon.

As a sculptor, however, Latham is best known for the magnificent monument to Archbishop Sheldon, 1683, in Croydon Parish Church, a work in which he was assisted by his partner, the obscure Boone. Unfortunately this was badly damaged when the church was destroyed by fire in 1869. He was also responsible for the monuments to Viscount Grandison, *c.* 1670, in Oxford Cathedral, and Thomas Brome, 1673, at Farnborough, Kent.

Latham was City mason from 1680 until his death, and, in 1689, Warden of the Masons' Company. He died in 1693, for at the end of the year his widow received payments for work he had been carrying out at the Royal Exchange (City Corporation Archives, Gresham Committee). She also carried on the business and, until 1697, continued working for the Mercers' Company, to whom her husband had been appointed mason in 1682.

Latham had been assisted by his son, Robert, at the Royal Exchange between 1691 and 1693, and the latter carried on the work for two years after his father's death. For some obscure reason he later left England, and in 1713 was living at Port Mahon in Minorca (Court Book, Masons' Company).

(Bodleian, Rawlinson MSS. 387; Diary of Robert Hooke; Wren Society's Publications; authorities cited in text.)

LAUGHTON, JOHN,
of Priors Cleeve
b. 1711, *d.* 1754

Several members of the Laughton family were masons by trade. John signs tombstones at Bretforton, Worcestershire, between 1741 and 1746, and at Welford-on-Avon, in Warwickshire, in 1750. His sons, William and Thomas Laughton, of Priors Cleeve, respectively sign tablets to Thomas Vale, 1769, at Elmley Castle, Worcestershire, and to John Slatter, 1785, at Bidford, Warwickshire.

Another member of the same family was Thomas Laughton, statuary and mason, who was born in 1790 and died in 1852.

LAURIE, W.
fl. 1846–1849

He exhibited at the Royal Academy in 1846 a model of a monument to Lord Haddington, and in the following year a design for a memorial to Shakespeare.

Laurie was living at Downham Market, Norfolk, in 1849, the year in which he published a book of designs for Gothic tombstones.

LAW, EDWARD, of Sheffield
b. 1798, *d.* 1838

He was born on 9 December, 1798, the fourth child of John Law of Sheffield and grandson of Thomas Law, a well-known silversmith of that town. Besides being a sculptor, Edward Law was a designer of some skill, working for Sheffield silversmiths and iron-founders. Among the objects he designed in 1825 was a bronze hexagonal stove with ormolu mountings for the Registrar's Office in Edinburgh. He was also one of the artists attached to the works of Hoole and Robson, where some years later Alfred Stevens was to be employed.

Law made a number of wax medallions between 1826 and 1827, including those of Shakespeare, Canning and William Wilson. He exhibited at the Royal Academy in 1829 and again in 1832, and died on 30 June, 1838.

Most of his work is to be found in Sheffield and includes busts of J. Rimmington (1821) and Earl Fitzwilliam (1834), both in the Cutlers' Hall; Frank Stone (1826) and Edward Rawson (1826), both in the Weston Park Museum; Thomas Waterhouse (1831) at the University; Thomas Rawson (1827) at the Royal Infirmary; Thomas Holy (1832) in the Carver Street Chapel; Henry Overend (1832) in the possession of the Literary Society; and Thomas Watson (1834) in the Cathedral. His medallions of William Staniforth (1835) and John Law (1838) are at the Royal Infirmary and the Free Masons' Hall respectively, and he also signs the monuments of John Greaves (1828) in the Cathedral, and of Mrs. Beard Holy (1838) in the Carver Street Chapel. Another bust of Earl Fitzwilliam (1829) was formerly at Wentworth Woodhouse, Yorkshire.

(Information, Sheffield Public Library.)

LAW, WILLIAM, of Camberwell
fl. 1775–1795

He signs large tablets in coloured marbles to Sarah Gretton, 1775, at Birchington, Kent, and to William Cody, 1795, in St. George-the-Martyr, Southwark.

LAWLOR, JOHN
b. 1820, *d.* 1901

He was born in Dublin and attended the Royal Dublin Society's Schools, studying sculpture under J. Smyth. He came to England in 1845 and, under J. Thomas (q.v.), made a number of statues for the Houses of Parliament. On Thomas's recommendation he joined the Royal Academy Schools two years later, giving his age as twenty-four, although Strickland's *Dictionary of Irish Artists*, which gives the date of his birth as 1820, would make him three years older.

Lawlor was made an Associate of the Royal Hibernian Academy in 1861 and exhibited at the Royal Academy, 1848–1879, showing groups of "Boy and Dog" (1844), "The Mourners" (1848), and "The Wrestlers" (1867); a statue of Titania (1868); and busts of Dr. Gully (1853), T. Kennedy (1854) and C. Cattermole (1873). In 1879 he had a disagreement with the Committee and refused to send any more works after that date. He also exhibited at the British Institution, 1840–1851, and at the Great Exhibition of 1851 showed his group of "The Bathers" which won a prize medal. H. Weekes (q.v.), in his *Treatise on the Fine Arts in the Great Exhibition* (page 97), wrote of this work that Lawlor was "not surpassed by any in the whole exhibition for the modelling of female flesh." The group was later purchased by the Prince Consort for the Royal Collection.

Lawlor's best-known work is the group representing "Mechanics" which he executed in 1864 for the Albert Memorial, while some of the plaques at the corners of the Memorial are also by him. His statue of "Poetry" (1870) was formerly at Manley Park, Manchester, and he is represented in Ireland by statues of Patrick Sarsfield (1889) at Limerick, and Dr. Delaney (1890) at Cork. His "Blind Girl" (1875) was sold at Christie's in 1877, while his busts of "Clio" (1864), "Summer" (1864) and "Hermione" (1865) were sent by an anonymous owner to the same salerooms on 10 June, 1904.

In 1886 Lawlor went to America, but returned two years later and died in London, in 1901. "He was well known and popular in artistic and literary society in London. His tall handsome figure, his fund of witty anecdotes, his genial manner and his fine baritone voice making him a welcome guest and a favourite of all who knew him. In his profession he was irregular, working only when he felt inclined or when necessity compelled him; and was thus unable to make much provision for his old age" (Strickland's *Dictionary of Irish Artists*).

(Authorities cited in text; various references, *Art Journal*.)

LAWRENCE, RICHARD
fl. 1760–1795

He was working for the Royal Palaces as early as 1760, for he is mentioned in a letter written in that year to the Duke of Ancaster by George Murray (q.v.). The latter, who had just succeeded James Richards (q.v.) as Master Sculptor and Carver to the Crown, complained bitterly that "the care of the limetree work" (i.e., the Grinling Gibbons carvings, etc.) "at His Majesty's Palace at Windsor" had been "taken from me without my knowledge, and given to one Lawrence a Carver who never had any Concern with His Majesty's work on any Acct." In another note Murray also states that Lawrence was receiving £50 a year which by right belonged to him (Archives, West of Alscot Park).

Later on Lawrence did a good deal of work at Greenwich Palace, where he carved large medallions and lions' heads in 1770, and three years later received £101 for "ten and three-quarter faces of Corinthian capitals and six pilasters," all the work being for the King Charles Building (P.R.O., Ad. MS. 68/876).

In 1784 Lawrence was entrusted with most of the stone-carving for the Chapel, which was being rebuilt after a disastrous fire. His work here included eight large mask-heads in Portland stone and eighty-three faces of Corinthian capitals for the exterior, while for the interior he executed "ten faces of very rich Corinthian capitals in statuary marble to the eight columns at the East and West end of the Chapel at £96 15s. per capital," and also "three hundred and twenty-one feet of large ogee carved in an antique ornament, very rich and sunk very deep" (P.R.O., Ad. MS. 68/813). Two years later he made "twenty-four faces of antique Ionic capitals in marble for the six columns to the organ gallery," and finally, in 1787, "thirty-two cantilivers on the North side of the Chapel, the fronts and ends very rich and very rich foliage on the side," costing £528 (P.R.O., Ad. MS. 68/819).

In 1778 Lawrence carved large ciphers and two large stars and garters for the Queen's lodge at Windsor (P.R.O. Works 5/66). In the previous year he had begun to work at Somerset House,

and continued there until 1791, carving in both wood and stone. Here his work included the Corinthian composite capitals in Portland stone for the back front, the east return building, and the west end of the main building. He also made "two large rich flowers in the soffit of the arch leading to the terrace" and "four goats' heads over the windows of the principal floor" (P.R.O., A.O. 1/2495).

At Westminster Hall he carved, in 1785, a rather complicated stone console with "a shell in front with a cross and five birds, lions on the sides, and over the console a Gothic cornice with sweeps and strawberry-leaves" (P.R.O., 5/70).

Lawrence also worked at a number of private houses, including Manor House, Milton, Berks, 1764–1773 (*Country Life*, 24 December, 1948); Inverary Castle, 1781–1782; and the Marquess of Buckingham's London house in Pall Mall, 1795. In 1791 he carved part of the column erected in that year at Colne Park, Essex, by Philip Hills (Soane Notebooks, Soane Museum).

LAWRENCE, RICHARD
fl. 1815–1840

He exhibited models of horses at the British Institution in 1815 and 1816, while in the former year the Royal Academy purchased a cast of his "restoration of a horse's head from Lord Elgin's marbles" (Royal Academy Archives).

He signs a monument to J. Alexander, 1839, at Broadstairs, Kent.

LAWSON, —

In 1692 he was paid £16 for a statue of Diana for Chatsworth (Chatsworth building account-book).

LEA, WILLIAM
b. 1776

He attended the Royal Academy Schools in 1797, having exhibited a "Model of Cupid" at the Academy three years previously.

LEADER, G.
fl. 1792–1804

He exhibited wax portraits at the Royal Academy, 1792–1804, the most interesting being those of the artists, George Stubbs (1792) and Paul Sandby (1792), and that of Admiral Bligh (1801).

LEADER, P. H.

He exhibited "models in wax" at the Royal Academy in 1797. His signed boxwood portrait-medallion of an unknown man is now in the Victoria and Albert Museum.

LEARMOUTH, J.

In 1836 he exhibited at the Royal Academy busts of Master D. Hanbury and of Murray, Bishop of Rochester.

LEDSHAM, EDWARD

Ledsham, who was probably a Llanfair crafts-man, received £10 12s. in 1679 for carving the great stone coat of arms above the hall door at Chirk Castle, Denbigh (Myddelton Archives).

LEE, JOHN, of Odiham
fl. 1797–1842

He signs a number of tablets in Hampshire, the best of which commemorate William Burgess, 1797, and Mrs. Nichols, 1821, both in Odiham Parish Church; and Richard Harrison, 1812, at South Warnston.

LEE, WALTER, of London
fl. 1716–1754

He was the son of a mason named Walter Lee and was apprenticed to his father in 1716. In 1724 he became free and later set up his yard in Oxford Road. As a mason he built a house in Marylebone for Thomas Warren in 1731 (Inventory of Directors of the South Sea Company), while about three years later he was working at Canons (Baker's *Duke of Chandos*, page 199). In 1740–1741 he was paid £114 for work at Canons for the second Duke of Chandos (Ipswich Public Library, S.I./2/100).

In 1742 Lee agreed to build Marylebone Chapel for £1,000 (Archives, West of Alscot Park), and he also seems to have been responsible for a tablet erected there in memory of James Gibbs the architect, who died in 1754. The latter stated in his will that he wished to be buried at Marylebone and "that a small monument of marble, to be made by Mr. Walter Lee, mason, to be put up against the wall within the said church" (*European Magazine*, 1789, page 169).

Lee was succeeded in the business by his son, George, who was apprenticed to him in 1740, became a member of the Masons' Company in 1757, and died in 1767. In the year before his death, his son, another Walter, had been bound apprentice to him.

LEGÉ, F. A.
b. 1779, *d.* 1837

About 1800 he was working for Messrs. Franceys (q.v.) of Liverpool and five years later carved the Royal coat of arms on the Union News Room in that city (*The Stranger in Liverpool*, 1815, page 76). In 1814 he exhibited in Edinburgh a colossal figure of "Satan." Apparently this work was not received with favour, for the *Scots Magazine* (1815, page 334) reported that "some intrusive Goth has dared to mutilate it."

When Legé came to London he was employed by Chantrey (q.v.) for whom he cut in marble the famous monument of the "Sleeping Children" which Sir Francis had already modelled. After the latter's death it was said by a number of people that Legé was responsible for the design of this monument, as well as for the carving, but this is, of course, absurd (*Notes and Queries*, 1850, page 94).

Legé exhibited at the Royal Academy, 1814–1825, showing a statue of "Psyche" (1824) and busts of Sir Francis Chantrey (1815); C. H. Smith, the sculptor (1822); and John Crossley (1825). His bust of the Rev. Robert Hawker (1829) was formerly in St. Andrew's Church, Plymouth.

His small marble figure of a lady reclining on a couch (signed and dated 1828) is in private possession. This enchanting and delicate work might at first sight be taken for contemporary French sculpture, for it has all the charm of that country. On closer examination, however, it shows that curious virginal English frigidity which seems to add to its beauty.

Legé's son, George, received a large Silver Medal from the Society of Arts in 1826, but does not seem ever to have exhibited, and died before his father. Legé himself died on 4 April, 1837, leaving two children, Ann, a governess in Russia, and Frederick, a private soldier (Archives, Artists' Annuity Fund).

LEGREW, JAMES
b. 1804, *d.* 1857

He was the son of the Vicar of Caterham and showed an aptitude for sculpture as a child, when he modelled figures of animals. His father placed him with Chantrey (q.v.) and in 1822 he joined the Royal Academy Schools, having in the same year been awarded the Silver Palette by the Society of Arts. In 1824 he won a Silver Medal at the Academy, and in 1829 the Gold Medal for a group entitled "Cassandra Dragged from the Altar." In 1830 he went to Rome and studied there for some years. On his return to England, he opened a studio in Pimlico.

In 1844 Legrew showed at Westminster Hall "The Last Prayer of Ajax" and "Milton Reciting to His Daughters." The former the *Literary Gazette* considered "finely proportioned, but yet the propriety of its attitude is liable to question," while it thought the latter "too smooth and yet an extremely pleasing performance." In 1850 the sculptor made a font for Morden Church in Surrey, and in the following year sent his group "The Murder of the Innocents" to the Great Exhibition.

Legrew exhibited at the Royal Academy, 1826–1857, and at the British Institution, 1829–1836. At the Academy he showed, among other works, a group entitled "Musidora" (1850) and busts of Prince George of Cumberland (1832); Mrs. George Smith, of Sanderstead Park (1833), W. Skelton (1837), the Bishop of Peterborough (1838); and Sir B. Frere (1857). His "Cupid," executed in 1839, was exhibited at the Birmingham Society of Artists, while a cast of his "Samson," dated 1843, was formerly at the Crystal Palace.

Legrew's taste was purely classical, but his work never met with the encouragement it deserved. He was a man of many attainments besides sculpture, and his linguistic ability was remarkable, not only in French, German and Italian, but also in Latin, Greek, Hebrew and Syriac. As a writer he published a work on *The Ancient Sculpture of the Jews* in 1855, and also a short life of Flaxman. Unfortunately towards the end of his life he became prone to delusions, a weakness which was aggravated by the deaths of his father and brother, and which ultimately led him to commit suicide at Kensington on 15 September, 1857.

His monuments in Surrey include those to Henry Hoare, 1828, at Morden; Robert Wright, 1832, in Wimbledon Parish Church; George Smith, 1836, at Sanderstead; and the Rev. J. Kendrick at Bletchingley. He also signs others to Edward Cranston, 1841, at East Grinstead, Sussex, and to Bishop Allen, 1845, with a life-size recumbent figure, in Ely Cathedral.

(*Art Journal*, 1857, page 348; various references, *Builder*.)

LEGTERIN,
or LOGTERIN, J. V.
fl. 1685–1708

He made the life-size statues of "Hera," "Apollo," "Artemis" and "Diana" for the quadrangle of Woburn Abbey (Bedford Archives).

LEIFCHILD,
HENRY STORMOUTH
b. 1823, *d.* 1884

He was the son of William Gerard Leifchild and studied in the sculpture galleries of the British Museum and at the Royal Academy Schools, which he joined in 1844 on the recommendation

of F. S. Cary. In 1848 he went to Rome and remained there studying for three years.

Leifchild's model won the competition for the Guards' Memorial at Chelsea Hospital, and he also designed the mortuary chapel near the entrance gates of Warriston Cemetery, Edinburgh, which contains his recumbent effigy of Mr. Robertson. At the Great Exhibition of 1851 he showed a group entitled "Rispah Watching Over the Dead Bodies of Her Sons," while to the Royal Academy, 1844–1882, he sent, among other works, busts of A. J. Scott (1851); the Rev. J. Leifchild (1852) and Mrs. Danson (1876). A bust of George Wilson, shown in 1871, is now in Manchester Town Hall, while his heroic seated figure of "Erinna," dated 1860, is at Holloway College.

After Leifchild's death on 11 November, 1884, his widow presented the models of his more important works to Nottingham Museum, but the only one remaining today is the "Jacob and the Angel," all the rest having been destroyed by a curator before 1929. Among these were a group of "Athene Repressing the Fury of Achilles," a figure of "Lot's Wife," and a design for a memorial to Lord Byron. (*Magazine of Art*, 1891; information, Nottingham Public Library.)

LE MASON, —,
of Paris and London

Le Mason, who was an Academician of France, in 1790 exhibited at the Royal Academy a bust of Sir William Chambers, the architect, and medallions of the latter's two daughters.

In the same year the sculptor was paid twenty-five guineas by the Duke of Bedford for two bas-reliefs, 3 ft. in diameter, for the exterior of the sculpture gallery at Woburn. These represented respectively "Spring sacrificing flowers presented to her by Zephyr" and "Summer leaning on a sheaf of corn and receiving flowers from a child." Le Mason, in a letter to the Duke, explained that he could not charge less than twenty-five guineas for the pair, "seeing that I shall have to pay for fresh fruit and flowers and other indispensable articles" (Woburn Abbey Archives).

LE PIPER, FRANCIS
d. 1698

He is chiefly known as a painter, but Buckridge in his article on Le Piper in *An Essay Towards An English School* (published 1706) has "in the latter part of his life he apply'd himself to the Study and Practice of Modelling in wax, in *basso-relievo*, in which he did abundance of things with good success. He often said he wish'd he had thought of it sooner, for that sort of work suited better with his genius than any. Had he lived longer he would have arriv'd to a great Perfection in it."

LESOW, or LESSOW, WILLIAM
d. 1738

He was mason to St. Thomas's Hospital from 1729 till his death in 1738. In 1734 he received £229 for the masonry of "the new building." William died in 1738 and the yard was carried on by his widow, Ursula, till her death in 1741 (Hospital Archives). Lesow was also working on the building of Guy's Hospital at the time of his death (Guy's Archives).

LESTER, EDWARD,
of Dorchester
fl. 1827–1837

He signs tablets in Dorset to Robert Pearson, 1827, at Maiden Newton; Joseph Symes, 1830, Long Bredy, and to the Rev. Middleton Onslow, 1837, at Bradford Peverell.

LEVEROTTI, G.

He exhibited a marble bust of a daughter of Lord Burghersh at the Royal Academy in 1838.

LEVERSUCH, RICHARD
fl. 1709–1725

From 1709 until 1718 he was one of the principal masons for building Queen's College, Oxford (College Archives). His monument to Robert Pescod, 1725, is in Winchester Cathedral.

Leversuch was succeeded by his son, Thomas, who became a bankrupt in 1755 (*London Magazine*, 1755, page 301).

LEWETT, —

He signs a tablet, with arched pediment, urn and flaming lamps, to William Clarke, 1727, at Warminster, Wilts.

LEWIS, JOHN, and FAMILY,
of Gloucester and Cheltenham
Firm *fl.* 1796–1860

The firm seems to have had its first premises in Gloucester, for the monuments are signed "John Lewis, of Gloucester" until about 1820. The founder was succeeded by a "C. Lewis," who was presumably his son, and this C. Lewis, in his turn, was followed by his son, another John, who has the designation "sculptor" after his name in contemporary directories. It was this second John Lewis who, in 1847, erected and carved the column at Southam, set up by Lord Ellenborough to commemorate the achievements of the British forces in India (*Builder*, 1847, page 29).

Tablets by the firm are in no way outstanding in design, rarely showing anything more ambitious than the conventional figure of a mourning widow or a fluted semi-urn against a pyramid. They are very frequent in Gloucestershire and its neighbouring counties, the best including those to Richard Morgan, 1796, at Lydney, Monmouth; Henry Parry, 1802, in Monmouth Parish Church; General Barnes, 1810, at Queenhill, Worcs; John Maggs, 1816, at Winchcombe, Glos; Richard Orlebar, 1819, at Podington, Beds; John Rose, 1821, and Peter Hunt, 1824, both in Cheltenham Parish Church; Robert Phillips, 1822, at Lugwardine, Hereford; and Henry Campbell, 1823, at Charlton Kings, Glos. Their monument at Poulton-le-Fylde, Lancs, to the Rev. Richard Buck, 1845, is copied from a design by Flaxman (q.v.).

LEYLAND, JOSEPH BENTLEY,
of Halifax
b. 1811, *d.* 1851

He was born at Halifax on 31 March, 1811, the second son of Robert Leyland, a distinguished naturalist. At the age of sixteen he began modelling, and attracted the attention of a wealthy collector, Mr. Christopher Rawson, who allowed the young man to study his collection of ancient Greek marbles.

Leyland's first independent work was a model of a greyhound which he showed at Manchester in 1833. In the following year he exhibited there a colossal statue of "Spartacus," and also sent a head of Satan to Leeds. These works were noticed by Mr. Illidge, a portrait-painter, and he advised the sculptor to try his fortune in London. Leyland acted on this advice and, while in London, studied anatomy under R. B. Haydon, who thought very highly of his work and declared him to be a genius.

The sculptor's most famous work is a group of African bloodhounds, executed in 1846. Landseer considered it "the noblest modern work of its kind," while the *Art Journal* thought it was "certainly not surpassed by any sculpture of modern times." The group, together with a "Thracian Falconer," also by Leyland, is now in the Salford Museum. He also executed for his native city a statue of "Kilmeny the Sinless Maiden" in 1840, and another of "An Anglo-Saxon Chief" erected in 1851, the year in which he died, at Halifax on 26 January.

Leyland signs monuments in Halifax to Bishop Ferrar, 1848, in the Parish Church, and to Mr.

and Mrs. Rawson, 1848, in Trinity Church. In Yorkshire he made the monument of James Fawthorp, 1843, at Thornton, and the recumbent figure of Dr. Beckwith, 1845, in York Minster. (*Art Journal*, 1851, page 140.)

LINES, W. R., of Birmingham
b. 1801, *d.* 1846

Lines, who was the second son of Samuel Lines of Birmingham (1778–1863), the well-known drawing-master, showed a figure of "Belisarius" at the Birmingham Society of Artists in 1827, following this two years later with busts of Mr. Thomas Hill and "An Infant Son of Mr. Rice Harris." He died on 27 July, 1846 (*Birmingham Gazette*, 3 August, 1846).

His brother Edward also exhibited at Birmingham at this time, showing figures of "Eve" in 1827 and "Musidora" in 1829.

LINTON, W., of London
fl. 1680–1720

He may be the son of William Linton of Norwich (q.v.). He signs the fine large monument to John Offley (*d.* 1678) in St. Pancras Old Church, and the architectural one in memory of Elizabeth Scrope, 1719, in Lincoln Cathedral. Another work by him is the monument of Anthony Sparrow, 1685, Bishop's Palace Chapel, Norwich.

LINTON, W., of Norwich
fl. 1666–1684

Signs a tablet to Edmond Hobart, 1666, at Holt, Norfolk. Another work by him, now destroyed, was the cartouche tablet to John Hall in the Church of St. Nicholas, Yarmouth.

LITTLE, J. S.

In 1843 he exhibited a bust of "The Late Tyrone Power" at the Royal Academy.

LOADMAN, MARK, of London
fl. 1761–1772

Between 1761 and 1767 he received nearly £4,000 for mason's work at Audley End, a sum which included £855 for the bridge which he built in 1763 (Essex Records, D/DBY.243).

Loadman was declared a bankrupt in 1772, his address at the time being given as Lamb's Conduit Street, Holborn (*London Magazine*, 1772, page 346).

LOCATELLI, JOHN BAPTIST
b. c. 1735, *d.* 1805

He was born in Verona about 1735, and worked there and also in Venice and Milan, many of his patrons being Englishmen making the Grand Tour. For the Cathedral of his native city he made statues of "Faith" and "Hope," and he also executed one of Pietro D'Abano for Padua.

About 1775 Locatelli went to London, but was in financial difficulties five years later, when the Royal Academy granted him £50 (Royal Academy Archives). According to J. T. Smith (*Nollekens and His Times*, Vol. II, page 61), Nollekens went to Harrogate for his health in 1780 and left Locatelli and his pupil, C. Rossi (q.v.), to carve the medallions on the façade of the Middlesex Sessions Hall, which had already been modelled by himself. In 1781 Locatelli received £64 for a "richly carved" chimney-piece for Somerset House (P.R.O., A.O.1/2495), while a year or so later he made a statue of "Venus" for the garden of Dr. Lettson at Camberwell (*European Magazine*, 1803, page 430). He also worked for Robert Adam, to whose design he executed a chimney-piece for Harewood House. At that architect's sale, held on 22 May, 1818, one of the lots was "six terra-cotta medallions of boys, modelled by Locatelli."

The sculptor later became a protégé of Lord Orford, who commissioned a colossal group of "Thesus and Hercules." The two figures when completed looked, according to Nollekens, like "the dried skins of two brick-makers stuffed with clotted flock from an old mattress," but Locatelli nevertheless had the effrontery to ask £2,400 for the work, a price which his patron firmly refused to pay. In 1788 it was examined by a jury of experts, including six sculptors, who reduced the charge to £1,350 (J. T. Smith, op. cit., Vol. II, page 59).

Locatelli also worked for Mrs. Coade (q.v.), for Hughson (*London*, Vol. IV, page 545) described "a female figure lying on a couch as large as life, modelled by Locatelli from nature" which was to be seen in the firm's showrooms at Lambeth. This may be a terra-cotta cast for the sculptor's original marble figure now at Stratfield Saye, or for the plaster reclining figure of Signora Bacelli at Knole. The former is signed on the head-band, the latter not signed at all, but all the same it is very possibly Locatelli's work, for he exhibited a head of the lady (then mistress of the Duke of Dorset and later of the Earl of Pembroke) at the Royal Academy of 1781, and the Knole figure only dates from a year or so later. In addition, the treatment is very similar to that of the signed work at Stratfield Saye. In 1796 Locatelli left England and settled in Milan, where he was patronized by Napoleon, who granted him a pension for life. At an anonymous sale held by Mr. Christie on 23 January, 1807, one of the lots was "a capital and well-known marble of exquisite sculpture of

PLATE XV

J. F. MOORE
William Beckford, *c.* 1767, Ironmongers' Hall.

PLATE XVI

CHARLES MANNING
Captain George Hardinge, 1808, St. Paul's Cathedral.

EDWARD MARSHALL
Lady Culpeper, 1638, Hollingbourne, Kent.

the "Cumbent Venus" by the celebrated artist Locatelli." This could be the figure now at Stratfield Saye.

At the sale by Mr. Christie of a "Man of Fashion" held on 14 May, 1793, there were sold two life-size statues of Apollo and Mercury by Locatelli. They were carved out of "Orco stone" and a note in the catalógue has "it is supposed that these are the only specimens in England of this fine stone which was discovered about twenty years ago in the Veronese State." Both lots were however passed (Archives, Messrs. Christie).

(Authorities cited in text.)

LOCHEE, JOHN CHARLES
b. 1751

He was born on 4 November, 1751, and joined the Royal Academy Schools in 1772, giving his name as "Joannes Carolus Lochees," though he soon anglicized it. In the same year he was awarded a Silver Medal by the Academy, and four years later won a premium of thirty guineas from the Society of Arts for a "Model of an Infant Representing Statuary."

In 1787 Lochee was employed by Wedgwood, modelling plaques from the gems, etc., at Stowe, and also medallion-portraits of the Princes Augustus, Adolphus and Ernest; the Princess de Ligne; William Pitt; Count Pinto, the Portuguese Ambassador; the Marchioness of Buckingham; Lord Hood; the Hon. Keith Elphinstone; Dr. Deman, "the famous midwife"; Mr. Dennis O'Kelly, "famous on the turf"; and the Duke of Brunswick (Archives, Wedgwood Museum).

Two of the medallions, those of Pitt and Count Pinto, are referred to in letters in the Wedgwood Archives. Apparently the sculptor was given permission to take the portrait of Pitt, for the Prime Minister's secretary wrote to Wedgwood on 16 November, 1787, to ask "what time it would be convenient for Mr. Lochee to call in Downing Street," while Lochee himself refers to the one of the Count in an appallingly misspelt letter dated 3 December of the same year, and directed to "Mr. Boyle at Mr. Wedgwood's." "I forgot to mention in my lettre," he says, "that I have been to the portugaiso embessador this morning wich is know wiser satisfied with the Likeness, but dont like to have it dress to much in the fashion so have been oblige to altered the hair."

Another letter from Charles Peart (q.v.), written on 26 March, 1788, to Mr. Byerley, Wedgwood's agent, tells him that "Mr. Waldin the artist at Stowe wishes me to inform you that Mr. Lochee last November applied to him from Mr. Wedgwood for the portrait of the Marquis of Buckingham which Mr. W. obtained and gave Mr. Lochee every assistance possible and gave him also the Marquis's mask in Plaister" (Wedgwood Archives).

A number of the busts which the sculptor had modelled for Wedgwood, including those of Mrs. Barnell, Princess de Lamballe and Count O'Kelly, were afterwards engraved as gems or cameos (Tassie's *Engraved Gems*, 1791).

In 1787 Lochee made a bust of the Duke of York which is now in the Royal Collection (another version is in the possession of Lord Sherwood), and in 1790 one of the Prince of Wales for the Society of Arts. For this he was awarded a silver medallion, and an engraving of it forms the frontispiece of Volume X of the Society's *Transactions*.

He exhibited at the Royal Academy, 1776–1790, showing busts of Prince Charles of Mecklenburg (1787); Prince Edward (1787); Dr. Herschell (1788); Prince William Henry (1788); and R. B. Sheridan (1790). He was declared a bankrupt in 1795 (*Universal Magazine*, 1795, page 238).

LOCKWOOD, JOSEPH,
of Doncaster
b. 1759, *d.* 1837

He became a Freeman of Doncaster on 21 November, 1794, on payment of twenty guineas. In 1807 he was elected to the Town Council and later was twice chosen Mayor (Corporation Archives). He died 14 February, 1837. His son, also Joseph, became a Freeman of Doncaster on 5 January, 1808.

Most of his tablets are neo-Hellenic in design, but that of Samuel Tooker, 1819, in Rotherham Parish Church, has a relief of fasces.

Other tablets in Yorkshire by Lockwood include those to John Nevile, 1804, at Badsworth; Charles Thellusson, 1820, at Brodswell; John Crosham, 1823, at Barnby-on-Don; Gilbert Hill, 1827, at Bawtry; Bartholomew Hodgetts, 1830, at Barnsley; and John Yarborough, 1836, at Campsell. He also signs tablets to the Rev. Thomas Denton, *c.* 1800, at Ashtead, Surrey; and to John Woodruff, *c.* 1800, and Thomas Peacock, 1827, both at Crowle, Lincolnshire.

LODGE, WILLIAM,
of Birmingham

His tablet commemorating Charles Richards, 1806, is in St. Paul's Church, Birmingham. His widow, Ann Lodge, signs tablets to Daniel Mathews, 1822, at Hagley, Worcs, and to William Clare, 1823, at Quat, Salop.

LOFT, JAMES
fl. 1820–1867

He was born at Hull about 1800, and at the age of twenty went to London, where he became a pupil of Chantrey (q.v.). He exhibited at the Royal Academy, 1825–1867, showing among other works busts of W. Graham (1831), J. Knight (1854), Sir Charles Napier (1855) and Sir E. Lyons (1856). In 1833 he made a statue of Daniel Sykes for the Mechanics' Institute in his native town.

Loft signs monuments to Samuel Russell, 1834, in Shepperton Parish Church; the Rev. John Scott, 1835 (with a medallion-portrait), in St. Mary's, Hull; and Major Mills, 1838, in St. Mary's, Bedford.

(Information, Hull Public Library.)

LONG, MRS.

In 1747 the *Gentleman's Magazine* (page 599) published an article on marble-staining and the practice of this art by W. Bird, of Oxford (q.v.). The author alleged that the art was not a lost one, "for we have lately been informed that the wife of Mr. Long, stonecutter at Bow Bridge, Essex, performs it in a very curious manner."

LONG, HENRY

He was apparently a worker in terra-cotta, for in 1690 he received £6 5s. for "a large vase of earth wrought with handles and festoons, painted and gilt," for Kensington Palace (P.R.O., E.351/3466).

LONG, MARK, and FAMILY, of Taunton
Firm *fl.* 1790–1845

The firm was founded by Mark Long, who was later joined by his wife, Maria. On Mark's death, his widow and son, Robert, carried on the business, the latter ultimately becoming the sole proprietor. It is for this reason that tablets made by the firm are signed either "M. Long," "M. and M. Long," or "R. Long." It was Robert Long who made the font for Trinity Church, Taunton, in 1842 (*Gentleman's Magazine*, May, 1842, Part II, page 190).

The firm's tablets include those to John Tripp, *c.* 1790, and Elizabeth Corfield, 1811, both in St. James's, Taunton; George Hart, 1813, and William Fraunciss, 1815, both in Taunton Parish Church; the Rev. Thomas Tucker, 1809, at Kingsdon, Som., Bridge Hamilton, 1824, at Broomfield, Somerset; and Hooker Bartelot, 1838, at Bishop's Hull in the same county.

LONGLEY, THOMAS, of Canterbury
Firm *fl.* 1802–1845

Longley was the best of the nineteenth-century Canterbury statuaries, and in 1802 succeeded Thomas White (q.v.) as master-mason of the Cathedral. He may also be the "Longley" who was employed on carving in the library of Lambeth Palace in 1829 (Cambridge University MS. 3928). His monument to Major Cairns, 1815, in Canterbury Cathedral is also signed by a "Robert and Mary Rushbrook," who may have designed it.

After Longley's death he was succeeded in the business by his son, John. Among the firm's monuments and tablets in Kent are those to Edward Brydges, 1809, at Wooton; Lady Sondes, 1818, and Christopher Milles, 1822, both at Nackington; William Hougham, 1828, in St. Martin's, Canterbury; Charlotte Hannam, 1831, at Minster; and Lord Sondes, 1836, at Sheldwich. They provided another monument to Lady Sondes, also dated 1818, at Rockingham in Northamptonshire.

LOSCOMB, —, of Reading

He signs a large wall-tablet to Sarah Terry, 1818, at Warfield, Berks.

LOUGH, JOHN GRAHAM
b. 1798, *d.* 1876

According to the Parish Register of Shotley, Northumberland, he was born in January, 1798, the third son of William Lough of Aycliff, Co. Durham, and his wife, Barbara Clementson, of Dalton, Northumberland, but Lough himself always seemed very uncertain about his age. When he joined the Royal Academy Schools in 1826 he gave it as twenty-three, and a year later, in an interview with the *Literary Gazette*, declared he had been born in 1803. The *Dictionary of National Biography*, however, gives the year of his birth as 1806.

Lough's father was a farmer near Hexham, and the boy was first apprenticed to a stonemason at Shotley Field. He later went to Newcastle-on-Tyne, where he found work as an ornamental sculptor and where he carved the decorations on the building of the Literary and Philosophical Society. In 1825 he persuaded the captain of a collier to give him a free passage and made his way to London by sea. Here he joined the Royal Academy Schools in 1826 on the recommendation of J. T. Smith, and made such rapid progress that in the same year he received a commission from the Duchess of Buckingham for a bust. In 1827 he was able to hold his first exhibition, which proved an instantaneous success.

Lough suffered all his life from being absurdly over-praised by one section of the Press and unfairly criticized by another, the extremes being represented by the *Literary Gazette* and the *Art Journal*. For example, when he held his first exhibition the *Literary Gazette* hailed him as an "extraordinary genius," whose works were of "perfectly miraculous power, productions as only the most exalted and powerful genius could conceive and execute." The *Art Journal*, on the other hand, described his group of "The Mourners," shown at Westminster Hall in 1844, as "maudlin sentimentality rarely outdone by the most drivelling essays," although the *Literary Gazette* considered that "nineteen out of twenty people would prefer it to any other work in the exhibition" and were "surprised that the artist is not among those to whom honour has been done by the Commission."

When the *Art Journal* heard that Lough had been given the commission for the statue of the Prince Consort at the Royal Exchange, their remark that there could "be no doubt of it being a failure" was mild compared with the abuse that greeted his model of the companion statue of the Queen, which he sent to the Royal Academy in 1845. This was damned out of hand as "an odiously coarse production, in which not one feature of the Queen is recognizable," while "for a public work" it was considered "a common disgrace, nothing so vulgar, worthless and unartist-like has ever been seen within these walls." When the unfortunate statue was erected the editor declared that its "gross vulgarity" exceeded "that of the worst production that ever has been publicly exhibited."

Lough, though attacked by the Press, was fortunate in his patrons, among whom may be numbered the Duke of Sutherland, Earl Grey and Sir Matthew Ridley. For the last-named he executed a large number of works, both for Blagdon in Northumberland and for the London house in Carlton House Terrace, which contained his ten marble statues representing characters from Shakespeare (later presented to the Corporation of Newcastle). At Blagdon, Lough made an even larger number of figures, busts, groups, etc., the best of these being the "Milo" and the four statues on the bridge near the house. The former was later placed by Sir Edwin Lutyens in the ornamental water on the west side of the building, and not only gains enormously in this new setting, but also proves that Lough was, at his best, a great sculptor.

Lough, who spent from 1835 until 1839 studying in Italy, exhibited at the Royal Academy, 1826–1863, and at the British Institution, 1833–1863. He sent his much-criticized group of "The Mourners" to the Great Exhibition of 1851.

He died on 8 April, 1876, and the *Art Journal* made rather tardy amends in its obituary which declared that "in private life no artist has been more largely esteemed and respected. His personal friends," the article continued, "were numerous, including many of the most famous men and women of the age in science, art and letters. There frequently assembled at his house persons not only high in rank, but renowned for intellectual and social worth; their regard for the man was great, as was their admiration of his genius as an artist. Few men have lived who will be more regretted by a very large circle."

Lough married a Miss North, daughter of the Duke of Kent's chaplain, who after her husband's death gave his models, etc., to the Corporation of Newcastle. They were first placed in Elswick Hall, but have since been distributed to other museums and buildings in the city.

(*Art Journal*, 1876, page 203; various references, *Art Union*, *Builder* and *Literary Gazette*.)

STATUES

1836	James Losh	Newcastle Literary and Philosophical Society
1845	Lord Collingwood	Tynemouth
1845	Queen Victoria	Royal Exchange
1846	Prince Consort	Royal Exchange
1847	Prince Consort	Lloyd's
1848	Marquess of Hastings	Malta
1853	Lady Diana Beauclerk	Exhibited Royal Academy
1858	Dr. Gilly	Durham
1862	Sir Henry Lawrence	St. Paul's Cathedral
1862	George Stephenson	Newcastle

BUSTS

1832	James Losh	Newcastle Literary and Philosophical Society
1839	Lord Reay	Exhibited Royal Academy
1840	Rev. William Ainger	St. Bees Church, Cumberland
1842	Sir Matthew Ridley	Blagdon, Northumberland
1843	Duke of Northumberland	Alnwick
1844	Lady Ridley	Blagdon, Northumberland
1845	Lord Collingwood	Exhibited Royal Academy
1845	Robert Southey	National Portrait Gallery
1850	Professor Forbes	Geological Museum

1855	Judge Talfourd	Crown Court, Stafford
1861	Edward Stanley	St. Bartholomew's Hospital
1875	Dr. Campbell de Morgan	For Middlesex Hospital

GROUPS AND IDEAL WORKS

1827	Milo	For Sir Matthew Ridley, Blagdon, Northumberland
1829	David	Howick, Northumberland
1832	Orpheus	For Sir Matthew Ridley, Blagdon, Northumberland
1834	Mercury and Argus	For Lord Brougham
1839	The Infant Lyrist	For the Duchess of Northumberland
c. 1850	Mercury and Pandora	For Sir Augustus Clifford
1851	Arie	For the Duke of Sutherland
1860	Puck	Bethnal Green Museum
1862	The Elder Brother in Comus	Mansion House
1863	Titania Sleeping	Bethnal Green Museum
1865	Jacques	Bethnal Green Museum

MONUMENTS

1838	Durham (St. Mary-le-Bow)	George Fennell
c. 1840	St. Paul's Cathedral	Middleton, Bishop of Calcutta
1841	Burnham Thorpe, Norfolk	Ann Everard
1846	Crosthwaite, Cumberland	Robert Southey (recumbent figure)
1847	Burnham Thorpe, Norfolk	William Everard
1848	Tonbridge, Kent	James Alexander
1849	Blockley, Glos	Hon. Anne Rushout
1850	Winchfield, Hants	Lord Frederick Beauclerk
1853	Canterbury (Cathedral)	Bishop Broughton (recumbent figure)
1856	Canterbury (Cathedral)	Frederick Mackeson
1857	Ledbury, Hereford	Edward Moulton-Barrett
1857	Norham, Durham	Dr. Gilly
1872	Toddington, Glos	Lord and Lady Sudeley (recumbent figures)
n.d.	Kensal Green Cemetery	Lady Bourchier (the sculptor's daughter; a life-size recumbent figure)

LOVE, NICHOLAS
fl. 1754–1773

He signs the large wall-monument in coloured marbles to John Frederick, 1773, at Wellingborough, Northants. In 1754 Henry Campion paid him £100 for repairing his London house, and in 1757 a further £80 (Archives, Campion of Danny, Sussex).

LOVELL, JAMES
fl. 1752–1778

He was a protégé of Horace Walpole's. In 1752 he made chimney-pieces for the state dining-room and the state bedroom at Stowe, and also "two cupids with branches in their hands" (Anon., *Guide to Stowe*, 1827). He made another chimney-piece for Hagley Hall, Worcestershire (Anon., *Guide to Hagley*, 1828). In 1767 he was paid £52 for two chimney-pieces for Sir Richard Lyttelton's house in Cavendish Square (Archives, Lord Brownlow).

Lovell's most important monument is that to Earl Fitzwalter, 1756, in Chelmsford Cathedral, a large and magnificent architectural work, with a white-marble urn set in an alcove of green marble. In 1760 he made the tablet to the memory of General Wolfe in Westerham Church, Kent (*Gentleman's Magazine*, 1760, page 201), and he also signs the monument to Thomas Trotman, 1777, at Bucknell, Oxon, and to the Montagu family 1756, Horton, Northants.

Lovell's yard was first situated "near Cavendish Square," but he later moved to Marylebone. He became a bankrupt in 1768 (*London Magazine*, 1768, page 711).

LOVETT, THOMAS, of Bath
fl. 1766–1795

Lovett, who was afterwards declared a bankrupt in 1795 (*Universal Magazine*, May, 1795, page 380), signs a wall-monument to Charles Shoare, 1766, at Warminster, Wiltshire.

LUCAS, RICHARD COCKLE
b. 1800, *d.* 1883

He was born at Salisbury on 24 October, 1800, and at the age of twelve was apprenticed to his uncle, who worked as a cutler in Winchester. Here he learnt to carve knife-handles and, finding that he had an aptitude in this direction, decided to adopt sculpture as a profession.

Lucas accordingly joined the Royal Academy Schools in 1828, on the recommendation of Sir Richard Westmacott (q.v.), and won Silver Medals in that year and in 1829, the latter for an architectural drawing of the "Elevation of a

Banqueting-House." In 1844 he exhibited groups of "Canute" and "Lilla and Edwin" at Westminster Hall. Though the *Literary Gazette* could give "no great praise" to the first of these works, it nevertheless considered that the second "embodies original ideas, is ably treated, and the group of the three figures tells well in several points of view."

In 1845 Lucas made a model of the Parthenon in its original state, which was 12 ft. in length and 6 ft. in width, while the sculptures were moulded in wax. This was purchased by the Trustees of the British Museum (*Builder*, 1845, page 598) and proved so successful that they ordered the sculptor to produce a second model, showing the building "immediately after the explosion of 1687" (op. cit., page 619).

Lucas was at his best in his smaller works, and his wax portraits and ivory carvings have great merit. A collection of the latter and also of small statuettes by him are in the Bethnal Green Museum, while his wax relief of "Leda and the Swan" is in the Victoria and Albert Museum.

A great deal of controversy has raged round the famous bust of "Flora" which was purchased by the Kaiser Friedrich Museum at Berlin and certified by Dr. Bode to be an authentic work by Leonardo da Vinci. The *Burlington Magazine*, however, set out to prove that the bust was modelled by Lucas from a picture attributed to Leonardo. The sculptor's son, Albert Dürer Lucas, supported them in this theory, but the matter has never been satisfactorily settled.

Lucas exhibited at the Royal Academy, 1829–1859, and at the Great Exhibition of 1851 showed ivory carvings and imitation bronzes. In 1854 he built himself a house at Chilworth, near Romsey, of which he wrote an account entitled "An Artist's Dream Realized; being a Residence designed and built by R. C. Lucas, Sculptor, 1854." Here he died of paralysis on 18 May, 1883.

Lucas was "a man of great originality and conversational powers, and a prolific writer in the periodical Press" (*D.N.B.*). He was a friend of Lord Palmerston, who obtained for him a Civil List Pension of £150 in 1865.

He signs two monuments, one (with a recumbent figure) to Count de Salis, 1836, at Harlington, Middlesex, and the other to the Hon. Charles Welbore-Ellis, 1855, in Harrow School Chapel. (Authorities mentioned in text.)

STATUES

1838	Dr. Johnson	Lichfield
1841	Sir Richard Colt Hoare	Salisbury Cathedral
1858	Isaac Watts	Southampton

BUSTS

1836	Sir David Baird	Exhibited Royal Academy
1836	Lady Stepney	Exhibited Royal Academy
1837	Lord Elcho	Exhibited Royal Academy
1840	D. C. Read	Ashmolean Museum, Oxford
1842	General Michell	Exhibited Royal Academy
1842	John Rokewood	Exhibited Royal Academy
1868	Self-portrait	National Portrait Gallery (plaster)

WAX PORTRAITS

1832	Earl of Stamford	Formerly Enville, Staffs
1832	Children of Lord Grey of Groby	Formerly Enville, Staffs
1849	Lady Madden	Exhibited Royal Academy
1849	Sir Frederic Madden	National Portrait Gallery
1850	Sir Anthony Panizzi	British Museum (replica at National Portrait Gallery)
1850	Richard Major	British Museum
1850	Sir Henry Rawlinson	National Portrait Gallery
1850	Rev. H. G. Liddell	Exhibited Royal Academy
1850	B. L. Vulliamy	Private possession
1851	Lord Anglesey	Exhibited Royal Academy
1851	Chevalier Bunsen	Bethnal Green Museum
1851	Henry Hallam	National Portrait Gallery
1851	Viscount Palmerston	Brooks's Club
1851	Viscount Palmerston	Possession author
1852	Rev. Canon Caris	Possession author
1856	J. W. Jones	British Museum
1856	Viscount Palmerston	National Portrait Gallery
1856	Sumner, Bishop of Winchester	Possession author
1858	Rev. C. Moore	Possession author
1858	Lord Lyndhurst	Bethnal Green Museum
n.d.	Earl of Stamford	Victoria and Albert Museum

LUFKIN, GEORGE and HENRY, of Colchester
fl. 1812–1855

As a monumental sculptor George Lufkin produced a number of tablets, the best being those to William Hawkins, 1812, at St. Leonard-at-Hythe, Essex, and to Thomas Walford, 1833, at Birdbrook in the same county. At one time he was in partnership with Slyth (q.v.), and together they sign a monument at Halstead, Essex, to John Manistre, 1826.

The elder Lufkin was succeeded by his son, Henry, who, in 1855, made the altar-piece of St. James's, Colchester (*Builder*, 1855, page 417), and also signs a number of tablets in Essex. These are all extremely dull, the least unattractive being those to the Rev. Peter Wright, 1839, at Mark's Tey; the Rev. Josias Robinson, 1843, at Alresford; and the Rev. Edward Green, 1844, at Lawford.

LUMLEY, JOHN,
of Northampton
d. 1721

Between 1706 and 1708 he made marble and stone urns for Lord Ashburnham's house at Ampthill in Bedfordshire. In 1707 the owner, in a letter to his neighbour in the county, Sir John Chester, writes: "Being informed you are about causing some works of marble to be done, I take the liberty to recommend to you Mr. John Lumley of Northampton, as a sound and very able workman" (Letter-book of the First Lord Ashburnham). On 7 November, 1706, Lord Ashburnham had written to Lumley: "Pray send the drafte of the great door and Pediment as agreed with the valuations" (op. cit.).

LUPTON, GEORGE
b. 1792

He was born in 1792 (Archives, Artists' Annuity Fund).

He was the underpaid assistant of Nollekens (q.v.) and in 1809 was sent down to Cambridge to erect his master's statue of Pitt. For this the University paid £1,000 of which Lupton received only £12 for "the working expenses" of the pedestal. He seems to have set up for himself before Nollekens' death, but nevertheless received £100 under the sculptor's will (J. T. Smith, *Nollekens and His Time*, Vol. I, page 369).

Lupton's tablets, which are not very distinguished, include those to John Eligé, 1814, at Nutfield, Surrey; Elizabeth Blake, *c.* 1815, at Swanton Abbots, Norfolk; Lettice Patten, 1817, in Marylebone Parish Church; Sarah Combe, 1817, at Wincanton, Somerset; General Charles Reynolds, 1819, and Isabella Bartlett, 1821, both in St. John's Wood Chapel; Drake Clerk, 1821, at Winchelsea, Sussex; the Hon. Mrs. George Montagu, 1821, at Bishopsbourne, Kent; John Pepper, 1822, at Great Dunmow, Essex; Andrew Crawford, 1824, in Winchester Cathedral; John Lloyd, 1826, at Cowden, Kent; and Mary Tritton, 1827, at Beddington, Surrey.

LYDYARD, WILLIAM,
of Keynsham

He signs a large marble tablet to the Holbeach family, 1732, at Whitchurch, Somerset.

LYON, EDWIN, of Liverpool
d. 1837

He was a native of Liverpool and in 1827 exhibited "Diomed Going to Meet the Council of the Grecians" at the British Institution, while at the Liverpool Academy he showed a number of wax busts, including those of Mr. Alexander Mosses and Mr. George Mosses in 1827; John Yates and Dr. Traill, in 1828; and Richard Butler, Joseph Lyon, Mrs. H. Leigh, John Leigh, Miss Eliza Leigh and the Rev. H. McNeile in 1837.

By 1834 Lyon was living in Dublin, and two years later was elected an Associate of the Royal Hibernian Academy. His wax bust of Mrs. Francis Beetham, executed in 1835, is in the Victoria and Albert Museum, while another of Sir William Cusack-Smith, dated 1837, is in the possession of the author.

(Strickland's *Dictionary of Irish Artists*.)

M

MACBRIDE, JOHN ALEXANDER PATTERSON, of Liverpool
b. 1819, d. 1890

Son of Archibald MacBride of Campbelltown, Argyll, he was trained under William Spence (q.v.), and went to London about 1841. In 1844 he exhibited a group entitled "Margaret of Anjou and Her Son" at Westminster Hall. The *Literary Gazette* considered Margaret "a virago" and her son "a poor attenuated, impudent lad," but Samuel Joseph (q.v.) was so impressed by the work that he took the sculptor into his studio as a pupil without charging his usual fee of five hundred guineas.

MacBride later became Joseph's chief assistant, but returned to Liverpool about 1852, where he became an enthusiastic supporter of the Pre-Raphaelite School. As Secretary of the Liverpool Academy, he was instrumental in awarding the annual prize of fifty guineas on two occasions to Holman Hunt and Millais.

MacBride's works included a statue of Dr. Adam Clarke for Portrush; statues of "The Four Seasons" for Sir John Gerrard; and busts of Philip Bailey (now Scottish National Portrait Gallery); Sir William Brown; Michael Whitby; Field-Marshal Lord Combermere; Dr. Raffles, for Great George Street Chapel, Liverpool; John Laird (1863), for Birkenhead Hospital; Colonel Peter Thomson; Sir A. B. Walker; and John Miller. He also carved the tablet in memory of Dr. Stevenson, 1854, in St. Mary's Church, Birkenhead. His last work was a statuette of H. M. Stanley, replicas of which were made by Messrs. Minton of Stoke-on-Trent.

MacBride exhibited at the Royal Academy, 1848–1853, and at the Liverpool Academy showed busts of C. M. Seddon in 1835, and the Rev. John Parke two years later. Models of his "Lady Godiva" were awarded by the Liverpool Art Union as one of their prizes in 1850. He died on 10 April, 1890. (*Liverpool Daily Post*, 11 April, 1890).

MACCARTHY, JOHN JAMES ALEXANDER
b. 1776

In 1851 when he applied to the A.G.B.I. for assistance he gave the following account of himself.

In 1805 he held a lieutenancy in the 1st Royal Regiment "expecting to prosecute the Army as a profession, but an increase of twins to the family" just as he was embarking for Cadiz induced his Colonel, the Duke of Kent, to send for him to Kensington Palace. Here in the course of conversation the Duke discovered MacCarthy's flair for art, and advised him to abandon the Army and turn to sculpture and painting. MacCarthy, according to his own account, painted pictures of the patron and George III and "modelled many subjects from the marbles at Christ Church College." John had a large family, most of whom were artists.

One son was Sexon John James MacCarthy (b. 1807), who carved a model of William IV's horse "Beauty," and whose wife exhibited at the Royal Academy, 1853–1858.

Two of John's daughters, the Misses Amelia and Gertrude MacCarthy, exhibited at the Royal Academy, 1838–1843, showing busts, etc.

MACCARTHY, HAMILTON and CARLTON, or CARLETON
Hamilton MacCarthy: b. 1809
Carlton MacCarthy: b. 1817

Sons of John James Alexander MacCarthy (q.v.), the brothers collaborated in executing a good deal of their work, for example their "St. George and the Dragon," exhibited at Westminster Hall in 1844. This the *Art Union* considered "on the whole a most spirited work" which exhibited "many of the finest points of sculpture," while the *Literary Gazette* described it as "a bold equestrian group and deserving of much praise."

The MacCarthys produced a great many models of horses and other animals; indeed, their address is given as Tattersalls in 1846. They appear to have been very successful at modelling racehorses and were employed by various owners, including Colonel Copeland, Lord William Beresford, Lady Dallas and Count Bathiany.

They exhibited at the Manchester Institution in 1846 "A Red Deer," "A Horse in a Lassoo" and "A Figure of Charles XII," while for the Great Exhibition of 1851 they produced an inkstand embodying figures of animals, "the base on which the stag stands" being "ingeniously designed as an envelope-box."

Hamilton MacCarthy exhibited independent work at the Royal Academy and British Institution, 1838–1867, while Carlton continued to show work until 1869. The former produced a number of busts towards the end of his life, including those of Mrs. Capron (1851), Mrs. Rae (1864) and Rev. Edward Irving (1867). His wife exhibited at the Royal Academy in 1857, while their son, Hamilton P. MacCarthy, was also a sculptor who modelled a number of busts, including those of Lord Derby (1871) and Wellington (1872) for the Merchant Taylors Company. He did not, however, begin to exhibit until after 1851, so his work is outside the scope of this book.

MACCARTHY, S.

He exhibited a small bust of the Duke of Wellington at the Royal Academy in 1839.

MACDONALD, LAWRENCE
b. 1799, *d.* 1878

He was born at Gask in Perthshire, on 15 February, 1799, and began to carve in stone at an early age while serving his apprenticeship to a local mason named Thomas Gibson. Macdonald's first recorded work, a statue of a boy supporting a vase on his head, dates from this period and is now in the garden at Moncreiffe, in Perthshire.

In 1822 he went to Edinburgh, where he entered the Trustees' Academy and later in the same year went to study in Rome, becoming one of the founders of the British Academy of Arts in that city. Four years later he returned to Edinburgh where he showed classical groups, a figure of "The Youthful Slinger," and a number of busts, including one of Charles Kemble. The *Literary Gazette* (1831, page 187) which described it as "as fine and energetic a head as ever was modelled," also considered that "Mr. Macdonald is one of the most distinguished ornaments of the British School of Sculpture." The year after this criticism was written the sculptor was back in Rome and here he remained almost continuously until his death on 4 March, 1878.

He was one of the most popular portrait-sculptors of his day. Indeed, a correspondent, writing to the *Art Journal* from Rome in 1851, describes his studio as "the peerage done into marble, a plaster galaxy of rank and fashion, row after row in room after room of noble and illustrious persons appear. All who ever figured in the Court Journal are here, looking as classical as drapery and hair-dressing can make them. Yet a patent family likeness pervades them all, a universal type reminding me of a bad dinner tasting as if every dish had been cooked in the same pot, insipid and unappetising, very." This criticism of Macdonald's work is not unfair, for though his earlier busts of women are made to look charming by the style of hairdressing fashionable at that time, he so consistently flattered his sitters that they all appear too noble, too handsome and too distinguished to be true. His most successful statue is that of the Countess of Winchelsea, in Eastwell Church, Kent, which shows the lady reclining, like Madame Recamier, on a day-bed. The work is graceful and charming and, though not carved until 1850, has all the distinction and elegance of the Regency.

Macdonald exhibited at the Royal Academy, 1828–1857, at the British Institution, 1832, at the Scottish Academy, 1827–1865, and at the Great Exhibition of 1851. At the Exhibition of Art Treasures of the United Kingdom held in Manchester in 1857 Lord Ward showed three of the sculptor's works in his possession, namely "A Bacchante," "Eurydice" and "Arethusa," while the Hon. A. D. Willoughby contributed another entitled "Venus."

(*D.N.B.; Art Journal*, 1851, page 351; Frederick Moncreiffe's *The Moncreiffes*, Vol. II, page 494.)

STATUES

1830	Girl with a Carrier Pigeon	Russell-Cotes Museum Bournemouth
1831	Ajax	Powerscourt, Ireland
1832	A Bacchante	Formerly possession of Charles Jenner
1832	Penelope	Exhibited Royal Academy
c. 1840	Elizabeth, Viscountess Powerscourt	Powerscourt, Ireland
1848	Andromeda Chained	For Earl of Aberdeen
1849	Eurydice	Powerscourt, Ireland
1849	Bacchante Weaving Her Hair	For Lord Ward
1850	Ulysses	For Earl of Kilmorey
1850	Andromeda	For Marquess of Abercorn
1852	Hyacinthus	Windsor Castle
1854	Venus	For Hon. A. D. Willoughby
1877	Young Fisherman	For Earl Fitzwilliam

BUSTS

1827	J. Gillespie Graham	Exhibited Royal Academy
1827	Duke of Atholl	Blair Atholl
1829	Robert Phillips	Exhibited Manchester Academy
1832	Earl of Errol	Exhibited Royal Academy
1837	Psyche	For George Dundas
1838	Viscountess Canning	Highcliffe Castle
1838	Marchioness of Waterford	Highcliffe Castle
1839	Lord Alexander Russell	Woburn Abbey
1839	Lady Ebury	Apsley House

1839	Lady James	Betteshanger House, Kent
1840	Lord Charles Montagu	Kimbolton Castle
1843	Sir Henry Taylor	National Portrait Gallery
1843	Lord Compton	Castle Ashby
1846	Duke of Cambridge	Windsor Castle
1848	Hon. Mrs. Sidney Herbert	Wilton House
1848	Viscountess Milton	Formerly Wentworth Woodhouse
1848	Miss Waterton	Walton Hall, Yorks
1849	Flora	Osborne
1853	Duke of Northumberland	Exhibited Royal Academy
1854	Earl Stanhope	Chevening, Kent
1861	Mrs. Watt	Bethnal Green Museum
1863	Watts Russell	Ilam Church, Staffs.
n.d.	Earl Stanhope	Chevening, Kent
n.d.	George Combe	National Portrait Gallery, Edinburgh

MACDONELL, FRANCIS
fl. 1843–1852

A deaf-and-dumb artist, he studied at the Royal Dublin Society's School, and exhibited at the Royal Academy, 1846–1852.

MACDOWELL, PATRICK, R.A.
b. 1799, *d.* 1870

He was born in Belfast on 12 August, 1799, and while still young lost his father, who died leaving very little money. In 1807 MacDowell was sent to a school kept by an engraver named Gordon, but four years later accompanied his mother to England where she had relations. They settled in Hampshire, and in 1813 the boy was apprenticed to a London coach-maker, but did not serve his full term as his master went bankrupt in 1817.

At that time MacDowell was lodging at the house of the sculptor P. Chenu (q.v.) and it was probably for this reason that he began to take an interest in modelling. His small figure of "Venus Holding a Mirror" so delighted Chenu that he purchased it, and by 1822 MacDowell was so advanced in his studies that he had a bust accepted for exhibition by the Royal Academy.

It was not until 1830, however, that he began, on the recommendation of John Constable, R.A., to attend the Academy Schools, but, once there, he made such rapid progress that only two years later he had a well-merited and secure reputation as a sculptor. One of his first patrons was Mr. T. W. Beaumont, at whose expense he went to study in Rome for eight months. He was also assisted by Sir Francis Chantrey (q.v.) and by Sir James Tennent, executing portrait-busts of the latter and of his wife.

MacDowell exhibited his "Girl at Prayer" at Westminster Hall in 1844. A replica of this work, which the *Literary Gazette* had described as "touching, simple and beautiful," is at Brynkinalt, Denbigh. Two years later he became a Royal Academician, having been elected an Associate as early as 1831. He exhibited at the Academy, 1822–1870, and at the Great Exhibition of 1851 showed a figure of "Early Sorrow." This apparently made a deep impression on H. Weekes (q.v.), for in his *Treatise on the Fine Art in the Great Exhibition* (page 65), he wrote: "MacDowell is an artist that England may well be proud of. He makes his appeal to our best and noblest feelings and while he continues to strike the chord of these, his reputation is safe."

J. M. Graham, however, does not rate the sculptor's talents nearly so highly, for in *British Literature and Art* he declares that "without any very elevated sentiment or feeling, MacDowell's works in poetic sculpture were mostly devoted to the representation of the female form. They were not equal to the masterpieces of Baily or Wyatt, but sufficiently attractive to the popular eye."

MacDowell signs two monuments; those to Catherine Spurway, 1845, at Milverton, Somerset, and to the Marchioness of Donegal, 1855, in the Castle Chapel at Belfast. In 1857 two owners lent works by him to the Exhibition of Art Treasures held in Manchester, Mr. G. W. Beaumont sending "Prayer" and "Virginius," and Mr. S. Ashton "The Summer Reverie" and "The Student."

MacDowell died in London on 9 December, 1870. On 7 July, 1877, his "Eve" was sold by an anonymous owner at Christie's for £189, while on 26 April, two years later, his "Daydream" went for £178 at the Joseph Arden sale. This later work appeared again at the Charles Seeley sale of 9 May, 1886, where it only fetched one hundred guineas (Archives, Messrs. Christie).

(*D.N.B.*; Strickland's *Dictionary of Irish Artists; Art Journal*, 1850, page 8; *ibid.*, 1871, page 41.)

STATUES

1827	Love of the Angels	For George Davidson of Belfast
1834	Procris and Cephalus	Markree Castle, Sligo
1838	A Girl Reading	For ◦Lord Ellesmere (replica at Brynkinalt, Denbigh)
1841	Girl Going to Bathe	For T. Wentworth Beaumont
1844	Love Triumphant	For T. Wentworth Beaumont
1846	A Nymph	Diploma Gallery, Royal Academy
1846	Lord Exmouth	Maritime Museum, Greenwich

1850	Earl of Warren	House of Lords
1850	Almeric	House of Lords
1850	Virginius and his Daughter	Great Exhibition
1851	Eve	Bethnal Green Museum
1851	Turner	St. Paul's Cathedral
1853	Day-dreams	Ny Carlsberg Glyptotek, Copenhagen
1855	Earl of Belfast	Free Library, Belfast
1856	The First Thorn	For Thomas Baring
1857	William Pitt	Palace of Westminster
1857	Earl of Chatham	Palace of Westminster
1858	Viscount Fitzgibbon	For Limerick (destroyed)
1858	Sir William Brown	St. George's Hall, Liverpool
1863	Lord Plunket	For Four Courts, Dublin
1866	Earl of Eglinton	For St. Stephen's Green, Dublin
1869	Leibnitz, Cuvier and Linnaeus	Civil Service Commission Buildings, Burlington Gardens
1870	Leah	Mansion House
1871	Europe	Albert Memorial

BUSTS

1826	Thomas Campbell	Exhibited Royal Academy
1833	J. Sheridan Knowles	Exhibited Royal Academy
1834	Robert Hall	Barking Parish Church
1835	G. Cartwright	Exhibited Royal Academy
1844	Sir James Carnac	Exhibited Royal Academy
1844	Lord Ashburton	Sold Christies, 5 December, 1950
1855	Lord Beaumont	Exhibited Royal Academy
1855	Earl of Belfast	St. Giles', Dorset
1856	Thomas Cubitt	Denbies, Dorking
1858	Lord Dufferin	Exhibited Royal Academy
1865	Sir Joshua Jebb	Bethnal Green Museum
1870	Mr. and Mrs. Perrott	Bethnal Green Museum

MACE, FREDERICK, of London
b. 1802

He attended the Royal Academy Schools in 1818 and exhibited at the Academy, 1820–1840, showing busts and a bas-relief executed for the library of the Duke of Leeds. In 1820 he was awarded the Silver Isis from the Society of Arts and a year later received their large Silver Medal for a "Bacchanalian Figure."

Mace signs monuments to the Rev. Thomas Chute, 1827, at South Pickenham, Norfolk, and to Thomas Keeton, 1840, in St. Thomas's Church, Bermondsey.

MACKENZIE, ALEXANDER, of London
fl. 1777–1790

He exhibited wax portraits at the Royal Academy, 1777–1790, and at the Free Society in 1782 and 1783. In 1789 he showed a "Bust of a Nobleman."

MAGNUS, —, of London
He signs a tablet to Henry Bunbury, 1811, at Great Barton, Suffolk.

MAINE, or MAYNE, JONATHAN
fl. 1680–1709

From 1696–1709 he was extensively employed at St. Paul's Cathedral, working both in wood and stone, and was paid £5 "for carving the capital of a composite Pilaster in Free Stone for the Inside of the Dome" and £13 for "carving the Bishops Coat of arms and Mitre with Mantling and other Ornaments under a window on the Outside of the Consistory" (Wren Society, Vol. XV, page 72). In 1706 he received £54 for "8 round Composite Capitals" and £48 for "two large Shields with Cherubims Heads and Drapery." For the four vases on the pediment he was allowed £6 (op. cit., page 138). For the interior of the Cathedral he was in 1703 responsible for 346 ft. of carved stone cornice above the Whispering Gallery, and two years later 631 ft. of "freeze" under the windows. (Op. cit., pages 99 and 129).

Maine was employed at a number of City churches and carved the font for St. Clement's, Eastcheap. He also worked at Eton and Christ's Hospital.

(Wren Society; Malcolm's *Londinium Redivivum*, Vol. III.)

MAINWARING, DANIEL, of Carmarthen
fl. 1809–1831

The monument at Rudbaxton, Pembroke, commemorating Sir Thomas Picton who fell at Waterloo in 1815, is by Mainwaring, as is also the one to the same General erected at Carmarthen 1826–1827. This "in its general design, particularly the shaft and entablature, resembles Trajan's Pillar in Rome," according to the *Gentleman's Magazine* (1828, Part II, page 265).

Mainwaring's work is above the usual provincial average, his monument to Admiral Laugharne, 1819, at Laugharne, Carmarthen, having delightful "Adam" details. He signs others to Thomas Jones, 1810, and Sir James Williams, 1829, both in Carmarthen Parish Church, and to the Rev. Charles Bowen, 1820, at Kidwelly in the same county.

His son John, who succeeded him in the business, signs a tablet to Henry Laurence, 1834, also in Carmarthen Parish Church.

MALCOT, or MALCOTT, JOHN, the Elder
d. 1766

He was described as the son of "William Mallcott, deceased of St. James's Westminster, carpenter" when in 1730 he was apprenticed to Robert Taylor the Elder (q.v.). He became free seven years later, but seems to have remained with his master as an assistant, and later worked under the latter's son, Sir Robert Taylor (Archives, Masons' Company).

Malcot was mason to the Royal College of Physicians in Warwick Lane from 1743 until 1766, the year of his death (Archives, Royal College of Physicians). In 1765 he was elected Renter Warden of the Masons' Company, but had to decline the post owing to ill-health.

Malcot's son, another John, was apprenticed to him in 1757, and in 1765 was admitted to the freedom of the Masons' Company by service with his father. In the following year he took the latter's place as mason to the Royal College of Physicians.

MALCOTT, or MALCOT, JOHN, the Younger
b. c. 1777

Son of the second John Malcot, and grandson of John Malcot the Elder (q.v.), he was apprenticed to Samuel Ireland in 1792 and became free in 1799.

He followed the family tradition by being appointed mason to the Royal College of Physicians, and was also the principal mason for building the National Gallery and the new Post Office. For the latter he carved 160 ft. of "egg and tongue, highly relieved on Grecian moulding," and also 147 ft. of "antique Grecian leaf and dart, high relieved," receiving a total of £203 for the work. In 1802 he and "E. Malcott" (presumably a brother) were appointed masons to the Ironmongers' Company. Malcott also worked at Stationers' Hall in 1820 and at St. Bartholomew's Hospital in 1835. His son, John Rowles Malcott, was apprenticed to him in 1823.

After the dismissal of Burnell (q.v.) in 1841, the Malcotts took his place as masons for the restora-

tion of the Temple Church. The firm was still in existence in 1862, for in that year they sign a tablet in that church to the memory of Allen Laing. In 1851 they made the font for St. James's, Clerkenwell. The *Builder* of 1845 (page 78) refers to the elder Malcott as a "practical mason who has been engaged for fifty years repairing old Churches and raising new buildings." As a contractor he built houses in Chelsea in 1804 (Middlesex building affidavits).

Malcott's monuments and tablets are mostly dull, although the best of them, to Sir Wharton Amcotts, 1807, at East Retford, Notts, is really rather a charming work. The tablet to William Hawes, 1811, in Islington Parish Church is illustrated in the *Gentleman's Magazine* of 1811 (Part I, page 313), which describes the sculptor as "an ingenious young artist." The same magazine (1821, page 505) also shows Malcott's tablet to Dr. Wells, formerly in St. Bride's, Fleet Street.

Other monuments and tablets by the same sculptor include those to Edward Pryce, 1807, in St. Stephen's, Walbrook; Clement Kynnersley, 1815, at Cheam, Surrey; Catherine Langstaff, 1820, in St. Martin's, Ludgate; James Carr, 1821, at Cheshunt, Herts; Benjamin Hawes, 1822, and Philip Green, 1823, both in St. Magnus-the-Martyr; Margaret Donovan, 1826, at Crowhurst, Surrey; Thomas Dalton, 1827, at Milton-by-Gravesend, Kent; Nathaniel Proctor, 1831, at Rye, Sussex; and Sarah Raven, 1837, in Streatham Parish Church.

(Archives of Companies, etc., cited in text.)

MAN, EDWARD

According to Streatfeild's *Hundred of Blackheath* (page 68), Man made in 1752 the very fine stone globes on the gate-piers at Greenwich Palace.

MANNING, CHARLES
b. 1776, *d.* 1812

Brother of Samuel Manning the Elder (q.v.), he attended the Royal Academy Schools in 1794, gaining a Silver Medal three years later. From 1801 until his death in 1812 he exhibited a number of busts at the Academy, including those of Dr. Jenner and J. Bacon the Younger (q.v.).

Charles Manning was responsible for the national monument in St. Paul's to Captain George Hardinge, 1808. This has been falsely attributed by some writers to his more prolific brother Samuel; it is by no means a masterpiece, but is nevertheless a far better work than that sculptor ever produced. Charles also signs the monument erected in the Cathedral in 1810 to the memory of Major-General Mackenzie and Brigadier-General

Langwerth, both of whom had fallen at Talavera in the previous year.

(Royal Academy Archives.)

MANNING, JOHN, the Elder
d. 1747

There were a good many masons and statuaries named Manning, all of whom appear to have been related to one another in various degrees. The two earliest members of this family whom I have been able to trace are Bryan and Christopher Manning, the former one of the chief masons for the additions to Whitehall Palace, 1685–1687, the latter carving the stone pinnacles for the south end of Westminster Hall in 1681. A William Manning, son of John Manning of Ketton, Rutland, mason, was apprenticed to John Young in 1683.

John Manning the Elder was best known as a maker of lead figures, although his obituary in the *Gentleman's Magazine* of 1747 (page 545) refers to him as "an ingenious statuary near Hyde Park Corner" (96, Piccadilly now stands on the site of his yard). In 1720 he made for Capt. Gough of Gough Park, Mx., lead statues of "Neptune" "Mercury" and "Fame," also "Two Boars" and "Two Vases." (Lawrence Weaver: English Leadwork, page 194.)

His son, John Manning the Younger, worked as a mason and stone-carver at St. Bartholomew's Hospital from 1752 until 1758. He also subscribed to the *Vitruvius Britannicus* in 1767.

MANNING, JOSHUA
b. 1810

He was the son of Samuel Manning the Elder (q.v.) and attended the Royal Academy Schools in 1830, having been recommended by J. Ward, R.A.

In the same year he received the Gold Isis Medal from the Society of Arts for an original model of a group. He exhibited at the Academy two years later, but all trace of him is lost after that date. Son of John Manning of Newman Street (1753-1845).

MANNING, SAMUEL, the Elder
b. 1788, *d.* 1842

He studied under J. Bacon the Younger (q.v.) and later became his partner.

Manning exhibited at the Royal Academy, 1806–1843, showing busts of Colonel Addenbrooke (1819), Princess Charlotte (1820), John Wesley (1825), Miss Hunter (1839), and the Rev. Charles Manning (1843). His bust of the Rev. Isaac Saunders (1838) was made for Blackfriars Church.

All Manning's monumental work, whether signed by himself alone or with Bacon (see under "Bacon and Manning"), is dull and uninspired and specimens of it are only too prevalent in England, for he had a very large practice. Monuments and tablets by him include those to Thomas Davies, 1818, in St. Mary's, Madras; Sir Jacob Astley, 1818, Melton Constable, Norfolk; John Addenbrooke, 1821, at Esher, Surrey; Sir John Prideaux, 1826, at Farway, Devon; Samuel Twyford, 1826, at Trotton, Sussex; the Rev. William Vivian, 1830, at Bushey, Herts; Octavia Harvey, 1833, at Gillingham, Kent; John Wilson, 1835, at Southborough, Kent; Samuel Smith, 1835, at Watton, Herts; the Rev. Isaac Saunders, 1836, in St. Andrew-by-the-Wardrobe; Robert Field, 1836, in the Chapel of Sidney Sussex College, Cambridge; Lancelot Haslope, 1838, in the Wesley Chapel, City Road; and George Tyrwhitt Drake, 1840, at Amersham, Bucks.

His best monument (with Bacon) is to Charles Grant, 1823, in St. George's, Bloomsbury, which was erected by the East India Company and shows the dying man supported by Faith.

MANNING, SAMUEL, the Younger
b. 1816, *d.* 1865

He was the son of Samuel Manning the Elder (q.v.) and was trained in the studio of John Bacon the Younger (q.v.), his father's partner. In 1831 he won a large Silver Medal from the Society of Arts for a model of a bust, and three years later was awarded the Gold Medal for his figure of "Prometheus Chained."

This work was acclaimed as a magnificent achievement by the critics, but their prophecy of a brilliant future for the sculptor was not fulfilled, for he never again produced anything so fine. In 1847 the *Art Union* remarked that "so fair a promise of future excellence affords matter for surprise that such a work should not have been followed by others of equal merit," but relented slightly by adding "that hopes are not always realized is more a default on the side of patrons than on that of artists." In 1851 "Prometheus Chained" was shown at the Great Exhibition.

Manning married on 13 August, 1846, at Marylebone, Honoria, daughter of Captain James William, of Stoke Damerel, Devon. He exhibited at the Royal Academy, 1831–1858, showing busts of John Manning (1845), John Bacon (1846), Samuel Manning (1847), Thomas Hawkins (1849), the Rev. John Wesley (1851), Samuel Rogers (1852), Lord Bloomfield (1853), and Dr. Hastings (1857).

His statue of Wesley, dated 1849, was executed or the Theological Institute at Richmond, Surrey, and his bust of the Rev. Charles Simeon is in the University Library at Cambridge.

Manning signs monuments to Francis Ede, 1849, at Sawbridgeworth, Herts; Edward Weller, 1850, at Amersham, Bucks; Sir John Edwards, Machynlleth, Wales; Sir Felix Booth, 1850, at Catsworth, Hunts; Sophia and Ellen Metcalfe, 1858, at Hawstead, Suffolk; Frances Thornton, 1862, at Blunham, Beds; and Elizabeth Trecothick, 1860, at Addington, Surrey. The memorial dated 1860 to the Officers and Men of the Shropshire Regiment in St. Chad's Church, Shrewsbury, is also his work.

MAPLETOFT, RICHARD,
of London
fl. 1699–1702

Described as a "stonecutter." He was paid £398 for work when Winslow Hall, Bucks, was built by Sir Christopher Wren for Mr. William Lowdnes (*Wren Society*, Vol. XVII, page 55).

MARCELLI, GIUSEPPE,
of Rome

In the Parish Church of Wotton-under Edge, Gloucestershire, is a monument with a lovely life-size figure of a youth, who leans on an urn and carries a down-turned torch in his hand. This commemorates William Taswell, 1775, and is signed "Giuseppe Marcelli, Scultore Romano." Local tradition insists that the monument was captured in a French ship by Mr. Taswell himself, who brought it home in triumph and kept it in readiness to be set up in the church after his death. A more probable and less romantic version of the story is that the figure was ordered direct from the sculptor by Mr. Taswell or his heir.

MARCHANT, NATHANIEL, R.A.
b. 1739, *d.* 1816

Marchant, who was born in Sussex and studied under Edward Burch (q.v.), is chiefly remembered as an engraver of gems and cameos. His work in this capacity is, of course, outside the scope of this book, but he did produce a few models in wax as well, though I have so far been unable to trace them.

He was held in high esteem during his lifetime and held various appointments, including those of assistant engraver to the Mint, gem sculptor to the Prince of Wales and the Duke of Gloucester, engraver to the King, and chief engraver of stamps. He became an Associate of the Royal Academy in 1791, and a full member in 1809. He exhibited at the Academy, 1781–1811, showing a large number of gems, cameos, intaglios, etc., and also busts of "Andromache" and Lord Downe in 1791 and 1810 respectively, and a model in wax of "A Nymph" in 1792.

Marchant also exhibited at the Society of Artists, 1765–1774, and was a member of the Academies of Venice and Stockholm. He died in Somerset Place, London, on 24 March, 1816, leaving to the Royal Academy three plaster busts, which he particularly requested in his will should "not be painted over with any colour but be suffered to remain as they are now." The diploma awarded to him by the Academy of Vienna in 1796 is now at Burlington House.

He was buried at Stoke Poges, where the tablet to his memory, carved by his executor, J. Flaxman (q.v.), stated that "his skill and industry as a Gem Engraver had supplied the place of patronage by enabling him to remove to Italy and cultivate an art to which his genius strongly inclined him." The epitaph also stated that the sculptor was buried at Stoke Poges owing to his friendship with Mr. John Penn, "the owner of the adjoining Mansion House." Marchant left £24,000 at his death.

(Lipscombe *History of Buckingham*, Vol. IV, page 565; Farrington's Diary, Vol. VIII, pages 62 and 118 and Royal Academy Archives.)

MARES, HENRY
b. 1813

In 1831 he joined the Royal Academy Schools on the recommendation of C. H. Smith (q.v.), and exhibited sculpture and pictures at the Academy, 1839–1851. His figure described as "part of a monument erected in the artist's ground at Kensal Green" was shown in 1840.

Four years later Mares exhibited at Westminster Hall a group entitled "Charles I Parting With His Children," the modelling of which the *Art Union* considered "extremely careless and coarse." The *Literary Gazette* went further when it remarked that the work was "perhaps the most curious sculpture ever perpetrated, the thin monarch with his quaint countenance and the young lady who seems to be intimating by a wink that it is not real but fun, are thoroughly grotesque."

The sculptor also signs the monument to the Rev. John Marshall, 1847, in Huddersfield Parish Church, Yorkshire.

MARMAN, JOHN, of Guildford

A Guildford statuary, he was paid £27 14s. in 1760 for the monument of James More Molyneux, which was erected in the north aisle of Haslemere Church, Surrey (Loseley Archives 1087/1796).

There was also a "Henry Marman" who was employed on marble chimney-pieces at Loseley House in 1782.

MARS, W., of Yarm

He signs a large Hellenic monument to Mary Langley, 1835, at Greatham, Durham.

MARSH, —, of Bristol and Ross

The fine monument erected in 1776 to the "Man of Ross," John Kyrle, in the Parish Church, is signed "Marsh of Ross." It is executed in coloured marbles with a medallion portrait, and is so good that it gives the impression of being London, rather than local, work.

MARSH, T., of London

fl. 1820–1842

His memorials, though pleasant, are not very distinguished. The best are to Barbara Murphy, 1822, in Paddington Parish Church, which takes the form of an amphora set in a niche, and to Hannah Allcroft, 1830, in St. Peter's, Worcester, which has the figure of a mourning woman.

Marsh also signs monuments to Brampton Dillingham, 1820, at Cranworth, Norfolk ; James Wildman, 1827, at Much Hadham, Herts; John Cope, 1825, in St. Paul's, Birmingham; Jacob Bosanquet, 1828, at Broxbourne, Herts; William Vawdrey, 1838, at Gwinear, Cornwall; the Browne family, 1840, at Esher, Surrey; Captain William Tucker, 1842, at East Wickham, Kent; and Rebecca Cotton, 1844, at Adderbury, Oxon.

MARSHALL and GRAY, of London

The firm, whose studio was in Mortimer Street, signs a large wall-tablet to John Manning, 1804, in St. Stephen's, Norwich. The design takes the form of a semi-urn (the handles formed of writhing snakes) set against a pyramid.

MARSHALL, EDWARD

b. 1598, *d.* 1675

Marshall, who worked under Nicholas Stone, became free of the Masons' Company in 1626 and of the Livery in 1631–1632. His yard was in Fetter Lane, and he was not only twice Master of the Masons' Company but was also appointed Master-Mason to the Crown in 1660.

He died on 10 December, 1675, and was buried at St. Dunstan's-in-the-West, where his epitaph stated that he had had fourteen children "whereof Joshua the eldest only survived him." "He was loyal to his King," the inscription continues, "useful in his Parish, charitable to the poor while he was living and left several memorials of it at his death."

Marshall's monuments are of the first importance, the finest perhaps being the noble recumbent effigy of Lady Culpeper, 1638, at Hollingbourne, Kent. He also engraved memorial brasses, and signs a magnificent one with portraits of Sir Edward and Lady Filmer, 1638, at East Sutton in the same county. In 1656 he was working at the Vyne, Hampshire; here he built the portico to the garden front of the house, being paid £13 for carving the capitals of the pillars and £11 for those of the pilasters. For the interior of the house he made two chimney-pieces of white marble and six of Portland stone (£101) and another of "Italian raunce" (£20). For the coat of arms above the portico Marshall received £3. (Archives, Sir Charles Chute.)

By his wife, Anne, who died in 1673, he had nine sons and five daughters, all of whom died before him except Joshua (q.v.). In 1659 Marshall advertised that his house at Barn Elms, Surrey, with "its pleasant walks by the Thames side" and "its spring water brought to the house in leaden pipes" was to let.

MONUMENTS

1618	Windsor (Parish Church)	Richard Braham
1628	Derby (All Saints')	William, Earl of Devonshire
1629	Stratford-on-Avon, Warwick	Earl of Totnes
1631	Swavesey, Cambs	Anne, Lady Cutts
1631	Westminster Abbey	Michael Drayton
1635	Spixworth, Norfolk	William and Alicia Peck
1637	Canterbury (St. Mary Magdalen)	Henry Saunders
1638	Amersham, Bucks	Henry Curwen
1639	Walkeringham, Notts	Francis Williamson
1641	Ightham, Kent	Dame Dorothy Selby
1644	Tottenham (Parish Church)	Sir Robert and Lady Barkham
1651	Withington, Glos	Howe Family
1655	Conington, Cambs	Sir Robert Cotton
1657	Silston, Herts	Bridget Gore
1658	Sotterly, Suffolk	Thomas Playters
1659	Dickleburgh, Norfolk	Lady Playters
1666	Windsor (Parish Church)	Mrs. Pagett

MARSHALL, JOSHUA

b. 1629, *d.* 1678

Marshall, who was the eldest son of Edward Marshall (q.v.), was Warden of the Masons' Company in 1666 and Master in 1670. He also succeeded to his father's appointment of Master-

Mason to the Crown, and in this capacity carried out a great deal of work at the Royal Palaces.

Between 1664 and 1667 he made a number of chimney-pieces for Whitehall, including one of stone "wrought after the Italian fashion" for the Duke of York's closet, and one of "white and Egyptian marble for Mad. Steward's (*sic*) lodging" (British Museum, Harleian 1618). Other chimney-pieces supplied for the Palace were two for the Duke of Monmouth's bedchamber and closet, one of Egyptian marble for the Queen's new closet (P.R.O., Works 5/6), one of white marble costing £17 5s. for the Countess of Castlemaine's lodging (P.R.O., Works 5/10), and one for Miss Howard's lodging at fifteen guineas (P.R.O., Works 5/9). Also in the Public Record Office in his contract for £16, dated 1668, for a chimney-piece for the same building (Works 5/145). This was to be "of clean white marble for the Queen's little bedchamber, 3 ft. 10 ins. wide and 3 ft. 4 ins. high in the clear, the marble 9 ins. in breadth and 6 ins. in thickness, according to the moulds given."

He also worked at Whitehall as a mason, receiving £465 for "ye front next ye Thames" in 1666 (P.R.O., Works 5/7), while between 1666 and 1667 he was employed at Greenwich Palace. Here he carved capitals (at £18 each) and pilasters for the north side, and made a white-marble chimney-piece costing £33 (P.R.O., E.331/3438). When working at the Customs House in 1671 he also carved a black-marble chimney-piece for the Council Chamber (P.R.O., A.O.1/2492).

Marshall received £1,500 as master-mason for the Monument (P.R.O., E.101/475/2) and also rebuilt, or helped to rebuild, several of the City churches after the Great Fire, among them being St. Mary, Aldermanbury; St. Stephen, Coleman Street; St. Peter, Cornhill; and St. Mary-at-Hill. For the tower of St. Clement Danes he was paid £2,525 (Westminster Public Library, MS. B.13/A. 47), while at St. Bride's, Fleet Street, his work included ten cherubim-heads and twelve shields. He was also employed at St. Swithun's, but died before the building was finished and the payments were made to his widow and executors, Henry Phillips and John Oliver (Bodleian, Rawlinson MSS., B.387). On 27 August, 1667, Joshua Marshall sent in an estimate for £592 10s. for repairs to Rochester Cathedral (Cathedral Archives, D. 236).

In 1675 he made the pedestal for the statue of Charles I at Charing Cross. The total cost of this was £230, which included £40 for "the two shields, arms and trophies" (P.R.O., Works 5/145).

Marshall died on 6 April, 1678, leaving a widow, Catherine, daughter of John George, and two children, Ann and Edward, the only survivors of their family of five. He was buried in St. Dunstan's-in-the-West, and in his will left £200 to the Masons' Company, the interest on which they were to use to provide pensions for needy widows of their members.

Marshall was one of the greatest statuaries of the seventeenth century, his finest work being the great monument to Lord and Lady Noel, 1664, at Chipping Campden, Gloucestershire. The design of macabre swathed figures in grave-clothes revealed by the open doors of the tomb is repeated in a very similar, though unsigned, monument to Sir Geoffrey and Lady Palmer, 1673, at East Carlton, Northamptonshire.

Sir John Cullum, writing in 1774 to Gough the antiquary, says of Marshall's signed monument to Richard Brownlow, 1638, at Belton, Lincolnshire, that "the bust is most excellently done: there is great life in the countenance, and the hands as well as the drapery are finely executed: in short it would be no discredit to any of our most modern artists" (Nichols's *Literary Anecdotes*, Vol. VIII, page 674). The monument to Sir William Thorold, 1649, formerly in St. Giles-in-the-Fields, was also signed by Marshall (*Miscellanea Genealogica et Heraldica*, Third Series, Vol. V, page 300), while in the same church still remains, though much mutilated, another commemorating Lady Frances Kniveton and Lady Anne Holbourne, 1663. This is mentioned in the latter's will, where she records that she has "agreed with one Mr. Marshall a stone-cutter in Shoe Lane" to execute it for £120, and that her own effigy, like that of Lady Frances, was to be shown in a winding-sheet. In the Vestry Minutes of St. Dunstan's-in-the-East is a note made in 1671 that the Churchwardens are to pay Marshall for the monument "made by him in commemoration of the Lady Dame Dyonis Williamson and her predecessors and to get the same as cheap as they can" (Wren Society, Vol. XIX, page 18).

In 1676 in the archives of Cleave's Almshouses, Kingston, Surrey, is a note of the payment of £8 to Marshall for a stone monument to William Cleave. There is also a further payment of 11s. for "drinke and victualls for Mr. Marshall's men att the setting upp the monument." According to Manning & Bray's *Surrey*, Vol. I, page 373, the monument was a ledger stone in Kingston Parish Church.

In 1670 Marshall also made the stone coat of arms (still in position) for the centre of the alms-houses.

Other monuments signed by Marshall include those to John Whatton, 1656, in Leicester Cathedral; Elizabeth Sherard, 1658, at North Witham

Lincolnshire; Henry Hammond, 1660, at Hampton Lovett, Worcestershire; Bishop Warner, 1666, in Rochester Cathedral; and John Turner, 1659, at Kirkleatham, Yorkshire. As Master-Mason to the Crown he also made in 1678 the monument in Westminster Abbey to Edward V and Richard, Duke of York, murdered in the Tower in 1483.

(Authorities cited in text.)

MARSHALL, T. and G., of Deptford
fl. 1790–1832

In the late eighteenth and early nineteenth centuries there was a school of minor statuaries at Deptford which included among its members Edward Pierce (q.v.) and the Marshalls.

This firm, whose earlier tablets have delightful details, signs memorials to William Board, 1790, at Lindfield, Sussex; the Rayley family, *c.* 1790, in the churchyard of Lee in Kent; Harriot Kruse, 1809, in Lewisham Parish Church; Oliver Stapleton, 1811, in Ealing Parish Church; Elizabeth Bland, 1816, in Isleworth Parish Church; Countess Winterton, 1831, at Westerham, Kent; and Stephen Groombridge, 1832, at Goudhurst, Kent.

MARSHALL, W., of London
fl. 1817–1830

Marshall signs tablets to Captain Fothergill, 1817, at St. Paul's Walden, Herts; Sir John Silvester, 1822, at Chingford, Essex; and to Dr. John Shaw, 1828, in Magdalen College Chapel, Oxford, the last-named being illustrated in the *Gentleman's Magazine* (1828, Part I, page 209).

He had yards in Westminster and Regent Street, and though he was declared a bankrupt in 1821 (*New Monthly Magazine*, 1821, page 84) continued working for some years after that date.

MARSHALL, WILLIAM CALDER, R.A.
b. 1813, *d.* 1894

He was born and educated in Edinburgh, but came to London in 1834. Here he studied under Chantrey (q.v.) and Baily (q.v.), and also joined the Royal Academy Schools, winning a Silver Medal in 1835. In the following year he went to study in Rome, but returned to England in 1839 and settled in London. In 1841 he gained a Gold Medal from Manchester for his "Bacchus and Ino," and in 1844 sent statues of Chaucer and "Eve" to Westminster Hall. The former was greatly admired by the *Literary Gazette*, which

considered that it stood "pre-eminently above any other contribution."

Marshall received a number of commissions from the *Art Union*. Models in plaster of his "Rebecca" and "The Girl With the Broken Pitcher" were awarded to their prize-winners, a reproduction of his "First Whisper of Love" was chosen by the £300 prize-winner in 1845, while the sculptor himself won a premium of £500 for his "Dancing Girl Reposing."

In 1857 Marshall won the first prize of £700 for his design for a national monument to the Duke of Wellington, but, in spite of this, only carved a series of bas-reliefs in the chapel at St. Paul's, the memorial itself being entrusted—perhaps fortunately—to Alfred Stevens.

Marshall exhibited at the Royal Academy, 1835–1891, at the British Institution, 1839–1857, and at the Royal Scottish Academy, 1836–1891. The last-named elected him an Associate in 1842, while in 1844 he became an Associate and in 1852 a full member of the Royal Academy. In 1857 he lent his "Ophelia" to the Exhibition of Art Treasures of the United Kingdom held in Manchester, while his "Sabrina" was sent by G. Moore, "Paul and Virginia" by the Earl of Ellesmere, and "Little Red Ridinghood" and "The Broken Pitcher" by F. Bennoch. The sculptor, who was nominated a Chevalier of the Legion of Honour in 1878, died in Ebury Street on 16 June, 1894.

Among other works by Marshall may be mentioned the sculpture on Bolton Town Hall, which he executed in 1870 (*Art Journal*, 1870, page 43), and he also signs a few monuments, including those to Mary Blacklock, 1852, in St. Michael's, Charleston, U.S.A.; Mrs. Adams, 1857, at Newport, Salop; and Lady John Manners, 1861, and Louisa Foljambe, 1871, at Tickhill, Yorks; the two last-named monuments both have recumbent figures.

Marshall was not a great sculptor. C. B. Scott said of him that he was "a man with some resources of a tangible Philistine sort, but with no more poetry, or fancy, or classic perceptions than a cow. One wonders how this sensible commonplace person has ever attempted to realize any ideals or to touch a modelling-tool; or how when he did attempt it, he had ever succeeded so far as he had."

(*Men of Our Times*, 1867; *D.N.B.*; *Art Journal*, 1894, page 286; various references *Art Union*, *Art Journal* and *Builder*.)

STATUES

| 1837 | Hebe | National Gallery, Edinburgh |

1847	Clarendon	Palace of Westminster
1849	Somers	Palace of Westminster
1852	Captain Coram	Foundling Hospital, Berkhamsted
1853	Sir Robert Peel	Manchester
1854	Ajax Praying for Light	Presented by Sculptor to Scottish Academy
1855	Thomas Campbell	Westminster Abbey
1858	Edward Jenner	Kensington Gardens
1859	Hume	Montrose
1862	Samuel Crompton	Bolton
1863	Sir George Grey	Cape Town
1865	7th Earl of Derby	Bolton
1868	Lady Godiva	Coventry

BUSTS

1843	Sir George Clerk	Exhibited Royal Academy
1844	Samuel Rogers	Exhibited Royal Academy
1850	Henry Beaufoy	City of London Schools
1858	Admiral Sir Hugh Pigot	Exhibited Royal Academy
1863	Dr. Thomas Alexander	For Netley Hospital
1866	Cordelia	Salford Art Gallery
1872	James Hopgood	Formerly Royal Free Hospital
1874	Sir Isaac Newton	Leicester Square

GROUPS, etc.

1838	Psyche	Arbroath
1839	Hero and Leander	For *Art Union* of London
1839	Hebe Rejected	National Gallery of Scotland
1843	The Fountain Glass	Exhibited Royal Academy
1846	The First Whisper of Love	For Sir Erskine Perry
1847	Paul and Virginia	Kelvingrove Art Gallery
1852	Infant Satyr	Diploma Gallery, Royal Academy
1855	Concordia	Paris Exhibition
1857	Imogen	Exhibited Royal Academy
1864	Agriculture	Albert Memorial
1864	Undine	Walker Art Gallery, Liverpool
1873	Ruth	Abroath
1874	The Venerable Bede	Salford Art Gallery
1880	Stepping-stones	Salford Art Gallery
1881	The Prodigal Son	Purchased Chantrey Bequest
n.d.	Self-portrait (bust)	Scottish National Portrait Gallery

MARSTON, R., of Norwich

He signs the tablet to Richard Boardman, 1785, in St. Mary Coslany, Norwich.

MARTEN, JOHN, of Tenterden
b. 1728, *d.* 1814

He executed good provincial work in a pleasantly typical eighteenth-century style, his tablets in coloured marbles having the usual semi-urn set against a pyramid with flaming lamps. He signs monuments to the Rev. Matthew Wallace, 1771, at Tenterden, Kent; to Arnold Nesbitt, 1779, at Icklesham, Sussex; and one to Thomas Holford, 1798, at Rye, in the same county.

Marten, who was married four times, is buried in Tenterden churchyard.

MARTIN, GEORGE, of Highgate
fl. 1827–1835

He signs the monument of the poet S. T. Coleridge, 1834, in Highgate Parish Church.

MARTIN, JOHN
d. 1691

He was the mason employed for rebuilding Brewers' Hall, 1669–1673 (Archives, Brewers' Company). He was buried in the graveyard of St. Mary's, Whitechapel, together with his wife, Mary (who had died in 1683), and ten of their children (Seymour's *London*, Vol. II, page 709).

MASON, JOHN
fl. 1827–1840

Mason, who lived at Twickenham, was awarded the Silver Isis Medal by the Society of Arts in 1827, and the large Silver Medal in the following year for a bust from life. He exhibited busts at the Royal Academy, 1827–1833, including those of two sons of Captain Probyn. A plaster copy of his bust of Mr. McKinsel, dated 1830, is at Brynkinalt, Denbigh.

He signs memorial tablets to Marie Espinasse, 1837, in Twickenham Parish Church, and to Elizabeth Palmer, 1838, at Sunbury, Middlesex.

MASON, JOHN, of London
fl. 1702–1726

He worked as an assistant to William Stanton (q.v.) and was later employed at various periods between 1702 and 1713 as a mason and stone-carver at Stonyhurst, Lancashire, where he was paid £1 a week (Account-books, Stonyhurst College). In 1704 he carved "a unicorn's head and a helmet" at the top of the stone stairs in the main court.

In 1726 he was employed by Edward Stanton (q.v.), who sent him down to Ditchley, in

Oxfordshire, to set up the chimney-pieces which he [Stanton] and his partner, Christopher Horsnaile (q.v.), had made for that house (Dillon Archives).

Mason's yard in London was situated in the parish of St. Sepulchre's. A Thomas Mason, who might have been a brother, was apprenticed to William Stanton in 1697 and became free ten years later.

MASON, ROBERT, of London
fl. 1678–1690

In 1678 he agreed with Richard Newdigate of Arbury, Warwickshire, that he "should well and finely carve the frontispiece of a Grotto according to a draught signed with both their hands," a work for which he was to receive £16 (Newdigate Archives).

His son, Robert Mason the younger, became free of the Masons' Company by patrimony in 1696.

MASSART, or MASSARET, J., of Paris

He is described as "sculptor in bas-relief to the Dauphin," and showed reliefs in alabaster at the Royal Academy in 1773 and 1774, and at the Society of Artists in the latter year.

MATHEWS, —, of Plymouth
fl. 1832–1837

He signs tablets to John Shearm, 1832, at Kilkhampton, Cornwall, and to Thomas Bond, 1837, at St. Martin's, in the same county.

MATZURA, P. J.

Matzura, whose address is given as 7, Chapel Street (*Annals of the Fine Arts, 1817*), exhibited a bust of Captain Hehl at the Royal Academy in 1816.

MAUGE, —, of Bath
fl. 1768–1783

He signs a large wall-monument in coloured marbles to James Long, 1768, at Urchfont, Wiltshire, and a smaller one, to Robert and Kerrenhappuch Bluett, 1783, at Holcombe, Devon.

MAY, GEORGE, of Romsey, Hants

He exhibited wax portraits at the Free Society of Artists in 1767. A Thomas May, also of Romsey, had exhibited a wax portrait at the Free Society in the previous year.

MEATYARD, M., of Blandford
fl. 1762–1774

He signs large tablets of good workmanship to Mary Russell, 1773, at Wimborne, Dorset, and to Sir William Phipard, 1774, at Poole, in the same county.

MEDCALF, T., of Liverpool

In 1838 he exhibited at the Liverpool Academy busts of W. Dawson, John Finch, Miss Dawson and T. Metcalf.

MELLIAN, C. MAXIMILIAN
d. 1769

He exhibited a bas-relief in metal at the Free Society in 1763 and another in the following year. One of these was described as representing "Venus and Cupid Being Offered a Coral by a Marine Deity."

MELLING, —

In 1833 a Mr. Melling held an exhibition of sculpture in London, showing among other works his "Comic Group of Falstaff, Mistress Doll and Bardolph." He excuses this artistic excursion in a foreword to his catalogue, asking: "Why should the chisel lead a melancholy life? Why should gravity have it all its own way?"

The *Literary Gazette* (1833, page 265), in its review of the exhibition, said that the sculptor "had not polluted his humour with vulgarity," but as he never exhibited at the Royal Academy and nothing more is known of him it is to be feared that he was more comic than successful.

MERCER, GEORGE
fl. 1740–1780

He was a subscriber to Kent's *Designs of Inigo Jones* and was employed at Longford Castle in 1740. In 1767 he made chimney-pieces for Milton Hall, Berks, receiving a total of £144 for the work (Archives of houses named).

Among the Hartwell archives is Mercer's estimate, dated 1740, for £95 for paving the hall at Hartwell Park, Bucks for Sir Thomas Lee. Mercer agreed to pay "Water carriadge to Edgworth and Wharfe and his Honour to pay land carriadge after." Mercer's address is given as "near Cavendish Square."

MERRETT, THOMAS HENRY
b. 1823

He entered the Royal Academy Schools in 1841, being recommended by W. Behnes (q.v.), and showed a relief of the "Combat Between the Centaurs and Lapithae" at the Academy three years later. He afterwards settled at Romford in Essex.

MERRIFIELD, THOMAS
b. 1797, *d.* 1833

He attended the Royal Academy Schools in 1815 and exhibited busts, wax portraits, models, etc., at the Academy from that year until 1822. He gained the Silver Medal from the Society of Arts in 1817, and the Gold Isis Medal in 1818, the latter for an original model of a figure. He died 1 May, 1833, leaving a widow, Charlotte, and three children (Archives, Artists' Annuity Fund).

MERRYMAN, JAMES, of Windsor
fl. 1805–1833

He was the son of John Merryman (q.v.) and in 1805 built the "new Gothic portico" designed by Wyatt on the south side of St. George's Chapel, receiving £249 for the work (Hope's *Windsor Castle*, Vol. II, page 408).

He also signs tablets to William Bonsor, 1830, at Upton, Bucks; to Louisa Legh, 1833, in Windsor Parish Church; and to the Rev. Joseph Morris, 1833, at Feltham, Middlesex.

MERRYMAN, JOHN, of Windsor
b. 1733, *d.* 1800

He was presumably the son of John Merryman of Windsor, mason, who built Baylies, Stoke Poges, for the Hon. Francis Godolphin in 1735 (Archives, Duke of Leeds).

The younger John was employed at St. George's Chapel from 1785 until 1792, doing mason's work and stone-carving both for the interior and exterior. His obituary in the *Reading Mercury* of 22 March, 1800, calls him a "stone-cutter and sculptor." He was buried at Stoke Poges.

MESSER, J., of Exeter
He signs a tablet with excellently carved details to Thomas Hore, 1765, at Spreyton, Devon.

MICALI, —, of Leghorn
His monument to Rear-Admiral Robert Reynolds (*d.* 1811) at St. Clement, Cornwall, has a medallion-portrait and, below it, a relief of a young soldier pointing to a memorial on which is depicted a naval battle. The work is, rather curiously, signed *"Micali direxit Liburni 1816"* instead of the more usual *"fecit."*

MICHENDEN, THOMAS
In 1718 he was paid £47 by Mr. Samuel Tufnell for carving "a architrave, arches in nib'd and gag'd work" at Langley, Essex (Account-book, Samuel Tufnell, of Langley).

MIDDLETON, CHARLES
fl. 1762–1772

He exhibited at the Society of Artists, 1762–1772, where his works included a model of a tablet for a chimney-piece.

MIDDLETON, JOHN, of Towcester
b. 1718, *d.* 1801

He signs the large ambitious monument to John Daye, 1767, at Church Stowe, Northamptonshire, and also a smaller one to Mary Hodges, 1759, at Towcester.

Middleton was probably the father of "John Middleton of Towcester, mason," who died in 1805 at the age of fifty-six (*Monthly Magazine*, 1805, Part I, page 191).

MILLARD, JAMES, of Gloucester
fl. 1790–1821

His monuments, like most of those executed by the Gloucester school of statuaries, are of excellent workmanship. Signed examples in the county include those to John James, 1790, at Eastington; Sarah Hawker, 1793, at Kings Stanley; Sir John Guise, 1794, and Anne Rudge, 1802, both in Gloucester Cathedral; Sir Howe Hicks, 1801, at Witcombe; and John Jones, 1801, at Brockworth. The monument to Thomas Smith, 1793, at Much Marcle, Hereford, is also his work.

Millard later went into partnership with James Cooke (q.v.), and together they sign five monuments in Gloucester Cathedral, to Mrs. Head, 1804; John Pitt, M.P., 1805; Sir Charles Hotham, 1811; Mrs. Stanford, 1812; and Joshua North, 1821, respectively. They made one in memory of Mrs. O'Malley, 1815, in Cheltenham Parish Church.

MILLER, FELIX MARTIN
b. 1820

Miller, who had been left fatherless at an early age, was brought up at the London Orphan School and joined the Royal Academy Schools in 1842, on the recommendation of H. Weekes (q.v.). At the exhibition of suggested works of art for the Houses of Parliament, held three years later, he showed "The Dying Briton" and "Orphans," the latter group being subsequently carved in marble and set up in the London Orphan Asylum.

Miller exhibited at the Royal Academy, 1842–

1880, and at the British Institution, 1847–1866, showing busts of Dr. Livingstone (1857) and S. T. Coleridge (1862), and no less than three versions of "Emily and the White Doe of Rylstone." What must have been a singularly unfortunate work was a model of "The Lover Overtasked," which could be adapted for a rose-stand, though the *Art Union* thought it would serve even better as an inkstand.

At the Great Exhibition of 1851 the sculptor showed bas-reliefs of "Titania," "The Spirit of Calm" and "Lycidas," while he sent the "Indian Siesta" to the International Exhibition of 1872. His statue of "The Archer" was bought for New South Wales, but was later destroyed in a fire in Sydney. His reliefs of "Cruising Among the Waterlilies" (1868) and "Ariel" (1870) were illustrated in the *Art Journal* of 1872 and 1873 respectively. In 1853 he carved the reredos for St. Barnabas's Church, Homerton, and in 1869 made the monument to Edward Jordan for Kingston Cathedral, Jamaica.

J. Foley, R.A. (q.v.), thought very highly of Miller and commissioned more than one of his works in marble, including "Titania Asleep" in 1853. When Foley died the *Art Journal* (1874, page 306) wrote that "the great artist was the principal patron of his struggling brother-artist," and added that Miller was "one of the few sculptors whose genius is manifest and who has produced works, chiefly bas-reliefs, that are unsurpassed by any productions of their class in modern art. It is his evil fortune to obtain much praise with little success or recompense."

(Authorities cited in text.)

MILLER, GEORGE, of Bedford

He signs a small wall-monument in the form of a sarcophagus to Philip Sanson, 1833, at Sharnbrook, Bedfordshire. A Samuel Miller of Bedford, "free-mason," was the master-mason employed in 1710 for building Hinwick House in the same county (Orlebar Archives).

MILLER, WILLIAM, and BOUCOCK, GEORGE
fl. 1787–1790

In the archives of Wanstead Church, Essex, is the contract drawn up between the parishioners and these two masons of "St. Martin's, Ludgate," for building the church. They later received £9,000 for the work, which they carried out between 1787 and 1790.

MILLIGAN, J., of London
fl. 1817–1834

Milligan exhibited busts at the Royal Academy,

1817–1824, including those of Sir J. Cotterell (1821) and Lady Mary Brownlow (1824).

He also signs a number of monuments, the best being one to the Rev. John Currey, 1824, at Dartford, Kent, which has a charming portrait-relief of a clergyman in a wig. Others commemorate Robert and Mary Wright, 1825, at Middle Claydon, Bucks; Neville Cameron, 1833, in Madras Cathedral; and Sophia Jervis, 1834, at Woking, Surrey.

MILLIGAN, W., of London
fl. 1845–1850

In 1850 he carved for Portsmouth the statues of Nelson and Wellington which had been commissioned by Lord Frederick FitzClarence. These do not seem to have been particularly successful, for the *Builder* of that year (page 243) commented on the "tasteless mistake" that had been made of "placing the Duke's foot on the Gallic cock," and later added (page 317) that "the impression of looking at them is one of discomfort."

Milligan also executed a bust of Nelson which realized £73 at the sale of the Peel heirlooms in 1900. Another fine work of his is the bust of Mary, Queen of Scots, at The Vyne, near Basingstoke.

MILLS, RICHARD, of Cirencester
fl. 1812–1839

He signs a monument to William Adams, 1812, at Cricklade, Wiltshire, while others in Gloucestershire commemorate Daniel Mills, 1814, at Miserden; William Hall, 1824, at Bibury; and John Poole, 1839, at Bourton-on-the-Water.

Mills is presumably the son of J. Mills, of Cirencester, who signs the tablet to John Howes, 1806, at Winson, in the same county.

MILLWARD, CHARLES, of Hereford
fl. 1761–1788

Millward, who became a Freeman of Hereford in 1761, signs the wall-tablet with an "Adam" semi-urn to Henry Davies, 1788, at Bredwardine, in the same county.

MILNES, THOMAS
b. 1813

In 1841 he joined the Royal Academy Schools on the recommendation of E. H. Baily (q.v.), and three years later exhibited at Westminster Hall a group entitled "The Death of Harold at the Battle of Hastings," called by the *Literary Gazette* "the strangest collection of short trunks and consumptive legs ever congregated together." In 1847 he was paid seven hundred guineas for the marble statue of Nelson erected at Norwich, and in the following year executed one of Wellington for the Tower of London, a work which was moved to the Royal Arsenal at Woolwich in 1863. In 1853 he carved a statue of Dr. Charlesworth for Lincoln Lunatic Asylum.

In 1854 Milnes made figures of a child and of a horse for the tomb of Alfred Cooke in Kensal Green Cemetery, and in 1857 a bust of William Rivers for Greenwich. In 1869 he carved four lions for the Mechanics' Institute at Saltaire.

He exhibited at the Royal Academy, 1842–1866, showing busts of Sir Michael Gibbs (1845), John Gurney (1848), William Martin (1848), Nelson (1850) and Thomas Wormald (1866). At the Great Exhibition of 1851 he showed a design for a monument to Lord George Bentinck, and to the International Exhibition of 1862 sent "Samson Slaying the Lion."

(Various references, *Art Journal* and *Builder*.)

MITCHARD, JOHN, of Salisbury
fl. 1812–1816

He signs tablets to Charles Pole, 1812, at Barford St. Martin, Wiltshire, and to Harriet Jukes, 1816, at Tisbury, in the same county.

MITCHELL, EDWARD
fl. 1672–1716

Mitchell, who was Master of the Masons' Company in 1692, had a yard at St Anne's, Westminster. In 1716–1717, John, son of "Joseph Kerridge of Ramsey, Hunts, inn-keeper," was apprenticed to him (P.R.O., I.R. 1/4).

When Mrs. Esdaile made her survey of the monuments in the Temple Church she found a bracket signed "N. Mitchell." She considered that the "N" stood for "Ned," and that the bracket had formed part of the monument to Sir William Morton, 1672—a work which had, at some earlier period, been taken down and stored in the triforium of the Church (Esdaile's *Temple Church Monuments*).

MITCHELL, GEORGE
b. 1815

He joined the Royal Academy Schools in 1835 and won a Silver Medal four years later. In 1836 he exhibited at the Academy "Hector Casting a Stone at Ajax."

MITCHELL, WILLIAM
d. 1762

In 1762 he won a premium of ten guineas from the Society of Arts for a bas-relief in clay of "Coriolanus and Volumnia." According to the Register of the Society, he died in the same year.

MITLEY, CHARLES, of York
b. 1705, *d.* 1758

In 1736 he was working at Castle Howard (Castle Howard Archives), and three years later made a statue of George II for the Market House at York. When the building was later pulled down the statue was moved to the Guildhall, but it has now disappeared.

Mitley, who became a Freeman of York in 1745, made with his partner Harvey in 1755 (he died in the same year) the monument, with its standing figure of Mrs. Ramsden, at Adlingfleet, Yorkshire. He also signs a tablet to Frances Graham, 1731, in Holy Trinity, Goodramgate, York; while another to Catherine and Christiana North, 1734, in the Belfry Church, is signed by him and another partner, E. Raper (q.v.).

Mitley died on 26 August, 1758, and was buried in St. Cuthbert's, York, where there is a cartouche-tablet to his memory (Drake's *York*, Vol. II, page 60).

MOCOCK, THOMAS, of Leyton

He signs an altar-tomb surmounted by an oval urn to Frances Sherburne, 1819, in the churchyard of Leyton Parish Church, Essex.

MOLE, LEONARD,
of Worcester
fl. 1770–1781

In 1763 he was apprenticed to his father, Leonard Mole, the Elder, mason and bricklayer, who had become a Freeman of Worcester in 1740

The younger Mole signs a large architectural wall-tablet to Mrs. Bodledge, 1781, in All Saints' Church, Evesham.

MONNOT, PETER STEPHEN,
of Rome
b. 1657, *d.* 1733

Monnot was employed by the fifth Earl of Exeter, for whom he carved a number of works which are now at Burghley. These include busts of the Earl and Countess, and of William Cecil, the Earl's brother; charming little figures of the "Sleeping Child" and the "Waking Child"; and a most lovely relief of the Virgin and Child, which is dated 1700.

On the death of Lord Exeter, in the same year, his widow commissioned Monnot to execute a huge monument with life-sized figures for St.

Martin's, Stamford. The work was finished in 1704 and set up in the church by W. Palmer (q.v.), who may also have carved the inscription. A note in the archives at Burghley, however, says that the monument was brought from Rome "among other exquisite works of art by the Earl himself," but this, for various reasons, seems improbable.

MONTI, RAFFAELLE
b. 1818, d. 1881

He was born in Milan and studied under his father, Gaetano Monti, of Ravenna, and also at the Imperial Academy, which awarded him a Gold Medal for a group entitled "Alexander Taming Bucephalus."

After exhibiting a group of "Ajax Defending the Body of Patroclus" in 1838, Monti was invited to Vienna, where he secured a number of patrons. He returned to Milan in 1842 and, after working there for four years, went to England in 1846. In 1847 he was back in Italy, where he joined the Popular Party and, as one of the chief officers of the National Guard, was sent on a mission to King Charles Albert. After the disastrous campaign of 1848 he fled to England and lived there until his death in 1881.

In 1854 he modelled for the Crystal Palace a replica of the sculpture in the pediment of the Parthenon (*Building Chronicle*, 1854, page 188), and in the following year made six colossal figures for the upper terrace and two fountains for the north nave. In 1857 he was responsible for the interior decoration of the great hall at Mentmore, Buckinghamshire (*Builder*, 1857, page 741), and in 1858 for the relievo over the proscenium arch of Covent Garden Opera House (*Builder*, 1858, page 347).

As a sculptor, Monti was fond of executing statues and busts which, though worked in solid marble, appeared to be covered by a transparent veil, an art brought to perfection about 1730 by an Italian, Antonio Corradini (d. 1752), who may also have been the originator of the idea. Statues of this type by Monti include "The Veiled Vestal" (1847), commissioned by the Duke of Devonshire, and "A Veiled Woman" (1850), now in the Wallace Collection. Other statues of his are "Eve" (1850) and "The Fisher Girls" (1851), made respectively for H. W. Eaton and Mrs. Ogle Hunt; "Truth Unveiling Herself" (1853), the model for which was formerly in the Crystal Palace; and an undated "Venus" now in the Birmingham Art Gallery. His finest work, however, is the equestrian statue of the Marquess of Londonderry in hussar uniform, executed for Durham in 1858. In 1869 he modelled the "Perseus" silver vase for H. E. Surtees.

Monti died on 16 October, 1881. He exhibited at the Royal Academy, 1854–1860, and showed "The Sleep of Sorrow and the Dream of Joy" and "The Reading Girl" at the International Exhibition of 1862. He also signs the monument with a recumbent figure of Lady de Mauley, 1848, at Hatherop, Gloucestershire, and another to William Poyntz, 1848, at Easebourne, Sussex.

(*Men of Our Times*, 1867; *Art Journal*, 1881; authorities cited in text.)

MOODY, ROBERT
b. 1807

He joined the Royal Academy Schools in 1830, on the recommendation of Sir T. Tyrwhitt, Bart., and exhibited busts at the Academy, including those of the Duke of Wellington and Lords Shaftesbury and Eldon, between 1836 and 1844. His bust of Viscount Melbourne, dated 1838, is in the Royal Collection.

MOON, CHRISTOPHER

He signs a large wall-tablet to Thomas Ogden, 1766, in Manchester Cathedral.

MOON, L., of Godalming
fl. 1824–1845

He signs tablets to William Sadler (d. 1824) at Chiddingfold, Surrey, and to Francis Annesley (d. 1845) at Shalford, in the same county.

MOORE, CHRISTOPHER
b. 1790, d. 1863

He was born in Dublin and when he was thirty came to London, exhibiting at the Royal Academy, and also at Brighton, his "Combat between the Archangel Michael and Satan," a work which he had already shown in Ireland.

He attended the Academy Schools in 1821 and soon established a practice in London, thereafter making it his permanent home, though he paid frequent visits to Ireland. He was elected a Member of the Royal Hibernian Academy in 1846 and died in Dublin on 17 March, 1863.

Moore also modelled a number of wax portraits and carved the lovely recumbent figure of a dead child, Isabella Cooper, in Goathurst Church, Somerset, 1835. He was successful with portrait busts—"they were well modelled and expressive likenesses; but his powers were unequal to larger or more important works, and in his statues and figure subjects he was not successful; his grotesque effigy of Thomas Moore, in College Street, Dublin, is an unfortunate memorial to the poet."

(Strickland's *Dictionary of Irish Artists*.)

He exhibited at the Royal Academy, 1821–1860, and at the British Institution, 1821–1834. At the Birmingham Society of Artists he showed busts of T. S. Goodenough (1838), Lord Stanley (1839) and Lord Morpeth (1839). For a list of his works in Ireland, see Strickland (op. cit.).

BUSTS

1823	Miss Grace Croft	Possession Edward Croft-Murray, Esq.
1826	Duke of Sussex	Exhibited Royal Academy
1828	Lord Nugent	Exhibited Newcastle
1828	Lord Denman	Exhibited Newcastle
1828	F. Danby, A.R.A.	Exhibited Liverpool Academy
1829	Sir James Mackintosh	For Lord Nugent
1829	Gotlemburger (a German painter)	Exhibited Liverpool Academy
1831	Sir Thomas Lawrence	Exhibited Royal Academy
1832	George Stephenson	Newcastle Literary and Philosophical Society
1832	William Mulready, R.A.	Exhibited Royal Academy
1832	George Stephenson	Exhibited Liverpool Academy
1833	Mrs. Evelyn	Wotton, Surrey
1836	Solomon Cox	Possession Colonel E. Goldsworthy
1836	Lord Brougham	Exhibited Royal Academy
1839	Lord Morpeth	Castle Howard
1841	Countess of Charlemont	Windsor Castle
1841	Lord Plunket (plaster)	Castle Howard
1842	Thomas Moore	National Portrait Gallery
1842	D. C. Golden, of New York	Exhibited Royal Academy
1842	Lady Dover	Castle Howard
1844	Lord Anglesey	For W. H. Curran
1845	T. N. Longman	Hampstead Parish Church
1848	Lord Palmerston	Exhibited Royal Academy
1849	Lord Clarendon	Exhibited Royal Academy
1850	Edmund Burke	Model formerly at Crystal Palace
1853	Lord Grey	Eton College
1853	Lord Denman	Law Institution
1853	Cardinal Wiseman	Exhibited Leeds
1853	Earl of Derby	For Lord Skelmersdale
n.d.	2nd Earl Fortescue	Barnstaple Infirmary

MOORE, JOHN, the Younger
fl. 1767–1788

Son of J. F. Moore (q.v.), he assisted his father and with him signs the monument to J. Hanway, 1786, in Westminster Abbey.

The younger Moore exhibited at the Free Society, 1767–1775, showing models of animals and marble medallions of Queen Anne, George II and George III.

MOORE, JOHN FRANCIS
d. 1809

Moore, who was born in Hanover, came to Britain about 1760, and six years later presented to the Society of Arts a relief of "Britannia reviver of Antique, prompter to Modern Art." In his day he seems to have been a popular artist, but has been unfairly treated by later writers. For example, Redgrave in his dictionary mentions only two of his works and adds that "neither of these says much for his ability." This is unjust, for Moore's statue of William Beckford, Lord Mayor in 1767, is a dramatic essay in baroque which gives ample proof of the sculptor's talents. The work stood for many years at Fonthill, but was presented by the Lord Mayor's son, the notorious "Vathek" Beckford, to the Ironmongers' Company in 1833, and in their possession it still remains.

Beckford's monument in the Guildhall, dated 1772, is also the work of Moore. This is engraved with the abrupt speech with which the Lord Mayor is said to have astonished George III and which, according to Horace Walpole, "made the King uncertain whether to sit still and silent or to pick up his robes and hurry into his private room." The speech (which was written by Horne Tooke) was, however, never really delivered.

Moore made a number of chimney-pieces for Audley End in 1761, including those for the north room, the Fish room and the gallery, while three years later he received £111 for one with Doric columns for the library. His work in this capacity seems to have attracted the attention of Monsieur Grosley, author of *A Tour of London*, published in 1772. In this work the Frenchman mentions having seen "at Mr. Moore's a piece of sculpture as remarkable on account of its high finishing as the oddness of the idea upon which it was executed. It was a chimney-piece of white marble for a country house belonging to Mr. Beckford, then Lord Mayor of London," the writer continues. "All the most remarkable deaths in the Iliad were represented in corresponding groups, the figures protuberant and almost starting from the marble; and these groups were intermixed with figures in basso-relievo representing the deaths of less consequence."

Moore's monuments are also far from contemptible, for they are well carved and a brilliant use is made of coloured marbles. The Beckford monument of 1772 has already been mentioned, but the most ambitious example of the sculptor's work is the huge group at Ettington, Warwick. This is dated 1775, and has a reclining figure of Mr. Shirley, flanked by standing figures of Lord and Lady Ferrers. Moore's statue of Mrs. Macaulay was unveiled in St. Stephen's, Walbrook, on 8 September, 1778, but was banished from the church shortly afterwards. The reason for its removal, however, had nothing to do with the sculptor, but was due to the extraordinary inscription carved on the base of the work by the eccentric rector, Thomas Wilson (who had ordered the figure), which gave the greatest offence to his parishioners. A later monument, with a spirited and exciting relief, commemorates Lord Hawke, 1781, the victor of Quiberon Bay, at North Stoneham, Hampshire.

Towards the end of his life (and presumably after the death of his son, John, q.v.) Moore went into partnership with a "J. Smith," and together they sign a number of monuments. As the latter signs with only his initial, and as there were three contemporary statuaries—James, Joachim and Joseph—who were all "J. Smith," it is impossible to be more specific, though I am inclined to think that the "J." stands for "James." Monuments signed by the partners commemorate Maria and John Chichester, 1791, at Arlington, Devon; Joseph Blunt, 1793, at Mapledurham, Oxon; Thomas Wildman, 1795, in Twickenham Parish Church; and Peter Oliver, 1795, in Marylebone Chapel.

Moore exhibited at the Free Society, 1766–1776, showing tablets for chimney-pieces, medallions, busts, etc., and also a marble statue of "Apollo" in 1769. His bust of Sir John Rushout, executed in the same year, is now in Worcester Infirmary. His death took place on 21 January, 1809, at Wells Street, Oxford Street.

(*European Magazine*, 1809, page 83; White's *History of Walbrook Ward*, page 387; authority cited in text.)

MONUMENTS

1753	Irnham, Lincs	Benedict Conquest
1757	Canterbury (St. Mildred's)	Windfrid Bridger
1767	Newington, Kent	James Brockman
1767	Bradford (Cathedral)	Faith Sawrey
1770	Bath (Abbey)	William Baker (drawing in Victoria and Albert Museum)
1771	Aldenham, Herts	Robert Hucks
1772	Worcester (Cathedral)	Margaret Rae
1772	Warrington (Parish Church)	Thomas Patten
1773	Cottesbrooke, Northants	Mrs. Langham
1773	Westminster Abbey	Lord Ligonier
1775	Ramsbury, Wilts.	William Jones
1775	Blockley, Glos	The Rushout family (3 busts by M. Rysbrack (q.v.))
1781	North Stoneham, Hants	Lord Hawke (two alternative designs for which are in the Victoria and Albert Museum, 4910/4–5)
1782	Symondsbury, Dorset	Edith Thew
1784	St. Stephen's, Walbrook	Rev. Thomas and Mrs. Wilson
1786	Westminster Abbey	Jonas Hanway
1786	Stafford (Parish Church)	Hon. Barbara Clifford
1786	Earsham, Norfolk	Lieutenant John Dalling
1788	Hatfield Broad Oak, Essex	John Barrington
1788	Harleston, Norfolk	John Wogan
1789	Winchester (Holy Cross)	Rt. Hon. Charles Cornwall
1797	Marylebone (Chapel)	Barbara, Countess of Scarborough
1801	Lewisham (Parish Church)	Lady Maria Churchill

MOORE, T., of Normanton

He signs a wall-tablet with a terra-cotta urn at Smalley, Derby, to Anthony Woodward, 1803.

MORE, J.

Probably a local worker, he signs a cartouche tablet at Warblington, Hants, to Thomas Sone, 1767. This, with its cherub-heads, wreaths and flowers, is a good copy, in stone, of a typical early eighteenth-century marble cartouche.

MOREHOUSE, —, of Dover
d. 1811

He signs an oval tablet at Stanford, Kent, to William Smythe, who died in 1768, although the tablet was not erected until 1791.

According to the *Gentleman's Magazine* (1811, Part II, page 589), Morehouse "dropped down in the market-place, Dover, and instantly expired, while going to his ordinary work."

MOREHOUSE, JAMES, of Greenwich

He was employed as master-mason at Greenwich Palace from 1759 until 1761 (P.R.O., Ad. 68/767).

His son, James Morehouse the younger, was apprenticed to Moses Waite in 1756, becoming free of the Masons' Company by redemption in 1760 and joining his father in the following year. I am uncertain whether it is the father or the son who signs the large wall-monument to Robert Austen, 1759, at Shalford, Surrey.

MORFITT or MORPHITT
fl. 1717–1721

In 1717 he made the font of Church Minshull, Cheshire, and in 1721 that of Holmes Chapel, also in the same county (Raymond Richards, *Old Cheshire Churches*).

MORGAN, E., of Llandaff
fl. 1791–1822

He signs a number of tablets between 1791 and 1822 in churches in Monmouthshire and Glamorganshire. The tablet to Henry Beauchamp, 1817, at Gwennap, Cornwall, is also his work.

MORGAN, W., of Exhall

He signs a large Hellenic tablet with well-cut details to Anne Brooks, 1839, at Exhall, Warwick.

MORILL, —
fl. 1775–1802

He was probably a Reading statuary and signs large wall-tablets in Berkshire to Elizabeth Shaw, 1775, at Kintbury; to Admiral Fowke, 1784, at Shaw; and to Mary Hartley, 1786, at Bucklebury.

MORISON, DAVID
fl. 1821–1850

In 1826 he was appointed "miniature modeller" to the Duke and Duchess of Gloucester, the Duchess of Cambridge and the Princess Augusta. He exhibited at the Royal Academy, 1821–1850, showing mostly miniature medallic portraits.

Morison's wax bust of George IV is in private possession, and he also executed the four wax portraits of the Abadon family which are now on loan from Mrs. Bate at the Victoria and Albert Museum.

MORLEY, MARTIN
fl. 1653–1669

In 1669 he received £45 for the monument to Thomas Windham erected in Felbrigg Church, Norfolk (Archives, Felbrigg Hall). He had become a Freeman of Norwich in 1653.

MORRIS, JOHN, of Lewes
fl. 1750–1775

His father, Arthur Morris, builder of Lewes Bridge in 1727 (*Sussex Archaeological Collections*, Vol. LXX, page 222), and son of Arthur Morris, a mason of that town, applied to become a "foreign member" of the London Masons' Company in 1712, and was admitted on payment of £1 16s. (Archives, Masons' Company). Between 1738 and 1743 the trustees of the Duke of Newcastle paid "Arthur Morris, Stonecutter," £592, this sum was probably for the building of the Duke's house in Lewes (British Museum, Ad. MSS. 33, 321).

John Morris did a great deal of work for Trevor, Bishop of Durham, at Glynde in Sussex. Between 1755 and 1760 he was the mason for building the east front of the house, also executing all the carved stonework and making a chimney-piece for the library. About the same time he built the stables, and a little later (1764–1765) the chapel, which had been designed by Sir Thomas Robinson (Archives, Brand of Glynde). From 1757 until 1761 he was employed on the rebuilding of Ashburnham Place, in the same county (Ashburnham Archives). In 1761–1763 he was paid £646 for building Lewes Sessions House, a charming building with a cupola. In 1786 he received £100 for rebuilding Riverhall Bridge (Town Archives).

He signs a wall monument to Mary Lushington, 1775, in Eastbourne Parish Church.

MORSE, S. F. B.
fl. 1813–1815

In 1813 he received the lesser Gold Medal from the Society of Arts for an original cast of "The Dying Hercules" and exhibited this work at the Royal Academy in the same year.

Morse, who was also a painter, showed pictures at the Academy in 1814 and 1815, but no other works of sculpture.

MORSSE, SYMON

In 1671 he made a marble chimney-piece, costing £31 17s., for the banking-house built by Alderman (afterwards Sir Robert) Clayton and his partner, Mr. Morris, in Old Jewry (Ledger of Sir Robert Clayton, Guildhall Library).

MORTIN, ELLIS, of Leicester
fl. 1785–1825

As "a stranger" but as a "stone mason and builder" he became a freeman of Leicester in 1799. His son Robert was apprenticed to William Firmadge (q.v.) in 1800, but was assigned to his father in 1804. Two other sons, Thomas and John, apprentices of their father, became freemen of Leicester in 1816 and 1824 respectively. Mortin signs a tablet to Jonathan Foster, died 1785, at Aylestone, Leics.

MOSS, W., of Canterbury
fl. 1780–1825

He signs a number of tablets in Kent, of which

the best are those to Elizabeth Denne, 1780, at Littlebourne, and to John Foote, 1800, at Bishopsbourne.

MOSSMAN, GEORGE
b. 1823, *d.* 1863

George Mossman, son of William (q.v.), and younger brother of John Mossman (q.v.), was born in Edinburgh, but was taken to Glasgow when still a child and later studied there under his father. When he was twenty-one he went to London and joined the Royal Academy Schools on the recommendation of William Behnes (q.v.). He worked in the latter's studio and also in that of J. Foley (q.v.), who thought highly of his powers, but apparently "the earnest night and day application with which he pursued the study of his art told seriously upon an organization never very robust" (*Art Journal*, 1864, page 12).

Mossman, who exhibited at the Royal Academy in 1846, later returned to Glasgow and shared a studio with his brother John, but died in 1863 at the age of forty. He left unfinished a life-size figure of "Hope," "a noble statue, giving evidence of true genius" (op. cit.). His statue of Alexander Wilson had been executed for Paisley in the previous year, while just before his death he had been given a commission for a monument to John Galt, which was to have been erected in Greenock Cemetery.

MOSSMAN, JOHN G.
b. 1817, *d.* 1890

He was the eldest son of William Mossman (q.v.), and studied under his father in Glasgow, where he spent practically all his life. Most of his works are to be found in Scotland, and of these his native city has a very large share, including the statues of Peel (1853), Livingstone (1876), Thomas Campbell (1877), Provost Lumsden, and Norman Macleod (1881), and the busts of William Connal (1856), Alexander Thomson (1877) and "Rosalind" (1879) in the Kelvingrove Art Gallery. In 1854 he made the monument to Henry Monteith in the Glasgow Necropolis (*Building Chronicle*, 1854, page 200), and in 1872 cast the bronze figure of "The Lady of the Lake" for the Loch Katrine fountain in West End Park. His statue of the Rev. Patrick Brewster, dated 1863, is in Paisley Cemetery, and in the same year he made a bust of the Duke of Hamilton for the Hamilton Monument at Cadzow.

Mossman exhibited at the Royal Academy, 1868–1879, and at the Royal Scottish Academy, 1840–1886, showing a number of busts, including those of James Lumsden (1840); Principal Cunninghame (1863); Norman Macleod (1868); and Sir Michael Shaw Stewart (1880). He was elected an Honorary Member of the Royal Scottish Academy in 1885. His bust of Henry Bell (1874) is in the National Portrait Gallery, Edinburgh.

MOSSMAN, WILLIAM
b. 1793, *d.* 1851

He was a pupil of Sir Francis Chantrey (q.v.) and practised for a time in London, but soon returned to his native city of Glasgow, where he spent the rest of his life.

In 1842 Mossman was employed by Blore the architect on "sculpture" for Glasgow Cathedral (Cambridge University Library, MS. 3955), and in 1848 he made a Gothic monument to Lord Cathcart in Paisley Abbey.

(Roger's *Monuments of Scotland*.)

MOUNTSTEVEN, ELEY GEORGE
fl. 1781–1791

He was born in the county of Meath and went to London in 1781. Here he exhibited at the Royal Academy between 1782 and 1791, showing wax portraits, including those of Barrington, Bishop of Salisbury; the Prince of Wales; the Duke of Orleans; and Sir Joshua Reynolds. He was also employed by Wedgwood, for whom he modelled portraits of Sir Eyre Coote and of Lord and Lady Auckland in 1788. His wax portrait of Benjamin West, dated 1791, is in private possession, while an undated one of John Henderson is in the Victoria and Albert Museum.

In 1791 Mountsteven left England for the Continent, where he died. "He was supposed to have brought this inferior department of statuary art" (i.e., wax modelling) "to a higher degree of perfection than ever it had attained before" (Walsh's *History of Dublin*, 1818, page 1187).

MOYER, HUMFREY
d. 1661

Moyer, who was apprenticed to Thomas Kingfield and became free in 1627, was an assistant of Nicholas Stone. With Stone he carved the famous monument of Dr. Donne with its shrouded figure—one of the few which survived when Old St. Paul's was destroyed in the Great Fire. He signs a monument to the Coston family, 1637, at Greenford, Middlesex.

"Remembrancer" Smith, in his obituaries, has an entry "5 September, 1661, Mr. Moyer, stonecutter in Little Britain, buried." He had previously noted the death of Mrs. Moyer on 11 November, 1659.

MULLANE, W.
fl. 1820–1840

One of the "New Road" statuaries, his tablets are ordinary and dull. The best are those to Robert Mackintosh, 1824, in St. Pancras Parish Church; Elizabeth Gulston, 1826, at West Clandon, Surrey; William Dawson, 1830, in Hammersmith Parish Church; Miss Belcher, 1832, in St. Martin's, Ludgate; and the Rev. Ellis Burroughs, 1838, at Stratton, Norfolk.

MUNDEN, CHARLES,
of Windsor
fl. 1761–1777

As a mason he was employed at Windsor Castle from 1772 until 1777. He signs a large tablet in coloured marbles to Ann Bidleson, 1762, at Bray, Berks. This has good details and is above the level of the ordinary provincial statuary's work.

MUNRO, ALEXANDER
b. 1825, *d.* 1871

His father was a stone-mason employed on the Duke of Sutherland's property in Scotland, and his artistic abilities were brought to the notice of Harriet, Duchess of Sutherland, wife of the second Duke, who assisted him in his education. In 1848 she brought the young man to London and introduced him to Sir Charles Barry, who employed him on the sculptured works intended for the Houses of Parliament, which were then being built.

Munro soon turned to portrait-sculpture and produced a number of busts. Redgrave says of his works that they were of "true genius and feeling and graceful and spirited, but sketchy in their execution." It was, however, as a sculptor of children that he excelled, and his groups of "The Ingram Children" (1853), "The Gathorne Hardy Children" (1859), "The Matheson Children" (1861) and "The Crompton Roberts Children" (1865) were all exhibited at the Royal Academy, while other child groups include "The Gladstone Children" (1856) at Hawarden, and "The Hardy Children" in Chilham Church, Kent. Here he showed "that refinement of sentiment and aesthetic feeling for grace and beauty which was nature to him" (Graham's *British Literature and Art*).

Munro suffered from a disease of the lungs and towards the end of his life had to leave Great Britain and live at Cannes, where he died on 1 January, 1871. His obituary in the *Art Journal* of that year (page 79) said that "few artists ever

numbered a larger, more various or more deeply attached circle of friends, by whom his memory will always be cherished as among the purest, sweetest and most lovable of men."

He exhibited at the Royal Academy, 1849–1870, the British Institution, 1850–1863, and at the Great Exhibition of 1851. His original plaster model for "The Sleeping Child" is in the Birmingham Art Gallery, and among his miscellaneous works may be mentioned the well-known fountain in Berkeley Square, executed in 1865, and the "Boy and Dolphin" fountain by Grosvenor Gate, Hyde Park, made about the same time. He also carved chimney-pieces for the Duke of Sutherland at Dunrobin Castle in 1849.

STATUES

1852	Francesca da Rimini	For the Rt. Hon. W. E. Gladstone
1857	Undine	Exhibited Art Treasures Exhibition, Manchester
1861	Mother's Joy	Exhibited Royal Academy
1862	Herbert Ingram	Boston, Lincs
1863	Mary II	For Houses of Parliament (now Central Criminal Court)
1863	Watt, Leibnitz, Hippocrates, Newton, Galileo and Davy	For Oxford Museum
1866	James Watt	Birmingham
1868	Ronald Munro Fergusson	Exhibited Royal Academy

BUSTS

1849	Mrs. Banks	Exhibited Royal Academy
1850	John Loch	Stoke College, Suffolk
1854	Peel	Oldham
1855	W. E. Gladstone	Exhibited Royal Academy
1857	Henry Acland	Bodleian, Oxford
1858	Adelaide Ristori	Exhibited Royal Academy
1860	Lord Ashburton	Exhibited Royal Academy
1860	Sir William Armstrong	Newcastle Literary and Philosophical Society
1861	Frederick Robb	Possession Major Eustace Robb
1866	Sir James Stephen	Exhibited Royal Academy
1867	Monsieur Victor Cousin	For Napoleon III
n.d.	R. Quain	Gravesend Town Hall (plaster)

MEDALLIONS

| 1853 | Lady Constance Grosvenor | Exhibited Royal Academy |

1854	Lady Alwyne Compton	Exhibited Royal Academy
1854	J. E. Millais	Ashmolean Museum, Oxford
1856	Henry Wellesley	Ashmolean Museum, Oxford
1859	Mrs. Tom Hughes	Exhibited Royal Academy
1860	Benjamin Woodward	University Museum, Oxford
1869	Duchess of Valembrossa	Exhibited Royal Academy
n.d.	George Macdonald	National Portrait Gallery, Edinburgh

MURRAY, GEORGE
d. 1761

In 1754 he made for Horace Walpole a chimney-piece "for the little parlour" at Strawberry Hill (Toynbee's *Strawberry Hill Accounts*). Three years later he was working at the Horse Guards in Whitehall, executing stone-carving "on the exterior front of the south pavilion" and "a carved statuary marble chimney-piece for the Secretary of War's apartments" which cost £23 (R.I.B.A. Library, MS. 725/18).

In 1760 Murray succeeded James Richards (q.v.) as Master Sculptor and Master Carver to the Crown, and on 15 February of the same year he wrote to the Duke of Ancaster about this appointment. In the letter he complains that "Your Honour was so good as to acquaint me with His Grace the Duke of Newcastle's promise that I was to enjoy the whole in the same manner as the Said James Richards which was by Pattent and a Warrant from the Lords of ye Treasury, for takeing care of the Limetree work" (i.e., the carving by Grinling Gibbons) "at His Majestys Palace at Windsor, which is taken from me without my Knowledge and given to one Lawrence a Carver who never had any Concern with His Majestys work on any Acct" (Archives, West of Alscot Park).

Murray also pointed out that if he received the same salary formerly paid to Richards he would have "four score pounds a year." From this, how-ever, £50 was being deducted as payment for Lawrence, while in addition "my pattent will cost me eighty pounds."

In 1760 Murray was paid £70 for work carried out at Ashburnham Place, Sussex, but he must have died in the following year, for the last payment, amounting to £95, was made to his executors by Lord Ashburnham in February, 1762 (Ashburnham Archives).

MUSCHAMP, W., of Liverpool

He signs a large wall-tablet, with a relief of "The Good Samaritan," to the Rev. David Simpson, 1799, in Christ Church, Macclesfield.

MUSCO, SALVATOR
fl. 1678–1700

In 1678 he was working for a "Mr. Sybert" (presumably C. G. Cibber, q.v.), for in that year a "general search" was made by the Masons' Company, and an entry in their Court Book included "Salvator Musco, Italian," among "Sybert's" assistants.

In 1698 Musco received £10 for carving the coat of arms on the north front of Burley-on-the-Hill (Pearl Finch's *History of Burley-on-the-Hill*), the seat of the Earl of Nottingham. A little later he was probably employed at Great Park, Ampthill; for the owner, Lord Ashburnham, mentions in a letter that he is thinking of employing the carver then working for Lord Nottingham. Indeed, most of the craftsmen at Burley seem to have entered Lord Ashburnham's employment as soon as they were free (Ashburnham Archives).

Musco's son, Joseph, was apprenticed to John Young (q.v.) in 1695, but was "turned over" to Thomas Stayner (q.v.) two years later.

MYERS, —

According to the *Gentleman's Magazine* of 1810 (Part II, page 203), Myers was responsible for "a very elegant monument of pyramidical form" erected in that year in "the new burying ground" at Calcutta to the memory of the Hon. John Hyde, who had died in 1796.

N

NADAULD, —
fl. 1699–1710

Francis Thompson, in his *History of Chatsworth* (page 36), says that "Nadauld, whose descendants continued to live at Ashford near Bakewell until quite recent years, was one of the Earl of Devonshire's numerous Huguenot protégés." It was apparently about 1700 that he replaced Cibber (q.v.) as sculptor of stone figures at Chatsworth.

In 1702 Nadauld was paid £150 for "the ornaments in the Great Frise & carving ornaments on each side of the two windows over the entrance of the West Front & carving 4 ciphers & coronetts upon 4 keystones in ye middle windows of ye West Front." Between 1700 and 1703 he carved the frost work on the grotto and the chimneypiece in the gallery; figures of "Mars," "Fortitude" and "Prudençe" of Roche Abbey stone for the Inner Court (£36), and statues at £22 each of "Cleopatra," "Amphitrite," "Antonius," "Two Rivers," "Pallas" "Pharsis" and "Two Muses"; also the "figures of Fluvius and 2 dolphins & 2 vauses for ye cascade." In the latter year he carved busts for the coping of the court and in 1704 received £24 for carving the figures in the niches on the west stairs and £60 for "carving the ornaments for the two gallerys on each side of the inner court."

From 1709–1710 Nadauld was working at Castle Howard, receiving £56 for "four statues" and £42 for "three figures" for the north front. In the interior of the house he carved the cornices in the saloon and also the two keystones in the Great Hall.

In 1704 he made the mural monument in Westminster Abbey to Lady Eland, granddaughter of the French Protestant Marquise de la Tour de Gouvernet.

(Building Accounts, Chatsworth and Castle Howard.)

NAPPER, GEORGE, of London
b. 1754, *d.* 1840

In 1828 when he applied to the A.G.B.I. he stated that he had worked "for the late Mr. John Bacon for forty years" and had also worked under J. E. Carew (q.v.) and W. Behnes (q.v.). Napper then apparently set up in business in Manchester and executed a number of monuments, including those to Mrs. Trafford, 1813, in Manchester Cathedral; the Rev. Samuel Bennett, 1823, at Hatfield Peverel, Essex; Master Astley, at Duckinfield, Cheshire; the Rev. Mr. Lock, at Newcastle, Co. Limerick; Archdeacon Cocker, at Glanmire, Cork; besides several for the West Indies. I have seen the first two mentioned monuments which have the usual contemporary classical details, but do not say much for Mr. Napper's powers as a sculptor.

NEALE, GEORGE, of Grantham
fl. 1811–1830

Neale seems to have had several partners, for tablets are signed "Neale and Wilson," and "Neale and Johnston." His best tablets are those to Beaumont Leeson, 1822, in Grantham Parish Church, and to James Faithfull, 1823, at Eastwell, Lincs.

Neale was succeeded in the firm by his son Joseph, who had a Mr. Dunn as his partner.

NEDOS, —
fl. 1705–1707

He was employed at Castle Howard in 1705, being paid £63 6s. for the "Tritons and Lions" and £6 10s. for the "Trophies," both for the south front. He was also paid £12 10s. for the "Trophies on the North Metop." In the following year he was paid £90 for carved stonework on the cupola, which included a "Frieze of Trophies" and "Four Keystones." He was also responsible for the "Frieze of Trophies" on the north front. It has been suggested that "Nedos" is a mis-spelling for "Nadauld" (q.v.), but the writing on the bill is quite clear.

NELSON, GEORGE
b. 1810, *d.* 1888

He was a relation of Thomas and James Nelson, of Carlisle (q.v.), and as a young man became assistant to M. L. Watson (q.v.), who was also a native of Cumberland.

At Watson's death in 1847 Nelson executed in marble those works which his master had only modelled in clay. These included the great group of Lords Eldon and Stowell, the statue of Flaxman and the monument to the 50th Regiment. The latter was erected in Canterbury Cathedral in the following year and was signed "George Nelson from a sketch by the late M. L. Watson." Nelson also exhibited a model of this work at the Great Exhibition of 1851.

His best-known original work was a statue of "Musidora," which was frequently engraved for Victorian art magazines. He exhibited at the Royal Academy, 1837–1869, showing among other things a bust of Lord Western and statues entitled "The Bather" and "The Captive." He also carved the recumbent figure in 1872 for the monument of Lord Stanley of Alderley. Other monuments signed by him include James M'Laughlan, 1848, St. Michael's, Dumfries; and Thomas Sheffield, 1853, and Thomas Elliot, 1859, both in Carlisle Cathedral.

(Various references *Art Journal* and *Builder*.)

NELSON, JAMES
d. c. 1811

One of the chief master-masons of his day, he received a great deal of employment from the architects Henry Holland and Sir John Soane. Under the former in 1767 he was working at Lord Bristol's house in St. James's Square, carving decorative details in Portland stone, and three years later making a chimney-piece. In 1769 he made a marble chimney-piece for Lord Guildford's London house and in 1784 marble tables for Sir Philip Yorke. In 1787 he was employed on the building of Fonthill (*Builder*, 1850, page 113).

In 1789 and 1790 Nelson was the master-mason for the building of, or repairs to, the houses of the Countess of Pembroke at Richmond, Sir Henry Peters in Park Street, and the Earl of Hardwicke in New Cavendish Street. Between 1792 and 1794 he was the master-mason for the rebuilding of Lord Hardwicke's seat at Wimpole, and also carved chimney-pieces for the house.

Between 1786 and 1796 he made a chimney-piece ("ornamented with flowers" and costing £32) for Peter Thelluson at Philpot Lane, and others for Sir Alexander Hood at Cricket St. Thomas, for William Pitt at Hollwood, and for the London houses of Lady Pembroke and Lord Buckingham in Charles Street and Pall Mall respectively. In 1791 he carved the stonework for the Temple at Audley End (Essex Records D/DBY/A.222).

Nelson's most important commission was the building of the Bank of England under Sir John Soane, where he was employed from 1791 until 1811. During the last five years he had Thomas Grundy (q.v.) as his partner. The statuary and carved work executed by him at the Bank included in 1793 an enriched marble chimney-piece for the centre room and another for the room adjoining, costing £75 and £43 respectively. In 1795 he received £72 for "ninety foot of enriched flute and dart," and in the following year eighteen guineas for "four antique angular honeysuckles with enriched faces on each." In 1801 his carved stonework for the exterior and interior of the building ranged from two antique caducei at £20, two swags of laurel wreaths and ribbons at £25, and one large drop of oak-leaves at £32, to a marble chimney-piece "with antique flowers" at £48.

In the years which followed Nelson worked unceasingly at the Bank, and the ledgers of Sir John Soane contain long lists of payments to him for capitals, friezes, Vitruvian scrolls, swags and lion-masks, besides a number of chimney-pieces. He also carved monuments designed by Soane, including one to Mrs. Bosanquet, erected in Leytonstone Parish Church in 1807 at a cost of £326, and another to the order of the Marquess of Abercorn in 1796, which I have so far failed to identify.

(Soane Note-books.)

NELSON, JOHN, of Shrewsbury
b. 1726, *d.* 1812

In 1777 he made the two lions outside the Lion Inn, Wyle Cop, Shrewsbury, and in 1795 a statue of Sir Rowland Hill for Hawkstone Park, Salop. His two sphinxes, also for Hawkstone, date from about the same time, while in 1796 he executed a statue of Roger de Montgomery for Shrewsbury Castle. This was subsequently removed from the Castle and stored in a basement, but some years later fell on a boy and broke his leg. It was thereupon relegated to the Corporation yard, whence, as might have been foreseen, it disappeared.

Nelson died on 17 April, 1812, and the *Gentleman's Magazine* of that year (Part I, page 492) said in its obituary of him that "his eminent abilities as a statuary will be long remembered in Shropshire and the neighbouring counties." The article continues that he, "having had a liberal education and possessing a fund of lively anecdote, was a very pleasant companion," and ends with some lines "to the worthy and aged Nelson," in which he is asked why he has not carved a bust of himself. The question is answered in another verse, the two last lines running as follows:

> "In busts to others' merits raised
> He has his own declared."

The *Salopian Journal* remarked on the same occasion that Nelson's "moral worth excited the esteem of all acquainted with him."

One of Nelson's account-books, giving details of his monumental work, etc., is now in Shrewsbury School Library. He signs monuments in Shropshire to Beatrice Peck, 1767, at Market Drayton;

M. Dorsett, 1779, at Llangedwyn; Sir Rowland Hill, 1784, at Hodnet; the Rev. Richard Lloyd, 1785, in St. Mary's, Shrewsbury; Thomas Prostam, 1788, in St. Julian's, Shrewsbury; Scarlett Lloyd, 1790, at Fitz; the Rev. Robert Jeffreys, 1800, at Baschurch; Mrs. Gardner, 1800, at High Ercall; Ann Corser, 1801, at Whitchurch; and Elizabeth Jones, 1801, at Oswestry. The monuments to Jane Vernon, 1799, in Chester Cathedral, and William Davies, 1800, in Montgomery Parish Church, are also the work of Nelson, while he signs others in Wales to the Rev. John Fletcher, 1777, at Bangor; David Davis, 1790, at Llanfair; and Thomas Hanmer, 1794, at Overton.

(Authorities cited in text.)

NELSON, JOHN HENRY
b. 1800, *d.* 1847

He was an Irishman, born in Sligo, who began his artistic career by painting portraits. These attracted the attention of two wealthy Irish landowners, Colonel Lloyd and Mr. Wynne, who in 1833 sent him to study in Paris. After spending four years there Nelson went to England and thence to Wales, where he painted a number of portraits. From Wales he moved to Bristol and about 1838 returned to Dublin.

It was not until 1844 that Nelson turned his attention to sculpture. In 1846 he produced a statue of "Venus Attiring," which he took to England in the following year, exhibiting it first at the Egyptian Hall in London, and later in Manchester. It was while he was in Manchester that he died, on 26 December, 1847, leaving a widow and four children totally unprovided for.

Of his "Venus Attiring" the *Builder* (1848, page 53) remarked that it had "cost him two years of unremitting toil," while the *Art Union* (1848, page 52) wrote that "the great talent displayed in the execution of his figure attracted the notice of many patrons of art who expressed much interest in the future prospects of the sculptor."

(Strickland's *Dictionary of Irish Artists.*)

NELSON, THOMAS, and JAMES
fl. 1829–1858

The Nelsons were brothers and joint owners of the Carlisle marble works, where they produced monumental tablets, chimney-pieces, etc. One of their advertisements in the *Builder* (1848, page 515) stated that "experienced workmen could be sent to any part of the kingdom to fix work at a reasonable rate."

They sign tablets to John Canning, *c.* 1830, at Ilmington, Warwick, and to the Rev. Christopher Hodgson, 1849, at Marholm, in the Isle of Ely.

In 1857 they carved various decorative details for the mausoleum built by Lord Lonsdale at Lowther.

NEWMAN, JAMES, of Sidmouth

He signs a large wall-tablet at Ottery St. Mary, Devon, to Thomas Hopkins, 1817.

NICHOLL, A., of London

He signs a large wall-monument of good workmanship to John Hopkins, 1793, at Harwell, Berkshire.

NICHOLL, WILLIAM GRINSELL
b. 1796. *d.* 1871

He attended the Royal Academy Schools in 1822, and in 1827 received £80 for carved stonework on the exterior of the Customs House in London (P.R.O., Works 5/119).

About 1830 Nicholl was employed by the architect Basevi to carry out his designs in marble, the most important of these being of sculpture for the Fitzwilliam Museum in Cambridge. In 1837 Nicholl accordingly carved the capitals, frieze and other decorative details and in the following year executed the sculpture in the pediment, the latter from a design by Eastlake. In 1839 he made the four lions at the foot of the staircase (*Architectural History of Cambridge*, Vol. III, page 210).

In 1838 he was responsible for the bas-reliefs above the windows of the Oxford and Cambridge Club in London, designed by Smirke, and in 1846, while working at Oxford, executed all the decorative carving on the exterior of the Taylor Institute (*Builder*, 1846, page 505). Two years previously he had exhibited a model of a statue of Captain Cook at Westminster Hall; this seems to have received scant attention, being referred to by the *Literary Gazette* as "a tame, crabbed looking person."

It was not, however, until 1850, when Cockerell selected him to carve the pediment of St. George's Hall, Liverpool, that Nicholl became well known to the public, and five years later he made the four recumbent lions for the exterior of the same building. After his death his friend, Henry Baker, in a letter to the *Builder* (1871, page 1002), described this particular period of the sculptor's life as follows: "When I first became acquainted with Nicholl he had, I think, never lost his courage, but patrons to sculptors are few and far between and I suspect that his progress was little better than a struggle for dear life until one day Cockerell, R.A., found him out, happily for both, one requiring most important work to be done, and well done, under his own eye, and the other sighing at once for fame and money, apparently so distant."

Other works by Nicholl include busts of H. Sass (1820) and Archdeacon Law (1827), the latter in Chatham Parish Church; the alabaster reredos for Waltham Abbey executed in 1862 (*Builder*, 1862, page 499) and the alabaster lectern made four years later for Worcester College Chapel, Oxford; and the statues of Lords Cornwallis and Clive (1867) for the India Office. He signs monuments to Sir John Hippisley, 1825, in the Temple Church; to John Turner, 1829, at Cold Overton, Leics.; to Henry Wootton, 1830, at Minster, Kent; to Sir George Don, 1832, in the Garrison Church, Gibraltar (from a design by Basevi); to Joseph Bonsor, 1835, at Great Bookham, Surrey; to Elizabeth Morley, 1837, in Walthamstow Parish Church; to Richard Stevenson, 1837, in Trinity College Chapel, Cambridge; and to the Rev. J. Murray, 1862 (with a recumbent effigy), in St. Andrew's, Well Street.

Nicholl exhibited at the Royal Academy, 1822–1861. He died at Acton on 8 December, 1871.

(Authorities cited in text.)

NICHOLSON, GEORGE,
of Durham

b. 1726, *d.* 1804

Ogle in his Diary says that "there lives in Bow Lane one George Nicholson who built the New Bridge, when to create a job for himself he made Dr. Sharp and the Dean and Prebends believe he could greatly add to the beauty of the Church (i.e., Durham Cathedral) by new chiselling it over on the outside and that he could add to the beauty of the ancient window by means of his own genius."

Nicholson did indeed persuade the Bishop and in 1799 was allowed to destroy the ancient tracery in the cloisters and replace it by his own poor and meaningless work. He also carved the sculpture of the Dun Cow on the Cathedral and was even permitted to remove the figures over the great window of the north transept, said to represent Friars Fossor and Castell, one the original builder and the other the restorer of the window. These he had the temerity to replace by full-length figures, executed by himself, of Bishop Pudsey and of a Prior in his chair.

At the time of his death in 1804 Nicholson was sword-bearer to the Provincial Grand Lodge of Freemasons, County Durham.

(Boyle's *Durham*, pages 207–209; *Universal Magazine*, 1804, page 573.)

NICHOLSON, JOHN, and
WOOD, —, of Newark

They sign a Hellenic wall-monument at East Stoke, Nottinghamshire, to the Hon. Lady Bromley, 1839.

NICHOLSON, THOMAS HENRY
d. 1870

He was first a modeller and later became a draughtsman on wood. As a young man he distinguished himself particularly in the modelling of horses, and when William Behnes (q.v.) was engaged on his group of Lady Godiva he required the services of an artist who had had experience of modelling animals, and Nicholson was recommended to him. The result of his association was a complete success. Count D'Orsay (q.v.), visiting Behnes' studio, was so struck by the modelling of a horse in the group that he engaged Nicholson to work for him. This partnership was unfortunate, for Nicholson, after D'Orsay's death, maintained that he did all the work and the Count took all the credit.

How much work each did will never now be known. Nicholson claimed that he completely modelled the statuettes, that when a visitor came to the Count's studio at Gore House he was hustled out of the room and that D'Orsay never acknowledged his assistance in any way. On the other hand, D'Orsay was undoubtedly an artist of considerable merit, and it seems unlikely that he would have foisted on to the public the work of another sculptor and called it his own. One of their most successful works was an equestrian statuette of the Great Napoleon, and Prince Louis Napoleon, then an exile in London, and a great friend of the Count, used to come to Gore House to give advice and to make suggestions about the details of the uniforms, etc. Later, as Emperor of the French, he remembered Nicholson and asked him to come and work for him in Paris; the offer was declined, as a year after the break up of Gore House, and D'Orsay's flight to France, Nicholson entirely abandoned modelling and devoted the rest of his life to drawing on wood.

The *Art Journal*, 1870 (page 204), in its obituary of Nicholson, says that "he was known only to a limited circle of artists and literary men, and so reserved were his habits of life that he seemed to shrink from public recognition. His reserve and retired habits militated against the acquisition of that reputation which he ought to have enjoyed."

Nicholson exhibited in the Royal Academy, 1838–1843, showing various models and sketches for historical groups. He died at Portland, Hants.

(Authority mentioned in text.)

PLATE XVII

JOHN VAN NOST
The Duke of Queensberry, 1711, Durisdeer, Dumfries.

PLATE XVIII

JOSEPH NOLLEKENS
George III, 1773, Royal Society.

ARNOLD QUELLIN
Sir John Cutler, 1683, Grocers' Hall.

J. M. RYSBRACK
Mr. and Mrs. Knight, 1733, Gosfield, Essex.

NICOLI, FREDERICO,
of London
fl. 1817–1820

His studio was in Mount Street, next door to that of Sir Richard Westmacott (q.v.). He exhibited at the Royal Academy in 1818 and 1819, showing in the former year a bust of the Princess Charlotte which was formerly in the Temple at Claremont. In 1819 he showed marble busts of Prince Leopold and Marshal Blücher; the latter, dated 1817, and a very fine work, is now at Windsor Castle.

Nicoli's undated bust of C. J. Fox is now in the National Maritime Museum at Greenwich.

NIXON, RICHARD
fl. 1730–1738

From 1730 until 1738 he was the chief mason for the building of Lamport Hall, Northampton-shire. His work there also included the chimney-piece for the Front Hall and a dial for a pedestal (Isham Archives, Lamport Hall).

NIXON, SAMUEL
b. 1803, *d.* 1854

He does not appear to have attended the Royal Academy Schools, nor to have studied under any master, although he first exhibited at the Academy at the age of twenty-three. In 1838 Nixon carved the statue of Richard Valpy for St. Lawrence's Church, Reading, out of Roche Abbey stone. The work was designed by Edward Charles Hakewill. (*Reading Mercury*, Saturday, 15 December, 1838.)

In 1840 he was employed by P. Hardwick, R.A., the architect of the Goldsmiths' Hall, to carve the decorative sculpture on the exterior of the building. This work is of great merit and includes the noble trophies of arms on the main front (Company's Archives). Four years later Nixon was selected to execute the colossal statue of William IV for King William Street in the City. The tender was for £2,200, but the material chosen was granite, and as the sculptor's obituary says (*Gentleman's Magazine*, 1854, page 406): "It is well known he and others considered he was not only inadequately remunerated, but that even his expenses were not paid. The statue was sculptured in Scotch granite, a material difficult to work and the expenses attending the conscientious execution of the contract severely crippled the artist." The work was given rather a mixed reception, the *Builder* (1845, page 26) considering it "coarse and clumsy and not likely to advance the reputation of the sculptor." It was later removed from its original position and is now at Greenwich.

Nixon was later much employed in executing monumental sculpture both for England and Canada. Some of these works are, to say the least of it, unfortunate, for he was always ready to accede to the whims and eccentricities of his patrons, to the detriment of his reputation. He defended this dangerous habit, according to the *Art Journal* (1854, page 230), by declaring "that a man had no right, artist though he might be, to enforce his own views to the subversion of those entertained by his patrons."

Nixon was employed by Blashfield (q.v.), for whom he designed the Shakespeare vase. Other works by him include statues of John Carpenter (1844) at the City of London School, and Sir John Crosby (1845) for Crosby Hall. In 1840 he executed figures of "The Four Seasons" for Gold-smiths' Hall, and four years later showed "The British Warrior" at Westminster Hall. His busts include those of the Rev. George Hatch (1837) for St. Matthew's, Friday Street; the Rev. William Rodber (1843) at St. Mary-at-Hill; and John Carpenter (1845) at the City of London School. He signs monuments to Philip Lucas, 1830, in Hackney Parish Church; to the Gillespie family, 1833, in St. John's Wood Chapel; to Samuel Whiteway, 1847, at Kingsteignton, Devon; to John Marshall, 1840, in Shoreditch Parish Church; and to the Rev. William Parker, 1843, in St. Ethelburga's, Bishopsgate.

Nixon exhibited at the Royal Academy, 1826–1846, at the British Institution, 1831–1832, and at the Great Exhibition of 1851. He died at Kennington on 2 August, 1854. His nephew, "Mr. Nixon, Jnr.," carved the capitals of the columns of St. Barnabas, Homerton, in 1845 (Godwin, *Buildings and Monuments*, page 24).

(Authorities cited in text.)

NIXSON, or NIXON, PAUL,
of Carlisle
b. 1766, *d.* 1850

In 1823 he carved the busts of Wren, West and Chantrey on the pediment of the Academy of Arts at Carlisle. In 1825 he was paid £130 10s. for marble chimney-pieces for the Council House, Bristol (City Archives). His monument to William Giles (*d.* 1814) is in Carlisle Cathedral.

NOAKES, —, and PEARCE, E.,
of London
fl. 1800–1820

Like the majority of the New Road statuaries, their work is of little interest and the designs of their tablets uninspiring. Their best works are those to Robert Usherwood, 1809, at Whitby,

Yorks; Sarah Ridehalgh, 1814, at Eccles, Cheshire; and Mrs. Falconbridge, 1816, in St. James's, Garlickhithe.

NOBLE, MATTHEW
b. 1817, *d.* 1876

He was born at Hackness in Yorkshire, and as a young man went to London, where he studied sculpture under John Francis (q.v.). He first exhibited at the Royal Academy in 1845, but the work which brought his name prominently before the public was the Wellington monument erected in Manchester in 1856. The commission for its execution had been awarded as the result of a competition, and the decision of the judges in favour of Noble—still a comparatively young and unknown man—aroused a considerable amount of ill-feeling and angry discussion, especially on the part of his fellow-artists. The statue, however, proved a success, and Noble soon became one of the most popular sculptors of his day.

Noble exhibited at the Royal Academy between 1845 and 1876, but died on 23 June in the latter year and was buried in Brompton Cemetery. He was of a delicate constitution, but his end appears to have been hastened by the death of his son, who was killed in a railway accident, while another son, who had shown great promise as a sculptor, had died two years before.

The *Art Journal* (1876, page 275), in its obituary of him, said that it seemed "surprising to those who knew him personally that he should have lived even the comparatively short period of his life, and yet more that he should have been able to continue his labours. Few men," the writer continued, "have been more esteemed and regarded, not alone for his great ability, the manifestations of talent that very closely approximated to genius, but for rare qualities of mind and heart. Generous in his acts and in his sympathies, amiable in his disposition, his nature was essentially kind and good. He was a gentleman of high rectitude, irreproachable in all the relations of life."

According to the sculptor's own wish, the unfinished works in his studio were completed by J. Edwards (q.v.), who had been his friend and assistant for twenty years. A number of his works were copied in "Parian" by Copeland, and his large bust of Queen Victoria (1856) in this ware is in the Bristol Art Gallery. His widow presented a collection of his models to the town of Newcastle and they were placed in Elswick Hall.

STATUES

1852	Peel	St. George's Hall, Liverpool
1853	Peel	Tamworth, Staffs
1853	Peel	Salford, Lancs
1853	Wellington	India Office
1854	Queen Victoria	Manchester
1856	Wellington	Manchester
c.1856?	Viscount Hill	Formerly Hawkstone, Salop
1856	Sir John Franklin	Waterloo Place, London
1858	Brotherton	Salford, Lancs
1858	Isaac Barrow	Trinity College, Cambridge
1858	Wellington	Leeds
1859	General Neill	Ayr
1860	Lord Lyons	St. Paul's Cathedral
1861	Marquess of Anglesey	Isle of Anglesey
1861	Duke of Sutherland	Dunrobin Castle
1862	Dr. Todd	Denmark Hill
1862	Mountstuart Elphinstone	St. Paul's Cathedral
1864	Lord Brougham	For Brown's Institute, Liverpool
1865	Prince Consort	Salford, Lancs
1865	Lord Eglinton	Ayr
1865	Prince Consort	Leeds
1865	Prince Consort	Manchester
1865	J. Foster	Assize Court, Manchester
1865	Juggoathjee Sunkerset	Bombay
1865	Sir James McGrigor	Millbank, London
1867	Cobden	Manchester
1867	Palmerston	Romsey, Hants
1868	Sir Peter Fairbairn	Leeds
1869	Duchess of Sutherland	Dunrobin Castle
1870	Prince Consort	Bombay
1870	Lee, Bishop of Manchester	Owen's College, Manchester
1870	Hunter, Hume and Davy	Civil Service Commission Building, London
1871	Sir James Outram	Embankment, London
1871	Lord Feversham	Helmsley, Yorks
1872	Queen Victoria	Bombay
1872	J. Ramsden	Barrow-in-Furness
1872	S. C. Lister	Bradford
1873	Lord Derby	Preston
1874	Queen Victoria	St. Thomas's Hospital
1874	Lord Derby	Parliament Square
1875	Cromwell	Manchester City Hall
1876	Peel	Parliament Square

BUSTS

1845	Archbishop of York	Exhibited Royal Academy
1847	J. Francis	Exhibited Royal Academy
1848	William Smith	University Museum, Oxford
1848	Professor Playfair	Geological Museum, London
1849	John Phillips	University Museum, Oxford

1850	Lord Nevill	Eridge Castle, Sussex
1850	W. Etty, R.A.	National Portrait Gallery
1851	Peel	National Portrait Gallery
1852	Nelson and Wellington	Grocers' Hall, London
1852	Earl and Countess Canning	Highcliffe Castle, Hants
1854	Marquess of Anglesey	Royal Collection
1855	Michael Faraday	Exhibited Royal Academy
1856	Queen Victoria	Manchester City Hall
1857	Duke of Newcastle	Formerly possession Earl Waldegrave
1857	Queen Victoria	For Lord Ellesmere
1857	Edward Brown	Ashton-under-Lyne Parish Church
1857	Lord Lyons	Exhibited Royal Academy
1858	Earl of Ellesmere	National Portrait Gallery
1859	Frances, Countess Waldegrave	Exhibited Royal Academy
1859	Prince Consort	Manchester City Hall
1859	7th Earl of Shaftesbury	St. Giles, Dorset
1860	Earl Canning	Possession Lord Allendale
1860	J. Brotherton	Manchester City Hall
1860	Dr. Todd	Royal College of Physicians
1860	Cromwell	Reform Club
1860	Lord Palmerston	Reform Club
1861	George Harcourt	Stanton Harcourt Church, Oxon
1862	Earl Canning	Guildhall, London (destroyed 29 September, 1940)
1862	Cromwell	Bethnal Green Museum
1863	Earl of Elgin	Exhibited Royal Academy
1863	Duke of Sutherland	For North Staffordshire Waterworks Company
1864	Cromwell	For Reform Club
1865	Lady Frere	Bombay
1865	James Heald	For Wesleyan Missionary Society
1867	Garibaldi	Bethnal Green Museum
1869	Cobden	Guildhall, London (destroyed 29 September, 1940)
1870	Harriet, Duchess of Sutherland	Castle Howard
1870	David Napier	Glasgow Art Gallery
1871	Earl of Derby	Guildhall, London (destroyed 29 September, 1940)
1873	Michael Faraday	Royal Society
1874	Cromwell	Manchester City Hall

1874	Earl of Aberdeen	Westminster Abbey
1874	Sir Thomas Potter	Manchester City Hall
1875	Sir John Franklin	Westminster Abbey
1876	James Hope Scott	Abbotsford
?	Alderman Goadsby	Manchester City Hall
?	Wellington	Walker Art Gallery, Liverpool

MONUMENTS

1847	Westminster Abbey	Sir John Franklin
1847	Stanton Harcourt, Oxon	Harcourt, Archbishop of York (recumbent figure)
1852	Stockport, Cheshire	John Marsland
1854	Kensal Green Cemetery	Thomas Hood
1855	York (Minster)	Harcourt, Archbishop of York (recumbent figure)
1855	St. Paul's Cathedral	Captain E. M. Lyons
1856	St. Paul's Cathedral	Officers and Men of the 77th Regiment
1860	York (Minster)	Musgrave, Archbishop of York (recumbent figure)
1860	Bombay (Cathedral)	Bishop Carr (recumbent figure)
1860	Limpsfield, Surrey	Lord Elphinstone (recumbent figure)
1861	Ashley, Staffs	Thomas Kinnersly
1861	Holme Lacy, Hereford	Lady Scudamore-Stanhope (with life-sized standing figure)
1863	Westminster Abbey	Sir James Outram
1864	Flitton, Beds	Earl de Grey (recumbent figure)
1867	Richmond, Yorks	Lady Charlotte Dundas
1868	Trentham, Staffs	Duchess of Sutherland (recumbent figure)
1868	Simonburn, Northumberland	Mr. and Mrs. Allgood
1869	Hereford (Cathedral)	Dean Dawes (recumbent figure)
1870	Bearwood, Berks	John Walter
1870	Newton, Cambs	Christopher Pemberton
1871	Holme Lacy, Hereford	Chandos Scudamore-Stanhope
1872	Biddulph, Staffs	William and Mary Heath
1872	Knowsley, Lancs	Earl of Derby (recumbent figure)
1874	Rufford, Lancs	Sir Thomas Fermor-Hesketh (recumbent figure)
1875	St. Paul's Cathedral	Rev. Henry Venn
1876	Brigstock, Northants	Lord Lyveden (d. 1873) (recumbent figure)

NOLLEKENS, JOSEPH, R.A.
b. 1737, d. 1823

He was the second son of Joseph Francis Nollekens (1702–1747), a painter commonly known as "Old Nollekens," and when young "was more remarkable for his fondness for ringing St. James's Church bells than for any more laudable exertion," according to a writer in the *European Magazine* (1788, page 385). This period of irresponsibility does not seem to have lasted long, for in 1750 the boy was apprenticed to Peter Scheemakers (q.v.), and "during that time abandoned his habits of dissipation and became very industrious and attentive in his profession" (op. cit.).

In 1759 Nollekens was awarded a premium by the Society of Arts for a drawing from plaster, and in 1760 their first premium for a model in clay of "Jeptha's Rash Vow." In the same year he went to Rome, sending from there two years later a marble relief of "Timocles Conducted before Alexander," which won him a prize of fifty guineas from the Society of Arts. Shortly after this he modelled a bust of David Garrick and, a little later, one of Laurence Sterne.

While he was in Rome he also began to deal in antique fragments, terra-cottas, etc., which he restored and then sold to English collectors. In 1770, however, he decided to return to London, but when passing through Paris found his father's brother "who had been reduced by misfortune" and "not only relieved his present wants, but settled on him a yearly stipend for the rest of his life" (op. cit.).

Nollekens' reputation as a sculptor had preceded him, and once he had set up his studio in Mortimer Street he began to receive commissions from the fashionable society of London. In fact he soon became to contemporary sculpture what Reynolds was to painting. In 1771 he made chimney-pieces for Harewood House, Yorkshire, and in 1773 a relief of "Cupid and Psyche" which is now at Burlington House. Four years later he received one hundred guineas for five keystones in Portland stone for the back front of Somerset House (R.I.B.A. Library, 335.A.).

Nollekens also seems to have worked in plaster, for in 1775 he was paid £280 "for modelling and casting the several figures in basso-relievo of the Great Hall" of Drapers' Hall (Court Book, Company's Archives). According to the *Gentleman's Magazine* (1778, page 585), the plaster-work consisted of two ceilings which he executed from designs by Richardson. For the Cordwainers' Hall he carved an urn and tablet to the memory of John Came (Allen's *London*, Vol. III, page 172),

while in 1780 he was responsible for the ornaments, etc., on the exterior of the Middlesex Sessions House, receiving £100. In 1793 he took a mould from the bust of Shakespeare in Stratford-on-Avon Church, from which "he made a mask and then a model" (*Historical Manuscripts Commission*, Earl of Charlemont, Vol. II, page 221).

In probably what is the most candid, pitiless and uncomplimentary biography in the English language, *Nollekens and His Times*, J. T. Smith, the sculptor's pupil, friend and disappointed executor, gives a picture of a grasping miser—or rather two misers, for Mrs. Nollekens, if anything, outdid her husband in parsimony. Yet unkind and biased as the book obviously is, it is nevertheless of the greatest value to all students of English sculpture, for not only does it paint a full-length portrait of Nollekens himself, but also gives in the second volume invaluable biographies, anecdotes and other details of contemporary artists, including a number of sculptors. Smith also recorded remarks made by Nollekens about sculptors he could remember in his youth, so that the whole book provides one of the most important sources of information on eighteenth-century English art in existence.

In all editions of Smith's book there is a list of the statues, busts and monuments executed by Nollekens. Curiously enough, this seems to omit a number of works, while others it does mention have since disappeared. The list given in the following pages is of those works of which I have personal knowledge.

The sculptor's "stock pieces" were the busts of Pitt and Fox. Of the latter there were two versions carved in 1791 and ca. 1802. Of the Pitt bust, based on a mask taken immediately after death, Nollekens is said to have sold seventy-four replicas at £120 each. He also made replicas of the mask itself, but in this case the original is in the possession of Earl Stanhope.

Nollekens, who exhibited at the Royal Academy, 1771–1816, was elected an Associate of the Academy in the former year, and a full member in 1772. His wife, Mary, the second daughter of a magistrate named Saunders Welch, predeceased him in 1817, and he himself died on 23 April, 1823, and was buried in Old Paddington churchyard. All his adult life had been passed in working and saving money, and he left behind him a fortune of £200,000.

On July 3, 1823, Mr. Christie held a sale of the contents of his studio and house. Casts of a number of his busts were sold, including those of Mr. Aufrere, Sir M. Sykes, Lord Brownlow, General Fitzpatrick, Lord Erskine, Lord St. Helens, Lord Mansfield, Mr. Busk, Mr. Holford, Marquis of

Donegal, Lord Petre, Lord George Cavendish, Sir W. W. Wynne, Mr. Le Merchant, Lord Dillon, Lord Leitrim, Lord Brooke, Mr. Justice and Mrs. Welch (Mrs. Nollekens's parents), Mr. Carr of York, Lord Cowper, Earls of Mulgrave, Egremont and Aberdeen, Dr. Baillie, Duchess of Argyll, Duke of Gordon, Mrs. Pelham, Lady Hartley, Mrs. Arkwright, Mr. Stonehewer, Miss Symmons, Lord Bessborough, Lord Rous, Gally Knight, Admiral Colpoys, Mrs. Maddocks, Duke of Bolton, Mr. Mathias, Mr. Gregory, Mrs. Braddyll, Miss Le Clerc, Lady St. Aubin and Mrs. Knight.

At the sale of David Garrick, held by Mr. Christie on 23 June, 1823, two of the lots were a terra-cotta of "a wounded infant borne on a Dolphin" and a marble "recumbent female figure" both by Nollekens (Archives of Messrs. Christie).

Nollekens' original model for the monument to Lord Robert Manners was sold at Christies on 4 July, 1823, while in the Victoria and Albert Museum are a number of his terra-cotta sketches, including one of Mrs. Howard, of Corby, his monumental masterpiece. Others in the Museum are "A Hero and Victory," "Venus and Adonis," "Juno Pronuba," and "Modesty"; there is also his terra-cotta of "The Judgment of Paris," lent by Mrs. M. Pott.

At the Peter Norton sale held by Christies on 11 January, 1869, the following terra-cottas by Nollekens were sold: "A Group of Adam and Eve," "Laocoon," "The Graces," "Venus at the Bath," "A Dancing Nymph" and "Susannah and the Elders."

(Authorities cited in text.)

STATUES

1761	Bacchus	Formerly Shugborough Hall, Staffs (sold 1842)
c. 1766	Boy and Dolphin	For Empress of Russia, now at Burghley House
1768	Castor and Pollux	Victoria and Albert Museum, South Kensington
c. 1770	Diana, Venus, Juno and Minerva	Wentworth Woodhouse (Warner's *Tour of the Northern Counties*, Vol. I, page 218)
1775	Trevor, Bishop of Durham	Bishop's Chapel, Bishop Auckland, Durham
1777	Sir Thomas and Lady Salusbury	Great Offley Church, Herts
1778	Venus Chiding Cupid	Usher Gallery, Lincoln

c.1782	Marquess of Rockingham	Mausoleum, Wentworth Woodhouse
1782	Cupid and Broken Bow	Formerly Mytton Hall, Yorks
1782	William Denison	Ossington Church, Notts
1783	Mercury	Usher Gallery, Lincoln
1785	Robert Denison	Ossington Church, Notts
1787	Mrs. Pelham	Mausoleum, Brocklesby
1808	William Pitt	Senate House, Cambridge (model Fitzwilliam Museum)
n.d.	Seated Venus	Petworth, Sussex
?	"Venus Pouring Ambrosia on her Hair"	Purchased by Russel Palmer for 220 guineas, Christies sale Nollekens' effects, 1823

BUSTS

1764	Medusa	Burghley House
1766	Duke of York	Royal Collection
1766	Laurence Sterne	National Portrait Gallery
1773	George III	Royal Society
1774	Bishop Johnson	Worcester Cathedral (on monument designed by Robert Adam)
1776	Earl and Countess Bathurst	Cirencester Church, Glos
1777	Dr. Johnson	Westminster Abbey (replica, Pembroke College, Oxford)
1778	Samuel Burroughs	Great Offley Church, Herts
1779	J. Mathias	Hyde Lodge, nr. Chalford, Glos
1780	Charles II	Royal Society
1784	Lord Rockingham	Dalmeny, Scotland
1784	Ann Simpson	St. Magaret, Lothbury
1784	Sir George Saville	Fitzwilliam Museum, Cambridge (replica, Victoria and Albert Museum)
1789	William Weddell	Ripon Cathedral
1790	Lord Robert Manners	Belvoir
1790	Earl of Mansfield	Belvoir
1792	Duke of Bedford	Holkham, Norfolk
1793	C. J. Fox	Possession Earl of Ilchester
1793	Earl of Bessborough	Derby Cathedral
1793	William Windham	Holkham, Norfolk
1795	John Lee	Staindrop Church, Durham
1796	Mrs. Maude	Great Offley Church, Herts
1797	Edwin, Lord Sandys	Ombersley Church, Worcs

1800	Dr. Willis	Greatford Church, Lincs
1802	Dr. Charles Burney	British Museum
1802	5th Duke of Bedford	Woburn
1803	Lord Robert Spencer	Woburn
1803	General Fitzpatrick	Woburn
1803	Marquess of Hastings	Holkham, Norfolk
1803	Earl Grey	Woburn
1803	8th Earl of Lauderdale	Scottish National Portrait Gallery, Edinburgh
1804	Lord Holland	Woburn
1804	James Hare	Woburn
1805	2nd Earl Grey	Southill, Beds
1805	Anna, Duchess of Bedford	Woburn
1806	William Pitt	Bayham Abbey, Kent
1806	4th Earl of Darnley	Cobham Hall, Kent
1807	Rev. Thomas Jones	Trinity College, Cambridge
1808	Louisa, Countess of Aylesford	Packington Hall, Warwick
1808	Marquess Wellesley	Windsor Castle (cast at Eton)
1808	6th Duke of Bedford	Woburn
1808	Earl of Yarborough	Victoria and Albert Museum
1809	Lady Louisa Hartley	Possession Mrs. Smyth
1810	Lord Grenville	Royal Collection
1810	William Windham	Felbrigg Church, Norfolk
1810	Lord Moira	Royal Collection
1810	George Grenville	Brasenose College, Oxford
1810	5th Duke and Duchess of Rutland	Belvoir
1810	Countess of Yarborough	Victoria and Albert Museum
1810	George Canning	Apsley House
1811	Lord Chatham	Belvoir
1811	John, Duke of Bedford	Windsor Castle
1812	Charles Townley	British Museum
1812	Thomas Finch	Taylor Institute, Oxford
1812	Duchess of Richmond	Goodwood
1812	6th Duke of Devonshire	Windsor Castle
1812	Lord George Cavendish	Compton Place, Eastbourne
1813	Duke of York	Windsor Castle
1813	Spencer Percival	Apsley House (replicas at Northwick Park and Harrow)
1813	Earl of Charlemont	Possession Mr. Crowther, Isleworth
1813	Duke of Wellington	Apsley House
1813	Lord Gwyder	Edenham Church, Lincs
1814	Duke of York	For Carlton House
1814	Samuel Whitbread	Drury Lane Theatre
1814	Marquess of Granby	Windsor Castle
1814	Duke of Cumberland	Windsor Castle
1814	Lady Brownlow	Possession Author

1814	Lord Lake	Windsor Castle (£157)
1814	Duke of Wellington	Castle Howard
1815	Lord Erskine	Windsor Castle
1815	Earl of Egremont	Petworth, Sussex
1816	Earl of Liverpool	Windsor Castle
1816	Lord St. Helens	Tissington, Derby
1818	Francis, Duke of Bedford	Windsor Castle
n.d.	5th Earl of Carlisle	Castle Howard, Yorks
n.d.	Matthew Baillie	Royal College of Surgeons
n.d.	Duke of Newcastle (replica)	Newark Town Hall
n.d.	Lord Morley	Saltram, Devon
n.d.	Lord Mansfield	Trinity Hall, Cambridge
n.d.	Marquess of Granby	Belvoir
n.d.	3rd Duke of Somerset	Belvoir
n.d.	William III	Belvoir
n.d.	George II	Belvoir
n.d.	Provost Drummond	Royal Infirmary, Edinburgh
n.d.	Sir George Saville	Holderness House, Hull
n.d.	Duke of Richmond	Goodwood
n.d.	Mrs. Welbore-Ellis	Shelford Church, Notts
n.d.	Dr. Johnson	Salisbury Museum

MONUMENTS

1759	Potterne, Wilts	Henry Kent
1766	East Horndon, Essex	Sir John Tyrell
1770	Throcking, Herts	Mrs. Elwes
1772	Kenilworth, Warwick	John Bird
1773	Ruabon, Denbigh	Lady Henrietta Williams Wynn
1774	St. Michael Penkevil, Cornwall	Edward Boscawen
1774	Westminster Abbey	Oliver Goldsmith
1776	Deptford (St. Paul's)	Admiral Sayer
1776	Chipping Ongar, Essex	Mrs. Mitford
1776	Barbados (Cathedral)	Richard Salter
1777	Rokeby, Durham	Sir Septimus Robinson (medallion portrait)
1778	Bruera, Cheshire	Sir Robert Cunliffe, Bart. (medallion portrait)
1779	Whiston, Northants	Lord and Lady Boston
c. 1780	Chester (Cathedral)	Samuel Peploe
c. 1780	Walton, Bucks	Sir Thomas Pinfold
1780	North Wraxall, Wilts	Mrs. Methuen
1781	Westminster Abbey	Charles Stuart
1782	Westminster Abbey	Captains Bayne, Blair and Lord Robert Manners (d. 1782)
1783	Great Brington, Northants	Earl Spencer (des. by Cipriani)
1785	Westbourne, Sussex	Henry Bardwell
1785	St. Margaret, Lothbury	Ann Simpson

1785	Goathurst, Somerset	Sir Charles Tynte
1787	Wisbech, Cambs	Edward Southwell
1787	Great Barrington, Glos	Mary, Countess Talbot
1787	Exton, Rutland	General Bennett Noel
1790	Bengeo, Herts	Daniel Minet
1790	Abingdon (St. Helen's)	Dr. John Crossley
1790	Wetheral, Cumberland	Hon. Mrs. Howard. Contract 23 March, 1790, at Corby Castle, Cumb
1790	Exton, Rutland	Earl of Gainsborough
1792	Whiston, Northants	Hon. Mary Irby
1792	St. Katherine's, Regent's Park	Elizabeth Grigg
1793	Bath (Abbey)	Colonel Alexander Champion
1793	St. Michael Penkevil, Cornwall	Viscountess Falmouth
1793	Helmingham, Suffolk	Lionel Tollemache
1793	Chester (Cathedral)	Anna Matthews
1793	Westminister Abbey	Sir John Pringle
1794	Titchfield, Hants	David Karr
1795	Maidstone, Kent	Sir Charles Booth
1795	Shalstone, Bucks	Anne Purefoy
1797	Isleworth, Middlesex	George Keate
1797	Greatford, Lincs	Mrs. Willis
1799	Marlow, Bucks	Richard Davenport
1799	Cobham, Surrey	Andrew Karr
1799	Petham, Kent	John Thomson
1800	Purley, Berks	Anthony Storer
1800	Westminster Abbey	James Steward MacKenzie
1800	Carlisle Cathedral	John Johnson
1800	Burnley, Lancs	Charles Townley
1800	Radley, Berks	Sir George Bowyer
1801	West Wycombe, Bucks	George Dashwood
1801	West Wycombe, Bucks	Sir George Dashwood-King
1802	Withyham, Sussex	John, Duke of Dorset
1802	Shobdon, Hereford	Viscount Bateman
1803	Hampreston, Dorset	Edward Greathed
1804	Helmingham, Suffolk	Countess of Dysart
1804	Westbourne, Sussex	Richard Bardwell
1805	Tittleshall, Norfolk	Mrs. Coke
1805	Shalstone, Bucks	Rev. George Jervoise
1806	Stoneleigh, Warwick	Hon. Mary Leigh
1806	St. Michael Penkevil, Cornwall	Hon. Frances Boscawen
1807	Cambridge (Trinity College Chapel)	Rev. Thomas Jones
1807	Greatford, Lincs	Rev. Francis Willis
1807	Standish, Lancs	Cecilia Towneley
1808	Batsford, Glos	Thomas Freeman
1808	Dogmersfield, Ha ts	Sir Henry Mildmay
1808	Shalstone, Bucks	Rev. Jervoise Jervoise
1810	Chatsfield, Sussex	John Fuller
1810	Whitkirk, Yorks	Lord Irwin
1810	St. James's, Hampstead Road	Lord Southampton
1812	Saxmundham, Suffolk	Charles Long
1812	Staindrop, Durham	Mary Lee
1812	Westminster Abbey	Countess of Beverley
1812	Westminster Abbey	Colonel Charles Macleod
1818	Abingdon (St. Helen's)	Clement Saxton

NORMAN, SAMUEL
fl. 1760–1778

In 1760 Norman was responsible for the enrichment of the walls and cornices, etc., of the state rooms at Woburn Abbey (Gladys Scott Thomson's *Family Background*, page 60).

In the list of artists given in Mortimer's *London Directory* for 1763 he is described as "sculptor and carver to Their Majesties and surveyor of the curious carvings in Windsor Castle." He was also, according to a bill-heading, "cabinet-maker and carver at the Royal Tapestry Manufactory in Soho Square."

NORRIS, —

In 1677 Robert Hooke "agreed for seven chimney-pieces for £80" for Montagu House with Norris (*Diary of Robert Hooke*, page 301, edited Robinson and Adams). A George Norris was employed on stone-carving work at Lord Ashburnham's house in St. James's Square in 1713 (Ashburnham Archives).

NORRIS, WILLIAM

In 1788 he was the builder of the Freemasons' Tavern, being responsible for the stone-carving (Freemasons' Archives). About the same time he became a partner of Daniel Pindar (q.v.).

NOST, or OST, JOHN van
d. 1729

Nost was an inhabitant of Mechelen and came to England, where Quellin (q.v.) employed him as foreman. After his master's death Nost married Quellin's widow and, as Vertue says, "became a master of reputation and left behind him a good fortune."

His yard was in the Haymarket and there he manufactured lead figures, urns, etc., and carved statues, monuments and chimney-pieces. His large school of assistants included Andrew Carpenter (q.v.).

One of Nost's earliest patrons was Thomas Coke, of Melbourne Hall, Vice-Chamberlain to Queen Anne, and the original of Pope's "Sir Plume." On 1 July, 1699, Nost writes to his patron: "I have set up two models of boys but they were not to my mind, and having had some extraordinary reasons which called me out of towne and which have been a great hindrance to my business; but I will now with all speed dispatch your boys with all the care." This letter presumably refers to the pairs of amorini still at Melbourne. Nost was paid for one such pair in 1706, receiving £10 10s. for "for two boys after Flamingo, modelled apurpose and cast in a hard metall." In 1700 Nost made a number of other figures for the gardens, including Perseus (£25), Andromeda (£20), and Mercury and Syca (Psyche) £50 the pair. Other payments to him include £10 "for a boy and swan for a fountain, the swan in proportion to the boy, no bigger than the young Triton"; £6 9s. for "a young Triton with a brass pipe in the middle," while a "duck and swan as big as ye life" came to £8. The two most important figures were the two kneeling slaves, "an Indian and a blackamore," which came to £30 and which, with nearly all the other figures mentioned above, still adorn the gardens at Melbourne.

Nost's grandest work at Melbourne and for which he received £100 in 1705 is the great "Vase of the Seasons," still standing in the garden where the long grass walks meet. It shows how high a standard of craftsmanship could be reached by the worker in lead. The vase is supported by four monkeys, the upper part bears four heads, emblematical of the seasons, while the middle is decorated with a masque of children playing and swinging; the basket which surmounts all is rich with fruit and flowers. For Melbourne Hall itself Nost made a number of chimney-pieces, including in 1701 one of "rich purple marble, with freeze and cornish and pallasters of white marble." Six years later he made less important ones for the "Pendilum room, the Clossett and stone-room."

Coke also employed Nost in London, paying him in 1699 £50 for a chimney-piece for his London house in St. James's Place, and in 1704 Nost received £8 10s. for a "marble basin with a brass socket and wooden pedestal" for Coke's apartments in St. James's Palace (Archives, Marquess of Lothian).

At Melbourne Hall also is Nost's copy of Serlio's *Five Books of Architecture, Englished by Robert Peake*, published in 1611 and bought by the sculptor in 1696, and later purchased by Coke for 15s. at the sale of Nost's effects. There is also among the Melbourne Hall Archives an estimate for lead figures which is interesting as howing the prices Nost asked. They include "The Sabine Rape,-£90"; "Hercules and Centoure, £70," and "Hercules and Anteus, £80." Though Nost wrote to his patron that he had "made as nice a calculation as can be and find it cannot be done under the prises that is rated above," Coke found them too expensive.

Nost was the sculptor of the statues on the pediment of Buckingham House, which must have been very well known to Londoners and are mentioned in all early eighteenth-century guidebooks to the capital. These statues, according to the *New View of London* (1708), were cast in metal and represented "Apollo, Equity, Liberty, Mercury, Secret Truth and the Four Seasons." Lord Ashburnham, writing to Brian Fairfax the younger in 1706, asked him to find out what Nost had charged for the "statues for the attic of the Duke of Buckingham's London house." Fairfax replied that they had cost £27 each. In a later letter Lord Ashburnham complained that Nost had raised his charges, which were now so excessive that the writer would have to find some other statuary for his house at Ampthill (Letter-book of the First Lord Ashburnham).

Nost did a good deal of carving, etc., for the Royal Palaces. In 1701–1702 his bill for work at Hampton Court included "several drawings of the King's statue for the marble fountain, £2. A model in clay for a fountain, four mermaids, each sitting on a dolphin and four shells between them and four dolphins in the middle, supporting a large shell, £10. For casting same in metal, £10" (P.R.O., Works 5/52). An alternative model for the fountain consisted of "four figures of young men each sitting on a dolphin and four swans between them, a pedestal of four scrowles in the middle and a Mercury on top of it." About the same time Nost was restoring "a little Venus of marble" at Hampton Court, receiving £10 for "half a foot and putting half a foot to the other leg, a hand, a nose and mending several parts" (P.R.O., Works 5/52). He also made "a blackamoor kneeling, 5 foot high, and holding a sundial, £30" (P.R.O., Works 5/52), for the same Palace. Similar figures are to be found at Dunham Massey, Cheshire, and Okeover, Staffs.

Also for Hampton Court, Nost made in 1700 four panels of Portland stone, 3 ft. 11 in. by 3 ft., "for ye new piers next the road fronting the long gravel walk, two carved with the King's coat of arms, two with laurel branches, sword, sceptre and crown." Later he made "six boys cast in hard metal, 3 ft. 4 ins. high to stand on top of the said piers, baskets of fruit, flowers and festoons about them" (P.R.O., Works 5/51). These were followed in 1701 by "a statue of Bacchus in hard metal, 6 ft. 2 ins. high" and "two marble pedestals for sundials, the plinth of black marble, carved with four cyphers and eight leaves in the manner of a capital." Pedestals for various statues included those of a Gladiator, Diana, Hercules and Apollo, while a more ambitious work costing £86 were the "great vauses" and the carving of "eight panels and the pedestals of the said two vauses with emblems relating thereunto" (P.R.O., Works 5/52).

For the interior of the Palace, Nost made in 1700 "two fine great marble tables" and a purple marble chimney-piece with "a frieze of the triumph of Venus and mask-heads each side cast in brass." This, which was for the King's Gallery, cost the very large sum of £235, while for the dove-coloured one in the Queen's Gallery the sculptor was only paid £30 (P.R.O., Works 5/52).

Nost was also employed at many of the great houses. For Canons, in 1722, he made vases for the south and east fronts of the house, and with C. Burchard (q.v.) an equestrian statue of George I. He worked at Chatsworth, where in 1698 he was paid £30 for "figures of a boy and a girl," at Stourhead, and at Boreham in Essex, while lead garden statues and groups by him are to be found at Rousham, Oxon; Seaton Delaval, Northumberland; and Chirk Castle, Denbigh (Archives of houses named).

Between 1703–1710 he was paid nearly £100 for lead figures for Castle Howard; these are presumably the ones which still stand in the South Garden (Castle Howard Archives).

Between 1705 and 1716 he made a number of statues for Sir Nicholas Shireburn at Stonyhurst, including "a Pegasus and Fame for ye fountain in ye high parterre," Diana on horseback, and groups of infants, representing Peace, Abundance, etc. In all Nost received £662 for this work, but the majority of the statues were later removed by the Duchess of Norfolk to Worksop and have presumably perished (Stonyhurst Archives). Two other patrons for whom he made lead figures were Humphrey Mildmay, of Moulsham Hall, Essex, in 1717, and the Duke of Kent in 1725. For the latter's garden at Wrest Park, Bedfordshire, he made two large vases and eight heads (Archives, Lady Lucas and Dingwall).

In 1720 three vases were ordered from Nost at a total cost of £80 for the Printing House at Oxford, but for some reason or other they do not seem ever to have been carried out.

In 1723 the sculptor agreed with the Ironmongers' Company to make a statue of "Sir Robert Geffery, six foote high in hard metall in a workmanlike manner, and to fix ye same in ye place provided for it at the Company's almshouses at Shoreditch, with ye proper ornaments of a Lord Mayor, and to give the Company a modell thereof in hard metall, neatly completed, all at £40" (Company's Archives). The statue is now at Mottingham and a replica of it has been placed over the door of the almshouses.

Other statues by Nost included those of William III and Queen Mary (c. 1700), presented to the Royal Exchange by the City of London; Venus (1702), now at Umberslade, Warwick; George I

(1717), for Essex Bridge, Dublin, which is now at the Barber Institute, Birmingham; Queen Mary (1720), at University College, Oxford; George I (1726), which was made for Grosvenor Square, but disappeared about 1838; and George II, executed for the Duke of Chandos' seat at Canons. When the contents of that house were sold the statue was purchased by an anonymous bidder, who had it erected in Golden Square on 14 March, 1753.

Nost undoubtedly made a number of very important monuments, though many attributed to him in various books and articles cannot be definitely established as his work. The only signed monument by him which I know of, that to the Earl of Bristol, 1698, is at Sherborne, Dorset. The bill for his magnificent baroque monument of the Duke of Queensberry, 1711, at Durisdeer, Dumfries, is in the archives of the Duke of Buccleuch.

Both the monument and its setting are among the most exciting and unexpected things I know. The monument stands in the Mortuary Chapel attached to, and coeval with, the Queen Anne Church, built by the Duke in a small and remote Lowland village. In the centre of the Chapel there towers above the Douglas Vault a great baldacchino, of pure-white marble, its domed canopy carved with angels' heads, and supported by four superb, twisted, white-marble Corinthian columns, wreathed with bay and based on those in the Raphael cartoons. Against the south wall is the tomb itself, with the life-size figures of the Duke and his wife, perfectly preserved. Queensberry, with his eyes open, lies on his side, his head resting on his hand, and gazing down at his Duchess, whose eyes are closed in death, for she had predeceased her husband by two years. It seems not improbable that the monument was ordered, and indeed erected before, the Duke's death, for the cutting of the inscription commemorating his death is by a different hand to that which, in more florid prose, remembers his Duchess.

Nost was also responsible for the very fine standing figure of Sir Hugh Wyndham (d. 1683), at Silton, Dorset. Captain William Wynde, the architect, writing to Lady Bridgeman on 23 July, 1692, informs her that "Mr. Noste ye carver is gone in ye country to set up ye monument to Judge Wyndham and will not be heer this fortnight." In a letter to Sir John Bridgeman dated 16 January, 1698, Wynde tells him that "laste weeke I was with Mr. Noste who schowed me a table of Italian marble for ye Duke of Devonshire, of ye same peece I tend one for your ladye" (Archives, Earl of Bradford).

Nost died on 26 April, 1729, and a sale of his effects was held in 1731 by his widow. An advertisement in the *Guardian* (No. 60, 20 May, 1731) informed the public that there remained "several extraordinary fine things belonging to the late famous sculptor Mr. John Nost, fine inlaid marble tables, marble chimney-pieces, figures, etc.," and that Mrs. Nost "designing to go beyond seas, will dispose of them at reasonable rates at her house near Hyde Park where attendance will be daily given."

(Authorities cited in text.)

NOST, JOHN van, the Younger
d. 1780

He was the nephew of John van Nost the Elder (q.v.), under whom he worked and, according to Vertue (*Walpole Society*, Vol. IV, page 35), "drove on the business, but never studied, nor did himself anything tolerable." About 1750 he settled in Dublin, where he found plenty of work and, having no rivals, soon enjoyed an almost complete monopoly of sculptural work in Ireland.

In 1753 he was commissioned by the Corporation of Dublin to make a statue of George II, and returned to London in order that the King might go to him for sittings. In the following year he was back in Dublin, and the statue, completed in 1756, was erected in the centre of St. Stephen's Green on 2 January, 1758 (*Gentleman's Magazine*, 1758, page 41).

In 1765 Nost went to England again, this time to make a model of George III for a statue which was subsequently set up in Dublin City Hall. In 1776 he made his last journey to London, where ill health forced him to remain for four years, and it was during this period that he exhibited a bust of the King at the Royal Academy in 1779. He returned to Dublin in 1780 and died there in 1787.

I know of no works by him in England, but a very full list of his works in Ireland is given in Strickland's *Dictionary of Irish Artists*. To this I would, however, add the statue of George, Earl of Bristol (*c.* 1778), at Down Hill, Northern Ireland; a bust of George III (1764), afterwards bought at David Garrick's sale (23 June, 1823) by a "Mr. Core"; and a monument to Viscount Loftus (1768) at New Ross, Co. Wexford.

Nost also took a mask of Garrick, from which he executed a bust. The mask later came into the possession of Charles Mathews, the comedian, while endless copies of the bust were afterwards put on the market; indeed, Macklin, the actor, said to Nollekens that one "was in every barber's shop-window, as a block for wigs" (J. T. Smith's *Nollekens and His Times*, Vol. II, page 207).

NOWELL, PHILIP
fl. 1806–1838

From 1806 until 1818 he was the master-mason under Wyatt for the additions to Longleat (Archives, Marquess of Bath), and in 1824 and 1825 was extensively employed as a mason during the restoration of Windsor Castle. His work here included carving various Gothic details, and in the two years he received over £9,300 (P.R.O., Works 5/125 and 19–30/1).

Nowell was also the mason for the building of the Duke of York's column, for which he was paid £15,760 (*Architectural Magazine*, 1834, page 192).

In 1828 he was employed on the restoration of, and additions to, Apsley House, receiving £7,624; while ten years later he was again working for the Duke of Wellington as master-mason for the alterations to Stratfield Saye, where he was assisted by his son, Philip Nowell the Younger (Archives, Duke of Wellington).

NURSEY, —

Presumably a Norfolk statuary, though I have so far failed to find his name in any contemporary directory. He signs a large wall-tablet with excellent details to the Hon. Charlotte Windham, 1827, at Earsham, Norfolk; and another to the Rev. Richard Dreyer, 1838, at Thwaite in the same county.

NUTCHER, J., of Swathling
fl. 1754–1762

Though Nutcher lived in a small Hampshire town, two of his signed monuments are of considerable importance. At Bursledon, in Hampshire, is his monument (erected in 1754) to Philemon Ewer, who, according to his epitaph, "during the late war with Spain built seven large ships of war" and was "an ingenious artist and an excellent workman." At the base of the monument is a high relief of a man-of-war in full sail.

Nutcher's other main work is to Anne Woodroffe (*d.* 1762), at Seale, Surrey. This is about 9 ft. high and has a curious design, embodying two cornucopiae from each of which springs a rose-tree in full bloom. The mantling of the coat of arms is elaborate and well-carved.

NUTT, JOHN, of Birmingham
fl. 1810–1837

He signs tablets at Sutton Coldfield, Warwick, to Will Pearson, 1810, and in St. Martin's, Birmingham, to Edward Bower, 1814. His large wall-tablet to Richard Craddock, 1837, at Eccleshall, Staffs, has two flaming lamps on each side of a pyramid.

O

OLDFIELD, JAMES, and TURNER, —, of London
fl. 1800–1811

The "Mr. Oldfield of London" who was employed to execute carved stonework at Castle Howard in 1801 (Castle Howard Archives) was probably the senior partner of Oldfield and Turner, and in 1810 the firm made two chimney-pieces for Coventry House, Piccadilly, costing £36 and £35 respectively. The first of these, in "Porto Veneri" marble, was for the "back parlour," while the second, of "dove-grey marble," was for the "eating-room" (Archives, Earl of Coventry).

In Cheltenham Parish Church is their large monument to Sir William Myers, 1811, a work 15 ft. in height. The design shows "Fame" pointing to a column inscribed with the word "Albuera," while behind it are flags and military trophies.

OLDFIELD, C., of Ashford, Derby

He signs a very attractive classical monument to William Burgoyne, 1835, at Sutton, Bedfordshire, a work in the form of a small sarcophagus with a medallion-portrait of Burgoyne in the centre.

OLIVER, JOHN
b. 1616, *d.* 1701

He was one of Wren's assistants, and in February, 1667, was appointed a member of the Commission entrusted with the rebuilding of London after the Great Fire of the previous year. He later became Assistant Surveyor of St. Paul's Cathedral, Surveyor to the Dean, and also a member of the Court of Christ's Hospital (Various references, Wren Society).

On 2 March, 1685-1686, Oliver was appointed Master-Mason to the Crown (*Wren Society*, Vol. XVIII, page 146), and in this capacity was working at Kensington Palace in 1697 (P.R.O., E.351/3466). Four years later he received £215 "for embossing and casting the imperial supporters, the Lion and Unicorn, in hard metal and two imperial shields with the Royal Garter about each of them for the gate of the Royal Palace at Hampton Court" (P.R.O., Works 5/52).

Oliver, who with Henry Phillips had been Executor of Joshua Marshall (q.v.), died in 1701. In his will he left bequests to his daughter, Grace Shaw, and her children, a legacy to Christ's Hospital, and desired to be buried under the choir of St. Paul's Cathedral.

OLIVER, SAMUEL EUCLID
fl. 1769–1774

He exhibited in 1769 "a portrait of a nobleman in wax" at the Royal Academy. In 1770 he was in partnership with James Hoskins (q.v.), but may have died in 1774, as in that year Hoskins took another partner, Benjamin Grant (q.v.).

OLIVER, SANDERS
b. c. 1719

He was apprenticed to Thomas Bull (q.v.) in 1733, and between 1748 and 1750 was the mason responsible for building Ironmongers' Hall (Company's Archives). In 1761 he carved the ornamental stonework for the Scotch meeting-house at London Wall (Guildhall MS. 4976).

In 1772 Oliver received a communication from the Court of Assistants of the Masons' Company which informed him "that not being free of the Company he did use and exercise the trade of masonry within the City of London or the Liberties thereof," he must attend the next meeting of the Court and take up his freedom, or pay a fine of £10.

His monuments, which are of good workmanship, include those to George Baker, 1765, at Mayfield, Sussex, and the Deschamps family, 1776, in St. Stephen's, Walbrook. Another, to Joseph Innes, 1779, in Lewisham Parish Church, has a portrait-bust.

OLIVIERI, DOMINICK ANDREW, or OLIVERI, of London
fl. 1820–1833

Olivieri's bust of William Pitt, based on the original work by Nollekens (q.v.), is in the National Portrait Gallery, and in the Thomas Robson sale of 1835 his three undated busts of George IV, the Duke of York and Washington were sold. His studio was in Berkeley Street, Lambeth. He exhibited busts of E. R. Colville and Miss Malcolm in 1833 at the Suffolk Street Galleries.

OLVERS, JACOB and THOMAS, of Falmouth
fl. 1811–1837

They sign tablets to John Pellew, 1811, and to James Burke, 1812, at Mylor, Cornwall, and a large

Hellenic wall-monument to the Rev. Lewis Mathias, 1837, in Falmouth Parish Church.

OSBORNE, JAMES, of Bristol
fl. 1729–1767

He became a Freeman of Bristol in 1729 on his marriage with Anne, daughter of George Britten, woolcomber. He signs a tablet to John Hast, 1763, in St. James's Church in that city, and two large wall-tablets of superior workmanship at Chard, Somerset, to Humphrey Ash and John Eveleigh, both of whom died in 1767.

(Bristol City Archives.)

OSBORNE, JAMES, of Mansfield
fl. 1743–1768

In 1743 he was in partnership with Thomas Ince, and with him was responsible for a great deal of building at Welbeck, Osborne being paid £93 in 1751 for work in the Great Hall. By 1757 he was working on his own, but later payments, amounting to £2,380, were made between 1767 and 1768 to him and his partner, Matthew Porter, for building the bridge (Welbeck Abbey Archives).

OSBORNE, JOHN, of Bath
d. c. 1838

He taught himself to model in clay, and later, with the help of a farmer, was able to go to London, where he worked in Bacon's (q.v.) studio. After many vicissitudes he settled in Bath and, about 1835, carved a figure of the Goddess of Sculpture and a colossal head of Jupiter, both in Bath stone. Of the latter, which weighed six tons and took the sculptor several years to complete, Walter Savage Landor wrote in a private letter: "Nothing of Michael Angelo's is nobler and nothing of Thorwaldsen's finer."

At his death Osborne left his widow destitute, her only asset being the Jupiter. This was purchased from her for £100 by the Corporation of Bath, but was left lying neglected until 1861, when Mr. Alderman Bush of Bath rescued both it and the Goddess of Sculpture and placed them in Victoria Park. At the same time he employed an architect named Wilson to design the pedestals for both works, which were later executed by Mr. H. Treasure.

Osborne signs tablets to Thomas Baines, 1821, at Queenhill, Worcestershire, and to Ann Tetherly, 1831, at Northam, Devon.

Granville, in his *Spas of England* (1841, page 424), refers to Osborne as follows: "Born in penury —a mere shepherd's boy—he died in misery—an admired genius and a statuary worthy of a place among the ablest chisels of either ancient or modern times."

OSBORNE, JOHN, of Oxford
d. c. 1785

There was a family of masons named Osborne at Oxford who were associated with the city for many years. The first of these, John Osborne the Elder, was apprenticed to William Townsend in 1706 and was presumably the father of John Osborne the Younger, who died about 1785. The latter signs tablets to the Rev. David Price, 1771, at Stockton, Wilts, and to Francis Emmett, 1784, at Great Milton, Oxon. In the account-books of St. John's College, Oxford, there is a payment made to him in 1780 for carving a chimney-piece.

John Osborne the Younger had two sons. The elder, William, became a Freeman of his native city in 1775, while the second (and much younger) son, John Hodges Osborne, was apprenticed in 1787 to his mother, Jane, who had been carrying on the business since the death of her husband

(City Archives.)

OSGOOD, RICHARD
d. 1728 (?)

In 1691 he made a "large Caesar's head" for the guard-room at Kensington Palace (P.R.O., E.351/3467). In 1696 he supplied two leaden ducks for the garden at Chatsworth and three leaden figures for "ye neeches in ye Bowling Green House," while two years later he also made a head and a bas-relief for which he received £32 (Devonshire Archives).

In 1700 Osgood was employed in mending statues at Hampton Court, and was paid £72 for "casting two new legs and two new arms of copper and the great part of the drapery and a new quiver of arrows for the Diana that stands in the Quadrangle Court and burning altogether and mending several other parts. For rifling and cleaning the figure with aquafort to make it look bright all alike." For the Hercules which had "been melted and broke by ye fire at Whitehall" he cast new feet, part of the legs, hands and the lion's skin. In the same year he was paid £40 for "casting a large piece of drapery of the great statue of Antinous" (P.R.O.; Works 5/51). In 1701 he was still working at Hampton Court, supplying at £20 each twelve large vases, 4 ft. 3 in. high, "with flutes and gadurnes (*sic*) and other ornaments," for the top of the two pavilions by the bowling-green.

In 1704 Osgood was employed by Colonel Child, making for him a "pair of shield boys, three antique Roman heads, two pairs of large flower-pots and eight vases," while two years later

Child purchased from him "two large Roman heads and bustos of hard metal and eight large vases" (Archives, Child's Bank).

In 1709 Osgood was back at Hampton Court, where he supplied "two new wings for the statue of Victory and two new trumpets for the statue of Fame" (P.R.O., A.O.1.2447). His last recorded work was for the same Palace, where in 1715 he was ordered to "model and cast in hard metal two large sea-horses and two large Tritons to spout the water in the great bason or fountain in Bushey Park at Hampton Court." For this he was paid £180.

OSMOND, WILLIAM,
of Salisbury
b. 1791, *d.* 1875

He was appointed mason to Salisbury Cathedral about 1818, and in the two following years made new pinnacles for the south-east and north-east corners of the tower. In 1843 he was paid for "columns and capitals for the south walk of the cloister" (Cathedral Archives).

Osmond was a friend of A. Welby Pugin, and there are copies of a number of letters written by that architect to him in Benjamin Ferrey's *Life of Pugin*. One, dated 1844, and written when Pugin was making a tour of France, ends: "Leave your blisters, leave your Doric porticos, leave all and follow me." Ferrey is careful to explain in a footnote that "blister" was the term used by Pugin to describe the tablets which Osmond "was in the habit of affixing to the walls of churches as memorials." Osmond was certainly influenced by Pugin and it is interesting to walk round Salisbury Cathedral and see how the style of his monuments swings violently from the classical to the Gothic. The most ambitious is that to Bishop Burgess, 1835, which is a copy of a fifteenth-century altar-tomb, while the majority of his later "blisters" are in the spikiest Gothic style.

Osmond is commemorated by a tablet in the cloisters of Salisbury Cathedral which records that he "was many years a lay-preacher and mason to this Cathedral." In the latter post he was succeeded by his son, William Osmond the Younger, who died in 1890 at the age of sixty-nine, and who was responsible, among other works, for the carving of the stone decorations of Sidney Herbert's Byzantine church at Wilton in 1845.

The elder Osmond made a slate sun-dial for Thruxton Church, Hampshire, in 1820. His monuments in Salisbury include those to Sarah Hayter (1822), John Jacob (1828), Bishop Fisher (1828), Wadham Wyndham (1835), Henry Hinxman (1841) and James Cobb (1858), all in the Cathedral; and to the Long family (1824), and the Rev. Herbert Hawes (1838), in the churches of St. Thomas and St. Edmund respectively. Elsewhere in Wiltshire he signs monuments to John Lampard (1824), at Barford St. Martin; Thomas King (1825), at Alvediston; the Rev. James Shuckburgh (1833), at Downton; William Locke (1835), at Seend; and Earl Nelson (1839), at Standlynch. Other memorials executed by him include those to Anne Kennicott (1830), in Windsor Parish Church; Henry Eyre (1830), in Winchester Cathedral; Lady Miles (1834), at Yateley, Hants; the Rev. Daniel Williams (1833), at Woolston, Hants; and Henrietta Thornycroft (1844), at Bodenham, Hereford.

OUGHTIBRIDGE, T.
fl. 1751–1756

At Hatfield, Yorks, is a large stone monument, 12 ft. high, decorated with rather crude carving of cherubs' heads, flowers, etc., to the memory of William Oughtibridge (*d.* 1756). This is signed "T. Oughtibridge, Engraver," a signature also found on a cartouche tablet in the same church to Thomas Johnson, 1751.

OUTRIDGE, A., of Petersfield

He signs a large wall-monument in coloured marbles to William Mitford (1777), at Tillington, Sussex. An Elizabeth Outridge signs a tablet to Harriet Godbold (1823), at Greatham, in the same county.

OWEN, T., of Liverpool
fl. 1812–1813

He was an assistant of G. Bullock (q.v.) and exhibited, at the Liverpool Academy of 1812, "Cupid Sleeping." A year later he also showed figures of "Pan" and "Music."

P

PAGE, GREGORY, of Horsham
b. 1773, *d.* 1834

He signs a wall-monument with a semi-urn against a rounded background to Henry Napper, 1803, at Wisborough Green, Sussex, and an oval tablet to Smith Whittby, 1816, at West Chiltington in the same county.

PAGE, GEORGE
d. 1853

In 1831 he received a Silver Medal from the Society of Arts for a model of a bust. He exhibited at the Royal Academy, 1841–1849, showing ideal works and a statuette of a child, and also showed models at the Society of British Artists in 1846. He became insane in 1852 and was placed in Colney Hatch, where he died in August, 1853 (Archives, Artists' Annuity Fund).

PAGE, ROBERT, of Norwich
b. 1707, *d.* 1778

Page is the best of the Norfolk statuaries and his monuments are important; indeed, his skilful use of coloured marbles, his details of rococo shields and groups of angels' heads make his work very similar, and in fact almost equal, to the contemporary monuments of Sir Henry Cheere (q.v.).

His monument to Nathaniel Mickelthwait, 1757, at Sprowston, Norfolk, has a fine portrait-bust, while he signs others in the county to Elizabeth Segrave, 1727, at Gateley; Mrs. Pell, 1732, at Dersingham; Sir Philip Astley, 1739, Melton Constable; Robert Daye, 1740, at Scoulton; Elizabeth Browne, 1741, at Colton; Bussy Greene, 1744, at Catton; Sir Jacob Astley, 1760, Melton Constable. In Norwich itself works by him commemorate John Moore, 1725, in the Cathedral; Mary Lubbock, 1729, in St. George Colegate; Edward Coleburne, 1730, in St. Peter Mancroft; Robert Bene, 1730, in St. Martin at Oak; Robert Snell, 1738, in St. Giles; and Thomas Crowe, 1751, in St. Andrew's. Page died in 1778 and was buried in St. John Timberhill, Norwich.

PAGET, JAMES
fl. 1720–1725

Between 1720 and 1725 he was building a house for the Master of the Rolls which had been designed by Colin Campbell and was situated next to the Rolls Chapel in Chancery Lane. Besides being generally responsible for the construction, he also carved the great door-case, Ionic capitals, lions' heads, masks and chimney-pieces (P.R.O., A.O. 407/2494).

PAINE, JAMES
b. 1745, *d.* 1829

He was the son of James Paine the architect (1725–1789) and was born in June, 1745 (Faring-ton Diary, Vol. VIII, page 26), and studied at St. Martin's Lane Academy. In 1764 he went to Rome for the first time, and though he was back in England by 1769, in 1774 he was again in Rome, this time accompanied by his wife. He seems to have remained in Italy for at least nine years, for as a subscriber to various books he gives his address as "Rome" up till 1783. By 1788, however, he had returned to London.

Paine exhibited sculpture and pictures at the Society of Artists, 1761–1773, where his work included a bust of Sir John Fielding. The most important of his monuments is that to William Powell, "one of the patentees of the Theatre Royal, Covent Garden," in Bristol Cathedral. This large work, dated 1769, is almost 17 ft. high and has a figure of "Fame" holding a medallion. Other works signed by Paine commemorate Lady Sondes, 1777, at Rockingham, Northants, and Sarah Proby, 1783, in Chatham Parish Church.

The drawing for the Sondes monument is in the Victoria and Albert Museum (*D.* 1551), and here, too, are drawings by Paine for monuments to Thomas Richardson (*D.* 1548) and Thomas Hirst (*D.* 1907). I have so far failed to trace these monuments, though, of course, it is quite possible that they were never erected.

Paine was well known as a maker of chimney-pieces, and also in the Victoria and Albert Museum are a number of his designs for these (*D.* 1540–1547), including two for a chimney-piece for the saloon at Brockett Hall, Hertford-shire, a magnificent work dated 1772, with a note in the artist's hand that the frieze is to represent "The Rape of Europa." There is also a drawing for a chimney-piece for "The Grove, Isle of Wight" (1775), and two undated ones for "Mr. Lloyd Baxendale" and "Lord Clifford, Ugbrooke, Devon." He also carved a chimney-piece for Lady Middleton of Peper Harrow in 1773.

When Sir William Chambers was building a

house for William Errington near Hexham, in Northumberland, he submitted some chimney-piece designs, but these apparently were not accepted and Mr. Errington instead expressed a wish for a special type of chimney-piece designed by Paine. In a letter written on 24 December, 1769, Sir William replied : "With regard to the chimney-piece you wish to substitute, I cannot give designs for them without breaking through an established rule they are the invention of Mr. Paine and he must be applied to for them. He lives in Salisbury Street by the Strand and will not only furnish you with the design, but likewise with the chimney-piece and he keeps statuary for the purpose" (British Museum Ad. MS. 41133).

On 12 March, 1830, Mr. Christie held a sale of the pictures, casts, books, etc., "the property of J. Paine, Esq., architect, deceased." Among the lots sold were the account-books of the sculptor, Nicholas Stone. These had originally belonged to Vertue and are now in the Sir John Soane Museum (Archives, Messrs. Christie).

PAINE, W., of Stratford-on-Avon

He was the son of a William Paine, of Stratford-on-Avon, mason, who died in 1800. In 1816 the younger Paine made eight chimney-pieces for the Judge's Lodging at Warwick (Warwick County Records, Class 24 [36]).

PALMER, BENJAMIN
fl. 1739–1778

After the death of his father, William Palmer (q.v.), in 1739, he took over the yard in Gray's Inn. In Eland's *Purefoy Letters* there is an entertaining series written by Mr. Henry Purefoy and Benjamin Palmer, concerning a most unsatisfactory purple-marble chimney-piece which William had supplied just before he died. In the end Benjamin had to take the blame for this and agree to its return.

His most ambitious work is the statue of Sir William Harpur over the old Grammar School at Bedford. He carved this in 1768 and at the same time made a monument with medallion portraits to the memory of Sir William and his wife, which was erected in St. Paul's Church, Bedford. For this and the statue he was paid a total sum of £200 (Bedford School MS. Account-book).

As a statuary Palmer is not as good as his father, and his monuments, though large, are not particularly distinguished. That to Arthur O'Keefe, 1756, in Westminster Abbey, has a portrait-bust, as has that to Sir Thomas Gage, 1742, at Hengrave, Suffolk.

Palmer signs monuments to Frances Legh, *c.* 1740, in Warrington Parish Church; Stephen

Master, 1741, at Daventry, Northants; Thomas Master, 1742, in Westminster Abbey; John Willis, 1744, at Malmesbury, Wilts; Arthur Bevan, 1749, at Laugharne, Carmarthen; Lord Stourton, 1753, in Cheam Old Parish Church; William Rose, 1753, at East Retford, Notts; Henry Uthwatt, 1757, at Lathbury, Bucks; Robert Johnson, 1769, and the Rev. Louis Monoux, 1771, both at Sandy, Beds; Margaret Sparhauke, 1770, at Graveley, Herts; and William Middlemore, 1772, at Grantham, Lincs.

Palmer retired in 1778, and a sale of his stock was held on 7 and 8 July in that year.

PALMER, J., of Manchester

He signs a Hellenic wall-tablet to John Baldwin, 1817, at Bowden, Cheshire.

PALMER, NATHANIEL
fl. 1829–1846

He exhibited at the Royal Academy, 1829–1844, showing various works, including busts of the Rev. Rowland Hill (1829) and Sir Robert Peel (1838).

His figure of Charles I, shown at Westminster Hall in 1844, was described by the acid Art Critic of the *Literary Gazette* as "a poor thing, as if the King was going to dance a corrante." In 1846 he applied for assistance to the Artists' General Benevolent Institution owing to "accute inflammation of the eyes."

PALMER, WILLIAM
b. 1673, *d.* 1739

He was the son of William Palmer, "late of St. Giles-in-the-Fields, coachman," and was apprenticed in 1687 to James Hardy (q.v.), but for some reason was turned over to Josiah Tully a few years later. In 1694 he became free and returned to work for Hardy, but by 1696 had left him and was serving under John Nost (q.v.). He may have worked for Thomas Hill (q.v.), as in November, 1704, Sir John Vanburgh, writing to Lord Godolphin about the misdemeanours of Thomas Hill, then master mason for the building of the Orangery at Kensington Palace, says, "I ask'd one of his (i.e. Hill) foreman who they work'd for, but he tould me One Palmer whom his master had made his Deputy" (*Wren Society*, Vol. VII, page 140).

Palmer gave a list of monuments he had "set up" to Le Neve for inclusion in the latter's *Monumenta Anglicana*. The phrase in all but one instance means "carved," the exception being the monument to the Earl and Countess of Exeter, which was ordered by the Countess from Pierre Monnot (q.v.) and executed by that sculptor in

Rome. In this case Palmer was only the mason who fitted the parts together and erected them in St. Martin's Church, Stamford, though he may also have carved the inscription. Mrs. Esdaile (*Antiquaries' Journal*, Vol. XXII), however, argued that "the only possible conclusion to be derived from this fact .is that Palmer went to Rome," where she supposed him to have worked as Monnot's assistant and to have cut the epitaph before the monument left Italy. On the other hand, it seems equally possible that he did whatever was necessary in England.

Palmer was certainly not abroad in 1706, for in that year Lord Ashburnham gave him an order for three marble chimney-pieces, two for his house at Ampthill in Bedfordshire, and one for the staircase-hall at Ashburnham House, Westminster. Palmer was then apparently not working on his own, for Lord Ashburnham refers to him as "chief man to Mr. Chapman, the marble-setter of Red Lion Square" (Ashburnham Archives). However, by 1710, he had his own yard in the Square, having by that time probably succeeded to, or perhaps purchased, Chapman's. In 1719 he made a chimney-piece for Knowsley in Lancashire (Derby Archives, 2005/1), while from 1718 until his death he held the post of mason to Lincoln's Inn, receiving £300 between 1730 and 1733 for work in connexion with the Chapel, Hall, etc. (Benchers' Archives).

Between 1727 and 1738 Palmer was working for Lord Folkestone at his London house, also in Red Lion Square (Archives, Earl of Radnor). In 1738 he made chimney-pieces for Mr. Edward Trotman of Shelswell and, in the following year, one for Mr. Henry Purefoy of Shalstone, Buckinghamshire (Eland's, *Purefoy Letters*, Vol. I, page 53, *et seq.*). He died towards the end of 1739, for Mr. Purefoy pays the bill for his chimney-piece to "Mrs. Anne Palmer," and Lord Folkestone's last payment in that year is made to "Mrs. Palmer, the mason's widow."

Palmer's monumental masterpiece is the very remarkable figure of the Hon. Margaret Watson, 1713, at Rockingham, Northamptonshire, a standing draped statue in the attitude of the Venus de Medici, a skull at her feet, and above her a canopy and a draped curtain which is bunched and tied back. The work is unsigned, but is included in the list which the sculptor gave to Le Neve. Other monuments by him, either signed or in that list, are those commemorating Anne Crispe (with a bust), 1708, at Birchington, Kent; Sir Roger Meredith, 1712, at Leeds, Kent; Richard Walburge, 1715, at Barholme, Lincs; Anne Gelthorpe, 1716, at Hillington, Norfolk; Elizabeth Hatten, 1724, Lincoln Cathedral; Richard Vaughan, 1724, in Carmarthen Parish Church; Mrs. Ann Crofts, 1727, at Little Saxham, Suffolk; William Chambers, 1728, Great Offley, Herts; Constantine Phipps, 1728, at White Waltham, Berks; John Barham, 1730, at Wadhurst, Sussex; William Games, 1731, at Upton, Northants; Mrs. Stepney, 1733, and Lady Stepney, 1733, both at Llanelly, Carmarthen; Gilbert Browne, 1737, at North Mimms, Herts; James Fortrye, 1737, at Northfleet, Kent; and Stephen Everard, 1738, at Faversham, Kent.

PAMPALONI, LUIGI
b. 1791, *d.* 1847

He was born in Florence and first attracted attention in 1827 when he executed a monumental group for a Polish lady. This represented a little girl sleeping and a boy with clasped hands and upturned face kneeling by her side. The figure of the boy, under the name of the "Praying Samuel," had a world-wide popularity and plaster copies of it were sold in immense numbers.

Pampaloni's best-known works in Italy are the figures of Arnolfo dei Lapi and Brunelleschi on the eastern side of the Cathedral in Florence. In England he signs the monument to Mrs. Gooch at Benacre, Suffolk, which was erected in 1840 and has a relief of an angel bearing the mother and her child heavenwards.

PANORMO, CONSTANTINE
b. 1805, *d.* 1852

Son of Francis Panormo, a professor of music, Constantine was born in London and, as a boy, went to Ireland, where he studied at the Royal Dublin Society's Schools and distinguished himself by gaining numerous prizes. In 1824 W. Behnes (q.v.), who had himself been a pupil at the school, offered to take two boys and instruct them for two years at £60 a year each. The Royal Dublin Society accepted the offer and sent over Panormo and Gallagher (q.v.). As Behnes's pupil, Panormo attended the Royal Academy Schools, gaining Silver Medals in 1825 and 1826. In the former years he also received the large Silver Medal of the Society of Arts for an entire figure.

The Royal Dublin Society then sent Panormo to study in Rome, but he was back in London in 1833, and by 1837 had returned to Dublin, where in 1842 he was elected an Associate of the Royal Hibernian Academy. In 1844 he sent a group of the "Liberation of Caractacus" to Westminster Hall and, two years later, finished the statue of George IV which the Dublin Society had ordered from Behnes, but which that sculptor had never been able to complete, owing to various financial difficulties.

PLATE XIX

NICHOLAS READ
Part of the monument of Admiral Tyrrell, 1766, Westminster Abbey.

PLATE XX

J. C. F. ROSSI
Lord Heathfield, 1825, St. Paul's Cathedral.

L. F. ROUBILIAC
Part of the monument of the Duke of Argyll and
Greenwich, 1748, Westminster Abbey.

Panormo exhibited at the Royal Academy in 1833 and 1834 and at the Royal Hibernian Academy in 1837–1849. At the former his works included ,busts of Sir Edward Antrobus, Lady Mary Leslie and Sir Richard Joddrell; for a list of his works in Ireland, see Strickland's *Dictionary of Irish Artists.*

(*New Monthly Magazine,* 1826, page 11; *Literary Gazette,* 1844, page 483; Strickland's *Dictionary of Irish Artists.*)

PANZETTA, JOSEPH
fl. 1789–1830

When he applied to the A.G.B.I. in 1830, Panzetta stated that he had been a pupil "of Mr. Joseph Wilton, who was also his godfather, and of J. B. Cipriani, and after a long residence in Italy for improvement returned to London in 1787." Panzetta then proceeded to give a list of his principal works, which included "A Monument in Westminster Abbey to Sir Archibald Campbell," "Vases for Somerset House," and "The Lions on the Terrace" (also for Somerset House), and the statue of Archbishop Tillotson in Yorkshire; "these were done for Mr. Wilton." Panzetta also said that he had "done in Portland stone for Mr. Banks" the relief in front of the Shakespeare Gallery in Pall Mall. He also claimed that he was responsible for the figures of Hercules and Justice on the Union Insurance Office. Panzetta worked for Mrs. Coade (q.v.) and her successors for twenty-six years, modelling the statue of George III at Lincoln Heath and a figure of Britannia at Plymouth. Other works carried out by him for Coade include the bas-relief in the pediment of Greenwich Hospital, which he executed in 1806, in collaboration with John Bacon the Younger (q.v.) (*European Magazine,* 1806, page 288). In 1817 he modelled the statue of Lord Hill which was supplied by the Coade works for the column at Shrewsbury (*Gentleman's Magazine,* 1817, Part II, page 393).

Panzetta exhibited at the Royal Academy, 1789–1810, showing bas-reliefs, ideal works, designs for monuments, etc.

If all that Panzetta said was true it would appear that he did the work and more famous sculptors got the credit and the cash; but what is more likely is that he merely carved in stone or marble the works which others had modelled and designed.

PAPERA, B.

As "Mr. Papera figure-maker" he supplied busts to Lord Bridport in 1802 (Soane Archives), while in the same year Wedgwood paid him for busts of Mrs. Siddons, Lord Nelson and Mrs. Deamour (Mrs. Dawson Damer ?), and also for "one vase with lamp" (Wedgwood Archives).

PAPERA, JAMES PHILIP
fl. 1829–1851

He was presumably the son of B. Papera (q.v.), and exhibited busts at the Royal Academy from 1829 until 1831. Twenty years later, when living at Cambridge, he sent to the Great Exhibition either statues or busts of Queen Elizabeth, Rubens, Cromwell, Charles I and Sir Robert Peel. A Louisa Papera is noted in the *London Directory* of 1828 as "figure maker" of 16, Marylebone Street.

PAPWORTH, EDGAR GEORGE
b. 1809, *d.* 1866

He was the only son of T. Papworth (q.v.), was born on 20 August, 1809, and at an early age became a pupil of E. H. Baily (q.v.). In 1826 he joined the Royal Academy Schools, gaining Silver Medals in 1829 and 1831 and a Gold Medal in 1833 for a group entitled "Ulysses Receiving the Scarf from Leacothea." In 1827 he had been awarded the Silver Palette by the Society of Arts for a bas-relief.

Papworth was elected to the Academy Travelling Scholarship in 1834 and went to Rome, but owing to ill health was forced to return to England after three years' study. In 1841 he exhibited "Poor Little Nell" at Birmingham and, three years later, showed at Westminster Hall a "Sleeping Girl" and "A Statue of Lord Brougham." Of the latter the *Art Journal* wrote: "it is a rough and unfinished statue, very easy, very good and very like." In 1848 he executed a stone figure of Minerva for the Royal Polytechnic in Regent Street (*Builder,* 1848, page 174).

In a competition held in 1857 to select the designer of the proposed Wellington monument in St. Paul's Cathedral, Papworth's model was awarded the third prize of £300. He also worked as a silver-designer and made the centre-piece presented "by the slave population of Jamaica" to the Marquess of Sligo in 1839.

Papworth married Caroline, daughter of his first master, E. H. Baily, and their son, another E. G. Papworth, was born in 1832. He also adopted sculpture as a profession, joining the Royal Academy Schools in 1848 and exhibiting at the Academy, 1852–1882. His "Startled Nymph," commissioned by J. Neeld, M.P., was lent to the Exhibition of Art Treasures of the United Kingdom held at Manchester in 1857; it is also illustrated in the *Art Journal* of the previous year (page 250).

In his latter years the elder Papworth's carelessness and extravagance led to his becoming financially embarrassed. He died on 26 September, 1866, and was buried in Highgate Cemetery.

He exhibited at the Royal Academy, 1832–1860, at the British Institution in 1840 and at the Great Exhibition of 1851. At the Academy his works included a group entitled "The Young Emigrant" (1861), and busts of Rowland Hill (1833), Dr. Latham (1857) and Sir Richard and Lady Burton (1865). His group of "Cupid and Psyche" was exhibited at the Birmingham Society of Artists in 1841, while others executed by him were: "The Moabitish Maiden" (1850), for the Prince Consort; "Martino" (1854) and "A Nymph of Diana" (1854), for the Crystal Palace; "Ruth" (1855), for Osborne; and "A Boy With a Bird's-nest" (1857), for a Mr. Joyce of Tulse Hill.

Papworth's bust of William Murdock (1839) is in the Birmingham Art Gallery, an undated one of Sir Henry de la Beche is in the Geological Museum, while those of Admiral Blake (1860), Locke (1862) and Captain Speke (1865) are in the Shire Hall, Taunton. He signs monuments to Alfred Tebbitt, 1838, in St. George's, Bermondsey; Thomas White, 1841, at Wethersfield, Essex; and John Mitchel, 1846, at Mancetter, Warwick. He also executed the one erected in Bunhill Fields in 1862 to commemorate John Bunyan.

(Various references, *Art Journal* and *Builder*.)

PAPWORTH, THOMAS
b. 1773, *d.* 1814

Son of John Papworth (1750–1799), master-plasterer to the Royal Palaces, Thomas continued his father's work and was the owner of the last stucco and plastering business carried on in London on a large scale.

He exhibited at the Royal Academy, 1794–1815, showing designs for ceilings, sketches of candelabra, and a number of busts, including those of Miss Mellon the actress, and of his brother, J. B. Papworth, the architect.

PARBURY, GEORGE
fl. 1760–1791

In the books of the Society of Arts he is described as "under twenty-two" and "son of the Keeper of the Royal Academy" when he won a premium from the Society for a "Model of Birds in Clay" in 1760. Next year he won a further premium, and a note in the list of the Society's prize-winners says that he later became a "metal-chaser."

Parbury exhibited wax portraits, models, etc. (chiefly of classical subjects), at the Society of Artists, 1764–1771, and at the Royal Academy, 1772–1791.

PARK, PATRIC
b. 1811, *d.* 1855

Both his father, Matthew Park, and his grandfather were statuaries and masons in Glasgow, and at the age of fourteen he was himself apprenticed to Mr. Connell, a mason. His master was at that time building Hamilton Palace, and here young Park, after working for two years as a stonecutter, was entrusted with the carving of the coat of arms above the main entrance. In 1828 he was employed by the architect Gillespie to carve decorative details at Murthly Castle.

In 1831 Park went to Rome and, after studying for two years under Thorwaldsen, returned home and began his career as a sculptor. In 1839 he submitted a fearsome design for the Nelson memorial, consisting of a heroic statue of the Admiral, supported by two figures representing "Manhood Mourning Nelson's Death" and "Honour Consoled by the Glory and Triumphs of Nelson," while as a crowning absurdity Nelson was shown grasping his sword by the blade. Two years after this he moved from Glasgow to Edinburgh, and in 1845 sent a figure of a "Greek Huntsman" to the exhibition held to select suitable works of art for the new Houses of Parliament.

In 1846 a statue of "Modesty Unveiled" was entered by Park for the *Art Union* competition, but he was not allowed to exhibit it and wrote furious letters of protest to the Press. The *Art Union*, however, justified their action on the ground that the work was "an offensive portraiture of a model, coarse in more than average degree; the lower limbs massive and ungraceful, the upper part of the figure exaggerated and sensual," and concluded firmly that they considered it "utterly deficient of every particle of beauty and elegance."

In 1850 Park formed the project of erecting a gigantic figure of Wallace on the hills near Edinburgh and prepared a model which stood 15 ft. high and required ten tons of clay. Lack of encouragement, however, led him to abandon the idea and he "destroyed with his own mallet the model he had so laboriously made" (*Builder*, 1866, page 733). Two years later he moved to Manchester, and on 16 August, 1855, died at Warrington railway station, where he had burst a blood-vessel in trying to help a porter to lift a heavy trunk.

Park was elected an Associate of the Royal Scottish Academy in 1849 and a full member two years later. He exhibited there, 1839–1855, at the Royal Academy, 1836–1855, and at the British Institution, 1837–1854. Among the works shown were statues of "Eliza" (1843) and "Alexander" (1845); and busts of the Duke of Newcastle (1836), Thomas Campbell (1839), John Landseer (1839), R. B. Haydon (1839), Charles Dickens (1842), the Earl of Dundonald (1848), and Sir Harry Smith (1848). His busts of Sir Archibald Alison (undated), Lord Jeffrey (1840), D. O. Hill (1842), James Jardine (1842) and Professor Simpson (1850) are in the Scottish National Portrait Gallery; those of James Oswald (1842) and Adam Smith (1845) are in the Glasgow Art Gallery; while undated ones of James Hutton and Sir James Hall are in the Geological Museum in London.

Other busts by Park include those of Mr. Huggins (1846) at Huggins College, Gravesend; Sir Charles Napier (1853), executed for Napoleon III; the Rev. Henry Grey (1853), at New College, Edinburgh; Sir John Potter (1854), at the Manchester Free Library; Napoleon III (1855), at the Victoria and Albert Museum; "A Scotch Lassie," National Gallery, Edinburgh; and undated ones of Charles Barry at the Reform Club, and Sir William Fairbairn at the Royal Society. He was also responsible for the statues of Michael Sadler (1837) and Charles Tennant (1841) in Leeds Parish Church and Glasgow Necropolis respectively, while he signs the monuments of Andrew Skene, 1836, in the New Calton Cemetery, Edinburgh, and Jane Richardson, 1839, at Sigglethorne, Yorkshire.

From the foregoing list it will be seen that Park was especially in demand as a sculptor of busts, a type of work at which he was at his best. Graham wrote in *British Literature and Art* (page 449) that "Park's appreciation of beauty in subjects of a more ideal kind was not equalled to his appreciation of character in portrait-busts," while the *Building Chronicle* (1855, page 236) considered that "all his works were marked by a vigorous originality, a grace of style and a delicate beauty of finish which few ever equalled."

His busts of Horatio McCulloch (1849) and of Sir John Watson-Gordon (1851) are in the Royal Scottish Academy, while his undated one of David Hamilton is in the Glasgow Museum.

(*Scottish Family History*, Vol. II, page 276; authorities cited in text.)

PARKER, RICHARD, of London
fl. 1769–1774

Parker, whose studio was in the Strand, was also employed by Wedgwood, and in the firm's archives there is an undated letter (written about 1769) from William Cox, the London agent, in which he informs Wedgwood that "Mr. Parker has cast the medallions off in the best manner him and I could well contrive. I should be glad of your notes respecting the propriety or Deserts of the Performance."

Parker apparently specialized in making casts, for the bill he sent in to Wedgwood has the following printed heading: "Mr. Parker having obtained from Joseph Wilton Esq. statuary to His Majesty various moulds of bas-reliefs and busto's made upon his original models, has the honour to acquaint the nobility and gentry that they may be accommodated with casts at the shortest notice. N.B. Those original casts can be had at no other place and although it may happen that some figure makers may clandestinely make moulds of any of those casts, they can produce at best but an impression void of every original touch" (Wedgwood Archives). In 1774 he was again working for Wedgwood, modelling "A Zingara, a Vestal and a Pug-dog" (Meteyard's *Wedgwood*, Vol. I, page 326).

At Ashburnham Place was a set of library busts by Parker based on works by well-known sculptors such as Roubiliac and Rysbrack. The set, which includes likenesses of Locke, Milton, Congreve, Prior, Inigo Jones, etc., is almost similar to one in the possession of Lord Trevor, at Brynkinalt, Denbigh.

PARKER, SAMUEL, of London
fl. 1820–1831

In 1822 he received eight hundred guineas for the chimney-piece for the saloon of the Royal Pavilion at Brighton. This is described by Brayley in his *History of the Royal Pavilion* (1838) as follows: "A sumptuous chimney-piece of statuary marble with enrichments of ormolu in each jamb, within a niche stands a Chinese figure; those figures, which are of metal, are highly painted and varnished and the dresses are finely pencilled." This is now in the yellow drawing-room at Buckingham Palace, a building where Parker was also employed and where, in 1829, he received £2,000 for statuary work (P.R.O., Works 19/3).

At the Great Exhibition of 1851 a Mr. Peachey showed a bronze bust of Sir Thomas Lawrence by Parker which was "made in London from a model produced at great cost and afterwards destroyed" (Catalogue of the Great Exhibition, Vol. II, page 841). Parker's small bronze busts of Lord Brougham (1831) and William IV (1831) are in the Scottish National Portrait Gallery.

PARKER, THEODORE

He was probably the father of Richard Parker (q.v.) and, like him, also worked for Wedgwood. In 1769 he modelled "statues of Flora, Seres (*sic*), Spenser, Hercules, Juno, Prudence, Milton, Shakespeare, a boy (on) a couch and three doggs" (Wedgwood Archives).

PARKINSON, ROBERT,
of Newmarket
fl. 1820–1840

He was the son of William Parkinson, a "statuary and mason" of Newmarket, and in 1833 married a Miss Jemima Well, a dressmaker of Grosvenor Square. He signs a tablet to John Isaacson, 1830, at Burwell, Cambridgeshire.

PARR, R.

According to Hutchins's *History of Dorset* (Vol. III, page 679), he signed the monument "with a pediment supported by two Corinthian pillars" to the Douch family, 1675, at Stalbridge, in that county.

PARS, ALBERT
fl. 1759–1767

He was the son of a silver-chaser, and in 1759, 1764 and 1765 received premiums for models in wax from the Society of Arts, while in 1767 a further award was made to him for a bronze cast.

Pars was the brother of William Pars, A.R.A., the portrait-painter, and of Henry Pars, the draughtsman and director of the well-known Art School in St. Martin's Lane.

PARSONS, —
fl. 1718–1720

He was probably a Gloucestershire mason and his monuments are excellent copies of contemporary London work. He signs two charming cartouche tablets in that county to Anne Millechamp, 1719, at Long Newton, and to Deborah Roche, 1720, at Tetbury, while his monument to Ferdinando Gorges, 1718, at Ashley, Wiltshire, has an inscription-tablet in the form of a heavy fringed curtain.

PARSONS, LATTER, of Lewes
Firm *fl.* 1788–1860

He took over the yard of R. Morris, of Lewes (q.v.), and as a mason built the County Hall in that town in 1808 (Town Archives).

Parsons' monuments and tablets, based on London work, are in excellent taste, that to Robert Durrant, 1799, at Framfield, Sussex, being in the manner of the younger Bacon, while a cartouche tablet to George Peckham, 1788, at Salehurst in the same county, is far above the ordinary provincial level in design and workmanship.

Parsons was later joined by his son, C. Parsons, who is responsible for some of the later tablets, and their yard in Eastgate, Lewes, continues to this day. The firm is no longer owned by the family, but its monuments are in the best manner and style, and worthily carry on the Parsons tradition, as the very dignified ledger to Viscount Gort, unveiled in 1950 in Penshurst Church, shows.

Other monuments and tablets executed by the Parsons in Sussex include those to William Chambers, 1808, at East Blatchington; William Constable, 1810, at Burwash; Odiarne Hooper, 1819, at Beckley; Richard Stone, 1824, at Mayfield; Mary Wright, 1831, at Framfield; the Rev. James Capper, 1835, at Wilmington; Ida Beauclerk, 1832, at Cowfold; and the Bishop of Sierra Leone, 1857, at Upper Dicker.

PARSONS, ROBERT, of Bath
b. 1717, *d.* 1790

In 1744 he was employed by the elder Wood as "a free stone-mason and one of the house-carvers" for the building of the Bristol Exchange, but he was chiefly known for his garden vases and ornaments carved from Bath stone, which he sent all over England.

In 1747 he carried out work of this kind for Lord Fitzwalter at Moulsham Hall, Essex; between 1745 and 1751 Henry Hoare paid him £110 for vases for Stourhead; and in 1759 and again ten years later he supplied others to Lord Folkestone. The two vases made in 1759 are still in the garden of Longford Castle, while a dozen more, made for Castle Hill, Devon, are also *in situ*. These particular vases cost £2 15s. each, and in Lord Fortescue's archives is Parson's original drawing for one of them. In 1766 he made six vases for the front of Corsham Court (Archives of Houses named).

In Parsons' manuscript Commonplace Book (now in private possession) is an account of how he went in 1764 to see Ralph Allen on the day before the latter's death, in order to show him designs for tombstone and memorials. Parsons, therefore, is presumably responsible for the pyramid in Claverton churchyard under which Allen lies buried.

Parsons became a Baptist minister about 1768, but "from the congregation he received no remuneration for his services and never relinquished his business as a stone-carver. He was removed to the Eternal World, February, 1790, and was buried in the Baptist Chapel at Walcot" (*Memoirs of the Rev. John Porter*). His obituary in the *Bath Chronicle* states that "for forty (*sic*) years he had been Pastor of the Baptist Congregation in Garrard Street, and it is to his disinterested zeal that the Society owed its origin and establishment." He published in 1772 *Letters of the Rev. Mr. Fletcher of Madely on the differences subsisting between him and the Hon. and Rev. Mr. Shirley.*

As a monumental mason Parsons was in partnership with Ford (q.v.), and together they sign a monument at Bucklebury, Berkshire, to Winchcombe Packer, 1747.

PARSONS, THOMAS, of Bath
b. 1744, *d.* 1813

He was the son of Robert Parsons (q.v.) and, like his father, a carver of stone vases and chimney-pieces. His book of designs is in the possession of the Bath Municipal Library and shows that he copied his vases from drawings by Hoare, Cipriani, Kent, Wedgwood, Mrs. Coade, etc. He made the famous vase for Mrs. (afterwards Lady) Miller into which verses were dropped by the wits of Bath. These she would pick out and read to her assembled guests, an amusement which terminated on the unfortunate day when a most indelicate ode polluted the urn.

Like his father, too, Thomas Parsons was a Baptist minister, and his published works include *Effusions of Paternal Affection on the Death of a Lovely Daughter* (1799) and *High Church Claims Exposed* (1808).

PASCO, JOSEPH
fl. 1754–1766

He lived at Hackney, where he carried out repairs to the Parish Church in 1754, and in 1765 was elected a churchwarden (Simpson's *Memorials of St. John at Hackney*).

Pasco signs monuments in Essex to Mrs. Anne Meade, 1758, at Great Easton, and to Samuel Bosanquet, 1765, in Leyton Parish Church.

PASSEY, J., of Tillingdon
He signs a stone wall-tablet which is painted to represent coloured marble, to Elizabeth Weaver, 1821, at Mansall Lacy, Hereford.

PATENT MARBLE WORKS, THE
Firm *est.* 1809

Their yard was in Westminster and they seem to have been mass producers of chimney-pieces and monuments, most of the latter being extremely dull and frequently ugly. One or two trained designers of taste must have been employed, however, for the firm occasionally turned out a good monument, and their best can be favourably compared with the work of contemporary sculptors. This is especially true of the fine, indeed noble, relief of three daughters mourning at a parent's tomb on the memorial to Thomas Bennion, 1840, at Overton, Flint. Other examples of their monumental work include those to Admiral Windham, 1833, at Felbrigg, Norfolk; Mary Mackinnon, 1833, in St. Mary Abbots, Kensington; James Seton, 1834, at Byculla, India; Phyllis Shirley, 1836, at Ettington, Warwick; John Holford, 1836, in St. John's Wood Chapel; Arthur Annesley, 1841, at Bletchington, Oxon; Francis Stewart-Mackenzie, 1844, in St. George's, Grenada, West Indies; Ann Burmester, 1848, in Holy Trinity, Tunbridge Wells; and Colonel Joseph Bradshaw, 1850, at Duffield, Derby.

In 1829 the firm received £122 for marble chimney-pieces for Lambeth Palace (Cambridge University Library MS. 3928). At the time of the Great Exhibition of 1851 the works were owned by a Mr. Thomas Hartley, who showed "a design for a Gothic monument."

PATERSON, ROBERT, of Galloway
b. 1712, *d.* 1801

Paterson, whose history and wayward mode of life suggested to Sir Walter Scott the novel of "Old Mortality," was the son of a free stone-mason and stone-cutter and followed in his father's footsteps.

In his time he carved hundreds of headstones for churchyards in Galloway and Wigtownshire, and many years after his death Messrs. Black, Scott's publishers, erected a tombstone to his memory in Caerlaverock churchyard in 1855.

Paterson had a son, Walter (1749–1812), who was also a stone-engraver.

(Ramage's *Drumlanrig and the Douglases.*)

PATIENCE, JOSEPH, of London
fl. 1798–1801

Son of Joseph Patience, architect, he exhibited at the Royal Academy in 1798 a bust and a bas-relief for a monument to the memory of his father, which was afterwards erected in the church of All Hallows, London Wall. In 1800 he showed two figures "designed for holding lights," and in the following year was declared a bankrupt (*Universal Magazine*, 1801, page 381).

PATTEN, C. T., of Bristol

According to the *Gentleman's Magazine* of 1796 (page 841), it was Patten who was responsible for "the very handsome marble monument" erected in Hardwick Church, Buckinghamshire, to the memory of the Rev. George Bridle, who had died in 1792.

PATTEN, FRANCIS, of Rochester

fl. 1791–1821

His father, Francis Smith Patten, was made a Freeman of Rochester by purchase in 1761, and became free of the Masons' Company in 1773. Patten himself, who became a Freeman of his native city by patrimony in 1791, was four times Mayor between 1812 and 1821 (Archives, City of Rochester).

With his partner, T. Brisley (q.v.), he built the cloisters at Cobham Hall, in Kent (Archives, Earl of Darnley), and he also signs a tablet to Thomas Brenchley, 1818, at Bredgar, in the same county.

PATTESON, JAMES and SAMUEL, of Manchester

Firm *fl.* 1790–1840

James Pattison was first in partnership with a Daniel Mathison, but the firm was declared bankrupt in 1792 (*Universal Magazine*, 1792, page 397), and after his discharge he took as partner his son Samuel.

Besides their monumental work, they also advertised themselves in 1840 as "manufacturers of marble mantelpieces." They sign Hellenic tablets to the Rev. Thomas Whitaker, 1818, at Bowden, Cheshire; to Thomas Wilkinson, 1832, at Middleton, Lancs; and to William Greenwood, 1834, at Burnley, in the same county.

PATY, JAMES, the Elder, of Bristol

fl. 1721–1746

He was not born in Bristol, for he paid £15 4s. 6d. on 15 April, 1721, to be admitted a Freeman of that city. In the following year, however, he was well established, taking Samuel Phillips, son of Maurice Phillips of Bursley, clothier, as an apprentice. In 1728 he carved the two "Jacks" on the tower of Christ Church, Bristol.

Paty's monument to Sir William Pendarves, 1726, at Camborne, Cornwall, is a large, important work, with a fine medallion head and shoulders of Sir William in armour and wig. He also signs a monument in St. Mary Redcliffe, Bristol, to the Rev. Richard Sandford, 1721. Paty was the principal mason and carver for Bristol Library, in King Street, 1739–1741. His will was proved 25 February, 1747.

(Bristol City Archives.)

PATY, JAMES, the Younger, of Bristol

b. c. 1746

He was presumably a son of James Paty (q.v.), and was apprenticed to Thomas Kilby on 23 February, 1760, becoming a Freeman of his native city on 9 March, 1768.

Paty signs a monument with a medallion-portrait of James Foy, 1771, in the church of St. Philip and St. Jacob, Bristol, while other works by him in the city commemorate John Rich, 1761, in St. Thomas's; Francis Colston, 1763, in All Saints; and Thomas Holmes, 1772, in Christ Church. He also signs the monuments of Francis Davis, 1766, at Chepstow, Monmouth, and of Henry Allen, 1767, in Monmouth Parish Church.

He was probably the brother of John Paty, of Bristol, who was born on 10 December, 1754, attended the Royal Academy Schools as a student of sculpture in 1772, and became a Freeman of Bristol on 7 December, 1778. There is also another "John Paty, architect," who became a Freeman on 22 April, 1789, on his marriage with Elizabeth, daughter of William Perry, of Bristol, "mariner."

PATY, THOMAS, of Bristol

b. 1713, *d.* 1789

He was employed by Wood as an "ornament-carver" during the building of the Royal Exchange at Bristol in 1744 (Wood's *Exchange of Bristol*), while between 1740 and 1747 he executed all the stone and wood-carving, both inside and out, for the Redland Chapel in the same city. In 1755, when the font was presented to the Chapel by John Cossins, its patron and builder, it was stated that this had been "designed and made by Mr. Thomas Paty, who is generally esteemed one of the best carvers in England, either in wood or stone, by whom all the rest of ye ornaments in the Chapel were designed and carved" (Archives, Redland Chapel, possession Messrs. Osborne, Ward and Co., Bristol). The most elaborate of these carvings are "the ornaments of the chancel and pulpit in limetree," for which he received £106 8s. in 1743. The work is admirable and quite equal to anything turned out by contemporary London craftsmen.

Paty was also the "freestone mason and carver" employed during the building of St. George's

Church, Kingswood, near Bristol, between 1752 and 1756 (Bristol City Archives), while in 1768 Mr. Henry Hoare engaged him to dismantle the famous Bristol Cross and to move it to Stourhead (Hoare Archives). In the Tredegar Archives is his letter to Mr. Charles Morgan, dated 1787, about a tablet to be erected to Mrs. Parry. He encloses a sketch of the work (an oval tablet with an urn in high relief) and informs Mr. Morgan that the price "will be £12, inclusive of the inscription and packing-case, letters will be 1¼d. each, but if the urn and part under it should be thought too plain it may be ornamented so as to make the monument look much better, which may be done from thirty shillings to five guineas."

Paty was best known as an architect, indeed the *European Magazine* of 1789 (page 424) refers to him only as such in its obituary notice. As a statuary he executed his most important work in memory of William Hilliard, who died in 1735. The monument, which is nearly 20 ft. high, stands in the Lord Mayor's Chapel, Bristol, and consists of a fine portrait-bust standing on a sarcophagus, while below is a tomb or cave with an arched entrance.

Other monuments signed by Paty include those to George Locke, 1735, at Frome, Somerset; John Price, 1736, and Walter Jeffreys, 1748, both in Brecon Cathedral; George Hussey, 1741, at Seend, Wilts; John Nelmes, 1742, at Wooton-under-Edge, Glos; the Hon. Rothesia Barrington, 1745, at Shrivenham, Berks; Edward Gore, 1748, at Barrow Gurney, Somerset; Mary Garlick, 1749, at Doulting, Somerset; Edward Southwell, 1755, at Henbury, Glos; William Rees, 1763, at Laugharne, Carmarthen; Judith Alleyne, 1763, in Bristol Cathedral; Thomas Bedingfield, 1764, in St. Mary's, Bury St. Edmunds, Suffolk; Mrs. Twyford, 1765, at Kilmerdown, Somerset; William Paston, 1769, at Horton, Glos; the Rev. John Rodgers, 1773, at Brixton Deverill, Wilts; Mrs. Hallings, 1775, at Ledbury, Hereford; the Morgan family, 1779, at Chepstow, Monmouth; M. Davis, 1783, at Abbots Leigh, Somerset; and John Morgan, 1784, in Carmarthen Parish Church. Paty died 4 May, 1789. His obituary in the *Bristol Journal* of 9 May refers to him as an architect "whose extensive virtues, professional abilities and strict integrity, will in this city ever be rever'd."

PATY, WILLIAM, of Bristol
b. 1758, *d.* 1800

Like his father, Thomas Paty (q.v.), he was an architect as well as a statuary, and was admitted to the Royal Academy Architectural Schools in 1775. He died on 11 December, 1800, and is buried in St. Augustine's, Bristol, where there is a tablet to his memory. His widow, Sarah, survived him, dying in 1807 at the age of fifty-three.

Paty's monument to Mrs. Heathcote, 1798, in St. John's, Devizes, has a medallion portrait-bust, while those to Daniel Cox, 1785, at Beaminster, and Thomas Harris, 1797, in the Lord Mayor's Chapel, Bristol, have bas-reliefs.

Of his other monuments, the early ones are frequently signed "Paty and Son," William Paty in such cases being the "son." They include those to William Springett, 1777, at Alderley, Glos; John Haviland, 1777, at Langford Budville, Somerset; Susanna Higfoot, 1779, at Chepstow, Monmouth; Margaret Sherston, 1779, and Abraham Elton, 1794, both in Wells Cathedral; Mrs. Martha Travell, 1780, at Upper Slaughter, Glos; Christian Alleyne, 1780, in St. George's, and Edward Jordan, 1791, in St. James's Church, Barbados; George Thorne, 1783, at Swimbridge, Devon; Elizabeth Holder, 1783, at Hinton Charterhouse, Somerset; Sarah Paget, 1784, at Shepton Mallet, Somerset; Richard Lockyer, 1789, at Falmouth, Cornwall; Henry Harvey, 1789, at Tetbury, Glos; Thomas Stokes, 1791, at Wickwar, Glos; James Lansdowne, at Radstock, Somerset; D. Bull, 1793, at Calne, Wilts; Mrs. Bragge, 1793, at Lydney, Monmouth; the Rev. Charles Selwyn, 1794, at Blockley, Glos; and the Griffith family in Barbados Cathedral. His monuments in Bristol commemorate Richard Nelmes, 1789, in St. Philip and St. Jacob; Mary Stretton, 1794, in St. Michael's; Sir Anthony Fitzherbert, 1798, in the Cathedral; and Mary McTaggart, 1799, in St. Augustine's.

PAYE, RICHARD MORTON
fl. 1773–1802

He exhibited wax models and a cast at the Royal Academy, 1773–1779. He continued to send works to the Academy until 1802, but in these later years only showed paintings.

PAYNE, —, of St. Ives, Hunts

He signs a tablet with an urn and cherub-heads to Robert Underwood, 1792, at Boxworth, Hunts.

PAYTON, JOHN MORRIS, of Bristol
fl. 1832–1842

He signs monuments to Sarah Major, 1836, at Hungerford, Berks; to James Williams, 1838, at Mathern, Monmouth; and to John Purnell, 1839, at Camerton, Somerset.

PEACOCK, WILLIAM,
of London ·

In 1810 he was paid £150 for "mason's and statuary work" at the New Mint (P.R.O., A.O.1/2500).

PEARCE, EDWARD, of London

He signs the arresting monument of the Duchess of Gloucester, 1848, in Kensal Green Cemetery. This consists of a sarcophagus with finely carved detail, set on a plain podium built of large blocks of stone.

PEARCE, or PIERCE, EDWARD
d. 1695

His father was Edward Pearce, a painter-stainer employed on the decorative paintings at Somerset House, St. Paul's Church in Covent Garden, and Belvoir. The elder Pearce died at Bottesford in 1658, while working for Lord Rutland, and was buried in the village churchyard.

Edward Pearce the younger was possibly apprenticed to Edward Bird, an artist whom Wren employed to execute painted decoration in the City churches. As a wood-carver Pearce worked for Sir Charles Wolseley at Wolseley Hall. He was apparently most successful, for, according to Plot (*Natural History of Staffordshire*, 1686, page 383), "of all the joiner's work I have met with in this County there is none comparable to that of the new dining-room of Sir Charles Wolseley at Wolseley, the carved work thereof is also very good, both done by one Pearce." He was also responsible for much of the wood-carving in the Church of St. Lawrence Jewry (unhappily destroyed by enemy action in 1940), while he received £4 for "carving a wooden dragon for ye model for ye vane of copper of St. Mary-le-Bow" (Bodleian, Rawlinson, B.387).

As a stone and marble-carver, Pearce made the font for St. Matthew, Friday Street, in 1685 (Guildhall MS. 3543), besides executing all the carved woodwork (*London and Middlesex Archaeological Society*, Vol. 3, page 378). Two years later he was paid for stone-carving (probably the shield-of-arms in the pediment) at the Bishop's Palace, Lichfield (Ecclesiastical Commissioners' MS. No. 123,828). He had carried out more work of the same kind in 1683, when he carved the coat of arms and pediment for Lord Craven's seat of Combe Abbey (Bodleian MS. Gough, Warwick 1).

Pearce was also employed at the Guildhall, receiving, between 1670 and 1673, £300 for "work in front of the Guildhall." On 16 May in the latter year he received a further £250 for "work about

the Guildhall and the public cistern in Pancras Lane" and, on 20 November, £112 in consideration of the same work (Guildhall MS. 184 SR/1–2). About 1690 he made four chimney-pieces for Castle Bromwich Hall, Warwick (Archives, Earl of Bradford).

Under Wren he built, or was employed at, the churches of St. Swithun, Cannon Street; St. Benet Fink; and St. Andrew, Holborn, where he received a total sum of £4,050 (Guildhall MS. 4256). He also worked at St. Paul's and, with his partner, Shorthose (q.v.), built St. Clement Danes between 1680 and 1681 (*Wren Society*, Vol. X, page 108).

For the City Companies he worked at the Coopers' Hall, 1671–1672 (Guildhall MS. 5606/4), and at the Grocers' Hall, 1680–1684, receiving there a total of £305. The final payment of £13 was made in 1698 to "John Pearce, executor of Edward Pearce (Archives, Grocers' Company).

Between 1689 and 1695 Pearce was employed at Hampton Court and Whitehall, executing seats for the latter and also "carving work done about ye fountain in ye Privy Garden," which included shells, festoons and scrolls.

Other decorative and architectural work carried out by him included the gate-posts at Horseheath, Cambridgeshire, for Lady Alington, in 1665 (R. T. Gunther's *Sir Roger Pratt*, page 130); "roses, festoons and other work about ye gates" at Clare College, Cambridge (Willis and Clark's *Architectural History of Cambridge*, Vol. I, page 104); the bronze dragons on the Monument, and the famous vases for Hampton Court. For these his bill runs as follows: "To Edward Pearce, more for a great vauze of white marble, all the figures enricht with leaves, and festoons of shells, and pedestal of Portland stone, £250. More for a white great marble urne with divers figures and other ornaments, £475 10s." (P.R.O., A.O.2482). The first "vauze," which has a relief of Amphitrite and the Nereids, now stands without its pedestal on the terrace at Windsor Castle. Apparently both were left unfinished at Pearce's death, for in 1700 a payment was made to John Nost (q.v.) "for fluting ye foot of ye vases that came from Mr. Pearce and polishing the plinth and moulding atop" (P.R.O., Works 5/51).

In 1685 Pearce made a statue of Queen Elizabeth for the Royal Exchange, the expense being borne by the Fishmongers' Company. He was also employed by the Skinners' for a similar purpose, for an entry in their Court Book, dated 1 October, 1685, reads: "At this Court Mr. Peirse appeared and informed the Court that the statue of Edward III was by him set up for the Company in the Exchange and finished—whereupon it is ordered that £60 be paid unto him by the Renter Warden" (Company's Archives). For the Goldsmiths' Company he made a statue of Henry V for which he received the same sum (Company's Archives). He had in the previous years made the statue of Sir Thomas Gresham for the same building and he also carved a wooden statue of Sir William Walworth for the Hall of the Fishmongers' Company. About 1690 he made the dial originally erected at Seven Dials, but which is now at Weybridge.

Busts by Pearce include those of Milton (c. 1656) at Christ's College, Cambridge; an undated terracotta one of Cromwell in the National Portrait Gallery, and another in bronze (1672) at the London Museum; Christopher Wren (c. 1673), at the Ashmolean Museum, Oxford; Baldwin Hamey (1680), at the Royal College of Physicians; and Thomas Evans (1680), in the possession of the Painter-Stainers' Company. He is also said to be responsible for the magnificent monument erected about 1670 to the memory of Lord and Lady Maynard, at Little Easton, Essex (Gentleman's Magazine, 1818, page 596).

Besides all his other work Pearce also found time to be a collector, his partner in this activity being a Mr. Manby. A notice in the London Gazette (No. 3156, 30 January–3 February, 1695/6) runs: "On Tuesday the 4th instant will be sold by auction at 4 in the afternoon Mr. Pearce, carver, and Mr. Manby, painter, their curious collection of books, drawings, prints, models and plaster figures."

Pearce married a widow named Anne Smith in 1651 and died in 1695. His death must have taken place early in the year, for probate of his will was granted on 27 April, according to the calendar of the Probate Court which still survives. The will itself, however, which was entered in the Register of Wills, Probate Court, Archdeaconry of Middlesex, "Vol. VII, Folio 2, Rector," no longer survives, for the volume was lost prior to 1858. Vertue is incorrect when he states that Pearce lived in Surrey Street and was buried in St. Mary-le-Strand, for he was buried in the neighbouring church of St. Clement Danes, and, according to the rate-books, lived in Arundel Street.

He must have had a very high reputation among his contemporaries, judging from a letter dated 1711 in the archives of the Marquess of Bath at Longleat. In it the writer, John Talman, describes to his father, William Talman, a party he had given in Rome, including the decoration of the room in which the entertainment was held. He mentions that around the walls were painted heads of famous Italian and English artists—

Palladio, Raphael and Bonaroti, on the one side, and Inigo Jones, Fuller and Pearce on the other. In the Soane Museum, British Museum and Ashmolean are a number of drawings for monuments formerly attributed to William Talman, but now identified by Mr. Howard Colvin as the work of Pearce. Two of these drawings were thought, by the late Mrs. Esdaile, to be the designs for the monuments to Lord and Lady Irwin at Whitkirk, Yorks, and to Mr. and Mrs. Withers at Arkesden, Essex, but the former is known to be by Nost.

(Mrs. Poole's Edward Pearce; Walpole Society, Vol. XI; Diary of Robert Hooke; Account-book, Royal College of Physicians; Authorities cited in text.)

PEARCE, J., of Frampton
fl. 1795–1812

He signs a large tablet with delicate details to John Cox, 1795, at Stone, Gloucestershire, and a charming one with a relief of a violin and an open music-book to Thomas Sinderby, 1812, at Westbury, in the same county.

PEARCE, THOMAS

According to the London Magazine of 1752 (page 575), Pearce executed in that year the Portland stone sculpture in the pediment of the Naval Hospital at Haslar. The relief, 48 ft. long and 11 ft. high, had in the centre a large Royal coat of-arms with figures of "Navigation" and "Trade" to left and right, while there were also various subsidiary figures and emblems, including "a sea-bird bringing an eel in its mouth to a sailor in distress." One could think of a great many things a shipwrecked mariner would have infinitely preferred.

PEARCE, W. H., of Truro
fl. 1826–1851

In 1848 he made, to the order of the Prince Consort, two columns of serpentine and a pedestal of steatite, with a porphyry and jasper base, for Osborne House (Builder, 1848, page 416).

Pearce's monuments and tablets are mostly neo-Hellenic, and signed examples of his work in Cornwall commemorate Frances Bettesworth, 1821, at St. Michael Carhays; Susannah Bayntun, 1826, at Mylor; Jonathan Passingham, 1833, and Colonel Pasmore, 1837, both at Helston; Benjamin Sampson, 1840, at Gwennap; the Earl of Falmouth, 1841, at St. Michael Penkevil. Another, to Thomas Teague, 1837, which is at Redruth, in the same county, has a medallion-portrait.

PEART, CHARLES
b. 1759, *d.* 1798

He was born at English Newton, Monmouth, on 22 December, 1759, and entered the Royal Academy Schools as a student in 1781. In the following year he was awarded the Gold Medal for a group entitled "Hercules and Omphale."

On leaving the Schools, Peart worked as assistant to Lochee (q.v.) and also modelled portraits for Wedgwood, including those of Sir William Chambers, two sons of George III, Hastings, Elliot and Lord Hillsborough in 1787. In the following year he wrote to Wedgwood from Stowe that he was "obliged to work 14 hours in a day which puts it out of my power to attend to anything else" (Wedgwood Archives).

In 1792 he carved the fine statue of Henry V for Monmouth, and three years later made a chimney-piece costing £51 16s. for the Marquess of Buckingham's house in Pall Mall (Soane MSS.). He exhibited at the Royal Academy, 1778–1798, showing wax-portraits, models, and busts of Sir Samuel Marshall and of "a nobleman, deceased." He died in 1798, and his widow, Elizabeth, was granted a small pension by the Academy in the following year.

Peart's signed monuments include those to Lt.-Colonel Joseph Moorhouse, 1791, in St. Mary's, Madras, and John Finch, 1791, at Dudley, Worcestershire.

(Heath's *Monmouth.*)

PEATTS, —, of Nottingham

He signs a large wall-tablet to the Rev. William Wild, 1827, at Costock, in that county.

PECK, HENRY WILLIAM
fl. 1816–1821

In 1816, while living at Shoreditch, Peck won a Silver Medal from the Society of Arts for a plaster-cast of "Adam and Eve," a work he showed at the Royal Academy a year later. He continued exhibiting at the Academy up till 1820 and also sent work to the British Institution from 1819 until 1821. In the former year his address is given as Hoxton.

PECK, J., of Loughborough
fl. 1770–1805

He signs a number of architectural tablets, the best being those to Benjamin Brookes, 1770, and the Rev. Francis Wilcox, 1798, both at Loughborough, Leics; Elizabeth Cropper, 1800, at Bunny, Notts; and the Rev. T. Hastings, 1804, at West Leake, Notts.

PECK, JOHN,
of Bishop's Stortford
d. 1834

He signs a wall-tablet to the Rev. Robert Tooke (*d.* 1776), at Lambourne, Essex. The date of his death is given by the *Essex and Herts Mercury* as 18 April, 1834.

PEDLEY, JOSEPH, of Warwick
b. 1677

As a young man he lived in Rocester, in Staffordshire, but settled in Birmingham in 1703, and about four years later was employed on the rebuilding of King Edward's Grammar School. *The Dugdale Society* (Vol. XII, page 93) quotes his deposition (made in 1713 when he was thirty-six) as to the mason's work he carried out there. He was apparently paid by instalments, and received in all a sum of £268.

In 1710 Pedley agreed to execute the stonework for St. Philip's Church, Birmingham, for "2½d. a foot and the mouldings at 7d. a foot, but if the Commissioners did find that 7d. per foot for the said mouldings be not enough, they to give something more." The Commissioners did decide that 7d. was insufficient, and three years later agreed to pay an extra "six-and-thirty pounds in consideration of the hard bargain made."

According to William Shenstone, Pedley "was a great sufferer by undertaking Birmingham New Church, which was, I think, a design of ye late Groom Porter" (i.e., Thomas Archer); "certain it is he has been a great sufferer by the Groom Porter himself, concerning which he relates a story not much to ye Groom Porter's honour" (Majorie Williams' *Letters of William Shenstone*).

In 1749 Pedley made stone urns for Lady Luxborough's garden at Barrells, Warwick, and in the same year was employed by Shenstone to build two "Gothick" turrets for his house, the Leasowes.

PEISLEY, BARTHOLOMEW,
the Younger, of Oxford
d. 1715

His father, Bartholomew Peisley the Elder, must have been born in 1620, for when he gave evidence in 1681 in a lawsuit between Thomas Wood (q.v.) and Richard Frogley, carpenter, he stated that "he was aged sixty-one and that he had erected a stone house in St. Giles's parish wherein Squire Bateman lately lived" (Vice-Chancellor's Archives, 1681, Mich.).

The younger Peisley was master-mason of Trinity College, Oxford, in 1691 (Wood's *Life and Times*, Vol. III, page 364). In 1708 he was working at Blenheim, where he carved capitals of columns. In his will, a copy of which is in the volume of Henry Joynes' papers in the British Museum (Ad. MS. 24327), Peisley left £400 to his daughter Elizabeth, and his property in Oxford to his son Bartholomew (q.v.). To his son-in-law, Henry Joynes the surveyor, he left £300, "to be paid within twelve months next, after the debt of £1,200 due to me for worke done at Blenheim House at Woodstock shall be paid to my Executor, or as soon as £300 of that debt shall be paid him."

Apparently most of the craftsmen employed at Blenheim found it difficult to get their money, for Joynes himself, writing to a Mr. Small in 1748, complained of his "hard fate of not being paid the amounts remaining due to me," adding "but the temper of the Duchess of Marlborough was such and I really know not for what or why, she would do everything that she could to prevent my being paid" (British Museum, op. cit.).

PEISLEY, BARTHOLOMEW, the Third
b. c. 1683, *d.* 1727

A mason like his father, he built the Great Bridge at Blenheim in partnership with William Townsend (q.v.), and in 1723 was paid £350 for the marble door-cases of the gallery of that house. Peisley died in 1727 and was buried in St. Giles's, Oxford.

PEPPER, W.

A Lincolnshire statuary, he signs a wall-tablet to Richard Quincey, 1767, at Rippingale, in that county.

PEPPER, W., the Elder, of Brighton
fl. 1830–1854

In 1846 Pepper made the model for the delightful fountain with its three intertwined dolphins which stands on the Steine at Brighton (*Gentleman's Magazine*, 1846, Part II, page 193). He exhibited busts at the Royal Academy, 1846–1854, and there is also one by him of F. W. Robertson, dated 1853, in the Bodleian at Oxford. His bust of William Seymour (1850) is in Brighton Town Hall.

His signed tablets include those to the Lidbetter children, 1831, and Mary Marla, 1838, both at Bramber, Sussex, while in Brighton Parish Church is his large monument with a relief-bust of J. Allen, 1851, and a charming miniature Gothic work to Mrs. Crozier, with a small figure of a woman mourning by an urn.

PEPPER, W., the Younger, of Brighton
b. 1831

Son of W. Pepper the Elder (q.v.), he joined the Royal Academy Schools in 1852, and exhibited busts at the Academy, 1851–1868. His bust of Lewis Slight, 1865, is in Brighton Town Hall.

His best monument, to Luke Flood (*d.* 1857), in St. Luke's, Chelsea, has a relief of a deathbed scene, while he signs others to the Rev. Richard Wake, at Courteenhall, Northamptonshire, and to William King, 1864, in St. George's, Brighton.

The "J. Pepper" who signs an undated bust of Sir Walter Scott in the Brighton Art Gallery was, I imagine, a member of the same family.

PERCIVALL, —, and RICKETTS, —, of Birmingham
fl. 1790–1800

They sign a large wall-tablet of simple, but good, design to Mary Scott, 1793, at Walsall, Staffordshire, and a smaller one to William Wakefield, 1798, at Curdworth, Warwick.

PERCY, FRANCIS
fl. 1676–1687

Between 1676 and 1679 he was working at Trinity College, Cambridge, where he cut capitals, festoons, shields and "thirteen great heads" (*Wren Society*, Vol. V, page 39). He was in Cambridge again in 1687, when he carved the College coat of arms above the hall door of Clare Hall (Willis and Clarke's *Architectural History of Cambridge*, Vol. I, page 107).

PERCY, JOHN FRANCIS
b. 1801

He was born in Dublin, the son of Edward H. G. Percy, who was described as an "artist," and entered the Dublin Society's Schools in 1816. He later exhibited in Ireland and also showed works at the Royal Academy from 1827 until 1839. His wax-relief of "Bacchus and Ariadne," dated 1827, was exhibited at Burlington House in the following year and is now in the Bethnal Green Museum.

Percy also worked as a designer and modeller of silver, and was employed in this capacity about 1835 by Messrs. Elkington, of London.

PERCY, SAMUEL
b. 1750, *d.* 1820

He was a native of Dublin and was trained at the Dublin Society's Schools, first exhibiting in

Ireland in 1772. About 1785 he came to London, where he lived, save for a few brief visits to Ireland, for the rest of his life. In 1806 he sent in a model for the City competition for the Guildhall monument to Nelson, offering to carry out the work for £4,000, but his design was not accepted (City Corporation Records, MSS. 95.2).

Percy's obituary in the *Annals of the Fine Arts* (1821, page 177) says that he died "of an apoplectic fit while finishing a portrait of Prince Leopold," and adds that "he was well known for his exquisite models in miniature size." He was, indeed, one of the best, if not the best, of the English wax-modellers, and exhibited many works at the Royal Academy between 1786 and 1804.

Percy's portraits of the Royal Family include those of George III and Queen Charlotte (1795), at Windsor Castle; Princess Charlotte (1814), at the National Portrait Gallery; and the Princess of Wales (1817) and Princess Charlotte (1817), in the Brighton Art Gallery. Other examples of his work are the wax scenes of "The Death of Voltaire" and "The Three Musicians," and the portraits of Lady Barrington and Sir Arthur Paget, all in the Victoria and Albert Museum; while the portrait of Sir Charles Morgan (1785) is at Tredegar Park, Monmouth.

An exhibition of his work was held at the Egyptian Hall where the works shown included a group of figures representing the progress of Inebriety, Frederick the Great in his last illness, a Blind Beggar and a dead Christ.

At the Alton Towers sale in 1857 over a hundred of his works were auctioned, including a full-length of Queen Caroline, and a set of "six groups of rustic figures" which, according to the catalogue, were "modelled and coloured with wonderful truth to nature." The *Connoisseur* of August, 1934, illustrated his wax portraits of Lady Menteith and Lord Rockingham.

On 31 January, 1800, Mr. Christie held a sale of his wax portraits and groups. Among the former were those of General Haviland, Admiral Roddam, Henderson, the actor, Lord Kenyon, Judge Butler, Tom Paine, Lord Thurlow, Duke of Richmond, Emperor and Empress of Russia (taken in 1788), Louis XVI, Judge Wilson, Judge Eyre, Lord Romney, Count Struenzee, the Duke of Leeds, etc. The forty-eight lots realized £172. (Archives, Messrs. Christie.)

A portrait of Percy was Lot 495 at the sale of the contents of Alton Towers, 10 July, 1857.

PERRY, JOHN, of Hackney
fl. 1797–1803

In 1797 he built the New Lodge, Hyde Park, which had been designed by Soane (Soane MSS.).

Perry, who was succeeded in the business by his son, Joseph William, signs a large tablet to Zipporah Sierra, 1803, in St. Albans Cathedral.

PEYMAN, HENRY PRINCE, of Abingdon
fl. 1825–1851

At the Great Exhibition of 1851 he showed "a font executed in marble," which may be the font now in St. Helen's Church, Abingdon.

His signed monuments include those to Thomas Herbert, 1825, at Faringdon, Berks; and to Richard Galloway, 1825, and the Rev. John Cleoburey, 1841, both in St. Helen's, Abingdon.

PHILIP, JOHN BIRNIE
b. 1824, *d.* 1875

Philip, who at the age of seventeen had entered the Government School of Design at Somerset House, was first employed on ornamental sculpture for the Houses of Parliament. However, he was soon able to start working on his own, and he rapidly became one of the most popular and prolific of mid-Victorian sculptors.

In 1852 he carved the arch of Caen stone erected in Welshpool Church over E. Richardson's (q.v.) recumbent figure of Lord Powis (*Gentleman's Magazine*, 1852, Part I, page 492). He was also employed at a number of churches, carving the reredos for Tamworth Parish Church in 1853, for Ely Cathedral in 1854, for St. George's Chapel, Windsor, in 1863 (the model for this is in Chelsea Public Library), and for Lichfield Cathedral in 1864. The relief of "Michael and Satan" in the tympanum of St. Michael's, Cornhill, was executed by him in 1857 and the four colossal statues of the Evangelists on the tower in 1858.

Philip's best-known work, however, is the frieze on the podium of the Albert Memorial, which represents the great architects and sculptors of the world. The eighty-seven figures contained in these two reliefs are admirably carved and grouped and, as the *Art Journal* of 1874 remarked, "he has so arranged the figures as to present a series of distinct groups, yet all forming one harmonious whole. There is not a single figure which will not repay close examination, while each leads the eye to a given point of special interest. All give evidence of close study, beauty of composition, and great artistic ability." Also for the memorial he modelled the bronze statues of "Geometry," "Geology," "Physiology" and "Philosophy," the canopy over Foley's (q.v.) figure of the Prince Consort, and the eight angels at the base of the cross which crowns the summit.

Other works executed by Philip include the

cornice in the morning-room at Caen Wood Towers; decorative sculpture at Crewe Hall, including the reredos in the private chapel; the capitals of the columns on Blackfriars Bridge; and the sculpture on the New Post Office at St. Martin's-le-Grand, the rebuilt Parish Church at Doncaster, and the restored Chapter House of Salisbury Cathedral. He also carved in 1858 the figures on the very ugly Peterhead granite Westminster column in Broad Sanctuary, designed by Sir Gilbert Scott. The St. George on the top, however, is the work, not of Philip, but of Clayton —who with his partner, Bell, is perhaps better known as a designer of stained-glass windows (*Art Journal*, 1861, page 159).

In addition to the statues for St. Michael's, Cornhill, Philip was also responsible for those of Richard Oastler (1866), at Bradford; Lord Elgin (1869) and Colonel Baird (1870), both at Calcutta; the Rev. Robert Hall (1870), at Leicester; and Colonel Akroyd (1875), at Halifax. In 1867 he made a number of statues representing various races of the Indian Empire for the India Office and, two years later, eight figures of Kings and Queens of England for the Royal Gallery at the Palace of Westminster. In 1870 and 1875 respectively he made others for the façade of Burlington House and for the front of the Foreign Office.

Just before his death Philip completed in plaster a statue of Sir Joshua Reynolds, which was formerly in Chelsea Town Hall, but was destroyed in 1940 by enemy action. The figure of "Peace" on the fountain in Smithfield Market was carved by him in 1873.

Philip was a popular monumental artist and executed a number of recumbent effigies. These include those of Earl Somers, 1854, at Eastnor, Hereford; Queen Katherine Parr, 1859, in the chapel of Sudely Castle, the Rev. W. H. Mill, 1860, in Ely Cathedral; and Lord and Lady Herbert of Lea, 1864, in Wilton Church. Other monuments by him include those to the first Duke of Wellington, 1854, in St. Nicholas', Brighton; the Elston family, 1857, in the churchyard of Christ Church, Doncaster; Sir Charles Hotham, 1858, in Melbourne, Australia; the Duchess of Gloucester, 1859, in Westminster Abbey; Countess Canning, 1864, at Calcutta; and Lord Elgin, 1868, in Calcutta Cathedral.

He exhibited at the Royal Academy from 1850 until 1875, and died of bronchitis at Merton Villa, King's Road, Chelsea, on 2 March of the latter year. He was buried in Bromfield Cemetery. Philip married Francis Black and one of his daughters became the wife of James A. M. Whistler, the painter.

(Various references, *Builder*, *Art Journal*, etc.)

PHILLIPS, JOHN,
of Haverfordwest
fl. 1796–1823

He signs a marble wall monument with Corinthian pillars, draped peers' robes, coronet, etc., to Lord Milford, 1823, in Haverfordwest Church, Pembroke. In 1796 he made a black-marble chimney-piece for Ffynone House, Pembroke (Colby Archives).

PHILLIPS, ROBERT

Almost certainly a local statuary. He signs the monument to Sir John Philipps, Bart., 1764, in Haverfordwest Church. This work, with its composite pillars and recessed pilasters of the same order, supporting a broken pediment, has considerable merit.

PHILLIPSON, —
d. 1785

On 12 December, 1785, Mr. Christie held a sale of the stock in trade of "Mr. Phillipson, statuary, deceased, of Great Castle Street, Cavendish Square." Among the lots sold was a bas-relief of the Forge of Vulcan, a bronze bust of a satyr, a bas-relief of the Marriage of Tobias, figures of Shakespeare, Milton and Newton, and busts of Lord Holland, Lord Ligonier and Garrick (Archives, Messrs. Christie).

PHYFFERS, THEODORE
fl. 1840–1872

A native of Louvain and a pupil of Charles Geerts, Phyffers was invited in 1844 by Sir Charles Barry to come to London and execute wood-carvings for the Houses of Parliament.

He then settled in England and later modelled the sculpture for the Byzantine Court of the Crystal Palace, also executing many of the ecclesiastical sculptures for the same building. His work for various churches included the decorative stone-carving at Harleston; the reredos for St. Marie, Sheffield; the lectern of Corsham stone at Birlingham; a series of reliefs, including the reredos in the private chapel, for the Jesuit Church in Farm Street, London; and statues of the Virgin and St. John for the exterior of the Roman Catholic Church of St. Mary, Rugby. For Carlisle Cathedral he restored the hammer-beam roof, for Salisbury the sculpture on the Chapter House, while for Canterbury he made the statues on the south porch in 1865.

Phyffers exhibited at the Royal Academy, 1850–1864, and at the British Institution in 1854, his bust of Alfred Rothschild being shown at the

Academy in 1863. His group entitled "Wounded at Scutari" was executed in 1858 for Florence Nightingale's friend, Mrs. Bracebridge, while his medallion of Sir Charles Napier, dated 1863, is at Landport. Four years later he made a statue of Sir Henry Ward for Kandy, Ceylon, and statues of Warren Hastings, Lord Teignmouth and four panels representing incidents in Indian history for the India Office. In 1859 he made a monument in the crypt of the Chapel at St. Augustine's, Canterbury, and in 1863 the Chesapeake Memorial at Portsmouth.

(Various references *Builder*, and *Art Journal*, especially 1858, page 48.)

PHYSICK, CHARLES
b. 1810

He was a brother of Robert Physick (q.v.), and in 1831 attended the Royal Academy Schools, to which he had been recommended by S. Joseph (q.v.).

He exhibited at the Academy "A Study in Marble" in 1832, and two years later showed "A Girl Fondling a Rabbit" at the British Institution. In 1842 he carved the font of St. Paul's, Knightsbridge.

PHYSICK, EDWARD
fl. 1810-1842

He exhibited at the Royal Academy, 1810–1842, and at the British Institution, 1824–1838, showing busts of Miss Freeman, H. G. Clough, George IV, Lt.-General Gordon and Lord Kingston.

Physick's earlier monuments are influenced by the neo-Hellenic school and many have well-designed and delicately chiselled reliefs. Perhaps his best work commemorates Captain Allen, 1841, at Tenby, Pembroke; this shows a seated mourning youth, on his shoulders a banner, whose folds fall behind him.

Other monuments signed by Physick include those to Lt.-General Thomas Trent, 1825, in St. Pancras Parish Church; Margaret Vaughan, 1826, at Little Gaddesden, Herts; James Bushel, 1826; Robert Fullerton, 1830; Lt.-General Gordon, 1832; and Richard Goodwin, 1836, all in Marylebone Parish Church; Mrs. Vaughan, 1828, at Sandal Magna, Yorks; Lady Grant, 1830, at Leigh, Glos; Mrs. Darnell, 1831, at Thrapston, Northants; Mrs. Woodall, 1831, in St. Mary's, Scarborough; the Rev. Isaac King, 1832, in High Wycombe Parish Church; Nathaniel Peach, 1835, at Ketteringham, Norfolk; Michael Sheepley, 1837, and Susanna Sheepley, 1840, both at Carshalton, Surrey; the Rev. Charles Wood, 1838, at Drayton Beauchamp, Bucks; General Sir Henry

King, 1839, at Winkfield, Berks; and Magens Dorrien Magens, 1849, at Brightlingsea, Essex.

PHYSICK, EDWARD GUSTAVUS
fl. 1823-1871

He was the son of Edward Physick (q.v.) and, in 1823, received a large Silver Medal from the Society of Arts for figures of "Telemachus" and "Narcissus," winning the same medal in the following year for the model of a group. In 1825 he won the Gold Isis Medal and, in 1826, the large Gold Medal.

In 1844 Physick showed his "Timidity" at Westminster Hall, of which the *Literary Gazette* remarked that they were "quite willing to give every praise for the creditable modelling of the figure, though reluctant to say as much for the drapery." In the following year he exhibited "Female and Child" at the Society of British Artists. To the Birmingham Society of Artists in 1839 he sent "Maternal Playfulness" and, in 1850, a "Head in Marble of the Dying Saviour," a work also seen at the Great Exhibition in the following year.

Physick carved, in 1854, the group above the portico of the Female Orphan School in St. John's Wood. He exhibited at the Royal Academy, 1822–1871, and at the British Institution, 1834–1866.

His monuments include those to Charles Manners-Sutton, 1845, at Addington, Surrey; James Brook, 1847, at Meltham Mills, Yorks; Thomas Brook, 1850, at Goodrich, Hereford; Christopher Pemberton, 1852, at Newton, Cambs; Thomas Brown, 1852, at Brent Eleigh, Suffolk; Sir John Tullock, 1860, in Kensal Green Cemetery; Captain Colby, 1853, at Manordivy, Cardigan; and Lt.-Colonel Louis Bazalgette, 1866, in St. Mary's, Warwick.

PHYSICK, EDWARD JAMES
b. 1829

Son of Edward Gustavus Physick (q.v.), he attended the Royal Academy Schools in 1847 on the recommendation of E. H. Baily (q.v.), and, in the same year, received a large Silver Medal from the Society of Arts for a figure of "Mercury." In 1850 he won the Royal Academy Gold Medal for a bas-relief of "The Rape of Proserpine," showing this work at the Great Exhibition in 1851.

Physick exhibited at the Academy, 1848–1863, and at the British Institution, 1849–1855. At the former he showed, among other things, busts of W. Westall, A.R.A., and R. B. Haydon, the latter for Philadelphia.

His monuments include those to Louisa Eardly, 1852, at Little Berkhamsted, Herts; Archibald Clevland, 1854, at Westleigh, Devon; the children of Lord. Paulett, 1857, at Hinton St. George, Somerset; Admiral Grace, 1859, in Kensal Green Cemetery; Edward Kemp, 1859, at East Hoathly, Sussex; Charles Vernon, 1863, at Wherstead, Suffolk; Mrs. Chichester, 1863, at Arlington, Devon; Mary Bolton, 1868, in the churchyard at Instow, Devon; and Blanch Astley, 1870, at Melton Constable, Norfolk.

PHYSICK, EDWARD WILLIAM
fl. 1830–1844

Son of Edward Physick (q.v.), he exhibited at the Royal Academy, 1830–1844, showing a bust of the Duke of Wellington and various designs for monuments, including, in 1839, the one to Lady Janet Grant erected in Cheltenham Parish Church.

Other monuments and tablets signed by him include those to Benjamin Bond, 1834, in St. John's Wood Chapel; Richard Goodwin, 1836, in Marylebone Parish Church; Lieut-Colonel By, 1836, and Mrs. By, 1838, both at Frant, Sussex; Miss Vaughan, 1838, at Sandal Magna, Yorks; and Margaret Bowes, 1842, in Tooting Parish Church.

PHYSICK, ROBERT
b. 1815

Brother of Charles Physick (q.v.), he attended the Royal Academy Schools in 1837 on the recommendation of Thomas Maisey, and there won a Silver Medal three years later. He exhibited at the British Institution, 1836–1840, and at the Academy, 1837–1856, showing busts of Sir Lewis Grant (1853) and Sir John Barrow (1854), among other works. His bust of Peel (1850) is in the possession of the Merchant Taylors Company, and that of Wellington (1852) in the Royal United Services Museum.

Physick's signed monuments include those to the Hon. Esther Ashburnham, 1848, at Frant, Sussex; John Lacon, 1848, at Ormesby St. Margaret, Norfolk; Sir James Kempt, 1850, in Kensal Green Cemetery; and Edward Jones, 1853, at Bayford, Herts.

PICKFORD, JOSEPH
fl. 1714–1762

In 1714 he was apparently working with G. B. Guelphi (q.v.), but later set up for himself at Hyde Park Corner. He is chiefly known as a carver of chimney-pieces, making in 1738 one for the drawing-room of Earl Fitzwalter's house in Pall Mall and, four years later, two for the dining-room

of the house in Berkeley Square designed for Lady Isabella Finch by William Kent (R.I.B.A., MS. 728–3). In 1743 Pickford was the mason for building the Rt. Hon. Henry Pelham's house in Arlington Street. Here he also received £126 for the "rich marble column chimney-piece" in the "Great Room" and £48 for carving a frieze with festoons of fruit and flowers (op. cit.). In 1738–1739 the Duke of Newcastle paid him £160 for work at Claremont (British Museum Ad. MSS. 33, 321).

In 1762 he supplied a chimney-piece for the second Earl of Ashburnham at Ashburnham Place, Sussex, sending down his workman, William Stoney, to fix it up in the dressing-room (Ashburnham Archives).

From a letter in the archives of Lord Falmouth, Pickford apparently made other chimney-pieces for Lord Duncannon and Admiral Boscawen, but he is best known for his work at Holkham, in Norfolk, where he was employed for nearly twenty years, not only carving chimney-pieces for most of the principal rooms, but the alabaster columns and capitals for the Great Hall, marble friezes, etc.

He also executed a number of monuments, the best being that of Sir John and Lady Bendish, *c.* 1740, at Steeple Bumpstead, Essex, which has medallion-portraits. He signs this, as well as the tablet to George Pyke, 1738, at Birdbrook, in the same county, jointly with his partner, W. Atkinson (q.v.). About 1740 he made the two busts to be added to the monument of Richard Hopkins (*d.* 1707) which stood at that time in St. Michael's Church, Coventry. These were of Hopkins' eldest son, Richard, a Member of Parliament and one of the Lords Commissioners of the Admiralty, and of his daughter-in-law, Anna Maria, widow of another son, Edward.

Two more of Pickford's monuments are those to the Roberts family, 1740, at Cranbrook, Kent, and to William Hanger, 1755, at Farningham, in the same county.

PICKMAN, W.
fl. 1825–1844

He exhibited at the Royal Academy, 1825–1844, where his works included a medallic portrait of J. C. Hobhouse (1825), a bust of Sir Francis Burdett (1833), and a medallion in wax of Mr. McKenzie, of Edinburgh (1841). At the Suffolk Street Galleries he showed wax busts of George IV and the Duke of York in 1828.

PIDDINGTON, JOHN, of Oxford
b. 1682, *d.* 1716

There were a number of statuaries and masons

of this name who worked at Oxford during the seventeenth and eighteenth centuries. The first of them, Richard, son of Humphrey Piddington, of Stanton St. John, was probably the "Piddington" who was in partnership with William Badger in 1639, and was paid £32 10s. for "paving the passage of the Congregation House and pitching the gutters" (Wood's *Life and Times*, Vol. IV, page 55).

Between 1657 and 1661 an Anthony Piddington was employed at Oriel (College accounts). He became a Freeman of the city in 1664 and had a son, Richard, whom he took as his apprentice. Richard, who died in 1724, built with his partner, George Smith, the south building of New College in 1700. He seems to have been well known, for in 1718 a Richard Curtin, son of a baker of Oxford of that name, was apprenticed to him (P.R.O., I.R. 1/6).

John Piddington, the subject of this biography, was Richard Piddington's elder son and was apprenticed to his father in 1698. He signs the monument with a portrait-bust to George Blackall, 1709, at Great Haseley, Oxon, and a tablet to Thomas Coghill and family, 1709, at Bletchington, in the same county. Another tablet by him commemorates Edmund Fettiplace, 1710, at Kingston Bagpuize, Berkshire.

Richard Piddington the Younger, second son of Richard Piddington, was apprenticed to his father in 1715 and died in 1752. The last of the family was John Piddington's son, another John, who, according to the *Royal Magazine* of 1764, was transported for seven years for stealing the club box of the Oxford Benefit Society.

PIERACHINI, PIETRO
fl. 1835–1839

He exhibited at the Liverpool Academy, 1835–1839, showing busts of Signor de Val (1835), William Roscoe (1836), William Ewart (1836), Thomas Gresham (1836), Queen Victoria (1838) and George Tyrer (1839).

PIERCE, or PEIRCE, EDWARD, of Deptford
fl. 1770–1790

Pierce was a competent minor statuary who made use of "Adam" details in some of his works. Monuments and tablets by him in Kent include those to James Hawley, 1777, at Leybourne; George Collard, 1782, in St. Martin's, Dover; and William Hardyman, 1784, in Farningham churchyard. He also signs others in Sussex to John Mittell, *c.* 1780, at East Hoathly; John Staples, 1789, at East Grinstead; and Charles Brown, 1789, at Frant. In 1778 he was paid £210 for a monument

designed by George Gibson, which was erected in Widford Churchyard, Essex, to the memory of Viscountess Falkland.

PIERCE, ROBERT, of Exeter
fl. 1803–1819

Three tablets signed by him in Devon are those to Peter Middleton, 1803, at Littleham, in coloured marbles; James Bell, 1805, in Exeter Cathedral, with a relief of a mourning woman; and William Burn, 1814, in Holy Trinity, Exeter, with a trophy of arms.

PINCAT, or PINCOT, DANIEL
d. 1797

In 1767 he is described as "artificial-stone manufacturer in Goulston Square, Whitechapel," and in that year exhibited at the Free Society "an antique bas-relief in artificial stone."

As Mrs. Coade (q.v.) did not open her factory at Lambeth until 1769, it seems that she and Pincat independently revived this lost art. However, by 1771 he was working for her, and in the same year he exhibited at the Society of Artists a copy of the Borghese Vase in artificial stone. A note in the catalogue states that, though it was contrary to the laws of the Society to admit any copies, yet "desirous of giving every encouragement in their power to merit and ingenuity, they have permitted the above to stand in the vestibule leading to their room in consideration of its being a very fine performance." Pincat died in 1797 and was buried in Bunhill Fields.

PINDER, DANIEL
b. ca. 1734, *d.* 1820

Between 1766 and 1798 he was mason to the Ironmongers' Company, and received similar appointments with the Royal College of Physicians and the Vintners' Company in 1768 and 1769. Three years later, however, he and William Pinder (q.v.) were summoned by the Court of Assistants of the Masons' Company to take up their freedoms or to pay a fine of £10.

In 1782 Daniel Pinder became mason to the Stationers' Company, and in the following year received £202 for masonry work in connexion with the statue of Lord Chatham in the Guildhall (Corporation of London Records, MS. 55.28). About 1784 he took William Norris (q.v.) into partnership, and from 1788 to 1790 they together rebuilt, under Dance, the south front of the Guildhall, being paid £900 (*Journal City Lands*, Vol. 81). In 1791 the firm was paid £129 for repairs to the steps of Surgeons' Hall.

In 1794, under Sir John Soane, they carried out repairs to Peter Thellusson's house in Philpot Lane. They were also masons to Child's Bank from 1785 until 1804, while in 1798 their bill for mason's work carried out during the rebuilding of East India House amounted to £6,770 (India Office Archives).

Pinder and his partner sign the large monument to Richard Sorbell, erected in 1784 at Great Warley, Essex.

(Archives of Companies, etc., mentioned in text; Soane Note-books.)

PINDER, WILLIAM
d. 1784

Son of William Pinder, Merchant Taylor and citizen of London, he was apprenticed in 1719 to Thomas Broomhall. In 1766 he made the chimney-piece for the vestry of St. Matthew's, Friday Street (Guildhall MS. 3543), and he also signs monuments to John Seale, 1777, at Cornworthy, Devon, and Daniel Sandford, 1779, at Castle Hedingham, Essex. He died in Falcon Square on 11 October, 1784 (*Gentleman's Magazine*, 1784, page 798). A sale of his stock-in-trade was held on 26 and 27 April, 1785.

Pinder had two sons, Samuel and William. The former was apprenticed to Thomas Bull (q.v.) in 1754, but was turned over to William Bull on his master's death two years later. The latter assisted his father, but was declared a bankrupt in 1789.

PINGO, —
fl. 1769–1800

His Christian name is unknown, but it is possible that he may be the John Pingo, son of Lewis Pingo (q.v.), who exhibited wax models, etc., at the Free Society, 1765–1774.

Pingo was employed as a modeller by Wedgwood, for whom he made a portrait of George III, and in 1769 medallions of the Battles of Plassey and Pondicherry (Meteyard's *Wedgwood*, Vol. I, page 441). In 1800 his wife, Theodosia, wrote to the firm as follows: "My husband who has long laboured under a severe illness being now reduced to that state as not to be able to attend any longer to business and myself and family destitute, Mr. Silvester who's knowledge and diligence are well known has obligingly engaged to give every assistance in conducting the business on my account" (Wedgwood Archives). "Mr. Silvester" is presumably the modeller of that name (q.v.) who exhibited at the Royal Academy in 1788. Redgrave states that it was Thomas Pingo who worked for Wedgwood, but as he died in 1776 this is obviously a mistake.

PINGO, LEWIS
b. 1743, d. 1830

Third son of Thomas Pingo, the medallist, he joined the Royal Academy Schools in 1770, having already been awarded premiums for medallions by the Society of Arts in 1759 and 1760. In 1776 he succeeded his father as an assistant engraver at the Mint, and three years later was appointed chief engraver, a post he held until 1815.

Pingo exhibited medals and wax portraits at the Society of Artists and at the Free Society, the wax portraits including likenesses of the King of Poland, Dr. Mead, Admiral Keppel and Lord Sandwich. He died at Camberwell on 26 August, 1830.

(*Gentleman's Magazine*, 1830, Part II, page 283.)

PINK, JAMES, of Lincoln
d. 1810

He either came from Bath or was working there before he settled in Lincoln, where he was employed on carving the ornaments of the altar-piece in the Cathedral in 1769. He later added the screen on each side of the altar-piece, and his signature is carved on the stonework of the south-west corner of the reredos.

Pink was also responsible for the small figures on the rood-loft, and repaired a great deal of the stone-carving both inside and outside the Cathedral. He had hoped to be appointed cathedral mason, but "being a Dissenter in religion eclipsed all his merits and he was rejected." He died in 1810 and was buried in the cemetery of the Old Baptist Chapel at Lincoln.

(*Lincoln Diocesan Magazine*, Vol. LXIII, page 212.)

PINK, W., of London
fl. 1828–1844

He exhibited busts at the Royal Academy, 1828–1844, including those of Mr. J. Pink and Mr. T. Wright in 1828 and 1829 respectively.

PIPER, THOMAS, the Elder
d. 1794

Son of William Piper, of Hampton, Middlesex, butcher, he was apprenticed to Charles Easton in 1767, becoming free in 1774, though he continued to work with Easton.

Piper was the chief mason for building the Fishmongers' Hall from 1788 until his death, executing also the carved stonework and supplying marble chimney-pieces. The work was completed for the Company by Piper's widow, Elizabeth, who took over the business (Archives, Fishmongers' Company). In 1799 and 1800 she carried out orders for marble chimney-pieces for the Mote, Maidstone, then being rebuilt by Lord Romney (Account-book for building the Mote, Maidstone Museum).

PIPER, THOMAS, the Younger, and Son

Firm *fl.* 1800–1850

Son of Thomas Piper the Elder (q.v.), he took over the family business from his mother about 1800, and was also appointed to his father's post as mason to the Fishmongers' Company (Company Archives).

Thomas's son, another Thomas, was bound apprentice to him in 1813, becoming a partner in the firm soon after he had gained his freedom in 1820. Father and son were the masons for rebuilding the Customs House, 1825–1827 (P.R.O., Works 5/119 and 5/125), and also for the restoration of the steeple of St. Antholin's, Budge Row, in 1829.

The third Thomas Piper's son, William, was apprenticed to him in 1833. It is this Thomas Piper who, I imagine, is responsible for the firm's later monuments. They include those to Sir Culling Smith, 1805, at Monken Hadleigh, Herts; the Rev. Charles Wakeman, 1822, at Bocking, Essex; Charles De Mauriel, 1823, at Henley, Oxon; the Russell family, 1841, in the churchyard of Sanderstead Parish Church; and the Williams family, 1849, in St. Magnus the Martyr, London Bridge.

PISTELL, WILLIAM, of London

fl. 1814–1844

One of the "New Road statuaries," many of his tablets, like those of his fellow-workers in the same street, are dull and obvious, though his monument to Maria Parratt, 1844, at Effingham, Surrey, has a very fine relief of a mother mourning at her daughter's deathbed, rather in the manner of Chantrey.

In its way the relief on Pistell's monument to Joseph Priestley, 1817, in Bradford Cathedral, is well carved and entertaining. This shows "navvies" excavating a canal down which a string of barges passes, while his monument to Colonel Ludow, 1821, in the Old Cathedral, Calcutta, consists of a sarcophagus, with a mourning woman on one side and a soldier with arms reversed on the other.

Other monuments and tablets signed by him include those to William Lee, 1814, at Alton, Hants; Major Balfour, 1817, in Marylebone

Parish Church; Jonathan Hammond, 1819, at Penshurst, Kent; Theodosia Crawley, 1820, at Luton, Beds; William Hickman, 1821, at Marlow, Bucks; the Rev. Edward Balm, 1822, and William Phillips, 1826, both in St. Pancras Parish Church; George Nassau, 1823, at Easton, Suffolk; John Cranston, 1823, at East Grinstead, Sussex; Richard Cray, 1825, in Ealing Parish Church; Robert Denn, 1828, at Shipdham, Norfolk; and James Burnet, 1840, at Chippenham, Wilts.

As a decorative carver he was employed by the Duke of Bridgewater at Ashridge Park, 1814–1817, receiving £180 (Archives, Lord Brownlow).

In 1808 he was paid £65 for chimney-pieces for the Royal Naval Asylum at Greenwich (P.R.O., Adm. 80/110).

PISTRUCCI, BENEDETTO

b. 1784, *d.* 1855

A Roman by birth, he settled in London in 1815 and started work at the Mint, where he modelled "St. George and the Dragon" for the gold coinage. In 1828 he was appointed chief medallist.

Pistrucci's chief works consist of carved cameos and designs for coins and medals, including those commemorating the Coronations of George IV and Queen Victoria. His wax medallion of Matthew Boulton is in the British Museum, and among his few busts may be mentioned one of Pozzo di Borgo and another of the Duke of Wellington, executed in 1832, which is now at Stratfield Saye. A copy of it, bought in 1836, is in the United Service Club, and a replica at the United Service Museum. Waagen, who saw the original in the sculptor's studio, considered it "by far the more like and the best I have seen and the more remarkable as the production of an artist accustomed to work on a very small scale" (*Art Treasures in Great Britain*, Vol. II, page 333).

In 1839 Pistrucci was one of those who competed for the commission to execute the memorial to Nelson, his model taking the form of a trident "with three graceful recumbent female figures on the base." The *Literary Gazette* (1839, page 393) was rightly appalled at the idea of "a monument all prongs and handles" standing like a great fork in the middle of Trafalgar Square, and the judges luckily seem to have been of the same opinion. Two years later Pistrucci, with various other sculptors, was invited to submit a model for the statue of Wellington to be erected in Glasgow.

He died at Flora Lodge, near Windsor, of inflammation of the lungs, on 16 September, 1855. In its obituary the *Art Journal* (1856, page 27) remarked on the fact that he had been commissioned to execute the medal for Waterloo, but

"George III died, still nothing certain was heard about it; George IV died, and collectors were still impatient; William IV died, and Mr. Hamilton assured us that it was in hand, would be a glorious work and well worth waiting for. Then came the Mint Commission of 1848, and it was not forthcoming. The medallist himself is now gone, but yet we hear nothing of his final and chief work."

(Wellesley's *Iconography of the First Duke of Wellington*; Authorities cited in text.)

PITCHES, WILLIAM

Probably a local craftsman, he was master-mason for the University Schools at Cambridge in 1732, carving "two heads, corbels" and other decorative details (Vice-Chancellor's accounts).

PITTS, JOSEPH
fl. 1830–1870

Son of William Pitts (q.v.), he was awarded the Silver Isis Medal for a bust by the Society of Artists in 1831, and five years later won the Silver Medal for a group of figures in bas-relief.

Pitts showed various busts, including those of Wellington, the Prince Consort, George Stephenson and Miss Symes, at the Royal Academy between 1842 and 1846. The bust of Stephenson, executed in the latter year, is now in the National Portrait Gallery.

PITTS, WILLIAM
b. 1790, *d.* 1840

He was apprenticed to his father, John Pitts, a silver-chaser, of Leicester, and in 1812 won the Gold Isis Medal of the Society of Arts for modelling two warriors. The first work to bring him fame was his chasing of the greater portion of the Wellington Shield, designed by Stothard, and he afterwards chased the shield of Achilles, from a design by Flaxman (q.v.). About the same time he made a silver model for Lord Arden of Le Soeur's equestrian statue of Charles I, while he later modelled the shields of Hercules and Aeneas. Indeed, between 1830 and 1840 he designed or modelled almost all the candelabra, épergnes and plate made for presentation, his works ranging from the vast masonic tribute presented to the Duke of Sussex, to the cup given to Charles Kemble on his retirement from the stage.

In 1829 Pitts contracted to carve reliefs for Buckingham Palace for the sum of £450, his guarantor being his father (P.R.O., Works 19/3). Here he worked for two years, carving reliefs of "Eloquence" for the picture-gallery, "Pleasure" for the blue drawing-room, "Harmony" for the music-room, "Peace and War" for the guard-room, and, in 1831, twelve panels with reliefs of children for the white drawing-room. Unfortunately he did not find it easy to obtain payment for this work, and, as he had married at the early age of nineteen and was seldom free from financial troubles, he was forced on 4 September, 1831, to write to the Lords of the Treasury that "my circumstances compel me to inform you that unless I receive further cash on account of my bill for work done at the Palace, which has been officially passed, I and my family will be ruined" (P.R.O., T. 1/3489). He had every reason to complain, for, out of £700 owing to him, he had only received £150.

In 1833 a model (now at Stratfield Saye) of the Duke of York's column was presented to the Duke of Wellington, the figure at the top being modelled by Pitts. Other works by him include reliefs of "Proserpine" and "The Nuptials of Pirithous and Hippodamia," made in 1829 for Mr. Simons of Regent's Park; a carving of "St. Martin and the Beggar," dated 1831, for the pediment of the vestry-room of St. Martin-in-the-Fields; and a relief of "The Muses between Greek and British Poets," executed eight years later for the Library Institution at Leicester. He also made three bas-reliefs for Sir W. A. Cooper, of Isleworth House, and three others entitled "The Triumph of Innocence," "Flora with the Seasons," and "The Pledges of Virtue," for George Harrison of Carlton Gardens.

Pitts exhibited at the Royal Academy, 1823–1840, and at the British Institution, 1824–1834. He also modelled a few busts, among them likenesses of Captain Fitzherbert, of Swinnerton, and Sir W. Horne. As a statuary he was responsible for the monuments to David Ricardo, 1823, in the churchyard of Hardenhuish, Wilts; Matty Chilton, 1828, in St. Giles-in-the-Fields; John Farhill, 1830, in Chichester Cathedral; Charles Young, 1830, Upper Chapel, Eton; Sir John Honywood, 1832, at Elmstead, Kent; Miss Wainwright, 1835, at Sandgate, Kent; and Charles Irby, 1836, at Morningthorpe, Norfolk.

He must have been an extremely versatile artist, for he also painted pictures and designed china, including a Davenport service ordered by William IV. In drawing and modelling he was ambidextrous and sometimes even used both hands at the same time.

Pitts died on 16 April, 1840. "A rash engagement, relative to a laborious and expensive work" which he had entered into, "preyed on his mind, and caused him to commit suicide by taking laudanum," according to the *Gentleman's Magazine* (1840, Part I, page 661), which also stated that "in subjects of pure classical taste he stood unrivalled and his talents were highly appreciated" by Flaxman, Westmacott and Chantrey. He left a widow and five children totally unprovided for, and a fund was opened, sponsored by Chantrey, G. Jones, R.A., and Storr and Mortimer, the silversmiths, to raise money for their support. In 1842 Mrs. Pitts also received a charitable donation of £30 from the Royal Academy. Of Pitts's children, Thomas (*b.* 1815) and James (*b.* 1821) assisted their father. Joseph is noticed separately.

(*Art Union*, 1840, page 101; Clifford Smith's *Buckingham Palace*; authorities cited in text.)

PLATT, JOHN, of Rotherham
b. 1728, *d.* 1810

He was born at Thrybergh, near Rotherham, "on Saturday, 9th March, 1727/8, about 10 o'clock at night" (Parish Register), the son of George Platt (1700–1743), who, about two years later, went to Rotherham to help his elder brother, the architect of St. Paul's, Sheffield.

On 8 September, 1762, John Platt agreed for £45 to "execute the carved work in ye pediment of the grand portico at Wentworth Castle new front, according to the model." In the same year he undertook to make for £110 the chimney-pieces in "My Lord's own room, My Lord and Lady's bedchamber, the library, My Lady's own room and the parlour on the third floor." Later he made another for the new dining-room (British Museum, Ad. MS. 22241). In 1776 he was responsible for the marble staircase at Aston Hall, Yorks, executing the one at Clifton Hall, near Rotherham, six years later.

Platt signs monuments to the Hopkins family, *c.* 1748, at Gainsborough, Lincs; and to Mrs. Catherine Buck (1778), Lieut.-Colonel Downes (1785), and Robert Cutforthay (1799), all in Rotherham Parish Church. The Downes monument has an urn of "blue john."

In his Journal (now in private possession) are notes on other monuments for which he was responsible and the extracts given below are taken from it. "August 1st, 1767: Putting up ye monument in Sheffield Church over Mrs. Bamford." In 1769 he erected monuments at Sprotboro to Mr. Copley, and at Leeds to Mr. Wolrich on 24 April and 1 December respectively, while on 13 April, 1778, he "altered ye drawing for ye monument in Wortley Chapel for Lady Bute." In 1783 he "fixed up at Sheffield Mr. Birk's monument" and also "got an order for a monument to put up in Ecclesfield Church to Miss Freeman." In December, 1790, he "set up a large monument for Mr. Foljambe of Aldwark over Esq. Hewett" (John

Hewett, *né* Thornhaugh, was Francis Foljambe's father-in-law), while three years later he "agreed for ye monument set up in Tankersley Church in memory of the late Rev. Mr. Francis Hall, £60."

In the late eighteenth century Platt took over the marble-works of Henry Watson (q.v.) at Ashford, in Derbyshire. These had been established about 1740 and were the first of their kind in England (Brewer's *Beauties of England*, Vol. III, page 484). In 1778 he sent in an estimate for repaving Lincoln Cathedral in black, Derbyshire grey and bird's-eye marbles. The Committee considered it "an ingenious design" which would have a "striking effect," but that "the execution of it would be very expensive" (Lincoln Cathedral Archives).

Platt died at Halifax and was buried in Rotherham churchyard. His tombstone could still be seen until 1950, when it was removed during "improvements." His will was proved by his son and daughter, George and Elizabeth.

Platt left three other sons, and was anxious that all four should follow his profession, though none, in fact, did so. John, the eldest (1763–1832), was sent to study architecture under F. Atkinson, of York, but abandoned it to join the Navy; Charles (1770–1817), articled to R. Westmacott the Elder (q.v.), and George (1779–1850), placed with an architect named Rawdon of York, both later entered the Army; while the third son, William (1775–1811), served his time with P. W. Tomkins, engraver to the King, and later set up in business in Golden Square.

(Information supplied by Mr. John D. Potts, of Ecclesfield; authorities cited in text.)

PLOWS, T., of Hertford
fl. 1763–1795

He signs tablets of careful workmanship to Margaret Lewin, 1763, and Elizabeth Hutton, 1769, at Broxbourne, Herts, and another to Matthew Martin, 1765, at Hunsdon, in the same county.

PLOWS, WILLIAM ABBEY, of York
b. 1789, *d.* 1865

Son of Benjamin Plows, marble-mason (1775–1824), he was apprenticed to his father in 1806. At the Great Exhibition of 1851 he showed a "sarcophagus with a Gothic canopy, marble tables and a figure of David carved in stone."

He, or his father, was responsible for monuments and tablets in Yorkshire, including those to

At Winslow Hall, Aylesbury, was a very fine pair of Nicholas Smith, 1815, all at Selby; to Richard Spofforth, 1824, at Howden; to Mary Clayton, 1828, at Kippax; to Sergeant-Major Polety, 1829, and Samuel Woodhead, 1834, both in All Saints', York; to the Rev. James Andrew, 1843, at Whitby; and to Seth Stables, 1848, at Pocklington. The large wall monument to John Strangways, 1840, at Well, in the same county, is signed by "T." Plows.

PLUMIÈRE, FRANÇOIS, or PIERRE DENIS
b. 1688, d. 1721

Plumière was an Antwerp sculptor, whose Christian name, according to Vertue, was Francis, although Thieme-Becker, in his "Künstler Lexicon," calls him Pierre Denis. He came to London at the suggestion of Lord Cadogan, bringing his family and workmen with him, but died of consumption in Westminster soon after his arrival.

Plumière, who was the master of P. Scheemakers (q.v.) and L. Delvaux (q.v.), executed the model for the monument of the Duke of Buckingham in Westminster Abbey. He also made casts of "Time" and "Truth" in the style of Michael Angelo, and statues for Lord Cadogan and the Earl of Castlemaine.

In Rysbrack's sale in 1766, Lot 68 was a "Figure of Hercules by Plumière," while at the Cassiobury Park sale of June, 1922, Lot 1174 was a "Reclining Venus," signed and dated 1717, by "D. Plumièr." Morley Wharrey, 1797, John Audus, 1809, and urns, also dated 1717, signed "D. Plumière," so if Thieme-Becker is correct in calling the sculptor Pierre Denis he must have signed his works with his second initial. There does not, however, seem to be any evidence for Vertue's calling him Francis.

(Walpole Society, *Vertue Notebook*, Vols. I and III.)

PLUMLEY, THOMAS
b. 1824

He attended the Royal Academy Schools in 1842 on the recommendation of Sir Richard Westmacott (q.v.), and two years later exhibited at Westminster Hall statues of Chaucer and Sir Thomas More, which the *Literary Gazette* considered "but feeble things."

Plumley exhibited at the Royal Academy in 1863, and in the following year carved eighteen heads for the interior and exterior of the Parish Church of Wootton St. Lawrence, Hampshire (Churchwardens' Accounts).

PLURA, GIOVANNI BATTISTA
d. 1756

In 1752 he was at Bath, where he carved five busts and the City Arms for the Grammar School. Contemporary letters in private possession suggest that it was Plura who was responsible for modelling the statue of Beau Nash in the Pump Room, although the credit for this has always been given to Prince Hoare (q.v.).

PLURA, GIUSEPPE
b. 1753

He was the son of Giovani Plura (q.v.) and joined the Royal Academy Schools in 1773. He exhibited at the Academy, 1782–1786, showing a "Bust of a Nobleman" in 1782, and one of "the Abbé Grant at Rome" four years later. He also modelled a few wax portraits, including a self-portrait which is now in the Victoria and Albert Museum.

POLLARD,—, of Quorn

He signs a wall-tablet to Benjamin Clarke, 1765, at Hardingstone, Northamptonshire.

POOLE, T. R.
fl. 1791–1809

He was "modeller to the Prince of Wales" and exhibited at the Royal Academy in 1799 and 1800, showing wax portraits, including one of Sir James Saunderson.

Other portraits in wax by Poole of the Rev. William Borrow, the Rev. Robert Aspland, the Rev. Rowland Hill and the Rev. Thomas Toller are on loan to the Victoria and Albert Museum. Another, of the Prince Regent (1804), is in the Royal Collection, while those of Edmund Burke (1791), George IV and Frederick, Duke of York, are at the National Portrait Gallery.

PORTER, THOMAS, of London
fl. 1814–1830

He signs tablets to Maurice Budgett, 1814, at Cheddar, Somerset; to George Parry, 1821, at Haverfordwest, Pembroke; and to Jacob Jones, 1830, at Wesley's Chapel, City Road.

POWELL, ROBERT, of Bristol

In 1705 he received £7 for the marble chimney-piece for Bristol Council House (City Archives).

POWELL, T., of Leominster

He signs a large wall-tablet with good details to Eleanor Morgan, 1763, at Boddenham, Hereford.

POWELL, WILLIAM,
of Hampton
fl. 1731

His father, Thomas Powell, of Hampton, who died in 1714, was mason for Hampton Court during the reign of William and Mary.

William Powell, who was a pupil of Sir Henry Cheere (q.v.), signs the very fine monument at Hampton, Middlesex, to Mrs. Susannah Thomas (*d.* 1731), although it is possible that most of the carving was actually done by his master, who allowed him to take the credit for it. Mr. Howard Colvin informs me that this important work, with its two life-size figures, was almost certainly designed by the architect, Thomas Archer, who was one of the executors of Mrs. Thornton's will.

Powell had a son, James, who was apprenticed in 1743 to William Perkins, citizen and mason of London. Other masons of the same name, who may also have been members of this family, are John Powell, who in 1743 received the balance owing to his late master, Robert Taylor the Elder, for work done at the Royal College of Physicians; Joseph Powell, apprenticed to Robert Wright in 1700; and Roger Powell, apprenticed in 1717 to John Harris.

POWLEY, JOHN

He signs the monument of Sir Andrew Fountaine (*d.* 1753) at Narford, Norfolk. The bust on this monument, however, seems to be based on Roubiliac's terra-cotta of Sir Andrew, and may or may not be the work of Powley.

POWNALL, JOHN, of Liverpool

He exhibited in 1813 a "Bust of a Lady" at the Liverpool Academy.

POYNTON, EDWARD,
of Nottingham
fl. 1722–1726

The inscription on the lead foundation-plate at Sutton Scarsdale House (now a ruin) reads: "This house was begun to be rebuilt in the year 1724 by order of the Rt. Honourable Nicholas, Earl of Scarsdale, Francis Smith, of Warwick, gentleman, Architect, Edward Poynton, of Nottingham, gentleman, carver." This means that Poynton was responsible, not only for carving the Corinthian capitals of the front, but also for the magnificent Leake coat of arms in the tympanum of the pediment.

As a statuary Poynton signs the large monument at West Stockwith, Nottinghamshire, to William Huntingdon, 1722, whom the epitaph describes as a "ship carpenter." Huntingdon is shown in life-size effigy, reclining on one elbow and holding in his hand a sheet of paper bearing the drawing of a ship. His second monument, at Bunny in the same county, has a miniature kneeling figure of Dame Anne Parkyns, who died in 1725.

POZZI, FRANCESCO,
of Florence
b. 1790, *d.* 1844

At the Vine in Hampshire is his bust of "The Youthful Hercules," signed and dated 1832, and he also signs the monument with a relief of "Charity," erected in 1833 to Anne Harper at Davenham, Cheshire.

Pozzi's best-known works in Italy are the colossal statue of Ferdinand III at Leghorn, and the Farinata degli Ubeati at the Uffizi in Florence.

PRATT, J., of Nottingham

He signs a tablet to John Entwisle, 1817, at Rempstone, Nottinghamshire.

PREECE, J., of London
fl. 1821–1822

In 1821 he received the Silver Palette from the Society of Arts for a copy of the Laocoon, and, in the following year, the Silver Isis Medal for a copy of a group. I have, however, found no evidence that Preece ever exhibited.

PREECE, JOHN, of Hereford
fl. 1809–1815

He became a Freeman of Hereford in 1814 and signs tablets in the county to Evan Lloyd, 1809, at Weobley; Nicholas Mason, 1811, at Bodenham; Joseph Clarke, 1812, at Walford; and William Money, 1815, at Much Marcle.

PRESTAGE, —
fl. 1754–1761

In 1754 he was employed by the Duke of Chandos both at Winchendon House and at Grosvenor Square, receiving £82 for the work done (Stowe Archives). In 1761 Lord Rockingham paid him £63 for two marble centaurs (Wentworth Woodhouse Archives).

PRICE, JOHN

In 1715 he carved the font of St. Mary-at-the-Wall, Colchester (Essex Archaeological Society, Vol. XXIII, Part II, page 319).

PRICE, THOMAS, of Ruthyn

In 1727 he made a Welsh-marble chimney-piece for Chirk Castle, Denbigh (Chirk Castle accounts).

PRITCHARD, THOMAS FARNOLLS

b. 1723, *d.* 1777

He may be the Thomas Pritchard, son of "Thomas Pritchard and Hester Wilding, his wife," who was born in 1718 and baptized at St. Chad's Church, Shrewsbury. He was the architect for the rebuilding of St. Julian's, Shrewsbury, and in 1769 was called in to advise on the rebuilding of Kinnerley Church, the state of which was causing anxiety. In the churchwardens' accounts is a payment to "Mr. Pritchard for coming over and drawing the Plan for ye Church."

In 1776 Pritchard sent in a design for an iron bridge at Coalbrookdale, and though his project was never carried out, owing to his death, he was nevertheless the first person to suggest building such a bridge in England. In 1765 he had sent in plans for repairing and widening the English Bridge at Shrewsbury, and was appointed Surveyor of the works a year later. For various reasons his temporary bridge was not a success and in 1768 he was superseded by John Gwynn, R.A.

Pritchard married, in 1751, Elinor Russell of the parish of St. Mary's, Shrewsbury. She died in 1768 and her husband in 1777, the latter being buried in St. Julian's, where a monument commemorates them and three of their children who died young.

Pritchard's monuments, in coloured marbles, are of the school of Henry Cheere (q.v.). They include those to Ann Wilkinson, 1756, at Wrexham, Denbigh; the Rev. John Lloyd, 1758, and Mary Morhall, 1765, both in St. Mary's, Shrewsbury; and Richard Corbet, 1770, at Moreton Corbet, Salop.

(A. W. Ward's *Bridges of Shrewsbury*; information supplied by Librarian, Shrewsbury Public Library.)

PRIVETT, WILLIAM, of Chilmark

fl. 1739–1770

He was employed at Stourhead, not only erecting, but also carving the stone details of many of the buildings in the garden and grounds. These included the grotto in 1740; the obelisk in 1748, for which he was paid £349; and the bridge a year later. In 1753 he built the Temple of Hercules and in 1755 the Palladian Temple, at a cost of £300 and £226 respectively. He was also responsible for some of the masonry at Stourhead House (Hoare Archives).

For Lord Folkestone, at Longford Castle, Privett made, in 1742, the "balustrade on ye walk" and "ye obelisk and ye pedestal." In 1743 he built the summer-house known as the "Flintery" and, in 1757, received £52 for "ye logio" and £50 for "ye piers." In 1769 he carved the four columns supporting the cupola under which was placed Rysbrack's statue of "Fame" (Longford Castle Archives).

In 1743 "William and Robert Privitt and Mr. Moore" were paid for their "bill of stonework done at Longleat in 1739" (Archives, Marquess of Bath), and in 1767 Privett received £100 for repairs to Britford Church (Longford Castle Archives).

PROCTOR, THOMAS

b. 1753, *d.* 1794

He was born at Settle, in Yorkshire, on 22 April, 1753, and was first apprenticed to a tobacconist in Manchester. In 1777 he went to London, where he entered the Royal Academy Schools and at first concentrated on painting. In 1782 he won a premium from the Society of Arts, following up this success by gaining the Academy's Silver Medal in 1783 and the Gold Medal a year later, all the awards being given for pictures.

It was not until 1785 that Proctor turned his attention to modelling and in that year produced his "Ixion," which was so highly praised by Benjamin West that it was purchased by Sir Abraham Hume. Horace Walpole was equally enthusiastic, writing to Sir Horace Mann about "Proctor, who is marvellous. He has gained the prizes in drawing, painting and sculpture; and now exhibits a model in terra-cotta of 'Ixion' less than life, which is a prodigy of anatomy, with all the freedom of nature." (*Letters of Horace Walpole*, ed. Cunningham, Vol. VIII, page 551.)

Encouraged by his success, Proctor spent twelve months on producing a larger work entitled "Diomedes Devoured by His Horses." This attracted a great deal of attention at the Royal Academy, but failed to find a purchaser, though the sculptor asked only fifty guineas for it. Bitterly disappointed, Proctor destroyed the group in a fit of despondency and turned again to painting. However, in 1792 he tried once more, showing "Pirithous Destroyed by Cerberus," which was also acquired by Hume.

In the following year the Academy selected Proctor as the student to be sent to Rome, but since 1790 he had exhibited without giving any address, and the President, Benjamin West, found him living in great privation in a miserable attic by Clare Market. West told the unfortunate man the good news and did all he could to relieve him, but the excitement was too much for Proctor. A few days later he broke a blood-vessel in the night and only lived a few hours. He was buried in Hampstead churchyard on 13 July, 1794.

A writer to the *New Monthly Magazine* (1816, page 423) says that "Proctor as a sculptor will ever be classed among the first, if not regarded as the very first, that ever appeared in this country. His Ixion is justly considered the finest piece of work ever produced by a Briton."

Nollekens, on the other hand, considered that Proctor "had less merit as a modeller than as a painter," but it is possible that this opinion might have been dictated by professional jealousy. Sir Richard Westmacott, when Professor of Sculpture at the Royal Academy, borrowed the "Ixion" and the "Pirithous Destroyed by Cerberus" from Hume and told his students in a lecture that they were works "of true genius and worthy of their deepest attention."

(*D.N.B.*; J. T. Smith's *Nollekens and His Times*; Hamilton's *English School*, Vol. III; *Georgian Era*, Vol. IV; *Farington Diary*, Vol. I, page 26.)

PROSPERI, CHRISTOPHER
fl. 1800–1815

His groups of "Venus and Cupid" and "Bacchus and Ariadne" were bought by, or presented to, the Duke of Wellington about 1812 and are now at Stratfield Saye. His bust of the Duke of Sussex (1811), a very fine work, is at Woburn Abbey, while another of the Duke of York was at Holland House.

Prosperi exhibited at the Royal Academy, 1810–1816, where his busts included those of Vestris, Lord Downe, Henry Hope, Miss Horatia Nelson and Lord Blandford. He signs a tablet to Edward Grant, 1812, at Lichborough, Northants.

PROST, V., of Dijon

His original signed drawings for the trophies of armour on the main gates of Petworth House are in the Wyndham archives at Petworth. These superb baroque trophies consist of great cuirasses and plumed helms and of their kind are almost without equal in England. As the house was built *c.* 1680–1690 the trophies are probably contemporary.

PULFORD, WILLIAM

Son of William Pulford the Elder, mason, he signs a tablet in coloured marbles to William Kemp, 1836, at Belton, Rutland.

PULHAM, JAMES
b. 1765, *d.* 1830

He was born at Woodbridge, Suffolk. He was first employed by a local bricklayer and plasterer called William Lockwood and succeeded so well that in a short time he became head foreman. Pulham was chiefly employed in the plastering side of the business modelling architectural details, but having acquired a book of prints called *Bowles' Passions of the Soul* he began to model grotesque faces and masks from it, which were used as keystones, etc., on various buildings. During the Napoleonic era Woodbridge was a military station, and a local architect called George Thompson, in 1806, designed a building known as "The Castle" both as a club for the officers and as a Lodge for the Woodbridge freemasons, and Pulham was employed to make in Roman cement all the details and also two statues which stood on the roof, while for the grotto in the garden he cast in the same material various busts and figures. In 1814 Pulham also made for a building called the "Little Castle" a statue of "Old Time." Pulham's employer, William Lockwood, had invented a kind of artificial stone which he called "Portland Stone Cement," and in 1816 moved to London where he opened a business in Tottenham called "The New Portland Stone Cement Agency." This was an instantaneous success, and Pulham, who was joined by his brother Obadiah, was kept busy modelling for his employer. Among the works carried out by them were the façade, with columns 40 ft. high, of the Female Orphan Asylum; the sign of the "Black Bull" at Holborn, and numberless Royal coats of arms, inn signs, and other architectural details, chiefly in the classical style, both for London and the country. In 1825 the brothers made busts of Alfred the Great and William Penn and groups of Adam and Eve and Romeo and Juliet.

James Pulham remained for many years with Lockwood, after which he seems to have set up on his own and patented a material called "Pulhamite" which probably was very similar to that discovered by Lockwood. His chief work in this medium was the laying out of the garden at Highnam Court, Glos, for Mr. T. Gambier-Parry. The use of "Portland Stone Cement" (which was quite different from "Portland Cement") seems to have died out in the middle of the last century. His bust by L. A. Goblet (q.v.) was exhibited at the Royal Academy in 1820.

(Lockwood, *Woodbridge in the Olden Times*, privately printed 1889; private information.)

Q

QUELLIN, or QUELING, ARNOLD

b. 1653, *d.* 1686

Sons of the famous Antwerp statuary, Artus Quellin, Arnold and his brother came to England, where the former proceeded to settle. The latter, however, went on to Copenhagen and, according to Vertue, "got great employment there and at Danzig and Hamburg, and, in about ten years' time, made his fortune, returned to Antwerp and there died, left a widow an Englishwoman who married another husband and ran it all out."

Vertue describes Arnold Quellin as "a tall well-shaped man" who "wore his own hair and lived in an old great house in Tower Street and there died in the prime of his days aged about thirty-three." His foreman was John Nost (q.v.), who later married his master's widow.

Quellin's greatest work was the altar-piece which he carried out in partnership with Grinling Gibbons for James II's Roman Catholic Chapel at Whitehall, Wren being responsible for the design. The bill for it (P.R.O., Works 5/54) runs as follows: "For the great altar-piece of white marble, veined, wrought according to a design and contract, finding all materials and workmanship, £1,800. Deduct one square white-marble pillar £14 18s.; more to them for two marble columns under the throne, fluted, with capitals and bases, £90. Total £1,875 2s."

This altar-piece with its "columns of purple Rance" and "statues and other sculpture" was taken down in 1694–1696 and sent to Hampton Court, where it remained in store until 1706, when Queen Anne presented it to Westminster Abbey, though when it was erected there it was deprived of its two chief figures. In 1820 a new altar-piece was set up in the Abbey and the old one was given to Walter King, Bishop of Rochester, who in 1826 had it placed in Burnham Church in Somerset, of which he was also Vicar. In the Victorian era it was decided that a huge white Italianate altar-piece, which incidentally blocked the east window, was quite unsuitable for a Gothic church and it was unfortunately dismantled. Only a few fragments, including two statues of angels and panels with figures of cherubs, exist today.

Like Pearce (q.v.), Quellin was also employed by City Companies to carve statues for presentation to the Royal Exchange. In all he made five: Henry VI for the Armourers, Edward IV for the Ironmongers (1685), Edward V for the Leather-

sellers, Henry VII for the Tallow Chandlers and Charles II for the Grocers. For the Royal College of Physicians he made statues of Charles II and Sir John Cutler in 1683, receiving £20 for each figure (College Archives). These statues are now at the Guildhall. In the same year he carved another and finer one of Cutler for the Grocers' Company, in whose Hall it still remains (Company Archives). He was also responsible for some garden ornaments for Carlton, County Kildare (*Country Life*, November, 1936).

The only monument which can be attributed to him with any certainty is the famous one in Westminster Abbey to Thomas Thynne, of Longleat, with its dramatic relief of "Tom of ten thousand's" murder in Pall Mall in 1682. This may be the one referred to in one of the Longleat account-books which has an entry: "1684. Paid Mr. Quellin in part for a monument." He also made another monument for the Thynne family, apparently that of the Duchess of Somerset, at Great Bedwyn, Wilts. In Lord Bath's archives is a letter from Quellin to Lord Weymouth, dated 8 October, 1685, which runs as follows: "My Lord, I have taken care to send down a man to set up Your Honour's monument which will be very careful in doing it, he is one that doeth all my business in this country and I do not doubt that he will give Your Honour content. This is all from Your Honour's humble servant to command, Arnold Quiling." It may be noticed how Quellin himself spells his name. Apparently some of his English employers had great difficulty with it, probably because of the pronunciation. In the Ironmongers' account-book it is given as "Collynes," while the Grocers, on the other hand, spell it "Collon." It is quite possible that the man sent down to set up Lord Weymouth's monument was the sculptor's foreman, John Nost.

In Rysbrack's sale on 24 and 25 January, 1760, the following works by Quellin were sold: Lot 37, "a basso-relievo of a pediment of the Stadhouse at Amsterdam"; Lots 44, 45 and 46, bas-reliefs of Mercury, Saturn and Jupiter; and Lot 61, a bas-relief of "The Judgment of Solomon."

In the Stowe sale of 1848, Lot 85 on the thirty-sixth day was "a set of four exquisite small marble figures of the Seaons by A. Quelinus." The Duke of Buckingham had given Well of Bond Street £250 for them, but at the sale they only cost "Mark Philips, Esq.," £89.

(Authorities cited in text.)

R

RACKSTROW, BENJAMIN
d. 1772

His museum at 197, Fleet Street was one of the sights of eighteenth-century London; for a sign it had the head of Sir Isaac Newton painted on a board, while inside were exhibited natural and artificial curiosities and anatomical figures (Timbs' *Curiosities of London*, page 599).

Rackstrow made "three bustos and a group" in 1748 for Arbury, in Warwickshire (Newdigate Archives, Arbury), and in 1750 received £3 13s. for two busts supplied to the Ironmongers' Company. A year later he was also paid six guineas for "a figure of King Edward VI," but this is no longer in the Company's possession (Company's Archives).

In 1763 he exhibited at the Free Society "a figure of a Gentleman, sitting; as large as life," and busts of the Marquess of Granby and Mr. Frye. His pupil, Mrs. Clark, showed in the same year "a cucumber vine; in composition."

RADBURN, STEPHEN, of London
fl. 1820–1836

Radburn, whose studio was at 44, South Audley Street, signs tablets to Sir William Smyth, 1823, at Thyedon Mount, Essex; James Sutherland, 1826, in Marylebone Parish Church; and John Butcher, 1835, in Paddington Parish Church.

RADCLIFF, —, of Nottingham
fl. 1758–1770

He signs a monument with mourning cherubs to Philip Bainbridge, 1769, at Lockington, Leicestershire, and a headstone to Elizabeth Cumberland, 1758, at Wilford, Nottinghamshire.

On Radcliff's death his yard was taken over by William Stretton (q.v.).

RAGGETT, HENRY, of Weymouth
fl. 1819–1840

He signs a wall-tablet to John Ruddock, 1819, in Weymouth Parish Church, and another to William Williams, 1839, at Little Bredy, Dorset.

RANDALL, CHARLES, of London
fl. 1808–1828

One of the "New Road statuaries," his tablets are neither better nor worse than those of his neighbours in the same street. His best work, which has a relief of two women mourning by an urn, commemorates Edmund Howard, 1827, in Marylebone Parish Church.

Other tablets signed by Randall include those to William Young, 1807, in Battersea Parish Church; John Field, 1815, at Barton, Beds; Robert Robinson, 1822, Denston, Suffolk; James Payn, 1822, at Cookham, Berks; Lady Smyth, 1826, at Berechurch, Essex; and Walter Meller, 1826, at Tuxford, Notts.

In 1808 he was paid £30 8s. 2d. for chimney-pieces for the Royal Naval Asylum at Greenwich (P.R.O., Adm. 80/110).

RANDLE, JOHN, of Gloucester

In the Gloucester County Archives (D. 177) is the agreement dated 1709 between John Randle of Gloucester, stone-cutter, and John Diggs of Newent. In it Randle promises to make "a freestone monument, full 6 feet high and 3 feet wide in which said monument there shall be fixed and placed in a workmanlike manner a good white oval marble table," and also to supply a ledger of "Pryor Cleeve blew stone." Diggs, on his part, agrees to "provide, entertain and accomodate" Randall, his servants and workmen, with "good meat and drink and lodging" during the whole time they are "erecting fixing up and painting" the monument.

RAPER, EDWARD, of York
fl. 1724–1738

Son of Edward Raper of Leyburn, York, he was apprenticed to George White of York in 1724 (City Archives). Between 1736 and 1738 he was working at Castle Howard, where he did most of the decorative stonework for the mausoleum. This included eight capitals for the interior, £64; the entablature, £30; modelling in the panels and the dome, £27; sixteen cherubim-heads, £11; forty-eight "flooroones," £25; and one hundred and forty-four roses in the panels of the dome, £28 (Castle Howard Archives).

With his partner, Charles Mitley (q.v.), Raper signs a tablet to Catherine and Christiana North, 1734, in St. Michael-le-Belfry, York.

RATHBONE, RICHARD
fl. 1784–1787

In 1784 he carved in wood the pediment in the

centre of the north front of Somerset House. This was 34 ft. long and 7 ft. high and showed two sea-horses with a figure of Amphitrite supporting naval arms, Rathbone receiving £87 for the work. Two years later he cut for the same building in Portland stone "twelve flowers in soffit of arches leading to the terrace" for £66, and also received £151 for sixteen faces of composite capitals in Portland stone for the south front of the loggia.

In 1789, at a cost of £140, he carved in Portland stone an ornament over the arch next the terrace, at the west end of the main building. This was 16 ft. long and 10 ft. 6 in. high, while the keystone consisted of a head of Neptune with dolphins, seaweed, naval arms, swags of laurel leaves, crown, etc., "the greatest part carved all round." In the following year he was paid £30 for an "ornament" in Portland stone, "carved with large bows of ribbands, swags and drops of laurel leaves," for the water-front of the lodge.

(Somerset House Building-accounts, R.I.B.A. Library, MS. 335A.)

RAWLINGS, DAVID, of Box
fl. 1760–1799

There was a West Country family of stone-masons and carvers of this name, the first member of whom I have found any record being a "Mr. Rawlings, freemason," who was paid in 1716 "for stone and work about my Lady Dutchess's monu-ment at Great Bedwin," the monument in question being that of the 2nd Duchess of Somerset (Longleat Archives).

It is probably this man's son who signs the monuments of Edward Baily, 1760, at Bradford-on-Avon, Wilts; Stephen Bowyer, 1795, at South Wraxall, Somerset; and Robert Fisher, 1785. at Bathampton, in the same county. These are excellent copies in local stone of contemporary marble works by London statuaries, and Rawlings makes good use of the swags, draperies, flaming lamps and winged cherubs so typical of the period.

RAWLINGS, JOHN, of Bruton
He signs a wall-monument with a draped urn to George Prince, 1817, at Bruton, Somerset.

RAWLINGS, JOHN,
of Maidstone
He made the ledger-stone of William Horsmon-den Turner (*d.* 1753) in Maidstone Parish Church. The bill for this is in Maidstone Museum.

RAWLINGS, SAMUEL,
of Shepton Mallet
fl. 1822–1827

He signs tablets in Somerset to the Rev. William

Provis, 1822, at Shepton Mallet; Sarah Lock, 1823, in Wells Cathedral; and Mary Jellard, 1827, at Milborne Port.

RAWLINS, NATHANIEL
fl. 1678–1707

In 1678, when the Masons' Company made a "General Search," Rawlins (who had become free of the Haberdashers' Company in 1670) was noted as working with Thomas Strong (q.v.). In the "Search" of 1694 he was working with Edward Strong, and about a year previously had succeeded Jasper Latham (q.v.) as one of the master-masons of St. Paul's Cathedral. Here he was employed until 1707 and carried out stone-carving in addi-tion to mason's work, receiving a total sum of £15,751.

RAWLINS, THOMAS, of Norwich
fl. 1747–1781

He was the son of Thomas Rawlins the Elder, a Norwich mason and statuary. He was trained in London, and became a Freeman of Norwich in 1747 (City Archives). In 1774 he was the mason responsible for the Gothic porch of St. Andrew's Hall, Norwich.

Rawlins as a monumental mason is in the front rank of the Norfolk statuaries, his only rival being R. Page (q.v.). His monuments in coloured marbles have delightful and delicately carved details, the best being that of Sir Thomas Churchman, 1781, in St. Giles Church, Norwich. This has a medallion portrait and a relief of "Fame Overthrowing Time" and compares favourably with the work of any London sculptor of the period. It is possible, indeed almost certain, that some of the earlier monuments given below were executed by Thomas Rawlins the Elder. They are all in Norfolk and include those to Edward Cooper, 1744, Bungay; Philip Stannard, 1747, in St. Giles, Norwich; William Rolfe, 1754, in Norwich Cathedral; William Rant, 1754, at Mendham; John Custance, 1756, and H. Custance, 1757, both in St. Andrew's, Norwich; John Drake, 1759, at Wymondham; Richard Oram, 1762, Smallburgh; Timothy Balderstone, 1764, in St. George Colegate, Norwich; William Stone, 1765, at Woodton; William Woodcocks, St. Swithin's, Norwich.

The younger Rawlins was also the author of *Familiar Dialogues on Architecture.*

(*Norfolk*, Anon., 1829, Vol. II, page 1194.)

READ, NICHOLAS
b. c. 1733, *d.* 1787

While Read was a pupil at St. Martin's Lane

Academy his father, knowing Roubiliac's great reputation, determined to get that sculptor to accept his son as a pupil. Roubiliac, however, when he first settled in England, had "determined never to take an apprentice," but the elder Read persisted and at last "prevailed with Mr. Roubiliac to take him into his house to instruct him in drawing and modelling."

"Some few weeks after, Mr. Roubiliac, working on a very fine bust of which he was particularly nice and would not permit anyone but himself to touch it, our young artist was daring enough in the absence of his master to attempt to finish, which he either nearly or quite accomplished." When Roubiliac returned he was so delighted with what Read had done that "from that moment he in his turn became a solicitor to Read's father to take him apprentice and they continued inseparable friends ever after and all distinction was lost in the affection he bore him" (Read's obituary, *Gentleman's Magazine*, 1787, Part II, page 644).

Vertue (*Walpole Society*, Vol. III, page 152) refers to Read in 1750 as: "A young man, an apprentice of Mr. Rubbillac, statuary, by a drawing I have seen of him; an academy figure shows great skill and fire and spirit extraordinary."

Read, while still apprenticed to Roubiliac, gained in 1762 a premium of one hundred guineas from the Society of Arts for a "life-sized figure in marble of Actaeon and his dog." Two years later he won a further premium of £147 for a "life-sized figure of Diana by a rock," these being the largest awards for sculpture hitherto granted by the Society. (Society's Archives.)

He assisted Roubiliac during the latter's lifetime, carving many of his works, including the skeleton on the famous monument of Lady Elizabeth Nightingale in Westminster Abbey, and, on his master's death, took over his studio at 66, St. Martin's Lane. J. T. Smith called Read "the most deficient in talent of all Roubiliac's pupils," while Nollekens, who disliked him, said that his figure of Admiral Tyrrell in Westminster Abbey looked "for all the world as if he was hanging from a gallows with a rope round his neck," a criticism probably coloured by the fact that the two men were rival sculptors.

In any case, Admiral Tyrrell's monument (1766), known from its swelling clouds as the "pancake monument," has been as virulently attacked by some writers as it has been absurdly over-praised by others. It was cruelly mutilated in the nineteenth century and it is now difficult, if not impossible, to form a true estimate of its worth. The relief, however, remains, and, as Mrs. Esdaile says, "in all the annals of sculpture was ever a ship so marvellously represented? The sails, the rigging, the port-holes, the poop and its balcony, the rich carving above, all these are technically among the most amazing things in English art." (Esdaile's *Roubiliac*, page 214.)

The Tyrrell monument having been dismembered, the most important of Read's untouched works is the huge mass of marble commemorating Nicholas Magens, 1779, at Brightlingsea, Essex, with its vast figure of "Fame" and its emblems of trade—bales of merchandise, anchor and rope, globe and bursting cornucopia, pouring forth a flood of fruits of the earth intermixed with golden guineas—while, above, angels tumble in heavy swirling clouds, defying all the laws of gravity.

Read died on 11 July, 1787. According to the *Gentleman's Magazine*, "his faculties were, from his great studies, impaired at a time of life when other men's are in their prime, and he became totally deprived of reason a short time before his death." After he died a sale of his effects was held, the more important lots being "a small monument complete," "a basso-relievo," "five plaster-casts of busts," and a "carved statuary tablet." He exhibited at the Society of Artists and at the Free Society, 1764–1780.

John Cheere (q.v.), who died in the same year, left Read in his will five guineas to buy a mourning-ring.

Other monuments executed by Read include those to Francis Hooper (with a bust), 1763, in Trinity College Chapel, Cambridge; James Kendall, c. 1765, at West Horsley, Surrey; Elizabeth and Stephen Niblett, 1766, at All Souls College, Oxford; Sir Thomas Morgan, 1767, at Kinnersley, Hereford; Mrs. Anne Simons, 1769, at Lechlade, Glos; the Duchess of Northumberland, 1776, in Westminster Abbey (from a design by Adam); the Rev. George Legh, 1776, in Halifax Parish Church; and James Poole, 1785, at Budworth, Cheshire.

REEVE, —

Possibly a Wiltshire stone-carver, he signs wall-tablets in that county of quite good workmanship to Lionel Seaman, 1760, at Upton Scudamore, and to Alice Wayte, 1768, at Dauntsey.

REEVE, STEPHEN
b. 1662, *d.* 1724

There was a family of craftsmen in Gloucestershire named Reeve during the seventeenth and eighteenth centuries. Members of it include Francis (1639–1715), described as "mason and carver," who is buried in St. Nicholas's Church, Gloucester; his son Joseph (1669–1716), also a carver, who is buried in the same church; and Stephen, who is buried in the church of St. John the Baptist, Gloucester, and who signs a large monument to Beata Johnson, 1722, at Barnwood, just outside that city (Fosbrooke's *Gloucester*, page 317, 369).

Reeves of a later generation were Joseph, "son of Joseph Reeve, stonecutter," who became free in 1751, and his two brothers, Nathaniel and Francis, who gained their freedom in 1761 and 1768 respectively (Corporation records).

REEVES and SONS, of Bath
Firm *fl.* 1778–1860

The firm was founded by William Reeves, who was succeeded by his son Charles, the latter, for a short period only, taking a Mr. Holland into partnership about 1825. Like the Kings of the same city, the firm was an extremely busy one and their tablets run into hundreds. Unfortunately they had a number of stock designs which they repeated almost incessantly and they relied almost entirely for decoration on the conventional weeping-willow or draped urn.

In 1824 and 1833 the firm made marble chimney-pieces for Stourhead, and in the latter year were also paid for shields for the gate piers of the same house. For these the material used was Bath stone, carved with the arms of Colt and Hoare (Hoare Archives).

Monuments and tablets signed by the Reeves in Somerset include those to Robert Perfect, 1778, and Moulton Messiter, 1786, both at Wincanton; Elizabeth Jeane, 1788, at Broomfield; Elizabeth Moffat, 1791, John Balfour, 1791, and Anne, Lady Cosby, 1817, all in Bath Abbey; Harry Atwood, 1814, at Batheaston; Ann Gunning, 1817, at Langridge; Archdeacon Turner, 1817, and Fridiswyde Broderip, 1825, both in Wells Cathedral; Alexander Luders, 1819, at Widcombe; and Admiral Holloway, 1826; in St. Cuthbert's, Wells. Others executed by them outside the county include those to Captain Stokes, 1786, at Yate, Glos; John Long, 1797, at Corhampton, Hants; the Rev. Edward Escourt, 1802, at Long Newton, Glos; Charles Cox, 1808, at Kemble, Glos; Mary Goodelen, 1812, at Over Compton, Dorset; Lady Spencer Wilson, 1818, at Charlton, near Greenwich; Stephen Ram, 1821, at South Stoneham, Hants; the Hon. Mrs. Long Wellesley, 1825, at Draycot Cerne, Wilts; James Wickens, 1827, in Salisbury Cathedral; and Sir Henry Mathias, 1832, at Haverfordwest, Pembroke. The firm also sent their work abroad and examples of it are to be found in Jamaica Cathedral, to Dr. Lee, 1822, and John Milward, 1822; at Byculla, in India, to

Lt.-Colonel Edward Woods, 1840; in St. Peter's Church, Colombo, to Augustus Marshall, 1841; and in Christ Church, Barbados, to Bishop Coleridge, 1849.

REGNART, CHARLES,
of London
b. 1759, *d.* 1844

Son of Philip Regnart (q.v.), he was born at Bristol and married a Miss Hunter of Hexham, by whom he had an only son, Charles, born in 1796. After his first wife died he married his cook, and she is presumably the "Jane Regnart" to whom the Royal Academy made a charitable gift in 1850 (Private information and Royal Academy Archives).

Regnart, who was buried in the Hampstead Road Cemetery, was an extremely competent monumental mason, whose work is to be found all over England. His masterpiece is the altar-tomb at Farthinghoe, Northants, to George Rush, 1806. Though nearly all recumbent figures of the Georgian era show the dead person in youth or in the prime of life, the sculpture shows Rush as an old, old man, thin and emaciated, clad in a loose robe with slippers on his feet and his Bible in his hand. He is at the point of death, and his closing eyes gaze towards Heaven. This effigy is, indeed, one of the most remarkable and unusual executed in England during the early nineteenth century, and Regnart exhibited a model of it and the tomb on which it rests at the Royal Academy in 1806. Regnart died 19 November, 1844.

MONUMENTS

1784	Stoke, near Guildford, Surrey	Ann Robertson
1793	Hadleigh, Suffolk	Sarah Johnson
1795	Tywardreath, Cornwall	Jane Rashleigh
1795	Hinxton, Cambs	William Vachell
1796	Eastnor, Hereford	Thomas Somers Cocks
1796	Mayfield, Sussex	Michael Baker
1796	Buxted, Sussex	George Medley
1796	Grays, Essex	Ann Cox
1797	Aldeburgh, Suffolk	William Sparkes
1797	Kentish Town (Parish Church)	John Finch
1797	Ilfracombe, Devon	Richard Bowen
1797	Hackney (Parish Church)	Henry Newcombe
1799	Kingston, Surrey	Henry Davidson
1799	Charlton, near Greenwich	General Morrison
1800	Ledbury, Hereford	Michael Biddulph
1800	Perranuthnoe, Cornwall	Humphrey Cole
1800	Carshalton, Surrey	Edward Beynon
1801	Orsett, Essex	Elizabeth St. Aubyn
1802	Hambledon, Bucks	Elizabeth Surtees

1802	St. Mary Aldermary	Margaret Bearsley
1803	Chesham, Bucks	Elizabeth French
1803	Battersea (Parish Church)	Thomas Astle
1804	Portsmouth (Cathedral)	Anthony Atcheson
1804	Barnet, Herts	Ann Corpe
1804	Grosvenor Chapel	John André
1806	Kentish Town (Parish Church)	Sarah Pepys
1809	Northampton (All Saints)	Charles Boycott
1810	Cookham, Berks	Admiral White
1811	Hackney (Parish Church)	Lieutenant Henry Sedgewick
1812	Hunton, Kent	Thomas Punnett
1814	Fordingbridge, Hants	Lieutenant Andrew Hay
1815	Stepney (Parish Church)	Rev. George Harper
1815	St. Margaret Pattens	John Bird
1815	Gissing, Norfolk	Sir John Kemp
1816	Mendlesham, Suffolk	Richard Chilton
1817	Carlisle (Cathedral)	Hugh James
1818	Jamaica (Cathedral)	David Milligan
1819	Goldington, Beds	Frances Addington
1820	Ickham, Kent	Captain John Wood
1821	Ealing (Parish Church)	Sir Jonathan Miles
1821	Roxwell, Essex	Marie Herlock
1823	Hartfield, Sussex	Richard Davies
1827	Battersea (Parish Church)	Thomas Ashness
1834	Kentish Town (Parish Church)	Henry Smith

REGNART, PHILIP
fl. 1760–1805

The family, whose badge was a fox, originally came from Flanders, and is said to be descended from Raginhart, a Gothic chief present with Alaric at the sack of Rome.

Philip Regnart was "under twenty-two and a pupil of his father" when in 1760 he won a premium from the Society of Arts for a "model of birds in clay" (Archives, Society of Arts). In 1761 and 1763 he gained further premiums and in 1764 was working with John Walsh (q.v.). A year later he was employed as an assistant by T. Ricketts, of Gloucester (q.v.), but later returned to London and set up as a statuary on his own account. He became bankrupt in 1805 (*Monthly Magazine*, 1805, Part I, page 276).

It is possible that he was responsible for some of the earlier monuments and tablets signed "Regnart" which I have attributed to his son Charles.

RENDALL, JOSEPH, of Bristol

He was a founder by trade, and in 1723 made the large lead statue of "Neptune" which now stands near the Broad Quay in Bristol (Latimer's *Annals of Bristol in the Eighteenth Century*, page 135).

RENNIE, GEORGE
b. 1802, *d.* 1860

He was born in Haddingtonshire, son of George Rennie the agriculturist (1749–1828), and nephew of John Rennie the engineer, and as a young man went to Rome to study sculpture. He first exhibited at the Royal Academy in 1828 (the year of his return to England), and in 1834 carved a series of bas-reliefs for the Dividend Office of the Bank of England, works which included representations of "Mercury," "Britannia," "Ceres," "The Thames," "Industry," "Calculation," etc.

In 1836 Rennie suggested to Sir William Ewart the formation of the Parliamentary Committee which led to the establishment of the School of Design at Somerset House, and he also assisted Joseph Hume in his efforts to obtain for the public freedom of access to all monuments and works of art in public buildings and museums. In 1841 he decided to enter Parliament, and was returned in the Liberal interest by Ipswich. Six years later he became Governor of the Falkland Islands, where he was an unqualified success. He died in London on 22 March, 1860.

Rennie's best-known sculpture is "The Archer," a statue executed in 1828 and now at the Athenaeum Club. The *New Monthly Magazine* of that year (page 256) considered that the figure showed an "admirable knowledge of anatomy," though it was forced to express surprise "in contemplating the excellencies of 'The Archer' to find that the very inferior statue of 'The Gleaner' is from the chisel of the same artist." The latter was exhibited at the Royal Academy in 1828, and from that year until 1837 Rennie continued to send works to Burlington House. These included groups of "Cupid and Hymen" and "The Conchologists" in 1831 and 1832 respectively, busts of John Rennie and Thorwaldsen in 1831, and a bust of David Wilkie in 1833. Another of William Jolliffe, dated 1832, is at Amerdown, in Somerset, while his statue of Lord Harris, executed three years later, is in Throwley Church, Kent. A figure of "Mars" and a bust of Alexander, both undated, are at Chatsworth.

It is interesting to remember that Rennie was one of the first artists to conceive the idea of bringing "Cleopatra's Needle" to London, for according to the design and plan he submitted for the competition in 1839 it was to be erected in Trafalgar Square as the main feature of the national monument to Nelson.

(*Athenaeum*, 31 March, 1860.)

REVITT, J., of Biggleswade, and Linford
fl. 1802–1803

He signs tablets to Mrs. Pigott, 1802, at Henlow, Bedfordshire, and to Robert Callinson, 1803, at Newport Pagnell, Buckinghamshire.

REX, —, of Salisbury

According to the *Builder* of 1848 (page 306), he made, about 1846, the ornamental figures "surmounting the pillars at the gate entrance to Wilton House."

REYNOLDS, GEORGE

In 1764, when "under twenty-two and apprenticed to Mr. Fest," he was awarded a premium of five guineas by the Society of Arts for a "model in clay of ornaments" (Archives, Society of Arts).

RHODES, ROBERT, of Leeds
fl. 1757–1802

Rhodes, who was apprenticed in 1757 to John Carr, an architect of York (City Archives), signs a large wall-tablet of various coloured marbles to Thomas Close, 1802, in Leeds Parish Church. He was succeeded in the business by his son Edward, who was working from 1817 until 1834.

A "John Rhodes" was one of the contractors for building St. Mary's Church, Bridgnorth, in 1792 (Archives, Lord Sandys).

RICE, THOMAS, of Brompton
fl. 1820–1840

He signs tablets to the Rev. Benjamin Wainewright, 1823, at East Bergholt, Suffolk; John Kennard, 1838, in Clapham Parish Church; and the Rev. John Hanley, 1840, at Amberley, Sussex.

RICE, W., of Barnstaple

He signs a wall-tablet with pilasters supporting a plain pediment to Mary Chichester, 1760, at Georgeham, Devon.

RICHARDS, J., of Exeter
fl. 1814–1830

He signs tablets in Devon to John Saltern, 1814, at Buckland Brewer; George Barbor, 1817, at Fremington; James Haynes, 1824, at Hartbury; and Hannah Beard, 1830, at Lifton.

RICHARDS, JAMES
b. 1671, *d.* 1759

In 1722, after the death of Grinling Gibbons (q.v.), George I appointed Richards by Letters Patent to "the Place & Office of Our Master Sculptor & Master Carver in Wood as well in All and singular Our Palaces Castles Honors Forts Houses and Buildings whatsoever wherein Wee now are or at any time whatsoever shall or are Accustomed to make Our Abode or to Abide as also all other Our Works whatsoever or wheresoever in any wise belonging to or touching or concerning the said Art of Sculpture or Carving in Wood." In addition to "the Fee or Wages of Eighteen Pence by the day," Richards was to receive "All and all manner of Fees Profits Rights Allowances Liberties Commodities and Advantages whatsoever to the said Office or Place belonging or any wise appertaining in as large and ample manner, as—Gibbons Gent, deceas'd," and also "One Robe yearly," to be taken "out of Our Great Wardrobe against the Feast of the Birth of Our Lord Jesus Christ by the hands of the Master Keeper or other Officer of Our said Wardrobe" (Copy in Archives of West of Alscot Park).

In this capacity Richards carved ornaments on the chimney-pieces at Kensington Palace (*Wren Society*, Vol. VII, page 194), while in 1750 and 1751 he executed the carved stonework (including pineapples, fasces, etc.) for the Horse Guards (R.I.B.A. Library, MS. 725/18).

He was also employed as a carver at Westminster School during the building of the New Dormitory between 1730 and 1733 (*Wren Society*, Vol. XI, page 44).

RICHARDS, L., of Hereford

He signs a large wall monument to Gilbert Abrahall (*d.* 1723), at Ross-on-Wye, Hereford. This architectural work (which was erected in 1728) is about 8 ft. high and has a semicircular pediment supported by four Corinthian pilasters, and is above the usual provincial standard.

RICHARDSON, CHRISTOPHER, of Doncaster
b. 1709, *d.* 1781

From 1748 until 1751 he was carving chimney-pieces for Welbeck Abbey, the most important being a Gothic one in Roach Abbey stone for the Great Hall, for which he was paid £44. He had previously, in 1747, been responsible for the carving of the "Alcove Room," and in 1750 he made a chimney-piece for the "daylight" room, also carving "six stags' heads" in wood. Seven years later he supplied a white veined-marble chimney-piece costing £42 for an unidentified room in the same house (Archives, Duke of Portland).

In 1756 Richardson executed the statue of

"Liberty" on top of the column in Gibside Park, County Durham (Boyles' *Durham*, page 597), and a year later was working at Alnwick and Berwick-on-Tweed.

At Berwick he cut the arms of the town on the Town Hall, taking the place of a Mr. Charles Litaneer who had originally been engaged to do the work. The account of this transaction given below is taken from minutes in the Guildbook dated 18 February and 22 March, 1757.

The first reads: "Works Committee. Called before them Mr. Charles Litaneer the carver and endeavoured to know from him the lowest price he could carve the Town Arms upon stone and also upon wood." After an interval of over a month the Committee then "reported that they did not approve of the model Mr. Litaneer made of the Corporation Arms and as Mr. Christopher Richardson, of Doncaster, carver, a person of known character who is now carving at Alnwick Castle, for the Rt. Hon. the Earl of Northumberland and at other parts of the north, has offered to carve our Arms with the ornaments as drawn by Mr. Gibson in his best style on stone which the Guild has seen and approved of, £42 (the stone being fixed up at Corporation expense). The Committee is authorized to employ him."

From 1756 until 1762 Richardson was working at Wentworth Woodhouse (Wentworth Woodhouse Archives), and two years later he was again at Welbeck, where he ornamented a cupola over the chapel clock. He died November, 1781, and was buried at Doncaster, his wife Sarah having predeceased him on 19 July, 1771, aged 56 (Registers, Doncaster Parish Church; information from Mr. H. M. Colvin; authorities cited in text).

RICHARDSON, EDWARD
b. 1812, *d.* 1869

In 1832 he attended the Royal Academy Schools on the recommendation of Sir Francis Chantrey (q.v.), and ten years later was allowed to restore the effigies of the Knights Templar in the Temple Church. The result of his work raised a chorus of disapproval, and he was refused admission to the Society of Antiquaries, while Augustus Hare called him "a charlatan who has planed down the effigies."

In 1844 Richardson sent his statue of John Gower to Westminster Hall, thereby causing the art critic of the *Literary Gazette* to remark that "men do strange things and how a man could be audacious enough to send such an abortion as this to a competition, must astonish everyone." In the same year, and again in 1846, he was working in Chichester Cathedral restoring first the monu-

ments of the Earl and Countess of Arundel (*Gentleman's Magazine*, 1848, Part II, pages 83 and 531), and later that of Richard de Wyche, for which he carved seven new statuettes. In 1847 he made the two bronze medallions, designed by Sir Augustus Calcott, for the monument of Sir Alexander Dickson at Woolwich.

In 1848 Richardson was again restoring ancient effigies, this time in Elford Church, Staffordshire, and also made two military monuments for Canterbury Cathedral, commemorating the officers and men of the 16th Lancers and the 31st Regiment respectively. Though the *Builder* of that year (page 310) considered these to be ably executed, it nevertheless felt "bound to say the designs ought to have been very different in character for the proposed situation."

Two years later the sculptor restored and replaced the statue of King Edward the Elder which had fallen from the west front of Wells Cathedral, narrowly missing the carriage of the Judge who was inside the building listening to the Assize sermon (*Builder*, 1853, page 560). In 1853 he carved the pulpit for St. Mary's, Shrewsbury, and was also commissioned to make, or to procure, casts of many of the sepulchral effigies for the Crystal Palace. In 1854 he restored the tomb of Sir Marmaduke Constable in Nuneaton Church, and in 1859 made the 30-ft. monument at Carmarthen erected to the memory of the officers and men of the Royal Welch Fusiliers who had fallen in the Crimea.

Richardson exhibited at the Royal Academy, 1829–1866, at the British Institution, 1840–1862, and at the Great Exhibition of 1851. At the Academy his works included busts of Richard Rothwell (1847) and Sir Edward Tierney (1857), while two others executed by him are of Dr. James Wylie (1853) at Madras, and of the Earl of Powis (1856) at Powis Castle.

Of his statues, "Mercury" (1839) was formerly at the Crystal Palace and another of a Bluecoat Boy (1854) is at the Bluecoat School, Chester. Besides the military monuments already mentioned, he also signs those to Catherine Lushington, 1846, in Madras Cathedral; John Abel-Smith, 1848 (with a recumbent effigy), in Chichester Cathedral; Sir Robert Dick, 1850, and Major George Broadfoot, 1851, both at Madras; Officers and Men of the North Lincoln Regiment 1851 (Lincoln Cathedral); Colonel McNeill, 1852, in St. Mary's Church, Madras; the Earl of Powis, 1853 (with a recumbent effigy), at Welshpool, Montgomery; the Dean of Lincoln, 1855, in St. Peter's, Guernsey; the Earl of Cork, 1856, at Frome, Somerset; Sir George Napier, 1857, at Geneva; the Earl of Bandon, 1859 (with a recumbent effigy), at Bandon, Ireland; the Marquess of Ormonde, 1860 (with a recumbent effigy), in Kilkenny Cathedral; the Officers and Men of the Duke of Cornwall's Light Infantry, 1861, in Exeter Cathedral; the Officers and Men of the 51st Regiment, 1863, in York Minster; and Sir Richard Shakespear, 1867, in St. Anne's Church, Indore. Richardson died on 17 May, 1869, at Milbury Terrace, Marylebone.

(Various references *Builder*, *Art Journal* and *Gentleman's Magazine*, especially 1850, Part I, page 619.)

RICHTER, JOHN AUGUSTUS
fl. 1764–1794

A native of Dresden, he came over to England before 1770. He was the senior partner in the firm of Richter and Bartoli, "Scagiolists," of Newport Street, and was employed by Horace Walpole at Strawberry Hill in 1774, where he made the mosaic work for the shrine of Capoccio (Toynebee's *Strawberry Hill Accounts*). This was purchased in the Strawberry Hill sale of 1842 by Sidney Herbert, who used some of the columns for the church he was then building at Wilton. Richter also made the marble chimney-piece for the round drawing-room at Strawberry Hill, the design for this being taken from the tomb of Edward the Confessor. About 1764 he made scagliola columns in imitation of porphyry, for the saloon at Holland House, Kingsgate, Kent (Ireland's *Kent*, Vol. I, page 526). He married Mary Haig and was the father of Henry Richter (1772–1857), the portrait painter. In 1794 father and son produced an edition of Milton's *Paradise Lost*, illustrated with engravings.

In 1777 the firm received £158 from Sir Rowland Wynn for, as their bill puts it, "two statuary tables inlaid of scagliola according to Messrs. Adams disaing for Nostel at 75 ghaneas each" (Brockwell's *The Nostel Collection*). They must have had a good reputation, for Sir William Chambers, in a letter written in 1773 to Mr. Kay, a master-builder in Edinburgh, said that they were the best makers of scagliola in London, and could "imitate almost any sort of marble and also make very beautiful ornaments" (British Museum Ad. MS. 41133).

About 1780 Richter made the chimney-piece for the state bed-dressing-room at Burghley. He apparently took a Mr. Hodgson as partner about two years later, for they exhibited together at the Free Society various "drawings in scagliola in a new manner." Independently Richter showed chimney-pieces at the Free Society in 1782 and 1783.

RICKETTS, JOHN, of Bath
fl. 1787–1796

He was presumably a member of the Gloucester family of statuaries and masons, and though his tablets are not outstanding, they have quite carefully carved details. He became a bankrupt in 1793 (*Universal Magazine*, 1793, page 471), but continued to work after that date.

Signed works by Ricketts in Gloucestershire include those commemorating Ann Trotman, 1787, at Winchcombe; Charles Barrow (with a portrait-medallion), 1789, at Minsterworth; Anne Cresswell, 1791, at Bibury; and John Scott, 1795, at Longborough. Two others in Berkshire are in memory of Jane Crosse, 1791, at Compton, and Thomas Crosse, 1795, at Kintbury.

RICKETTS, JOHN, the Elder, of Gloucester
d. 1734

He first lived in Cheltenham, but had moved to Gloucester by 1710, for in that year he petitioned the Corporation to be made a Freeman of the city and offered to execute a stone statue of Queen Anne in return. His proposition was agreed to, and he duly became a Freeman of Gloucester on 11 September, 1711, receiving in the following year £23 in part payment for his statue. This first stood in Southgate, near the Wheat Market, but was removed in 1782 to the park of Mr. John Pitt. In 1839, however, it returned to the city and was erected on College Green, near the Cathedral (Gloucester Corporation Archives; *Gentleman's Magazine*, 1839, Vol. I, page 631).

Ricketts signs monuments in Gloucestershire to William Guise, 1716, at Elmore, and to William Lisle, 1723, in the Cathedral; the latter is an important work, with a fine bust. He may also have worked at Bristol, for in 1711 and 1712 a "Mr. Ricketts" was one of the chief masons for building All Saints Church in that city.

He died on 16 July, 1734, and in his will (proved on 31 January of the following year) left his effects to his son Thomas and also mentioned a son named William. His eldest son, James Ricketts, became a Freeman of Gloucester in 1734, but does not seem to have worked in the family business.

RICKETTS, JOHN, the Younger, THOMAS, the Elder, (*d.* 1780) and THOMAS, the Younger, of Gloucester
Firm *fl.* 1729–1795

John Ricketts was a younger son and apprentice of his father, John Ricketts the Elder (q.v.),

and became a freeman of Gloucester on 23 May,
1741 (Gloucester Corporation Archives). Vertue,
who visited the city in 1729, wrote of a "Mr.
Rickett, stone-carver at Gloucester, a son—a
hopeful young man" (*Walpole Society*, Vol. XX,
page 61). This is presumably a reference to John
Ricketts the Younger, the member of the family
who was also responsible for the stone-carving on
Gloucester "Tolsey" or Guildhall, which included
the City Arms on the north and south fronts and
"the city regalia and other ornaments on the east
front pediment" (Corporation Archives). He
exhibited a statue of William Beckford at the Free
Society in 1771.

Ricketts' monuments are above the average
provincial level. That commemorating Sir Thomas
Snell, 1754, at Upton St. Leonards, Gloucestershire, is a large architectural work, while those of
Lady Strachan, 1770, in Gloucester Cathedral,
and Elizabeth Charlett, 1746, at Fladbury,
Worcestershire, have a portrait medallion and a
bust respectively.

John Ricketts' successor was his son Thomas,
grandson of the founder of the firm, which was
later taken over by a member of the fourth generation, Thomas Ricketts the Younger, son of the
elder Thomas.

In the accompanying list of monuments
executed by the firm the earlier ones are the work
of John Ricketts the Younger. They include those
to the Rev. Prideaux Sutton, 1748, at Bredon,
Worcs; Robert Thomas, 1756, at St. Bride's
Major, Glamorgan; Ellis, Bishop of St. David's,
1761, and James Benson, 1785, both in Gloucester
Cathedral; Sarah Boucher, 1762, at Barnsley,
Glos; Sir William Osbaldeston, 1765, at Chadling-
ton, Oxon; the Williams family, 1767, at Llantwit,
Glamorgan; Samuel Sheppard, 1770, at Minchin-
hampton, Glos; Mrs. Prinn, 1771, and John
Whitehouse, 1797, both at Charlton Kings,
Glos; Captain Dansey, 1775, at Little Hereford,
Hereford; Admiral Sayer, 1776, at Sandford St.
Martin, Oxon; Henry Perrot, 1778, at North
Leigh, Oxon; Elizabeth Coxe, 1783, at Kemble,
Glos; and Mrs. Warren, 1792, in Worcester
Cathedral.

RING, JAMES, of Reading
fl. 1751–1766

He signs tablets of white and coloured marbles
to Thomas Shaw, 1751, at Bramley, Hants; and to
John Baker, 1760, and Nathaniel Butler, 1766,
both at Farnham, Surrey.

Ring was dead by 1774, the year in which his
son, Moses, was apprenticed to Thomas Burnell
(q.v.) (Archives, Masons' Company).

RINGWOOD, R.
fl. 1835–1843

He exhibited busts and medallions at the Royal
Academy, 1835–1843, including those of "a noble
lord and lady" and "an artist." His studio was at
26, Albany Street.

RIPPINGILLE, EDWARD VILLIERS
b. 1798, *d.* 1859

He is chiefly known as a painter, but he exhibited
two works of sculpture, "Head of a Sleeping
Child" and "Sympathy," at the Birmingham
Society of Artists in 1829.

RITCHIE, ALEXANDER HANDYSIDE
b. 1804, *d.* 1870

He was born at Musselburgh, near Edinburgh,
the son of James Ritchie, a brickmaker, and after
studying architecture turned to sculpture. He
then went to Rome, where he became a pupil of
Thorwaldsen, and in 1844 exhibited "Sophronia
and Olinda at the Stake" in Westminster Hall.
The *Literary Gazette* was sparing in its praise of
this group, remarking that "while some parts
have had great care bestowed upon them, there
are others, for instance the drapery about the
foot, as slovenly as any we have ever witnessed."

Ritchie was elected an Associate of the Royal
Scottish Academy in 1846. In the same year he
carved the figures for the tympanum of the Commercial Bank in Glasgow which were highly
praised by the *Art Union* (1846, page 284). The
critic was particularly impressed by the three
figures of children, considering not only "that they
would do credit to the chisel of any sculptor," but
also that Ritchie himself "must be a man of fine
sympathies and of gentle nature, as well as high
genius, who can represent the innocence of childhood so successfully."

Ritchie was also responsible in Edinburgh for
the ornamental figures on the Commercial and
British Linen Banks, for a group of children (1848)
for the Western Bank, and for decorative details
on the office of the Life Association of Scotland
(1859). In London he was employed under J.
Thomas (q.v.) on decorative sculpture for the
Houses of Parliament.

He exhibited at the Royal Academy, 1830–1868,
and at the Royal Scottish Academy, 1825–1869,
showing, among other works, busts of Sir John
Hope (1825), Thorwaldsen (1830), the Countess
of Lincoln (1837), the Marquess of Huntley (1838),
James Callender (1843), Sir David Milne (1846)

and Sir Charles Eastlake (1866). He also carved the busts of the Rev. Charles Finlater (1836), for Newlands Church; Dr. Andrew Thomson (1837), for the Presbyterian Hall, Edinburgh; and the Rev. George Lee (1838), for the Mechanics' Institute, Hull; while those of George Kemp (1845) and David Stow (1852) are in the Scottish National Portrait Gallery and the Kelvingrove Art Gallery respectively.

Ritchie also executed a number of statues, including those of Sir Walter Scott (1839), at Selkirk; Mr. Ferguson of Raith (1843), at Dirlton, Haddington; Prince Charles Edward Stuart (1844), for the Scott Memorial in Edinburgh; Eustace de Vesci and William de Mowbray (1848), at the House of Lords; Queen Victoria (1851), at Holyrood Palace; Peel (1852), at Montrose; Dr. Moir (1853), at Musselburgh; Hugh Miller (1858), at Cromarty; and Wallace (1858), at Stirling. He also made a number of statues in 1845 for the New Physicians' Hall in Edinburgh, and, in 1858, those of Knox, Melville, Henderson, Renwick, and Ebenezer Erskine for Stirling Cemetery. His group of the Rev. David Dickson blessing children (1844) is outside St. Cuthbert's, Edinburgh.

His monument to Charles Marjoribanks, 1836, is at Coldstream, and his tablet to the Rev. John Patterson, 1838, in Falkirk Church. For the Hamilton Palace Mausoleum he carried out a pair of lions in 1852, and heads of "Time," "Death" and "Eternity" in 1863.

(*D.N.B.*; various references *Builder*, *Art Union* and *Art Journal*.)

RITCHIE, JOHN
b. 1809, *d.* 1850

He was the brother of Alexander Handyside Ritchie (q.v.), and studied sculpture at home, producing a few models which attracted but little notice. He later became Alexander's assistant when the latter returned from Rome.

In 1840 John Ritchie exhibited at the Royal Academy a group entitled "The Deluge" which he had modelled in clay in 1832. Some years later this was brought to the notice of a Mr. Davidson, of London, who was so impressed that he commissioned the sculptor to execute the group in marble and so gave him the chance to fulfil his long-cherished wish to visit Rome. Ritchie left Scotland for Italy in September, 1850, and began work on his arrival. Soon afterwards he went with some friends on a visit to Ostia, but neglected to observe all the usual precautions against malaria and died on 30 November, 1850, of the disease after a few days' illness.

His chief works in Scotland are the statue of

Scott at Glasgow, and the figure of the Last Minstrel (1844) made for the Scott Memorial in Edinburgh. He exhibited the statue of Scott, together with one of Lord Byron, in Bond Street in 1833, while his marble statue of "A Poetess" was shown after his death at the Great Exhibition of 1851 (*Art Journal*, 1851, page 44).

RIVERS, CHARLES AUGUSTUS
b. 1811

In 1830 he attended the Royal Academy Schools on the recommendation of E. H. Baily (q.v.), and in the following year won the large Silver Medal from the Society of Arts for an original model of a group. In 1837 he also received a Silver Medal from the Academy.

Rivers exhibited at Westminster Hall in 1844 figures of Richard I and John Rennie. The former the *Literary Gazette* declared to be "of small merit," although the *Builder* considered it a "work of animation." There is a cabinet statue of Benjamin Babington by Rivers at the Royal College of Physicians.

The sculptor also exhibited at the Royal Academy, 1831–1847, showing a large number of busts, including those of Sir Thomas Lawrence (1833), Sir W. Blizard (1835), Madame Malibran (1837), Queen Victoria (1838), Miss Helen Faucit (1841) and John Bright (1847). At the Suffolk Street Galleries he showed a bust of Mrs. Fry in 1832.

ROACH, A.

He exhibited at the Royal Academy a figure of "Lady Godiva" in 1830.

ROBERTS, —, of Exeter

He signs a wall-tablet with a relief of a mourning woman to Elizabeth Gartside, 1813, at Topsham, Devon.

ROBERTS, C., of Sheffield
fl. 1800–1809

He signs the monument of Mary Mort, 1800, in St. James's Church, Sheffield, and a tombstone with finely cut military emblems commemorating Richard Walker, a trumpeter (*d.* 1800), in the churchyard of the Cathedral (Holland's *Our Old Churchyard*). He also executed the capitals of the eight pillars supporting the pulpit in Carver Street Chapel, Sheffield.

ROBINS, or ROBBINS, FRANCIS, of Bath
fl. 1755–1794

He may belong to the same family as George

Robins, a mason of Bristol, whose son Samuel, also a mason of that city, became free in 1739.

Francis Robins was declared a bankrupt in 1770, being described at the time as "statuary, mason and penant man." His best work, the monument to Sir Boucher Wray, 1784, at Tawstock, Devon, takes the form of a large square pedestal surmounted by an urn, and he signs others commemorating Charles Biggs, 1755, at Backwell, Somerset; the Rev. Henry Lockett, 1778, at Crowcombe, Somerset; Anne Acton, 1780, at Camborne, Cornwall; Sir James Long, 1794, at Draycot Cerne, Wilts, and of Henry Dickanson, 1796, at Bathampton, Somerset. (*Universal Magazine*, 1770, page 335.)

ROBINSON, —,
of Saffron Walden

According to the *Gentleman's Magazine* of 1791 (Part I, page 780), he designed and executed the memorial tablet at Ashdon, Essex, to the Rev. Nathaniel Salter, who died in that year.

ROBINSON, CHARLES B.,
of Liverpool
b. 1806, *d.* 1894

At the Liverpool Academy of 1836 he showed a bust of Nicholas Robinson, and in 1843 a bas-relief of "A Greek Warrior and His Horse" at the Royal Hibernian Academy. In 1844 he sent a statue of William IV to the exhibition in Westminster Hall, and in the two following years showed busts of William Lowe, W. Hodgson and T. Tobin at the Royal Manchester Institution.

Robinson also signs the monument to John Hodgkinson, 1836, in Prescot Church, Lancashire.

ROBINSON, JOHN

In 1834 he exhibited "Venus, a bas-relief in marble" at the exhibition of the Royal Northern Society held at Leeds.

ROBINSON, JOHN, of London

He was employed at the Board of Trade Buildings in 1825, where he carved, among other details, two capitals costing £90. In the same year a new building was being erected to house the offices of the Privy Council, and here Robinson received £400 for ten Corinthian capitals and £152 for the "enrichment in the architrave" (P.R.O., Works 5/125).

ROBINSON, L., of Barnstaple
fl. 1801–1802

He signs tablets in Devon to Elizabeth Hale,

1801, at South Molton, and to Samuel Chappell, 1802, at Fremington.

ROBINSON, LEWIS
fl. 1763–1764

He was "under twenty-two and an apprentice of Mr. Grepel, of Rathbone Place" when in 1763 he won a premium from the Society of Arts for a "model of ornaments in clay." According to a manuscript note in the Records of the Society, he was working on his own in the following year.

ROBINSON, T., of Chudleigh
fl. 1805–1809

He signs pretty wall-tablets in coloured marbles to Robert Sutton, 1805, at Littleham, Devon, and to Edward Kershaw, 1809, at Dawlish, in the same county.

ROBINSON, THOMAS, of Oxford
fl. 1675–1709

He was possibly a son of that Thomas Robinson, of Oxford, who was employed on the building of the north side of Christ Church quadrangle in 1641, and was also a master-mason for the Sheldonian between 1664 and 1669 (Hiscock's *A Christ Church Miscellany*).

There are a number of payments to Robinson in the Vice-Chancellor's accounts. In 1670 he was paid £40 10s. 8d. for "ye winter house for ye Physic Garden" and in 1671–1672 received £23 5s. 2d. for mason's work at the Printing House. In 1674–1676 he was paid £100 "for stone works and setting up of 40 Pinnacles about St Marie's church at £2 10s. per Pinnacle." In 1684–1685 he was paid £110 for "ye conduit at Carfax," and in 1693–1694 £122 for work at "the Physick Garden." In 1681 he and Christopher Kempster (q.v.) were master-masons for building Tom Tower.

Other works carried out by Robinson at Oxford were in connexion with the conduit at Carfax in 1686, for which he received £110; the Physic Gardens in 1692; and the Divinity School ten years later. In 1709 he was one of the master-masons for building Queen's College (Wood's *Life and Times*, Vol. IV).

ROBINSON, WILLIAM
fl. 1729–1758

Presumably a Yorkshire mason, he built the mausoleum at Castle Howard between 1729 and 1737, his bill for this including carved stonework. Robinson, who was later joined by his son, Christopher, also received £109 for building the steps to the south front of Castle Howard. In 1753–1758 he was the mason for building the "New Wing" to the house (Castle Howard Archives).

ROGERS, —, of Tavistock

He signs a wall-tablet, with a relief of a seated mourning woman, to John Carpenter, 1813, in the church at Tavistock, Devon.

ROGERS, PHILIP, of Swansea

According to the *Gentleman's Magazine* (1838, Vol. I, page 596), he made in 1837 both a monument and a tombstone in memory of the Rev. Edward Davies, at Bishopston, near Swansea. The relief on the monument took the form of sprigs of oak and mistletoe.

ROGERSON, W., of London
fl. 1794–1800

Rogerson, whose yard was in Gerrard Street, was declared a bankrupt in 1800. His monument to George Madocks, 1794, at Gresford, Flint, has a fine portrait-bust, and he signs others to Captain James Thresher, 1794, at Fareham, Hants; John Bull, 1794, in St. Thomas's Church, Lewes; and the Keane family, 1796, in Barbados Cathedral.

ROPER, WILLIAM, of Preston

In 1782 he built an obelisk, 33 ft. high, which stood in the old Market Place at Preston until 1853, when it was taken down (Borough Archives).

His son, R. Roper, signs a tablet to Edward Buckley, 1816, at Penwortham, Lancashire.

ROSE, JOSEPH, the Elder
fl. 1721–1735

He was born about 1696, the son of John Rose, a gunsmith of High Wycombe, Buckinghamshire. In 1710 he was apprenticed to James Paget (q.v.) and became free in 1721.

Rose's two signed monuments—grand and imposing works with life-size reclining figures and elaborate architectural settings—place the sculptor in the front rank of early eighteenth-century statuaries. The first, to Sir John Packington, 1727, at Hampton Lovett, Worcestershire, has a reclining figure in contemporary costume, while from an arched pediment behind falls a curtain inscribed with the epitaph. The second, to Richard Ladbroke, 1730, at Reigate, Surrey, is described as follows in the *Topographer* of 1798 (Vol. III, page 274): "The base is ornamented with skulls, bones, etc. Between the two very lofty variegated marble pillars of the composite order, is the figure of an elderly man, in a reclining posture, supporting himself by his right arm, and in his left hand is a celestial crown; on one side is Justice and on the other Truth, both as large as life; above are two angels with trumpets and palm-branches, and in the centre is a resplendent sun. On a pyramid which forms part of the background is the inscription."

Rose's yard was at Cow Lane, West Smithfield; he was declared a bankrupt in 1735 (*London Magazine*, 1735, page 100).

ROSE, JOSEPH, the Younger
b. 1744

He was the third generation of his family to be called Joseph, his grandfather being Joseph Rose the Elder (q.v.), and his father that Joseph who became a freeman of the Masons' Company in 1733.

In 1765 Rose was awarded a premium of ten guineas by the Society of Arts, in whose journal it is stated that he was then living with his father "opposite Portland Chapel, Cavendish Square." He joined the Royal Academy Schools in 1770, but went to Italy in the same year. From Rome he sent a bas-relief to the Academy, and in 1771 exhibited "A Sacrifice to Hymen."

ROSS, H.
fl. 1851–1867

He showed wax statuettes of Wellington and Peel at the Great Exhibition of 1851, and at the International Exhibition of 1862 a group entitled "Home Sweet Home."

Ross exhibited at the Royal Academy, 1858–1867, showing busts, and also a model of a marble figure for a church at Clapham. His colossal bust of Wellington was formerly at the Crystal Palace.

ROSSETER, JAMES MARMADUKE, of the Borough
fl. 1777–1800

Son of "Thomas Rosseter, Gentleman, of the Bank of England," he was apprenticed to Robert Clemens in 1777, becoming free in 1784. Seven years later he took his son, Richard Baker Rosseter, as an apprentice, and his name continues to appear in local directories until 1818.

It is the elder Rosseter who signs a large wall-tablet to Anthony Hall, 1799, in St. George the Martyr, Southwark.

ROSSI, FREDERICK ORTON
b. 1812, *d.* 1851

He was a son of J. C. F. Rossi (q.v.) by his second wife, and in 1830 was awarded the Silver

Isis Medal by the Society of Arts for the model of a figure. In 1831 he joined the Royal Academy Schools, where he won a Silver Medal in the same year.

Rossi exhibited at the Academy, 1830–1848, showing a bust of his father in 1838. From 1847 until his death four years later, he received a yearly pension of £11 from the Academy (Royal Academy Archives).

ROSSI, HENRY
b. 1791, *d.* 1844 (?)

He was a son of J. C. F. Rossi (q.v.) and attended the Royal Academy Schools in 1811, receiving a Silver Medal four years later for a copy of a plaster-cast.

In 1818 Henry Rossi was sharing a house in Lisson Grove with his father, but set up for himsehf in the New Road in 1820. He first exhibited in 1813, when he showed a medallion of Prince Rupert at the Liverpool Academy, while his bust of Canova was in the Royal Academy of 1817. In the following year he began to exhibit at the Academy the models of cricketers for which he was later so well known. "The Batsman" and "The Bowler," shown as models at the Academy in 1824 and 1825 respectively, were later executed in marble for the Duke of Bedford and are now in the Sculpture Gallery at Woburn. Replicas are at Stourhead, and in the possession of the Merchant Taylors Company, for, owing to the popularity of the figures, a number of casts were made.

In 1819 Rossi assisted his father with the terracotta decoration of St. Pancras Church, for which they received £4,300; three years later he was appointed sculptor to the Duke of Gloucester. Besides exhibiting at the Royal Academy, 1817–1827, and at the British Institution, 1820–1829, he was also one of the foundation members of the Society of British Artists, to whose exhibitions he sent work up till 1837. He probably died in 1844, as his name does not figure in the list of members after that date.

ROSSI, JOHN CHARLES FELIX, R.A.
b. 1762, *d.* 1839

He was born on 8 March, 1762, at Nottingham, the son of an Italian from Sienna who practised medicine. As a young man Rossi studied sculpture under Locatelli (q.v.) and, at the expiration of his apprenticeship, remained with his master for a short time at the meagre wage of eighteen shillings a week. In 1788 he was working at the Derby China Works and in 1789 was with Vulliamy the clock-maker.

He later joined the firm of Coade (q.v.) at Lambeth, where he gained considerable experience in the art of modelling in terra-cotta. During his later career as a sculptor he frequently worked in this medium; indeed, according to the *Gentleman's Magazine* (1827, Part II, page 395), he invented a composition of terra-cotta which "it is hoped will rival in firmness and durability the same description of material of the ancients." In 1781 he first attended the Royal Academy Schools and three years later won a Gold Medal for a group entitled "Venus Conducting Helen to Paris."

In 1785 Rossi won the Academy Travelling Studentship and went to Rome for three years. Here he carved a marble relief for the Academy Exhibition, but after its arrival at Burlington House he received a letter from the Council informing him that they were "of opinion that his time would be more properly employed in modelling than in working in marble" (Royal Academy Archives). Notwithstanding this admonition, he also made a marble statue of "Mercury" for Lord King (*Art Union*, 1839, page 22).

Soon after his return to London the sculptor went into parternership with J. Bingley (q.v.). It was to this episode in his career that he referred when he told Joseph Farington "that he became a partner with a mason-sculptor in John Street by which he lost much money" (*Farington Diary*, Vol. III, page 94). In 1796 the partners made the terra-cotta statues of "Music" and "Dancing" for the Assembly Rooms at Leicester. In 1790 Rossi had been paid £240 for "modelling, moulding, casting in plaster and executing in Portland stone two colossal lions 10 ft. 3 in. long erected at the western water-gate" of Somerset House (R.I.B.A. Library MS. 335A), and four years later he won a premium of fifty guineas from the Society of Arts for his group of "King Edward I and Queen Eleanor." In 1798 he was elected an Associate of the Royal Academy, becoming a full member in 1802.

During his lifetime Rossi was a popular sculptor and as such was selected to design and execute several of the national monuments in St. Paul's Cathedral. In this he was not particularly successful and his work aroused a good deal of adverse criticism. Flaxman said of his monument to Captains Moss and Riou that "it was rather mason's work than that of a sculptor," while Farington added that "Rossi had by employing ordinary men at low wages got much money by it, but had greatly suffered in reputation" (op. cit., Vol. III, page 238). The diarist also noted the opinion of N. Marchant that the monuments were "very badly designed and executed. Rossi could do nothing without Smirke's designs" (op. cit., Vol. III, page 182).

In 1806 Rossi sent in a design for the Guildhall monument to Pitt, but to his chagrin the commission was awarded to his pupil, Bubb (q.v.). Rather tactlessly the Committee then wrote to the sculptor asking him for his opinion of Bubb. In his reply Rossi confessed he had received their letter with "considerable mortification" but continued that his "resentment gradually changed into a settled contempt for civic taste and civic liberality." Of the unfortunate Bubb he coldly remarked that "the young man concerning whose abilities they are now anxious to be informed it is true was a pupil of mine, but not having been employed during his continuance with me upon anything by which he could acquire any practical skill in the execution of such works as the one proposed, and as I have had no communication with him or knowledge of his progress since he left me, I cannot conceive myself authorized to give any opinion as to the executive ability of Mr. Bubb" (City Corporation Records, MS. 95.2).

In 1816 King Christophe of Hayti invited Rossi to come out to the island and execute sculpture for the palaces which the King was then building. Rossi was tempted by this offer for, according to Farington, he had "of late been very unfortunate, being without a professional commission for a year and a half past" (op. cit., Vol. VIII, page 76). However, the terms of the contract seemed so vague and uncertain that he decided to remain in England. Curiously enough, one of his sons, Charles Rossi, later emigrated to the Barbados and set up as a monumental mason. Here he executed a number of tablets between 1819 and 1830, including those to Jane Edwards, 1819, A. M. Clinton, 1820, H. J. Lorraine, 1821, and J. W. Fletcher, 1824, all in Barbados Cathedral.

In 1819 Rossi and another son, Henry (q.v.), entered into a contract to execute the terra-cotta decorations of the new church of St. Pancras for £4,300, their chief contribution consisting of the four colossal female caryatids which form so prominent a feature on the north side of the building. Each figure bears in one hand a ewer and in the other an inverted torch—the latter a symbol of death, for between them are the folding iron doors leading to the catacombs. Inwood, the architect of the church, obtained permission to take complete casts of the caryatids of the Erechtheum in Athens, and these were then copied by Rossi in terra-cotta. The figures were made in pieces and then cemented round the cast-iron pillars which are the real supporters of the entablature (Britton and Pugin's *Public Buildings of London*, Vol. I, page 160).

In 1797 Rossi had been appointed sculptor to the Prince of Wales, afterwards George IV, a post he held until the latter's death in 1830, when he became sculptor in ordinary to William IV. His bust of the Prince was apparently very successful, for Farington quotes Flaxman as saying that "it was worth all that Nollekens had done" (op. cit., Vol. III, page 55). For Buckingham Palace he carried out a good deal of work in artificial stone, receiving £560 in 1827 and £1,766 two years later (P.R.O., Works 19/3 and 5/119). Two friezes executed in this material depicted "The Progress of Navigation" and "The Seasons," the latter pleasing "George IV so much that he directed Mr. Nash, the architect, to give Rossi any part of the sculpture he wanted" (*Gentleman's Magazine*, 1839, Part I, page 548).

Rossi exhibited at the Royal Academy, 1782–1834, and at the British Institution, 1806–1834. In 1835 a sale of the contents of his studio was held by Robins the auctioneer and a list of the more important lots sold is given below, the sum paid in each case following in brackets: "Eve at the Fountain, recumbent figure slightly less than natural size" (200 guineas); "Parental Affection, a Father Protecting His Child from a Wolf" (£19 18s. 6d.)—a terra-cotta model, now in the Soane Museum; "Marble Bust of Nelson" (45 guineas); "Marble Statue of Mercury" (£190); "Group of Zephyrus and Aurora" (£150); "The Poet Thomson in His Study, Marble Statue, life-sized" (£320, bought by Sir Robert Peel); "Bronze Equestrian Figure of Wellington Attended by Fame and Victory, 32 inches high" (96 guineas); and a "Marble Chimney-piece, 4 foot high with bronze group of Shepherds and Nymphs" (180 guineas).

B. R. Haydon, the painter, says in his autobiography that he lodged with Rossi in 1817. He calls him "a singular man" who "had made by commissions £10,000, but he had such an appetite for bricks and mortar he would let no tenant repair his house." After the sculptor's death on 21 February, 1839, the *Art Union* (1839, page 221), however, wrote that "our Nobility have no space for masses of hewn stone and Mr. Rossi found but few patrons . . . and he bequeathed to his family nothing but his fame." The family was, in truth, an extremely large one, for Rossi had married twice and had had eight children by each wife. Indeed, in 1834 he had been forced to write to the Royal Academy "stating his great distress and urging the Council to afford him immediate assistance," and in 1835 had been granted the pension of a superannuated member—one hundred guineas a year. In 1842 the Academy made a gift of £10 to his widow, and in the following year one of £20 to his unmarried daughter (Royal Academy Archives).

(Authorities cited in text.)

WORKS IN TERRA-COTTA AND ARTIFICIAL STONE

1794	Justice and Mercy	Pediment of Stafford County Hall (Richardson's *Vitruvius Britannicus*, Vol. II, page 2)
1799	Britannia	Liverpool Exchange (*Monthly Magazine*, 1799, page 904)
1800	Hindu Temple	Melchet Park, Wilts (illustrated *Gentleman's Magazine*, 1841, Part II, page 243)
1800	Sir Edward Coke	Stoke Poges, Bucks (Lipscomb's *Buckinghamshire*, Vol. IV, page 552)
1801	Prince Regent	For Brighton (*Monthly Magazine*, 1802, page 91). Removed 1819
1804	Decorative Work	Royal Stables, Brighton (Roberts' *History of the Royal Pavilion*, page 28)
1809	Thalia	For Covent Garden Theatre
1810	Justice	For Hotel at Stamford
1811	Royal Coat of Arms	Royal College of Surgeons (300 guineas). (College Archives)
1815	Four tripods	Royal College of Surgeons (£65). (College Archives)
1817	Statues of Henry II, Henry III and Edward II	Inner Temple Hall (destroyed enemy action 1941)
1819– 1822	Caryatids, Columns, Friezes, etc.	New St. Pancras Church, London
1823	Coat of Arms	Portico of Royal College of Surgeons (£100). (College Archives)
1824	Frieze	Assembly Room, York (Allen's *Yorkshire*, Vol. I, page 415)
1832	Apollo and Diana	Pediment, Buckingham Palace
1837	Royal Coat of Arms	Private entrance, Windsor Castle

BUSTS

1792	Mrs. Siddons	Exhibited Royal Academy
1797	J. Wyatt	National Portrait Gallery
1801	Lord Thurlow	Windsor Castle (replica for Inner Temple)
1802	George Dance	Diploma Work, Royal Academy
1804	Prince Regent	Exhibited Royal Academy
1807	Viscount Pery	Trinity College, Dublin
1815	Prince Regent	County Hall, Carlisle
1823	John Nash	Exhibited Royal Academy

MISCELLANEOUS WORKS

1809	Shakespeare	For Covent Garden Theatre (yellow marble). (Britton and Pugin's *London*, Vol. I, page 154)
1809	Tragedy	For façade, Covent Garden Theatre
1813	Chimney-piece	Longleat (£250). (Archives, Marquess of Bath)
1820	Chimney-piece	Chatsworth (Devonshire Archives)
1820	Celadon and Amelia	Petworth
1820	St. Anthony of Padua	For Mr. Beckford (sold 1845 in Beckford's sale)
1825	Lord Heathfield	St. Paul's Cathedral (statue)
1828	The British Pugilist	Petworth
1829	Musidora	For Sir Augustus Clifford, Westfield, Isle of Wight
?	Signs of the Zodiac, etc.	For Oxford Observatory
?	King Alfred (relief)	Arundel Castle

MONUMENTS

1793	East Grinstead, Sussex	Gibbs Crawfurd
1793	Wilton, Wilts	Elizabeth, Countess of Pembroke
1797	Canons Ashby, Northants	Sir John Dryden
1797	St. Paul's Cathedral	Captain Faulkner
1800	Weston-under-Lizard, Salop	Earl of Bradford
1802	St. Paul's Cathedral	Captains Moss and Riou
1805	Tottenham Court Road Cemetery	Bishop of Down (Epitaph by C. J. Fox; *Gentleman's Magazine*, 1805, page 1169)
1807	Lydd, Kent	Robert Cobb
1807	St. Paul's Cathedral	Marquess Cornwallis
1808	Upper Slaughter, Glos	Rev. Ferdinando Travell
1811	St. Paul's Cathedral	Admiral Lord Rodney

1812	Much Hadham, Herts	Rev. Anthony Hamilton
1812	Tillington, Sussex	Lieutenant John Ayling
1812	St. Paul's Cathedral	General le Marchant (designed by James Smith)
1815	Great Dunmow, Essex	Sir George Beaumont
1815	Prestwold, Leics	Major Robert Packe
1815	Newton, Cambs	Anne Pemberton
1817	Corsham, Wilts	Elizabeth Harrington
1817	Adlestrop, Glos	Rev. Thomas Leigh
1817	Ecton, Northants	Catherine Whalley
1819	Lydd, Kent	David Denne
1819	Cirencester, Glos	Maria Master
1819	Newcastle (Cathedral)	Lord Collingwood
1821	Hampton, Middlesex	John Deverell
1821	Chelsea Old Church (churchyard)	Elizabeth Tyndale
1823	Cirencester, Glos	Thomas Master
1823	Henbury, Glos	Elizabeth Battersby
1837	Marylebone (Parish Church)	Mary and Frances Swinney
1838	Llanelly, Carmarthen	Emma Chambers

ROUBILIAC, LOUIS FRANCOIS
b. 1705 (?), *d.* 1762

He was born at Lyons and was apprenticed to Permoser (1651–1732), who was then living at Dresden as sculptor to the Elector of Saxony. He later became assistant to Nicholas Coustou, and in 1730 received the second Grand Prix for a group (now lost) representing "Daniel Saving Susannah when she was Condemned to Death."

Roubiliac seems to have come to England about 1732 and here he was employed by either Benjamin (q.v.) or Thomas Carter (q.v.). The foundation of his fortune, however, was laid by a lucky chance. When returning from Vauxhall one evening he came upon a pocket-book containing bank-notes and valuable papers and, having discovered that it was the property of Sir Edward Walpole, returned it to its owner. Walpole was so struck by the young man's honesty and also by the specimens of sculpture shown to him that he promised his patronage. He kept his word by introducing Roubiliac to Sir Henry Cheere (q.v.), who thereupon engaged him as an assistant.

In 1735 Roubiliac married Catherine Helot and two years later received his first independent commission—the famous statue of Handel for Vauxhall Gardens, the original terra-cotta of which is in the Fitzwilliam Museum, Cambridge. He received three hundred guineas for it (a large sum for a practically unknown sculptor), and it proved so overwhelming a success that in a year he was able to set up for himself in a studio in St. Martin's Lane. Here he executed commissions for busts and also carved a number of monuments for

country churches, but it was not until 1748 that he received an order for a monument for Westminster Abbey, that of the Duke of Argyll and Greenwich. This work, Vertue considered, not only showed "the greatness of his genius in his invention, design and execution, in every part equal, if not superior, to any others," but also outshone "for nobleness and skill all those before done by the best sculptors this fifty years past" (*Walpole Society*, Vol. IV, page 146).

A year or so later Roubiliac was employed for a short period as a modeller at the Chelsea china factory, and in 1752 he married for the second time, his first wife having died before 1751. However, he was soon a widower again, for his bride (Elizabeth Crosby, of Deptford, a considerable heiress) appears to have died shortly after their marriage. Towards the end of 1752 he travelled to Italy in the company of various other artists, visited Rome, and in Florence was joined by J. Wilton (q.v.).

Roubiliac, who in 1745 had been appointed lecturer on sculpture at the St. Martin's Lane Academy, became in 1755 a member of the Committee formed to bring the works of English artists to the notice of the public. About five years later he married again, his third wife being Nicole Reignier. He died on 11 January, 1762, and was buried in the graveyard of St. Martin-in-the-Fields.

Roubiliac was probably the greatest sculptor to work in England during the eighteenth century. His busts are unsurpassed, for he had the seeing eye, as well as the skilled hand. Sir Joshua Reynolds remembered the sculptor's comments when he was making a bust of Pope from life and how he observed "that the poet's countenance was that of a person who had been much afflicted with headaches and he should have known the fact from the contracted appearance of the skin above the eyebrows, though he had not otherwise been apprised of it" (Prior's *Life of Malone*, page 429). Vertue (op. cit., page 162) probably gave the best description of Roubiliac's work when he said that "his models of statues, monuments, bustos are very curious and excellent, with great skill and variety. His inventions very copious and free—pictoresque —so light and easy—as painting."

At the sculptor's sale, held from 12–15 May in the year of his death, a number of his casts and models were purchased by Dr. Matthew Maty and presented on 28 May following to the British Museum. The details of this gift were as follows: "Socrates, Plato, Demosthenes, Tully from the antique; Marcus Aurelius from a cast brought from Rome; Charles I, Oliver Cromwell and Shakespeare, models in terra-cotta; Milton, Pope,

Dr. Mead, Mr. Folkes, Lord Chesterfield, casts in plaster; Ray Willoughby, Dr. Barrow and Dr. Bentley, original models in terra-cotta, from which the marble busts in Trinity College, Cambridge, were executed."

Mrs. Esdaile, in her outstanding and important *Life of Roubiliac*, gives a very full list of all his works. In the briefer one which follows, I have only noted those which I have myself seen and found signed, or which are indisputably the work of the sculptor. I have ignored those which are attributed to him by Mrs. Esdaile on perhaps not absolutely unimpeachable evidence.

His most famous monument, of course, is that to Lady Elizabeth Nightingale in Westminster Abbey. It has been attacked as theatrical and over-dramatic, but the late Lord Mamhead told the writer that Lady Elizabeth was frightened by a sudden flash of lightning when walking on the terrace at Mamhead, Devon, on 17 August, 1731, and that the sudden shock caused the premature birth of her child and her own death—a story which throws light on the sculptor's design of the skeleton Death with his pointed dart striking his victim down. The inscription on the monument (which was not erected until thirty years later) gives the date of Lady Elizabeth's death as 1734, a curious blunder, for the actual date is not in question and, as additional proof, her husband's will, signed 25 October, 1731, directs that he is to be buried near her in the Abbey.

Since Mrs. Esdaile's book was written, a few other facts about the sculptor's works, etc., have come to light.

At the sale of — Phillipson (q.v.), one of the lots sold was "a bust of Time by Roubiliac" (Archives, Messrs. Christie). At Mr. Christie's sale of the property of "A Gentleman" held on 25 April, 1804, one of the principal lots was "Bust of Shakespeare by Roubiliac. This delightful work of sculpture was executed by that distinguished artist himself from the celebrated painting then belonging to Mr. Keck, and since then to the Chandos family. He never parted with his fine performance, but it remained with him till the time of his death." The work fetched 170 guineas. On 29 March, 1805, Christie held a sale for a "Man of Fashion." One of the lots was "Tarquin and Lucretia, a singularly fine model in terra-cotta by the celebrated Roubiliac, undoubted, with glass shade." At the same sale were his terra-cotta models for busts of Handel and Pope.

At the sale of a "Mr. Jackson" held by Mr. Christie on 22 July, 1807, Lot 88 was "Roubiliac's model of the Nightingale monument." (Archives, Messrs. Christies.) The model of Hogarth's dog

"Trump" was Lot 238 in James Brindley's sale in 1819, and was bought by someone giving his name as "Triphook." At the Shugborough Hall sale of 1842 the following busts were sold as by Roubiliac (the amount each fetched and the name of the purchaser being given in brackets): Shakespeare (36 guineas, Lord Derby); Locke (62 guineas, Colnaghi); Demosthenes (27 guineas, Woodin); Homer (30 guineas, Colonel Anson); and Mark Anthony (25 guineas, Brown). In the sale of the Peel heirlooms, held by Robinson and Fisher on 10 May, 1900, were included the sculptor's busts of Pope (£535); Racine (£178); Molière (£325); Voltaire (£267); and Rousseau (£110). Roubiliac's terra-cotta statuette of Shakespeare, dated 1757, is in the Victoria and Albert Museum, while at Kimbolton Castle was a signed bust of Cromwell, but in my opinion this is a later copy based on a lost original.

(Mrs. Esdaile's *Life of Roubiliac*; authorities cited in text.)

STATUES

1738	Handel	Possession of Messrs. Novello
1751	John Cass	Cass Institute, Aldgate
1752	Sir Thomas Molyneux	Armagh Cathedral
1752	Lord President Forbes	Advocate's Library, Edinburgh
1755	Newton	Trinity College, Cambridge
1758	Shakespeare	British Museum
1761	Religion	Formerly Gopsal, Leics, now Leicester Museum

BUSTS

c. 1735	Sir Edward Walpole	?
1738	Pope	
1739	Handel	Windsor Castle (terra-cotta, in National Portrait Gallery)
1741?	Pope	National Portrait Gallery
1744	Admiral Vernon	Maritime Museum (Greenwich)
1745	Lord Chesterfield	?
1746	Lady Grizel Baillie	Possession Earl of Haddington
1747	Sir Andrew Fountaine	Wilton
1747	Martin Folkes	Wilton
1747	Countess of Pembroke	Wilton
1750	9th Earl of Pembroke	Wilton (terra-cotta in Fitzwilliam Museum, Cambridge)
c. 1750	Lord Ligonier	Windsor Castle (terra-cotta in National Portrait Gallery)

1751	Archbishop Chichele	All Souls College, Oxford (50 guineas)
1751	Newton	Trinity College, Cambridge
1751	John Ray	Trinity College, Cambridge
1751	Francis Bacon	Trinity College, Cambridge
1751	Francis Willoughby	Trinity College, Cambridge
1756	Dr. Bentley	Trinity College, Cambridge
1756	Isaac Barrow	Trinity College, Cambridge
1757	Sir Edward Coke	Trinity College, Cambridge
1757	Sir Robert Cotton	Trinity College, Cambridge
1757	Lord Whitworth	Trinity College, Cambridge
1757	Lord Trevor	Trinity College, Cambridge
1757	Dr. Frewen	Christ Church Library, Oxford
c. 1757	Colley Cibber	National Portrait Gallery
1759	Lord Leicester	Tittleshall Church, Norfolk
1760	Joseph Wilton	Burlington House (terra cotta)
1760	L. F. Roubiliac	National Portrait Gallery
?	Edward VI	Sold Sotheby, 6 February, 1948
?	Isaac Newton	Royal Society

MONUMENTS

1737	Derby (Cathedral)	Thomas Chambers
1740	Highclere, Hants	Thomas Milles, Bishop of Waterford
1742	Hempsted, Essex	William Harvey
1746	Worcester (Cathedral)	Bishop Hough
1746	Condover, Salop	Roger Owen
1747	Framlingham, Suffolk	Mrs. and Miss Kerridge
1748	Westminster Abbey	Duke of Argyll and Greenwich (model in Victoria and Albert Museum)
1750	Wrexham, Denbigh	Miss Mary Myddelton
1750	St. Botolph's Aldersgate	Elizabeth Smith
1750	Westminster Abbey	Field-Marshal Wade (*Gentleman's Magazine*, 1752, page 379)
c. 1751	Westminster Abbey	General Fleming
1752	Lancaster (St. Mary's)	William Stratford
1752	Warkton, Northants	Duke of Montagu
1753	Warkton, Northants	Duchess of Montagu
1753	Battersea Old Church	Lord Bolingbroke (*London Magazine*, 1753, page 437)

1753	Hertingfordbury, Herts	Spencer Cowper
1753	Westminster Abbey	Sir Peter Warren
c. 1753	Cambridge (Trinity College Chapel)	Daniel Lock
c. 1753	Tonbridge, Kent	Richard Children
1754	Port Royal, Jamaica	Lieutenant Stapleton
1755	Walton-on-Thames, Surrey	Viscount Shannon
1756	Wrexham, Denbigh	Dr. and Mrs. Myddelton
1757	Newark, Notts	Mrs. Taylor
1757	Westminster Abbey	General Hargrave
1760	Southwick, Northants	George Lynn
1761	Westminster Abbey	Lady Elizabeth Nightingale
1761	Westminster Abbey	George Frederick Handel
1761	Earls Colne, Essex	John Wale

ROUCH, ARTHUR
b. 1779, *d.* 1839

He exhibited wax models, etc., at the Royal Academy, 1818–1833, and at the British Institution, 1821–1832. One of these showed a "Providential Escape in Hunting the Tiger of a European who was torn from the Back of an Elephant and carried several Miles by the ferocious Animal." As a widower he married at St. James's, Clerkenwell, on 12 December, 1833, Frances Moore, a widow. Rouch died 11 August, 1839 (Archives, Artists Annuity Fund).

ROUW, HENRY
fl. 1795–1834

Son of Peter Rouw the Elder (q.v.), and brother of Peter Rouw the Younger (q.v.), he is presumably the Henry Rouw who exhibited paintings at the Royal Academy from 1796 until 1803.

As a statuary Henry was not the equal of his brother. His best works are the monuments to Jane Akers, 1804, at Yalding, Kent, and to the brothers Colonel Aubrey and Captain Thomas Aubrey, 1806, in Paddington Parish Church. The former has a relief of an angel bearing a child heavenwards, while the latter has a figure of Victory standing by a sarcophagus on which are medallion portraits of the two officers.

Other monuments signed by Henry Rouw include those to Mrs. Gazeley, 1795, in Hornsey Parish Church; Rev. R. Henning, 1798, Great Canford, Dorset; Mary Burton, 1801, at North Cave, Yorks; Eleazar Davey, 1803, at Yoxford, Suffolk; Elizabeth and Joanna Cure, 1804, at Bovinger, Essex; Diana Miller, 1805, in Exeter Cathedral; Charles Purvis, 1808, at Darsham,

Suffolk; Edward Pocock, 1813, in Twickenham Parish Church; James Hill, 1814, at Uppingham, Rutland; the Rev. George Burvill, 1819, at Charing, Kent; Elizabeth Fowke, 1820, at Chelsworth, Suffolk; and John Fuller, 1834, at Brightling, Sussex.

ROUW, PETER, the Elder
fl. 1787–1793

Between 1787 and 1793 he exhibited wax portraits and a figure for a chimney-piece at the Royal Academy. The former included those of A. Carlini, R.A., and Lord Fife.

ROUW, PETER, the Younger
b. 1770, *d.* 1852

He was born on 17 April, 1770, the son of Peter Rouw the Elder, and attended the Royal Academy Schools in 1788. The younger Rouw and his work link the two centuries, for he first exhibited at the Academy in 1794 and lived long enough to send a collection of his wax portraits to the Great Exhibition of 1851.

In 1807 he was appointed "sculptor-modeller of gems to H.R.H. the Prince of Wales." In 1816 he received £23 for carving the tablet designed by Soane recording the history of Daylesford Church which had been rebuilt by Warren Hastings; the bill for this work is in the Soane Museum.

Rouw's monuments are in the classic style; they are all well carved and a number of them have medallion portraits. He was a most versatile artist, for besides working as a statuary, modelling wax portraits, and cutting gems and cameos, he also designed medals, including one of Wilberforce. In 1823 he showed at the Royal Academy "a device proposed for an Indian coinage from a design by John Flaxman, R.A."

Between 1825 and 1829 Rouw executed a series of bronze busts for Sir John Thorold's library at Syston Hall. His wax portraits of James Watt (1802) and William Pitt (1809) are at the National Portrait Gallery, while others at the Victoria and Albert Museum are of C. J. Fox (1808), the Prince Regent (1812), Thomas Sheldon (1812), Matthew Boulton (1814), Lucien Bonaparte (1814), Wellington (1818) and the Princess Charlotte (1818).

Rouw was a friend of Nollekens (q.v.), who left him £100 and a slab of marble in his will, while Mrs. Rouw received a legacy of £20. In 1842 Rouw seems to have been in financial difficulties, for the Royal Academy granted him £30 as a "charitable gift" (Royal Academy Archives). He died at Pentonville on 9 December, 1852, having lost the sight of one eye in 1840.

MONUMENTS

Year	Place	Person
1799	Shute, Dorset	Sir John de la Pole
1801	Standlake, Oxon	Maximilian Western
1802	Little Torrington, Devon	Henry Stevens
1804	Standlake, Oxon	Elizabeth Western
1804	Birmingham (Cathedral)	Francis Rogers
1804	Birmingham (Cathedral)	Moses Haughton
1804	Birmingham (St. Martin's)	Robert Coales
1806	Niton, Isle of Wight	G. Arnold
1808	Shute, Dorset	Lady de la Pole
1809	Hammersmith (Parish Church)	Sir Elijah Impey
1810	Springfield, Essex	Thomas Brograve
1810	Mitcham, Surrey	John Hyde
1810	Iver, Bucks	Christopher Tower
1811	Widworthy, Devon	James Marwood
1811	Marylebone (Parish Church)	Rev. John Vardill
1812	Hartland, Devon	Paul Orchard
1813	Finchingfield, Essex	Thomas Ruggles
1814	Bocking, Essex	Joseph Green
1816	Streatham (Parish Church)	Elizabeth Laing
1818	Otterden, Kent	Granville Charles Wheler
1819	Salehurst, Sussex	Jane Micklethwait
1820	Bovinger, Essex	Capel Cure
1822	North Cave, Yorks	Robert Burton
1822	Weybridge, Surrey	William Merle
1823	Hougham, Lincs	Rev. George Thorold
1825	Weybridge, Surrey	Elizabeth Merle
1826	St. John's Wood Chapel	John Farquhar
1827	Abington Pigott, Cambs	Foster Pigott
1827	Paddington (Parish Church)	Stephen Pellet
1828	Otterden, Kent	Granville Wheler
1828	St. George's, Bloomsbury	Mrs. Creswell
1830	Honiton, Devon	Rev. William Tucker
1830	Widworthy, Devon	Rev. Thomas Tucker
1830	Brightling, Sussex	William Shield
1832	Whitchurch, Oxon	Jemima Pigou
1832	Rivenhall, Essex	Sarah Hawkins
1832	Shute, Dorset	Lady de la Pole
1833	Marylebone (Parish Church)	Sir John Sewell
1834	Worth, Sussex	John Ewart
1835	Worth, Sussex	Catherine Ewart
1837	Shute, Dorset	Mrs. Schemberg
1837	Otterden, Kent	Mrs. Tattershall
1838	St. John's Wood Chapel	William Richardson
1838	Widworthy, Devon	Thomas White (with bust)
1839	St. Katherine's, Regent's Park	Sir Herbert Taylor
1840	Kensal Green Cemetery	William Money

ROWE, SIMON, of Exeter
fl. 1840–1850

His work seems to have been confined to Devonshire, where in 1842 he executed all the ornamental stonework for Exwick Chapel (*Gentleman's Magazine*, 1842, Part II, page 523) and in the following year the font for Exeter Cathedral (*Builder*, 1843, page 372). The font and pulpit for Holy Trinity, Barnstaple, were carved by him in 1845 (*Gentleman's Magazine*, 1845, Part II, page 186), and in 1846 he carried out the freestone work at Heavitree Church, near Exeter (*Builder*, 1846, page 393).

ROYAL, THOMAS

He exhibited wax portraits at the Society of Artists, 1770–1776. His address is given as "At Mr. Brown, hairdresser, in St. Clement's churchyard."

ROYCE, N., of Bury St. Edmunds

He signs the large and important monument to Jacob Harvey, 1723, at Cockfield, Suffolk. This is nearly 18 ft. high and has, as its central feature, a sarcophagus on which is set a well-carved bust of a young man, clad in a coat and scarf and wearing his own hair. The setting is architectural, with Corinthian pillars and pilasters of variegated marble supporting a heavy triangular pediment with a large coat of arms at the apex.

It is curious that there is no trace of his name in the apprentices' or Freemans' lists of Bury St. Edmunds, nor do I know any other work by him, yet Harvey's monument shows that Royce was a skilled and competent statuary.

RUSH, —, or RUST, of Norwich

He signs a large wall-tablet to Isaac Preston, 1708, at Beeston St. Lawrence, Norfolk. This is an ambitious work, 9 ft. high, with an urn surmounting a curved pediment and flaming lamps to left and right. The coat of arms at the base has elaborate mantling.

RUSHWORTH, —, of Beverley

He signs a large wall-tablet to Anna Fox, 1811, at Etton, Yorkshire.

RUSSELL, T. H.
b. 1809

He lived in Birmingham, where he showed "Achilles" and a "Bust of a Lady" at the exhibition of the Society of Artists held in 1829. In 1832 he joined the Royal Academy Schools, exhibiting "Innocence" at the Academy in the same year.

RYLEY, —

According to Augustus Hare (*Walks in London*, Vol. I, page 285), he executed the monument erected in St. Peter's, Cornhill, to the memory of the seven children of Mr. and Mrs. Woodmason, who in 1782 were burnt to death in their beds in their father's house in Leadenhall Street.

RYLEY, E.
fl. 1833–1837

He exhibited various busts at the Royal Academy, 1833–1837, including those of George Birkbeck, Daniel Harvey, M.P., and Andrew Amos, the last-named being for University College. In 1836 he showed a bust of the Rev. J. Yates at the Liverpool Academy.

RYSBRACK, JOHN MICHAEL
b. 1694, *d.* 1770

His father, Peter Rysbrack, was a landscape painter and etcher of Antwerp who apparently worked in England, until the outcry against Catholics following the "discovery" of the Popish Plot forced him to leave the country and settle in Paris. He later returned to his native city, where he died in 1728, aged eighty.

Rysbrack himself was trained as a sculptor under Van der Voort. Vertue has the following entry in his notebook under the date October, 1720: "Came into England Michael Rysbracht, statuary (son of . . . Rysbracht of Antwerp, an excellent landskape painter), his moddels in clay are very excellent and shows him to be a great Master, tho young (about 26 years old); he is of Antwerp and there and at Brussels has lived till he came to England. He was recommended to Mr. Gibbs, architect" (*Walpole Society, Vertue*, Vol. I, page 76).

Vertue considered that Gibbs underpaid his assistant, and gave as an instance the monument to Prior in Westminster Abbey, which Gibbs designed and for which Rysbrack carved the figures, though the bust is by Coysevox. "He [Gibbs] will give him no more than £35 for each statue to be cut in marble," he remarks, "while others have above £100, and Gibbs is to have of my Lord Harley upwards of £100 for each of these statues. Many other things of this kind he has done by him. 'Tis an unreasonable gripeing usage to a most ingenious artist (in his way) far more merit than Gibbs will ever be mr. (master) of." (Op. cit., Vol. III, page 17.)

However, Rysbrack was fortunate enough to make a bust of Lord Nottingham which attracted a good deal of attention, and the indefatigable Vertue, when he visited his studio in 1732, found over sixty busts of historic and contemporary notabilities, ranging from Palladio, Cromwell, Spenser and the Black Prince, to Tillemans, the Dukes of Argyll and Kent, and Mr. Dahl the portrait-painter (op. cit., Vol. III, page 56). Many of these cannot be identified, though "Mr. John Straughan, surveyor of Bristol," may be one of a pair in Redland Chapel, Bristol, the builder of which was John Cossins, for whom Strachan had designed the neighbouring Redland Court.

Rysbrack was the acknowledged head of his profession, and reigned unchallenged until P. Scheemakers (q.v.) carved his statue of Shakespeare for Westminster Abbey. This, Vertue says, established the latter's reputation, "but at the same time obliterated in some degree that of Rysbrack insomuch that he feels the effects in a decline of business." In addition, Rysbrack's lowest fee for a bust was thirty-five guineas, while Scheemakers "wd and dos for near ten gns. less; but that is the difference every one can distinguish tho in point of skill, likeness, etc., there is difference sufficient to those who know better" (op. cit., Vol. III, page 116).

Rysbrack's famous statue of Hercules, now at Stourhead, was begun in 1747, according to Vertue (though not paid for till 1757). The sculptor found "himself somewhat at leisure, business not being so brisk (as had been with him some years before). He therefore set himself about a Model of Hercules" (op. cit., Vol. III, page 121). Walpole says the statue was "compiled from various parts and limbs of seven or eight of the strongest and best made men in London, chiefly the bruisers and boxers of the then flourishing amphitheatre for boxing; the sculptor selecting the parts which were most truly formed in each." Vertue later says it took the sculptor "the study and labour of five years to complete."

Rysbrack retired from business in 1765, and on 8 January, 1770, died at Vere Street, Oxford Street (where he had lived for many years), and was buried in Marylebone churchyard. His will was proved 26 January, 1770. A three-day sale of his prints and drawings was held by Messrs. Christies, 7–9 February, 1774.

In an undated sale catalogue of the effects of "A Person of Note Abroad" (c. 1735), auctioneer Mr. Miller, the following lots are described as being by Rysbrack: "Marble basso-relievos of his late Majesty King George and Inigo Jones, two basso-relievos after the antique, two models of boys."

In Rysbrack's own sale, held by Langford on 24 and 25 January in the year after his retirement, part of his collection of models, drawings, etc., were auctioned, and among the models of monu-

ments sold were those of Mr. Knight, Chief Baron Ward, William Young, the Duke of Beaufort, and Sir John Dutton. Other sales followed in 1767 and 1770. At the first Mr. Hoare bought five terra-cotta bas-reliefs, now at Stourhead, while Lord Radnor paid £59 for a statue of "Fame," which is now at Longford Castle.

One of the earlier notices relating to Rysbrack in the Press appeared in the *Free Briton* on 16 August, 1733, and runs as follows: "I do not wonder to see Rysbrack encouraged by so many of the British nobility. It hath been allowed in his praise that he never undertook any great work but with an industry which far exceeded his reward, and always showed that he wrought more for Reputation than any other Recompense." Later in the same article the writer says: "I know not whether Rysbrack be Whigg or Tory. I know him to be a good statuary and believe him to be an honest man, an impartial sculptor. If he hath made a busto of Sir Robert Walpole, he hath made a monument for the late Daniel Pulteney."

In the *Gentleman's Magazine* of 1735 (30 June) the following paragraph occurs: "Her Majesty has ordered Mr. Risbrack to make the bustos in marble of all the Kings of England from William the Conqueror in order to be placed in her new buildings in the gardens at Richmond," while the *London Magazine* states in the same year (page 390) that he is carving statues of the Black Prince and King Alfred for the "octagon in the garden of the Princess of Wales in Pall Mall." According to Pyne's *Royal Residences* (Vol. III, page 2), the figures were later to be found at Old Carlton House. (See Guelfi, G. B.)

In the accounts of the trust estates of the Earl and Countess of Oxford with Sir Francis Child is a payment to Rysbrack, dated August, 1740, of £63 13s. 8d. and another of £47 7s. 4d. on 9 July, 1741, while in the "schedule of debts" of Lord and Lady Oxford there is a note of a bill of the sculptor's amounting to £191 1s. (Archives, West of Alscot Park). Some of these payments must be almost certainly for the busts of Lady Margaret Harley and an infant son of Lord and Lady Oxford, both of which are now at Welbeck Abbey.

Writing to Sir Edward Littleton in 1756, Rysbrack says that he is making two marble chimney-pieces for the saloon of the Duke of Bedford "with Women, Thermes, Ornamented with festoons of Fruit and Flowers, and Friezes with Cornucopias of Fruit and Flowers, and a Ram's Head in each, Ornamented with Flowers as rich as can be." Rysbrack also says that he is making a chimney-piece for the Earl of Hopetoun "near 10 feet long, and 6 feet and near 10 inches high, with Women, Thermes, cloathed with drapery; almost Round" (Esdaile, *The Art of Rysbrack in Terracotta*, page 11).

At Alscot Park is Rysbrack's marble bust of Shakespeare. In 1758 Joseph Greene, schoolmaster of Stratford-on-Avon, wrote to James West at Alscot that "if Mr. Rysbrack carves your Shakespeare from ye mask you had of me, I am very sure it answers exactly to our original bust, for Heath ye carver and I took it down from ye chancel wall and laid it exactly in a horizontal posture, before we made ye cast which we executed with much care, so that no slipping of the materials could occasion ye unnatural distance in the face which he mentions." On 11 July, 1763, the sculptor wrote to James West that "the last time you did me the pleasure to call at my house, you said there must be some letters put on the pedestal of the bust for Shakespeare, which have been finished a long while since, I desire you will please to let me have them and they shall be put on the pedestal directly. As I have nothing to live on but my business, I want money and am at too. great expenses to continue where I am without business. I must therefore retire for my own best advantage. If you do not want any letters put on the pedestal, I will send it home as it is." West seems to have ignored this rather sad letter, for there is still no inscription on the pedestal of the bust save the words "Genio Loci."

Rysbrack's terra-cotta bust of the first Earl of Shaftesbury, executed about 1732, is at St. Giles' House, Dorset, while the marble of it is in the parish church. In 1772, "a bust of Dr. Sharp by Rysbrack" was in the saloon of Ditchley Park, Oxfordshire, according to the inventory taken in that year on the death of the third Earl of Lichfield (Dillon Archives). At Blockley in Gloucestershire is the large monument to the Rushout family, executed by J. F. Moore (q.v.) and erected about 1775. This has five busts, those of Sir James and Sir John Rushout and the Countess of Northampton being by Rysbrach. In the P.R.O. (c.107/126) is the contract (1728) between Francis Seymour, Rysbrach and Walter Lee (q.v.) for the monument to Sir Edward Seymour at Maiden Bradley, Wilts.

In 1730, when Lord Westmorland was trying to decide on a suitable sculptor to make a monument in memory of his wife, his cousin, John Fane of Mereworth, wrote to tell him that he had approached Guelfi (q.v.) and also that "the other man I writ to (whose name is Rysbrack) and to whom I sent a copy of the same draught, instead of sending an estimate of the charge of it, as I desired, sent me back a draught of his own, a very bad one, and an estimate of that amounting to £155" (Archives, Earl of Westmorland).

In the Newdigate Archives is Rysbrack's bill for £132, dated 1732, for "the monument and bustow of Sir Richard Newdigate" erected in Harefield Church, Middlesex, while at Barkwày, Hertfordshire, is his monument to Admiral Sir John Jennings. Apparently the original idea of the Admiral's son, George, had been to set up a memorial in Westminster Abbey, and in 1743 he wrote to Mr. West asking him to see Rysbrack about it. The size of this work as first contemplated meant asking Lady Oxford's permission to remove "part of the rail" round the monument to her father the Duke of Newcastle, and it was probably because she refused that the whole project had to be abandoned. (Archives, West of Alscot.)

There are a number of the sculptor's sketches and designs for monuments in the Victoria and Albert Museum, including those of Sir Watkins Williams Wynn, Lord Foley, Admiral Vernon, Sir Edward Prideaux, Nicholas Rowe, Earl Stanhope, Milton, Viscountess Folkestone and Brian Duppa.

Horace Walpole thought very highly of Rysbrack and described him in *Anecdotes of Painting* as "the greatest master the islands have seen since Le Sueur." This is perhaps rather exaggerated praise, although the sculptor's work was, as Vertue said, "beautifully and masterly done, admired by all artists and lovers of art."

Rysbrack's fellow artists seem to have collected his works, as at the sale by Messrs. Christie, 3 and 4 April, 1770, of Peter Vanina, "figure-maker of Dover Street," two of the lots were "Judgment of Hercules, by Rysbrack, a basso-relievo," and a "Bust of Virgil." Again at the sale of Edward Stevens, architect, on 7 February, 1776, a number of Rysbrack's works were sold, including "the original terra-cotta by Rysbrack of the Duke of Marlborough taking prisoner the Marshall Tallard"; a bust of Milton in terra-cotta and "boys in terra-cotta, the original design for the Great Saloon at Bedford House."

The sale of Joseph Vanhaecken, "drapery painter," was held by Langford in Covent Garden in 1751 on 11 February, and the following fourteen evenings. Original works by Rysbrack included "Head of Proserpine," "King William on Horseback," busts of "Palladio, Inigo Jones and Bacchus," "Two termes" and "original models of Rubens, Van Dyck and Fiamingo." At the sale of George Vertue on 17 May, 1757, lot 27 was a "small head of Milton, finely modell'd by Mr. Rysbrack in an oval frame."

At the sale of Matthew Nulty on 27 March, 1783, Lot 88 was "a fine bust of Gibbs by Rysbrack," and in the same year at the great sale of the contents of Sir Gregory Page's house at

Blackheath, which began on 23 April, Lots 50–53 on the fifth day were nine unnamed marble busts, "very capital sculpture by Rysbrack." An MS. note in the catalogue gives the name of the purchaser of all the busts as "Lloyd." At the sale of Thomas Hudson of Twickenham on 25 February, 1785, two lots by Rysbrack were a plaster cast of King William on Horseback and two terracotta angels from the Duke of Marlborough's monument at Blenheim. Three years later when Mr. Christie sold the belongings of Mr. Lyde Brown on 30 May, 1788, one of the items was "the original terracotta model for the great bas relief on the Duke of Marlborough's monument aṭ Blenheim" (Archives, Messrs. Christie). At the sale of "An Eminent Publisher retiring from Business" held by Mr. Christie on 24 February, 1809, one of the lots was a "marble bust of John Hadley by Rysbrack."

(Archives, Messrs. Christie, Information from Mrs. M. Webb; authorities cited in text.)

STATUES

1730	Earl of Strafford	For Wentworth Castle
c. 1730	Queen Caroline	Stowe
Before 1732	George II	For Royal Exchange
1735	George II	Greenwich
1736	William III	Bristol
c. 1736	Neptune and Britannia	Houghton, Norfolk
1737	Sir Hans Sloane	Physic Garden, Chelsea
1738	Queen Anne	Blenheim (*Gentleman's Magazine*, 1738, page 349)
1739	George I	Law Library, Cambridge
1744	Dr. Radcliffe	Radcliffe Library Oxford (£220)
c. 1744	Palladio, Inigo Jones and Fiamingo	For Chiswick House
1751	Bacchus	Stourhead (£71)
1756	Duke of Somerset	Senate House, Cambridge
1756?	Hercules	Stourhead
1756	Henry Grenville	For Barbados
1757	Locke	Christ Church, Oxford (*London Magazine*, 1757, page 41)
1761	Flora	Stourhead (£400)
?	John Willett	For Merley House, Dorset

BUSTS

1722	Earl of Sunderland	Blenheim
c. 1724	Earl of Nottingham	Formerly Burley-on-the-Hill
1726	James Gibbs	Radcliffe Camera, Oxford (terracotta)
1726	James Gibbs	St. Martin-in-the-Fields (marble)
1727	Inigo Jones	For Henry Hoare, Stourhead
1727	Richard Miller	Queen's College, Oxford (terracotta)
1727	Richard Miller	St. Martin-in-the-Fields (marble)
c. 1730	Sir Isaac Newton	Possession Earl of Portsmouth
c. 1730	Sir Robert Walpole	Houghton
c. 1730	1st Earl of Radnor	Longford Castle
c. 1730	Edward Bouverie	Longford Castle (the pair of busts, £113)
c. 1730	Lord Folkestone as a Boy	Longford Castle
1730	Marlborough	Blenheim (another version at the Ashmolean, Oxford)
c. 1730	George II	Sold Christie's, June, 1859
1730	Pope	Athenaeum Club
1732?	Seven Deities for Saxon Temple	Stowe
1733	Locke, Newton, Woolaston, Boyle	Kensington Palace
1733?	Seven Busts in Temple of British Worthies	Stowe
1737	Lord Bolingbroke	Lydiard Park, Swindon
1737	Lord Bolingbroke	Petworth
1738	Milton as a Young Man	Stourhead
1738	Milton Blind	Stourhead
1738	Milton	Fitzwilliam Museum, Cambridge
1738	Sir Robert Walpole	National Portrait Gallery
1738	Robert Freind	Christ Church, Oxford
1738	George II and Queen Caroline	Windsor Castle (terracottas and marbles)
1739	Sir Isaac Newton	Trinity College, Cambridge
1739	Dr. Arthur Johnston	Scottish National Portrait Gallery, Edinburgh
c. 1739	Queen Caroline	Wallace Collection
c. 1740	John and Martha Cossins	Redland Chapel, Glos (Shiercliff's *Bristol Guide*, 1789)
1741	Francis (?) Smith	Ashmolean Museum, Oxford
1743	Van Dyck	Althorp
1743	Called "Villiers, Duke of Buckingham"	Formerly possession Countess Peel
1746	Rubens and Van Dyck	Hagley Hall, Worcs
1748	Hercules	Lot 468, Wentworth Woodhouse sale, 1948
1750	Charles, Duke of Marlborough	Blenheim

PLATE XXI

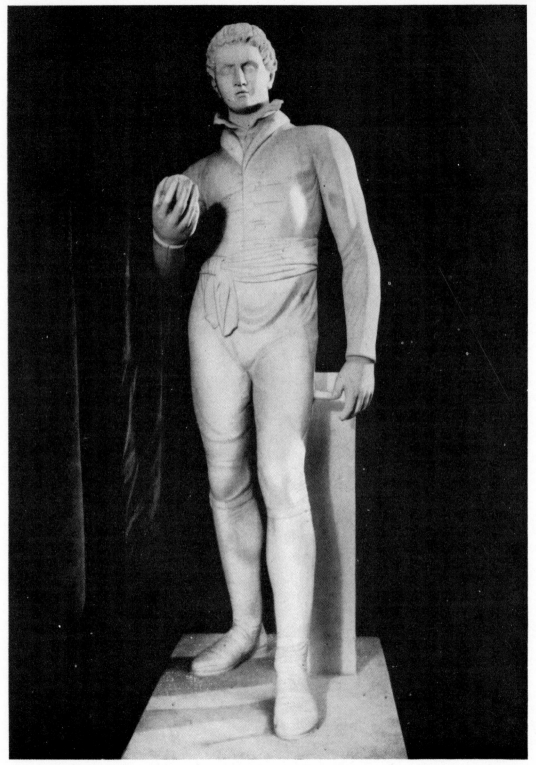

HENRY ROSSI
"The Bowler," 1825, Woburn Abbey, Bedfordshire.

PLATE XXII

JOSEPH ROSE THE ELDER
Richard Ladbroke, 1730, Reigate, Surrey.

1751	Bacchus	Formerly Stourhead (sold 1883)
c. 1754	Duke of Cumberland	Possession Earl of Ilchester
1755	Bacon	National Maritime Museum
1757	Ralegh	National Maritime Museum
1757	Cromwell	National Maritime Museum (these three busts, with four others of Newton, Milton, Pope and Locke, were made between 1755 and 1757 for Sir Edward Littleton, whose descendant, Lord Hatherton, sold them in 1932)
1757	Locke	Welbeck Abbey (see Cromwell above)
1757	Pope	Fitzwilliam Museum, Cambridge (see Cromwell above)
1760	George II	Victoria and Albert Museum
1764	King Alfred	Stourhead (£100)
n.d.	George I and George II	Christ Church, Oxford
n.d.	3rd Earl of Coventry	Badminton
n.d.	Sir Hans Sloane	British Museum
n.d.	2nd and 4th Dukes of Beaufort	Badminton

RELIEFS

1723	Roman Marriage	Kensington Palace
c. 1728	Reliefs	Great Hall, Clandon Park, Surrey
1730	Britannia Seated by the Sea, Receiving the Homage of India	India Office (£100) (Archives)
c. 1736	Reliefs, etc.	Great Hall, Houghton, Norfolk (H.M.C. *Duke of Portland*, Vol. IV, page 171)
1745	Children Engaged in Navigation and Husbandry	For Foundling Hospital
1755	Sacrifice to Apollo	Woburn Abbey (limestone)
1755	Sacrifice to Diana	Woburn Abbey (limestone)
?	Five bas-reliefs	Purchased at Rysbrack's sale, 1766; now at Stourhead

CHIMNEY-PIECES

1732	Dining-room	Houghton, Norfolk (H.M.C. *Duke of Portland*, Vol. IV, page 161)
1738	Two chimney-pieces	Longford Castle (£57 14s.) (Archives, Earl of Radnor)
1744	Chimney-piece	Longford Castle (£266 15s.) (Archives, Earl of Radnor)
1756	Two chimney-pieces (for saloon)	Woburn Abbey (£195) (Archives, Duke of Bedford)

VARIOUS

1732	Water God (£7 7s.)	For Davenport House, Salop (*Country Life*, 27 June, 1952)
c. 1734	Inigo Jones	Royal Institute of British Architects (statuette)
1739	Pegasus	Inner Temple (£100)
1754	Pedestal for statue of Lady Walpole	Westminster Abbey
1757	Pedestal for figure of Hercules	Stourhead (£83) (Archives, Hoare's Bank)
1762	Pedestal for statue of Flora	Stourhead (£82) (Archives Hoare's Bank)
?	Figure of Goat	Chatsworth
?	Boys and Young Satyrs	Formerly Wanstead House (life-size group, sold 1822) (£88 4s.)
?	Genius of Architecture	Formerly Wanstead House (sold 1822, £46 4s.)

MONUMENTS

after 1720	Westminster Abbey	John Methuen (*d.* 1706)
after 1720	Stoke Doyle, Northants	Chief Baron Ward (*d.* 1714)
after 1720	Westminster Abbey	Nicholas Rowe (*d.* 1717)
c. 1721	North Kirkby, Yorks	Sir John Wentworth (*d.* 1720)
1721	Westminster Abbey	Matthew Prior (designed by Gibbs)
1722	St. Germans, Cornwall	Edward Eliot
1726	Aston, Birmingham	Sir John Bridgeman
1728	Westminster Abbey	Dr. John Freind (bust)
1728	Westminster Abbey	Benjamin Johnson
1728	Maiden Bradley, Wilts	Sir Edward Seymour
1729	Bristol (All Saints)	Edward Colston
1730	Westminster Abbey	Sir Godfrey Kneller (*d.* 1723) (bust)
1730	Westminster Abbey	Mrs. Oldfield
1731	Westminster Abbey	Sir Isaac Newton
1732	Stapleford, Leics	Earl of Harborough
1732	Barkby, Leics	Charlotte Pochin
1732	Whitley, Worcs	Lord Foley
1732	Westminster Abbey	Daniel Pulteney (*Gentleman's Magazine*, 1733, page 422)
1732	Westminster Abbey	John Gay
1733	Blenheim, Oxon	Duke of Marlborough

1733	Westminster Abbey	Earl Stanhope
1733	Gosfield, Essex	Mr. and Mrs. Knight
1733	Normanton, Rutland	Sir Gilbert Heathcote (Bentham's *Baronetage*, Vol. III, page 220)
1734	Heydour, Lincs	Sir John Newton
1734	Edgcote, Northants	Richard Chauncy
1734	Ockham, Surrey	Lord King
1736	Westminster Abbey	Sir Richard Kane
1737	Clifton Camville, Staffs	Sir Richard Pye
1737	Clifton Camville, Staffs	Sir Charles Pye
1737	Bradford-on-Avon, Wilts	Anthony Methuen
1737	Westminster Abbey	John Milton (with bust)
c. 1737	Westminster Abbey	Ben Jonson
1738	St. Margaret Pattens	Sir Peter Delme
1738	Hollingbourne, Kent	Baldwin Duppa
c. 1740	Edgcote, Northants	Children of Toby Chauncy
c. 1740	Edgcote, Northants	William Chauncy
1740	Warbleton, Sussex	Sir John Lade (with bust; drawing in Victoria and Albert Museum)
1742	Goathurst, Somerset	Sir John Tynte
1742	Hollingbourne, Kent	Lord Colepepper
1743	Nunnington, Yorks	Lord Widdrington (designed by Gibbs)
1743	Barkway, Herts	Admiral Sir John Jennings (with bust)
1745	Hinton St. George, Somerset	Earl Poulett (d. 1743; with bust)
1745	Salisbury (Cathedral)	Lord Wyndham
1746	Ashby-de-la-Zouch, Leics	Earl of Huntingdon
1746	Hardingstone, Northants	Bartholomew Clarke
1746	Alvediston, Wilts	John Wyndham
1746	West Grinstead, Sussex	William Powlett
1747	Lymington, Hants	Charles Colborne (with bust)
1749	Ruabon, Denbigh	Sir Watkin Williams Wynn
1749	Sherborne, Glos	Sir John Dutton (d. 1742)
1750	St. Michael's, Paternoster Royal	Sir Samuel Pennant (with bust)
1751	Westminster Abbey	Hon. John Hay

1751	Coleshill, Berks	Viscountess Folkestone (d. 1750)
1751	Stratford-upon-Avon, Warwick	James Kendall (with bust)
1751	Chartham, Kent	Sir William Young
1751	Twickenham (Parish Church)	Sir Chaloner Ogle
1752	Throcking, Herts	Robert Elwes
1752	Birdsall, Yorks	Thomas Southeby
1752	Canterbury (Cathedral)	John Sympson
1752	Llanyblodwell, Salop	Sir John Bridgeman
1753	Eling, Hants	Susanna Serle
1753	Aston, Birmingham	Robert Holden
1753	Addington, Bucks	Rev. Thomas Busby
1753	Carshalton, Surrey	John Braddyll
1754	Great Badminton, Glos	2nd and 3rd Dukes of Beaufort
1756	Great Badminton, Glos	4th Duke of Beaufort
1758	Sacombe, Herts	Thomas Rolt
1760	Hatfield, Herts	Sir James and Lady Read (with busts)
1760	Edgcote	Richard Chauncy
1760	Derby (All Saints)	Lady Bessborough
1760	Chislehurst, Kent	Roger Townsend
1761	Greenwich (St. Alphege)	In west portico is a monument signed by Rysbrack, but with the inscription-tablet removed and a modern one inserted, commemorating benefactions of John Roan
1761	Heydour, Lincs	Margaret, Countess of Coningsby
1761	Ecton, Northants	John Palmer (with bust)
1763	St. Michael Penkevil, Cornwall	Admiral Boscawen (d. 1761; designed by Adam)
1763	Westminster Abbey	Admiral Vernon (d. 1757)
1764	Hollingbourne, Kent	Baldwin Duppa
1765	Kedleston, Derby	Sir Nathaniel Curzon (d. 1758; designed by Adam)
1776	Mold, Flint	William Wynn
?	Armagh (Cathedral)	Dean Drelincourt

S

SABIN, THOMAS,
of Ashby-de-la-Zouch
d. 1702.

He was the mason for building Sir John Moore's School at Appleby, Leicestershire, in 1697, where he was also responsible for all the carved stonework (*Wren Society*, Vol. XI, page 100).

ST. GEORGE, JOSEPH

At the exhibition of the works of Scottish artists held in Edinburgh in 1815 he showed a bust of Wellington. It was favourably noticed by the *Scottish Magazine* of that year (page 100) as being "freely modelled and the drapery very well cast." The critic also added that "this young artist appears to be making rapid advancement and to feel his art."

SALE, A.

He signs an altar-tomb to the Rev. John Jeffreys, 1824, in the churchyard of Barnes Parish Church, Surrey.

SALISBURY, JOHN, of London

Although I know of no work by him, his name is in Pigot's *London Directory* of 1827 as "statuary of Highgate." In the churchyard of West Malling, Kent, is the tombstone of Elizabeth, "wife of John Salisbury, statuary in this town and formerly both of Exeter," who died in 1832 at the age of forty.

SALT, JAMES

He signs a tablet to Richard Roberts, 1738, at Pelynt, Cornwall. This is a small, architectural work with broken pediment and urn, and with a coat of arms at the base.

SAMS, THOMAS, of Piccadilly
fl. 1810–1837

His yard was in Down Street and in 1810 he was the mason for the rebuilding of Coventry House, Piccadilly, also receiving sixty guineas for "five veined marble chimney-pieces" (Archives, Earl of Coventry).

Sams' tablets, which are classical in design, include those to Charles Pieschell, 1821, and August Pieschell, 1822, in St. John's Wood Chapel; and to Thomas Hunter, 1831, and Frances Lincoln, 1836, both in Holy Trinity, Brompton.

SANDERS, J. J.
fl. 1812–1846

He was the son of "J. Sanders, a mason," but as there are several craftsmen with this name and initial who might fill the bill, it is impossible to be more specific. There is, for example, a Joseph Sanders who joined the Royal Academy as "a sculptor" in 1775, but against whose name is an entry "to be discharged" (Royal Academy Archives); while a James Sanders, son of Joseph Sanders, goldsmith of Maiden Lane, was apprenticed to Samuel Newton in 1754 and became free in 1762.

J. J. Sanders was the mason who carried out repairs to St. John's Church, Westminster, in 1812 (Churchwardens' Accounts). In 1846 he carved the tablet to the memory of Mr. John Lydeker which was placed in the Royal Exchange (*Illustrated London News*, 1846, page 208). His monuments and tablets are dull and uninteresting, the best being that to Walter Strickland, 1839, at Standlake, Oxon.

Other tablets signed by Sanders include those to Thomas Dampier, 1812, in Eton College Chapel; Henry Whitfield, 1813, at Rickmansworth, Herts; Thomas Gibson, 1822, at Shalford, Surrey; Mary Cullum, 1830, at Hawstead, Suffolk; Christina Kidd, 1831, at Hartfield, Sussex; Mariana Brouncker, 1833, at Cranborne, Dorset; Emma Faulkner, 1833, at Whiteparish, Dorset; Catherine Filmer, 1834, at East Sutton, Kent; Frances Strickland, 1836, at Standlake, Oxon; Major Keighly, 1837, at Idlicote, Warwick; and Evan Roberts, 1837, in St. Matthew's, Brixton.

SANDS, WILLIAM, of Spalding
d. 1751

He signs a tablet at Crowland Abbey to Elizabeth Cox, 1735. Sands himself was buried in Spalding Church, where a monument to his memory was erected by his pupil, Edward Hutchinson, but this disappeared when the church was restored.

SANGIOVANNI, BENEDETTO,
of London
fl. 1827–1847

He exhibited at the Royal Academy, 1827–1847, showing models of animals and various works of a romantic nature, including statuettes of bandit chiefs and brigands of Calabria.

In 1844 the *Art Union* (page 97) described him as "an Italian gentleman who has been compelled by circumstances to adopt as 'a business' the occupation which he long followed as an accomplishment." In the following year Sangiovanni exhibited his "Contadina of the Province of Salerno" at the Academy, which the same journal (1845, page 78) described as "perfect in costume and character and modelled with the utmost nicety of execution."

SANSBY, R., of Hull
fl. 1815–1831

He signs three large wall-tablets at North Cave, Yorkshire, to Captain Barnard, 1815, Henry Barnard, 1815, and Sarah Barnard, 1831. The monument to Captain Barnard, who fell at Waterloo, has a well-cut trophy of arms.

SANTLER, RICHARD
b. 1761

He was born on 28 September, 1761, and attended the Royal Academy Schools in 1780, winning a Silver Medal two years later.

Santler exhibited wax portraits at the Royal Academy, 1785–1787, including those of George III and the Princess Royal.

SAUNDERS, F.

In Hereford Town Hall is his bust of Nelson, signed and dated 1842.

SAUNDERS, P., of Windsor

He signs a large wall-tablet to William Cook, 1828, at Horton, Middlesex.

SAUNDERS, RICHARD
d. 1735

Saunders, who was apprenticed to Johnathan Maine (q.v.) in 1675 and became free in 1682, later lived in King Street, Cheapside. He did a great deal of work for the Corporation of the City of London and also served as Captain in the City Trained Bands. In 1705 his name occurs in the minutes of the Committee appointed to undertake repairs to the Guildhall, where it is recorded that "Captain Saunders appeared again about the carving work to be done on the front of the chapel. He proposes to finish all the imagery, scrolls, pediments, arms, etc., for £45." He is later mentioned as carving "dragons," and in the end seems to have received a total sum of £72 (City Corporation Records MS. 117/3).

Saunders' most famous works were the statues of Gog and Magog, carved in fir-wood, which stood in the Guildhall until they were destroyed by enemy action in the Second World War. The figures were ordered on 17 December, 1709, and though it is generally supposed that the Stationers' Company presented them to the City, an entry in the City Cash Account (1/27) in 1713 seems to indicate that it was the Corporation who paid for them. The entry reads as follows: "Richard Saunders in full of his bill for making and carving the Giants and other work in the Guildhall and his time and expenses in and about the same by order of the Committee for repairing the Guildhall, £65." In 1711 he had also received £25 for "carving about the City eighteen-oared barge" (op. cit.).

In 1710 Saunders was employed by Lord Ashburnham, who paid him £68 for work in connexion with the house then building in St. James's Square, and a further £10 for carving, four years later (Accounts of the first Earl of Ashburnham).

SAUNDERS, SAMUEL
d. 1743

He was presumably a brother of Richard Saunders (q.v.), and like him worked for Lord Ashburnham, who employed him at Ashburnham House, Westminster, in 1708 (Ashburnham Archives).

Saunders, who in 1717 took as an apprentice Thomas, son of Thomas Thompson of Waltham Abbey, Essex (P.R.O., I.R.1/6), was Renter Warden of the Masons' Company in 1721 and Master five years later. He was also an officer in the City Trained Bands, and his death as "Colonel Saunders" is noted in the Court Book of the Company in 1743 (Archives, Masons' Company).

SAUNDERS, WILLIAM
fl. 1748–1754

In the Westminster Poll-Book of 1748 his address is given as Windmill Street. In 1754 he was working as a mason on repairs to Coutts' Bank in the Strand (Bank Archives).

Saunders must have died before 1767, for in that year his widow and son William were noted as living in St. Pancras when the latter was apprenticed to John Hinchliff. He became free in 1774 (Archives, Masons' Company).

SCHADOW, RUDOLPH
b. 1786, *d.* 1822

Son of the famous German sculptor, J. G. Schadow, he signs the monument erected in 1819 at Wimborne St. Giles, Dorset, to the memory of Barbara, Countess of Shaftesbury, who had died eight years previously.

SCHEEMAKERS, HENRY

d. 1748

He was the brother of Peter Scheemakers (q.v.) and was born in Antwerp. Some time after 1720 he came to England and went into partnership with Henry Cheere (q.v.). Together they were responsible for the vast monument to the first Duke of Ancaster at Edenham, Lincolnshire, with its architectural background and life-size figure of the Duke in Roman costume. Faussett the antiquary, writing in 1757, says that the cartouche tablet at Westbere, Kent, to Hammond Twyman, 1727, is also the joint work of Cheere and Scheemakers (Faussett Archives, private possession); it is, however, only signed by the former.

Henry Scheemakers left England about 1733 and, after living in Paris, died in Antwerp in 1748. According to Vertue, he was a small man, even shorter than his brother.

His three signed monuments, all of importance, commemorate Richard Graves, 1729, at Mickleton, Glos; Sir· Francis and Lady Page, 1730, at Steeple Aston, Oxon; and John Bradbury, 1731, at Wicken Bonhunt, Essex. The first of these has a medallion portrait, the second reclining figures of Sir Francis and his wife—he in his judge's robes, she, on a lower stage, looking up at him. The Bradbury monument is most surprising and unusual, and far excels in delicacy and refinement of carving anything executed by the sculptor's more famous brother. It has a baroque frame and a bas-relief of a youth in classical drapery, while the cherub-heads in the clouds above him are particularly striking.

SCHEEMAKERS, PETER

b. 1691, *d.* 1781

He was the son of Peter Scheemakers the Elder (1640–1713), a sculptor of Antwerp, and first worked as a journeyman in Copenhagen, where illness reduced him to poverty. He was, however, determined to study sculpture in Rome, and as he had no money for travel, realized his ambition by walking to Italy. After a short stay in Rome he went to London, and was employed by Francis Bird (q.v.) and Plumière (q.v.). During this period he became friends with his fellow-workman, L. Delvaux (q.v.), and together they executed various monuments (listed under "Delvaux, L.").

In 1728 Scheemakers, with Delvaux and the painter Angelis, revisited Italy and remained there for several years. According to Vertue, he was "very assiduous in his studies in Rome" and "the number of models, busts, etc., so neatly and curiously finisht, besides others works shows his great application to study, which in some measure surprised the Italian sculptors and other artists from England who do not usually use so much diligence in their studies now adayes. Among the number of these models I well remember," Vertue continues, "the Faunus, the Young Bacchus, the Centaur with Cupid on his Back, the Venus Crouching, the Venus and Cockle-shell, the Gladiator, the Flora, and the Ceres; the Hermaphrodite and Woman one groupe, they well deserve to be made of more durable matter than clay" (*Walpole Society,* Vol. III, page 45).

When Scheemakers returned to England he brought with him, not only the models in clay, but also two or three marble statues copied from the antique. These were all carefully examined by Vertue, who declared his conviction that "no one master heretofore had brought so many complete works in that perfection of their own studies into England."

The sculptor first settled in St. Martin's Lane, whence he moved first to Old Palace Yard and then, in 1741, to Vine Street. His most successful work was the statue of Shakespeare in Westminster Abbey which, as Vertue said, "was so much spoke of in all conversations and in publick print" that it "effectually established his credit and reputation and at the same time obliterated in some degree that of Rysbrake." Both artists Vertue considered to be "certainly ingenious men," but "Rysbrake has long been at the top of fortune's wheel here, whilst the other has been (with the great labour, polish and finishing of his works gains upon the minds of most people) labouring below and broken with great fatigue to rise. At length, by this takeing object Shakespeare (the publick favourite of all English playwrites), tossd this sculptor above on the summit of the wheel and so became the admiration of the publick, immediately brought him into considerable employments of profit and honour and joynd to that some subtilitys nature had given to Scheemaker in the management of his affairs, boldness and also always underworking the other's price, added to his success" (op. cit., Vol. III, page 116).

Praise, however, seems to have turned Scheemakers' head and he was apparently very rude to Lord Oxford. Vertue records the incident and adds "this little fellow [Scheemaker] since he had done Shakespear mont. [monument] thinks himself above all others, and tells several such bold-faced stories of his own assurance without reserve, and the truest is when he sayes I am a little impudent fellow, no matter, I can't help it" (op. cit., Vol. III, page 108).

On 10 December, 1753, a sale was held of the sculptor's prints and drawings for, according to the catalogue, he "intended to retire from business."

Three years later, on 10 and 11 March, 1756, a further sale of his "models, marbles and pictures" was held at Langford's auction-room in the Great Piazza, Covent Garden. Lots in the earlier sale included "two models of lions in the Villa Medici," "Cupid on a Sphinx," and busts of "Flora," Cicero and Caracalla, while at the second auction were sold the model for the statue of Edward VI, busts of Locke, Dryden and Inigo Jones, and heads of a "Vestal Virgin" and "Zingara," both of which were purchased by Lord Radnor. The highest sums—£43 and £69 respectively—were paid for a statue of Shakespeare and a group of "The Laocoon," the latter being bought by Lord Lincoln. Yet another sale was held in 1757, but it is uncertain in which of the three were included the sketch-books with drawings, figures, etc. These were at one time in the possession of J. Nollekens (q.v.) and some of them are now in the library at Burlington House.

In spite of his declared intention to retire, however, Scheemakers continued working in England until 1771, when he finally settled in Antwerp, dying there on 12 September, ten years later. According to Nollekens, he grew so fat at the end of his life "that when he was kneeling down to say his prayers he placed his legs under him with his hands" (J. T. Smith's *Nollekens and His Times*, Vol. II, page 40).

Scheemakers' busts of Milton, Spenser, Shakespeare and Dryden were presented by Frederick, Prince of Wales, to Pope who, in his turn, bequeathed them to the first Lord Lyttelton. In 1857 the sculptor's busts of Swift and Milton were in the possession of the Rt. Hon. H. Labouchère.

According to Pyne (*Royal Residences*, Vol. II), Old Carlton House "possessed several massive chimney-pieces sculptured by Scheemakers, which were carefully removed by a Frenchman called Gaubier, and probably now decorate other mansions."

Of the sculptor's many monuments, those commemorating Charles Wathen, 1721, Anne Colleton, 1741, and Francis Sherwood, 1744, were destroyed or damaged when All Hallows, Barking, was burnt out during the Second World War, his monument to Samuel Mead *d.* 1733, is outside the Temple Church.

Dr. Richard Mead, his brother, was a patron of Scheemakers, as at the Doctor's sale, held in 1755 on 11 March and following days, the sculptor's busts of Shakespeare, Milton, Pope and Alexander and a statue of Zingara were among the lots auctioned. At the sale of the collection of the Earl of At the sale of the collection of the Earl of Bessborough held by Mr. Christie on 7 April, 1801, one of the lots was "a beautiful small copy of

Lacoon in terra-cotta, modelled by the late Mr. Scheemaker." (Archives, Messrs. Christie). At the sale of Nollekens' effects held by Mr. Christie on 3 July, 1823, two of the lots were "Piping Faun" and "Saturn and Child" by Scheemakers.

(Authorities cited in text; Sale catalogues, British Museum; Archives, Earl of Radnor.)

STATUES

1734	Thomas Guy	Guy's Hospital (unveiled 11 February)
1734	William III	Hull
c. 1735	Lycurgus, Socrates, Homer and Epaminondas	Stowe
1737	Sir John Barnard	For Royal Exchange
1737	Edward VI	St. Thomas's Hospital
1739	Marwood Turner	Kirkleatham, Yorks
1741	Shakespeare	Westminster Abbey
1743	Shakespeare	Wilton (£75 18s. 4½d.)
1743	Lion Attacking a Horse	Rousham, Oxon
1743	Dying Gladiator	Rousham, Oxon
1762	A Faun	For Lord Rockingham (£31) (Wentworth Woodhouse Archives)
1764	Sir George Pococke, Lord Clive and General Laurence	India Office
?	Venus and Adonis	Stowe
?	Cain Killing Abel	For Gallery, Chiswick House
?	Muse and Apollo	For Gardens, Chiswick House
?	A Satyr	For Gardens, Chiswick House (for these three, see Faulkner's *Brentford*, pages 428, 412 and 430 respectively)
?	George II	Formerly on a Corinthian pillar in gardens at Stowe

BUSTS

1731	Dryden	Westminster Abbey (a replica was Lot 164 at the Erlestoke sale in 1832)
1733	Antoninus Pius	For Earl Fitzwalter (8 guineas)
1733	Seven busts in Temple of Friendship	Stowe
1737?	Sir Justinian Isham	Lamport Hall, Northants (replica Lamport Church)
1739	Dr. Harvey	Royal College of Physicians
1740	Earl Temple	Stowe

1743	Shakespeare, Locke, Homer, Cicero and Milton	Trinity College, Dublin
1747	Edward VI	King Edward's School, Birmingham
1758	Dr. Robert Smith	Trinity College, Cambridge
1758	Roger Cotes	Trinity College, Cambridge
1763	Nymph	Corsham Court, Wilts
1764	Sir Paul Methuen	Corsham Court, Wilts
1766	James Jurin	Trinity College, Cambridge
1766	Edward Wortley Montagu	Trinity College, Cambridge
?	3rd and 4th Earls of Shaftesbury	St. Giles, Dorset
?	Ceres	For Charles Jennens
?	Head of a Girl	For Charles Jennens (for both see Dodsley's *London*, Vol. V, page 96)
?	James Ussher	Trinity College, Dublin
?	Six members of the Shirley family	Staunton Harold, Leics
?	Milton, Spenser, Dryden and Shakespeare	Hagley Hall, Worcs
?	Viscount Cobham	Victoria and Albert Museum
?	Antoninus Pius	Rousham, Oxon
?	Ceres	Rousham, Oxon

VARIOUS

1733	Chimney-piece of "statuary marble with mask and carved egg and anchor"	For Drawing-room, Moulsham Hall, Essex (£28 12s.) (Fitzwalter Archives)
1736	Chimney-piece	St. Thomas' Hospital (£16 16s.) (Hospital Archives)
1747	Chimney-piece	King Edward's School, Birmingham (School Archives)
1764	Chimney-piece	For Picture Gallery, Corsham Court, Wilts (£225) (Methuen Archives)
1765	(Relief) *Et in Arcadia Ego*	Shugborough Staffs
1765	Chimney-piece	For Red Drawing-room, Corsham Court, Wilts (Methuen Archives)
?	Chimney-piece	For Green Damask Drawing-room, Ditchley, Oxon
?	Chimney-piece	For Velvet Bed-chamber, Ditchley, Oxon (for these see *England Displayed*, Vol. I, page 269)

?	Two vases with reliefs of the Sacrifices of Apollo and the Sacrifice of Iphigenia	For Wanstead House (they were Lots 369 and 370 in the Wanstead sale, 1822, and were purchased for Leigh Court, Somerset, for £84 and £78 15s. respectively)
?	Relief of "Alexander Visiting Darius"	Stowe (Lipscomb's *Bucks*, Vol. III, page 89)
?	Relief on pediment	Temple of Concord and Victory, Stowe

MONUMENTS

c. 1730	Beverley (Minster)	Sir Michael Warton (*d.* 1725)
c. 1730	Amersham, Bucks	Montague Drake (*d.* 1728)
c. 1730	Westminster Abbey	Dr. Woodward (*d.* 1728)
1730	Westminster Abbey	General Monck (*d.* 1670)
1731	Westminster Abbey	Sir Henry Belasyse
1732	Barnby-on-Don, Yorks	Sir Thomas Hodgson (with bust)
1732	Reading (St. Laurence's)	William Douglas
1733	Harrow (Parish Church)	Thomas Graham
1733	Blunsdon St. Andrew, Wilts	Sir John Potenger
1734	Westminster Abbey (cloisters)	Francis Meyrick
1735	Windsor (Parish Church)	Sir Thomas and Lady Reeve
1736	Exeter (Cathedral)	Bishop Grant
1736	Westminster Abbey (cloisters)	Thomas Jordan
1736	Kingston, Surrey	James Belcher
1737	Heydour, Lincs	Lady Newton
1737	Kedleston, Derby	Sir Nathaniel and Lady Curzon
1737	Twickenham (Parish Church)	Nathaniel Pigott
1737	Ely (Cathedral)	Charles Fleetwood
1737	Stoughton, Leics	Sir George Beaumont
1737	St. Mary-le-Bow	Matthew Howard
1737	Lamport, Northants	Sir Justinian Isham
1738	Wandsworth (Parish Church)	Samuel Palmer
1738	Drumcondra, Co. Dublin	Marmaduke Coghill
1739	Bray, Berks	Mary Hanger
1739	Ledsham, Yorks	Lady Elizabeth Hastings
1739	Mapperton, Dorset	Richard Brodrepp
1739	Wheatfield, Oxon	John Rudge
1740	Betteshanger, Kent	Admiral Morrice
1740	Faulkbourne, Essex	John Bullock
1740	Westminster Abbey	Lord Aubrey Beauclerk

1740	Westminster Abbey	William Shakespeare
1741	Stow Bardolph, Norfolk	Susanna Hare
1741	Westminster Abbey	General Kirk
1742	Bradford (Cathedral)	Abraham Sharp
1742	Boughton Monchelsea, Kent	Sir Christopher Powell
1742	Pusey, Berks	Jane Pusey
1743	Westminster Abbey	Sir Charles Wager
1744	Westminster Abbey	Admiral Balchen
1745	Wanstead (Parish Church)	David Petty
1746	Heydour, Lincs	Sir Michael Newton
1746	Gloucester (St. Mary)	Dorothy Snell
1746	Chittlehampton, Devon	Samuel Rolle
1747	Soberton, Hants	Thomas Lewis
1747	Westminster Abbey	Magdalen Walsh
1747	Reading (St. Laurence)	Anne Haydon
1748	Reading (St. Giles)	Horwood Aubrey
1749	Bruton, Somerset	Hon. William Berkeley (d. 1733)
1750	Benenden, Kent	Admiral Sir John Norris
1750	Cardington, Beds	John Whitbread
1751	Grendon Underwood, Bucks	John Pigott
1752	Goodnestone, Kent	Brook Bridges
1753	Clewer, Berks	Roger Jenyns
1753	Urchfont, Wilts	Mr. and Mrs. Tothill (with busts)
1754	Kintbury, Berks	Sir Jemmet Raymond
1754	Boston, U.S.A. (King's Chapel)	Mrs. Shirley
1754	Westminster Abbey	Dr. Mead (with bust)
1754	High Wycombe, Bucks	Lord Shelburne
1755	Downton, Wilts	Lady Feversham
1756	Abbots Langley, Herts	Lord Raymond
1757	Westminster Abbey	Admiral Watson (designed by Stuart)
1758	Westminster Abbey	Viscount Howe
1759	Richmond, Surrey	Sir Matthew Decker
1759	Studley, Warwick	George Petre
1759	Wimpole, Cambs	Hon. Mrs. Charles Yorke
1763	Downham, Wilts	George Duncombe
1766	Wimpole, Cambs	Earl of Hardwicke
1770	Wimpole, Cambs	Hon. Charles Yorke
?	Windsor (Parish Church)	Topham Foot (with bust) (d. 1712)
n.d.	Prestbury, Cheshire	William Watts

SCHEEMAKERS, THOMAS
b. 1740, d. 1808

He was born in July, 1740, the son of Peter Scheemakers (q.v.) and worked in his father's studio, although he did attend the Royal Academy Schools for a short period in 1772.

In 1769 he received £42 from Lord Radnor for a "basso-relievo" for Longford Castle (Archives,

Earl of Radnor) and in 1775 was paid £72 by the Drapers' Company for "executing the ornaments in the pediment of the Company's Hall in Portland stone from the design of the Company's surveyor Mr. John Gorham" (Court-Book, Drapers' Company). In 1777 he was working at Coleshill, Berks, while in 1779 and 1780 he supplied chimney-pieces at a total cost of £118 for West Wycombe Park (Dashwood Archives). He seems also to have carved a number of tablets for chimney-pieces.

Scheemakers was apparently an architect as well as a sculptor, for in 1779 Lord Le Despencer engaged him to design the portico for the Parsonage House at Mereworth, Kent. In the same year he executed busts of his patron and of Admiral Keppel. He exhibited at the Free Society, 1756–1783, and at the Royal Academy, 1780–1804, showing models for monuments and a bust of General Honywood (1782). His terra-cotta figure of "Arion" is in the Victoria and Albert Museum.

Scheemakers, who was a Roman Catholic, died on 15 July, 1808, and was buried in St. Pancras churchyard; the inscription on his tombstone (Cansick's *Epitaphs*, Vol. I, page 164), shows that he spelt his name "Sheemakers," and that his wife Barbara, who died at the age of sixty-three, survived him by two years and was buried in the same grave.

As a statuary, he worked in collaboration with James Stuart (1713–1788), and the latter is responsible for the design of several of the more important monuments. These include those to the fourth Earl of Shaftesbury, 1771, at Wimborne St. Giles, Dorset; Thomas Steavens, c. 1773, at Preston-on-Stour, Warwick; Ralph Freman (with medallion portraits), c. 1773, at Braughing, Herts; Mrs. Mary Cocks, 1779, and Joseph Cocks, 1775, both at Eastnor, Hereford; and Thomas Bentley, 1780, in Chiswick Parish Church.

Scheemakers' best independent monument is the enchanting one to the memory of Mrs. Russell, 1786, at Powick, Worcestershire, which has a relief of a mother teaching her child music. Others executed by him include those to Jemmet Raymond (with busts), 1773, at Kintbury, Berks; Joseph Cocks, 1777, at Eastnor, Hereford; the Rev. William Langhorn, 1778, at Folkestone, Kent (the bill for this is in the Longford Castle archives); the Archbishop of Cashel, 1779, in Kilkenny Cathedral; Charles Fortescue, 1779, in St. Peter's Droitwich; Sir John Honywood, 1781, at Elmstead, Kent; Lord Feversham, 1784, at Downton, Wilts; Mrs. Cocks and Mrs. Neale, 1785, at North Mimms, Herts; William Hendley, 1785, at Otham, Kent; the Hon. and Rev. George

Talbot, 1786, at Guiting, Glos (*Gentleman's Magazine*, 1786, Part I, page 439); Lady Mary Wortley Montagu, 1789, in Lichfield Cathedral; Sir William Fagg, 1792, at Chartham, Kent; and Thomas and Catherine Wilson, undated, in Holy Trinity, Bungay.

Mr. Christie held a sale of his effects on 21 May, 1805—a number of plaster casts of the sculptor's busts were sold including those of "Mr. Robertson, Admiral Keppel, General Honeywood, Dr. James, Filmer Honeywood and Lord Le Despencer"— also sold was the model of his monument to Mrs. Ogilvy. (Archives, Messrs. Christie.)

SCHROWDER, BENJAMIN
b. 1757, *d.* 1826

Schrowder, who was supposed to be a descendant, on his mother's side, of the poet Milton, was born at Winchelsea on 15 November, 1757. In 1772 he joined the Royal Academy Schools and in 1781 exhibited various wax portraits at the Academy.

He later settled in Dublin, where he assisted Edward Smyth to carve the keystone (representing Irish rivers) for the new Customs House (Strickland's *Dictionary of Irish Artists*).

SCOTT, J., of Penzance
fl. 1813–1825

His tablets are carefully carved and carried out. Examples of his work in Cornwall include those commemorating James Pascoe, 1813, and Philothea Thompson, 1825, both at Gulval; William Nicholls, 1815, at Madrom; and Mary Harrison, 1820, and John Rogers, 1821, both at Helston.

SCOTT, JOHN
fl. 1760–1765

He was "under twenty-two and a pupil of Mr. Cuenot" when in 1760 he received a premium from the Society of Arts for a "model of birds." For the next four years he won further prizes from the Society for models of ornaments, festoons of flowers, etc. He exhibited at the Free Society, 1761–1762.

SCOTT, ROBERT
fl. 1742–1762

He was a son of Thomas Scott the Younger (q.v.) and became free of the Masons' Company by patrimony in 1742. Three years later he was working as a mason at the Hampstead house of Mr. Christopher Arnold, one of the partners in Hoare's Bank (Bank archives).

In 1748 Scott made the monument of Mr. John

Nichol, father of the Marchioness of Carnarvon, which was erected in a church near London, possibly Colney. The bill for this is in the Stowe archives. In 1762 Scott took his son Edward as an apprentice.

SCOTT, THOMAS, the Elder
b. c. 1678, *d. c.* 1723

He was apprenticed to Anthony Leonard in 1692 and became free of the Masons' Company in 1703. In 1714 he was appointed mason to the Inner Temple, receiving in the same year the sum of £80 for repairing the garden wall. Between 1719 and 1721 he carried out repairs to Hoare's Bank (Bank archives).

In 1722 Scott's son William was apprenticed to him, but he probably died in the following year, as his son Thomas is described as the "son of the late Thomas Scott" in 1724.

SCOTT, THOMAS, the Younger
b. c. 1703, *d.* 1757

Son of Thomas Scott the Elder (q.v.), he was apprenticed to John Lucas in 1717, and became free of the Masons' Company in 1724. Between 1730 and 1742 he was mason to the Inner Temple, an appointment which had also been held by his father. Here his work included the circular steps "at the great gate of the Great Garden" in 1729 and, in 1741, "the Portland stone obelisks and posts" on the terrace (Inderwick's *Inner Temple Records*). He also signs the large monument to John Elliston, 1741, at Gestingthorpe, Essex.

Scott was Master of the Masons' Company in 1745, and his death in 1757 is noted in their Court Book. He had two sons, Robert and John, who became free "by patrimony" in 1742 and 1753 respectively, while a James Scott became free in 1758 "by service with Thomas Scott" (Archives, Masons' Company).

SCOULAR, WILLIAM
d. 1854

He studied under Mr. John Graham at the Trustees' Academy in Edinburgh and, about 1814, travelled to London, where he became a pupil of Sir Richard Westmacott (q.v.).

In 1816 Scoular received a Silver Medal from the Society of Arts for a statue of "Faunus" and, in 1820, the Isis Gold Medal for a group of "Brutus and His Son." He had already gained the Royal Academy Gold Medal in 1817 for a relief of "The Judgment of Paris." In 1825 he won the Academy Travelling Scholarship and went to study in Rome, remaining for some years in the city, though the

Literary Gazette (1829, page 649) declared that his "modest and retired habits estrange him from his countrymen visiting Rome." In the same article mention was made of the works at that time in the sculptor's studio, including "The Deluge," "Adam and Eve," "Narcissus" and "A Girl Playing a Guitar." The "Adam and Eve" was later purchased for £300 by the "Association for Promoting the Fine Arts in Scotland." In 1823 he was appointed sculptor to the Duke and Duchess of Clarence, having carved in 1821 a small recumbent figure of their child, the infant Princess Elizabeth, which is now at Windsor Castle.

Scoular exhibited at the Royal Academy, 1815–1846, and at the British Institution, 1816–1843, showing at the Academy a marble statue of Sir Walter Scott, and various busts, groups, etc., including a figure of Narcissus. Of this the *Literary Gazette* (1825, page 428) declared that "we have scarcely ever seen a more beautiful model, chaste in design, just in its proportions and graceful in action." The *Art Union* (1844, page 171), on the other hand, asserted that the sculptor's bust of the Prince Consort was "among the worst of the portraits we have seen."

In 1840 Scoular's statue of an "Italian Peasant Boy" was one of the prizes awarded by the Scottish Art Union, while in the following year he exhibited his figure of "A Girl Playing a Guitar" in Edinburgh and sold it for one hundred guineas. In 1843 he made the medallion of John Hampden for the memorial erected on the site of the battle of Chalgrove Field. His bust of Sir John Dashwood King is at West Wycombe Park. His statue of James Watt, which he had shown at the Birmingham Society of Artists, fetched £136 when it was sold at Christie's on 9 May, 1889.

Scoular died on 23 July, 1854, at Dean Street, Soho.

(Redgrave's *Dictionary of Artists; Scottish Magazine*, 1816, page 207; *Gentleman's Magazine*, 1854, Part II, page 316.)

SCURRY, J.
fl. 1850–1852

From 1850 until 1852 he exhibited busts and medallions at the Royal Academy. The former included those of Professor Rodgers, William Essex and Miss Louisa Pyne.

SEABORNE, —, of Birmingham
fl. 1812–1816

He signs a wall-tablet in the form of a sarcophagus to Benjamin Wilson, 1812, at Burton-on-Trent, Staffs, and a large Gothic monument to Isaac Spooner, 1816, at Elmdon, Warwick.

SEAGER, PETER, of Coventry
fl. 1816–1830

He may be the son of the Seager of Rugby who signs a wall-tablet to Thomas Benn, 1788, at Clifton, Warwick.

Seager himself signs tablets in the same county to Thomas Lant, 1816, at Berkswell; Frances Prince, 1825, at Solihull; Edward Wise, 1826, and Edward Hobson, 1830, both in St. Paul's Church, Birmingham; and George Yates, 1828, at Aston, near Birmingham. At Watford, Northants, is his tablet to Richard Abbey, 1821.

SEALEY, THOMAS

He was employed as a marble mason under Wyatt at the rebuilding of Longleat in 1810 (Archives, Marquess of Bath). He signs the monument with a relief of "Hope" to Mrs. Kent, 1810, in Paddington Parish Church.

SEALY, JOHN
b. 1749, *d.* 1813

Sealy, who was a cousin of Mrs. Coade (q.v.) on her father's side, became her partner in the terracotta manufactory at Lambeth (for a list of their works, see under "Coade and Sealy"). His son and namesake exhibited at the British Institution in 1809 and at the Royal Academy in 1810 and 1811, and died 1817, aged twenty-eight; while another son, Thomas, employed at Lambeth, died on 7 January, 1804, as the result of an accident. He was only twenty when "passing through Pedlar's Acre in the evening, it being very dark, he unfortunately ran against a short post which, striking him, occasioned his death" (*Universal Magazine*, 1804, page 70).

The elder John Sealy (who died 22 October, 1813), and his wife Elizabeth, who predeceased him in 1807, are both buried at Lambeth, where a large monument in Coade artificial stone covers the family vault in the churchyard.

SEARES, DANIEL, of Maidstone
fl. 1810–1830

Seares, whose yard was in Stone Street, signs a few tablets in Kent, the best being one of Mrs. Crispe, 1825, at Sutton Valence.

SEARS, —

Of "9 Strand, London," he signs a large marble tablet to the Dugdale family, 1828, in Handsworth Parish Church, every letter of the long inscription it bears being cast in bronze.

SEDDON, C. M., of Liverpool
fl. 1824–1858

Seddon exhibited at the Liverpool Academy, showing a bust of Richard Jones in 1824 and a medallion of Sir Walter Scott in 1837. He also signs a large monument with a relief of a mourning widow to Richard Phillips, 1824, at St. Martin's, Salop.

SEDERBACH, VICTOR ALEXANDER

Apparently a worker in terra-cotta, as J. Talbot, writing to his architect, Sanderson Miller, in January, 1756, about his improvements to Laycock Abbey, Wilts, says: "The Foreigner who has been here ever since May has executed his Performance in a very Workmanlike manner and your Niches are filled by a set of Inhabitants worthy such Repositories. I presume you are acquainted with the method of making Models for Statues. He proceeds on the same principles, only Bakes them afterwards, by which means they become of a Red Colour and ring like a Garden Pot. . . . I fancy Lord Shelburn will employ him on his arrival at London, where he goes next week; however, as so many of your friends are Connoisseurs, I would advise them seeing his Performances, which are both Easy and not Expensive. His name is sonorous, no less than Victor Alexander Sederbach and yet lodges at one King's a grocer in Green Street, near Castle Street, Leicester Fields. I am sorry he did not show all his Performances to the Gentleman you sent a note by, but on asking the Reason, was told that someone the day before had Broke a Figure, which made him extremely Captious." (*An Eighteenth Century Correspondence*, edited by Lilian Dickins and Mary Stanton, page 308.)

The work carried out by Sederbach may have been in the old Refectory, as J. Britton, writing in 1812 (*Beauties of Wilts*, Vol. III, page 242), states that "at the sides are small niches, containing a number of small statues and busts in terra-cotta, allusive to the history of the monastery."

SEELEY, JOHN
b. 1789

Seeley, who joined the Royal Academy Schools in 1808, later went into partnership about 1840 with Felix Austin (q.v.), and together they carried out various monumental works (for a list of these, see under "Austin").

Like his partner, Seeley chose good designers for his works, and like him, too, dealt in terra-cotta, although he called his material "artificial limestone." He executed a number of fountains, including those for Tottenham Park, the seat of the Marquess of Ailesbury; the dairy at Blenheim; and the market at Birkenhead. Another, for the Marquess of Hertford, was designed by Smirke, while two at Brighton—in Queen's Park and the Steyne—were made from the designs of Barry and Papworth respectively (*Builder*, 1851, page 474).

Seeley signs tablets to Anna Forster, 1829, at Walsall, Staffordshire, and to John Gosling, 1848, in St. John's Wood Chapel.

SEEST, CHRISTIAN CARLSEN
fl. 1734–1757

He left his native country of Denmark in 1734, being described on his passport as "sculptor-apprentice." He travelled to Germany, Holland and other countries and was in Paris in the 1740s and in London from 1750–1757. Presumably he had been there earlier as Vertue (*Walpole Society*, Vol. III, page 154) says "a bust, a modell done of my own portrait, a head only, by one who was workman to Mr. Rubilliac (bust done Michaelmas, 1750). This man came from Denmark and had been some years in . . . and Holland, but first in England and lately has returned to England again. Now constantly works for Mr. Rubilliac, his name is Siste. He is an ingenious man, draws very well and modells in good taste." As far as I know the bust of Vertue has disappeared. Seest also worked for Roubiliac on the statue of Sir Isaac Newton for Trinity College, Cambridge.

On 16 September, 1748, Seest was appointed Danish Court Sculptor. From London he had sent drawings for monuments, etc., to the Danish King, Frederick V, and a bust of that monarch, probably his work, is at Ledreborg Castle.

(Weilbach's *Kunsteerlexikon*, Vol. III.)

SELLERS, JOSEPH, of Stoke

He signs a wall-tablet at Bunbury, Cheshire, to Thomas Acton, who died in 1803.

SEPHTON, DANIEL, of Manchester
b. 1714, *d.* 1759

Sephton, who was the son of Henry Sephton (q.v.), was the best of the eighteenth-century Manchester statuaries. His monument to William Wright, 1753, at Stockport, Cheshire, is a large architectural work, nearly 20 ft. high, with a portrait-bust, while the side consoles are delicately carved with beetles, butterflies, etc. He signs other monuments to Sarah Jarvis, 1748, in Chester Cathedral; Francis Massy, 1748, in Warrington Parish Church; Francis Price, 1749, at Overton, Flint; and Thomas Barron, 1751, at Prescot, Lancs.

Sephton died on 11 January, 1759, and was commemorated on the same tablet as his father in Walton Church, the epitaph describing him as "eminent in carving." His wife survived him and died in 1770.

SEPHTON, HENRY,
of Manchester
b. 1686, *d.* 1756

He was one of the principal masons for building Knowsley (Earl of Derby's Archives, DDK. 2002/1-7) and also signs a cartouche tablet, with excellent detail, to Robert Scarisbrick, 1737, at Ormskirk, Lancashire.

Sephton died on 2 June, 1756, and was buried in Walton Church, Liverpool, but the monument to his memory was presumably lost when the church was destroyed by enemy action. His epitaph, however, described him as an "architect" and stated that his wife, Esther, died in 1750

SERVANT, —

According to the catalogue of the Society o Free Artists, published in 1762 and now in the library of the Victoria and Albert Museum, Servant exhibited in that year a "Statue of Ceres in white marble." This work is ignored by Graves in his *Exhibitors at the Society of Artists and Free Society*, though he does mention a "— Servant" exhibiting pictures in 1764.

SETTLE, JOHN
fl. 1679–1692

According to Brayley's *Westminster Abbey* (Vol. II, page 234), Settle signed the monument to Sir Lumley Robinson, 1684, which was originally situated between the "third and fourth pillars from the cloyster gates westward," but which now lies dismantled in the triforium. The work, which is illustrated in Dart's *Westmonasterium* (Part II, No. 117), is described as follows in an anonymous guide to the Abbey, published about 1840: "The columns are supported by Death's heads, and the arms upon the base by a cherub. On the top is a vase and rising to the pediments, enrichments of laurel branches, etc."

Settle also signed the monument to Albert Faber, 1685, in St. Dunstan's-in-the-West. In 1679 he had received £214 for work in the Mercers' Chapel (Archives, Mercers' Company).

SHARLAND, JOHN, of Torquay
fl. 1823–1835

His tablets are mostly neo-Hellenic, the best being those to the Viscountess Kilcoursie, 1823, at

Tormohun, Devon; Elizabeth Hague, 1830, at Barrow Gurney, Somerset; and the Rev. John Edwards, 1834, at Berry Pomeroy, Devon.

SHARMAN, EDWARD,
of Peterborough
b. 1773, *d.* 1805

His obituary in the *Gentleman's Magazine* (1805, page 686) says of him that "his goodness of heart was rarely equalled and his natural genius was far above his opportunity of cultivating it."

Sharman's monuments and tablets are good provincial work, the best being that to George Pochin, 1798, at Bourne, Lincs, which has a relief of a mourning woman. Other signed works by him include those to the Judd family, 1791, in St. Martin's, Stamford; William Whitsed, 1796, at Peakirk, Northants; and George Digby, 1797, at Bourne, Lincs.

SHARP, GEORGE, of Gloucester

He signs a wall-tablet with naval trophies at St. Magnus, London Bridge, to John Sharp, 1822.

SHARP, THOMAS
b. 1805

He attended the Royal Academy Schools in 1831, on the recommendation of Sir Francis Chantrey (q.v.) and gained a Silver Medal three years later. He had already exhibited at the Academy his "Boy and the Lizard" in 1831, a figure which was praised in the *Library of Fine Arts* (1831, page 431). In the course of the article the writer drew attention to the fact that "it was probably in utter unconsciousness of his own power" that the sculptor "had chosen a piece of marble so veiny and imperfect as to offend the eye; thus, while we see all around abominations in the purest white marble, here is a work that would have done credit to almost any artist carved in the most objectionable material, and consequently scarcely noticed." The work was purchased by Lady Colbourne who, in 1855, lent it to the Exhibition of English Art held in Paris.

Sharp exhibited at the Royal Academy, 1830–1869, and at the British Institution, 1831–1861, showing among other things a statue of David in 1835, and busts of Lord Augustus FitzClarence (1832), the Rev. J. Reynolds (1863) and the Earl of Lauderdale (1869). There is a bust executed by him of Lord Palmerston at Broadlands, dated 1844, and a statue of the same statesman at Southampton, dated 1868. Two of the sculptor's groups, "Christ's Charge to Peter" and "*Non Angli sed Angeli*" were shown respectively at the

Great Exhibition of 1851 and the International Exhibition of 1862. He signs two monuments, that of Anne Hardinge, *c.* 1830, at Crowhurst, Sussex, and of Elizabeth Grape, 1832, in Windsor Parish Church. Sharp was also a silver-chaser and showed a silver medallion of St. Martin in 1835, and a Shakespeare cup in 1842.

SHARPE, EDWARD, of Stamford
fl. 1714–1749

He became a Freeman of Stamford in 1714 on payment of £4. His large monument to Sir Brownlow Sherrard, 1736, is at North Witham, Lincolnshire, and takes the form of a sarcophagus with lion-clawed feet, while behind it stands a pyramid.

Sharpe's son, another Edward, was apprenticed to him and later became a Freeman of Stamford in 1749. The business must have been a considerable one, for two earlier apprentices, Thomas Burbridge and William Bolland, had both become Freemen of the town in 1732 (Stamford Archives).

SHARPE, P.

Apparently a local artist, he exhibited at the Liverpool Academy in 1813 a "Bust of Master Betty in Achmed."

SHAW, DANIEL, of King's Lynn
fl. 1628–1675

In 1628 he became a Freeman of King's Lynn and later executed a certain amount of work for that town. In 1660 he carved the Town Arms on the schoolhouse and seven years later made figures of a unicorn and of a boy. The latter was probably for the exterior of a Charity School, and in this case the sculptor also provided the stone. In 1675 he carved a stone lion for the Town Cross (Chamberlain's Accounts, King's Lynn Archives).

SHAW, J., of Reading
fl. 1815–1837

He signs tablets in Berkshire to the Hon. Henry Bennett, 1815, at Easthampstead, and to Martha Fisher, 1837, at Basildon.

SHAW, JAMES
fl. 1776–1787

He exhibited wax models at the Royal Academy from 1776 until 1787.

SHEFFIELD, WILLIAM

In 1758 when "under twenty-two and apprenticed to Mr. Wildsmith" (q.v.) he was awarded a premium by the Society of Arts for a "Model of Birds," receiving a further premium in the following year.

SHENTON, HULL and POLLARD, of Leicester
Firm *fl.* 1807–1828

The best of their tablets (all in Leicestershire) are those to Katherine Aynsworth, 1807, at Sileby; Thomas Smith, 1812, at Bitteswell; Ann Parkinson, 1818, at Cosby; and Charles Packe, 1828, at Prestwold. The last of these, however, is only signed "Hull and Pollard."

SHENTON, HENRY CHAWNER
b. 1825, *d.* 1846

He came of a family of artists, his father being Henry Shenton (1803–1866), the engraver, and his uncle Luke Clennell, the artist, while his maternal grandfather was Charles Warren, the line-engraver.

Young Shenton was a pupil of Behnes (q.v.) and attended the Royal Academy Schools in 1843. In the same year he showed a group of "Christ and Mary" at the Academy and in 1844 received a Silver Medal from the Society of Arts for a model of "Sabina." Also in 1844 he exhibited his "Burial of the Princes in the Tower" at Westminster Hall, following this with a figure of Archbishop Cranmer in 1845, and a relief of "The Penitent" at the Academy in the same year.

Apparently Shenton worked under very difficult conditions, for his first group was "modelled in a stable with a roof so low that the ground had to be dug away to the depth of several feet, while the only light came through a narrow window in the wall; to the damps and chill of this fireless workroom his friends attribute the first insinuation of that disease which has laid the sculptor in an early grave" (*Athenaeum*, 1846, page 72). His death took place on 7 February, 1846.

(Authority cited in text.)

SHEPHERD, EDWARD, of Plymouth
fl. 1818–1832

In 1818 he made a "variegated pavement composed of 1,238 pieces of marble further enriched by 102 brass figures" for the Duke of Bedford's Temple of the Graces at Woburn (*New Monthly Magazine*, 1818, page 173). In 1826 he executed a fountain of black-and-white Devon marble for the Emperor of Brazil, a vast work 25 ft. high and weighing 18 tons (*Gentleman's Magazine*, 1826, Part II, page 78).

Shepherd's tablets are dull, the best in Cornwall being those to Sally Graham, 1818, at Saltash; Joseph Ede, 1823, at Liskeard; and Jane Michel, 1824, at Lostwithiel. Others in Devon are to James Glencross, 1825, at St. Budeaux; Richard King, 1829, at Tamerton Foliot; and the Rev. W. Manley, 1832, at Stoke Fleming.

SHEPHERD, VINCENT
b. 1750, *d.* 1812

He was architect to the Duke of Northumberland and also carried out a considerable amount of stone-carving for his patron. In the choir of Alnwick Church he executed "a piece of Gothic trellis work, which for elegance of fancy and superiority of workmanship has seldom been equalled and perhaps never excelled" (*Gentleman's Magazine*, 1812, page 601). He died at Alnwick in 1812.

SHERWOOD, JAMES, of Derby
fl. 1800–1821

His best work is the delightful monument in Derby Cathedral to Thomas Swanwick, 1814, who had been a schoolmaster for thirty years. The monument, which was erected by Swanwick's pupils, has a relief of a master teaching a small boy who is seated on a pile of books, while above are terrestrial and celestial globes.

Sherwood signs other monuments to William Mills, 1802, at Leek, Staffs; Thomasine Buxton, 1809, at Tissington, Derby; and the Rev. James Falconer, 1821, in Lichfield Cathedral.

SHORTHOSE, JOHN
d. 1704?

Son of Thomas Shorthose, citizen and mason, he came on the Livery in 1662 and later received £130 for work at the Guildhall and Sessions House (P.R.O., E.101. 475/2). With his partner, Robert Mortimer, he was the master-mason for the rebuilding of the Coopers' Hall, 1668–1672 (Company's Archives).

Shorthose was also employed under Wren on several of the City churches. He was the mason-contractor for building St. Olave's, Jewry, where his work included "roses, cherubim, festoons and the shield over the steeple door," and in the same capacity he, and his partner John Crooke, built Christ Church, Newgate. Here they received £130 for ten composite capitals, £20 for four pineapples, and £36 for four urns for the steeple (Bodleian, Rawlinson, B.387). In 1680 he was the master-mason with Edward Pearce (q.v.) for St. Clement Danes (*Wren Society*, Vol. X, page 108).

Shorthose was Warden of the Masons' Company in 1676 and 1681, and Master in 1686. He married Mary, daughter of Humphrey Moyer (q.v.). She died 1706.

SHOUT, BENJAMIN and ROBERT
Firm *fl.* 1778–1823

Benjamin Shout and his son Robert made a few busts and a large number of monuments. In 1806 they made the plaster busts for Lord Bridport's library which had been designed by Soane, and in 1827 they executed others for Salters' Hall; these, however, were destroyed when the Hall was burnt in 1940. Their bust of an unknown man, in the possession of the writer, shows careful modelling.

In 1819 the firm made casts of Canova's "Hebe," "Venus," "Paris" and "Perseus" (*Annals of the Fine Arts*, 1819, page 632), a type of work for which they were apparently well known, for Shelley writes of Leigh Hunt's studio, that

"His room no doubt
Is still adorned with many a cast from Shout."

The early monuments and tablets carried out by the firm are well carved, but the later ones are dull, the unadventurous designs rarely going beyond reliefs of widows mourning by urns, or figures of "Religion" pointing heavenwards. The family yard was in Holborn and in 1809 Robert took as an apprentice his son, Charles Lutwyche Shout.

The firm's monuments and tablets include those to John Webber, 1778, at Bampton, Devon; Frances Lester, 1778, at Poole, Dorset; Charles Bushby, 1789, at Arundel, Sussex; Captain Baldon Swiney, 1790, at Hartfield, Sussex; Mrs. Lomax, 1793, and Elizabeth Cooper, 1793, both at Sleaford, Lincs; Thomas Knight, 1794, and Harriett Knatchbull, 1794, both at Godmersham, Kent; Mrs. Burrows, 1795, at Chalk, Kent; William Carter, 1799, in St. Dunstan's, Canterbury; Elizabeth Pinnell, 1800, at Fittleworth, Sussex; Alexander Hoskins, 1800, Melling, Lancs; the Rev. Stephen Barrett, 1801, at Hothfield, Kent; Sarah Jeaffreson, 1804, at Dullingham, Cambs; Sir Matthew Blakiston, 1806, at Lymington, Hants; John Hinde, 1806, at Milton Regis, Kent; Sir Wolstan Dixie, 1807, at Market Bosworth, Leics; Harriet Stewart, 1807, in Portsmouth Cathedral; Sir William Yeo, 1808, at Wiveliscombe, Somerset; Mary Croft, 1808, at Dullingham, Cambs; Samuel Johnson, 1809, at St. Ives, Hunts; Thomas Cockayne, 1809, at Ickleworth, Herts; John Stapleton, 1809, at Ottery St. Mary, Devon; Grace Sutton, 1814, at Stockton,

Durham; William Bennet, 1820, in Emmanuel College Chapel, Cambridge; Martin Wilshere, 1821, at Welwyn, Herts; and Olive Western, 1826, at Rivenhall, Essex.

SHOUT, WILLIAM, of York
fl. 1720–1750

In 1720 and 1721 he built the north and south gateways at Castle Howard. For the house he carved vases and cartouches, while for the grounds he erected the fluted obelisk which formerly stood by the south front, but which has now disappeared (Castle Howard Archives).

In 1749 he built a small temple in the grounds of Hovingham Hall, Yorks, for Thomas Worsley (Archives, Sir William Worsley, Bart.).

SHOUT, WILLIAM, of York
b. 1750, *d.* 1826

Son of Henry Shout, of York, he was appointed master-mason to the Minster in 1794, and here he renewed and recut the figures of the west end in 1813.

Shout was buried at Huntington, near York, where his epitaph states that "for forty years with credit to himself and satisfaction to his employers he conducted the repairs and restoration of York Minster."

SHROPSHIRE, JOHN

He signs a large architectural tablet with excellently cut details to John Smallwood, 1771, at Market Drayton, Salop.

SIBSON, HENRY
fl. 1826–1863

In 1844 he exhibited statues of Marlborough and Bacon at Westminster Hall. The *Literary Gazette* called them "pretty pieces of costume," while the *Art Union* remarked that though there was "life and movement" in the figure of Marlborough, "whatever merit it possessed was annihilated by the heavy and graceless boots."

Sibson exhibited at the Royal Academy, 1826–1863. At the Great Exhibition of 1851 he showed a recumbent life-size figure with the odd title of the "Dying Shipwrecked Sea Boy."

SIDNELL, MICHAEL, of Bristol
fl. 1714–1745

Sidnell was an architect as well as a statuary, and his monuments are consequently architectural in design; he also makes much use of heraldic shields and coats of arms. His best work, commemorating James Lyde, 1738, is at Stanton Drew,

Somerset, and stands about 12 ft. high, with Doric pilasters supporting a broken pediment.

Other monuments signed by him include those to Henry Grinsteed, 1714, at Yatton, Somerset; Cornelius Lyde, 1717, and Anna Maria Lyde, 1729, at Stanton Drew, Somerset; Captain Jacob Knight, 1720, at Westbury, Glos; Anne Luttrell, 1731, at Dunster, Somerset; Christopher Devonshire, 1731, at Alderley, Glos; Charles Pearson, 1732, at Bredon, Worcs, and Anthony Ellesdon, 1737, Charmouth, Dorset. Examples of his work in Bristol are to be found in the churches of St. Stephen's, to John Frankland, 1731; St. James's, to Thomas Edwards, 1733; St. Michael's, to Robert Earle, 1736; and St. Augustine's, to Freeman Partridge, 1738, while he also signs the great monument to Edward Colston, 1729, in All Saints'. In this case, however, the semi-recumbent figure is known to be the work of Rysbrack (q.v.), so it seems possible that Sidnell either executed the architectural part of the monument, or else erected it when it was sent down from London.

In 1742 the sculptor became a bankrupt. (*London Magazine*, 1742, page 518), but he seems to have continued to work. Between 1743 and 1745 he was the architect responsible for building Westbury Court, Gloucestershire, for Maynard Colchester, and is described at that time as "of the City of Bristol, master-workeman and architect" (Archives, Sir Francis Colchester-Wemyss).

A "Daniel Sidnell of Bristol, stonecutter," became free of that city on 18 June, 1739, on his marriage with "Sarah, daughter of James Tanner, weaver, deceased," while a "J. Sidnell" was working under Thomas Paty (q.v.) in 1744 at Redland Chapel, Bristol.

SIEVIER, ROBERT WILLIAM
b. 1794, *d.* 1865

Sievier, who was born in London on 24 July, 1794, decided to become an engraver in 1812 when the Society of Arts awarded him a Silver Medal for a pen-and-ink drawing. After studying first under John Young and later under Edward Scriven, he joined the Royal Academy Schools in 1818; shortly after this he began engraving portraits and produced a number of works of considerable merit.

In 1823 Sievier turned his attention to sculpture, and in the following year Lord Chancellor Eldon sat to him for a bust. His gift of "rapidly improving his great facility of seizing the likeness and characteristic expression of his sitters, led many persons of distinction to his studio," but his success in two separate branches of art did not satisfy him, and in 1840 he became interested in science. He was soon absorbed in his new pursuit to the neglect of his artistic work and "built a large manufactory for the production of elastic fabrics, made great improvement in the manufactory of carpets, was associated with the original india-rubber works and rendered good early service to electric telegraphy." He was, however, a great artist, and it is sad to think that he did not take to sculpture until he was thirty and that he abandoned it before he was fifty.

Sievier exhibited at the Royal Academy, 1822–1844, and at the British Institution, 1825–1831, showing at the Academy (among other works) a group entitled "Musidora" (1831), and busts of the Countess of Sheffield (1829) and Lord Brougham (1831). His statue of Dr. Jenner (1825) is in Gloucester Cathedral and that of Charles Dibdin at Greenwich, while for the Foundling Hospital he executed one of Sir William Curtis and a statuette of Captain Coram. The latter, which is dated 1833, is now in the office of the Hospital in Brunswick Square. Of his groups, "Boy with Tortoise" (1826) is in private possession, and "Two Bacchantes" at Chatsworth; he also carved one of his few chimney-pieces for the dining-room of the same house (*Handbook to Chatsworth*, 1846). In 1829 he made a statue of "Undine" for the conservatory at the Colosseum (*Literary Gazette*, 1829, page 43).

In addition to the busts already mentioned, Sievier also executed those of Sir John Silvester (1823) and Richard Clarke (1829) for the Guildhall, the latter being destroyed by enemy action on 29 September, 1940; John Latham (1824) and John Abernethey (1828), both in St. Bartholomew's Hospital; the Earl of Eldon (1824) at St. Giles, Dorset (a plaster bust of the same sitter, dated 1827, is at Windsor Castle); Sir George Paul (1825) in Gloucester Cathedral; Earl Harcourt (1828) and the Prince Consort (1842), both at Windsor Castle; Sir Thomas Lawrence (1830) in the Soane Museum; Turton, Bishop of Ely (1831), in the Divinity School, Cambridge; the Rev. James Lyon (1836) at Prestwich, Lancs; and Sir William Bolland (?) at Trinity College, Cambridge.

Sievier's monuments have great charm and delicacy of carving; his designs are unusual, while his early training as an engraver enabled him to cut scenic bas-reliefs and to set a whole scene in a small space. The monument to Robert Chessher, 1831, at Peckleton, Leicestershire, has, for example, a relief of a graveyard, each altar-tomb and stone minutely shown, shadowed by weeping-willows. The pedestal of Lord Harcourt's statue, 1832, in St. George's Chapel, Windsor, has four battle-scenes, while the monument to the Rev.

James Lyon, 1836, at Prestwich, Lancashire, shows him at the altar-rail of his church, administering the Communion to his flock.

Other monuments signed by Sievier include those to Andrew French, 1825, in Madras Cathedral; Jacob Dearden, 1825, at Rochdale, Lancs; Sir George Alderson, 1826, in Paddington Parish Church; the Countess of Cardigan, 1826, at Deene, Northants; Isabella Fairlie, 1830, in Marylebone Parish Church; Earl Harcourt, 1832, at Stanton Harcourt, Oxon; Earl Harcourt, 1832, at Clewer, Berks; John Saint John Long, 1834, in Kensal Green Cemetery; Lieutenant Michael Smith, 1834, in Holy Trinity, Marylebone; Thomas Simpson, 1835, in St. Matthew's, Brixton; Ann Sykes, 1835, St. John's, Islington; Mary Barnard, 1836, at Wolverstone, Suffolk; William Blathwayt, 1839, at Dyrham, Glos; Elizabeth Mott, 1842, at Banstead, Surrey; and Charles Bridge, 1843, at Harwich, Essex.

Sievier died on 28 April, 1865, and is buried in Kensal Green Cemetery. His son, Robert Moore Sievier, born in 1827, studied sculpture at the Royal Academy Schools in 1845.

(Redgrave's *Dictionary of Artists*; various references *Art Journal*.)

SILVESTER, —
fl. 1788–1800

He exhibited at the Royal Academy in 1788 busts of Lord Hood, the Duke of York, Lord Rodney and John Wesley. The last-named is possibly the bust now in the National Portrait Gallery (see under "Pingo").

SIMMONDS, —, of Swindon

He signs a curious monument, erected in 1802 at Lambourne, Berks, to the memory of the three children of John and Maria Fortescue. This consists of a pyramid against which stand miniature statuettes about nine inches high of the three children in contemporary costume. Simmonds also signs a tablet to Joseph Walker, 1803, at Bampton, Oxon.

SIMPSON, —, of London Bridge
Firm *fl.* 1799–1817

He was mason to the Skinners' Company, 1801–1804, but apparently died before 1808, as in that year a Mary Simpson of the same address, presumably his widow, was paid for repairs to the Fishmongers' Hall.

Simpson's two signed monuments, to Miles Stringer, 1799, in St. Magnus, London Bridge, and Mrs. Thomas White, 1805, in St. James, Garlickhithe, are pleasant and well-carved works.

PLATE XXIII

ABRAHAM STOREY
Lord and Lady Crofts, *c.* 1678, Little Saxham, Suffolk.

PLATE XXIV

WILLIAM STANTON
Sir John and Lady Brownlow, *c.* 1679, Belton, Lincs.

R. W. SIEVIER
Earl Harcourt, 1832, Stanton Harcourt, Oxon.

THOMAS SCHEEMAKERS
Part of the monument of Ralph Freman, *c.* 1773,
Braughing, Hertfordshire.

SINGLETON, ROBERT, of Bury St. Edmunds and Norwich

fl. 1706–1740

In 1737 he received thirty guineas from the 1st Earl, of Bristol for the coat of arms on the front of the latter's house at Bury St. Edmunds, and two years later made a chimney-piece for Ickworth (Account-book of the 1st Earl of Bristol).

As a monumental sculptor, Singleton takes high rank. His monument to Colonel Edmund Soames, 1706, at West Dereham, Norfolk, is an exciting and remarkable work, with a standing life-sized figure of the Colonel in armour, his helmet at his feet and his right hand holding his great military cloak, which billows out and falls in folds behind him. The cartouche tablet to Richard Manty, 1720, in St. Martin's at Palace, Norwich, is a delightful work, while that to Thomas Pindar, 1721, at St. George Colegate in the same city, has a large figure of a cherub, an hour-glass in his hand and with his head resting on a skull.

Singleton also signs tablets to Sir Dudley Cullum, 1720, at Hawstead, Suffolk, and to Mary Bateman, 1721, in St. Gregory's, Norwich. About 1729 he went into partnership with George Bottomley (q.v.) and they carved a few monuments together (for these see under "Bottomley").

SINGLETON, THOMAS, of Bury St. Edmunds

b. 1715, *d.* 1792

Son of Robert Singleton (q.v.), he was employed by Mr. Ambrose Crowley in 1753 on repairs to Barking Hall, Suffolk (Ashburnham Archives). In 1775 he worked under Robert Adam at Bury St. Edmunds, where he built the Town Hall and was also responsible for carving the delightful reliefs on the exterior (Bury St. Edmunds Town Archives). In 1789, under Soane, he repaired the Mansion House in the same town (Soane Note-book).

Singleton, who had been a widower since 1788, died in 1792, leaving his daughter Sarah as his executrix. According to his obituary in the *Bury Post* (24 October, 1792), he was at an advanced age at the time of his death and had served as one of the Burgesses of the Common Council. The writer added that "few men have passed through a long life of active business more distinguished for ingenuity and integrity."

His monuments and tablets, which are not nearly as good as his father's, include those to the Rev. Thomas Knight, 1740, at Bluntisham, Hunts; Simon Kerrich, 1748, at Harleston, Norfolk; Valentine Muntee, 1750, at Horringer,

Suffolk; and the Lake family (undated) at Goudhurst, Kent.

SKAE, PETER

b. 1808

He attended the Royal Academy School in 1826 and later became an assistant of H. Hopper (q.v.). He is responsible for a few inferior busts.

SKELTON, MATTHEW, of York

b. 1772, *d.* 1844

One of the least distinguished of the York statuaries, the majority of his tablets are neo-Hellenic in design. In Yorkshire the best of these are to Joseph Emmot, 1820, at Keighley; Francis Edmunds, 1825, at Worsborough; Elizabeth Alexander, 1832, at Halifax; James Brooke, 1837 at Barwick in Elmet; Thomas Bland, 1840, at Kippax; Francis Duffield, 1841, in Bradford Cathedral, and Christopher Oldfield, 1843, in York Minster. He also signs a tablet to Ann Sleigh, 1835, at Stockton, Durham.

SKIKELTHORPE, L., of Abridge

He signs a wall-tablet in Wimbledon Parish Church to Emma Grosvenor, 1842.

SKUTT, WILLIAM, of York

fl. 1719–1722

He was employed as a master-mason in 1719 at Castle Howard. He also carved pedestals and vases for the bowling green and a number of chimney-pieces for the house (Castle Howard Archives). Skutt is probably a mis-spelling of Shout (q.v.).

SLATER, J. R.

He exhibited at the Royal Academy, showing busts of J. McRone and Harrison Ainsworth in 1834 and 1836 respectively.

SLATER, PETER, of Edinburgh

b. 1809

He attended the Royal Academy Schools in 1831 on the recommendation of W. Collins, R.A. In 1844 he exhibited at Westminster Hall "Canute Reproving his Flatterers," a work which caused the *Literary Gazette* to observe tartly "we must decline being one," while the *Art Union* thought "the general execution is coarse."

In 1853 Slater made the statue of James Watt for Adams Square, Edinburgh, but this was not an original work, being a copy of one by Chantrey (q.v.). His statue of George Heriot was executed in the following year and was placed on the south-west niche of the Scott monument in Princes Street, while the monument of Dr. Carson, 1855, in St. Giles, is also his work.

Slater exhibited at the Royal Academy, 1846–1870, showing mainly busts of Scottish worthies.

SLINGSBY, JOHN
d. 1808

He was the son of that Thomas Slingsby who had been master-mason at Windsor Castle and in 1778 (the year of his retirement or death) had carved the stonework of the portico of the north front (P.R.O., Works 5/66). John in his turn became master-mason and held the post for twenty years.

During the remodelling of the Castle he was responsible for a considerable amount of mason's and stonecarver's work. In 1781 he made a chimney-piece for the Prince of Wales's room, and in 1794 received £200 for the carved-stone moulding of the windows in the picture gallery.

Under Wyattville he was naturally much employed, working on the Royal tomb-house in 1800 and in 1805. At this time he was paid over £4,000, a sum which included £28 for a marble reeded chimney-piece; £25 for one of dove-grey marble; and £20 for another with pilasters of red marble.

After Slingsby's death in 1808 the business was carried on by his widow, Hannah, who in that year received £60 for a "red-marble chimney-piece with pilasters for the library." (Hope's *Windsor Castle*; P.R.O., Works 5/67.)

SLYTH, ISAAC, of Colchester
d. 1800

He was in partnership with Messrs. Roper and Doughty, of Ipswich, but became a bankrupt a few months after he had left the firm in 1799. He died on 24 December, 1800 (*Monthly Magazine*, 1801, page 93).

Slyth was succeeded by his son James, who in 1812 advertised in the *Chelmsford Chronicle* that he had "imported some very beautiful Italian marble and laid in a quantity of the newly discovered British marble," and also that he had a "quantity of chimney-pieces fitted up for inspection." The same paper reported James Slyth's death on 12 June, 1816, the obituary stating that his widow intended to "carry on the business for her children's benefit."

Since that time there have been several generations of the family who followed the same trade; indeed, the firm lasted into this century; but none of their tablets or gravestones ever rose above a low provincial level.

SMALLMAN, J.

He signs a large wall tablet with an arched pediment surmounted by an urn to Thomas Smyth, 1780, at Much Wenlock, Salop.

SMART, JAMES, of Guildford
fl. 1800–1835

Between 1802 and 1804 he was the master-mason for building Albury House, near Guildford, which had been designed for Samuel Thornton by Soane (Soane Archives).

Smart signs tablets in Surrey to William Smith, 1826 (with a relief), at Stoke-by-Guildford; Colonel Berkeley, 1826, at Wotton; and Colonel Charles Somerset, 1835, at Old Woking.

SMITH, —, of Stamford
fl. 1828–1837

His tablets are mostly neo-Hellenic, the best being those to Francis Waters, 1828, at Rippingale, Lincs; George Parker, 1831, at Eddenham, Lincs; Emma Mason, 1837, at Kingscliffe, Northants; and the Rev. William Hardyman, 1837, at North Luffenham, Rutland.

SMITH, BERNARD
b. 1820, *d.* 1885

He attended the Royal Academy Schools in 1840 and exhibited at the Academy, 1842–1851. Here he showed busts and medallion portraits, including those of Sir James Ross (1844); Edward Doubleday (1845); Rowland Hill (1845); William Rathbone (1847); and Christopher Rawdon (1847).

SMITH, CHARLES HARRIOTT
b. 1792, *d.* 1864

He was born in London on 1 February, 1792, the son of Joseph Smith (q.v.) of Portland Road, and was taken from school at the age of twelve to work in his father's yard. He was later befriended by Bonomi, the architect, at whose suggestion he joined the Royal Academy Schools in 1814, and here he won the Gold Medal for architecture three years later. A remarkable feature of his career is the fact that he passed through all the Schools of the Academy by drawings of the human figure—apparently the only student ever to do so.

Smith next turned his attention to architectural sculpture and carved the Corinthian capitals and other ornaments for University College, the

National Gallery and the Royal Exchange (*Builder*, 1850, page 305). He also did decorative carving at Bridgewater House in 1848, for which he received £1,349 (Archives, Earl of Ellesmere), while four years later he was responsible for the ornamental work on the façade of Dorchester House, Park Lane (*Builder*, 1852, page 550). His carving of the capital of Nelson's Column in Trafalgar Square dates from 1850 (*Builder*, 1850, page 169).

When Sir Charles Barry was appointed to build the new Houses of Parliament he felt it would be difficult to find enough stone of good quality for so vast an undertaking. He therefore proposed to the Government that a Royal Commission should be appointed to visit, not only possible quarries, but also the ancient cathedrals and castles of Britain, in order to discover which type of stone had best stood the test of time. C. H. Smith was one of the four members of this Commission whose "report won the admiration of the profession as a great addition to professional knowledge," while he himself "secured the lasting goodwill and esteem of his colleagues by his zeal, intelligence and cheerful co-operation."

He exhibited at the Royal Academy, 1809–1823, showing architectural designs and in 1824 a bust of "The Hon. and Rev. E. J. Turnour." His undated statue in Portland stone of the Farnese Hercules is at the Geological Museum.

Smith also took an interest in science and wrote a number of papers on a variety of subjects. He said of himself that he was "a strange mongrel of art, science, literature and business." When he died on 27 October, 1864, the *Builder* in its obituary (page 802) quoted a remark made by one of his former workmen on hearing of his death: "He never grasped for money, but he did for knowledge which he held fast but nevertheless gave away abundantly."

As a monumental sculptor, Smith was influenced by Winckelmann and neo-Hellenism. One of his most beautiful designs, which he repeated several times, is of an Attic plumed helmet in high relief, with a great Homeric shield below it and crossed swords behind. A strictly classical work, without a hint of any emblem of Christianity.

His signed monuments include those to Giles Earle, 1811, and Nathaniel Crichton, 1814, both at Hendon, Middlesex; Robert Cotton, 1821, at Reigate, Surrey; Lt.-Colonel FitzGerald, 1821, Rebecca Phipps, 1830, Henry Moreton-Dyer, 1841, and Countess Beauchamp, 1846, all in Marylebone Parish Church; Elizabeth Peters, 1822, and John Francis, 1824, both at Badby, Northants; Lt-General George Deare, 1823, in St. John's Wood Chapel; Charles Higginson, 1824,

in Madras Cathedral; Margaret Randall, 1824, at Erith, Kent; the Stuckey family, 1824, at Langport, Somerset; the Rev. Charles Tower, 1825, at South Weald, Essex; William Sleigh, 1825, at Stockton, Durham; Georgina Chamier, 1826, at Stoke next Guildford, Surrey; Anthony Parker, 1827, at Churchgate Street, Essex; the Rev. Edward Meyrick, 1839, at Ramsbury, Wilts; Richard Alsager, 1841, at Tooting, Surrey; the Rev. Francis Goode, 1842, in Clapham Parish Church; A. R. Freebairn, 1847, in Highgate Cemetery; John Pereira, 1853, in Kensal Green Cemetery; John Garden, 1855, at Ringsfield, Suffolk; and Henry Hickman, 1855, at Newnham, Northants.

SMITH, CHARLES R.
b. 1798, *d.* 1888

He was the son of James Smith (q.v.) and attended the Royal Academy Schools in 1816, winning the Silver Medal in 1821. From the Society of Arts he had received the Silver Isis Medal for an original model in 1817, and the Gold Isis Medal for a group of two figures four years later; finally, in 1822, he was awarded the Large Gold Medal for his group, "The Fight for the Body of Patroclus."

Smith's chief work was a series of heroic figures of English Kings and Queens and the notable personages of their reigns, which he executed for Sir Robert Newman between 1838 and 1842. These are in Caen stone and still line the long corridor at Mamhead Park, Devon. In 1841 he made for Lord Lansdowne the life-size figures of Michelangelo and Raphael which now stand in niches by the front door of Bowood.

In 1852 he made a pair of bronze stags costing £52 for the front of Pynes, near Exeter, and in the same year he was paid £43 for a fountain for the gardens (Archives, Earl of Iddesleigh). Smith is also responsible for the great fountain of St. George and the Dragon at Holkham, Norfolk.

Smith exhibited at the Royal Academy, 1820–1840, and at the British Institution, 1829–1833, showing busts of Mr. Ricci (1820); Edward Goldsmith (1827); Colonel Dalrymple (1830); George Campbell, of New York (1831); and Winthrop Mackworth Praed (1841). In the latter year he also made a bust of the Rev. Thomas Gisborne for Durham University.

Of his monuments the most important are the life-sized figure of the Rev. Thomas Whitaker, 1822, at Whalley, Yorks, and the semi-recumbent effigy of Jacob Britton, 1839, in Durham Cathedral, both of which are carved in stone. He signs others to Major Sayer, 1823, at Clare, Suffolk; George

Holroyd, 1827, at Reigate, Surrey; James Hudson, 1827, at Newington-by-Sittingbourne, Kent; William Williams, 1828, in Chichester Cathedral; Elizabeth Rose, 1829, at Carshalton, Surrey; the Countess of Clonmell, 1829, in Marylebone Parish Church; Mary Walker, 1830, at Sand Hutton, Yorks; the Rev. Thomas Stephens, 1832, and Jane Farquhar, 1834, both in St. John's Wood Chapel; the Rev. Hugh Bailye, 1833, at Hanbury, Staffs; and Margaret Joliffe, 1839, Worth, Sussex.

SMITH, EDWIN, of Sheffield
b. 1810, *d.* 1889

He was born in Sheffield, the son of an engraver named James Smith. At first he studied sculpture locally, and it was not until 1836 that he went to London to join the Royal Academy Schools on the recommendation of E. Hawkins. About four years later he returned to his native city and set up there as a sculptor.

In 1846 Smith made a model of Jerusalem, on the scale of eighteen inches to a mile, which was exhibited in London and later purchased by Lord Fitzwilliam. He also executed busts for various buildings in Sheffield, including those of James Silk Buckingham (1834), James Montgomery (1843), William Jeffcock (1845), and Samuel Hadfield (1854), all in the Cutlers' Hall. For the Cathedral and the Bluecoat School he made busts of Thomas Sutton, dated 1853 and 1861 respectively, while in the Royal Infirmary is one of the Rev. James Wilkinson (1839), and also one of his few wax medallions, that of William Younge (1837).

Smith's monuments to Charles Favell, 1846, in St. Paul's, Sheffield, and Samuel Gilett, 1862, at Norton, Derbyshire, have medallion portraits. In 1841 he carved the monument in Rotherham Parish Church erected to the memory of "fifty young persons who awfully perished at the launching of a vessel at Masborough, 5 July, 1841." Other signed works commemorate Frederick Wilkinson, 1845, at Newcastle-under-Lyme; William Bagshawe, 1851, at Norton, Derby; Elizabeth Peel, 1851, at Wellow, Notts; and Margaret Coward, 1854, in Rotherham Parish Church.

SMITH, FRANCIS, of Warwick
b. 1672, *d.* 1738

He was born on 4 January, 1671/2, the third son of Francis Smith the Elder, of Warwick, "bricklayer," and with his elder brother William rebuilt the tower and nave of St. Mary's Church,

Warwick, after the fire of 1694. In 1702 he married Anne Lea, a native of the same town.

Smith, who was the master-mason for building the Court House at Warwick in 1724, also designed and built a number of houses in Shropshire, Derbyshire and Northamptonshire. In Worcestershire he worked between 1723 and 1727 for Samuel Sandys as the master-mason (and presumably the architect) of Ombersley Court, and there are a number of receipts for payments made to him for this work among Lord Sandys' Archives. The first, dated 4 December, 1723, reads: "Received then of Samuel Sands, Esq. at several times by ye hands of Mr. Cooks, the sum of four hundred pounds towards building Ombersley by us William Smith and Francis Smith." This is the only receipt signed by both brothers, for William died on 21 August, 1724, and Francis continued the work alone. The house took four years to complete, and receipts still extant show that he received £632 in 1723, £170 in 1724, £570 in 1725, and £260 in 1726, while a final payment of £100 was made in 1730. He was also almost certainly responsible for the chimney-pieces.

In 1732 Smith supplied two chimney-pieces for Lamport Hall, Northamptonshire, one of dove-grey marble and the other "of various coloured marbles with a cornice and two side-scrolls," which cost £38 10s. Four years later he received £87 for the monument in Lamport Church to Sir Justinian Isham, who had died in 1730 (Isham Archives). This is an architectural work with Corinthian pillars supporting an open pediment.

(Archives of houses mentioned in text.)

SMITH, FREDERICK WILLIAM
b. 1797, *d.* 1835

He was born in Pimlico, the second son of Anker Smith the engraver (1759–1819), and joined the Royal Academy Schools in 1815. In the following year he was awarded the Silver Isis Medal by the Society of Arts for an alto-relievo of "The Death of Pallas," and in 1821 received the Academy Gold Medal for a group entitled "Haemon and Antigone." In 1823 Smith showed his bust of Allan Cunningham at the Academy. Flaxman, who was arranging the works of art at Somerset House, said on seeing it that he would "give this bust the best place in the exhibition, for in sentiment it surpasses any head I have seen here for some years."

Smith was the first pupil of Sir Francis Chantrey (q.v.) and later remained with his master as one of his chief assistants. He showed various works at the Royal Academy between

1818 and 1828, including busts of Chantrey, Keats and Brunell; the first-named, dated 1826, is now at Burlington House. The sculptor's death took place at Shrewsbury on 18 January, 1835.

In the church of St. Margaret's, Lothbury, is a marble bust of Alderman Boydell, signed "Banks del. F. Smith sc." The original model for this was exhibited at the Academy by Banks as early as 1791, although Smith did not carve it in marble until 1820. It was then erected in St. Olave's, Jewry, in accordance with instructions given in the will of Mrs. Nichol, Boydell's niece, but when that church was destroyed was removed to St. Margaret's.

(*Athenaeum*, 1835, page 75; *Builder*, 1863, page 112.)

SMITH, GEORGE
fl. 1820–1823

About 1820 he carved "a new entablature, balustrade, bassi-relievi, and statues" for the principal entrance of the Royal Exchange (Elmes' *Metropolitan Improvements*, Vol. I, page 158). Three years later he made the altar-piece for St. Michael's Church, Queenhithe (op. cit.).

SMITH, H. A.
fl. 1827–1844

He exhibited at the Royal Academy, 1827–1844, showing among other works a bust and a wax portrait of Mrs. Marsh.

As Charles Smith (q.v.) and H. A. Smith are noted as living at the same address, they were presumably father and son, in which case the latter was the brother of Raymond Smith (q.v.).

SMITH, JOHN, of Rye
fl. 1815–1852

Smith's tablets are based on minor works by John Bacon the Younger (q.v.), but considering he lived and worked in a small Sussex town they are surprisingly good and well above the average of the contemporary provincial sculptor. The best, all in Sussex, are those to Sarah Woodham, 1822, William Woodham, 1826, and Thomas Langford, 1845, all at Udimore; and to the Rev. John Lettice, 1832, at Peasmarch.

In 1851 Smith and his son built the delightful and romantic Gothic railway station at Battle, in the same county. In 1815 he had made a few chimney-pieces for Battle Abbey (Archives, Mrs. Harbord, of Battle Abbey).

SMITH, JAMES
b. 1775, *d.* 1815

He was a pupil of Locatelli (q.v.) and attended the Royal Academy Schools in 1795, winning the Gold Medal two years later for his group of "Venus Wounded by Diomede." When he left the Schools he was first employed by C. Rossi (q.v.), but later became an assistant of Flaxman (q.v.), with whom he remained for eight years, and for whom he worked upon the figure of Lord Mansfield in Westminster Abbey (*Farington Diary*, Vol. III, page 229). He also assisted Mrs. Damer (q.v.) in many of her works.

Smith's chief work, indeed almost his only important independent work, is the cenotaph of Lord Nelson in the Guildhall, an inferior mass of marble which cost £4,442 7s. 4d. and was unveiled in 1810. A number of models were submitted for this memorial, but the choice ultimately lay between those of C. Rossi and Smith. The final voting at the Common Council was thirty-two for Smith and twenty-seven for Rossi, but the votes were cast not so much on the artistic merits of the two designs, but rather in an attempt to spite Boydell and the Court of Aldermen who favoured Rossi. The latter, however, subsequently acquitted Smith of any part in this affair, telling Farington (op. cit., Vol. III, page 212) that he (Smith) "was a quiet man and not likely to have carried a point by intrigue." Smith later found it difficult to get the Corporation to pay him for the cenotaph, and wrote: "I am drained of all the money I had the honour of last receiving from the Corporation and I am now really left destitute of means to provide for the remaining sums that must be paid by the latter end of the present month" (City Records, MS. 95.2).

In 1813 Mrs. Siddons sat to him for her bust. An advertisement which appeared in the Press at the time stated that "Mr. Smith sculptor having been honoured by Mrs. Siddons with several sittings has just finished a full-sized bust of that inimitable actress," and announced that the bust, "which is the only one of Mrs. Siddons modelled from the life," could be inspected at her house. This bust was exhibited at the Royal Academy and afterwards placed in the Green Room of Drury Lane Theatre. A replica of it was at Guy's Cliff, Warwick. A year later the sculptor exhibited a bust of Robert Southey at the Academy.

Smith signs tablets to the Hon. G. F. Lake, 1808, in Westminster Abbey; to Caroline Shuckburgh, 1809, at Shuckburgh, Warwick; and to Thomas Barwis, 1815, in Wandsworth Parish Church. He also designed the monument of General le Marchant for St. Paul's Cathedral, but died before he could begin to carve it in marble and the work was executed by Rossi, who, however, sent Mrs. Smith a present of £200.

Smith died on 28 April, 1815, at the age of

forty-three, according to his obituary in the *Gentleman's Magazine* (1815, Part I, page 567), but he really seems to have been three years younger, for the Royal Academy Register records that he was born in 1775.

(*Gentleman's Magazine*, 1819, Part I, page 43, and 1839, Part I, page 547.)

SMITH, JOACHIM
fl. 1758–1803

In 1758, when "under twenty-two years of age" and an "untaught designer and modeller," he received a premium of ten guineas from the Society of Arts for a wax portrait. A later note in the records of the same Society states that Smith had "invented a composition in which colours being mixed up to the various tints and shades of human features, was rendered fit, from the fine texture and intimate commixtion of the ingredients to model portraits in miniature to a degree of delicacy," and adds that "the invention is now being carried on in an improved practice by the discoverer in Berners Street, near Middlesex Hospital."

In 1763 Smith made a model, about four inches long, of the infant Prince of Wales, showing "him naked lying on a couch of crimson velvet," according to the *London Magazine* of that year (page 56), which described the work at length and noted that "this amazing piece of art is done with a composition of wax in natural colours." His wax portraits of the Prince and of Frederick, Duke of York (1766), are in the Royal Collection.

In 1773 Smith began to model wax portraits which were copied and produced by Wedgwood and Bentley in white biscuit-ware, and later in white terra-cotta. Among these were likenesses of John Bradley, Wedgwood, Thomas Bentley, Dr. Foster, and Lady Charlotte Finch and her daughter. On 8 February, 1775, he wrote to Wedgwood that "the many accidents I have had with several moulds as well as with some of the models has been attended with a considerable loss of time and deprived me of the possibility of sending you anything for some months past. But there is a difficulty which naturally awaits on everything in its infancy—which with a little indulgence I hope to get the better of" (Wedgwood Archives). His wax portrait of Viscount Fitzmaurice is at Bowood.

Smith became a director of the Free Society of Artists in 1772, and Treasurer four years later. He exhibited wax portraits at the Society of Artists, 1760–1783, and wax portraits and busts at the Royal Academy, 1781–1803. A number of his portraits, including those of the Duke and Duchess of Gloucester, Mrs. Fitzherbert, and Governor and Mrs. Johnstone, were used as models by gem-cutters and cameo-engravers.

SMITH, JOHN, of Darnich

According to the *Gentleman's Magazine* of 1817 (Part I, page 621), he carved the colossal statue of Wallace erected at Dryburgh in that year by Lord Buchan.

SMITH, JOSEPH
fl. 1792–1800

His large monument to Lady Chapman, 1800, at Barkway, Hertfordshire, has as its predominant feature a sarcophagus surmounted by an urn.

SMITH, LEONARD, of York
fl. 1725–1733

In 1725 he and his partner, James Disney, repaired the Barr Wall at York, and in 1729 Smith, on his own account, carved a chimney-piece for York Guildhall (City Archives). In the same year he was appointed master-mason for building the Assembly Rooms, but was discharged for "being negligent" early in 1731.

His successor, however, was even more unsatisfactory, and within the year Smith was reinstated and ordered to set up the portico and to carve its capitals "according to my Lord Burlington's designs," while in 1733 he made the chimney-piece for the "circular room" (Minute-book, York Assembly Rooms).

SMITH, NATHANIEL
b. c. 1741, *d.* after 1800

He was born at Eltham Palace, the son of a Shropshire clothier, and with his playfellow, Joseph Nollekens (q.v.), went to Shipley's Academy in the Strand to study drawing. On 7 August, 1755, he was apprenticed to L. F. Roubiliac (q.v.) and assisted his master on some of the latter's monuments in Westminster Abbey.

Between 1758 and 1762 Smith was awarded six premiums by the Society of Arts. His prize-winning "Model of Animals" (1760) was formerly in the possession of Lord Maynard, while "The Continence of Scipio," which was successful in the following year, was later owned by Lord Rockingham. In 1762 he exhibited at the "Society for the Encouragement of the Arts" a relief of "The Meeting between Coriolanus and Volumnia" (*London Magazine*, 1762, page 174).

After Roubiliac's death Smith became the assistant of J. Wilton (q.v.) and carved the figures on the latter's cenotaph of General Wolfe in

Westminster Abbey, a work which took him three years to complete, according to J. T. Smith, the sculptor's son (*Nollekens and His Times*, Vol. II, page 110). The author also asserts that his father executed a great deal of the sculpture on Somerset House for which Wilton received the money.

About 1788 the elder Smith became the principal assistant of Nollekens, and therefore spent most of his life working for other sculptors. Apparently his only independent works were the heads of three "River Gods" (designed by Cipriani) for Somerset House, and the signed monument to Sir Merrik Burrell, 1787, with its fine medallion portrait, at West Grinstead, Sussex.

Smith exhibited at the Society of Free Artists, 1761–1763. His terra-cotta model for a statue of the Earl of Chatham was Lot 1097 in Mr. Peter Norton's sale at Christie's in 1869.

Smith's wife, who was a Miss Tarr and a Quakeress, died in 1779.

(*Gentleman's Magazine*, 1833, Part I, page 641; authorities cited in text.)

SMITH, RAYMOND
fl. 1842–1876

He is presumably the son of Charles Smith (q.v.), and carried on his father's work, completing the series of statues for Mamhead.

In 1842 he carved a figure of "A Falconer" for Mr. Bulteel of Flete, and this, together with a statue of Raphael, he exhibited in Westminster Hall two years later. (In the catalogue of the exhibition the Raphael is attributed to him, although by a coincidence Charles Smith had executed a similar figure for Lord Lansdowne in 1841.) Both works were well received by the critics, the *Literary Gazette* considering that the "Falconer" was "talented and full of pictorial character," while the *Art Union* thought that the Raphael had "much merit." In 1851 the sculptor showed a statue of Lady Danberry at the Great Exhibition.

In 1852 Smith modelled reliefs of "Peace" and "War" for Bylaugh Hall, Norfolk (*Builder*, 1852, page 517), and in the same year made two large groups for Eaton Hall, one showing the "Gros Veneur," or head-huntsman, of the Norman Duke seated on horseback and accompanied by four dogs, the other representing the "Death of the Stag." For the garden he made statues of Odo, Bishop of Bayeux, Sir Robert de Grosvenor, Engulphus de Aquila and Joan of Eaton (*Builder*, 1852, page 595), and in 1856 carved a large fountain in Portland stone with a group of "St. George and the Dragon." A "large column of water" was apparently thrown up by the dragon,

which was "in the agonies of death" (*Art Journal*, 1856, page 383). About 1854 he had made two Egyptian lions, also in Portland stone, for the terrace of Sir Augustus Clifford's house, Westfield, Isle of Wight (*Description of Westfield*, privately printed, 1862). In 1865 he executed the figures of "The Principal Races of the Indian Empire" for the façade of the India Office.

Smith also made a number of monuments, the most important being the recumbent figure of Grace Darling, which was placed over her grave at Bamburgh, Northumberland, in 1846, and that to Winthrop Mackworth Praed (*d.* 1839) in Kensal Green Cemetery, which has a medallion portrait. Tablets signed by him include those to the Rev. Baptist Turner, 1836, at Denton, Lincs; William St. Croix, 1842, in the Cloisters of St. George's Chapel, Windsor; Countess Cadogan, 1845, in St. Luke's, Chelsea; Henry Baring, 1848, at Felbrigg, Norfolk; and Thomas Tryon, 1872, at Bulwich, Northants.

Graves, in his *Exhibitors at the Royal Academy*, includes, not only a "Raymond Smith," but a "C. Raymond Smith." This, however, seems incorrect and I have therefore attributed all exhibited works to Raymond.

(Authorities cited in text.)

SMITH, ROBERT ORMEROD
b. 1819

He attended the Royal Academy Schools in 1838, but afterwards lived chiefly in Rome, whence he sent a bust of Theophilus Smith to the Academy in 1855. His statue of "Rebekah" (then in the possession of T. Agnew, Esq.) was shown at the Exhibition of Art Treasures of the United Kingdom held in Manchester in 1857.

SMITH, THOMAS
b. 1800

Son of James Smith (q.v.), and younger brother of Charles R. Smith (q.v.), he attended the Royal Academy Schools in 1817 and won a large Silver Medal in 1822 from the Society of Arts for a group entitled "Oedipus and Antigone." In 1830 he was appointed "Modeller of Wax Medallic Portraits" to William IV.

Smith, who exhibited at the Academy, 1827–1852, and at the British Institution, 1829–1831, also had a considerable practice as a monumental sculptor. His best works are the tablets to Robert Bevan, 1837, at Monmouth, and Eliza Russell, 1838, at North Ockendon, Essex, both of which have medallion portraits. His monuments to Sir Thomas Salusbury, 1835, at Great Offley, Herts, and to Sir Edward Banks, 1835, at Chipstead,

Surrey, have busts, while the latter also has reliefs of Waterloo, Southwark and London Bridges, all built by Banks. Other monuments executed by Smith are those to Lady Elizabeth Russell, 1828, at North Ockendon, Essex; Gilbert Jolliffe, 1833 (with a replica at Merstham, Surrey), at Worth, Sussex; Whitlock Nicholl, 1838, in Wimbledon Parish Church; and Nicholas Mori, 1839, in Kensal Green Cemetery.

SMITH, W.

A "W. Smith" was the master-mason for building St. George's Church, Liverpool, in 1715 (City Archives).

SMITH, W.

Probably a Durham artist, he signs the altar-tomb with a life-size recumbent figure of Michael Matthen, 1689, at Whitburn, in that county. The figure is carved in stone and shows Matthen in contemporary costume with a book in his hand.

SMITH, WILLIAM, of Warwick
b. 1705, *d.* 1747

Son of Francis Smith, of Warwick (q.v.), he built the Georgian front of Thame Park, and in 1737 was appointed joint mason with William Townesend (q.v.) for building the Radcliffe Library, Oxford.

In 1737 he also made a dove-grey marble chimney-piece for Lamport Hall, Northants (Isham Archives).

SMITH, WILLIAM
b. 1808

He attended the Royal Academy Schools in 1826 on the recommendation of J. Wood, winning Silver Medals in the following year and again in 1830. His bust of Sir Francis Chantrey (1826) is at Burlington House.

SMITH, WILLIAM, and ELSWORTH, JOHN, of York
fl. 1703–1719

They were the principal masons for building Castle Howard from 1703 onwards, receiving as much as £4,034 in 1705. Another partner was Major or Mauger Smith, perhaps the son of William Smith, who, by 1710, is not mentioned in the bills. The younger Smith and Elsworth were also responsible for a good deal of carved stone-work, including in 1715 vases for the mulberry garden, for the gateway of the Back Court and for those on the "circular corridor." They were also paid for "angular" vases for the North Wing (Castle Howard Archives).

SMITH, WILLIAM

He may be the William Smith, son of Samuel Smith, of Rochester, who was apprenticed in 1765 to Thomas Vidgeon. Three years later he was "by order of the Lord Mayor and Court of Aldermen discharged from the said Thomas Vidgeon," who had "neglected to enroll him," and was apprenticed instead to George Freshwater. Smith's new master, however, "turned him out of his service and refused to receive him therein again," so that he had finally to finish his apprenticeship with John Wynne (Court Book, Masons' Company).

A William Smith signs the large architectural tablet with a broken pediment and flaming lamps to Ralph Manning (*d.* 1769), at Westerham, Kent.

SMITH, WILLIAM
b. c. 1758

Son of John Smith, of Dunchurch, Warwick, he was apprenticed to Thomas Beard (q.v.) in 1772 and became free of the Masons' Company in 1785. His yard was in Jermyn Street, and he signs a very pretty tablet to Matthew Armstrong, 1801, at St. Magnus, London Bridge.

SMOUT, or SMOOTE, JOHN
fl. 1704–1715

He was chiefly a carver of marble chimney-pieces, and in 1704 made five for the rooms in the west front at Chatsworth (Archives, Duke of Devonshire). About 1706 he became master-mason to the Royal Palaces and supplied a marble and Portland-stone chimney-piece for Whitehall and another in Reigate and Portland stone for the Palace of Westminster (P.R.O., E.351/3312). Smout provided other chimney-pieces for the Tower of London and Denmark House in 1709, and for St. James's Palace in 1710. In the latter year he also made two veined-marble tables for the Queen's closet at Newmarket Palace, and in 1715 the "great marble bason" in Bushy Park (P.R.O., A.O.1.2248/149).

In 1708 he built a "New Summerhouse at the lower end of the Garden" at Kensington Palace. This, according to the Wren Society's Publications (Vol. VII, page 189), is probably the famous alcove now removed to the Fountain Garden at the head of the Serpentine.

In 1712 he was paid for Purbeck paving at the lodging of Rt. Hon. Thos. Coke, Vice-Chamberlain to Queen Anne at St. James's Palace (Archives, Marquis of Lothian).

SMYTHE, JAMES,
of Woodbridge
b. 1771, *d.* 1836

He signs a pretty architectural tablet, with an urn and cockle-shells to left and right, at Grundis-burgh, Suffolk, to John Higgs, 1816. Smythe's widow, Ann, died a few weeks after her husband.

SOANES, JOSEPH

He was an assistant of J. F. Moore (q.v.) and in 1764 made marble chimney-pieces for Audley End (Essex Record Office, D./DBY. 243).

SOWARD, JOHN
fl. 1802–1838

He was possibly a son of George Soward, who, according to the Westminster Poll Book of 1748, had a mason's yard in Chapel Street and who carried out considerable repairs to St. Anne's, Soho, in 1761 (Westminster Public Library, A.2312).

John Soward's yard was in Tottenham Court Road. His monuments and tablets are not very exciting, his best works being the large altar-tomb of Eliza Harris, 1802, in Hillingdon churchyard, Middlesex, and the tablet to Lady Sondes, 1818, at Norton, Kent, which has a well-carved relief of two angels guiding the deceased to heaven. Other tablets executed by him include those to Shadrach Brise, 1810, at Cavendish, Suffolk; the Rev. Joseph Jefferson, 1821, at Witham, Essex; Charlotte Prendergrass, 1821, in St. Giles-in-the-Fields; James Spawforth, 1824, at Horbury, Yorks; Mrs. Pedley, 1827, at Everton, Beds; Anne Burley, 1831, at Basing, Hants; Miss Livermore, 1831, in Hackney Parish Church; and James Sparrow, 1838, at Gosfield, Essex, which is signed "J. Soward and Son."

Soward was also a herald-painter and in 1831 executed the two hatchments of the 4th Earl of Darnley, one for Cobham Hall and the other for his London house (Archives, Earl of Darnley).

SPANG, MICHAEL HENRY
d. 1762

He was a native of Denmark who came over to England about 1756, and two years later received a premium of thirty guineas for modelling the "seal of the Society of Arts used for letters" from a design by Cipriani.

In 1759 Spang made the chimney-pieces for the four principal rooms at Kedleston at a total cost of £990 (Kedleston Archives). In 1760 he carved the dolphins and prows of ships on the stone screen of the Whitehall entrance to the Admiralty, and in the same year executed three statues for the front of Lord Spencer's house in St. James's Park (Timbs's *Curiosities of London*).

His monument to James Thomson, who died in 1748, was erected in Westminster Abbey about 1760. It has a life-size figure of Thomson and enchanting reliefs of the four seasons, com-memorating his most famous poem.

Spang exhibited at the Society of Artists, 1760–1762. His bronzed terra-cotta statuette of Hogarth is in the Victoria and Albert Museum, and at the sale of the effects of G. M. Moser, R.A., held on 21 May, 1783, Lot 19 was "Spang's anatomy figure in bronze, restored by Mr. Moser."

The sculptor left little or no money at his death. A sale of his belongings was held at Little Stanhope Street on 21 December, 1762. Among the lots were various models and a marble bust. In 1768 the Society of Artists had to provide eleven guineas in order to apprentice his son, Henry, to a peruke-maker (Archives, Society of Artists). Spang's widow, Mary, married a Mr. Brown shortly after the death of her first husband, but on the recommendation of Sir William Chambers drew a pension from the Royal Academy from 1769 until her death in 1785 (Royal Academy Archives).

(Archives, Society of Arts; authorities cited in text.)

SPANGEN, RICHARD,
of Camberwell

In the writer's possession is a letter from Spangen, dated 19 December, 1749, addressed to a Mr. Hooper of Hailsham, Sussex, and enclosing three drawings for monumental tablets.

Spangen writes that "the enclosed sketches I have made according to your direction, the expense will be about what you mention; they are drawn to a small scale but when executed will be about 8 ft. high and breadth proportionate. Materials to be of the best white and veined and statuary marble," he continues, "the inscription to be engraved and painted black, and the coat of arms in proper colours and executed in a work-manlike manner." I do not know if Mr. Hooper ever ordered one of these monuments, but there is certainly no sign of any work resembling them in Hailsham Church today.

He may be the same as the "Mr. Spangor" who made the monument of Lord Trevor at Bromham, Beds, in 1732. The Rev. Benjamin Rogers, whose diary is quoted in Harvey's *Hundred of Willey*, has "Some of the marble cost Mr. Spangor the Statuary in the block in Italy 18s. per foot, which stood him in 26s. per foot when brought to London, this was black with yellow veins."

SPARROW, GEORGE,
of Stamford
fl. 1782–1811

Sparrow, who was possibly a son of James Sparrow (q.v.), signs tablets to Thomas Smith, 1782, and Mrs. Thompson, 1805, both in St. George's, Stamford; Henry Sheild, 1792, at Preston, Rutland; Mary Arundell, 1802, at Irnham, Lincs; and George Hill, 1808, at Rothwell, Northants. His best monuments, however, are both at Rockingham, Northamptonshire, and commemorate the first and second Lords Sondes, who died in 1795 and 1806 respectively.

SPARROW, JAMES, of Stamford
b. c. 1716

According to the town archives, he was born about 1716, at Radcliffe-on-Trent. He signs slate headstones to Ann Hall, 1744, Granby, Notts, and to John and Mary Langston, 1753, in Grantham churchyard, Lincolnshire; and to Henry Green, 1776, at Flintham, Nottinghamshire.

SPENCE, BENJAMIN EDWARD
b. 1822, *d.* 1866

He was born in Liverpool, the son of William Spence (q.v.), and in 1846 was awarded the Heywood Silver Medal by the Royal Manchester Institution for his model of "The Death of the Duke of York at Agincourt." Two years previously he had exhibited this work at Westminster Hall, when the *Builder* described it as an "exquisite specimen of artistic feeling." The *Literary Gazette*, on the other hand, considered it "very laboured" and also complained that "the figure of the Duke of York is naked."

Spence's father was an old friend and fellow-student of John Gibson (q.v.), who in 1846 persuaded him to send his son to Italy. Young Spence accordingly went to Rome, where he entered the studio of R. J. Wyatt (q.v.), and also received considerable help from Gibson himself. It was Spence who later carved, just before his own death, the monument erected over Gibson's grave in the Protestant cemetery in Rome.

When Wyatt died Spence completed his unfinished works and also took over the studio, indeed he spent nearly all his working life in Italy, only going to England about once a year to visit the Royal Academy Exhibition. He exhibited at the Academy, 1849–1866.

Spence died on 21 October, 1866, while on a visit to Leghorn. The *Art Journal* of the same year (page 364) said in its obituary that "Mr. Spence, though not a great sculptor attained a highly honourable position among the artists of our time. His works are characterized by great purity of feeling and general elegance of expression rather than by much originality of design or vigorous treatment."

Spence signs the monument of Lieutenant James Marshall, 1855, in Leeds Parish Church. He also made a few busts, including those of Mr. and Mrs. Brassey which were formerly at Normanhurst Court, Sussex. At the Exhibition of Art Treasures of the United Kingdom, held at Manchester in 1857, Spence's statue of "The Favourite" was lent by H. N. Sandbach and "Psyche" by W. Jackson. Other works of his in the exhibition were the four figures of "The Seasons" and "Girl at the Fountain," the property of John Pender and Thomas Critchley respectively.

In 1870 Messrs. Christie held a sale in London of works from Spence's studio in Rome. The *Art Journal* (1870, page 221), reporting the results, said that "the sale only confirms what we have frequently had occasion to remark, that there is little or no taste for, and less desire to acquire, ideal sculpture on the part of our patrons in art. Portraits, statues and busts are as plentiful as blackberries, they gratify one's vanity, or may proclaim our good deeds, and English sculptors manage to live by them, but imaginative works are but little more than drugs in the market. We feel ashamed to note down the prices paid for Spence's examples." The chief works sold (the names of the buyers and the prices paid being in brackets) were "Sabrina" (Bowring, 210 guineas); "Oberon and Titania" and "Highland Mary" (Vokins, 200 and 121 guineas respectively); and "Flora Macdonald" and "Psyche" (Agnew, 173 guineas for the two). A total sum of £1,425 was paid for nineteen works. On 10 February, 1894, at the R. C. Naylor sale at Christie's, "Venus and Cupid" by Spence fetched 300 guineas.

(*Art Journal*, 1849, page 95; Graham's *British Literature and Art*, page 457; authorities cited in text.)

STATUES, etc.

1849	Lavinia	For Mr. Holme, of Liverpool
1850	Ophelia	For Thomas Brassey, M.P.
1853	Innocence	Illustrated *Art Journal*, 1853
1854	Highland Mary	Osborne (replica Sefton Park, Liverpool)
1854	Liverpool	Formerly Crystal Palace
1855	Venus and Cupid	Formerly Hooton Hall, Cheshire

1856	Spring	Illustrated *Art Journal*, 1856
1856	Archdeacon Brooks	St. George's Hall, Liverpool
1860	Rebecca at the Well	Walker Art Gallery, Liverpool
1862	The Finding of Moses	International Exhibition, 1862 (purchased by J. Naylor, of Liverpool)
1862	Jeanie Deans before Queen Caroline	International Exhibition, 1862
1863	The Angel's Whisper	For James Smith, of Liverpool
1863	The Lady of the Lake	Balmoral
1865	Marine Venus	Hereford Town Hall
?	Parting of Hector and Andromache	Formerly Normanhurst Court, Sussex
?	Flora Macdonald	Stanley Park, Liverpool

SPENCE, WILLIAM
b. 1793, *d.* 1849

He was born in Chester in 1793 and showed artistic talent at an early age. He later went to Liverpool to study under Mr. Pether, a woodcarver and teacher of drawing, and while he was there formed a friendship with John Gibson (q.v.), who was then working for the firm of Franceys (q.v.). Gibson persuaded his employers to agree to give Spence a trial, his confidence in his friend soon being justified, for the young man quickly distinguished himself both as a modeller and designer.

Spence exhibited "Young Hymen" at the Liverpool Academy in 1812 and "Cupid Riding on a Dolphin" and a bust of William Roscoe in the following year. The bust attracted considerable attention and the sitter and his friends were anxious to send the sculptor to Rome, but Spence preferred to remain in Liverpool with Messrs. Franceys. He later became a partner in the firm and also held the appointment of Professor of Drawing at the Liverpool Academy for many years.

Spence exhibited at the Royal Academy, 1821–1844, at Manchester, where he showed figures of "A Greek Soldier" and "Pegasus" in 1832, and at the Liverpool Academy from 1812 until the year of his death. Here (besides those already mentioned) his works included a statue of William Roscoe (1832) and busts of Thomas Leyland (1822), John Gladstone (1824); Benjamin Heywood (1824); Mr. Secretary Canning (1824); William Hope (1827); John Foster (1827); George Canning (1828)—called "stiff and priggish" by the *Saturday Advertiser*; J. B. Hollinshead (1828); Robert Preston (1834); Lord Sandon (1836); and

Sir Walter Scott (1837). His busts of Foster and George Canning are now in the Walker Art Gallery, Liverpool. In 1844 he sent his "Caractacus Before Claudius Caesar" to the exhibition held in Westminster Hall. The *Literary Gazette* described this work as "a group of idiotic beggars," although the *Builder* thought it "fine."

One of Spence's patrons was Benjamin Hicks, of Mytton Hall, Yorkshire, who commissioned from him a portrait-bust, medallions of Scott, Shakespeare and Roscoe, and a delightful marble relief of three Cupids, all of which are illustrated in the privately printed *Catalogue of Mytton Hall* (1893).

As a monumental sculptor Spence is dull, his best monuments being those to the Rev. James Archer, 1832, at Middleton, Lancs, with a life-size figure of "Faith," and to John Gore, 1830, in St. James's Cemetery Chapel, Liverpool, which has a well-carved relief. Tablets executed by him include those to Rachel Roe, 1819, in Christ Church, Macclesfield; Edward Rowland, 1828, at Ruabon, Denbigh; Mary Williams, 1829, at Corwen, Denbigh; Margarrette Golightly, 1831, and Anne Goodwin, 1842, both at Gresford, Denbigh; John and Henry Fletcher, 1834, at Overton, Flint; Michael Heathcote, 1835, at Ormskirk, Lancs; Catherine Shufflebotham, 1836, at Betley, Staffs; Harriet Vyse, 1836, at Holmes Chapel, Cheshire; Sarah Vawdrey, 1837, at Middlewych, Cheshire; Margaret Hoskins, 1838, Melling, Lancs; Elizabeth Latham, 1839, at Sandbach, Cheshire; Thomas Parker, 1842, at Colne, Lancs; Milborne Tynte, 1845, at Goathurst, Somerset; and Henry Swetenham, Astbury, Cheshire. The monument of Joseph Bradbury, 1845, in Huddersfield Parish Church, is signed "Spence and Sons."

(*Gentleman's Magazine*, 1849, Part II, page 435; *Art Journal*, 1849, page 75.)

SPENCER, EDWARD, and RICHARD, of Chester
fl. 1775–1800

The Spencers of Chester were a family of masons, the first being Richard, whose son and apprentice, Thomas, became a Freeman in 1738–1739. On 3 September, 1770, and 7 April, 1784, respectively, Edward and Richard, sons of Thomas, in their turn became Freemen of Chester (Archives, Mason's Company of Chester).

Their monuments and tablets are typical of the period, the "Adam" details being carried out in coloured marbles. The best are those to Samuel Manning, 1775, at Wrenbury, Staffs; Priscilla Laurence, 1788, in St. Mary's, Chester; Sidney

Lee, 1788, in St. John's, Chester; the Spencer family, 1790, in Chester Cathedral; and Sir Robert Townshend, 1790, at Gresford, Denbigh.

SPILL, THOMAS

In 1697 he carved a marble chimney-piece for Kensington Palace (P.R.O., E.351/3466).

SPILLER, JOHN
b. 1763, *d.* 1794

Spiller was a brother of James Spiller the architect, and was born on 23 December, 1763. He attended the Royal Academy Schools in 1781 and later became a pupil of J. Bacon, R.A. (q.v.).

His best-known work was the statue of Charles II, executed in 1793, which occupied the centre of the Piazza of the Royal Exchange and escaped the fire of 1838. In 1792 he made two chimney-pieces for the Earl of Hardwicke at Wimpole Hall, one of "enriched veined marble, £40," and the other "of enriched statuary marble, £35" (bills in private possession). He also carved the monument of Phillip Chauncy, erected in the Mercers' Hall in 1791 (*Gentleman's Magazine*, 1794, page 592).

He died at Croydon 17 May, 1794 of consumption, his wife, who is said to have been very beautiful, dying of the same disease a few months later. The elder Disraeli said of him that "the energy of his labour and the strong excitement of his feelings had already made fatal inroads on his constitution and he only lived to finish his statue of Charles II."

(Malcom's *Londonium Redivivum*, Vol. II, page 442; *Builder*, 1868, page 415.)

SPILLER, ROBERT
fl. 1794–1827

A younger brother of John Spiller (q.v.), he was much employed by various architects for chimney-pieces and ornamental details. Under Soane he made a chimney-piece for Mr. Thomas Lewis's house at Palmer's Green in 1794; one for Lord Hardwicke at Wimpole in 1796; and three others in marble for the Bank of England in 1799, at a cost of £102. He also made a marble chimney-piece costing £46 for Lord Eliot's house at Down Ampney in the same year, while in 1801 he supplied one at £42 6s. 6d. for Albury House, Surrey, which was then being built by Soane for Mr. Samuel Thornton.

In 1803 Spiller built the Portland-stone obelisk at Reading for Mr. Edward Simeon, receiving £310 for the work, while in the same year Mr. Cartwright paid him £109 for chimney-pieces at Aynho Park. Other chimney-pieces made by him were for Bushy Park and for Lord Le Despencer's London house.

When Dance rebuilt the Royal College of Surgeons in 1807, Spiller was the master-mason and was also responsible for all the carved work and the chimney-pieces. Ten years later he made the "termes" for the busts of Sir E. Home and Sir W. Blizard for the same building, and finally in 1827 received £58 19s. 6d. for the chimney-piece in the library. He also worked as Dance's master-mason during the rebuilding of Ashburnham Place, Sussex, 1815–1818, besides providing some of the smaller chimney-pieces.

(Soane's Notebooks, Soane Museum; Archives of the Royal College of Surgeons; Archives at Ashburnham Place.)

SPITTLE, —

Probably a Leicester statuary, he signs a tablet at Hungerton, in that county, to John Goodhall, 1828.

SPRATT, WILLIAM
b. c. 1709

Son of William Spratt of Stepney, Middlesex, he was apprenticed to Thomas Stayner (q.v.) in 1723, becoming free in 1730.

He signs the fine architectural monument to Mrs. Mary Dawkins, 1741, at South Mimms Herts.

SPRINGALL, ROBERT
of Bletchington
b. 1625

In a lawsuit between Thomas Wood (q.v.) and Richard Frogley, a carpenter, in 1681, Springall gave evidence. He said that he was "fifty-six years old; that he had worked as a master workman in Windsor Castle where for twenty weeks he had the command over twenty workmen; that he had worked for the late Duke of Richmond and now for the Lord Privy Seal at Bletchington, and likewise for Esquire Coghill there, for Chancellor Hyde at Cornbury, for Sir Thomas Chamberlaine at Northbrooke, Esquire Dormer at Rowsam, and for Mr. Carter at Brill" (Oxford, Vice-Chancellor's Archives, 1681, Mich.).

SQUIRE, RICHARD,
of Worcester
b. 1700, *d.* 1786

In 1724 he was paid for repairing the statue of King Charles I on the front of the Worcester Guildhall (City Archives). In 1758 he made a marble table and a freestone font for the church at Upton-on-Severn (Churchwardens' accounts). Squire was one of the best of the Worcestershire statuaries. His monuments, which are architectural in design, are often carried out in coloured marbles with well-designed and cut detail. He died on 1 August, 1786, and was buried in the aisle of All Saints' Church, Worcester, where his epitaph on a ledger of touch commemorates "Richard Squire, one of the master builders of this church, which with many memorial works here and throughout this county will be a lasting monument of his skill and ability."

Squire's son, Robert, was apprenticed to him in 1750. His monuments in Worcestershire include those to Elizabeth Cave, 1728, at Evesham, and Benjamin Scarlett, 1739, at Hampton; Christianus Kendrick, 1746, at Eckington; Thomas Hopwood, 1758, in St. Andrew's, Droitwich; Josiah Weston, 1765, at Powick; William Amphlett, 1768, at Hadzor; and Dorothy Holbeche, 1771, at Dodderhill. In Worcester itself his works include monuments to James Smyth (1740), Edward Lowbridge (1742), and C. Draper (1765), all in All Saints' Church; and Henry Hope (1753), in St. Swithun's. In All Saints' there is also an inscription concerning Queen Anne's Bounty, executed by Squire in 1762, while his monuments outside the county include those to John Middlemore, c. 1740, at King's Norton, Warwick; the Mann family, 1749, in Tewkesbury Abbey, Glos; and Thomas Morres, 1752, at Burford, Salop.

STAFFORD, FRANCIS,
of Norwich
fl. 1740–1744

His architectural monuments are well carved, the most interesting being to Mrs. Hodgson, 1743, at Dersingham, Norfolk, which has a central Corinthian column standing in front of a pyramid.

Other works signed by Stafford in the same county commemorate John Baron, 1739, at Saxlingham Nethergate; Robert Wiggett, c. 1740, at Guist; Ann Holmes, 1740, at Wymondham; and T. Gurdon, 1744, at Cranworth.

STAFFORD, T., of Norwich
b. 1728, *d.* 1796

He was the son of Francis Stafford (q.v.), and signs tablets in Norfolk to Fysher Colman, 1758, at Great Ellingham; Hannah Curteis, 1760, at Aylsham; and Robert Cremer, 1778, at Wymondham.

Stafford later went into partnership with G. Athow (q.v.), and together they sign tablets in the same county to Abraham Robertson, 1777, in St. Swithun's, Norwich; Bartholomew Dey, 1780, at Wicklewood; Robert Plumptre, 1788, in Norwich

Cathedral; and William Fell, 1795, at Horsham St. Faith.

STAIG, —, of London
fl. 1826–1830

Staig, whose yard was in the Old Kent Road, signs the neo-Hellenic monument with a relief of a mourning angel to Sarah Drew, 1826, in Streatham Parish Church, and a wall-tablet to Beriah Drew, 1829, in Bermondsey Parish Church.

STAINES, WILLIAM, SIR
b. 1725, *d.* 1807

In 1774, when "a stone-mason and pavior," he designed and built the church of St. Alphage, Cripplegate, a work for which he received £1,350, "the parish deeming the expense of an architect unnecessary" (Allen's *History of London*, Vol. III, page 473).

Staines, who was an Alderman of the City of London (1793–1807), is described in the directory of 1787 as "statuary of 23 Barbiccan." He was also mason to the Royal Exchange, receiving nearly £1,700 between 1768 and 1772. In 1784 he rebuilt the Barbican Chapel, Cripplegate. Staines died 10 September, 1807.

STANBOROUGH, WILLIAM
d. 1695

Stanborough, who carved the font of St. Christopher le Stocks in 1673, died in 1695 and is buried in the north aisle of St. Mary's, Whitechapel (*Wren Society*, Vol. XIX, page 15; Seymour's *London*, Vol. II, page 708).

STANLEY, CHARLES
b. 1703, *d.* 1761

Simon Carl Stanley, to give him his baptismal name, was born in Copenhagen of British parents on 12 December, 1703, and in 1718 he was apprenticed to Sturmberg, the Danish stuccoist.

He came to England in 1727, and during the time he spent in England executed two most important monuments. The first of these, to Thomas Maynard, 1742, at Hoxne, Suffolk, is nearly 18 ft. high, with a life-size statue of Maynard in Roman dress, his left arm resting on an urn, while his right hand holds a book. The base of the pedestal which supports the urn is decorated with charming reliefs of "Justice," "Charity," "Faith," etc.

Stanley's second work, the huge monument commemorating Lord Maynard and his ancestors, at Little Easton, Essex, is on an even grander scale and was erected in 1745. This shows Lord

Maynard in semi-Roman dress leaning upon an urn, while around him are busts and medallions of his family and forebears; on the base of the monument is a large relief.

While in England Stanley also worked as a decorator in plaster at Compton Place in Sussex, Langley Park in Norfolk, and other houses, but his work in this capacity is, of course, outside the scope of this book. In the year that his second monument was finished he was invited by Frederick V to return to Denmark as court sculptor, a post he held until his death on 17 February, 1761.

Stanley was an artist of varied talent, for while in Denmark he designed not only monuments and garden statues, but ceilings, stoves, picture-frames and china. He was also well-read in history, translated various books (which he illustrated himself) and was keenly interested in music.

His first wife, an Englishwoman named Anna Allen, whom he married in 1730, died five years later, and in 1737 he married Magdalene Margrethe Lindemann, who survived him, dying in 1763. His son by his second wife, Carl Frederick Stanley, was born in Westminster in 1738 and returned to Denmark with his father. He adopted sculpture as a profession, studying in Copenhagen, Paris and Rome, and in 1777 adopted Danish nationality and was elected a member of the Royal Danish Academy. He died in Copenhagen in 1813.

(Information from Director, Frederiksborg Castle, Denmark.)

STANLEY, ROWLES

He signs the monument of William Knight, 1786, at Stroud, Glos. This is a very pretty work, which takes the form of a medallion-portrait hanging against a pyramid.

STANTON, EDWARD
b. 1681, d. 1734

He and his brother Thomas were apprenticed to their father, William Stanton (q.v.), and were admitted by patrimony to the Masons' Company in 1702. During the next few years Edward made several chimney-pieces for Aynho Park, Northamptonshire, including in 1704 one for "ye south-west chamber," and in 1707 another for "ye closet over ye white parlour" (Cartwright Archives). In the following year he received £13 for a marble chimney-piece for an unidentified room in the same house. He made a chimney-piece for Knowsley, Lancashire, in 1724 (Derby Archives).

In 1707 Stanton had also been working at the Temple Church, receiving £127 (Inderwick's

Inner Temple Records, Vol. III, page 406), and in 1709 he was employed by Sir Nicholas Shireburn at Stonyhurst, where he carved "ye crest at ye head of ye hall stairs" for £6, and his patron's arms on the almshouses at Cartington for a further £10 (Stonyhurst College Archives). In 1711 he was paid £273 for work he had carried out at the Guildhall and £520 for building "Three Cranes stairs" (City Cash Account 1/27). In 1721 he was working at Leicester House, London (Archives, Lord De L'Isle, while between 1726 and 1730 he was the mason responsible for building the New Dormitory at Westminster School (*Wren Society*, Vol. XI, page 43).

In 1720 Stanton was appointed Mason to Westminster Abbey, a post he held until his death. His chief work as Abbey Mason was rebuilding the north front. Indeed, between 1720 and 1723 he received no less than £6,038. He was responsible for all the carved stonework, including the Capitals, Pinnacles, Cherubim Heads, etc., and in 1722 he was paid for carving "The College Arms" and "Two Portcullis and Chains." On 11 October, 1722, Stanton acquainted the sub-commissioners "That He had entered into an Agreement in writing with the Lord Bishop of Rochester for doing repairs of the Church and had given a bond in penalty of £2,000" (Westminster Abbey Archives).

Stanton was Warden of the Masons' Company in 1713 and 1716, and Master in 1719. He married three times, his first wife being a daughter of Samuel Fulkes (q.v.), and his third the daughter of Robert Churchill, mason and bricklayer. He died in 1734, and in his will (proved on 20 June of the same year) desired to be buried "by daylight in the north churchyard of St. Andrew's, Holborn, towards the enginehouse door."

He was one of the most prolific of English statuaries, as can be seen from the long list of works (ranging from life-sized effigies to cartouche tablets and ledgers) which he gave his friend Le Neve for the latter's "Monumenta Anglicana."

Stanton's brother Thomas spent nearly all his life in Italy. In 1734 he was living at Leghorn and in 1742 was removed from his post of Assistant to the Masons' Company, "having been one of the Court of Assistants of the Company for forty years and has very seldom attended them, and in the last twelve years has not been to any" (Archives, Masons' Company). Another brother, William, was made Beadle of the Company and died in 1753, when his widow was granted a pension.

Thomas's son, another Edward Stanton who had become a linen-draper in Fleet Street at the Golden Key, petitioned the Company in 1755 for the return of his Livery fine of £5, "on account of his necessities and indigent circumstances," a request which was refused. A year later he lodged a similar petition, but this was again turned down. Another member of the family, also William, had a mason's yard "near Bloomsbury Church" in 1763, while a "Mrs. Stanton, widow," was a pensioner of the Company until her death in 1785. (Esdaile, *Archaeological Journal*, Vol. LXXXV, pages 149–169; Esdaile, *Antiquaries' Journal*, Vol. XXII; authorities cited in text.)

MONUMENTS

1699	Mitton, Yorks	Richard and Isabel Shireburn
1703	Barkway, Herts	Mary Chester
1704	Kelvedon, Essex	Sir Anthony Abdy
1704	Warminghurst, Sussex	Ann Barnham
1705	Strensham, Worcs	Sir Francis Russell
1705	Blunham, Beds	Thomas Bromsal
1705	Wisbech, Cambs	Thomas Edwards
1705	Lichfield (Cathedral)	John Hutchinson
1705	Knebworth, Herts	Sir William Lytton
1706	Bishop's Tachbrook, Warwick	Lady Wagstaffe
1706	Faringdon, Berks	Jane Pye
1706	Ardeley, Herts	Henry Chauncey
1706	Grantham, Lincs	William Bury
1707	Braughing, Herts	Sir Thomas Brograve (ledger)
1707	Wooton, Beds	Sir Philip Monoux
1707	Knebworth, Herts	Sir George Strode
1707	Winwick, Northants	Sir William Craven (ledger)
1707	Charterhouse Chapel	James Sidgrave (ledger)
1707	Chawton, Hants	William Fisher
1707	Barkway, Herts	Rev. Thomas Smoult
1707	Ely (Cathedral)	Bishop Patrick
1708	Bishop's Tachbrook, Warwick	Sir Thomas Wagstaffe
1708	Twickenham (All Hallows')	Edward Tyson
1709	Sutton, Beds	Sir John Burgoyne
1710	Edmondthorpe, Leics	Lady Smith
1710	West Ham (Parish Church)	The Buckeridge family
1710	Keel, Staffs	John Sneyd
1710	Southill, Beds	Nathaniel Fowler
1710	Gissing, Norfolk	Sir Robert Kemp
1710	Theydon Mount, Essex	Sir Edward Smyth
1710	Sudbury, Derby	George Vernon
1710	Dallington, Northants	Thomas Rayner
1711	Greenford, Middlesex	Sibill Brown
1711	Blunham, Beds	Ralph Bromsal
1712	Thaxted, Essex	Thomas Swallow
1713	Harlestone, Northants	Sir Salathiel Lovell
1713	Lamport, Northants	Lady Isham
1713	Hunsdon, Herts	Felix Calvert
1713	St. Mary-at-Hill	Isaac Milner
1714	Ivinghoe, Bucks	Henry Cooley
1714	Chichester (Cathedral)	Elizabeth Manningham
1716	Longdon, Staffs	Thomas Orme
1718	Harlestone, Northants	Lady Lovell

STANTON, JAMES, of London

He signs a tablet to Theodosia Richards, 1810, at Sidmouth, Devon.

STANTON, THOMAS
b. 1610, *d.* 1674

He was an uncle of William Stanton (q.v.) and was apprenticed to Christopher Kingsfield. He became free in 1631 and was Master of the Masons' Company in 1660.

Stanton's finest work is the monument to Dame Jane Bacon, at Culford, Suffolk, the agreement for which is published in the Report of the Historical Manuscripts Commission on the collection of the Earl of Verulam (page 54). The monument, which was erected in 1654, was to cost £300 and was to be executed "according to the best skill of a stone-cutter, alle in whit and black marble without the addition of any other ston whatsoever."

Other signed works by Stanton include those commemorating Judith Combe, 1649, at Stratford-upon-Avon, Warwick; Jane Robinson, 1665, at Pangbourne, Berks; and Sir Thomas Lyttelton, 1666, in Worcester Cathedral.

STANTON, WILLIAM
b. 1639, *d.* 1705

His father was Edward Stanton, who died in 1686 and may possibly be the craftsman who made the chimes at the Royal Exchange (*Builder*, 1846, page 2), while his uncle was the statuary, Thomas Stanton (q.v.).

In 1686 he was employed by Sir John Brownlow as the master-mason for building Belton, receiving a total of £5,091. Some of his bills are still in existence and show that he received £30 for "five cornishes with freezes to ten chimney-pieces"; £100 for paving the hall and staircase, while for the "cornish in ye withdrawing-roome" he was paid £8 and £26 for "two scollop shells." He also made a number of chimney-pieces, receiving £50 for six which are not described. For Belton Church he made the monument of Sir John and Lady Brownlow which cost £100. This large work has columns supporting a broken pediment and in the centre are half-figures of Sir John and his wife, set on a slab of black Belgian marble (Archives, Lord Brownlow).

William Stanton, who is the greatest sculptor of the three Stantons of Holborn, became free of the Masons' Company in 1663. In 1678 he received £10 for the monument in Chirk Church (now fixed to a pillar) commemorating Dr. Walter Balcanqual (Chirk Castle Archives), and two years later was paid £20 for "making and erecting the pillars in the Cloister of the Inner Temple (Inderwick's *Inner Temple Records*, Vol. III, page 157).

In the archives of Lord Monson is the bill: "Rec'd John Archer, Esq., in full for a monument and grave stone sett up in the parish church of Coopersaile in Essex the sume of therty pounds and all other accounts by me"—7 July, 1683. This refers both to the monument which is on the east wall of the chancel and the gravestone in the floor of the aisle in memory of John Archer (*d.* 1682) in Theydon Garnon Church, Essex.

In 1699 Stanton executed the monument to Lady Isham in Lamport Church, Northants. The agreement in the Isham Archives reads as follows: "It is agreed by Sir M. Dayrell on behalfe of Sir Just Isham on the one part and William Stanton, Stone-Cutter of the other part that the sd Will Stanton shall make the pillars of the Monument, Twisted pillars of the best Dove coloured Marble and the Trusses underneath the sd pillars likewise of the best dove coloured Marble and it is agreed that the large plate·for the Inscription shall be full 2 Inches and halfe thick of the best white marble & the said William Stanton for the fashon of the said twisted pillars is to have foure pds over and above the former bargen Wittnesse the hand of the said Will stanton this 16th day of Febr 1699."

The monument cost £64 and, in a later letter, Stanton says he is sending it down by wagon with his man, John Summers, who will set it up.

Two years later Stanton was working at Stonyhurst, where Sir Nicholas Shireburn paid him £4 16s. for "Reigate stone lions," and £160 in 1703 for the monument to Richard Shireburn. This lovely work is in Mitton Church and has a pathetic figure of the last of the Shireburns, a boy of nine, who starts back in fear from a skull and crossbones. It has been incorrectly attributed by most writers to Edward Stanton (q.v.). Also in 1703 Stanton made the lions and eagles on the court stairs at Stonyhurst for £30, while the front-door shield cost the same sum.

In the Elford Hall MS. (now in the Birmingham Reference Library) is Stanton's receipt, dated 24 September, 1703, for £35 paid by Lady Diana Howard for a "monument sett up for Mr. Howard in Ashteed Church." The work referred to commemorates Thomas Howard, who died in 1701, and is to be found in the chancel of Ashtead Church, Surrey.

In 1704 Stanton began carving the fine monument to the fourth Earl of Leicester in Penshurst Church, Kent, but died before finishing it. For some reason it was completed, not by his son Edward, but by William Woodman (q.v.), as the bill at Penshurst Place shows (Sidney Archives). Stanton also made the bust of Hugh Saxey on the Saxey Hospital at Bruton, Somerset.

In 1688 and 1689 he was Master of the Masons' Company, but when asked to serve again in the following year wrote a refusal on 24 June, adding that he would "be willing to submit to what fine the Company shall think fit." His wife, Dorothy, survived him and died in 1707 at the age of sixty-seven. She was called "a prudent tender wife and mother" on the family gravestone, formerly at St. Andrew's, Holborn.

(Authorities cited in text.)

MONUMENTS

1665	Bengeo, Herts	John Byde
1670	Westminster Abbey	Hon. Penelope Egerton
1674	Worcester (Cathedral)	John Bromley
1674	Westminster Abbey	Carola Harsnett
1675	Quainton, Bucks	Sir John and Lady Dormer
1678	Monken Hadleigh, Herts	Elizabeth Davies
1679	Belton, Lincs	Sir John Brownlow
1679	Besford, Worcs	Sir Edward Sebright
1680	Westminster Abbey	Ann Filding (Lady Morland)
1683	Colne, Lancs	William Emmott
1683	Hurst, Berks	Sir Richard and Lady Harison
1684	Gretton, Northampton	The Ladies Hatton
1685	Harefield, Middlesex	Sir Richard and Lady Newdigate
c. 1685	Hythe, Kent	Mrs. Elizabeth Beane
c. 1689	Clapham (St. Paul's)	Sir Richard and Lady Atkins
1690	Ragnell, Notts	William Mellish
1694	Macclesfield, Cheshire	Lord Rivers (erected September, 1696)
1695	Oxford (St. Mary's)	Charles Holloway
1695	Blithfield. Staffs	Lady Bagot
1696	Brecon (Christ Church)	Rev. Richard Lucy
1696	Harefield, Middlesex	Abraham Stanyon
1697	Downham, Lancs	Sir John Assheton
1697	Hitchin, Herts	Ralph Skynner
1697	Brecon (Christ Church)	Chancellor Lucy
1699	Elmley Castle, Worcs	Earl of Coventry
1699	Hethersett, Norfolk	Isaac Motham
1699	Monkwearmouth, Durham	Lady Williamson
1700	Lowther, Westmorland	Lord Lonsdale
1702	Norwich (Cathedral)	Dean Fairfax
1702	Barkway, Herts	Judith Chester
1703	Wrexham, Denbigh	Owen Bold

PLATE XXV

HENRY SCHEEMAKERS
Sir Francis and Lady Page, 1750, Steeple Aston, Oxon.

PLATE XXVI

PETER SCHEEMAKERS
AND L. DELVEAUX
Sir Samuel Ongley, 1726, Old Warden, Bedfordshire.

ROBERT SINGLETON
Colonel Edmund Soames, 1706, West Dereham,
Norfolk.

STAVELEY, —, of Woodstock

He signs a monument to Edward Perrott, 1731, at North Leigh, Oxon.

STAVELEY, CHRISTOPHER, 'of Melton Mowbray

b. 1727, d. 1801

Staveley, who married Dorothy Loasby in 1741 (who died 23 September, 1780, aged fifty-two), was the builder in 1783 of Stapleford Church, and also executed some good architectural monuments with excellent lettering. The best are at Grantham, Lincolnshire, and include works commemorating the Rev. Richard Stevens, 1751, Randulph Clarke, 1751, and Jane Stevens, 1771, all in the Parish Church, while in the churchyard are the altar-tombs of Richard Huthwaite, 1752, and Joseph Osbourn, 1772, and the tombstones of James Rubins, 1761, and Mary Blower, 1781, the last with a charming relief of "Charity." A "Stephen Staveley" signs a slate monument to John Hopkinson, 1728, Hickling, Notts, and was also employed at Melbourne Hall, Derbyshire, in 1740 (Archives, Marquess of Lothian). Christopher died 31 January, 1801.

(*Monthly Magazine*, 1801, page 189.)

STAYNER, or STAINER, —, of Warwick

fl. 1730–1751

A "Mr. Stayner, carver," was paid in 1730 for the coat of arms on the front of the Court House at Warwick, and in 1751 was still living in the town.

STAYNER, or STAINER, THOMAS

b. c. 1668, d. 1731

He was the son of Thomas Stayner, "late of St. Giles-in-the-Fields, mason," and was apprenticed to Michael Todd in 1682, becoming free in 1690. By 1694 he had two apprentices, one of them his brother Anthony. Stayner must have married very young, for his son, another Thomas, was apprenticed to him as early as 1702 and became free in 1709.

Stayner made rapid progress in the Masons' Company, for he was an Assistant in the year after he became free, Renter Warden in 1703, Upper Warden in 1706, and Master in 1709. In the Court Book of the Company in 1720 there is, however, the following curious entry: "Ordered that Mr. Thomas Stainer, a member of this Court be summoned to appear at the next Court to show cause why he should not be discharged from

being an assistant for the misdemeanour by him committed in affronting the Master Wardens and Company at the public dinner on the Lord Mayor's Day last." Stayner appeared before the Court and "purged his offence" by a payment of 6s. 8d.

In 1697 Stayner was living in Goodmans Fields, but by 1715 he had moved to Bow Bridge in Essex, where he died in 1731. In his will he left his property to his son Thomas, who was still living there in 1750 (Court Book, Masons' Company).

As a sculptor Stayner is of great importance. His earliest monument is the signed altar-tomb with recumbent effigies of Richard and Anne Winwood, 1691, at Quainton, Bucks. Much later comes his most ambitious work, the remarkable monument, with its two standing figures, to Dr. Turner, 1714, at Stowe-Nine-Churches, Northants. This is followed in 1717 by that of Sir Henry Bendyshe at Steeple Bumpstead, Essex, with twisted barley-sugar columns and a reclining effigy of Sir Henry with a babe beside him. In 1723 he made the architectural tablet, also with twisted columns, to Lady Goselin, at Morningthorpe, Norfolk, and two years later the monument to Sir Richard Hoare in St. Dunstan-in-the-West, the bill for which is in the archives of Hoare's Bank. In the Delme-D.E.3574) is Stayner's contract with Edward D.E.3574) is Stayner's contract with Ralph Radcliffe, dated 31 August, 1721, for the monument to Sir Ralph Radcliffe which was erected in Hitchin Church.

On 13 February, 1727, Mr. Rice Williams wrote to Samuel Sandys, M.P., from Pyrgo informing him that "upon inquiry I found that Mr. Stayner, a stone-cutter upon Bowbridge was the person who lay'd the stone upon Mrs. Cheeke in Pyrgo Chapel." The writer continues: "He called upon me this morning and I came with him hither in case you and Mr. Archer approve of it. The dimensions of the stone are six foot six inches by three foot two inches, so that the whole stone will be near twenty foot, which at ten shillings a foot, a penny a letter for cutting and about three pounds for the coat of arms brings the whole to about 14 pounds if you have the same sort of stone with (*sic*) Mrs. Cheeke. . . . If you please to stop on Bow Bridge you may talk with this Mr. Stayner yourselves and I think he may be brought a little lower in his prices" (Archives, Lord Sandys). The letter refers to the ledger stone in Pyrgo Chapel, Essex, for Samuel's mother-in-law, Lady Tipping, who was herself a daughter of Thomas Cheke of Pyrgo. Both monuments were formerly in the private chapel attached to the house.

In the declared accounts of the directors of the

South Sea Company, published in 1721, is a payment made to Stayner by Ambrose Page, which appears to be for work done at the latter's brewery at Bow.

(Authorities cited in text.)

STEAD, SAMUEL, of Ludlow

He signs a large wall-tablet to Thomas Green, 1828, at Ashford Bowdler, Salop.

STEAD, WILLIAM, of York
fl. 1773–1815

He was apprenticed to Joseph Atkinson, of York (q.v.), and became free in 1773. He signs tablets in the county to Henry Bubb, 1792, in Holy Trinity, York; Samuel Lister, 1793, and Charles Sharp, 1804, both in Bradford Cathedral; James Lord, 1799, at Sowerby; and William Markham, 1815, at Aberford. He also executed the tablet to Mary Boucher, 1791, at Chesterfield, Derbyshire.

STEELL, SIR JOHN
b. 1804, *d.* 1891

He was the son of John Steell, a carver and gilder, and was born in Aberdeen on 18 September, 1804. His family moved to Edinburgh about a year after his birth, and at the age of fourteen he was apprenticed to a wood-carver and also studied at the Trustees' Academy.

On the expiration of his apprenticeship Steell decided to become a sculptor, and with this end in view went to Rome, where he lived and studied for several years. In 1827 he carved a colossal statue in wood for the North British Fire and Insurance Corporation, and in 1833 modelled the group entitled "Alexander Taming Bucephalus," which at once attracted attention. In 1829 he had become a member of the Royal Scottish Academy, and in 1838 was appointed sculptor to the Queen in Scotland.

Sir Francis Chantrey (q.v.) urged Steell to come to London, but he preferred to remain in his native country and devote himself to the improvement of Scottish art. He therefore spent the rest of his life in Scotland, and his seated figure of Sir Walter Scott in Princes Street, Edinburgh, is said to be the first marble statue ever commissioned in that country from a native artist. He was also the first to introduce artistic bronze casting into Scotland, and built at his own expense a foundry, so that not only his works, but those of other artists, could be reproduced in metal.

Steell was knighted on the occasion of the inauguration of his statue of the Prince Consort by Queen Victoria in 1876. He exhibited at the Royal Scottish Academy, 1827–1880, and at the Royal Academy, 1837–1876. In 1868 he carved a group for the tympanum of the Bank of Montreal in Canada, and executed another of the parable of "The Ten Virgins" for the Standard Assurance Office, Dublin. He died on 15 September, 1891, and was buried in the Old Calton Cemetery.

(*D.N.B.*; Rinder and McKay's *The Royal Scottish Academy*; various references, *Builder* and *Art Journal*.)

STATUES

1840	Lord de Saumarez	National Maritime Museum, Greenwich
1844	Professor Blaikie	West Church, Aberdeen
1844	Queen Victoria	Royal Institution, Edinburgh.
1846	Sir Walter Scott	Princes Street, Edinburgh
1849	Countess of Elgin	Jamaica
1850	Allan Ramsay	Edinburgh
1852	Wellington	Edinburgh
1855	Lord Jeffrey	Parliament House, Edinburgh
1856	Professor Wilson	Princes Street, Edinburgh
1856	Lord President Boyle	Parliament House, Edinburgh
1857	Lord Melville	Edinburgh
1863	Sir David Baxter	Dundee
1864	Lord Dalhousie	Calcutta
1865	Professor Wilson	Dean Cemetery, Edinburgh
1865	James Wilson	Calcutta
1868	Earl of Shrewsbury	Ingestre Church, Staffs (recumbent figure)
1870	Sir Walter Scott	New York
1871	Dr. Chalmers	Free Church College, Edinburgh
1874	Burns	New York
1876	Prince Consort	Edinburgh
1878	Dr. Chalmers	George Street, Edinburgh
1880	Burns	Dundee
1883	Alexander taming Bucephalus (modelled 1832)	Edinburgh
1884	Burns	Embankment, London

BUSTS

1831	David Scott	Diploma Work, Royal Scottish Academy
1838	Wardlaw Ramsey	For Scottish Missionary Society's Hall, Edinburgh
1838	Lady Stuart of Allenbank	Scottish National Portrait Gallery

1839	Earl Grey	Council Hall, Edinburgh
1843	Lord Campbell	Scottish National Portrait Gallery
1843	Wellington	Cirencester Park
1845	Wellington	Upper School, Eton
1846	Wellington	Apsley House
1846	Duchess of Buccleuch	Dalkeith Palace
1857	Lord Cockburn	Parliament House, Edinburgh
1859	Florence Nightingale	Royal United Service Institution
1859	Sir John McNeill	Scottish National Portrait Gallery
1859	James Wilson	National Gallery of Scotland
1862	Florence Nightingale	Derby Art Gallery (replica National Portrait Gallery)
1876	Thomas de Quincey	Scottish National Portrait Gallery
1879	Dr. Warburton Begbie	Royal College of Physicians, Edinburgh
1885	Robert Burns	Westminster Abbey

MONUMENTS

1843	Jamaica (Cathedral)	Countess of Elgin
1845	Edinburgh (St. Paul's)	Dr. Alison
1845	Edinburgh (St. Giles')	78th Highland Regiment
1854	Edinburgh (Dean Cemetery)	John Wilson
1864	Blair Atholl, Perth	Duke of Atholl
1866	Uphall, Linlithgow	Colonel Drysdale
1866	Edinburgh (Free High Church)	Rev. Dr. Gordon
1869	Glasgow (Cathedral)	Officers and Men of the 93rd Highlanders
1872	Dunkeld (Cathedral)	Officers and Men of the Black Watch
1875	Edinburgh (St. John's)	Dean Ramsay

STEGGLES, WILLIAM, of Bury St. Edmunds
b. 1767, *d.* 1859

Steggles signs tablets in Suffolk to the Rev. Beriah Brook, 1809, at Stansfield, and to James Oakes, 1829, in St. Mary's, Bury St. Edmunds; he also executed a ledger to Thomas Robins, 1834, at Isleham, Cambridgeshire. He was assisted in the business by his son, William Henry Steggles, who died in 1843 at the age of thirty-one.

STEPHAN, PIERRE

In the Wedgwood Archives is a letter from Stephan to Josiah Wedgwood, written from Wirksworth and dated 9 May, 1774. In it Stephan says: "I was informed some time agoe by several persons (particularly Mr. Gardiner of Derby the architect) that you gave great encouragements to Artists in Modelling branch, at which time I was then engag'd with Mr. Duesbury of Derby and since then with the china factory at Wirksworth, both which I am now disengaged from and have some thought of goeing to London, but first take the liberty of informing you that if I coud meet with agreeable Employment and that encouragement my work may deserve, I should be glad to have an Opportunity of being Employ'd by persons of taste and meriets (*sic*) which I hear is the Character of your Manufactory, but at the same time should chuse to have some part of my Employment in London on account of having a greater Opportunity of improveing my Ideas in the art of Modelling; but hope you will be so kind as to favour me with a line as soon as possible as I shall leave this Plase in a fortnight or three weeks at the farthest. N.B. I work in figures, vasses, or any sort of Useful as Business may require."

Stephan was later employed by Wedgwood and modelled for him a variety of things, including two wax models of "Hope" and "The Conquer'd Province." Wedgwood, however, does not seem to have thought much of these, for he wrote to Bentley in 1774 that "the drapery is hard and unfinished and the characters of the faces are those of common mortals of the lower class."

STEPHENS, EDWARD BOWRING
b. 1815, *d.* 1882

He was born in Exeter on 10 December, 1815, the son of James Stephens, a native of that city. He first studied art under John Glendall, a landscape painter (1790–1865), but his master saw that his real interest was in sculpture, and persuaded the elder Stephens to allow his son to go to London and work under E. H. Baily (q.v.).

In 1836, the year in which he joined the Royal Academy Schools, Stephens won a Silver Medal from the Society of Arts for a model of a figure. In 1837 he was awarded the Academy Silver Medal for his original model of "Ajax Defying the Gods," and in the following year executed his first commission, a bust of Miss Blanche Sheffield. In 1839 he went to Italy, where he remained for two years, and on his return to Exeter in 1841 he carved the statue of Lord Rolle.

In 1842 Stephens moved to London, where he again attended the Academy Schools and gained the Gold Medal for his relief entitled "The Battle of the Centaurs and Lapithae." In 1844 he exhibited his "Hagar and Ishmael" at Westminster Hall, a work praised by the *Art Union* which considered it possessed "very high merit and does credit to one of the most rising sculptors of the day, one whom we confidently expect to see

placed in the highest seat the profession supplies."
In 1845, the year in which Stephens sent his
"Pastoral Apollo" to Westminster Hall, he was
employed on decorating the Summer Pavilion in
the grounds of Buckingham Palace. Here he made
two reliefs of "The Attendant Spirit Disguised as
Thyrsis" and "The Lady from Comus." In 1846
he also carved a marble chimney-piece for the
same building.

In 1857 Stephens made a marble sarcophagus
for Lord Lonsdale's Mausoleum at Lowther and,
two years later, the bronze relief of Balaclava for
the memorial to Colonel Morris on Hatherleigh
Down in Devonshire. He became an Associate of
the Royal Academy in 1864, although at the time
it was believed that his election was the result of
his name having been confused with that of Alfred
Stevens, the sculptor of the Wellington monument
in St. Paul's. In 1868 he carved a relief of the
"Raising of the Widow's Son" for Kenton
Church, Devon.

Stephens exhibited at the Academy, 1838–1883,
and at the British Institution, 1838–1853. In 1857
he lent his "Preparing for the Chase" to the
Exhibition of Art Treasures held in Manchester.

He died of bronchitis on 9 November, 1882.
"He was one of those genuine, unpretending,
honest beings that are always appreciated. He
took the greatest interest in his native city and
county. He was kind-hearted and liberal; was
always among the first, often the first, to help a
brother artist in difficulty, or to render justice
when justice was due but not accorded" (Pycroft's
Art in Devonshire, page 140).

(Various references *Builder* and *Art Journal*;
D.N.B.; authority cited in text.)

STATUES

1841	Lord Rolle	Lupton, Devon (replica at Bicton, Devon)
1847	Comus Offering the Cup	For T. H. Hippesley, of Shobrooke Park, Devon
1848	Diana	For Mr. Soames, Beech Hill, Essex
1851	Satan Vanquished	Great Exhibition
1851	Satan Tempting Eve	Great Exhibition
1859	Lord Saltoun	Fraserborough, Inverness
1859	Maternal Love	Illustrated in *Art Journal*, 1859
1860	Dr. Priestley	Oxford Museum
1861	Sir Thomas Dyke-Acland	Exeter
1863	Earl Fortescue	Exeter
1863	Alfred the Great	Egyptian Hall, Mansion House
1863	Earl of Lonsdale	Mausoleum, Lowther

1864	Duke of Bedford	Tavistock, Devon
1864	John Dinham	Exeter
1868	Prince Consort	Exeter Art Gallery
1871	Zingari	For Captain Hill, Brighton
1873	Leonardo da Vinci, Wren and Sir Joshua Reynolds	Façade of Burlington House
1878	Alfred Rooker	Plymouth
1878	Sir John Burrows	Brighton
1878	The Deer Stalker	Exeter
1878	The Bathers	Russell Cotes Museum, Bournemouth
1879	The Earl of Devon	Exeter
1879	Science and Literature	Melbourne, Australia
1882	Shielding the Helpless	Burlington House

BUSTS

1841	Sir John Bayley	Meopham Church, Kent
1842	Earl of Devon	Powderham Castle, Devon
1843	Baldwin Fulford	Fulford Park, Devon
1847	General Sir B. D'Urban	Exhibited Royal Academy
1850	Sir John Bayley	Upper School, Eton
1851	Viscount Palmerston	Broadlands, Hants
1851	Bishop of Madras	Calcutta Cathedral
1854	William Courtney	Powderham Castle, Devon
1861	3rd Earl Fortescue	Barnstaple Infirmary
1870	Sir John Bowring	Exhibited Royal Academy
1873	Lord Lister	St. Thomas's Hospital
1881	R. S. Gard	Exeter Art Gallery

MONUMENTS

1843	Aylesbeare, Devon	Edward Kenyon
1843	Ruabon, Denbigh	Edward Lloyd Kenyon
1846	Sandford, Devon	Sir Humphrey Davie
1869	Powderham, Devon	Countess of Devon (recumbent effigy)
1879	C. C. Whiteford	For Plymouth Town Hall (with bust)

STEPHENS, JOSEPH, the Elder, and JOSEPH, the Younger, of Worcester

Joseph Stephens the Elder: *b.* 1773, *d.* 1834
Joseph Stephens the Younger: *b.* 1808

Joseph Stephens the Elder was the son of
William Stephens (q.v.), but his monuments and
tablets have little of the charm of those designed
and carved by his father. He died on 14 July, 1834,
and was buried in St. Andrew's Church, Worcester. His wife, Elizabeth, predeceased him, dying
on 13 August, 1809, at the age of thirty-six.

Joseph Stephens the Younger was born in 1808
and attended the Royal Academy Schools, on the

recommendation of Chantrey (q.v.), in 1828. In the following year he received a large Silver Medal from the Society of Arts for a bust, and in 1830 exhibited at the Birmingham Society of Artists a model of a monument for St. Nicholas' Church, Worcester. He exhibited busts at the Royal Academy, 1833–1852; in 1853 he took casts of the monuments in Worcester Cathedral for the sculpture gallery at the Crystal Palace.

Both father and son were prolific statuaries. The elder Stephens's best work commemorates Joseph Roberts, 1806, at Saintbury, Glos, and has a relief of "Hope" standing by an altar. Good tablets by his son are those to Frances Brace, 1840, at Leominster, Hereford, and Edward Corles, 1866, in Worcester Cathedral, both of which have well-carved reliefs. Other tablets executed by the firm in Worcestershire include those to Catherine Yarndel, 1800, at Malvern; Captain Norbury, 1800, at Dodderhill; Mrs. Palmer, 1808, at Spetchley; the Rev. Slade Nash, 1823, in St. Peter's, Droitwich; the seventh Earl of Coventry, 1831, and the eighth Earl of Coventry, 1843, both at Croome; Jane Perrott, 1835, at Fladbury; Viscount Valentia, 1841, at Upper Arley; and Lady Winnington, 1854, at Stanford. Others to R. Wilkes, 1824, at Enville, Staffs, and Edward Wallwyn, 1831, at Much Marcle, Hereford, are also their work.

STEPHENS, WILLIAM HUMPHRIES, of Worcester
b. 1737

He was the son of Joseph Stephens, a stone-cutter, and was apprenticed to his father in 1751, becoming free in 1760. Early in his career he was in partnership with a Mr. Bott, and tablets belonging to this period are signed with both their names, including one to Richard Canwardine, 1763, at St. John in Bedwardine, Worcestershire. Later Stephens was joined by his son Joseph (q.v.) when the latter became free. The tablet to the Rev. Hudson Boyce (*d.* 1786) at Fladbury in the same county, which is signed "Stephens and Co.," is probably their joint work. Another William Stephens, who may have been a relation, was one of the master-masons responsible for building Ombersley, near Worcester, 1724–1727 (Archives, Lord Sandys).

William Stephens is the best of the Worcester school of statuaries. His tablets, with their various-coloured marbles and well-carved details, are a delight to the eye and are models of eighteenth-century good taste. In Worcester itself his monuments and tablets include those to Robert

Woodward, 1780, Mary Astley, 1782, Mary Hall, 1794, and Bishop Hurd, 1808, all in the Cathedral; Patience Turner, 1786, and John Williams, 1793, both in All Saints' Church; and Joseph Berwick, 1798, in St. Nicholas' Church. Works by him in Worcestershire commemorate Thomas Parker, 1751, at Longden; Thomas Dunn, 1777, in All Saints, Evesham; Arthur Charlett, 1779, at Fladbury; the Rev. James Gyles, 1792, at Powick; and the Rev. George Martin, 1796, at Overbury. Others in Gloucestershire include those to William Hankins, 1771, at Dymock; Robert Bateson, 1779, at Bourton-on-the-Water: Mary Clarke, 1792, and Richard Clarke, 1796, both in Gloucester Cathedral; and Daniel Ellis, 1797, at Elmore. Other signed monumental works by Stephens include those to Mrs. Sarah Hall, 1780, at Ledbury, Hereford; William Bach, 1785, at Leominster, Hereford; Jonathan Green, 1792, at Ashford Bowdler, Salop; and Lord Somers, 1808, at Eastnor, Hereford.

(Worcester Corporation Archives.)

STEPHENS, WILLIAM and JOSEPH, of Exeter
firm *fl.* 1810–1833

Their tablets are the usual provincial productions of the period, the best being one commemorating Sir Boucher Wray, 1826, at Tawstock, Devon, which has well-carved classical details. Others executed by the firm include those to the Rev. William Hole, 1822, at Swimbridge, Devon; and the Hawkesley family, *c.* 1830, and Samuel Wills, 1833, both at Crewkerne, Somerset.

STEPHENSON, WILLIAM, of Liverpool
fl. 1752–1756

In 1752 it was decided to add a bas-relief to the pediment of Liverpool Town Hall and the Council engaged Stephenson to carry out the work. On its completion, however, they were not at all satisfied and offered the sculptor eighty guineas, instead of the larger sum which they had originally mentioned.

In 1756 Stephenson petitioned the Council for a further £20, but they refused his request, considering that the relief was "ill-executed" and that "Mr. Stephenson had been already paid more than he deserved and that they would pay him no more" (City Archives).

STEWART, JAMES

In 1767 he exhibited "A Marble Bust of a Lady" at the Free Society.

STEWART, JOHN GUISE
d. 1844

His widow, Mary Ann, applied to the A.G.B.I. after her husband's death. She stated that Stewart had worked for W. G. Nicholl (q.v.), Samuel Nixon (q.v.) and "Mr. Smith of New Road." Stewart exhibited a "Group of Flowers in Wax" in 1844. He died on 20 June, 1844, leaving, besides his widow, four children.

STEWART, RICHARD
d. 1847

He applied to the A.G.B.I. in 1846 and stated that he had left Dublin in 1843 to come to London, bringing with him his work "King John Signing Magna Charta," but he failed to sell this work or indeed to find employment in London. Stewart also stated that he had executed "several works at Windsor under Sir Jeffery Wyatville," and had made stone figures for the Duchess of Leinster. He had also given instructions in modelling to the "Countess of Verulam, Earl of Auckland and many others of the Nobility." As a specimen of his work he sent to the A.G.B.I. a model "of a work designed to be set up in Lloyd's Coffee Room, Royal Exchange." Stewart died in April, 1847, leaving a widow, Jane.

STEWART, ROBERT
fl. 1777–1784

He exhibited at the Society of Artists, showing wax portraits, and also medallions of Lord Thurlow and the Duchess of Devonshire.

On 27 March, 1784, Mr. Christie held the sale of "Mr. Stewart, statuary and mason, quitting business, at his house, No. 14, on the west side of Princes Street, near Great George Street, Westminster." Among the lots were, "50 drawings for tablets, tombs, etc." and "drawings for chimneypieces." Four marble chimney-pieces by Stewart were also sold.

A "Stewart" signs a fine monument to Bishop Preston, 1787, at Ferns, Co. Wexford.

STIRLING, EDWIN
b. 1819, *d.* 1867

He was born at Dryburgh, in Scotland, on 27 July, 1819, and when quite a child modelled some clay figures which were shown to Sir David Erskine, who lived in the neighbourhood. Erskine was so impressed by the boy's work that he had him apprenticed to a stone-carver at Darnick, and after he had become free Stirling went to Edinburgh to study at the School of Art.

He later settled in Liverpool, where he first worked for an architectural carver named Canavan, and afterwards became his partner. In 1857 he executed most of the decorative carving on the offices of the Liverpool and London Insurance Company in Liverpool (*Builder*, 1857, page 40), and he was also responsible for the statues on the south front of Horton Hall, Cheshire (*Art Journal*, 1867, page 84), and for the memorial to the Prince Consort erected at Hastings in 1863.

Stirling died on 6 January, 1867, and was buried in Liverpool Necropolis, where a monument commemorates him and his infant son.

(Information, Liverpool Public Library.)

STOREY, ABRAHAM
d. c. 1696

He was admitted to the livery of the Masons' Company in 1662, and in the same year was employed on repairs to St. James's Palace. By 1669 he was apparently his own master, for he sent in a tender for the masonry work for Brewers' Hall, then about to be rebuilt after the Great Fire (Archives, Brewers' Company).

In 1672 he received £15 for a marble chimneypiece for Wrest Park, in Bedfordshire (Archives, Lady Lucas and Dingwall), while two years later he was paid for work at the Royal College of Physicians. As a master-mason under Wren he built the Church of St. Edmund the King, 1677–1679, receiving £2,884 (Bodleian, Rawlinson, B.387). He was Warden of the Masons' Company in 1673 and 1677, and Master in 1680.

Storey's monuments are of great importance, his finest being one commemorating Lord and Lady Crofts at Little Saxham, Suffolk, which was erected about 1678. This has a life-sized, semi-recumbent figure of Lord Crofts in full peer's robes, while his wife reclines on a lower table (Gage's *Hundred of Thingoe*, page 159). He signs the large, elaborate architectural monument to Sir Thomas Hewytt, who died in 1662, at Sawbridgeworth, Hertfordshire.

STOREY, GEORGE, of Norwich
fl. 1733–1759

Andrews Jelfe (q.v.), who was working at Holkham from 1742 until 1743, wrote in the latter year to Brettingham the architect that "after I had parted with you at Norwich, I talked to George Storey, who I don't like and will have no further dealings with" (British Museum, Ad. MS. 27587).

Storey signs monuments to Thomas and Mary Till, 1733, in St. Peter Mancroft, Norwich, and John Newdigate, 1743, Holt, Norfolk; also a larger one to D. Durrant, 1759, at Scottow, Norfolk. This a clumsy work, 18 ft. high, consisting of a pyramid with an urn at the apex, and is only impressive because of its size.

An Andrew Storey, who may have been a son of George Storey, was apprenticed to Robert Page (q.v.) in 1774.

STOREY, WILLIAM, of London
fl. 1800–1826

Storey, whose yard was in Mount Street, carried out repairs in 1805 to Lord Radnor's house at 6, Grosvenor Street (Archives, Longford Castle). Two years later he was the master-mason for building Mr. Coutts's house at the corner of Stratton Street and Piccadilly, and here he also supplied marble chimney-pieces (Archives, Coutts Bank).

His tablets are mostly classical, the best being those to John Croft, 1805, at Woodbridge, Suffolk; Mrs. Wilkes, 1806, in the Grosvenor Chapel; Hugh Dive, 1812, and Solomon Knobel, 1817, both in Paddington Parish Church; Colonel William Kelly, 1818, at Chilton Foliat, Berks; Sarah Hugford, 1822, at Tonbridge, Kent; Elizabeth de Beauvoir, 1822, at Basildon, Berks; and Hugh Shortrudge, 1823, at Great Bookham, Surrey.

STOTHARD, ALFRED JOSEPH
b. 1793, *d.* 1864

Alfred Stothard, who was the son of Thomas Stothard, R.A. (1755–1824), in 1828 contracted to supply four bas-reliefs for Buckingham Palace from designs by his father, each relief being about 20 ft. long with the figures about half the size of life. The designs were published in book form in 1829 (*Literary Gazette,* 1829, page 555), and in the same year the sculptor received £584 for the work (P.R.O., Works 19/3).

Stothard exhibited medallic portraits at the Royal Academy, 1821-1845, and his wax portrait of an unknown clergyman is now on loan from Mrs. Bate to the Victoria and Albert Museum. His monuments to Charles Lane, 1827, at Arundel, Sussex, and to Richard Collins, 1831, at Fareham, Hants, both have medallion portraits. The original design for the former is now in the possession of the writer, while that for the latter was exhibited at the Royal Academy in 1832. Stothard also signs a tablet to D. Rhudde, 1819, at East Bergholt, Suffolk.

STOTHARD, HENRY
b. 1795, *d.* 1847

Henry Stothard was born in 1795 (Archives,

Artists' Annuity Fund), and was the third son of Thomas Stothard, R.A., and a brother of Alfred Stothard (q.v.), was a pupil of Flaxman (q.v.) and attended the Royal Academy Schools in 1811. In 1813 he won a Silver Medal at the Academy, but later became incapacitated through paralysis and was forced to give up sculpture. The influence of Queen Adelaide secured him admission to the Charterhouse, where he died on 26 February, 1847.

His younger brother, Robert Thomas Stothard, who was born in 1797, also attended the Academy modelling school in 1823.

(Authority cited in text.)

STOWERS, CHARLES
fl. 1810–1821

He was the son of Thomas Stowers, a painter who exhibited landscapes at the Royal Academy, 1778–1811. The younger Stowers also showed works at the Academy from 1811 until 1821, including busts of "A Nobleman" and of "W. Bromet, M.D." He signs three undistinguished tablets to Mary Hughes, 1810, at Merstham, Surrey; Elizabeth Randolph, 1811, in Walcot Church, Bath; and Mary Glendining, 1817, at Lympston, Devon. In 1819 he was paid £177 8s. for the tablet erected in Lincoln's Inn Chapel to the memory of Spencer Perceval (Inn Archives).

STRETTON, WILLIAM, of Nottingham
b. 1755, *d.* 1828

He was the son of Samuel Stretton (1731–1811), a builder of Nottingham, who erected Colwick Hall in 1776 and the grandstand on Nottingham racecourse in the following year. In 1778 the younger Stretton took over Radcliff's (q.v.) yard at Nottingham, and advertised in the local press that he made "monuments, chimney-pieces, marble sideboards, Indian inkstands, etc."

About 1787 he joined his father, and together they were responsible for a number of buildings, including Arkwright's cotton-mill at Hockley in 1790 and the Park Gateway for Lord Middleton at Wollaton Hall. In Nottingham itself they built the Assembly Rooms in 1790 (the architect being Carr of York), the seven-arched bridge over the Trent in 1796, and the barracks from 1792 until 1799, the last named at a total cost of £20,000. On his own account William Stretton built the church of St. James's, Standard Hill, Nottinghamshire. He also rebuilt the Nottingham Exchange in 1815, besides being responsible for all the carved stonework.

He signs the well-executed wall-monument, with

roundels of "blue john" at its base, to Mary Bambrigge, 1779, at Lockington, Leicestershire. According to the "Stretton Manuscripts" he was also responsible for tablets in Nottinghamshire to John Lindley, 1797, at Skegby; Jane Francis, 1787, and Mary Williamson, both at Ruddington; while at Nuthall he executed "two tablets to the memory of the present and late Rectors."

Stretton was also an antiquary and collector. His obituary in the *Nottingham Journal* stated that in him "antiquarians had lost a fund of general and useful knowledge."

(*Stretton Manuscripts* privately printed, Nottingham, 1910.)

STRONG, EDWARD, the Elder
b. c. 1652, *d.* 1724

Clutterbuck, in his *History of Hertfordshire* (Vol. I, page 187), gives a copy of an MS. history of the Strong family written by Edward Strong. From this it appears that the writer's grandfather, Timothy Strong, was born in Wiltshire, but settled at Little Barrington, in Gloucestershire, and there became a quarry-owner. About 1630 he built the south front of Cornbury House, Oxon, and died about 1644. Timothy had one son, Valentine, who married Anne, daughter of Edward Margetts, of Charlbury, Oxon, about 1631 or 1632. Valentine first assisted his father, and later, about 1656, built a house for William Whitmore at Slaughter, Gloucestershire. Between 1651 and 1653 he built Sherborne for Sir John Dutton. He died in 1662 while erecting a house for Andrew Barker at Fairford, Gloucestershire, and was buried in Fairford churchyard.

Edward Strong, one of Valentine's sons, became free of the Masons' Company by redemption in 1680. In the following year he became mason-contractor for building the churches of St. Bennet's, Paul's Wharf, and St. Austin-by-St. Paul's, on the death of his brother, Thomas Strong (q.v.), who had left them unfinished.

On his own account Edward Strong was responsible for the masonry of St. Mildred's, Bread Street; St. Mary Magdalen's, Old Fish Street; St. Clement's, Eastcheap, and St. Michael Royal; but his most important work was concerned with the building of St. Paul's, where, in 1694, sixty-five of his masons were employed. During all this period he was paid for carved stonework, though presumably the actual carving was done by his assistants. The payments include "fourteen spandril flowers, 18 guineas," at St. Mary Magdalen's, and £24 "for carving ye vine and two pineapples" at St. Mildred's. At St. Clement's, Eastcheap, he received payment for "two death's

heads," and at St. Michael Royal for "cherubim heads and keystones." Photographs of his carved stonework at St. Paul's are among the publications of the Wren Society.

Between 1682 and 1686 Strong was working at Winchester Palace, where he was paid for making "pilasters and columns" and for "ornaments on several pilasters and carving ye tops of ye capitals" (P.R.O., E.351/3460). In 1688 he made a chimney-piece of Egyptian marble for the Queen's withdrawing-room at the Palace of Whitehall (P.R.O., Works 5/42). He was employed at Greenwich Palace from 1698 (P.R.O., Admiralty Records); and from 1705 until 1712, with his son, Edward Strong the Younger, was the contractor for Blenheim Palace, being responsible for a great deal of carved stonework. In 1715 the Strongs were working for the Duke of Chandos at Canons, where they built the north front of the house (Baker's *James Bridges, First Duke of Chandos*, page 123). Strong also received £25 in 1707 "for the pedestal for the dial in the great garden steps" of the Inner Temple (*Inner Temple Records*, Vol. III, page 406). In 1717 he took as an apprentice, John "son of John Strong of Fainton near Burford."

Strong died on 8 February, 1723-1724, and was buried in St. Peter's Church, St. Albans, where there is a monument with a bust to his memory. His long epitaph states that he worked at St. Paul's "even from its foundations to his laying the last stone," and adds that, with Wren and Compton, Bishop of London, "he shared the felicity of seeing both the beginning and finishing of that stupendous fabrick." He married Martha, sister of Ephraim Beauchamp (q.v.).

(Knoop and Jones's *London Masons of the Seventeenth Century*; *Wren Society*, various volumes; *Builder*, 1862, page 563, and 1864, page 500; Bodleian, Rawlinson MS. 387.)

STRONG, EDWARD, the Younger
b. 1676, *d.* 1741

He was apprenticed to his father, Edward Strong the Elder (q.v.), in 1691, and in 1698 became free of the Masons' Company. In the same year he went abroad and travelled through France, Italy and Holland with Christopher Wren, son of the architect.

Strong, who worked as his father's assistant or partner at Greenwich and Blenheim, was also with him at St. Paul's, where in 1706 he began to build the lantern on his own account. According to the Strong family MS. quoted in Clutterbuck's *History of Hertfordshire* (Vol. I, page 168), he was the mason responsible for the towers of St.

Vedast's, Foster Lane; St. Stephen's, Walbrook; and St. James's, Garlickhithe; besides rebuilding the tower of St. Michael's, Cornhill, and the upper part of the tower of St. Christopher's, Threadneedle Street. The same source also records that he executed "the ornaments or lanthorn upon the square tower of Christ Church, London, and the stonework of Dr. Draper's house in Surrey."

In 1712 Strong was working at Marlborough House (Malcolm's *Londinium Redivivum*, Vol. IV, page 317), while five years later he was the mastermason for building the Queen's House at Greenwich (P.R.O., Ad. MS. 68/874). Here, in 1719, he received £217 for the west colonnade of the Palace, and £14 for the "doorcase the south side of the officers' hall" (P.R.O., Ad. MS. 68/875). In 1712 he was paid £728 for masonry-work at the Chapter House of St. Paul's (*Notes and Queries*, fifth Series, Vol. X, page 463).

He also worked with Edward Tufnell (q.v.) and with him built the churches of St. Alphege, Greenwich, 1712–1714 (where they were responsible for the four · delightful stone altars, with cherubs and festoons, standing in front of the portico); St. Anne's, Limehouse, 1712–1724; St. Paul's, Deptford, 1712–1730; St. John's, Westminster, 1714–1728; and St. George's, Wapping, 1715–1723 (P.R.O., A.O.1.437/2).

Strong had married Susanna Roberts in 1699, and left four daughters on his death in 1741, the eldest—Susannah, wife of Sir John Strange, the Master of the Rolls—being his heiress. He died 10 October, 1741, his will being proved in the same month.

(Knoop and Jones's *The London Mason in the Seventeenth Century*; R.I.B.A. Library, MS. 726.54.)

STRONG, THOMAS
d. 1681

Eldest son of Valentine Strong, and brother of Edward Strong the Elder (q.v.), he completed the house which his father had been building for Mr. Barker at Fairford at the time of his death in 1662. In the following year he built the stables at Cornbury for the Earl of Clarendon, and about 1665 was responsible, under Wren, for the "Lodging for Scholars" · at Trinity College, Oxford (Clutterbuck's *History of Hertfordshire*, Vol. I, page 167).

In 1667 Strong went up to London to help with the rebuilding of the City devastated by the Great Fire in the previous year. "He also took up masons with him to London to work with him, to serve the City in what they wanted in his way of trade, and continued there in that employment many years till most of the houses and halls were built"

(op. cit.). With his partner, C. Kempster (q.v.), he was the contractor for St. Stephen's, Walbrook, in 1672, where they were paid £122 for sixteen Corinthian capitals and £1 10s. for the "mask-head to the west door" (Bodleian, Rawlinson MS. 387), though Strong alone was responsible for the font (White's *History of Walbrook Ward*, page 376).

Strong also built the churches of St. Bennet and St. Austin, besides doing a great deal of work at St. Paul's. In 1681 he contracted to carve for the Cathedral the "great capitals of the pilasters for £15 a face," and in the same year received £60 for "ten festoons between the impost capitals" and £120 for "carving twenty-seven great pannells in the sofetes of the two arches of the nave of the Church." For the north-west vestry he was paid £294 for "forty-nine faces of impost capitalls," and £7 for "one ffestoon in the splay of the vestry lookeing to the dome."

In 1675 Strong "built a front of stone betwixt the wings of Lord Craven's house at Hempstead Marshall, in Berkshire (Clutterbuck's *History of Hertfordshire*, Vol. I, page 168). He died unmarried at about midsummer, 1681, leaving "all his employment to his brother Edward, whom he made his sole executor" (op. cit.).

(Wren Society's Publications; authorities cited in text.)

STUBINGTON, JAMES,
of Bishops Waltham
fl. 1748–1753

He signs an architectural tablet about 7 ft. high, with an urn at the apex of a triangular pediment, to Mrs. James Wright, 1753, at Bishops Waltham. He was also responsible for the tablet to Edward Wynn, 1748, at Southwick, Hampshire.

STURDY, WILLIAM,
of Romford
fl. 1825–1841

He signs tablets at Dagenham, Essex, to William Ford, 1825, with a relief of two charity children playing by a tombstone; to William Stone, 1839, with a well-carved relief of a woman mourning by an urn; and a classical one to the Fanshawe family, dated 1841.

Sturdy may possibly be the son of the "Mr. Sturdy a mason of Romford" who died in 1800 (*Monthly Magazine*, 1800, page 199).

SUMMERS, CHARLES
b. 1827, *d.* 1878

He was born on 27 July at East Charlton,

Somerset, the son of a mason named George Summers, and was erecting a monument at Weston-super-Mare when he attracted the attention of Henry Weekes (q.v.), who took him into his studio. Summers also had lessons from M. L. Watson (q.v.), and after the latter's death helped to complete the colossal group of Lord Eldon and Lord Stowell which is now in the library of University College, Oxford. In 1851 he was awarded, not only the Royal Academy Silver Medal, but the Gold Medal as well, this for a group entitled "Mercy Interceding for the Vanquished." He was apparently the first student of sculpture to win both prizes simultaneously, and he also received a grant of £500 to enable him to continue his studies in Rome.

For some unknown reason, however, Summers suddenly abandoned the brilliant career that lay before him, and in 1853 went to Australia to dig for gold. Here he had little success and later found employment as a modeller for the Houses of Parliament which were then being built in Melbourne. In 1866 he returned to England, and in the following year went to Rome, where he spent most of the rest of his life. He died in Paris on 30 November, 1878, and was buried in the Protestant Cemetery in Rome.

Summers exhibited at the Royal Academy, 1849–1876, showing in 1871 a bust of Professor Owen, while to the Great Exhibition of 1851 he sent the figure of "A Boy Playing with a Shell." His undated statue of "Rebecca" is in the Exeter Art Gallery, an undated bust of Henry Weekes, R.A., is at Burlington House, and a bust of Bishop Perry (1876) is in the Speech-Room at Harrow School. He also signs the monument with a recumbent figure of Mrs. MacLeay, 1870, at Godstone, Surrey.

Summers' work for Australia included statues of Shakespeare (1863); Burke and Wills (1872), which cost £4,000; and the Prince and Princess of Wales (1876), all for Melbourne, the last named being in the Public Library. In the city's Art Gallery is his bust of the Duke of Edinburgh (1873), while he also executed statues of Linceus and Hypermnestra for Sydney in 1875, but these were destroyed in the fire of 1883.

(*D.N.B.*; *Builder*, 1852, page 23.)

SUMPTER, —, of Irthlingborough
fl. 1784–1792

According to the *Gentleman's Magazine* of 1799 (pages 939 and 1103), he made the tablet at Finedon, Northamptonshire, to John Perkins, who died in 1784 and who was "for twenty-seven years organist of the Church." Sumpter signs a stone

tablet with a basket of fruit at the top to Thomas Wylde, 1792, at Yeldon, Huntingdonshire, while in 1799 he built the obelisk at Finedon for Sir English Dolben.

SUTTON, JAMES, the Elder, and JAMES, the Younger, of Maidstone
James Sutton the Elder: *b.* 1774, *d.* 1828
James Sutton the Younger: *b.* 1798

The elder Sutton signs a number of tablets in Kent, the best being those to Ann Argles, 1813, at Maidstone, and to Thomas Turner, 1821, at Hunton. He died in 1828 and is buried in the churchyard of Maidstone Parish Church.

He was succeeded in the business by his nephew James, "son of Mary Sutton of Maidstone, widow," who had been apprenticed to him in 1812 (Town Archives). The younger Sutton was a prolific statuary, whose better works in Kent include tablets to Edward Usborne, 1828, at Staplehurst; Robert Rugg, 1831, and Joseph Sharpe, 1831, both at Detling; and George, sixth Viscount Torrington, 1832, at Mereworth.

SWAN, WILLIAM
In 1730 he received £200 for decorative stone-work at Queen Anne's Court, Greenwich. This included the carving round the windows in the attic cornice and also shields at £3 each (P.R.O., Ad. MS. 68/711).

SWEET, W., and MILES, M.
They sign the large monument with its life-size reclining figure of Sir Edward Hales, 1665, at Tunstall, Kent. They were probably local craftsmen, for the carving of the effigy is rather crude and coarse.

SWINTON, ARCHIBALD, of Cambridge
He signs a wall-tablet to John Whitechurch, 1728, at Harlton, Cambs.

SWITZER, STEPHEN
b. c. 1618, *d. c.* 1669

He was apprenticed to Guy Glandinning in 1632 and was Warden of the Masons' Company in 1660 and 1664, becoming Master in the following year. In 1664 he was the mason responsible for building Clarendon House in Piccadilly and a year later he and his partner, Thomas Wise (q.v.), were working at Greenwich Palace, where they executed a certain amount of carved stonework, including in 1667 "a carved capital of a pilaster,

£13" for the "south end towards the park" (P.R.O., Works 5/9). Switzer had himself been sent to Portland in 1660 to select suitable stone for building the Palace (P.R.O., A.O.1, 2487/357).

He may have been the father of that Stephen Switzer who was one of the apprentices of Thomas Burman (q.v.) and was left 40s. under his master's will.

(Knoop and Jones's *The London Mason in the Seventeenth Century*.)

SYMONDS, THOMAS,
of Hereford
d. 1791

Symonds, who became a freeman of Hereford in 1753, was an excellent provincial statuary. His large monument to Thomas Symonds, 1760, at Sellack, Hereford, has a fine medallion portrait, while that to Anne Somerset, 1764, at Pauntley, Glos, is an impressive architectural work with a sarcophagus set against a pyramid.

Other monuments and tablets executed in Herefordshire by Symonds include those to John Davies, 1752, at Bullingham; Isabella Davies, 1760, at Kingsland; William Bach, 1766, and William Tolderly, 1789, both at Leominster; the Rev. Josiah Smart, 1769, at Bodenham; Edmund Brydges, 1772, at Tyberton; William Barnesley, 1773, at Eardisley; Bridget Monnington, 1775, at Sarnesfield; John Woodcock, 1781, at Byford; and Mary Trahern, 1788, at Lugwardine.

T—U

TACONET, CHARLES
b. 1766, *d.* 1793

He joined the Royal Academy Schools in 1789, winning a Silver Medal in the same year and the Gold Medal for his figure of Samson in 1790. Taconet exhibited at the Academy, 1790–1792. He died in 1793 and his widow, Martha, was granted a small pension by the Academy (Academy Archives).

TAIRE, —, of Kendal

He signs a large tablet at Skipton, Yorkshire, to Margaret Chippindale, 1817, a work which has the heavenly crown, descending dove, palm branches, Bibles, etc., so typical of the period.

TALLEMACH, WILLIAM
See Tollemache, William

TARAGNOLA, CHEVALIER G.
fl. 1815–1820

He exhibited various works at the Royal Academy, 1815–1820, among them a model for a monument and a bas-relief of "Victory Presenting two Dying British Heroes to Britannia."

TARRANT, —, of Swindon

He signs a large stone wall-tablet to Frances Tyrell, 1782, at Harwell, Berkshire.

TATE, CHRISTOPHER J. A., of Newcastle-on-Tyne
b. 1812, *d.* 1841

He was apprenticed to R. G. Davies of Newcastle (q.v.), and after he became free worked as assistant to David Dunbar the Younger (q.v.). After a few years in the latter's studio, he decided to set up for himself as a sculptor and produced first a "Dying Christ Suitable for Catholic Chapels," and later a statue of "Blind Willie."

Tate then turned his attention to busts, and carved, among others, likenesses of the Duke of Northumberland, Sheridan Knowles, Lord Byron and H. Phillips, the singer. Apparently he met with some success, for the *Gentleman's Magazine* in its obituary (1841, Part II, page 102) considered that "for execution, precision and arrangement" they could "scarcely be surpassed." The same article also mentioned his "Judgment of Paris" and "Musidora" which, the writer thought, "would

have done credit to an artist of greater experience."

In 1838 the sculptor carved the very fine Royal coat of arms in the pediment of the theatre at Newcastle. At the time of his death he was working on a statue of the Duke of Northumberland, to be erected in front of the Master Mariners' Asylum at Tynemouth, but the figure had to be completed by his former master, R. G. Davies.

Tate, who was a consumptive, went to Malta in an attempt to regain his health, but sailed for home when he realized that his end was near. He died on 22 March, 1841, soon after his ship reached London, his widow and children being left totally unprovided for. According to the obituary notice already quoted, "his store of information was inexhaustible and whatever the subject under discussion, Mr. Tate was always able to take a prominent part."

(*Local Records of Newcastle, 1832–1857*, page 138; *Magazine of Art*, 1894, page 258.)

TATE, W. K., of London
fl. 1828–1834

He exhibited at the Royal Academy in 1828 and 1829, showing a number of busts, including those of the Hon. George Agar-Ellis and Major Bridgeman. His small bronze bust of Henry Philip Hope, dated 1834, is in the possession of the writer.

TATHAM, FREDERICK
b. 1805, *d.* 1878

Eldest son of Charles Heathcote Tatham (1772–1842), the architect, he received a Silver Palette from the Society of Arts in 1824, but it was not until 1833 that he joined the Royal Academy Schools on the recommendation of J. Phillips, R.A. He exhibited at the Academy, 1825–1836, and at the British Institution, 1828–1829, showing various busts, including those of Lord Eldon (now in the National Portrait Gallery), John Colley, the Hon. George Neville, Edward Irving and Edward Walpole. His bust of Charles Tatham, dated 1837, is at Lord Northampton's Almshouses, Greenwich.

Graves, in his *Exhibitors at the Royal Academy*, says that Tatham also showed miniatures at the Academy until 1854. He was the close friend of William Blake and his wife (see Gilchrist's *Life of Blake*). In 1829 he made a statue of Lord Eldon for the Eldon Schools, Vauxhall.

TATHAM, BENJAMIN and WILLIAM, of Folkingham
fl. 1811–1839

They sign tablets to Mary Eastland, 1811, at Folkingham, Lincolnshire, and to George Wakefield, 1839, at East Stoke, Nottinghamshire.

TAUNTON and BROWN

They sign a large oval tablet with a relief of "Religion" seated by an urn to John Barnfather, 1793, in St. Giles-in-the-Fields.

TAYLOR, H.
b. 1805

He joined the Royal Academy Schools in 1825, and in 1843, when living in Dover Street, showed a model of a horse at the Academy.

TAYLOR, MICHAEL, of York
b. 1760, *d.* 1846

He was born at Felton in Northumberland and became a Freeman of York in 1803. From 1802 until 1810 he did a large amount of stone-carving at York Minster, including figures of Percy and Vavasour for the central doorway in 1802 and a statue of Henry VI for the organ-screen in 1810. From 1814 to 1818 he was working on repairs to Skelton Church, Yorkshire, where he was responsible for all the stone-carving. A writer to the *Builder* (1846, page 317) who saw him just before he died, describes him as "a man well skilled in Gothic art and accustomed to it from boyhood."

Taylor also produced a large number of monuments and tablets, the best being those to the Duke of Kingston, *c.* 1806, at Holme Pierrepont, Notts, which has a relief of a mourning woman; to the Rev. Henry Goodriche, 1801, which has charming swags of flowers, and to Sir Walter Vavasour, 1810. The two last-named are both at Sutton-in-the-Forest, Yorkshire, the former in the Parish Church, the latter in the Roman Catholic Chapel.

Other tablets executed by Taylor in Yorkshire, commemorate Susanna Lloyd, 1797, at Swillington; John Lea, 1800, at Sowerby; James Saunders, 1803, in All Saints', York; Christopher Oxley, 1803, and Thomas Kilvington, 1809, both in Ripon Cathedral; Lady Mary Hore, *c.* 1804, and the Hon. Dorothy Langley, 1824, both in York Minster; Emily Cleaver, 1806, at Nunnington; Samuel Waterhouse, 1807, at Halifax; the Rev. William Comber, 1810, at Stonegrave; John Babley, 1820, and Countess Harcourt, 1833, both at Masham; John Raper, 1824, at Aberford;

Thomas Norcliffe, 1828, at Langdon; and Thomas Eadon, 1835, at Selby.

(Allen's *Yorkshire*, Vol. I, page 284; Hargroves' *York*, Vol. II, page 77.)

TAYLOR, ROBERT
b. c. 1690, *d.* 1742

He was apprenticed to Richard Garbut, "citizen and mason," and became free in 1712. In 1722 he was working for the Ironmongers' Company and two years later he carved a chimney-piece, costing £40, for Stourhead. In 1732 he received £150 and in 1733 £98 for unidentified works in the same house, probably chimney-pieces, although Taylor might have had something to do with the building of Alfred's Tower in the grounds, or with the carving of King Alfred's statue (Archives, Hoare's Bank). In 1732 also he made a chimney-piece for Masons' Hall, while from the Grocers' Company he received £69 for decorative carving undertaken in 1735–1736. For the Barber Surgeons he seems to have acted as master-mason when their theatre was rebuilt from designs by Lord Burlington.

From 1725 until 1739 Taylor was the mason for the Royal College of Physicians and was also responsible for a good deal of the building of St. Bartholomew's Hospital between 1728 and 1740. Here his decorative work included carving "leaves at the bottom of the scrolls" and a chimney-piece for which he was paid £62 in 1730. Two years previously he had rented "two tenements in Duck Lane" from the Governors of the Hospital.

As a statuary Taylor is important. His masterpiece is the magnificent monument with its reclining figure of Thomas Deacon, 1721, in Peterborough Cathedral. Others signed by him include those to Michael Askill, 1713, at Chadshunt, Warwick; Mrs. Jane Brewer, 1716, at West Farleigh, Kent; the Raymond family, 1720, at Belchamp Walter, Essex; Sir John Garrard, *c.* 1720, at Wheathampstead, Herts; Abraham Hill, 1721, Sutton-at-Hone, Kent; Francis Barrell, 1724, in Rochester Cathedral; Sir Nathaniel Napier, 1725, at Minterne Magna, Dorset; Lady Pennyman, 1727, at Stainton, Yorks; John Fisher, *c.* 1730, at Hayes, Middlesex; and Robert Chester, 1732, at Hunsdon, Herts.

Taylor, who was also a Captain in the City Trained Bands, made a large fortune out of his business, but wasted it by living extravagantly in a house in Essex and died leaving little except debts. His death is noted in the Court Book of the Masons' Company. (*Builder*, 1846, page 505; Archives of City Companies, etc., mentioned in text.)

TAYLOR, SIR ROBERT
b. 1714, *d.* 1788

The son of Robert Taylor, *d.* 1742 (q.v.), he was apprenticed to Henry Cheere (q.v.). On becoming free young Taylor went to study in Rome, but he had only been a short time in Italy when he heard that his father was ill and decided to return home. Europe was then at war and, finding it almost impossible to get a passport, Taylor disguised himself as a Franciscan monk and so passed safely through the enemy's lines. He was very proud of this exploit, and kept the habit he had worn until the day of his death, often showing it to his friends and telling the story of his adventures.

When he arrived in England Taylor found that his father had died heavily in debt, and the young man decided to set up as a statuary on his own account, although he once told a friend many years later that he had only eighteen pence in his pocket at the time. However, some assistance from the Godfrey family of Woodford in Essex, together with his own efforts, soon started him on his successful career and by 1744 he had made such a name for himself that he was entrusted with the Abbey monument to Captain Cornewall, for which Parliament had voted a sum of money. In the same year he became free of the Masons' Company by patrimony.

Taylor later carved the figure of Britannia in the centre of the principal façade of the old Bank of England, and the sculpture in the pediment of the Mansion House, for which he received £420. Roubiliac (q.v.) and Cheere (q.v.) had also sent in models for this work, but when Lord Burlington was asked to select the winning design he refused, observing acidly that "any sculptor would do well enough for such a building as that." According to Taylor's obituary in the *Gentleman's Magazine* (1788, page 930), his practice on this and other occasions was "to hew out his heads from the block and except for some few finishing touches, to leave the rest to his workmen."

As a mason Taylor carried out repairs to Mr. Du Cane's house in St. James's Square in 1750, when he received £267 (Essex Records, D/DDC.A. 18). In the same year he was paid £131 by Lord Folkestone for chimney-pieces, etc., at Longford (Longford Castle Archives).

About 1753 Taylor practically abandoned sculpture for architecture, but his work as an architect is, of course, outside the scope of this book. He was Sheriff of London, 1782–1783, when he was knighted. He died on 27 September, 1788, from a chill caught at the funeral of his friend Sir Charles Asgill, and was buried on 9 October, in a vault near the north-east corner of St. Martin-in-the-Fields. A cenotaph was later erected in Westminster Abbey which records that his "works entitle him to a distinguished rank in the first Class of British architects. He was eminently useful to the Public as an active and impartial Magistrate."

Taylor was a hard-working man who "never slept after four in the morning. When he had a journey to make, he did it in the night and thus never, but in a carriage, slept at all." Unlike his father, he died extremely well off, leaving the bulk of his large fortune of £180,000 to his son Michael Angelo for life, and then to the University of Oxford to endow a foundation for teaching modern European languages.

Taylor's finest monumental work is the statue in Grendon Church, Warwick, of Miss Mary Chetwynd, who died in 1750 at the age of ninety-one. His monuments commemorating Robert Shippen, 1745, in Brasenose College Chapel, Oxford; Christopher and John Emmott, 1746, at Colne, Lancs; William Phipps, 1748, at Westbury, Wilts; and Lieut.-General Joshua Guest, 1752, in Westminster Abbey, all have portrait-busts, while that to his early patrons the Godfrey family in Woodford churchyard takes the form of a large marble column with a Corinthian capital. Other works signed by him include those to Thomas Marsh, 1739, at Womenswold, Kent; Sir James Pennyman, 1745, at Stainton, Yorks; Thomas Panuwell, 1749, at Tonbridge, Kent; Daniel Adey, 1752, at Wotton-under-Edge, Glos; Charles Pyott, 1753, in St. Martin's, Canterbury; Elizabeth Townsend, 1754, at Thorpe, Surrey; the Rev. Alexander Young, 1755, at Wickham-breaux, Kent; Richard Emmott, 1761, at Colne, Lancs; and Edmund Auberry, 1767, at Pinner, Middlesex.

(*Builder*, 1846, page 505; authorities cited in text.)

TAYLOR, ROBERT,
of Melton Mowbray
fl. 1706–1710

As a mason he was employed to build a house in Melton Mowbray, in 1708 for Thomas Coke, but apparently had difficulty in getting paid, as he writes to Coke: "I was fain to hire many men when your Honour was down and I have paid them as far as I am able and I desire you to consider my condition and relieve me, as I have not neglected your business night nor day, but have left all business to serve you. I beg you to send me an order as speedily as you can" (Archives, Marquess of Lothian). While working at Melbourne, Taylor seems to have taken his son, Robert Taylor, the younger, into partnership, as various bills are made out to them both.

TAYLOR, THOMAS,
of Nottingham
fl. 1738–1745

As a carver in "marble, stone and wood" he was employed at Welbeck Abbey from 1743 until 1745. Here he executed ornamental work, including a carved stone doorcase and two chimney-pieces, one for the alcove room costing £41 and another at £127. The latter must have been of some importance, for the decoration consisted of "lions' heads, snakes, two shields and two columns and capitals" (Archives, Welbeck Abbey).

Taylor signs a large monument with a medallion portrait of Sir John Bennett, *c.* 1740, at Melton Mowbray, Leicestershire.

TAYLOR, THOMAS,
of Stratford-on-Avon

He signs a tablet to Robert Middleton, 1833, at Snitterfield, Warwick. An "E. Taylor of Stratford-on-Avon" signs a tablet to Philip Wren, 1829, at Wroxall in the same county.

TAYLOR, W. H., of Birmingham

In 1830 he showed a model of George IV at the Birmingham Society of Artists. A "Mr. Taylor of Birmingham"—a different person according to the catalogue—exhibited at the same time a "Model of James Watt."

TAYLOR, WILLIAM, of London

He signs a wall-tablet to Mrs. Slingsby, 1837, in All Saints, St. Pancras.

TEASDALE, JOHN, the Elder,
and JOHN, the Younger
John Teasdale the Younger: *b.* 1777

The elder Teasdale was born at Greystoke in Cumberland and in 1780 was brought to the notice of the Duke of Norfolk, who had him trained under a London sculptor. About ten years later he began work as "a sculptor of ornaments in marble" at Arundel Castle, which was then being rebuilt, and here he was responsible for much of the ornamental work (Dallaway's *Western Sussex*, Vol. II, Part I, page 162).

John Teasdale the Younger attended the Royal Academy Schools in 1801. He and his father were two of the chief stone-carvers employed during the restoration of King Henry VII's Chapel in Westminster Abbey in 1809 (Brayley's *Westminster Abbey*, Vol. I, Part II, page 26). A Michael Teasdale, who may have been a relation, was awarded a Silver Palette for sculpture by the Society of Arts in 1823. He later settled in Bath and is described as "a sculptor" in the directory of 1842.

TEMPLETON, GEORGE
fl. 1811–1847

He was born in Liverpool, and was living there in Olive Street when he exhibited a figure of "Venus Rising From the Sea" at the Liverpool Academy in 1811.

In 1844 Templeton exhibited at Westminster Hall a figure of St. John the Divine, which the *Literary Gazette* considered "exactly like Westall's 'Spirit of the Storm,' " and the Art Union "poor and faulty to a degree."

The sculptor (whose initials are incorrectly given in Grave's *Exhibitors at the Royal Academy*) showed a marble bust there in 1847.

TEMPLETOWN, LADY
b. 1747, *d.* 1823

She was Elizabeth, daughter of Shuckburgh Boughton of Poston, Co. Hereford, and married in 1769 Clotworthy Upton, who was created Lord Templetown in 1776. Lady Templetown made a number of designs for Wedgwood between 1783 and 1787. Her busts of the first Marquess of Bristol (her son-in-law) and Lady Augusta Seymour are at Ickworth Park, Suffolk. (Wedgwood Archives; *Art Journal*, 1864, page 256.)

TENERANI, PIETRO
b. 1789, *d.* 1870

Tenerani, who was born near Carrara and worked under Thorwaldsen, exhibited at the Royal Academy a marble statue of "Psyche" in 1846, and a bust of Lady Arbuthnot in 1854. His bust of Prince Woronzow is at Wilton, and his statue of "Flora," dated 1848, in the Royal Collection. In Castle Ashby Church, Northamptonshire, is his monument to Margaret, Marchioness of Northampton, 1830, a work which has a charming relief, although his heroic angel commemorating the second Marquess, 1866, in the same church is rather overpowering.

Tenerani was an indefatigable sculptor and produced a vast number of works. He was General Director of the museums and galleries of Rome, and six years after he died a special museum was opened in that city containing more than four hundred and fifty of his statues, groups, busts, etc. (*Men of Our Times*, 1869).

TERNOUTH, JOHN
b. 1795, *d.* 1849

He attended the Royal Academy Schools in

1820, gaining a Silver Medal two years later. In 1844 he exhibited at Westminster Hall a statue of "A Penitent," described variously by the *Literary Gazette* as "being very carelessly done and wanting in feeling" and by the *Art Union* as "treated in a spirit which appeals to our sympathies."

In 1847 Ternouth carved figures of St. George and Britannia flanking a shield for the centre of the east front of Buckingham Palace (Clifford Smith's *Buckingham Palace*, page 55). His best-known work is the great bronze relief of the Battle of Copenhagen at the base of the Nelson Column in Trafalgar Square. He exhibited at the Royal Academy, 1819–1849, where he showed a number of busts, including those of John Cam Hobhouse (1825); Sir Francis Burdett (1827); Sir John Tyrell (1829); Viscount Melbourne (1837); Sir Ronald Ferguson (1839); Lord John Russell (1841); and Lord Bridport (1842). His bust of John Ireland, Dean of Westminster, is in the Abbey, while those of Peter Fraser (1828) and John Kaye, Bishop of Lincoln (1834), are at Christ's College, Cambridge, and Brasenose College, Oxford, respectively. His statues include those of Dean Shipley (1829) in St. Asaph's Cathedral; the Duke of Atholl (1835) at Dunkeld; and General Conway (1844) in Madras Cathedral.

Apparently Ternouth produced very little work towards the end of his life, and a report went round that he had died. This he hastened to correct and the *Athenaeum* of 14 November, 1846, reported that "Mr. Ternouth has written to say he is not dead and we give him the benefit of the assertion."

Ternouth's monuments are uninteresting, the symbolism being hackneyed, obvious and uninspired; for example, the monument of Frances Popham, 1839, at Chilton Foliat, Bucks, has a relief of a hand breaking a lily. His most ambitious work commemorates Henry Davidson, 1827, in the parish church of Kingston-on-Thames, which has a life-size seated figure in high relief. Another, to the Bennett family, 1821, in St. Mary Abbots, Kensington, has a well-carved relief of an angel ascending to heaven. Other signed works by him include those to William Kinnersly, 1823, at Ashley, Staffs; Sir John Filmer, Bart., 1824, at East Sutton, Kent; Lady Tyrell, 1825, at Boreham, Essex; Admiral Sir James Morris, 1830, at Marlow, Bucks; Jean Miller, 1831, in the Colonnade at Kensal Green Cemetery; Colonel Mark Wilks, 1831, in the Grosvenor Chapel; the Rev. Henry Ridley, 1832 at Hambleden, Bucks; Elizabeth Arbuthnot, 1834, at Ockley, Surrey; Jeremiah and Rose Milles, 1835, at Sawbridgeworth, Herts; Pelham Warren, 1835, at Worting,

Hants; John Phillips, 1836, at Wotten Warren, Warwick; Sir Peter and Lady Warburton, 1837, at Budworth, Cheshire; Susannah Newton, 1837, at Great Hallingbury, Essex; the Rev. William Heath, 1838, in St. George's, Grenada; Marianne Maurice, 1840, in St. Peter's, Marlborough; Thomas Lane, 1844, in Madras Cathedral; Prudence Lamb (*d.* 1843, monument erected 1848), at Meeth, Devon, and Lady Madden, 1849, at Jacobstowe in the same county.

THEAKSTON, CHARLES DELATRE

b. 1804

Theakston, who may have been a son of Joseph Theakston (q.v.) attended the Royal Academy Schools in 1820, and in the following year received the Silver Isis Medal from the Society of Arts for a copy of the "Laocoon." In 1825 he exhibited a bust of Edward Hind at the Academy, and in 1831 a cabinet statue of the Duke of Wellington.

J. H. Theakston, who was possibly a relative, showed a bust at the Academy in 1832.

THEAKSTON, CHRISTOPHER, of Doncaster

fl. 1762–1783

He was an apprentice, and later an assistant, of C. Richardson (q.v.) and together they were employed at Wentworth Woodhouse in 1762 (Fitzwilliam Archives). On 6 July, 1774, Theakston became a Freeman of Doncaster and in the same year carved the figure of "Justice" for Newark Town Hall. On 14 February, 1765, he married Harriet Richardson, daughter of his former master. She died 19 January, 1808, aged 61. In 1773 Theakston, now working on his own account, received £73 for two chimney-pieces for the front hall of Nostell, Yorks (Brockwell's *The Nostell Collection*, page 19). Ten years later he was again engaged at Wentworth Woodhouse. He signs a monument to William Bilbie, 1777, at Blidworth, Notts.

(Doncaster and Newark Corporation Archives.)

THEAKSTON, JOSEPH

b. 1772, *d.* 1842

His father, John Theakston of St. Michael's, Spurriergate, York, died when young Theakston was a child and his mother, Sarah Theakston, apprenticed him in 1786 to John Fisher (q.v.). He became free in 1794 and shortly afterwards went to London, where he entered the studio of John Bacon the Elder (q.v.). He later worked as assistant both to John Flaxman (q.v.) and E. H.

PLATE XXVII

EDWARD STANTON
Sir Francis Russell, 1705, Strensham, Worcestershire.

THOMAS STAYNER
Dr. Turner, 1714, Stowe-Nine-Churches, Northants.

CHARLES R. SMITH
Rev. Thomas Whitaker, 1822, Whalley, Yorkshire.

PLATE XXVIII

WILLIAM TYLER
Samuel Vassall, 1766, King's Chapel, Boston, U.S.A.

JOHN WALSH
Bust of Lady Lechmere, part of the monument to
Sir Thomas Robinson and his wife, the Dowager
Lady Lechmere, c. 1778, Westminster Abbey.

HENRY WEEKES
Robert Southey, 1843, Westminster Abbey.

Baily (q.v.), but spent the last twenty-four years of his life in the employment of Sir Francis Chantrey (q.v.), carving most of the drapery, etc., for the latter's statues and groups.

In 1821 the *English Chronicle* of 20 December reported that the iron railings in Westminster Abbey "which obstructed the view of the monuments in this beautiful edifice are now removed preparatory to Mr. Theakston the sculptor beginning his Herculean task of cleaning and restoring them." In that year also he executed a statue of Mr. S. Watson for Weymouth Guildhall, which was followed by another of the Duke of Sutherland for Golspie, Sutherland, in 1838.

In 1829 Theakston received £1,000 for the sculptured-marble chimney-piece and clock-frame in the grand hall of Buckingham Palace. This is perhaps the most imposing chimney-piece in the building, with its winged female figures supporting a roundel fitted with a clock, the whole being surmounted by a bust of George IV (P.R.O., Works 19/3). He exhibited at the Royal Academy, 1809–1837, and at the British Institution, 1813–1819, showing busts of R. Walker (1813); Mr. Schwanfelder, "animal painter to H.R.H. the Prince Regent" (1818); and Queen Victoria (1830); also a number of models and sketches for monuments to national heroes.

Theakston died on 14 April, 1842, and was buried in Kensal Green Cemetery. Peter Cunningham, who knew him well, wrote in the *Builder* of 1863 (page 112) that he was "a fine, venerable, kind-hearted man, ever prompt with a kind word and a kind smile," and that in his work with Chantrey "he was a consummate master in making marble convey the qualities and surfaces of silks and satins, velvets and ermines." His obituary in the *Gentleman's Magazine* (1842, Part I, page 672) said of him that "he was, perhaps, the ablest drapery or ornamental carver of his time, as he was certainly the most rapid. When he began to carve a statue he knew perfectly well what was required of him and cut away the superfluous marble at once. He had not to try again and again, like most artists, and by frequent touching and retouching accomplish his object."

Theakston's monuments are mostly Hellenistic. The one commemorating William Davey, 1827, at Redruth, Cornwall, has a medallion portrait, while another to the Rev. Roger Carus Wilson, 1839, in Preston Parish Church has a relief of the five churches in that city which were built through Wilson's efforts.

Other signed monuments by Theakston include those to Reymundo Putt, 1812, at Gittisham, Devon; Sir William Herschell, 1822, at Upton, Bucks; Anthony Hamond, 1822, Westacre,

Norfolk; Robert Dorner, 1823, at Budbrook, Warwick; Peter Elmsley, 1825, and Bishop Lloyd, 1829, both in Oxford Cathedral; Lady Sophia Heathcote, 1825, at Normanton, Rutland; Thomas Hethrington, 1825, in Walthamstow Parish Church; Bishop Heber, 1826, in St. Peter's, Colombo; Mary Inglis, 1827, at Wartling, Sussex; Sophia Matlock, 1828, at Bramley, Surrey; Archbishop Manners Sutton, 1828, at Addington, Surrey; Georgiana Serocold-Pearce, 1828, and Ann Pearce, 1835, both at Cherry Hinton, Cambs; Frances Goring, 1830, at Wiston, Sussex; John Christie, 1831, at Broxbourne, Herts; Marmaduke Ramsay, 1831, in Jesus College Chapel, Cambridge; the Rev. Charles Platt, 1833, at Forthampton, Glos; Frederick Page, 1834, at Speen, Berks; and Anne Wynter, 1839, at Lanlivery, Cornwall.

(York Apprentice Books; British Museum Ad. MS. 39, 784; *Builder*, 1863, page 113; authorities cited in text.)

THEED, WILLIAM, the Elder
b. 1764, *d.* 1817

He was the son of a wig-maker in Wych Street and entered the Royal Academy Schools in 1786. He began his career as a painter, and exhibited both portraits and classical subjects at the Academy from 1789 until 1805. About 1791 he went to Rome where he remained for four or five years.

In 1799 Theed began to model for Messrs. Wedgwood, and in the archives of the firm there is a letter to him dated 26 December of that year by the younger Wedgwood. In it the writer considers that "upon further consideration it appears very desirable that we should know each other better before we bind ourselves to one another for three years. You will be better able to understand what are *our* wants and expectations, and we should have a probability of their being fulfilled." The letter continues: "To induce you till this is done is to break up your former connexion and might eventually be an act of cruelty. After this fair, open and deliberate understanding has taken place we shall come together with a greater certainty of mutual satisfaction." The matter was settled and Theed worked for the Wedgwoods until 1804, when he left them for Messrs. Rundell and Bridge, for whom he designed gold and silver plate until his death in 1817. In 1811, however, he was again employed by Wedgwoods and modelled for them a portrait of Thomas Byerley.

Theed was elected a Royal Academician in 1813, depositing as his Diploma Work a "Bacchanalian Group in bronze," which has since disappeared from Burlington House. His work which is best known to Londoners is the spirited group of "Hercules Capturing the Thracian Horses" on the pediment of the Royal Mews facing Buckingham Palace Road. Other works executed by him include the group entitled "The Prodigal Son" which was formerly in the possession of Lord Yarborough and is now in the Ussher Art Gallery, Lincoln, and another in 1812 of "Thetis Returning from Vulcan with Arms for Achilles" which is in the Royal Collection. His fine monument of Thomas Westfaling, 1814, with its portrait-bust and relief of "Charity Teaching Children" is in the parish church of Ross-on-Wye, Herefordshire.

After his death in 1817, Theed's widow (*née* Rougeot) applied to the Royal Academy for a pension and was granted £50, but she died in the following year (Academy Archives).

(Sanby's *Royal Academy of Arts*, Vol. I, page 382.)

THEED, WILLIAM, the Younger
b. 1804, *d.* 1891

The younger Theed was born at Trentham in Staffordshire, the son of William Theed (q.v.) who was then working for Wedgwood, and a French-woman named Rougeot, whom his father had married in Naples in 1794. He attended the Royal Academy Schools and also worked for five years in the studio of E. H. Baily (q.v.). In 1820 he won the Silver Palette from the Society of Arts for a figure of Hercules and, two years later, their Silver Isis Medal.

In 1826 Theed went to Rome and studied under Thorwaldsen, Gibson and Wyatt, sending over several busts to the exhibitions of the Royal Academy. In 1844 the Prince Consort asked John Gibson (q.v.) to send him designs by English sculptors working in Rome for marble statues to be placed in Osborne House, which had been recently acquired by the Queen. Two designs by Theed were accepted and in 1848 he returned to London. Here he soon received a large number of commissions, chiefly for public statues. He was also chosen by Queen Victoria to take the death-mask of the Prince Consort in 1861.

Between 1853 and 1859 Theed made a series of twelve bas-reliefs for the Prince's chambers at the Palace of Westminster. In 1856 he made a "series of variegated marble pedestals and busts of classic form" for the State Rooms of Buckingham Palace (*Art Journal*, 1856, page 192), two reliefs for the banqueting-room, and others of "The Birth of Venus" and "Venus Bringing Armour to Achilles" for the dining-room gallery. He also carved four classical busts for the Palace in the same year. In 1858 he made models of seated figures repre-

senting "Morning" and "Evening" for Queen's Gate, Hyde Park, but for some reason they were never cut in marble.

In 1865 he designed a statue of the Prince Consort which was executed in terra-cotta for the Bishops Waltham Infirmary, and in the following year modelled the figures for the baptismal silver group presented to Prince Victor by his grand-mother, Queen Victoria.

In 1867 Theed carved the reredos for St. John's Church, Croydon, and in 1872 he exhibited at the International Exhibition reliefs of the "Four Acts of Mercy" which he had made some years previously for the monument of the Duchess of Gloucester in St. George's Chapel, Windsor. On the window-sill of the parish church of Churchgate Street, Essex, is the figure of a dead child signed by Theed and dated 1862; his bust of an unknown man signed "W. Theed fecit Roma 1848" is at St. George's Hospital.

Theed exhibited at the Royal Academy, 1824–1885; at the British Institution, 1852 and 1853; and at the Great Exhibition of 1851, where he showed a statue of "Prometheus." His "Rebekah," then in the possession of S. Ashton, was shown at the Exhibition of Art Treasures held in Manchester in 1857, while the sculptor himself lent his "Narcissus" and "Ruth." His "Prodigal's Return" was in Miss Webb's sale held at Christie's on 3 March, 1878, when it realized £143. Theed died 9 September, 1891.

(*D.N.B.*; *Art Journal*, 1891, page 352; various references *Builder* and *Art Journal*.)

STATUES

c. 1840	Lady De L'Isle and Dudley	Penshurst Church, Kent
1847	Psyche	Royal Collection
1847	Narcissus	Royal Collection
1849	Charles Norris	Bombay Cathedral
1853	Humphrey Chetham	Manchester Cathedral
1854	John Dalton	Manchester
1856	Five Statues of "Cities"	New Wing, Somerset House
1857	Hon. Evelyn Pelham	Exhibited Royal Academy
1857	The Bard	Mansion House
1857	Boadicea	For Sir M. Peto
1857	Sir Isaac Newton	New College, Oxford
1857	James Watt	Manchester
1858	Edmund Burke	Palace of Westminster
1859	Sir Isaac Newton	Grantham
1860	Sir William Peel	Maritime Museum, Greenwich
1861	Sir William Peel	Sandy Church, Beds
1863	Sir William Peel	Calcutta
1863	Prince Consort	Balmoral
1863	Henry Hallam	St. Paul's

1864	Duchess of Kent	Frogmore
1864	Africa	Albert Memorial
1865	Prince Consort	Rosenau, Coburg
1866	Prince Consort	Sydney, Australia
1866	Musidora	For Marlborough House
1867	George IV and William IV	For Palace of Westminster (now Sessions House, Old Bailey)
1868	Queen Victoria and the Prince Consort as Ancient Saxons	Windsor Castle
1868	Earl of Derby	Liverpool
1869	Locke, Bacon and Adam Smith	Façade of Burlington House
1871	Two Angels	Private Chapel, Windsor Castle
1872	Earl of Derby	Junior Carlton Club
1873	Sir Robert Peel	Huddersfield
1876	Hon. C. P. Villiers	Manchester Town Hall
1876	Hagar and Ishmael	Formerly possession Lord Cowdray
1877	John Bright	Manchester Town Hall
1878	Gladstone	Manchester
?	Dancing Girl	Dunorlan Park, Tunbridge Wells

BUSTS

1839	Duke of Lucca	Ducal Palace, Lucca
1839	Princess of Capua	Exhibited Royal Academy
1852	John Gibson	Conway Church (unveiled 1866)
1855	Periander	Osborne
1856	Clyte	Royal Collection
1858	Flora	Bowood
1859	Prince Consort	Buckingham Palace
1860	Queen Victoria and the Prince Consort	Grocers' Hall
1860	Queen Anne	Windsor Castle
1861	Sir John Lawrence	Grocers' Hall
1861	Crown Prince of Prussia	Buckingham Palace
1861	Prince Consort	Society of Arts
1861	Prince Frederick of Prussia	Royal Collection
1862	Prince Consort	Windsor Castle
1864	Henry Hallam	Royal Collection
1866	Prince Consort	For Surrey County Hospital
1868	Earl of Derby	Knowsley
1869	Sir William Tite	Guildhall, Bath
1873	Sir Henry Holland	National Portrait Gallery
1874	Baron Van de Weyer	Windsor Castle
1875	Sir Charles Lyell	Westminster Abbey
1877	Lady Augusta Stanley	Windsor Castle
1879	Duke of Sussex	Windsor Castle
1879	Pitt (after Nollekens)	Lincoln's Inn

1879	Sir Francis Goldsmid	Benchers' Hall, Lincoln's Inn
1881	Rowland Hill	Manchester City Hall
1885	Lord Salisbury	Exhibited Royal Academy
1886	General Gordon	Guildhall
1887	J. P. de Gex	Lincoln's Inn

MONUMENTS

1824	Felbrigg, Norfolk	Mrs. Windham
1828	Little Berkhampstead, Herts	Robert Hanbury
1834	Stow Bardolph, Norfolk	Lady Hare
1837	Penshurst, Kent	Sir John Shelley-Sidney
1849	Essendon Herts	Robert and Laura Hanbury (figures of two children)
1851	Gresford, Denbigh	John Williams (figure of "Resignation")
1853	Trent, Somerset	Rev. William Turner (recumbent figure)
1855	Westminster Abbey	Sir James Mackintosh (d. 1832)
1856	Harlington, Middlesex	Countess de Salis (recumbent figure)
1857	Kensal Green Cemetery	Louisa Bright
1860	Little Berkhampstead, Herts	Lady Eardley
1860	Oxford (All Souls)	Henry Denison
1862	Doddington, Kent	Sir John Croft
1863	Thundridge, Herts	Caroline Hanbury
1864	Whippingham, I.O.W.	Prince Consort
1864	Belton, Lincs	Hon. and Rev. Richard Cust
1865	Wrenbury, Cheshire	Lord Combermere
1867	Thundridge, Herts	Robert Culling-Hanbury
1868	Westminster Abbey	Sir Herbert Edwardes
1874	Prestwold, Leics.	Lt.-Colonel George Packe

THEWS, —

He signs a large and ambitious wall-tablet at Hascombe, Surrey, to William Diddlesfold, 1785.

THOM, JAMES
b. 1802, *d.* 1850

He was born at Lochlee on 17 April, 1802, and as a boy was apprenticed to a builder at Kilmarnock who employed him on ornamental carving. Though he had never had any lessons, Thom executed a bust of Burns in 1827, and when this was widely praised determined on a more ambitious work. Without so much as a preliminary sketch, he proceeded to hew out of the local grey-stone life-size figures of "Tam O'Shanter" and "Souter Johnnie." The statues were at once secured for the Burns monument at

Alloway and were then sent on tour. A large sum was raised by charging a shilling for admission, the net profit amounting to nearly £2,000 after all expenses had been paid. In 1829 the figures came to London where the critics at once hailed them as inaugurating a new era in sculpture. Emboldened by his success, Thom showed two new works in London in 1834, but these did not meet with such a favourable reception.

Two years later the sculptor set off to America in pursuit of his agent, a fellow Scotsman, who had gone over to exhibit some of his works, but who had kept all the proceeds. Thom at last tracked the man down in Newark, New Jersey, where he forced him to disgorge most of the embezzled money; he then decided to stay and work in America and accordingly settled down in Newark. It was he who discovered the quarries at Little Falls, which later furnished stone for a number of important buildings. One of these was Trinity Church in New York, for which Thom did most of the Gothic stone carving, although he left before the building was completed, owing to a disagreement with the architect. Having amassed a considerable fortune, he bought a farm at Ramapo, Rockland County. He died in New York on 17 April, 1850.

Besides the two statues which first attracted attention (replicas of which are at Beauport Park in Sussex), Thom's other works in Scotland include a group entitled "Old Mortality" at Maxwelltown in Dumfries, and a statue of Wallace at Ayr, of which he executed a replica for Lord Grey's seat of Kinfauns Castle, Perth. At Burns' cottage at Alloway are the figures of "The Landlord" and "The Landlady." Of these he also made several replicas, including those for Lord Cassillis, who had them sent to his house near London "where his Lordship intends to have them placed in a building representing an old Scotch ale-house" (Swan's *Views of the River Clyde*, page 158).

Thom's works in America include a statue of Burns, another replica of his "Old Mortality" group for Laurel Hill Cemetery, Philadelphia, and various ornamental pieces for gardens.

(*Gentleman's Magazine*, 1850, Part II, page 98; *Builder*, 1851, page 48; *Building Chronicle*, Vol. II, page 66.)

THOM, ROBERT, of Glasgow
b. 1805, *d.* 1895

According to the *Art Union* of 1839 (page 153), he was the sculptor of the monument erected in that year at Drumclog to commemorate the victory of the Scottish Covenanters over the forces of Graham of Claverhouse. It is described as being 23 ft. high and in the Gothic style. Robert was the brother of James Thom (q.v.), and as a boy was apprenticed to Howie and Brown, builders, of Kilmarnock.

THOMAS, MARY, of Exmouth
fl. 1814–1817

She signs a large wall-tablet to the Heathfield family, 1816, at Cullompton, Devon. Her tablet to Charles Fanshawe, 1814, was formerly in the Temple Church, but was destroyed by enemy action.

THOMAS, C., of Sherborne
b. 1742, *d.* 1805

He signs wall-tablets to John Gaisford, 1775, at Axbridge, Somerset, and to Thomas Pearson, 1785, at Queen Camel in the same county. According to Hutchins' *Dorset* (Vol. IV, page 124), he signed a monument to the Rev. William Preston, 1785, at Bradford Abbas, but this no longer exists.

Thomas was succeeded in the business by his son, J. Thomas, who repaired the monuments of the Williams family at Wotton Glanville, Dorset, in 1805 (*Monthly Magazine*, 1805, Part I, page 197), and also signs a tablet to the Rev. William Owen, 1830, at Castleton in the same county.

THOMAS, JOHN
b. 1813, *d.* 1862

Thomas was born at Chalford, Gloucestershire, and was left an orphan at the age of thirteen. He became the apprentice of a stone-mason in a neighbouring village, but on the expiration of his term went to Birmingham, where he had a brother practising as an architect. Soon after his arrival he secured a contract for erecting a Gothic monument in Huntingdon and this work was later brought to the notice of Sir Charles Barry, then building Birmingham Grammar School. Barry was so impressed by Thomas's talent that he at once engaged him to execute all the ornamental and carved-stone and wood work at the school, a task which took him three years to complete.

When his work for Barry had ended, Thomas was employed by the architect Blore to carve coats of arms and heraldic devices for Crewe Hall and Capesthorne Hall which the latter was then building. After this he went to various towns on the new North Midland Railway to execute appropriate coats of arms on the stations then in course of erection. Meanwhile Barry had not forgotten him, and, as soon as the building of the Houses of Parliament was far enough advanced, engaged him to superintend the stone-carving in the entire structure. Thomas, whose industry must have been amazing, was himself responsible for a prodigious amount of work, including the statues on the north and south fronts, the panels with the arms of the Kings and Queens of England from William the Conqueror to Queen Victoria, the statues and bosses for the Victoria Tower and the bosses in St. Stephen's Hall. He later made the bronze statues of Stephen Langton, Archbishop of Canterbury, and William, Earl of Salisbury, for the House of Lords.

In 1845 he carved the statue of St. Michael and a pulpit for Sowton Church, Devon; in 1846 he made a font for Bolton-le-Moors, and in 1847 another for St. John's, Westminster. In 1848 the Prince Consort commissioned him to execute two large reliefs of "Peace" and "War" for Buckingham Palace, and in the same year he carved the two lions, each measuring 25 ft. in length and weighing 80 tons, for the Britannia Bridge, Menai Straits. In 1849 he supplied a chimney-piece for Mr. Brunel's "Shakespeare room," a series of bas-reliefs for Euston Station of the chief cities and towns connected with the North-Western Railway, and a group in high relief of "Britannia Supported by Science and Industry" for the same building.

Before 1850 Thomas had executed architectural sculpture for the National Bank in Glasgow, the Imperial Fire Office in London and the Bristol Law Courts. The life-size wooden figures of British Judges, etc., which he carved for the dining-hall of Lincoln's Inn also date from about the same time. In 1850 he restored a chimney-piece in the Royal Pavilion at Brighton and carved decorative details for Bridgewater House. In the following year he made the High Cross at Bristol.

It is impossible to give here all the sculpture executed by Thomas during the last twelve years of his life, but among his numerous works may be mentioned the fountain, etc., at Preston Hall, Maidstone (1851); decorative sculpture at Windsor railway station and statues on St. Martin's Church, Birmingham (1853); decorative work at the Crystal Palace (1854); sculpture on the façade of the Free Trade Hall, Manchester; a bronze bas-relief of "Ariel" for Balmoral; and a statue of the Duke of Sussex, presented by the sculptor to the Royal Free Hospital in London (1856); a statue of "Rachel," now in the Bethnal Green Museum; all the decorative sculpture for the Fine Arts Academy at Bristol (1857); the frieze round the United Service Club, London, and sculpture on the West of England Bank, Bristol (1858); a statue of Thomas Attwood at Birmingham (1859); and a statue of Queen

Victoria at Maidstone (1863). Other works carried out by him during those years were the coats of arms on the funeral car of the Duke of Wellington; the pediment and figures for the Great Western Hotel, Paddington; the great fountain at Castle Howard; sculptural decoration for the Sultan's Palace at Constantinople; and decorative sculpture on the piers of the entrance gates of Buckingham Palace. In 1861 he made the figures and vases for the new works at the Serpentine, Hyde Park.

In Edinburgh Thomas was responsible for the carving on the Life Assurance Building, a group for the Masonic Hall, and a fountain at Holyrood. At Glasgow he designed the mausoleum erected in 1854 by Mr. John Holsworth and also carved for it groups of "Faith," "Hope" and "Charity." In 1859 he made a chimney-piece for the same patron.

At the time of his death the sculptor was working on a chimney-piece for Windsor Castle, which had been ordered by the Prince Consort. It must have been rather a peculiar work, for it is described as having "bas-reliefs from the Midsummer Night's Dream, busts of two children, and a figure of Little Red Ridinghood." About the same time he finished another chimney-piece, also with reliefs from *A Midsummer Night's Dream*, for Mr. Lucas the contractor.

Thomas's ideal works include "Musidora"; "Una and the Lion" (reproduced in Parian china); "Lady Godiva" (the model for which is in Maidstone Museum); "A Naiad" for Queen Victoria; and "Boadicea" for Sir Morton Peto. Of his portrait statues, those of Sir Hugh Myddelton, for Islington, and Joseph Sturge, for Birmingham, were both unfinished at the time of his death. He also carved in 1845 the statue of Queen Victoria on the south end of Lincoln's Inn Library; it is, however, practically impossible to see this as it is a hundred feet above the pavement.

Thomas made a bust of the Prince Consort for the Birmingham Midland Institute, while others by him include those of three Royal Academicians, D. Maclise, J. Philip and W. Frith; the last-named, which was executed in ivory, is now in the Tate Gallery. His monuments include those to Lieutenant Richard Creed, 1841, in Westminster Abbey; Dr. Arnold, 1844, in Rugby School Chapel; and John Brooks, 1851, at Prestwich, near Manchester. His last work was the colossal Shakespeare monument for the International Exhibition of 1862. The difficulties he encountered over its admission to the Fine Art Gallery of the Exhibition hastened his end.

Incredible though it may seem, Thomas also worked as an architect and prepared designs for the National Bank of Glasgow; the Royal Dairy at Windsor; the Regent's Park Chapel; Headington House, Oxford; and the Print Room at Windsor Castle. For Sir Morton Peto he designed Somerleyton Hall and also executed a considerable amount of decorative carving for the house.

Thomas exhibited at the Royal Academy, 1842–1861, at the British Institution, 1850, and at the Great Exhibition of 1851, where he showed various works, including a statue of "Rosamunda" and a fountain. He died on 9 April, 1862.

(*Art Journal*, 1849, page 340, and 1862, page 144; *Illustrated London News*, 30 August, 1862; Catalogue of the International Exhibition, 1862; various references, *Art Journal* and *Builder*.)

THOMAS, JOHN EVAN

b. 1810, *d.* 1873

He was born at Brecon, the eldest son of John Thomas of Castle Street and his wife, Jane Evans, of Aberedw, Radnor. At a very early age he began to show an interest in sculpture, carving fruit and flowers in stone, and his father accordingly sent him to London to study under Sir Francis Chantrey (q.v.). Thomas later studied on the Continent and in 1844 exhibited at Westminster Hall his model for the statue of the second Lord Londonderry. This had a mixed reception from the critics, the *Literary Gazette* considering that it was "without intellect in the head and without dignity in the attitude," while the *Art Union* pronounced that it had "very considerable merit." The statue was later executed in marble and placed in Westminster Abbey in 1850. In 1848 Thomas carved the statues of Henri de Londres, Archbishop of Dublin, and William, Earl of Pembroke, for the House of Lords; in the same year he won the premium for sculpture at the Abergavenny Eisteddfod.

At the Great Exhibition of 1851 (of which he was one of the original guarantors) Thomas showed the model of his colossal statue of the Marquess of Bute, which was carried out in marble and erected in Cardiff later in the same year. He also exhibited "Science Unveiling Ignorance," the original model for which is now in the Cardiff City Hall. Two years later he repaired the ancient monuments of the Herberts in Cardiff Church.

About 1857 the sculptor left London, although he still kept his studio in Pimlico, and for the rest of his life lived mostly in Brecknockshire where he filled the office of High Sheriff in 1868. He had a considerable practice as a monumental sculptor, several of his works have well-cut medallion portraits, while his monument to the Rev. Thomas

Watkins (*d.* 1829) in Brecon Cathedral, has a lovely relief of two angels watching by a death-bed. The mausoleum of the Pearce family, 1856, in Llanspyddid churchyard is also his work.

Thomas exhibited at the Royal Academy, 1838–1870, showing a large number of works, chiefly portrait busts. He died on 3 October, 1873, and was buried in Brompton Cemetery.

(Poole's *Brecknockshire*, page 322; *Builder*, 1873, page 856; *Art Journal*, 1874, page 26.)

STATUES

1840	Wellington	For Joseph Bailey, of Glanusk
1851	Sir Charles Morgan	Newport
1853	Sir Joseph Bailey	Glenusk
1854	Wellington	Brecon
1857	James Vivian	Swansea
1857	Prince of Wales	Welsh Schools, Ashford, Middlesex
1863	Prince Consort	Tenby

BUSTS

1838	Daniel Jones	Cardiff Infirmary
1840	Sir W. Williams-Wynn	For Welsh Institution, London
1840	Sir Charles Morgan	Tredegar Park, Monmouth (another version in the same house is dated 1841)
1845	Lord Clive	Powis Castle
1852	Joseph Bailey	Hereford Cathedral
1856	Clement Swanston	Lincoln's Inn
1862	Charles Williams	Town Hall, Cardiff

MONUMENTS

1831	Mitcham, Surrey	William Bailey
1834	Brecon (Cathedral)	Roderick Jones
1835	Eye, Suffolk	Sir Charles Cunningham
1837	Cowbridge, Glamorgan	Mary Powell
c. 1840	Shrewsbury (St. Mary's)	Admiral Benbow
1840	Brecon (Cathedral)	Marquess Camden
c. 1840	Brecon (Cathedral)	John Powell
1841	Kirkling, Cambs	Maria, Marchioness of Bute
1842	Windsor (St. George's Chapel Cloisters)	Lt.-Colonel Basset
1845	Carew, Pembroke	Hannah Bowen
1846	Bassaleg, Monmouth	Sir Charles Morgan
1848	Kirkling, Cambs	Marquess of Bute (*d.* 1840)
1849	Luton, Beds	Rev. William McDouall
1850	Little Hereford, Hereford	Joseph Bailey
1851	Brecon (Cathedral)	Sophia Watkins
1852	Clapham (St. Paul's)	Rev. W. Borrows
1854	Renhold, Beds	Robert Polhill
1858	Gwennap, Cornwall	Michael Williams

THOMAS, WILLIAM MEREDYTH
b. 1819, *d.* 1877

Like his older brother, J. E. Thomas (q.v.), he was born at Brecon and studied under Sir Francis Chantrey (q.v.). The younger Thomas exhibited at the Royal Academy, 1839–1871, where his works included busts and a bas-relief of "Ariel." At Westminster Hall in 1844 he showed a statue of Prince Henry which the *Literary Gazette* called a "feeble and unsightly production." Other works by him include "The Racket Player," "Sabrina Rising from the Severn," "The Welsh Harper" and "The Lament of Llewellyn Over his Dog Gelert."

For over thirty years Thomas acted as his brother's assistant, and on the latter's death in 1873 completed the unfinished sculpture in the studio. Thomas himself died four years later and is buried in the family vault in Brompton Cemetery.

(Poole's *Brecknockshire*, page 323.)

THOMASON, SIR EDWARD
b. 1769, *d.* 1849

He was a Birmingham manufacturer and inventor and is best known for his jewellery, medals, coins, gilt and painted buttons, and tokens in gold, silver and bronze. He also produced a number of works of art, including facsimiles in bronze of the Warwick Vase which took seven years to complete.

For the city of Birmingham Thomason cast the life-size statue of George IV, which was acknowledged to be an excellent likeness "by all who have witnessed the progress of the model, standing as it does in all the majesty of Truth and exhibiting a noble specimen of the near approach of art to the stamp of nature"—to quote a contemporary report. Unfortunately this remarkable work has disappeared and was probably melted down by the ungrateful citizens of Birmingham. It may perhaps have been this statue which Thomason sent to Westminster Hall in 1844 and which was dismissed by the *Literary Gazette* (1844, page 466) as "Brummagen and contemptible." He also made a bronze bust of the Duke of Wellington, which his widow presented to the "Cavalry of England" and which is now in the Cavalry Barracks at Canterbury.

In 1845 Thomason wrote his Memoirs, an amazing two-volume production, consisting mainly of descriptions and illustrations of the orders, medals and presents he had received from foreign sovereigns.

(*Gentleman's Magazine*, 1849, Part II, page 430; Information, Birmingham City Library.)

THOMPSON, CHARLES and WILLIAM
Firm *fl.* 1800–1845

Thompson, who was later assisted by his son William, had his studio in Osnaburgh Street. The productions of the firm are typical of their period, with heavily draped urns, branches of cypress and reliefs of weeping widows. Monuments and tablets by them include those to Josias Du Pre, 1800, at Beaconsfield, Bucks; George Cuthbert, *c.* 1800, in Portsmouth Cathedral; John Prettejohn, 1803, in St. George's, Barbados; Dorothy Twopenny, 1822, at Tunstall, Kent; Martha Lovibond, 1828, at Hatfield Peveril, Essex; Amelia Barnett, 1828, at Great Hormead, Herts; Sir Richard King, 1834, at Eastchurch, Kent; Lady Duckworth, 1837, in Paddington Parish Church; and Charles King, 1841, at Sutton, Surrey. In 1845 he provided casts of classical figures for the Colosseum, in Regent's Park.

THOMPSON, or TOMPSON, JOHN
d. 1700

Thompson, who was apprenticed to Francis Clarke and became free in 1667, was the contractor, under Wren, for several of the City churches and was also paid for carved decorative stonework. With George Dowderswell he built St. Magnus, where he received £24 for eight Ionic capitals and £32 for two Portland stone scrolls, 10 ft. long and 6 ft. broad; and with Thomas Cartwright (q.v.) the tower of St. Mary-le-Bow, where his work included four pinnacles and carving costing £250, and four urns with flames, £20 (Bodleian, Rawlinson MS. B.387). In 1685 he was paid £600 for repairs to the chapel of Lincoln's Inn (Inn Archives). In 1686 he was the master-mason under W. Stanton (q.v.), for building Belton.

On his own account Thompson built All Hallows', Lombard Street, where the ornaments of the frieze cost £10; St. Bartholomew by the Exchange, where he carved eight cherub-heads for £6; and St. Dionis Backchurch, where he executed four great festoons on the east front costing £15 (op. cit.). In 1683 he was employed at Winchester Palace, and in 1691 carried out work at a total cost of £1,308 in the gardens of Hampton Court. In 1685 he was paid £600 for rebuilding Lincoln's Inn Chapel (Inn Archives).

From 1688 until 1700 Thompson was working at St. Paul's, his most important contribution to the building being the great doorcase at the west end of the Cathedral, though he also received £60 for "four large festoones on each side of the two windows in the tower" and £100 for setting "ye great tribune over the west end of the chappell and carving ye same."

Thompson was Master of the Masons' Company in 1700, but, according to the Court Book of the Company, died during his year of office.

(Various references, Wren Society's publications; Archives, Lord Brownlow.)

THOMPSON, JOHN, of Lichfield

He signs a wall-tablet to John Fern, 1801, in St. Chad's, Lichfield. He may be the same "Thompson" who signs a charmingly carved tombstone, with a relief of a dove bearing an olive-branch, to Jane Bannister, 1780, at Hanbury, Staffordshire.

THOMPSON, MARY
fl. 1843–1852

She exhibited busts, etc., at the Royal Academy, 1843–1852, and at the British Institution in 1849.

THOMPSON, WILLIAM,
of Birmingham
fl. 1785–1811

He signs a tablet about 12 ft. high in coloured marbles to Gilbert Walmesley, 1785, in Lichfield Cathedral. Other works by him commemorate Rebecca Grice, 1790, and Sobieski Brookshaw, 1811, both in Birmingham Cathedral; Jane Simpson, 1802, at Dudley, Worcs; Thomas Brooke, 1802, at Aston, Birmingham; and the Rev. Richard Yates, 1805, at Solihull, Birmingham.

THORNE, —

He signs the large wall-monument to William Burkitt, 1703, at Dedham, Essex, which has an inscription-panel in the form of a heavy, gold-fringed curtain bunched at the corner. The large acanthus leaf at the base of the monument is boldly carved.

THORNTHWAITE, JOHN
fl. 1772–1776

Son of Andrew Thornthwaite, an architect, he exhibited wax portraits, including one of the Duke of Gloucester, at the Society of Artists, 1772–1776.

THORNTON, HERBERT,
of Gainsborough

He signs a wall-tablet with pretty details to Gervase Cole, 1792, at Kettlethorpe, Lincolnshire.

THORNYCROFT, MARY
b. 1814, *d.* 1895

She was born at Thornham, Norfolk, the daughter of the sculptor, John Francis (q.v.), and was trained in her father's studio. She first exhibited at the Royal Academy in 1835 at the age of twenty-one, and four years later showed "The Orphan Flowergirl," described by the *Art Union* as "sweetly conceived, delicately arranged, and executed with much knowledge, skill and ability." In 1840 she married the sculptor, Thomas Thornycroft (q.v.), and together they went to Italy, where they lived and worked for some years in Rome.

The first work which Mrs. Thornycroft exhibited under her married name was a bust of John Lander, the African traveller, but it was her model of "A Sleeping Child" which impressed John Gibson (q.v.). Indeed, he was so much struck by it, that when Queen Victoria asked him to suggest a suitable sculptor to model portraits of her children he at once recommended Mary Thornycroft, who returned to London and was engaged by the Queen. The work took the form of life-size statues of the Royal children, the four eldest representing "The Seasons." These were a great success and engravings of them appeared in most art publications of the period. One stern teetotaller, however, was much distressed by the fact that Prince Alfred, who personified "Autumn," was shown holding a bunch of grapes. "To connect childhood with intoxicating wine is repugnant to our feelings," he wrote.

Mrs. Thornycroft also executed a number of busts of the Royal Family, including those of the Duchess of Gloucester; Queen Victoria (1840); the Prince of Wales (1846); the Duchess of Kent (1847); the Princess Royal (1858); Princess Alice (1861); Princess Louise (1870); Prince Albert of Schleswig-Holstein (1870); Princess Helena (1874); and the Duchess of Edinburgh (1876). These, and the statues previously referred to, are all in the Royal Collection.

In 1863 she was allowed to make the first bust of Alexandra, Princess of Wales, and copies of this work in "Parian" porcelain were one of the *Art Union's* prizes for 1864. In 1877 she carved statues of the Princesses Victoria, Maud and Louise, daughters of the Prince and Princess of Wales. Her statue of "The Skipping-Rope" is at Osborne, and her bust of Lady Peel was at Avington Park, Hants.

Mary Thornycroft assisted her husband in so many of his works that it is difficult to distinguish her own independent productions, though one of them is almost certainly the recumbent figure of

Lady Braye, 1865, at Stanford-on-Avon, Northampton. She exhibited at the Royal Academy, 1835–1871, and at the British Institution, 1845–1864. Mrs. Thornycroft died on 1 February, 1895.

(Various references, *Art Journal*, *Builder*, etc.)

THORNYCROFT, THOMAS

b. 1815, *d.* 1885

He was born in Cheshire and educated at Congleton Grammar School. As a young man he was apprenticed to a local surgeon, but soon discovered that he was unfitted for the work and that his real interest lay in art. His mother accordingly sent him to London to study under John Francis (q.v.) and it was here that he met and married the sculptor's daughter, Mary, in 1840.

Thornycroft exhibited at Westminster Hall in 1844 "The Jealousy of Medea" which the *Literary Gazette* called "a Juno-like matron exhibiting forcibly her insulted mind." In 1848 he carved statues of Henry, Earl of Hereford, and Roger, Earl of Norfolk, for the House of Lords, and in 1849 the bust of "Medea" which is now in the Royal Collection. At the Great Exhibition of 1851 he showed an "Equestrian Statue of Queen Victoria" and in 1857 with his wife executed the recumbent figure of the child John Hamilton-Martin (*d.* 1851), which is now in Ledbury Church, Hereford.

In 1857 he made the statue for Wolverhampton of Mr. G. B. Thorneycroft, the first mayor of that town, and in 1858 his work included a statue of Lady Anna Chandos-Pole. In 1864 came the equestrian statue of the Prince Consort for Halifax and a year later the group of "Commerce" for the Albert Memorial, while another statue of the Prince Consort, this time for Wolverhampton, followed in 1866. In 1867 the sculptor, assisted by his wife, executed two statues of James I and Charles I for the Houses of Parliament. These are now in the Sessions House, Old Bailey.

In 1868 and 1870 Thornycroft made statues of the Prince Consort and Queen Victoria for Liverpool, the two works costing £10,000. In 1869 his statue of the second Marquess of Westminster was erected in Chester, but the frosts of the following winter loosened a large piece let into the left shoulder, which not only spoilt its appearance, but also annoyed the inhabitants, who had understood that the work was carved from a single block of marble (*Art Journal*, 1870, page 86). Another unfortunate error was the abbreviation of the word "second," so that the inscription read "2d Marquess of Westminster," a title which the *Builder* rightly considered open to misconstruction

(1869, page 414). In 1875 his statue of Lord Mayo was sent to Calcutta.

Thornycroft's best-known work in London is the great group of Boadicea at the northern end of Westminster Bridge. He began work on this in the 1850s and in the early stages received much encouragement from the Prince Consort, who wished to see it placed on the central arch of the entrance to Hyde Park, but the model occupied the sculptor for fifteen years and the Prince was dead before it was finished. After Thornycroft's own death it was presented to the nation by his son, Sir John Thornycroft, and a sum of money was raised to have it cast in bronze. The group was not, however, unveiled until 1902. In 1875 Thornycroft made the Poets' Fountain, a work in which he was assisted by another son, Sir Hamo Thornycroft (1850–1925), who carved the figures of Shakespeare, "Comedy" and "Fame." This fountain formerly stood at the junction of Park Lane and Hamilton Place, but was damaged in the Second World War and later removed. In 1836 he made the monument of William Dickinson at Twycross, Leics.

Thomas Thornycroft died on 30 August, 1885, and was buried at Chiswick. He exhibited at the Royal Academy, 1836–1874, and at the British Institution, 1840–1860.

(*D.N.B.*; various references, *Art Journal*.)

THORPE, JOHN, of Bakewell

fl. 1706–1728

He was much employed by Thomas Coke of Melbourne Hall, Derbyshire. In 1706 Mr. Sergeant, Coke's Derbyshire agent, wrote to his master in London: "John Thorpe has brought three chimney-pieces from Bakewell." Two years later Coke agreed with Thorpe for "two moulded chimney-pieces of ye grey marble, ye same size and moulding as ye black chimney-piece in ye stone-room." In 1723 Thorpe received £11 6s. 3d. for another chimney-piece which was apparently for Coke's London house in St. James's Place, as Coke writes to Mr. Sergeant that it is to be "carefully putt up and to be sent by water to London directed to me" (Archives, Marquess of Lothian).

In 1712 Thorpe was working at Castle Howard, where he made a chimney-piece for the saloon costing £23 and another for the "bewfett" at £37. He was also paid for a double doorcase for the dining-room and another of marble for the drawing-room (Archives, Castle Howard). In 1721 he supplied marble for the building of Knowsley (Lancashire County Archives, D.D.K. 2002/1).

In 1727 he was employed by Lord Bingley at Bramham Park, Yorkshire. Here the steward addressed him as "Mr. Thorpe, marble-cutter," and informed him that: "My Lord will pay your bill if you will come hither on the five and twentieth day of September, but you must be punctual to your time because you cannot have your money before and within three or four days after My Lord goes to London" (Lane-Fox Archives).

THORWALDSEN, BERTEL
b. 1770, *d.* 1843

The famous Danish sculptor was living in Rome from 1797 until 1838 and it was during this period that he executed a number of busts for English patrons. The sitters included Lord Dover (1817), the second Duke of Sutherland (1818), Lord Pembroke (1819), Lord Taunton (1828), Lord Wriothesley Russell (1829), Sir Walter Scott (1832), Lord de Dunstanville, Lord Valletort, Lord and Lady Breadalbane, William Haldiman, Colonel Thomas Bonar, the three daughters of Lord Lucan, and Thomas Divett, M.P. Sir George Barlow, Bart., who died in 1847, left instructions in his will that his bust by Thorwaldsen should descend with the title as an heirloom.

Besides the busts Thorwaldsen also carved "A Shepherd" (1817) for Lord Cowley; "Mercury" (1818) for Lord Ashburton; "Venus" (1824) for Lord Lucan; a vase with bas-reliefs (1825) for Lord Taunton, and a bas-relief of "Charity" for the Marquess of Lansdowne. A number of these have since been purchased by the Thorwaldsen Museum and are now in Copenhagen. The sculptor's famous statue of Lord Byron was finished in 1829, but Dean Ireland refused to allow it to be erected in Westminster Abbey and it lay in the vaults of the Customs House until 1842. In that year it was again offered to the Abbey, but was refused by Dean Turton, and in 1843 it was finally placed in the Library of Trinity College, Cambridge.

Thorwaldsen also signs three monuments in England: those of Charles and Ann Garrard, 1832, at Wheathampstead, Herts; Lady Lawley, 1828, at Escrick, Yorks, and the Earl of Newburgh, 1814, in the Roman Catholic Church at Slindon, Sussex.

THRUPP, FREDERICK
b. 1812, *d.* 1895

He was born on 20 June, 1812, the youngest son of Joseph Thrupp of Paddington Green, and attended the academy of Henry Sass in Bloomsbury, where he studied modelling and drawing. In 1829 he won a Silver Medal from the Society of Arts for a drawing, and a year later attended the Royal Academy Schools. In 1837 he went to

Rome for five years. In 1844 he showed in Westminster Hall two groups entitled "A Hindu Throwing a Javelin" and "Arethusa"; his "Hunter Returning Home With a Child on His Back" appeared at another exhibition at Westminster in the following year.

In 1846 a competition was held to choose a sculptor for the statue of Sir Fowell Buxton which was to be erected in Westminster Abbey. One of the five judges was G. Richmond, R.A., a personal friend of Thrupp, so when the latter received the commission it was rumoured in artistic circles that undue influence had been brought to bear to get his model chosen, especially as it does not seem to have been a very outstanding performance. The *Art Union* (1846, page 264), indeed, called it "the worst statue of all" and added that "it is such proceedings as these which disgust our best artists with competitions."

In 1848 Thrupp executed statues of Robert, Earl of Oxford, and Robert FitzWalter for the House of Lords, and five years later "Timon of Athens" for the Mansion House. In 1854 he finished his statue of Wordsworth for Westminster Abbey, the face being modelled from the death-mask of the poet taken by Chantrey. This commission aroused almost as much ill-feeling as the one for the Buxton statue, and Thrupp was again accused of securing it through favouritism. The *Art Journal* (1851, page 222) remarked on "the sudden removal of Mr. Thrupp's model as soon as the decision was declared without the other competitors having had an opportunity of seeing it" and also noted that "after the decision it is said the successful artist had been recommended to amend his design." The writer was forced to the conclusion that "there must have been some lack of fair play when the successful artist is not successful enough to show his design."

In 1853 the sculptor had made a bas-relief for St. Martin's Hall, Long Acre, and in 1868 he executed a pair of bronze doors ornamented with ten subjects from the *Pilgrim's Progress* for the same building; these are now in the Bunyan Chapel at Bedford. Another pair of doors with bronze panels illustrating George Herbert's poems are also his work. They were placed in the Divinity School at Cambridge in 1888. He was also responsible for the reredos of St. Clement's Church, York, the monument to Lady Coleridge at Ottery St. Mary, Devon, and the recumbent effigy of Canon Pearson, 1883, at Sonning, Berks.

Thrupp exhibited at the Royal Academy, 1832–1880, at the British Institution, 1837–1862, and at the Birmingham Society of Artists, where in 1849 he showed a figure of "Ariel" and a small marble statue of the Magdalen. At the Great Exhibition of 1851 he showed "The Maid and the Mischievous Boy," and at the International Exhibition of 1862 "Nymph and Cupid" and a relief of "Hamadryads" which the *Art Journal* (1862, page 230) called "one of the most classic and correct bas-reliefs in the Exhibition." He lent his "Boy and the Butterfly" to the Exhibition of Art Treasures held in Manchester in 1857.

Thrupp died on 21 March, 1895, and was buried at Torquay. In the previous year he had given the works in marble and plaster in his studio to the City of Winchester and they had been placed in the ancient Abbey building adjoining the Guildhall. In 1911, however, they were returned to the sculptor's family, who then presented them to the Torquay Corporation.

(Various references, *Art Journal* and *Builder*.)

THURLOW, THOMAS, of Saxmundham
b. 1813, *d*. 1899

He was the son of a mason named John Thurlow (1785–1850) and was born at Saxmundham in Suffolk, a county in which he spent all his life and where most of his work is to be found. In 1847 he made a bust of the poet Crabbe for Aldeburgh Church, and in 1873 executed the reredos for his own parish church of Saxmundham.

Thurlow's largest work, in Kelsale Church, is the statue of Samuel Clouting, 1852, which, with its beaky nose and almost military type of cloak, bears a curious resemblance to the Duke of Wellington. Other monuments and tablets by him in Suffolk include those to Sir Charles Blois, 1840, at Yoxford; Robert King, 1842 (with a medallion portrait), at Witnesham; William Shuldham, 1850, at Marlesford; Sir Thomas Gooch, 1851 (with a relief of "Faith, Hope and Charity"), at Benacre; Susanna Mayhew, 1853, and John Crampin, 1869, both at Saxmundham; and Richard Garrett, 1866 (with a bust), at Leiston.

Thurlow exhibited at the Royal Academy, 1846–1872, and at the British Institution, 1841. He died in 1899 and is buried in Saxmundham churchyard.

TILNEY, J., of York
fl. 1822–1841

His tablets are mostly neo-Hellenic in design, the best (all in Yorkshire) being those to Toft Richardson, 1827, at Riccall; Isabella Serjeantson, 1834, at Snaith; Henry Sidgwick, 1835, at Brompton; John Todd, 1837, in St. Michael-le-Belfry, York; and Harriet Carr, 1841, at Horbury.

Tilney took his son Charles as an apprentice in 1833.

TILSTON, JOHN, of Chester
b. 1671, *d*. 1723

Son of Modland Tilston, of Gresford, Denbigh, he was apprenticed to Thomas Davies, of Chester, and became a Freeman of that city in 1695. Tilston, who carved the statue of Queen Anne for the front of Chester Exchange, died in 1723 and was buried in the south aisle of St. John's Church.

His grandson, John Tilston, was also a carver and became free of the Masons' Company of Chester in 1732.

(Archives, City of Chester.)

TIMBRELL, HENRY
b. 1806, *d*. 1849

He was born in Dublin, the son of James Timbrell, "Clerk in the Ordinance." He studied under the Irish sculptor, John Smyth. In 1825 he entered the Schools of the Royal Dublin Society and after winning various prizes and exhibiting at the Royal Hibernian Academy, 1827–1829, went to London in 1830. Here he entered the studio of E. H. Baily (q.v.), but apparently did not stay there long, for when he put down his name for the Royal Academy Schools, to which he had been recommended by T. Denman (q.v.), he gave his address as "40, Via Laurina, Rome."

Timbrell attended the Academy Schools, where he won the Gold Medal for a group entitled "Mezentius Tying the Living to the Dead." In 1843 his "Hercules Throwing Lycas into the Sea" gained him the Travelling Scholarship and he accordingly made a second journey to Rome. When he had been there nearly two years he executed a life-size marble group of a mother teaching two children which he sent in to the Royal Academy, but the ship carrying the work was wrecked on its way to England and the group almost completely ruined.

Timbrell died of pleurisy in Rome on 10 April, 1849, leaving unfinished statues of Richard, Earl of Clare, and William, Earl of Aumale, for the House of Lords and another of "The Lamp of the Ganges" for Queen Victoria. Had he lived there is little doubt that he would have reached the highest rank in his profession. John Gibson (q.v.) admired his work and recommended him to the Queen, who commissioned the statue already mentioned for Osborne. During his second stay in Rome he also executed two bas-reliefs for the garden house of Buckingham Palace.

Timbrell exhibited at the Royal Academy, 1833–1843, at the British Institution, 1843, and at

Westminster Hall, 1844, where he showed his "Hercules." He married, on 3 February, 1838, at St. Pancras, Miss Susan Flather (Archives, Artists' Annuity Fund).

(*Art Journal*, 1849, page 198; and 1855, page 260.)

TIMBRELL, JAMES C.
b. 1807, *d.* 1850

He was a younger brother of Henry Timbrell (q.v.) and entered the Schools of the Royal Dublin Society in 1825, where he studied painting. Five years later he went to London, but it was not until 1848 that he turned his attention to sculpture, showing in that year "a bas-relief, part of a monument to be erected in marble" at the Royal Academy.

Timbrell died at Portsmouth on 5 January, 1850. He apparently left very little money, for his widow was given a grant of £10 by the Royal Academy shortly after his death (Royal Academy Archives).

TINKLER, —, of Derby

He signs a ledger, with a coat of arms at the top, to the Herrick family, 1759, at Barrow-on-Soar, Leicestershire.

TOGNOLI, GIOVANNI, of Rome
b. 1786, *d.* 1862

He was drawing-master to Canova and made the font (which he signs) at Escrick, Yorkshire, in 1844. This is a charming work, in the form of two angels supporting a bowl.

TOLLEMACHE, WILLIAM
d. 1817

Tollemache studied at the Royal Academy Schools, where in 1805 he won the Gold Medal for his group entitled "Prometheus Chained to the Rock." In 1813 his bronze cast of "Venus" gained him a Silver Medal and a premium of twenty guineas from the Society of Arts. He exhibited at the Academy, 1812–1814, and at the British Institution, 1814–1816, showing various small models to be cast in bronze. His signed monument commemorating Amelia Gooch (*d.* 1807) is at Beaconsfield, Bucks.

In the year of Tollemache's death his widow wrote to the Academy "stating her great distress and petitioning for assistance." The Committee awarded her a grant of ten pounds (Minute-book, Royal Academy). She had, as Harriot Gilchrist, married Tollemache at St. James's, Piccadilly,

on 21 August, 1804. She died in Liverpool on 28 October, 1841 (Archives, Artists' Annuity Fund).

TOLMIE, JAMES
d. 1866

As an ornamental stone-carver, he was employed at the Whitehall Club, New City Club, Inns of Court Hotel and the hotel at Buxton. He was also responsible for some of the carving of the Prince Consort's mausoleum.

Tolmie died at Lambeth, leaving unfinished two statues for the interior of St. George's Hall, Bradford.

(*Art Journal*, 1867, page 56.)

TOMBLING, JOHN, of London
fl. 1794–1817

He may possibly have been a son of the "Mr. Robert Tombling, mason," who worked at Corsham Court, Wiltshire, on various occasions between 1769 and 1786 (Archives, Lord Methuen).

John Tombling's studio was in Mount Street and under Soane he was employed at Lord Delaval's house in Hanover Square. He also worked for the Duke of Leeds, for whose house in St. James's Square he made in 1795 "three marble tables with moulded edges" (Sir John Soane's Account-book, Soane Museum). He signs a Hellenic wall-tablet to Mrs. Faran, 1803, in the Grosvenor Chapel. As a mason he worked at Lord Brownlow's house in Hill Street in 1794 (Archives, Lord Brownlow).

TOMLINSON, J., of Uxbridge
fl. 1806–1819

Most of his monuments and tablets are in the Regency style, although that commemorating Mary Auberry, 1813, at Pinner, Middlesex, is a copy of the monument by Sir Robert Taylor erected in 1767 to Edmund Auberry in the same church. Other monumental works by Tomlinson include those to Mrs. Barry, 1806, at East Bedfont, Middlesex; Lt.-Colonel Hillard, 1811, at Cowley, Middlesex; Henry Pye, 1813, at Pinner, Middlesex; and Arabella Popple, 1819, at Burnham, Bucks.

TOMLINSON, R.
b. 1779

He joined the Royal Academy Schools in 1798 and won a Silver Medal in 1805. From 1806 until 1810 he exhibited at the Academy, showing busts, including a fine marble one of William Beckwith, dated 1807, which is now in the office of the Foundling Hospital in Brunswick Square.

Tomlinson's relief of a shipwreck (which he also showed at the Academy) afterwards formed part of his monument erected at Itchen (Pear Tree Green), Hampshire, to the memory of Captain Robert Scott, commander of H.M.S. *Boreas*, which went down off Guernsey in 1807.

TOMSON, EDWARD and THOMAS, of Cambridge

Edward Tomson: *b.* 1773, *d.* 1829
Thomas Tomson: *b.* 1775, *d.* 1849

In 1803 Edward Tomson carved the pedestal, designed by Flaxman, for a Greek statue of "Ceres," which had been presented to Cambridge by Messrs. Clarke and Cripps (*Monthly Magazine*, 1803, Part II, page 87). In 1815 he was employed in the University on masonry work at Clare Hall.

He was also assisted by his brothers Thomas and Lewis (1783–1832) and it was the former who was working under Soane at Caius College in 1792. He later altered the west front of Clare Hall in 1815, and ten years later built Gisborne Court at Peterhouse (Willis and Clarke's *Architectural History of Cambridge*, Vol. I, pages 111 and 39).

Edward Tomson's best monumental work is the large wall-tablet in coloured marbles to Joseph Clarke (*d.* 1790) at Wethersfield, Essex; he also executed those of Charles Matthews, 1811, in St. Benet's Church, Cambridge, and of Sir Thomas Hatton, 1812, at Long Stanton, Cambridgeshire. With his brother Thomas he signs a tablet to Samuel Knight, 1806, at Milton in the same county.

Thomas on his own account signs tablets to Thomas Sennett, 1819, at Newton, Cambs; George Maltby, 1820, at Buckden, Hunts; Thomas Marten, 1821, at Stow-cum-Quy, Cambs; Mary Jennyns, 1832, at Bottisham, Cambs; and Charlotte Gibbons, 1833, at West Wratting, Suffolk.

Edward Tomson died in 1829, and was buried in St. Botolph's Church, Cambridge, the business being carried on by Thomas and his sons.

An "Edward Tomson, stone cutter" (presumably an ancestor) was paid £5 3s. 10d. in 1754 for repairing the Market Cross at Cambridge (City Sessions Book).

TOVELL, GEORGE and ROBERT, of Ipswich

Robert Tovell: *b.* 1778, *d.* 1840

They were sons of Edward Tovell, stone-mason, and they sign a good many tablets in Suffolk, though none of these is outstanding. The best executed by George commemorate George Booth,

1821, in St. Clement's, Elizabeth Trotman, 1821, in St. Peter's, and Elizabeth Cobbold, 1824, in St. Mary-at-Tower, Ipswich; and James Ellis, 1832, at Hunston.

Robert's tablets include those to Robert Green, 1818, at Debenham, and the Rev. John Longe, 1834, at Coddenham. His wife, Sarah Thurston, also of Ipswich, whom he married in 1812, died in 1831 at the age of thirty-seven. Another Robert Tovell, "stonemason," died 27 October, 1786, and was buried at St. Margaret's, Ipswich.

TOVEY, WILLIAM
d. 1771

In 1725 Tovey became a member of the Masons' Company "by virtue of an order of the Court of the Lord Mayor and Aldermen." In 1749 he sent in an estimate for £1,203 for the mason's work for the principal storey at the Mansion House, but was turned down in favour of Christopher Horsnaile Jnr. (q.v.), who offered to do it for £900.

Tovey, who was mason to the Ironmongers' Company from 1758 until 1767 (Company's Archives), left a widow (or perhaps a daughter) named Sarah when he died in 1771 (Court-book, Masons' Company). She proceeded to carry on the business in partnership with a Mary Wheeler and their firm carried out mason's work at Skinners' Hall in 1773. This is the only example I know of in the eighteenth century of two women being partners and running a mason's business.

TOWNE, JOSEPH
b. 1808, *d.* 1879

He was born at Royston on 25 November, 1808, and at the age of seventeen made a model of a human skeleton for Guy's Hospital. This was so delicate and well-executed a piece of work that the Governors offered the young man the post of anatomical modeller to the hospital, a position he held for fifty-three years. During that time he won an international reputation and received orders for models from countries all over the world, including America, Russia and Australia. In 1826 he was awarded a medal by the Society of Arts and, ten years later, he made a bust of Sir Astley Cooper, for which Sir Astley's medical students paid £400.

In 1837 Towne made a small equestrian statue of the Duke of Kent for Queen Victoria and, a year later, another of Wellington, which is now in Guy's Hospital. In 1836 he had carved a bust of Nelson and in 1842 he executed one of Wellington, both of which are in the Junior United Service Club. His bust of Bishop Otter, dated 1844, was placed in Chichester Cathedral in 1861. In 1841 he made a bas-relief of "Christ Healing the Blind" which was erected in the Clothworkers' Hall. In Guy's Hospital are his busts of William Babbington, 1834; Thomas Addison, 1852; and Sir Astley Paston Cooper, 1841. The last named has a large pedestal with a fine relief, also carved by Towne, of three youths carrying a sick man.

Towne exhibited at the Royal Academy, 1834–1866, showing a marble statue of Wellington in 1835. He signed the tablet to Randal Jackson, 1837, formerly in the Temple Church.

Thomas Hodgkin, in a lecture on Towne and his anatomical models, said of him that "he was an artist, who had the signal merit of having both created his art for himself and arrived at such a proficiency in it that his works, already numerous, rival, if not surpass, those of the best and most distinguished masters of Florence and Bologna." Towne died 25 June, 1879.

(*Guy's Hospital Gazette*, 22 September, 1947; *Gentleman's Magazine*, 1842, Part I, page 639; *Builder*, 1861, page 696.)

TOWNESEND, GEORGE,
of Bristol
d. 1719

He was the eldest son of John Townesend the Elder of Oxford (q.v.) and became a Freeman of Bristol on 8 July, 1706, on his marriage with Margaret, widow of Malachi Harford. In 1709 he drew a "frontispiece" for the Bristol Council House, having already carved a chimney-piece for the same building in 1705 (City Archives). In 1716 he completed the tower of All Saints' Church, Bristol, and is, therefore, presumably responsible for the carving of the charming urns and vases (Churchwardens' Accounts).

Townesend signs a monument to Sir Hugh Smyth, who died in 1680 (although the monument was erected later), and another to Lady Smyth, who died in 1715, both in Long Ashton Church, Somerset. The design in each case is more or less the same and consists of Corinthian pilasters, supporting a pediment on which recline mourning cherubs. The coats of arms, swags and other details are well carved.

TOWNESEND, JOHN, the Elder,
of Oxford
b. 1648, *d.* 1728

He was the son of Thomas Townesend of Oxford and was apprenticed to Bartholomew Peisley in 1664. From 1688 until 1712 he was the college mason of Queen's, but retired in the latter year and was succeeded by his son William (q.v.). He was

also the father of George Townesend of Bristol (q.v.) and John Townesend of London (q.v.).

The elder Townesend, who was one of the masons for building Blenheim in 1709, was elected Mayor of Oxford in 1682, and again in 1720. Apparently he was not a popular character, for Hearne in his *Collections* (Vol. VII, page 171), recording the election, also adds the Mayor was "commonly called 'Old Pincher' from his pinching his workmen." When Townesend died on 23 May, 1728, Hearne writes (Vol. X, page 15): "Yesterday died of a dropsy old Mr. Townesend of Oxford, mason. He was near four-score, a strong hearty man till of late. He was good for nothing."

TOWNESEND, JOHN,
the Younger, of London
d. 1742

Son of John Townesend the Elder of Oxford (q.v.), his yard was in London at St. Paul's Wharf, and from 1714 until 1717 he and his brother William were the mason contractors for building the church of St. Mary-le-Strand. In 1738 "Mr. John Townsend, citizen and haberdasher, Mr. Christopher Horsnaile and Mr. Robert Taylor, citizens and masons, did jointly propose to perform the mason's work of the Mansion House" (City Corporation Records, Mansion House Committee Papers, Box I).

John Townesend's death is noted in the *London Magazine* of April, 1742, as follows: "Died, Mr. John Townesend, one of the Common Council men for Castle Baynard Ward and brother to the late Mr. Townesend of Oxford, well known for his many noble structures in that place." An Edward Townesend, who may be a relation, became free in 1721, was Steward of the Masons' Company in 1727 and Master in 1738.

TOWNESEND, JOHN,
the Younger, of Oxford
d. 1746

He was the son of William (q.v.) and the grandson of John Townesend the Elder of Oxford (q.v.), and in 1737 received £1,900 for mason's work at Queen's College. This sum included £25 for the carving in the pediment and other payments for "two lions and two unicorn-heads, large gilloss-flowers in the centre of the arch, sixty-four octagon panels and carving a flower in the middle of each" (Bodleian, Rawlinson, D.912, Folio 528). Also for the College, he carved in 1745 the console round the niche where the statue of Queen Philippa stood (College Archives).

In 1739 Townesend succeeded his father as

college mason of Christ Church and as one of the mason-contractors for the Radcliffe Camera, though he had already been a "stone-carver" there since work on the building had begun two years previously. Here his payments for stone-carving included £384 for thirty-two Corinthian capitals; £32 for eight festoons between columns; £105 for forty-five Ionic capitals; £60 for forty-eight roses; £120 for "carving ye compartments"; and £187 for "twenty oblesques and lamps round the Library" (Building Account, Radcliffe Library, Bodleian).

In 1742 he made a chimney-piece for the Hall of St. John's College, and in the following year made the screen, which had been designed by Gibbs and cost £120 (College Archives).

Townesend signs monuments to John Stamp, 1728, at Wantage, Berkshire, and to John Clark, 1740, at Fighledean, Wiltshire.

TOWNESEND, JOHN, the Third
d. 1784

In 1746 Townesend was working at Welbeck (Archives, Duke of Portland). In 1757 he made a marble shield for Mrs. Sarah Holmes to be added to the monument to her husband in the Chapel of St. John's College, and in the following year he carved two pots of flowers for the College garden gate (St. John's College Archives).

In Oxford itself he signs the monuments of Henrietta, Countess of Pomfret, 1761, in St. Mary's, and of Henry Bowles, 1765, in New College Chapel. His monument to Richard Wykeham, 1768, is at Swalcliffe in the same county.

I am uncertain of his exact relationship to the other Townesends of Oxford and London, though he could be the "John Townesend son of Christopher Townesend of Stepney, mariner," who was apprenticed on 30 October, 1704, to Edward Edwards and became free in 1711.

TOWNESEND, WILLIAM, of Oxford
b. c. 1669, *d.* 1739

Son of John Townesend the Elder (q.v.), he was apprenticed to his father and was college mason of Christ Church in 1704. In 1707 he received £15 for work at Carfax (Vice-Chancellor's Accounts), and two years later began to build the west side of the front quadrangle of Queen's College, the Chapel and Hall following in 1714. His bills for stone-carving included £36 for eighteen Corinthian capitals in 1716; £3 for four cherubim-heads for two niches in the Chapel; and £18 for two lions. In 1718 he made the grand entablature between

the Hall and the Chapel, and in the following year received £293 for the marble altar-piece. Later, in 1733, he was paid £1,045 for the cupola (Queen's College Archives).

About 1721 Townesend and Bartholomew Peisley the Younger (q.v.) were working at Blenheim, and the former received a letter from the Duchess of Marlborough telling him that she thought herself "very hapy (*sic*) that I have got two so able and honest men to carry on my buildings as you and Mr. Peisley."

In the same year he built the famous bridge at Blenheim and also the triumphal arch. Hawksmoor, writing to him on 14 November, 1722, informs him that "when Bat. Peasley (*sic*) was in Town I gave him the designs of the Gate for Woodstocke Park together with the mouldings and cornices of the same."

Townesend was also responsible for the marble work in the Chapel, and in 1727 executed the memorial column in the Park, which had been designed by Flitcroft. The cutting of the long inscription caused trouble, and in 1730 the Duchess wrote to him complaining of the inferior quality of the marble he had used, and remarking that she could not "help wondering that you could not see the Fault when you were in Town, who are so much used to marble. I hope," she continued, "you will take effectual care that there is no more Blonders made—For it will be a most terrible thing, if there is, to me; who have so long set my heart upon this pillar's being well performed." (Birmingham and Midland Institute, Transactions, 1884–1885.)

In 1712 Townesend had begun to erect the Clarendon Building, receiving £2,000 in 1712 and 1713 (Archives, All Souls College). He also did a considerable amount of work at All Souls, beginning in 1719 when the Chapel was "beautified" and he was paid £85 for his share of the work. In 1729 he agreed to build the Hall, buttery, kitchen, etc., for £2,500, and his carved stonework included the magnificent screen in the Hall, "4 coats of arms on the South side," and "the shield between the two pinacles" (Archives, All Souls College). He was also employed at many of the other Colleges in Oxford; indeed Hearne (*Collections*, Vol. VII, page 171) describes John Townesend the Elder on his election as Mayor in 1720 as "father to Townesend who hath a hand in all the buildings in Oxford and gets a vast deal of money that way."

Between 1721 and 1725 Townesend was employed at Radley House, Berkshire, where he was responsible for a good deal of the carved stonework. In 1737 he was again working in Oxford, where he and William Smith, of Warwick (q.v.), were appointed masons for building the Radcliffe Library.

According to W. G. Hiscock (*A Christ Church Miscellany*, pages 61 and 62), Townesend executed the monument to James and John Narborough, 1708, in Oxford Cathedral; the busts of John Wallis, 1703, and David Gregory, 1708, in St. Mary's Church; and the mitre-like monument to the memory of his father erected in 1728 in St. Giles's churchyard. He also made the monument to Sir Thomas Powell, 1706, at Llanbadarn, near Aberystwyth (Gunther's *Early Science in Oxford*, Vol. IX).

Townesend's death is noted in the *London Magazine* of 1739, where the obituary for September (page 465) has the following entry: "At Oxford, Mr. Townesend, the great mason and builder."

TRENTANOVA, R., of Rome
b. 1792, *d.* 1832

His works in England include the fine bust of Sir John Elley, *c.* 1815, in St. George's Chapel, Windsor; another of Napoleon, dated 1824, at the United Service Club; a group of "Venus and Cupid," signed and dated 1825, in private possession; and a "Vestal" at Chatsworth.

Trentanova's bust of the Duke of Buckingham and Chandos and his copy of Canova's statue of Princess Pauline Borghese were formerly at Stowe.

TRIGG, JOHN,
of Kingston-on-Thames
fl. 1837–1843

He signs tablets in Surrey to Edward Woods, 1837, at Shere; Henry Diggle, 1841, at Esher; and William Sells, 1843, at Kingston-on-Thames.

TROSCHEL, G., of Rome
b. 1806, *d.* 1863

His statue of "La Filatrice," 1840, is at Windsor Castle and he was also responsible for two monuments in England, those commemorating Gilbert Shuldham, 1839, at Lea, Lincs; and Lady Elizabeth Feilding, 1846, at Laycock, Wilts.

TROYES, —
He signs the wax portrait, *c.* 1820, of Henrietta, Countess of Stamford, in the possession of the Earl of Stamford.

TRUBSHAW, CHARLES COPE,
of Stafford
b. 1715, *d.* 1772

He was born on 13 September, 1715, the son of Richard Trubshaw (1689–1745), the mason who built Bangor-Iscold steeple in 1726. Charles Trubshaw trained in London under P. Scheemakers (q.v.), but later returned to Stafford where he set up for himself. He made a good many marble chimney-pieces for houses in the neighbourhood, including those for Mr. Sneyd, of Keele Hall, Lord Ward at Himley, Mr. Talbot at Hoarcross, and for the Raven Inn at Shrewsbury.

In 1765 Rysbrack made a figure of a goat for Sir Edward Littleton, but the plinth and one of the animal's horns were broken on the way from London to Teddseley. Rysbrack, in a letter to Sir Edward, written on 30 November of the same year, assured him that he need not "be uneasy about the goat, because when Mr. Trubshaw has mended it, it will be just the same as it was before" (Littleton Archives).

Trubshaw signs a large wall-monument to Acton Moseley, 1745, at Enville, Staffordshire.

(Susannah Trubshaw's *Family Records*; Eva Whitehouse's *History of Haywood*.)

TRUBSHAW, JAMES
b. 1777, *d.* 1853

Trubshaw, who was a son of James Trubshaw the Elder (1746–1808) and a grandson of Charles Cope Trubshaw (q.v.), studied sculpture in London under Sir Richard Westmacott (q.v.), who afterwards found him a post as foreman of the masons then building Fonthill Abbey. He was later employed at Windsor Castle and also at Buckingham Palace, where he fixed the grand staircase.

Trubshaw subsequently returned to Stafford, and it was during this period that he built Ilam Hall for Mr. Watts Russell, Weston House in Warwickshire and, in 1827, the bridge over the Dee at Chester, which, when finished, had the largest arch in Europe.

He was apparently a man of great physical strength and when he was working at Ilam his employer, Mr. Watts Russell, matched him in a race with the young Russells' tutor. On being told that his opponent was a weedy creature, Trubshaw offered to run with Sir Francis Chantrey (q.v.) on his back, the latter being a guest of the family at the time. This was agreed to and, in spite of so great a handicap, he won the race.

Trubshaw signs various wall-tablets in Staffordshire, including those to John Collins, 1820, at Hints; John Sparrow, 1821, at Colwich; and Ralph Moreton, 1834, at Wolstanton. The tablet to the Hales family, 1841, in Stoke-on-Trent Parish Church is signed "J. and C. Trubshaw."

(Susannah Trubshaw's *Family Records*.)

TRUEMAN, EDWARD, of Worcester

fl. 1800–1815

He signs a wall-tablet to Ann Wickens, 1812, in All Saints' Church, Worcester. His son, George Clewer Trueman, was apprenticed to him and became free in 1807.

TUFFNELL, JOHN and EDWARD

John: *b.* 1643, *d.* 1697
Edward: *b.* 1678, *d.* 1719

John Tuffnell and his son Edward were members of a family of masons and master-builders. The elder Tuffnell, born in 1643, may have been the son of Edward Tuffnell and Catherine Moorecocke, of Christ Church, Newgate, London, who were married at St. Martin-in-the-Fields on 8 October, 1638. In 1671 "John Tuffenell" was paid 15s. for the sundial (still in position) on Cleave's Almhouses, Kingston, Surrey (Archives, Cleave's Almhouses).

John was the master-mason at Westminster Abbey for twenty-three years and was also employed on repairs to St. Margaret's, Westminster, in 1674 and again later. He died on 18 February, 1697, and was buried "near the east end of the south Cloister" of the Abbey. His wife, Dorothy Smythe, whom he had married in 1672/3, afterwards became the wife of a Mr. Noble and died in 1720.

Edward Tuffnell, who succeeded his father as Abbey mason, was baptized at St. Margaret's, Westminster, on 21 February, 1678, and in 1697 married Anne Browne, "daughter and coheir of Samuel Browne of St. Margaret's, Westminster, Gent."

He worked at the Abbey as master-mason for twenty-two years and during that time, according to his epitaph, restored and redecorated the south and east sides of the building. In 1702 he received £12 15s. for masonry work when the Royal vault in Henry VII's Chapel was opened to receive the coffin of William III (P.R.O., Works 5/53).

He died on 2 September, 1719, and, like his father, was buried in the cloisters, where a large monument with a portrait-bust (presumably the work of his son Samuel) was erected to his memory. His widow remarried in 1721 a merchant named Thomas Mytton, of St. Leonard's, Shoreditch, and died seven years later.

(J. L. Chester's *Westminster Abbey Registers.*)

TUFFNELL, SAMUEL

d. 1765

Son of Edward (q.v.), he was the master-mason

for building St. John's, Horsleydown, from 1728 until 1733. He also made marble chimney-pieces, including one for Lord Derby's new house at Knowsley, Lancashire, in 1719 (Derby Archives), and another (designed by Nicholas Dubois) for Stanmer Park, Sussex, in 1725 (Newcastle Archives).

In 1737 William, and in 1743 Samuel, became directors of the Westminster Fire Company (Company's Archives).

Samuel Tuffnell signs a number of monuments, usually architectural in character, including those to Henry Phillips, 1714, at Aylesbury, Bucks; Newdigate Owsley, 1714, at Leyton, Essex; Bishop George Hooper, 1727, and Abigail Hooper, 1728, both in Wells Cathedral; and Francis Wilkinson, 1728, at Feltham, Middlesex. His monument to the Cart family was formerly in St. Mary-le-Bow, but was destroyed when the church was bombed in 1940. According to Allen's *London* (Vol. III, page 437), this was "a plain sarcophagus surmounted by a well-executed bust of the deceased in the undress costume which marks the likeness of Thomson and other poets. At the back of the bust are four Corinthian Columns, sustaining a broken elliptical pediment. On the base is J. Potter arch. S. Tuffnell sculp."

Edward and Samuel Tuffnel had another brother, William (1680–1733), who worked as a master-builder and bricklayer for the New River Company.

The family seem to have had the right to be buried in the Abbey, for as late as 1832 Ann White, Samuel's granddaughter, was buried in the west cloister, and her grave was reopened in 1839 on the death of her daughter, Emmeline-Eliza (J. L. Chester, *Westminster Abbey Registers*).

TURNBULL, ROBERT

fl. 1748–1750

About 1750 he built the grotto and circular Corinthian temple at Ascot Park, Berks. "The carving with which he has enriched the Corinthian Temple and a Gothic seat at no great distance from it gives very sufficient proof of his skill and ingenuity" (Hakewill's *Windsor*, page 293).

Turnbull's yard was in Brick Street, Piccadilly (Westminster Poll Book, 1748).

TURNER, JOSEPH, of Chester

b. 1729?, *d.* 1807

He was admitted a Freeman of Chester by Order of Assembly on 22 October, 1774, and in 1782 became a Sheriff of the city. In the same year he was the architect for building Bridge Gate (Hemingway's *Chester*, Vol. I, page 369).

DES—2C

He was an alderman of Chester and died on 6 February, 1807. He was buried at Harwarden Church, Flintshire, where there is a tablet to his memory, which records that "the many splendid and Publick Works in which he was concerned in the counties of Flint, Denby and Chester, will be a lasting memorial of his taste and abilities as an architect."

Turner's monuments are mostly architectural in character, the most imposing being that commemorating Sir Lynch Cotton, 1777, at Wrenbury, Cheshire, which has a large urn set against a pyramid. Other signed monuments by him include those to Charles Legh, 1785, at Prestbury, Cheshire; J. Harrison, 1789, at Aldford, Cheshire; George Hawkshaw, 1792, in Chester Cathedral; Susanna Price, 1796, at Llangollen, Denbighshire; and John Hughes, 1798, at Ruthen, Denbigh.

(Chester Corporation Archives.)

TURNER, THOMAS, of London

He signs a Hellenic wall-tablet to Elizabeth Peters, 1837, in St. Luke's, Chelsea. His yard was in Somerset Place, Whitechapel.

TURNER, WILLIAM, of London
fl. 1804–1820

He exhibited busts at the Royal Academy, 1804–1819, including those of J. Shaw (1815) and Mrs. Phillips, of Tean Hall (1819). In the latter year he received £42 12s. for a veined-marble chimney-piece for the Bank of England (Soane Account-books).

Turner signs a Hellenic wall-tablet carried out in coloured marbles to the Countess of Mount Edgcumbe, 1806, at Maker, Cornwall, and a smaller one to Anne Grant, 1814, at Farnborough, Hants.

TURNERELLI, PETER
b. 1774, *d.* 1839

He was born in Dublin, the son of James Tognarelli, an Italian modeller and figure-maker, and an Irishwoman. He first studied in a Roman Catholic seminary with a view to entering the priesthood, but in 1793 followed his family to London and decided to train there as a sculptor. He first worked in the studio of P. F. Chenu (q.v.) and also joined the Royal Academy Schools, his name in the admission-book being spelt "Taguarelli." In 1799 he won a Silver Medal from the Academy.

Turnerelli's first patron was the second Lord Heathfield, for whom he made a bust of Sir Francis Drake modelled on a painting. This was so successful that he received a further commission for a bust of his employer's father, the famous defender of Gibraltar. Sir Thomas Lawrence also took an interest in the sculptor and recommended him to the Princess of Wales, who engaged him to teach her modelling. Shortly after this, Turnerelli was appointed teacher and sculptor to the Queen and the Princesses and consequently was frequently at Windsor. He held the post for three years and, at the end of that time, became Sculptor-in-Ordinary to the Royal Family. He was also offered a knighthood, which he declined.

His work for the Royal Family naturally led to the sculptor being given permission to make the Jubilee bust of George III in 1810. The work was an instantaneous success and he received orders for eighty copies in marble from the nobility of England and the Colonies. In 1816 he went to France, where Louis XVIII sat to him for a bust at the Tuileries. In the same year he was paid £472 10s. by the Prince Regent for busts of Wellington, Platoff and Blücher, which were intended for Carlton House (P.R.O., L.C. 9/367). Apparently Turnerelli had already made a bust of Wellington, for Farington in his diary (Vol. VII, page 194) mentions that "Nollekens complained much of the conduct of Turnarelli, the sculptor, who, he said, had copied his (Nollekens') bust of Lord Wellington and now sold it as his own performance."

Shortly afterwards Turnerelli went to Ireland, where he made his famous bust of Grattan in eleven hours. It was this work which Canova, when on a visit to London, described as the best modern bust he had seen in England. He next received commissions for a "nuptial bust" of the Princess Charlotte and also for one of her future husband, Prince Leopold. The latter sat to him in the Pavilion at Brighton and was so anxious to see the work completed that he even found time for a sitting on his wedding morning.

Between 1828 and 1830 Turnerelli paid several visits to Ireland. Here he modelled the bust of Daniel O'Connell, which was so popular that ten thousand plaster copies of it are supposed to have been sold. He also made a white-marble altar for Marlborough Street Church, Dublin.

As a sculptor of busts, Turnerelli was the first to portray his subjects in contemporary dress instead of in conventional classic costume, an innovation suggested to him by Benjamin West when they were instructing the Royal Family at Windsor. On the accession of George IV he was again offered a knighthood, and again declined it. He died in London on 18 March, 1839, and was buried in the graveyard of St. John's Wood Chapel. His first wife was Margaret Tracy, a claimant of the Tracy peerage (*d.* 1835), and his second, whom he married at St. Thomas's, Dublin, on 28 December, 1835, Mary O'Connor. By his first marriage he had a son, Peter Turnerelli (1813–1890) (see *D.N.B.*).

According to his obituary in the *Gentleman's Magazine* (1839, Part I, page 548), Turnerelli was also "a charming singer with a voice of singular quality and sweetness." He exhibited at the Royal Academy, 1802–1838, showing no less than one hundred and eight works, including "Caro, a favourite Venetian greyhound for the Countess of Breadalbane" (1811), and "Sacrifice, being part of a work to be executed for Spetchley Hall, near Worcester, the seat of R. Berkley, Esq." (1813).

His work as a monumental sculptor is very uneven; for example, his tablet to Lady Nelson, 1831, at Littleham, Devon, is more like the work of a "New Road statuary" than of a distinguished sculptor.

(*European Magazine*, 1821, Part I, page 387, etc.; Strickland's *Dictionary of Irish Artists*; Archives, Artists' Annuity Fund.)

STATUES

1813	George III	Exhibited Royal Academy (presented to King's College, London, 1842)
1816	Robert Burns	Dumfries (national monument)
1819	St. Peter and St. Paul	For Roman Catholic Chapel at Bath

BUSTS

1801	Lord Hood	Possession Lord Bridport
1802	Princess Charlotte	Royal Collection (plaster)
1805	Nelson	Plaster-cast at Lewes Town Hall, Sussex
1807	Lord Melville	Exhibited Royal Academy
1808	Sir Thomas and Lady Proctor	Formerly Langley Park, Norfolk
1809	George III	Newark Town Hall
1809	Colonel Burr, "late Vice-President of America"	Exhibited Royal Academy
1810	George III	Windsor Castle (replicas possession Duke of Richmond, Lord Normanton, etc.)
1812	William III	Bank of England
1812	George III	Bank of England
1812	Bishop Douglass	Roman Catholic Chapel, Ware, Herts
1812	Grattan	National Gallery of Ireland

1814	Sir Joseph Banks	Royal College of Surgeons (£105) (replica National Maritime Museum)
1814	Wellington	Guildhall
1814	Wellington	Walmer Castle, Kent
1815	Blücher	Windsor Castle
1815	Count Platoff	Windsor Castle
1815	Wellington	India Office (another version at Goodwood, dated 1817)
1816	Count Platoff	Hermitage, Leningrad (?)
1816	Louis XVIII	Exhibited Royal Academy
1816	Wellington	Ombersley Court, Worcs
1816	Duke of Cumberland	For Trinity College, Dublin
1817	Princess Charlotte	Windsor Castle
1818	George III	For Maynooth College, Ireland
1820	Duke of Kent	Royal Collection
1820	Lord and Lady Audley	Exhibited Royal Academy
1821	Lady Caroline Lamb	Exhibited Royal Academy
1828	Lord Anglesey	Windsor Castle
1829	Queen of Portugal	Exhibited Royal Academy
1829	Doyle, Bishop of Kildare	Exhibited Royal Academy
1830	Charles Kendal Bushe	Exhibited Royal Academy
1835	Viscount Frankfort de Montmorency	Exhibited Royal Academy
1838	1st Marquess of Normanby	Exhibited Royal Academy
n.d.	Duke of Kent	Scottish National Portrait Gallery

MONUMENTS

1808	Canterbury (Cathedral)	Lt.-Colonel John Stuart
1815	Great Canford, Dorset	John Willett
1816	Bristol (Redland Chapel)	Mrs. Parry
1816	Harrow, Middlesex	James Edwards
1816	Shandon, Co. Cork	Bishop Moynan
1817	Dublin (St. Michael and St. John)	Rev. Thomas Betagh
1818	Dunblane (Cathedral)	John and Patrick Stirling
1820	Penang (Cathedral)	Samuel Moorat
1820	Westminster Abbey	Admiral Sir George Hope
1826	Cheltenham, Glos	Rev. Charles Jervis
1833	St. Mary, Boltons, Kensington	T. Roper

TYLER, WILLIAM, R.A.
d. 1801

In 1762 it was decided to erect a statue of

George III in the Royal Exchange and Tyler accordingly wrote to the Committee begging "leave to offer himself as a candidate to execute the statue of the King." In his letter he described himself as "the son and grandson of a citizen and many years student under the late Mr. Roubiliac" (City Records, MS. 167.13).

In 1765 he became a director of the Society of Artists, and on the foundation of the Royal Academy in 1768 he was nominated one of the original forty members and later Auditor.

In 1772 he made a marble chimney-piece for Milton Hall, near Peterborough, from a design by Sir William Chambers. The latter, when enclosing Tyler's bill for £282 in a letter to Lord Fitzwilliam, suggests that: "If it is convenient to your Lordship, Mr. Tyler will, I believe, be very thankful for the money as he told me in confidence he was as poor as could be" (British Museum, Ad. MS. 41133). Three years later the sculptor was paid for repairing the monument of Sir Richard Hoare in St. Dunstan-in-the-West (Archives, Hoare's Bank). In 1765 he was paid £37 6s. 6d. for the monument of Sir Wyndham Knatchbull, which was erected in Mersham Church, Kent (Archives, Lord Brabourne).

The Dictionary of National Biography, in its short and sterile notice of Tyler, says that in sculpture "he displayed no great ability," an unjust criticism, for his busts are extremely well modelled and his monuments have great charm. Two good examples of these commemorate Lord Ashbrook, 1780, at Shellingford, Berks, and Saville Cust, 1772, in St. George's, Stamford. The design for the former, two cherubs draping an urn with a floral swag, was later copied by Nollekens; while the latter features an heroic urn of yellow and red brescia set in a white-marble curtained niche. The sculptor was apparently at one time in partnership with his former pupil, Robert Ashton, for they sign together monuments to Elizabeth Yorke, 1779, at Marchwiel, Flint; William Pym, 1788, at Sandy, Bedfordshire; and William Franks, 1790, in the parish church of Kentish Town. (See also Ashton, Robert.)

Tyler exhibited at the Society of Artists, 1760–1768, and at the Royal Academy, 1769–1786, showing a number of architectural designs and various busts, including one of Bishop Pearse (1777). He died in his house in Caroline Street, Bedford Square, on 6 September, 1801.

(Sandby's *Royal Academy of Art*, Vol. I, page 120.)

MONUMENTS

1756	Oxford (Queen's College)	Joseph Smith (with bust)
1759	Guisborough, Yorks	Thomas Spencer
1761	Oxford (Cathedral)	Francis Gastrell
1762	Earsham, Norfolk	Ann Wyndham
1765	Northallerton, Yorks	Thomas Crosfield
1766	Boston, U.S.A. (King's Chapel)	Samuel Vassall (with bust)
1766	Finchingfield, Essex	Thomas Marriott (with bust)
1766	Crowcombe, Somerset	Thomas Carew
1767	Chichester (Cathedral)	Richard Smith
1769	Chiswick (Parish Church)	Charles Holland
1770	Belton, Lincs	Sir John Cust
1770	Clifton, Bristol	Robert Dinwiddie
1770	Southwark (Cathedral)	Thomas Jones (with bust)
1771	Kensington (St. Mary Abbots)	Francis Colman
1772	Spelsbury, Oxon	3rd Earl of Lichfield
1772	Westminster Abbey	Barton Booth
1772	Bletchingley, Surrey	Mrs. Thomas
1772	Belton, Lincs	Lady Cust
1773	St. Osyth, Essex	Countess of Rochford
1773	Marchwiel, Flint	Anne Yorke
1774	Westminster Abbey	Dr. Zachary Pearce
1775	Westminster Abbey	General Lawrence
1775	Dunchideock, Devon	General Lawrence
1775	Lincoln (Cathedral)	Bishop Smyth
1775	Sandy, Beds	William Pym
1775	Everton, Beds	Richard Astell
1776	Spelsbury, Oxon	4th Earl of Lichfield (designed by Henry Keene)
1776	Georgeham, Devon	John Harris (with bust)
1777	Eastry, Kent	Sarah Boteler
1777	Old Radnor, Radnorshire	Thomas Lewis
1778	Saxmundham, Suffolk	Charles and Mary Long
1780	Laleham, Middlesex	George Perrott
1781	Sevenoaks, Kent	Admiral Amherst
1785	Saxmundham, Suffolk	Beeston Long
1797	Sevenoaks, Kent	Lord Amherst

TYLEY, JAMES, and THOMAS, and Sons, of Bristol

Firm *fl.* 1792–1864

The "Tyley of Colerne" who signs a tablet at Corsham, Wiltshire, to John Leir, 1784, may be related to this Bristol family of statuaries and masons, of whom the elder, Thomas, signs a tablet, with a relief of a mourning woman, to John Tucker, 1792, at St. Dogwell's, Pembroke.

A younger Thomas Tyley won a Silver Isis Medal in 1811 from the Society of Arts for a group entitled "Christ Healing the Sick." In 1830 he carved the dove on the pediment of Trinity Church, Clifton (Chilcott's *Bristol*, page 273), and in 1839 made a statue for Clifton of Sir Charles Wetherell (*Gentleman's Magazine*, 1846, Part II, page 430). Another member of this generation was

James Tyley the Younger, who was apprenticed to John Dunn on 14 March, 1807.

The firm was still active in 1864, for in that year it received a commission from Mr. R. A. Kinglake for busts of Bishop Ken and the Rev. Henry Byam for a proposed sculpture gallery of British worthies (*Builder*, 1864, page 783).

Monuments and tablets executed by the Tyleys are very frequent in the West Country, the best being that to Major William Gore, 1814, in Bristol Cathedral, which has a medallion portrait between two figures of officers in full regimentals. Their later works in the Cathedral are inferior by comparison and include a tablet with a relief of a dead child commemorating Georgiana Worrall, 1832, and the monuments of Elizabeth Cookson, 1852 (with a fantastic rococo frame), and John Eagles, 1855 (with a medallion portrait).

MONUMENTS

1798	Bristol (St. Augustine's)	The Shiercliffe family
1804	Barbados (St. George's)	H. Trotman
1809	Penally, Pembroke	Laurence Cook
1810	Llandovery, Brecon	Caroline Rice
1813	Waterford Cathedral	Bishop Stock
1817	Wraxall, Somerset	John Lucas
1818	Wells (Cathedral)	Susanna Henning
1818	Chester (Cathedral)	Charles Hawker
1819	Bristol (St. Stephen's)	Captain John Gardes (with a relief)
1819	Bideford, Devon	James Ley
1820	Barnstaple, Devon	William Mullins
1825	Hinton St. George, Somerset	Thomas Beazly
1827	Cherington, Glos	John George
1830	Alford, Somerset	John Thring
1832	Henbury, Glos	Lord de Clifford
1833	Tenby, Pembroke	Catherine and Grace Hickman
1835	Hartland, Devon	The Wolferston family
1837	Aldenham, Herts	George Hibbert
1837	Hope-under-Dinmore, Hereford	Sophia Phillips
1840	Lilleshall, Salop	William Phillips
1845	Almondbury, Glos	Margaret Lippincott
1856	Sierra Leone (Cathedral)	Rev. M. Leacock

U

UNWINS, T., of Liverpool

He exhibited at the Liverpool Academy in 1831, showing a bust of Nathaniel Philips.

V

VALENTINE, J., of Birmingham

He exhibited a bust of the Rev. E. Dales at the Birmingham Society of Artists in 1829.

VALORY, —, of Rome

He carved the statue of Catherine, Lady Walpole (d. 1737), first wife of Sir Robert Walpole, the Prime Minister, which her son Horace erected in Westminster Abbey in 1754, although it had been executed some years previously. The pedestal of the statue was the work of J. M. Rysbrack (q.v.) (*Letters of Horace Walpole*, ed. Cunningham, Vol. I, page lxxiv).

VAN DER HAGEN, —, of Shrewsbury

b. ca. 1732, *d.* 1790

He was presumably the son of Alexander van der Hagen (q.v.) and about 1767 settled in Shrewsbury, where he soon succeeded in establishing himself as a monumental sculptor. His most important works (both with medallion portraits) commemorate Maria Lloyd, 1780, at Corwen, Merioneth, and William Vaughan, 1786, at Llanddwywe in the same county, while his large wall-monument to Richard Lyster (d. 1766) at Alderbury, Salop, is exactly like, and very nearly equal to, the work of Sir Henry Cheere (q.v.).

Other signed works by van der Hagen include those to Thomas Jenkins, 1767, in the Abbey Church, Shrewsbury; John Corser, 1770, in the parish church of Moreton Say, Salop, and Sir John Markham, 1778, in the churchyard; Mrs. Hanmer, c. 1770, and Owen Wynne, 1780, both at Overton, Flint; Margaret Vaughan, 1772, at Llanddwywe, Merioneth; Thomas Trevor, 1778, at Oswestry, Salop; and Lewis Nanney, 1779, at Dolgelley, Merioneth.

VAN DER HAGEN, ALEXANDER

d. c. 1775

According to Vertue (*Walpole Society*, Vol. III, page 135), van der Hagen worked for Rysbrack (q.v.) and "has done several head portraits in ivory very well, but not meeting with proper encouragement, did not continue." In 1763 he received £63 for carving two figures in Hopton stone for Kedleston Hall, but apparently this was too much, for a note on the bill made by Robert Adam, the designer of the house, states that the amount should have been only £50 (Curzon Archives). In 1767 Lord Radnor paid him £7 for a bust of King Alfred (Longford Castle Archives).

Van der Hagen exhibited a marble bas-relief at the Free Society in 1766, and an ivory bust of the Duke of Cumberland in the following year. He seems to have fallen on hard times, for from 1769 until 1775 he received a small pension from the Royal Academy. In the latter year he presumably died and the payments were continued to his widow until her own death in 1781 (Royal Academy Archives).

VAN DER MEULEN, JOHN FERDINAND

fl. 1765–1780

In 1765 he received a premium of fifty guineas from the Society of Arts for a bas-relief in marble of the "Supplication of Volumnia to her Son Coriolanus." In 1767 he won a further premium of thirty guineas for a bas-relief in clay of "Abimelech Restoring Sarah to Abraham," and exhibited both these works at the Society of Artists in the same year. In 1768 he sent in a model for the statue of Sir William Harpur to be erected at Bedford School, but was unsuccessful and the commission was given to B. Palmer (q.v.). (School Archives.)

Van der Meulen exhibited at the Free Society, 1767–1780, and at the Society of Artists, 1778–1780, showing a number of tablets for chimney-pieces, wax portraits, etc. His son exhibited marble busts and wax portraits at the Society of Artists and also at the Free Society between 1772 and 1780.

VAN DER MEULEN, LAURENS

b. 1645, *d.* 1719

He was a statuary of Malines who came over to England and worked under Grinling Gibbons. In the P.R.O. (*Domestic Entry Book*, Car. II, Vol. LI, page 77) is the "License to Forainers employed at Windsor to remaine here wth. out molestation" dated 16 November, 1678. Among the names mentioned are "Laurence Vandermulen and Antony Verhencke servants to Mr. Grinling Gibbons, the carver." Another assistant of Gibbons was Dievot (q.v.) and, according to Vertue (*Walpole Society*, Vol. I, page 61), Van der Meulen was employed with him on the bronze statue of James II which had been ordered from their master.

Nothing further seems to be known of Van der Meulen's work in England and in 1691 he left the country for Mechelen.

VAN DER STEIN, JOHN
fl. 1678–1700

In 1678 he was working at Windsor Castle where he received £197 for carver's work for the Royal Throne; this included "Three large figures called Slaves, £90," "a figure called Justice, £20," and "two figures called Fame, £60." He was also paid "for drawing and making of several designs, models and figures in clay for ye pedestall under His Majesty's statue and for carving ye stone eagles that the brasse dyall is set upon" (Hope's *Windsor Castle*, Vol. I, page 318). In the P.R.O. (*Domestic Entry Book*, Car. II, Vol. LI, page 77) is the "License to Forainers employed at Windsor to remaine here wth. out molestation"—it is dated 16 November, 1678—among the names mentioned are "John Vanderstaine, stone-carver; John Oastes and Arnold Luellan, his servants; and— Gocisen, his housekeeper."

About 1692 van der Stein went to Oxford and was employed at the Physick Garden, where his work included in 1695 "cutting the Earle of Danby's statue £7 12s." (Vice-Chancellor's Accounts). In the previous year he had been paid £26 10s. for unidentified work in the same place (op. cit.). A year or so later he was at Queen's College, where he received £4 for the models of Aristotle and Plato and a similar sum for those of Socrates and Seneca. In 1694 he was paid for "fretwork in the New Library," and about 1696 for carving the eight statues on the west front of the building, and also for "two eagles and eight keystones" (Archives, Queen's College).

VANGELDER,
PETER MATHIAS
b. 1739, *d.* 1809

He was born in Amsterdam, and as a young man came over to England where he entered the employment of Thomas Carter (q.v.). John Deare (q.v.), who later worked for Carter himself, wrote to his father in 1776 that "Vangelder who cut that large figure in our shop and is considered one of the best hands in London at foliage, was seven years in saving a thousand pounds by keeping men at work at his own house, while he got two guineas a week at Mr. Carter's" (J. R. Smith's *Nollekens and His Times*, Vol. II, page 237).

It was not until 1769 that Vangelder attended the Royal Academy Schools, gaining a Silver Medal in the same year and winning the Gold Medal in 1771 for his bas-relief entitled "The Choice of Hercules." In 1778 he was paid twenty guineas for a chimney-piece for the Drapers' Hall (Company's Archives) and about the same time made two chimney-pieces for Sir John Rushout, who was at that time improving his family seat of Northwick Hall in Gloucestershire (*Gentleman's Magazine*, 1793, page 298).

From 1789 until 1792 Vangelder was working at the Fishmongers' Hall, receiving £296 for work which included four Portland stone capitals for the colonnade, £60; carving in wood the King's Arms over the Master's chair, £38; and "two boys holding two dolphins, £24" (Company's Archives). In 1794 he made a marble plaque for the library at Audley End (Essex Records, D/DBY A.225), and in 1800 was paid £370 for a chimney-piece for the Grocers' Hall (Company's Archives). In 1809 he made another chimney-piece, this time for the house of Mr. Coutts in Stratton Street, Piccadilly, but died in the same year and the money was paid to his Executors in 1810. As a contractor he built houses in Bedford Square (1781), Riding House Lane (1786) and Devonshire Place (1793) (Middlesex Building Affidavits).

Vangelder had a considerable practice as a statuary, his finest work being the tablet to Mrs. Frampton in Moreton Church, Dorset. This, with its lovely frame of wild and garden flowers, is one of the most enchanting works of art in any English church. Hutchins, in his *History of Dorset* (Vol. II, page 146), says that it is "esteemed by connoisseurs one of the completest pieces of sculpture in this Kingdom" and rightly remarks on the "exquisite art" of the carving.

A number of monuments carried out by Vangelder were designed by Robert Adam, the most magnificent being that to the Duchess of Montagu (*d.* 1771) at Warkton, Northants, which is really more like a stage set, with its background and semicircular apse. Others are to Major André in Westminster Abbey and Robert Child, 1782, at Heston, Middlesex. André was hanged as a spy in America in 1780, and his tomb bears a finely carved relief of Washington receiving the petition in which the prisoner vainly asked for a soldier's death; the Child monument has well-executed candelabra on either side of a pyramid.

Other signed works by Vangelder include those to the Rev. John Fulham, 1778, at Compton, Surrey; Henry Read, 1786, and Frances Read, 1801, both at Ramsbury, Wilts; Mrs. Newland, 1786, at Havant, Hants; Lady Orde, 1796, at Hanwell, Middlesex; Henry Southby, 1797, at Buckland, Berks; Lord Northwick, 1800, at Blockley, Glos; John Fleming, 1802, at North Stoneham, Hants; Robert Davies, 1802, and Richard Puleston, 1804, both at Wrexham,

Denbigh; and Newton Barton, 1808, at Broadwater, Sussex. According to Malcolm's *Londinium Redivivum* (Vol. I, page 167), Vangelder was responsible for the monument of Alexander Hume, 1800, in the churchyard of Wormley, Herts.

Vangelder died on 3 September, 1809, in Upper Norton Street (*Gentleman's Magazine*, 1809, Part II, page 392). His widow survived him, dying on 6 March, 1814, at Upper George Street, Portman Square (ibid., 1814, Part II, page 414).

(Archives, Messrs. Coutts; authorities cited in text.)

VANINA, or VANNINI, PETER
fl. 1761–1770

In 1761 he made two "statues" (probably of plaster) for Trevor, Bishop of Durham. These were for the Bishop's house at Glynde in Sussex, but they are now no longer in existence (Archives, Mr. Humphrey Brand of Glynde).

On 3 and 4 April, 1770, Mr. Christie held two sales of Vanina's stock-in-trade at the latter's house in Dover Street on the occasion "of his going abroad." Among the lots sold were busts of Prior, Congreve, Milton, Ralegh and the Duke of Cumberland; equestrian statues of Louis XIV and William III; a relief of the "Virgin Mary Visiting St. Elizabeth" and "original statues" of Apollo, Venus de Medici, Mercury, Antinous, Brutus and Celeste. At a further sale on 3 July, 1770, Flaxman the Elder (q.v.) purchased a statue of Flora and busts of Venus and Tiberius (Archives, Messrs. Christie).

Also sold were statuettes of Rubens and Vandyck, which are probably copies of those by Rysbrack. Vanina certainly worked for that sculptor, as writing to Sir Edward Littleton in 1758 Rysbrack says that he has "Enquired of Mr. Vannini, the Caster in Plaster of Paris (Whom I Employ when I want) what the Expense of a Mould off of your Honours Bust, and each Cast out of it; it being a thing entirely out of my way" (Mrs. Esdaile—*The Art of Rysbrack in Terra-cotta*).

VAN PENNEN, THEODORE

In May, 1725, he made two statues for the Duke of Chandos's house at Canons (Collins-Baker's *The First Duke of Chandos*, page 142).

VANPOOK, —, of Brussels

He made the noble monument, with its magnificent relief, to Anne Petrie (*d.* 1787) in Lewisham Parish Church. This was sent over from Brussels about 1790 and was erected on the north side of the organ. The sculptor engaged to fix it in position was Thomas Banks (q.v.), who, five years later, was himself responsible for a companion monument to Mrs. Margaret Petrie, placed on the south side of the organ in the same church.

VAN SPANGEN
fl. 1800–1828

Van Spangen was a Dutchman who started a terra-cotta manufactory at Bow in competition with Coade and Sealy (q.v.). Here he made in 1801 statues of "Faith," "Hope" and "Charity" for the Freemasons' Charity School in St. George's Fields, Southwark, the last-named for the top of the building, the others for niches in two of the sides (*European Magazine*, 1801, page 205).

The firm later became van Spangen, Powell and Co., and manufactured terra-cotta keystones, ornamental moulded panels, tombstones, statues, etc. It went out of business about 1828.

A van Spangen made the font (designed by Gibbs) for Dulwich College in 1729 (Young's *History of Dulwich College*, Vol. II, page 346).

VARDY, JOHN

Vardy designed the tomb of Bishop Sherlock (*d.* 1761) in Fulham churchyard, which was visited by Cole, the antiquary, in 1764, shortly after its erection. Apparently it did not meet with his approval, for he described it as a "very clumsy and heavy altar-tomb of Portland stone and black marble on which is placed a most monstrous and awkward kind of sarcophagus, in no sort of taste or in the very worst" (Feret's *Fulham Old and New*, Vol. I, page 297). (See, Dixon, John.)

VARDY, THOMAS
fl. 1755–1773

In 1755 Vardy offered to do all the carving of the "Great Hall" of the Mansion House for £450, but his estimate was not accepted (City Corporation Records, Mansion House Building Accounts). In 1767 he carved two tablets for chimney-pieces for Hill Park, then being built for Lord Hillsborough by Henry Holland, the architect (Holland's account-book, Soane Museum). He also made several chimney-pieces for Cobham Hall in Kent, including a very pretty one for the blue damask room in 1773 (Archives, Earl of Darnley).

VASSALLI, —

In 1723 Sir John Dutton paid "Sig. Vassalli" £20 9s. for fourteen busts (Archives, Lord Sherborne). He is presumably the "Francis Vessali" who was responsible for the plaster-work at Sutton Scarsdale, Derbyshire, in the following year.

VEALE, —, of Plympton St. Mary

He signs the monument to John Harrys, 1725, at Plymstock, Devon.

VEALE, JOHN RICHARD, of Plymouth
fl. 1747–1774

The most notable features of his large architectural monuments in every case are the elaborate and well-carved shield and coat of arms at the base. Signed examples of his work commemorate Adrian Swete, 1747, at Ermington, Devon; John Clarke, 1749, at St. Dominick, Cornwall; and Thomas Saltern, 1753, at Parkham, Devon.

VERE, WILLIAM, of Stratford-by-Bow
fl. 1775–1790

Son of Thomas Vere, a corn-factor of Barking, he was apprenticed to Thomas Vidgeon in 1762 and became free in 1775. Ten years later he was appointed Steward of the Masons' Company, but asked to be allowed to refuse the office as he had met with an accident and had hurt his leg. The Court, however, would not accept this excuse and ordered their Clerk to write "peremptorily to him to attend."

Vere signs a large monument to Samuel Feake, 1790, at Henham, Essex. This work is 12 ft. high and consists of a pyramid, in front of which stands a large urn with a well-carved relief of an East Indiaman in full sail.

VERNON, JOHN

In 1713 the Earl of Strafford paid Vernon for carving a pair of stone griffins. No place is mentioned, but it seems almost certain that these were intended for Wentworth Woodhouse (British Museum, Ad. MS. 22,257).

VERSCHAFFEN, or VERSCHAFFELT, —
fl. 1765–1767

He was described as "Chief Sculptor to His Serene Highness the Elector Palatine" when, in 1765, he exhibited a large marble relief at the Free Society. Two years later Lord Rockingham paid him £52 for busts of Homer and Mithridates (Archives, Wentworth Woodhouse).

VICK, —
fl. 1807–1825

He signs tablets in Herefordshire, both with well-carved details, to Lacon Lambe, 1807, at Dilwyn, and to Thomas Woodward, 1822, at Ledbury.

VIDLER, JOHN, of Battle

There was a family of this name who, for several generations, were the leading masons in Battle, Sussex. In 1780 John Vidler was paid £300 for building the Webster family vault in Battle churchyard. He was succeeded by his son, Thomas, who, between 1811 and 1818, was responsible for all the alterations and additions to Battle Abbey, and also in 1817 for building the stables. Vidler was paid £1,950 by Sir Godfrey Webster in the first year or two, but after that found it impossible to extract any more money from his patron; as late as 1827 he was writing to the Webster lawyer in London trying to get his claim settled. Vidler appears also to have been an architect, as in the same letter he stresses that his claim on Sir Godfrey also included "superintending the whole of the works at Battle Abbey from the year 1812 and drawing all plans and working drawings." Vidler was succeeded by his son, John (Archives, Mrs. Harbord of Battle Abbey). In 1775 "Messrs. Inskip and Vidler" repaired the House of Correction at Battle, Sussex (County Archives, Lewes).

VIDLER, JOHN, of Westminster
fl. 1796–1804

He was variously employed at Richmond Palace in 1796, and also carved the capitals of the piers for the gateway into the Botanic Gardens. In 1804 he claimed £1,255 for work carried out at the White Lodge, Richmond (P.R.O., Works, 19.25/9).

He may be the same "Vidler" who signs the very pretty monument, with a medallion portrait of William Lowndes (d. 1775), at Astwood, Bucks.

VIDLER, MAJOR, of Hastings
fl. 1823–1839

He signs a series of rather dull tablets, all of which are in Sussex, to Edmund Cartwright, 1823, at Battle; Elizabeth Barnouin, 1826, in All Saints', Hastings; and Richard Greenland, 1839, at Winchelsea.

VIERPYL, SIMON
b. c. 1725, d. 1810

Vierpyl was born in London and, after studying under Peter Scheemakers (q.v.), went to Rome about 1750. Here he met Lord Charlemont, who employed him to make copies of the antique statues in the art galleries and private collections of the city, while for the Rev. Edward Murphy,

Charlemont's tutor and travelling-companion, he made in terra-cotta twenty-two statues and seventy-eight busts of Roman emperors. About 1774 Murphy wrote to Vierpyl, asking various questions about the value, etc., of these works. The sculptor, in his reply, asserted that he was "certain that no eminent artist will hereafter stand four years, winter and summer, as I have done, in the chilling Capitoline museum to model so many busts and statues with his own hand." A later Lord Charlemont afterwards presented this series to the Royal Irish Academy in 1868.

Vierpyl, after his first patron had left Rome, still continued to work for him, and also executed commissions for Lord Huntingdon and Lord Brudenell, carving for the latter a bust of Pythagoras.

In 1756 he went to Ireland and was again employed by Lord Charlemont, this time on the decoration of the Casino for the latter's seat, "Marino," designed by Sir William Chambers.

A statue of a "Dying Gladiator" by Vierpyl is, or was, at Wilton (Kennedy's *Description of Wilton*, 1769, page 38); for a list of his other works in Ireland, see Strickland's *Dictionary of Irish Artists*. (*Historical Manuscripts Commission*, Earl of Charlemont, Vol. I.)

VINE, JAMES, and THOMAS
Thomas: *b*. 1788, *d*. 1840
James: *b*. 1798, *d*. 1831

They were the sons of "Mr. Vine, of Bury, mason," who died in 1827 at the age of seventy; together they sign the monument to Sir Thomas Cullum, 1830, in Hawstead Parish Church, Suffolk. (Their obituaries are noted in the *Bury Post*.) .

VINER, C., of Bath
fl. 1780–1806

His monuments, although quite well carried out, are not particularly interesting, the best being that commemorating Lady Dundonald, 1779, at Weston, Somerset, which is a large work in coloured marbles.

Other signed tablets in Somerset executed by Viner include those to Robert Coe, 1788, at Walcot, Bath; Theophilus Ponting, 1791, at Norton St. Philip; Charlotte Wicker, 1795, at Weston; and John Taylor, 1806, at Newton St. Loe.

In the Throckmorton archives at Coughton Court is the diary of Sir Charles Throckmorton which contains the following entry: "14 April, 1795. Agreed with Mr. Viner, of Morford Street, Bath, to erect a marble monument in the Abbey Church

of Bath to the memory of Mr. Metcalfe according to the draught given in, for £15." (*Country Life*, 25 May, 1951.)

VOUSDEN, SAMUEL,
of Clapham
fl. 1827–1838

He signs a few Hellenic tablets, of which the three best (all in Greater London) are those to William Charrington, 1832, and Thomas Withington, 1838, both in Streatham Parish Church; and Katherine Cancellor, 1823, in St. Matthew's, Brixton.

VOYEZ, JOHN
fl. 1765–1773

In 1768 Voyez was offered employment by Wedgwood, who apparently had great hopes of him, for he wrote to his partner, Bentley, that he had "hired a modeller for three years, the best I am told in London. He served his time with a silversmith, has worked several years at a china works, has been two or three years carving in wood and marble for Mr. Adam the famous architect, is a perfect master of the antique style in ornaments, vases, etc., and works with equal facility in clay, wax, wood or stone."

Wedgwood treated Voyez extremely well, paying his debts in London and transporting him and his wife to Burslem. Voyez, indeed, seemed sensible of this, for when he wrote to Wedgwood's London agent, Mr. Cox, on 19 August, 1768, he spoke of "Mr. Wedgwood's exceeding genteel behaviour to me, who, on my arrival here, entertained us in his own house until our house was gotten ready which was by the usiall diligance or rather delays of joiner Show kept back longer than it otherwise might have been."

In spite of this good beginning, Voyez was in trouble in less than a year and was sentenced to three months' imprisonment at the Stafford Assizes. Even then Wedgwood was not free of him, for he later set up as a modeller of inferior seals and cameos, which he sold as from the Wedgwood factory, even going so far as to forge the name of the firm on the back of his productions. Cox, writing to Bentley in June, 1769, indignantly informs him that "I have not seen Mr. Voyez and have desired our people to keep him out of here if he should dare to call when I am out."

Voyez exhibited intaglios, etc., at the Free Society in 1772, when he described himself as "a carver and manufacturer of composition at Cowbridge, near Newcastle, Staffs." A number of his works are in the Bristol Art Gallery.

(Wedgwood Archives.)

W

WADDILOVE, J.

He signs a large wall-tablet with an "Adam" urn and well-carved detail, to Martha Tate, 1795, at Mitcham, Surrey.

WADE, JOSEPH
b. ca. 1664, *d.* 1743

From 1726 until 1728 he was in partnership with Bartholomew Chichley (q.v.), and in the following year was employed on his own at Greenwich Palace, receiving £101 for decorative work on the South Pavilion of Queen Anne's Court. This sum included £8 a face for Corinthian capitals; £21 10s. for forty-three "Modilions"; and £3 each for two scrolls, carved to a depth of 2 ft. (P.R.O., Ad. 68/708).

A John Wade was the carver of the doorway of St. Michael's Church, Cornhill, in 1717.

WAKE, J. HALL

He acted as foreman to Henry Wood (q.v.) and in 1792 was working at Woburn, where he was paid £100 for stone-carving (Woburn Archives).

WALDIN,
or WALLDIN, SAMUEL,
of Winchester
b. c. 1730, *d.* 1804

He was the son of Samuel Waldin, a farmer of Winchester, and was apprenticed to John Blake in 1744, although he did not trouble to take up his freedom until thirty years later. In 1781 he was employed on repair work at Winchester Palace, and he also signs the monument of Robert Eyre (*d.* 1770) in the Cathedral.

On Waldin's death his son, Samuel Waldin the Younger, took over the business (*Monthly Magazine*, 1804, Part II, page 370).

WALKER, —, of Kendal
fl. 1825–1841

He signs a large tablet with a relief of "Hope" to Thomas Parkin, 1825, at Ecclesfield, Yorks, and another, with a relief of mourning soldiers, to Captain Considine, 1841, in Chester Cathedral.

The monument of Nathaniel Bowen (*d.* 1839) in St. Michael's Church, Charleston, South Carolina, is signed "Walker" and is said to be the work of an English statuary.

WALKER, A. E.

He exhibited a medallic portrait at the Royal Academy in 1830. In 1841 a Mrs. Theresa Snell Walker showed at the Academy two models of Australian subjects.

WALKER, R., of Bristol
fl. 1830–1836

He signs an ambitious monument to Lucy Palmer, 1834, at Brixton, Devon, which has a life-size figure of a woman kneeling by an urn. The tablet at Cold Ashton, Glos, to Elizabeth Kater, 1835, is also his work.

An "R. Walker" of Bath signs the monument to John Rundall, 1852, in St. Mary's Church, Madras.

WALLIS, JAMES, of Newark
b. 1748, *d.* 1824

He was apprenticed to Christopher Staveley (q.v.) in 1761, and later set up for himself as an "architect and marble and stone-mason" in Newark. His monuments and tablets are neat and pleasant works, mostly in coloured marbles, the best being that to Richard Fydell, 1780, in Boston Parish Church, Lincolnshire, which has a medallion portrait. Other signed works by him in Nottinghamshire commemorate Thomas and Mary Kelham, *c.* 1770, at Great Gonerby; Gilbert Charlton, *c.* 1770, at Staunton-in-the-Vale; Joseph Sykes, 1778, at Balderton; the Rev. John Ferrand, 1779, at Messingham; Francis Foss, 1792, at Everton; the Rev. Thomas Wakefield, 1798, at East Stoke; and Margaret Spragging, 1803, and Thomas Spragging, 1814, both in Newark Parish Church. The monument to the Rev. B. Clarkham, 1798, at Sleeford, Lincs, is also his work.

Wallis later went into partnership with R. Marshall and together they sign tablets to George Smith, 1806, at Fulbeck, Lincs; Elizabeth Withers, 1817, at Barnby, Notts; Mary Boucher, 1819, at Coddington, Notts; and William Underwood, 1820, at Melton Mowbray, Leics. On Wallis's death on 6 January, 1824, his partner erected a large tomb to his memory in Newark churchyard; he also carried on the business, and signs wall-tablets to Slingsby Duncombe, 1831, at Langford, Notts, and James and Mary Dyson, 1843, in Newark Parish Church.

WALLIS, JOHN
fl. 1789–1791

As a mason and stone-carver he was employed at Carlton House from 1789 until 1790 (P.R.O., H.O. 73/24). In the following year he received £89 for marble chimney-pieces for some of the bedrooms at Woburn Abbey (Bedford Archives).

WALMSLEY, JOHN, of Liverpool

He signs a tablet to John Plumb, 1796, at Aughton, Lancs. His yard was in Berry Street.

WALSH and DUNBAR, of Leeds
Firm *fl.* 1816–1840

The firm produced heavy, unexciting monuments and tablets at their yard in Park Row, the best being those to Charles Brackenbury, 1816, at Scremby, Lincs; John Allcott, 1824, at South Kirby, Yorks; Anne Lindley, 1825, at Whitkirk, Yorks; Sir John Beckett, 1826, at Torrington, Lincs; and John Ramsden, 1836, at Brotherton, Yorks.

There was also a firm in Leeds named "Walsh and Lee" which flourished 1830–1860, and had a yard in Waterloo Road. Their best works (all in Yorkshire) include a large Gothic monument to Sir John Ramsden, Bart., 1839, at Brotherton; tablets to John Starkey, 1844, and Thomas Pearson Crossland, 1845, both in Huddersfield Parish Church; and a Hellenic wall-monument to John Wilkinson, 1850, at Barwick-in-Elmet. They were also responsible for the Crimean War memorial in Leeds Parish Church.

WALSH, JOHN
fl. 1757–1778

He was an apprentice and pupil of T. Carter (q.v.), and in 1775, when living in South Street, Berkeley Square, became free of the Masons' Company by redemption. In 1757 he exhibited a model (based on a work by Scheemakers) of a "Dying Gladiator" at the Society of Arts and showed it again four years later at the Free Society. Also in 1761 he received a premium of five guineas from the Society of Arts for a model in clay copied from a cast in the Duke of Richmond's Gallery.

Walsh later set up for himself as a carver of chimney-pieces and was apparently employed by a Mr. Errington, whose new house near Hexham in Northumberland was designed by Sir William Chambers. The latter, writing to Errington about the interior decoration in 1762, says that he believes "Mr. Walsh's proposals about the chimney-pieces are reasonable and if he will send me the size of the tablet, I will make a drawing. In a day or two I shall have the drawings done for your other two chimney-pieces, and I will send for Mr. Walsh to hear his proposals. I think he will execute them very well" (British Museum, Ad. MS. 41133). In 1764 Trevor, Bishop of Durham paid Walsh £26 for carving his coat of arms in Portland Stone. This was placed on the exterior of the Chapel at Glynde, Sussex, which had been designed by Sir Thomas Robinson in the same year. (Archives, Brand of Glynde.)

Walsh signs a number of architectural monuments of some importance, the best being that commemorating Sir Thomas Robinson (the architect already mentioned) and his wife, the Dowager Lady Lechmere. This was erected in Westminster Abbey about 1778 and has two portrait-busts. Other signed monuments by Walsh include those to Thomas Amphlett, 1763, at Enville, Staffs; Joseph Percival, 1764, in St. Michael's, Bristol; Sir Ralph Assheton, 1765, at Middleton, Lancs; Henry, Earl of Stamford, 1768, at Enville, Staffs; Pratt Mawbey, 1770, at Chertsey, Surrey; Sir John Rous, 1771, at Wangford, Suffolk; and Stephen Soame, 1771, at Little Thurlow, Suffolk. The last-named has a portrait-medallion of Mrs. Soame and her child.

WALSHA, GEORGE, of Wakefield
fl. 1814–1818

He signs a number of tablets in Yorkshire, the best being those commemorating George Clerk, 1814, at Barnsley, and Thomas Cotton, 1816, at Darton.

WALTERS, RICHARD
fl. 1690–1701

In 1691 Walters, together with his partners, Thomas Hill (q.v.) and John Thompson (q.v.), received £2,321 for various works which they had carried out at Kensington Palace. This included ninety-six chimney-pieces in Portland stone, and twenty-five chimney-pieces, three tables and "a cisterne," all in marble (*Wren Society's Publications*, Vol. VII, page 177).

In 1701 Walters was paid £14 for another marble chimney-piece, this time for "my Lord's bedchamber" at Powys House (P.R.O., Works 5/51).

WALTON, FREDERICK, of Staines
b. 1799, *d.* 1834

Two monumental works by Walton in Surrey

are the large wall-tablet to Henry Wood, 1827, at Chertsey and a square Hellenistic tomb with an urn to Alexander Urquhart, 1829, in Long Ditton churchyard.

Walton himself is buried in the churchyard of Kingston-upon-Thames under a tomb of his own design, for the inscription states that beneath it lies "Frederick Walton, by whom this tomb was composed and erected." His wife, Charlotte, survived him and died in 1839.

WARD, ROBERT, of Liverpool
fl. 1827–1829

He was living in Harford Street when in 1827 he exhibited busts of William Huskisson and General Gascoyne at the Liverpool Academy. Two years later he showed busts of Dr. Birkbeck and the Rev. E. Hull.

WARD, W., of Scarborough
He signs a wall-tablet to E. Musham, 1820, at Burton Agnes, Yorkshire.

WARREN, JOSIAH, of Southampton
fl. 1808–1828

Warren seems to have started business in Southampton, but later moved to Wareham, in Dorset, where he signs a tablet to John Card, 1822. He signs others to Eliza Stewart, 1808, at North Stoneham, Hants, and Sarah Wilt, 1814, at East Stoke, Dorset.

WARREN, WILLIAM, of Hitchin
fl. 1790–1828

In 1826 he was employed by Countess de Grey at Wrest Park in Bedfordshire, where he received £90 for repairing the statues and £75 for carving and erecting the stone piers for the gates. Two years later he made vases, columns and statues in Portland stone for the Bowling Green House in the garden (Wrest Archives).

Warren signs a large wall-tablet to the Wilshire family, *c.* 1790, at Welwyn, Herts, and another with a sculptured urn to Catherine Price, 1820, at Knebworth in the same county.

WATERWORTH, THOMAS, the Elder, and THOMAS, the Younger, of Doncaster
Thomas, the Elder, *b.* 1753, *d.* 1829
Thomas, the Younger, *b.* 1788, *d.* 1835

Thomas, the Elder, was the son of Thomas Waterworth of Sutton-on-Derwent who had married in 1740 Rebecca Whittal and who had died in 1755, aged 54, and was buried at Hemingborough, Yorks.

The elder Waterworth was responsible for all the decorative stone-carving of the mausoleum which was erected in 1788 at Wentworth Woodhouse by Lord Rockingham (Fitzwilliam Archives). He also signs a monument, with a portrait-bust, to William Dixon, 1783, at Loversall, Yorks, and another to the Rev. John Simpson, 1784, at Babworth, Notts.

It is presumably the younger Waterworth who signs the monument at Tuxford, Notts, to Captain Charles White, 1814, which has a relief of the graves of the Captain and his brother-officers at Bayonne.

The firm is also responsible for a tablet to John Jarrett, 1800, at Bradford, Yorks, and for the monument commemorating Lord Effingham, 1816, at Rotherham, in the same county. The elder Waterworth married Harriet, daughter of Christopher Richardson (q.v.), who may well have been his master; she had been previously married to Christopher Theakston (q.v.). The younger Waterworth died 21 December, 1835, aged 47, and was buried at Doncaster. His widow died 11 September, 1837, aged 42.

(Doncaster Corporation Archives.)

WATKINS, HENRY, of Newport
fl. 1835–1852

At the Great Exhibition of 1851 he showed a marble group entitled "The Death of Llewllyn, the last Prince of Wales." The large wall-tablet to Martha Davies, 1838, in Newport Church, Monmouthshire, is also his work.

Watkins either died or left Newport in 1852, for his name ceases to appear in local directories after that date.

WATKINS, JOHN, of Ringwood
fl. 1795–1813

He signs the architectural monument about 8 ft. high to James Mowbray, 1801, in Ringwood Church, Hampshire. This, with its "Adam" urn and gadrooned base, is an extremely competent piece of carving for a local craftsman. Watkins is also responsible for the circular wall-tablet to the Hackman family, 1811, in the same church.

WATKINS, JOHN
He was presumably a local carver and signs a tablet to Catherine and James Davies, 1780, at Lyonshall, Herefordshire.

WATSON, HENRY
b. 1714, *d.* 1786

He was born at Heanor, Derbyshire, and according to Glover (*Derbyshire*, Vol. II, page 260) was the son of Samuel Watson (q.v.), although Francis Thompson (*History of Chatsworth*, page 115) suggests that he was the elder Watson's grandson or great-nephew. I am, however, inclined to agree with Glover, whose information came from White Watson (q.v.), the last member of the family.

In 1749 Henry Watson was working at Welbeck Abbey, where he made a marble chimney-piece, costing £65 10s., for the "North-East Room" (Portland Archives). In 1779 he laid the tessellated floor of black-and-white marble squares in the Painted Hall at Chatsworth (Francis Thompson, op. cit., page 115).

At Welbeck, Chatsworth, and the Derby County Library are a number of Watson's original drawings for monuments and other works, with brief notes in his own handwriting. The monumental drawings include a cartouche tablet for a Mr. Turnbull to be erected in Bedsworth Church, dated 1733 (I have been unable to identify this village); a monument, dated 1736, at Didsbury, near Manchester, apparently commemorating Sir John Bland; and another undated one to a "Mr. Murgatroyd" in Dewsbury Church; also a tablet, dated 1740, to be erected at Wakefield to a "Mr. Fairfax"; and a sketch of an undated monument to "Mr. Bagshaw's family in Norton Church."

A design, dated 1738, for a carved wooden chimney-piece with a broken pediment is annotated: "This design was made by Mr. Leoni, the ornaments I performed in wood for Peter Bold, Esq.," and there are other sketches of vases carried out in "blue john" for "Mrs. Legge of Grindlesmith Gate, Nottingham."

WATSON, JAMES, the Elder, and JAMES, the Younger, of Norwich
Firm *fl.* 1793–1851

The elder Watson's tablets are quite well carved, but in no way outstanding, the best being those to Elizabeth Clarke, 1793, and Peter Stoughton, 1805, both at East Dereham, Norfolk.

The firm was later carried on by James Watson the Younger, whose work is competent. His tablets in Norfolk include those to the Rev. John Warren, 1824, at Tacolneston; Thomas Talbot, 1832, at Wymondham; George Smith, 1841, at Mattishall; Samuel Stone, 1848, in St. Andrew's, Norwich; and Lord Berners, 1851, at Ashwellthorpe. He also signs a tablet to the Rev. Bartholo-

mew Riston, 1835, in Lowestoft Parish Church, Suffolk.

Watson's wife, Susan, died in 1830.

WATSON, JOHN
fl. 1808–1829

He did a considerable amount of work at the Royal Palace at Greenwich, building the "New Helpless Ward" in 1808 and the Infirmary four years later. Here he was responsible for all the carved stonework and the marble chimney-pieces, including one of "veined marble" costing £20 16s., and another of "black marble" at £16 4s. Between 1812 and 1814 he completed the west front of King Charles's Building, and in 1815 received £7,000 for "new offices, eastward of Greenwich Palace."

In 1825 Watson built the Out Pension Office at St. Mary Axe, and in 1828–1829 the Royal Hospital Schools at Greenwich. (P.R.O., Ad. 882–Ad. 887.)

WATSON, MUSGRAVE LEWTHWAITE
b. 1804, *d.* 1847

He was born on 24 January, 1804, near Carlisle, and was educated at the village school. From an early age he showed artistic talent, carving in wood and engraving on metal; indeed, he wished to take up art as a profession, but his father decided that he should practise law and articled him to a solicitor in Carlisle. Here Watson remained for two years, but fortunately his employer, a Major Mounsey, had a good collection of pictures and the young man was given every opportunity to study them, so that his time was not entirely wasted.

On the death of his father in 1823 Watson left Carlisle and went to London, where he sought the advice of Flaxman. On the latter's recommendation he entered the Royal Academy Schools and at the same time became a pupil of R. Sievier (q.v.). This arrangement did not last long, for Watson soon set out for Italy (again acting on Flaxman's advice) and remained there for three years.

In 1828 he returned to London and then revisited Carlisle, where he carved a bust of the naturalist, J. Heysham, which was shown in the same year at the Carlisle Exhibition of Painting and Sculpture. However, he was soon back in London and took a studio near the British Museum. Here he produced various poetical works, including compositions from Homer, Chaucer and Spenser.

In 1833 Sir Francis Chantrey (q.v.) engaged

Watson as a modeller and employed him on the monument of Mrs. Digby which was later erected in Worcester Cathedral. The association did not last, for Watson very soon asked for a rise in wages and left when his request was refused, in spite of the fact that Allan Cunningham, who super-intended Chantrey's studio, had given it his support.

Watson next worked for W. Behnes (q.v.) and E. H. Baily (q.v.), modelling for the former the figure (but not the head) of the statue of Dr. Babbington for St. Paul's Cathedral. About this time he was also employed by W. Croggan (q.v.) at the terra-cotta works at Lambeth. Here he designed and modelled friezes for the Wyndham family, statues of "Aesculapius" and "Hygeia" for a hall in Liverpool, and groups for Dublin.

By 1842 he was more or less independent and working on his own account, and in that year carved the frieze on the façade of Moxhay's "Hall of Commerce" in Threadneedle Street. Shortly afterwards he received the commission for what was to prove his greatest work, the colossal group of the brothers, Lord Eldon and Lord Stowell. The second Lord Eldon had originally intended to entrust the work to Chantrey, but after the latter's death was persuaded by Allan Cunningham to allow Watson to model it. The sculptor soon had a number of orders for other works, so the group was not finished when he died and it was left to his pupil and friend, G. Nelson (q.v.), assisted by Charles Summers (q.v.), to complete it. It is now in the Library of University College, Oxford, and is undoubtedly one of the most important portrait groups of the nineteenth century.

In 1844 Watson exhibited a relief of "Death and Sleep Bearing off the Body of Sarpedon," at the Royal Academy. This was acclaimed by all the art critics of the time, and from contemporary engravings appears to have been a work of great beauty. Among his other works were statues of Flaxman (1843), for University College, London; Queen Elizabeth (1844), for the Royal Exchange; the Earl of Lonsdale (1845) and Major Aglionby (1845), both for Carlisle; and "Hebe" and "Iris" (1847), for the gates at Bowood. His terra-cotta relief entitled "Little Children Come Unto Me" was executed in 1845 for Little Holland House, and two years later he made the font for Ryde Church in the Isle of Wight. The bronze relief of the Battle of St. Vincent, at the base of the Nelson Column in Trafalgar Square, was unfinished at the time of his death. His four monuments are those of his friend, Allan Cunningham, 1843, one in Kensal Green Cemetery and another in St. Michael's, Dumfries; the Rev. W. Fletcher (with a bust), 1847, at Dalston, Cumberland; and Dr.

Cameron, 1847, in the Chapel Royal, Savoy; the last-named was, however, destroyed by fire in 1864.

Watson died of heart disease at his home, 13, Upper Gloucester Place, on 28 October, 1847, and was buried in Highgate cemetery. Had he lived he would assuredly have been one of the greater sculptors of the nineteenth century. In Carlisle Cathedral is a tablet to his memory with a portrait relief and the inscription that he was "second son of Thomas Watson of the Bogs Sebergham." The epitaph ends: "The elegance, simplicity and purity of his works are sufficient to impose all that by his death, art has lost one of her most gifted exponents."

He appears, in his biography by Lonsdale, to have been temperamental and difficult to deal with, quarrelling with his patrons and employers and "wanting in equanimity"; one day falling "the victim of doubts, depressions and despond-ency," the next rising "with hopes and lofty aspirations." Nor, according to the same author, were "his domestic arrangements of a nature to give him a place in society," for he lived "with a young female, the daughter of a publican in Carlisle, but never married her."

On 14 September, 1848, a sale of sketches, casts, etc., was held in Watson's studio. Shortly before his death the sculptor had apparently destroyed a number of works which did not satisfy him, but among the lots sold were two sketches in plaster of Sir David Wilkie and "A Study of the Mother of Lord Brougham," neither of which seems ever to have been carved in marble.

Eight years after Watson's death an open letter on the selection of artists for public monuments was addressed to Sir Benjamin Hall, Chief Commis-sioner of Works, and signed by all the leading British sculptors of the time. This contained the following paragraph: "A sculptor of the name of Watson recently died. He was an industrious artist, and a competitor for most of the public monuments erected in his day. He never attained a commission, but the rejected models which he exhibited on such occasions are now sought for with avidity and studied by living artists."

(Lonsdale's *Life of Watson; Art Union*, 1848, page 27; *Art Journal*, 1856, page 379.)

WATSON, R., of Dartford
fl. 1802–1822

His best work is the large wall-tablet to George Sharp, 1810, at Stone, Kent, which has a relief of a wreathed urn on a column; another tablet in the same church, to Thomas Heathcote, 1802, has good details and a coat of arms engraved on brass.

Other signed works by Watson commemorate Enoch Holden, 1809, at Crayford, Kent; and Lady Gordon, 1811, and Miss Pritchard, 1818, both at West Tilbury, Essex.

WATSON, SAMUEL
b. 1663, *d.* 1715

He was born at Heanor in Derbyshire and, according to a statement made by his grandson, White Watson (q.v.), to the Rev. Daniel Lysons early in the last century, was "a pupil of Charles Oakey, carver, in the parish of St. Martin's in the fields" (Lysons's *Derbyshire*, page 153)

Watson is chiefly remembered for the immense amount of work he did at Chatsworth, for he first went there when he was twenty-six and was still doing carving for the house at his death in 1715. In 1698 he received £20 for two large festoons and for carving two pedestals in the garden, while a year later his bill was for "carving basons in Willow Tree grove, two vauses on ye peers at ye bird-house and carving two dragons."

Also among the Chatsworth Archives is the agreement between Watson and the Earl of Devonshire for stone-carving on the west front of the house. This is dated 2 September, 1701, and stipulates that he is to receive £4 10s. for each column capital and £3 for each pilaster capital; £4 each for the ornaments over the windows; £1 each for "serpents in a twisted knot"; and 12s. a head for "lyons heads in the cornish." In the same year he was paid for fourteen mask-heads in the terrace wall; for "two flower potts set upon ye two peers going to ye bowling-green"; and for eight urns for the Hall front.

Other works carried out by Watson at Chatsworth include the cornice, doorcase and niches on the west staircase, the coat of arms on the west front (for which he received £55 in 1704), and "ten terms in the garden" in 1711.

In 1706 he wrote to Thomas Coke, of Melbourne Hall, Derbyshire: "I have according to your order sent you two designs of vases, which I take to bee something after ye manner your worship spoke of att Melborn; but if you would have any alteration in either of them as to cartouches instead of festoons or in any other part, be pleased to give me your directions which shall bee observed to my uttermost power" (Archives, Marquess of Lothian). There are still in the gardens of Melbourne a number of stone vases which could be the work of Watson.

Watson even found time to execute a number of monuments, and in the Chatsworth Archives is a payment of £17 made to him in 1698 for "cutting a monument in alabaster for His Grace the Duke of Newcastle," while a book containing original drawings and sketches for monuments, etc., made by him and his family is now in the library of the Derby County Council. It is not possible to identify the majority of these sketches with complete certainty, but one is undoubtedly the preliminary drawing for the monument at Tamworth, Staffordshire, which commemorates John Ferrers and his son Humphrey. This is an interesting discovery, for the monument with its kneeling baroque figures is one of the most dramatic in England.

Watson died on 31 March, 1715, and was buried at Heanor, where the epitaph on his monument reads:

> "Watson is gone, whose skilful art display'd
> To the very life whatever nature made.
> View but his wonderous works on
> Chatsworth Hall
> Which are so gaz'd at and admir'd by all."

(Francis Thompson's *History of Chatsworth*; Chatsworth Archives; Glover's *Derbyshire*, Vol. II, pages 255–258; R. Gunnis, *Country Life*, 9 February, 1951.)

WATSON, WHITE
b. 1760, *d.* 1835

Grandson of Samuel (q.v.) and nephew of Henry Watson (q.v.), he carved the Manners coat of arms in Hopton stone, which was formerly in front of the Rutland Arms Inn at Bakewell. In 1792 he made the font and, a year later, a sundial, for Bakewell Church.

Watson's most important monumental work is the semi-Corinthian column, 15 ft. high, with a central inscription-tablet in the form of a parchment, which commemorates Sir Sitwell Sitwell, 1811, in Eckington Church, Derby. Signed tablets by him in the same county include those to Richard Roe, 1795, and the Rev. Richard Chapman, 1816, both at Bakewell; John Sutton, 1803, at Heanor; and Emma Sgambella, 1821, at Bradley. He also signs others to Richard Jackson, 1799, at Sandbach, Cheshire; Frances Kirkby, 1823, at Broadwater, Sussex, and Thomas Rawson, 1826, at Ecclesfield, Yorks.

WAUDBY, JOHN, of Hull
fl. 1830–1850

His tablets are mostly heavy and clumsy works in the Hellenic manner. The best (all in Yorkshire) are those to Joseph Eggington, 1830, at Kirk Ella; Henry Bell, 1839, at Eastrington; Charlotte Willoughby, 1845, and Henry Willoughby, 1849, both at Birdsall; and Robert Dunn, 1847, at Howden.

WEALE, WILLIAM,
of Wolverhampton

He signs a small monument, with a well-carved relief of an angel leading a woman to heaven, to Sarah Riley, 1835, at Bilston, Staffordshire.

WEARING, JOHN, of London

He was a London mason employed at Chatsworth, where in 1699 he was paid £20 "in part for mason's worke done in finishing the marble fountaine and stairs," and £55 "for finishing the staircase in the west court and fountaine in the inner court and steps in the gatehouse" (Chatsworth Archives).

WEBB, EDWARD WILLIAM
b. 1811

He attended the Royal Academy Schools in 1829 and won a Silver Medal four years later. An "R. D. Webb," of 12, Charles Street, was awarded a Silver Palette by the Society of Arts for figures in 1826 and a Silver Isis Medal in 1827. Neither of these artists seems to have exhibited at the Academy, nor is any further trace of them to be found.

WEBB, T.
fl. 1776–1786

Webb, who was presumably a local statuary, signs two monuments in Tetbury Church, Gloucestershire. The first, with a marble portrait-bust, commemorates Sir William Romney (*d.* 1611), and was erected *c.* 1776, while the second, to Joseph Wickes (*d.* 1786), has an urn and a draped pyramid.

WEBBER, HENRY
b. 1754, *d.* 1826

He was born in July, 1754, the son of Abraham Webber, a Swiss sculptor, who had settled in England at the age of twenty-four and married an Englishwoman named Maria Quandt.

Henry Webber, who was a pupil of J. Bacon the Elder (q.v.), attended the Royal Academy Schools in 1772 and won a Silver Medal two years later. In 1776 he was awarded the Gold Medal by a unanimous vote for a relief of "The Judgment of Midas," a work now in the Soane Museum (Royal Academy Archives).

In 1784 Sir Joshua Reynolds and Sir William Chambers recommended Webber to Wedgwood, with whom he signed a seven-year contract on 17 January, 1785, and who appointed him head of the ornamental department at Etruria. In a letter he wrote to Byerley, Wedgwood's London agent,

in 1786, Webber tells him that he "left London, as it is said many people do England, in too great a hurry even to pay their debts." He modelled a number of reliefs, vases, chimney-pieces for Wedgwood, and in 1787 the firm sent him ·to Rome to make drawings of the works of art in the Capitoline Museum, the terms of their agreement making it clear that Webber was there "for the purpose of making models, drawings and other improvements in the art of modelling and designing for the benefit of the said Josiah Wedgwood." He later travelled home via Switzerland and Paris with his employer's eldest son, who had also been in Rome at that time.

On his return to England in 1789 Webber was employed on the Barberini, or Portland, vase and also modelled bas-reliefs from the sketches he had made while in Italy. Although he only seems to have been paid twelve guineas a month, he nevertheless remained at Etruria until Wedgwood's death.

In 1795, on the sudden death of J. Hickey (q.v.), the sculptor originally chosen for the work, Webber was given the commission for the monument to David Garrick to be erected in Westminster Abbey. This was unveiled in May, 1797, and in general met with only qualified praise, although the *Universal Magazine* (1797, Part II, page 73) did consider it worthy of the sculptor's "improved talents" and also that it afforded "a happy earnest of what in future may be expected from them."

The monument is the "Harlequin figure" which Charles Lamb describes in the following passage: "Taking a turn the other day in the Abbey I was struck with the affected attitude of a figure which I do not remember to have seen before, and which upon examination proved to be a whole length of the celebrated Mr. Garrick. Though I would not go so far, with some good Catholics abroad, as to shut players altogether out of consecrated ground, yet I own I was not a little scandalized at the introduction of theatrical airs and gestures into a place set apart to remind us of the saddest realities."

Webber's other signed monument commemorates Henry Askew in the Cathedral of Newcastle-on-Tyne and was erected in 1801. He exhibited at the Society of Artists, 1773, and at the Royal Academy, 1775–1779. His model in clay of "Hercules Holding Cerberus" is also in the Soane Museum.

Webber died on 7 August, 1826, and on the following day a Captain William Small wrote to Josiah Wedgwood the Younger begging "leave to communicate to you the death of my friend, Mr. Henry Webber. He died at three o'clock yesterday at Mrs. Kincade's, 11, South Crescent, Bedford Square. I went to Messrs. Coutts and find by his will that you are one of the Executors." The letter is signed "William Small, Captain late 37th Regiment, a very old friend of Mr. Webber's."

(Wedgwood Archives; Redgrave's *Dictionary of Artists*; Brayley's *Westminster Abbey*, Vol. II, page 253; authorities mentioned in text.)

WEBSTER, C., of Lichfield

His monument to John Perrott, 1802, at Brewood, Staffordshire, has a pyramid, from which hangs a coat of arms.

WEBSTER, FRANCIS, and SONS, of Kendal

Firm *fl.* 1790–1850

According to local directories, the firm started business before 1790 as "Webster and Howe, Builders and Marble-cutters," but by 1811 the sole proprietor was "Francis Webster, Stonemason." Before 1828 the name was changed again to "Francis Webster and Sons, Sculptors," and in 1829 to "George and Francis Webster, Sculptors" (presumably on the death of the senior partner).

The Websters made a number of chimney-pieces in the local Westmorland marble, including one for the Union News-room at Liverpool in 1801 (Anon, *History of Liverpool*, 1810, page 347), and in 1826 another for Sir Charles Ibbetson (private information).

Their monuments and tablets follow the usual trend of Hellenic and Gothic taste of the time; a late one, commemorating James Thompson, 1850, at Clitheroe, Lancs, has a portrait-bust. They sign other monumental works to Nicholas Halsted, 1808, at Burnley, Lancs; Thomas Hinde, 1819, and Frances Parke, 1822, both in Lancaster Parish Church; Thomas Ireland, 1817, and Anne Moffett, 1828, both in Kendal; William Steele, 1822, at Market Drayton, Salop; William St. Clare, 1822 and William Pritchard, 1829, both in Preston Parish Church; the Rev. Christopher Goodwill, 1822, in Richmond Parish Church, Yorks; Strethill Harrison, 1823, at Holmes Chapel, Cheshire; Elizabeth Rawstorne, 1823, at Penwortham, Lancs; Countess of Lonsdale, 1824, Lowther; Elizabeth Crawshay, 1825, in Llandaff Cathedral; Richard Hankins, 1829, at Ledbury, Herefordshire; Richard Orford, 1830, at Prestbury, Cheshire; Rev. Thomas Watson, 1833, Edenhall, Cumberland; William and Mary Sugden, 1834, at Keighley, Yorks; Richard Haydon, 1837, at Boughton, Oxon; Philip Bedingfield, 1841, at Northallerton, Yorks; and Lady Gardener, 1842, at Whalley, Yorks.

In Kirkby Lonsdale Church, Westmorland, is a charming classical monument (by Webster?) to "Jane, wife of Francis Webster, architect, and daughter of George Slater of Spital, yeoman, died 26 August, 1805, aged 34."

WEEKES, HENRY, R.A.
b. 1807, *d.* 1877

He was born at Canterbury, the only son of Capon Weekes, a bank clerk, and was educated there at the King's School. In 1822 he was apprenticed to William Behnes (q.v.), and in the following year joined the Royal Academy Schools, where he won a Silver Medal in 1826.

In 1827 Weekes became one of Chantrey's (q.v.) assistants and received a legacy of £1,000 on his employer's death. He then took over the sculptor's studio in Buckingham Palace Road and completed many of the unfinished works, including the equestrian statue of Wellington outside the Royal Exchange. His first independent commission for a bust was for one of Lord Harris, and in 1838 he made another of Queen Victoria, the first to be executed after her accession to the throne. He is, indeed, chiefly known as a portrait-sculptor and his busts have considerable merit. He did, however, find time for other work, including, in 1829, the marble column for a sundial erected on the "Dane John" Hill, Canterbury, and in 1869 a chimney-piece for Crewe Hall.

Weekes exhibited at the Royal Academy, 1828–1877, and at the British Institution, 1850–1866. He was elected an Associate of the Academy in 1850 and a full member in 1862, when he deposited as his Diploma work a bust of Henry Green, the Academy Professor of Anatomy. In 1869 he joined the staff himself as Professor of Sculpture.

At the International Exhibition of 1862 Weekes showed his figure of "The Young Naturalist," while two years later he executed the group which represents "Manufactures" at one of the corners of the Albert Memorial. In the possession of his descendant, Mrs. Van Maurik, are a number of his busts, including those of his father, Capon Weekes (1851); Mrs. Catherine Pfiel; Mary Weekes (afterwards Mrs. Knight); Caroline Weekes (afterwards Mrs. Collard); Sir William Arbuthnot; and Lord Hammond (1873).

He also had a considerable practice as a monumental sculptor, his best-known work being the group commemorating Shelley in the Priory Church at Christchurch, Hampshire. This was erected in 1854 by Sir Francis Shelley, son of the poet, and shows the drowned man lying amid pieces of broken rock, as if just washed ashore, while his wife supports his head and gazes intently into his face. At the former Royal Female Orphan Asylum at Beddington, Surrey, is Weekes tablet to the Duke of Cambridge, President of the institution, which was erected about 1850. This is a charming work, with the inscription tablet flanked by weeping female orphans and surmounted by a profile relief of the Duke himself.

Weekes also figured as an art critic, and his essay on the Fine Arts Section of the Great Exhibition of 1851 won him a Gold Medal in the following year. He finally retired in 1876 and went to live at Ramsgate, but died on 28 June, 1877. At the sale of his remaining works held by Messrs. Christie on 29 May, 1880, his figure of a "Sleeping Child" fetched £152. The Introduction to his *Lectures on Art* which were published in the same year, describes him as "about the middle height, his head large, the forehead high and square, features rugged and irregular but thoughtful and expressive."

(Authority cited in text; various references *Art Journal*.)

STATUES

1836	J. S. Lushington	Madras Cathedral
1841	Cranmer, Ridley and Latimer	Martyrs' Memorial, Oxford
1842	Bishop Daniel Corrie	Madras Cathedral
1843	Edward Tatham	All Saints' Church Oxford
1845	Marquess Wellesley	India Office
1845	Dr. Goodall	Upper Chapel, Eton College
1845	Sir Francis Bacon	Trinity College, Cambridge
1846	Sir Edward Barnes	Colombo, Ceylon
1847	Earl of Auckland	Calcutta
c. 1850?	Flaxman	Tate Gallery
1861	Sardanapalus	Mansion House
1864	John Hunter	Royal College of Surgeons
1864	Dr. Harvey	University Museum, Oxford
1865	The Sleeping Child	Possession Sir Archibald Weigall
1870	Charles II	For Palace of Westminster (now Sessions House, Old Bailey)
1870	The Young Naturalist	Leeds Art Gallery
1875	Queen Victoria	Calcutta
1876	Linacre, Harvey and Sydenham	Portico of Royal College of Physicians
?	Mother and Child	Southill, Beds

BUSTS

1828	John Plumptree	Exhibited Royal Academy
1829	Lord Darnley	Cobham Hall, Kent
1830	Bagot, Bishop of St. Asaph	Exhibited Royal Academy
1834	S. Lushington	For the Canterbury Philosophical Society
1835	Earl of Winchilsea	Formerly Eastwell Park, Kent
1838	Zachary Macaulay	Westminster Abbey
1838	J. Martin	Exhibited Birmingham Society of Artists
1839	Thomas Watson	Royal Infirmary, Sheffield
1840	Viscountess Midleton	Exhibited Royal Academy
1842	Allan Cunningham	Scottish National Portrait Gallery
1843	Baboo Tagore	Calcutta
1843	6th Earl of Shaftesbury	St. Giles, Dorset
1844	H. T. Prinsep	Victoria Hall, Calcutta
1844	Earl of Auckland	Victoria Hall, Calcutta
1845	5th Duke of Richmond	Goodwood
1845	Charles Greenlaw	Town Hall, Calcutta
1845	Sir Astley Cooper	Royal College of Surgeons
1846	Duchess of Marlborough	Blenheim
1848	Charles Buller	Westminster Abbey
1849	Sir George Gipps	Canterbury Cathedral
1849	Lord Abinger	Exhibited Royal Academy
1853	James Arnott	Royal College of Surgeons
1854	Horace Cust	Boughton, Northants
1856	William Buckland	Westminster Abbey
1856	Sir Charles Bell	Royal College of Surgeons
1856	Lord Truro	Exhibited Royal Academy
1858	William Buckland	University Museum Oxford
1859	Duke of Marlborough	Blenheim
1860	William Buckland	Geological Museum
1860	Mary Wollstonecraft	Exhibited Royal Academy
1861	Duke of Buccleuch	Boughton, Northants
1863	Sir Benjamin Brodie	Royal College of Surgeons
1863	J. H. Green	Burlington House
1864	Sir George Lewis	Westminster Abbey
1864	W. H. Whitbread	Exhibited Royal Academy
1865	J. H. Green	Royal College of Surgeons
1865	Sir Tatton Sykes	Exhibited Royal Academy
1866	Thomas Martin	Town Hall, Reigate
1867	Sir William Lawrence	St. Bartholomew's Hospital
1868	Sir Randolph Crewe	Crewe Hall, Cheshire

1868	Bishop Crewe	Crewe Hall, Cheshire
1868	T. Stothard	For National Gallery
1870	George Jones	Burlington House
1871	W. Cheselden and Dr. Mead	St. Thomas's Hospital
1871	Sir Roderick Murchison	Geological Museum (replica Royal Geographical Society)
1872	John South	St. Thomas's Hospital
1873	Sir George Pollock	Merchant Taylors Company
1873	Lord Hammond	Foreign Office
1874	Sir Joshua Reynolds	Leicester Square
1877	Tait, Archbishop of Canterbury	St. Peter's Orphanage, Kent
?	Richard Ansdell	Walker Art Gallery, Liverpool
?	Elizabeth Cust	Boughton, Northants

MONUMENTS

1830	Sandwich, Kent	Joseph Stewart (d. 1828)
1836	Peper Harrow, Surrey	Viscount Midleton (recumbent figure)
1837	Colombo (St. Peter's)	Corrie, Bishop of Madras
1840	Brixton (St. Matthew's)	Charles Kemp
1842	Mitcham, Surrey	Henry Hoare
1843	Westminster Abbey	Robert Southey
1844	Tooting, Surrey	Richard Gibbs
1844	Weston-super-Mare, Somerset	Emily Pigott
1845	Amersham, Bucks	Ann Tyrwhitt-Drake
1845	Madras (Cathedral)	John Dent
1846	Battersea (Parish Church)	Sir George Wombwell
1847	Willingdon, Sussex	Inigo Thomas
1849	Cardington, Beds	Samuel Whitbread (life-size figures)
1849	Beckenham, Kent	Earl of Auckland
1850	Cromford, Derby	Charles Arkwright
1852	Great Billing, Northants	Robert Elwes
1852	Amersham, Bucks	Thomas Tyrwhitt-Drake (semi-recumbent figure)
1853	Leyton, Essex	Mary Innes
1858	Willesley, Leics	Sir Charles Abney Hastings
1859	Morden, Surrey	Charles Hoare
1863	Canterbury Cathedral	Archbishop Sumner (recumbent figure)
1864	Brixton (St. Matthew's)	Richard Gibbs
1875	Winchester (Cathedral)	Bishop Sumner

WEIGALL, HENRY
b. 1800 (?), *d.* 1883

Weigall executed several busts of the Duke of Wellington. The first—a small bronze work of which a number of replicas were made—dates from 1829, while in 1851 came the life-size bust, also in bronze, which the sculptor exhibited at the Royal Academy two years later. In the catalogue this is described as "done from sittings." It was, indeed, the last bust for which the Duke sat, the sittings being given on 6, 9 and 11 August, and 18 November, 1851. A replica is now at the United Service Club, and another, dated 1864, in the Birmingham Art Gallery (Wellesley's "Iconography of the First Duke of Wellington").

Weigall showed a relief of Canning at the Royal Hibernian Academy in 1829, and a bust of James Stewart, the historical engraver, at the Suffolk Street Galleries three years later. He exhibited at the Royal Academy, 1837–1854, where his busts included those of Sir Harris Nicholas (1837), Thomas Carlyle (1848), Samuel Warren (1849), Sir David Davies (1849) and Viscount Mandeville (1850). His bust of S. Jarratt (1848) is in the University Museum at Oxford, and one of the 6th Earl of Shaftesbury is at St. Giles, Dorset. At the Crystal Palace were his busts of Carlyle and Warren, together with that of William Yarrell, the naturalist (*Handbook to the Crystal Palace*, 1854).

WELLS, THOMAS
fl. 1786–1791

His studio was in Holborn and he exhibited wax portraits at the Royal Academy, 1786–1791.

WESSEL, GERHARD GEORGE
b. 1744, *d.* 1811

He was born in Hollenstede and studied in Berlin before he came to England in 1773, under the patronage of George III. On his arrival he entered the Royal Academy Schools and gained a Silver Medal three years later. He exhibited at the Academy, 1781–1787, showing wax portraits and a figure of "Argus" in terra-cotta.

In 1787 Wessel left England for Osnabrück, and in the following year the decorative artist Vernona wrote to the Hofmarschall, Count von Münster, that "Her Royal Highness has just told me to inform you that she has sent from London to Osnabrück a very accomplished sculptor named Wessel; he has worked for fourteen years in London, but is a native of Osnabrück and prefers to work here."

Wessel was employed under Vernona, but his chief collaborator was the architect Hollenberg. He carried out a good deal of work at the Royal Palace in Osnabrück, then belonging to the English Crown, and various reliefs and wax portraits by him are now in the local museum.

(Information, Director of Osnabrück Museum.)

PLATE XXIX

R. J. WYATT
Part of the monument of Ellen Legh, 1831, Winwick, Lancashire.

PLATE XXX

JOSEPH WILTON
Admiral Holmes, 1761, Westminster Abbey.

WESTMACOTT, CHARLES MOLLOY

b. 1782 *d.* 1868

He was the illegitimate son of Richard Westmacott (q.v.), his mother being Susan Molloy, a widow and landlady of the "Bull and Horns" at Fulham. Charles was educated at St. Paul's and Oxford and is best known as the author of the *English Spy* and editor of *The Age* and *Records of the Fine Arts*. In 1822 he exhibited a bust of J. P. Kemble at the Royal Academy.

WESTMACOTT, GEORGE

fl. 1799–1827

He was a brother of Sir Richard Westmacott (q.v.) and exhibited busts, etc., at the Royal Academy, 1799–1820. He also seems to have assisted his brother Henry (q.v.), for the payments for the base of the "Achilles" statue in Hyde Park are made to them jointly.

Another of the Westmacott brothers was Thomas, who died on 3 December, 1798, three weeks after receiving the Royal Academy Silver Medal for Architecture (*Gentleman's Magazine*, 1798, page 1153).

WESTMACOTT, HENRY

b. 1784, *d.* 1861

Henry Westmacott, thirteenth child of Richard Westmacott (q.v.), was employed at Kensington Palace, and in 1808 received £1,399 for work carried out in the apartments of the Princess of Wales. This included four chimney-pieces, the most important, "of statuary marble with circular reeded profiles, moulded cornice and panelled frieze," costing £100, while the one for the music-room cost £40. Two others were "of spar marble inlaid with mouldings and ornaments of statuary marble in the frieze" (£50), and of "bardiglio" marble respectively. In the following year he received a further £222 for chimney-pieces, which included £86 for two in marble "with circular reeded profiles and bronze metal columns." Three years later he was again at Kensington, this time supplying seven chimney-pieces for £267. (P.R.O. Works, 5/97–5/101.)

Between 1806 and 1810 Henry Westmacott was paid £173 for work in connexion with Nelson's tomb in St. Paul's. As a mason he was employed at Somerset House in 1810 and at the Fleet Prison two years later. In 1814 he was at Greenwich Palace, where he received £450 for six Corinthian capitals of Portland stone and £990 for eighteen pilaster capitals, all for the front of King Charles's Quadrangle (P.R.O., Ad. 68/884). In 1816 he was working at Cobham Hall, Kent, carrying out repairs to the pyramid of the mausoleum at a total cost of more than £500 (Archives, Earl of Darnley). Two years later he was at Lord Carrington's house at Whitehall (Soane Note-book), and in 1822 was working at Brighton Pavilion, receiving £32 for a marble plinth and £448 for a marble chimney-piece in the following year. In 1825 he built part of the Royal Mews at Pimlico and was also employed at Buckingham Palace. In 1823 he and his brother George (q.v.) had been paid £801 for the base of the "Achilles" statue in Hyde Park, the statue itself being the work of Sir Richard Westmacott.

About 1830 Henry Westmacott moved to Edinburgh and exhibited at the Royal Scottish Academy, 1830–1836, where his busts included those of Paganini, Sir Walter Scott and General Jackson, President of the United States. In 1836 he showed "a model of a cenotaph in granite, surmounted by a bust in marble, in memory of the Bard of Abbotsford, to be erected by subscription in New York." He also exhibited at the Royal Academy, 1833–1835, and at the Liverpool Academy in 1831 showed busts of a "Young Midshipman of the East India Company's Service, The Duke of Kent, Dr. Valpy and a deceased artist," the last three being in wax. His bust of Scott was Lot 59 in the J. M. Oppenheim sale at Christies in 1864. Henry married firstly at St. George's, Hanover Square, on 1 May, 1810, Eliza Brodie Stewart, daughter of the Town Clerk of Montrose. By her he had five sons and four daughters. He married secondly at St. Clement Danes on 8 December, 1827, Hannah Wilkinson Rowe, a descendant of Nicholas Rowe (1673–1718), the Poet Laureate.

His monuments and tablets are competent, but not outstanding, the best being that to Lord William Gordon, 1824, at Whitkirk, Yorks, which has a delightful small full-length relief of Lord William in Highland dress. At the Scottish Academy of 1832 he exhibited the model of "a marble medallion erected by the inhabitants of St. Elizabeth, West Indies, to Andrew Miller, Esq."

(Authorities cited in text; private information.)

MONUMENTS

c. 1796	Stadhampton, Oxon	Sarah Beavis
1796	Swanscombe, Kent	Henry Roberts
1798	Chertsey, Surrey	Sir Joseph Mawbey
1799	Eastnor, Hereford	John Cocks
c. 1800	Beddington, Surrey	Sir Nicholas Carew
1800	Hambleden, Bucks	John D'Oyly
1800	Lambeth (Parish Church)	The Goodbehere family
1807	Horningsham, Wilts	Thomas Davis
1807	Chichester (St. Olave's)	Martha Dear

1808	Chichester (Cathedral)	Ernest Udny
1808	Wyddial, Herts	Mary Heaton
1808	Norwood, Middlesex	Robert Donald
1809	Harwich, Essex	Lt.-Colonel Donaldson
1811	Beddington, Surrey	Elizabeth Tchitchagoff
1811	Lamport, Northants	John Isham (£113 10s.) (Isham Archives)
1812	Mitcham, Surrey	James Garth
1812	Hartnest, Suffolk	Lt. Harrington
1812	Westminster Abbey	John Beresford
1813	Crowhurst, Sussex	Jeremiah Dyson
1814	Shipton Moyne, Glos	Edmund Estcourt
1814	Heavitree, Devon	Dudley Wyatt
1814	Jamaica (Montego Bay)	Mrs. Kerr
1815	Hambleden, Bucks	Georgiana Reay
1815	Teddington, Surrey	Thomas Cuff
1816	Cheam, Surrey	Philip Antrobus
1817	East Carleton, Leics	Thomas Palmer
1817	East Carleton, Leics	Sir John Palmer
1818	Broxbourne, Herts	Henrietta Peere-Williams
1818	Hampstead Marshall, Berks	John James
1819	Southover, Sussex	Louisa Baldock
1820	Witham, Essex	Rev. Andrew Downes
1820	North Elmham, Norfolk	Richard Milles
1820	Barford, Warwick	William Mills
1821	Itchen (Pear Tree Green), Hants	George Ede
1821	Little Stukeley, Hunts	Lucy Bayley
1821	Nether Worton, Oxon	William Wilson
1822	Newport, Essex	Joseph Smith
1822	Windsor (St. George's Chapel)	Sir Isaac Head
1823	Clifton Camville, Staffs	Sarah Stokes
1829	Penshurst, Kent	Richard Allnutt

WESTMACOTT, JAMES SHERWOOD

b. 1823, *d.* 1900

He was born 27 August, 1823 (Archives, Artists' Annuity Fund), and was the son of Henry Westmacott (q.v.) by his first marriage. He studied sculpture with Sir Richard, and in 1844 exhibited at Westminster Hall figures of "Alfred the Great" and "Richard I Planting the Standard of England on the Walls of Acre." The *Literary Gazette* considered that both these works evinced "much knowledge of the figure and spirit of execution," while the German art critic, Dr. Forster, thought that the "Alfred" was "one of the most eminent works of the Exhibition."

In 1845 Westmacott won a Gold Medal from the Royal Academy of Dresden for a figure of "Victory," which he exhibited at Burlington House in the following year. In 1848 he made the statues of Geoffrey, Earl of Gloucester, and Saher, Earl of Winchester, for the House of Lords (the latter being subsequently shown at the Great Exhibition of 1851). In 1849 he went to Rome, and shortly afterwards executed the figure of "Satan Overthrown" for Mr. Theophilus Burnand; replicas of this work (in the form of bronze statuettes) were produced in large numbers by Messrs. Elkington in 1853. In 1855 Westmacott showed his marble figure of "The Peri at the Gates of Paradise" at the Paris Exhibition. This later became very popular and was illustrated in the *Art Journal* and other periodicals of the time.

In 1858 he made the font for St. Mary's, Stoke Newington, and in 1863 carved the figure of Alexander, now in the Mansion House. Two years later he executed a statue of Bomanjee Hormasjee for the Coorla Spinning Company of Bombay. In 1868 he carved the reredos for Little Wolston Church, Buckinghamshire, and in the following year the statues of Galen, Cicero and Aristotle for the façade of the Civil Service Commission buildings in Burlington Gardens. He also modelled all the figures for the reredos of Newcastle Cathedral. In 1870 came his figure of "The Guardian Angel," commissioned by Mr. Burnand of Lowndes Square.

Westmacott exhibited at the Royal Academy, 1846–1885, and at the British Institution, 1852–1867, where his busts included those of George Barnard (1854), the Marquess of Anglesey (1858) and J. Langton Down (1883). His "Fountain Nymph" is illustrated in the *Art Journal* of 1861 (page 216). He signs the monuments of Sir Gilbert East, 1866, at Hurley, Berkshire; to Owen Wethered, 1862, and Martha Wethered, 1867, both at Marlow, in the same county; and John Francis Bassett, 1869, at Illogan, Cornwall. The altar-tomb of the Rev. George Vanbrugh, 1856, at Augton, Lancashire, is also his work. He probably died in 1888.

(Various references *Art Journal* and *Builder*; private information.)

WESTMACOTT, RICHARD, the Elder

b. 1747, *d.* 1808

Westmacott was educated at Brasenose College, Oxford, but "gave up all pursuit of the learned professions early in life and took to the business of a statuary" (*Gentleman's Magazine*, 1856, Part II).

He married Sarah, daughter of John Vardy (*d.* 1765), the architect.

Although he worked chiefly as a monumental sculptor, he also made a number of chimney-pieces, and in 1777 published a series of twenty engraved designs for chimney-pieces with classic ornaments. In 1778 he made a magnificent one, with life-size figures of a shepherd boy and a dancing girl, for the music-room at Cobham Hall, Kent (Archives, Earl of Darnley), and in 1780 supplied one for Corsham Court. A year later he laid down the marble floor in the Methuen Chapel in the aisle of North Wraxall Church, Somerset (Methuen Archives).

Other chimney-pieces executed by Westmacott include one for the state bedroom at Warwick Castle (Anon, *History of Warwick*, 1815, page 193), and an unspecified number for Gorhambury, Herts, where he was paid £89 (Hertford County Archives, B.XI.66). In 1788 he received £260 for chimney-pieces for the Admiralty, including one of "rich statuary marble" adorned with "bassorelievo, tablet, rich swags of fruit and foliage," costing £84, and another of "rich statuary marble with Siena columns and carved frieze, £63" (P.R.O., Ad. 17/1). Two years later the Duke of Bedford paid him £37 for one of marble for Woburn Abbey (Bedford Archives). In 1796 he was granted the Royal Appointment of Mason for Kensington Palace.

Westmacott also designed chimney-piece tablets for Wedgwood, and one of these with "birds in a nest and with festoons of flowers" fetched £98 at the Sibson sale at Christies in 1877. It was he, not George Westmacott, as stated by Graves, who exhibited a "model of a boy for a monument" at the Society of Artists in 1775. He became a bankrupt in 1803 (*Monthly Magazine*, 1803, Part II, page 58), and died five years later.

Westmacott's most important monument was erected in 1791 in Sherborne Church, Gloucestershire, to the memory of James Dutton, who had died in 1778. This is nearly 18 ft. high and has a life-size figure of an angel with outspread wings who tramples underfoot a prostrate figure of Death, represented by a realistic and macabre skeleton.

In addition to the monuments he made independently, Westmacott also executed others designed by James Wyatt, the architect; together they sign those commemorating William, Viscount Barrington, 1793, at Shrivenham, Berks; Henry, tenth Earl of Pembroke, 1794, at Wilton, Wilts; John Oglander, 1794, at New College, Oxford; and Margaret May, 1796, at Hale, Hants.

MONUMENTS

1770	Devizes, Wilts	George Willy
1771	Margaretting, Essex	Richard Benyon
1773	Bowden, Cheshire	Thomas Ashton
1774	Shimpling, Suffolk	Elizabeth Plampin
1778	Dullingham, Cambs	Mrs. Jeaffreson
1779	Devizes, Wilts	Prince Sutton

1780	Britwell Baldwin, Oxon	William Lowndes-Stone (*d.* 1772)
1780	Bristol (St. Mary Redcliffe)	Mary Edwards
1781	Rotherfield Greys, Oxon	Sir Thomas Stapleton
1782	Lingfield, Surrey	Sir James Burrow
1782	Grosvenor Chapel	Charles Rich
1782	Little Linford, Bucks	Matthew Knapp
1784	High Wycombe, Bucks	Mrs. Shrimpton
1784	Chipstead, Surrey	Rev. James Tattershall
1785	Chartham, Kent	Lady Fagg
1786	Kelvedon Hatch, Essex	John Luther
1787	Longcot, Berks	Elizabeth King
1787	Morden, Surrey	Richard Garth
1787	Lichfield (Cathedral)	Catherine Buckridge
1788	Newark, Notts	William Handley
1789	Dullingham, Cambs	Christopher Jeaffreson
1790	Aston, Birmingham	Sir Lister Holte
1790	Fareham, Hants	Rev. Thomas Woolis
1790	Fringford, Oxon	Anthony Addington
1791	Devizes, Wilts	James and Mary Sutton
1791	Whitchurch, Denbigh	Richard Heaton
1792	Woking, Surrey	Rev. Edward Emily
1793	Bredwardine, Hereford (churchyard)	George Jarvis
1795	Ealing (Parish Church)	Henry Beaufoy
1795	Oxford (St. John's College)	Samuel Dennis
1795	Landwade, Cambs	Sir John Cotton
1796	Margaretting, Essex	Richard Benyon
1796	Jamaica (Montego Bay)	Dr. William Fowle
1797	Lichfield (Cathedral)	John Fletcher
1797	Stamford (St. Martin's)	Cyril Jackson
1797	Brompton Chapel	Richard Harrison (*Gentleman's Magazine*, 1797, page 10)
1798	Mitcham, Surrey	Maria Tate
1799	Badminton, Glos	Duchess of Beaufort
1799	Weybridge, Surrey	Mrs. Bunbury
1802	St. Michael's, Cornhill	John Platt
1802	Paddington (Parish Church)	John Colborne
1803	St. Giles-in-the-Fields	Mrs. Goulburn
1805	Linton, Cambs	Elizabeth Owen
1805	Fawsley, Northants	Lucy Knightley

WESTMACOTT, SIR RICHARD, R.A.

b. 1775, *d.* 1856

He was born in 1775, the son of Richard Westmacott the Elder (q.v.), and studied under his father. In 1793 he went to Rome, where he became a pupil of Canova. Here he made such rapid progress that he was not only elected a Member of the Academy of Florence in 1795, but also won the first Gold Medal of the Academy of St. Luke (offered by the Pope) for a bas-relief of "Joseph and His Brethren" on 28 May in the same year. In 1797 he returned to England, after an adventurous journey, during which he fell into the hands of Italian bandits, who robbed him of everything he possessed and wounded him in the shoulder.

On his arrival Westmacott set up for himself in a studio near his father, and in 1798 married Dorothy, daughter of Dr. Wilkinson of Jamaica. He soon had a large practice of his own, which in course of time became second only to that of Chantrey; indeed, as early as 1803 Farington notes that he had commissions amounting to £16,000. Besides his monumental and other work, he also made a number of chimney-pieces, including one in 1805 in dove-grey marble for the Queen's drawing-room at Windsor, and two large ones, costing £140, which had been designed by Wyatt for Carlton House (P.R.O., Works 5/94). Two years later he received £192 for four chimney-pieces of grey marble, two for the drawing-room and two for the saloon of the Duke of York's apartments in Kensington Palace (P.R.O., Works 5/96). Like his father, he was also employed at Cobham Hall, Kent, where he was paid £275, a sum which probably included payments for chimney-pieces, in 1804. (Archives, Earl of Darnley.)

For the chimney-piece in the music-room of the Royal Pavilion at Brighton, Westmacott received no less than £1,244. This is described by Parry (*Coast of Sussex*, page 128) as "having a really noble effect, the projecting sweep of cornice is supported on the wing of an expanding dragon and the massive, though short, oriental columns with statuary carved capitals and still larger bases of inverted lotus are in the best possible style." In fact, the writer considered it "by far the most stately in the Pavilion."

In 1816 Westmacott made copies in plaster-of-Paris for the Phigalian Marbles for the Royal Academy (Academy Archives), and two years later the relief on the Temple of Liberty at Woburn Abbey and the chimney-piece for the inner library (Woburn Archives). In 1828 he carved reliefs for the north side of the Marble Arch and also executed two others of "The Death of Nelson" and "The Meeting of Wellington and Blücher," for the parapet. These, however, were never used until 1832, when Blore placed them in the attic storey of the grand entrance to Buckingham Palace.

The Waterloo Vase which now stands in the Palace Gardens is also the work of Westmacott. The blocks of marble from which it is made had originally been seen by Napoleon when he was passing through Tuscany on his way to the

Russian campaign, and he had ordered them to be preserved so that a trophy commemorating his anticipated victory could be carved from them. After the Emperor's downfall the Grand Duke of Tuscany presented the blocks to George IV, who commissioned Westmacott to make them into a vase to commemorate Waterloo. When it was finished the vase weighed twenty tons and, as it was far too heavy for the Waterloo Gallery at Windsor, the King ordered it to be placed in the National Gallery (*Gentleman's Magazine*, 1836, page 186). It was not placed in its present position until 1906. The reliefs on it show George IV on his throne and Napoleon dismounted from his horse, while the rest of the space is filled with allegorical figures (*Naval and Military Magazine*, 1828, pages 368–373).

In 1825 he carved the monument, erected on the bank of the Tiber, near Rome, to the memory of Rosa Bathurst, unfortunate daughter of an unfortunate father; for, as the epitaph says, she "was accidentally drowned in the Tiber on the 16th March, 1824, whilst on a riding party, owing to the swollen state of the river and her spirited horse taking fright. She was the daughter of Benjamin Bathurst, whose disappearance when on a special mission to Vienna some years since was as tragical as it is unaccountable, no positive account of his death ever having been received by his distracted wife." The truth of the disappearance of Mr. Bathurst at Perleberg, in Brandenbourg, in 1809 has never been solved.

Westmacott's last work of importance was the group of sculpture in the pediment of the British Museum. Here he was persuaded to follow the fashion of the day by introducing a slight touch of colour, and so tinted the tympanum blue and gilded some of the ornaments.

He exhibited at the Royal Academy, 1797–1839, and was elected an Associate in 1805 and a full member in 1811. In 1827 he succeeded Flaxman (q.v.) as Academy Professor of Sculpture; ten years later he was knighted.

Westmacott died on 1 September, 1856, and was buried at Chastleton, Oxon, where his third son was Rector. The *Art Journal*, in its obituary, sums up his work by saying that "if he never reached the highest point of grandeur or beauty, he was always chaste, dignified and impressive." Canova (q.v.), however, said of Westmacott's figure of the negro on the Abbey monument to C. J. Fox that neither in England nor out of England had he seen any work which surpassed it.

(*European Magazine*, Vol. 82, page 493; *Art Journal*, 1856, page 316; *Gentleman's Magazine*, 1856, Part II, page 509.)

STATUES

1799	La Madonna della Gloria	For Fonthill
1804	Viscount Duncan	St. Paul's Cathedral
1806	Addison	Westminster Abbey
1809	5th Duke of Bedford	Russell Square
1809	Robert Milligan	West India Dock
1809	Nelson	Birmingham (unveiled 25 October)
1810	Sir Charles Turner	Kirkleatham Mausoleum, Yorks
1810	Nelson	Barbados
1814	William Pitt	Westminster Abbey
1814	Edward VI	Ashridge Park, Herts
1815	Queen Elizabeth	Ashridge Park, Herts
1815	Nelson	Liverpool (with M. C. Wyatt)
1815– 1823	Eight statues of Founders and Benefactors	Ashridge Park, Herts
1816	Charles James Fox	Bloomsbury Square
1819	William Pitt	For National Debt Office
1822	George III	Liverpool
1822	Achilles	Hyde Park
1828	Warren Hastings	Calcutta
1830	Lord Erskine	Old Hall, Lincoln's Inn
1830	Duke of Montpensier	Exhibited Royal Academy
1831	George III	Windsor Great Park
1831	Mrs. Rawson	Exhibited Royal Academy
1832	Canning	Parliament Square
1833	Dr. Alderson	Hull Hospital
1834	Locke	University College, London (plastercast at Woburn)
1834	Duke of York	Carlton House Terrace
1835	Lord William Bentinck	Calcutta
1839	Lady Susan Murray	Exhibited Royal Academy
n.d.	Mary, Queen of Scots	For Hardwicke Hall
?	Venus Attiring	Castle Howard
?	Venus and Cupid	Formerly Trentham Hall
?	Pandora	Castle Howard

BUSTS

1797	Sir William Chambers	Exhibited Royal Academy
1807	T. Newton	Exhibited Royal Academy
1810	Viscount Sidmouth	Exhibited Royal Academy
1810	Unknown Man	Exeter Art Gallery (bronze)
1815	Hon. Georgiana Holland	Millbrook Church, Beds

1816	David Williams	*Gentleman's Magazine,* 1816, Part II, page 90
1818	C. J. Fox	Alscot Park, Warwick
1827	11th Earl of Pembroke	Wilton Church, Wilts
c. 1830	Lord and Lady Holland	Millbrook Church, Beds
1834	Dorothy Westmacott	Brighton Parish Church
1838	Sir Abraham Hume	Wormley Church, Herts
1843	Lord George Russell	Woburn Abbey
1846	George Byng	Woburn Abbey

IDEAL WORKS, GROUPS AND RELIEFS

1811	Jupiter and Ganymede	Diploma Work, Burlington House
c. 1820	The Fighting Gladiator	Woburn Abbey (bronze cast)
c. 1820	The Dying Gladiator	Woburn Abbey (bronze cast)
1821	Hector Reproaching Paris	Woburn Abbey (relief)
1821	Hero and Leander	Petworth (relief)
1822	The Distressed Mother	For Lord Lansdowne (replica for Mrs. Fergusson of Raith)
1822	Psyche	Woburn Abbey
1823	Cupid	Woburn Abbey
1823	Dream of Horace	Petworth (relief)
1827	Nymph and Cupid	Petworth
1828	Nymph and Zephyr	For Earl Grosvenor
1828	Nymph Unclasping her Zone	For Earl of Carlisle
1832	The Gypsy	Exhibited Royal Academy
1837	Euphrosyne	For Duke of Newcastle
1837	Mercury and Vulcan	Bowood (relief)
?	Sleeping Infant	For Countess of Dunmore

MONUMENTS

c. 1796	Sonning, Berks	William Barker (d. 1758)
1796	Swanscombe, Kent	Henry Roebuck
1796	Jamaica (St. James's)	Dr. William Fowle
1796	Monmouth (Parish Church)	Joseph Price
1796	Ashbourne, Derby	George Errington
1797	Gresford, Denbigh	John Parry
1797	Monken Hadleigh, Herts	Catherine Pennant
1797	Preston-on-Stour, Glos	James West
1798	Whiteford, Flint	Thomas Pennant
1798	Mitcham, Surrey	Martha James
c. 1799	St. Anthony-in-Roseland, Cornwall	Sir Richard Spry
1799	Oxford (St. Mary's)	Dorothy Eveleigh
1799	Ruscombe, Berks	Sir James Eyre
1799	Swinbrook, Oxon	Thomas Fettiplace
1799	Grenada (St. George's)	Ninian Home

1799	Pembridge, Hereford	Rev. Henry Evans
1799	Barbados (St. John's)	Mrs. Pinder
1800	Stepney (Parish Church)	Benjamin Kinton
1800	Streatham (Parish Church)	Peter Brown
1800	Battersea (Parish Church)	Russell Manners
1800	Achurch, Northants	Lord Lilford
1800	Westminster Abbey	Warren, Bishop of Bangor
1801	Devizes, Wilts	James Sutton
1801	Wimpole, Cambs	Hon. John Yorke
1801	Stockport, Cheshire	Sir George Warren
1802	Grenada (St. George's)	Mather Byles
1802	Farley, Wilts	Earl of Ilchester
1802	Madras (Cathedral)	Hon. Mrs. Bruce
1803	Badminton, Glos	5th Duke of Beaufort
1803	Prescot, Lancs	Sir William Atherton
1803	Gresford, Denbigh	Rev. Henry Newcombe
1803	Ruthen, Denbigh	Elizabeth Hughes
1803	Weyhill, Hants	John Gawler
1803	Bidborough, Kent (churchyard)	Countess of Darnley
1804	Cuckfield, Sussex	Mary Sergison
1804	Walsingham, Norfolk	Henry Lee-Warner
1804	Ketteringham, Norfolk	Edward Atkyns
1804	Abingdon (St. Helen's)	M. Champain
1804	Marchwiel, Flint	Philip Yorke
1805	Horsham, Sussex	Captain Marriott
1805	Sheldwich, Kent	Mary Hill
1805	St. Paul's Cathedral	Captain John Cooke
1805	Shute, Devon	Hon. Mrs. Cocks
1805	Mylor, Cornwall	Hon. Reginald Cocks
1805	Whalley, Yorks	Sir James Gardener
c. 1806	Winchester (Cathedral)	Bishop Tomline
1806	Brasted, Kent	John Turton
1806	Little Samford, Essex	William Savage
1806	Frampton, Dorset	Frances Browne
1806	Ilmington, Warwick	Francis Canning
1806	Lichfield (Cathedral)	Andrew Newton
1806	Westminster Abbey	William Pitt
1807	Antony, Cornwall	Jemima Pole-Carew
1807	Titchfield, Hants	Richard Veale
1807	Belton, Lincs	Lord Brownlow
1807	Madingley, Cambs	John Cotton
1807	Westminster Abbey	Duc de Montpensier
1808	Longworth, Oxon	William and Ann Bowles
1808	York (Minster)	William Burgh
1808	Hawkesbury, Glos	Earl of Liverpool
1808	Overton, Flint	Philips Lloyd-Fletcher
1808	Bassalleg, Monmouthshire	Lady Morgan
1808	St. Andrew, Jamaica	General Villettes
1808	Westminster Abbey	General Villettes
1809	St. Paul's Cathedral	Sir Ralph Abercrombie
1809	Orsett, Essex	Lady Trafford
1809	Hayes, Middlesex	The Blencowe family
1809	Waltham St. Laurence, Berks	Hon. Henry Neville
1809	Marston St. Lawrence, Northants	William Walmesley
1809	Rokeby, Durham	John Morritt
1810	Brasted, Kent	Mary Turton
c. 1810	Bathford, Somerset	John Symons
1810	Weybridge, Surrey	George Mangles
1810	Barbados (St. George's)	George Hall
1811	Finchingfield, Essex	Anne Marriott
1811	Fareham, Hants	Captain Newman
1811	Staunton-in-the-Vale, Notts	Job Charlton
1811	Oxford (Oriel College)	George Carter
1812	Upminster, Essex	James Esdaile
1812	Chelsea (Duke of York's School)	Colonel Williamson
1813	Cheam, Surrey	John Antrobus
1813	Cheam, Surrey	Rev. Henry Peach
1813	St. Paul's Cathedral	Lord Collingwood
1813	Slindon, Sussex	Edward Long
1813	St. Paul's Cathedral	Generals Packenham and Gibbs
1813	Long Newton, Durham	Sir Henry Vane-Tempest
1813	North Perrott, Somerset	William Hoskins
1813	Clitheroe, Lancs	Thomas Wilson
1813	Clayworth, Notts	Francis Otter
1814	Crayford, Kent	Mrs. Cottrell
1814	Teddington (Parish Church)	William Stretton
1814	Sidmouth, Devon	John Hunter
1814	Ledbury, Hereford	Robert Biddulph
1815	Westminster Abbey	Charles James Fox (d. 1806)
1815	Preston-on-Stour, Glos	Harriett West
1815	Buxted, Sussex	Rev. Mathias D'Oyly
1815	Millbrook, Beds	Hon. Miss Holland
1815	Buxted, Sussex	Sir Francis D'Oyly
1815	Berkswell, Warwick	John Eardley-Wilmot
1816	Clapham (Parish Church)	John Thornton
1816	Petworth, Sussex	Charles Dunster
1816	Wrexham, Denbigh	William Lloyd
1816	Westminster Abbey	Mrs. Warren ("The Distressed Mother")
1816	Thorpe Constantine, Staffs	Henrietta Madam
1816	Storrington, Sussex	Sir Henry Bradford
1816	Calcutta (St. John's)	Michael Cheese
1816	Pewsey, Wilts	Rev. J. Townsend
1816	Westminster Abbey	Spencer Perceval (d. 1812)
1816	Blithfield, Staffs	Captain H. Bagot
1817	Hampton, Middlesex	Selina Smith
1817	Halifax (Parish Church)	H. Coulthurst
1817	Ledbury, Herefordshire	George Woodyatt
1817	Kenilworth, Warwick	Caroline Gresley

1818	Berkswell, Warwick	Elizabeth Eardley-Wilmot
1818	Crayford, Kent	Sir Stephen Cottrell
1818	Colwich, Staffs	Viscount Anson
1818	Ledbury, Herefordshire	Penelope Biddulph
1818	Cambridge (Trinity College)	Charles Fox-Maitland
1818	Burford, Salop	Lady Caroline Rushout
1819	Walsingham, Norfolk	Anne Lee-Warner
1819	Penang (St. George's)	John Bannerman
1819	Bicester, Oxon	Hon. Charlotte Coker
1819	Hinton St. George, Somerset	Vere, 3rd Earl Poulett
1819	Hinton St. George, Somerset	John, 4th Earl Poulett
1820	Lacock, Wilts	James Shottowe
1820	Loughborough, Leics	Benjamin Tate
1820	Llandegai, N. Wales	Lord Penrhyn
1820	Stockport, Cheshire	Rev. Charles Prescott
1820	Weobley, Hereford	Anne Birch
1821	Feltham, Middlesex	Rev. Colston Carr
1821	Calcutta (Cathedral)	Alexander Colvin
1821	Feltham, Middlesex	Sir Henry Carr
1821	Mitcham, Surrey	Mrs. Tate
1821	Honington, Warwick	Lady Elizabeth Townsend
1821	Marylebone (Parish Church)	Richard Cosway
1821	Methley, Yorks	Countess of Mexborough
1821	Darley Abbey, Derby	Arthur Evans
1822	Burford, Salop	Caroline Rushout
1822	Calcutta (Old Cathedral)	George Cruttenden
1822	Markham Clinton, Notts	Georgiana, Duchess of Newcastle
1823	Jamaica Cathedral	Elizabeth Burton
1823	Framfield, Sussex	Mrs. Sarah Woodward
1823	Burton Bradstock, Dorset	William Daniell
1823	Little Gaddesden, Herts	John, Earl of Bridgewater
1823	St. Germans, Cornwall	First Earl of St. Germans
1823	Knutsford, Cheshire	Elizabeth Leigh
1824	Campsey Ash, Suffolk	John Sheppard
1824	Walthamstow (Parish Church)	William Raikes
1824	Dullingham, Cambs	Lt.-General Jeaffreson (recumbent figure)
1824	Belton, Lincs	Caroline, Countess Brownlow
1824	Hale, Hants	Mary May
1824	Marylebone (Parish Church)	Augusta Kirkland
1824	Egloshayle, Cornwall	Sir Arscott Molesworth
1824	Woburn, Beds	Hon. Charlotte Seymour
1825	Twickenham (Parish Church)	Lady Margaret Wildman
1825	Ledbury, Hereford	Daniel Saunders
1825	Calcutta (Old Cathedral)	John Adam
1825	Marylebone (Parish Church)	William Fairlie
1825	Burton-on-Trent, Staffs	Lady Fowler
1825	Bedale, Yorks	Henry Peirse
1826	Chenies, Bucks	Edward Morris
1826	Dullingham, Cambs	Viscountess Gormanston
1826	Haynes, Beds	Lord Carteret
1826	Halifax (Parish Church)	John Rawson
1826	Honington, Warwick	Gore Townsend
1827	Farnham, Surrey	Sir Nelson Rycroft
1827	Frome, Somerset	The Ladies Lucy and Louisa Boyle
1827	Hampton, Middlesex	Elizabeth Mallet
1827	Storrington, Sussex	Major Falconar
1827	Bainton, Northants	Isabella Peyton
1827	Orsett, Essex	Richard Baker
1827	Burford, Salop	Elizabeth Rushout
1828	Ealing (Parish Church)	Charles Hutchinson
1828	Shalstone, Bucks	Mary Hawes
1828	Halifax (Parish Church)	William Rawson
1828	Madingley, Cambs	Commander Cotton
1829	Feltham, Middlesex	Mrs. Knyvett and Mrs. Aldous
1829	Streatham (Parish Church)	Jane Brown
1829	Hampstead (Parish Church)	George Todd
1829	Packwood, Warwick	Wilson Roberts
1830	Brighton (Parish Church)	Frances Crosbie
1830	Derby (Cathedral)	Mrs. Chichester
1830	Malvern, Worcs	John Dandridge
1831	Chilham, Kent	Sir Thomas Mantell
1831	Nunton, Wilts	John Batt
1832	Kew (Parish Church)	Timothy Tyrrell
1832	Great Finborough, Suffolk	Roger Pettiward
1833	Calcutta (Old Cathedral)	Walter Nisbet
1834	Marlow, Bucks	Sir William Clayton
1834	Beddington, Surrey	Sir Benjamin Carew
1834	Ledbury, Hereford	Augusta Biddulph
1834	Astbury, Cheshire	Charles Shakerley
1834	Wanstead (Parish Church)	Joshua Knowles
1835	Birdsall, Yorks	6th Lord Middleton
1835	Woolaton, Notts	6th Lord Middleton
1835	St. Asaph (Cathedral)	Sir John Williams
1835	Illogan, Cornwall	Lord de Dunstanville
1835	Brixton (St. Matthew's)	George Brettle
1835	Catton, Norfolk	Frances Ives
1837	Mitcham, Surrey	William Myers
1837	Longborough, Glos	Sir Charles Cockerell

1837	North Wraxall, Wilts	Paul Methuen
1838	Stratford-on-Avon, Warwick	James Dennis
1838	Wormley, Herts	Lord and Lady Farnborough
1838	Saxmundham, Suffolk	Lord Farnborough
1839	Wyke Regis, Dorset	Mary Warrington
1840	Kew (Parish Church)	Francis Bower
1842	Staindrop, Durham	Duke of Cleveland (recumbent figure)
n.d.	Oxford (Cathedral)	John James, Bishop of Calcutta

WESTMACOTT, RICHARD, the Younger, R.A.

b. 1799, d. 1872

He was the eldest son of Sir Richard Westmacott (q.v.) and in his youth wanted to become a barrister. However, he yielded to his father's wishes and trained as a sculptor in the latter's studio. In 1818 he attended the Royal Academy Schools, and in 1820 went to Italy, where he spent six years studying the remains of Greek and Roman art.

On his return young Westmacott worked with his father in South Audley Street and in 1829 was paid £600 for two chimney-pieces for Buckingham Palace (P.R.O., Works 19/3). In the following year he set up for himself at 21, Wilton Place.

About 1840 Westmacott and R. Sievier (q.v.) made two chimney-pieces for the dining-room of the north wing at Chatsworth. The Duke of Devonshire, in his privately-printed Handbook of Chatsworth (1846, page 83), said of them: "They are clever and well-executed, but do not nearly approach the idea I wish to see realized. I wanted more abandon, and joyous expression. I find these baccanali too composed and sedate." Westmacott was also responsible for a chimney-piece for Stafford House, London, the supporting figures on either side being likenesses of two daughters of the Duchess of Sutherland.

His only important work in London, however, is the relief in the pediment of the Royal Exchange, which he executed between 1842 and 1844. About 1862 he made a fountain for Regent's Park with a figure of a woman and two swans.

Westmacott exhibited at the Royal Academy, 1827–1855, and was elected an Associate in 1838. In 1849 he became a full member, and in 1857 succeeded his father as Professor of Sculpture. He died on 19 April, 1872. The Art Journal of that year (page 167) said of him in its obituary that "as a sculptor his works generally must rank below those of his father, yet they are by no means without merit, graceful rather than powerful, but manifesting careful study and matured knowledge.

He was indeed learned in art and accepted as an authority on all matters connected with it."

As a monumental sculptor Westmacott produced competent, though uninspired, work. His best is perhaps the recumbent figure of the fifteen-year-old Eton boy, Charles Packe (d. 1842), in Prestwold Church, Leicestershire.

(Builder, 1872, page 380; authorities cited in text.)

BUSTS

1829	Sir Sidney Smith	Exhibited Royal Academy
1830	George Tierney	Westminster Abbey
1830	John Lodge	Exhibited Liverpool Academy
1833	Davies Gilbert	Pembroke College, Oxford
1833	Lord King	Ockham Church, Surrey
1835	Rev. Sidney Smith	Exhibited Royal Academy
1839	Archdeacon Berners	Wolverstone Church, Suffolk
1839	Mrs. Henry Milman	Exhibited Royal Academy
1840	Viscount Fordwich	Exhibited Royal Academy
1841	Cardinal Newman	Exhibited Royal Academy
1842	Wilbraham Egerton	Tatton Park, Cheshire
1842	Miss Egerton	Tatton Park, Cheshire
1843	Lord John Russell	Woburn Abbey
1844	Lord Wriothesley Russell	Woburn Abbey
1844	Marianne Packe	Prestwold Church, Leics
1844	Marquess of Tavistock	Woburn Abbey
1845	Sir Francis Burdett	Possession author
1847	Sir Roderick Murchison	Scottish National Portrait Gallery
1847	7th Duke of Bedford	Woburn Abbey
1847	Earl Talbot	Exhibited Royal Academy
1849	Lord Wharncliffe	Exhibited Royal Academy

RELIEFS, etc.

1831	Venus Carrying off Ascanius	Bridgewater House
1836	Bluebell	For Earl of Ellesmere
1837	Paolo and Francesca	Bowood
1838	Venus Instructing Cupid	Bridgewater House
1840	The Captive	For Lord Amherst
1849	Go and Sin No More	Diploma work, Burlington House
?	Cupid and Wasp	Eaton Hall
?	The Cymbal Player	For the Duke of Devonshire

MONUMENTS

1820	Worcester (Cathedral)	William Burslem
1828	Exeter (Cathedral)	Sacharissa Hibbert
1828	Newton, Cambs	Rev. William Pemberton
1830	Winchester (Cathedral)	Tomline, Bishop of Winchester
1831	Leeds (Parish Church)	Roger Leigh
1831	Bickleigh, Devon	Sir Mannaseh Lopes
1833	Storrington, Sussex	Countess of Carnwath
1833	Wistow, Leics	Lady Halford
1833	Rugby (School Chapel)	Dr. Wooll
1834	Medmenham, Bucks	Emma Scott
1835	Harrow (Parish Church)	Joseph Drury
1835	Moccas, Hereford	Sir George Cornewall
1837	Lutterworth, Leics	Wycliffe Memorial
1837	Wistow, Leics	Sir John Vaughan
1837	Chelsea (St. Luke's)	Mary Denman
1838	Cambridge (St. Benet's)	William Hayward
1838	Oxford (Brasenose College)	James Smith
1838	Preston-on-Stour, Glos	James Roberts West
1839	Prestwold, Leics	Charles James Packe
1839	Westonbirt, Glos	Robert and George Holford
1840	Cobham, Surrey	William Cooper
1841	Buckland Monachorum, Devon	Lady Drake
1842	Prestwold, Leics	Charles Packe (recumbent figure)
1843	Frome, Somerset	Isabella, Countess of Cork
1843	Lowick, Northants	5th Duke of Dorset
1844	Wistow, Leics	Sir Henry Holland
1844	Wimpole, Cambs	3rd Earl of Hardwicke (recumbent figure)
1844	Limerick (Cathedral)	Lord Glentworth (recumbent figure)
1845	Rostherne, Cheshire	Charlotte Egerton (recumbent figure)
1846	South Harting, Sussex	Sir Henry Featherstonehaugh
1846	Weobley, Hereford	Ann Birch
1848	Worcester (Cathedral)	Earl of Stafford and Officers of the Worcestershire Regiment
1848	Canterbury (Cathedral)	Archbishop Howley (recumbent effigy)
1849	Ingestre, Staffs	Earl Talbot (recumbent effigy)
1852	Shalstone, Bucks	Geraldine and Henry Jervoise
1852	Well, Yorks	Lady Margaret Milbank
1856	Nether Alderley, Cheshire	Lord Stanley of Alderley (recumbent effigy)
1857	Lincoln (Cathedral)	Kaye, Bishop of Lincoln (recumbent effigy)

WESTON, —

In 1704 Browne Willis, the antiquary, when he was at Bletchley, paid "Weston the carver for new cutting over the Lord Grey's monument, £3." Weston was also paid for "two black marble stones laid over the bodies of Thomas Willis, Esq. and Alice his wife and cutting the arms and inscription" (*Records of Bucks*, Vol. XII, page 246).

The monument recut was that commemorating Lord Grey of Wilton, who died in 1447. The armorials on the tombs of Mr. and Mrs. Willis are surprisingly well carved.

WESTON, —, of Exeter
fl. 1696–1733

In spite of the fact that Weston was one of the most remarkable of the provincial statuaries, a careful search through the archives of his native city has revealed no trace of either his apprenticeship or freedom. All his monuments are important and have an extraordinary range, both in style and execution. Most of them are well up to the best provincial standards of the early eighteenth century, but four equal, if they do not surpass, the finest contemporary London productions.

The monuments in question are those which commemorate John Kelland, 1712, at Ashprington, Devon; Jonathan and Elizabeth Ivie, 1717, in St. Petrock's Church, Exeter; Francis Pengelley, 1722, Whitchurch, Devon; and Henry Scobell, 1729, at St. Blazey, Cornwall. Each is distinguished by having on the base the most remarkable relief of the Last Judgment, in which the figures have all the grace and movement of the Italian Renaissance, while the design anticipates the work of William Blake. The Ivie monument, originally a much larger work, was first erected in St. Kerrian's, Exeter, but when the church was pulled down the relief only was moved to its present position. According to Cresswell (*Churches of Exeter*, page 147), it was signed by Weston, the architectural surround was probably similar to those of the Kelland and Scobell monuments which still exist. Of these the former is architectural in design, about 10 ft. high, and consists of a large pediment surmounted by an urn, with a cartouche inscription-tablet below. The latter is more elaborate, standing about 12 ft. high, with Corinthian pillars supporting a curved pediment with reclining angels on either side; beneath is a fringed inscription-tablet under a baldacchino. The tablet to Francis Pengelley is also an architectural composition, though flanking the monument are symbolic figures of Learning and Justice.

Other signed monuments by Weston in Devonshire include an architectural work commemorating Roger Vavasour, 1696, at Dartmouth; another, with a portrait-bust and an enchanting relief of a ship at the base, to Benjamin Dollen, 1700, in Exeter Cathedral; a life-size kneeling figure of Philip Hooper in robes and wig, dated 1715, in St. Martin's Church, Exeter; and a fine cartouche tablet to the Rev. John Newte, 1715, at Tiverton.

Two more elaborate examples of his monumental work commemorate Edward Hobbs, 1718, at Gerrans, Cornwall, and Joseph Taylor, 1733, at Denbury, Devon. The first has a central baldacchino from which hang curtains, raised on either side by female figures to reveal the inscription-tablet they are holding; at the base is a shield with a mixture of spades, scythes, coronets and crowns turned upside down, skull and cross-bones, etc. The second is in memory of a sailor, and has a medallion-portrait, naval trophies in the shape of an anchor, sextant, chart and globe, and medals of Queen Anne and George I. At the base is a fine relief of Taylor's ship engaging four triremes, probably Moorish pirates. At Honiton Clyst, in the same county, is a fragment of what must once have been an important monument by Weston, but all that now remains are two mourning cherubs, a coat of arms, and the sculptor's signature beneath. This may be part of the "elegant marble monument" to Francis Weller, mentioned by Polwhele in his *Devonshire* (Part II, page 199).

WHEELER, JOHN, of Beaulieu

He signs a neo-Hellenic wall-tablet to Lady Cope, 1806, at Eversley, Hampshire. He also signs tablets at South Wanborough, Hants.

WHITE, C., of London

He signs a monument with a relief to John Hooper, 1808, at Shoreham, Sussex.

WHITE, SIMON, of Oxford
fl. 1656–1669

He was the principal stone-carver for the library and chapel at Brasenose College, Oxford, 1656–1658; and is also described as a "carver" for "marbles" when he received a payment of £30 from the College in 1665. A year later he was paid a further £52 for "laying the marbles" (E. W. Allfrey's *Brasenose Quatercentenary Monographs*, No. 3, pages 20–22). In 1669 White received £5 for a "marble altar," which was placed with the Arundel Marbles (Wood's *Life and Times*, Vol. IV, page 69).

WHITE, THOMAS, of Canterbury
fl. 1764–1801

From 1764 until 1801 he was the master-mason of Canterbury Cathedral, and in 1791 carried out extensive repairs, receiving £271 for his work on "Bell Harry" (Treasurer's Accounts, Cathedral Library). In the previous year he had been paid £890 for rebuilding Brookland Church.

WHITE, THOMAS, of Worcester
b. c. 1674, *d.* 1748

He was a native of Worcester, but seems to have gone to London as a boy and to have been apprenticed to a statuary in Piccadilly. He must have returned to Worcester about 1709, for in that year the City Chamber "ordered that Thomas White be and is admitted a Freeman of this City, making a handsome effigie of the Queen to ye well-liking of the Mayor and Aldermen for the time being, but that he be not sworne before the effigie be done." This is the statue of Queen Anne now in the centre of the façade of the Guildhall. Three years later White received £10 for "carving and beautifying the statue of Charles I," but this probably only means that he recut the old statue.

Between 1721 and 1724 White was working at Worcester Guildhall, which dates from this time. Here he was responsible for most of the decorative carving; the great trophy of arms in the pediment is signed by him and dated 1722. Green, in his *History of Worcester* (Vol. II, page 89), says that White was also responsible for the figure of Britannia on a house in the city, the bust of George II on Edgar's Tower, and another of Bishop Hough at the east end of All Saints' Church. He apparently "lived in easy circumstances" and is said to have died a bachelor.

In his Will, White left to Worcester Infirmary "all and every sum of money that shall appear to be due to me at the time of my decease from the Corporation . . . on account of the annuity due to me." This "annuity" had been granted to him by the Corporation in 1724 in recognition of his work at the Guildhall.

White also worked as a statuary. His most important monument is that to Admiral Skynner, 1725, at Ledbury, Herefordshire, with its life-sized busts. Other signed monuments and tablets by him include those to Adam Cave, 1698, in All Saints, Evesham; Mrs. Nanfan, 1704, at Birtsmorton, Worcs; Sir John Turton, 1707, at Alrewas, Staffs; Bishop Thomas, *c.* 1710, and Henrietta Wrottesley, 1720, both in Worcester Cathedral; Sir John Bridgeman, 1719, and Roger

Mathews, 1746, both at Llanbodwell, Salop; the Rev. Josiah Foster, 1727, at Aston, Birmingham; Mary Lyster, 1730, in St. Mary's, Shrewsbury; John Holte, 1735, at Ripple, Worcs; George Peyton, 1742, in Tewkesbury Abbey; and John Brydges, 1742, at Bosbury, Hereford. He must have had a yard in Shrewsbury as well as in Worcester, for the monuments at Llanbodwell are signed "of Salop," although the drawings in the archives of the Earl of Bradford are signed "of Worcester." (Rev. Buchanan-Dunlop's *Thomas White*; Worcestershire Archaeological Society, 1943; Worcester City Archives.)

WHITEHEAD, JAMES,
of London
fl. 1817–1828

In 1817 he was paid £123 for marble chimney-pieces at Battle Abbey (Archives, Mrs. Harbord, of Battle Abbey).

His studio was in the New Road, and he signs a tablet to Lieutenant-General William St. Leger, 1818, in Marylebone Parish Church. A "John Whitehead of the New Road," who is presumably a relation (although the "John" may be a misprint for "James"), received a Silver Palette from the Society of Arts in 1814 for a plaster-cast of "Aeneas Flying from Troy." A "W. Whitehead of London" signs the monument of the Hon. George Fox-Strangways, 1859, at Farley, Wilts, and "J. and M. Whitehead" sign a tablet, with the figure of a mourning woman, in Kentish Town Parish Church.

WHITELAW, WILLIAM,
of London
fl. 1805–1843

From 1807 until 1812 he was making chimney-pieces for Longleat, receiving £182 from the Marquess of Bath (Longleat Archives). In the latter year he did similar work at Ombersley Court, Worcestershire (Archives, Lord Sandys).

As a monumental statuary Whitelaw was prolific, but most of his works are dull. His monument to Lord St. Vincent, 1823, at Stone, Staffs, has a portrait-bust, and he signs others commemorating Mrs. Forrester, 1805, in All Saints', Leicester; Richard Sowdon, 1816, in St. Mary's, Reading; Frederick Pitcher, 1816, in St. James's, Hampstead Road; Robert Powney, 1817, in Marylebone Parish Church; Edward Tew, 1817, in Upper Chapel, Eton College; Thomas Taylor, 1818, at Debden, Essex; Lady Bayly, 1818, Stoke d'Abernon, Surrey; James Grave, 1820, at Baldock, Herts; Hon. Samuel Ongley, 1822, at

Sandy, Beds (and also in Christ Church, Dublin); Sir Thomas Reid, 1824, St. Michael's, Dumfries; General Sir Edward Howorth, 1827, at Banstead, Surrey; Charles Gordon, 1829, at Berkhamsted, Herts; the Rev. John Templer, 1832, at Teigngrace, Devon; Edward Jacob, 1837, at Faversham, Kent; and Lucy Monoux, at Evershot, Beds.

WHITING, JOHN,
of Northampton
b. 1782, *d.* 1854

He settled in Northampton and became a Freeman of that borough by purchase on 15 March, 1806. His monumental work is scattered over Northamptonshire and the neighbouring counties and is mostly very uninteresting. His tablet to William Kerr, 1824, in the Church of the Holy Sepulchre, Northampton, has a relief of the County Hospital at the top; while that to Thomas Samwell, 1835, at Upton, Northants, has a well-cut relief of a mourning woman.

Whiting also signs works in the same county commemorating Katherine Thornton, 1807, at Brockhall; Daniel Knightley, 1808, and Benjamin Laver, 1810, both at Hardingstone; Robert Fleetwood, 1810, in St. Peter's, Northampton; John Yates, 1824, at Brackley; the Rev. E. Isham, 1814, and Sir Justinian Isham, 1818, both at Lamport; and Mary Hayne, 1838, at Spratton. Others by him include those to Thomas Foster, 1821, at Newport Pagnall, Bucks; Mary Dawson, 1829, at Clapham, Beds; and Joseph Brookes, 1840, at Clifton-Reynes, Bucks.

WHITING, ROBERT,
of Cambridge
He signs a large wall-tablet to Thomas Price at Astwell in Northants. This is undated, but, from its style, was probably erected about 1790.

WHITTLE, BENJAMIN,
of Liverpool
He signs a large wall-tablet with an urn, coat of arms, etc., to the Rev. W. Keyt, 1816, at Runcorn, Cheshire.

WHITTON, ROBERT, of Ripon
fl. 1830–1841

He signs two large Hellenic tablets with well-cut details to Edward and Frederick Oxley, 1830, and to John Small, 1834, both in Ripon Cathedral.

WICKSTEAD,
or WICKSTEED, JAMES
fl. 1779–1824

He exhibited engraved gems, etc., at the Royal

Academy, 1779–1824, and at the Suffolk Street Galleries showed a bas-relief of "Mary Magdalene Anointing Christ's Feet" in 1824.

WILD, H.

Probably a Manchester mason, he signs a wall-tablet to George Clarke, 1777, at Stockport, Cheshire.

WILDING, R.

He was presumably a Shrewsbury artist and signs a curious monumental tablet to Thomas Jones, 1714, in St. Alkmund's, Shrewsbury. This takes the form of a brass plate with a long inscription, while above are three repoussé coats of arms very well cast in bronze.

WILDSMITH, JOHN
fl. 1757–1769

He may have been an apprentice of Thomas Carter (q.v.). As "mason and carver" he became a bankrupt in 1769, and on 31 July and 1 August of the same year a sale of his stock-in-trade was held at his yard "near St. James's Church, Piccadilly." Among the marble chimney-piece tablets sold were those of "Diana," "Shepherd and Wolf" and "Boys and Sheep." Another lot was "3 marble boxes inlaid with different sorts of marble." In 1763 he was paid £90 for chimney-pieces for Sir Richard Littleton's house in Piccadilly (Archives, Lord Brownlow).

WILKES, —, of Birmingham
fl. 1830–1838

He signs monuments commemorating Abraham Spooner, 1830, and the Countess of Rosse, 1838, both at Elmdon, Warwickshire.

WILKINS, —, of Beaminster
fl. 1830–1840

He signs a few tablets in Dorset, the best commemorating Captain Bowles, 1837, at Netherbury, which has military trophies. The large, heavy monument to Edmund Hall, 1839, at Broadwindsor, in the same county, has a relief of a dragoon and his horse, and is also the work of Wilkins.

WILLEMS,
or WILLIAMS, JOSEPH
d. 1766

He was born in Brussels and about the middle of the eighteenth century came over to England, where he worked as a modeller in the Chelsea china factory. In Mortimer's *Universal Directory* for 1763 (Part I, page 19) he is described as "Willems, Joseph, Modeller, at the Brussels Coffee-house, Chelsea. This artist teaches drawing, modelling and has modelled for the Chelsea china factory for many years."

Willems, who anglicized his name to "Williams," exhibited at the Society of Artists, 1761–1766, where his works included a bust of Mr. Martinelli (1761), an emblematic figure of "Honour" (1763), a bust of "A Gentleman" (1764), and models of "Charity" and "Sincerity" in 1765 and 1766 respectively.

Willems left England in 1766 and settled in Tournai, where he died on 1 November of the same year.

(W. H. Tapp's *Joseph Willems; Connoisseur*, April, 1938, page 176.)

WILLIAMS, —, of Brighton
fl. 1800–1829

He signs a few tablets in Sussex, the best being those to John Ingram, 1803, at Chailey, and John Payne, 1805, at Patcham, the latter carried out in coloured marbles.

WILLIAMS, —, of Plymouth
fl. 1808–1818

Of his three tablets in Egg Buckland Church, Devon, the best commemorates William Harris, 1816.

WILLIAMS, EDWARD,
of Cowbridge
b. 1746, *d.* 1826

He signs an undated oval wall-tablet to Anthony Jones at Llantwit, Glamorgan; this was erected about 1800 and is exactly like the contemporary work of T. King of Bath (q.v.).

He is best known as a poet and antiquary (see D.N.B.).

WILLIAMS, EMANUEL

He became a bankrupt as "mason and carver of Tooley Street, Southwark," in 1778. On 18 and 19 January in the following year a sale of his stock-in-trade was held; the lots auctioned included a great deal of marble, chimney-pieces, monuments, tablets, etc., and it would seem as if Williams must have had a considerable business. Between 1774–1777 he built the west wing of Guy's Hospital (£1,425), and in 1777–1778 the centre building (£1,474) (Hospital Archives).

WILLIAMS, HUGH, of Holyhead
According to the *Cambrian Magazine* (Vol. III,

page 507) he made the monument commemorating Gromo Owen, 1831, in Bangor Cathedral.

WILLIAMS, RICHARD
b. 1799

He was the son of Solomon Williams, an Irish historical portrait painter, and studied in Dublin under James Smyth, the Irish sculptor. Here he exhibited various works in 1815, 1817 and 1819, and in 1816 won the first prize for sculpture at the Dublin Society's Schools.

In 1820 Williams came to London and joined the Royal Academy Schools, winning Silver Medals in 1820 and 1823. He exhibited at the Academy, 1822–1832, where his works included a bust of Charles Rossi, R.A., in 1824 and "Haidée Recovering Juan" in 1832. He was elected a member of the "Artist Annuity Fund" in 1822. He became blind in 1841 (Archives, A.G.B.I.).

(Strickland's *Dictionary of Irish Artists.*)

WILLIAMS, W.
fl. 1824–1839

He exhibited architectural plans and portrait-busts at the Royal Academy, 1824–1839. He also signs the monument to John Mortimer, 1829, in Huddersfield Parish Church.

WILLIAMS, W., of Merthyr
He signs an oval wall-tablet to Lewis Thomas, 1804, in Brecon Cathedral.

WILLIAMS, WILLIAM and THOMAS, of Middleton Stoney
fl. 1706–1724

In 1706 they carved the capitals for the greenhouse at Aynho, Northants. In 1715 and 1716 they made chimney-pieces for the same house, one in Warwickshire stone for "the little parlour" and the other for an unidentified room (Cartwright Archives).

The Williams sign the large and important monument at Kirtlington, Oxon, erected to the Dashwood family in 1724. This impressive architectural work has a broken pediment with a fluted urn in the centre, and two mourning cherubs standing at the base of the inscription-tablet. It is an extremely advanced and elaborate production for provincial (indeed, almost village) masons.

WILLOUGHBY, G., of Malton
b. ca. 1767, *d.* 1835

He signs a large Hellenic monument to the Worsley family, 1812, at Hovingham, Yorks, and

a tablet with naval trophies at the base to Nathaniel Bruton, 1815, at Stockton, Durham.

WILLOUGHBY, W., of Howden
He signs a large wall-tablet with careful and well-cut details to John and Ann Whitaker, 1798, at Howden, Yorks.

WILLSON, DANIEL WILLIAM, of London
fl. 1824–1834

His yard was at Bath Place, New Road. His best monuments are those to Elizabeth Bainbridge, 1824, at Chobham, Surrey, and to Mary Sikes, 1828, at Balderton, Notts; the former has a relief of a seated mourning woman in the manner of John Bacon the Younger (q.v.), while the latter has figures of Hope and Faith. Other signed works by Wilson include those to Francis Peach, 1832, at Ketteringham, Norfolk, and Benjamin Burton, 1834, in Marylebone Parish Church. He also signs a small tablet to Lord Colchester, 1829, in the Parish Church of East Grinstead, Sussex.

WILSON, —, of Wellingborough
According to the *Gentleman's Magazine* of 1799 (page 939), he made the monumental tablet to Mrs. Roberts (*d.* 1781) at Fineden, Northants.

WILSON, J. T.
fl. 1837–1838

He exhibited medallion portraits in marble at the Royal Academy in 1837, and showed a bust of Sir Robert Inglis, Bart., in the following year.

WILSON, SIR WILLIAM
b. 1641, *d.* 1710

He was the son of a Leicester baker and in 1670 was working as a carver at Sudbury Hall, Derbyshire (then being rebuilt by George Vernon), where he was responsible for the elaborate sculpture of the entrance-porch (*Country Life*, 15, 22, 29 June, 1935). In or about 1671 he made the Wilbraham family monuments in Weston Church, Staffordshire, for Lady Elizabeth Wilbraham, who recorded the agreement in her copy of Palladio, now in the possession of the Earl of Bradford (see *Wren Society*, Vol. XI, page 109).

About nine years later Wilson made the equestrian statue of the Duke of Newcastle which was placed over the door of the north-east front of Nottingham Castle. The work was supposed to have been carved from a single block of stone, but when the castle was sacked by rioters in 1831 they took away with them as a trophy one of the horse's legs, which was then discovered to be made of wood.

Deering, the historian of Nottingham, who is quoted by Throsby (*Town of Nottingham*, 1795, page 26), says that Wilson "was an ingenious artist of whom it was remarkable that after this performance (i.e., the statue of the Duke) he was for a time spoiled for a statuary because a Leicestershire widow lady, the Lady Pudsey, who was possessed of a very large jointure, falling deeply in love with him, got him knighted and married him. But he living up to the extent of his apronstring estate and his lady dying before him, Sir William returned to his former occupation and the public recovered the loss of an eminent artist." Wilson married Mrs. (not "Lady") Jane Pudsey, widow of Henry Pudsey, of Langley Hall, Warwick. About 1677 the sculptor had made the monument (with two busts) of Pudsey for Sutton Coldfield Church, Warwick, so that it is possible he first met his future wife when discussing the form this memorial should take.

A writer in the *Gentleman's Magazine* (1761, page 401) rather over-praises this monument when he describes the curtains, which are drawn back to disclose the busts, as being "so well designed in their folds and executed with such an easy flowing of the drapery as would not have disgraced a Roubiliac."

About 1680 Wilson probably made the statue of Charles II for the exterior of Lichfield Cathedral. In 1701 he executed the statue of Sir John Moore at Appleby School, Leicester, receiving £50 and another £5 for the coat of arms on the exterior of the School (Historical Manuscripts Commission, Tenth Report, Appendix Part IV, Captain Stewart's MS., page 139). In 1707 he made a statuette of Edward VI, costing £25, for Birmingham Grammar School (Nicholas Carlisle's *Endowed Grammar Schools*, 1818, Vol. 2, page 644). As an architect he was responsible for part of St. Mary's Church, Warwick, and in September, 1700, was also paid for "carving work" and in 1706 a further payment was made to him for "carving church windows." In the following year is Wilson's receipt for £10 and "for the Marble Monuments on which the two brass figures are fixt in the Church of St. Maryes in Warwick over against the South Isle in the sd. Church." (P.R.O., c.104/97.)

Owing to his wife's efforts, Wilson was knighted at Whitehall on 8 March, 1681/1682. He died on 3 June, 1710, and is commemorated by a tablet in Sutton Coldfield Church. According to a work entitled *The History of Sutton Coldfield by an Impartial Hand* (London, 1762), Wilson's lowly birth so offended his wife's relations that they refused to contemplate his being buried in the same vault with her. Wilson was aware of this and, when a friend commiserated with him, facetiously replied that he was not worried, for he would be buried outside the church, directly opposite the Pudsey vault. Then, he said, "there will be only a single stone wall betwixt us, and as I am stonemason there will be no kind of labour or difficulty in cutting my road through the wall to my old bedfellow."

(*Wren Society*, Vol. XI, pages 109–112, and authorities cited in text.)

WILTON, JOSEPH, R.A.
b. 1722, *d.* 1803

He was born in London on 16 July, 1722, the son of a worker in ornamental plaster who had a large manufactory near Charing Cross. The elder Wilton was responsible, among other works, for the ceilings at the Foundling Hospital (*Builder*, 1859, page 849), and it was in his father's studio that the young man received his first grounding in decorative art. He had, however, a strong natural inclination towards sculpture, and although his father wished him to become a civil engineer he ultimately got his own way and became a pupil of L. Delvaux (q.v.), at Nivelle, in Brabant.

From Nivelle Wilton went in 1744 to study at the Academy in Paris then directed by J. B. Pigalle (1714–1785). Here he learnt to work in marble and won a Silver Medal. In 1752 he set out with L. F. Roubiliac (q.v.) to study in Rome, and three years later received the "Jubilee" Gold Medal from Pope Benedict XIV.

While he was in Rome Wilton met his first patron, William Locke, of Norbury, and the two soon became inseparable, travelling about Italy together in a search for antiquities. Later he moved to Florence and worked there for four years, receiving a number of orders for marble copies of statues from the antique. He was apparently already making a name for himself, for Horace Walpole, writing to Sir Horace Mann in 1753, refers to a remark made by the latter in a previous letter about Wilton's being "mentioned with encomiums" (*Letters of Horace Walpole*, edited by Cunningham, Vol. II, page 358).

In 1755 Wilton returned to England, in company with Sir William Chambers, the architect, Cipriani, the decorative painter, and Capitsoldi, the sculptor (q.v.). He settled in his father's house in London and soon had a large number of commissions. Three years later he and Cipriani were appointed directors of the gallery of painting and sculpture opened for the use of students by the Third Duke of Richmond at Whitehall. Wilton was also appointed coach-carver to the King and was responsible for some of the designs and carving of the State Coach used by George III at his Coronation; in 1764 he was appointed "Sculptor to His Majesty."

On his father's death he inherited a very considerable fortune and lived in a sumptuous, indeed extravagant, manner, with a house in town, another in the country, and "a family coach, a phaeton, and numerous saddle-horses for himself and his sons, to whom he gave a University education" (J. R. Smith's *Nollekens and His Times*, Vol. II, page 105).

Wilton was paid for a great deal of decorative carving at Somerset House, though Smith, who is not always reliable, says that John Atkins (q.v.) and Nathaniel Smith (q.v.) "modelled and carved the whole of them for Wilton, immediately from the drawings, he never having put a tool to them" (op. cit., Vol. II, page 110). Whether this is the truth or not, Wilton was credited with a long list of works, including, in 1776, "six relieved high-finished colossal heads cut in Portland stone, £126"; in 1778, four colossal statues of "Europe, Asia, Africa and America, erected on the attic of the inner front of the Royal Academy"; and, in 1780, chimney-pieces for the principal rooms at a total cost of £1,097, which included payments for two with "enriched tablets of griffins and urns" for the Royal Academy Council Room. In the following year he supplied "two semi-circular niches in Portland stone," and in 1784 and 1786 respectively received further sums of £940 and £835 for chimney-pieces. In 1788 he made chimney-pieces for the rooms allotted to the Treasurer of the Navy in Somerset House. One intended for the "eating-room" had a tablet carved with a head of "Flora" and cost £60, while two others, for the drawing-room and withdrawing-room, cost £55 each. In 1787 he had made "eight large vases with Tritons and other emblematical figures and ornamented with festoons and trophies allusive to different offices" for which he received £640, and in 1790 he was paid £200 for two colossal lions in Portland stone, each 10 ft. 3 in. in length, which were to be placed on the eastern watergate of the great terrace (R.I.B.A. Library, MS. 335A; P.R.O., A.O.1/2495–2498).

Wilton also produced a number of richly carved chimney-pieces for various mansions, including Blenheim, where he supplied one, designed by Sir William Chambers, for the dressing-room of the Duchess of Marlborough in 1772 (British Museum, Ad. MS. 41133); Sandbeck Park, the seat of Lord Scarborough (Miller's *Doncaster*, page 311); Kirkleatham, Yorkshire (*England Displayed*, Vol. II, page 158); and about

1770 one for Peper Harrow House, Surrey, with a tablet to "Bacchus and Tiger." Some of the houses for which he worked had been built, or altered, by his friend Chambers, and it was from the latter's design that he made keystones for the bridge at Woburn Abbey in 1771 (British Museum, Ad. MS. 41133). In the same year he executed the monument to the Earl and Countess of Mountrath for Westminster Abbey. This was also from a design by Chambers, who later wrote asking for the £50 owing to him for the work, remarking that he would "be glad to have my share, being now in want of the needful" (British Museum, Ad. MS. 41133).

One of Wilton's most lavish patrons was Lord Charlemont, a man of great culture, of whom Henry Grattan said that "the very rabble grew civilized as it approached his person." He employed Wilton to carve a variety of objects, both for his house in Dublin and for his lovely seaside villa "Marino." One of the most elaborate was a table in lapis-lazuli which cost £150. This was apparently more than he had anticipated, for Wilton, writing to him on 17 May, 1773, says: "I wish it had been in my power to have made the table come less expensive, as it has far exceeded my first computation" (*Historical Manuscripts Commission*, Earl of Charlemont, Vol. I, page 314).

One of the sculptor's finest, though least known, works is the statue of Archbishop Tillotson in Sowerby Church, Yorkshire. The figure in its alcove has a curious air of bravura rather out of keeping with its subject and, of all Wilton's productions, reflects most clearly the influence of his foreign training. According to the inscription, it was erected to the memory of the primate by his two great-nieces, but the original model (still in the possession of the Stansfeld family) is inscribed: "To George Stansfeld, Esq., under whose direction the marble statue of Archbishop Tillotson was executed and erected in Sowerby Church, this model in sincerest gratitude is respectfully dedicated by Joseph Wilton, R.A., Statuary to the King and Keeper of His Majesty's Royal Academy in London. The Year of Our Lord MDCCXCVI."

Wilton was also responsible for two statues of George III, one of lead and the other of marble. The first, which was modelled by A. Beaupré (q.v.) under Wilton's direction, showed the King on horseback, and formerly stood in Berkeley Square. The second, which was ordered for the Royal Exchange by the City Corporation, received so much adverse criticism when it was unveiled in 1764 that the sculptor felt bound to explain why he did not retaliate. He accordingly wrote to the Committee which had commissioned the statue, saying that though "some gentlemen were very earnest that I should publish a defence against the criticisms which have been wantonly made upon it," yet "on mature deliberation such appeal to the public seems to me neither reasonable nor necessary," giving as his reason that "an altercation with thousands of people who understand nothing of the matter might not only endanger my reputation, but would naturally give occasion to careless and malicious pens to work my ruin by construing away the best meaning by the usual arts of equivocation" (City Corporation MS. 167.13). The offending statue was badly damaged when the Royal Exchange was burned in 1838 and it was later sold for £11 15s.

In 1766 Wilton made a statue of George II, which is now in the Senate House, Cambridge. In the same year his statue of the elder Pitt was erected in New York; this was mutilated during the War of Independence and is now the property of the New York Historical Society. A second statue of Pitt, executed for Cork Town Hall, is in the Crawford School of Science and Art, Emmet Place, Cork. Copies of classical statues made by Wilton include the "Venus de Medici," for Lord Charlemont; "Venus" and "Apollo," for Lord Pembroke, both of which are now at Wilton; "Flora" and "Bacchus," for Lord Tilney, which were formerly at Wanstead; "Apollo" and "Isis," for Lord Rockingham (1762); and the "Apollo Belvedere," for the Duke of Richmond (1758).

According to Nichols' *Literary Anecdotes* (Vol. VIII, page 679), Wilton made the bust of Richard Gipps in West Harling Church, Norfolk. The same authority (page 637) quotes a letter from the Rev. E. Tyson, Vicar of Lambourne, Essex, written to Gough the antiquary on 15 November, 1778, in which Tyson says that "one of the most elegant modern monuments I ever saw was last week put up in my church to (John) Lockwood— a figure of Hope leaning on an antique urn in alto-relievo by Wilton." The sculptor also submitted a design for the monument to Thomas Guy and was paid thirty guineas for his model, although the commission was given to Bacon (Archives, Guy's Hospital).

Two very fine unidentified marble busts, signed by Wilton and dated 1766, were bought at the Duke of Newcastle's sale at Clumber and are now in the Fitzwilliam Museum, Cambridge. According to Throsby (*Leicestershire*, Vol. I, page 173), who wrote in 1791, Wilton's bust of Cromwell was at that time at Castle Donington in the possession of Lord Rawdon, and it was the carving of this bust which "had secured the artist an honourable employment under his present Majesty."

Wilton was one of the original foundation-members of the Royal Academy and exhibited there from 1769 until 1783. Finding that the taste for ornamental and monumental sculpture was declining, and also that his extravagant mode of living had caused him to exceed his income, he decided in 1786 to sell his premises and property by public auction and to retire into private life. In June, 1793, he was declared a bankrupt (*Universal Magazine*, 1793, Vol. I, page 472), but seems to have paid off his creditors very quickly. Three years previously he had been appointed Keeper of the Royal Academy and held the post until his death, which took place on 25 November, 1803. He was buried at Wanstead.

Allan Cunningham gives the following picture of Wilton: "Tall, portly and personable, a perfect gentleman in manners, a warm friend and an agreeable companion. He went always dressed in the extremity of fashion, with a gold-headed cane and a bag-wig plentifully be-powdered" (*Lives of the Painters*, 1830, Vol. III, page 80). Redgrave, in his *Dictionary of Artists*, considers the sculptor's "works are skilfully executed and coldly correct— sometimes graceful. His groups are crowded in their composition, yet not without grandeur of conception."

At a sale "of a man of fashion" held on 2 June, 1779, by Mr. Christie, the following lots by Wilton were sold; busts of Laocoon, Homer, Caracalla, Faustine, Sir Isaac Newton, Lepidus, Alexander, Julius Caesar, and a statue of Hermaphroditus. At the sale of the property of "a gentleman brought from his seat in Norfolk" on 16 February, 1781, held by Mr. Christie, one of the lots was "a bust of Alexander, very capital, from the antique, executed at Rome from the original by Wilton" (Archives, Messrs. Christie). At the Earl of Bessborough's sale of the contents of his house at Roehampton, held by Mr. Christie on 7 April, 1801, Wilton's statues of Apollo and Venus fetched £130 and £105 respectively. (Archives, Messrs. Christie).

(Authorities cited in text.)

BUSTS

1749	Chatham	National Portrait Gallery, Edinburgh (replica Peper Harrow, Surrey)
1758	Laocoon	Victoria and Albert Museum
1758	Thomas Sydenham	Royal College of Physicians (£73)
1758	Bearded Immortal	Formerly Wentworth Woodhouse
c. 1760	Wolfe	Dalmeny, Scotland
1761	Roubiliac	Exhibited Society of Artists

PLATE XXXI

—WESTON
Part of the monument of Jonathan and Elizabeth Ivie, 1717, St. Petrock's Church, Exeter.

PLATE XXXII

RICHARD WESTMACOTT THE ELDER
James Dutton, 1791, Sherborne, Gloucestershire.

1762	Sir Isaac Newton	Bodleian Library, Oxford
1767	Lord Camden	Exhibited Society of Artists
1767	Sir Robert Long	Draycote Cerne Church, Wilts.
1771	Alfred the Great	For Lord Radnor (£51 18s.), who presented it to University College, Oxford
1772?	Lord Chesterfield	British Museum
n.d.	4th Earl of Bristol	Ickworth Park, Suffolk

MONUMENTS

1755	Antony, Cornwall	Admiral Graves
1756	Buntingford, Herts	Pyke Crouch
1757	Westminster Abbey	Admiral Temple West
1761	Westminster Abbey	Stephen Hales
1761	Westminster Abbey	Admiral Holmes
1761	Winchester (Cathedral)	Bishop Hoadly (*Royal Magazine*, 1763, page 244)
1762	Harpham, Yorks	Charlotte St. Quentin
1763	Chelsea Old Church (churchyard)	Sir Hans Sloane
1764	Okeover, Derby	Mary Okeover
1764	Westminster Abbey	Pulteney, Earl of Bath
1768	Hale, Hants	Henry Archer
1769	Addington, Surrey	Grace Trecothick
1769	Chenies, Bucks	Duke of Bedford
1769	Dartrey, Co. Monaghan	Lady Anne Dawson
1771	Westminster Abbey	Earl and Countess of Mountrath (designed by Sir William Chambers)
1771?	Bicester, Oxon	Sir Edward and Lady Turner
1772	Westminster Abbey	General Wolfe
1772	Crowan, Cornwall	Sir John St. Aubyn
1774	Hillington, Norfolk	William Browne
1774	Worcester (Cathedral)	Sir Thomas Street
1777	Horsford, Norfolk	Jane Day
1778	Methley, Yorks	Earl of Mexborough (life-size figure)
1778	Lambourne, Essex	John Lockwood
c. 1780	West Harling, Norfolk	Richard Gipps
1780	Jamaica (Cathedral)	Sir Basil Keith
1780	Westminster Abbey	Sir James Denham
1781	Chelsea Old Church	The Misses Wilton (daughters of the sculptor)
1782	Linton, Cambs	Elizabeth Bacon
1783	Wroxton, Oxon	The Three Wives of the 1st Earl of Guilford
1786	Great Brickhill, Bucks	Rev. Philip Barton
1788	Brenchley, Kent	Stephen Hooker
1795	Westminster Abbey	Sir Archibald Campbell

WINBURY, —
fl. 1690–1710

He either carved the statue of Charles I at Worcester or re-cut an earlier one, the entries in the City Archives being not quite clear on this point. In 1690 there is an order that Mr. Alderman Haines "doe agree with Winbury the stone-cutter for the takinge downe of the King's picture and setting it up againe," while in the audit of accounts for that year there is a payment of £5 to Winbury for "work done to and setting up the King's picture" In 1710 he received a further payment for putting a new hand on the statue (Worcester City Archives).

WINCHESTER, WILLIAM
b. c. 1715, *d.* 1772

Son of Henry Winchester of Wimbledon, he was apprenticed to Thomas Dunn (q.v.) in 1729 and became free in 1739. According to the Court Book of the Masons' Company, he died in 1772.

Winchester signs a large monument to James Adams, 1765, in the Churchyard of Stanford-le-Hope in Essex, a work illustrated in Palin's *Stifford and Its Neighbourhood* (1872).

WINDOVER, or WENDOVER, J., of Andover
fl. 1810–1830

He signs a large wall-tablet with fluted pilasters supporting a plain pediment to John Carter, 1810, at Kingsclere, Berkshire, and a smaller one to the Rev. John Blair, 1830, at Whitchurch, Hampshire. He was later assisted by his son, James Wendover the Younger.

WINFIELD, JAMES, of Leicester
fl. 1790–1800

Winfield was one of the best of the Leicestershire slate-workers and his productions are frequently found in that county. They include signed tablets to Lucretia King, 1795, at Barrow-on-Soar, and to Langley Bankes, 1796, at Loughborough.

WING, JOHN, of Bedford
b. 1756, *d.* 1826

He is presumably the son of the "Mr. Wing, architect of Leicester," who died at Bedford in 1794 (*Gentleman's Magazine*, 1794, Part II, page 675). He was employed as a mason during the rebuilding of Woburn Abbey, 1789–1792, receiving nearly £5,000 for masonry and carved stonework and also erected the main entrance-lodge and the stables (Bedford Archives).

Wing's tablets are architectural and occasionally have well-carved details carried out in coloured marbles. Examples in Bedfordshire include those commemorating Henry Palmer, 1786, at Northill; Robert Battisson, 1788, and the Rev. John Crowe, 1794, both in Bedford Parish Church; George Edwards, 1797, and Richard Raynsford, 1800, both at Henlow; Martha Monoux, 1803, at Sandy; and William Wright, 1807, at Aspley Guise. The signed tablet to Mrs. Bull (d. 1794), at Godmanchester, Hunts, is also his work.

The younger Wing also designed and built Bedford bridge between 1811 and 1813.

WINSER, EDWARD,
of Newton Abbot
fl. 1810–1817

He signs two tablets at Townstal, Devon, one to the Banfill family, 1810, and the other to William Banfill, 1817.

WIRMADGE, —, of Leicester

He was a worker in slate, and signs a slab, with a well-carved figure of "Hope" at the top, to Henry Payne, 1786, at Market Bosworth, Leicestershire.

WISE, THOMAS, the Elder
d. 1686

He was admitted to the freedom of the Masons' Company by redemption in 1672 and became Master in 1681. He also held the post of Master Mason to the Crown. In 1664 he was working at Greenwich with Stephen Switzer (q.v.). In 1681 he was engaged at the Tower of London, where he received £13 for a white-marble chimney-piece for Lord Alington's apartment (P.R.O., Works 5/36).

For "King Charles's new building" at White-hall, Wise made marble chimney-pieces in 1682 (P.R.O., Works 5/37) and, in the following year, one of black-and-yellow marble for the "eating-room." In 1684 he supplied another of white marble for the Duke of Grafton's lodging in the Palace (P.R.O., Works 5/38), and in 1685 he made the arch on the great staircase, carving the keystone and a wreath of laurel above the oval window. He was working at Whitehall up till the time of his death, for the last payments in 1686 (including that for the "rance-marble" chimney-piece for the "Duchess Mazarin's lodging") are made to his executors (P.R.O., Works 5/54).

Wise also worked under Wren during the building of the City churches, receiving payments for carved stonework which included four Ionic capitals for St. Michael's, Wood Street; the four urns at the corners of the steeple of St. Nicholas Cole Abbey; and two palm branches for St. Benet Grace (Bodleian, Rawlinson, 387). He was also employed at St. Paul's, and his various contracts for work in the Cathedral (including one for carving the great capitals) are given in the *Wren Society's Publications*, Vol. XVI. In 1685 he was paid £50 for the "Neece" for the statue of Charles II on Southwark Town Hall. (Rentals of the Bridge House, Corporation of London Record Office.)

WISE, THOMAS, the Younger
fl. 1670–1706

He was the son of Thomas Wise the Elder (q.v.) and did a great deal of work as a mason-contractor at St. Paul's with his partner, T. Hill (q.v.). Between them they received £24,509, while the carved stonework executed by Wise included scrolls, festoons, capitals at £15 a face, "window scrowles" at £6 each, and the keystone of the great window on the inside of the portico. Shields carved by him for the Cathedral are illustrated in the *Wren Society's Publications*, Vol. XV, Plate 64.

Wise, who was Master of the Mason's Company in 1695, was also a "merchant of Portland stone," and in this capacity supplied stone for the new buildings at Hampton Court.

(Various references, *Wren Society's Publications*.)

WISE, WILLIAM
fl. 1673–1703

He was the second son of Thomas Wise the Elder (q.v.) and was apprenticed to his father in 1673, becoming free in 1680. He was Renter Warden of the Masons' Company in 1695, Upper Warden in 1696 and Master in 1703.

In 1683 he and his partner, Samuel Fulkes (q.v.), were working as masons at Winchester Palace (*Wren Society*, Vol. VII, page 36).

WITHENBURY, JAMES,
of Worcester

In A. Tindal Hart's *Life of Lloyd, Bishop of Worcester*, is printed (page 258) the contract between the bishop's widow and Withenbury for a monument to her husband. The monument was to be of marble, to cost £140, to be finished by 1 August, 1718, to be erected in Fladbury Church, Worcs, and to consist of a half figure of the bishop in an architectural setting. At the restoration in 1865 of Fladbury Church the monument was unfortunately dismembered.

WITHERS, ROBERT

He signs a wall-tablet, with a draped urn in front of a pyramid, to William Davison, 1777, at Milverton, Somerset.

WOLFE, or WOOLFE, BARTHOLOMEW
b. c. 1654, *d.* 1720

He was the son of Bartholomew Woolfe, of Bromley, Kent, yeoman, and was apprenticed to John Palmer in 1668, becoming free in 1675. He later became one of the leading City masons and worked for several of the City Companies, including the Fishmongers.

Wolfe died in 1720, for his executors received the payment for work done at the Fishmongers' Hall during the latter part of that year (Prime Warden's Accounts).

WOOD, GEORGE, of Gloucester
fl. 1785–1828

His best work is the monument to Charles George, 1807, at Rodmorton, Gloucestershire, which has a pretty relief of a mourning widow standing by an urn, while her little daughter clutches at her skirt. Other signed works by him in the county include those to John de la Bere, 1785, and Alexander Jaffray, 1818, both in Cheltenham Parish Church; Dr. John Bosworth, 1785, at Tortworth; John Smyth, 1809, in Gloucester Cathedral; Edward Rogers, 1810, at Dowdeswell; Martha Taylor, 1817, at Charlton Kings; Capel Molyneux, 1821, at Prestbury; and Lady Robert Somerset, 1823, and the Duchess of Beaufort, 1828, both at Badminton. At Stanton, Worcestershire, is his monument to Reginald Wynniatt, 1819.

Wood, who also had a yard at Cheltenham, became a bankrupt in 1820 (*European Magazine*, 1820, page 561).

WOOD, H.

Wood, who was presumably a Yorkshire craftsman, signs a large tombstone in the churchyard of Wentworth, Yorkshire. This has a well-cut angel's head at the top and commemorates Hannah Jennet, 1769, "late Housekeeper to the Most Hon. the Marquis of Rockingham."

WOOD, HENRY, of Bristol
fl. 1801–1830

He is described as "architect and statuary of London" in 1801, when he bought the yard and business of Thomas Paty, of Bristol (q.v.), and may presumably be a son of Henry Wood the Elder (q.v.) of London.

Wood's monuments and tablets, which are quite pleasant, must have been much admired in his day, for they are not only found all over England, but also in Ireland and the West Indies. The best commemorates Charles Tottenham (*d.* 1795), at New Ross, Co. Wexford, and has a relief showing three sons mourning by a medallion portrait of their father.

Other signed monumental works by Wood include those to Catherine Smith, 1801, and M. J. Ward, 1829, both in Barbados Cathedral; William Clarkson, 1802, at Alvington, Monmouth; Mrs. Tottenham, 1806, at New Ross, Co. Wexford; the Rev. Thomas Pentycross, 1808, at Wallingford, Berks; Thomas Browne, 1811, at Church Stoke, Salop; Thomas Taylor, 1815, at Marlow, Bucks; Clement Tudway, 1815, in St. Cuthbert's, Wells; Francis Smith, 1815, at Shepton Mallet, Somerset; Frances and Lucy Ireland, 1816, in Christ Church, Bristol; Arabella Schaw, 1819, in St. Mary Redcliffe, Bristol; Richard Turville, 1820, at Ewenny, Glamorgan; Richard Goodlad, 1821, at Droxford, Hants; Sir Hugh Smyth, Long Ashton, Somerset; and Gertrude Allen, 1825, at Jeffreston, Pembroke.

Wood's son, Henry Wood the Younger, signs tablets to General Kinsey, 1837, at Abergavenny, Monmouth; Lant Carpenter (with a medallion portrait), 1840, in Lewins Mead Chapel, Bristol; and S. M. Alleyne, 1847, in St. Thomas's, Barbados.

WOOD, HENRY, the Elder, of London
fl. 1771–1801

Wood worked under Henry Holland, the architect, at Lord Clive's house at Claremont, 1771–1772, carving four Corinthian capitals for the columns and six for the pilasters. He also made six lions' heads in the frieze on the portico, as well as "two thermes" and three masks of satyrs (Notebook of Henry Holland, Soane Museum). In 1775 he was employed by Lord Craven at Benham, where he carved six Ionic capitals for the pilasters on the front of the house.

Between 1783 and 1789 Wood was at Carlton House, supplying a chimney-piece for the bow room costing £80, and another, "very highly finished" for the lower eating-room at £42 10s. He was also paid £55 for "a rich stove in veined marble for the lower octagon" and also for the carved stonework of the riding-house. The total sum he received during this period amounted to £1,050 (P.R.O., H.O.73/24).

In 1789 he went to Woburn Abbey, where he worked for two years. In 1790 he built the balustrade to the south front of the house, and in 1791 the quadrangle, as well as an entrance-lodge. Between 1790 and 1792 he received nearly £1,600 for stone and wood-carving and other work at Woburn. In 1796 he was paid £34 2s. by the Duke of Bridgewater for two French marble chimney-pieces for Cleveland House, London (Archives, Duke of Bedford and Lord Brownlow).

In 1801 he received £423 for marble chimney-pieces for the Mote, which was then being built near Maidstone for Lord Romney (Romney Archives, Maidstone Museum).

WOOD, JOSEPH

He signs a large architectural wall-tablet, about 8 ft. high, to Catherine Hornby, 1772, at Blyth, Notts. The work is in stone and marble with Doric pilasters supporting a plain pediment surmounted by an urn, while flaming lamps stand to left and right.

WOOD, LANCELOT EDWARD, of Chelsea
fl. 1804–1829

In 1809 he received £22 for "a veined-marble chimney-piece with reeded pilasters" and, three years later, £30 for another with a "water-leaf design," both being for Hampton Court (P.R.O., Works 5/99).

Wood's tablets are competent but dull, the best being those which commemorate Lady Caroline Leigh, 1804, at Adlestrop, Glos; Josiah Tead, 1807, Bridport, Dorset; John Manfield, 1808, at Portisham, Dorset; Levett Ibbetson, 1809, at Castor, Northants; George Gregory, 1822, at Harlaxton, Lincs; and Bishop Richard Beadon, 1824, in Wells Cathedral. His yard was in the King's Road.

WOOD, THOMAS, of Bingham
b. 1760, *d.* 1841

He carved a number of tombstones in Nottinghamshire and examples of his work can be seen at Bingham (1794), Whatton (1815) and Lowdham (1785, 1799, 1820, 1826). Wood was buried at Bingham, where his epitaph describes him as "well-known for more than half a century as an ingenious carver of tombs and gravestones."

WOOD, T., of Hereford
fl. 1787–1800

He signs tablets in Herefordshire, the best being those to Elizabeth Allen, 1787, at Kinnersley, and Thomas Lane, 1799, at Leominster. He may possibly be the Thomas Wood, son of John Wood, "citizen and mason of London," who was apprenticed to his father in 1774, but did not take out his freedom until 1796.

An "R. Wood" of Leominster signs a tablet to J. Phillips, 1826, at Dilwyn, in the same county.

WOOD, THOMAS, of Oxford
b. 1646 *d.* 1695

In 1676 Wood was paid "for the anticks and other worke about Adam Brome's Chapell" in St. Mary's, Oxford, and three years later was engaged by Richard Frogley, a carpenter of the city, to do the mason's work for the Bishop of Oxford's new palace at Cuddesdon, which Frogley had contracted to build. Besides doing the stonework of the walls, etc., Wood also supplied the door-case of Burford stone in front of the house, but he was unable to get his money, and in 1680 brought an action against his employer. In the course of the evidence it appeared that Frogley had also commissioned a stone chimney-piece from Wood for "Esquire Lenttall's" house at Hasely (Archives, Vice-Chancellor's Court, Misc. 1681). In the Vice-Chancellor's accounts are also payments of £87 19s. 2d. in 1675–1676 for "laying ye marbles in St. Maire's Church, which marble was the gift of Dr. Ralph Bathurst, Vice-Chancellor." In the following year there is a payment of £1 10s. 0d. for "cutting Oriel College Arms in Adam Brome's Chapell."

From 1679 until 1683 Wood was the mason responsible for building the Ashmolean, receiving nearly £2,000; in 1682 he was paid for a "stained marble" chimney-piece (Vice-Chancellor's Accounts), and in 1693 received £10 for setting up "at Water Eaton for the Lord Lovelace a white-marble chimney-piece" (British Museum, Ad. MS. 22,188).

In 1671 he carved the tablet commemorating Mr. John Myddelton for the cloisters of Brasenose College (Chirk Castle Archives), and in 1680 made the monument erected to F. Junius in St. George's Chapel, Windsor, at the charge of the University (Vice-Chancellor's Accounts, 1680).

Wood was described as "aged twenty-two" and "of St. Peter's in the East, Oxford, Sculptor," when, in 1668, he took out a licence to marry Alice Beach, of Patchall, Herefordshire, at St. Margaret's, Westminster.

(Wood's *Life and Times*, Vol. IV.)

WOOD, THOMAS, of London
b. c. 1760

He was the son of John Wood, mason, "of

Rose Street, St. Luke's, Old Street," who had become free by redemption in 1770. Young Wood was bound apprentice to his father in 1774 and later went into partnership with John Gilliam (q.v.). From 1793 onwards they did a great deal of masonry work at Somerset House, receiving a total payment of £1,797 for that year alone, a period when they were also employed at the Rolls House (P.R.O., Works 5/82).

From 1808–1810 Wood (now on his own) was employed at Whitehall Chapel, where he received £1,695 for work which included "pedestalls, ballustrades, and the coping to the north end of the Chapel." In 1808 he made a marble chimney-piece for the Palace of Westminster, and from 1812 until 1815 worked under James Wyatt in the same building, executing a small amount of carved stonework (P.R.O., A.O. 435/2499).

WOODALL, C., of Carlisle

He signs a tablet with a portrait relief to William Hildebrand, 1832, in Carlisle Cathedral.

WOODALL, JOHN
b. ca. 1670, *d.* 1735

Woodall was assistant to Benjamin Jackson (q.v.) during the building of Drayton Hall, Northamptonshire, and signs receipts for payments and probably himself was responsible for some of the carved work (Archives, Colonel Stopford-Sackville).

Woodall worked as a mason at several of the Royal Palaces and in 1715 carved a marble chimney-piece for the Countess of Schulemberg's apartment at St. James's Palace (P.R.O., A.O.1, 3448/149). He was also the mason responsible for the repairs to Hicks Hall (the Middlesex Sessions House) from 1723 until 1728 (Parliamentary Report, 1731).

In the Earl of Westmoreland's archives there is a letter from John Fane, of Mereworth, written in 1730 to Lord Westmoreland about a matter to which they had been giving some thought, namely, a sculptor for the monument to Lady Westmoreland. "It is but just come into my head," he says, "and I will send by the next post to Mr. Woodall my mason, the same draught and order him to make an estimate of it."

"Mr. Woodall Master-Mason to George I" who died on 4 September, 1735 and was buried at Kingston-on-Thames. (*Gentleman's Magazine*, 1735, page 559).

WOODINGTON, WILLIAM FREDERICK
b. 1806, *d.* 1893

He was born on 10 February, 1806, at Sutton Coldfield, in Warwickshire, but was brought to London at an early age and about 1820 was apprenticed to R. W. Sievier (q.v.), who was then working as an engraver. In the same year he gained a Silver Medal from the Society of Arts, but in 1823 decided to follow his master in abandoning engraving in favour of sculpture.

In his new profession Woodington apparently worked for Croggan (q.v.), who succeeded Coade (q.v.) as a manufacturer of artificial stone. In 1951 the latter's trade-card and a sheet of paper inscribed "Mr. Woodington, sculptor, 24 May, 1837, Princess Victoria's birthday," were found in a bottle inside the artificial stone lion which for many years had stood on top of a brewery on the South Bank, but which was taken down when the building was demolished to make way for the Festival Hall (*The Times*, 9 March, 1951).

In 1844 Woodington exhibited "The Deluge" and "Milton Dictating to his Daughters" at Westminster Hall. The *Literary Gazette* of that year (page 466) considered them "able groups, designed with much skill and beautifully executed. The mother and son in the first are finely imagined, and there is a calm earnestness in Milton and a sweet simplicity in the daughters which are extremely pleasing." Four years later the sculptor made statues of William, Earl of Arundel, and Hubert, Earl of Kent, for the House of Lords, while in 1850 came the work for which he is best known—the great bronze relief of the Battle of the Nile at the base of the Nelson Column in Trafalgar Square.

In 1846 he had executed a bust of George III, based on a work by John Bacon, R.A. (q.v.), for the Upper School at Eton, while ten years later he made a colossal one of Sir Joseph Paxton for the Crystal Palace and a statue of James Steel for Carlisle. His bust of Patrick Macdowell, R.A., dated 1862, is now at Burlington House.

The second premium of £500 for the Wellington memorial was won by Woodington, and in 1861 he carved the reliefs for the Consistory Chapel in St. Paul's, where the monument (executed by Alfred Stevens) was placed. In 1867 he made statues of Columbus, Galileo, Drake, Cook, Raleigh and Mercator for the new Liverpool Exchange, and was later responsible for the sculpture in the pediment, which represented "Wisdom sending forth her Messengers to the Nations of the Earth." In 1870 he was chosen to execute statues of Plato, Archimedes and Justinian for the Civil Service Commission Buildings in Burlington Gardens.

Woodington also worked as a painter as well as a sculptor, and showed a number of pictures at the Royal Academy. In 1851 he was appointed Curator of the School of Sculpture, and in 1876 became an Associate of the Academy. He exhibited there, 1825–1882, and at the British Institution, 1827–1832. He died on 24 December, 1893, and was buried in Norwood Cemetery.

(*Art Journal*, 1894, page 60; various references *Builder* and *Art Journal*.)

WOODLEY, —, of Torquay
fl. 1840–1866

He not only made monuments in his yard at St. Mary Church, near Torquay, but also carried on a flourishing business in local marbles, manufacturing "columns, vases, chimney-pieces and a variety of other ornamental articles" (*Art Journal*, 1856, page 4).

Woodley signs a number of minor monuments and tablets, the most important commemorating Mary Bloxsome, 1840, at Dursley, Gloucestershire. This has a relief of a woman leaning on a broken column, the Corinthian capital of which lies at her feet.

WOODMAN, WILLIAM, the Elder
b. c. 1654, *d.* 1731 (?)

Woodman was first apprenticed to Francis Devonshire, citizen and haberdasher, in 1668, but later decided to be a mason and was turned over to William Matthews, becoming free in 1678. In 1687 he built the "resurrection gate" of St. Giles-in-the-Fields, the remarkable wooden carving being executed by an unknown artist named Love (*Notes and Queries*, Third Series, Vol. V, page 67). In 1689 he became an Assistant in the Masons' Company and was afterwards Renter Warden in 1703 and Master in 1708.

In 1704 Woodman put the finishing touches to the fine monument to the 4th Earl of Leicester in Penshurst Church, Kent, which had been left incomplete at the death of William Stanton (q.v.). He was also employed at the Dowager Lady Leicester's house in London, where he made a marble cistern (Sidney Archives). In 1705 he and his son, William Woodman the Younger, built a house for Lord Ashburnham at Brockborough Park (Ashburnham Archives).

As a monumental statuary, Woodman did extremely important work, his masterpiece being the signed monument to Lord and Lady Newhaven, 1728, at Drayton Beauchamp, Bucks. Here Lord Newhaven, in his Peer's robes, reclines on a sarcophagus, while his wife (a superbly carved figure) sits for ever at his feet, gazing at her husband. This remarkable work in its little-visited church is one of the most outstanding monuments in England, and deserves to be better known and appreciated.

Woodman also signs monuments to Edward Mansell (*d.* 1681) and Monck, Bishop of Hereford (*d.* 1661, monument erected 1723), both in Westminster Abbey; and to John Nicholas, 1711, in Winchester Cathedral. Woodman's cartouche tablet to Elizabeth Calnent, 1715, is in Maidstone Parish Church, Kent.

In the Court Book of the Masons' Company there is a curious minute made in 1719 which desires Woodman to visit a certain Mr. Robinson "who alleges to have discovered an art to glaze cornerstones for chimneys and prevail with him if he can to produce a specimen to the Company of one of these stones 4 ft. long, and then this Court will further consider of the proposition by him made to the Company."

WOODMAN, WILLIAM, the Younger
fl. 1713–1741

He was the son of William Woodman the Elder (q.v.) and carried on the family business after the death of his father. He signs the monument with a life-size standing figure of Daniel Dobson (*d.* 1741), at Cheshunt, Herts. In 1713 he and his father made the marble pavement for the chancel of Whitchurch Church, Salop, but it was not till many years later that Woodman the Younger sent in his account for £46; writing to Alexander Duncombe in October, 1733, he explained that "being under an extream fitt of the Gout, I could not go to render the bill and was forc'd to send one of my Dautrs who this day recd the money" (Bridgewater Archives).

WOODRUFF, FRANCIS
b. c. 1657

Son of John Woodruff, citizen and mason, he was apprenticed to his father in 1671, but on the latter's death was turned over to William Hammond and became free in 1679. The younger Woodruff must have died after 1693, for in that year he received £31 for carving work at Brewers' Hall (Archives, Brewers' Company).

In the account-book of Sir Charles Kemeys, Bart. (in the possession of the writer), is a payment to Francis Woodruff for a chimney-piece for an unnamed house. He also signs an architectural monument to Edward Cotton, 1682, at Wokingham, Berks.

There are several other masons and carvers of this name, including Edward Woodruff of Oxford and John Woodruff of Windsor. The former was to be admitted a Freeman of Oxford in 1667 without fine if he could "in a workmanlike manner cutt or carve the King's Arms or such other signes for the use of the Citty as the Mayor or his brethren shall direct" (Oxford Council Acts, 1666–1701, Oxford Historical Society, page 6), while the latter was paid £23 by Lord Weymouth for work at his house in Old Windsor (Longleat Archives). John Woodruff died in 1728 and was buried in Windsor Parish Church, the family business being carried on by his son, John. There is a letter dated 1743 to the younger Woodruff from Thomas Gayfere the Younger (q.v.) reminding him that he owes Andrews Jelfe (Gayfere's master) money. "My master imagines," he writes, "that it may have slipt your memory, so desires you would order ye payment and send him word by next post" (British Museum, Ad. MS. 27, 587).

WOODS, T., of Titchfield

He signs a large wall-tablet to G. A. Thomas, 1804, at Wickham, Hants.

WOODWARD, —, of Bakewell

He signs a large tablet at Wortley, Yorks, to Benjamin Newton, 1818.

WOODWARD, EDWARD, of Chipping Campden
b. c. 1697, *d.* 1766

His father was Thomas Woodward of Chipping Campden, who built the tower of Blockley Church in 1728 (*Gentleman's Magazine*, 1793, page 297) and died in 1748 at the age of seventy-six.

Edward Woodward, who was working at Alscot Park, Gloucestershire, from 1751 until 1765 (West Archives), also signs a number of monuments and tablets, including those to Edward Croft (*d.* 1711) at Blockley, Glos; John Graves, 1719, at Mickleton, Glos; Robert Martin, 1720, at Pebworth, Glos; and John Brandis, 1724, at Alcester, Warwick. They are usually architectural works, with standing cherubs, etc., although the one commemorating his grandfather, Thomas Woodward (*d.* 1716), at Mickleton, is a cartouche tablet.

Edward Woodward died in 1766 and was buried in the churchyard of Chipping Campden under a tomb which he had built himself. His son Richard (*fl.* 1723–1755) built St. Anne's Church, Bewdley, in 1745, while another son, Edward, carried on the family business, but became a bankrupt in 1777 (*London Magazine*, 1777, page 51).

A John Woodward was paid for cutting stone for the University Schools, Cambridge, in 1728. Eight years previously he executed the carved woodwork for the "Dome Room," receiving £4 "for two pillaster cappatalls, very large, after the Corinthian order" and £24 for six similar double pilasters (Vice-Chancellor's Accounts).

(H. M. Colvin, *Architectural Review*, 1948.)

WOOLES, WILLIAM
b. 1804, *d.* 1835

He was the son of William Wooles, a surveyor in Bristol, and as a boy came to London, where he entered the studio of E. H. Baily (q.v.). In 1827 he won a Gold Medal from the Society of Arts for an original model of a historical group, and two years later joined the Royal Academy Schools, gaining Silver Medals in 1830 and 1833.

Wooles exhibited at the Suffolk Street Galleries in 1832 and at the Academy, 1830–1833, showing busts and medallic portraits. He died on 4 May, 1835.

(*Gentleman's Magazine*, 1835, Part I, page 667.)

WOOLNER, THOMAS, R.A.
b. 1825, *d.* 1892

Woolner was born at Hadleigh, in Suffolk, on 17 December, 1825, and from an early age showed a decided talent for art. He first went to school in Ipswich, but his father later received an appointment in the Post Office and the family then moved to London, where the boy was sent to study under Behnes the painter. The arrangement was soon terminated by the latter's death, but young Woolner had made so good an impression that William Behnes the sculptor (q.v.), brother of his late master, offered to take him into his studio without a premium, only stipulating that when he was sufficiently advanced he should work for a short time without wages, and afterwards, during his term, for rather less than the ordinary rate of pay.

When four years had elapsed it was on Behnes's suggestion that Woolner joined the Royal Academy Schools in 1842, though he still continued to carve for his master. In 1843 he sent a group entitled "Eleanor Sucking Poison from Prince Edward's Wounds" to the Academy, and in the following year exhibited a group of "The Death of Boadicea" at Westminster Hall. This work was "produced under extraordinary disadvantages," according to the *Literary Gazette* (1844, page 483), which accepted it "as an earnest of better things." In 1845 Woolner won the Silver Medal from the Society of Arts for a bas-relief entitled "Affection." Two years later he met Rossetti and through him became one of the Pre-Raphaelite Brotherhood, which he joined as sculptor-member.

In 1848 Woolner exhibited "Titania and the Indian Boy" at the British Institution, but its reception did not encourage him to continue with idealistic sculpture and he turned instead to making medallion portraits. In 1850 he modelled one of Mrs. Coventry Patmore, wife of the poet. This was apparently a great success, for Patmore wrote in a letter: "The more I look at your medallion of my wife, the more I admire it, and the more I feel the great obligation you have put me under in doing it." In the following year Woolner made a medallion of Carlyle and, having already carved a medallion of Wordsworth, entered for the competition held to choose the sculptor for the poet's memorial. This he fully expected to win, but his model was rejected and this rebuff, coupled with an unfortunate love-affair, made him decide that there was no future in sculpture and that he must seek his fortune elsewhere. In 1852 he set sail from Gravesend, bound for the Australian goldfields, and among the Pre-Raphaelites who went to see him off was Ford Madox-Brown, whose noble picture "The Last of England" was inspired by seeing the emigrants on the ship.

Woolner, however, soon discovered that it was not easy to make money in the goldfields and started to work as a sculptor in Australia. He opened a studio in Melbourne and made a number of medallions of notabilities of the time, including the Governor-General, Sir Charles FitzRoy.

In 1854 he returned to England, where his fellow Pre-Raphaelites were able to assist him, for their work was now accepted in artistic circles. The turning-point in his career came with his bust of Tennyson and the portrait-medallion of Carlyle, both executed in the year following his return, while in 1856 he made an equally popular medallion of Browning. This is now in the Birmingham Art Gallery, while a plaster-cast of the Carlyle medallion is in the National Portrait Gallery. In 1858 Woolner modelled four figures in alto-relievo for the pulpit of Llandaff Cathedral, and later came his bust of Cardinal Newman and the Gladstone monument for the Bodleian, with three fine bas-reliefs from the Iliad inserted into the base of the pedestal.

In 1871 he exhibited a bust of Dickens at the Royal Academy, based on the death-mask he had taken at Gadshill, and in the same year he made four bas-reliefs of "The Acts of Mercy" for the fountain in memory of Mrs. George Moore, erected at Wigton. In 1872 he executed the memorial to Sir John Simeon for Newport, Isle of Wight, and in 1880 he made a medallion of Joseph Chamberlain for the fountain outside Birmingham City Hall. For Birmingham also he made a statue of George Dawson, but this was later taken down and is now housed in the City Library.

Woolner exhibited at the Royal Academy, 1843–1893. He was elected an Associate of the Academy in 1871 and a full member three years later, when he deposited as his Diploma work a relief entitled "Achilles and Pallas Shouting From the Trenches." In 1877 he was appointed Professor of Sculpture on the death of Weekes (q.v.), but never lectured, and resigned in 1879. His last work was "The Housemaid," a life-size figure of a servant-girl wringing out the cloth with which she washes the doorstep. After his death this was cast in bronze and exhibited at the Academy in 1893.

Woolner died on 7 October, 1892, and was buried in Hendon churchyard. According to his obituary in *The Times* "his workmanship was as thorough as his study, his time and labour were freely expended in the pursuit of perfection, without regard to the pecuniary considerations that too often take precedence of all else. . . . In life, as in art, he was the uncompromising foe of sham, of claptrap and of superficiality."

(Amy Woolner's *Thomas Woolner, Life and Letters; Art Journal*, 1894).

STATUES

1857	Lord Bacon	University Museum, Oxford
1862	Emma and Arthur Fairbairn	Tunbridge Wells Cemetery
1864	Prince Consort	University Museum, Oxford
1865	John Godley	New Zealand
1866	Lord Macaulay	Trinity College Chapel, Cambridge
1867	Mother and Child	For Sir Walter Trevelyan
1867	Thirteen statues	Manchester Assize Court
1868	William III	For Palace of Westminster (now Sessions House, Old Bailey)
1869	David Sassoon	Bombay
1872	Sir Bartle Frere	Bombay
1873	Dr. Whewell	Trinity College Chapel, Cambridge
1875	Bluecoat Boy Group	Christ's Hospital, Horsham
1875	Lord Lawrence	Calcutta
1876	Lord Palmerston	Parliament Square
1876	Sir Cowasjee Readimoney	Bombay
1877	Edwin Field	Law Courts, London
1878	Sir Thomas White	For Merchant Taylors Company
1879	J. S. Mill	Thames Embankment
1879	Captain Cook	Sydney, Australia
1880	Lord Chief Justice Whiteside	For Four Courts, Dublin
1883	Queen Victoria	Birmingham

| 1887 | Sir Stamford Raffles | Singapore |
| 1888 | Bishop Fraser | Manchester |

BUSTS

1857	Lord Tennyson	Trinity College, Cambridge
1859	Sir William Hooker	For Linnean Society (plaster-cast National Portrait Gallery)
1860	Professor Sedgwick	Trinity College, Cambridge
1861	Rev. F. D. Maurice	Westminster Abbey
1861	Julius Hare	Trinity College, Cambridge
1861	J. S. Henslow	Botany School, Cambridge
1865	Richard Cobden	Westminster Abbey (replica Brighton Art Gallery)
1865	John Kemble	Trinity College, Cambridge
1866	Cardinal Newman	Keble College, Oxford
1867	Henry Christy	British Museum
1867	Captain Fowke	Exhibited Universal Exhibition, Paris
1868	Gladstone	Bodleian Library, Oxford
1868	Sir Henry Frere	National Portrait Gallery (plaster-cast)
1868	Dr. William Hey	Leeds Infirmary
1868	Thomas Carlyle	For Louisa, Lady Ashburton
1869	Edward Wilson	Public Library, Melbourne
c. 1870	J. F. Pollock	Inner Temple
1873	John Keble	Westminster Abbey
1873	Rev. F. D. Maurice	Senate House, Cambridge
1873	Dr. Henry Jones	Royal Institution
1874	John Hunter	Leicester Square
1875	Charles Kingsley	National Portrait Gallery (plaster-cast)
1875	T. K. Key	University College
1876	Lord Tennyson	Later placed in Westminster Abbey (replica Adelaide, Australia)
1876	Charles Kingsley	Westminster Abbey
1877	T. Huxley	Charing Cross Hospital
1877	E. L. Lushington	Glasgow University (replica Maidstone Museum)
1878	Sir John Quain	Middle Temple
1878	Sir John Simon	Royal College of Surgeons
1879	William George Clark	Trinity College, Cambridge
1880	Sir Redman Barry	Public Library, Melbourne
1880	Dr. Percival	Clifton College
1881	Lord Lawrence	Westminster Abbey

1882	E. M. Barry	Burlington House
1882	Gladstone	National Portrait Gallery (bronze)
1883	Gladstone	Guildhall, London
1883	Earl Russell	Sydney, Australia
1885	Earl of Derby	Sydney, Australia
1886	Professor Munro	Trinity College, Cambridge
1889	Professor Harrison	Muir College, Allahabad
1890	Sir Thomas Elder	Adelaide University, Australia
n.d.	Sir James Brooke	National Portrait Gallery
n.d.	William Spottiswoode	Royal Society
n.d.	Richard Quain	Royal College of Surgeons

MONUMENTS

1851	Grasmere, Cumberland	William Wordsworth (medallion)
1867	Wrexham, Denbigh	Mrs. Peel (d. 1863)
1867	Bockleton, Worcs	Mr. Prescott (recumbent figure)
1873	St. Paul's Cathedral	Sir Edwin Landseer
1875	Oxford (Merton College Chapel)	Bishop Patteson
1875	Ramsgate (St. Laurence's)	Mrs. Froude
1881	Kensal Green Cemetery	Hepworth Dixon
1882	St. Paul's Cathedral	Sir Edwin Landseer
1885	Cartmel, Lancs	Lord Frederick Cavendish (recumbent figure)
1887	St. Paul's Cathedral	Bishop Jackson (recumbent figure)

WRIGHT, —

In 1680 he received £120 from the Duke of Newcastle for chimney-pieces in cedar-wood, and was also paid £52 for others in marble for Nottingham Castle (Throsby's *Nottingham*, page 22).

A "William Wright," possibly the same man, was apprenticed to John Shorthose (q.v.) and became free in 1672.

WRIGHT, JOHN, of Chester
fl. 1820–1830

As a mason he was responsible for building St. Bridget's Church, Chester, in 1827, executing the work "in a superior style of elegance" (Hemingway's *Chester*, Vol. II, page 116).

His monuments are Hellenistic in design and uninspiring in workmanship, although Hemingway (op. cit., page 118), calls the tablet to the Shaw family, 1829, in St. Bridget's Church "a beautifully executed work." Other signed tablets by Wright in Chester include those to Margaret Hallon, 1824, in the Cathedral, and Simeon Leet, 1826, in St. Oswald's Church.

WYATT, EDWARD

b. 1757, *d.* 1833

Wyatt, who had a shop at 360, Oxford Street, chiefly worked as a wood-carver and gilder, and in this capacity was employed at Windsor Castle for many years, repairing cabinet work, picture-frames, etc. In 1808 he carved a "rich frize" for the Queen's Audience Chamber "emblematically describing two of the Elements, Land and Water." He was also responsible for most of the wood-carving at Carlton House.

As a worker in stone, Wyatt was paid in 1808 for "carving for the entrance-gate to St. James's Park in six panels, and nine lion-heads and a rich pattern of twenty-four flowers" (P.R.O., Works 5/98). In 1815 he was paid £200 for carving at Ashridge Park (Archives, Lord Brownlow). He died in 1833 and was buried at Merton in Surrey, a district in which he owned property.

WYATT, JAMES

b. 1808, *d.* 1893

Wyatt, who was a son of M. C. Wyatt (q.v.), exhibited a statue of Richard Coeur de Lion at Westminster Hall in 1844. The *Literary Gazette* of that year (page 482) described the work as "a bold and spirited horse and rider, the former amazingly life-like, the action of the King just and appropriate," while the *Builder* (1844, page 367) considered it to be "of considerable beauty."

At the Great Exhibition of 1851 Wyatt showed a model of a quadriga designed for a triumphal arch, and equestrian statues of Queen Victoria and the Prince Consort. *The Times* said of the Prince's horse that it was "admirably modelled and comes nearer to life than any which quite recent art has produced," and the statue was later purchased by the owner of the Coliseum, who displayed it outside the building. Wyatt also carved an equestrian statuette of Viscount Hardinge and a group of figures for the Bank of Scotland in Edinburgh.

He exhibited at the Royal Academy, 1838–1844, showing various works, including a marble statue entitled "Lila Asleep." He assisted his father on many occasions and, after the latter's death, completed the unfinished sculpture in the studio.

WYATT, MATHEW COTES

b. 1777, *d.* 1862

Son of James Wyatt (1746–1813), the architect, he was educated at Eton and obtained employment at Windsor Castle when he was quite young, owing to his father's position as Surveyor General. He decorated thirty-three ceilings in the

Castle and was also commissioned to paint twenty-eight full-length figures of various Knights of the Garter from the time of Edward I for the Robing Room; for this he received £1,173 (P.R.O., Works 5/103). Wyatt soon became a favourite of the King and Queen and received from the latter the present of a large silver tea-service.

His first public commission was for the Nelson Monument to be erected in the quadrangle of the Mansion House in Liverpool. He designed the work in 1813, although most of the modelling was carried out by Sir Richard Westmacott (q.v.) (*Builder*, 1866, page 835), and he also executed mural paintings for the Liverpool Town Hall.

In 1816 Wyatt was employed on decorative work at the Royal Mint (P.R.O., Works 5/112), and four years later he designed and carved the famous cenotaph to the Princess Charlotte in St. George's Chapel, Windsor. This work, which was paid for by subscription limited to a shilling, was over-praised at the time of its unveiling in 1824, but has been unnecessarily attacked during the present century. It is only fair to the sculptor to remember that the monument is now seen in a hard, clear light, whereas his original design provided for yellow glass in the side windows, so as to cast a golden glow over the marble. Indeed, the writer can remember the coloured glass being in position in 1912, when he was a boy at Eton.

Wyatt's next work was the statue of George III in Cockspur Street. Here the pendulum swung the other way, for the statue when erected was the target of the critics who objected, not only to the King's pigtail, but also to the fact that the work had not been the subject of an open competition, but had been given to Wyatt in 1822 by a Committee of which Lord Liverpool was Chairman. Today the statue and the pigtail are regarded with affection by all Londoners and it was one of the two statues removed to the country for safety during the Second World War.

Wyatt's original design, which took him twelve months of "intense exertion" to create, consisted of the King standing in a quadriga accompanied by "Fame" and "Victory," while "Faction," represented by a hydra-headed monster, "is levelled in the dust" (*Gentleman's Magazine*, 1822, Part I, which also gives a Plate). As nothing like enough money was forthcoming for this grandiose scheme, the Committee luckily decided to be content with an equestrian statue, but owing to various delays it was not until 1836 that it was ready to be unveiled.

The site chosen in the first instance was Waterloo Place, but it was then discovered that this meant that the Duke of York on his column would be turning his back on his royal father. A site in Cockspur Street was next decided upon, but on the eve of the statue's erection the Chairman of the Committee (now Lord Kenyon) put a mysterious notice in the Press, stating that "a calamitous event had caused them (the Committee) extreme mortification and the artist employed severe loss and distress," adding that "the calamity had been produced by some unaccountable accident or by some malicious design, the motive for which we do not pretend to assign or ascribe to any person in particular." "Malicious design" was apparently the root of the trouble for, in a speech at the unveiling, Sir Frederick Trench said that "the mischief was *not* accidental, it *could not* be accidental; this was confirmed by the most scientific men of the country."

The statue having been repaired, a further difficulty arose when Mr. Williams of the firm of Ransom and Co., Bankers, considered "that an injury would be done to his premises" by its erection opposite his bank and made an affidavit to this effect in the Vice-Chancellor's court. It was only after "two months of tedious and expensive litigation" that the Lord Chancellor removed the injunction, and even then Mr. Williams had the last word, for he firmly shut his bank and drew all the blinds "as if for public mourning" on the day that the statue (then "a gorgeous gold colour") was unveiled by the Duke of Cumberland (*Literary Gazette*, 1836, page 507).

Wyatt did a great deal of work for the Duke of Rutland, his most important commission being for the monument to the Duchess. This was unveiled in the mausoleum at Belvoir Castle in 1828 and shows the Duchess rising from the tomb with extended arms, her face turned towards the clouds in which are seen four cherubs, representing the children who predeceased her. The group, like the one at Windsor, depends largely for its effect on the lighting, which in this case comes through stained-glass windows placed above, and on either side of, the monument and is thus "judiciously contrived so not to be obvious to the visitor" (Eller's *Belvoir Castle*, page 252). Wyatt painted the ceiling of the "Elizabeth saloon" at Belvoir and carved the marble statue of the Duchess which it contains. He also made a side-table of the same material for a punch-bowl "covered in appearance with a table-napkin, the folds of which are so accurately represented in the marble as to require a close inspection to convince the observer of the solidity of the material" (op. cit., page 315).

In 1834 Wyatt held an exhibition of his works, the *pièce de résistance* being the figure of the Newfoundland dog "Bashaw," belonging to Lord Dudley, which had taken the sculptor three years to complete and was carried out in various coloured marbles. The catalogue describes it as being "the most elaborate of a quadruped ever produced by ancient or modern art." Certainly no expense was spared; even the eye of the dog was "with great fidelity copied by the insertion of a gem in colour and lustre almost equalling nature," while the pedestal on which the figure stood was of black marble "with panels decorated with festoons of fruit, imitated in gems" (*Literary Gazette*, 1834, page 120). "Bashaw" was auctioned by Messrs. Christie at the Dudley sale of 1887, but was bought in.

A certain amount of drama was undoubtedly attached to several of Wyatt's works, and in this category must be included the group of "St. George and the Dragon," commissioned by George IV. It had been originally intended for St. George's Hall, Windsor, but only the horse and dragon had been modelled at the time of the King's death, and the group was left on the sculptor's hands incomplete. In this state it was cast in bronze and shown at the Great Exhibition, where it failed to find a purchaser. In 1865, however, James Wyatt (q.v.), the sculptor's son, sold it to the Second Duke of Wellington for £750 and it was placed in the gardens of Apsley House. In 1950 the Seventh Duke had the group brought to Stratfield Saye and erected in front of the building.

Wyatt's last work probably raised the bitterest storm of opposition and was the target of more ridicule than any other statue ever erected in London. It was a statue of Wellington designed for the top of Decimus Burton's arch at Hyde Park Corner. The idea had originally been suggested by the Court of Common Council and a Committee was formed which collected a large sum of money (stated by one paper to amount to nearly £30,000) for the purpose. Wyatt, assisted by his son James (q.v.) worked on it from 1838 until 1846, when it was cast in bronze. The result was an equestrian statue nearly 30 ft. high, showing the Duke with a huge Roman nose and with his right hand stiffly pointing a baton between his horse's ears. The huge mass was hauled into position with considerable difficulty and then the storm broke. The Press had already disapproved when a wooden model had been tried out on the arch in 1839, but now they attacked in full force. Nobody had a good word for the statue; even the mild Mr. Burton thought it would ruin his arch, while the Institute of Architects protested, questions were asked in Parliament and newspapers of every shade of political opinion were filled with angry letters. Even *Punch* joined in the fray, publishing jokes and cartoons ridiculing "The Arch Duke." Lord Morpeth, Chief Commissioner of Works, however, stood firm and in course of time the agitation lessened, although it never completely died down. In 1883 the unwanted statue was removed from the arch and banished to Caesar's Camp on the sandy, scrubby heaths of Surrey, where it now stands on a small hillock in a copse, the Duke's baton ever pointing over Copenhagen's head.

Wyatt also carved an equestrian statuette in ivory of Lord Anglesey, and two small bronze portraits of horses in high relief for George IV. His bust of the Duchess of Rutland (1826) is at Castle Howard, while one of George III, which stood for many years in the Board Room of the Treasury, has now been lent to the British Embassy at Lisbon. His undated bust of the Princess Charlotte is in private possession and is a replica of the one sent to her husband, Prince Leopold, shortly after her death.

Besides the two monuments already mentioned, Wyatt signs those to the Rt. Hon. Isaac Corry, 1813, at Newry, Co. Down; to Charlotte Pigott, 1823, at Quainton, Bucks; and to Richard Thompson, *c.* 1834, at Escrick, Yorks.

He exhibited at the Royal Academy, 1800–1814, and at the British Institution, 1808–1822. He died at his home in the Harrow Road, London, on 3 January, 1862, and was buried in Highgate Cemetery.

(Information, Miss E. Wyatt; *Art Journal*, 1862, page 86; *Country Life*, 25 May and 15 June, 1951; authorities cited in text.)

WYATT, RICHARD JAMES
b. 1795, *d.* 1850

He was born on 3 May, 1795, the son of Edward Wyatt (q.v.) and a cousin of M. C. Wyatt (q.v.). In 1809 he was apprenticed to J. C. F. Rossi (q.v.) and three years later joined the Royal Academy Schools, where he won a Silver Medal in 1815.

Wyatt first exhibited at the Academy in 1818 and shortly afterwards met Sir Thomas Lawrence who was impressed by the young sculptor's work and took an interest in him. When Canova came over to England, Lawrence introduced him to his protégé and the Italian was interested enough to promise Wyatt his protection and permission to work in his studio should he ever go to Italy.

Nothing would now satisfy Wyatt except a chance to work in Rome. He first travelled to Paris, where he studied for a short time under the distinguished Italian sculptor Bozio, and finally arrived in Rome in 1821. Here he found that Canova had not forgotten him and that there was a place for him in the studio. Wyatt became very devoted to his master and remained with him until he (Canova) died. He then worked for a short time in Thorwaldsen's studio and finally decided to set up on his own account, but was for a long time completely neglected and did not get his first commission for five years.

Once he had gained recognition, however, he soon became one of the most sought-after sculptors in Rome and his ideal statues and groups were eagerly purchased by English and foreign visitors to the city. A visitor to Rome in 1829 records in the *Literary Gazette* (page 476) that among the works in Wyatt's studio were a statue for Sir Matthew Ridley, monuments to the memory of Lady Barrington and Mrs. Buller and a group for Sir Robert Lawley. Among his patrons was the Duke of Devonshire, for whom he executed one of his best-known and most frequently illustrated works, the statue of Musidora, which is now at Chatsworth. For Lord Charles Townsend he made a statue of a "Girl at the Bath"; for Earl de Grey two figures of nymphs, still at Wrest Park, Bedfordshire; while for Miss Webb he carved "Ino and Bacchus," and for Lord Otho Fitzgerald "Cupid and Psyche." These two works fetched £199 and £106 respectively when they were sold at Christies on 2 May, 1878; and 10 May, 1884. The statue of "Glycera," now at Eaton Hall, was executed for Lord Grosvenor, and a "Bacchante and Child" for Sir Robert Peel.

Wyatt, who was an extremely hard worker, was in his studio from dawn until long after midnight, and the longer he lived in Rome, the more he adored the city. Indeed he only revisited England once, in 1841, when he was given a commission by Queen Victoria for a statue of "Penelope," now in the Royal Collection. He lived a very retired life, his only interest being his work, but all who did meet him spoke highly of his character. The end of his life was clouded by unhappiness. During the attack on Rome a shell struck his studio and burst only four feet from him. This, coupled with the fact that he was told to leave the studio, preyed on his mind, and the woman who came to clean his rooms found him one day lying on the floor in an apoplectic fit. He died a few hours later, on the morning of 28 May, 1850.

Wyatt was highly thought of by his contemporaries, and a very large number of tributes were paid to his work in the Press. His friend, John Gibson (q.v.), said that he had "acquired the purest style and his statues were highly finished. Female figures were his forte and he was clever in composition and the harmony of lines. No sculptor in England has produced female statues to be compared to those by Wyatt" (Eastlake's *Life of Gibson*, page 130). A writer in the *Gentleman's Magazine* (1850, page 99) considered that he had "surpassed all living artists in representing the pure and delicate beauty of the female form."

Wyatt carved a few busts, including those of Sir Thomas and Lady Cullum, now in the Public Library at Bury St. Edmunds, and one of George Lushington, a cast of which is at Raby Castle, Durham. His busts of Lady Sydney and Lord Anglesey were exhibited at the Royal Academy.

As a monumental sculptor, he was responsible for a fine relief to Mrs. Buller, 1831, in Poltimore Church, Devon; an even finer one to Ellen Legh, 1831, at Winwick, Lancs; and a third, erected by Mrs. Cook, widow of the circumnavigator, to members of her family in Merton Church, Surrey, in 1832. He also signs the classical monument to Elizabeth Bayley, 1838, at Meopham, Kent.

Ideal works by Wyatt not already mentioned are "Girl With a Kid" which was in the Manley Hall sale of 1875; "Hebe," sold at Christies in June, 1885; "Flora," shown at the Great Exhibition of 1851; a "Shepherd Boy," for the Duke of Sutherland; "Nymph Leaving the Bath" (1847), for Lord Canning; "Venus and Cupid" (1847), for Mr. Holford; and "Glycera" (1848), in the Royal Collection.

At the time of his death a number of unfinished works were left in his studio and were completed by J. Gibson (q.v.) and B. E. Spence (q.v.). These included "A Huntress of Diana," for Queen Victoria; "A Nymph Taking a Thorn out of a Greyhound's Foot," for Lord Charles Townsend; and "A Nymph Bathing," for Mr. Foot, of Read Hall, Lancs.

Gibson carved the medallion-bust placed over Wyatt's grave in Rome and also composed the rather unfortunate inscription which reads more like a testimonial to the sculptor's attainments than a Christian epitaph: "His works were universally admired for their purity of taste, grace and truth of nature. The productions of his genius adorn the Royal Palaces of England, St. Petersburg and Naples, as well as the residences of the nobility and gentry of his own country" (*Art Journal*, 1851, page 232).

(*Gentleman's Magazine*, 1844, Vol. II, page 71; and 1850, Vol. II, page 99; *Art Union*, 1846, pages 298 and 304; *Art Journal*, 1850, page 249; 1854, page 352; and 1862, page 23.)

WYNNE, ROBERT, of Ruthin
d. 1731 ?

Wynne lived at Ruthin from 1715 until 1731 and there are various payments to him in the Chirk Castle Archives for work carried out for the Myddeltons. This included, in 1723, carving Robert Myddelton's coat of arms in the new seat in Ruthin Church, and "beautifying the coats of arms and other ornaments of the old monuments of Chirk Church" five years later. Wynne was also responsible for the monument erected in the same church by Mary Myddelton, of Croesnewydd, to the memory of her father, mother and brother. This striking work, with its three life-size effigies, is unsigned, but in the family archives there is a payment in 1721 of £180 to "Mr. Robert Wynne, stone-cutter in Ruthin . . . being ye remainder of £400 in full for ye monument in Chirk." Wynne signs a small well-carved tablet to Thomas Powell, 1705, at Llanbadarnfawr, Cardigan.

The impressive monument to the Wynn family in Ruabon Church, Denbigh, is a signed work by the same hand and was erected about 1719. Here again there are three life-size figures: the blind Henry Wynn, who died in 1671, stands in the centre in his lawyer's robes, his hands extended in blessing over the kneeling figures of Jane and John Wynn, who died in 1675 and 1718 respectively.

In the records of the London Masons' Company for 1669 the apprenticeship is entered of Simon Wynne, "son of Gualloth Wynne, of Lambold, Denbigh, gentleman, to Peter Roberts, Citizen and Mason of London." It is possible that Simon and Robert were one and the same, for there is no trace of Robert's ever having been apprenticed in London, although the carving of his figures seems to indicate City training.

WYON, EDWARD WILLIAM
b. 1811, *d.* 1885

He was the son of Thomas Wyon (1767–1830), chief engraver of the Seals, and joined the Royal Academy Schools in 1829, on the recommendation of E. H. Baily (q.v.). Two years later he exhibited a bust of General Maitland at the Academy, following this with another of Sir George Chetwynd in 1833. His busts of Shakespeare and Milton, both dated 1850, are now in the Birmingham Art Gallery.

At the Great Exhibition of 1851 Wyon showed "A Tazza Modelled from a Greek Design for the Art Union of London." In the following year he made a bust of Wellington for Wedgwood for reproduction in "Parian"; other models executed for the firm included "Titania," "Oberon,"

"Hope," and "The Nubian Water-Carrier." In 1853 he made a statuette of Lord Dalhousie for the Nepalese Ambassador (*Illustrated London News*, 22 January, 1853).

Wyon is represented by several statues in London. In 1866 he made one in bronze of Richard Green, having already executed in 1863 a bust of the shipowner and philanthropist, which is now at Kenswick Manor, Worcestershire. The statue, erected at Poplar, is of considerable merit, and shows Green sitting in an armchair caressing a Newfoundland dog, whose head rests on his knee. In 1869 the sculptor carved statues of Galileo, Goethe and La Place for the Civil Service Commission Building in Burlington Gardens; his statue of "Britomartis" is at the Mansion House.

When the Drapers' Hall was rebuilt in 1866 Wyon was chosen to carry out all the decorative carving. This included a series of reliefs in the inner courtyard and two statues of Edward III and Queen Philippa for the façade; these were placed in position in 1871. In 1874 he executed two heroic caryatids for the main first-floor entrance of the Fitzwilliam Museum, Cambridge.

Wyon exhibited at the Royal Academy, 1831–1876, showing nearly one hundred works. Among his portrait-busts were those of W. C. Ross, the miniaturist (1840); the Duchess of Sutherland (1853); Robert Stephenson (1855), now in possession of the Newcastle Literary Society; Dr. Livingstone (1858); Joseph Locke, M.P. (1859); I. K. Brunel (1862); Sir Joseph Paxton (1864); Robert Napier (1867), now in the Glasgow Art Gallery; and Henry Bessemer (1868). At the Birmingham Society of Artists he showed busts of the Rev. W. Orme (1830); General Maitland (1832); Sir George Chetwynd (1835); a wax portrait of Baron Blome (1835); and a medallion portrait of Sir Edward Lytton-Bulwer (1838). His wax portraits of William Wordsworth (1835) and Robert Southey (1835) are now in the National Portrait Gallery, while a cast of his bust of John Wichcord (1860) is in the Maidstone Museum.

Wyon's delightful monument to Caroline Stevens (*d.* 1840) is in Bradfield Church, Berks. It was designed by H. Corbould and takes the form of a copper relief showing Mrs. Stevens kneeling in prayer. Other monuments by Wyon commemorate the Rev. Watts Wilkinson, 1844, in St. Margaret's, Lothbury, and the Rev. Josiah Pratt, 1846, in St. Stephen's, Coleman Street. In 1853 he cast two bronze plaques, one showing the Rev. Frederick Robertson preaching, and the other teaching in a Mechanics' Institute; these were commissioned as part of the monument to Robertson erected in Brighton Cemetery.

(Various references, *Art Journal* and *Builder*.)

Y

YATES, D., of Leicester
fl. 1830–1840

He signs two undistinguished tablets to John Pares, 1831, at Scraptoft, Leicestershire, and to Thomas Whiteman, 1836, at Peckleton in the same county.

YATES, J., of Hereford
fl. 1801–1822

He signs a large Hellenic wall-monument at Burghill, Herefordshire, to Thomas Farrington, 1801, and a tablet to William Hardwick, 1811, at Madley in the same county. There is also a small tablet to John Berrow, 1809, at Burghill, which is signed by "T. Yates, Junior."

YEOMANS, T., of Bodenham
fl. 1797–1830

A village mason, he signs a number of stone wall-tablets in Wellington Church, Herefordshire. These are dated between 1797 and 1830 and are of pleasant, though rather crude, workmanship.

Yeomans was succeeded in the business by his son Richard, who signs other tablets in the same church.

YOUNG, J.

He signs a monument to William Tabburn, 1788, in Portsmouth Cathedral.

YOUNG, J., of Ewell
fl. 1814–1832

He signs a large wall-tablet with carefully cut details to Sir George Glyn, Bart., 1814, at Ewell, Surrey, and another smaller one to William Payne, 1832, at Sutton, in the same county.

YOUNG, JOHN
d. 1695

Having been "made sinisterly free of ye Weavers," Young was taken and presented for disfranchisement together with his master in 1635/6. He made his peace with the Masons' Company and agreed to pay £5 for his translation from the Weavers (Knoop and Jones' *The London Mason in the Seventeenth Century*, page 31).

In 1638 Young was working at the Inner Temple, receiving £140 for repairs to the Temple Church, and a further £400 for building the Temple Bridge two years later; in 1655 he was paid for work "about the Garden Gate and Stairs" (Inderwick's *Inner Temple Records*, Vol. II). In 1652, and again in 1655, he was Warden of the Masons' Company and was appointed Master in 1657.

From 1665 Young and his partner, Joshua Marshall (q.v.), were working at Greenwich Palace, building first the north end and later the east front (P.R.O., A.O.1 2487/357). Between 1665 and 1667 they were also responsible for a great deal of carved stonework at the Palace, receiving, for example, £15 for each Corinthian capital (P.R.O., Works 5/9). In the latter year Young built the "ballastrades and rails" of the Pavilion on his own account.

From 1667 until 1675 he was the master-mason for building the Mercers' Hall and chapel, although for part of the time he was assisted by T. Cartwright the Elder (q.v.). In 1669 he made the Great Gateway, and in the following year the Court Minute Book records a payment of £50 to "John Young and his sonne Nicholas Young for ye figures of Faith, Hope and Charity." When the Hall was rebuilt in 1878 the gateway and its figures were bought for Swanage and now form the front of the Town Hall.

In 1670 Young was working at St. Dunstan's-in-the-East (*Wren Society*, Vol. XIX, page 18). In 1675 he was employed at Bethlem Hospital, for Robert Hooke notes in his diary on 1 April of that year that he had "signed Young's bills for carvings" (*Diary of Robert Hooke*, page 156).

Young had two sons, Nicholas (q.v.) and John, both of whom followed their father's craft. The latter became free of the Masons' Company by patrimony in 1671, and was Warden in 1686 and 1687. In 1695 he was Master of the Company, but died during his year of office. In 1684 Mr. Thomas Thynne paid him £15 for a marble chimney-piece (Longleat Archives).

YOUNG, NICHOLAS
fl. 1663–1686

Nicholas Young, who was admitted to the Masons' Company in 1662/3, was the son of John Young the Elder (q.v.), with whom he worked as assistant or partner. Inderwick (*Inner Temple Records*, Vol. II, page 21) quotes an agreement dated 1 August, 1663, between Sir Heneage Finch,

Treasurer of the Inner Temple, and "John Young and Nicholas Young his son, Citizens and Freemasons" for repairs to the Temple Bridge, while the Court Book of the Mercers' Company notes a payment of £50 to "John Young and his sonne Nicholas" in 1670.

Under Wren, Nicholas Young was employed as a master-builder at several of the City churches, including St. Andrew-by-the-Wardrobe and St. Michael's, Cornhill. He also executed a certain amount of stone-carving, making a festoon, 18 ft. long, for the front of St. George's, Botolph Lane, and four pillars costing £120 for St. Martin's,

Ludgate Hill (*Wren Society*, Vol. XIX). He was Warden of the Masons' Company in 1674 and Master in 1682. Nicholas's finest work is the bust of Gideon De Laune in the possession of the Apothecaries' Company.

YOUNG, WILLIAM

The *Daily Post* of 23 April, 1731, refers to him as "that ingenious statuary at the Eagle and Rock, near Hyde Park Corner." He may be the "Mr. Young" to whom Henry Hoare paid six guineas on 20 December of the same year (Archives, Hoare's Bank).

INDEX OF PLACES

Abbotsford (Scotland), 94, 275
Abbots Langley (Herts), 29, 98, 344
Abbots Leigh (Som), 36, 295
Aberdeen, 77
  University, 63
  West Church, 27, 370
Aberford (Yorks), 370, 381
Abergavenny (Mon), 66, 220, 439
Aberystwyth (Cardigan), 95, 140
Abingdon (Berks), 181
  Market House, 225
  St. Helen's, 175, 200, 279, 300, 426
  St. Nicholas, 200
Abington (Northants), 115
Abington Pigotts (Cambs), 31, 332
Achurch (Northants), 15, 426
Acle (Norfolk), 233
Acrise (Kent), 196
Acton (Middx), 30
Acton Scott (Salop), 203
Adderbury (Oxon), 76, 220, 254
Adderley (Salop), 32, 63, 81, 188
Adderley Hall (Salop), 80
Addington (Bucks), 209, 338
Addiŝuton (Surrey), 253, 302, 385, 437
Adelaide (Australia), 445
Adlestrop (Glos), 329, 440
Adlingfleet (Yorks), 261
Alberbury (Salop), 57
Albury (Surrey), 68
Albury House (Surrey), 149, 354, 364
Alcester (Warwicks), 51, 96, 443
Aldbourne (Wilts), 61
Aldeburgh (Suffolk), 317, 395
Aldenham (Herts), 36, 65, 116, 212, 264, 405
Alderbury (Salop), 406
Alderley (Glos), 295, 351
Aldford (Ches), 402
Alford (Som), 405
Alfreton (Derby), 142, 146
Allahabad, Muir College, 445
Allesley (Coventry), 184
Allington (Lincs), 108, 185
Alloway (Scotland), 388
Almondbury (Glos), 405
Alnwick (Northumb), 80, 243, 320, 350
Alnwick Castle, 219, 249, 320
Alresford (Essex), 246
Alrewas (Staffs), 430
Alscot Park (Warwicks), 335, 425, 443
Alsley (Warwicks), 15
Altarnum (Cornwall), 71
Althorp, 336
Alton (Hants), 306
Alton Towers (Staffs), 22, 77, 205, 207
Alvediston (Wilts), 64, 285, 338
Alvington (Mon), 439
Alwington (Devon), 225
Amberley (Surrey), 319
Amerdown (Som), 318

Amersham (Bucks), 29, 30, 31, 32, 83, 99, 128, 252, 253, 254, 343, 420
Amesbury (Wilts), 54
Ampney Crucis (Glos), 210
Ampthill (Beds), 288
  Cooper's Hill, 108
Ampthill House (Beds), 96, 188, 268
Anglesey, Isle of, 274
Anstey (Leics), 62
Ansty (Warwicks), 206
Anthony (Cornwall), 65, 86, 426, 437
Antigua (West Indies), 28
Appleby (Leics), 339, 434
Appleton (Berks), 57, 114, 175
Arbroath (Scotland), 257
Arbury (Warwicks), 15, 16, 141, 194, 203, 228, 258, 314
Ardeley (Herts), 367
Arkesden (Essex), 204, 297
Arlesey (Beds), 132
Arlington (Devon), 264, 303
Armagh (Ireland), Cathedral, 29, 96, 330, 338
Armley (Yorks), 178
Arreton (I.o.W.), 191
Arundel (Sussex), 104, 108, 328, 350, 375, 383
Ascot Park (Berks), 401
Ash by Gravesend (Kent), 31
Ashbourne (Derby), 38, 40, 41, 195, 425
Ashburnham (Sussex), 73
Ashburnham Place (Sussex), 21, 84, 108, 139, 174, 265, 268, 291, 303, 364
Ashbury (Berks), 158
Ashby-de-la-Zouch (Leics), 338
Ashby St. Ledgers (Northants), 27, 195, 198
Ashdon (Essex), 324
Ashford (Kent), 84, 113
Ashford (Middx), Welsh Schools, 390
Ashford Bowdler (Salop), 21, 370, 373
Ashley (Staffs), 96, 206, 275, 384
Ashley (Wilts), 292
Ashprington (Devon), 429
Ashridge Park (Herts), 15, 51, 60, 65, 306, 425, 446
Ashtead (Surrey), 168, 209, 241, 368
Ashton Keynes (Wilts), 150
Ashton-under-Lyne (Lancs), 128, 208, 275
Ashurst (Sussex), 150
Ashwellthorpe (Norfolk), 414
Aspley Guise (Beds), 438
Assington (Suffolk), 31
Astbury (Cheshire), 229, 363, 427
Asthall (Oxon), 217
Astley (Worcs), 27, 29, 30
Aston (Birmingham), 141, 207, 337, 338, 346, 392, 423, 431

Aston (Yorks), 108
Aston Flamville (Leics), 206
Aston Hall (Birmingham), 206
Aston Hall (Salop), 68
Aston Hall (Yorks), 308
Aston Rowant (Oxon), 209
Aston-sub-Edge (Glos), 204
Astwell (Northants), 431
Astwood (Bucks), 409
Aswanby (Lincs), 77, 137
Athens (Greece), 93
Attingham Park (Salop), 129
Audlem (Cheshire), 63, 157
Audley End (Essex), 81, 106, 129, 147, 208, 240, 263, 270, 361, 407
Aughton (Lancs), 412, 422
Avington Park (Hants), 62, 392
Axbridge (Som), 208, 388
Axminster (Devon), 105, 170
Aylesbeare (Devon), 372
Aylesbury (Bucks), 401
  Free School, 213
  Museum, 58, 213
Aylesford (Kent), 21, 109, 195
Aylestone (Leics), 265
Aylsham (Norfolk), 13, 209, 215, 365
Aynho (Northants), 66, 364, 366, 433
Ayr, 274, 388

Babworth (Notts), 413
Backwell (Som), 324
Badby (Warwicks), 355
Badger (Salop), 95, 150, 173
Badminton (Glos), 14, 140, 141, 337, 338, 423, 426, 439
Badsworth (Yorks), 56, 241
Bagshot (Surrey), 31
Bainton (Northants), 427
Bakewell (Derby), 185, 416
Balderton (Notts), 411, 433
Baldock (Herts), 36, 431
Balmoral (Scotland), 63, 363, 386, 389
Bamburgh (Northumb), 359
Bampton (Devon), 137, 350
Bampton (Oxon), 352
Bampton (Westmorland), 14
Banbury (Oxon), 190
Bandon (Eire), 321
Bangor, Cathedral, 151, 271
Banstead (Surrey), 30, 352, 431
Barbados (W.I.), 226, 336, 425
  Cathedral, 29, 57, 150, 173, 201, 278, 295, 325, 439
  Christ Church, 317
  Codrington College, 181
  St. George's, 391, 405, 426
  St. James's, 295
  St. John's, 150, 426
  St. Thomas's, 439
Bardwell (Suffolk), 125
Barford (Warwicks), 66, 228, 422

Barford St. Martin (Wilts), 261, 285
Barholme (Lincs), 288
Barkby (Leics), 212, 337
Barking (Essex), 202, 250
Barking Hall (Suffolk), 353
Barkway (Herts), 100, 118, 226, 335, 338, 358, 367, 368
Barnack (Northants), 175
Barnard Castle (Durham), 156
Barnby (Notts), 411
Barnby-on-Don (Yorks), 241, 343
Barnes (Surrey), 44, 99, 200, 339
Barnet (Herts), 318
Barnsley (Glos), 322
Barnsley (Yorks), 241, 412
Barnstaple (Devon), 17, 43, 191, 225, 405,
  Holy Trinity, 333
  Infirmary, 47, 263, 372
Barnwood (Glos), 317
Barrells (Warwicks), 111, 298
Barrow Gurney (Som), 295, 348
Barrow-in-Furness, 274
Barrow-on-Soar (Leics), 396, 437
Barsham (Suffolk), 138
Barton (Beds), 314
Barwick in Elmet (Yorks), 353, 412
Baschurch (Salop), 81, 271
Basildon (Berks), 104, 201, 349, 375
Basing (Hants), 150, 361
Bassaleg (Mon), 109, 390, 426
Batcombe (Som), 155
Bath (Som), 161, 180
  Abbey, 27, 30, 52, 58, 86, 96, 150, 151, 162, 165, 229, 264, 279, 317, 410
  Art Gallery, 94, 149, 161
  Cross Bath, 122
  Grammar School, 154, 309
  Guildhall, 47, 52, 204, 387
  Hospital, 204
  Lansdowne Monument, 191
  Municipal Library, 293
  Pump Room, 191, 203, 204, 309
  Roman Catholic Chapel, 403
  St. Mary's, 52
  St. Michael extra Muros, 191
  Victoria Park, 284
Bathampton (Som), 155, 189, 315, 324
Batheaston (Som), 317
Bathford (Som), 155, 426
Batsford (Glos), 279
Battersea Parish Church, 31, 68, 108, 131, 223, 314, 318, 331, 420, 426
Battle (Sussex), 409
Battle Abbey (Sussex), 108, 357, 409, 431
Battlefield (Salop), 80
Bawtry (Yorks), 241
Bayford (Herts), 96, 303
Bayham Abbey (Kent), 47, 94, 278
Beaconsfield (Bucks), 175, 391, 396
Beaminster (Bristol), 295
Bearwood (Berks), 275
Beauport Park (Sussex), 388
Beauséjour Museum, New Brunswick (Canada), 109
Beckenham (Kent), 15, 150, 200, 420
Beckford (Glos), 112

Beckington (Wilts), 97, 229
Beckley (Sussex), 292
Bedale (Yorks), 122, 427
Beddington (Surrey), 30, 246, 419, 421, 422, 427
Bedford, 438
  Bunyan Chapel, 394
  Old Grammar School, 287, 406
  St. Mary's, 242
  St. Paul's, 287
Bedingham (Norfolk), 125
Bedsworth, 414
Bedwardine (Worcs), 373
Beech Hill (Essex), 372
Beeston St. Lawrence (Norfolk), 61, 333
Belchamp St. Paul (Essex), 90, 187
Belchamp Walter (Essex), 381
Belfast, Castle Chapel, 249
  Free Library, 250
Bell Rock Lighthouse, 222
Belton (Lincs), 27, 78, 82, 94, 95, 98, 99, 210, 367, 368, 387, 391, 404, 426, 427
Belton (Rutland), 144, 174, 312
Belview House (Co. Galway), 107
Belvoir Castle (Leics), 90, 102, 122, 277, 278, 296, 447
Benacre (Suffolk), 47, 288, 395
Benenden (Kent), 344
Bengeo (Herts), 15, 279, 368
Benham (Berks), 439
Bentley Priory (Middx), 66, 156, 166
Berechurch (Essex), 141, 314
Berkhamsted (Herts), 27, 188, 431
Berkswell (Warwicks), 27, 127, 346, 426, 427
Berlin (Germany), Kaiser Friedrich Museum, 245
Bermondsey (London), Free School, 115
  St. George's, 290
  St. James's, 131, 202, 365
  St. Thomas's, 250
Bermuda (West Indies), 49
Berry Pomeroy (Devon), 114, 348
Berwick-on-Tweed, 320
Berwick St. John (Wilts), 138, 228
Besford (Worcs), 368
Betchworth Castle (Surrey), 53
Bethnal Green (London), Museum, 35, 45, 49, 70, 244, 245, 249, 250, 275, 299, 389
Betley (Staffs), 57, 363
Betteshanger (Kent), 343
Betteshanger House (Kent), 249
Beverley (Yorks), Minster, 100, 109, 111, 146, 193, 343,
  St. Mary's, 30
Bewdley (Worcs), St. Anne's, 443
Bewdley Bridge, 80
Bexley (Kent), 19, 61, 231
Bibury (Glos), 260, 321
Bicester (Oxon), 45, 76, 126, 427, 437
Bickleigh (Devon), 231, 429
Bicton (Devon), 372
Bidborough (Kent), 31, 426
Biddulph (Staffs), 275
Bideford (Devon), 225, 405
Bidford (Warwicks), 235

Bifrons (Kent), 159
Bilston (Staffs), 417
Bingham (Notts), 440
Birchington (Kent), 45, 235, 288
Birdbrook (Essex), 229, 245, 303
Birdsall (Yorks), 338, 416, 427
Birkenhead (Cheshire), Hospital, 247
  Market, 347
  St. Mary's, 247
Birmingham, 207, 267, 301, 389, 391, 425, 444
  Art Gallery, 206, 221, 262, 267, 290, 420, 444, 449
  Barber Institute, 281
  Bluecoat School, 181, 206
  Bull Ring, 207
  Calthorpe Park, 206
  Cathedral, 206, 207, 298, 332, 392
  City Hall, 154, 206, 444
  Dispensary, 207
  Exchange, 205
  General Hospital, 206
  Institution for Promoting the Fine Arts, 207
  King Edward's Grammar School, 298, 343, 434
  Library, 104
  Midland Institute, 389
  Post Office, 205
  Queen's College, 206
  St. Margaret's, 206
  St. Martin's, 206, 282, 332, 389
  St. Paul's, 206, 241 254, 346
  St. Philip's, see Cathedral
  School of Medicine, 206
  Soho House, 207
  Town Hall, see City Hall
Birr (Eire), 154
Birtsmorton (Worcs), 430
Bisham (Berks), 32
Bishop Auckland (Durham), 222, 277
  Palace, 197
Bishopsbourne (Kent), 220, 246, 266
Bishop's Castle (Salop), 80
Bishop's Cleeve (Glos), 66
Bishop's Hull (Som), 242
Bishop's Lydiard (Som), 229
Bishops Tachbrook (Warwicks), 367
Bishops Tawton (Devon), 178, 219
Bishopston (Glam), 325
Bishops Waltham (Hants), 61, 192, 377, 386
Bitterswell (Leics), 349
Blagdon (Northumb), 131, 243, 244
Blair Atholl (Perth), 248, 371
Blair Castle, 84
Blandford (Dorset), 203
Blenheim Palace (Oxon), 16, 37, 88, 99, 152, 169, 194, 299, 336, 337, 347, 376, 398, 399, 419, 435
Blessington (Co. Wicklow, Eire), 228
Bletchingley (Surrey), 30, 110, 118, 238, 404
Bletchington (Oxon), 181, 293, 304, 364
Blewbury (Berks), 104, 175
Blidworth (Notts), 384
Blithfield (Staffs), 368, 426

Blockley (Glos), 244, 264, 295, 335, 407, 443
Bloomsbury, St. George's, *see* London
Bloxham (Oxon), 83
Blunham (Beds), 30, 253, 367, 376
Blunsdon St. Andrew (Wilts), 343
Bluntisham (Hunts), 353
Blyth (Notts), 186, 440
Boarhunt (Hants), 90
Bocking (Essex), 31, 164, 306, 332
Bockleton (Worcs), 445
Bodelwyddan (N. Wales), 206
Bodenham (Heref), 285, 309, 310, 379
Bodicote (Oxon), 76
Bodmin (Cornwall), 47, 48
Bolsover (Derby), 55
Bolton (Lancs), 257
    Town Hall, 256
Bolton-le-Moors, 389
Bombay (India), 29, 49, 93, 154, 274, 275, 422, 444
    Cathedral, 30, 31, 275, 386
    Town Hall, 93
Bonar Bridge, 80
Boreham (Essex), 384
Boreham Hall (Essex), 99, 107, 113, 135, 178, 195, 201
Bosbury (Heref), 431
Boston (Lincs), 267, 411
Boston (U.S.A.), Athenaeum, 89, 212
    King's Chapel, 99, 344, 404
    Merchants' Exchange, 212
    Public Library, 47
    State House, 93
Bottisham (Cambs), 28, 397
Boughton (Northants), 77, 419, 420
Boughton (Oxon), 418
Boughton Monchelsea (Kent), 21, 91 344
Bourne (Lincs), 348
Bournemouth, Russell-Cotes Museum, 34, 248, 372
Bourton-on-the-Water (Glos), 260, 373
Bovinger (Essex), 131, 331, 332
Bow (London), 370
Bowdon (Cheshire), 83, 208, 287, 294; 423
Bowood, 63, 75, 84, 85, 99, 176, 355, 358, 387, 415, 425, 428
Boxley (Kent), 226
Boxted (Suffolk), 125
Boxworth (Hunts), 295
Brackley (Northants), 52, 431
Bradfield (Berks), 450
Bradford (Yorks), 274, 301, 413
    Cathedral, 29, 145, 150, 177, 264, 306, 344, 353, 370
    St. George's Hall, 396
Bradford Abbas (Dorset), 388
Bradford-on-Avon (Wilts), 315, 338
Bradford Peverell (Dorset), 239
Bradley (Derby), 416
Bradwell (Essex), 195
Braintree (Essex), 90
Bramber (Sussex), 108, 299
Bramham Park (Yorks), 81, 393
Bramley (Hants), 322
Bramley (Surrey), 385
Brampton (Hunts), 228

Brampton Ash (Northants), 212
Bramsdean (Hants), 224
Bramston (Lincs), 86
Brasted (Kent), 426
Braughing (Herts), 344, 367
Braunton (Devon), 219
Bray (Berks), 65, 105, 267, 343
    Fishmongers' Almshouses, 139
Brayton (Yorks), 146
Brecon, 390
    Cathedral, 29, 151, 295, 368, 390, 433
    Christ Church, 368
Brede (Sussex), 220
Bredgar (Kent), 294
Bredon (Worcs), 322, 351
Bredwardine (Heref), 260, 423
Brenchley (Kent), 437
Brent Eleigh (Suffolk), 134, 302
Brentford (Middx), St. Laurence's, 29, 109, 151, 208, 227
Brereton (Staffs), 143
Bretforton (Worcs), 234
Brettenham (Suffolk), 59
Brewood (Staffs), 418
Bridestowe (Devon), 183
Bridgnorth, St. Mary's, 319
Bridport (Dorset), 440
    Town Hall, 185
Briggens (Herts), 83, 88
Brightling (Sussex), 94, 332
Brighton, 93, 156, 328, 372
    Aquarium, 56
    Art Gallery, 300, 445
    Cemetery, 450
    Church Street School, 80
    Parish Church, 299, 425, 427
    Pavilion, 61, 107, 116, 291, 389, 421, 424
    Queen's Park, 347
    Roman Catholic Church, 79, 80
    Royal Stables, 328
    St. George's, 299
    The Steyne, 299, 347
    Town Hall, 299
Brigstock (Northants), 275
Brill, 364
Brinkworth (Wilts), 158, 208
Brislington (Som), 156
Bristol, 336
    All Saints, 151, 294, 321, 337, 351, 398
    Art Gallery, 34, 35, 94, 274, 410
    Bank of England, 182
    Broad Quay, 318
    Cathedral, 35, 36, 61, 95, 96, 128, 202, 286, 295, 405
    Christ Church, 294, 439
    Commercial Rooms, 67
    Council House, 34, 103, 273, 309, 398
    Cross, 295
    Exchange, 52, 67, 170, 180, 294
    Fine Arts Academy, 389
    General Hospital, 74
    High Cross, 389
    Institution, 34
    Law Courts, 389
    Lewins Mead Chapel, 439
    Library, 294
    Literary Institute, 32

Lord Mayor's Chapel, 95, 103, 119, 295
Mansion House, 14
Masonic Hall, 32
Portland Square, 107
Redland Chapel, 161, 184, 294, 334, 336, 403
St. Augustine's, 133, 156, 295, 351, 405
St. James's, 34, 36, 284, 351
St. Mary Redcliffe, 17, 133, 191, 294, 423, 439
St. Michael's, 48, 295, 351, 412
St. Nicholas's, 103
St. Philip and St. Jacob, 220, 294, 295
St. Stephen's, 351, 405
St. Thomas's, 294
West of England Bank, 389
Britford (Wilts), 32, 129, 311
Britwell Baldwin (Oxon), 423
Brixton (Devon), 411
Brixton (London), Freeman's Orphan School, 198
    St. Matthew, 123, 163, 199, 339, 352, 410, 420, 427
Brixton Deverill (Wilts), 295
Broadlands (Hants), 348, 372
Broadstairs (Kent), 236
Broadwater (Sussex), 45, 408, 416
Broadway (Worcs), 91
Broadwindsor (Dorset), 170, 432
Brockborough Park, 442
Brocket Hall (Herts), 60, 286
Brockhall (Northants), 213, 220, 431
Brocklesby, 277
Brockworth (Glos), 112, 199, 259
Brodswell (Yorks), 241
Brome (Suffolk), 191
Bromfield (Salop), 45
Bromham (Beds), 204
Bromham (Wilts), 155, 189
Bromley (Kent), 91
Brompton (London), Chapel, 423
    Holy Trinity, 339
Brompton (Yorks), 395
Brookland, 430
Broome (Worcs), 151
Broomfield (Som), 242, 317
Broomham (Beds), 361
Broseley (Salop), 142
Brotherton (Yorks), 174, 412
Broughton (Oxon), 64
Broughton (Staffs), 157
Broxbourne (Herts), 84, 151, 254, 308, 385, 422
Broxted (Essex), 213
Bruera (Cheshire), 189, 278
Bruton (Som), 315, 344
    Saxey Hospital, 368
Bryncoed-Ivor (N. Wales), 141
Brynkinalt (Denbigh), 77, 187, 249, 257, 291
Buckden (Hants), 35, 397
Buckingham Church, 42
Buckland (Berks), 108, 407
Buckland Brewer (Devon), 319
Buckland Filleigh (Devon), 151
Buckland Monachorum (Devon), 28, 31, 429
Bucklebury (Berks), 209, 265, 293

Bucklebury House (Berks), 200
Bucknell (Oxon), 244
Budbrook (Warwick), 385
Budworth (Cheshire), 316, 384
Bugbrook (Northants), 114
Bulkington (Warwicks), 194, 195
Bullingham (Heref), 379
Bulwich (Northants), 359
Bunbury (Ches), 347
Bungay (Suffolk), 315
  Earlsham Hall, 125
  Holy Trinity, 345
  St. Mary's, 233
Bunny (Notts), 30, 298, 310
Buntingford (Herts), 21, 116, 437
Burford (Salop), 166, 365, 427
Burghill (Heref), 65, 451
Burghley House (Northants), 107,
  113, 163, 164, 261, 277, 321
Burley-on-the-Hill (Rutland), 96,
  268, 336
Burnham (Bucks), 27, 66, 396
Burnham (Som), 313
Burnham Hall (Norfolk), 125, 156
Burnham Thorpe (Norfolk), 150,
  244
Burnley (Lancs), 116, 157, 279, 294,
  418
Bursledon (Hants), 282
Burslem (Staffs), Wedgwood Insti-
  tute, 56
Burton Agnes (Yorks), 146, 413
Burton Bradstock (Dorset), 427
Burton Hall (Lincs), 194
Burton-on-Stather (Lincs), 30, 31,
  145
Burton-on-Trent (Staffs), 72, 185,
  427
Burton Overy (Leics), 144
Burwash (Sussex), 57, 87, 151, 292
Burwell (Cambs), 292
Bury (Lancs), 34
Bury St. Edmunds, 353, 449
  Mansion House, 353
  St. Mary's, 125, 295, 371
  Town Hall, 77, 253
Busbridge, 85
Buscot (Berks), 112
Bushey (Herts), 136, 252
Bushley (Worcs), 200
Bushy Park (Middx), 360, 364
Buxted (Sussex), 317, 426
Buxted Park (Sussex), 176
Buxton (Derby), 396
Byculla (India), 293, 317
Byfield (Northants), 231
Byford (Heref), 218, 379
Bylaugh (Norfolk), 31
Bylaugh Hall (Norfolk), 359
Bywall, St. Peter's, 122

Cade Street Chapel (Sussex), 188
Cadzow (Scotland), 266
Cairo, Grand Hotel, 56
Caistor (Northants), 174, 440
Calcutta, 29, 34, 93, 95, 96, 104,
  127, 149, 153, 154, 268, 301,
  370, 386, 393, 419, 425, 444
  Asiatic Society of Bengal, 95
  Botanical Gardens, 40
  Cathedral, 30, 58, 372, 427

Metcalfe Hall, 35
Mint, 154
Old Cathedral, 306, 427
St. John's, 30, 426
St. Paul's Cathedral, 47
Town Hall, 419
Victoria Hall, 419
Callington (Cornwall), 72
Calne (Wilts), 52, 295
Camberwell (London), 151, 163, 240
Camborne (Cornwall), 36, 71, 294,
  324
Cambridge, 154, 161
  All Saints, 95
  Anatomical Museum, 49
  Assize Courts, 122
  Botany School, 445
  Caius College, 397
  Christ's College, 89, 297, 384
  Clare College, 296
  Clare Hall, 182, 299, 397
  Divinity School, 114, 352, 394
  Emmanuel College, 152, 351
  Fitzwilliam Museum, 35, 47, 74,
    91, 94, 154, 164, 271, 277, 329,
    330, 336, 337, 436, 450
  Jesus College, 51, 151, 385
  King's College, 88
  Law Library, 336
  Magdalene College, 111
  Market Cross, 397
  New Library, 22
  Pembroke College, 94
  Peterhouse, 397
  St. Benet's, 397, 429
  St. Clement's, 174
  St. John's College, 34, 35, 52, 71,
    94, 95, 192, 222
  Senate House, 59, 88, 277, 436,
    445
  Sidney Sussex College, 252
  Town Hall, 49, 74, 123
  Trinity College, 26, 34, 35, 47,
    48, 51, 74, 94, 102, 151, 169,
    182, 272, 274, 278, 279, 299,
    316, 330, 331, 336, 343, 347,
    352, 394, 419, 427, 444, 445
  Trinity Hall, 88, 278
  University Library, 253
  University Schools, 307, 443
Cambridge (Mass., U.S.A.), Mount
  Auburn Cemetery, 212
Camerton (Som), 17, 295
Campsall (Yorks), 150, 241
Campsey Ash (Suffolk), 105, 427
Campton (Beds), 132
Canford (Dorset), 27, 28, 68, 331,
  403
Canford Magna (Dorset), 189
Canons (Middx), 70, 82, 88, 237,
  281, 376, 408
Canons Ashby (Northants), 328
Canterbury, Cathedral, 31, 59, 110,
  127, 151, 158, 184, 202, 242,
  244, 269, 320, 338, 403, 419,
  420, 429, 430
  Cavalry Barracks, 391
  Dane John Hill, 418
  Holy Cross, 113, 184
  Philosophical Society, 419
  St. Augustine's, 302

St. Dunstan's, 350
St. Margaret's, 159
St. Martin's, 242, 382
St. Mary Magdalen, 254
St. Mildred's, 27, 264
St. Paul's, 113
Capel St. Mary (Suffolk), 109
Cape of Good Hope, 93, 95
Capesthorne Hall, 388
Cape Town, 257
Cardiff, Church, 390
  City Hall, 390
  Infirmary, 390
  Town Hall, see City Hall
Cardington (Beds), 28, 195, 344, 420
Carew (Pembroke), 390
Carlisle, 154, 415, 441
  Academy of Arts, 273
  Cathedral, 39, 134, 230, 270, 273,
    279, 301, 318, 441
  County Hall, 328
  St. Cuthbert's, 134, 217, 230
Carlton (Co. Kildare, Eire), 313
Carlton House (nr. Kirkcudbright),
  119
Carmarthen, 32, 122, 133, 156, 215,
  250, 251, 288, 295, 320
Carshalton (Surrey), 70, 190, 228,
  302, 317, 338, 356
Carshalton House, 121
Cartmel (Lancs), 445
Castle Ashby (Northants), 56, 249,
  383
Castle Bromwich Hall (Warwick),
  296
Castle Cary (Som), 155
Castle Hedingham (Essex), 305
Castle Hill (Devon), 47, 99, 292
Castle Howard (Yorks), 47, 77, 82,
  100, 133, 141, 158, 160, 190,
  224, 261, 263, 269, 275, 278,
  281, 283, 314, 324, 351, 353,
  360, 389, 393, 425, 448
Castleton (Dorset), 388
Catfield (Norfolk), 181
Catherington (Hants), 57
Catton (Norfolk), 286, 427
Catworth (Hunts), 115, 253
Cavendish (Suffolk), 361
Caverswall (Staffs), 93
Cawthorne (Yorks), 179, 180, 200
Chadlington (Oxon), 66, 322
Chadshunt (Warwicks), 381
Chailey (Sussex), 432
Chalfont St. Giles (Bucks), 70
Chalgrove, 346
Chalk (Kent), 350
Chalton (Hants), 187
Chard (Som), 284
Charing (Kent), 332
Charlecote Park (Warwicks), 47
Charleston (S.C., U.S.A.), College,
  110
  St. Michael's, 174, 256, 411
Charlton (London), 94, 131, 317
Charlton Kings (Glos), 229, 239,
  322, 439
Charmouth (Dorset), 351
Chartham (Kent), 113, 338, 345,
  423
Chastleton (Oxon), 162, 424

Chatham (Kent), Dockyard, 179
New Storehouse, 179
Parish Church, 272, 286
Chatsfield (Sussex), 279
Chatsworth, 22, 50, 51, 65, 77, 94, 96, 101, 122, 166, 173, 177, 193, 217, 236, 269, 281, 284, 318, 328, 337, 360, 400, 414, 416, 428, 448
Chawton (Hants), 367
Cheam (Surrey), 36, 116, 127, 189, 251, 287, 422 426
Checkheaton (Oxon), 192
Cheddar (Som), 309
Chelmsford (Essex), 34, 178
Cathedral, 244
Town Hall, 107
Chelsea (London), 131, 169, 251
Duke of York's School, 426
Hospital, 14, 17, 142, 201, 238
Old Church, 17, 329, 437
Physic Garden, 336
St. Luke's, 95, 116, 118, 299, 359, 402, 429
Town Hall, 136, 301
Chelsworth (Suffolk), 332
Cheltenham (Glos), 66, 239, 259, 283, 303, 403, 439
Hospital, 78
Chenies (Bucks), 55, 427, 437
Chepstow (Mon), 294, 295
Cherrington (Glos), 405
Cherry Hinton (Cambs), 150, 385
Chertsey (Surrey), 57, 127, 151, 412, 413, 421
Chesham (Bucks), 29, 30, 318
Cheshunt (Herts), 184, 251, 442
Chester, 393
Bluecoat School, 320
Bridge, 224, 400
Bridge Gate, 401
Cathedral, 31, 39, 40, 57, 80, 157, 170, 195, 206, 271, 278, 279, 347, 364, 402, 405, 411, 445
Exchange, 395
Lunatic Asylum, 192
St. Bridget's, 445
St. John the Baptist, 224, 364
St. Mary on the Hill, 63, 363
St. Michael's, 63
St. Oswald's, 445
St. Peter's, 157
Chesterfield (Derbys), 56, 146, 370
Chester-le-Street (Durham), 222
Chesterton (Warcs), 103
Chettle (Dorset), 159
Chevening (Kent), 26, 33, 92, 96, 226, 249
Chew Magna (Som), 31
Chichester, Cathedral, 31, 65, 79, 80, 148, 150, 151, 173, 189, 200, 202, 224, 226, 307, 320, 356, 367, 397, 404, 422
St. Olave's, 421
Chicksands Priory, 51
Chiddingfold (Surrey), 262
Childwall (Lancs), 174
Chilham (Kent), 61, 96, 184, 267, 427
Chilton (Bucks), 231
Chilton Foliat (Berks), 375, 384

Chingford (Essex), 209, 256
Chippenham (Wilts), 306
Chipping Campden (Glos), 255
Chipping Ongar (Essex), 278
Chipstead (Surrey), 65, 110, 359, 423
Chirk (Denbigh), 449
Aqueduct, 80
Parish Church, 73, 157, 368, 449
Chirk Castle (Denbigh), 63, 133, 140, 237, 281, 311, 449
Chislehurst (Kent), 65, 95, 139, 338
Chiswick (Middx), 95, 344, 404
Chiswick House (Middx), 20, 336, 342
Chittlehampton (Devon), 344
Chobham (Surrey), 209, 433
Cholesbury (Bucks), 161
Christchurch (Hants), 95, 151, 189, 203, 418
Churchgate Street (Essex), 355, 386
Church Minshull (Ches), 265
Church Stoke (Salop), 439
Church Stowe (Northants), 259, 369
Cirencester (Glos), 158, 277, 329
Cirencester Park, 371
Claines (Worcs), 206
Clandon (Surrey), 267
Clandon Park (Surrey), 337
Clapham (Beds), 431
Clapham (London), 99, 128, 218, 325, 426
Parish Church 30, 36, 134, 157, 319, 355
St. Paul's, 96 368, 390
Clarborough (Notts), 146
Clare (Suffolk), 355
Claremont (Surrey), 273, 303, 439
Claydon Hall (Bucks), 51
Clayworth (Notts), 426
Clerkenwell (London), 207
St. James's, 251
Clewer (Berks), 344, 352
Clifden House, 56
Cliffe Pypard (Wilts), 61, 129, 158
Clifton (Bristol), 404
College, 445
Trinity Church, 404
Clifton Campville (Staffs), 48, 338, 422
Clifton Hall (nr. Rotherham), 308
Clifton-on-Teme (Worcs), 170
Clifton Reynes (Bucks), 18, 132, 431
Clinton (Northants), 52
Clitheroe (Lancs), 418, 426
Clovelly (Devon), 229
Cloyne (Eire), Cathedral, 196
Cobham (Kent), 41, 108
Cobham (Surrey), 279, 428, 429
Cobham Hall (Kent), 51, 61, 112, 121, 129, 278, 294, 361, 408, 419, 421, 423, 424
Cocanada (Madras), 74
Cockfield (Suffolk), 333
Cockley Cley (Norfolk), 143
Coddenham (Suffolk), 397
Coddington (Notts), 411
Colchester (Essex), All Saints, 138
St. Botolph's, 141
St. James's, 246
St. Mary at the Wall, 310

Cold Ashton (Glos), 232, 411
Cold Overton (Leics), 272
Coldstream, 323
Coleham Head, Bridge, 80
Coleshill (Berks), 109, 338, 344
Coleshill (Warwicks), 218
Colne (Lancs), 157, 363, 368, 382
Colne Park (Essex), 129, 236
Colney (Herts), 345
Coln Roger (Glos), 112
Coln St. Aldwyn (Glos), 118
Colombo (Ceylon), 154, 317, 385, 419, 420
Colton (Norfolk), 286
Colwich (Staffs), 36, 158, 400, 427
Combe Abbey, 296
Combe Hay (Som), 155
Comber (N. Ireland), 220
Compton (Berks), 321
Compton (Surrey), 407
Compton Place (Sussex), see Eastbourne
Condover (Salop), 331
Congleton (Ches), 157, 195
Conington (Cambs), 168, 170, 254
Constantinople, Sultan's Palace, 389
Conway (Carnarvon), 63, 387
Cookham (Berks), 151, 209, 314, 318
Coopersale (Essex), 368
Copenhagen (Denmark), 394
Glyptotek, 35, 103, 149, 250
Corfe (Som), 209
Corhampton (Hants), 317
Cork (Eire), 27, 154, 235, 436
South Parish Church, 196
Cornbury (Oxon), 364, 376, 377
Cornworthy (Devon), 305
Corrington (Lincs), 48
Corscombe (Dorset), 101
Corsham (Wilts), 404
Corsham Court (Wilts), 14, 22, 114, 187, 203, 292, 329, 343, 423
Corwen (Merioneth), 363, 406
Cosby (Leics), 202, 212, 349
Cossington (Leics), 212
Costock (Notts), 298
Cotterstock (Northants), 52, 61
Cottesbrooke (Northants), 30, 31, 87, 264
Courteenhall (Northants), 115, 299
Courtown (Co. Wexford), 77
Coventry, 257
Holy Trinity, 213
St. Michael's, 203, 303
Cowbridge (Glam), 390
Cowden (Kent), 246
Cowfold (Sussex), 292
Cowley (Middx), 396
Craig Ellachie, Bridge, 80
Cranborne (Dorset), 339
Cranbrook (Kent), 100, 113, 303
Cranford St. John (Northants), 199
Cranworth (Norfolk), 254, 365
Crayford (Kent), 30, 163, 416, 426, 427
Creech St. Michael (Som), 220
Crewe Hall (Ches), 301, 388, 418, 419, 420
Crewkerne (Som), 170, 373
Cricket St. Thomas (Som), 161, 270
Cricklade (Wilts), 260

Croft (Yorks), 40, 156
Cromarty, 323
Cromer (Norfolk), 57
Cromford (Derby), 96, 420
Croome (Worcs), 30, 228, 373
Croome Park (Worcs), 108
Croscombe (Som), 119
Crosthwaite (Westmorland), 244
Crowan (Cornwall), 48, 437
Crowcrombe (Som), 324, 404
Crowhurst (Surrey), 251
Crowhurst (Sussex), 349, 422
Crowland Abbey, 339
Crowle (Lincs), 241
Croxall (Staffs), 96
Croydon (Surrey), Parish Church, 234
St. John's, 386
Crystal Palace, 26, 49, 56, 58, 124, 166, 227, 238, 262, 290, 301, 320, 325, 362, 373, 389, 420, 441
Cuckfield (Sussex), 15, 30, 72, 150, 426
Cuddesdon (Oxon), 440
Culford (Suffolk), 35, 367
Cullompton (Devon), 225, 388
Cults (Fife), 95
Culverthorpe Hall (Lincs), 59
Culworth (Northants), 72
Curdworth (Warwicks), 299
Currey Rivel (Som), 220

Dagenham (Essex), 377
Dalham (Suffolk), 125
Dalkeith Palace, 77, 170, 371
Dallington (Northants), 367
Dalmeny (Scotland), 277, 436
Dalston (Cumberland), 415
Darleston (Staffs); 206
Darley Abbey (Derbys), 185, 427
Darsham (Suffolk), 331
Dartford (Kent), 260
Dartmouth (Devon), 225, 430
Darton (Yorks), 179, 412
Dartrey (Co. Monaghan, Eire), 437
Datchworth (Herts), 203
Dauntsey (Wilts), 316
Davenham (Ches), 63, 157, 310
Davenport House (Salop), 337
Daventry (Northants), 57, 287
Dawlish (Devon), 137, 150, 151, 209, 225, 324
Daylesford Church, 104, 116, 332
Daylesford House, 27, 38
Deane (Hants), 30, 117
Debden (Essex), 107, 125, 229, 392, 431
Debenham (Suffolk), 397
Dedington (Oxon), 76
Deene (Northants), 183, 352
Deepdene (Surrey), 41, 46, 128, 149
Delgany (Co. Wicklow, Eire), 200
Denbury (Devon), 430
Denham (Bucks), 68, 103, 213
Denmark Hill (London), 274
Denstone (Suffolk), 125, 314
Denton (Lincs), 179, 359
Deptford (London), St. Nicholas, 97, 168
St. Paul, 27, 115, 175, 278, 377
Derby, All Saints, see Cathedral

Arboretum, 57
Art Gallery, 104, 109, 173, 371
Cathedral, 64, 96, 180, 185, 254, 331, 350, 427
County Library, 414
Infirmary, 109
Museum, 109
Prison, 65
St. Werburgh's, 96
Town Hall, 94
Dersingham (Norfolk), 41, 174, 175, 286, 365
Desborough (Northants), 108
Detling (Kent), 378
Devizes (Wilts), 35, 97, 204, 295, 423, 426
Devonport, 14
Dewsbury (Yorks), 414
Dickleburgh (Norfolk), 254
Didsbury (Lancs), 414
Dilwyn (Heref), 409, 440
Dingestow (Mon), 141
Dingley (Leics), 142
Dinton (Bucks), 229
Dirlton (Haddington), 323
Disley (Ches), 165
Diss (Norfolk), 15, 191
Ditchley (Oxon), 97, 232
Ditchley Park (Oxon), 190, 203, 210, 258, 335, 343
Ditton (Kent), 100
Ditton Park, 40
Dodderhill (Worcs), 365, 373
Doddington (Kent), 387
Dodleston (Ches), 224
Dogmersfield (Hants), 76, 279
Dolgelley (Merioneth), 35, 406
Doncaster (Yorks), 216, 301
Mansion House, 43
Dorchester, St. Peter's, 170, 203
Dorking (Surrey), Denbies, 250
Dornoch (Sutherland), 93, 158
Doultin (Som), 295
Dover (Kent), Parish Church, 91, 100
St. Martin, 304
Dowdeswell (Glos), 210
Down Ampney, 364
Downham (Lancs), 368
Down Hatherley (Glos), 112
Down Hill (N. Ireland), 282
Downton (Wilts), 285, 344
Draycot Cerne (Wilts), 229, 317, 324, 437
Drayton Beauchamp (Bucks), 302, 442
Drayton House (Northants), 77, 120, 216, 441
Drinkstone (Suffolk), 226
Drogheda (Eire), St. Peter's, 200
Droitwich, St. Andrew's, 365
St. Peter's, 344, 373
Droxford (Hants), 439
Drumclog, 388
Drumcondra (Co. Dublin), 434
Dryburgh, 358
Dublin, 46, 107, 154, 230, 415
Bank of Ireland, 29
Christ Church Cathedral, 98, 431
City Hall, 93, 282
College Green, 169

College Street, 262
Customs House, 38, 81, 345
Essex Bridge, 281
Four Courts, 250, 444
Marino, 16, 435
Marlborough Street Church, 402
Merrion Square, 107
National Gallery of Ireland, 221 234, 403
Royal College of Physicians, 154
Royal Hibernian Academy, 79
St. Michael and St. John, 403
St. Patrick's Cathedral, 34
St. Stephen's Green, 250, 282
Standard Assurance Office, 370
Trinity College, 46, 199, 328, 343, 403
Dudleston (Salop), 174
Dudley (Worcs), 206, 207, 229, 298, 392
Duffield (Derbys), 293
Dukinfield (Ches), 269
Dullingham (Cambs), 350, 423, 427
Duloe (Cornwall), 15, 215
Dulwich (London), College, 56, 408
Picture Gallery, 123
Dumfries, 403
Observatory, 119
St. Michael's, 134, 270, 415, 431
Dummer (Hants), 175
Dunblane, Cathedral, 403
Duncarrey (Eire), 227
Dunchideock (Devon), 404
Dunchurch (Northants), 57, 136
Dundee, 370
Corn Exchange, 63
Dunfermline, Abbey, 154
Dunham Massey (Ches), 280
Dunkeld, 384
Bridge, 80
Cathedral, 371
Dunkeswell (Devon), 27
Dunrobin Castle, 63, 94, 158, 267, 274
Dunstable (Beds), 179
Dunster (Som), 351
Durham, 243, 262
Durham, Cathedral, 96, 122, 145, 172, 177, 272, 355
St. Mary le Bow, 244
University, 355
Durisdeer (Dumfries), 281
Dursley (Glos), 112, 442
Dymock (Glos), 373
Dyrham (Glos), 352

Ealing (Middx), 208, 256, 306, 318, 423, 427
Pitshanger Manor, 108
Eardisley (Heref), 379
Earlham (Norfolk), 264
Earls Colne (Essex), 210, 331
Earsham (Norfolk), 282, 404
Earsham Hall (Norfolk), 125, 129
Eartham (Sussex), 150
Easebourne (Sussex), 95, 262
East Barnet (Herts), 27
East Bedfont (Middx), 57, 208, 396
East Bergholt (Suffolk), 319, 375
East Blatchington (Sussex), 292

Eastbourne (Sussex), 265
Compton Place, 34, 278, 366
East Carleton (Leics), 422
East Carlton (Northants), 255
Eastchurch (Kent), 391
East Dereham (Norfolk), 56, 150, 414
East Farleigh (Kent), 223
East Grinstead (Sussex), 238, 304, 306, 328, 433
East Haddon (Northants), 114, 115
East Ham (Essex), 195
Easthampstead (Berks), 349
East Hoathly (Sussex), 303, 304
East Horndon (Essex), 278
Eastington (Glos), 186, 229, 259
East Langdon (Kent), 113
East Malling (Kent), 21
Eastnor (Hereford), 317, 344, 373, 421
Easton (Suffolk), 306
Easton Neston (Northants), 35, 36
East Retford (Notts), 251, 287
Eastrington (Yorks), 416
Eastry (Kent), 27, 28, 65, 404
East Stoke (Dorset), 413
East Stoke (Notts), 216, 272, 381, 411
East Sutton (Kent), 175, 254, 339, 384
Eastwell (Kent), 248
Eastwell (Lincs), 269
Eastwell Park (Kent), 419
East Wickham (Kent), 254
Eaton Hall (Ches), 95, 103, 359, 428, 448
Ebrington Park (Glos), 15
Eccles (Lancs), 29, 274
Ecclesfield (Yorks), 195, 206, 308, 411, 416
Eccleshall (Staffs), 282
Eckington (Derbys), 365, 416
Ecton (Northants), 35, 329, 338
Edenhall (Cumberland), 418
Edenham (Lincs), 97, 189, 278, 341, 354
Edgbaston (Birmingham), 206, 207, 228
Edgcote (Northants), 76, 209, 338
Edinburgh, 62, 63, 77, 93, 155, 323, 370
Adam Square, 353
Advocates' Library, 330
Bank of Scotland, 446
British Linen Bank, 322
Commercial Bank, 322
Council Hall, 371
Dean Cemetery, 370, 371
Free Church Institution, 370
Free High Church, 371
George Street, 370
Holyrood Palace, 323, 389
Life Association of Scotland, 322
Life Assurance Building, 389
Masonic Hall, 389
National Gallery of Scotland, see Scottish National Gallery
New Calton Cemetery, 291
New College, 291
New Physicians' Hall, 323
Parliament House, 62, 370, 371
Presbyterian Hall, 323

Prince Consort Memorial, 62
Princes Street, 354, 370
Register Office, 120, 235
Royal Bank of Scotland, 77
Royal College of Physicians, 371
Royal Infirmary, 278
Royal Institution, 370
Royal Scottish Academy, 257
St. Cuthbert's, 63, 150, 323
St. Giles's, 63, 354, 371
St. John's, 63, 371
St. Paul's, 371
Scottish Missionary Societies Hall, 370
Scottish National Gallery, 222, 223, 256, 257, 291, 371, 428
Scottish National Portrait Gallery, 14, 63, 77, 94, 95, 196, 197, 218, 222, 223, 247, 249, 257, 266, 268, 278, 291, 323, 336, 370, 371, 403, 419, 436
Sessions House, 93, 94
University, 63, 222
Warriston Cemetery, 63, 238
Western Bank, 322
Edington (Wilts), 95
Edmondthorpe (Leics), 367
Edmonton (Middx), 188
Edwardstone (Suffolk), 30, 31
Effingham (Surrey), 306
Egg Buckland (Devon), 432
Egham (Surrey), 35, 65, 151
Egloshayle (Cornwall), 427
Eldersfield (Glos), 66
Elford (Staffs), 320
Elgin, General Anderson's Institution, 127
Eling (Hants), 141, 338
Elmdon (Warwicks), 432
Elmley Castle (Worcs), 235, 368
Elmore (Glos), 373
Elmstead (Kent), 209, 307, 344
Eltham (Kent), 32
Elton (Northants), 52
Elton (Notts), 78, 185
Elvaston (Derby), 78, 108
Elvetham (Hants), 188, 223
Ely (Cambs), Cathedral, 100, 182, 210, 238, 300, 343, 367
Enderby (Leics), 144
Enfield (Middx), 204
Englefield Green (Surrey), Holloway College, 238
Enville (Staffs), 121, 373, 400, 412
Epsom (Surrey), 30, 96, 150, 175
Eridge Castle (Sussex), 275
Erith (Kent), 96, 355
Erlestoke Park (Wilts), 34, 171
Ermington (Devon), 409
Escrick (Yorks), 146, 394, 396, 448
Esher (Surrey), 98, 151, 252, 254, 400
Etchingham (Sussex), 224
Eton College (Bucks), 26, 28, 47, 49, 54, 77, 95, 104, 167, 250, 263, 278, 307, 339, 371, 372, 419, 431, 441
Etruria (Staffs), 128, 147
Ettington (Warwicks), 264, 293
Etton (Yorks), 333
Etwall (Derby), 209

Evenley (Bucks), 57
Everingham (Yorks), 60
Evershot (Beds), 431
Eversley (Hants), 170, 430
Everton (Beds), 361, 404
Everton (Notts), 411
Evesham (Worcs), 365, 373
All Saints, 205, 261, 430
Ewell (Surrey), 40, 451
Ewelme (Oxon), 72
Ewenny (Glam), 439
Exeter, 372
Art Gallery, 136, 372, 378, 425
Bridge, 131
Cathedral, 93, 95, 96, 106, 116, 209, 225, 304, 321, 331, 333, 343, 429, 430
Exchange, 207
Guildhall, 110, 225
Holy Trinity, 304
St. Kerrian's, 429
St. Laurence's, 28
St. Leonard's, 204
St. Martin's, 35, 430
St. Petrock's, 429
St. Stephen's, 110
St. Thomas's, 28, 146
Exhall (Warwicks), 265
Exton (Rutland), 170, 279
Exwick (Devon), Chapel, 333
Eydon (Northants), 30
Eye (Suffolk), 390

Fairford (Glos), 66, 376
Falkirk, 155, 323
Falmouth (Cornwall), 214, 284, 295
Polytechnic Hall, 71
Fareham (Hants), 74, 163, 192, 325, 375, 423, 426
Holy Trinity, 36, 127, 150
Faringdon (Berks), 300, 367
Farleigh Hungerford (Som), 52
Farley (Hants), 59, 426, 431
Farnborough (Hants), 402
Staff College, 74
Farnborough (Kent), 234
Farne Island, St. Cuthbert's Chapel, 122
Farnham (Surrey), 151, 154, 187, 322, 427
Town Hall, 56
Farnham Royal (Bucks), 20
Farningham (Kent), 303, 304
Farnley Hall (Yorks), 145
Farthinghoe (Northants), 317
Farway (Devon), 137, 252
Faulkbourne (Essex), 90, 343
Faversham (Kent), 20, 57, 288, 431
Fawley (Northants), 173, 423
Faxton (Northants), 115, 213
Felbridge (Sussex), 156
Felbrigg (Norfolk), 51, 161, 265, 278, 293, 359, 387
Feltham (Middx), 44, 259, 401, 427
Fen Stanton (Hunts), 108
Ferns (Co. Waterford, Eire), 374
Fetcham (Surrey), 63
Ffynone (Pembroke), 108, 133, 162, 301
Fiddown (Co. Kilkenny), 22, 228
Fighledean (Wilts), 127, 399

Filby (Norfolk), 199
Finchcox (Kent), 191
Finchingfield (Essex), 332, 404, 426
Finchley (Middx), 16, 113
Finedon (Northants), 378, 433
Fingask Castle (nr. Perth), 17, 18
Finglas (Co. Dublin), 36
Finningham (Suffolk), 28, 175
Fittleworth (Sussex), 70, 350
Fitz (Salop), 271
Fladbury (Worcs), 322, 373, 438
Fleetwood (Lancs), 70
Flintham (Notts), 362
Flitton (Beds), 39, 42, 132, 143, 220, 224, 275
Flixton (Suffolk), 49
Florence (Italy), Cathedral, 288
  Uffizi Gallery, 43, 310
Folkestone (Kent), 344
Folkingham (Lincs), 381
Fonthill (Wilts), 38, 149, 263, 270, 400, 425
Fordingbridge (Hants), 318
Forfar, 18
Forthampton (Glos), 385
Fowlmere (Cambs), 15
Foxton (Leics), 212
Foxton (Northants), 30
Framfield (Sussex), 292, 427
Framlingham (Suffolk), 105, 331
  Agricultural College, 136
Frampton (Dorset), 117, 155, 426
Frant (Sussex), 303, 304
Fraserburgh (Inverness), 372
Freetown (Sierra Leone), Cathedral, 35, 49, 405
Fremington (Devon), 319, 324
Friern Barnet (Middx), 30
Fringford (Oxon), 423
Frogmore, 387
Frome (Som), 69, 113, 232, 233, 295, 320, 427, 429
Fulbeck (Lincs), 36, 411
Fulford Park (Devon), 372
Fulham (London), 73, 113, 114, 118, 131, 170, 209, 408
Funtington (Sussex), 205

Gaddesby (Leics), 177
Gaddesden (Herts), 51
Gainsborough (Lincs), 308
Galway (Eire), 154
Gamlingay (Cambs), 52
Gamston (Notts), 113
Garstang (Lancs), 157
Gateley (Norfolk), 286
Gateshead (Durham), 134, 222
Gautby (Lincs), 234
Gayton (Norfolk), 124
Gaze Dore (India), 151
Geddington (Northants), 42, 115
Geneva (Switzerland) 320
Georgeham (Devon), 319, 404
George Nympton (Devon), 178, 229
Gerrans (Cornwall), 430
Gestinthorpe (Essex), 345
Gibraltar, Garrison Church, 272
Gibside Park (Durham), 320
Gilling (Yorks), 177, 180
Gillingham (Dorset), 41, 232
Gillingham (Kent), 252

Gissing (Norfolk), 318, 367
Gittisham (Devon), 385
Glanmire (Co. Cork, Eire), 269
Glasgow, 62, 93, 149, 154, 306, 323, 389
  Art Gallery, 34, 63, 275, 291, 450.
    See also Kelvingrove Art Gallery
  Cathedral, 95, 185, 217, 371
  College, 93
  Commercial Bank, 322
  Kelvingrove Art Gallery, 62, 257, 266, 323. See also Art Gallery
  Life Insurance Building, 62
  Merchants' Hall, 172
  National Bank, 389, 390
  Necropolis, 144, 155, 266, 291
  Royal Exchange, 144
  University, 445
  West End Park, 266
Glatton (Hunts), 110
Glemsford (Suffolk), 187
Glenaladale (Inverness), 180
Glenham Hall (Suffolk), 131, 190
Glentworth (Lincs), 213
Glenusk, 390
Glevering Hall (Suffolk), 15
Gloucester, 321, 322
  Cathedral, 34, 66, 104, 150, 179, 229, 259, 321, 322, 352, 373, 439
  St. John, 158
  St. Mary, 344
  St. Nicholas, 66
Glynde (Sussex), 60, 99, 265, 408, 412
Goathurst (Som), 209, 262, 279, 338, 363
Godmanchester (Hunts), 438
Godmersham (Kent), 350
Godstone (Surrey), 27, 53, 114, 378
Gogmagog (Cambs), 218
Goldington (Beds), 318
Golspie (Sutherland), 385
Goodnestone (Kent), 344
Goodrich (Heref), 112, 218, 302
Goodwood (Sussex), 16, 26, 120, 278, 419
Goostrey (Cheshire), 116, 208
Gordon Castle, 191
Gorhambury (Herts), 40, 41, 60, 107, 192, 423
Gosfield (Essex), 338, 361
Göttingen University, 25
Goudhurst (Kent), 56, 75, 256, 353
Grafton Regis (Northants), 48, 151
Graig (Glam), 141
Granby (Notts), 362
Grantham (Lincs), 52, 98, 99, 111, 200, 232, 269, 287, 362, 367, 369, 386
Grasmere (Cumberland), 445
Graveley (Herts), 287
Graveley (Cambs), 131
Gravesend (Kent), Huggins College, 291
  Town Hall, 267
Grays (Essex), 317
Great Amwell (Herts), 209
Great Barrington (Glos), 279
Great Barton Suffolk), 250
Great Bedwyn (Wilts), 313, 315

Great Billing (Northants), 74, 151, 420
Great Bookham (Surrey), 63, 86, 272, 375
Great Brickhill (Bucks), 223, 437
Great Brington (Northants), 96, 115, 151, 279
Great Bromley (Essex), 30, 31
Great Canford, see Canford
Great Casterton (Rutland), 174
Great Dunmow (Essex), 108, 210, 246, 329
Great Easton (Essex), 293
Great Ellingham (Norfolk), 365
Great Finborough (Suffolk), 125, 427
Greatford (Lincs), 278, 279
Greatford (Worcs), 160
Great Gaddesden (Herts), 150
Great Gonerby (Lincs), 411
Great Hallingbury (Essex), 384
Greatham (Co. Durham), 152, 222, 254
Greatham (Sussex), 285
Great Harrowden (Northants), 199
Great Haseley (Oxon), 304
Great Horkesley (Essex), 229
Great Hormead (Herts), 226, 391
Great Leighs (Essex), 131
Great Milton (Oxon), 284
Great Oakley (Northants), 158
Great Offley (Herts), 277, 288, 359
Great Somerford (Wilts), 61, 229, 232
Great Tew (Oxon), 96
Great Waltham (Essex), 90
Great Warby (Essex), 305
Great Wenham (Suffolk), 20
Great Whitcombe, 66
Great Yeldham (Essex), 28
Greenford (Middx), 266, 367
Greenhithe (Kent), St. Michael's, 152
Greenock, 93, 266
Greenwich (London), 88, 261, 336, 352, 376
  Church, see St. Alphege
  Hospital, 27, 48, 64, 91, 135, 289
  King William Building, 64
  Lord Northampton's Almshouses, 380
  National Maritime Museum, 230, 249, 273, 330, 337, 370, 386
  Palace, 41, 44, 94, 100, 104, 106, 107, 108, 129, 134, 201, 218, 221, 236, 251, 255, 378, 411, 414, 421, 451
  Queen Anne's Court, 378
  Queen's House, 377
  Royal Chapel, 47, 109, 129
  Royal Hospital Schools, 414
  Royal Naval Asylum, 306, 314
  St. Alphege, 88, 221, 338, 377
Grenada (B.W.I.), 46, 293, 384, 425, 426
Grendon (Warwicks), 382
Grendon Underwood (Bucks), 344
Gresford (Denbigh), 57, 63, 140, 157, 325, 363, 364, 387, 425, 426
Gretton (Northants), 368
Greystock (Cumberland), 174, 232

Grimesthorpe, 211
Grindon (Durham), 122
Grinshill (Salop), Church, 80
Grove, the (I.o.W.), 286
Grundisburgh (Suffolk), 361
Guernsey, 96, 135, 320
Guildford (Surrey), St. Nicholas, 91
Guilsborough (Northants), 114
Guilsfield (Montgomery), 154
Guisborough (Yorks), 404
Guist (Norfolk), 365
Guiting (Glos), 345
Gulval (Cornwall), 43, 345
Gumley (Leics), 134
Guy's Cliff (Warwicks), 357
Gwennap (Cornwall), 65, 265, 297, 390
Gwinear (Cornwall), 254

Hacconby (Lincs), 187
Hackney (London), Parish Church, 80, 88, 273, 293, 317, 318, 361
Hadenham (Norfolk), 119
Hadleigh (Suffolk), 317
Hadley (Herts), 74, 75. *See also* Monken Hadley
Hadzor (Worcs), 365
Hafod (Cardigan), 92, 108
Hagley (Worcs), 241
Hagley Hall (Worcs), 244, 336, 343
Hailsham (Sussex), 188, 361
Hainton (Lincs), 30
Halberton (Devon), 68
Hale (Denbigh), 157
Hale (Hants), 423, 427, 437
Halesowen (Worcs), 40
Halifax (Yorks), 135, 301, 353, 381, 393
  All Saints, 178
  Parish Church, 60, 113, 146, 208, 239, 316, 426, 427
  Trinity Church, 240
Halstead (Essex), 246
Hamble (Southampton), Sydney Lodge, 64
Hambleden (Bucks), 189, 317, 384, 421, 422
Hamilton Palace, 290, 323
Hammersmith (London), Parish Church, 72, 226, 267, 332
Hampden House (Bucks), 184, 214
Hampreston (Dorset), 279
Hampstead (London), 345, 427
  Caen Wood Towers, 301
  Parish Church, 30, 31, 144, 181, 226, 263
Hampstead Marshall (Berks), 377, 422
Hampton (Middx), 44, 57, 98, 201, 226, 310, 329, 426, 427
Hampton (Worcs), 365
Hampton Court Palace, 17, 56, 99, 103, 104, 122, 142, 170, 201, 205, 216, 280, 283, 284, 296, 310, 313, 391, 438, 440
Hampton Gay (Oxon), 231
Hampton Lovett (Worcs), 256, 325
Hanbury (Staffs), 206, 356, 392
Hanbury (Worcs), 96, 210

Handsworth (Birmingham), Parish Church, 36, 93, 95, 149, 206, 207, 346
Hanmer (Flints), 30
Hanwell (Middx), 31, 407
Hanworth (Norfolk), 13
Hardenhuish (Wilts), 307
Hardingstone (Northants), 213, 309, 338, 431
Hardwick (Bucks), 294
Hardwicke Hall, 425
Harefield (Middx), 29, 70, 165, 168, 170, 194, 202, 335, 368
Harewood (Yorks), 146, 195
Harewood House (Yorks), 111, 240, 276
Harlaxton (Lincs), 188, 440
Harleston (Norfolk), 264, 301, 353
Harlestone (Northants), 30, 367
Harlington (Middx), 245, 387
Harlton (Cambs), 378
Harmondsworth (Middx), 70
Harpham (Yorks), 146, 226, 437
Harrietsham (Kent), 188
Harrow (Middx), 151, 209, 278, 343, 403, 429
  School, 34, 154, 217, 245, 378
Hartburn (Northumb), 96
Hartbury (Devon), 319
Hartfield (Sussex), 110, 127, 318, 339, 350
Hartland (Devon), 190, 225, 332, 405
Hartlebury Castle (Worcs), 176
Hartnest (Suffolk), 422
Hartwell House (Bucks), 97, 258
Harwell (Berks), 96, 271, 380
Harwich (Essex), 162, 352, 422
Hascombe (Surrey), 387
Haselbury Plucknett (Dorset), 209
Hasely, 55
Haslar, Naval Hospital, 297
Haslemere (Surrey), 253
Hastings, 374
  All Saints, 409
Hatfield (Herts), 29, 39, 64, 110, 338
Hatfield (Yorks), 285
Hatfield Broad Oak (Essex), 113, 151, 264
Hatfield Peverel (Essex), 114, 269, 391
Hatherleigh Down (Devon), 372
Hatherop (Glos), 262
Havant (Hants), 192, 407
Haverfordwest (Pembroke), 43, 72, 210, 301, 309, 317
Haverhill (Suffolk), 21
Havering-atte-Bower (Essex), 189
Hawkchurch (Dorset), 101
Hawkesbury (Glos), 426
Hawkstone Park (Salop), 270, 274
Hawstead (Suffolk), 27, 30, 32, 35, 125, 253, 339, 353, 410
Hayes (Middx), 381, 426
Haynes (Beds), 427
Hazelbeach (Northants), 75, 213
Heacham (Norfolk), 188
Heanor (Derbys), 185, 416
Heathfield (Sussex), 188
Heavitree (Devon), 333, 422
Heckfield (Hants), 32, 64
Hedington (Wilts), 204

Helmingham (Suffolk), 279
Helmsley (Yorks), 274
Helston (Cornwall), 127, 297, 345
Hempsted (Essex), 209, 331
Hemsby, 21
Henbury (Glos), 13, 43, 86, 103, 132, 170, 295, 329, 405
Hendon (Middx), 75, 151, 204, 355
  Police College, 46
Hengrave (Suffolk), 287
Henham (Essex), 409
Henham Hall (Suffolk), 108, 110
Henley (Oxon), 54, 55, 306
  Bridge, 120
Henlow (Beds), 319, 438
Hereford, Cathedral, 218, 275, 390
  Museum, 219
  Town Hall, 340, 363
Herrenhausen (Hanover), 95
Hertingfordbury (Herts), 127, 331
Heston (Middx), 22, 35, 127, 407
Hethersett (Norfolk), 368
Heworth (Durham), 222
Hexham (Norfolk), 287
Heydour (Lincs), 338, 343, 344
Hickling (Notts), 369
Highclere (Hants), 331
Highcliffe Castle (Hants), 248, 275
High Ercall (Salop), 271
Highgate (Middx), Cemetery, 48, 140, 355
  Parish Church, 257
Highnam Court (Glos), 312
High Offley (Staffs), 70
Highworth (Wilts), 228
High Wycombe (Bucks), 81, 302, 344, 423
Hilborough (Norfolk), 215
Hillersden (Bucks), 98
Hillingdon (Middx), 28, 361
Hillington (Norfolk), 175, 209, 288, 437
Hill Park, 408
Himley (Staffs), 400
Hingham (Norfolk), 215
Hinton Charterhouse (Som), 52, 61, 229, 295
Hinton St. George (Som), 303, 338, 405, 427
Hints (Staffs), 228, 400
Hinwick House (Beds), 212, 260
Hinxton (Cambs), 317
Hitchin (Herts), 90, 368, 369
Hoarcross (Staffs), 400
Hockley (Notts), 375
Hockwold (Norfolk), 215
Hodnet (Salop), 80, 81, 96, 271
Holcombe (Devon), 258
Holderness House (Hull), 278
Holkham Hall (Norfolk), 21, 37, 85, 94, 95, 125, 198, 218, 277, 278, 303, 355
Holland House (Kingsgate, Kent), 321
Hollingbourne (Kent), 254, 338
Holloway (London), St. Mary's, 229
Hollwood, 270
Holme Lacy (Heref), 275
Holme Pierrepont (Notts), 43, 150, 151, 381

Holmes Chapel (Ches), 265, 363, 418
Holmhurst (nr. Hastings), 53, 54
Holsworthy (Devon), 225
Holt (Norfolk), 240, 374
Holton (Oxon), 228
Holywell (Flint), 151
Homerton (London), St. Barnabas, 260, 273
Honington (Warwicks), 427
Honiton (Devon), 231, 332
Honiton Clyst (Devon), 430
Hooton Hall (Cheshire), 24, 362
Hope-under-Dinsmore (Heref), 405
Hopton Wafers (Salop), 36
Horbury (Yorks), 361, 395
Horne (Surrey), 188
Horningsham (Wilts), 97, 421
Hornsey (Middx), Parish Church, 48, 331
Horringer (Suffolk), 353
Horseheath (Cambs), 296
Horsford (Norfolk), 437
Horsham (Sussex), 188, 426
    Christ's Hospital, 169, 444
    Gaoler's House, 219
Horsham St. Faith (Norfolk), 365
Horsmonden (Kent), 74
Horstead (Norfolk), 41
Horton (Bucks), 44
Horton (Glos), 295
Horton (Middx), 340
Horton (Northants), 244
Hothfield Place (Kent), 107, 350
Hougham (Lincs), 111, 332
Houghton Hall (Norfolk), 218, 336, 337
Hove, Museum, 78
Hovingham (Yorks), 204, 433
Hovingham Hall (Yorks), 351
Howden (Yorks), 45, 64, 146, 309, 416, 433
Howick (Northumb), 45, 77, 244
Hoxne (Suffolk), 95, 365
Hoxton (London), Aske's Hospital, 159
Huddersfield (Yorks), 253, 363, 387, 412, 433
Hughenden (Bucks), 47, 164
Hull, 137, 342
    Bank of England, 182
    Central Museum, 137, 227
    Christ Church, 227
    Holy Trinity, 29, 48, 137, 138, 227, 230
    Hospital, 221, 425
    Infirmary, 227
    Maisters' House, 99
    Mechanics' Institute, 137, 227, 242, 323
    Minerva Lodge, 138
    St. James's, 227
    St. John's, 227
    St. Mary's, 138, 242
    St. Paul's, 227
    Smith's Bank, Whitefriars Gate, 137
    Town Hall, 227
    Trinity Almshouses, 137
    Trinity House, 188
Hungerford (Berks), 30, 189, 200, 295
    Chilton, 85

Hungarton (Leics), 40, 364
Hunsdon (Herts), 308, 367, 381
Hunston (Suffolk), 397
Huntingdon, St. Mary's, 110
Huntley, 62
Hunton (Kent), 318, 378
Hurley (Berks), 105, 151, 422
Hursley (Hants), 213
Hurst (Berks), 189, 368
Hurstbourne Tarrant (Hants), 170
Hurstmonceaux (Sussex), 227
Hurstpierpoint (Sussex), 150
Hyde Lodge (nr. Chalford, Glos), 277
Hythe (Kent), 368

Ickenham (Middx), 40, 70
Ickham (Kent), 318
Icklesham (Sussex), 257
Ickleworth (Herts), 138, 350
Ickworth (Suffolk), 132, 193
Ickworth Park (Suffolk), 41, 47, 108, 125, 149, 176, 187, 353, 383, 437
Idlicote (Warwicks), 339
Ifield (Sussex), 219
Ightham (Kent), 254
Ilam (Staffs), 96, 173, 249, 400
Ilfracombe (Devon), 317
Illogan (Cornwall), 422, 427
Ilmington (Norfolk), 426
Ilmington (Salop), 190
Indore (India), St. Anne's, 321
Ingatestone (Essex), 178
Ingestre (Staffs), 96, 230, 370, 429
Ingres Abbey (Kent), 194
Instow (Devon), 225, 303
Inverary (Argyle), Manse, 63
Inverary Castle, 217, 236
Ipplepen (Devon), 190
Ipswich, St. Clement's, 397
    St. Helen's, 132
    St. Mary-at-Tower, 397
    St. Peter's, 397
Irnham (Lincs), 264, 362
Isleham (Cambs), 371
Isleworth (Middx), 55, 84, 108, 177, 184, 191, 208, 256, 278, 279
Islington (London), 24, 389
    Parish Church, 251
    St. John's, 352
Itchen (Pear Tree Green), 32, 96, 141, 164, 285, 397, 422
Iver (Bucks), 57, 96, 202, 332
Ivinghoe (Bucks), 367

Jacobstowe (Devon), 384
Jamaica, 34, 370
    Cathedral, 29, 76, 155, 317, 318, 371, 427, 437
    Halfway Church, 100
    Kingston Cathedral, 27, 28, 260
    Lucea, 150
    Montego Bay, 27, 422, 423
    St. Andrew's, 426
    St. James's, 425
    Spanish Town, 26
    Spanish Town Cathedral, 28
Jeffreston (Pem), 439
Jersey, St. Helier, 27

Kandy (Ceylon), 302
Kedleston (Derby), 41, 64, 111, 142, 185, 194, 338, 343, 361, 406
Keele (Staffs), 367, 400
Keighley (Yorks), 353, 418
Kelmarsh (Northants), 75, 95, 118
Kelsale (Suffolk), 395
Kelvedon (Essex), 64, 367
Kelvedon Hatch (Essex), 423
Kemble (Glos), 66, 317, 322
Kempton (Beds), 132
Kendal (Westmorland), 146, 418
    Parish Church, 15
    Roman Catholic Church, 133
Kenilworth (Warwicks), 278, 426
Kenninghall (Norfolk), 124
Kennington (London), Licensed Victuallers' Asylum, 137
Kensal Green Cemetery (London), 47, 64, 75, 80, 119, 154, 198, 206, 232, 244, 261, 275, 296, 302, 303, 332, 352, 355, 359, 360, 384, 387, 415, 445
Kensington (London), 202, 216
    St. Mary Abbots, 57, 151, 170, 183, 186, 293, 384, 404
    St. Mary Boltons, 403
Kensington Gardens, 257
Kensington Palace, 103, 142, 201, 242, 283, 287, 319, 336, 337, 360, 364, 412, 421, 424
Kenswick Manor (Worcs), 450
Kentish Town (London), Parish Church, 20, 78, 96, 317, 318, 404, 431
Kenton (Devon), 225, 372
Ketteringham (Norfolk), 151, 302, 426, 433
Kettlethorpe (Lincs), 392
Ketton (Rutland), 145, 199
Kew (Surrey), 110, 131, 427, 428
    Gardens, 49
    Palace, 17, 56
    Temple, 95
Keynsham (Som), 108, 180
Keyworth (Notts), 58
Kidwelly (Carmarthen), 74, 251
Kildrought (Co. Kildare), 86
Kilkenny (Eire), Cathedral, 321, 344
Kilkhampton (Cornwall), 101, 258
Kilmerdown (Som), 204, 295
Kilmington (Devon), 189
Kilnasoola (Co. Clare, Eire), 228
Kilnwick Hall (Yorks), 98, 99
Kilverstone (Norfolk), 21
Kimbolton (Hunts), 115
Kimbolton Castle (Hunts), 98, 128, 187, 249, 330
Kinfauns Castle (Perth), 388
Kingsbridge (Devon), 151
Kingsbury (Warwicks), 182
Kingsclere (Berks), 437
Kingscliffe (Northants), 174, 354
Kingsdon (Som), 170, 242
Kingsland (Heref), 379
King's Lynn (Norfolk), 349
    St. Margaret's, 143
King's Norton (Warwicks), 365
King's Stanley (Glos), 259
Kingsteignton (Devon), 273

Kingsthorpe (Northants), 115
Kingston, Church, 56
Kingston (Som), 180
Kingston Bagpuize (Berks), 59, 304
Kingston-on-Thames (Surrey), 54, 93, 150, 255, 317, 343, 384, 400, 413.
Cleave's Almshouses, 401
Kingswood (Som), St. George, 294–5
Kington (Heref), 218
Kinlet (Salop), 80, 81
Kinnerley (Salop), 31
Kinnersley (Heref), 316, 440
Kinsbury (Warwicks), 213
Kintbury (Berks), 265, 321, 344
Kippax (Yorks), 309, 353
Kirby Fleetham (Yorks), 151
Kirkby (Westmorland), 219
Kirkby Lonsdale (Westmorland), 418
Kirkby Mallory (Leics), 70
Kirk Deighton (Yorks), 145
Kirk Ella (Yorks), 30, 50, 138, 227, 416
Kirkheaton (Yorks), 183
Kirkleatham (Yorks), 256, 342, 425, 435
Kirkling (Cambs), 390
Kirklington (Yorks), 145
Kirkmichael (Ayrshire), 185
Kirkthorpe (Yorks), 150, 183
Kirtlington (Oxon), 23, 98, 100, 433
Kislingbury (Northants), 213
Knebworth (Herts), 19, 367, 413
Knights' Enham (Hants), 189
Knole, Sevenoaks (Kent), 68, 230, 240
Knowsley (Lancs), 130, 275, 288, 348, 366, 387, 393, 401
Knutsford (Ches), 427
Kyre Wyard (Worcs), 203

Lacock (Wilts), 232, 347, 400, 427
Lakenham (Norfolk), 117
Laleham (Middx), 404
Lambeth (London), Coade's Factory, 26
Palace, 103, 242, 293
St. Mary, 48, 94, 108, 109, 150, 421
Lambourn (Berks), 352
Lambourne (Essex), 150, 298, 437
Lambton Castle, 46
Lamport (Northants), 356, 367, 368, 422, 431
Lamport Hall (Northants), 50, 102, 115, 273, 342, 343, 356, 360
Lanark, 155
Lancaster, Parish Church, 145, 418
St. Mary's, 331
Landport, 302
Landwade (Cambs), 423
Langdon (Yorks), 381
Langford (Norfolk), 210
Langford (Notts), 411
Langford Budville (Som), 229, 295
Langham (Essex), 32
Langley (Essex), 259
Langley Burrell (Wilts), 229
Langley Marish (Bucks), 44, 108

Langley Park (Norfolk), 56, 366
Langleys (nr. Chelmsford, Essex), 633
Langport (Som), 355
Langridge (Som), 317
Langtoft (Lincs), 199
Lathbury (Bucks), 287
Laugharne (Carmarthen), 108, 142, 162, 211, 250, 287, 295
Laughton (Leics), 144
Launcells, 101
Launceston (Cornwall), 225
Lavington (Suffolk), 191
Lawford (Essex), 141, 246
Lawhitton (Cornwall), 108
Laxton (Northants), 116
Lea (Lincs), 138, 400
Leamington, 206
Leasowes (Staffs), 111, 298
Leatherhead (Surrey), 210
Lechlade (Glos), 316
Ledbury (Heref), 112, 150, 180, 244, 295, 317, 373, 393, 409, 418, 426, 427, 430
Ledreborg Castle (Denmark), 347
Ledsham (Yorks), 87, 343
Lee (London), 108, 109, 256
Leeds (Kent), 288
Leeds (Yorks), 274, 308, 429
Art Gallery, 177, 330, 419
Infirmary, 47, 93, 138, 445
Literary Society, 177
Moot Hall, 82
Parish Church, 22, 82, 151, 177, 291, 319, 362, 412, 429
St. John's, 82
Leek (Staffs), 29, 65, 185, 350
Leghorn (Italy), 310
Leicester, 122, 301
All Saints', 196, 207, 431
Assembly Rooms, 326
Cathedral, 27, 212, 255
Library Institution, 307
Museum, 330
Prison, 144
St. Margaret's, 185, 202
St. Mary's, 31, 127, 212
St. Mary's School, 106
Leigh (Glos), 162, 302
Leigh Court (Som), 343
Leiston (Suffolk), 395
Lemmington (Northumb), 156
Leningrad, Hermitage, 403. See also St. Petersburg
Leominster (Heref), 218, 373, 379, 440
Letheringsett (Norfolk), 31
Letton Hall (Norfolk), 125, 233
Lewes (Sussex), 265
County Hall, 108, 209, 292
Prison, 144
Riverhall Bridge, 265
St. Michael's, 116
St. Thomas's, 325
Sessions House, 265
Sussex Archaeological Museum, 188
Town Hall, 209, 403
Lewisham (London), Parish Church, 36, 40, 113, 150, 226, 256, 264, 283, 408

Lewknor (Oxon), 114
Lexington (Va., U.S.A.), 154
Leybourne (Kent), 304
Leyton (Essex), 19, 151, 200, 261, 293, 401, 420
Leytonstone (Essex), 270
Lichborough (Northants), 312
Lichfield (Staffs), 245
Bishop's Palace, 296
Cathedral, 35, 92, 94, 95, 96, 146, 195, 206, 300, 345, 350, 367, 392, 423, 426, 434
Liddington (Wilts), 175
Lifton (Devon), 319
Lilleshall (Salop), 405
Lillingstone Dayrell (Bucks), 189
Limerick (Eire), 235, 250
Cathedral, 34, 429
Limpsfield (Surrey), 275
Lincoln, Abbey, 305
Asylum, 261
Cathedral, 22, 194, 240, 288, 305, 308, 320, 404, 429
Usher Gallery, 277, 386
Lincoln Heath, 289
Lindfield (Sussex), 256
Lingfield (Surrey), 423
Linton (Cambs), 423, 437
Linton (Kent), 33, 35, 36
Lisbon (Portugal), British Embassy, 448
Lisburn (Co. Antrim), Cathedral, 154
Liskeard (Cornwall), 65, 215, 350
Liston (Essex), 209
Little Berkhampstead (Herts), 303, 387
Littlebourne (Kent), 266
Little Bredy (Dorset), 314
Little Cressingham (Norfolk), 125
Little Easton (Essex), 297, 365
Little Gaddesden (Herts), 20, 74, 302, 427
Little Glenham (Suffolk), 172
Little Hadham (Herts), 117
Littleham (Devon), 137, 225, 304, 324, 403
Little Hereford (Heref), 322, 390
Little Linford (Bucks), 423
Little Missenden (Bucks), 70, 117
Little Sampford (Essex), 426
Little Saxham (Suffolk), 288, 374
Little Stukeley (Hunts), 422
Little Thurlow (Suffolk), 412
Little Torrington (Devon), 35, 178, 332
Little Wolston (Bucks), 422
Liverpool, 69, 93, 154, 387, 393, 415, 425
Academy, 105
Bank of England, 182
Brown's Institute, 274
Christ Church, 95
Custom House, 172
Exchange, 107, 181, 199, 328, 441
Great George Street Chapel, 247
Liverpool and London Insurance Co., 374
Mansion House, 446
Necropolis, 172
Public Library, 217

Renshaw Chapel, 173
Royal Institution, 124, 173
Royal Insurance Office, 224
St. George's, 174, 360
St. George's Hall, 14, 122, 173, 224, 250, 271, 274, 363
St. James's Chapel, 96, 173, 177, 363
St. John's, 170
Stanley Park, 363
Town Hall, 93, 373, 446
Union News Room, 237, 418
Walker Art Gallery, 14, 41, 136, 172, 173, 177, 217, 221, 257, 275, 363, 420
Llanbadarn Fawr (Cardigan), 35, 151
Llanbadon (Aberystwyth), 400
Llanbedr (Denbigh), 157
Llanbodwell (Salop), 80, 338, 431
Llandaff, Cathedral, 418, 444
Llandegai (N. Wales), 427
Llandovey (Brecon), 220, 405
Llandwywe (Merioneth), 406
Llanelly (Carmarthen), 288, 329
Llanfair (Denbigh), 80, 174, 271
Llangadock (Carnarvon), 133
Llangedwyn (Salop), 271
Llangollen (Denbigh), 402
Llanlivery (Cornwall), 385
Llanspyddid, 390
Llantwit (Glam), 322, 432
Lockington (Leics), 59, 314, 376
London, Admiralty, 33, 40, 107, 129, 361, 423
Ailesbury House, Clerkenwell, 87
Albert Hall, 135
Albert Memorial, 49, 153, 154, 235, 250, 257, 300, 387, 393, 418
Alford House, 56
All Hallows, Barking, 342
All Hallows, Bread Street, 159
All Hallows the Great, 186
All Hallows, Lombard Street, 391
All Hallows, London Wall, 293
All Souls, Langham Place, 117
Apsley House, 14, 94, 158, 173, 223, 248, 278, 282, 371, 447
Argyll House, 129
Arlington Street, 40, 303
Army and Navy Club, 64
Ashburnham House, Dover Street, 139
Ashburnham House, Westminster, 288, 340
Athenæum Club, 34, 93, 197, 198, 318, 336
Austin Friars, 40, 234
Bakers' Hall, 117
Bank of England, 38, 40, 98, 107, 174, 182, 213, 270, 364, 382, 402, 403
Barbican Chapel, Cripplegate, 365
Bedford House, 129
Bedford Square, 407
Berkeley Square, 44, 267, 435
Berners Street, 26
Bethlem Hospital, 28, 102, 451
Bishopsgate, 210

"Black Bull," Holborn, 312
Blackfriars Bridge, 131, 301
Blackfriars Church, 252
Bloomsbury Square, 425
Board of Trade, Whitehall, 90, 117, 324
Brewers' Hall, 257, 374, 442
Bridgewater House, 355, 389, 428
British Museum, 29, 77, 89, 93, 94, 112, 120, 146, 154, 158, 200, 245, 278, 297, 306, 330, 337, 424, 437, 445
Broad Sanctuary, 301
Brooks' Club, 245
Buckingham Palace, 15, 27, 33, 45, 46, 51, 56, 66, 79, 94, 95, 116, 117, 123, 127, 138, 148, 157, 173, 181, 280, 291, 307, 327, 328, 372, 375, 384, 385, 386, 387, 389, 395, 400, 421, 424, 428
Bunhill Fields Cemetery, 108, 290, 304
Burlington House, 34, 39, 81, 90, 94, 95, 122, 136, 172, 173, 276, 301, 331, 342, 357, 360, 372, 378, 387, 419, 420, 425, 428, 441, 445. See also Royal Academy.
Cannon Street Hotel, 56
Carlton House, 29, 85, 107, 129, 166, 187, 200, 278, 402, 412, 424, 439, 446
Carlton House Terrace, 66, 243, 425
Carpenters' Hall, 26
Cartwright Gardens, Euston, 104
Cass Institute, Aldgate, 330
Cavendish Square, 77, 84 97, 132, 244
Chapel Royal, Savoy, 415
Charing Cross, 255
Charing Cross Hospital, 445
Charing Cross Hotel, 56
Charles Street, Berkeley Square, 61, 66, 270
Charterhouse Chapel, 48, 95, 367
Cheapside, 121
Chester Terrace, Regent's Park, 67
Child's Bank, 305
Christ Church, Newgate Street, 350, 377
Christ Church, Spitalfields, 117, 121, 134, 150
Christ's Hospital, 21, 69, 117, 169, 250
City of London School, 24, 47, 136, 257, 273
Civil Service Commission, 250, 274, 422, 441, 450
Clarendon House, Piccadilly, 378
Cleveland House, 53, 213, 440
Clothworkers' Hall, 69, 398
Cockspur Street, 446
Colonial Office, 136
Coopers' Hall, 296
Cordwainers' Hall, 276
Cornbury House, 128
Cornhill, Union Assurance Office, 108
Coutts Bank, Strand, 93, 129

Covent Garden Theatre, 149, 328
Coventry House, Piccadilly, 16, 283, 339
Cripplegate, 68
Crosby Hall, Bishopsgate, 117, 273
Cumberland Street, Hyde Park, 56
Cumberland Terrace, 67
Customs House, 67, 271, 306
Danish Church, Wellclose Square, 102, 103
Denmark House, 360
Devonshire Place, 202, 407
Dorchester House, 217, 355
Dover Street, 20
Drapers' Hall, 87, 158, 173, 276, 344, 407, 450
Drury Lane Theatre, 34, 79, 100, 120, 163, 278, 357
Duke of York's Column, 282
East India House, 27, 59, 305
Egyptian Hall, Piccadilly, 161
Emmanuel Hospital, Tothill Fields, 123
Euston Station, 389
Farm Street, Jesuit Church, 301
Female Orphan Asylum, 312
Fife House, 182
Fishmongers' Hall, 106, 107, 297, 305, 439
Fleet Prison, 174, 421
Fleet Street, 66
Foreign Office, 49, 301, 420
Founders' Hall, 44
Foundling Hospital, 35, 46, 108, 128, 193, 257, 337, 352, 396, 434
Fountain Court, 66
Free Society of Artists, 58
Freemasons' Charity School, Southwark, 408
Freemasons' Hall, 34, 94, 135, 136, 158, 182
Freemasons' Tavern, 20, 279
Garrick Club, 136
G.P.O., 251, 301
Geological Museum, 71, 158, 243, 290, 291, 354, 419, 420
Gloucester Gate, Regent's Park, 135
Golden Square, 281
Goldsmiths' Hall, 273
Gower Street, 202
Great St. Helen's, Bishopsgate, 48
Grocers' Hall, 108, 117, 275, 296, 313, 387, 407
Grosvenor Chapel, 20, 27, 150, 202, 318, 375, 384, 396, 423
Grosvenor Square, 156, 281, 310
Grosvenor Street, 53, 375
Guildhall, 14, 26, 47, 49, 67, 69, 93, 120, 123, 136, 263, 275, 296, 300, 304, 313, 340, 352, 357, 387, 403, 445
Guildhall Museum, 102, 103
Guy's Hospital, 26, 35, 40, 121, 128, 239, 342, 397, 398, 432
Haberdashers' Hall, 87
Hand Alley, 234
Hanover Square, 85, 93, 396
Harrow Road, 132

Haymarket, Opera House, 67
Hertford Street, 131
Hicks' Hall, 441
Hill Street, 396
Hoare's Bank, Fleet Street, 122, 210, 345
Holborn Circus, 24
Holland House, 312
Horse Guards, 84, 218, 268
House of Lords, 250, 323, 390, 393, 394, 395, 422, 441
Houses of Parliament, 171, 217, 267, 300, 301, 322, 355, 388, 393
Hyde Park, 267, 300, 386, 389, 421, 425
Hyde Park Corner, 198, 447
Imperial Fire Office, 389
India Office, 26, 39, 94, 149, 272, 274, 302, 337, 342, 359, 403, 419
Inner Temple, 46, 50, 68, 72, 87, 135, 165, 210, 328, 337, 345, 376, 445, 451
Inns of Court Hotel, 396
Ironmongers' Hall, 22, 283
Jeffrye Museum, 128
Junior Carlton Club, 387
Junior United Service Club, 95, 112, 397
King's Bench Prison, 129
King's College, 403
King William Street, 273
Langham Place, 61, 116
Lansdowne House, Berkeley Square, 85
Law Courts, 444. See also New Courts of Judicature
Law Institution, 263
Law Society, 95
Leicester House, 366
Leicester Square, 70, 136, 257, 420, 445
Lincoln's Inn, 47, 184, 221, 288, 375, 387, 389, 390, 391, 425
Lincoln's Inn Fields, 50, 85, 108, 111
Little Holland House, 415
Lloyd's, 243, 374
Lombard Street, 128
London Museum, 297
London Orphan Asylum, 259
London Wall, 283
Long Acre, 109
Ludgate, 117
Ludgate Hill, 67
Mansion House, 15, 35, 40, 128, 134, 136, 137, 154, 158, 187, 198, 210, 244, 250, 372, 382, 386, 394, 397, 398, 408, 419, 422, 450
Marble Arch, 32, 33, 66, 93, 148, 198, 424
Marlborough House, 37, 230, 377, 387
Marylebone Cricket Club, 122
Masons' Hall, 381
Mercers' Hall, 87, 364, 451
Merchant Taylors' Hall, 34
Metropolitan Cattle Market, 49
Middlesex Hospital, 244
Middlesex Sessions House, 111, 240, 276

Middle Temple, 46, 47, 122, 445
Millbank, 274
Monument, 103, 255, 296
Moorfields, R.C. Church, 112
Moorgate, 87
National Debt Office, 425
National Gallery, 33, 148, 169, 251, 355, 420, 424
National Portrait Gallery, 14, 27, 29, 34, 35, 39, 46, 47, 70, 77, 94, 95, 129, 130, 136, 142, 149, 153, 154, 158, 162, 173, 176, 198, 222, 243, 245, 249, 263, 275, 277, 283, 297, 300, 307, 309, 328, 330, 331, 332, 336, 352, 371, 380, 387, 444, 445, 450
New Cavendish Street, 156, 166, 270,
New City Club, 396
New Courts of Judicature, 117, 182
Newgate, 87, 102, 103, 128
Northumberland House, 84, 118
Old Bailey, Sessions House, 73, 267, 387, 393, 419, 444
Old Carlton House, 334, 342
Old Jewry, 37, 119, 234, 265
Old Street, 19
Oxford and Cambridge Club, 271
Pall Mall, 38, 85, 107, 108, 120, 156, 236, 270, 289, 298, 334
Pancras Lane, 296
Pantheon Bazaar, 22
Park Lane, 20, 211, 393
Park Street, 53, 270
Parliament Square, 274, 425, 444
Pentonville Chapel, 108
Philpot Lane, 270, 305
Piccadilly, 85, 107, 432
Pimlico Gardens, 172
Polytechnic, Regent Street, 289
Portland Place, 89, 149, 161, 182, 211
Powys House, 412
Privy Council Office, 324
Quadrant, Regent Street, 61
Queenhithe, 69
Record Office, 136
Red Lion Square, 175, 211, 288
Reform Club, 47, 158, 275, 291
Regent's Park, 198, 217, 391, 428
Regent's Park Chapel, 390
Regent Street, 67, 182
Riding House Lane, 407
Rolls Chapel, 126, 286
Royal Academy, 81, 95, 136, 154, 249, 253, 257. See also Burlington House
Royal College of Physicians, 19, 47, 94, 101, 116, 117, 135, 186, 208, 251, 275 297, 310, 313, 323, 342, 374, 381, 419, 436
Royal College of Surgeons, 13, 35, 47, 74, 77, 94, 117, 122, 149, 197, 206, 278, 328, 364, 403, 419, 445
Royal Exchange, 46, 67, 73, 79, 87, 93, 102, 168, 222, 234, 243, 281, 296, 336, 339, 342, 355, 357, 364, 367, 404, 415, 418, 435

Royal Free Hospital, 257, 389
Royal Geographical Society, 420
Royal Institute of British Architects, 337
Royal Institution, 136, 445
Royal Mews, Buckingham Palace Road, 386, 421
Royal Mews, Charing Cross, 37, 128, 218
Royal Mint, 296, 446
Royal Society, 94, 95, 122, 154, 163, 275, 277, 291, 331, 445
Royal Society of Arts, 81
Royal Society of Medicine, 26
Royal United Service Institution, 371
Royal United Services Museum, 303, 306
Russell Square, 425
Sailors' Home, Wells Street, 136
St. Alphage's, Cripplegate, 365
St. Andrew by the Wardrobe, 28, 31, 252, 452
St. Andrew's, Holborn, 296
St. Andrew's, Wells Street, 272
St. Anne's, Limehouse, 88, 121, 377
St. Anne's, Soho, 157, 228, 361
St. Anne and St. Agnes, 186, 201
St. Antholin, 87, 306
St. Austin by St. Paul's, 376
St. Bartholomew by the Exchange, 142, 391
St. Bartholomew the Less, 53
St. Bartholomew's Gate, Smithfield, 54
St. Bartholomew's Hospital, 18, 47, 181, 244, 251, 252, 352, 381, 419
St. Benet Fink, 87, 181, 296
St. Benet Grace, 438
St. Benet's, Paul's Wharf, 376
St. Botolph's, Aldersgate, 18, 20, 112, 331
St. Bride's, Fleet Street, 142, 159, 251, 255
St. Christopher le Stocks, 365, 377
St. Clement Danes, 255, 296, 350
St. Clement's, Eastcheap, 250, 376
St. Dionis Backchurch, 391
St. Dunstan in the East, 44, 152, 255, 404, 451
St. Dunstan in the West, 348, 369
St. Edmund the King, Lombard Street, 27, 36, 374
St. Ethelburga's, Bishopgate, 273
St. George's, Bloomsbury, 32, 59, 219, 224, 228, 252, 332
St. George's, Botolph Lane, 452
St. George's, Hanover Square, 88, 152
St. George the Martyr, Southwark, 157, 190, 235, 325
St. George's Hospital, 14, 47, 386
St. George's Road, S.E., 74
St. Giles's, Cripplegate, 27, 39
St. Giles in the Fields, 90, 116, 128, 202, 255, 307, 361, 381, 423, 442

St. James's, Garlickhithe, 225, 274, 352, 377
St. James's, Hampstead Road, 29, 30, 80, 108, 121, 279, 431
St. James's, Piccadilly, 150, 169, 228
St. James's Palace, 129, 218, 280, 360, 441
St. James's Park, 100, 217, 361, 446
St. James's Place, 149, 280, 393
St. James's Square, 26, 29, 88, 122, 131, 179, 182, 218, 227, 270, 279, 340, 382, 396
St. James's Street, 85
St. John, Horsleydown, 59, 121, 401
St. John's, Westminster, 88, 339, 377, 389
St. Katherine's, Regent's Park, 90, 209, 279, 332
St. Lawrence Jewry, 135, 296
St. Luke's, Old Street, 59, 88, 121
St. Magnus the Martyr, 251, 306, 348, 352, 360, 391
St. Margaret Lothbury, 116, 143, 159, 277, 279, 357, 450
St. Margaret Pattens, 159, 202, 318, 338
St. Margaret's, Westminster, 16, 55, 401
St. Martin-in-the-Fields, 88, 307, 336
St. Martin's, Ludgate, 251, 267, 452
St. Martin's Hall, Long Acre, 394
St. Mary Abchurch, 142, 225
St. Mary Aldermanbury, 78, 159, 255
St. Mary Aldermary, 29, 66, 318
St. Mary at Hill, 163, 228, 255, 273, 367
St. Mary Axe, Out Pension Office, 414
St. Mary le Bow, 38, 39, 87, 122, 296, 343, 391, 401
St. Mary le Strand, 226, 398
St. Mary Somerset, 225
St. Mary Woolnoth, 121, 134
St. Mary Magdalen, Old Fish Street, 376
St. Matthew's, Friday Street, 273, 296, 305
St. Michael Bassishaw, 152
St. Michael's, Cornhill, 109, 181, 300, 301, 377, 411, 423, 452
St. Michael's, Crooked Lane, 186
St. Michael Paternoster Royal, 338, 376
St. Michael's, Queenhithe, 357
St. Michael's, Wood Street, 438
St. Mildred's, Bread Street, 376
St. Mildred's, Poultry, 277
St. Nicholas Cole Abbey, 438
St. Olave's, Hart Street, 74
St. Olave's, Jewry, 350, 357
St. Olave's, Southwark, 59, 128, 210
St. Pancras, 31, 65, 107, 228, 267, 302, 306, 326, 327, 328
St. Pancras Old Church, 240
St. Paul's Cathedral, 14, 26, 30, 31,

33, 34, 35, 43, 44, 46, 53, 54, 55, 57, 67, 77, 83, 93, 95, 149, 150, 151, 159, 161, 169, 198, 201, 209, 225, 226, 234, 243, 244, 250, 251, 256, 266, 274, 283, 289, 296, 315, 326, 328, 329, 357, 372, 376, 377, 386, 391, 415, 421, 425, 426, 438, 441, 445
St. Paul's, Covent Garden, 150, 179, 296
St. Paul's, Knightsbridge, 302
St. Paul's School, 26
St. Peter's, Cornhill, 255, 333
St. Peter-le-Poer, 69
St. Stephen's, Coleman Street, 255, 450
St. Stephen's Hall, 49, 79, 154
St. Stephen's, Walbrook, 29, 225, 251, 264, 283, 377
St. Swithin's, Cannon Street, 159, 255, 296
St. Thomas's, Southwark, 87
St. Thomas' Hospital, 87, 88, 94, 169, 274, 342, 343, 372, 420
St. Vedast, Foster Lane, 377
Salters' Hall, 21, 67, 350
Senior United Service Club, 77
Seven Dials, 297
Skinners' Hall, 26, 68, 397
Sloane Street, 201
Smithfield Market, 224, 301
Soane Museum, 39, 94, 107, 127, 148, 149, 164, 177, 297, 352, 417
Society of Antiquaries, 25
Society of Arts, 387
Soho Square, 103
Somerset House, 16, 21, 26, 38, 74, 81, 89, 99, 129, 166, 174, 180, 192, 194, 236, 240, 276, 289, 296, 314, 326, 359, 386, 421, 435, 441
Southwark Cathedral, 15, 113, 404
Southwark Town Hall, 74, 438
Stafford House, 66, 428
Star and Garter Hotel, 56
Stationers' Hall, 251
Steelyard, 103
Stratford Place, 38
Stratton Street, 174, 375, 407
Sun Fire Office (Charing Cross), 56
Surgeons' Hall, 17, 304
Tallow Chandlers' Hall, 87
Tate Gallery, 173, 222, 389, 419
Temple, see Inner Temple; Middle Temple
Temple Bar, 72, 224, 231, 234
Temple Bridge, 451, 452
Temple Church, 68, 72, 110, 122, 142, 150, 210, 251, 261, 272, 320, 342, 366, 388, 398, 451
Threadneedle Street, 415
Tottenham Court Road, 202, 328
Tower, 111, 128, 179, 218, 261, 360, 438
Trafalgar Square, 14, 34, 46, 79, 93, 104, 137, 355, 384, 415, 441
Treasury, 448

Trinity House, 27, 28, 91, 94
Union Insurance Office, 289
United Service Club, 14, 149, 222, 306, 389, 400, 420
University College, 34, 122, 127, 148, 333, 354, 415, 425, 445
Vauxhall Gardens, 329
Victoria and Albert Museum, 15, 26, 36, 37, 56, 85, 94, 102, 110, 120, 126, 149, 167, 173, 176, 183, 184, 193, 196, 199, 237, 245, 246, 265, 266, 277, 278, 286, 291, 300, 309, 330, 332, 335, 337, 343, 344, 361, 375, 436
Victoria Embankment, 74, 274, 370, 444
Vintners' Hall, 108, 186, 214
Wallace Collection, 336
Warwick Lane, 87
Warwick Street, Church of the Assumption, 79
Waterloo Place, 48, 49, 154, 274
Watermen's Hall, 107
Watlingford House, 234
Weavers' Hall, 87
Welsh Institution, 390
Wesley Chapel, City Road, 71, 252, 309
West India Docks, 106, 108, 425
Westminster Abbey, 19, 20, 24, 26, 27, 29, 30, 31, 34, 35, 36, 39, 40, 46, 48, 51, 54, 55, 58, 59, 63, 68, 71, 73, 77, 78, 81, 86, 90, 92, 93, 94, 95, 96, 98, 99, 100, 108, 118, 121, 122, 126, 139, 148, 149, 150, 151, 154, 160, 161, 166, 168, 170, 173, 175, 183, 184, 195, 202, 210, 211, 213, 217, 222, 254, 256, 257, 263, 264, 269, 275, 277, 278, 279, 287, 301, 309, 313, 316, 329, 330, 331, 333, 334, 337, 338, 341, 342, 343, 344, 357, 358, 359, 361, 366, 368, 371, 382, 383, 384, 385, 387, 389, 390, 394, 401, 403, 404, 406, 407, 412, 417, 419, 420, 422, 425, 426, 428, 435, 437, 442, 445
Westminster Bridge, 166, 218, 393
Westminster Cemetery, 36
Westminster Hall, 166, 198, 236, 252, 271, 309, 383
Westminster Palace Hotel, 135
Westminster, Palace of, 13, 34, 79, 91, 154, 250, 257, 360, 386, 387, 419, 441, 444
Westminster School, 210, 319, 366
Westminster Sessions House 103
Whitehall, 87, 91, 142, 169, 252, 255, 296, 313, 360, 376, 421, 438, 441
Whitehall Club, 396
Wyndham's Club, 224
Long Ashton (Som), 103, 232, 398, 439
Longborough (Glos), 321, 427
Long Bredy (Dorset), 239
Longbridge Deverill (Wilts), 96
Long Buckby (Northants), 57, 115, 212

Longcot (Berks), 423
Longden (Worcs), 373
Long Ditton (Surrey), 413
Longdon (Staffs), 206, 367
Longford (Derby), 158, 185
Longford Castle, 16, 40, 84, 85, 88, 97, 99, 117, 129, 138, 193, 220, 221, 258, 292, 311, 334, 336, 337, 344, 382
Longleat (Wilts), 15, 47, 62, 112, 229, 282, 311, 328, 346
Long Melford (Suffolk), 187
Long Newton (Durham), 22, 426
Long Newton (Glos), 292, 317
Long Stanton (Cambs), 50, 397
Long Whatton (Leics), 203
Long Wittenham (Berks), 189
Longworth (Oxon), 426
Lostwithiel (Cornwall), 215, 350
Loughborough (Leics), 298, 427, 437
Loversall (Yorks), 413
Lowdham (Notts), 440
Lower Basildon (Berks), 151
Lowestoft, Parish Church, 21, 414
Lowick (Northants), 429
Lowther (Westmorland), 146, 271, 368, 372
Lowther Castle, 134
Lucca (Italy), Ducal Palace, 387
Lugwardine (Heref), 239, 379
Lupton (Devon), 372
Luscombe Castle (Devon), 149
Luton (Beds), 114, 187, 306, 390
Lutterworth (Leics), 207, 429
Lydd (Kent), 149, 328, 329
Lydiard Park (Swindon), 336
Lydney (Glos), 133, 208, 229, 239, 295
Lyme Regis (Dorset), 170
  Belmont, 106
  The Cobb, 185
Lymington (Hants), 28, 110, 164, 208, 338, 350
Lympstone (Devon), 137, 375
Lyndhurst (Hants), 150
Lyonshall (Heref), 413
Macclesfield (Ches), 368
  Christ Church, 27, 268, 363
Machynlleth (Wales), 253
Madehurst (Sussex), 226
Madingley (Cambs), 151, 426, 427
Madley (Heref), 451
Madras, 39, 49, 93, 320
Madras, Cathedral, 35, 95, 127, 136, 151, 173, 260, 320, 352, 355, 384, 419, 426
  St. Mary's, 30, 31, 104, 150, 151, 154, 252, 298, 320, 411
  St. Thomas's, 96
Madresfield (Worcs), 20
Madrom (Cornwall), 345
Maidenhead, Town Hall, 113
Maiden Newton (Dorset), 74, 239
Maidstone (Kent), 21, 209, 279, 315, 378, 389, 443
  Museum, 115, 445, 450
  Preston Hall, 389
Maisemore (Glos), 66
Maker (Cornwall), 225, 402
Mallwyd (Montgomery), 174
Malmesbury (Wilts), 61, 287

Malta, 243
Malvern (Worcs), 112, 373, 427
  Priory, 205, 206
Malvern Hall, 156
Mamhead (Devon), 193, 355, 359
Mancetter (Warwicks), 290
Manchester, 257, 274, 386, 387, 445
  Art Gallery, 35, 78, 198
  Assize Court, 274, 444
  Cathedral, 30, 34, 60, 62, 262, 269, 386
  City Hall, 238, 274, 275, 387
  Collegiate Church, see Cathedral
  Free Library, 291
  Free Trade Hall, 389
  Manley Park, 235
  Owen's College, 274
  Royal Institution, 93
  St. Ann's, 157
  St. John's, 151
  Town Hall, see City Hall
Manordivy (Cardigan), 302
Mansoll Lacy (Heref), 293
Mapledurham (Oxon), 175, 264
Mapperton (Dorset), 343
Marham-church (Cornwall), 101
Marholm (Northants), 145, 271
Market Bosworth (Leics), 350, 438
Market Drayton (Salop), 80, 141, 206, 270, 351, 418
  Pelwall House, 80, 182
Market Lavington (Wilts), 61, 150, 200
Markham Clinton (Notts), 427
Markree Castle (Sligo), 249
Mark's Tey (Essex), 246
Markyate (Herts), 31
Marlborough (Wilts), St. Mary's, 143
  St. Peter's, 61, 155, 191, 384
Marlesford (Suffolk), 80, 118, 395
Marlow (Bucks), 30, 113, 127, 279, 306, 384, 422, 427, 439
Marston (Lincs), 111, 210
Marston House, Somerset, 16
Marston Lea (Warwick), 108, 206
Marston St. Lawrence (Northants), 72, 76, 210, 426
Marsworth (Bucks), 232
Marylebone, Chapel, 39, 132, 237, 264
  Holy Trinity, 127, 192, 352
  Parish Church, 30, 32, 40, 63, 110, 202, 209, 230, 246, 302, 303, 306, 314, 329, 332, 352, 355, 356, 427, 431, 433
Masham (Yorks), 146, 381
Mathern (Mon), 180, 295
Mattishall (Norfolk), 414
Mawgan in Meneage (Cornwall), 41
Maxwelltown (Dumfries), 388
Mayfield (Sussex), 188, 283, 292, 317
Maynooth (Eire), College, 403
Mayo (Eire), 154
Medmenham (Bucks), 429
Meeth (Devon), 384
Melbourne (Australia), 372, 378, 445

Melbourne Hall (Derbys), 129, 156, 179, 185, 211, 217, 222, 279, 369, 382, 393, 416
Melbury Osmond (Dorset), 196
Melbury Sampford (Dorset), 96
Melchet Park (Wilts), 328
Melfield (Hants), 154
Melksham (Wilts), 62, 204
Melling (Lanes), 350, 363
Meltham Mills (Yorks), 302
Melton Constable (Norfolk), 30, 109, 252, 286, 303
Melton Mowbray (Leics), 383, 411
Menai Strait, Britannia Bridge, 389
Mendham (Suffolk), 315
Mendlesham (Suffolk), 318
Menheniot (Cornwall), 137
Mentmore (Bucks), 262
Meopham (Kent), 43, 372, 449
Mere (Wilts), 97, 232
Merevale (Warwicks), 202
Mereworth (Kent), 344, 378
Merley House (Dorset), 336
Mersham (Kent), 85, 404
Mersham Hatch (Kent), 211
Merstham (Surrey), 209, 360, 375
Merthyr Tydfil, 140
Merton (Surrey), 449
Messingham (Notts), 411
Methley (Yorks), 57, 145, 427, 437
Micheldever (Hants), 151
Mickleham (Surrey), Church, 19
Mickleton (Glos), 113, 155, 341, 443
Middle Claydon (Bucks), 35, 98, 189, 260
Middleton (Lancs), 195, 294, 363, 412
Middleton St. George (Durham), 69
Middlewych (Ches), 363
Mid Lavant (Sussex), 73
Midsomer Norton (Som), 97, 180
Milborne Port (Som), 209, 315
Milborne St. Andrew (Dorset), 110
Mildenhall (Suffolk), 31, 124
Millbrook (Beds), 425, 426
Milton (Berks), Manor House, 236
Milton (Cambs), 151, 397
Milton (Kent), see Milton-by-Gravesend
Milton Abbey (Dorset), 81, 82, 107
Milton Abbot (Devon), 199
Milton-by-Gravesend (Kent), 57, 251
Milton Ernest (Beds), 115
Milton Hall (Berks), 258
Milton Hall (Northants), 16, 52, 85, 129, 404
Milton Regis (Kent), 220, 350
Milverton (Som), 249, 489
Minchinhampton (Glos), 90, 322
Minehead (Som), 55
Minster (Kent), 242, 272
Minsterworth (Glos), 321
Minterne Magna (Dorset), 381
Mistley (Essex), 66
Mitcham (Surrey), 118, 189, 332, 390, 411, 420, 422, 423, 425, 427
Mitton (Yorks), 367, 368
Moccas (Heref), 429
Moggerhanger House (Beds), 108, 132

Mold (Flint), 98, 170, 174, 338
Monaco, Palace, 90
Moncreiffe (Perth), 248
Monken Hadley (Herts), 201, 306, 368, 425. *See also* Hadley
Monkton (Pemb), 30
Monkton Combe (Som), 52
Monkwearmouth (Durham), 368
Monmouth, 239, 294, 298, 359, 425
Montford Bridge (Salop), 80
Montgomery, 271
Monticello (Va., U.S.A.), 89
Montreal (Canada), 107, 370
Montrose, 257, 323
Montserrat, St. Andrew's, 108
Morcott (Rutland), 175
Morden (Surrey), 80, 238, 420, 423
Moreton (Dorset), 185, 407
Moreton Corbet (Salop), 80, 311
Moreton Say (Salop), 57, 81, 406
Morningthorpe (Norfolk), 307, 369
Morpeth, Town Hall, 154
Mortlake (Surrey), 228
Morvill Hall (Salop), 203
Moseley (Birmingham), 35, 206, 207
"Mote, The" (nr. Maidstone), 21, 306, 440
Mottingham (Kent), 281
Mottram (Lancs), 165
Moulsham Hall (Essex), 82, 85, 99, 113, 281, 292, 343
Mountsorrel (Leics), 203, 212
Much Hadham (Herts), 35, 254, 329
Much Marcle (Heref), 66, 218, 259, 310, 373
Much Wenlock (Salop), 354
Murthly Castle, 290
Musselburgh, 323
Mylor (Cornwall), 214, 283, 297, 426
Mytton Hall (Yorks), 363

Nackington (Kent), 195, 242
Nacton (Suffolk), 127
Nantes, Museum, 90
Narford Hall (Norfolk), 121, 126, 310
Navestock (Essex), 30, 47, 48, 116, 131
Neath (Glam), 132
Nether Alderley (Ches), 429
Netherbury (Warwicks), 432
Nether Whitacre (Warwicks), 195
Nether Worton (Oxon), 422
Netley (Hants), Hospital, 257
Newark (Notts), 44, 48, 190, 331, 411, 423
    Town Hall, 278, 384, 403
Newbold-on-Avon (Northants), 213
Newby Hall (nr. Ripon), 234
Newcastle, 34, 233, 243
    Bank of England, 182
    Cathedral, 27, 35, 122, 134, 146, 151, 329, 417, 422
    Elswick Hall, 243, 274
    Literary and Philosophical Society 34, 95, 161, 242, 243, 263, 267, 450
    Public Library, 35
    St. Andrew's, 122
    Theatre, 380

Newcastle (Co. Limerick, Eire), 269
New Haven (Conn., U.S.A.), Yale Art Gallery, 212
Newington (Kent), 29, 76, 264, 356
Newington (London), Fishmongers' Almshouses, 138
Newington (Oxon), 113
Newlands Church, 323
Newmarket (Suffolk), Jockey Club Room, 220
    Palace, 360
Newnham (Northants), 355
Newport (Essex), 422
Newport (I.o.W.), 444
Newport (Mon), 133, 390, 413
Newport (Salop), 256
Newport Pagnell (Bucks), 319, 431
New Ross (Co. Wexford, Eire), 282, 439
Newry (Co. Down, Ireland), 448
Newton (Cambs), 59, 174, 275, 302, 329, 397, 429
Newton Blossomville (Bucks), 18
Newton-in-Makerfield (Lancs), 165
Newton St. Cyres (Devon), 225
Newton St. Loe (Som), 204, 410
Newtown (Montgomery), 141
New York, 370, 436
    Historical Society, 58, 89, 94, 110, 436
    Metropolitan Museum of Art, 89
    Museum, 110
    Public Library, 89
    Trinity Church, 212, 388
New Zealand, 444
Niton (I.o.W.), 332
Nocton (Lincs), Dunston Pillar, 107
Norham (Durham), 244
Normanhurst Court (Sussex), 362, 363
Normanton (Rutland), 127, 213, 338, 385
Northallerton (Yorks), 141, 404, 418
Northam (Devon), 178, 225, 284
Northampton, All Saints', 114, 115, 212, 213, 318
    Holy Sepulchre, 431
    St. Giles's, 114, 115, 213
    St. Peter's, 57, 114, 115, 213, 431
    Town Hall, 93
North Bradley (Wilts), 155
Northbrooke, 364
North Cadbury (Som), 20
North Cave (Yorks), 65, 137, 331, 332, 340
North Cray (Kent), 96
North Elmham (Norfolk), 422
North Ferriby (Yorks), 137
Northfleet (Kent), 288
Northill (Beds), 438
North Kirkby (Yorks), 337
North Leigh (Oxon), 15, 192, 322, 369
North Luffenham (Rutland), 52, 354
North Lydbury (Salop), 80
North Marston (Bucks), 118
North Mimms (Herts), 28, 36, 288, 344
North Molton (Devon), 229

North Ockendon (Essex), 47, 359, 360, 367
North Otterington (Yorks), 141
North Perrott (Som), 426
North Stoke (Som), 155
North Stoneham (Hants), 95, 208 264, 407, 413
North Walsham, 13
Northwick Park (Glos), 117, 124, 278, 407
North Witham (Lincs), 210, 255, 349
North Wraxall (Wilts), 278, 423, 427
Norton (Derby), 146, 356
Norton (Durham), 122, 152
Norton (Kent), 361
Norton (Northants), 46, 47
Norton (Sheffield), 196
Norton St. Philip (Som), 410
Norwich, 14, 261
    Bank of England, 124, 182
    Bishop's Palace Chapel, 240
    Blackfriars Bridge, 125
    Cathedral, 59, 93, 215, 286, 315, 265, 268
    Octagon Chapel, 21
    Old Meeting House, 215
    St. Andrew's, 286, 315, 414
    St. Andrew's Hall, 315
    St. George Colegate, 30, 49, 179 215, 286, 315, 353
    St. Giles's, 98, 286, 315
    St. Gregory's, 179, 353
    St. John Maddermarket, 119, 125
    St. John de Sepulchre, 188
    St. Martin at Palace, 353
    St. Mary Coslany, 59, 215, 257
    St. Peter Mancroft, 17, 41, 286, 374
    St. Saviour's, 56, 119
    St. Simon and St. Jude, 233
    St. Stephen's, 125, 215, 233, 254
    St. Swithin's, 315, 365
Norwood (Middx), 422
Noseley (Leics), 115
Nostell Priory (Yorks), 128, 321, 384
Nottingham, 217
    Assembly Rooms, 375
    Castle, 433, 445
    Exchange, 375
    St. Mary's, 59
    St. Nicholas's, 59
Nowton (Suffolk), 30
Nuneaton (Warwicks), 320
Nunnington (Yorks), 338, 381
Nunton (Wilts), 64, 427
Nutfield (Surrey), 110, 246
Nuthall (Notts), 376
Nynehead (Som), 114

Oadby (Leics), 227
Oakley (Bucks), 42
Ockham (Surrey), 29, 338, 428
Ockley (Surrey), 384
Odell (Beds), 30
Odiham (Hants), 237
Offchurch (Warwicks), 178
Okeover (Derbys), 280, 437
Old Alresford (Hants), 47
Oldham (Lancs), 267
Old Radnor, 150, 404
Old Swinford (Worcs), 206

Old Warden (Beds), 126
Old Weston (Hunts), 110
Old Windsor (Berks), 109, 443
Old Woking (Surrey), 354
Olney (Bucks), 18
Ombersley (Worcs), 55, 277
Ombersley Court (Worcs), 186, 203, 356, 373, 403, 431
Orlingbury (Northants), 115
Ormesby St. Margaret (Norfolk), 303
Ormesby St. Michael (Norfolk), 30, 180
Ormskirk (Lancs), 157, 348, 363
Orpington (Kent), 61, 95, 205
Orsett (Essex), 317, 426
Orton Longueville (Hunts), 96
Osborne (Isle of Wight), 49, 157, 187, 249, 290, 297, 362, 386, 387, 392, 395
Osnabrook (Germany), 420
Ossington (Notts), 277
Oswestry (Salop), 63, 80, 157, 271, 406
Otford (Kent), 30
Otham (Kent), 344
Otley (Yorks), 84, 146
Otterden (Kent), 185, 223, 332
Ottery St. Mary (Devon), 29, 231, 271, 350, 394
Oundle (Northants), 52, 158, 213
Overbury (Worcs), 112, 373
Over Compton (Dorset), 317
Overstone (Northants), 21, 213
Overton (Flint), 45, 63, 140, 271, 293, 347, 363, 406, 426
Over Whitacre (Warwicks), 15
Ovingham (Northumberland), 31
Ovington (Hants), 224
Owston (Yorks), 95, 96, 145, 146
Oxford, All Souls' College, 26, 55, 98, 229, 316, 331, 387, 399, 419
   Ashmolean Museum, 55, 245, 268, 297, 336
   Balliol College Chapel, 31
   Bodleian Library, 83, 94, 233, 267, 299, 336, 437, 444, 445
   Brasenose College, 95, 126, 202, 217, 278, 382, 384, 429, 430, 440
   Carfax, 324, 399
   Cathedral, 35, 98, 234, 385, 400, 404, 428. *See also* Christ Church
   Christ Church, 25, 26, 51, 55, 93, 94, 214, 225, 230, 324, 331, 336, 337, 399. *See also* Cathedral
   Clarendon Building, 55, 98, 399
   Congregation House, 304
   Corpus Christi, 94
   Divinity School, 55, 127, 324
   Examinations Schools, 149
   Infirmary, 56
   Keble College, 445
   Laboratory, 127
   Magdalen College, 34, 59, 118, 256
   Martyrs' Memorial, 419
   Merton College, 59, 445
   Museum, 95, 136, 267, 372
   New College, 55, 127, 209, 304, 386, 399, 423

Observatory, 26, 27, 328
   Oriel College, 47, 426
   Pembroke College, 277, 428
   Physic Garden, 324, 407
   Printing House, 281, 324
   Queen's College, 97, 98, 164, 231, 239, 324, 336, 398, 399, 404, 407
   Radcliffe Camera, 130, 336, 360, 399, 400
   St. Edmund Hall, 55
   St. Giles, 400
   St. John's College, 126, 201, 284, 399, 423
   St. Mary's, 89, 134, 150, 217, 324, 368, 399, 400, 425, 440
   St. Michael's, 55
   St. Peter in the East, 57
   Sheldonian Theatre, 55, 97, 126, 324
   Taylorian Institution, 271, 278
   Tom Tower, 324
   Town Hall, 181
   Trinity College, 298, 377
   University College, 54, 55, 150, 151, 281, 378, 415, 437
   University Museum, 34, 268, 274, 419, 420, 444
   Worcester College, 272

Packington Hall (Warwicks), 278
Packwood (Warwicks), 218, 427
Padbury, 42
Paddington, Great Western Hotel, 389
   Parish Church, 30, 47, 57, 109, 116, 117, 254, 314, 331, 332, 346, 352, 375, 391, 423
Padua (Italy), 240
Painswick (Glos), 158
Paisley, 266
   Abbey, 266
   County Hall, 144
Palmer's Green (Middx), 64, 364
Pangbourne (Berks), 367
Parham Park (Sussex), 124
Paris, National Institute, 95
Parkham (Devon), 409
Patcham (Sussex), 432
Patshull (Staffs), 100
Paul (Cornwall), 175, 214
Paulton (Som), 180
Pauntley (Glos), 112, 379
Peakirk (Northants), 20, 213, 348
Peasmarsh (Sussex), 31, 357
Pebworth (Glos), 443
Peckleton (Leics), 212, 451
Pelynt (Cornwall), 116, 339
Pembridge (Heref), 103, 426
Penally (Pem), 405
Penang (Malaya), 151
   Cathedral, 403
   St. George's, 47, 427
Penicuik House (Midlothian), 17, 218
Penn (Bucks), 96, 200
Penpont House, 71
Penrith (Cumberland), 230
Penshurst (Kent), 222, 292, 306, 368, 386, 422, 442

Penshurst Place (Kent), 94, 223, 387
Pentney (Hants), 141
Penwortham (Lancs), 157, 325, 418
Penzance (Cornwall), 44, 214
Peper Harow (Surrey), 286, 420, 435, 436
Perdiswell Hall (Worcs), 107
Perivale (Middx), 15
Perranuthoe (Cornwall), 317
Pershore Abbey (Worcs), 66
Perth, 62
   County Place, 18
Peterborough Cathedral, 52, 143, 179, 381
   St. John's, 52, 151, 195
Petersfield (Hants), 110, 150, 199, 213
Petham (Kent), 279
Petworth (Sussex), 34, 46, 70, 79, 80, 94, 149, 150, 164, 204, 223, 277, 278, 312, 328, 336, 425, 426
Pewsey (Wilts), 189, 426
Philadelphia (U.S.A.), 302
   Christ Church, 112
   Laurel Hill Cemetery, 388
Pennsylvania Academy of Fine Arts, 89
Pinner (Middx), 382, 396
Pishiobury (Herts), 27
Pitsford (Northants), 114
Plumstead (London), 116, 226, 228
Plymouth, 289, 372
   Duke of Cornwall's Hotel, 56
   Library, 71
   St. Andrew's, 39, 65, 237
   Town Hall, 372
Plympton (Devon), 17, 96, 108, 215
Plympton St. Mary (Devon), 125
Plympton St. Maurice (Devon), 215
Plymstock (Devon), 409
Pocklington (Yorks), 309
Podington (Beds), 209, 213, 239
Poltimore (Devon), 449
Pontcysylte Aqueduct, 80
Ponteland (Northumb), 108, 222
Poole (Dorset), 203, 258, 350
Poplar (London), 450
   St. Matthias, 72, 150
Porchester (Hants), 192
Portisham (Dorset), 440
Port Royal (Jamaica), 331
Portsea (Hants), 192
Pott Shrigley (Ches), 165
Portsmouth Cathedral, 141, 192, 318, 350, 391, 451
   Chesapeake Memorial, 302
   New Storehouse, 179
Potsdam (Germany), 139
Pott (Ches), 28, 57
Potterne (Wilts), 35, 278
Poulton-le-Fylde (Lancs), 133, 239
Powderham (Devon), 372
Powderham Castle (Devon), 47, 163, 180, 372
Powerscourt (Eire), 51, 248
Powick (Worcs), 344, 365, 373
Powis Castle, 320, 390
Prees (Salop), 81
Prescot (Lancs), 36, 324, 347, 426
Prestbury (Ches), 344, 402, 418
Prestbury (Glos), 439

Preston (Lancs), 274, 325, 418
    Art Gallery, 133
    Literary Institute, 133
    Parish Church, 385
    St. Augustine's, 133
    St. George's, 133
    St. John's, 133
    Town Hall, 133
Preston (Rutland), 174, 212, 362
Preston (Yorks), 227
Preston-on-Stour (Glos), 344, 425, 426, 429
Prestonpans, 62
Prestwich (Lancs), 352, 389
Prestwold (Leics), 29, 329, 349, 387, 428, 429
Pulborough (Sussex), 173
Puncknowle (Dorset), 186
Purley (Berks), 279
Purley Hall, 83
Purton (Wilts), 158
Pusey (Berks), 55, 344
Putney (London), 131
Pynes (Devon), 94, 355
Pyrgo (Essex), Chapel, 369

Quainton (Bucks), 368, 369, 448
Quat (Salop), 241
Queen Camel (Som), 388
Queenhill (Worcs), 239, 284
Quidenham (Norfolk), 143

Raby Castle (Co. Durham), 47, 149, 449
Rackheath (Norwich), 96, 119
Radbourne (Derbys), 170
Radley (Berks), 279
Radley House (Berks), 399
Radstock (Som), 295
Ragnell (Notts), 368
Rainham Hall (Norfolk), 143
Ramsbury (Wilts), 57, 208, 229, 264, 355, 407
Ramsey Abbey, 57
Ramsgate (Kent), 209
Ramsgate (Kent), St. Laurence, 445
Ranworth (Norfolk), 119
Reading (Berks), 108, 151, 364
    St. Giles's, 28, 217, 344
    St. Lawrence's, 273, 343, 344
    St. Mary's, 30, 431
Redbourn (Herts), 68
Redbourne (Lincs), 96
Redgrave (Suffolk), 179
Redlynch House (Som), 214
Redruth (Cornwall), 297, 385
Reigate (Surrey), 29, 110, 325, 355, 356, 419
Rempstone (Notts), 310
Rendlesham (Suffolk), 114
Renhold (Beds), 390
Repton (Derbys), 142, 185
Rettendon (Essex), 91
Riccall (Yorks), 395
Richmond (Surrey), 17, 151, 183, 334, 344
    Palace, 409
    Theological Institute, 252
    White Lodge, 409
Richmond (Yorks), 31, 36, 116, 146, 156, 275, 418

Rickmansworth (Herts), 150, 339
Riddlesworth (Norfolk), 15
Ridge (Herts), 28
Ridlington (Rutland), 212
Ringsfield (Suffolk), 355
Ringwood (Hants), 210, 413
Ringwould (Kent), 232
Rio de Janeiro (Brazil), Palace, 108
Ripon, 82
    Cathedral, 145, 146, 186, 191, 229, 277, 381, 431
    Town Hall, 152
Rippingale (Lincs), 299, 354
Ripple (Worcs), 162, 431
Rise (Yorks), 156
Rivenhall (Essex), 103, 332, 351
Roch (Pem), 108
Rochdale (Lancs), 110, 145, 157, 352
Rochester, Cathedral, 30, 38, 62, 108, 138, 150, 170, 222, 255, 256, 381
    Travellers' House, 127
Rock (Northumb), 141
Rockingham (Northants), 126, 242, 286, 288, 362
Rodmarton (Glos), 66, 439
Rokeby (Durham), 278, 426
Rolleston (Staffs), 144, 185
Rome, Capitoline Museum, 177
    Protestant Cemetery, 173, 362
Romsey (Hants), 72, 274
Romsey Abbey (Hants), 151
Rosenau (Coburg), 387
Ross, 254
Rossie Priory, 77
Ross-on-Wye (Heref), 319, 386
Rostherne (Ches), 20, 27, 31, 60, 208, 429
Rotherfield Greys (Oxon), 32, 423
Rotherham (Yorks), 151, 241, 308, 356, 413
Rothley (Leics), 212
Rothwell (Northants), 362
Rousham (Oxon), 281, 342, 343, 364
Roxwell (Essex), 318
Royal Collection, 35, 47, 49, 77, 94, 142, 149, 162, 173, 187, 235, 241, 262, 275, 277, 278, 309, 358, 383, 386, 387, 392, 393, 403, 448, 449
Roydon (Norfolk), 143
Royston (Herts), 66
Ruabon (Denbigh), 157, 278, 338, 363, 372, 449
Rudbaxton (Pembroke), 250
Rudby (Yorks), 69, 146, 208
Ruddington (Notts), 58, 376
Rufford (Lancs), 151, 275
Rugby, 93, 203
    St. Mary's Roman Catholic Church, 301
    School Chapel, 96, 389, 429
Runcorn (Ches), 27, 28, 181, 187, 199, 431
Runwell (Essex), 88
Ruscombe (Berks), 150, 425
Rushden (Herts), 103
Ruthin (Denbigh), 157, 402, 426, 449
Ruyton (Salop), 80
Ryde (I.o.W.), 415

Rye (Sussex), 30, 32, 150, 251, 257
Ryton (Durham), 15, 57
Ryton-on-Dunsmore (Warwicks), 43

Sacombe (Herts), 23, 151, 338
St. Albans (Herts), Cathedral Abbey, 96, 118, 300
    St. Stephen's, 118
St. Anthony in Roseland (Cornwall), 209, 425
St. Asaph, Cathedral, 63, 384, 427
St. Austell (Cornwall), 215
St. Bees (Cumberland), 243
St. Blazey (Cornwall), 209, 429
St. Brides (Glam), 162, 232
St. Bride's Major (Glam), 322
St. Budeaux (Devon), 17, 215, 350
St. Clement (Cornwall), 259
St. Columb Major (Cornwall), 215
St. David's Cathedral, 66
St. Dogwell's (Pemb), 404
St. Dominick (Cornwall), 409
St. Ewe (Cornwall), 44, 215
St. Germans (Cornwall), 427
St. Giles (Dorset), 250, 275, 335, 343, 419, 420
St. Gluvias (Cornwall), 229
St. Helena, Island of, 150
St. Ives (Cornwall), 163
St. Ives (Hunts), 350
St. John in Bradwardine (Worcs), 189
St. John's Wood (London), Chapel, 23, 47, 57, 96, 127, 246, 273, 293, 303, 332, 339, 347, 355, 356
    Female Orphan School, 302
St. Kitts (British West Indies), Trinity, Palmetto, 29
St. Leonard's (Bucks), 52, 72
St. Leonard at Hythe (Essex), 245
St. Martin by Looe (Cornwall), 13, 258
St. Martin's (Salop), 42, 80, 347
St. Mellion (Cornwall), 160
St. Michael Carhays (Cornwall), 107, 109, 297
St. Michael Penkevil (Cornwall), 214, 278, 279, 297, 338
St. Osyth (Essex), 404
St. Pancras (London), All Saints, 383. See also London (St. Pancras)
St. Paul's Walden (Herts), 256
St. Peter's-in-Thanet (Kent), 30, 31
    Orphanage, 420
St. Petersburg, Royal Mint, 207. See also Leningrad
Saintbury (Glos), 373
Salehurst (Sussex), 292, 332
Salford (Lancs), 208, 274
    Art Gallery, 49, 122, 165, 257
    Museum, 239
Salisbury, Cathedral, 27, 55, 64, 80, 96, 138, 150, 151, 189, 224, 229, 245, 285, 301, 317, 338
    Guildhall, 112, 117
    Museum, 278
    St. Edmund, 285
    St. Martin's, 64, 151, 229
    St. Thomas's, 138, 285

Sall (Norfolk), 215
Saltaire, Mechanics' Institute, 261
Saltash (Cornwall), 183, 350
  St. Nicholas, 215
  St. Stephen, 215
Saltram (Devon), 84, 85, 278
Samlesbury (Lancs), 226
Sandal Magna (Yorks), 302, 303
Sandbach (Ches), 363, 416
Sandbeck Park (Yorks), 111, 435
Sanderstead (Surrey), 238, 306
Sandford (Devon), 372
Sandford St. Martin (Oxon), 322
Sandgate (Kent), 307
Sand Hutton (Yorks), 146, 356
Sandon Park, 47, 77
Sandwich (Kent), 420
  St. Clement's, 29
Sandy (Beds), 20, 127, 287, 386, 404, 431, 438
Sans Souci (Germany), 139
Sarnesfield (Heref), 379
Sawbridgeworth (Herts), 65, 253, 374, 384
Saxlingham Hall (Norfolk), 125
Saxlingham Nethergate, 365
Saxmundham (Suffolk), 279, 395, 404, 428
Scarborough (Yorks), 302
Scone Palace, 183
Scottow (Norfolk), 375
Scoulton (Norfolk), 286
Scraptoft (Leics), 72, 451
Scrapton (Leics), 144
Scremby (Lincs), 412
Scrivelsby (Lincs), 22
Scrooby (Notts), 130
Sculcoates (St. Mary's), 138
Seal (Kent), 21, 92
Seale (Hants), 44, 282
Seasalter (Kent), 220
Seaton Delaval (Northumb), 48, 105, 281
Sedgbrook (Lincs), 53, 111
Seend (Wilts), 62, 155, 189, 285, 295
Sefton (Lancs), 156, 157, 171
Sefton Park (Liverpool), 362
Selattyn (Salop), 157
Selborne (Hants), 232
Selby (Yorks), 23, 60, 309, 381
Selkirk, 119, 323
Sellack (Heref), 218, 379
Sellinge (Kent), 113
Sevenoaks (Kent), 80, 83, 404
  Montreal House, 22
Shalford (Surrey), 28, 64, 262, 264, 339
Shalstone (Bucks), 42, 104, 279, 288, 427, 429
Shandon (Co. Cork, Eire), 403
Shap Wells Spa (Westmorland), 56
Shardeloes (Bucks), 85
Sharnbrook (Beds), 151, 260
Sharsted Court (Kent), 208
Shaw (Berks), 265
Shawbury (Salop), 80
Sheffield (Yorks), 71, 308
Sheffield, Art Gallery, 141
  Bluecoat School, 356
  Carver Street Chapel, 235, 323

Cathedral, 94, 96, 141, 235, 323, 356
  Cemetery, 49
  Cutlers' Hall, 141, 235, 356
  Freemasons' Hall, 235
  Literary Society, 235
  Parish Church, 91
  Royal Infirmary, 94, 235, 356, 419
  St. James's, 323
  St. Marie's, 301
  St. Paul's, 94, 308, 356
  University, 235
  Weston Park Museum, 235
Sheldwich (Kent), 242, 426
Shelford (Cambs), 59
Shelford (Notts), 96, 278
Shellingford (Berks), 150, 404
Shelswell, 288
Shenley (Herts), 218
Shenstone (Staffs), 220
Shepperton (Middx), 242
Shepton Mallet (Som), 295, 315, 439
Sherborne Castle, 218
Sherborne (Dorset), 86, 281
Sherborne (Glos), 28, 30, 66, 71, 338, 376, 423
Sherborne St. John (Hants), 209
Shere (Surrey), 66, 400
Sherrington, 18
Sheviock (Cornwall), 116, 214
Shillingston (Dorset), 95
Shimpling (Suffolk), 163, 423
Shinfield (Berks), 201, 216
Shipdham (Norfolk), 306
Shipton Moyne (Glos), 140, 422
Shirley (Derby), 185
Shirwell (Devon), 178
Shobdon (Heref), 279
Shobrooke (Devon), 137
Shobrooke Park (Devon), 372
Shoreditch (London), Church, 54, 55, 134, 273
  Fishmongers' Almshouses, 281
Shoreham (Kent), 98
Shoreham (Sussex), 209, 430
Shorwell (I.o.W.), 150
Shouldham (Norfolk), 181
Shrewsbury, 107, 289
  Abbey, 112, 406
  Castle, 270
  Claremont Buildings, 80
  English Bridge, 311
  Lion Inn, Wyle Cop, 270
  Prison, 26
  Raven Inn, 400
  St. Alkmund's 80, 81, 432
  St. Chad's, 80, 94, 95, 253
  St. Julian's, 80, 271, 311
  St. Mary's, 34, 80, 112, 271, 311, 320, 390, 431
  Welsh Bridge, 80
Shrivenham (Berks), 127, 150, 221, 295, 423
Shrublands (Suffolk), 67
Shuckburgh (Warwicks), 36, 50, 65, 150, 151, 213, 357
Shudy Camps (Cambs), 86
Shugborough (Staffs), 342
Shustoke (Warwicks), 233
Shute (Devon), 97, 332, 426
Sidmouth (Devon), 230, 367, 426

Sierra Leone, see Freetown
Sigglethorne (Yorks), 137, 291
Silchester (Hants), 188
Sileby (Lincs), 349
Silston (Herts), 254
Silton (Dorset), 281
Simonburn (Northumb), 275
Simpson (Bucks), 27, 42
Singapore, 445
  Raffles Institution, 95
Sisted (Essex), 36
Skegby (Notts), 376
Skelton (Yorks), 381
Skipton (Yorks), 146, 380
Slaughter (Glos), 376
Sleaford (Lincs), 52, 350, 411
Sledmere (Yorks), 107
Slindon (Sussex), 394, 426
Smallburgh (Norfolk), 315
Smalley (Derby), 264
Smarden (Kent), 220
Snaith (Yorks), 60, 82, 93, 152, 395
Snettisham (Norfolk), 112
Snitterfield (Warwicks), 127, 383
Soberton (Hants), 344
Solihull (Warwicks), 346, 392
Somerley (Hants), 64
Somerleyton Hall (Suffolk), 135, 390
Sonning (Berks), 394, 425
Sotterly (Suffolk), 254
Soulbury (Bucks), 108, 115, 170
Southam, 239
Southampton, 245, 348
Southborough (Kent), 252
South Burstead (Sussex), 80
South Cave (Yorks), 138
Southfleet (Kent), 175
South Harting (Sussex), 429
Southill (Beds), 278, 367
Southill Park (Beds), 100, 163, 164
South Kirby (Yorks), 412
South Littleton (Worcs), 36
South Mimms (Middx), 127, 364
South Molton (Devon), 178, 324
  Town Hall, 60
Southover (Sussex), 422
South Park, Penshurst, 154
South Petherton (Som), King Ina's Palace, 97
South Pickenham (Norfolk), 215, 250
Southrepps (Norfolk), 13
South Stoneham (Hants), 30, 36, 43, 317
Southwark, see London
South Warnborough (Hants), 48, 430
South Warnston (Hants), 237
South Weald (Essex), 127, 160, 218, 355
Southwell Cathedral, 51, 185
Southwick (Hants), 141, 377
Southwick (Northants), 331
South Wooton (Hants), 141
Sowerby (Yorks), 145, 370, 381, 435
Sowton (Devon), 389
Spalding, 213
Speen (Berks), 27, 78, 187, 385
Speldhurst (Kent), 30, 109, 127
Spelsbury (Oxon), 404
Spetchley (Worcs), 373, 403

Spilsby (Lincs), 24
Spixworth (Norfolk), 254
Spratton (Northants), 115, 208, 213, 431
Spreyton (Devon), 225, 259
Springfield (Essex), 332
Sprotboro, 308
Sprowston (Norfolk), 30, 286
Stadhampton (Oxon), 421
Stafford, County Hall, 328
  Crown Court, 244
  Parish Church, 264
Staindrop (Durham), 112, 113, 277, 279, 428
Staines (Middx), 230
Stainton (Yorks), 186, 381, 382
Stalbridge (Dorset), 292
Stamford, 328
  All Saints, 52
  St. George's, 27, 362, 404
  St. John's, 108, 175
  St. Martin's, 52, 53, 174, 189, 262, 288, 348, 423
  St. Mary's, 189
  Town Hall, 199
Standard Hill (Notts), St. James's, 375
Standish (Lancs), 30, 170, 279
Standlake (Oxon), 332, 339
Standlynch (Wilts), 285
Stanford (Kent), 264
Stanford (Worcs), 373
Stanford-le-Hope (Essex), 50
Stanford-on-Avon (Northants), 393
Stanford-on-Soar (Notts), 97, 160
Stanmer (Sussex), 188, 401
Stanmore (Middx), 27, 65, 147
Stansfield (Suffolk), 371
Stanstead Abbots (Herts), 30, 32, 227
Stanstead Mountfitchet (Essex), 160
Stanton (Worcs), 439
Stanton Drew (Som), 156, 220, 229, 351
Stanton Harcourt (Oxon), 275, 352
Stapleford (Leics), 65, 107, 337, 369
Stapleford (Notts), 29
Staplehurst (Kent), 378
Stapleton (Glos), 150
Staunton (Glos), 199
Staunton Harold (Leics), 343
Staunton-in-the-Vale (Notts), 137, 411, 426
Stedham (Sussex), 189
Steep (Hants), 61
Steeple Ashton (Wilts), 155, 204, 229
Steeple Aston (Oxon), 151, 182, 341
Steeple Bumpstead (Essex), 303, 369
Steeple Langford (Wilts), 232
Stepney (London), 212, 220, 318, 426
Steveton (Hants), 209
Stifford (Essex), 437
Stillington (Yorks), 146
Stirling, 323
Stockport (Ches), 14, 32, 63, 157, 158, 208, 275, 347, 426, 427, 432
Stockton (Durham), 350, 353, 355, 433
Stockton (Wilts), 284

Stoke (nr. Guildford, Surrey), 30, 36, 150, 317, 354, 355
Stoke Abbott (Dorset), 170
Stoke-by-Nayland (Suffolk), 31
Stoke Climsland (Cornwall), 190
Stoke College (Suffolk), 267
Stoke D'Abernon (Surrey), 431
Stoke Doyle (Northants), 95, 209, 337
Stoke Edith (Heref), 57, 62
Stoke Fleming (Devon), 350
Stoke Newington, Abney Park. Cemetery, 34
  Church, 40, 422
Stoke-on-Trent, 122
  Parish Church, 47, 48, 149, 209, 400
Stoke Park, 16
Stoke Poges (Bucks), 151, 328
  Baylies, 59, 259
Stoke Poges House, 124
Stoke Rochford (Lincs), 57
Stone (Glos), 297
Stone (Kent), 415
Stone (Staffs), 206, 431
Stonegrave (Yorks), 381
Stoneleigh (Warwicks), 279
Stoneleigh Abbey, 41
Stonham Aspal (Suffolk), 55
Stonor Park (Oxon), 113
Stonyhurst (Lancs), 70, 257, 281, 366, 368
Stony Stratford (Bucks), 189
Storrington (Sussex), 426, 427, 429
Stoughton (Leics), 343
Stoulton (Worcs), 116
Stourhead (Wilts), 16, 22, 84, 88, 99, 106, 164, 176, 195, 203, 214, 218, 292, 295, 311, 317, 334, 336, 337, 381
Stourton (Wilts), 189, 214
Stow Bardolph (Norfolk), 121, 344, 387
Stow-cum-Quy (Cambs), 397
Stowe (Bucks), 41, 89, 101, 126, 241, 336, 342, 343, 400
Stowe-Nine-Churches (Northants), 369
Stowmarket (Suffolk), 125
Stow-on-the-Wold (Glos), 105
Stratfield Saye (Hants), 13, 14, 77, 94, 107, 151, 158, 161, 172, 181, 187, 240, 241, 282, 306, 307, 312, 447
Stratford-le-Bow, 134
Stratford-on-Avon (Warwicks), 50, 99, 182, 254, 276, 338, 367, 428
  New Place, 38
Stratton (Norfolk), 101, 267
Stratton Audley (Oxon), 29, 31
Strawberry Hill (Middx), 85, 106, 107, 120, 165, 268, 321
Streatham (London), Parish Church, 47, 61, 65, 109, 151, 251, 332, 365, 410, 426, 427
Strensham (Worcs), 367
Stroud (Glos), 229, 366
Studley (Warwicks), 344
Studley Royal (Yorks), 143
Sudbury (Derby), 158, 367
Sudbury Hall (Derby), 433

Sudbury (Suffolk), St. Gregory's, 29, 125, 187
Sulacoats (Hull), 48
Sunbury (Middx), 209, 257
Sunderland, 24, 134
Sundridge (Kent), 120
Sutton (Beds), 283, 367
Sutton (Surrey), 391, 451
Sutton-at-Hone (Kent), 381
Sutton Coldfield (Warwicks), 182, 282, 434
Sutton-in-the-Forest (Yorks), 381
Sutton-on-Hull (Yorks), 137
Sutton Place (Guildford), 157
Sutton Scarsdale House (Derby), 310, 408
Sutton Valence (Kent), 65, 346
Swaffham (Norfolk), 141
Swalcliffe (Oxon), 399
Swallowfield (Berks), 48
Swanage, Town Hall, 451
Swanscombe (Kent), 421, 425
Swansea, 390
Swanton Abbots (Norfolk), 246
Swavesey (Cambs), 254
Swillington (Yorks), 146, 381
Swimbridge (Devon), 295, 373
Swinbrook (Oxon), 18, 55, 425
Swithland (Leics), 202
Sydling St. Nicholas (Dorset), 232
Sydney (N.S.W.), 34, 378, 387, 444, 445
Symondsbury (Dorset), 264
Syston (Glos), 225
Syston Hall, 332

Tackley (Oxon), 28
Tacolneston (Norfolk), 414
Tamerton Folliott (Devon), 215, 350
Tamworth (Staffs), 274, 300
Tanjore (India), 149, 151
Tankersley (Yorks), 308
Tanworth (Warwicks), 200
Tardebrigge (Worcs), 96
Tarvin (Ches), 57
Tattingstone (Suffolk), 151
Tatton Park (Ches), 428
Taunton (Som), 202
  Parish Church, 242
  St. James's, 242
  Shire Hall, 290
  Trinity Church, 242
Tavistock (Devon), 157, 325, 372
Tawstock (Devon), 51, 71, 137, 219, 229, 324, 373
Teddington (Middx), 53, 209, 422, 426
Tehidy Park (Cornwall), 106
Teigngrace (Devon), 109, 225, 431
Tenbury Wells (Heref), 32
Tenby (Pemb), 166, 302, 390, 405
Tenterden (Kent), 257
Terling Place (Essex), 197
Terrington St. Clement (Norfolk), 127, 230
Tetbury (Glos), 229, 292, 295, 417
Teversal (Notts), 226
Tew Park, 95
Tewkesbury Abbey (Glos), 365, 431
Thame Park, 360
Thames Ditton (Surrey), 30, 31, 35

Thaxted (Essex), 367
Theddingworth (Leics), 195
Theddlethorp All Saints (Lincs), 83
Thetford (Norfolk), Guildhall, 107
Theydon Garnon (Essex), 29, 368
Theydon Mount (Essex), 314, 367
Thirkleby (Yorks), 150
Thirsk (Yorks), 146
Thoresby, 101
Thorndon Hall (Essex), 216
Thorndon Park (Essex), 143
Thorne (Yorks), 146
Thorney (Cambs), 174
Thornham Magna (Suffolk), 226
Thornhill (Yorks), 40
Thornton (Yorks), 240
Thornton-le-Moors (Ches), 224
Thornton-le-Street (Yorks), 146
Thorpe (Middx), 112, 382
Thorpe (Norfolk), 109
Thorpe Achurch (Northants), 190
Thorpe Constantine (Staffs), 426
Thrapston (Northants), 302
Throcking (Herts), 278, 338
Throwley (Kent), 151, 318
Thruxton (Hants), 285
Thundridge (Herts), 387
Thurcaston (Leics), 62
Thwaite (Norfolk), 282
Ticehurst (Sussex), 179
Tichborne (Hants), 80
Ticklehill (Yorks), 114, 256
Tillington (Sussex), 80, 202, 209, 285, 329
Tinworth (Rutland), 110
Tisbury (Wilts), 261
Tissington (Derby), 55, 278, 350
Titchfield (Hants), 96, 112, 224, 279, 426
Titchmarsh (Northants), 52, 110
Tittleshall (Norfolk), 21, 279
Tiverton (Devon), 225
    Town Hall, 140
Toddington (Beds), 73
Toddington (Glos), 244
Todmorden (Yorks), 154
Tonbridge (Kent), 68, 108, 244, 331, 375, 382
Tooting (London), 29, 30, 45, 303, 355, 420
Topcliffe (Yorks), 69
Topsham (Devon), 95, 323
Tormohun (Devon), 348
Toronto (Canada), 62
Torquay (Devon), 395
Torrington (Devon), 43, 225
Torrington (Lincs), 412
Tortworth (Glos), 439
Totnes (Devon), 164
Tottenham, New Chapel, 56
Tottenham (Middx), Parish Church, 35, 254
Tottenham Park, 347
Totteridge (Herts), 30, 204
Towcester, 259
Townstal (Devon), 438
Towyn (Merioneth), 98
Tranby Park (Yorks), 137
Tredegar Park (Mon), 141, 300, 390
Trefont (Wilts), 64
Tregynon (Montgomery), 28

Trent (Som), 225, 387
Trentham (Staffs), 93, 275
Trentham Hall, 425
Tring (Herts), 66
Trinidad, Cathedral, 96
    Roman Catholic Cathedral, 96
Trotton (Sussex), 252
Trowbridge (Wilts), 35
Trumpington (Cambs), 127
Truro (Cornwall), 71
    Cathedral, 143
    Town Hall, 71
Tsarskoe Selo (U.S.S.R.), 38
Tunbridge Wells, Cemetery, 444
    Dunorlan Park, 387
    Holy Trinity, 48, 209, 293
    Hospital, 47
Tunstall (Kent), 378, 391
Turvey (Beds), 213
Turville (Bucks), 113
Tutbury (Staffs), 185, 187
Tuxford (Notts), 32, 214, 314, 413
Twickenham (Middx), 29, 427
    All Hallows, 138, 213, 367
    Argyll House, 107
    Parish Church, 53, 54, 204, 257, 264, 332, 338, 343
Twycross (Leics), 393
Twyford (Hants), 151
Twyning (Glos), 162, 189
Tyberton (Heref), 229, 379
Tynemouth, 122, 243, 380
Tyringham (Bucks), 48, 160
Tywardreath (Cornwall), 317

Udimore (Sussex), 202, 357
Uffington (Berks), 35
Ufford (Northants), 52
Ugbrooke (Devon), 286
Ulcombe (Kent), 32, 160
Umberslade (Warwicks), 281
Uphall (Linlithgow), 371
Upminster (Essex), 426
Up Park (Sussex), 164
Upper Arley (Worcs), 373
Upper Dicker (Sussex), 292
Upper Penn (Staffs), 150
Upper Sheringham (Norfolk), 32
Upper Slaughter (Glos), 66, 295, 328
Uppingham (Rutland), 332
Upton (Bucks), 36, 65, 259, 385
Upton (Northants), 23, 114, 288, 431
Upton Grey (Hants), 100, 104, 170
Upton Hall (Northants), 212
Upton-on-Severn (Worcs), 364
Upton St. Leonards (Glos), 322
Upton Scudamore (Wilts), 316
Urchfont (Wilts), 258, 344
Uxbridge (Middx), Treaty House, 70

Vaudreuil (Quebec), 150
Vauxhall (London), Eldon Schools, 380
Venice, S. Lazaro dei Mendicanti, 72
Versailles (France), 221
Vyne, The (Hants), 56, 85, 86, 254, 260, 310

Wadhurst (Sussex), 188, 288
Wakefield (Yorks), 414
    Cathedral, 60, 227
Walcot (Bath), 375, 410
Walcot (Berks), 189
Waldershare (Kent), 179
Walford (Heref), 218, 310
Walkeringham (Notts), 254
Wallingford (Berks), 210, 439
    St. Leonard's, 104
Wallington (Northumb), 97
Walmer (Kent), 30, 42, 403
Walsall (Staffs), 141, 299, 347
Walsingham (Norfolk), 21, 426, 427
Walsoken (Norfolk), 18
Waltham Abbey (Essex), 226, 272
Waltham St. Lawrence (Berks), 426
Walthamstow (Essex), 45, 91, 220, 272, 385, 427
Walton (Bucks), 71, 278
Walton Hall (Yorks), 249
Walton-le-Dale (Lancs), 133
Walton-on-Thames (Surrey), 31, 86, 96, 141, 177, 331
Wandsworth (Surrey), 116, 343, 357
Wangford (Suffolk), 47, 412
Wanstead (Essex), Parish Church, 30, 95, 260, 344, 427
Wantage (Berks), 55, 399
Wapping (London), St. George, 377
Warbleton (Sussex), 188, 338
Warblington (Hants), 192, 205, 226, 264
Warblington (Sussex), 224
Warboys (Hunts), 27
Ward End (Birmingham), 206
Wardington (Oxon), 228
Ware (Herts), 29, 114, 203, 228
    Roman Catholic Chapel, 403
Wareham (Dorset), 203
Wareham (Hants), 225
Warfield (Berks), 32, 209, 242
Warkton (Northants), 77, 331, 407
Warminghurst (Sussex), 210, 367
Warminster (Wilts), 189, 239, 244
Warnford (Oxon), Asylum, 206
Warrington (Lancs), Parish Church, 229, 264, 287, 347
Wartling (Sussex), 32, 127, 160, 385
Warwick, Castle, 423
    Court House, 356, 369
    Judge's Lodging, 287
    St. Mary's Church, 43, 111, 134, 188, 203, 302, 356, 434
    St. Nicholas's, 48
    Shire Hall, 228
Washington (Sussex), 202
Washington (U.S.A.), Supreme Court, 89
Water Eaton, 440
Waterford (Eire), Bridge, 220
    Cathedral, 220, 228, 405
Wateringbury (Kent), 100, 226
Waterloo (Belgium), 93
Waterferry (Oxon), 95
Watford (Herts), 116, 175
Watford (Northants), 346
Wath (Yorks), 146, 151
Watton (Herts), 27, 252
Weald Hall (Essex), 128
Wednesbury (Staffs), 206, 207

Weekley (Northants), 42
Welbeck Abbey, 53, 85, 121, 132, 214, 284, 319, 334, 337, 383, 414
Welcombe (Stratford-upon-Avon), 102
Welford (Berks), 30
Welford-on-Avon (Warwick), 234
Well (Yorks), 309, 429
Wellingborough (Northants), 213, 244
Wellington (Heref), 81, 103, 451
Wellington (Salop), 206
Wells, Cathedral, 30, 41, 96, 229, 295, 315, 317, 320, 401, 405, 440
St. Cuthbert's, 214, 317, 439
Welshpool (Montgomery), 300, 320
Welton (Northants), 115
Welwyn (Herts), 351, 413
Wendover (Bucks), 20
Wentworth (Yorks), 439
Wentworth Castle, 59, 191, 308, 336
Wentworth Woodhouse (Yorks), 26, 104, 145, 146, 200, 235, 249, 277, 320, 384, 409, 413, 436
Weobley (Heref), 310, 427, 429
Wereham (Norfolk), 144
Westacre (Norfolk), 144, 385
Westbere (Kent), 97
West Bilney (Norfolk), 141
Westbourne (Sussex), 205, 279
West Brompton, Cemetery, 75
Westbury (Glos), 179, 297, 351
Westbury (Wilts), 213, 382
Westbury Court (Glos), 56, 60
West Chiltington (Sussex), 286
West Dean (Wilts), 64
West Dereham (Norfolk), 353
West Drayton (Middx), 14, 29, 30, 127
Westerham (Kent), 244, 256, 360
West Farleigh (Kent), 381
Westfield (I.o.W.), 51, 66, 328, 359
West Grinstead (Sussex), 150, 338, 359
West Ham (Essex) Parish Church, 367
West Harling (Norfolk), 436, 437
West Horsley (Surrey), 316
West Leake (Notts), 298
Westleigh (Devon), 132, 220, 303
West Malling (Kent), 228, 339
Westminster, see London
West Molesey (Surrey), 31
Weston (Heref), 60
Weston (Salop), 205
Weston (Som), 410
Weston (Staffs), 433
Weston (Wilts), 204
Westonbirt (Glos), 429
Weston Favell (Northants), 115
Weston-super-Mare (Som), 378, 420
Weston Underwood (Bucks), 18, 132
West Stockwith (Notts), 310
West Tilbury (Essex), 228, 416
West Wickham (Kent), 48, 220
West Wratting (Cambs), 397
West Wycombe (Bucks), 26, 55, 344, 346
West Wycombe Park (Bucks), 15, 99, 107, 126, 279

Wetheral (Cumb), 278
Wethersfield (Essex), 290, 397
Weybridge (Surrey), 96, 190, 297, 332, 423, 426
Weyhill (Hants), 170, 426
Weymouth (Dorset), 107, 178, 185, 196, 314, 385
Whalley (Lancs), 36, 146, 355, 418, 426
Whalton (Northumb), 35, 36
Whatton (Notts), 440
Wheatfield (Oxon), 104, 231, 343
Wheathampstead (Herts), 155, 381, 394
Whepstead (Suffolk), 220
Wherstead (Suffolk), 303
Whickham (Durham), 222
Whippingham (I.O.M.), 387
Whiston (Northants), 128, 278, 279
Whitburn (Durham), 360
Whitby (Yorks), 146, 273, 309
Whitchurch (Bucks), 163, 173
Whitchurch (Denbigh), 423
Whitchurch (Devon), 429
Whitchurch (Hants), 437
Whitchurch (Middx), 98, 169
Whitchurch (Oxon), 332
Whitchurch (Salop), 271, 442
Whitchurch (Som), 246
Whitechapel, St. Mary, 39
Whiteford (Flint), 425
Whiteparish (Dorset), 339
White Waltham (Berks), 288
Whitkirk (Yorks), 112, 209, 279, 297, 412, 421
Whitley (Worcs), 337
Whitstone (Cornwall), 189
Whittlebury (Northants), 96
Wickham (Hants), 443
Wickhambreaux (Kent), 382
Wicklewood (Norfolk), 365
Wickwar (Glos), 295
Widcombe (Som), 317
Widford (Essex), 304
Widford (Som), 133
Widworthy (Devon), 27, 332
Wigton, 444
"Wilderness, The," 21
Wilford (Notts), 97, 314
Willesley (Leics), 420
Willey (Salop), 81, 142
Williamsburg (Va., U.S.A.), 194
Willian (Herts), 23
Willingdon (Sussex), 420
Willoughby-on-the-Wolds (Notts), 97
Wilmington (Kent), 208
Wilmington (Sussex), 292
Wilmslow (Ches.), 220
Wilton (Wilts), 328, 330, 423, 425
Wilton House (Wilts), 249, 319, 342, 383, 410, 436
Wimbledon (Surrey), 134, 228, 238, 353, 360
Parish Church, 36
Wimborne (Dorset), 258
Wimborne St. Giles (Dorset), 340, 344
Wimpole (Cambs), 28, 39, 83, 127, 151, 156, 166, 344, 364, 426, 429
Wimpole Hall, 364

Wincanton (Som), 214, 246, 317
Winchcombe (Glos), 66, 112, 239, 321
Winchelsea (Sussex), 246, 409
Winchendon House, 310
Winchester, 55
Cathedral, 30, 57, 95, 96, 98, 150, 175, 224, 239, 246, 285, 411, 420, 426, 429, 437, 442
College, 103
County Buildings, 47
Holy Cross, 264
Palace, 55, 376, 391, 411, 438
Winchfield (Hants), 244
Windsor, 154, 344, 374, 389, 390, 424
Windsor Castle, 14, 29, 34, 37, 43, 44, 46, 47, 51, 77, 81, 93, 94, 95, 103, 104, 108, 109, 120, 135, 147, 157, 167, 169, 176, 198, 199, 214, 236, 248, 249, 263, 267, 273, 278, 279, 282, 296, 300, 328, 330, 336, 346, 352, 354, 364, 387, 389, 390, 400, 403, 446
Great Park, 425
Guildhall, 104
Parish Church, 29, 44, 61, 65, 254, 259, 285, 343, 344, 349
Royal Mausoleum, 56
St. George's Chapel, 55, 107, 116, 135, 151, 209, 259, 300, 359, 386, 390, 400, 422, 440, 446
Wingrave (Bucks), 70
Winkfield (Berks), 44, 302
Winslow (Bucks), 15, 96
Winslow Hall (Bucks), 158, 253, 309
Winterbourne Came (Dorset), 66
Winthorpe (Notts), 90
Winwick (Lancs), 63, 367, 449
Wirksworth (Derbys), 20
Wisbech (Cambs), 18, 202, 279, 367
Wisborough Green (Sussex), 286
Wiston (Sussex), 96, 108, 385
Wistow (Leics), 429
Witcombe (Glos), 259
Witham (Essex), 163, 210, 361, 422
Withington (Glos), 254
Withyham (Sussex), 96, 102, 279
Witnesham (Suffolk), 395
Wiveliscombe (Som), 164, 350
Woburn (Beds), 427
Woburn Abbey (Beds), 77, 80, 85, 93, 95, 107, 126, 129, 131, 149, 158, 163, 164, 194, 198, 200, 238, 248, 278, 279, 312, 326, 337, 349, 411, 412, 423, 424, 425, 428, 435, 437, 440
Woking (Surrey), 260, 423
Wokingham (Berks), 442
Wollaston (Northants), 114
Wollaton (Notts), 30, 375
Wolseley Hall (Staffs), 296
Wolstanton (Staffs), 400
Wolverhampton, 393
Wolverley House (Worcs), 147, 149, 150, 152
Wolverstone (Suffolk), 352, 428
Wombourn (Staffs), 96
Womenswold (Kent), 382
Wonersh (Surrey), 65

Wonston (Hants), 175
Woodbridge (Suffolk), 375
  The Castle, 312
Woodbury (Devon), 190, 225
Woodchester (Glos), 100, 158
Woodeaton Hall, 20
Woodeaton Manor (Oxon), 108
Woodford (Essex), 27, 106, 163, 382
Woodnesborough (Kent), 30
Woodstock (Oxon), 88. *See also*
  Blenheim
Woodstone (Hunts), 143
Wootton (Norfolk), 125, 315
Woolaton (Notts), 427
Woolley (Som), 229
Woolston (Hants), 141, 285. *See also*
  Itchen (Pear Tree Green)
Woolwich (London), 49, 320
  Dockyard, 115
  Parish Church, 15
  Royal Arsenal, 261
  Royal Foundry, 179
  Royal Military Academy, 105
Wooton (Kent), 242
Wootton (Beds), 367
Wootton Bassett (Wilts), 158
Wootton Glanville (Dorset), 388
Wootton St. Lawrence (Hants), 309
Wootton Wawen (Warwicks), 384
Worcester, 437
  All Saints, 365, 373, 401, 430
  Cathedral, 30, 31, 96, 204, 264,
    277, 322, 331, 367, 368, 373,
    415, 429, 430, 437
  Guildhall, 36, 364, 430
  Infirmary, 264
  St. Nicholas's, 373
  St. Peter's, 254

St. Swithin's, 27, 365
Workington (Cumb), 134
Worksop (Notts), 111, 281
Worlington (Suffolk), 124, 209
Worlingworth (Suffolk), 31
Wormley (Herts), 408, 425, 428
Worsborough (Yorks), 353
Worth (Sussex), 332, 356, 360
Worting (Hants), 170, 384
Wortley (Yorks), 150, 151, 308, 443
Wotton (Surrey), 86, 91, 99, 168,
  263, 354
Wotton-under-Edge (Glos), 35, 119,
  121, 253, 295, 382
Wragby (Yorks), 96, 151
Wraxall (Som), 315, 405
Wreary (Cumb), 134
Wrenbury (Ches), 29, 30, 31, 363,
  387
Wrensbury (Staffs), 402
Wrest Park (Beds), 61, 79, 83, 112,
  130, 143, 182, 230, 233, 281,
  374, 413, 448
Wrexham (Denbigh), 63, 133, 311,
  331, 368, 407, 426, 445
Wrington (Som), 35
Writtle (Essex), 98, 127
Wroxall (Warwicks), 383
Wroxton (Oxon), 150, 437
Wroxton Abbey, 203
Wycken Bonant (Essex), 341
Wyddial (Herts), 198, 422
Wyke Regis (Dorset), 113, 178, 185,
  196, 428
Wymondham (Norfolk), 315, 365,
  414

Yalding (Kent), 15, 331

Yardley (Warwicks), 206
Yarmouth, 93, 107
  St. Nicholas's, 240
Yarnton (Oxon), 231
Yarrow, St. Mary's Lake, 119
Yate (Glos), 317
Yateley (Hants), 285
Yatton (Som), 351
Yaxley (Hunts), 18, 174
Yeldon (Hunts), 378
Yelvertoft (Northants), 115
Yelverton (Norfolk), 127
York, All Saints, 309, 381
  Art Gallery, 222
  Assembly Rooms, 42, 328, 358
  Barr Wall, 358
  Belfry Church, *see* St. Michael-le-
    Belfry
  Bishopthorpe, 22
  Guildhall, 42, 261, 358
  Holy Trinity, 22, 261, 370
  Market House, 261
  Micklegate Bar, 42
  Minster, 45, 51, 55, 60, 99, 145,
    146, 170, 183, 202, 240, 275,
    321, 353, 381, 426
  Philosophical Society, 145
  St. Clement, 394
  St. Crux, 23, 146
  St. Dennis, 145
  St. Helen's, 193
  St. Mary's, Bishophill Senior,
    82
  St. Michael-le-Belfry, 146, 152,
    261, 314, 395
  School for the Blind, 222
Youghal (Eire), 116
Yoxford (Suffolk), 331, 395

INDEX OF NAMES

Abadon family, 265
Abbey, Harriot, 137
Abbey, Richard, 346
Abbott, Mrs. George, 13
Abdy, Sir Anthony, 367
Abel-Smith, John, 320
Abercorn, Marquess of, 94, 270
Abercrombie, Sir Ralph, 426
Aberdeen, Earl of, 29, 275, 277
Abernethy, John, 94, 181, 252
Abinger, Lord, 419
Abrahall, Gilbert, 319
Abraham, Mrs., 31
Acland, Henry, 267
Acland, Sir Thomas Dyke, 372
Acton, Anne, 324
Acton, Edward, 203
Acton, Elizabeth, 95
Acton, Thomas, 347
Acton, William, 116
Adam, John, 427
Adam, Robert, 211
Adams, Clarke, 115
Adams, Dr., 63
Adams family, 228
Adams, J. C., 71
Adams, James, 437
Adams, Mrs., 256
Adams, Rev. William, 229
Adams, William, 127, 260
Adamson, Christopher, 144
Addenbrooke, Col., 252
Addenbrooke, John, 252
Adderley, Charles, 206
Adderley, Lettice, 108
Addington, Dr., 39
Addington, Anthony, 423
Addington, Frances, 318
Addison, John, 133
Addison, Joseph, 211, 425
Addison, Samuel, 206, 207
Addison, T. B., 133
Addison, Thomas, 208, 398
Adelaide, Queen, 95
Aderson, Sir George, 352
Adey, Daniel, 382
Adkin, Thomas, 164
Adolphus, Prince, 241
Adye, Major-Gen., 15
Affleck, Sir James, 125
Agar-Ellis, Hon. George, 380
Agge family, 112
Aglionby, Major, 415
Ailesbury, Countess of, 120
Ainger, Rev. William, 243
Ainsworth, Harrison, 353
Airedale, Lord, 177
Aislabie, Benjamin, 122
Akers, Aretas, 15
Akers, Jane, 331
Akroyd, Col., 301
Akroyd, Jonathan, 178
Albemarle, 1st Duke of, 73, 343
Albert, Prince Consort, 13, 14, 24,
    43, 49, 62, 97, 135, 136, 137, 153,

154, 157, 158, 243, 274, 275, 307,
    346, 352, 370, 372, 374, 386, 387,
    389, 390, 393, 444, 446
Albert of Schleswig-Holstein, Prince,
    392
Albuquerque, Marquess of, 161
Alcock, Mrs., 75
Aldersey, William, 150
Alderson, Dr., 221, 425
Alderson, John, 48
Aldous, Mrs., 427
Aldrich, Henry, 98
Aldridge, Richard, 158
Alexander the Great, 137, 318, 342,
    422, 436
Alexander I, Tsar, 161
Alexander, Dr., 62
Alexander, Dr. Thomas, 257
Alexander, Elizabeth, 353
Alexander, J., 236
Alexander, James, 244
Alexandra, Princess of Wales, 392
Alfred the Great, King, 19, 61, 166,
    225, 312, 328, 334, 337, 372, 381,
    422, 437
Alice, Princess, 392
Alison, Dr., 371
Alison, Rev. Archibald, 198, 223
Alison, Sir Archibald, 291
Allardyce, Mrs., 27
Allcott, John, 412
Allcraft, Henry, 189
Allecroft, Hannah, 254
Allen, Bishop, 238
Allen, Capt., 302
Allen, Elizabeth, 440
Allen, Gertrude, 439
Allen, Henry, 294
Allen, J., 299
Allen, James, 208
Allen, Margaret, 219
Allen, Ralph, 176, 204
Allen, Samuel, 175
Allen, Sir Thomas, 16
Allen, Thomas, 70
Alleyne, Christian, 295
Alleyne, Judith, 295
Alleyne, S. M., 439
Allgood, Mr. and Mrs., 275
Allison, Mr., 197
Allnutt, Richard, 422
Allsopp, Samuel, 185
Allwood, Miss, 135
Alsager, Richard, 355
Alston, Thomas, 30
Althorp, Lord, 75
Amcotts, Sir Wharton, 251
Amherst, Admiral, 404
Amherst, Lord, 404
Amherst, Sir Jeffery, 176
Amos, Andrew, 333
Amphlett, Thomas, 412
Amphlett, William, 365
Ancaster, 1st Duke of, 97, 341
Ancaster, 3rd and 4th Dukes of, 189

Anderson, Dr., 29, 93
Anderson, Sir Charles, 138
Anderson, Rev. George, 146
Anderson, James, 95
Anderson, Robert, 134
Anderson, Lieut. Robert, 217
André, Major, 407
André, John, 318
Andrew, Francis, 29
Andrew, James, 100
Andrew, Rev. James, 309
Andrew, John, 155
Andrew, Robert, 30
Anglesey, (Marquesses of), 114, 206,
    207, 245, 263, 274, 275, 403, 422,
    448, 449
Anne, Queen, 53, 54, 55, 59, 82,
    121, 198, 263, 321, 336, 387, 395,
    430
Annersley, Sir James, 154
Annersley, Arthur, 293
Annersley, Francis, 262
Annesley, Rev. Francis, 30
Ansdell, Richard, 420
Ansell, Richard, 138
Anson, Viscount, 427
Anson, Anne, Viscountess, 158
Anson, Frederick, 118
Anspach, Margrave of, 9, 78
Anstey, Christopher, 211
Anstey, Helen, 127
Anthony, Mary, 175
Anthony of Padua, St., 328
Antonie, William, 151
Antoninus Pius, 342, 343
Antrobus, Sir Edward, 289
Antrobus, John, 426
Antrobus, Philip, 422
Appleyard, John, 138
Apthorp, Charles, 99
Arabin, Gen., 127
Arbuthnot, Lady, 383
Arbuthnot, Mrs., 29
Arbuthnot, Elizabeth, 384
Arbuthnot, Sir William, 418
Archer, Lord, 200
Archer, Lady Mary, 29
Archer, Henry, 437
Archer, Rev. James, 363
Archer, John, 30, 368
Archimedes, 441
Argles, Ann, 378
Argyll, Duchesses of, 120, 277
Argyll, Dukes of, 63, 152, 222, 329,
    331
Aristotle, 99, 407, 422
Arkwright, Mrs., 96, 277
Arkwright, Charles, 420
Arkwright, Sir Richard, 41, 109, 133
Armston family, 202
Armstrong, Matthew, 360
Armstrong, Sir William, 267
Arnold, G., 332
Arnold, Richard, 52
Arnold, Thomas, 47

Arnold, Dr. Thomas, 389
Arnott, James, 419
Arundel, Earl and Countess of, 320
Arundel, William, Earl of, 441
Arundell, Mary, 362
Ash, Humphrey, 284
Ash, William, 182
Ashbrook, 2nd Viscount, 404
Ashbrook, 3rd Viscount, 150
Ashbrook, Deborah, Viscountess, 151
Ashburnham, Hon. Esther, 303
Ashburnham, William, 73
Ashburton, Lord, 154, 250, 267
Ashby, George, 75
Ashby, Shuckburgh, 40
Ashe, Thermuthis, 229
Ashley, Lady, 170
Ashley, Isaac, 115
Ashley, John and Jane, 27
Ashley, Joseph, 198
Ashley, Moses, 195
Ashness, Thomas, 318
Ashton, Edward, 110
Ashton, Thomas, 423
Ashton, William, 115
Askel, Michael, 381
Askew, Dr. Anthony, 101
Askew, Henry, 417
Asperne, Mrs., 109
Aspland, Rev. Robert, 309
Assheton, Sir John, 368
Assheton, Sir Ralph, 412
Astell, Richard, 404
Astle, Thomas, 318
Astley, Blanch, 303
Astley, Sir Jacob, 252, 286
Astley, Mary, 373
Astley, Master, 269
Astley, Sir Philip, 286
Astley, Rhoda and Sofia, 30
Atcheson, Anthony, 318
Athelstan, 111
Atherton, Sir William, 426
Athlone, Countess of, 23
Atholl, Dukes of, 248, 371, 384
Atkins, Sir Richard and Lady, 368
Atkinson, James, 193
Atkinson, Robert, 114
Atkinson, Rev. William, 175
Atkyns, Edward, 99, 426
Attwood, Thomas, 206, 389
Atwood, Harry, 317
Auberry, Edmund, 382
Auberry, Mary, 396
Aubrey, Col., 331
Aubrey, Horwood, 344
Aubrey, Mary, 189
Aubrey, Capt. Thomas, 331
Auckland, Earl of, 419, 420
Auckland, Lord and Lady, 266
Audis, John, 309
Audley, Lord and Lady, 403
Aufrere, Mr., 276
Augusta, Princess, 157
Augusta, Princess of Saxe-Gotha, 176
Augustus Caesar, 120
Augustus, Prince, 241
Aumale, William Earl of, 395
Austen, Edward, 231

Austen, Richard, 76
Austen, Robert, 28, 264
Austin, Mrs., 29
Austin, Rev. James, 209
Austria, Emperor of, 132
Awdry, Priscilla, 178
Aylesford, Louisa Countess of, 278
Ayling, Lieut. John, 329
Aynsworth, Katherine, 349
Ayre, Dr., 227

Babbington, Dr., 415
Babbington, William, 398
Babclay, Jacob, 204
Babington, Dr., 45
Babington, Benjamin, 323
Babington, Stephen, 93
Babington, William, 47
Babley, John, 381
Bacelli, Signora, 240
Bach, William, 373, 379
Bache, Miss Josephine, 70
Back, Mr., 184
Backwell, Richard, 115
Bacon, Lord, see Bacon, Francis
Bacon, Elizabeth, 437
Bacon Francis, 34, 43, 198, 211, 331, 337, 351, 387, 419, 444
Bacon, Jane, 367
Bacon, John, 251, 252
Bacon, John, (R.A.), 29
Bacon, Thomas, 115
Badcock, John, 175
Badcock, Lovell, 117
Badger, Mr., 45
Badger, Thomas, 206
Badley, John, 206
Bagnell, Maria, 161
Bagot, Bishop of St. Asaph, 419
Bagot, Lady, 368
Bagot, Capt. H., 426
Bagot, Lewis, 94
Bagshaw family, 414
Bagshaw, Elizabeth, 56
Bagshaw, Richard, 146
Bagshawe, William, 356
Bailey, John, 20, 174
Bailey, Sir Joseph, 390
Bailey, Philip, 247
Baillie, Lady Grizel, 330
Baillie, Dr. Matthew, 94, 277, 278
Baily, Mr. (father of E. H. Baily), 34
Baily, Edward, 315
Baily, E. H., 131
Baily, Elizabeth, 113
Bailye, Rev. Hugh, 356
Bainbridge, Elizabeth, 433
Bainbridge, Joseph, 35
Bainbridge, Mary, 376
Bainbridge, Philip, 195, 314
Bainbridge, Thomas, 209
Bainbrigge, Elizabeth, 59
Baines, John, 95
Baines, Sir Thomas, 89
Baines, Thomas, 284
Baird, Col., 301
Baird, Sir David, 245
Baker family, 61
Baker, Admiral, 55

Baker, Charles, 36
Baker, Edward, 229
Baker, George, 283
Baker, John, 322
Baker, Joseph, 200
Baker, Michael, 317
Baker, Richard, 427
Baker, William, 96, 264
Balcanqual, Dr. Walter, 368
Balchen, Admiral, 344
Balderstone, Timothy, 315
Baldock, Louisa, 422
Baldwin, Dr., 199
Baldwin, Mr., 72, 167
Baldwin, Joseph, 161
Baldwyn, Bernard, 204
Baldwyn, Catherine, 80
Bale, H., 61
Balfe, M., 220
Balfour, Major, 306
Balfour, John, 317
Ball, Mrs. Frances, 201
Ball, John and Elizabeth, 114
Ball, Rev. Thomas, 151
Ballard, Charlotte, 180
Balm, Rev. Edward, 306
Balme, Abraham, 150
Bamford, Mrs., 308
Bamford, Charles, 138
Bampfylde, Copplestone, 180
Banbury, Earl of, 224
Bandon, Earl of, 320
Banfill family, 438
Banfill, William, 438
Bankes, Sir Joseph, 39
Bankes, John, 181
Bankes, Langley, 437
Banks, Mrs., 267
Banks, Sir E., 110
Banks, Sir Edward, 359
Banks, Sir Joseph, 93, 94, 120, 147, 164, 403
Banks, George, 177
Bannerman, John, 427
Bannister, Jane, 392
Bansall, George, 142
Barbar, George, 319
Barber, George, 206
Barclay, Miss Ada, 63
Bardwell, Henry, 279
Bardwell, Richard, 279
Baretti, Giuseppe, 39
Barfott, Capt. John, 72
Barham, John, 288
Bariatinsky, Princess, 30
Baring, Lady, 151
Baring, Henry, 359
Barker, John, 225
Barker, William, 425
Barkham, Sir Robert and Lady, 254
Barkly, Aeneas, 229
Barlow, Rev. John, 136
Barlow, Peter, 105
Barlow, William, 215
Barnard, Capt., 340
Barnard, Sir John, 342
Barnard, Rev. B., 20
Barnard, E. G., children of, 104
Barnard, George, 422
Barnard, Mary, 352
Barnard, Sarah, 340

Barnell, Mrs., 241
Barnes, Gen., 239
Barnes, Sir Edward, 419
Barnes, Edward, 46
Barnesley, William, 379
Barnett, Amelia, 391
Barnfather, John, 381
Barnham, Ann, 367
Barnouin, Elizabeth, 409
Baron, John, 365
Baron, Nathaniel, 65
Barran, John, 177
Barras, Alice, 152
Barrell, Francis, 381
Barrett, John, 158
Barrett, Rev. Stephen, 350
Barrington, Admiral, 150
Barrington, Bishop, 96
Barrington, Bishop of Durham, 45
Barrington, Bishop of Salisbury, 266
Barrington, Hon. Rothesia, 295
Barrington, Hon. Russell, 127
Barrington, Viscountess, 300, 448
Barrington, Viscount, 46, 264
Barrington, William Viscount, 423
Barron, Barbara, 29
Barron, Thomas, 347
Barrow, Charles, 321
Barrow, Sir George, 24
Barrow, Isaac, 274, 330, 331
Barrow, Sir John, 303
Barry, Sir Charles, 154
Barry, Sir Redman, 445
Barry, Mrs., 396
Barry, Charles, 47, 291
Barry, E. M., 445
Barry, Mrs. Smith, 165
Barrymore, Mr., 111
Bartelot, Hooker, 242
Bartholomew, Rev. Moses, 76
Bartlett, Isabella, 246
Barton, Newton, 408
Barton, Rev. Philip, 437
Barwis, Thomas, 357
Baseley, John, 119
Basnett, Rev. John, 81
Basset, Lt.-Col., 390
Bassett, John Francis, 422
Bastard, John, 203
Batchelor, Thomas, 59
Bateman, Viscount, 279
Bateman, 2nd Baron, 118
Bateman, Edmund, 114
Bateman, Mary, 353
Bateman, Richard, 96
Bateman, Thomas, 205
Bateman, William, 217
Bates, John, 175
Bates, Joshua, 47
Bateson, Robert, 373
Bath, Marquess of, 96
Bath, Pulteney, Earl of, 437
Bath, Rachel, Countess of, 71
Bathurst, Earl and Countess, 277
Bathurst, Lord, 176
Bathurst, Bishop, 93
Bathurst, Bishop of Norwich, 157
Bathurst, Ann, 208
Bathurst, Poole, 229
Bathurst, Rosa, 424
Batt, John, 427

Batt, William, 64
Battersby, Elizabeth, 329
Battisson, Robert, 438
Batton, William, 164
Batty, Richard, 28
Baugh, Rev. Joseph, 162
Baverstock, Mrs. Hinton, 189
Baxter, Sir David, 370
Baxter, Mrs., 229
Bayley, Sir John, 372
Bayley, Elizabeth, 449
Bayley, Francis, 35
Bayley, Lucy, 422
Bayley, Thomas, 29
Bayly, Lady, 431
Bayne, Capt., 278
Bayntun, Susannah, 297
Bayston, Peter, 214
Bazalgette, J. W., 74
Bazalgette, Lt.-Col. Louis, 302
Beach, Thomas, 229
Beadon, Bishop Richard, 440
Beale, Rev. and Mrs., 71
Bean, Major George, 31
Beane, Mrs. Elizabeth, 368
Beard, Hannah, 319
Bearsley, Margaret, 29, 318
Beauchamp, Earl, 20
Beauchamp, Countess, 355
Beauchamp, Henry, 265
Beauclerk, Lord Aubrey, 343
Beauclerk, Lady Diana, 243
Beauclerk, Lord Frederick, 244
Beauclerk, Ida, 292
Beaufort, Dukes of, 14, 140, 334
Beaufort, 2nd Duke of, 337, 338
Beaufort, 3rd Duke of, 338
Beaufort, 4th Duke of, 337, 338
Beaufort, 5th Duke of, 426
Beaufort, 6th Duke of, 140
Beaufort, Duchesses of, 141, 423, 439
Beaufoy, Miss, 170
Beaufoy, Henry, 257, 423
Beaufoy, John, 100, 104
Beaumont, Francis, 211
Beaumont, Sir George, 329, 343
Beaumont, Lord, 250
Beaumont, Sir Richard and Lady, 184
Beaumont, Richard, 183
Beaumont, Thomas, 179
Beaumont, William, 210
Beavis, Sarah, 421
Beazly, Thomas, 405
Beckett, Sir John, 412
Beckett, Capt., 151
Beckett, Mrs., 115
Beckett, Rev. John, 48
Beckford, William, 263, 322
Beckham, George, 292
Beckwith, Dr., 240
Beckwith, William, 396
Bede, the Venerable, 224, 257
Bedford, Ann, Duchess of, 198
Bedford, Anna, Duchess of, 278
Bedford, Dukes of, 55, 158, 164, 277, 372, 437
Bedford, 5th Duke of, 278, 425
Bedford, 6th Duke of, 278
Bedford, 7th Duke of, 278, 428
Bedford, John, Duke of, 278

Bedford, Sarah, 44
Bedingfield, Philip, 418
Bedingfield, Thomas, 295
Bedwell, Bernard, 175
Beechey, Sir W., 34
Beetham, Mrs. Francis, 246
Beevor, Rev. John, 137
Begbie, Dr. Warburton, 371
Belasyse, Sir Henry, 343
Belcher, Miss, 267
Belcher, James, 343
Belfast, Earl of, 77, 250
Belfield, Eleanor, 150
Belgiosa, Count, 90
Belgrave, William, 174
Bell, Sir Charles, 419
Bell, Dr. Andrew, 48
Bell, Henry, 266, 416
Bell, James, 304
Bell, John, 70
Bellamont, Earl of, 202
Bellamy, John, 150
Benbow, Admiral, 390
Benbow, Rev. Edward, 36
Bendish, Sir John and Lady, 303
Bendish, Heigham, 195
Bendyshe, Sir Henry, 369
Bendyshe, Richard, 229
Bene, Robert, 286
Benet, Lady, 210
Benezet, William, 141
Benfield, Paul, 127
Bengough, Henry, 95
Benn, Thomas, 346
Bennet, Michael, 47
Bennett family, 384
Bennett, Hon. Henry, 349
Bennett, James, 20
Bennett, Sir John, 383
Bennett, John, 17
Bennett, Richard, 219
Bennett, Samuel, 206
Bennett, Rev. Samuel, 269
Bennett, William, 196, 351
Bennion, Thomas, 293
Bensley, Sir William, 30
Benson, Mrs., 55
Benson, Elizabeth, 54
Benson, James, 322
Bentham, Jeremy, 121, 136
Bentinck, Lord George, 34, 77, 261
Bentinck, Lord William, 425
Bentley, Dr., 330, 331
Bentley, Thomas, 344, 358
Benyon, Mrs., 115
Benyon, Richard, 423
Beresford, Lady, 46
Beresford, Lord, 209, 222
Beresford, John, 422
Beresford, Marianne, 31
Berkeley, Col., 354
Berkeley, Hon. George, 31
Berkeley, Hon. M., 199
Berkeley, Hon. William, 344
Bernard, Sir Robert, 228
Berners, Archdeacon, 428
Berners, Lord, 414
Berrow, John, 451
Berry, Jeremiah, 233
Bertie family, 83
Berwick, Joseph, 373

Bessborough, Countess of, 338
Bessborough, Earl of, 277
Bessemer, Henry, 450
Best, Martha, 209
Betagh, Rev. Thomas, 403
Betenson, Sir Edward, 139
Bethell, Richard, 138
Bethell, William, 156
Bettesworth, Frances, 297
Bettesworth, Capt. George, 107
Betty, Master, 69
Bevan, Arthur, 287
Bevan, Robert, 359
Bevan, Thomas, 221
Beverley, Countess of, 279
Bewes, Edward, 215
Bewes, Henry, 15
Bewick, Thomas, 34
Bewicke, Calverly, 35
Beynon, Edward, 317
Bickerton, Sir Richard, 96
Bickley, Henry, 212
Biddulph, Augusta, 427
Biddulph, Benjamin, 65
Biddulph, Michael, 317
Biddulph, Penelope, 427
Biddulph, Robert, 426
Biddulph, Rev. T., 34
Biddulph, Thomas, 34
Biddulph, Rev. Thomas, 36
Bidleson, Ann, 267
Bigg, Rev. John, 187
Biggs, Charles, 324
Biggs, Edward, 202
Bilbie, William, 384
Bindley, James, 226
Bingham, Rev. Peregrine, 228
Bingham, William, 151
Bingley, Lady, 81
Birch, Ann, 429
Birch, Anne, 427
Birch family, 42
Bird, Edward, 94
Bird, John, 278, 318
Birk, Mr., 308
Birkbeck, Dr., 413
Birkbeck, George, 333
Birnie, Sir Richard, 131
Birtwhistle, John, 146
Bishop, Joseph, 101
Black Prince, 334
Black Watch, 371
Blackall, George, 304
Blackburne, Rev. Thomas, 157
Blacket, Sir Edward, 186
Blackett, Mary, 31
Blackie, Prof., 63
Blacklock, Mary, 256
Blacknall, Mr., 181
Blackshaw, Mary, 150
Blackstone, Sir William, 26
Blackwood, Sir Henry, 48
Blaikie, Prof., 370
Blair, Capt., 278
Blair, President, 93
Blair, Rev. John, 437
Blake, Admiral, 290
Blake, Elizabeth, 246
Blake, John, 151
Blake, Richard, 137
Blake, William, 130

Blakestone, Arthur, 35
Blakeway, Rev. J. B., 80
Blakiston, Sir Matthew, 350
Bland, Sir John, 414
Bland, Elizabeth, 256
Bland, Joseph, 29
Bland, Thomas, 353
Blandford, Marquess of, 312
Blathwayt, William, 352
Blayney, Arthur, 28
Bleamire, William, 226
Blegborough, Henry, 156
Blencoe, Sir John, 210
Blencoe, Elizabeth, 76
Blencowe family, 426
Blencowe, John, 72, 76
Blenkarne, Thomas, 48
Blessington, Countess of, 132
Blicke, James, 53
Bligh, Admiral, 109, 236
Blisset, Troth, 151
Blizard, Sir William, 94, 323
Blizard, Thomas, 13
Blizard, W., 364
Blois, Sir Charles, 395
Blomberg, Rev. Dr., 104
Blome, Baron, 450
Bloomfield, Sir Thomas, 226
Bloomfield, Lord, 252
Blower, Mary, 369
Bloxsome, Mary, 442
Blücher, Marshal, 161, 187, 273, 402, 403, 424
Bluett, Robert and Kerrenhappuch, 258
Blundell, Henry, 156, 171, 227
Blunt, Joseph, 264
Board, William, 256
Boardman, Richard, 257
Bodledge, Mrs., 161
Body, Sarah, 65
Bohun, John and Mary, 213
Bold, Owen, 368
Bolingbroke, Viscount, 331, 336
Bolithoe, Thomas, 110
Bolland, Sir William, 352
Bolton, Duke of, 277
Bolton, 6th Duke of, 150
Bolton, Mary, 303
Bonar, Col. Thomas, 394
Bond, Anne, 13
Bond, Benjamin, 303
Bond, Thomas, 258
Bone, Henry, (R.A.), 94
Bonham, Edward, 43
Bonnell, Jane, 45
Bonner, Ann, 97
Bonney, Mrs., 174
Bonsal, Mr., 95
Bonsor, Joseph, 272
Bonsor, William, 259
Boorn, Major Richard, 72
Booth, Lt.-Col., 127
Booth, Sir Charles, 279
Booth, Sir Felix, 253
Booth, Sir George, 61
Booth, Barton, 404
Booth, George, 397
Booth, Lt.-Col. Henry, 141
Booth, John, 108, 206
Booth, Langham and Henry, 83

Booth, Philip, 32
Booth, Walter, 116
Booth, William, 195
Boothby, Lady, 41
Boothby, Penelope, 38, 40
Borghese, Princess Pauline, 76, 77, 400
Boringdon, Lord, 125
Borlase, Capt., 163
Borlase-Warren, Admiral Sir John, 31
Borrett, Mr. and Mrs., 98
Borrett, Anne, 98
Borrow, Rev. William, 309
Borrows, Rev. W., 390
Bosanquet, Sir J., 141
Bosanquet, Mrs., 270
Bosanquet, Charles, 141
Bosanquet, Jacob, 254
Bosanquet, Joseph, 86
Bosanquet, Samuel, 293
Bosanquet, William, 151
Boscawen, Admiral, 338
Boscawen, Edward, 278
Boscawen, Hon. Frances, 279
Bostock, J., 217
Boston, Lord and Lady, 278
Boswell, Sir Alexander, daughter of, 93
Bosworth, Dr. John, 439
Boteler, Lt.-Col. Richard, 65
Boteler, Sarah, 404
Botetourt, Lord, 194
Botfield, Beriah, 47
Botfield, Charlotte, 45, 46
Botfield, Thomas, 36
Bott, Sarah, 45
Boucher, Rev. John, 175
Boucher, Mary, 370, 411
Boucher, Sarah, 322
Boughton, Sir William and Lady, 213
Boulter, Archbishop of Armagh, 98
Boulton, Mrs., 96
Boulton, Matthew, 149, 306, 332
Bourchier, Lady, 244
Bourgeois, Sir Francis, 123, 182
Bourke, Sir Richard, 34
Bourne, John, 48
Bouverie, Admiral D., 193
Bouverie, Edward, 336
Bovell, Frances, 173
Bovill, John, 65
Bowditch, Nathaniel, 212
Bowen, Rev. Charles, 251
Bowen, Hannah, 390
Bowen, Nathaniel, 411
Bowen, Richard, 317
Bower, Edward, 282
Bower, Frances, 157
Bower, Francis, 428
Bowes, Gen., 95
Bowes, Major-Gen., 109
Bowes, Margaret, 303
Bowes, Thomas, 146
Bowker, William, 52
Bowles, Capt., 432
Bowles, George, 95
Bowles, Henry, 399
Bowles, William, 21, 90

Bowles, William and Ann, 426
Bowring, Sir John, 121, 372
Bowyer, Sir George, 279
Boyce, Rev. Hudson, 373
Boycott, Charles, 318
Boydell, Alderman, 357
Boydell, Mary, 57
Boyle, Archbishop of Armagh, 228
Boyle, Lord President, 370
Boyle, Lady Louisa, 427
Boyle, Lady Lucy, 427
Boyle, Robert, 100, 211, 336
Boys, William, 29
Brace, Frances, 373
Brackenbury, Charles, 412
Bradbury, John, 341
Bradbury, Joseph, 363
Braddyll, Mrs., 277
Braddyll, John, 338
Bradford, Bishop of Rochester, 98
Bradford, Countess of, 205
Bradford, Earl of, 328
Bradford, Lady, 96
Bradford, Sir Henry, 426
Bradley, John, 358
Bradshaw, Charlotte, 96
Bradshaw, Col. Joseph, 293
Bragge, Mrs., 295
Braham, Richard, 254
Braham (singer), 103
Braithwaite, John, 150
Brame, William, 36
Bramston, William, 117
Brand, Rev. T., 151
Brandenburg-Anspach, Christian,
    Margrave of, 19, 78
Brandis, John, 443
Brandreth, Joseph, 157
Brandwood, Edward, 141
Brassey, Mr. and Mrs., 362
Brassey, Thomas, 220
Bray, William, 66
Braye, Lady, 393
Breadalbane, Lord and Lady, 394
Breay, Rev. George, 206
Breeres, Rev. W., 231
Brenchley, Thomas, 294
Brenton, Mr., 93
Brettle, George, 427
Brewer, Mrs. Jane, 381
Brewster, Sir David, 62
Brewster, Frances, 152
Brewster, Rev. Patrick, 266
Brewster, Richard, 222
Brideoake, Bishop of Chichester, 55
Bridge, Charles, 352
Bridge, Lt.-Col. Cyprian, 162
Bridgeman, Sir John, 337, 338, 430
Bridgeman, Major, 380
Bridger, Windfrid, 264
Bridges, Brook, 344
Bridges, H., 193
Bridges, Col. Robert, 36
Bridges, William, 30
Bridgewater, John, Earl of, 427
Bridle, Rev. George, 294
Bridport, Viscount, 384
Bridport, Viscountess, 161
Brigade of Guards, 48, 49
Briggs, H. P., 196
Bright, Hester, 80

Bright, John, 71, 323, 387
Bright, Louisa, 387
Brind, Walter, 175
Brindle, Mr., 77
Brise, Shadrach, 361
Bristol, Earl of, 281
Bristol, 4th Earl of, 176, 437
Bristol, Frederick, Earl of, 125
Bristol, George, Earl of, 282
Bristol, Isabella, Countess of, 132
Bristol, Marchioness of, 41
Bristol, 1st Marquess of, 47, 383
Britton, Jacob, 355
Broadbelt, Francis, 28
Broadfoot, Major George, 320
Broadly, John, 27
Brocas, Anne, 190
Brocas, Thomas, 229
Brockman, James, 264
Brockman, Rev. Ralph, 29
Broderip, Fridiswyde, 317
Brodie, Sir Benjamin, 47, 419
Brodrepp, Richard, 343
Brograve, Sir Thomas, 367
Brograve, Thomas, 332
Broke, Sir Philip, 127
Brome, Thomas, 234
Brome, Viscount, 36
Bromet, W., 375
Bromley, Hon. Lady, 272
Bromley, John, 368
Bromsal, Ralph, 367
Bromsal, Thomas, 367
Brook, Rev. Beriah, 371
Brook, James, 302
Brook, Thomas, 302
Brooke, James, 353
Brooke, Jonas, 27
Brooke, Joseph, 175
Brooke, Lord, 277
Brooke, Sir James, 445
Brooke, Sir Richard, 158
Brooke, Sir Richard (4th Bt.), 27
Brooke, Sir Richard (5th Bt.), 28
Brooke, Thomas, 31, 187, 392
Brooker, William, 64
Brookes, Benjamin, 298
Brookes, Joseph, 431
Brooks, Anne, 265
Brooks, Archdeacon, 363
Brooks, John, 389
Brooks, Rev. Jonathan, 222
Brooks, Thomas, 36
Brookshaw, Sobieski, 392
Broome, Lord, 33
Broome, Richard, 158
Brothers, James, 138
Brotherton, 274
Brotherton, J., 275
Brougham, 1st Lord, 14, 34, 47, 114,
    124, 132, 158, 175, 178, 184, 188,
    197, 222, 263, 274, 289, 291, 352
Broughton, Bishop, 244
Broughton, Sir Thomas, 157
Brouncker, Mariana, 339
Brown, Sir William, 247, 250
Brown, Gen., 80
Brown, Charles, 304
Brown, Edward, 275
Brown, Francis, 108
Brown, George, 62

Brown, James, 208
Brown, Jane, 427
Brown, John, 217
Brown, Peter, 426
Brown, Rev. Robert, 181
Brown, Sibill, 367
Brown, Stephen, 315
Brown, Thomas, 302
Brown, William, 14
Browne family, 254
Browne, Elizabeth, 286
Browne, Frances, 426
Browne, Francis, 117
Browne, Gilbert, 288
Browne, Isaac, 95, 151
Browne, Jane, 150
Browne, John, 94, 155
Browne, P., 233
Browne, Robert, 155
Browne, Thomas, 439
Browne, William, 144, 437
Browning, Robert, 444
Brownlow, Lady, 278
Brownlow, Lord, 276, 426
Brownlow, Caroline, Countess, 427
Brownlow, Sophia, Countess, 78
Brownlow, Alice, Lady, 210
Brownlow, Mary, Lady, 260
Brownlow, Richard, 255
Brownlow, Sir John, 368
Brownlow, Sir John 367
Brownlow, William, 210
Brownsmith, Francis, 115
Bruce, Hon. Mrs., 426
Bruce, Gen. the Hon. Robert, 154
Bruce, Robert, 155
Brudenell, Hon. Mrs. 151
Brudenell, Margaret, 111
Brunel, I. K., 357, 450
Brunelleschi, 288
Brunswick, Duke of, 241
Brunswick, Ferdinand, Duke of, 176
Bruton, Nathaniel, 433
Brutton, Henry, 225
Brutus, 99
Bryan, Capt., 30
Bryan, James, 108
Bryans, James, 97
Bryant, John, 158
Bryant, William, 21
Brydges, Edmund, 379
Brydges, Edward, 242
Brydges, Frances, 229
Brydges, John, 431
Brydges, William, 229
Bubb, Henry, 370
Buccleuch, Duchess of, 77, 371
Buccleuch, Duke of, 77, 419
Buchan, Earl of, 197
Buchan, William, 151
Buchanan, Elizabeth, 206
Buck, Ann, 18
Buck, Mrs. Catherine, 308
Buck, George, 225
Buck, Rev. Richard, 239
Buck, Samuel, 151
Bucker, Richard, 65
Buckeridge family, 367
Buckingham and Chandos, Duke of,
    400
Buckingham, Duke of, 309

Buckingham, Villiers, Duke of, 336
Buckingham, Duchess of, 242
Buckingham, Marchioness of, 241
Buckingham, James Silk, 356
Buckland, William, 419
Buckley, Edward, 325
Buckridge, Catherine, 423
Budd, Richard, 123
Budgett, Maurice, 309
Bulkeley, Samson, 65
Bull, Mrs., 438
Bull, Catherine, 150
Bull, D., 295
Bull, Capt. James, 214
Bull, John, 325
Buller, Sir Edward, 215
Buller, Mrs., 448, 449
Buller, Charles, 419
Buller, James, 146
Bullock, Augusta, 203
Bullock, John, 343
Bullock, William, 21
Bulstrode, John, 58
Bunbury, Mrs., 423
Bunbury, Henry, 250
Bunning, James, 136
Bunny, Elizabeth, 191
Bunsen, Chevalier, 245
Bunyan, John, 290
Burdett, Sir Francis, 14, 303, 384, 428
Burdett, Mary, 229
Burdett-Coutts, Baroness, 14, 63
Burges, Amelia, 156
Burgess, Bishop, 285
Burgess, John, 229
Burgess, Capt. Richard, 40
Burgess, William, 237
Burgh, William, 426
Burghersh, Lord, daughter of, 239
Burgoyne, Sir John, 367
Burgoyne, William, 283
Burchill, William, 392
Burke, Edmund, 154, 200, 263, 309, 386
Burke, James, 283
Burke, Robert, 378
Burke, William, 62
Burland, John, 30
Burland, Mary, 138
Burley, Anne, 361
Burlton, Charles, 209
Burmester, Ann, 293
Burn, William, 304
Burnard, Nevil Northey, 71
Burnet, James, 306
Burnet, John, 144
Burnet, Bishop, 190
Burney, Charles, 161, 175, 278
Burns, John, 149
Burns, Robert, 18, 126, 134, 370, 387, 388, 403
Burr, Col., 403
Burr, Mrs., 30
Burrard, Paul, 164
Burrell, Sir Merrick, 359
Burrell, Sir William, 150
Burrell, Lady, 104
Burrell, Mrs., 200
Burrell, Percy, 30
Burroughs, Rev. Ellis, 267

Burroughs, Samuel, 277
Burrow, Sir James, 423
Burrows, Sir John, 372
Burrows, Mrs., 350
Burrows, Rebecca, 137
Burslem, William, 429
Burton, Elizabeth, 427
Burton, Sir Richard and Lady, 290
Burton, Benjamin, 433
Burton, Francis, 230
Burton, Mary, 331
Burton, Capt. Richard, 31
Burton, Robert, 332
Burwill, Rev. George, 332
Bury, Mrs., 110
Bury, William, 367
Busby, Dr. Richard, 55
Busby, Rev. Thomas, 338
Bush, Alderman, 284
Bush, Thomas, 213
Bushby, Charles, 350
Bushe, Charles Kendal, 403
Bushel, James, 302
Bushman, Joseph, 28
Bushnell, John, 104
Busk, Mr., 276
Butcher, John, 314
Bute, Lady, 308
Bute, Maria, Marchioness of, 390
Bute, Marquess of, 390
Butler, Alexander, 157
Butler, Bishop, 34
Butler, Catherine, 190
Butler, Rev. Dr., 104
Butler, Edward, 423
Butler, Judge, 300
Butler, Nathaniel, 322
Butler, Richard, 246
Butt, Dr., 229
Butt, Ann, 116
Butt, John, 189
Buxton, Sir Fowell, 49, 394
Buxton, Thomasine, 350
By, Lt.-Col. and Mrs., 303
Byam, Rev. Henry, 405
Byard, Thomas, 17
Byde, John, 368
Bye, John, 116
Byerley, Thomas, 385
Byles, Mather, 426
Byng, George, 425
Byron, Lord, 34, 49, 121, 161, 180, 238, 323, 380, 394

Cadogan, Col., 185, 197
Cadogan, Col. Henry, 95
Cadogan, Countess, 359
Cadogan, Emily, 177
Cadogan, Hon. and Rev. William, 28
Cairns, Major, 242
Caldecott, Ellen, 163
Caldecott, Georgiana, 36
Caldwell, Ralph, 215
Call, Sir John, 108
Callender, James, 322
Callinson, Robert, 319
Calnent, Elizabeth, 442
Calthorpe, Lord, 228
Calthorpe, Reynolds, 188
Calvert, Anthony, 30

Calvert, Felix, 367
Cambridge, Duchess of, 45, 46
Cambridge, Duke of, 14, 221, 249, 419
Camden, Marquess, 94, 390
Camden, Marquess, family of, 92
Camden, Earl, 39, 47, 176
Camden, John, 108
Came, John, 276
Cameron, Dr. 415
Cameron, Alexander, 192
Cameron, Neville, 260
Campion, John, 18
Campbell, Lord, 198, 371
Campbell, Lord Frederick, 197
Campbell, Lord John, 222
Campbell, Sir Archibald, 289, 437
Campbell, Mrs., 39
Campbell, Rev. A., 217
Campbell, Archibald, 144
Campbell, George, 355
Campbell, Henry, 239
Campbell, John, 205, 209
Campbell, Thomas, 34, 197, 250, 257, 266, 291
Campden, Viscount, 170
Cancellor, Katherine, 410
Candlish, John, 24
Cann family, 225
Canning, Earl, 154, 275
Canning, Earl and Countess, 275
Canning, Countess, 301
Canning, Viscountess, 248
Canning, Col., 93
Canning, Francis, 426
Canning, George, 29, 34, 93, 94, 121, 157, 180, 235, 278, 363, 420, 425
Canning, John, 271
Canova, 142
Canwardine, Richard, 373
Capel, Lady Harriet, 116
Capel, Sarah, 96
Capper, Rev. James, 292
Capron, Mrs., 248
Capron, Thomas, 209
Capua, Princess of, 387
Caracalla, 106, 191, 342, 436
Caractacus, 154
Card, John, 413
Cardigan, Countess of, 116, 352
Carew, Lord, 220
Carew, Sir Benjamin, 427
Carew, Mary, 86
Carew, Sir Nicholas, 421
Carew, Richard, 95
Carew, Thomas, 404
Carey, Anne, 204
Carhampton, Earl of, 182
Cariboo, Princess, 161
Carleton, Viscountess, 30
Carlini, A., 332
Carlisle, Earls of, 113, 154, 221, 224.
Carlisle, 5th Earl of, 278
Carlisle, 7th Earl of, 154
Carlyle, Rev. Alexander, 197
Carlyle, Thomas, 63, 420, 445
Carnarvon, Countess of, 98
Carnac, Sir James, 250
Carnwath, Countess of, 429

Caroline, Queen, 98, 198, 300, 336
Carpender, John, 175
Carpenter family, 157
Carpenter, James, 97
Carpenter, John, 273, 325
Carpenter, Lant, 439
Carpenter, William, 154
Carpue, Dr., 47
Carr, Bishop, 275
Carr, Sir Henry, 427
Carr, Lady Charlotte, 137
Carr, Mr., 277
Carr, Rev. Colston, 427
Carr, Harriet, 395
Carr, James, 251
Carr, John, 222
Carr, Mary, 28
Carr, Ralph, 222
Carrick, 4th Earl of, 36
Carruthers, William, 158
Carsan, Charles, 108
Carson, Dr., 354
Cart family, 401
Carter, Abigail, 66
Carter, George, 426
Carter, John, 437
Carter, William, 213, 350
Carteret, Lord, 427
Carteret, Hon. Philip, 121
Cartwright, Major, 104
Cartwright, Edmund, 409
Cartwright, G., 250
Cary, Hon. George, 146
Cary, Rt. Hon. Walter, 22
Carylon, Thomas, 209
Casement, Sir William, 232
Cashel, Archbishop of, 344
Cass, Christopher, 88
Cass, John, 330
Castell, John, 30
Castlereagh, Viscount, 94
Caswell, Elizabeth, 151
Catalini, Mme., 161, 175
Cathcart, Lord, 266
Catherine, Empress of Russia, 70
Catherine of Braganza, 72
Cattell, Frances, 228
Cattermole, C., 235
Cave, Adam, 430
Cave, Elizabeth, 365
Cave, Isabella, 43
Cavendish, Lord Frederick, 445
Cavendish, Lord George, 277, 278
Cavendish family, 55
Cavendish-Spencer, Capt. Sir
  Robert, 96
Cawdor, Earl, 217
Cawley, Rev. John, 54, 55
Caxton, 135
Caygill, Jane, 113
Caygill, John, 208
Cayley, Ann, 146
Cecil, William, 261
Chabot, Mr., 144
Chafin, Thomas, 159
Challnor, William, 174
Chalmers, Dr., 370
Chamberlain, Joseph, 444
Chamberlain, Mason, 27
Chamberlayne, Charlotte, 96
Chamberlayne, William, 96

Chamberlen, Dr. H., 126
Chambers, Emma, 329
Chambers, Ephraim, 195
Chambers, John, 215
Chambers, Major, 21
Chambers, Sir Robert, 150
Chambers, Thomas, 331
Chambers, Sir William, 238, 298, 425
Chambers, William, 288, 292
Chamier, Anne, 173
Chamier, Georgina, 355
Champain, M., 426
Champion, Col. Alexander, 279
Champion, Anthony, 150
Champneys, Frances, 226
Chandos, Duchess of, 31
Chandos, Duke of, 169
Chandos-Pole, Lady Anne, 393
Chaning, Charlotte, 74
Chantrey, Sir Francis, 196, 237, 273, 357, 360
Chapman, Lady, 358
Chapman, Rev. Charles, 17
Chapman, Rev. Richard, 416
Chapman, Thomas, 208
Chappell, Samuel, 324
Chardin, Sir John, 98
Charlemont, Earl of, 278
Charles I, 69, 73, 253, 255, 287, 289, 307, 329, 364, 393, 437
Charles II, 36, 72, 73, 103, 168, 169, 214, 234, 277, 313, 364, 419, 434
Charles, Prince, of Mecklenburg, 241
Charles Edward Stuart, Prince, 18, 180, 323
Charlesworth, Dr., 261
Charlett, Arthur, 373
Charlett, Elizabeth, 322
Charlotte, Queen, 69, 142, 176, 300
Charlotte, Princess, 113, 164, 187, 197, 252, 273, 300, 332, 402, 403, 446, 448
Charlton, Gilbert, 411
Charlton, Job, 426
Charrington, John, 212
Charrington, William, 410
Chase, Thomas, 57
Chatham, William Pitt, Earl of, 25, 26, 27, 39, 47, 106, 250, 278, 304, 359, 436
Chaucer, Geoffrey, 100, 156, 186, 211, 309
Chauncey, Lady, 367
Chauncy, Phillip, 364
Chauncy, Richard, 338
Chauncy, Toby, children of, 338
Chauncy, William, 338
Cheese, Michael, 426
Cheney, Col. Edward, 177
Cheney, Harriet, 173
Cherry, Martha, 57
Cheselden, W., 420
Chessher, Robert, 352
Chester, Henry, 114
Chester, Judith, 368
Chester, Mary, 367
Chester, Robert, 381
Chesterfield, Earls of, 203, 330, 437

Chetham, Humphrey, 386
Chetwynd, Sir George, 450
Chetwynd, Mary, 382
Chew, William, 179
Chichele, Archbishop, 331
Chichester, Bishop of, 24
Chichester, Mrs., 209, 303, 427
Chichester, Maria and John, 264
Chichester, Mary, 319
Child, Mary, 200
Child, Robert, 407
Childe, William, 81
Children, George, 68
Children, Richard, 331
Chilton, Matty, 307
Chilton, Richard, 318
Chippindale, Margaret, 380
Chiswell, Richard, 229
Chivers, William, 109
Cholmeley, Sir Montagu, 57
Cholmley, Catherine, 146
Cholmley, Nathaniel, 146
Cholmondeley, Dr., 186
Cholmondeley, George, 161
Cholmondley, Rev. Hugo, 95
Chowne, Gen., 64
Christian, Edward, 151
Christie, James, 46
Christie, James II, 70
Christie, John, 385
Christopher, William, 122
Christy, Henry, 445
Chuke, Stephen, 101
Church family, 64
Churchill, 44
Churchill, Admiral, 170
Churchill, Major-Gen., 226
Churchill, Mrs., 225
Churchill, George, 203
Churchill, Maria, 264
Churchman, Sir Thomas, 315
Churchman, Thomas, 98
Chute, Chaloner, 85, 86
Chute, Rev. Thomas, 250
Chute, William, 209
Cibber, Colley, 331
Cicero, 83, 158, 191, 211, 329, 342, 343, 422
Cipriani, 39
Clare, Richard Earl of, 395
Clare, Mary, 212
Claremont, Countess of, 263
Clarendon, Earls of, 49, 55, 98, 221, 263
Clarendon, 257
Clark, Dr., 49
Clark, John, 399
Clark, Thomas, 226
Clark, Dr. William, 74
Clark, William George, 445
Clarke, Dorothy Lady, 170
Clarke, Sir Simon, 150
Clarke, Dr., 80, 183
Clarke, Dr. Adam, 247
Clarke, Bartholomew, 338
Clarke, Benjamin, 309
Clarke, E. D., 94
Clarke, Edward, 151
Clarke, Elizabeth, 414
Clarke, George, 432
Clarke, Canon James, 80

Clarke, John, 40, 409
Clarke, Joseph, 310, 397
Clarke, Mary, 373
Clarke, Nathaniel, 206
Clarke, Randulph, 369
Clarke, Richard, 352, 373
Clarke, Rev. Sloughter, 195
Clarke, Thomas, 70
Clarke, William, 215, 239
Clarkham, Rev. B., 411
Clarkson, Rev. Isaac, 206
Clarkson, Thomas, 45, 46, 47
Clarkson, William, 439
Claudius, 187
Clavering, Jacob, 222
Clavering, Margaret, 122
Clayton, Sir Robert and Lady, 118
Clayton, Sir Thomas, 169
Clayton, Sir William, 427
Clayton, Lady, 404
Clayton, Mary, 30, 309
Cleave, William, 255
Cleaver, Emily, 381
Clement XIV, Pope, 199
Clement, John, 61
Clements, Harriet, 110
Clennell, Luke, 122
Cleoburey, Rev. John, 300
Clerc, Pierre, 228
Clere, William, 241
Clerk, Sir George, 257
Clerk, Drake, 246
Clerk, George, 412
Clermont, Earl of, 125
Cleveland, Duke of, 428
Cleveland, Duchess of, 47
Cleveland, Augustus, 220
Clevland, Archibald, 303
Clifford, Sir Augustus, 51, 178
Clifton, Sir Robert, 217
Clifford, Hon. Barbara, 264
Clifford, George, 70
Cline, Henry, 94
Clint, G. (R.A.), 34, 70
Clinton, Gen. Sir William, 118
Clinton, Lady Beatrice, 136
Clinton, A. M., 327
Clinton, George, 89
Clitherow, Ann, 29
Clive, Lord, 272, 390
Clive, Elizabeth, 81
Clode, Sir Richard, 61
Clonmel, Countess of, 356
Clootwyk, Jane, 229
Close, Thomas, 319
Clough, Mrs., 170
Clough, H. G., 302
Clouting, Samuel, 395
Clowes, Rev. John, 151
Clowes, William, 60
Clutton, Rev. John, 218
Clutton, John, 218
Clyde, Lord, 14, 154, 160
Coade, Robert, 170
Coales, Robert, 332
Coates, George, 145
Coates, Peter, 220
Coates, W. Martin, 159
Cobb, Lady, 204
Cobb, James, 285
Cobb, Robert, 328

Cobbett, William, 154
Cobbold, Elizabeth, 397
Cobden, Richard, 14, 71, 274, 275, 445
Cobham, Viscount, 343
Cockayne, Thomas, 350
Cockburn, Lord, 62, 63, 271
Cocker, Archdeacon, 269
Cockerell, Sir Chas., 104, 427
Cocks, Hon. Reginald, 426
Cocks, Hon. Mrs., 426
Cocks, Mrs., 344
Cocks, Rev. John, 344
Cocks, John, 421
Cocks, Joseph, 344
Cocks, Mary, 344
Cocks, Thomas Somers, 317
Codd, John, 229
Codrington, Christopher, 98, 181
Cody, William, 235
Coe, Robert, 410
Coffin, Sir Isaac, 46
Coffin, A. J., 165
Coffin, Richard, 108
Cogcombe, Thomas, 189
Coghill, Marmaduke, 343
Coghill, Mary, 191
Coghill, Thomas, and family, 304
Coke, Sir Edward, 328, 331
Coke, Lady Mary, 176
Coke, T. W., 94
Coker, Hon. Charlotte, 427
Colborne, Charles, 338
Colborne, John, 423
Colby, Capt., 302
Colchester, Lord, 433
Colchester, Maynard, 179
Colchester, Susanna, 112
Cole, Major-Gen. Sir Barry, 151
Cole, Gen. Sir Lowry, 222
Cole, Gervase, 392
Cole, Humphrey, 317
Cole, John, 110
Colebrooke, Henry, 94
Coleburne, Edward, 286
Coleman, Henry, 144
Colepepper, Lord, 338
Coleridge, Bishop, 317
Coleridge, Lady, 394
Coleridge, Lord, 49
Coleridge, James, 231
Coleridge, S. T., 20, 257, 260
Colet, Dean, 26
Collard, Mrs., 418
Collard, George, 304
Colleton, Anne, 342
Colley, John, 189, 380
Colley, Priscilla, 17
Collier, Lt.-Col., 125
Collingwood, Lord, 243, 329, 426
Collins, John, 218, 400
Collins, Richard, 375
Collins, Thomas, 204
Collins, William, 148, 150
Colman, Edward, 134
Colman, Francis, 404
Colman, Fysher, 365
Colmore, Charles, 151
Colnaghi, Mr., 142
Colpitts, Thomas, 156
Colpoys, Admiral, 277

Colquitt, Scrope, 174
Colston, Alexander, 66
Colston, Edward, 337, 351
Colston, Francis, 294
Columbus, Christopher, 177, 441
Colvile, Emma, 125
Colville, Clare, 35
Colville, E. R., 283
Colvin, Alexander, 427
Combe, George, 249
Combe, Judith, 367
Combe, Sarah, 246
Comber, Rev. William, 381
Comberbach, Robert, 63
Combermere, Viscount, 247, 387
Compton, Lord, 249
Compton, Lady Alwyne, 268
Comyns, Sir John, 98
Conduitt, John, 98
Coney, Caroline, 209
Congreve, William, 54, 55, 211, 291, 408
Coningsby, Margaret Countess of, 338
Connal, William, 266
Connell, Elizabeth, 134
Connolly, Mr. Speaker, 86
Conquest, Benedict, 264
Considine, Capt., 411
Constable, Sir Marmaduke, 320
Constable, John, 122
Constable, William, 292
Conway, Lady Caroline, 120
Conway, Gen., 176, 384
Conway, Henry Seymour, 176
Conyers, Miss, 176
Conyngham, Countess, 164
Conyngham, Lady Albert, 19
Cook family, 449
Cook, Esther, 209
Cook, Capt. James, 39, 147, 271, 441, 444
Cook, Laurence, 405
Cook, William, 340
Cooke, Gen. Sir George, 202
Cooke, Alfred, 261
Cooke, Bryan, 96
Cooke, Capt. Edward, 29
Cooke, Edward, 80
Cooke, Frances, 95
Cooke, Capt. John, 426
Cooke, Julia, 145
Cooke, Mary, 146
Cooke, Rev. William, 109
Cookson, Elizabeth, 405
Cooley, Henry, 367
Cooper, Sir Astley, 34, 397, 419
Cooper, Sir Astley Paston, 398
Cooper, Sir Astley and Lady, 51
Cooper, Sir Frederick, 209
Cooper, Mr., 49
Cooper, C. H., 74
Cooper, Edward, 315
Cooper, Elizabeth, 350
Cooper, Hannah, 181
Cooper, Isabella, 262
Cooper, John, 181
Cooper, Samuel, 74
Cooper, Thomas, 207
Cooper, Rev. William, 209
Cooper, William, 428, 429

Coote, Sir Eyre, 39, 266
Cope, Lady, 430
Cope, John, 254
Cope, Robert, 178
Copleston, Edward, 47
Copley, Mr., 308
Coram, Capt., 257, 352
Corbet, Sir Corbet, 81
Corbet, John, 80
Corbet, Mary, 80
Corbet, Richard, 311
Corbould, Henry, 224
Corfield, Elizabeth, 242
Cork, Earl of, 232, 320
Cork, Isabella, Countess of, 429
Corles, Edward, 373
Cornewall, Sir George, 429
Cornewall, Capt., 100, 382
Cornwall, Rt. Hon. Charles, 264
Cornwallis, Marquesses, 26, 29, 35, 39, 151, 272, 328
Cornwallis, Earl, 35
Cornwallis, Julia, Countess, 36
Cornwallis, Sir William, 154
Corpe, Ann, 318
Corrance, Elizabeth, 212
Corrie, Bishop of Madras, 420
Corrie, Bishop Daniel, 419
Corrigan, Sir Dominic, 154
Corry, Rt. Hon. Isaac, 448
Corser, Ann, 271
Corser, John, 57, 406
Coryton, William, 160
Cosby, Anne Lady, 317
Cossins, John and Martha, 336
Coston family, 266
Cosway, Mrs., 39
Cosway, Richard, 427
Cotes, Roger, 343
Cotterell, Sir J., 260
Cottesloe, Lord, 14
Cotton, Admiral Sir Charles, 151
Cotton, Sir John, 423
Cotton, Sir Lynch, 402
Cotton, Sir Robert, 254, 331
Cotton, Admiral, 215
Cotton, Commander, 427
Cotton, Edward, 442
Cotton, Harriot, 45
Cotton, Rev. Holford, 220
Cotton, Rev. H. S., 124
Cotton, John, 426
Cotton, Rebecca, 254
Cotton, Robert, 168, 170, 355
Cotton, Sarah, 235
Cottrell, Sir Stephen, 427
Cottrell, Mrs., 426
Cottrell, Samuel, 114
Coulson, Juliana, 209
Coulthurst, H., 426
Courtail, Rev. John, 151
Courtauld, Samuel, 153
Courten, William, 170
Courthope, George, 179
Courtis, John, 101
Courtney, William, 372
Courtown, Countess of, 77
Cousin, Victor, 267
Coutis, Mr., 93
Coventry, Earls of, 30, 368
Coventry, 3rd Earl of, 337

Coventry, 7th Earl of, 373
Coventry, 8th Earl of, 373
Coventry, John Lord, 168
Coventry, Sir Henry, 228
Coventry, Hon. Francis, 228
Coward, Margaret, 356
Coward, Thomas, 155
Cowley, Abraham, 73
Cowper, Lord, 277
Cowper, Hon. F. W., 217
Cowper, Spencer, 331
Cowper, William, 150
Cox, Hon. Mrs., 66
Cox, Ann, 317
Cox, Charles, 317
Cox, Daniel, 295
Cox, David, 206
Cox, Elizabeth, 339
Cox, John, 297
Cox, Solomon, 263
Cox, Thomas, 221
Coxe, Anne, 66
Coxe, Charles, 66
Coxe, Elizabeth, 322
Coytmore, George, 63
Cozens, Elizabeth, 170
Crabbe, 395
Crabbe, Rev. G., 35
Craddock, Richard, 282
Cradock, Mrs., 188
Craggs, James, 183
Crammer, Josiah, 185
Crampin, John, 395
Cranmer, Archbishop, 349, 419
Cranston, Edward, 238
Cranston, John, 306
Cranford, Emma, 96
Craven, Sir William, 367
Craven, R., 227
Crawford, Gen., 31
Crawford, Dr., 63
Crawford, Andrew 246
Crawford, Gibbs, 328
Crawley, Theodosia, 306
Crawshay, Elizabeth, 418
Cray, Richard, 306
Creed, Mrs., 110
Creed, Col. John, 52
Creed, Lieut. Richard, 389
Cremer, Robert, 365
Cressiner, George, 210
Cresswell, Anne, 321
Creswell, Mrs., 332
Creuzé, Elizabeth, 30
Crewe, Sir Randolph, 419
Crewe, Bishop, 420
Crichton, Nathaniel, 355
Cripple, Elizabeth, 58
Crispe, Mrs., 346
Crispe, Anne, 288
Croft, Sir John, 228, 387
Croft, Edward, 443
Croft, Grace, 263
Croft, John, 375
Croft, Mary, 350
Crofts, Lord and Lady, 374
Crofts, Mrs. Ann, 288
Croker, John Wilson, 230
Crome, John, 49
Crompton, Elizabeth, 142
Crompton, Samuel, 257

Cromwell, Agnes, 150
Cromwell, Elizabeth, 213
Cromwell, Oliver, 39, 130, 211, 274, 275, 289, 297, 329, 330, 334, 337
Cropper, Elizabeth, 298
Crosbie, Gen., 30
Crosbie, Frances, 427
Crosby, Sir John, 117, 273
Crosfield, Thomas, 404
Crosham, John, 241
Cross, Mary, 225
Crosse, Jane, 321
Crosse, Thomas, 321
Crossfield, Thomas, 203
Crossland, Thomas Pearson, 412
Crossley, Frank, 135
Crossley, Dr. John, 279
Crossley, John, 237
Crouch, Pyke, 437
Crowe, Rev. John, 438
Crowe, Thomas, 286
Crowe, William, 117
Crowther, Edward, 206
Crowther, Thomas and William, 31
Crozier, Mrs., 299
Cruikshank, George, 47, 165
Crumbleholme, William, 97
Cruttenden, George, 427
Cubitt, Lieut. Thomas, 181
Cubitt, Thomas, 250
Cuff, Thomas, 422
Cullin, Rev. Edward, 80
Culling-Hanbury, Robert, 387
Cullum, Sir Dudley, 353
Cullum, Sir Thomas, 125, 410
Cullum, Sir Thomas and Lady, 449
Cullum, Lady, 77
Cullum, Mary, 339
Cullurpe, Anne, 61
Culpeper, Lady, 254
Cumberbatch, Mrs., 116
Cumberland, Duke of, 45, 47, 81, 97, 278, 337, 403, 406, 408
Cumberland, William Duke of, 176
Cumberland, Bishop, 179
Cumberland, Elizabeth, 314
Cumberland, Richard, 213
Cunliffe, Sir Robert, 278
Cunliffe, Francis, 80
Cunningham, Sir Charles, 390
Cunningham, Allan, 144, 356, 415, 419
Cunninghame, Principal, 266
Cunynghane, Col., 185
Curc, Capel, 332
Cure, Elizabeth and Joanna, 331
Curran, John, 79
Currey, Rev. John, 260
Curteis, Caroline, 32
Curteis, Charlotte, 127
Curteis, Hannah, 365
Curteis, Herbert, 160
Curtis, Sir William, 209, 352
Curtis, Rev. Canon, 245
Curtis, Augustine, 41
Curtis, Elizabeth, 232
Curwen, Henry, 254
Curzon, Viscount, 96
Curzon, Lady, 343
Curzon, Sir Nathaniel, 338, 343
Cusack-Smith, Sir William, 246

Cust, Sir John, 404
Cust, Sir Richard and Lady, 27
Cust, Lady, 184, 404
Cust, Hon., and Rev. Richard, 387
Cust, Elizabeth, 420
Cust, Hon. Etheldred, 27
Cust, Horace, 419
Cust, Saville, 404
Custance, H., 315
Custance, John, 315
Cutforthay, Robert, 308
Cuthbert, George, 391
Cutler, Sir John, 313
Cutts, Anne, Lady, 254
Cuvier, 250

d'Abano, Pietro, 240
da Costa, Hippolyte, 105
Daer, Lord, 39, 95
Dahl, Michael, 334
Daintry, John, 29
Dales, Rev. E., 406
Dalhousie, Lord, 370, 450
Dalkeith, Earl of, 77
Dalling, Lieut. John, 264
Dallingham, Brampton, 254
Dalrymple, Col., 355
Dalrymple, John, 77
Dalton, Dr., 78
Dalton, Francis, 141
Dalton, John, 93, 386
Dalton, Thomas, 251
Damer, Hon. Lionel, 66
Damer, Anne Seymour, 120, 289
Damer, John, 120
Dampier, Thomas, 339
Danberry, Lady, 359
Danby, Earl of, 407
Danby, F., 263
Danby, William, 146
Dance, George, 328
Dandridge, John, 427
Daniell, William, 427
Dansey, Capt., 322
Danson, Mrs., 238
D'Anvers family, 72
Danvers, Sir Joseph, 202
Darby, Mary, 146
Darcy of Navan, Lord, 180
Dargan, Mr., 221
Darker, John, 53
Darker, Mark, 53
Darling, Grace, 122, 134, 259
Darling, William, 134
Darlington, 2nd Earl of, 112
Darlington, Katherine Countess of, 113
Darlington, Margaret Countess of, 112–13
Darnell, Mrs., 302
Darnley, Lord, 419
Darnley, 4th Earl of, 278
Darnley, Countess of, 426
Darrell, Hugh, 55
Darwin, Dr., 109
Dash, Mrs. Ann, 184
Dashwood family, 433
Dashwood, Sir Francis, 26
Dashwood, Lt.-Col., 23
Dashwood, Caroline, 160
Dashwood, George, 279

Dashwood, Richard, 143
Dashwood-King, Sir George, 279
Davenport, Sir Thomas, 146
Davenport, John, 53
Davenport, Richard, 279
Davey, Eleazar, 331
Davey, William, 385
Davidson, Elizabeth, 157
Davidson, Henry, 317, 384
Davidson, Susannah, 195
Davie, Sir Humphrey, 372
Davies, Sir David, 420
Davies, Catherine and James, 413
Davies, Rev. Edward, 325
Davies, Elizabeth, 368
Davies, Henry, 260
Davies, Isabella, 379
Davies, John, 174, 379
Davies, Martha, 413
Davies, Mary, 113
Davies, Richard, 318
Davies, Robert, 98, 407
Davies, Susannah, 103
Davies, Thomas, 31, 252
Davies, William, 271
Davis, Mrs., 141
Davis, David, 271
Davis, Francis, 294
Davis, M., 295
Davis, Peter, 41
Davis, Thomas, 421
Davison, William, 439
Davy, Sir Humphry, 120, 197, 267, 274
Dawes, Dean, 275
Dawes, Richard, 121, 222
Dawkins, Mrs. Mary, 364
Dawson, Lady Anne, 437
Dawson, Dr., 34
Dawson, Miss, 258
Dawson, Mrs., 44
Dawson, Edward, 203
Dawson, George, 444
Dawson, Gertrude, 125
Dawson, John, 215
Dawson, Rev. Josias, 157
Dawson, Mary, 431
Dawson, Pudsey, 174
Dawson, Thomas, 30
Dawson, W., 258
Dawson, William, 267
Dawtrey, Thomas, 204
Day, Jane, 437
Daye, John, 259
Daye, Robert, 286
Daylis, John, 112
Dayrell, Mrs. Elizabeth, 86
Dayrell, Rev. John, 189
Dayrell, Richard, 189
Deacon, Thomas, 381
Dealtry, Bishop Thomas, 136
Dealtry, John, 145
Deane, Mrs., 59
Deane, Robert, 113
Dear, Francis, 150
Dear, Martha, 421
Dearden, Jacob, 352
Deare, Lt.-Gen. George, 355
Debary, Sarah, 170
de Beauvoir, Elizabeth, 375
de Burgh, Augustus, 14

de Burgh, Catherine, 30
de Burgh, Fysh, 29
Decker, Sir Matthew, 344
de Clifford, Lord, 405
de Coussemaker, John, 230
de Dunstanville, Lord, 394, 427
Deeble, Rev. Samuel, 116
de Gex, J. P., 387
degli Uberti, Farinata, 310
de Grey, Earl, 275
de Grey, Countess, 224
De Grey, Henrietta Countess, 143
dei Lapi, Arnolfo, 288
de la Beche, Sir Henry, 290
de la Bere, John, 439
de Lamballe, Princess, 241
de la Motte, Gen. Peter, 75
Delaney, Dr., 235
de Lannay, Rev. Thomas, 113
Delany, Mrs., 176
de la Pole, Sir John, 332
de la Pole, Lady, 332
de Ligne, Princess, 241
De L'Isle and Dudley, Lady, 223, 386
Delme, Sir Peter, 338
Delves, Elizabeth, 31
de Lys, Gabriel, 206
Deman, Dr., 241
de Manley, Lady, 262
de Mauriel, Charles, 306
de Montmorency, Viscount Frankfort, 403
de Morgan, Dr. Campbell, 244
Demosthenes, 100, 329, 330
Dendy, Richard, 110
Denham, Sir James, 437
Denison, Sir Thomas, 195
Denison, Henry, 387
Denison, Robert, 277
Denison, William, 277
Denman, Lord, 77, 221, 263
Denman, Mary, 429
Denn, Robert, 306
Denne, David, 329
Denne, Elizabeth, 266
Dennis, James, 428
Dennis, Samuel, 423
Denny, Hon. Mary, 116
Denshire, Mr. and Mrs., 52
Denshire, George, 52
Dent, John, 420
Denton, Sir Alexander and Lady, 98
Denton, Rev. Thomas, 241
Denys, Peter, 36
de Quincey, Thomas, 371
Derby, Earls of, 248, 263, 274, 275, 387, 445
Derby, 7th Earl of, 257
de Roll, Baron, 31
de Salis, Count, 245
degli Salis, Countess, 387
de Saumarez, Lord, 370
de Saumarez, Capt. Philip, 98
Deschamps family, 283
de Triqueti, Baron, 135
de Val, Signor, 304
Deverell, John, 329
de Vesci, Eustace, 323
Devon, Earl of, 372

Devon, Countess of, 372
Devonshire, Duchess of, 147
Devonshire, Dukes of, 51, 77, 197
Devonshire, 6th Duke of, 193, 278
Devonshire, William Earl of, 254
Devonshire, Christopher, 351
Dew, Hon. Mrs., 218
Dewer, George, 189
Dey, Bartholomew, 365
Dibdin, Charles, 352
Dick family, 61
Dick, Sir Robert, 320
Dick-Lauder, Sir Thomas, 62
Dickanson, Henry, 324
Dickens, Charles, 152, 291, 444
Dickens, John, 193
Dickinson, Elizabeth, 130
Dickinson, John, 143
Dickinson, William, 393
Dickson, Sir Alexander, 320
Dickson, Rev. David, 323
Dickson, Maria, 13
Diddlesfold, William, 387
Digby, Capt., 209
Digby, Mrs., 415
Digby, Charlotte, 96
Digby, George, 348
Digby, James, 160
Digby, John, 52
Diggle, Henry, 400
Dillon, Lord, 277
Dinham, John, 372
Dinwiddie, Mrs., 20
Dinwiddie, Robert, 404
Dirdoe, Henry, 41
Disraeli, Benjamin, 47
Dive, Hugh, 375
Divett, Thomas, 394
Dixie, Sir Wolstan, 350
Dixon, Edward, 229
Dixon, Hepworth, 445
Dixon, John, 22
Dixon, Sophia, 36
Dixon, William, 413
Dobree, Samuel, 34
Dobson, Daniel, 442
Dobson, Elizabeth, 115
Dobson, John, 60
Docton, Elizabeth, 215
Dodd, Benjamin, 88
Dodd, William, 65
Dodsley, James, 150
Dodson, Rev. Christopher, 150
Dolben, Sir English, 378
Dollen, Benjamin, 430
Dollond, Ann, 32
Dollond, Sir George, 163
Dollond, John, 163
Dolphin, Lucy, 66
Domett, Sir William, 101
Don, George, 272
Donald, Robert, 422
Donaldson, Lt.-Col., 422
Donegal, Marchioness of, 249
Donegal, Marquess of, 277
Donkin, Alderman, 35
Donne, John, 266
Donovan, Margaret, 251
Doorman, Hannah, 30
Dorchester, Countess of, 81
Dormer, Sir John and Lady, 368

Dorner, Robert, 385
Dorrien, John, 27
D'Orsay, Count, 47, 132
Dorset, Arabella, Duchess of, 96, 230
Dorset, 5th Duke of, 429
Dorset, Earl and Countess of, 102
Dorset, John, Duke of, 279
Dorsett, M., 271
Doubleday, Edward, 354
Douce family, 228
Douch family, 292
Doughty, George, 203
Doughty, Henry, 175
Doughty, Robert, 13
Douglas, Marquess of, 197
Douglas, Bishop, 403
Douglas, William, 343
Douro, Marchioness of, 77
Dover, Lady, 263
Dover, Lord, 28, 394
Dowdeswell, William, 200
Dowling, M. G., 116
Down, Bishop of, 328
Down, J. Langton, 422
Down, Richard, children of, 30
Downe, Lord, 93, 312
Downe, Henry, 225
Downes, Lt.-Col., 308
Downes, Rev. Andrew, 422
Downes, Bridget, 165
Downes, Edward, 57
Downes, Peter, 28
Dowson, John, 232
Doyle, Bishop of Kildare, 403
Doyle, Edward, 138
D'Oyly, Sir Francis, 426
D'Oyly, Mr. and Mrs., 96
D'Oyly, John, 421
D'Oyly, Rev. Mathias, 426
Drake, Sir Francis, 28, 402, 441
Drake, Lady, 429
Drake, Mrs., 224
Drake, Rev. Charles, 31
Drake, Elizabeth, 29, 99
Drake, George Tyrwhitt, 252
Drake, John, 315
Drake, Montagu, 83, 343
Drake, Rachel, 29
Drake, Thomas Tyrwhitt, 30
Drake, William, 29, 128, 170
Draper, Mrs., 27
Draper, C., 365
Drayton, Michael, 254
Drelincourt, Dean, 338
Drew, Beriah, 365
Drew, Sarah, 365
Dreyer, Rev. Richard, 282
Drinkwater, Thomas, 208
Drummond, Provost, 278
Drummond, Henry, 77
Drury, Ann, 65
Drury, Frances, 151
Drury, Joseph, 429
Dryden, Sir John, 328
Dryden, John, 100, 211, 342, 343
Drysdale, Col., 371
Duckworth, Admiral Sir John, 95
Duckworth, Lady, 391
Duckworth, George, 95
Ducrow, Andrew, 119, 211
Dudley, Lord, 113

Duff, Capt. George, 30
Dufferin, Lord, 250
Duffield, Francis, 353
Dugdale family, 346
Dugdale, Dugdale, 202
Duke of Cornwall's Light Infantry, 321
Dunbar, Edith, 134
Duncan, Viscount, 425
Duncan, Admiral Viscount, 91, 128, 425
Duncan, Charles, 30
Duncan, J., 30
Duncan, J. S., 130
Duncan, Jonathan, 31
Duncan, William, 209
Duncannon, Viscount, 228
Dunch, M., 55
Duncombe, George, 344
Duncombe, Slingsby, 411
Duncombe, Thomas Slingsby, 208
Duncumb, Mrs., 188
Dundas, Baron, 198
Dundas, Lady Charlotte, 275
Dundas, Gen., 30
Dundas, Henry, 176
Dundas, Robert, 93
Dundonald, Earl of, 291
Dundonald, Countess of, 410
Dunfermline, Lord, 63
Dunkellin, Lord, 154
Dunn, Rev. J., 133
Dunn, John, 146
Dunn, Robert, 416
Dunn, Thomas, 373
Dunster, Charles, 426
Duppa, Mrs., 208
Duppa, Baldwin, 338
Duppa, Baldwin, the Younger, 338
Duppa, Brian, 71, 335
Du Pre, Josias, 391
D'Urban, Gen. Sir B., 372
Durrant, D., 375
Durrant, Robert, 292
Dutton, Sir John, 334, 338
Dutton, James, 423
Dutton, John, 71
Dwarris, Fortunatus, 27
Dyer, Sir Thomas, 224
Dyke, William, 127
Dykes, Rev. Thomas, 227
Dymoke, Lewis, 22
Dysart, Countess of, 279
Dyson, James and Mary, 411
Dyson, Jeremiah, 422

Eadon, John, 152
Eadon, Thomas, 381
Eagle, Thomas, 15
Eagles, John, 405
Eardley, Lady, 27, 387
Eardley, Lord, 96
Eardley-Wilmot, Elizabeth, 427
Eardley-Wilmot, Sir John, 127
Eardley-Wilmot, John, 426
Eardly, Louisa, 303
Earle family, 150
Earle, Ann, 138
Earle, Giles, 355
Earle, H., 206
Earle, Henry, 46, 47

Earle, Robert, 351
Earle, William, 150, 173
East, Sir Edward Hyde, 93
East, Sir Gilbert, 422
East, Augustus, 32
East, William, 210
Eastlake, Sir Charles, 323
Eastland, Mary, 381
Easton, Thomas, 15
Eaton, Peter, 90
Ebrington, Lady, 47
Ebrington, Lord, 47
Ebury, Lady, 248
Eccleston, Mary, 68
Ede, Francis, 253
Ede, George, 422
Ede, Joseph, 350
Edgcumbe, Arthur, 199
Edgell, Harry, 229
Edgworth, John, 189
Edinburgh, Duchess of, 392
Edinburgh, Duke of, 24, 378, 392
Edings, James, 52
Edmonds, William, 20
Edmunds, Francis, 353
Edward the Elder, King, 320
Edward I, 117, 137, 326
Edward II, 328
Edward III, 102, 225, 296 450
Edward IV, 313
Edward V, 256, 313
Edward VI, 87, 168, 314, 331, 342, 343, 425, 434
Edward, Prince, 241
Edward, Black Prince, 334
Edward, Duke of Kent, 142
Edwardes, Mrs., 174
Edwardes, Sir Herbert, 387
Edwardes, John Pusey, 202
Edwards, Sir John, 253
Edwards, Lady, 57
Edwards, Charlotte, 162
Edwards, George, 105, 438
Edwards, James, 403
Edwards, Jane, 327
Edwards, Rev. John, 348
Edwards, Mary, 423
Edwards, Thomas, 351, 367
Edwards, Rev. Thomas, 157
Edwards, William, 132
Effingham, Earl and Countess of, 28
Effingham, 4th Earl of, 413
Egerton, Hon. Penelope, 368
Egerton, Dr., 39
Egerton, Miss, 428
Egerton, Mrs., 177
Egerton, Charlotte, 429
Egerton, Samuel, 27
Egerton, Wilbraham, 428
Eggington, Joseph, 416
Eglinton, Earl of, 250, 274
Egremont, Earl of, 34, 46, 80, 164, 277, 278
Eland, Lady, 269
Elcho, Lord, 245
Elder, Sir Thomas, 445
Elder, Charles Bamford, 138
Eldon, Lord, 36, 46, 47, 95, 262, 269, 351, 352, 378, 380, 415
Eldridge, James, 110

Eleanor, Queen, 326
Elford, Sir W., 69
Elgin, Earls of, 47, 275, 301
Elgin, Countesses of, 370, 371
Eligé, John, 246
Eliot, Edward, 337
Elizabeth, Princess, 346
Elizabeth I, Queen, 113, 289, 296, 415, 425
Ellard, John, 170
Ellenborough, Lady, 96
Ellenborough, Lord, 95, 187
Ellesdon, Anthony, 351
Ellesmere, Earl of, 256, 275
Ellesmere, Lord Chancellor, 224
Elley, Sir John, 400
Ellice, Capt., 44
Elliot, 298
Elliot, Hon. Elizabeth, 222
Elliot, George, 108
Elliot, Thomas, 270
Elliott, Ebenezer, 71
Elliott, Capt. R. J., 136
Ellis, Bishop of St. David's, 322
Ellis, Sir Henry, 31
Ellis, Hon. Mrs., 151
Ellis, Charles Heaton, 198
Ellis, Daniel, 373
Ellis, Elizabeth, 151
Ellis, James, 397
Ellis, John, 198
Ellis, Rev. William, 227
Ellison, C., 173
Ellison, George, 127
Elliston, John, 345
Elmsley, Peter, 385
Elmslie, John, 61
Elphinstone, Lord, 154, 275
Elphinstone, Miss, 224
Elphinstone, Keith, 241
Elphinstone, Mountstuart, 93, 274
Elston family, 301
Elsworth, Mrs., 48
Elton, Abraham, 295
Elverson, Ann, 227
Elwes, Mrs., 278
Elwes, Caroline, 151
Elwes, Robert, 338, 420
Elwyn, Dr., 36
Elwyn, Mrs., 95
Emily, Rev. Edward, 423
Emmett, Francis, 284
Emmot, Joseph, 353
Emmott, Christopher and John, 382
Emmott, Richard, 382
Emmott, William, 368
Encombe, Lord, 104
Enfield, Rev. W., 21
Engleheart, George, 208
Engelphus de Aquila, 359
Entwisle, John, 310
Enys, John, 229
Epaminondas, 342
Ernest, Prince, 241
Errington, George, 425
Errol, Earl of, 248
Erskine, Lord, 276, 278, 425
Erskine, Hon. Francis, 30
Erskine, Ebenezer, 323
Escourt, Rev. Edward, 317

Esdaile, James, 426
Espinasse, Marie, 257
Essex, Alfred, 142
Essex, William, 346
Essington, Sir William, 116
Estcourt, Edmund, 422
Estcourt, Eleanor, 140
Estlin, John, 35
Ethelred, King, 61
Eton, Mr., 74.
Etty, W., 275
Euclid, 136
Eugénie, Empress, 221
Euston, Countess of, 151
Evans, Arthur, 427
Evans, George, 114
Evans, Harriet, 57
Evans, Rev. Henry, 426
Evans, Mary, 215
Evans, Morgan, 133
Evans, T. E., 221
Evans, Thomas, 297
Evans, Walter, 185
Eveleigh, Dorothy, 425
Eveleigh, John, 284
Evelyn, Sir John, 91
Evelyn, Mrs., 263
Evelyn, Edward and Julia, 156
Evelyn, Henry, 30
Evelyn, Jacob, 53
Everard, Ann, 244
Everard, Stephen, 288
Everard, William, 244
Ewart, Catherine, 332
Ewart, John, 332
Ewart, William, 177, 304
Ewbank, Margaretta, 202
Ewer, Philemon, 282
Ewin, William, 151
Exeter, Earl and Countess of, 287
Exeter, 5th Earl and Countess of, 261
Exmouth, 1st Viscount, 249
Exmouth, 2nd Viscount, 160
Exon, Sarah, 220
Eyles family, 204
Eynead, Anthony, 213
Eyre, Sir James, 74, 425
Eyre, Judge, 300
Eyre, Mrs. 55
Eyre, Henry, 285
Eyre, Robert, 411
Eyton, Rev. Hope, 174
Eyton, Mary, 63

Faber, Albert, 348
Fagg, Sir William, 345
Fagg, Lady, 423
Fairbairn, Sir Peter, 274
Fairbairn, Emma and Arthur, 444
Fairbairn, William, 291
Fairborne, Sir Palmes, 73
Fairfax family, 146
Fairfax, Dean, 368
Fairfax, Mr., 414
Fairfax, Thomas, 177
Fairlie, Isabella, 352
Fairlie, William, 427
Faithfull, James, 269
Falconar, Major, 427
Falconbridge, Mrs., 274

Falconer, Hugh, 49, 74
Falconer, Rev. James, 350
Falkland, Viscount, 208
Falkland, 2nd Viscount, 49
Falkland, Viscountess, 69, 304
Falkner, Rev. William, 41
Falmouth, 2nd Earl of, 297
Falmouth, Viscount, 214, 279
Fane, Sir Henry, 36
Fane, Lady Georgiana, 80
Fanshawe family, 377
Fanshawe, Charles, 388
Faraday, Michael, 34, 154, 275
Faran, Mrs., 396
Farhill, Rev. George, 189
Farhill, John, 307
Farmer, Henry, 127
Farnaby, Sir John, 220
Farnborough, Lord, 94
Farnborough, Lord and Lady, 428
Farquhar, Jane, 356
Farquhar, John, 332
Farquharson, Mrs., of Invercauld, 63
Farren, Miss, 120
Farrington, Mary, 143
Farrington, Thomas, 451
Faucit, Helen, 154, 323
Faudel, Henry, 24
Faulkener, Capt., 67
Faulkner, Capt., 328
Faulkner, Emma, 339
Faustina, 105, 191, 436
Favanti, Signora, 221
Favell, Charles, 356
Faversham, of Downton, Lady, 344
Faversham, Lord, 274
Fawcett, Rev. John, 217
Fawkener, Sir Everard, 52
Fawkes, Francis, 84, 146
Fawkes, Walter, 146
Fawks, Henry, 97
Fawssett, Rev. William, 209
Fawthorp, James, 240
Featherstonehaugh, Sir Henry, 429
Feilde, Paul, 30
Feilding, Lady Elizabeth, 400
Feilding, William, 192
Fell, William, 365
Fenn, Sir John, 28
Fennell, George, 244
Ferdinand III, 310
Ferguson, Mr., 155, 323
Ferguson, Sir Robert, 221
Ferguson, Sir Ronald, 384
Fergusson, Ronald Munro, 267
Fermor, Sir John, 83
Fermor-Hesketh, Sir Thomas, 275
Fern, John, 392
Ferrand, Rev. John, 411
Ferrar, Bishop, 239
Ferrers, Earl and Countess, 264
Ferres, Alderman, 138
Ferris, Solomon, 141
Fetherston, Sir Henry, 50
Fettiplace family, 55
Fettiplace, Sir George, 18
Fettiplace, Edmund, 304
Fettiplace, Thomas, 425
Fiamingo, 335, 336
Field, Edwin, 444

Field, John, 314
Field, Mary, 80
Field, Robert, 252
Fielden, John, 154
Fielding, Sir John, 286
Fielding, Dr. George, 227
Fife, Lord, 332
Figg, Mary, 199
Filding, Ann, 368
Filmer, Sir Edward and Lady, 254
Filmer, Sir John, 384
Filmer, Catherine, 339
Filmer, Dorothy, 175
Filmore, Egerton, 137
Finch, Sir John, 89
Finch, Lady Charlotte, 96, 358
Finch, John, 258, 298, 317
Finch, Thomas, 278
Finlater, Rev. Charles, 323
Finlay, Kirkham, 172
Firmadge, Anne, 144
Fisher, Bishop, 285
Fisher, Bishop of Salisbury, 226
Fisher, John, 381
Fisher, Martha, 349
Fisher, Robert, 315
Fisher, William, 367
Fisk, Mr., 232
Fitch, John, 221
FitzClarence, Lord Augustus, 348
FitzGerald, Lord, 35
FitzGerald, Lord Henry, 117
FitzGerald, Lt.-Col., 355
Fitzgerald, Mrs., 46
Fitzgibbon, Viscount, 250
Fitzharris, Viscountess, 151
Fitzherbert, Sir Anthony, 295
Fitzherbert, Capt., 307
Fitzherbert, Mrs., 55, 80, 358
FitzMaurice, Viscount, 358
Fitzpatrick, Gen., 276, 278
Fitzroy, Lord James, 48
Fitzroy, Sir Charles, 444
Fitzroy, Hon. Charles, 181
Fitzwalter, Earl, 244
Fitzwalter, Robert, 394
Fitzwilliam, Earls, 49, 146, 235
Fitzwilliam, First Earl, 145
Flavell, Elizabeth, 138
Flaxman, John, 34, 121, 127, 149, 222, 269, 415, 419
Flaxman, Miss, 149
Fleetwood, Bishop, 210
Fleetwood, Charles, 343
Fleetwood, Robert, 431
Fleming, Gen., 331
Fleming, John, 407
Fleming, Thomas, 34
Fletcher, Sir Richard, 35
Fletcher, Sir Thomas, 57
Fletcher, Lady, 189
Fletcher, Hon. Eileen, 209
Fletcher, Mrs., 198
Fletcher, J. W., 327
Fletcher, Rev. John, 271
Fletcher, John, 211, 423
Fletcher, John and Henry, 363
Fletcher, Rev. W., 415
Fletcher, William, 231
Flood, Luke, 299
Floyd, Gen. Sir John, 80

Fludyer, Henry, 104
Fluelling, Thomas, 142
Foley, Lord, 335, 337
Foley, Edward, 57
Foljambe, Mr., 308
Foljambe, Louisa, 256
Folkes, Martin, 20, 330
Folkestone, Viscount, 336
Folkestone, Viscountess, 335, 338
Follett, Sir William, 45
Foot, Samuel, 138
Foot, Topham, 344
Foote, John, 266
Foote, Robert, 21
Foote, Samuel, 26
Forbes, Sir Charles, 93
Forbes, Sir William, 197, 198
Forbes, Lord President, 330
Forbes, Maj.-Gen., 154
Forbes, Professor, 243
Forbes, Prof. Edward, 71
Forbes, Jacob, 27
Forbes, James, 62
Forbes, John and Richard, 30
Forbes, William, 17
Ford, John, 157
Ford, William, 377
Fordwich, Viscount, 428
Forester, Lord, 81
Foresti, Sir Spiridon, 93
Forrester, Mrs., 431
Forrester, Alexander, 207
Forrester, William, 196
Forster, Anna, 347
Forster, Edward, 146
Forster, Jane, 52
Fortescue, Earls, 47, 372
Fortescue, 2nd Earl, 263
Fortescue, 3rd Earl, 372
Fortescue, Ann, 151
Fortescue, Charles, 344
Fortescue, Francis, 31
Fortescue, John, children of, 352
Fortescue, Mary, 145
Fortescue, Sarah, 35
Fortrye, James, 288
Foss, Francis, 411
Foster, Rt. Hon. J., 164
Foster, Dr., 358
Foster, C. S., 206
Foster, J., 274
Foster, James, 65, 206
Foster, John, 137, 363
Foster, Jonathan, 265
Foster, Rev. Josiah, 431
Foster, Samuel, 200
Foster, Thomas, 431
Foster, William, 233
Fothergale, Mr., 147
Fothergill, Capt., 256
Fothergill, Mr., 146
Fothergill, John, 221
Foulis, Charles, 27
Foulkes, Sir Martin, 134
Fountaine, Sir Andrew, 310, 330
Fountaine, Rev. William, 69
Fowke, Admiral, 265
Fowke, Capt., 445
Fowke, Elizabeth, 332
Fowle, Dr. William, 423, 425
Fowler, Lady, 98, 427

Fowler, Nathaniel, 367
Fox, Anna, 333
Fox, Charles James, 34, 109, 120, 147, 157, 164, 273, 276, 277, 332, 425, 426
Fox-Maitland, Charles, 427
Fox-Strangways, Hon. George, 431
Foxall, Zachariah, 18
Foy, James, 294
Foyster, Samuel, 31
Frampton, Mrs., 407
Frampton, James, 185
France, Elizabeth, 157
Francesca da Rimini, 267
Francis, Clement, 215
Francis, J., 274
Francis, Jane, 376
Francis, John, 355
Frankland, Sir Thomas, children of, 150
Frankland, Admiral, 151
Frankland, John, 351
Franklin, Sir John, 24, 121, 274, 275
Franklin, Sir William, 222
Franklin, Benjamin, 89
Franklin, William, 147
Franks, William, 20, 404
Fraser, Bishop, 445
Fraser, Col., 69
Fraser, George, 31
Fraser, Peter, 384
Fraser, Capt. Thomas, 192
Fraunciss, William, 242
Frederick V of Denmark, 347
Frederick the Great, 300
Frederick of Prussia, Prince, 387
Frederick, Prince of Wales, 97
Frederick, John, 244
Freebairn, A. R., 355
Freeman, Miss, 302, 308
Freeman, Mrs., 120
Freeman, Sarah, 30
Freeman, Thomas, 279
Freer, John, 207
Freind, Robert, 336
Freke, Samuel, 409
Freman, Ralph, 344
Fremeaux, Margaret, 115
French, Andrew, 352
French, Elizabeth, 318
Frere, Sir Bartle, 238, 444
Frere, Sir Henry, 445
Frere, Lady, 275
Frere, J. H., 92
Frere, Susanna, 143
Frewen, Dr., 331
Friend, Dr. John, 337
Frith, W., 389
Fromantal, Daniel, 59
Froude, Mrs., 445
Fry, Mrs., 228, 323
Fry, William, 61
Frye, Mr., 314
Fryer, Henry, 52
Fulford, Baldwin, 372
Fulham, Rev. John, 407
Fuller, Lieut. James, 127
Fuller, John, 94, 279, 332
Fullerton, George, 36
Fullerton, Mary, 36

Furness, Sir Henry, 179
Furniss, Mrs., 68
Fuseli, H., 34
Fydell, Richard, 411

Gage, Sir Thomas, 287
Gainsborough, Earl of, 279
Gaisford, John, 388
Galen, 422
Galileo, 267, 441, 450
Gall, Dr., 124
Galloway, Richard, 300
Galsworthy, Thomas, 225
Galt, John, 198, 266
Gambier, Lord, 202
Games, William, 288
Garaway, Miss, 69
Gard, R. S., 372
Garden, John, 355
Gardener, Sir James, 426
Gardener, Lady, 418
Gardener, Mr., 211
Gardes, Capt. John, 405
Gardiner, Sir John, 28
Gardner, Mrs., 271
Garibaldi, 275
Garlick, Mary, 295
Garneys, Charles, 119
Garrard, Sir Jacob, 210
Garrard, Sir John, 381
Garrard, Sir Samuel, 155
Garrard, Charles and Ann, 394
Garrard, G. (A.R.A.), 20
Garrard, Thomas, 155
Garrett, Richard, 395
Garrick, David, 162, 176, 211, 276, 301, 417
Garside, Elizabeth, 323
Garth, James, 422
Garth, Richard, 423
Garthshore, Dr., 29
Garvey, Capt. John, 29
Gascoyne, Gen., 413
Gaskell, Charlotte, 181
Gastrell, Francis, 404
Gataker, Mary, 124
Gatley, Rev. Charles, 232
Gawler, John, 426
Gay, John, 337
Gay, Thomas, 178
Gazeley, Mrs., 331
Gee, Sir Orlando, 55
Gee, family, 95
Gee, William, 95
Geffery, Sir Robert, 281
Geldart, Rev. James, 145
Gell, Richard, 133
Gell, William, 118
Gelthorpe, Anne, 288
George I, 70, 121, 126, 176, 281, 334, 336, 337
George II, 97, 176, 261, 263, 278, 281, 282, 336, 337, 342, 430, 436
George III, 25, 26, 29, 44, 69, 80, 81, 93, 94, 95, 105, 107, 120, 142, 158, 176, 185, 196, 247, 263, 277, 282, 289, 300, 305, 340, 402, 403, 404, 425, 435, 441, 446, 448
George IV, 34, 46, 92, 93, 94, 95, 137, 157, 161, 176, 181, 187, 196, 207, 222, 230, 265, 283, 288, 302,

303, 309, 328, 332, 383, 385, 391
George, Prince, of Cambridge, 47
George, Prince, of Cumberland, 47, 238
George, Prince, of Hanover, 45
George, Charles, 439
George, John, 405
George, Thomas and Catherine, 119
Gericke, Rev. Christian, 150
German, Thomas, 133
Gery, William, 52
Gibbons, Charlotte, 397
Gibbs, Sir Michael, 261
Gibbs, Gen., 426
Gibbs, James, 237, 335, 336
Gibbs, Mary, 36
Gibbs, Richard, 420
Gibson, George, 137
Gibson, John, 387
Gibson, Thomas, 339
Giffard, Rev. Dr., 192
Gilbert, Davies, 222, 428
Gilbert, Jefferay, 110
Gilbert, John Graham, 62, 63
Gildart, Mrs., 204
Giles, William, 273
Gilett, Samuel, 356
Gilkes, Peter, 228
Gillespie family, 273
Gillespie, Sir Robert, 93, 220
Gillingham (murderer), 161
Gilby, Dr., 243, 244
Gilpin, Sawrey, 164
Gipps, Sir George, 419
Gipps, Richard, 436, 437
Girtin, Thomas, 164
Gisborne, Rev. Thomas, 355
Gladstone, John, 363
Gladstone, W. E., 71, 267, 387, 444, 445
Glaze, Major, 178
Gleadall, Rev. J. W., 193
Glegg, John, 208
Glenbervie, Lord, 197, 198
Glencross, James, 350
Glendining, Mary, 375
Glentworth, Lord, 429
Glossop, Robert, 227
Gloucester, Duchess of, 39, 296, 301, 386, 392
Gloucester, Dukes of, 69, 112, 199, 392
Gloucester, Duke and Duchess of, 358
Gloucester, Geoffrey Earl of, 422
Glyn, Sir George, 451
Glyn, Sir Richard, 34
Goadsby, Alderman, 275
Goblet, Henry, 175
Godbold, Harriet, 285
Goddington, James, 207
Godfrey family, 382
Godfrey, Elizabeth, 151
Godfrey, Thomas, 30
Godley, John, 444
Godolphin, Earl of, 55
Godschall, Sir Robert, 68
Godson, William, 32
Godwin, George, 193
Goethe, 450
Golden, D. C., 263

Goldfinch, Sir Henry, 193
Golding, Mary, 100
Golding, William, 15
Goldney, Gabriel, 161
Goldsmid, Sir Francis, 387
Goldsmith, Edward, 355
Goldsmith, Oliver, 19, 46, 153, 154, 278
Golightly, Margarette, 363
Gomm, Elizabeth, 224
Gonsalvo, Cardinal, 77
Gooch, Sir Thomas, 47, 395
Gooch, Mrs., 288
Gooch, Amelia, 396
Goodall, Dr., 419
Goodall, Joanna, 141
Goodbehere family, 421
Goode, Rev. Francis, 355
Goode, Rev. William, 31
Goodelen, Mary, 317
Goodenough, T. S., 263
Goodhall, John, 364
Goodlad, Richard, 439
Goodriche, Rev. Henry, 381
Goodwill, Rev. Christopher, 418
Goodwin, Anne, 363
Goodwin, Richard, 302, 303
Gordon, Dukes of, 77, 197, 277
Gordon, Lord William, 421
Gordon, Lady, 416
Gordon, Sir Alexander, 198
Gordon, Gen., 387
Gordon, Lt.-Gen., 302
Gordon, Rev. Dr., 371
Gordon, Caroline, 184
Gordon, Charles, 431
Gore, Gen., 95
Gore, Bridget, 254
Gore, Edward, 220, 295
Gore, John, 363
Gore, Major William, 405
Gorges, Ferdinando, 292
Goring, Sir Harry, 202
Goring, Charles, 96
Goring, Frances, 385
Goring, Sarah, 108
Gormanston, Viscountess, 427
Gorsuch, Thomas, 100
Gort, Viscount, 292
Goselin, Lady, 369
Gosling, John, 347
Gosselin, Christian, 20
Gosset, Gideon, 176
Gostling, George, 29, 151
Gostling, Lydia, 35
Gothemburger, 263
Gott, Benjamin, 177, 178
Gough, Viscount, 14, 35, 154
Goulburn, Mrs., 423
Gouldsmith, Harriet, 131
Gower, John, 320
Gowland, Jane, 122
Grabe, W. E., 55
Grace, Admiral, 303
Graffitt, William, 211
Grafton, Duke of, 176
Graham, Lady, 146
Graham, 197
Graham, Frances, 261
Graham, J. Gillespie, 248
Graham, Margaret, 137

Graham, Mary, 174
Graham, Sally, 350
Graham, Dr. Thomas, 62
Graham, Thomas, 343
Graham, W., 242
Grahame, Rev. James, 198
Grainger, Edward, 206
Granard, Earl of, 74
Granby, Marquess of, 90, 278, 314
Grandison, Viscount, 234
Grant, Sir Charles, 32
Grant, Sir F., 132
Grant, Sir Lewis, 303
Grant, Lady, 302
Grant, Lady Janet, 303
Grant, Bishop, 343
Grant, Abbé, 309
Grant, Anne, 402
Grant, Charles, 252
Grant, Edward, 312
Grant, Rev. John, 108
Grantham, Lady, 224
Grantham, Sir Thomas, 126
Granville, Earl, 176
Grape, Elizabeth, 349
Grattan, Henry, 79, 93, 154, 402, 403
Grave, Sir William, 136
Grave, Edward, 230
Grave, James, 431
Graves, Hon. Cassandra, 66
Graves, Admiral, 27, 437
Graves, Henry, 70
Graves, John, 443
Graves, Mary, 202
Graves, Morgan, 155
Graves, Richard, 341
Graves, Mrs. Robert, 105
Graves, Samuel, 14
Graves, Walwyn, 113
Gray, Bishop, 36
Gray, John, 138
Gray, Rev. Robert, 134
Gray, Thomas, 27
Greathed, Edward, 279
Greatrex, Thomas, 207
Greaves, Anna, 95
Greaves, John, 235
Greaves, Sophia, 45
Gredge, William, 205
Green, Sir William, 116
Green, Rev. Edward, 246
Green, Edward, 141
Green, Henry, 362
Green, J. H., 419
Green, Jonathan, 373
Green, Joseph, 209, 332
Green, Philip, 251
Green, Richard, 180, 450
Green, Robert, 397
Green, Thomas, 108, 370
Greene, Bussy, 286
Greenland, Richard, 409
Greenlaw, Charles, 419
Greenough, George, 71
Greenwood, William, 294
Greg, Samuel, 220
Gregory, Mr., 277
Gregory, David, 400
Gregory, George, 188, 440
Gregory, Olinthus, 105

Gregory, Rev. William, 184
Gregson, Matthew, 170, 278
Grenville, Lord, 112
Grenville, Sir Bevil, 101
Grenville, George, 176, 208, 278
Grenville, Henry, 336
Gresham, Sir Thomas, 46, 73, 297
Gresham, Thomas, 304
Gresley, Sir Nigel, 229
Gresley, Caroline, 426
Greswolde, Edmund, 206
Grey, 2nd Earl, 278
Grey, Earls, 34, 45, 46, 77, 114, 157, 184, 263, 278, 371
Grey of Groby, Lord, children of, 245
Grey of Wilton, Lord, 429
Grey, Sir George, 257
Grey, Rev. Henry, 291
Grice, Joseph, 206
Grice, Rebecca, 392
Griffin, Robert, 186
Griffith family, 295
Grigby, George, 226
Grigg, Elizabeth, 279
Grimston, Thomas, 99
Grinsteed, Henry, 351
Groby, Charles, 80
Groombridge, Stephen, 256
Grosvenor, Sir Robert de, 359
Grosvenor, Lady Constance, 267
Grosvenor, Emma, 353
Grosvenor, Thomas, 185
Grote, George, 24, 47
Guest, Sir John, 140
Guest, Lt.-Gen., 382
Guilford, Earls of, 104, 150
Guilford, wives of 1st Earl of, 437
Guilford, 2nd Earl of, 149
Guinness, Sir Benjamin Lee, 154
Guise, Sir John, 259
Guise, John, 26
Guise, William, 55, 321
Gully, Dr., 235
Gulston, Elizabeth, 267
Gunning, Ann, 317
Gunning, John, 232
Gurdon, Rev. Philip, 31
Gurdon, T., 365
Gurdon, William, 32
Gurney, Henry, 217
Gurney, John, 261
Gurwood, Col., 223
Guthrie, Dr., 63
Guthrie, George, 122
Guthrie, Rev. John, 140
Guy, Thomas, 27, 342, 436
Gwyder, Lord, 278
Gyles, Rev. James, 373

Hackman family, 413
Haddington, Lord, 235
Hadfield, Samuel, 356
Hadley, George, 42
Hadley, John, 336
Haffey, Henry, 189
Hague, Elizabeth, 348
Haldiman, William, 394
Hale, Mrs., 220
Hale, Elizabeth, 324
Hale, Hannah, 157

Hale, Warren Stormes, 24
Hales family, 400
Hales, Sir Edward, 378
Hales, Robert, 219
Hales, Stephen, 437
Halford, Lady, 429
Halford, Sir Henry, 94
Halford, Mrs., 115
Halifax, Earl of, 27
Hall, Sir James, 291
Hall, Ann, 362
Hall, Anthony, 325
Hall, Edmund, 432
Hall, Edward, 150
Hall, Rev. Francis, 308
Hall, George, 426
Hall, Rev. Henry, 187
Hall, Henry, 46
Hall, Hugh, 208
Hall, Humphrey, 15
Hall, John, 240
Hall, Mary, 373
Hall, Rev. Robert, 301
Hall, Robert, 202, 250
Hall, Rev. Samuel, 157
Hall, Samuel Carter, 70
Hall, Mrs. Sarah, 373
Hall, Thomas, 136, 179, 215
Hall, William, 260
Hallam, Henry, 245, 386, 387
Hallam, John, 116
Halliday, John, 40
Hallifax, Mrs., 40
Hallings, Mrs., 295
Hallon, Margaret, 445
Hallyburton, Lord Douglas, 75
Halsey, Agatha, 150
Halsted, Nicholas, 418
Halton, Sir Thomas, 50
Hamey, Baldwin, 297
Hamilton, Duke of, 266
Hamilton, Lord Archibald, 197
Hamilton, Alexander, 89, 212
Hamilton, Rev. Anthony, 329
Hamilton, Bridge, 242
Hamilton, Gavin, 199
Hamilton, John, 195
Hamilton-Martin, John, 393
Hamlyn, Lady, 229
Hammerton, William, 173
Hammond, Lord, 47, 418, 420
Hammond, Sir Andrew, 230
Hammond, Sir Francis, 220
Hammond, Henry, 256
Hammond, Rev. Horace, 141
Hammond, Jonathan, 306
Hammond, Maria, 199
Hammond, William, 173
Hamond, Sir A., 94
Hamond, Anthony, 385
Hampden, 130
Hampden, Viscount, 197
Hampden, John, 154, 346
Hamper, Will, 104
Hanbury, Caroline, 387
Hanbury, D., 237
Hanbury, Edward, 225
Hanbury, Robert, 387
Hanbury, Robert and Laura, 387
Hanbury, William, 95
Hancock, John, 162

Hand, Anne, 39
Handel, George Frederick, 147, 329, 330, 331
Handley, Mrs., 199
Handley, William, 423
Hanger, Mary, 343
Hanger, William, 303
Hankins, Richard, 418
Hankins, William, 373
Hanley, Rev. John, 319
Hanmer, Sir Thomas, 122
Hanmer, Sir Waldon, Bt., 27
Hanmer, Mrs., 406
Hanmer, Thomas, 271
Hannam, Charlotte, 242
Hanson, Gertrude, 19
Hanson, Henry, 30
Hanson, William, 31
Hanway, Jonas, 263, 264
Harborough, Earl of, 337
Harcourt, Earl, 352
Harcourt, Countess, 381
Harcourt, Archbishop of York, 275
Harcourt, George, 275
Hardinge, Viscount, 153, 154, 446
Hardinge, Anne, 349
Hardinge, Capt. G., 30
Hardinge, Capt. George, 251
Hardwick, Thomas, 227
Hardwick, William, 451
Hardwicke, Earls of, 39, 344
Hardwicke, 3rd Earl of, 429
Hardy, Sir Thomas, 47
Hardy, Admiral Sir Thomas, 98
Hardy, Children, 267
Hardyman, Rev. William, 354
Hardyman, William, 304
Hare, Lady, 387
Hare, Mrs., 121
Hare, David, 34
Hare, Gilbert, 230
Hare, James, 278
Hare, Julius, 445
Hare, Susanna, 344
Harford, Mary, 150
Hargrave, Gen., 331
Hargraves, Isaac, 47
Hargreaves, Rev. John, 116, 157
Harison, Sir Richard and Lady, 368
Harley, Lady Margaret, 334
Harold, 137
Harold, Lord, 132
Harper, Anne, 310
Harper, Rev. George, 318
Harper, Richard, 21
Harper, William, 52-3
Harpur, Sir William, 287
Harpur, Lady, 287
Harpur, Rev. Henry, 108
Harrington, Lieut., 422
Harrington, Elizabeth, 329
Harris, Lord, 318, 418
Harris, Hon. Charles, 151
Harris, Dr., 176
Harris, Eliza, 361
Harris, Jacob, 27
Harris, John, 404
Harris, Rice, son of, 240
Harris, Rev. Robert, 133
Harris, Thomas, 295
Harris, William, 43, 432

Harrison, Mr. (architect), 76
Harrison, Prof., 445
Harrison, J., 402
Harrison, Rev. John, 90
Harrison, Lane, 15
Harrison, Mary, 345
Harrison, Richard, 48, 237, 423
Harrison, Strethill, 418
Harrison, Thomas, 96
Harrowby, Earl of, 47
Harrowby, Countess of, 77
Harrys, John, 409
Harsnett, Carola, 368
Hart, George, 242
Hart, Thomas, 133
Hart-Davis, R., 34
Hart-Davis, Richard, 70
Hartley, Lady, 277
Hartley, Lady Louisa, 278
Hartley, Mary, 265
Hartley, Samuel and Mary, 177
Hartley, Rev. W., 209
Hartopp, Sir Edward, 206
Harty, Rev. Wm., 131
Harvey, 419
Harvey, Admiral Sir Eliab, 209
Harvey, Sir Henry, 30
Harvey, Capt., 29
Harvey, Dr., 342, 419
Harvey, Daniel, 135, 333
Harvey, David, 108
Harvey, Henry, 42, 295
Harvey, Jacob, 333
Harvey, Jemima, 160
Harvey, Capt. John, 28
Harvey, John, 228
Harvey, Octavia, 252
Harvey, Richard, 42
Harvey, William, 136, 211, 331
Harvey-Bathurst, Sir Felton, 65
Harwood, John, 30
Haslope, Lancelot, 252
Hast, John, 284
Hastings, 298
Hastings, Marquess of, 127, 131, 149, 243, 278
Hastings, Sir Charles Abney, 420
Hastings, Lady Elizabeth, 343
Hastings, Dr., 252
Hastings, Rev. T., 298
Hastings, Warren, 31, 39, 149, 298, 302, 425
Haswell, Capt. John, 214
Hatch, Rev. George, 273
Hatchard, Mr., 192
Hatsell, James, 114
Hatten, Elizabeth, 288
Hatton, Sir Thomas, 397
Hatton, the Ladies, 368
Haughton, Rev. John, 195
Haughton, Moses, 332
Haultain, Theodore, 52
Havelock, Sir Henry, 14, 45, 47
Havers, Mr., 136
Haviland, Gen., 300
Haviland, John, 295
Haviland, Gen. William, 200
Hawarden, Lord, 225
Hawes, Dr., 161
Hawes, Benjamin, 251
Hawes, Rev. Herbert, 285

Hawes, Mary, 427
Hawes, Thomas, 19
Hawes, William, 251
Hawke, Lord, 264
Hawker, Charles, 405
Hawker, Rev. Robert, 237
Hawker, Sarah, 259
Hawkesley family, 373
Hawkey, Lieut., 215
Hawkins, Mrs., 200
Hawkins, Gertrude, 182
Hawkins, Sarah, 332
Hawkins, Thomas, 252
Hawkins, William, 141, 245
Hawkshaw, George, 402
Hawksley family, 59
Hawksmoor, Nicholas, 218
Hawley, James, 304
Hawtrey, Rev. Charles, 117
Hay, Hon. John, 338
Hay, Gen., 209
Hay, Lieut. Andrew, 318
Hay, Joseph, 109
Haydon, Anne, 344
Haydon, R. B., 34, 291, 302
Haydon, Richard, 418
Hayes, Miss Catherine, 152
Hayley, John, 204
Hayley, Thomas, 150
Hayne, Mary, 431
Haynes, James, 319
Hayter, Sarah, 285
Hayward family, 195
Hayward, Leonard, 105
Hayward, Robert, 200
Hayward, Samuel, 66
Hayward, William, 429
Hazeldene, William, 95
Hazledine, William, 80
Head, Sir Edmund, 150
Head, Sir Isaac, 422
Head, Sir Richard, 170
Head, Mrs., 259
Headlam, Thomas, 222
Heald, James, 275
Hearle, Edmond, 215
Hearne, Joseph, 75
Heath, Rev. William, 384
Heath, William and Mary, 275
Heathcote, Sir Gilbert, 338
Heathcote, Lady, 127
Heathcote, Lady Sophia, 385
Heathcote, Mrs., 295
Heathcote, Godfrey, 146
Heathcote, Michael, 363
Heathcote, Thomas, 415
Heathfield family, 388
Heathfield, Lord, 28, 328, 402
Heathfield, 2nd Lord, 31
Heathfield, Mary, 225
Heaton, John, 198
Heaton, Mary, 422
Heaton, Richard, 423
Heaviside, John, 39
Heber, Bishop, 93, 96, 385
Heber, Mary, 81
Heberden, William, 29
Hedges, Ann, 163
Hehl, Capt., 258
Helena, Princess, 392
Hemans, Felicia, 152

Henderson, 300, 323
Henderson, Mr., 196
Henderson, John, 266
Hendley, William, 344
Heneage, Frances, 30
Henniker, Lord, 108, 226
Henniker, John, Lord, 30
Henniker, Lord and Lady, 226
Henniker, Lady, 38, 108
Henniker, Admiral Hon. Jacob, 160
Henniker, Dame Ann, 108
Henning, John, 198
Henning, Rev. R., 331
Henning, Susanna, 405
Henri de Londres, Archbishop of
    Dublin, 390
Henry II, 328
Henry III, 328
Henry V, 297, 298
Henry VI, 26, 54, 313, 381
Henry VII, 313
Henry VIII, 54
Henry, Prince, 391
Henshaw, Thomas, 78
Henslow, J. S., 445
Herbert of Lea, Lord, 154
Herbert of Lea, Lord and Lady, 301
Herbert, Hon. Mrs. Sidney, 249
Herbert, Thomas, 300
Hereford, Henry Earl of, 393
Heriot, George, 353
Herlock, Marie, 318
Herney, Ann, 202
Herrick family, 396
Herries, Charles, 94
Herring, John, 30
Herringman, Henry, 228
Herschel, Sir John, 35
Herschell, Sir William, 147, 149,
    385
Herschell, Dr., 100, 241
Herschell, Dr. Solomon, 13
Hertford, Marquess of, 96
Hervey, Hon. Barbara, 193
Hesilrige, Sir Arthur, 115
Hesilrige, Sir Thomas, 95
Hesketh, Lady, 151
Hesketh-Fleetwood, Sir Peter, 70
Heslewood, Mary, 227
Hethrington, Thomas, 385
Hewer, William, 158
Hewitt, Thomas, 20, 374
Hey, W., 69, 134
Hey, Dr. William, 93, 445
Hey, William, 47
Heyrich, Rev. Samuel, 212
Heyrick, John, 212
Heysham, J., 414
Heywood, Benjamin, 363
Hibbert, George, 405
Hibbert, Sacharissa, 429
Hichens family, 163
Hickman, Catherine and Grace,
    405
Hickman, Henry, 355
Hickman, William, 306
Hicks, Sir Howe, 259
Hicks, Fowler, 146
Hicks Beach, Sir Michael, 118
Hickson, Rev. John, 28
Higfoot, Susanna, 295

Higgins, Bartholomew, 18
Higgins, John, 132
Higginson, Charles, 355
Higgs, John, 361
Hildebrand, William, 441
Hill, Viscount, 274
Hill, Lord, 80, 107, 209, 289
Hill, Sir John, 81
Hill, Sir Richard, 80
Hill, Sir Roger, 68
Hill, Sir Rowland, 205, 206
Hill, Sir Rowland, Bart., 270, 271
Hill, Recorder, 206
Hill, Abraham, 381
Hill, Anne, 151
Hill, D. O., 291
Hill, Miss E. W., 196
Hill, George, 362
Hill, Gilbert, 241
Hill, James, 332
Hill, John, 80
Hill, M. Davenport, 206
Hill, Mary, 426
Hill, Col. Noel, 209
Hill, Peter, 127
Hill, Rev. Rowland, 106, 130, 188,
    287, 309
Hill, Rowland, 290, 354, 387
Hill, Thomas, 205, 240
Hill, William, 162
Hillard, Lt.-Col., 396
Hillersdon, Edward, children of, 151
Hillhouse, Ann, 220
Hilliard, Mary, 204
Hilliard, William, 295
Hillman, William, 108
Hillsborough, Lord, 298
Hilton, Major, 170
Hilton, Mary, 174
Hind, Edward, 384
Hinde, John, 350
Hinde, Robert, 90
Hinde, Robert, jnr., 90
Hinde, Thomas, 418
Hinxman, Henry, 285
Hippisley, Sir John, 272
Hippocrates, 267
Hitchcock, Mary, 76
Hoadly, Bishop, 176, 437
Hoare, Lady, 150
Hoare, Sir Richard, 200, 404
Hoare, Sir Richard Colt, 245
Hoare, Charles, 420
Hoare, Henry, 80, 99, 189, 238, 369,
    420
Hoare, Prince, 58, 164
Hoare, Sophia, 151
Hoare, William, 96
Hobart, Bishop, 212
Hobart, Edmond, 240
Hobbs, Edward, 430
Hobhouse, Sir Benjamin, 94
Hobhouse, John Cam, 303, 384
Hobson, Edward, 346
Hockin, Hugh, 190
Hoclin, Edward, 190
Hodges, Catherine, 112
Hodges, Mary, 259
Hodgetts, Bartholomew, 241
Hodgkinson, John, 324
Hodgson, Anne Lady, 210

Hodgson, Sir Thomas, 343
Hodgson, Mrs., 41, 365
Hodgson, Rev. Christopher, 271
Hodgson, Marmaduke, 229
Hodgson, W., 324
Hodson, John, 170
Hogarth, William, 136, 177
Hogg, Rev. James, 42
Hogg, James, 119
Hogg, Thomas, 178
Hoghton, Gen., 95
Holbeach family, 246
Holbeche, Dorothy, 365
Holbourne, Lady Anne, 255
Holden, Enoch, 416
Holden, Robert, 338
Holder, Elizabeth, 295
Hole, Rev. William, 373
Holford, Mr., 276
Holford, John, 293
Holford, Robert and George, 429
Holford, Thomas, 257
Holiday, Ann, 72
Holland, King of, 220
Holland, Lord, 157, 158, 278, 301
Holland, 3rd Lord, 36
Holland, Lord and Lady, 425
Holland, Hon. Georgiana, 425
Holland, Hon. Miss, 426
Holland, Sir Henry, 387, 429
Holland, Benjamin, 103
Holland, Charles, 404
Holland, Henry, 164
Holles, John, Duke of Newcastle, 54
Holliday, Thomas, 215
Hollins, John, 206
Hollins, William, 206
Hollinshead, J. B., 363
Holloway, Admiral, 317
Holloway, Charles, 368
Holloway, Thomas, 206
Holmes, Sir L. Worsley, 191
Holmes, Admiral, 437
Holmes, Ann, 365
Holmes, John, 138
Holmes, Thomas, 294
Holmes, William, 137
Holroyd, George, 355–6
Holroyd, Sarah, 220
Holt, Lord Justice, 179
Holte, Sir Lister, 423
Holte, Jacob, 110
Holte, John, 431
Holy, Mrs. Beard, 235
Holy, Thomas, 235
Home, 39
Home, Sir E., 364
Home, John, 206
Home, Ninian, 425
Homer, 61, 99, 100, 183, 191, 330, 342, 343, 409, 436
Hone, Sir Edward, 94
Honeywood, Gen., 345
Honeywood, Filmer, 345
Honywood, Sir John, 307, 344
Honywood, Lady, 209
Honywood, Gen., 344
Hood, Lord, 241, 352, 403
Hood, Lady, 161
Hood, Admiral Sir John, 209
Hood, Thomas, 122, 275

Hook, Rev. Walter, 227
Hooke, Sir Thomas, 331
Hooker, Sir William, 445
Hooker, Richard, 165
Hooker, Stephen, 437
Hooper, Bishop George, 401
Hooper, Abigail, 401
Hooper, Elizabeth, 213
Hooper, Francis, 316
Hooper, John, 430
Hooper, Odiarne, 292
Hooper, Philip, 430
Hooper, Robert, 209
Hope, Sir George, 403
Hope, Sir John, 322
Hope, Gen., 27
Hope, Alexander, 46
Hope, Henry, 41, 312, 365
Hope, Henry Philip, 380
Hope, John, 44, 185
Hope, Samuel, 36
Hope, William, 363
Hopetoun, 4th Earl of, 77
Hopgood, James, 257
Hopkins family, 308
Hopkins, Anna Maria, 303
Hopkins, Henry, 104
Hopkins, John, 271
Hopkins, Rev. Maurice, 170
Hopkins, Richard, 303
Hopkins, Thomas, 60, 271
Hopkinson, John, 369
Hopkinson, Rev. Samuel, 187
Hopson, William, 220
Hopwood, John, 145
Hopwood, Thomas, 365
Horace, 100, 211
Hore, Lady Mary, 381
Hore, Thomas, 259
Hormasjee, Bomanjee, 422
Hornby, Catherine, 440
Hornby, family 96
Hornby, Geoffery, 226
Horne, Sir W., 307
Horne, Mr., 36
Horner, Francis, 93, 94, 197, 198
Hornor, Charles, 13
Horrocks, John, 133
Horsmonden, William, 115
Horton, Eusebius, 96
Hoskins, Alexander, 350
Hoskins, Frances, 114
Hoskins, Margaret, 363
Hoskins, William, 426
Hoste, Sir William, 77
Hotham, Sir Charles, 259, 301
Hotham, Robert, 145
Hough, Bishop, 331, 430
Hougham, William, 242
Houghton family, 20
Houstoun, Robert, 70
How, Elizabeth, 226
Howard, Hon. Mrs., 278
Howard, Mrs., 277
Howard, Edmund, 314
Howard, Henry, 149
Howard, John, 26, 208
Howard, Mary, 137
Howard, Matthew, 343
Howard, Robert, 63
Howard, Thomas, 368

Howe family, 254
Howe, 1st Earl, 39, 47, 91, 149, 150
Howe, Viscount, 344
Howell, James, 31
Howell, Mark, 103
Howell, Rev. R. W., 232
Howes, John, 260
Howland, Johanna, 21
Howley, Archbishop, 429
Howorth, Gen. Sir Edward, 431
Hucks, Robert, 264
Hudson, James, 356
Hugford, Sarah, 375
Huggins, Mr., 291
Hughes, Elizabeth, 35, 426
Hughes, Hannah, 133
Hughes, John, 174, 402
Hughes, Mary, 375
Hughes, Mrs., 66
Hughes, T., 74
Hughes, Mrs. Tom, 268
Hulbert, James, 138, 139
Hull, Rev. E., 413
Hulme, Joseph, 60
Hulse, Sir Charles, 154
Hulse, Sir Edward, 208
Hulse, Col. William, 212
Hulton, William, 165, 206
Hume, Baron, 94
Hume, Sir Abraham, 425
Hume, Bishop John, 229
Hume, Alexander, 408
Hume, David, 257, 274
Humfrey, Edmund, 91
Humfrey, Thomas, 175
Hunt, Edward, 225
Hunt, Henry, 108
Hunt, Joseph, 225
Hunt, Leigh, 136
Hunt, Peter, 239
Hunt, Rev. Philip, 209
Hunt, Thomas, 136
Hunter, 274
Hunter, Frances, 151
Hunter, John, 94, 149, 419, 426, 445
Hunter, Susannah, 113
Hunter, Thomas, 339
Huntingdon, Earl of, 55, 338
Huntingdon, William, 310
Huntley, Marquess of, 322
Hurd, Bishop, 176, 373
Hurlock, Joseph, 40
Hurnard, Thomas, 215
Hurrell, Mary, 174
Hurst, Thomas, 286
Husey, George, 155
Huskisson, Mrs., 173
Huskisson, William, 79, 172, 223, 413
Hussey, Charles, 155
Hussey, George, 295
Hutcheson, Francis, 176
Hutchinson, Charles, 427
Hutchinson, George, 187, 219
Hutchinson, John, 367
Hutchinson, William, 30, 146
Huthwaite, Richard, 369
Hutt, Capt., 29
Hutton, Dr., 161
Hutton, Miss, 141
Hutton, Charles, 95

Hutton, Elizabeth, 308
Hutton, James, 291
Hutton, William, 206
Huxley, T., 445
Hyatt, Rev. J., 161
Hyde, Hon. John, 268
Hyde, John, 332

Ibbetson, Lady, 151
Ibbetson, Levett, 440
Ikerrin, Viscount, 188
Ilchester, Countess of, 96
Ilchester, Earl of, 426
Iles, Joseph, 90
Illidge, Thomas Henry, 36, 117
Image, Rev. John, 52
Impey, Sir Elijah, 332
Ince, Charles, 75
Ince, James, 74, 75
Inceldon, Elizabeth, 191
Ingestre, Lord, 96
Inglis, Sir Robert, 433
Inglis, Mary, 385
Ingram, Herbert, 267
Ingram, John, 432
Inman, Charles, 155
Innes, Joseph, 283
Innes, Mary, 420
Irby, Charles, 307
Irby, Edmund, 128
Irby, Hon. Mary, 279
Ireland, Frances and Lucy, 439
Ireland, John, Dean of Westminster, 94, 384
Ireland, Thomas, 418
Ireson, Miss, 214
Irvine, Lord and Lady, 297
Irvine, Rev. Edward, 20
Irving, Rev. Edward, 248
Irving, Edward, 380
Irving, Henry, 63, 217
Irwin, Lord, 279
Isaacson, John, 292
Isham, Sir Justinian, 342, 343, 356, 431
Isham, Lady, 367, 368
Isham, Rev. E., 431
Isham, John, 422
Ives, Edward, 112
Ives, Frances, 427
Ivie, Jonathan and Elizabeth, 429
Ivory, Rebecca, 213
Ivyleafe, Richard, 225

Jackson, Bishop, 445
Jackson, Gen., 154
Jackson, Gen. Andrew, 421
Jackson (pugilist), 75
Jackson, Cyril, 93, 94, 423
Jackson, Elizabeth, 56
Jackson, Henry, 127
Jackson, John, 30, 36
Jackson, Joshua, 60
Jackson, Randal, 398
Jackson, Richard, 416
Jackson, William, 27
Jacob, Edward, 431
Jacob, John, 285
Jadis, Martha, 57
Jaffray, Alexander, 439
James I, 69, 168, 393

James II, 74, 130, 168, 169, 233, 406
James, John, Bishop of Calcutta, 428
James, Lady, 249
James, Dr., 93, 198, 345
James, Edward, 57
James, George, 173
James, Hugh, 318
James, Isaac, 48
James, John, 259, 422
James, Martha, 425
James, Thomas, 96
Jameson, Mrs., 173
Jardine, James, 291
Jarratt, S., 420
Jarrett, John, 413
Jarvis, George, 423
Jarvis, Sarah, 347
Jay, Rev. —, 161
Jay, John, 89
Jeaffreson, Lt.-Gen., 427
Jeaffreson, Mrs., 423
Jeaffreson, Christopher, 423
Jeaffreson, Sarah, 350
Jeane, Elizabeth, 317
Jebb, Bishop of Limerick, 34, 36
Jebb, Sir Joshua, 250
Jeffcock, William, 356
Jeffcutt, Nicholas, 115
Jefferson, Joseph, 361
Jefferson, Thomas, 89, 110
Jeffrey, Lord, 62, 197, 291, 370
Jeffreys, Henry, 170
Jeffreys, Rev. John, 339
Jeffreys, Rev. Robert, 271
Jeffreys, William, 295
Jelfe family, 218
Jellard, Mary, 315
Jenkings, Mrs., 220
Jenkins, Silvanus, 214
Jenkins, Thomas, 406
Jennens, Charles, 194, 195
Jenner, Dr., 34, 251, 352
Jenner, Catherine, 207
Jenner, Edward, 257
Jennet, Hannah 439
Jennings, Admiral Sir John, 335, 338
Jennings, John, 30
Jennings, William, 189
Jennings-Clerke, Sir Charles, 150
Jenny, Abigail, 119
Jennyns, Mary, 397
Jenyns, Roger, 344
Jenyns, Soame, 28
Jephson, Dr., 206
Jerdan, William, 136
Jeremie, Sir John, 35
Jerrold, Douglas, 34, 35, 152
Jerrold, W. Blanchard, 165
Jersey, Countess of, 46
Jerweys, Richard, 32
Jervis, Sir John, 122
Jervis, Rev. Charles, 403
Jervis, Sophia, 260
Jervoise, Rev. George, 279
Jervoise, Geraldine and Henry, 429
Jervoise, Rev. Jervoise, 279
Jervoise, Richard, 104
Jesse, E., 144
Jewell, William, 21
Joan of Eaton, 359
Jocelyn, Robert, 30

Joddrell, Sir Richard, 289
Jodrell, Henry, 31
Jodrell, Richard, 114
John of Beverley, St., 111
John, King, 374
Johnes, Mr. and Mrs., 39
Johnes, Marianne, 92
Johnson, Bishop, 277
Johnson, Beata, 317
Johnson, Benjamin, 337
Johnson, George, 157
Johnson, John, 27, 217, 279
Johnson, Robert, 287
Johnson, Sarah, 317
Johnson, Thomas, 285
Johnson, Dr. Samuel, 26, 34, 107, 147, 211, 245, 277, 278, 350
Johnston, Dr. Arthur, 336
Johnston, Francis, 122
Johnston, Joseph, 109
Johnstone, Governor and Mrs., 358
Johnstone, Miss, 202
Johnstone, George, 151
Johnstone, John, 104
Johnstone, John F., 208
Joliffe, Hilton, 110
Joliffe, Margaret, 356
Jolliffe, Christopher, 170
Jolliffe, Gilbert, 360
Jolliffe, William, 318
Jones, Sir Harford, 130
Jones, Sir John, 46
Jones, Sir Richard, 45
Jones, Sir Thomas, 81
Jones, Sir William, 26, 150
Jones, Algernon, 191
Jones, Anthony, 432
Jones, Daniel, 390
Jones, Rev. E., 157
Jones, Edward, 303
Jones, Elizabeth, 271
Jones, George, 420
Jones, Dr. Henry, 445
Jones, Inigo, 26, 131, 166, 291, 334, 335, 336, 337, 342
Jones, J. W., 245
Jones, Jacob, 309
Jones, John, 154, 162, 259
Jones, Mary, 43
Jones, Rev. Noah, 57
Jones, Richard, 47, 347
Jones, Roderick, 390
Jones, Sarah, 90
Jones, Rev. Thomas, 278, 279
Jones, Thomas, 251, 404, 432
Jones, William, 264
Jonson, Ben, 211, 338
Jopling, Robert, 122
Jordan, Mr., 201
Jordan, Mrs., 93
Jordan, Edward, 260, 295
Jordan, Thomas, 343
Joy, Baron, 46
Judd family, 348
Judd, Peter, 182
Jukes, Harriet, 261
Julius Caesar, 436
Jurin, James, 343
Justinian, 441

Kane, Sir Richard, 338

Karr, Andrew, 279
Karr, David, 279
Karslake, William, 229
Katencamp, Herman, 30
Kater, Elizabeth, 411
Kay, William, 66
Kaye, Bishop of Lincoln, 384, 429
Kean, Edmund, 222
Kean, Edward, 79
Keane family, 325
Kearsey, Thomas, 124
Keate, George, 279
Keats, Sir Richard, 47
Keats, John, 357
Keble, George, 30
Keble, John, 445
Keeble, Edward, 105
Keeton, Thomas, 250
Kehall, Elizabeth, 127
Keighly, Major, 339
Keith, Sir B., 76, 437
Keltham, Thomas and Mary, 411
Kelland, John, 429
Kelly, Maria, 111
Kelly, Col. William, 375
Kemble, Charles, 74, 122, 248
Kemble, Henry, 65
Kemble, John, 149, 445
Kemble, John Philip, 69, 147, 173, 202, 421
Kemeys, Eleanor, 133
Kemp, Sir John, 318
Kemp, Sir Robert, 367
Kemp, Charles, 420
Kemp, Edward, 303
Kemp, George, 323
Kemp, William, 144, 312
Kempenfelt, Admiral, 30, 192
Kempt, Sir James, 303
Kempt, Gavin, 192
Ken, Bishop, 405
Kendall, James, 316, 338
Kendrick, Christianus, 365
Kendrick, Rev. J., 238
Kenmare, Countess of, 128
Kennard, John, 319
Kennedy, John, 78
Kennedy, T., 235
Kennicott, Anne, 285
Kent, Duke of, 29, 46, 158, 161, 247, 397, 403
Kent, Duchess of, 45, 122, 387, 392
Kent, Hubert, Earl of, 441
Kent, Lady Sophia, 46
Kent, Mrs., 346
Kent, Henry, 278
Kenyon, Lord, 30, 300
Kenyon, Edward, 372
Kenyon, Edward Lloyd, 372
Kenyon, Henry, 81
Keppel, Admiral, 90, 305, 344, 345
Ker, John, 170
Kernan, John, 156
Kerr, Lady Caroline, 104
Kerr, Mrs., 422
Kerr, William, 431
Kerrich, Simon, 353
Kerrich, Rev. Thomas, 174
Kerridge, Mrs. and Miss, 331
Kerrison, John, 119
Kerry, Earl and Countess of, 68

Kershaw, Edward, 324
Kettlewell, Simon, 145
Key, T. K., 445
Keynton, Samuel, 114
Keyt, Rev. W., 431
Kidd, Benjamin, 213
Kidd, Christina, 339
Kilcoursie, Viscountess, 348
Kildare, Earl of, 98
Killeen, Lady, 135
Killett, William, 124
Killigrew, Robert, 55
Kilmorey, Francis, Earl of, 32
Kilmorey, Viscount, 188
Kilmorey, Robert Viscount, 32
Kilvington, Thomas, 381
Kinaston, William, 80
King, Lord, 338, 428
King, Bishop, 94
King, Gen. Sir Henry, 302
King, Sir John Dashwood, 346
King, Sir Richard, 391
King, Mrs., 80
King, Charles, 175, 391
King, Elizabeth, 423
King, Harriet, 80
King, Rev. Isaac, 302
King, John, 57
King, Lucretia, 437
King, Richard, 350
King, Robert, 395
King, Thomas, 64, 285
King, Unedale, 218
King, William, 299
Kingdom, Richard, 225
Kingsley, Charles, 445
Kingston, Duke of, 381
Kingston, Lord, 302
Kingston, Robert, 214
Kinnaird, Lord, 63
Kinnaird, Lady, 62
Kinnaird, Hon. A., 77
Kinnersly, Elizabeth, 206
Kinnersly, Thomas, 96, 275
Kinnersly, William, 384
Kinsey, Gen., 439
Kinton, Benjamin, 426
Kipling, Mr., 231
Kipling, John, 21
Kirby, Sir Richard, 74
Kirby, Mark, 190
Kirby, Richard, 76
Kirk, Gen., 344
Kirkby, Frances, 416
Kirkland, Augusta, 427
Kirkpatrick, J. A., 30
Kirkpatrick, Lt.-Col. James, 30
Kirkpatrick, John, 65
Kirkwood, Joseph, 228
Kanpp, Matthew, 423
Knatchbull, Harriett, 350
Kneller, Sir Godfrey, 337
Knight, Mr. and Mrs., 334, 338
Knight, Mrs., 277, 418
Knight, Charles, 136
Knight, Elizabeth, 151
Knight, Gally, 277
Knight, Helen, 150
Knight, J., 242
Knight, Capt. Jacob, 351
Knight, John, 105

Knight, R. Payne, 29
Knight, Samuel, 213, 397
Knight, Rev. Thomas, 353
Knight, Thomas, 350
Knight, William, 366
Knightley, Lady, 173
Knightley, Daniel, 431
Knightley, John, 178
Knightley Lucy, 423
Knighton, Sir William, 34
Knipe, Mrs., 165
Kniveton, Lady Frances, 255
Knobel, Solomon, 375
Knowles, Joshua, 427
Knowles, Rev. Richard, 110
Knowles, Sheridan, 117, 250, 380
Knox, John, 155, 323
Knyvett, Mrs., 427
Kruse, Harriot, 256
Kyd, Col., 40
Kynnersley, Clement, 251
Kyrle, John, 254

la Beche, Sir Henry, 35
Labouchere, Henry 62
Lacon, John, 303
Laconwood, Mrs., 146
Lacy, George and Mary, 47
Ladbroke, Sir Robert, 150
Ladbroke, Richard, 325
Lade, Sir John, 338
Laing, Allen, 251
Laing, Rev. David, 152
Laing, Elizabeth, 332
Laing, Malcolm, 28
Laird, John, 247
Lake family, 353
Lake, Lord, 278
Lake, Hon. G. F., 357
Lamb, Lady Caroline, 403
Lamb, Hon. Peniston, 120
Lamb, Hon. W., 226
Lamb, Prudence, 384
Lambard, Thomas, 31
Lambe, Lacon, 409
Lambry, William, 18
Lambton, Hon. Charles, 45, 46
Lampard, John, 285
Lamplugh, Archbishop, 170
Lancaster, Ann, 141
Lander, John, 392
Lander, Richard, 71
Landor, W. S., 173
Landseer, Sir Edwin, 445
Landseer, Thomas, 291
Lane, Charles, 375
Lane, Edward, 233
Lane, Ralph, 52
Lane, Thomas, 28, 384, 440
Langdon, Mr. and Mrs., 13
Langford, Thomas, 357
Langham, Sir John and Lady, 87
Langham, Sir William, 31
Langham, Lady, 30
Langham, Marianne, 30
Langham, Mrs., 264
Langhorn, Rev. William, 344
Langley, Hon. Dorothy, 381
Langley, Mary, 254
Langstaff, Catherine, 251
Langston, John and Mary, 362

Langton, Archbishop Stephen, 389
Langwerth, Brig.-Gen., 251–2
Lansdowne, Marquess of, 49, 197
Lansdowne, Baron, 191
Lansdowne, James, 295
Lant, Thomas, 346
Laplace, 450
Lascelles, W., 158
Latham, Dr., 290
Latham, Elizabeth, 363
Latham, John, 352
Latimer, Bishop, 419
Latimer, Bishop of Worcester, 62
Latimer, Thomas, 97
La Touche, David, 200
Lauderdale, Earls, 94, 197, 198
Lauderdale, 8th Earl of, 278
Laugharne, Admiral, 250
Launder, Francis, 185
Laurence, Anna, 151
Laurence, Henry, 251
Laurence, Priscilla, 363
Laurence, Robert, 63, 80
Laurie, Sir Peter, 161
Laver, Benjamin, 431
Lavington, Lord, 28
Law, Bishop, 39
Law, Archdeacon, 272
Law, John, 235.
Lawes, James, 100
Lawford, Sir John, 127
Lawley, Lady, 394
Lawley, Sir Robert, 228
Lawley, Sir Robert and Lady, 39, 228
Lawrence, Lord, 444, 445
Lawrence, Sir Henry, 77, 243
Lawrence, Sir John, 387
Lawrence, Sir Thomas, 34, 263, 291, 323, 352
Lawrence, Sir William, 419
Lawrence, Gen., 404
Lawrence, Mrs., 152
Lawrence, Thomas, 151
Lawson, Charles, 30
Lawson, William, 60
Layng, Rev. William, 199
Layton, Bartholomew, 210
Lea, John, 381
Leacock, Rev. M., 405
Leake, Col., 47
Leake, Stephen, 80
Lechmere, Dowager Lady, 412
Le Clerc, Miss, 277
Le Despencer, Lord, 29, 344, 345
Lee, Bishop, of Manchester, 274
Lee, Hon. Mrs., 29
Lee, Dr., 317
Lee, Mrs., 144
Lee, Rev. George, 323
Lee, George, 227, 237
Lee, Dr. John, 58
Lee, John, 277
Lee, Mary, 279.
Lee, Richard, 42, 116
Lee, Sidney, 363–4
Lee, William, 306
Lee-Warner, Anne, 427
Lee-Warner, Henry, 426
Leeds, Duke of, 300

Leeson, Beaumont, 269
Leet, Simeon, 445
Lefevre, Charles, 64
Legard, Miss, 49
Legard, Henry, 50
le Geyt, Maria, 110
Legg, Richard, 61
Legh, Anna, 208
Legh, Charles, 402
Legh, Ellen, 449
Legh, Frances, 287
Legh, Rev. George, 316
Legh, Mary, 165
Legh, Thomas, 165
Leibniz, 250, 267
Leicester, Coke, Earls of, 21, 158, 185, 198, 331
Leicester, Countess of, 279
Leicester, Dudley, Earls of, 43
Leicester, Sidney, 4th Earl, 368, 442
Leifchild, Rev. J., 238
Leigh, Lady Caroline, 440
Leigh, Mrs. Eliza, 246
Leigh, Elizabeth, 427
Leigh, Mrs. H., 246
Leigh, John, 246
Leigh, Louisa, 259
Leigh, Hon. Mary, 279
Leigh, Roger, 429
Leigh, Rev. Thomas, 329
Leighton, Francis, 80
Leir, John, 404
Leith, Sir James, 226
Leitrim, Lord, 277
Leman, John, 27
Le Marchant family, the, 96
Le Marchant, Gen., 329, 357
Le Merchant, Mr., 277
Lemon, Sir Charles, 71
Leonardo da Vinci, 372
Leopold I of Belgium, 135
Leopold, Prince, 273, 402
Leopold, Prince, of Belgium, 157
Lepidus, 436
Leslie, Lady Mary, 289
Leslie, Archdeacon, 151
Lester, Frances, 350
Lett, Thomas, 94
Lettice, Rev. John, 357
Lever, Joan, 35
Leverton, Thomas, 226
Levins, Humphrey, 122
Levinz, William, 195, 201
Lewin, Margaret, 308
Lewis, Sir George, 419
Lewis, Sir William, 95
Lewis, John, 150
Lewis, Owen, 142
Lewis, Thomas, 138, 344, 404
Lewys, Sir John and Lady, 87
Ley, James, 405
Leyland, Thomas, 363
Lichfield, 3rd Earl of, 404
Lichfield, 4th Earl of, 404
Liddell, Rev. H. G., 245
Ligonier, Lord, 264, 301, 330
Lilford, Lord, 426
Linacre, 419
Lincoln, Countess of, 322
Lincoln, Dean of, 320
Lincoln, Frances, 339

Lind, Jenny, 132, 136
Lindley, Anne, 412
Lindley, John, 376
Linley, Thomas, 229
Linnaeus, 250
Lintott, Anna, 141
Linwood, Miss, 185
Lippincott, Margaret, 405
Lisle, William, 321
Lister, Lord, 372
Lister, Mary, 145
Lister, S. C., 274
Lister, Samuel, 370
Liston, Mr., 222
Liston, Robert, 77
Little, Archibald, 65
Little, George, 112
Littlehales, John, 30
Littleton, E. J., 207
Littleton, Fisher, 176
Livermore, Miss, 361
Liverpool, Countess of, 93
Liverpool, Earl of, 278, 426
Liverpool, 2nd Earl of, 187
Livingstone, David, 63, 260, 266, 450
Lloyd, Bishop, 385
Lloyd, Mrs., 132
Lloyd, Anna Maria, 133
Lloyd, Charles, 206
Lloyd, Evan, 310
Lloyd, George, 127
Lloyd, Henry, 189
Lloyd, Rev. John, 311
Lloyd, John, 68, 133, 246
Lloyd, Maria, 406
Lloyd, Maurice, 80
Lloyd, Philip, 215
Lloyd, Rev. Richard, 271
Lloyd, Robert, 63
Lloyd, R. W., 80
Lloyd, Scarlett, 271
Lloyd, Susanna, 381
Lloyd, Thomas, 177
Lloyd, William, 426
Lloyd-Fletcher, Philips, 426
Loch, John, 267
Lock, Daniel, 331
Lock, Rev. Mr., 269
Lock, Sarah, 315
Locke, John, 100, 183, 211, 290, 291, 330, 336, 337, 342, 343, 387, 425
Locke, Joseph, 450
Locke, William, 285
Lockett, Rev. Henry, 324
Lockwood, John, 437
Lockyer, Richard, 295
Locock, Henry, 114
Lodge, Ann, 241
Lodge, John, 428
Loftus, Viscount, 282
Lomax, Mrs., 350
Lombe, Sir John, 31
Londonderry, Marquess of, 262
Londonderry, 2nd Marquess, 390
Long family, 285
Long, Sir James, 229, 324
Long, Sir Robert, 437
Long, Beeston, 404
Long, Charles, 279

Long, Charles and Mary, 404
Long, Edward, 44, 426
Long, Henry, 155
Long, James, 258
Long, John, 204, 317
Long, John St. John, 352
Long, Walter, 151
Longe, Rev. John, 397
Longman, T. N., 263
Lonsdale, Earls of, 94, 134, 271, 368, 372, 415
Lonsdale, Countess of, 418
Lonsdale, Viscounts, 146
Lonsdale, Mr., R.A., 175
Lonsdale, James, 35
Lopes, Sir Manasseh, 429
Lord, James, 370
Lorraine, H. J., 327
Lort, Sir Gilbert, 213
Lort, R., 166
Losh, Catherine, 134
Losh, James, 243
Loten, Gen., 40
Loughborough, Lord, 200
Louis XIV, 408
Louis, XVI, 110, 300
Louis, XVIII, 402, 403
Louis Philippe, King, 220
Louise, Queen of Belgium, 157
Louise, Princess, 392
Louise, of Saxe-Weimar, 94
Louth, Bishop of London, 176
Love, Jane, 196
Loveday, Dr., 59
Loveden, Elizabeth, 112
Loveden, Margaret, 112
Lovell, Lady, 367
Lovell, Sir Salathiel, 367
Lover, Samuel, 153
Lovett, Eleanor, 108
Lovett, Peter, 219
Lovett, Robert, 170
Lovett, Thomas, 157
Lovibond, George, 114
Lovibond, Martha, 391
Lowbridge, Edward, 365
Lowe, John, 165
Lowe, William, 324
Lowndes, Louisa, 30
Lowndes, Mr., 95
Lowndes, Robert, 115
Lowndes, T., 133
Lowndes, William, 409
Lowndes-Stone, William, 423
Lownes, John, 157
Lowth, George, 115
Lowther, Sir W., 146
Lowther, Hon. Barbara, 151
Loxham, Rev. William, 157
Lubbock, Sir John, 13
Lubbock, Mary, 286
Lucan, Lord, daughters of, 394
Lucas, Charles, 199
Lucas, John, 57, 405
Lucas, Joseph, 90
Lucas, Philip, 273
Lucas, Richard, 174
Lucas, Richard C., 245
Lucas, Thomas, 114
Lucca, Duke of, 387
Luce, James, 17

Lucy, Chancellor, 368
Lucy, Rev. Richard, 368
Luders, Alexander, 317
Ludford family, the, 206
Ludford, John, 206
Ludow, Col., 306
Lukin, Paul, 158
Lumsden, Provost, 266
Lumsden, James, 266
Lushington, Dr., 70
Lushington, Catherine, 320
Lushington, E. L., 445
Lushington, George, 449
Lushington, J. S., 419
Lushington, James, 151
Lushington, Louisa, 31
Lushington, Mary, 265
Lushington, S., 419
Luther, John, 423
Luttrell, Anne, 351
Lydeker, John, 339
Lyde, Anna Maria, 351
Lyde, Cornelius, 351
Lyde, Elizabeth, 229
Lyde, James, 351
Lyell, Sir Charles, 387
Lyndhurst, Lord, 47, 132, 245
Lyne, Samuel, 225
Lyne, William, 213
Lynn, George, 331
Lyon, Capt., 130
Lyon, Rev. James, 352
Lyon, John, 151
Lyon, Joseph, 246
Lyons, Lord, 274, 275
Lyons, Sir E., 242
Lyons, Capt. E. M., 275
Lyster, Mary, 431
Lyster, Richard, 57, 406
Lyttelton, Sir Thomas, 367
Lyttleton, Lady, 112
Lytton, Sir William, 367
Lytton-Bulwer, Sir Edward, 450
Lyveden, Lord, 275
16th Lancers, 320

Mabletoft, Mrs., 190
Macalister, John, 47
Macaulay, Lord, 71, 199, 444
Macaulay, Mrs., 264
Macaulay, Rev. Auley, 212
Macaulay, John, 185
Macaulay, Zachary, 419
McCarthy, Dr., 196
McDivitt, John, 220
Macdonald, Lady Sophia, 143
Macdonald, Flora, 18
Macdonald, George, 268
McDouall, Rev. William, 390
MacDougall, Sir Duncan, 14
Macdowell, Patrick, 441
McFarquhar, George, 27
McGrigor, Sir James, 274
Mackenzie, Major-Gen., 251
McKenzie, Mr., 303
Mackenzie, Rev. Alexander, 94
Mackenzie, Mrs. Christian, 57
Mackenzie, Elizabeth, 131
Mackenzie, Henry, 222
MacKenzie, James Steward, 279
McKinsel, Mr., 257

Mackerell, Charles, 215
Mackeson, Frederick, 244
Mackie, John, 44
Mackinnon, Gen., 31
Mackinnon, Mary, 293
Mackintosh, Sir James, 70, 263, 387
Mackintosh, Robert, 267
Mackworth, Sir Robert, 132
McLaughlan, James, 270
Maclean, Gen., 176
MacLean, Lt.-Col. Thomas, 127
MacLean, Mrs., 378
Macleod, Col. Charles, 279
McLeod, M. Bentley, 199
Macleod, Norman, 266
Maclise, Daniel, 122, 389
McMahon, Sir Thomas, 141
McNeile, Rev. H., 246
McNeile, Hugh (Dean of Ripon), 14
McNeill, Sir John, 371
McNeill, Col., 320
MacNeill, Hector, 197, 198
Macome, Ebenezer, 197
Maconochie, Capt., 142
McPherson, Gen., 128
Macready, W., 104
Macready, William, 205
McRone, J., 353
McTaggart, Mary, 295
Madam, Henrietta, 426
Madden, Sir Frederick, 245
Madden, Lady, 245, 384
Madden, Edward, 31
Maddock, Matthew, 115
Maddocks, Mrs., 277
Maddox, Bishop, 204
Madocks, George, 325
Madras, Bishop of, 372
Magens, Magens Dorrien, 302
Magens, Nicholas, 316
Maggs, John, 239
Magnay, Sir William, 221
Maister, Henry, 137
Maitland, Gen., 130, 449, 450
Maitland, Mrs., 110
Major, James, 204
Major, Richard, 245
Major, Sarah, 295
Malcher, Thomas, 115
Malcolm, Sir John, 93,
Malcolm, Admiral Sir Pultney, 34
Malcolm, Miss, 283
Malibran, Mme., 323
Mallet, Elizabeth, 427
Malmesbury, 1st Earl of, 96
Maltby, Dr., 198
Maltby, George, 397
Maltby, William, 47
Manchester, Dean of (1948), 19
Mandeville, Viscount, 420
Manfield, John, 440
Mangin, Susan, 209
Mangles, George, 426
Mangles, Laetitia, 31
Manifold, Susanna, 52
Manistre, John, 246
Manley, Henry, 68
Manley, Rev. W., 350
Mann family, 365
Mann, Lieut. C. J., 36
Mann, Maria, 35

Manners, Lady John, 256
Manners, Lord George, 102
Manners, Lord James, 52
Manners, Lord Robert, 277, 278
Manners, Russell, 426
Manners-Sutton, Charles, 302
Manning, Rev. Charles, 252
Manning, Hester, 180
Manning, John, 252, 254
Manning, Ralph, 360
Manning, Samuel, 252, 363
Manning, Thomas, 15
Manningham, Gen., 30
Manningham, Elizabeth, 367
Manockjee, Cursetjee, 49
Mansel, Sarah, 114
Mansell, Edward, 442
Mansfield, Earl of, 34, 148, 150, 176, 276, 277, 278, 357
Mantell, Sir Thomas, 427
Manty, Richard, 353
Mapletoft, Messrs., 231
Mapletoft, Sarah, 150
Marchant, Nathaniel, 151
Marcus Aurelius, 105, 191, 329
Margaret of Anjou, 247
Marjoribanks, Charles, 323
Mark Antony, 122, 330
Markham, Archbishop of York, 29
Markham, Sir John, 406
Markham, Mary, 31
Markham, Robert, 39
Markham, William, 370
Marks, John, 233
Marla, Mary, 299
Marlborough, Dukes of, 40, 83, 121, 155, 198, 335, 336, 337, 351, 419
Marlborough, Charles Duke of, 336
Marlborough, Duchess of, 419
Marrack, Grace, 214
Marriott, Capt., 426
Marriott, Anne, 74, 426
Marriott, Thomas, 404
Marryat, Capt., 47, 80
Marryat, Joseph, 46
Marsh, Sir Henry, 154
Marsh, Dr., 78
Marsh, Mrs., 357
Marsh, John, 150
Marsh, Richard, 96
Marsh, Thomas, 382
Marshall, Augustus, 317
Marshall, Elizabeth, 225
Marshall, Lieut. James, 362
Marshall, Rev. John, 253
Marshall, John, 273
Marshall, Samuel, 298
Marsham, Rev. Thomas, 110
Marshland, John, 275
Marston, Rev. Thomas, 110
Marten, Thomas, 397
Martin, Lady, 154
Martin, Gen., 39
Martin, Rev. George, 373
Martin, J., 419
Martin, John, 228
Martin, Matthew, 308
Martin, Robert, 443
Martin, Samuel, 27
Martin, Thomas 419
Martin, William, 261

Martineau, Elizabeth, 109
Marwood, James, 27, 332
Mary, Queen, 55
Mary I, Queen, 168
Mary II, Queen, 155, 267, 281
Mary Queen of Scots, 260, 425
Mash, Henry, 227
Mason, Lady, 193
Mason, Emma, 354
Mason, Nicholas, 310
Mason, Richard, 189
Mason, Rev. W., 108
Mason, William, 28
Massey family, 60
Massy, Francis, 347
Master, Maria, 329
Master, Stephen, 287
Master, Thomas, 287, 329
Masters, Katherine, 43
Masters, Mrs. Mary, 113
Mathew, Thomas, 170
Mathews, Charles, 65, 222
Mathews, Daniel, 241
Mathews, Roger, 430–31
Mathias, Sir Henry, 317
Mathias, J., 277
Mathias, Rev. Lewis, 284
Matlock, Sophia, 385
Matterface, William, 225
Matthen, Michael, 360
Matthew, Father, 80, 154
Matthews, Anna, 40, 279
Matthews, Charles, 397
Maud, Princess, 392
Maude, Mrs., 277
Maude, Janet, 226
Maude, Margaret, 32
Maule, George, 110
Maule, Thomas, 188
Maurice, Rev. F. D., 445
Maurice, Marianne, 384
Mawbey, Sir Joseph, 127, 421
Mawbey, Emily, 151
Mawbey, Pratt, 412
Maxse, John, 156
Maxwell, Capt., 189
Maxwell, Margaret, 222
May, Margaret, 423
May, Dame Mary, 73
Maydwell, Matilda, 150
Maydwell, Thomas, 115
Mayhew, Susanna, 395
Maynard, Lord, 176, 365
Maynard, Lord and Lady, 297
Maynard, Thomas, 365
Mayne, John, 64
Mayo, Lord, 393
Mayo, William, 115
Mead, Dr., 106, 305, 330, 344, 420
Mead, Richard, 342
Meade, Miss, 112
Meade, Mrs. Anne, 293
Meade, Robert, 112
Meadows, Lady Frances, 150
Mealy, Rev. Pearce, 151
Medley, Admiral, 99
Medley, George, 317
Medlycott, Sir William, 209
Meetkerke, Adolphus, 103
Melbourne, Lady, 120
Melbourne, Lord, 94 95, 157, 384

Meller, Walter, 314
Mellish, Joseph, 186
Mellish, William, 368
Mellon, Miss, 290
Melton, Henry, 219
Melville, Lord, 93, 155, 370, 403
Melville, Andrew, 323
Mendelssohn, 206
Menteith, Lady, 300
Mercator, 441
Meredith, Sir John, 29
Meredith, Sir Roger, 288
Merewether, William, 61
Merle, Elizabeth, 332
Merle, William, 332
Messiter, Moulton, 317
Metcalf, T., 258
Metcalfe, Lord, 34, 35
Metcalfe, Sir Thomas, 44
Metcalfe, Christopher, 32
Metcalfe, Frances, 32
Metcalfe, Lucy, 27
Metcalfe, Philip, 32
Metcalfe, Sophia and Ellen, 253
Methuen, Sir Paul, 343
Methuen, Hon. Paul, 35
Methuen, Mrs., 278
Methuen, Anthony, 338
Methuen, John, 337
Methuen, Paul, 427
Mexborough, Earl of, 145, 437
Mexborough, Countess of, 57, 427
Meylor, Jeremiah, 208
Meyrick, Rev. Edward, 355
Meyrick, Francis, 343
Michel, Jane, 350
Michelangelo, 149, 355
Michell, Gen., 245
Michell, Catherine, 213
Mickelthwait, Nathaniel, 286
Micklefield, William, 228
Micklethwait, Jane, 332
Micklethwait, Lady Maria, 30
Middlemore, John, 365
Middlemore, William, 287
Middleton, 5th Lord, 30
Middleton, 6th Lord, 427
Middleton, Bishop of Calcutta, 244
Middleton, Mrs., 35
Middleton, Peter, 304
Middleton, Robert, 383
Midleton, Viscount, 420
Midleton, Viscountess, 419
Milbank, Lady Margaret, 429
Milbanke, Eleanor, 156
Milbanke, Sophia, 156
Milbanke, William, 156
Milborne, Mary, 66
Mildmay, Sir Henry, 279
Mildmay, Lady, 76
Mildmay, Harvey, 86
Miles, Lady, 285
Miles, Sir Jonathan, 318
Miles, Mary, 195, 212
Miles, Philip, 36
Miles, William, 150
Milford, Lord, 301
Mill, Dr., 95
Mill, Rev. Arthur, 15
Mill, J. S., 444
Mill, Rev. W. H., 301

Millais, J. E., 268
Millard, Benjamin, 180
Millbank, Cornelia, 40
Millechamp, Anne, 292
Miller, Lady, 27
Miller, Dr., 103
Miller, Diana, 331
Miller, Edward, 75
Miller, Hugh, 63, 323
Miller, Jean, 384
Miller, John, 247
Miller, Capt. Ralph, 150
Miller, Richard, 336
Miller, Thomas, 133
Miller, W. H., 165
Milles, Bishop of Waterford, 331
Milles, Christopher, 242
Milles, J., 27
Milles, Richard, 422
Milles, Rose, 384
Milligan, David, 318
Milligan, Robert, 425
Millington, Edward, 61
Mills, Major, 242
Mills, Daniel, 260
Mills, Jane, 66
Mills, Jeremiah, 384
Mills, William, 350, 422
Milman, Mrs. Henry, 428
Milne, Sir David, 322
Milner, Isaac, 367
Milner, Joseph, 29
Milton, Viscountess, 249
Milton, John, 27, 100, 136, 147, 211,
    291, 292, 297, 301, 329, 335, 336,
    338, 342, 343, 408, 449
Milward, John, 317
Minet, Daniel, 279
Minor, Lucy, 80
Minshull, William, 96
Mitchel, John, 290
Mitchell, Mr., 163
Mitchell, William, 15
Mitford, Charles, 209
Mitford, Mrs., 278
Mitford, William, 285
Mithridates, 409
Mittell, John, 304
Moffat, Elizabeth, 317
Moffett, Anne, 418
Mohun, Lall, 221
Moir, Dr., 323
Moira, Lord, 278
Moises, Rev. Hugh, 151
Molesworth, Sir Arscott, 427
Molesworth, Sir William, 47
Molière, 330
Molyneux, Sir Francis, 226
Molyneux, Sir Thomas, 330
Molyneux, Col., 91
Molyneux, Capel, 439
Molyneux, James More, 253
Moncenigo, Alviso, 72
Monck, Bishop of Hereford, 442
Monck, Gen., 343
Monck, John, 151, 160
Money, Sir James Kyrle, 218
Money, Col. James, 114
Money, William, 310, 332
Monk, Miles, 205
Monnington, Edward, 379

Monoux, Sir Philip, 367
Monoux, Rev. Louis, 287
Monoux, Lucy, 431
Monoux, Martha, 438
Monson, Charles, 84
Montagu family, 244
Montagu, Duke of, 331
Montagu, Duchesses of, 331, 407
Montagu, Lord Charles, 249
Montagu, Lady Mary Wortley, 345
Montagu, Hon. Mrs. George, 246
Montagu, Edward Wortley, 108,
    343
Montagu, Capt. James, 150
Montagu, James, 232
Montesquien, Baron, 105
Monteith, Henry, 266
Montgomery, James, 49, 141, 356
Montpensier, Duke of, 425, 426
Moody, Catherine, 192
Moody, William, 232
Moorat, Samuel, 403
Moore, Sir John, 30, 149, 164, 169,
    434
Moore, Rev. C., 245
Moore, Mrs. George, 444
Moore, James, 108
Moore, John, 286
Moore, Richard, 52
Moore, Col. Thomas, 86
Moore, Thomas, 215
Moore, Thomas (Poet), 230, 262,
    263
Moorhouse, Lt.-Col. Joseph, 298
Morceau, Mr., 196
Mordaunt, Lord, 73
More, Sir Thomas, 309
More, Hannah, 35, 161
Moreton, Ralph, 400
Moreton-Dyer, Henry, 355
Morewood, George, 146
Morgan family, 295
Morgan, Sir Charles, 109, 300, 390
Morgan, Sir Thomas, 316
Morgan, Lady, 121, 426
Morgan, Gen., 187
Morgan, Col., 30
Morgan, Aaron, 113
Morgan, Eleanor, 309
Morgan, John, 295
Morgan, Lewis, 141
Morgan, Richard, 239
Morgan, Rev. Robert, 157
Morgan, Thomas, 52
Morgan, William, 151
Morhall, Mary, 311
Mori, Nicholas, 360
Morland, Lady, 368
Morland, the Ladies, 368
Morley, Lord, 278
Morley, Mrs., 141
Morley, Elizabeth, 272
Morley, Robinson, 146
Morley, Sarah, 150
Morpeth, Lord, 47, 263
Morphew, Mary, 127
Morrah, James, 196
Morrall, Charles, 174
Morres, Thomas, 365
Morrice, Admiral, 343
Morris, Admiral Sir James, 384

Morris, Lt.-Gen., 154
Morris, Col., 372
Morris, Edward, 427
Morris, George, 150
Morris, Rev. Joseph, 259
Morris, Lt.-Col. Roger, 150
Morris, Sophia, 74
Morris, William, 163
Morrison, Gen., 317
Morrison, Charlotte, 225
Morrison, Thomas, 225
Morritt, J. S. B., 152
Morritt, John, 426
Morse, Gen. Robert, 110
Morse, Mary, 66
Mort, Mary, 323
Mortimer, Eliza, 35
Mortimer, Rev. G. F. W., 24
Mortimer, John, 433
Morton, Sir William, 261
Morton, Hon. John, 28
Morton, Rev. George, 143
Moseley, Acton, 400
Mosley, Hannah, 146
Mosley, Rev. John, 185
Moss, Capt., 326, 328
Mosses, Alexander, 246
Mosses, George, 246
Motham, Isaac, 368
Motherwell, William, 144
Mott, Elizabeth, 352
Moulton Barrett, Edward, 244
Mounsay, Sally, 174
Mounsey, George, 230
Mount Edgcumbe, Countess of, 402
Mountrath, Earl and Countess of,
    435, 437
Mousley, Archdeacon, 151
Mousley, John, 48
Moutray, James, 58
Mowbray, James, 413
Mowbray, William de, 323
Moynan, Bishop, 403
Muilman. Peter, 229
Mulgrave, Earl of, 277
Muller, W. J., 61
Mullins, William, 405
Mulready, William, 263
Munden, Joseph, 34
Mundy, Francis, 94
Munro, Sir Thomas, 93
Munro, Prof., 445
Muntee, Valentine, 353
Muntz, George, 104
Murchison, Sir Roderick, 420, 428
Murdock, William, 95, 290
Mure, Col., 144
Mure, Frederica, 96
Murgatroyd, Mr., 414
Murphy, Prof., 152
Murphy, Barbara, 254
Murray, Bishop of Rochester, 237
Murray, Sir George, 226
Murray, Hon. George, 29
Murray, Hon. William, 57
Murray, Hon. Mrs., 172
Murray, Lady Susan, 425
Murray, Admiral, 217
Murray, Rev. J., 272
Musgrave, Archbishop of York, 275
Musgrave, Bishop of Hereford, 74

Musgrave. Sir James, 15
Musgrave, Anne, 222
Musgrave, C., 209
Musham, E., 413
Myddelton family, 449
Myddelton, Sir Hugh, 222, 389
Myddelton, Sir Thomas and Lady, 73
Myddelton, Elizabeth, Lady, 73
Myddelton, Dr. and Mrs., 331
Myddelton, Mary, 331
Myers, Sir William, 57, 226, 283
Myers, William, 427
Myres, Miles, 133

Nairn, Charles, 100
Nanfan, Mrs., 430
Nanney, Lewis, 406
Naper, William, 28
Napier, Admiral Sir Charles, 14
Napier, General Sir Charles, 14, 217, 242, 291, 302
Napier, Sir George, 320
Napier, Sir Nathaniel, 381
Napier, Sir Robert, 186
Napier, Sir William, 14
Napier, Hon. George, 161
Napier, David, 275
Napier, Robert, 144, 450
Napoleon I, 39, 90, 112, 132, 164, 272, 400
Napoleon III, 291
Napper, Henry, 286
Narborough, James and John, 400
Narrien, Prof., 74
Nash, Beau, 309
Nash, J., 47
Nash, John, 328
Nash, Richard, 203, 204
Nash, Rev. Slade, 373
Nash, Thomas, 219
Nassau, George, 306
Naylor, Georgiana, 227
Naylor, Mary, 158
Neale, Mrs., 344
Neale, Josiah, 174
Neame, George, 113
Neate, John, 61
Neate, Rachel, 61
Neave, Sir Richard, 160
Neech, Henry, 44
Needham, Samuel, 137
Neill, Gen., 274
Nelmes, John, 295
Nelmes, Richard, 295
Nelson, Lord, 33, 34, 48, 68, 69, 79, 91, 93, 94, 106, 107, 109, 119, 120, 121, 128, 148, 149, 151, 161, 175, 217, 230, 260, 261, 275, 285, 289, 290, 300, 306, 340, 357, 397, 403, 421, 424, 425, 446
Nelson, Lady, 403
Nelson, Rev. Edmund, 150
Nelson, Miss Horatia, 158, 312
Nelson, James, 63
Nelson, William, 63
Nero, 187, 206
Nesbitt, Arnold, 257
Nesbitt, William, 109
Nesham, Margaret, 65
Nesserwanjee, Manochjee, 154

Neuiville, Mrs., 27
Nevile, John, 241
Nevill, Lord, 275
Nevill, William, 224
Neville, Hon. George, 380
Neville, Hon. Henry, 426
Neville, Richard, 150
Newbold, Ann, 178
Newburgh, Earl of, 77, 394
Newcastle, Dukes of, 47, 54, 55, 136 176, 275, 278, 291, 433
Newcastle, Georgiana Duchess of, 427
Newcomb, Joseph, 163
Newcombe, Rev. Henry, 426
Newcombe, Henry, 317
Newcombe, John, 114
Newdegate, Hester, Lady, 29
Newdigate, Sir Richard, 170, 335
Newdigate, Ladies, 168, 170, 194 368
Newdigate, Lady, 168, 170, 194
Newdigate, John, 374
Newhaven, Lord and Lady, 442
Newland, Mrs., 407
Newling, Rev. John, 206
Newman, Cardinal, 428, 444, 445
Newman, Sir Robert, 193
Newman, Capt., 426
Newman, John, 29
Newman, Thomas, 193
Newte, Rev. John, 225, 430
Newton, Lady, 343
Newton, Bishop, 38, 39
Newton, Sir Isaac, 34, 43, 100, 130, 136, 160, 183, 211, 217, 257, 267, 301, 330, 331, 336, 337, 347, 386, 436, 437
Newton, Sir John, 338
Newton, Sir Michael, 59, 344
Newton, Andrew, 426
Newton, James, 32
Newton, John, 183
Newton, Rev. Robert, 36, 71
Newton, Susannah, 384
Newton, T., 425
Niblett, Elizabeth and Stephen, 316
Nichol, John, 345
Nicholas, Sir Harris, 420
Nicholas, Charlotte, 150
Nicholas, John, 442
Nicholl, Whitock, 360
Nicholls, William, 345
Nichols, Mrs., 237
Nichols, John, 167
Nichols, Peter, 127
Nicholson, Brig., 154
Nicholson, Charles, 124
Nicholson, William, 96
Nightingale, Lady Elizabeth, 316, 330, 331
Nightingale, Florence, 371
Nike, John, 110
93rd Highlanders, 371
Nisbet, Walter, 427
Noble, Col. John, 96
Noel, Lord and Lady, 255
Noel, Gen. Bennett, 279
Noel, Katherine, 70
Nolan, Hon. Michael, 195
Nollekens, Joseph, 47, 94

Norbury, Capt., 373
Norcliffe, Thomas, 381
Norfolk, Duke of, 175
Norfolk, Duchess of, 125
Norfolk, Roger Earl of, 393
Norman, George, 47
Normanby, 1st Marquess of, 403
Normanton, Earl of, 31
Norris, Admiral Sir John, 344
Norris, Charles, 386
Norris, James, 192
Norris, Mary, 202
Norris, William, 60
North, Lord, 47, 176
North, Bishop, 96
North, Hon. Mrs., 150
North, Lt.-Col., 229
North, Catherine and Christiana, 261, 314
North, Dudley, 172
North, Esther, 47
North, John, 124, 209
North, Joshua, 259
North Lincoln Regiment, 320
Northage, Anne, 164
Northampton, Marquess of, 19
Northampton, Margaret, Marchioness of, 383
Northampton, Countess of, 29
Northbourne, Lord, 173
Northcote, Sir Henry, 219
Northcote, J., 34, 94
Northcote, James, 46, 58, 93, 96
Northcote, Samuel, 39
Northrop, William, 29
Northumberland, Duke of, 380
Northumberland, Duchess of, 316
Northwick, Lord, 407
Norton, Ann, 20
Norton, Hon. Mrs., 74, 205
Nott, Sir William, 122
Nottedge, Josias, 31
Nottidge, Anne, 164
Nottidge, Thomas 164
Nottingham, Earl of, 333, 336
Nugent, Lady, 92
Nugent, Lord, 263
Nugent, Michael, 80

Oakes, Elizabeth, 30
Oakes, James, 371
Oakley, Sir Charles, 96
Oakley, Capt., 48
Oakley, John, 80
Oakley, Richard, 156
Oastler, Richard, 301
O'Brien, Sir Donat, 228
O'Callaghan, Sir Robert, 34
O'Connell, Daniel, 132, 154, 221 402
O'Connor, Arthur, 121
O'Connor, Daniel, 121
Octavius, Prince, 176
Odo, Bishop of Bayeux, 359
Offley, John, 240
Ogden, George, 195
Ogden, Thomas, 262
Ogilvy, Mr., 345
Oglander, John, 59, 423
Ogle, Sir Chaloner, 338
Ogle, Chaloner, 174

Ogle, John, 35, 36
Ogle, Richard, 108
Ogle, Sara, 36
O'Keefe, Arthur, 287
Okell, Benjamin, 115
O'Kelly, Count, 241
O'Kelly, Dennis, 241
Okeover, Mary, 437
Old, William, 163
Oldfield, Christopher, 353
Oldfield, Mrs., 337
Olive, James, 162
Oliver, Martha, 206
Oliver, Peter, 264
O'Malley, Mrs., 259
Ongley, Sir Samuel, 126
Ongley, Hon. Samuel, 431
Onslow, Rev. Middleton, 239
Opie, Amelia, 121
Oram, Richard, 315
Orcagna, 43
Orchard, Paul, 225, 332
Orde, Lady, 407
Ordoyne, Garret, 190
Orford, Richard, 418
Orleans, Duke of, 266
Orlebar, Diana, 213
Orlebar, Richard, 209, 239
Orme, Thomas, 367
Orme, Rev. W., 450
Ormonde, Duke of, 97
Ormonde, Marquess of, 32, 321
Osbaldeston, Sir William, 322
Osborn, John, 132
Osborne, Mrs., 22
Osbourn, Joseph, 369
Oswald, James, 291
Otter, Bishop, 397
Otter, Francis, 426
Oughtibridge, William, 285
Oughton, Sir James, 195
Ouseley, Sir Gore, 127
Outram, Sir James, 153, 154, 274, 275
Outram, Archdeacon, 207
Outram, Edmund, 207
Outybridge, Thomas, 146
Overend, Henry, 235
Overend, William, 141
Owen, Sir Hugh, 30
Owen, Prof., 34, 35, 378
Owen, A., 98
Owen, David, 207
Owen, Elizabeth, 423
Owen, Rev. Evan, 141
Owen, Gromo, 433
Owen, Roger, 331
Owen, Rev. William, 388
Owens, Thomas, 150
Owsley, Newdigate, 401
Oxford, Robert Earl of, 394
Oxford, Lord, infant son of, 334
Oxley, Christopher, 381
Oxley, Edward and Frederick, 431

Packe, Charles, 349, 428, 429
Packe, Charles James, 429
Packe, Lt.-Col. George, 387
Packe, Marianne, 428
Packe, Major Robert, 329
Packe, Robert, 209

Packenham, Gen., 426
Packington, Sir John, 325
Paganini, 421
Page, Sir Francis and Lady, 341
Page, Francis, 151
Page, Frederick, 385
Page-Turner, Sir Edward, 45
Paget, Sir Arthur, 300
Paget, Sarah, 295
Pailliet, Susanna, 174
Paine, Tom, 300
Painter, John, 61
Paisley, Admiral Sir Thomas, 160
Palladio, 131, 334, 335, 336
Palmer, Sir Geoffrey and Lady, 255
Palmer, Sir John, 422
Palmer, 39
Palmer, Miss, 176
Palmer, Mr., 96
Palmer, Mrs., 373
Palmer, Elizabeth, 180, 257
Palmer, George, 114
Palmer, Henry, 438
Palmer, John, 43, 338
Palmer, Rev. Joseph, 209
Palmer, Lucy, 411
Palmer, Robert, 189
Palmer, Rosa, 27
Palmer, Samuel, 343
Palmer, Thomas, 422
Palmerston, Lord, 14, 136, 140, 151, 217, 221, 245, 263, 274, 275, 348, 372, 444
Panizzi, Sir Anthony, 245
Panton, Elizabeth, 57
Panton, Paul, 151
Panuwell, Thomas, 382
Paoli, Pasquale di, 70, 90, 149
Papillon, Mrs., 196
Papp, Capt. William, 18
Papworth, J. B., 290
Pares, John, 451
Paris, J. A., 217
Paris, John, 47
Park, Sir James, 36
Park, H., 173
Park, Mungo, 119
Parke, Frances, 418
Parke, Rev. John, 247
Parke, John, 115
Parker, Anthony, 355
Parker, Charles, 29
Parker, Daniel, 109
Parker, Elizabeth, 104
Parker, George, 354
Parker, John, 227
Parker, Peter, 70
Parker, Thomas, 363, 373
Parker, Rev. William, 273
Parker, Winchcombe, 293
Parkes, Dr. E., 122
Parkes, Joseph, 208
Parkhurst, Rev. John, 150
Parkin, Thomas, 411
Parkinson, Ann, 349
Parks, Henry, 58
Parkyns, Sir Thomas, 30
Parkyns, Dame Anne, 310
Parr, Queen Katherine, 301
Parr, Rev. S., 104
Parratt, Maria, 306

Parry, Sir Edward, 161
Parry, Mrs., 295, 403
Parry, Caleb, 161
Parry, George, 309
Parry, Henry, 239
Parry, John, 425
Parry, Nicholas, 117
Parry, William, 35
Parsloe, Mary, 232
Partridge, Freeman, 351
Parsons, John, Bishop of Peterborough, 31
Parsons, John, 97
Pascoe, James, 345
Pashley, George, 186
Passingham, Jonathan, 297
Pasmore, Col., 297
Paston, William, 295
Pate, William, 157
Patmore, Mrs. Coventry, 444
Patrick, Bishop, 367
Patrick, Josiah, 189
Patten, Dorothea, 229
Patten, Lettice, 246
Patten, Thomas, 264
Patterson, Rev. John, 323
Patteson, Bishop, 445
Pattison, Hannah, 163
Patton, W., 124
Paul, Sir George, 352
Paul, Rev. John, 63
Paul, John, 229
Paulett, Lord, children of, 303
Paxton, Sir Joseph, 57, 441, 450
Payn, James, 314
Payne, Henry, 438
Payne, John, 116, 432
Payne, William, 451
Paynter, Eliza, 36
Paynter, Samuel, 36
Peabody, George, 178
Peace, Thomas, 213
Peach, Francis, 433
Peach, Harriot, 151
Peach, Rev. Henry, 426
Peach, Nathaniel, 302
Peach, Thomas, 142
Peacock, Thomas, 122, 241
Pearce family, 390
Pearce, Ann, 385
Pearce, Thomas, 158
Pearce, Bishop Zachary, 91, 404
Pears, William, 175
Pearse, Bishop, 404
Pearson, Canon, 394
Pearson, Charles, 351
Pearson, Robert, 239
Pearson, Thomas, 388
Pearson, Will, 282
Pease, Joseph, 138
Peck, Beatrice, 270
Peck, Edward, 134
Peck, William and Alicia, 254
Peckham, Sarah, 189
Pedley, Mrs., 361
Peel, Sir Robert, 13, 18, 34, 46, 51, 94, 133, 162, 173, 178, 206, 221, 257, 266, 267, 274, 275, 287, 289, 303, 323, 325, 387
Peel, Sir William, 386
Peel, Lady, 392

Peel, Mrs., 445
Peel, Elizabeth, 356
Peel, Joseph, 72
Peel, Mary, 225
Peere-Williams, Henrietta, 422
Peet, Stephen, 212
Peirse, Henry, 427
Pelham, Bishop, 35
Pelham, Hon. Evelyn, 386
Pelham, Mrs., 277
Pelham, Henry, 176
Pell, Mrs., 286
Pellet, Stephen, 332
Pellew, John, 283
Pemberton, Mrs., 187
Pemberton, Anne, 329
Pemberton, Christopher, 275, 302
Pemberton, Rev. Jeremy, 90
Pemberton, Rev. William, 429
Pembroke, William Earl of, 390
Pembroke, 9th Earl of, 330
Pembroke, Henry, 10th Earl of, 423
Pembroke, 11th Earl of, 425
Pembroke, Countess of, 330
Pembroke, Elizabeth, Countess of, 328
Pendarves, Sir William, 294
Pendarves, Edward, 36
Pengelley, Francis, 429
Penleaze, J., 203
Penn, William, 312
Pennant, Sir Samuel, 338
Pennant, Catherine, 425
Pennant, Thomas, 425
Penneck, Rev. John, 43
Pennefather, Sir John, 14
Pennington, Samuel, 213
Pennyman, Sir James, 50, 382
Pennyman, Lady, 150, 381
Penrhyn, Lord, 427
Pentland, Joseph, 121
Penton, Elizabeth, 137
Pentycross, Rev. Thomas, 439
Peploe, Samuel, 278
Pepper, Lt.-Col. Hercules, 104
Pepper, John, 246
Pepys, Mrs., 74
Pepys, Sarah, 318
Perceval, Spencer, 93, 94, 161, 278, 375, 426
Percival, Dr., 445
Percival, Joseph, 412
Percy, 381
Percy family, 80
Pereira, John, 355
Perfect, Elizabeth, 108
Perfect, Robert, 317
Perkens, John, 213
Perkins, Augustus, 191
Perkins, John, 378
Perkins, Sarah, 196
Perkins, Col. Thomas, 46
Perrot, Edward, 192
Perrot, Henry, 322
Perrott, Mr. and Mrs., 250
Perrott, Edward, 369
Perrott, George, 404
Perrott, Jane, 373
Perrott, John, 418
Perry, Bishop, 378
Pery, Viscount, 328

Pescod, Robert, 239
Peterborough, Bishop of, 238
Peters, Elizabeth, 355, 402
Peters, Henry, 53
Petre, Lord, 277
Petre, Hon. Catherine, 23
Petre, Hon. Edward, 158
Petre, George, 344
Petrie, Anne, 408
Petrie, John, 150
Petrie, Margaret, 40, 408
Petrie, Robert, 29
Pettiward, Roger, 427
Pettus, Sir Horatio and Lady, 96
Petty, David, 344
Peyton, George, 431
Peyton, Isabella, 427
Pfiel, Mrs. Catherine, 418
Pheleps, John, 96
Philip, J., 389
Philip, John (R.A.), 63
Philippa, Queen, 398, 450
Philippa of Hainault, 118
Philipps, Sir John, 210
Philips, Nathaniel, 405
Phillips, Sir John, 301
Phillips, Hon. B. S., 24
Phillips, Mrs., 402
Phillips, Elinor, 72
Phillips, Elizabeth, 155
Phillips, George, 92
Phillips, H., 380
Phillips, Henry, 401
Phillips, J., 440
Phillips, John, 274, 384
Phillips, Joseph, 174
Phillips, Owen, 43
Phillips, Richard, 80, 347
Phillips, Robert, 239, 248
Phillips, Sophia, 405
Phillips, William, 306, 405
Phillipson, Rev. Charles, 141
Phipard, Sir William, 258
Phipps, Constantine, 288
Phipps, William, 382
Phipson, William, 206
Picton, Sir Thomas, 32, 161, 162, 250
Pierce, Charlotte, 190
Pierrepont, Lady Sophia, 43
Pierrepont, Hon. Evelyn, 150
Pierrepont, Augusta, 172
Pierson, Major, 27
Pieschell, August, 339
Pieschell, Charles, 339
Piess, William, 109
Pigeon, Susan, 190
Piggon, Edward, 13
Pigot, Lord, 100
Pigot, Admiral Sir Hugh, 257
Pigot, Sir Robert, 100
Pigot, Harriet, 173
Pigott, Mrs., 319
Pigott, Charlotte, 448
Pigott, Emily, 420
Pigott, Foster, 332
Pigott, John, 344
Pigott, Mary, 31
Pigott, Nathaniel, 343
Pigon, Jemima, 332
Pike, Thomas, 189

Pilkington, Lady, 125
Pillans, Richard, 56
Pinchnay, Philip, 138
Pinckney, Gen. Charles, 110, 174
Pindar, Thomas, 353
Pinder, Mr., 150
Pinder, Mrs., 426
Pinfold, Sir Thomas, 278
Pink, J., 305
Pinnell, Elizabeth, 350
Pinnell, Thomas, 61
Pinto, Count, 241
Pitcher, Frederick, 431
Pitt, Sir William (d. 1809), 32
Pitt, James, 66
Pitt, John, M.P., 259
Pitt, William, 28, 29, 67, 93, 94, 149, 161, 163, 164, 241, 246, 250, 276, 277, 278, 283, 332, 387, 425, 426
Pitt-Rivers, George, 121
Pitts, Noble, 66
Pius VI, Pope, 90
Pius VII, 142
Plampin, Elizabeth, 423
Plato, 99, 329, 407, 441
Platoff, Count, 402, 403
Platt, Rev. Charles, 385
Platt, John, 423
Playfair, Prof., 274
Playters, Lady, 254
Playters, Thomas, 254
Plenderleath, Dr., 30
Pleydell, Robert, 210
Plumb, John, 412
Plumer, Sir Thomas, 46
Plumptre, Robert, 365
Plumptree, Elizabeth, 189
Plumptree, John, 419
Plunket, Lord, 250, 263
Plymouth, Lord, 96
Pochin, Charlotte, 337
Pochin, Francis, 175
Pochin, George, 212, 348
Pocock, Sir George, 27
Pocock, Sir Isaac, 151
Pocock, Edward, 332
Pointing, Caleb, 180
Poland, King of, 305
Pole, Sir William, 97
Pole, Charles, 261
Pole, German and Anne, 170
Pole-Carew, Jemima, 426
Polety, Sgt.-Major, 309
Polhill, Charles, 30
Polhill, John, 87
Polhill, Robert, 390
Pollock, Sir Frederick, 136
Pollock, Sir George, 136, 420
Pollock, J. F., 445
Pollock, T., 208
Pomfret, George, 3rd Earl of, 35
Pomfret, Henrietta Countess of, 399
Ponsonby, Sir W., 35
Ponsonby, Sir William, 33
Ponsonby, Rt. Hon. Mr., 175
Ponsonby, Rt. Hon. George, 79
Ponting, Theophilus, 410
Poole, James, 316
Poole, John, 131, 260
Poore, Edward, 80

Pope, Alexander, 54, 147, 204, 211, 329, 330, 336, 337, 342
Pope, Rev. S., 48
Popham, Frances, 384
Popple, Arabella, 396
Porson, Prof., 167
Porson, Richard, 47, 94
Portarlington, Countess of, 66
Porteus, Bishop, 114
Portington, John, 115
Portland, Duke of, 26
Portugal, Queen of, 403
Postlethwaite, Elizabeth, 175
Postlethwaite, John, 127
Potenger, Sir John, 343
Pott, Arthur, 32
Pott, Percival, 206
Potter, Sir John, 291
Potter, Sir Thomas, 275
Pottinger, Sir Henry, 221
Poulett, Earl, 338
Poulett, Vere, 3rd Earl, 427
Poulett, John, 4th Earl, 427
Pounsett, Margaret, 68
Powell, Sir Alexander and Lady, 138
Powell, Sir Christopher, 344
Powell, Sir Thomas, 400
Powell, Judge, 179
Powell, John, 390
Powell, Mary, 390
Powell, Thomas, 449
Powell, William, 56, 286
Powerscourt, Elizabeth Viscountess, 248
Powis, Earl of, 320
Powis, Lord, 300
Powlett, William, 338
Powney, Robert, 431
Powys, Sir Thomas, 190
Powrys, Maria, 15
Poynder, Sarah, 209
Poyntz, Lady, 367
Poyntz, Hon. Elizabeth, 95
Poyntz, William, 262
Pozzo di Borgo, 306
Praed, James, 48
Praed, William, 48
Praed, Winthrop Mackworth, 355, 359
Pratt, Rev. Josiah, 450
Prendergast, Catherine, 154
Prendergrass, Charlotte, 361
Prescott, Mr., 445
Prescott, Rev. Charles, 427
Prescott, William, 75
Preston, Bishop, 374
Preston, Lady, 61
Preston, Isaac, 333
Preston, Ralph, 155
Preston, Robert, 363
Preston, Rev. William, 388
Prettejohn, John, 391
Prevost, Gen., 27
Prevost, Lt.-Gen. Sir George, 95
Price, Sir Charles, 116
Price, Catherine, 413
Price, Rev. David, 284
Price, Elizabeth, 220
Price, Francis, 45, 347
Price, Francis Parry, 63
Price, John, 295

Price, Joseph, 425
Price, Susan, 140
Price, Susanna, 402
Price, Thomas, 431
Price, William, 115, 184
Prideaux, Sir Edmund, 98
Prideaux, Sir Edward, 335
Prideaux, Sir John, 252
Priestley, Joseph, 90, 306, 372
Priestman, Admiral Henry, 55
Prince Regent, see George IV
Prince, Frances, 346
Prince, George, 315
Princess Royal, 392
Pring, George, 226
Pringle, Sir John, 278
Prinn, Mrs., 322
Prinn, William, 229
Prinsep, H. T., 419
Prior, Matthew, 211, 291, 333, 337, 408
Pritchard, Miss, 416
Pritchard, Mrs., 195
Pritchard, William, 418
Pritchett, Rev. D., 66
Probert, Hester, 213
Proby, Sarah, 286
Probyn, Capt., sons of, 257
Probyn, Mary, 66
Proctor, Sir Thomas and Lady, 403
Proctor, B. W., 154
Proctor, Nathaniel, 251
Proctor, Thomas, 14
Prosser, Richard, 145
Prosset, Samuel, 180
Prostam, Thomas, 271
Provis, Rev. William, 315
Prowse, Abigail, 208
Prowse, Thomas, 208
Prussia, King of, 157
Prussia, Crown Prince of, 387
Pryce, Edward, 251
Pryce, Richard, 112°
Pryse, Hon. Harriet, 151
Puckering, Sir Henry, 188
Pudsey, Bishop, 272
Pudsey, Henry, 434
Puget, John, 30
Pughe, Elizabeth, 66
Puleston, Philip, 63
Puleston, Richard, 407
Pulleyn, Mary, 146
Pulteney, Daniel, 334, 337
Pulton, Mary, 108
Punnett, Thomas, 318
Purefoy, Mrs., 42
Purefoy, Anne, 279
Purnell, John, 295
Purvis, Arthur, 74
Purvis, Charles, 331
Pusey, Jane, 344
Putt, Lucretia, 225
Putt, Reymundo, 385
Pybus, Martha, 116
Pye, Sir Charles, 338
Pye, Sir Richard, 338
Pye, Henry, 396
Pye, Jane, 367
Pye, John, 70
Pyke, George, 303
Pyke, Lucia, 61

Pyke, William, 229
Pym, Francis, 127
Pym, Sophia, 23
Pym, William, 20, 404
Pyne, Louisa, 346
Pyott, Charles, 382
Pythagoras, 410

Quain, Sir John, 445
Quain, R., 267
Quain, Richard, 445
Quantock, John, 202
Queensberry, Duke of, 281
Quicke, Andrew, 225
Quin, James, 229
Quincey, Richard, 299

Racine, 330
Radcliffe family, 215
Radcliffe, Sir Edward, 369
Radcliffe, Dr., 336
Radcliffe, John, 54
Radnor, Earls of, 193, 336
Radstock, Lord, 46, 47
Rae, Mrs., 248
Rae, Margaret, 264
Raeburn, Sir Henry, 77
Raffaelle, 149
Raffles, Sir Stamford, 93, 95, 445
Raffles, Dr., 124, 217, 247
Raffles, Rev. Thomas, 217
Raglan, Lord, 140, 291
Raikes, William, 427
Raincock, F., 122
Raine, Charlotte, 70
Ralegh, Sir Walter, 408, 441
Ralegh, Walter, 337
Ram, Stephen, 317
Ramsay, Dean, 371
Ramsay, Allan, 370
Ramsay, Marmaduke, 385
Ramsden, Sir John, 412
Ramsden, Mrs., 261
Ramsden, J., 274
Ramsden, John 412
Ramsey, Wardlaw, 370
Rand, Capt. Charles, 116
Randall, Margaret, 355
Randolph, Archibald, 35
Randolph, Cornelia, 110
Randolph, Elizabeth, 375
Ranelagh, Viscountess, 113
Rankin family, 66
Rant, William, 315
Raper, John, 381
Raphael, 355, 359
Rashleigh, Jane, 317
Rathbone, William, 122, 154, 217, 354
Rattray, Col. David, 57
Raven, Sarah, 251
Ravenshaw, Thomas, 209
Rawdon, Christopher, 354
Rawlinson, Sir Henry, 245
Rawson, Mrs., 425
Rawson, Mr. and Mrs., 240
Rawson, Edward, 235
Rawson, John, 427
Rawson, Mary, 146
Rawson, Thomas, 235, 416
Rawson, William, 427
Rawstorne, Elizabeth, 418

Ray, John, 330, 331
Rayley family, 256
Raymond family, 381
Raymond, Lord, 98, 344
Raymond, Sir Jemmet, 344
Raymond, Mr., 163
Raymond, Hugo, 15
Raymond, Jemmet, 344
Raymond, William, 127
Raynal, Abbé, 106
Rayner, Thomas, 367
Raynsford, Mrs., 30, 115
Raynsford, John, 213
Raynsford, Richard, 438
Read, Sir James, 338
Read, Lady, 338
Read, D. C., 245
Read, Deborah, 146
Read, Edward, 232
Read, Frances, 407
Read, Henry, 407
Reade, Sir Thomas, 160
Readimoney, Sir Cowasjee, 444
Ready, Rev. Robert, 112
Reay, Lord, 243
Reay, Georgiana, 422
Redfearn, Francis, children of, 150
Redfern, James, 78
Redhead, Mary and Richard, 136
Reed, Rev. Andrew, 154
Reepington, Barbara, 189
Rees, William, 295
Reeve, Sir Thomas, 343
Reeve, Lady, 343
Reeves, Pelsant, 146
Reid, Sir Thomas, 431
Reid, Sir William, 49
Reid, Mrs. Sarah, 192
Reigley, Sir William, 211
Renaud, David, 192
Renda, Thomas, 210
Rendlesham, Eliza, Lady, 114
Rennell, James, 184
Rennell, Sarah, 224
Rennell, Thomas, 57
Rennie, John, 94, 318, 323
Renwick, 323
Repton, Humphrey, 164
Reynolds, Sir Joshua, 29, 39, 90, 147, 149, 266, 301, 372, 420
Reynolds, Gen. Charles, 246
Reynolds, Rev. J., 348
Reynolds, Rear-Admiral Robert, 259
Reynolds, Robert, 157
Rhodes, Anna, 29
Rhudde, D., 375
Ribblesdale, Lady, 29
Ricardo, David, 307
Ricci, Mr., 355
Rice, Caroline, 405
Rice, Henry, 100
Rice, John, 29
Rice, Mary, 30
Rich, Charles, 423
Rich, John, 294
Richard I, 323, 422, 446
Richard, Duke of York, 256
Richards, Sir Richard, 35
Richards, Charles, 241
Richards, Theodosia 367

Richardson, Mr., 152
Richardson, Rev. Benjamin, 52
Richardson, Jane, 291
Richardson, Thomas, 286
Richardson, Toft, 395
Richardson, William, 146, 332
Richmond, Dukes of, 62, 120, 160, 278, 300
Richmond, 5th Duke of, 419
Richmond, Duchess of, 278
Richmond, Anne Duchess of, 183
Richmond, Elizabeth, 112
Richmond, Rev. L., 63
Ridehalgh, Sarah, 274
Ridley, Bishop, 419
Ridley, Sir Matthew, 151, 243, 244
Ridley, Lady, 243
Ridley, Rev. Henry, 384
Ridley, Matthew, 27
Rigby, George, 198
Riland, Rev. Richard, 182
Riley, Sarah, 417
Rimmington, J., 235
Riou, Capt., 326 328,
Ripley, Hugh, 191
Riston, Rev. Bartholomew, 414
Ristori, Adelaide, 267
Rivers, Lord, 151, 368
Rivers, William, 261
Roach, Robert, 227
Robb, Mrs., 115
Robb, Frederick, 267
Roberts family, 303
Roberts, Mrs., 433
Roberts, D., 70
Roberts, Evan, 339
Roberts, Hannah, 95
Roberts, Henry, 421
Roberts, John, 195
Roberts, Joseph, 373
Roberts, Richard, 339
Roberts, Rev. Thomas, 35
Roberts, Wilson, 427
Robertshaw, Mr., 109
Robertson, Lord, 198
Robertson, Mr., 238, 345
Robertson, Abraham, 365
Robertson, Ann, 317
Robertson, Col. Francis, 27
Robertson, Rev. Frederick, 450
Robins, Thomas. 371
Robins, Walter, 178
Robinson family, 125
Robinson, Archbishop of Armagh, 26, 69
Robinson, Sir George, 199
Robinson, Sir Lumley, 348
Robinson, Sir Septimus, 278
Robinson, Sir Tancred, 23
Robinson, Sir Thomas, 265, 412
Robinson, Hon. Frederick, 220
Robinson, Rev. Charles, 151
Robinson, Rev. George, 185
Robinson, Jane, 367
Robinson, Rev. Josias, 246
Robinson, Nicholas, 324
Robinson, Robert, 314
Robinson, Rev. Thomas, 31
Robinson, Rev. W., children of, 92, 95
Roche, Dr., 79

Roche, Deborah, 292
Rochejacquelin, Marquess de la, 162
Rochford, Countess of, 404
Rockingham, Marquess of, 277, 300
Rockingham, Earl of, 126
Rockliffe, John, 69
Rodber, Rev. William, 273
Roddam, Admiral, 300
Roden, 2nd Earl of, 65
Rodgers, Prof., 346
Rodgers, Rev. John, 295
Rodick, Thomas, 124
Rodney, Ann, 86
Rodney, Lord, 26, 328, 352
Roe, Charles, 27
Roe, Emily, 189
Roe, Rachel, 363
Roe, Richard, 416
Roebuck, Arthur, 141
Roebuck, Henry, 425
Roger de Montgomery, 270
Rogers, Capt., 28
Rogers, Edward, 439
Rogers, Francis, 332
Rogers, Rev. Hugh, 71
Rogers, John, 61, 190, 345
Rogers, Samuel, 48, 252, 257
Rogers, W. G., 142
Rogers, William, 210
Rokeby, Lord, 29
Rokewood, John, 245
Rolfe, Mr., 104
Rolfe, William, 315
Rolle, Lady, 219
Rolle, Lord, 371, 372
Rolle, Samuel, 344
Rollinson, Thomas, 295
Rollo, Lord, 74
Rolls, William, 224
Rolt, Andrew, 189
Rolt, Thomas, 338
Romaine, Rev. William, 28
Romilly, Lord, 136
Romilly, Sir Samuel, 161
Romilly, Sir Samuel and Lady, 197
Romney, Lord, 300
Romney, Sir William, 417
Ronalds, Sir Francis, 122
Rooker, Alfred, 372
Roper, T., 403
Roscoe, Mrs., 173
Roscoe, W., 69, 217
Roscoe, William, 93, 171, 173, 304, 363
Rosdew, Richard, 96
Rose, Miss, 39
Rose, Elizabeth, 356
Rose, John, 239
Rose, William, 287
Ross, Sir James, 354
Ross, Sir John, 121
Ross, Gen., 226
Ross, Charles, 31
Ross, F. W. L., 136
Ross, W. C., 450
Rosse, Earl of, 154
Rossetti, Dante Gabriel, 186
Rossi, Charles, 433
Rosslyn, Earl of, 197

Rosson, Mr., 174
Rosson, John, 220
Rothschild, Alfred, 301
Rothwell, Rev. Richard, 157
Rothwell, Richard, 68, 320
Roubiliac, L. F., 331, 436
Rous, Lord, 277
Rous, Sir John, 412
Rouse, Thomas, 119
Rousseau, J. J., 146, 147, 330
Rouw, Master T., 222
Rowe, Jane, 30
Rowe, Milward, 202
Rowe, Nicholas, 335, 337
Rowe, William, 65
Rowland, Anne, 157
Rowland, Edward, 363
Rowland, John, 144
Rowley, Admiral Sir Wm., 31
Rowney, Alderman, 181
Roxby, Henry, 146
Royal Princess, 340
Roy, Rajah Ramohun, 104
Royds, John, 146
Rubens, Peter Paul, 61, 160, 289, 335, 336, 408
Rubins, James, 369
Ruddiman, William, 23
Rudding, Martha, 226
Ruddock, John, 314
Rudge, Anne, 259
Rudge, John, 343
Rudge, Samuel, 104
Rudman, James, 225
Rugg, Robert, 378
Ruggles, Thomas, 332
Rumbold, Sir Thomas, 27
Rundall, John, 411
Rupert, Prince, 326
Rush, Sir William, 228
Rush, George, 317
Rushbridge, Eleanor, 217
Rushout family, 264, 335
Rushout, Sir John, 264, 335
Rushout, Lady Caroline, 427
Rushout, Hon. Anne, 244
Rushout, Caroline, 427
Rushout, Elizabeth, 427
Rushout, Harriot, 166
Russ, John, 155
Russell, Lord Alexander, 248
Russell, Lord Cosmo, 159
Russell, Lord George, 425
Russell, Lord John, 157, 158, 206, 384, 428, 445
Russell, Lord Wriothesley, 394, 428
Russell, Sir Francis, 367
Russell, Sir Henry, 48
Russell, Lady Elizabeth, 360
Russell, Lady Louisa, 93
Russell, Admiral, 189
Russell amily, 306
Russell, Mrs., 344
Russell, Ann, 149
Russell, Edward, children of, 60
Russell, Eliza, 359
Russell, Elizabeth, 35
Russell, Jane, 30
Russell, John, 47
Russell, Joseph, 47

Russell, Mary, 258
Russell, Samuel, 242
Russell, Sarah, 36
Russell, W. Congreve, 206
Russell, Watts, 249
Russell, William, 206
Russia, Emperor of, 132
Russia, Emperor and Empress of, 300
Rutland, Duke of, 122
Rutland, 5th Duke and Duchess of, 278
Rutland, Duchess of, 447, 448
Rutland, 8th Earl and Countess, 102
Rycroft, Sir Nelson, 427
Ryder, Bishop, 94, 96
Ryder, Henry, Bishop of Lichfield, 207

Sabine, Sir Edward 136
Sackville, Lady Caroline, 77
Sackville, Thomas, 102
Sadler, Mr., 69
Sadler, John, 158
Sadler, Michael, 291
Sadler, William, 262
Sainsbury family, 200
Sainsbury, John, 150
Sainsbury, Thomas, 150
St. Albans, Duchess of, 96
St. Aubyn, Lady, 277
St. Aubyn, Sir John, 48, 437
St. Aubyn, Elizabeth, 317
St. Barbe, Charles, 110
St. Clare, William, 418
St. Croix, William, 359
St. Germans, 1st Earl of, 427
St. Helens, Lord, 276, 278
St. John, Sophia, 160
St. Leger, Lt.-Gen. William, 431
St. Pol de Leon, Bishop of, 161
St. Quentin, Charlotte, 437
St. Quintin, William, 226
St. Vincent, Earl, 35
St. Vincent, Admiral Lord, 91, 128, 431
St. Vincent, Countess, 93
Sale, Thomas, 141
Salisbury, William Earl of, 389
Salisbury, Marquess of, 387
Salisbury, Sir Thomas, 359
Salisbury, Sir Thomas and Lady 277
Salisbury, Elizabeth, 339
Salter, Rev. Nathaniel, 324
Salmon, William, 35
Salomons, Sir David, 47
Salomons, David, 122
Salter, John, 70
Salter, Richard, 278
Saltern, John, 319
Saltern, Thomas, 409
Saltmarshe, Arthur, 45
Saltmarshe, Elizabeth, 146
Saltmarshe, Philip, 64
Saltoun, Lord, 372
Saltrey, William, 151
Sambrook, Thomas, 52
Sampson, Benjamin, 297
Samwell, Sir Thomas, 114

Samwell, Frances, 23
Samwell, Thomas, 431
Sandby, Paul, 236
Sandes, William, 213
Sandford, Daniel, 305
Sandford, Rev. Richard, 294
Sandon, Lord, 363
Sands, William, 339
Sandwich, Lord, 305
Sandys, Archbishop, 185
Sandys, Edwin Lord, 277
Sandys, Samuel, 55
Samford, Mrs., 114
Sanson, Philip, 260
Sardanapalus, 419
Sargeant, Mrs., 115
Sargeant, Dorcas, 115
Sarsfield, Patrick, 235
Sass, H., 272
Sassoon, David, 444
Saunders, Daniel, 427
Saunders, Edward, 21
Saunders, Emma, 108
Saunders, Henry, 254
Saunders, Rev. Isaac, 252
Saunders, J. C., 167
Saunders, James, 381
Saunderson, Elizabeth, 213
Saunderson, Sir James, 309
Savage, Richard, 91
Savage, William, 426
Savile, Sir George, 40, 145, 277
Savile, Hon. Henry, 57
Savill-Onley, Caroline, 36
Saville, Sir George, 278
Sawle, Joseph, 214
Sawrey, Faith, 264
Saxe-Coburg, Duke and Duchess of, 157
Saxey, Hugh, 368
Saxton, Clement, 279
Saye and Sele, 10th Lord, 64
Saye and Sele, 11th Lord, 64
Sayer, Admiral, 278, 322
Sayer, Henry, 27
Sayer, Major, 355
Sayer, Mary, 207, 208
Scarborough, Barbara, Countess of, 264
Scarisbrick, Elizabeth, 22, 230
Scarisbrick, Robert, 348
Scarlett, Benjamin, 365
Schaw, Arabella, 439
Schemberg, Mrs., 332
Scholefield, William, 206
Scholes, Robert, 143
Schoolcroft, William, 204
Schreiber, Mrs., 116
Schroeter, J. C., 39
Schultz, George, 228
Schwanfelder, Mr., 385
Schwartz, Christian, 151
Scobell, Henry, 429
Scott, Lord John, 136
Scott, Sir Walter, 92, 94, 95, 180, 222, 299, 323, 346, 347, 363, 370, 394, 421
Scott, Sir William, 197
Scott, Gen., 109
Scott, A. J., 238
Scott, Rev. Alexander, 134

Scott, David, 370
Scott, Emma, 429
Scott, Rev. George, 80
Scott, James Hope, 275
Scott, Rev. John, 242
Scott, John, 321
Scott, Mary, 299
Scott, Richard, 80
Scott, Capt. Robert, 397
Scott, Rev. Thomas, 215
Scott, William, 124
Scrase, Elizabeth, 188
Scrope, Elizabeth, 240
Scudamore-Stanhope, Lady, 275
Scudamore-Stanhope, Chandos, 275
Seale, Bernard, 90
Seale, John, 305
Sealy, William, 108
Seaman, Sir Peter, 179
Seaman, Lionel, 316
Seare, John, 232
Seaton, Lord, 14
Sebright, Sir Edward, 368
Seddon, C. M., 247
Sedgwick, Prof., 445
Sedgwick, Lieut. Henry, 318
Sedgwick, Rev. James, 220
Segrave, Elizabeth, 286
Selby, Dame Dorothy, 254
Selden, 154
Selfe, Jacob, 204
Sells, William, 400
Sellwood, Robert, 175
Selsey, Lord, 226
Selwin, William, 113
Selwyn, Rev. Charles, 295
Selwyn, George, 176
Selwyn, Rev. John, 189
Selwyn, William, 95
Seneca, 99, 131, 191, 407
Sennett, Thomas, 397
Sergison, Charles, 15
Sergison, Mary, 426
Serjeantson, Isabella, 395
Serocold, Capt., 150
Serocold-Pearce, Georgiana, 385
Serle, Susanna, 338
Seton, James, 293
Sewell, Sir John, 332
Sewell, Rev. Samuel, 36
Seyer, Richard, 48
Seymour, Lady Augusta, 383
Seymour, Lady Mary, 96
Seymour, Lord Webb, 197, 198
Seymour, Admiral Sir Michael, 34
Seymour, Hon. Charlotte, 427
Seymour, William, 299
Sgambella, Emma, 416
Shadwell, Thomas, 55
Shaftesbury, 1st Earl of, 335
Shaftesbury, 3rd Earl of, 343
Shaftesbury, 4th Earl of, 343, 344
Shaftesbury, 6th Earl of, 419, 420
Shaftesbury, 7th Earl of, 262, 275
Shaftesbury, Barbara Countess of, 340
Shakealey, Peter, 229
Shakerley, Charles, 427
Shakespear, Richard, 321
Shakespeare, Wm., 24, 49, 69, 99, 100, 235, 292, 301, 328, 329, 330,

334, 335, 341, 342, 344, 363, 378, 389, 393, 449
Shannon, Earl of, 223
Shannon, Viscount, 331
Sharp, Archbishop, 55
Sharp, Dr., 335
Sharp, Abraham, 344
Sharp, Charles, 370
Sharp, George, 415
Sharp, Granville, 94, 95
Sharp, Henry, 132
Sharp, John, 348
Sharp, William, 177
Sharpe, Joseph, 378
Sharpe, Rev. Lancelot, 184
Shavington, Carter, 132
Shaw family, 445
Shaw, Elizabeth, 265
Shaw, J., 402
Shaw, Dr. John, 256
Shaw, Thomas, 322
Shearm, John, 258
Sheepley, Michael, 302
Sheepley, Susanna, 302
Sheffield, Countess of, 352
Sheffield, Sir Charles, 145
Sheffield, Sir John, 31
Sheffield, Blanche, 371
Sheffield, Penelope, 30
Sheffield, Thomas, 270
Sheild, Rev. Henry, 212
Sheild, Henry, 362
Shelburne, Countess of, 81, 176
Shelburne, Earl of, 344
Sheldon, Archbishop, 97, 234
Sheldon, Thomas, 332
Shelley, Percy B., 418
Shelley-Sidney, Sir John, 387
Shephard, Francis, 29
Shepherd, Prof., 26
Shepherd, William, 31
Sheppard, John, 105, 427
Sheppard, Samuel, 322
Sherard, Sir John, 210
Sherard, Sir Richard, 210
Sherard, Rev. C., 110
Sherard, Elizabeth, 255
Sherborn, William, 57
Sherburne, Frances, 261
Sheridan, R. B., 92, 95, 164, 241
Sheridan, Mrs. R. B., 109
Sherlock, Bishop, 131, 408
Sherrard, Sir Brownlow, 349
Sherston, Dodington, 229
Sherston, Margaret, 295
Sherston, Peter, 229
Sherwood, Francis, 342
Shield, W., 68
Shield, William, 332
Shiercliffe family, 405
Shiers, Sir George, 63
Shipley, Dean, 384
Shipley, Mrs., 151
Shipley, Anna Maria, 151
Shippen, Robert, 382
Shipton, Dr. John, 114
Shireburn, Richard, 368
Shireburn, Richard and Isabel, 367
Shirley, Bishop of Sodor and Man, 185
Shirley, Mr., 264

Shirley, Mrs., 344
Shirley, Hannah, 128
Shirley, Phyllis, 293
Shoare, Charles, 244
Short, Catherine, 32
Shorte, Col., 104
Shortgrave, Mary, 213
Shorting, Sharan, 191
Shortrudge, Hugh, 375
Shottowe, James, 427
Shovel, Sir Cloudesley, 54, 70
Showers, Capt. C. L., 58
Shrewsbury, Earls, 207, 224, 370
Shrewsbury, Earl and Countess of, 77
Shrewsbury, Countess of, 71
Shrimpton, Mrs., 423
Shuckburgh, Sir John, 213
Shuckburgh, Sir Richard, 50
Shuckburgh, Lady, 65
Shuckburgh, Caroline, 357
Shuckburgh, Gertrude, 36
Shuckburgh, James, 285
Shuckburgh-Evelyn, Sir George, 151
Shuckburgh-Evelyn, Lady, 150
Shuldham, Gilbert, 400
Shuldham, Lemuel, 118
Shuldham, Wilham, 395
Shuttleworth, Rev. Barton, 144
Shufflebotham, Catherine, 363
Sibthorp, Humphrey, 225
Sibthorpe, Dr., 150
Siddons, Mrs., 69, 77, 120, 147, 197, 198, 200, 289, 328, 357
Sidgrave, James, 367
Sidgwick, Henry, 395
Sidmouth, Viscount, 425
Sidney, 130
Sidney, 2nd Viscount, 65
Sidney, William, 113
Sierra, Zipporah, 300
Sierra Leone, Bishop of, 292
Sikes, Mary, 433
Silvester, Sir John, 256, 352
Simcoe, John, 52
Simeon, Sir John, 444
Simeon, Rev. Charles, 253
Simon, Sir John, 445
Simons, Mrs. Anne, 316
Simpson, Sir James, 62, 63
Simpson, Lady Ann, 209
Simpson, Dr., 146
Simpson, Prof., 291
Simpson, Ann, 277, 279
Simpson, Rev. David, 268
Simpson, Jane, 392
Simpson, John, 80, 94
Simpson, Rev. John, 413
Simpson, Margaret, 108
Simpson, Thomas, 352
Sims, Capt. Rodney, 187
Simson, Mrs., 92
Sinclair, Duncan, 198
Sinderby, Thomas, 297
Singleton, Henry, 200
Sitwell, Sir Sitwell, 416
Skelton, W., 238
Skene, Andrew, 291
Skerrett, Gen., 95
Skevington, Thomas, 18

Skinner, Lt.-Gen., John, 35
Skipp, Anne, 112
Skottowe, Nicholas, 29, 30
Skrine, Henry, 31
Skynner, Admiral, 430
Skynner, Ralph, 368
Slade, Augusta, 31
Slade, Mary, 203
Slatter, John, 235
Slatson, Mary, 215
Sleigh, Ann, 353
Sleigh, William, 355
Slight, Lewis, 299
Slingsby, Mrs., 383
Sloane, Sir Hans, 336, 337, 437
Sloane, Lady Gertrude, 92
Sloane, Rev. Stephen, 95
Slocombe, Thomas, 229
Sloper, Amelia, 151
Small, Alexander, 18, 132
Small, Charles, 18
Small, John, 431
Smallwood, John, 351
Smart, Sir George, 19
Smart, Rev. Josiah, 379
Smart, Capt. Thomas, 84
Smart, William, 66
Smeaton, John, 112
Smirke, Sir Robert, 77
Smirke, Thomas, 34
Smith, Sir Gulling, 306
Smith, Sir Harry, 14, 291
Smith, Sir James, 69
Smith, Sir Sidney, 121, 230, 428
Smith, Lady, 367
Smith, Hon. Mary, 222
Smith, Dean, 39
Smith, Miss, 146, 197
Smith, Adam, 291, 387
Smith, Alexander, 63
Smith, Benjamin, 157
Smith, C. H., 237
Smith, Catherine, 439
Smith, Charles, 13
Smith, Charlotte, 30
Smith, Christiana, 140
Smith, Christopher, 96
Smith, Elizabeth, 331
Smith, Francis, 336, 439
Smith, George, 238, 411, 414
Smith, Mrs. George, 238
Smith, Grice, 116
Smith, Henry, 318
Smith, J. T., 94
Smith, James, 18, 202, 217, 429
Smith, Jane, 150
Smith, Lieut. John, 78
Smith, John, 90, 97, 213
Smith, Joseph, 404, 422
Smith, M., 18
Smith, Mary, 66
Smith, Lieut. Michael, 352
Smith, Nicholas, 309
Smith, Mrs. Oswald, 61
Smith, Peter, 100
Smith, Richard, 217, 404
Smith, Robert, 155
Smith, Dr. Robert, 343
Smith, Rev. Samuel, 165
Smith, Samuel, 17, 252
Smith, Sarah, 192

Smith, Mrs. Sarah, 27
Smith, Selina, 426
Smith, Rev. Sidney, 197, 198, 428
Smith, Theophilus, 359
Smith, Thomas, 157, 208, 259, 349, 362
Smith, Thomas, wife and children of, 62
Smith, W. H., 136
Smith, William, 51, 274, 354
Smoult, Rev. Thomas, 367
Smyth, Bishop, 404
Smyth, Sir Edward, 367
Smyth, Sir Hugh, 398, 439
Smyth, Sir William, 314
Smyth, Lady, 314
Smyth, Lady, 398
Smyth, Lady Georgina, 150
Smyth, Henry, 141
Smyth, James, 365
Smyth, John, 150, 439
Smyth, Sarah, 150
Smyth, Thomas, 354
Smyth, William, 35
Smythe, William, 264
Snell, Sir Thomas, 322
Snell, Dorothy, 344
Snell, Robert, 286
Sneyd, John, 367
Soame, Stephen, 412
Soames, Col. Edmund, 353
Soames, Samuel, 144
Soane, Sir John, 94
Soane, George, 39
Soane, John, 193
Socrates, 100, 166, 329, 342, 407
Solander, Dr., 147
Solly, Richard, 30
Soloman, Edward, 232
Somers, 257
Somers, Earls, 301
Somerset, Dukes of, 169, 336
Somerset, 3rd Duke of, 278
Somerset, Duchess of, 313
Somerset, 2nd Duchess of, 315
Somerset, Lady Emily, 46
Somerset, Lady Robert, 439
Somerset, Anne, 379
Somerset, Col. Charles, 354
Somerville, Lord, 164
Somerville, Mrs., 121
Somerville, Mary, 95
Somes, Joseph, 220
Sondes, Lady, 242, 286, 361
Sondes, Lord, 242
Sondes, 1st and 2nd Lords, 362
Sone, Thomas, 264
Sorbell, Richard, 305
South, John, 420
South, Joseph, 81
Southampton, Lord, 279
Southampton, Lord and Lady, 46
Southby, Anne, 57
Southby, Henry, 407
Southby, Thomas, 338
Southey, Robert, 35, 95, 243, 244, 420, 450
Southgate, Rev. Richard, 202
Southwell, Hon. Catherine, 86
Southwell, Sir Edward, 170
Southwell, Edward, 279

Southwell, Edward, 295
Sowdon, Richard, 431
Spackman, Thomas, 129
Spaldin, Mr. and Mrs., 48
Sparhawke, Margaret, 287
Sparkes, Emma, 64
Sparkes, William, 317
Sparks, Samuel, 170
Sparre, Amelia, 146
Sparrow, Anthony, 240
Sparrow, Elizabeth, 36
Sparrow, James, 361
Sparrow, John, 400
Spawforth, James, 361
Spearing, John, 35
Speke, Capt., 290
Speke, John, 162
Spencer family, 364
Spencer, Earl, 157, 279
Spencer, Countess, 151
Spencer, Lord Charles, 231
Spencer, Lord Robert, 278
Spencer, Lady Elizabeth, 231
Spencer, Benjamin, 207
Spencer, Christiana, 180
Spencer, John, 179, 180, 200
Spencer, Thomas, 404
Spenser, Edmund, 100, 156, 211, 334, 342, 343
Spode, Josiah, 48, 209
Spofforth, Richard, 309
Spong family, 109
Spooner, Abraham, 432
Spooner, Isaac, 346
Spottiswoode, William, 445
Spragging, Margaret, 411
Spragging, Thomas, 411
Sprat, Thomas, Bishop of Rochester, 55
Springett, William, 295
Spry, Sir Richard, 425
Spry, Admiral, 209
Spurway, Catherine, 249
Squire, Agnes, 151
Squire, Jane, 52
Stables, Col., 226
Stables, Seth, 309
Stafford, Marquess of, 94, 112
Stafford, Earl of, 429
Stafford, John Howard, Earl of, 90
Staines, G., 146
Stains, Robert, 184
Stamford, Earl of, 245
Stamford, Henry Earl of, 412
Stamford, Henrietta Countess of, 400
Stamp, John, 399
Stanfield (artist), 103
Stanford, Mrs., 259
Stanhope, Earls, 249, 335, 338
Stanhope, Earl (third), 226
Stanhope, Lady, 109
Stanhope, Lady Frederica, 33, 92, 96
Stanhope, Anna Maria, 77
Staniforth, William, 235
Stanley, Lord, 263
Stanley of Alderley, Lord, 270, 429
Stanley, Lady Augusta, 387
Stanley, Rev. Edward, 134
Stanley, Edward, 244

Stanley, H. M., 247
Stanley, Henry, 74
Stanley, John, 63
Stanley, Robert, 42
Stannard, Philip, 315
Stanyon, Abraham, 368
Staples, John, 304
Stapleton, Sir Thomas, 32, 423
Stapleton, Lady Elizabeth, 82
Stapleton, Hon. Antonia, 29
Stapleton, Lieut., 331
Stapleton, John, 350
Stapleton, Oliver, 256
Stark, J., 196
Starkey, Eleanor, 31
Starkey, John, 412
Starkey, Thomas, 29
Staunton, Sir George, 95, 96
Steavens, Thomas, 344
Stede, Alicia, 188
Stede, Constance, 188
Steel, James, 441
Steele, William, 418
Steer, Jane, 170
Steevens, George, 150
Stephen, Sir James, 267
Stephens, Nathaniel, 229
Stephens, Rev. Thomas, 356
Stephenson, George, 136, 173, 243,
    263, 307, 450
Stepney, Lady, 245, 288
Stepney, Mrs., 288
Sterne, Laurence, 147, 211, 276, 277
Stevens, Alfred, 141
Stevens, Caroline, 450
Stevens, Henry, 332
Stevens, Jane, 369
Stevens, Rev. Richard, 369
Stevens, Richard, 113
Stevens, Thomas, 178
Stevens, William, 142
Stevenson, Dr., 247
Stevenson, George, 189
Stevenson, John, 59
Stevenson, Richard, 272
Stevenson, Robert, 222
Stevenson, W., 69
Stevenson, William, 125
Stewardson, Anne, 15
Stewart, Sir Michael Shaw, 266
Stewart, Prof., 222
Stewart, Alexander, 70
Stewart, Dugald, 198, 223
Stewart, Eliza, 413
Stewart, Harriet, 350
Stewart, James, 420
Stewart, John, 208
Stewart, Joseph, 420
Steward-Mackenzie, Francis, 293
Stibbert, Lt.-Gen., 30
Stirling, John and Patrick, 403
Stock, Bishop, 405
Stokes, Capt., 317
Stokes, Lucy, 104
Stokes, Sarah, 422
Stokes, Thomas, 295
Stone, Frank, 235
Stone, George, 125
Stone, Richard, 292
Stone, Samuel, 414
Stone, William, 315, 377

Stonehewer, Mr., 277
Stonehouse, Frances, 189
Stonestreet, Griffin, 29
Storace, Stephen, 40
Storer, Anthony, 279
Story, John, 200
Stothard, T., 420
Stothard, Thomas, 34
Stoughton, Peter, 414
Stourton, Lord, 287
Stow, David, 323
Stowe, Harriet Beecher, 135
Stowell, Lord, 46, 95, 269, 378, 415
Stracey, Harriet, 119
Strachan, Lady, 322
Strachan, James, 47
Strachey, Sir Henry, 31
Stradbroke, 1st Earl of, 47
Strafford, Earl of, 336
Strangways, John, 309
Stratford, Dorcas, 213
Stratford, Edward, 213
Stratford, Frances, 213
Stratford, William, 331
Stratton, Charles, 57
Stratton, John, 208
Stratton, William, 158
Street, Sir Thomas, 437
Stretton, Mary, 295
Stretton, William, 426
Strickland, Frances, 339
Strickland, Walter, 100, 339
Stringer, Miles, 352
Stringer, Thomas and Katherine,
    183
Stringer, William, 56
Strode, Sir George, 367
Strode, Gen., 195
Strode, Elizabeth, 27
Strode, Thomas, 215
Strode, William Lytton, 19
Strutt, William, 109
Struenzee, Count, 300
Stuart, Archbishop of Armagh, 96,
    187
Stuart of Allenbank, Lady, 370
Stuart, Hon. J., 154
Stuart, Charles, 278
Stuart, Lt.-Col. John, 403
Stuart-Pleydell, Mark, 109
Stuart-Wortley, Hon. James, 151
Stubbs, George, 236
Stubbs, Rev. John, 206
Stuckey family, 355
Studley, Benjamin, 170
Stukely, Dr., 131
Sturge, Joseph, 389
Sturges, Charles, 115
Style, Sir Thomas, 100
Style, Charles, 226
Styleman, John, 19
Styleman, Mary, 112
Styleman, Nicholas, 188
Sudeley, Lord and Lady, 244
Sugden, William and Mary, 418
Sullivan, Sir Henry, 31
Sullivan, Sir Richard, 30
Sullivan, Rt. Hon. John, 184
Sulyard, Edward, 88
Sumner, Bishop of Winchester. 245
    420

Sumner, John B., Archbishop, 14,
    420
Sunderland, Earl of, 336
Sunkerset, Juggoathjee, 274
Surtees, Elizabeth, 317
Sussex, Duke of, 34, 94, 176, 186,
    212, 263, 312, 387, 389
Sutherland, Dukes of, 93, 94, 158,
    274, 275, 385
Sutherland, 2nd Duke of, 157, 394
Sutherland, Duchesses of, 274, 275,
    450
Sutherland, Harriet Duchess of, 275
Sutherland, Lady, 104
Sutherland, Andrew and Alexander,
    229
Sutherland, James, 314
Sutton, Archbishop Manners, 385
Sutton, Rev. Evelyn, 96
Sutton, Grace, 350
Sutton, James, 426
Sutton, James and Mary, 423
Sutton, John, 113, 416
Sutton, Rev. Prideaux, 322
Sutton, Prince, 423
Sutton, Robert, 324
Sutton, Thomas, 356
Swabey, Maurice, 44
Swaffield, John, 196
Swale, Elizabeth, 31
Swale, John, 31
Swallow, Thomas, 367
Swan, James, 212
Swanston, Clement, 390
Swanwick, Thomas, 350
Swedenborg, Emanual, 139
Sweetland, Harriet, 116
Swete, Adrian, 409
Swete, Rev. John, 225
Swetenham, Henry, 363
Swift, Jonathan, 211, 342
Swiney, Capt. Baldon, 350
Swinfen, Edward, 115
Swinney, Mary and Frances, 329
Swyer, Herbert, 208
Sydenham, 419
Sydenham, Thomas, 436
Sydney, Lady, 449
Sydney, Rt. Hon. Thomas, 138
Syers, George, 217
Sykes family, 138
Sykes, Sir Francis, 151
Sykes, Sir M., 276
Sykes, Sir Tatton, 419
Sykes, Ann, 352
Sykes, Daniel, 242
Sykes, Joseph, 30, 227, 411
Sylvester, Charles, 104
Symes, Miss, 307
Symes, Joseph, 239
Symmons, Miss, 277
Symons, John, 426
Symons, Thomas, 379
Symons, William, 108
Sympson, John, 338
Shropshire Regiment, officers and
    men of, 253
93rd Sutherland Highlanders, offi-
    cers and men of, 63

Taburn, Wilbram, 451

Tagore, Baboo, 419
Tait, Archbishop A. C., 420
Talbot, Earl, 428, 429
Talbot, Countess, 230
Talbot, Mary, Countess, 279
Talbot, Hon. and Rev. George, 344–5
Talbot, John, 96
Talbot, Roger, 146
Talbot, Thomas, 414
Talfound, Judge, 244
Tallents, William, 44
Talman, Mr., 74
Tamworth, Lord, 69
Tanjore, Rajah of, 149
Tarrant, Catherine, 158
Tassie, William, 184
Taswell, William, 253
Tate, Mrs., 427
Tate, Benjamin, 118, 189, 427
Tate, George, 118
Tate, Martha, 411
Tate, Sophia, 189
Tatham, Charles, 380
Tatham, Edward, 419
Tattershall, Mrs., 332
Tattershall, Rev. James, 423
Tattershall, Rev. John, 223
Taunton, Lord, 394
Tavistock, Marquess of, 428
Taylern, Charles, 217
Taylor, Sir Henry, 249
Taylor, Sir Herbert, 222, 332
Taylor, Sir Simon, 95
Taylor, Col. Charles, 30
Taylor, Gen., 202
Taylor, Mrs., 39, 331
Taylor, Ann, 17
Taylor, David, 35
Taylor, Edward, 182
Taylor, Emilius Watson, 34
Taylor, John, 410
Taylor, Joseph, 430
Taylor, Martha, 439
Taylor, Michael Angelo, 222
Taylor, Robert, 35
Taylor, Thomas, 431, 439
Taylor, William, 91, 133
Tchitchagoff, Elizabeth, 422
Tead, Josiah, 440
Teague, Thomas, 297
Teale, Thomas, 138
Teast, Mary, 132
Tebbitt, Alfred, 290
Teignmouth, Lord, 302
Telford, Thomas, 34, 127, 197
Temperance, Charlotte, 230
Temple, Earl, 343
Temple, William, 121
Templer, Capt., 109
Templer, James, 109
Templer, Rev. John, 431
Tennant, Charles, 291
Tennant, Mrs. Charles, 144
Tennent, Lady, 249
Tennent, Sir James, 249
Tennyson, Lord, 63, 445
Terry, Ellen, 63
Terry, John, 175
Terry, Sarah, 242
Terwin, William, 116

Tetherly, Ann, 284
Tew, Edward, 431
Thackeray, John, 36
Thackeray, W. M., 71, 130, 136
Thellusson, Charles, 241
Thelwall, Richard, 63
Theobald, Mrs. Elizabeth, 131
Thew, Edith, 264
Thickness, Mr., 200
Thirkell, Ann, 213
Thirlwall, Bishop of St. Davids, 122
Thomas, Bishop, 430
Thomas, Bishop of Rochester, 29
Thomas, Sir George, 226.
Thomas, Archdeacon, 162
Thomas, Mrs. Susannah, 310
Thomas, Miss, 98
Thomas, Mr., 74
Thomas, Francis, 124
Thomas, G. A., 443
Thomas, Inigo, 420
Thomas, Lewis, 433
Thomas, Maria, 48
Thomas, Robert, 322
Thomas, Samuel, 29
Thomas, Rev. Vaughan, 206
Thomond, Lord, 74
Thompson, Admiral Sir Charles, 150
Thompson, Lady, 74
Thompson, Capt., 14
Thompson, Miss, 206
Thompson, Mrs., 362
Thompson, Beilby, 146
Thompson, James, 418
Thompson, Joseph, 146
Thompson, Philothea, 345
Thompson, Richard, 448
Thompson, Sophia, 205
Thompson, William, 219
Thomson, Alexander, 266
Thomson, Dr. Andrew, 323
Thomson, James, 327, 361
Thomson, John, 279
Thomson, Col. Peter, 247
Thoresby, 82
Thorn, John, 51
Thorne, George, 295
Thornhill, Clare, 15
Thornhill, John, 65
Thornton, Dr., 209
Thornton, Gen., 220
Thornton, Frances, 253
Thornton, Giles, 133
Thornton, Godfrey, 30
Thornton, John, 426
Thornton, Katherine, 431
Thornycroft, Sir John, 83
Thornycroft, G. B., 393
Thornycroft, Henrietta, 285
Thorold, Rev. George, 332
Thorold, Sir John, 111
Thorold, Sir William, 255
Thorwaldsen, 318, 322
Thresher, Capt. James, 325
Thring, John, 405
Thrupp, J., 51
Thurlow, Lord, 80, 176, 300, 328
Thurnham, William, 230
Thursby, Downhall, 115

Thursby, J. H., 115
Thursby, Richard, 115
Thursby, William, 115
Thynne, Thomas, 313
Tiberius, 408
Tichborne, Sir Henry, 80
Tierney, Sir Edward, 320
Tierney, George, 46, 428
Tiley, John, 191
Till, Thomas and Mary, 374
Tillemans, Peter, 334
Tillotson, Archbishop, 100, 289, 435
Tillyer, Mrs., 70
Tilyard, Robert, 21
Timson, Frances, 151
Tindal, Chief Justice, 33, 34
Tipper, William, 62
Tipping, Lady, 369
Tippitts, Henry, 43
Tite, Sir William, 387
Tobin, T., 324
Todd, Dr., 274, 275
Todd, Miss, 137
Todd, George, 427
Todd, John, 57, 138, 395
Todd, Rev. Robert, 137
Tolderly, William, 379
Tollemache, Lionel, 279
Toller, Rev. Thomas, 309
Tomkins, Thomas, 95
Tomkinson, William, 63
Tomline, Bishop of Winchester, 426, 429
Tomlinson, John, 47
Tomlinson, Joseph, 114
Tonnancour, Madame, 150
Tooke, John Horne, 39, 91
Tooke, Rev. Robert, 298
Tooke, William, 122
Tooker, Samuel, 241
Toosey, Margaret, 208
Torriano, John, 186
Torriano, William, 160
Torrin, Robert, 64
Torrington, George, 6th Viscount, 378
Tothill, Mr. and Mrs., 344
Totnes, Earl of, 254
Tottenham, Charles, 439
Tottenham, Mr., 161
Tottenham, Mrs., 439
Totty, Admiral, 29
Toulmin, William, 190
Tower, Admiral, 127
Tower, Rev. Charles, 355
Tower, Christopher, 332
Towneley, Cecilia, 279
Townley, Charles, 278, 279
Townsend, Lady Elizabeth, 427
Townsend, Elizabeth, 382
Townsend, Gore, 427
Townsend, Rev. J., 426
Townshend, Sir Robert, 364
Townshend, Lord John, 80
Townshend, Charles, 94, 176
Townshend, Lt.-Col. Roger, 139
Townshend, Roger, 86, 338
Townshend, Thomas, 176
Towry, Elizabeth, 30
Tracton, Lord, 27
Trafford, Lady, 426

Trafford, Mrs., 269
Trahern, Mary, 379
Traill, Dr., 246
Traill, Sarah, 215
Traill, Dr. Stewart, 124
Travell, Rev. Ferdinando, 328
Travers, Benjamin, 47
Travers, William, 140
Treadway, Rev. Ligonier, 124
Trecothick, Elizabeth, 253
Trecothick, Grace, 437
Trelawney, Sir John, 116
Tremaine, Mrs., 64
Trent, Lt.-Gen. Thomas, 302
Treslove, Thomas, 115
Trevanion, Charlotte, 109
Trevenen, John, 127
Trevor, Lord, 331, 361
Trevor, John, Lord, 204
Trevor, Richard (Bishop of Durham), 26, 176, 277
Trevor, Mr., 161
Trevor, Thomas, 406
Trigge, Sir Thomas, 31
Trimmell, Elizabeth, 213
Tripp, John, 242
Tritton, Mary, 246
Trotman, Ann, 321
Trotman, Elizabeth, 397
Trotman, H., 405
Trotman, Thomas, 244
Trotter, Alexander, 48
Trotter, Rev. Henry, 131
Trower, George, 219
Truman, John, 52
Truman, Thomas, 189
Trumbull, John, 212
Truro, Lord, 419
Truslove, Ann, 224
Tryce, Richard, 52
Tryon, Thomas, 359
Tuam, Archbishop of, 154
Tubb, Mrs., 232
Tucker, Mrs., 189
Tucker, John, 404
Tucker, Rev. Thomas, 242, 332
Tucker, Capt. William, 254
Tucker, Rev. William, 332
Tudway, Clement, 439
Tullock, Sir John, 302
Tully, see Cicero
Tunno, John, 47
Tupper, Martin, 47
Turnbull, Mr., 414
Turner, Sir Charles, 146, 425
Turner, Sir Edward and Lady, 437
Turner, Archdeacon, 317
Turner, Dr., 369
Turner, Rev. Baptist, 359
Turner, Edmund, 52
Turner, Frances, 66
Turner, J. M. W., 34, 250
Turner, John, 272
Turner, Marwood, 342
Turner, Patience, 373
Turner, Thomas, 112, 378
Turner, Rev. W., 34
Turner, Rev. William, 387
Turner, William Horsmonden, 315
Turney, John, 111
Turnour, Sir John, 256

Turnour, Hon. and Rev. E., 355
Turton, Bishop of Ely, 352
Turton, Sir John, 430
Turton, John, 426
Turton, Mary, 426
Turville, Richard, 439
Twenlow, John, 113
Twisden, Sir John, 21
Twopenny, Dorothy, 391
Twyford, Mrs., 295
Twyford, Samuel, 252
Twyman, Hammond, 97, 341
Tyler, Thomas, 97
Tyndale, Elizabeth, 329
Tynte, Sir Charles, 279
Tynte, Sir John, 338
Tynte, Lady, 209
Tynte, Elizabeth, 209
Tynte, Milborne, 363
Tyrconnel, Viscount, 99
Tyrell, Lady, 384
Tyrell, Sir John, 278, 384
Tyrell, Edmund, 125
Tyrell, Frances, 380
Tyrer, George, 304
Tyres, Ann, 229
Tyrrell, Admiral, 316
Tyrrell, Mrs. Edward, 152
Tyrrell, Timothy, 427
Tyrwhitt, Arthur, 32
Tyrwhitt-Drake, Ann, 420
Tyrwhitt-Drake, Thomas, 420
Tyson, Edward, 367

Udney, Sarah, 151
Udny, Ernest, 422
Underwood, Robert, 295
Underwood, William, 411
Unett, Thomas, 206
Upcher, Abbot, 32
Upcher, Elizabeth, 30
Urquhart, Alexander, 413
Usborne, Edward, 378
Usher, James, 343
Usherwood, Robert, 273
Uthwatt, Henry, 287

Vachell, William, 317
Vale, Thomas, 235
Valembrossa, Duchess of, 268
Valentia, Viscount, 373
Valentia, Viscountess, 181
Valentine, T., 113
Valletort, Lord, 394
Valpy, Richard, 273
Vanbrugh, Rev. George, 422
Van Cortlandt, Pierre, 110
Van de Weyer, Baron, 387
Van Dyck, 335, 336, 408. See also Vandyke
Vandyke, 61. See also Van Dyck
Vane, Sir Henry, 22
Vane, Lady, 22
Vane-Tempest, Sir Henry, 426
Vanhattem, Elizabeth, 229
Van Mildert, Bishop, 172
Vardill, Rev. John, 332
Varley, Rev. John, 146
Vassall, Samuel, 404
Vassall, William, 223
Vaughan, Sir John, 429

Vaughan, Sir Thomas, 218
Vaughan, Miss, 303
Vaughan, Mrs., 140, 302
Vaughan, Felix, 39
Vaughan, Margaret, 302, 406
Vaughan, Richard, 288
Vaughan, William, 92, 406
Vaux, W. S., 146
Vavasour, 381
Vavasour, Sir Walter, 381
Vavasour, Roger, 430
Vawdrey, Sarah, 363
Vawdrey, William, 254
Veale, Richard, 426
Venables, Joseph, 157
Venn, Rev. Henry, 275
Verney, Catherine, 35
Verney, Countess, 98
Verney, Earl, 51
Vernon, Lord and Lady, 158
Vernon, Admiral, 330, 335, 338
Vernon, Charles, 303
Vernon, George, 36, 367
Vernon, Jane, 271
Vernon, Thomas, 96, 210
Vespasian, 187
Vespucci, Amerigo, 89
Vestris, 312
Victoria, Princess, 392
Victoria, Queen, 41, 45, 47, 49, 62, 63, 95, 97, 114, 135, 136, 137, 138, 157, 158, 171, 173, 221, 224, 243, 274, 275, 304, 323, 370, 385, 387, 389, 392, 393, 418, 419, 444, 446
Vigors, Urban, 230
Villettes, Gen., 426
Villiers, Hon. C. P., 387
Virgil, 100, 335
Virtue, George, 141
Vitoria, Duke of, 165
Vivian, Lord, 143
Vivian, Sir Vyell, 41
Vivian, James, 390
Vivian, Rev. William, 252
Voltaire, 106, 223, 330
Von Holst, Theodore, 212
Vulliamy, B. L., 245
Vyse, Harriet, 363
Vyse, Rev. Wm., 195

Wachul, Dr., 167
Waddington, James, 60
Wade, Field-Marshal, 331
Wade, William, 229
Wager, Sir Charles, 344
Waghorne, Mary, 105
Wagner, Dr., 80
Wagstaffe, Lady, 367
Wagstaffe, Sir Thomas, 367
Wagstaffe, Mrs., 44
Wainewright, Rev. Benjamin, 319
Wainhouse, Anne, 155
Wainwright, Miss, 307
Wainwright, John, 115
Wainwright, Rev. Latham, 223
Waite, Edward, 201
Waite, Henry, 146
Wake, Sir Charles, 115
Wake, Rev. Richard, 299
Wakefield, Edward, 136

Wakefield, George, 216, 381
Wakefield, Rev. Thomas, 411
Wakefield, William, 299
Wakeman, Sir Henry, 206
Wakeman, Rev. Charles, 306
Wakeman, William, 112
Walburge, Richard, 288
Walcot, William, 158
Waldegrave, Earl, 28
Waldegrave, 1st and 2nd Earls, 131
Waldegrave, 7th Earl, 48
Waldegrave, Frances, Countess, 275
Waldegrave, Hon. Edward, 30
Waldo, Peter, 170
Wale, Gregory, 59
Wale, John, 331
Wales, Princes of, 71, 224, 241, 266, 358, 390, 392
Wales, Frederick Prince of, 176
Wales, Prince and Princess of, 378
Wales, Princess of, 173, 197, 300
Walford, James, 229
Walford, Oliver, 48
Walford, Samuel, 50
Walford, Thomas, 245
Walker, Sir A. B., 247
Walker, Capt., 151
Walker, Henry, 119
Walker, John, 205
Walker, Joseph, 352
Walker, Mary, 356
Walker, R., 385
Walker, Richard, 323
Walkinshaw, William, 144
Wallace, Lord, 77
Wallace, Sir William, 155
Wallace, Rev. Matthew, 257
Wallace, William, 290, 323, 358
Waller, John, 34
Waller, Thomas, 114
Wallis, John, 214, 400
Wallwyn, Edward, 373
Walmesley, Gilbert, 392
Walmesley, William, 426
Walmley, Anne, 199
Walpole, Sir Edward, 330
Walpole, Sir Robert, 49, 334, 336
Walpole, Catherine, Lady, 337, 406
Walpole, Edward, 380
Walpole, Rev. Henry, 15
Walsh, Sir John, 32
Walsh, Magdalen, 344
Walsh, Robert, 229
Walsham, Vokes, 143
Walter, John, 275
Walter, Mary, 163
Walton, Frederick, 413
Walworth, Sir William, 297
Wandesforde, Lady Sarah, 160
Wanostrocht, Nicholas, 151
Warburton, Bishop, 229
Warburton, Sir Peter and Lady, 384
Ward family, 155
Ward, Sir Henry, 302
Ward, Chief Baron, 334, 337
Ward, Dr., 81
Ward, Edward, 96
Ward, James, 154
Ward, M. J., 439
Warden, Capt., 30
Warden, John, 72

Wardle, John, 228
Wardon, Mrs., 95
Warminster, John, 101
Warner, Bishop, 256
Warner, Dr., 39
Warner, Fanny, 61
Warnford, Rev. Dr., 206
Warnford, Rev. Samuel, 206
Warre, John, 150
Warre, Susan, 96
Warren, 420
Warren, Earl of, 250
Warren, Bishop of Bangor, 426
Warren, Sir George, 426
Warren, Sir Peter, 331
Warren, Hon. Frances, 158
Warren, Miss, 29
Warren, Mrs., 322, 426
Warren, Charles, 141
Warren, George, 41
Warren, George Borlase, 29
Warren, Rev. John, 414
Warren, Pelham, 384
Warren, Samuel, 138, 420
Warrington, Earl and Countess of, 83
Warrington, George, 63
Warrington, Mary, 428
Warton, Sir Michael, 343
Warton, Joseph, 150
Warwick, Earl of, 183
Warwick, Ambrose, Earl of, 43
Wasdale, John, 57
Wasey, Rev. George, 209
Washington, George, 89, 90, 93, 139, 283
Waterford, Marchioness of, 248
Waterhouse, Samuel, 381
Waterhouse, Thomas, 235
Waters, Francis, 354
Waterton, Miss, 249
Wathen, Charles, 342
Watkins, Rev. John, 48
Watkins, Sophia, 390
Watkins, Rev. Thomas, 390
Watlington, George, 65
Watson, Hon. Margaret, 288
Watson, Admiral, 344
Watson, Holland, 195
Watson, James, 127
Watson, Joseph, 202
Watson, Thomas, 235
Watson, Margaret, 105
Watson, S., 385
Watson, Thomas, 419
Watson, Rev. Thomas, 418
Watson, William, 213
Watt, James, 92, 93, 95, 121, 188, 196, 197, 207, 267, 346, 353, 386
Watt, Richard, 30
Watt, Mrs., 249
Watten, Mary, 100
Watts, Alarick, 24
Watts, David Pike, 96
Watts, Isaac, 34, 39, 145
Watts, J., 163
Watts, John, 109
Watts, Richard, 138
Watts, William, 344
Waveney, Lady, 49
Way, Gregory, 28

Way, John, 30
Way, Rev. William, 103
Wayte, Alice, 316
Weaver, Elizabeth, 293
Webb, John, 66
Webb, Samuel, 133
Weber, Carl Maria von, 226
Webbe, Josiah, 151
Webber, John, 350
Webster family, 409
Webster, Thomas, 136
Weddell, William, 277
Wedderburn, Elizabeth, 69
Wedgwood, Josiah, 122, 149, 358
Weech, John, 164
Weekes, Capon, 418
Weekes, Caroline, 418
Weekes, Mary, 418
Welbore-Ellis, Hon. Charles, 245
Welbore-Ellis, Mrs., 278
Welby, Lady, 185
Welby, Richard, 179
Welch, Mr. Justice and Mrs., 277
Weld, George, 142
Weller, Edward, 253
Weller-Poley, George, 125
Wellesley, Marquess, 29, 278, 419, 158
Wellesley, Lord Charles, 14
Wellesley, Hon. and Rev. Gerald, 14
Wellesley, Henry, 268
Wellesley, Hon. Mrs. Long, 317
Wellington, Duchess of, 173
Wellington, Duke of, 13, 34, 47, 49, 77, 79, 93, 94, 95, 97, 103, 114, 132, 155, 158, 161, 162, 164, 181, 187, 197, 208, 212, 248, 260, 261, 262, 274, 275, 278, 289, 301, 303, 306, 307, 325, 332, 370, 371, 372, 384, 390, 391, 397, 402, 403, 418, 420, 424, 447, 449
Wellington, 2nd Duke of, 14
Wells, Dr., 251
Wells, Rev. Joseph, 200
Wellwood, Sir Henry, 198, 222
Wemyss, Hon. Charles, 92
Wentworth, Sir John, 337
Wentworth, Lady Henrietta, 73
Wentworth, T. Watson, 183
Wenyade, Elizabeth, 59
Wesley, John, 71, 179, 207, 252, 352
West, Lady, 209
West, Lady Georgina, 96
West, Benjamin, 39, 46, 94, 113, 164, 266, 273
West, Harriett, 426
West, James, 425
West, James Roberts, 429
West, Admiral Temple, 437
Westall, W., 302
Westcar, John, 173
Westcott, Capt., 40
Western, Lord, 103, 270
Western, Admiral, 151
Western, C. C., 208
Western, Elizabeth, 332
Western, Maximilian, 332
Western, Olive, 351
Westfaling, Thomas, 386
Westlake, Richard, 101
Westmacott, Dorothy, 425

Westminster, Marquess of, 95
Westminster, 2nd Marquess of, 393
Westmorland, 6th Countess of, 335
Westmorland, 7th Earl of, 15, 22
Weston, Lt.-Col. John, 58
Weston, Josiah, 365
Weston, Samuel, 113
Westropp, Walter, 187
Wethered, Martha, 422
Wethered, Owen, 422
Wetherell, Sir Charles, 404
Wetherell, Rev. Nathan, 151
Wettenhall, Nathaniel, 63
Whalley, Catherine, 329
Whalley, Elizabeth, 146
Whalley, Rev. Thomas, 35
Wharncliffe, Lord, 428
Wharrey, Morley, 309
Wharton, Richard, 146
Whately; Richard, 47
Whatton, John, 255
Wheeler, Benjamin, 72
Wheeler, William, 133
Wheler, Granville, 332
Wheler, Rev. Granville, 223
Wheler, Granville Charles, 332
Wheler, Sibylla, 185
Whewell, Dr., 444
Whewell, William, 35
Whichcote, Lady, 77
Whinyates, Mrs., 96
Whipham, William, 52
Whitaker, John and Ann, 433
Whitaker, Rev. Thomas, 294, 355
Whitbread, Harriet, 195
Whitbread, John, 344
Whitbread, Samuel, 28, 278, 420
Whitbread, W. H., 419
Whitby, Michael, 247
White, Sir Thomas, 444
White, Admiral, 318
White, Capt. Charles, 413
White, Gilbert, 232
White, Henry, 95
White, Henry Kirke, 95
White, James 61
White, John, 113
White, Samuel, 181
White, Thomas, 290, 332
White, Mrs. Thomas, 352
Whitechurch, John, 378
Whiteford, C. C., 372
Whitehouse, John, 322
Whiteman, Thomas, 451
Whiteside, Lord Chief Justice, 444
Whiteway, Samuel, 273
Whitfield, Henry, 339
Whitsbee, William, 348
Whitson, John, 103
Whittam, Henry, 146
Whittby, Smith, 286
Whittington, Sir Richard, 79
Whitton, Edward, 115
Whitwell, Sophia, 213
Whitwell, Thomas, 143
Whitworth, 1st Earl, 80
Whitworth, Lord, 331
Whytell, Miss, 27
Wichcord, John, 450
Wickens, Ann, 401
Wickens, James, 317

Wicker, Charlotte, 410
Wickes, Joseph, 417
Wickham, Sarah, 175
Wickham, William, 202
Wickins, John, 150
Widdrington, Lord, 338
Wiggett, Elizabeth, 215
Wiggett, Robert, 365
Wigley, Ann, 72
Wigram, Sir James, 131
Wilberforce, Agnes, 223
Wilberforce, William, 164, 222, 332
Wilbraham family, 433
Wilcocks, Dean, 98, 99
Wilcox, Rev. Francis, 298
Wild, Rev. William, 298
Wildash, Isaac, 76
Wildman, Lady Margaret, 427
Wilde, H., 162
Wildman, James, 96, 254
Wildman, Thomas, 264
Wilkes, Mrs., 375
Wilkes, Edward, 206
Wilkes, John, 121
Wilkes, John, 150
Wilkes, R., 373
Wilkie, Sir David, 222, 223
Wilkie, David, 318
Wilkie, Rev. David, 95
Wilkie, Henrietta, 27
Wilkins, Charles, 162
Wilkins, John, 70
Wilkins, William (R.A.), 34
Wilkinson, Dr., 69
Wilkinson, Ann, 311
Wilkinson, Francis, 401
Wilkinson, Frederick, 356
Wilkinson, Rev. J., 91
Wilkinson, James, 94
Wilkinson, Rev. James, 356
Wilkinson, John, 412
Wilkinson, Thomas, 294
Wilkinson, Rev. Watts, 450
Wilks, Col. Mark, 384
Wilks, Mary, 145
Willes, Mr. Justice, 27
Willes, Charlotte, 30
Willett, Augustus, 132
Willett, Catherine, 28
Willett, John, 336, 403
William the Conqueror, 334
William III, 26, 29, 97, 98, 169, 278, 281, 335, 336, 342, 403, 408, 444
William IV, 58, 94, 95, 129, 158, 161, 198, 222, 273, 291, 324
William II (King of the Netherlands), 97
William Henry, Prince, 241
William of Wykeham, 55, 103
Williams family, 306, 322, 388
Williams, Sir James, 251
Williams, Sir John, 427
Williams, Lady, 177
Williams, Archdeacon, 140
Williams, Caroline, 65
Williams, Charles, 65
Williams, Charles, 390
Williams, Rev. Daniel, 285
Williams, David, 425
Williams, Elizabeth, 112
Williams, Rev. Harry, 218

Williams, Rev. Henry, 80
Williams, James, 295
Williams, John, 373, 387
Williams, Rev. John, 178
Williams, Mary, 363
Williams, Matthew, 35
Williams, Michael, 390
Williams, William, 29, 140, 215, 314, 356
Williamson, Lady, 28, 368
Williamson, Lady Dyonis, 255
Williamson, Col., 426
Williamson, Anne, 222
Williamson, Edward Retchford, 109
Williamson, Francis, 254
Williamson, Hugh, 110
Williamson, John, 175
Williamson, Mary, 376
Williamson, Robert, 134
Willis, Bishop, 98
Willis, Dr., 164, 278
Willis, Mrs., 279
Willis, Alice, 429
Willis, Rev. Francis, 279
Willis, John, 160
Willis, John, 287
Willis, Admiral Richard, 80
Willis, Thomas, 429
Willoughby, Charlotte, 416
Willoughby, Francis, 330, 331
Willoughby, Henry, 416
Wills, Samuel, 373
Wills, Thomas, 115
Wills, William, 378
Willy, George, 423
Wilmore, William, 55
Wilmot, Robert, 108
Wilshere, Martin, 351
Wilshire family, 413
Wilson, Bishop, 47
Wilson, Lady Spencer, 317
Wilson, Alderman, 134
Wilson, Judge, 300
Wilson, Mr. and Mrs., 264
Wilson, Prof., 95, 144, 370
Wilson, Alexander, 266
Wilson, Benjamin, 346
Wilson, Catherine, 345
Wilson, Edward, 445
Wilson, George, 238
Wilson, Henry, 158
Wilson, James, 370, 371
Wilson, John, 96, 206, 209, 252, 371
Wilson, Rev. Roger Carus, 385
Wilson, Sarah, 150
Wilson, Sybil, 145
Wilson, Thomas, 345, 426
Wilson, William, 235, 422
Wilt, Sarah, 413
Wilton, Joseph, 331
Wilton, the Misses, 437
Winchelsea, Countess of, 248
Winchester, Saher Earl of, 422
Winchilsea, Earl of, 419
Windham, Hon. Charlotte, 282
Windham, Admiral, 293
Windham, Mrs., 387
Windham, Thomas, 265
Windham, William, 125, 161, 277, 278
Winfield, Sarah, 160
Winford, Harriot, 29

Winford, Sarah, 27
Wing, Eleanor, 53
Wing, Robert, 18
Wingfield, Hon. Emily, 160
Wingfield, Anthony, 55
Winnington, Lady, 373
Winn, Sir Rowland, 151
Winn, John, 96
Winstanley, Thomas, 57
Winterton, Countess, 121, 256
Wintringham, Sir Clifton, 40
Winwood, Richard and Anne, 369
Wise, Edward, 346
Wise, John, 164
Wiseman, Cardinal, 105, 263
Wishart, Jacob, 210
Withering, William, 207
Withers, Mr. and Mrs., 297
Withers, Elizabeth, 411
Withers, Joseph, 27
Wogan, John, 264
Wolfe, Gen. James, 78, 81, 176, 244, 358, 436, 437
Wolfe, Thomas, 204
Wolferston family, 405
Wolff, Dr., 74
Wollaston, William, 125
Wollstonecraft, Mary, 419
Wolmer, John, 27
Wolrich, Mr., 308
Wolsey, Cardinal, 55, 181
Wolstenholme, Mary, 62
Wombwell, Sir George, 420
Wood, Dr., 34
Wood, Col. Cornelius, 52
Wood, Rev. Charles, 302
Wood, Henry, 413
Wood, Rev. Henry, 97
Wood, Capt. John, 318
Wood, Rev. John, 97
Wood, M., 68
Wood, Mary, 212
Wood, Mr. and Mrs. Seth, 52
Wood, Vincent, 184
Woodall, Mrs., 302
Woodbine, John, 56
Woodcock, John, 379
Woodcocks, William, 315
Woodford, Sir Ralph, 96
Woodham, Sarah, 357
Woodham, William, 357
Woodhead, Samuel, 309
Woodhouse, Dean of Lichfield, 48
Woodhouse, Rev. George, 218
Woodhouse, Mercy, 195
Woodifield, Elizabeth, 122
Woodmason children, 333
Woodroffe, Anne, 282
Woodruff, John, 241
Woods, Edmund, 80
Woods, Lt.-Col. Edward, 317
Woods, Edward, 400
Woodward, Dr., 343
Woodward, Anthony, 264
Woodward, Benjamin, 268
Woodward, Elizabeth, 150

Woodward, Robert, 373
Woodward, Mrs. Sarah, 427
Woodward, Thomas, 409
Woodyatt, George, 426
Woodyatt, Thomas, 206
Woolaston, Mr., 183
Woolaston, 336
Woolis, Rev. Thomas, 423
Wooll, Dr., 429
Woollett, Elizabeth, 30
Woollett, John, 32
Woollett, William, 39
Woolley, Hannah, 220
Woolley, William, 227
Woolston family, 76
Woolston, Ann, 115
Wootton, Henry, 272
Wordsworth, John, 48
Wordsworth, William, 94, 394, 445, 450
Wormald, Thomas, 261
Woronzow, Prince, 383
Worral, Mrs., 202
Worrall, Georgiana, 405
Worsley family, 433
Wortley, John Stuart, 150
Wortley-Mackenzie, Hon. Mrs., 151
Wrags, Adam, 189, 219,
Wren, Christopher, 273, 297, 372
Wren, Jane, 55
Wren, Philip, 383
Wrench, Edward, 57
Wrench, Thomas, 189
Wrey, Anne Lady, 229
Wrey, Sir Boucher, 324, 373
Wrey, Sir Cecil and Lady, 86
Wrey, Florence Lady, 219
Wright, Mrs. James, 377
Wright, Mary, 203, 292
Wright, Rev. Peter, 246
Wright, Robert, 59, 238
Wright, Robert and Mary, 260
Wright, Stephen, 72
Wright, Rev. Stephen, 174
Wright, T., 305
Wright, Thomas, 21
Wright, William, 347, 438
Wrottesley, Henrietta, 430
Wyatt, Dudley, 422
Wyatt, J., 328
Wyatt, R. J., 173
Wyatville, Sir Jeffrey, 95
Wyche, Cyril, 215
Wyche, John, 64
Wyche, Richard de, 320
Wycliffe, William, 429
Wykeham, Richard, 399
Wykeham-Martin, Lady Jemima, 36
Wykes, William, 213
Wyld, Mary, 187
Wyld, Thomas, 27
Wyldbore, William, 195
Wylde, Thomas, 378
Wylie, Dr. James, 320

Wyndham, Lord, 338
Wyndham, Sir Hugh, 281
Wyndham, Ann, 404
Wyndham, George, 57
Wyndham, John, 338
Wyndham, Henry, 80
Wyndham, Thomas, 161
Wyndham, Wadham, 285
Wynn, Sir W. W., 277
Wynn, Sir Watkin Williams, 335 338
Wynn, Lady Henrietta Williams, 278
Wynn family, 449
Wynn, Edward, 377
Wynn, William, 338
Wynne, Lutherell, 31
Wynne, Owen, 406
Wynne, Rev. Richard, 144
Wynniatt, Reginald, 439
Wynter, Anne, 385
Wynyard, Emily, 209

Yarborough family, 150
Yarborough, Earls of, 138, 278
Yarborough, Countess of, 278
Yarborough, John, 241
Yarndel, Catherine, 373
Yarrell, William, 420
Yates, George, 346
Yates, Rev. J., 333
Yates, John, 246, 431
Yates, Rev. Richard, 392
Yeo, Sir William, 350
Yonge, Sir George, 149
York, Archbishop of, 274
York, Dukes of, 34, 45, 47, 77, 95, 129, 162, 176, 180, 196, 241, 277, 278, 282, 283, 303, 312, 352, 362, 425
York, Duchess of, 96
York, Edward Duke of, 176
York, Frederick Duke of, 309, 358
Yorke, Hon. Charles, 127, 344
Yorke, Hon. Mrs. Charles, 151, 344
Yorke, Hon. and Rev. James, 57
Yorke, Hon. John, 426
Yorke, Anne, 404
Yorke, Charles, 176
Yorke, Elizabeth, 20, 404
Yorke, John, 30
Yorke, Martin, 30
Yorke, Philip, 426
Young, Sir John and Lady, 36
Young, Sir William, 338
Young, Mr. (of Covent Garden), 46
Young, Rev. Alexander, 382
Young, Arthur, 164
Young, Charles, 307
Young, Mary, 115
Young, William, 314, 334
Younge, William, 356

Zenogle, Mrs., 20
Zetland, Earl of, 138
Zingara, 342